THE TROTTING & PACING GUIDE

The Official Handbook of Harness Racing

Now in its 45th Edition
Published Annually by

The United States Trotting Association

Corwin M. Nixon - President
Paul A. Fontaine - Chairman of the Board
Francis X. Ready - Executive Vice President

Compiled and Edited by

John Pawlak

"World Records" provided by
David Carr

With staff assistance from
**Bruce Brinkerhoff
Paul Ramlow
Corky Visminas
Karen Yager**

And the Harness Publicists of North America

*Cover photo of Beach Towel by Ed Keys
Inside photos from the USTA files*

The United States Trotting Association

**750 Michigan Avenue
Columbus, Ohio 43215**

Main Switchboard	(614) 224-2291
Harness Racing Hotline	(614) 228-1821
Automatic "Fax"	(614) 228-1385

*(Publicity, Hoof Beats, Information & Research,
Data Processing, and Race Track System)*

Automatic "Fax"   (614) 224-4575
(All other departments)

(c) - Copyright USTA, 1991

INTRODUCTION

TABLE OF CONTENTS

The U.S. Trotting Association

About the USTA 4
USTA Officers and Directors 5

The Tracks

Directory of Tracks 7
Roster of Major Tracks 8
Other North American Tracks 37
Grand Circuit Fairs 42
Major Training Centers 45
Alphabetical Listing of
  Track Abbreviations 46
Top Tracks by Purses 51
Top Tracks by 2:00 and 1:55 Miles 53
Speed Ratings for North American Tracks 55
Track Trotting and Pacing Records 57
The Business of Racing, 1990 80

Organizations

Harness Tracks of America 91
Harness Racing Communications 92
American Horse Council 92
American Horse Racing Federation 92
Canadian Trotting Association 93
Canadian Standardbred Horse Society 93
Breeders Crown 94
Hambletonian Society 94
Grand Circuit 94
Hall of Fame of the Trotter 95
Delvin Miller Amateur Drivers Association 95
North American Amateur
  Drivers Association 95
United States Harness Writers Association 96
Harness Publicists Association 96
Harness Horsemen International 97
Standardbred Breeders and
  Owners Organizations 98
Harness Horse Youth Foundation 99
Association of Racing
  Commissioners International 100
North American Judges and
  Stewards Association 100
Other Harness Racing Organizations 100
State and Provincial Racing Commissions 101

Sire Stakes Information Sources 103
World Trotting Councils 104

Race Dates

Pari-Mutuel and County Fair
  Racing Dates for 1991 107
Grand Circuit Dates for 1991 113
Major Races for 1991 114
$100,000 Open Races for 1991, by
  Division, & 1990 Winners 137

World Records

USTA World Championship Records 143
North American Race Records 148
Mile Records by the World
  Champion Trotters and Pacers 163
History of Record Speed: 1890-1990 165

The Crowns

Charts of the 1990 Triple Crown Races 167
Triple Crown Champions 172
Winners of Two Legs of the Triple Crown 175
Charts of the 1990 Breeders Crown Races 177
Breeders Crown Statistics &
  Leading Breeders Crown Drivers 181

Awards and Earnings

Beach Towel: 1990 Harness
  Horse of the Year 186
Previous Horse of the Year Winners 187
Divisional Winners in Horse of
  the Year Balloting 188
Previous Divisional Winners 192
Owners, Trainers, Drivers &
  Breeders of Horses of the Year 197
USTA Horse of the Month 200
Leading Single-Season
  Moneywinning Horses 201
Leading Moneywinning Horses, All-Time 202
Leading Moneywinning Horses,
  by Gait, 1890-1990 204
Average Earnings by Age 206
Leading Moneywinning Horses, 1990 207

INTRODUCTION

Dashes and Speed

History of the 2:00 Mile 210
Leading Dashwinning Horses in 1990 211
Leading Dashwinning Horses, 1946-90 213
Fastest Miles by Gait and Track Size 214
Ten Fastest Miles: Age, Sex and Gait 216
The Fastest Miles by Gait, 1990 218
The 1:58 Trotters of 1990 219
The 1:54 Pacers of 1990 222
1:55 Trotters and 1:52 Pacers, All-Time 227
Top Single-Season 2:00 Horses 231
Leading 2:00 Performers, 1990 and
 All-Time 232
Top 1:55 Performers, 1990 and All-Time .. 233
1990 Season's Champions 234

Leading Drivers

John Campbell 237
HTA Driver of the Year 238
Leading Dashwinning Drivers in 1990 241
Previous Leading Dashwinning Drivers 240
Leading Dashwinning Drivers, All-Time   240
Leading Moneywinning Drivers in 1990 245
Previous Leading Moneywinning Drivers   246
Leading Moneywinning Drivers, All-Time 247
Leading Drivers in 1990, The
 Universal Driver Rating System 250
Previous UDR Champions 251
Leading 2:00 Drivers, 1990 and All-Time   253
Leading 1:55 Drivers, 1990 and All-Time   254
Major Wins by Top Drivers 255
Leading Drivers, by Various Milestones 265
Leading Drivers at North
 American Tracks 266
The World Driving Championship 284
The World Cup of Amateur Driving 284

Breeding and Sales

Leading Moneywinning Sires 286
Leading Sires by Average Earnings 287
Leading Juvenile Sires 287
Leading First Crop Sires 288
Previous Leading Moneywinning Sires 289
Leading Moneywinning Sires, All-Time 289
Stud Fees of Leading Stallions 289
Sires of $100,000 Winners 290
Two-Minute Sires 291
Leading Stallions by State 292
Percentage Sires 293
"Early Speed" Sires 295
Broodmare Sires and Broodmares 296
Leading 2:00 Producing Broodmares 297
Leading Breeders in 1990 298
Results of Major Sales 300
Yearling Price Averages: 1952-1990 301
Top-Priced Yearlings of 1990 302
Leading Sires of $100,000
 Yearlings in 1990 303
Top-Priced Yearlings, 1944-1989 304
Record Prices for Horses sold at Auction   305
1991 Standardbred Sale Dates 306

Chronicles

Chronicles of Rich and Historic Events 308
The Major Races of 1990 - Chronological 359
The Richest Events of 1990 and All-Time 376
1990 European Grand Circuit Results 378
Chronicles of Discontinued Events 379

General Information

Members of the Hall of Fame 387
The Writers' Corner of the Hall of Fame   389
Members of the United States
 Harness Writers Association 390
Proximity Achievement Award Winners   394
The "Red Smith Caretaker
 of the Year" Award 394
John Hervey and Broadcasters Awards 395
Harness Racing Books and Periodicals 396
An Album of "Pop" Records 399
Fastest Performers by Age 402
Leading Double-Gaited Performers 402
USTA Services to the Media 403
Need to Know More? 404
Excerpts from the USTA Rule Book 405
Harness Racing Hotlines 419
A Handy List of Telephone Fax Numbers 420
Harness Racing Tack and Equipment 422

*New, revised, or expanded sections are
shown in* **boldface** *type*

INTRODUCTION

THE UNITED STATES TROTTING ASSOCIATION

The United States Trotting Association, now in its 52st year of operation, was created in 1939 to unify a fragmented Standardbred industry. Prior to that time, the American, National and United Trotting Associations governed harness racing in separate sections of the country, while the American Registry Association was responsible for maintaining the Standardbred Stud Book.

Francis X. Ready
Executive Vice-President

Corwin Nixon
President

Although its first offices were located in Goshen, New York, the USTA has been based in Columbus, Ohio since 1948. The USTA serves the entire United States and much of the Maritime provinces of Canada. The basic objectives of the USTA are:

1. **Establish and enforce the rules and regulations for the conduct of harness racing.**
2. **License owners, trainers, drivers, and officials.**
3. **Maintain racing information and records.**
4. **Serve as the registry for the Standardbred breed.**
5. **Promote the sport of harness racing.**

In addition, the USTA makes a substantial contribution to other segments of the Standardbred industry, such as donating funds for research on a variety of equine health questions, and sponsoring training seminars for racing officials. The USTA offices are open between the hours of 8:00 a.m. and 5:00 p.m. (eastern) every Monday through Friday, except holidays. For specific information, contact the individual below by calling: (614) 224-2291.

Department (Extention)	Contact	Department (Extention)	Contact
Executive V.P. (209)	Francis X. Ready	Membership (210)	Carol Van Bibber
Administrative (250)	John Gouch	Photo Lab (223)	Ed Keys
Blood Typing (247)	Harold Gerhardt	Program/Eligibility (206)	Al Buongiorne
Colors Registration (206)	Carla Kamberling	Publicity (226)	John Pawlak
Customer Services (249)	Ron Fabiano	Race Track System (249)	Ron Fabiano
Data Processing (242)	Larry Cordell	Officials (203)	Dennis Nolan
Driver Licencing (220)	Al Buongiorne	Registrar (205)	Robert Luehrman
Hoof Beats (226)	Dean Hoffman	Security (230)	Ken Brown
Hoof Beats Circulation (227)	Ardith Carlton	Stakes Guide (233)	Carol Cramer
Hoof Beats Adv. (254)	Richard Dakin	Track Department (203)	Dennis Nolan
Information/Research (239)	David Carr	Tattoo (280)	Sally Robinson
Legal (212)	Don Pontius	Treasury (207)	Dennis Fisher

INTRODUCTION

THE USTA BOARD OF DIRECTORS

There are about 43,000 members of the USTA who work and/or participate in harness racing. The USTA is located in Columbus, Ohio at 750 Michigan Avenue, 43215-1191. The telephone number, for all departments, is: (614) 224-2291. Facsimile (fax) service is also available; for Publicity, Information & Research, Data Processing, Customer Services, and *Hoof Beats* magazine, dial: (614) 228-1385. For all other departments, the fax number is: (614) 224-4575.

Officers

Corwin M. Nixon	President
Paul A. Fontaine	Chairman of the Board
Francis X. Ready	Exec. Vice-President
Frank O. White	Treasurer
Bonnie Kern	Secretary

Directors

District 1 - Ohio
Richard J. Buxton	Urbana (92)
Robert C. Sidley	Painsville (93)
Thomas M. Aldrich	Northfield (92)
Corwin M. Nixon	Lebanon (92)
Donald W. Hoovler	Pataskala (94)
Richard Brandt, Jr.	Logan (93)

District 2 - Indiana & Michigan
Kenneth E. Marshall	Livonia, MI (94)
Robert W. Huff	Durand, MI (92)
John L. Surbrook	Rives Junction, MI (94)
Jerry G.E. Landess	Portland, IN (93)
James A. Young	Jackson, MI (94)
John E. Schuberg	LaSalle, MI (93)

District 3 - AK, AZ, CA, CO, HI, ID, MT, NV, NM, OR, UT, WA, WY
Richard E. Crow	Carmichael, CA (93)
Charles H. Meyers	Escondido, CA (94)
Ivan L. Axelrod	Los Angeles, CA (92)

District 4 - At Large
James D. Coulter	New Sharon, IA (92)

Sub-District 4-A - AR, IA, KS, MO, NE, OK, TX
Kermit L. Hinshaw	Richland, IA (92)

Sub-District 4-B - MN, ND, SD, WI
James R. Laird	Appleton, WI (94)

District 5 - Illinois
John C. Cisna	Sherman (93)
W.H. Johnston, Jr.	Hinsdale (94)
F. Phillip Langley	Olympia Fields (94)
Kim P. Hankins	Bolingbrook (93)
Dr. Kenneth L. Walker	Maple Park (94)

District 6 - AL, FL, GA, KY, LA, MS, NC, SC, TN, WV
Charles W. Clark	Orlando, FL (92)
John A. Cashman, Jr.	Pompano Bch., FL (94)
Martha Brown	Lexington, KY (92)
Brooks Wells	Ashland, KY (94)

District 7 - Pennsylvania
George L. Beinhauer	Scenery Hill (92)
Hans G. Enggren	New Oxford (94)
John M. Swiatek	Meadow Lands (93)
Walter Dunn	Cochranton (93)

District 8 - Upstate New York
Richard Manzi	Smallwood (93)
Lon V. Frocione	Syracuse (92)
Creighton W. Brittell	Clifton Park (94)
Philip W. Tully	Monticello (94)
Frank O. White	Hamilton (93)
Barbara P. Samberg	Batavia (93)

District 8-A - Metro New York City
Joseph A. Faraldo	Kew Gardens (92)
Douglas J. Warren	New York (94)
Robert J. Galterio	Yonkers (94)
Michael Santa Maria	Westbury (93)
Arthur J. Rooney, Jr.	Pittsburgh, PA (93)

District 9 - CT, ME, MA, NH, RI, VT
Bert M. Fernald	West Poland, ME (92)
Paul A. Fontaine	Woonsocket, RI (94)
Wallace H. Tefft	Epping, NH (93)
Joseph J. Ricci	Falmouth, ME (92)

District 10 - Maritime Canada
Frank G. Daniels	Truro, NS (92)
Norman L. Reeves	Summerside, PEI (94)

District 11 - DE, DC, MD, VA
Dale Massey	Berlin, MD (92)
H.W.G. "Grady" Speers	Churchland, VA (94)

District 12 - New Jersey
Anthony T. Abbatiello	Colts Neck (94)
Sam Anzalone	East Rutherford (94)
Alan J. Leavitt	Bedminster (92)
Ronald S. Dancer	New Egypt (92)

Tracks

TRACKS

DIRECTORY OF TRACKS IN THE TRACK ROSTER SECTION

Track	(Phone)	Page
Arlington at Maywood	(708) 343-4800	21
Assiniboia Downs	(204) 885-3330	8
Associates at Maywood	(708) 343-4800	21
Atlantic City at Freehold	(201) 462-3800	15
Avalon Raceway	(709) 745-6822	8
Balmoral Park	(708) 568-5700	9
Bangor Raceway	(207) 947-3313	9
Barrie Raceway	(705) 726-9400	37
Batavia Downs	(716) 343-3750	10
Hipp. Blue Bonnets	(514) 739-2741	10
Buffalo Raceway	(716) 649-1280	11
Calgary Stampede Park	(403) 261-0214	33
Charlottetown Dr. Park	(902) 892-6823	11
Chicago Downs	(708) 242-1121	32
Clinton Raceway	(519) 482-7729	37
Cloverdale Raceway	(604) 576-9141	37
Hipp. Connaught	(819) 771-6111	12
Delaware Cty. Fair	(614) 363-6000	42
Delmarva Downs	(301) 641-0600	12
Dover Downs	(302) 674-4600	13
Dresden Raceway	(519) 683-4466	37
Du Quoin State Fair	(618) 542-3000	42
Edmonton Northlands	(403) 471-7379	25
Egyptian at Maywood	(708) 343-4800	21
Elmira Raceway	(519) 669-8036	38
Exhibition Park	(506) 633-2020	13
Fairmount Park	(618) 345-4300	14
Flamboro Downs	(416) 627-3561	14
Fredericton	(506) 458-8819	15
Freehold Raceway	(201) 462-3800	15
Garden State Park	(609) 488-8400	16
Goderich Raceway	(519) 524-2431	38
Goshen	(914) 294-5333	43
Greenwood Raceway	(416) 698-3131	16
Hanover Raceway	(519) 364-2860	38
Harrington Raceway	(302) 398-3269	17
Hawthorne	(708) 780-3700	17
Hazel Park Harness	(313) 398-1000	18
Historic Track	(914) 294-5333	43
Indiana State Fair	(317) 927-7589	43
Inverness Raceway	(902) 258-2648	38
Jackson at Northville	(313) 349-1000	25
Jackson Raceway	(517) 788-4500	18
Kawartha Downs	(705) 939-6316	19
Kingston Pk. Raceway	(613) 549-2314	39
Ladbroke @ Meadows	(412) 225-9300	22
Leamington Raceway	(519) 326-1885	39
Lebanon Raceway	(513) 932-4936	19
Los Alamitos	(714) 995-1234	20
Louisville Downs	(502) 964-6415	20
Maywood Park	(708) 343-4800	21
The Meadowlands	(201) 935-8500	21
The Meadows	(412) 225-9300	22
Miami Valley	(513) 932-4936	19
Mid-Am. Racing Assn.	(614) 491-2515	31
Mohawk Raceway	(416) 854-2255	22
Monticello Raceway	(914) 794-4100	23
Muskegon Racecourse	(616) 798-7123	23
New Brunswick Downs	(506) 857-9600	24
Northfield Park	(216) 467-4101	24
Northlands Park	(403) 471-7379	25
Northville Downs	(313) 349-1000	25
Orangeville Raceway	(519) 941-6961	39
Pocono Downs	(717) 825-6681	26
Pompano Park	(305) 972-2000	26
Quad City Downs	(309) 972-0202	27
Hippodrome de Quebec	(418) 524-5283	39
Queensbury Downs	(306) 527-2674	40
Quinte Raceway	(613) 968-3266	40
Raceway Park	(419) 476-7751	27
The Red Mile	(606) 255-0752	28
Rideau Carleton	(613) 822-2211	28
Riverside Downs	(502) 827-5641	29
Rosecroft Raceway	(301) 567-4000	29
Saginaw Harness Rcwy.	(517) 755-3451	30
Sandown Park	(604) 656-1631	40
Saratoga Raceway	(518) 584-2110	30
Scarborough Downs	(207) 883-4331	31
Scioto Downs	(614) 491-2515	31
Sports Creek Raceway	(313) 635-3333	32
Sportsman's Park	(708) 242-1121	32
Springfield, IL	(217) 782-2239	44
Stampede Park	(403) 261-0214	33
Suburban Downs	(708) 780-3700	17
Sudbury Downs	(705) 855-9001	40
Summerside Raceway	(902) 436-7221	33
Syracuse Mile	(315) 487-7711	44
Tartan Downs	(902) 564-8465	34
Toledo-Maumee	(419) 476-7751	27
Hipp. Trois Rivieres	(819) 374-6734	41
Truro Raceway	(902) 893-8075	34
Vernon Downs	(315) 829-2201	35
Western Fair Raceway	(519) 438-7203	35
Windsor Raceway	(519) 969-8311	36
Woodstock Raceway	(519) 537-8212	41
Yonkers Raceway	(914) 968-4200	37

TRACKS

Assiniboia Downs (AsD 13/16)

Track located in Winnipeg, Canada.

Address: 3975 Portage Avenue
Winnipeg, Manitoba R3K 2C7

Phone: (204) 885-3330
Results Hotline: (204) 831-0321
Fax Number: (204) 831-5348

Sponsored by: Race Track Management

Dates: January 1 - April 14
October 19 - December 29

Post Time: 7:00 p.m. each Wednesday, Friday and Saturday;
1:30 p.m. on Sundays and Holidays

Track Officials
President:	Robert H. Wright
Racing Secretary:	Darrell Stephansson
Publicity Director:	Sharon Gulyas

Track Facts
Track Opened:	1958
Speed Rating:	2:03 4/5
Length of Homestretch:	950'
Width of Homestretch:	80'
Starters Behind the Gate:	8
General Admission:	$2.50
Clubhouse Admission:	None
General Parking:	$1.00
Grandstand Capacity:	1,500
Clubhouse Capacity:	1,000
Parking Capacity:	1,200

1990 Attendance and Handle
Number of Race Programs:	89
Gross Handle:	$18,246,107
Gross Attendance:	118,476
Average Handle:	$205,012
Average Attendance:	1,331
Percapita Wagering:	$154.02

Record Business
Handle:	$307,049	April 21, 1985
Attendance:	3,647	November 11, 1981

Leading Drivers (Meets Combined)
Wins:	Doug Shaw (Win.)	56
	Doug Shaw (Fall)	38
UDR:	Roland Rey (Win.)	.433
	Roland Rey (Fall)	.372
Purses:	Doug Shaw (Win.)	$76,792
	Greg Manning (Fall)	$77,224

Leading Trainer
Wins:	Roland Rey ('89-'90)	60

Avalon Raceway (StJhn 1/2)

Track located in St. John's, Newfoundland.

Address: c/o Goulds Post Office
General Delivery
St. John's, Nfld A1C 5L4

Phone: (709) 745-6822

Sponsored by: St. John's Trotting Park

Dates: May 12 - October 27

Track Officials
President:	Denis P. Galway
General Manager:	Denis P. Galway
Race Secretary:	James Flynn
Publicity Director	William Driscoll

Track Facts
Track Opened:	1964
Speed Rating:	2:13 4/5
Starters Behind the Gate:	6
Length of Homestretch:	440'
Width of Homestretch:	65'
General Admission:	$1.00
Clubhouse Admission:	$1.00
General Parking:	Free
Grandstand Capacity:	500
Parking Capacity:	700

1990 Attendance and Handle
Number of Race Programs:	43
Gross Handle:	$779,772
Gross Attendance:	13,596
Average Handle:	$18,566
Average Attendance:	324
Percapita Wagering:	$57.35

Record Business
Handle:	$42,079	July 2, 1989
Attendance:	2,000	July, 1981

Leading Drivers
Wins:	Gary McDonald	44
UDR:	Gary McDonald	.393
Purses:	Gary McDonald	$8,965

Leading Trainer
Not Reported

TRACKS

Balmoral Park (BmlP 1 mile; 5/8)

Track located in Crete, Illinois along Rt. 394, the Calumet Expressway S., or Rt. 1, Dixie Highway, about 38 miles from Chicago's loop.

Address: Rte. 1 & Elms Court Lane
P.O. Box 159
Crete, Illinois 60417
Phone: (312) 568-5700 and
(708) 672-7544
Results "Hotline:" (708) 672-7544
Fax Number: (708) 672-5932
Sponsored by: Balmoral Racing Club, Inc. & Balmoral Park Trot, Inc.
Dates: January 1 - December 31
Post Time: 8 p.m.

Track Officials
President:	William H. Johnston, Jr.
General Manager:	John Johnston
Racing Secretary:	Ben Wessels
Publicity Director:	Jim Hannon

Track Facts
Track Opened:	1926
One Mile Track Added:	1989
Speed Ratings:	(mile) 1:59 1/5; (5/8) 2:00 3/5
Length of Stretch:	(mile) 1,360' - (5/8) 720'
Width of Homestretch (both):	80'
Starters Behind the Gate (both):	9
Hubrail (both)?:	Yes
General Admission:	Free
Clubhouse Admission:	$2.00
General Parking:	Free
CLubhouse Capacity:	2,000
Grandstand Capacity:	8,281
Parking Capacity:	15,000

1990 Attendance and Handle
Number of Race Programs:	99
Gross Handle:	$28,006,174
Gross Attendance:	221,680
Average Handle:	$282,891
Average Attendance:	2,239
Percapita Wagering:	$126.35

Record Business
Handle:	$1,724,234	February 4, 1990
Attendance:	Not Kept	

Leading Drivers
Wins:	Dan Knox (Win.)	49
	Jim Maxwell (Fall)	38
UDR:	Ernie Adam (Win.)	.449
	Doug Hamilton (Fall)	.352
Purses:	Dan Knox (Win.)	$214,873
	Jim Maxwell (Fall)	$130,121

Leading Trainer
Wins:	Ed Holdeman	52

Bangor Raceway (Bang 1/2)

Track located at Bangor, Maine at the corner of Main & Buck Streets. Interstate 95 To Front Entrance.

Address: 100 Dutton Street
Bangor, Maine 04401

Phone: (207) 947-3313

Sponsored by: Bangor Parks & Recreation Department

Dates: May 24 - July 26
October 11 - October 27

Track Officials
Chairperson:	Patricia Blanchette
General Manager:	Dale W. Theriault
Race Secretary:	Frank Hall, Jr.
Publicity Director:	Owen W. Butler

Track Facts
Track Opened:	1849
Speed Rating:	2:05
Starters Behind the Gate:	8
General Admission:	$1.00
Clubhouse Admission:	$1.00
General Parking:	Free
Grandstand Capacity:	3,750
Clubhouse Capacity:	100
Parking Capacity:	3,000+

1990 Attendance and Handle
Number of Race Programs:	44
Gross Handle:	$3,380,651
Gross Attendance:	(est.) 47,494
Average Handle:	$80,492
Average Attendance:	1,131
Percapita Wagering:	$71.16

Record Business
Handle:	$143,547	July 16, 1989
Attendance:	8,950	July 28, 1984

Leading Drivers
Wins:	Gary Hall	68
UDR:	Bob Sumner	.419
Purses:	Gary Hall	$51,873

Leading Trainer
Not Reported

TRACKS

Batavia Downs (Btva 1/2)

Track located west of city limits of Batavia, New York on Route 5, and 1/2-mile from New York State Thruway Exit 48; 25 miles from Buffalo and Rochester.

Address: 8315 Park Road
Batavia, NY 14020
Phone: (716) 343-3750
Fax Number: (716) 343-7773

Sponsored by: Genesee-Monroe Racing Association

Dates: February 28 - April 20
July 31 - November 30
Post Times: 7:30 - Sundays 1:30 p.m. - Mondays 4:15 p.m.

Track Officials
President:	Barbara P. Samberg
C.O.B & Exec. V.P.:	Donna P. Warner
Race Secretary:	Peter Koch
Publicity Director:	Mike McDonald

Track Facts
Track Opened:	September 20, 1940
Speed Rating:	2:02 3/5
Length of Homestretch:	500'
Width of Homestretch:	66'
Starters Behind the Gate:	8
Hubrail?:	No
General Admission:	$2.00
Clubhouse Admission:	$1.00
General Parking:	$1.00
Grandstand Capacity:	9,000
Clubhouse Capacity:	600
Parking Capacity:	5,000

1990 Attendance and Handle
Number of Race Programs:	133
Gross Handle:	$19,562,305
Gross Attendance:	202,825
Average Handle:	$147,085
Average Attendance:	1,525
Percapita Wagering:	$96.45

Record Business
Handle:	$625,399	December 2, 1967
Attendance:	15,228	August 26, 1966

Leading Drivers
Wins:	Rod Laframboise (Win.)	53
	Sam Schillaci (Fall)	80
UDR:	Bob Bompczyk (Win.)	.443
	Tom Agosti (Fall)	.361
Purses:	R. Laframboise (Win.)	$81,125
	Tom Swift (Fall)	$145,577

Leading Trainer (Meets Combined)
Wins:	Brenda Ohol	28

Hippodrome Blue Bonnets (BB 5/8)

Track located in Montreal, Quebec. Easy access by public transport.

Address: 7440 Decarie Boulevard
Montreal, Quebec H4P 2H1

Phone: (514) 739-2741
Results Hotline: (514) 340-2018/2026
Fax Number: (514) 340-2025

Sponsored by: Hippodrome Blue Bonnets, Incorporated

Dates: January 4 - December 30

Post Time: 7:30 p.m.; Sundays 1:30 p.m.

Track Officials
President:	Andre Marier
General Manager:	Andre Marier
Director of Racing:	Jean Dube
Race Secretary:	Yvon Giguere
Publicity Director:	Rene Tessier

Track Facts
Track Opened:	1907
Speed Rating:	2:01 3/5
Length of Homestretch:	690'-2"
Width of Homestretch:	85'
Starters Behind the Gate:	9
Hubrail?:	Yes
General Admission:	$3.25
Clubhouse Admission:	$4.50
General Parking:	$2.00
Grandstand Capacity:	30,000
Clubhouse Capacity:	5,000
Parking Capacity:	7,000

1990 Attendance and Handle
Number of Race Programs:	253
Gross Handle:	$238,512,429
Gross Attendance:	1,228,628
Average Handle:	$942,737
Average Attendance:	4,856
Percapita Wagering:	$194.13

Record Business
Handle:	$1,983,176	August 20, 1989
Attendance:	41,578	July 1, 1970

Leading Drivers
Wins:	Rick Zeron	368
UDR:	Rick Zeron	.375
Purses:	Rick Zeron	$1,941,021

Leading Trainer
Wins	Robert MacKenzie	269

TRACKS

Buffalo Raceway (BR 1/2)

Track located in Hamburg, New York on McKinley Parkway, 12 miles south of Buffalo, four miles east of Lake Erie, Just off U.S. Route 20 or Exit 56 or 57 of the New York State Thruway, between Buffalo and Erie.

Address: P.O. Box 38
5600 McKinley Parkway
Hamburg, New York 14075

Phone: (716) 649-1280
Fax Number: (716) 649-0033
Sponsored by: Erie County Agricultural Soc.
Dates: January 2 - February 24
April 24 - July 28
December 4 - December 31

Track Officials
President:	Frank Newton
General Manager:	Bruce Munn
Race Secretary:	Peter Koch
Publicity Director:	Darrell Wood
Pub. Consultant:	Chuck Burr

Track Facts
Track Opened:	1942
Speed Rating:	2:02 3/5
Length of Homestretch:	640'
Width of Homestretch:	80'
Hubrail?:	Yes
Starters Behind the Gate:	8
General Admission:	$2.00
Clubhouse Admission:	$3.00
General Parking:	$.75
Grandstand Capacity:	6,000
CLubhouse Capacity:	700
Parking Capacity:	3,000

1990 Attendance and Handle
Number of Race Programs:	128
Gross Handle:	$23,315,222
Gross Attendance:	226,217
Average Handle:	$182,150
Average Attendance:	1,767
Percapita Wagering:	$103.08

Record Business
Handle:	$602,821	July 8, 1972
Attendance:	12,799	July 15, 1966

Leading Drivers
Wins:	Rod Laframboise (Win.)	46
	Rod Laframboise (Sum.)	77
UDR:	Tom Agosti (Win.)	.383
	Gerry Sarama (Sum.)	.314
Purses:	R. Laframboise (Win.)	$75,290
	Patsy Rapone (Sum.)	$245,905

Leading Trainer
Wins:	Bob Johnson (Sum.)	25
	Tom Agosti (Win.)	13

Charlottetown Driving Pk. (Chrtn 1/2)

Track located in Charlottetown, Prince Edward Island.

Address: P.O. Box 308
Kensington Road
Charlottetown, P.E.I. C1A 7K7

Phone: (902) 892-6823
Results "Hotline": (902) 566-4408
Fax Number: (902) 368-8856

Sponsored by: Charlottetown Driving Pk. and Provincial Exhibition Association

Dates: January 1 - December 28

Post Times: 7:30 p.m. - Matinees 1:30 p.m.

Track Officials
President:	Dr. Erwin Howatt
General Manager:	Jack Hynes
Race Secretary:	John "Buddy" Campbell
Publicity Director:	Kevin "Boomer" Gallant

Track Facts
Track Opened:	December, 1889
Speed Rating:	2:07 4/5
Length of Homestretch:	625'
Width of Homestretch:	60'
Starters Behind the Gate:	7
Hubrail?:	No
General Admission:	$2.00
Clubhouse Admission:	$1.00
General Parking:	Free
Grandstand Capacity:	1,500
Clubhouse Capacity:	550
Parking Capacity:	4,500

1990 Attendance and Handle
Number of Race Programs:	113
Gross Handle:	$6,083,677
Gross Attendance:	70,426
Average Handle:	$53,838
Average Attendance:	623
Percapita Wagering:	$86.38

Record Business
Handle:	$302,429	August 19, 1989
Attendance:	17,600	August 18, 1990

Leading Drivers
Wins:	Paul MacDonald	86
UDR:	Joe Smallwood	.450
Purses:	Paul MacDonald	$49,224

Leading Trainer
Not Kept

TRACKS

Hippodrome Connaught (Conn 1/2)

Track located in Aylmer, Quebec, five miles from downtown Ottawa, Ontario.

Address: P.O. Box 37
Ayhlmer, Quebec J9H 5E4

Phone: (819) 771-6111, or
(819) 770-7044
Fax Number: (819) 778-1708

Sponsored by: Hippodrome Connaught

Dates: January 1 - June 30
December 1 - December 29

Post Time: 7:30 p.m.; 1:30 weekends

Track Officials
President:	Joseph Gorman
General Manager:	Joseph Gorman
Race Secretary:	Caroline Mace
Publicity Director:	Don DuJay

Track Facts
Track Opened:	April 1912
Speed Rating:	2:04 3/5
Starters Behind the Gate:	9
Length of Homestretch:	700'
Width of Homestretch:	100'
General Admission:	$2.50
Clubhouse Admission:	$2.50
General Parking:	$3.00
Grandstand Capacity:	4,000
Parking Capacity:	5,000

1990 Attendance and Handle
Number of Race Programs:	116
Gross Handle:	$20,424,926
Gross Attendance:	144,144
Average Handle:	$176,007
Average Attendance:	1,243
Percapita Wagering:	$141.70

Record Business
Handle:	$350,000	May 24, 1982
Attendance:	4,870	July 9, 1970

Leading Drivers
Wins:	Gilles Plourde	138
UDR:	Gilles Plourde	.380
Purses:	Gilles Plourde	$227,884

Leading Trainer
Wins:	Bob O'Dwyer	NR

Delmarva Downs (DMV 1/2)

Track located four miles west of Ocean City, Maryland, on Route 50.

Address: Routes 50 & 589
P.O. Box 11
Berlin, Maryland 21811

Phone: (301) 641-0600
Results "Hotline:" (301) 567-5800
Fax Number: (301) 641-2711

Dates: May 24 - September 2

Post Time: 7:20 p.m.; Sundays at 6:20 p.m.

Track Officials
Trustee:	James J. Murphy
Race Secretary:	Rick Bonekemper
Publicity Director:	TBA

Track Facts
Track Opened:	1949
Speed Rating:	2:02 3/5
Length of Homestretch:	(est.) 440'
Width of Homestretch:	(est.) 70'
Starters Behind the Gate:	8
Hubrail?:	No
General Admission:	$2.00
Clubhouse Admission:	$3.00
General Parking:	$1.00
Grandstand Capacity:	4,650
Clubhouse Capacity:	350
Parking Capacity:	5,000

1990 Attendance and Handle
Number of Race Programs:	72
Gross Handle:	$16,233,954
Gross Attendance:	149,621
Average Handle:	$225,472
Average Attendance:	2,078
Percapita Wagering:	$108.50

Record Business
Handle:	$342,159	July 7, 1990
Attendance:	9,975	August 17, 1953

Leading Drivers
Wins:	Bill Long	89
UDR:	Walter Callahan	.347
Purses:	Bill Long	$142,776

Leading Trainer
Wins:	D.W. Camac	25

TRACKS

Dover Downs (DD 5/8)

Track located within city limits of Dover, Delaware, on east side of Route 13 (DuPont Highway).

Address: P.O. Box 843
1131 N. DuPont Highway (19901)
Dover, Delaware 19901

Phone: (302) 674-4600
Results "Hotline:" (302) 678-3212
Fax Number: (302) 734-3124

Sponsored by: Dover Downs, Inc.

Dates: January 1 - March 23
November 17 - December 31
Post Time: 7:30 p.m.; Sundays 1 p.m.

Track Officials
President:	Denis McGlynn
General Manager:	Jerry Dunning
Race Secretary:	Herman Brickel
Publicity Director:	Al Robinson

Track Facts
Track Opened:	November 10, 1969
Speed Rating:	2:01 4/5
Length of Homestretch:	500'
Width of Homestretch:	60'
Starters Behind the Gate:	8
Hubrail?:	Yes
General Admission:	$2.00
Clubhouse Admission:	$3.00
General Parking:	$.50
Grandstand Capacity:	4,200
Clubhouse Capacity:	500
Parking Capacity:	12,000

1990 Attendance and Handle
Number of Race Programs:	100
Gross Handle:	$11,789,072
Gross Attendance:	121,690
Average Handle:	$117,891
Average Attendance:	1,217
Percapita Wagering:	$96.87

Record Business
Handle:	$515,177	February 4, 1973
Attendance:	5,971	February 4, 1973

Leading Drivers
Wins:	Jim Dennis (Win.)	77
	Bret Brittingham (Fall)	17
UDR:	John Littleton, Jr. (Win.)	.443
	Eddie Davis (Fall)	.391
Purses:	Jim Dennis (Win.)	$73,203
	Jim Dennis (Fall)	$12,532

Leading Trainer
Wins:	Ty Case III ('89-'90)	30

Exhibition Park (EPR 1/2)

Track located in Saint John, New Brunswick.

Address: McAllister Drive
P.O. Box 284
Saint John, New Brunswick E2L 3Y2

Phone: (506) 633-2020
Results "Hotlines:" (506) 633-2054 or 2056
Fax Number: (506) 633-0802

Sponsored by: Exhibition Association of the City and County of Saint John.
Dates: January 1 - December 28

Post Time: Wednesdays 7:30, Sundays 1:30

Track Officials
President:	Milton Downey
Director of Racing:	Willard Jenkins
Racing Secretary:	James Mason
Publicity Director:	Ingham Palmer

Track Facts
Track Opened:	1910
Speed Rating:	2:05
Length of Homestretch:	N/A
Width of Homestretch:	75'
Starters Behind the Gate:	8
Hubrail?:	Yes
General Admission:	$2.00
Clubhouse Admission:	$2.00
Sulky Room Lounge:	$5.00 add'l
General Parking:	Free
Grandstand Capacity:	3,200
Clubhouse Capacity:	430
Parking Capacity:	3,500

1990 Attendance and Handle
Number of Race Programs:	103
Gross Handle:	$5,621,968
Gross Attendance:	59,637
Average Handle:	$54,582
Average Attendance:	579
Percapita Wagering:	$94.27

Record Business
Handle:	$217,977	August 29, 1980
Attendance:	5,500	September 2, 1983

Leading Drivers
Wins:	Steve Mahar	158
UDR:	Dan O'Brian	.404
Purses:	Steve Mahar	$131,167

Leading Trainer
Wins:	Steve Mahar	92

TRACKS

Fairmount Park (FP 1)

Track located on Interstate 70 & U.S. 40, ten miles east of St. Louis, Missouri, at Collinsville, Illinois.

Address: Route 40
Collinsville, Illinois 62234

Phone: (618) 345-4300
(314) 436-1516 (in Missouri)
Fax Number: (618) 344-8218

Sponsored by: Ogden-Fairmount, Inc.

Dates: January 1 - April 7
December 5 - December 31

Post Time: 7:30 p.m.; Tuesdays 1:30 p.m.

Track Officials
President:	John K. MacAniff
General Manager:	Brian Zander
Race Secretary:	Ozzie Cole
Publicity:	Mary Ozanic

Track Facts
Track Opened:	1925
First Harness Meet:	November, 1966
Speed Rating:	2:01 3/5
Length of Homestretch:	1,050'
Width of Homestretch:	80'
Starters Behind the Gate:	9
Hubrail?:	Yes
General Admission:	$2.00
Clubhouse Admission:	$3.00
General Parking:	$1.00
Grandstand Capacity:	2,400
Clubhouse Capacity:	1,000
Parking Capacity:	4,200

1990 Attendance and Handle
Number of Race Programs:	78
Gross Handle:	$23,405,657
Gross Attendance:	152,676
Average Handle:	$339,212
Average Attendance:	1,957
Percapita Wagering:	$173.33

Record Business
Handle:	$808,202	March 2, 1985
Attendance:	6,727	March 2, 1985

Leading Drivers
Wins:	Dean Magee (Win.)	65
	Dean Magee (Fall)	47
UDR:	John Reese (Win.)	.322
	Chris Loney (Fall)	.359
Purses:	Dean Magee (Win.)	$223,753
	Dean Magee (Fall)	$137,985

Leading Trainer
Wins:	Roy Saul ('89-'90)	51

Flamboro Downs (FlmD 1/2)

Track located ten miles north of Hamilton on Highway 5, 42 miles west of Toronto on QEW. Exit #6 Highway to #5 Highway west. Special buses from Toronto and Hamilton.

Address: P.O. Box 8220
967 Highway 5
Dundas, Ontario L9H 5G1

Phone: (416) 627-3561
Results "Hotline:" (416) 525-2426
Fax Number: (416) 627-3561

Sponsored by: Flamboro Downs Holdings
Dates: January 1 - December 30
Post Time: 7:30 p.m., August 25 1:30 p.m.

Track Officials
President:	Charles Juravinski
General Manager:	Richard Jacob
Race Secretary:	Neil McCoag
Marketing:	Gary Holloway
Publicity:	Ken Hornick

Track Facts
Track Opened:	April 9, 1975
Speed Rating:	2:03 4/5
Starters Behind The Gate:	8
Length of Stretch:	600'
Width of Homestretch:	80'
Hubrail?:	No
General Admission:	$3.25
Clubhouse Admission:	$5.50
General Parking:	$2.50
Grandstand Capacity:	7,000
Clubhouse Capacity:	400
Parking Capacity:	5,000

1990 Attendance and Handle
Number of Race Programs:	215
Gross Handle:	$47,617,970
Gross Attendance:	380,967
Average Handle:	$221,479
Average Attendance:	1,772
Percapita Wagering:	$124.99

Record Business
Handle:	$787,946	August 28, 1989
Attendance:	8,282	August 28, 1988

Leading Drivers
Wins:	Callie Rankin	216
UDR:	Callie Rankin	.344
Purses:	Callie Rankin	$533,395

Leading Trainer
Wins:	Terry Grant	139

TRACKS

Fredericton Raceway (Frdtn 1/2)

Track located in Fredericton, New Brunswick.

Address: P.O. Box 235, Station "A"
Smythe & Saunders Streets
Fredericton, New Brunswick E3B 4Y9

Phone: (506) 458-8819
Fax Number: (506) 458-9294

Sponsored by: Fredericton Exhibition, Ltd.

Dates: March 30 - December 31
Racing Mondays and Thursdays
Post Time: 7:30 p.m.; 1:30 p.m. Holidays & Weekends

Track Officials
President:	Murray Wilson
General Manager:	Brian Embleton
Race Secretary:	Brian Embleton
Promotions Director:	Dianne Quigg

Track Facts
Track Opened:	1887
Speed Rating:	2:07 1/5
Starters Behind the Gate:	6
Length of Homestretch:	660'
Width of Homestretch:	100'
Hubrail?:	Yes
General Admission:	$2.00
Clubhouse Admission:	Free
General Parking:	Free
Grandstand Capacity:	2,500
Clubhouse Capacity:	500
Parking Capacity:	2,000

1990 Attendance and Handle
Number of Race Programs:	34
Gross Handle:	$1,403,918
Gross Attendance:	17,422
Average Handle:	$41,292
Average Attendance:	512
Percapita Wagering:	$80.58

Record Business
Handle:	$73,986	Not Recorded
Attendance:	1,550	Not Recorded

Leading Drivers
Wins:	Steve Mahar	63
UDR:	Steve Mahar	.383
Purses:	Steve Mahar	$51,518

Leading Trainer
Wins:	Drew Campbell	40

Freehold Raceway (Fhld 1/2)

Track located at outskirts of Freehold NJ, at intersection of Rt. 33 & 9. Track 15 miles from Asbury Park; 10 miles from Hightstown, Exit 8 on NJ Turnpike; 35 miles south of NY City via Jersey Turnpike.

Address: P.O. Box 111
Routes 9 and 33
Freehold, New Jersey 07728

Phone: (201) 462-3800
Results "Hotline:" (900) 740-5555
Fax Number: (201) 462-3807
Dates: January 1 - May 27
August 16 - December 31
Post Time: 1 p.m., Dark Mondays

Track Officials
President:	Kenneth R. Fischer
General Manager:	Ed Ryan
Race Secretary:	Frank Ferone
Publicity Director:	Steven Wolf

Track Facts
Date Track Opened:	1853
Re-opened After 1984 Fire:	1986
Speed Rating:	2:02
Length of Stretch:	480'
Width of Homestretch:	80'
Starters Behind the Gate:	8
Hubrail?:	No
General Admission:	$2.00
General Parking:	$1.00
Grandstand Capacity:	1,000
Clubhouse Capacity:	1,000
Parking Capacity:	2,800

1990 Attendance and Handle
Number of Race Programs:	235
Gross Handle:	$82,623,226
Gross Attendance:	523,140
Average Handle:	$531,588
Average Attendance:	2,226
Percapita Wagering:	$157.95

Record Business
Handle:	$1,311,929	October 22, 1988
Attendance:	15,747	August 28, 1973

Leading Drivers
Wins:	Cat Manzi (Spr.)	199
	Jack Moiseyev (Sum.)	160
UDR:	Cat Manzi (Spr.)	.339
	Jack Moiseyev (Sum.)	.334
Purses:	Cat Manzi (Spr.)	$796,875
	Herve Filion (Sum.)	$889,685

Leading Trainers
Wins:	Jeff LaPoff (Comb.)	121

TRACKS

Garden State Park (GSP 1)

Track located six miles from downtown Philadelphia, Pennsylvania at the intersection of St. Route 70 and Haddonfield Road

Address: Route 70 & Haddonfield Road
Cherry Hill, New Jersey 08034-0649

Phone: (609) 488-8400
Results "Hotline:" (900) 786-8880
Fax Number: (609) 488-3776

Dates: September 4 - December 7

Post Time: 7:30 p.m.

Track Officials
President:	Robert J. Quigley
Racing Secretary:	Joe DeFrank
Publicity Director:	Bill Fidati

Track Facts
First Harness Race:	September 1, 1985
Speed Rating:	1:59 2/5
Length of Homestretch:	960'
Width of Homestretch:	80'
Starters Behind the Gate:	10
Hubrail?:	Yes
General Admission:	$2.00
Clubhouse Admission:	$3.00
General Parking:	$1.00
Grandstand Capacity:	19,000
Clubhouse Capacity:	7,000
Parking Capacity:	11,000

1990 Attendance and Handle
Number of Race Programs:	76
Gross Handle:	$24,802,596
Gross Attendance:	277,031
Average Handle:	$326,350
Average Attendance:	3,645
Percapita Wagering:	$89.53

Record Business
Handle:	$1,616,560	November 29, 1985
Attendance:	21,326	November 14, 1986

Leading Drivers
Wins:	Jack Moiseyev	116
UDR:	Jack Moiseyev	.336
Purses:	John Campbell	$813,225

Leading Trainer
Wins:	Rosemary Smutz	28

Greenwood Raceway (GrR 5/8)

Track situated in Toronto on an 80-acre tract on the banks of Lake Ontario. ten minutes from downtown Toronto.

Address: 1669 Queen Street, East
Toronto, Ontario M4L 1G5

Phone: (416) 698-3131
Fax Number: (416) 698-1230

Sponsored by: The Ontario Jockey Club

Dates: January 1 - March 16
May 27 - August 31
December 6 - December 31
Post Times: 7:30 p.m.; Fridays 5 p.m. (Win.)
Saturday & Sunday 1:30 p.m. (Winter)

Track Officials
President:	J. H. Kenney
Race Secretary:	Barry Hewson
Publicity Director:	Kathy Wade

Track Facts
Track Opened:	1874 (1954 Modern)
Speed Rating:	2:01 3/5
Length of Homestretch:	746'
Width of Homestretch:	80'
Starters Behind the Gate:	8
Hubrail?:	Yes
General Admission:	$3.25
Clubhouse Admission:	$7.00
General Parking:	$3.00
Grandstand Capacity:	12,000
Clubhouse Capacity:	6,000
Parking Capacity:	5,000

1990 Attendance and Handle
Number of Race Programs:	145
Gross Handle:	$246,174,987
Gross Attendance:	1,038,632
Average Handle:	$1,697,759
Average Attendance:	7,163
Percapita Wagering:	$237.02

Record Business
Handle:	$3,279,802	August 12, 1990
Attendance:	18,389	August 12, 1972

Leading Drivers
Wins:	Doug Brown (Comb.)	197
UDR:	Tony Kerwood (Win.)	.323
	Tony Kerwood (Sum.)	.346
	John Holmes (Fall)	.407
Purses:	D. Brown (Comb.)	$2,571,179

Leading Trainer
Wins:	Bill Robinson	44

TRACKS

Harrington Raceway (Har 1/2)

Track located one mile south of Harrington, Delaware on U.S. Route 13, 60 miles south of Wilmington Delaware.

Address: U.S. Rte. 13
P.O. Box 28
Harrington, Delaware 19952

Phone: (302) 398-3269
Results "Hotline:" (302) 398-5038
Fax Number: (302) 398-5030

Sponsored by: Harrington Raceway, Inc.

Dates: March 24 - May 19
September 5 - November 16
Post Times: 7:30 p.m.; Sundays 6:30 p.m.

Track Officials
President:	Thurman Adams, Jr.
General Manager:	F. Gary Simpson
Race Secretary:	Barney Breslow
Publicity Director:	Dennis Hazzard

Track Facts
Track Opened:	August 15, 1946
Speed Rating:	2:03 4/5
Length of Homestretch:	213'
Width of Homestretch:	100'
Starters Behind the Gate:	8
Hubrail?:	No
General Admission:	$2.00
Clubhouse Admission:	Free
General Parking:	$.50
Grandstand Capacity:	4,500
Clubhouse Capacity:	400
Parking Capacity:	1,200

1990 Attendance and Handle
Number of Race Programs:	41
Gross Handle:	$3,782,964
Gross Attendance:	40,496
Average Handle:	$92,267
Average Attendance:	988
Percapita Wagering:	$93.39

Record Business
Handle:	$241,766	September 29, 1974
Attendance:	4,077	September 29, 1974

Leading Drivers
Wins:	Jim Dennis	48
UDR:	Ray Robinson, Jr.	.356
Purses:	Jim Dennis	$42,328

Leading Trainer
Wins:	Don Brittingham & Russell Thomas, Jr.	NR

Hawthorne Racecourse (Haw 1)

Track located in Cicero, Illinois, eight miles from Chicago.

Address: 3501 South Laramie Avenue
Cicero, Illinois 60650

Phone: (708) 780-3700
Results "Hotline:" (708) 976-8200

Sponsored by: Suburban Downs, Inc.

Dates: January 1 - February 18

Post Time: 1:00 p.m. matinees
8:00 p.m. evenings

Track Officials
President:	Thomas F. Carey
General Manager:	Beulah G. Dygert
Race Secretary:	Robert Larry
Publicity Director:	Phil Georgeff

Track Facts
Track Opened:	1891
First Harness Race:	1969
Speed Rating:	2:01 3/5
Length of Homestretch:	1,340'
Width of Homestretch:	60'
Starters Behind the Gate:	9
Hubrail?:	Yes
General Admission:	$1.50
Clubhouse Admission:	$3.25
General Parking:	$1.50
Grandstand Capacity:	8,000
Clubhouse Capacity:	5,000
Parking Capacity:	10,000

1990 Attendance and Handle
Number of Race Programs:	66
Gross Handle:	$37,301,631
Gross Attendance:	227,752
Average Handle:	$565,176
Average Attendance:	3,451
Percapita Wagering:	$163.77

Record Business
Handle:	$2,430,466	February 17, 1985
Attendance:	17,758	1982

Leading Drivers
Wins:	Walter Paisley	87
UDR:	Walter Paisley	.404
Purses:	Walter Paisley	$652,689

Leading Trainer
Not Reported

TRACKS

Hazel Park Harness (HP 5/8)

Track located on Ten Mile Rd., two miles east of Woodward (U.S. 10) intersection, and one mile east of I-75. 12 miles due north from center of Detroit on I-75.

Address: 1650 East Ten Mile Road
Hazel Park, Michigan 48030

Phone: (313) 398-1000
Results "Hotline:" (313) 546-0155
Fax Number: (313) 398-5236

Sponsored by: Hazel Pk. Harness Raceway

Dates: April 3 - October 12

Post Time: 7:30 p.m., Dark Sundays

Track Officials
President:	Herbert Tyner
Operations Director:	Michael J. Collins
Race Secretary:	Ken Marshall, Jr.
Publicity Director:	Gordon Waterstone

Track Facts
Track Opened:	1953
Speed Rating:	2:03
Length of Homestretch:	615'
Width of Homestretch:	80'
Starters Behind the Gate:	9
Hubrail?:	Yes
General Admission:	$2.50
Clubhouse Admission:	$3.50
General Parking:	$1.50
Grandstand Capacity:	9,200
Clubhouse Capacity:	3,000
Parking Capacity:	8,000

1990 Attendance and Handle
Number of Race Programs:	168
Gross Handle:	$129,522,215
Gross Attendance:	721,122
Average Handle:	$770,966
Average Attendance:	4,292
Percapita Wagering:	$179.63

Record Business
Handle:	$1,425,478	July 12, 1975
Attendance:	15,372	July 12, 1975

Leading Drivers
Wins:	Peter Wrenn	159
UDR:	Kevin Wallis	.458
Purses:	Peter Wrenn	$772,931

Leading Trainer
Wins:	Mike Gorshe	98

Jackson Harness Raceway (Jack 1/2)

Track located Jackson County Fairgrounds five blocks north of downtown Jackson

Address: 200 W. Ganson St. (49201)
P.O. Box 881
Jackson, Michigan 49201

Phone: Jackson (517) 788-4500
Results "Hotline:" (517) 783-3783
Fax Number: (517) 788-6772

Dates: April 3 - June 23
August 21 - October 12
Jackson at Northville Oct. 14 - Dec. 31

Post Time: 7:30 p.m.; 3 p.m. Sundays
At Northville 7:30 p.m.

Track Officials
President:	Nanette Slavin
General Manager:	James A. "Chic" Young
Director of Racing:	E. Ann Butt
Publicity Director:	Jill Bohne'

Track Facts
Track Opened:	1948
Speed Rating:	2:04 4/5
Length of Homestretch:	600'
Width of Homestretch:	50'
Starters Behind the Gate:	6
General Admission:	$2.00
General Parking:	$1.00
Grandstand Capacity:	6,500
Dining Room Capacity:	250
Parking Capacity:	1,000

1990 Attendance and Handle (at Jackson)
Number of Race Programs:	73
Gross Handle:	$13,562,913
Gross Attendance:	107,788
Average Handle:	$185,793
Average Attendance:	1,477
Percapita Wagering:	$125.83

Record Business
Handle:	$346,557	May 18, 1986
Attendance:	6,812	August 16, 1975

Leading Drivers
Wins:	Terry Buter (Spr.)	83
	Terry Buter (Fall)	.41
UDR:	Jeff Stimer (Spr.)	.417
	Jim Jones	.394
Purses:	Terry Buter (Spr.)	$82,386
	Peter Wrenn (Fall)	$55,527

Leading Trainers (Jackson)
Not Reported

TRACKS

Kawartha Downs (KD 5/8)

Track located on Highway 28 at Highway 115, Peterborough, Ontario.

Address: General Delivery
Fraserville, Ontario K0L 1V0

Phone: (705) 939-6316
Fax Number: (705) 939-6342

Sponsored by: Kawartha Downs, Ltd.

Dates: May 4 - November 30

Post Time: 7:30 p.m.

Track Officials
President:	Harvey Ambrose
General Manager:	Grant C. Wade
Race Secretary:	Grant C. Wade
Publicity:	Grant C. Wade

Track Facts
Track Opened:	July 22, 1972
Speed Rating:	2:04
Length of Stretch:	550'
Width of Homestretch:	85'
Starters Behind The Gate:	8
Hubrail?:	Yes
General Admission:	$3.00
General Parking:	Free
Preferred Parking:	$2.00
Grandstand Capacity:	1,500
Clubhouse Capacity:	200
Parking Capacity:	1,200

1990 Attendance and Handle
Number of Race Programs:	55
Gross Handle:	$6,426,577
Gross Attendance:	74,784
Average Handle:	$116,847
Average Attendance:	1,360
Percapita Wagering:	$85.94

Record Business
Handle:	Not Kept
Attendance:	Not Kept

Leading Drivers
Wins:	Allan Nicholls	56
UDR:	Wayne Dowson	.413
Purses:	Murray Brethour	$78,089

Leading Trainer
Wins:	Lorne Brethour	20

Lebanon Raceway (Leb 1/2)

Track located on north corporation limits of Lebanon, Ohio, halfway between Cincinnati and Dayton on State Route 4.

Address: 655 N. Broadway
P.O. Box 58
Lebanon, Ohio 45036

Phone: (513) 932-4936
Fax Number: (513) 932-5358

Sponsored by: Miami Valley Trotting, Inc.
January 4 - May 4
Lebanon Trotting Club, Inc.
September 20 - December 28

Post Time: 7:30 p.m.

Track Officials
President:	Louis E. Carlo
General Manager:	Keith Nixon
Race Secretary:	Ron Giehls
Publicity Director:	Jerry Nardiello

Track Facts
Track Opened:	May, 1948
Speed Rating:	2:03 2/5
Length of Homestretch:	461'
Width of Homestretch:	64'
Starters Behind the Gate:	8
Hubrail?:	Yes
General Admission:	$1.50
General Parking:	$1.00
Grandstand Capacity:	3,000
Parking Capacity:	2,600

1990 Attendance and Handle
Number of Race Programs:	132
Gross Handle:	$27,387,220
Gross Attendance:	167,152
Average Handle:	$204,479
Average Attendance:	1,266
Percapita Wagering:	$163.89

Record Business
Handle:	$463,255	December 30, 1988
Attendance:	5,295	April 8, 1967

Leading Drivers
Wins:	David Miller (Win.)	103
	David Miller (Fall)	61
UDR:	"Chip" Noble (Win.)	.393
	David Miller (Fall)	.345
Purses:	David Miller (Win.)	$142,521
Purses:	David Miller (Fall)	$112,859

Leading Trainer
Wins:	Randy Owens	NR

TRACKS

Los Alamitos Harness (LA 5/8)

Track located on Katella Avenue in Cypress, 24 miles from downtown Los Angeles. May be reached via all freeways. Take 605 freeway to Katella Avenue off-ramp and go east.

Address: 4961 Katella Avenue
Los Alamitos, California 90720
Phone: (714) 995-1234
Results "Hotline:" (714) 995-2222
Fax: (714) 995-6276

Sponsored by: Los Alamitos Racing Assn.

Dates: February 8 - July 27

Post Time: 7:30 p.m.

Track Officials
President:	Lloyd Arnold
General Manager:	Lloyd Arnold
Director of Racing:	Fred Kuebler
Race Secretary:	Ron Goldman
Publicity Director:	Dick Feinberg

Track Facts
Track Opened:	1951
First Harness Meet:	1972
Speed Rating:	2:03
Length of Homestretch:	558'
Width of Homestretch:	90'
Starters Behind the Gate:	9
Hubrail?:	Yes
General Admission:	$2.25
Clubhouse Admission:	$4.00
General Parking:	$1.50
Grandstand Capacity:	18,000
Clubhouse Capacity:	3,000
Parking Capacity:	8,500

1990 Attendance and Handle
Number of Race Programs:	122
Gross Handle:	$67,767,855
Gross Attendance:	364,205
Average Handle:	$555,474
Average Attendance:	2,985
Percapita Wagering:	$186.09

Record Business
Handle:	$1,606,238	March 13, 1987
Attendance:	15,205	March 13, 1987

Leading Drivers
Wins:	Ross Croghan (Win.)	68
	Joe Anderson (Fall)	61
UDR:	Ross Croghan (Win.)	.356
	Joe Anderson (Fall)	.357
Purses:	Ross Croghan (Win.)	$338,814
	Joe Anderson (Fall)	$378,443

Leading Trainer
Wins:	Robert Gordon ('89-'90)	24
	Paul Blumenfeld (Fall '90)	32

Louisville Downs (LouD 1/2)

Track located at Watterson Expressway and Poplar Level Road.

Address: 4520 Poplar Level Rd.
P.O. Box 32457
Louisville, Kentucky 40213
Phone: (502) 964-6415
Results "Hotline:" (900) 420-6789
Fax Number: (502) 969-3735

Sponsored by: Louisville Downs, Inc.
Dates: March 1 - April 25
July 2 - September 2
October 1 - October 26
Post Time: 6:45 p.m. Tue.-Fri.;
1:15 p.m. Sun.; 5:45 p.m. Sat. (Spring);
6:45 p.m. Sat. (Summer & Fall)

Track Officials
President:	Ched Jennings
General Manager:	David B. Pierce
Race Secretary:	Don Knapton
Publicity Director:	Jeff Crawford

Track Facts
Track Opened:	July 14, 1966
Speed Rating:	2:03 4/5
Length of Homestretch:	512'
Width of Homestretch:	80'
Starters Behind the Gate:	8
Hubrail?:	Yes
General Admission:	$2.00
Clubhouse Admission:	$3.00
General Parking:	$2.00
Grandstand Capacity:	5,500
Clubhouse Capacity:	3,200
Parking Capacity:	5,000

1990 Attendance and Handle
Number of Race Programs:	160
Gross Handle:	$15,511,677
Gross Attendance:	351,814
Average Handle:	$96,948
Average Attendance:	2,199
Percapita Wagering:	$44.09

Record Business:
Handle:	$511,030	September 10, 1988
Attendance:	8,376	August 31, 1966

Leading Drivers
Wins:	Roger Cullipher (Win.)	87
	Roger Cullipher (Sum.)	51
	Steve Martz (Fall)	28
UDR:	Roger Cullipher (Win.)	.363
	Allen Harris (Sum.)	.412
	Earl Spalding (Fall)	.462
Purses:	E.Morgan,Jr.(Comb.)	$313,608

Leading Trainer
Wins:	Roger Cullipher	NR

TRACKS

Maywood Park (May 1/2)

Track in Maywood, Illinois, a west suburb of Chicago, at intersection of North and First.

Address: 8600 W. North Ave.
P.O. Box 308
Maywood, Illinois 60153

Phone: (708) 343-4800, 4801 (Race Dept.)
Fax Number: (708) 343-4800, ext. 352
Sponsored by: Arlington at Maywood; Egyptian Racing Assn.; Associates Racing Assn.; and Maywood Park Trotting Assn.
Dates: February 19 - May 16
October 7 - December 31
Post Time: 8:00 p.m.

Track Officials
Pres., "Associates:"	Lester H. McKeever
Pres., "Egyptian:"	William Johnston III
Pres., "Maywood:"	William Johnston III
General Manager:	Bill Moore
Racing Secretary:	Doc Narotsky
Publicity:	Jim Hannon

Track Facts
Track Opened:	1946
Speed Rating:	2:00 1/5
Length of Homestretch:	594'
Width of Homestretch:	70'
Starters Behind the Gate:	8
Hubrail?:	Yes
General Admission:	$2.00
Clubhouse Admission:	$3.25
General Parking:	$2.00
Grandstand Capacity:	10,847
Clubhouse Capacity:	16,000
Parking Capacity:	21,000

1990 Attendance and Handle
Number of Race Programs:	150
Gross Handle:	$60,874,390
Gross Attendance:	405,071
Average Handle:	$405,829
Average Attendance:	2,700
Percapita Wagering:	$150.31

Record Business
Handle:	$1,748,432	June 3, 1989
Attendance:	20,133	September 27, 1980

Leading Drivers
Wins:	Dave Magee (Spr.)	107
	Dave Magee (Fall)	80
UDR:	Ron Marsh (Spr.)	.318
	Bea Erdman (Fall)	.380
Purses:	Dave Magee (Spr.)	$680,177
	Dave Magee (Fall)	$543,787

Leading Trainer (Meets Combined)
Wins:	Ed Holdeman (Comb.)	63

The Meadowlands (M 1)

Located in East Rutherford, New Jersey, six miles west of New York City on Routes Routes 3 and 20. Special buses nightly from New York City, Westchester and all of northern New Jersey

Address: 50 St. Route 20
East Rutherford, New Jersey 07073
Phone: (201) 935-8500
Results "Hotline:" (201) 460-4002
Fax Number: (201) 460-4080

Sponsored by: New Jersey Sports & Exposition Authority
Dates: January 1 - August 18
December 26 - December 31
Post Time: 7:30 p.m.; 1:00 August 3

Track Officials
Pres. & C.E.O.	Robert Mulcahy III
Exec. V.P. & G.M.:	Sam Anzalone
Race Secretary:	Joseph DeFrank
Dir. of Media Relations:	Ellen Harvey

Track Facts
Track Opened:	September 1, 1977
Speed Rating:	1:58 3/5
Length of Homestretch:	990'
Width of Homestretch:	90'
Starters Behind the Gate:	10
Hubrail?:	No
General Admission:	$2.00
Clubhouse Admission:	$3.00
General Parking:	$2.00
Total Capacity:	40,000
Parking Capacity:	25,000

1990 Attendance and Handle
Number of Race Programs:	202
Gross Handle:	$339,806,554
Gross Attendance:	2,084,852
Average Handle:	$1,682,211
Average Attendance:	10,321
Percapita Wagering:	$162.99

Record Business
Handle:	$4,612,013	July 19, 1985
Attendance:	52,974	June 11, 1982

Leading Drivers
Wins:	John Campbell	434
UDR:	John Campbell	.353
Purses:	John Campbell	$6,070,474

Leading Trainer
Wins:	Brett Pelling	117

TRACKS

Ladbroke at The Meadows (Mea 5/8)

Track located in Washington County Pennsylvania, ten miles south of Pittsburgh on U.S. Route 19 and I-79, four miles north of Washington, Pennsylvania.

Address: Race Track Road
P.O. Box 499
Meadow Lands, Pennsylvania 15347
Phone: (412) 225-9300
Results"Hotline:" (900) 420-5444
Fax Number: (412) 225-0298

Sponsored by: Mount Laurel Racing & Washington Trotting Assn.

Dates: January 3 - December 29
Post Times: 7:30 p.m. - Sundays 7:00 p.m.

Track Officials
President:	David Goodwill
General Manager:	John M. Swiatek
Racing Secretary:	Tom Leasure
Publicity Director:	Bob Sabot

Track Facts
Track Opened:	June 28, 1963
Speed Rating:	2:02 1/5
Length of Homestretch:	608'
Width of Homestretch:	80'
Starters Behind the Gate:	9
Hubrail?:	Yes
General Admission:	Free
Clubhouse Admission:	Free
General Parking:	Free
Grandstand Capacity:	4,500
Clubhouse Capacity:	1,150
Parking Capacity:	4,500

1990 Attendance and Handle
Number of Race Programs:	216
Gross Handle:	$42,891,212
Gross Attendance:	532,239
Average Handle:	$198,570
Average Attendance:	2,464
Percapita Wagering:	$80.59

Record Business
Handle:	$870,071	August 11, 1990
Attendance:	14,672	August 4, 1975

Leading Drivers
Wins:	Dave Palone	427
UDR:	Dave Palone	.383
Purses:	Dave Palone	$1,035,126

Leading Trainer
Wins:	Mickey Burke	100

Mohawk Raceway (Moh 5/8)

Track located on a 450-acre tract at Exit 38 of the McDonald-Cartier Freeway near Campbellville, 25 miles west of Toronto.

Address: R.R. 1
Campbellville, Ontario L0P 1B0

Phone: (416) 854-2255
Fax Number: (416) 854-2255

Sponsored by: The Ontario Jockey Club

Dates: March 17 - May 26
September 1 - December 3

Post Time: 7:30 p.m.

Track Officials
President:	J.H. Kenney
Race Secretary:	Barry Hewson
Publicity Director:	Kathy Wade

Track Facts
Track Opened:	April 26, 1963
Speed Rating:	2:01 3/5
Length of Homestretch:	608'
Width of Homestretch:	85'
Starters Behind the Gate:	8
Hubrail?:	Yes
General Admission:	$3.25
Clubhouse Admission:	$7.00
General Parking:	$2.00
Grandstand Capacity:	10,000
Clubhouse Capacity:	5,000
Parking Capacity:	4,276

1990 Attendance and Handle
Number of Race Programs:	119
Gross Handle:	$167,343,269
Gross Attendance:	819,598
Average Handle:	$1,406,246
Average Attendance:	6,887
Percapita Wagering:	$204.18

Record Business
Handle:	$1,939,152	October 28, 1988
Attendance:		14,606 September 22, 1984

Leading Drivers
Wins:	Doug Brown (Spr.)	647
	Doug Brown (Fall)	73
UDR:	Doug Brown (Spr.)	.320
	Doug Brown (Fall)	.307
Purses:	Doug Brown (Spr.)	$717,866
	Doug Brown (Fall)	$1,030,840

Leading Trainer
Wins:	Bill Robinson	51

TRACKS

Monticello Raceway (MR 1/2)

Track located Monticello, New York. May be reached via Routes 17 & 17-B.

Address: Routes 17 & 17B
Monticello, New York 12701

Phone: (914) 794-4100
Results "Hotline:" (900) 786-8883
Fax Number: (914) 794-0523

Sponsored by: Berenson Pari-Mutuel of New York

Dates: January 1 - December 31

Post Time: 7:30 p.m.; Sundays 1:05 p.m.

Track Officials
President:	Richard Berenson
General Manager:	William J. Sullivan
Race Secretary:	Larry Miller
Publicity Director:	John Manzi

Track Facts
Track Opened:	1958
Speed Rating:	2:02 2/5
Length of Homestretch:	500'
Width of Homestretch:	90'
Starters Behind the Gate:	8
Hubrail?:	No
General Admission:	$1.50
Clubhouse Admission:	Free
General Parking:	Free
Grandstand Capacity:	4,500
Clubhouse Capacity:	500
Parking Capacity:	5,000

1990 Attendance and Handle
Number of Race Programs:	230
Gross Handle:	$44,725,474
Gross Attendance:	348,535
Average Handle:	$194,459
Average Attendance:	1,515
Percapita Wagering:	$128.36

Record Business
Handle:	$1,040,636	May 29, 1974
Attendance:	17,495	June 20, 1980

Leading Drivers
Wins:	Bill Parker, Jr.	339
UDR:	Bill Parker, Jr.	.337
Purses:	Bill Parker, Jr.	$537,085

Leading Trainer
Wins:	Craig Mosher	77

Muskegon Racecourse (MRc 5/8)

Track located on Harvey Street, between Hile and Ellis Roads, southeast of Muskegon. Take I-96 to the Hile Road exit, proceeding west on Hile, then south on Harvey.

Address: 4800 Harvey Street
Fruitport, Michigan 49415

Phone: (616) 798-7123
Fax Number: (616) 798-3997

Sponsored by: Muskegon Race Track, Inc.

Dates: May 3 - October 27
Post Time: 7:00 p.m.

Track Officials
Executive V.P.:	Dominick L. Marotta
General Manager:	Gary Buxton
Race Secretary:	TBA
Marketing Director:	Don Marotta

Track Facts
Track Opened:	May 25, 1989
Speed Rating:	2:03 3/5
Length of Homestretch:	550'
Width of Homestretch:	80'
Starters Behind the Gate:	9
Hubrail?:	Yes
General Admission:	$3.00
Clubhouse Admission:	$4.00
General Parking:	$1.50
Grandstand Capacity:	7,000
Clubhouse Capacity:	3,500
Parking Capacity:	3,800

1990 Attendance and Handle
Number of Race Programs:	88
Gross Handle:	$16,931,635
Gross Attendance:	209,769
Average Handle:	$192,405
Average Attendance:	2,384
Percapita Wagering:	$80.71

Record Business
Handle:	$321,661	October 7, 1990
Attendance:	10,149	July 4, 1989

Leading Drivers
Wins:	Larry Stalbaum	88
UDR:	Larry Stalbaum	.336
Purses:	Larry Stalbaum	$100,943

Leading Trainer
Not Reported

TRACKS

New Brunswick Downs (NBD 5/8)

Located near Moncton, New Brunswick.

Address: 500 Gauvin Road
Dieppe, New Brunswick E1A 1M8

Phone: (506) 857-9600
Results "Hotline:" (506) 857-7223
Fax Number: (506) 857-9940

Sponsored by: New Brunswick Downs, Ltd.

Dates: March 30 - December 31

Post Time: 7:30 p.m.

Dark: Racing Tuesdays and Saturdays, and July 8, 10 and 11

Track Officials
President:	Peter Cattoni
Operations Manager:	Peter Cattoni
Race Secretary:	Kim Hobert
Publicity Director:	Brad Donnolly

Track Facts
Track Opened:	1984
Track Re-named:	1989
Speed Rating:	2:03 4/5
Length of Homestretch:	660'
Width of Homestretch:	80'
Starters Behind the Gate:	8
Grandstand Admission:	$2.00
Clubhouse Admission:	$2.00
General Parking:	Free
Grandstand Capacity:	5,000
Clubhouse Capacity:	500
Parking Capacity:	2,500

1990 Attendance and Handle
Number of Race Programs:	69
Gross Handle:	$4,074,682
Gross Attendance:	48,555
Average Handle:	$59,053
Average Attendance:	704
Percapita Wagering:	$83.92

Record Business
Handle:	$274,733	October 14, 1989
Attendance:	4,556	June 15, 1985

Leading Drivers
Wins:	Frank Fagan, Jr.	68
UDR:	Dan O'Brian	.348
Purses:	Steve Mahar	$79,983

Leading Trainer
Not Kept

Northfield Park Harness (Nfld 1/2)

Track located between Cleveland and Akron on Route 8 in Northfield, Ohio.

Address: 10705 Northfield Rd.
P.O. Box 374
Northfield, Ohio 44067

Phone: (216) 467-4101
Fax Number : (216) 468-2628

Sponsored by: Northfield Park Associates

Dates: January 1 - December 29

Post Time: 7:30 p.m.; Matinees 1 p.m. Sun. 1:30 p.m.; Sundays in July 6:30 p.m.

Track Officials
President:	Carl Milstein
General Manager:	Thomas Aldrich
Race Secretary:	Gregg Keidel
Publicity Director:	Ken Warkentin

Track Facts
Track Opened:	August 23, 1957
Speed Rating:	2:02 2/5
Length of Homestretch:	440'
Width of Homestretch:	80'
Starters Behind the Gate:	8
Hubrail?:	Yes
General Admission:	$1.50
Clubhouse Admission:	$3.00
General Parking:	$1.00
Grandstand Capacity:	4,300
Clubhouse Capacity:	1,500
Parking Capacity:	6,000

1990 Attendance and Handle
Number of Race Programs:	211
Gross Handle:	$90,793,424
Gross Attendance	733,031
Average Handle:	$430,301
Average Attendance:	3,474
Percapita Wagering:	$123.86

Record Business
Handle:	$859,234	June 2, 1990
Attendance:	14,085	July 18, 1963

Leading Drivers
Wins:	Mitch Sahely	202
UDR:	Don O'Dwyer	.350
Purses:	Mitch Sahely	$460,331

Leading Trainer
Wins:	Jerry Ross, Sr.	145

TRACKS

Northlands Park (Edm 5/8)

Located within city limits, west of Capiliano Freeway, 75th St., and 115th Avenue. Five minutes from downtown.

Address: 76th St. & 115th Ave.
P.O. Box 1480
Edmonton, Alberta T5J 2N5
Phone: (403) 471-7379
Results "Hotline:" (403) 493-9000
Fax Number: (403) 471-7134

Sponsored by: Edmonton Northlands

Dates: March 1 - May 27
September 20 - December 2
Post Time: 7 p.m. Weekdays;
1:30 p.m. Sunday & Holidays

Track Officials
President:	Dale Cole
General Manager:	Colin Forbes
Racing Manager:	Jack Nicholl
Race Secretary:	Carl Walczak
Publicity Director:	Don Fleming

Track Facts
Track Opened:	July, 1925
Speed Rating:	2:03 1/5
Length of Homestretch:	567'
Width of Homestretch:	70'
Starters Behind the Gate:	8
Hubrail?:	No
General Admission:	$2.00
Clubhouse Admission:	$3.25
General Parking:	$3.00
Grandstand Capacity:	8,000
Clubhouse Capacity:	1,000
Parking Capacity:	7,000

1990 Attendance and Handle
Number of Race Programs:	99
Gross Handle:	$56,606,879
Gross Attendance:	269,872
Average Handle:	$571,787
Average Attendance:	2,726
Percapita Wagering:	$209.75

Record Business
Handle:	$928,492	October 13, 1990
Attendance:	9,622	November 1, 1984

Leading Drivers
Wins:	Keith Clark (Spr.)	51
	Keith Clark (Fall)	78
UDR:	Issac Tougas (Spr.)	.391
	Keith Clark (Fall)	.407
Purses:	Keith Clark (Spr.)	$228,796
	Keith Clark (Fall)	$380,305

Leading Trainer
Wins:	Keith Clark	129

Northville Downs (Nor 1/2)

Located in Northville, Michigan, northwest of Detroit. Can be reached via I-96 & M-14 and Sheldon north to Seven Mile Road.

Address: 301 South Center Street
Northville, Michigan 48167

Phone: (313) 349-1000
Results "Hotline:" (313) 349-1528
Fax Number: (313) 348-8955

Sponsored by: Northville Downs

Dates: January 3 - March 31
October 14 - December 31 (Jack @ Nor)
Post Time: 7:30 p.m.
Saturday Matinees: 1:00 p.m.

Track Officials
Executive Manager:	Margaret J. Zayti
Director of Operations:	Louis E. Carlo
Race Secretary:	Harry Peterson
Publicity Director:	Michael Janchick

Track Facts
Track Opened:	August 4, 1944
Speed Rating:	2:03 3/5
Length of Homestretch:	440'
Width of Homestretch:	80'
Starters Behind the Gate:	8
General Admission:	$2.50
Clubhouse Admission:	$3.50
General Parking:	$1.00
Grandstand Capacity:	5,200
Clubhouse Capacity:	2,000
Parking Capacity:	2,500

1990 Attendance and Handle (Jack & Nor)
Number of Race Programs:	156
Gross Handle:	$78,361,285
Gross Attendance:	391,394
Average Handle:	$502,316
Average Attendance:	2,509
Percapita Wagering:	$200.21

Record Business
Handle:	$935,067	March 28, 1986
Attendance:	9,610	May 15, 1950

Leading Drivers (Incl. Jack & Nor)
Wins:	Keith Crawford (Nor)	73
	Vince Copeland (Jack)	59
UDR:	Keith Crawford (Nor)	.408
	Art McIlmurray (Nor)	.444
Purses:	Keith Crawford (Nor)	$237,797
	V. Copeland (Jack)	$190,069

Leading Trainer
Not Reported

TRACKS

Pocono Downs (PcD 5/8)

Located two miles northeast of Wilkes-Barre, Pennsylvania on Route 315, five miles from Exit 36 of the Pennsylvania Turnpike.

Address: Route 315
Wilkes-Barre, Pennsylvania 18702

Phone: (717) 825-6681
Results "Hotline:" (717) 824-7511
Fax Number: (717) 823-9407

Sponsored by: Pocono Downs, Inc.
Dates: March 1 - November 30

Post Time: 7:30 p.m.; Holidays 1:30 p.m.

Track Officials
President:	Joseph B. Banks
Operations Manager:	Dale Rapson
Race Secretary:	Phil Wentworth
Publicity Director:	John Zimich

Track Facts
Track Opened:	July 15, 1965
Speed Rating:	2:02
Length of Homestretch:	490'
Width of Homestretch:	90'
Starters Behind the Gate:	8
Hubrail?:	Yes
General Admission:	$2.00
Clubhouse Admission:	Free
General Parking:	$1.00
Grandstand Capacity:	5,000
Clubhouse Capacity:	1,000
Parking Capacity:	8,000

1990 Attendance and Handle
Number of Race Programs:	150
Gross Handle:	$26,007,271
Gross Attendance:	282,854
Average Handle:	$173,382
Average Attendance:	1,886
Percapita Wagering:	$91.93

Record Business
Handle:	$654,274	September 4, 1967
Attendance:	15,186	September 10, 1966

Leading Drivers
Wins:	Bill Lambertus	192
UDR:	Carmine Vitale	.340
Purses:	Bill Lambertus	$331,875

Leading Trainer
Wins:	Jim Groff	64

Pompano Park Harness (PPk 5/8)

Track located just off Atlantic Blvd. Exit west off I-95 and near Interchange 24 of Florida Turnpike.

Address: 1800 S.W. 3rd Street
Pompano Beach, Florida 33069

Phone: (305) 972-2000
Results "Hotline:" (900) 820-1777
Fax Number: (305) 972-7894

Sponsored by: Pompano Park Limited Associated Partnership

Dates: January 1 - April 27
October 5 - December 31 (Tentative)
Post Time: 7:30 p.m.

Track Officials
President:	John A. Cashman, Jr.
General Manager:	Harold Duris
Race Secretary:	Ted Leonard
Publicity Director:	Allen J. Finkelson
Communications Director:	Joe Hartmann

Track Facts
Track Opened:	February 4, 1964
Speed Rating:	2:01 2/5
Length of Homestretch:	608'
Width of Homestretch:	80'
Starters Behind the Gate:	9
Hubrail?:	Yes
General Admission:	$1.50
Clubhouse Admission:	$3.00
General Parking:	$1.00
Grandstand Capacity:	7,500
Clubhouse Capacity:	2,250
Parking Capacity:	10,000

1990 Attendance and Handle
Number of Race Programs:	156
Gross Handle:	$68,730,814
Gross Attendance:	672,479
Average Handle:	$440,582
Average Attendance:	4,311
Percapita Wagering:	$102.20

Record Business
Handle:	$1,340,574	November 13, 1987
Attendance:	18,451	December 27, 1980

Leading Drivers
Wins:	Don Harmon (Win.)	107
	Wally Hennessey (Fall)	63
UDR:	Kevin Wallis (Win.)	.356
	John Hogan (Fall)	.366
Purses:	Don Harmon (Win.)	$331,911
	Jo. Campbell (Fall)	$1,021,815

Leading Trainer
Wins:	Robert Duncan ('89-'90)	76

TRACKS

Quad City Downs (QCD 5/8)

Track located at Illinois Routes 5 and 92 just two miles west of the junction of I-80 and East-West Tollway, East Moline.

Address: 5005 Morton Drive
P.O. Box 368
East Moline, Illinois 61244

Phone: (309) 792-0202, or
(800) 747-3696
Results "Hotline:" (309) 792-3557
Fax Number: (309) 792-4143

Sponsored by: Quad City Downs, Inc.
Dates: April 11 to October 27
Post Time: 7:30 p.m. Wed. thru Sat.
1:30 p.m. Sundays and Holidays

Track Officials
President:	Ed Duffy
General Mgr.:	William Mosenfelder
Marketing Dir.	Roger Derby
Race Secretary:	Eric Warner
Publicity Director:	Robin Parker

Track Facts
Track Opened:	June 1973
Speed Rating:	2:02 1/5
Length of Homestretch:	488'
Width of Homestretch:	80'
Starters Behind the Gate:	9
Hubrail?:	Yes
General Admission:	$2.00
Clubhouse Admission:	$3.00
General Parking:	$1.00
Grandstand Capacity:	4,000
Clubhouse Capacity:	1,780
Parking Capacity:	2,200

1990 Attendance and Handle
Number of Race Programs:	131
Gross Handle:	$17,897,001
Gross Attendance:	253,123
Average Handle:	$136,618
Average Attendance:	1,932
Percapita Wagering:	$70.71

Record Business
Handle:	$543,862	September 17, 1978
Attendance:	7,807	September 17, 1978

Leading Drivers
Wins:	Dean Magee	205
UDR:	Dean Magee	.357
Purses:	Dean Magee	$316,180

Leading Trainer
Not Reported

Raceway Park (RP 5/8)

Located five miles from downtown Toledo, at Telegraph Road (U.S. 24) and Alexis Rd. St. Route 184), one-half mile south of the Michigan-Ohio line.

Address: 5700 Telegraph Road
Toledo, Ohio 43612

Phone: (419) 476-7751
Results "Hotline:" (419) 476-7759
Fax Number: (419) 476-7979

Sponsored by: Raceway Park and Toledo-Maumee Raceways, Inc.
Dates: March 16 - December 7
Dark: Mon., Tues., and Thursday
Post Time: 7:30 p.m.

Track Officials
President:	Arnold Stansley
General Manager	Arnold Stansley
Race Secretary:	Dennis Haskell
Publicity Director:	Brent Nelson

Track Facts
Track Opened:	1959
First Harness Race:	June 15, 1962
Speed Rating:	2:02 3/5
Length of Homestretch:	700'
Width of Homestretch:	85'
Starters Behind the Gate:	9
Hubrail?:	Yes
General Admission:	$2.25
Clubhouse Admission:	$1.50 add'l
General Parking:	Free
Grandstand Capacity:	5,000
Clubhouse Capacity:	700
Parking Capacity:	2,500

1990 Attendance and Handle
Number of Race Programs:	152
Gross Handle:	$35,531,511
Gross Attendance:	344,609
Average Handle:	$233,760
Average Attendance:	2,267
Percapita Wagering:	$103.11

Record Business
Handle:	$658,888	December 3, 1989
Attendance:	6,936	April 21, 1978

Leading Drivers
Wins:	Charlie Brown	143
UDR:	Charlie Brown	.309
Purses:	Jay Cross	$188,315

Leading Trainer
Wins:	Rick Redder	47

TRACKS

The Red Mile (Lex 1)

Track located one mile from downtown Lexington on South Broadway.

Address: 1200 Red Mile Road (40504)
P.O. Box 420 (40585)
Lexington, Kentucky (Zip as above)

Phone: (606) 255-0752 or (800) 354-9092
Fax Number: (606) 231-0217

Sponsored by: Lexington Trots Breeders Association

Dates: April 26 - June 29
September 10 - October 4

Post Time: 7:00 p.m.; Matinees 1:00 p.m.

Track Officials
President:	John Cashman, Jr.
General Manager:	Curt Greene
Race Secretary:	Donald Knapton
Publicity Director:	Paulette Welch

Track Facts
Track Opened:	September 28, 1875
Speed Rating:	2:00 3/5
Length of Homestretch:	850'
Width of Homestretch:	115'
Starters Behind the Gate:	9
Hubrail:	Yes
General Admission:	$3.00
Clubhouse Admission:	$3.00
General Parking Fee:	Free
Grandstand Capacity:	6,000
Clubhouse Capacity:	500
Parking Capacity:	3,000

1990 Attendance and Handle
Number of Race Programs:	58
Gross Handle:	$9,203,900
Gross Attendance:	143,404
Average Handle:	$158,688
Average Attendance:	2,472
Percapita Wagering:	$64.19

Record Business
Handle:	$389,384	September 30, 1988
Attendance:	24,082	May 30, 1988

Leading Drivers
Wins:	Jay Picciano (Spr.)	46
	John Campbell (Fall/GC)	12
UDR:	Dan Shetler (Spr.)	.407
	Jan Johnson (Fall/GC)	.448
Purses:	Jay Picciano (Spr.)	$77,588
	M.Lachance (Fall/GC)	$194,737

Leading Trainer
Wins:	Roger Cullipher (Spr.)	22

Rideau Carleton (RidC 5/8)

Track located in Gloucester, Ontario.

Address: 4837 Albion Road
P.O. Box 904
Gloucester, Ontario K1G 3N3

Phone: (613) 822-2211 Track
(613) 822-0247 Race Office
Results "Hotline:" (613) 822-2260
Fax Number: (613) 822-1586

Sponsored by: Rideau Carleton Raceway Holdings, Ltd.
Dates: July 1 - November 30
Post Time: 7:30 p.m.;
Matinees, Thanksgiving & Sundays in November 1:30 p.m.

Track Officials
President:	Glenn Pearson
General Manager:	Glenn Pearson
Race Secretary:	Glenn Pearson

Track Facts
Track Opened:	September, 1962
Speed Rating:	2:03 3/5
Length of Homestretch:	585'
Width of Homestretch:	90'
Starters Behind the Gate:	8
Hubrail?:	No
General Admission:	$3.00
Clubhouse Admission:	$1.00
General Parking:	1.50
Grandstand Capacity:	4,500
Clubhouse Capacity:	1,000
Parking Capacity:	4,000

1990 Attendance and Handle
Number of Race Programs:	105
Gross Handle:	$18,966,690
Gross Attendance:	188,916
Average Handle:	$180,635
Average Attendance:	1,799
Percapita Wagering:	$100.40

Record Business
Handle:	$447,555	July 22, 1984
Attendance:	6,000	July 20, 1984

Leading Drivers
Wins:	Howard Portelance	107
UDR:	Bob O'Dwyer	.359
Purses:	Howard Portelance	$181,373

Leading Trainer
Wins:	Robert O'Dwyer	42

TRACKS

Riverside Downs (Hend 1/2)

Track located on U.S. 41, on north edge of Henderson, Kentucky; six miles south of downtown Evansville, Indiana

Address: 3003 Sunset Lane
P.O. Box 1549
Henderson, Kentucky 42420

Phone: (502) 826-9746
Fax: (502) 827-1120

Sponsored by: Riverside Downs, Inc.

Dates: April 26 - June 29
October 25 - December 7

Post Time: 6:30 p.m.

Track Officials
President:	M.L. Vaughan
General Manager:	Jack Myers
Race Secretary:	Ozzie Cole
Publicity Director:	Alvey Albin

Track Facts
Track Re-opened:	1990
Speed Rating:	2:04 4/5
Length of Homestretch:	NR
Width of Homestretch:	NR
Starters Behind the Gate:	8
General Admission:	$1.00
Clubhouse Admission:	$2.50
General Parking:	Free
Grandstand Capacity:	2,000
Clubhouse Capacity:	600
Parking Capacity:	2,000

1990 Attendance and Handle
Number of Race Programs:	39
Gross Handle:	$1,979,607
Gross Attendance:	30,104
Average Handle:	$50,759
Average Attendance:	772
Percapita Wagering:	$65.75

Record Business
Handle:	$206,265	April 15, 1980
Attendance:	4,508	June 2, 1972

Leading Driver
Wins:	Ed Morgan, Jr.	46
UDR:	Paul Shelton	.416
Purses:	Ed Morgan, Jr.	$39,184

Leading Trainer
Not Reported

Rosecroft Raceway (RcR 5/8)

Track located seven miles southeast of Washington, D.C. in Oxon Hill, Maryland on Capital Beltway (Route 95) at Exit 4A.

Address: 6336 Rosecroft Drive
Fort Washington, Maryland 20744-1999

Phone: (301) 567-4000
Results "Hotline:" (301) 567-5800
Fax Number: (301) 567-9267

Dates: January 11 - December 21

Post Time: 7:30 p.m., Sundays 6:30 p.m.

Track Officials
Trustee:	James J. Murphy
General Manager:	Tom Barry
Race Secretary:	William J. Perkins III
Publicity Director:	Jerry Connors

Track Facts
Track Opened:	1949
Speed Rating:	2:00 4/5
Length of Homestretch:	402'
Width of Homestretch:	90'
Starters Behind the Gate:	9
Hubrail?:	No
General Admission:	$2.00
Clubhouse Admission:	$2.00
General Parking:	$1.00
Grandstand Capacity:	9,000
Clubhouse Capacity:	6,000
Parking Capacity:	5,850

1990 Attendance and Handle
Number of Race Programs:	248
Gross Handle:	$112,057,388
Gross Attendance:	748,683
Average Handle:	$451,844
Average Attendance:	3,019
Percapita Wagering:	$149.18

Record Business
Handle:	$1,195,681	July 17, 1990
Attendance:	13,158	June 17, 1965

Leading Drivers
Wins:	Don Irvine, Jr.	281
UDR:	Steve Warrington	.371
Purses:	Don Irvine, Jr.	$1,351,318

Leading Trainer
Wins:	Roger Hans	112

TRACKS

Saginaw Harness Raceway (SgVy 1/2)

Track located at the Saginaw County Fairgrounds.

Address: 2701 East Genesee Street
Saginaw, Michigan 48601

Phone: (517) 755-3451
Results "Hotline:" (517) 752-2464
Fax Number: (517) 755-1300

Dates: April 10 - August 25

Post Time: 7:00 p.m., 6:00 p.m. Sundays

Track Officials
Preisdent:	Marshall Davis
General Manager:	Eugene T. Budd
Race Secretary:	TBA
Public Affairs Director:	David Karoub

Track Facts
Track Opened:	June 16, 1980
Speed Rating:	2:02 4/5
Length of Homestretch:	600'
Width of Homestretch:	70'
Starters Behind the Gate:	8
Hubrail?:	Yes
General Admission:	$2.50
General Parking:	$1.00
Grandstand Capacity:	2,500
Clubhouse Capacity:	250
Parking Capacity:	5,000

1990 Attendance and Handle
Number of Race Programs:	86
Gross Handle:	$17,131,973
Gross Attendance:	135,730
Average Handle:	$199,209
Average Attendance:	1,578
Percapita Wagering:	$126.24

Record Business
Handle:	$471,945	August 18, 1985
Attendance:	6,600	June 16, 1980

Leading Drivers
Wins:	Dan Rathka	78
UDR:	Clay Faurot	.440
Purses:	Joe Putnam	$126,858

Leading Trainer
Wins:	Dale Peterson	NR

Saratoga Harness (Stga 1/2)

Located in the southeastern outskirts of Saratoga Springs, New York, two miles from downtown. From Northway (I-87), take Exits 13N or 14.

Address: Nelson Avenue
P.O. Box 356
Saratoga Springs, New York 12866-0356

Phone: (518) 584-2110
Fax Number: (518) 583-2169 (Publicity);
583-1056 (Race Office)

Sponsored by: Saratoga Harness Racing
Dates: January 11 - November 30
Post Times: 7:45 Evenings;
1:15 p.m. Matinees

Track Officials
President:	Frank Fernandez
General Manager:	Warren DeSantis
Race Secretary:	Ralph Swalsky
Publicity Director:	George W. "Skip" Carlson

Track Facts
Track Opened:	1941
Speed Rating:	2:02 1/5
Length of Homestretch:	550'
Width of Homestretch:	92'
Starters Behind the Gate:	8
Hubrail?:	No
General Admission:	$1.75
Clubhouse Admission:	$3.00
General Parking:	$1.00
Grandstand Capacity:	2,000
Clubhouse Capacity:	1,700
Parking Capacity:	4,000

1990 Attendance and Handle
Number of Race Programs:	179
Gross Handle:	$28,970,064
Gross Attendance:	351,322
Average Handle:	$161,844
Average Attendance:	1,963
Percapita Wagering:	$82.45

Record Business
Handle:	$505,857	July 12, 1975
Attendance:	14,200	June 30, 1971

Leading Drivers
Wins:	Kim Crawford	199
UDR:	Wally Hennessey	.380
Purses:	Kim Crawford	$421,849

Leading Trainer
Wins:	David Spagnola	63

TRACKS

Scarborough Downs (Scar 1/2)

Track located eight miles from Portland, Maine.

Address: U.S. Route One
P.O. Box 468
Scarborough, Maine 04074

Phone: (207) 883-4331
Fax Number: (207) 883-2020
Race Office: (207) 883-9521

Sponsored by: Davric-Maine, Inc.

Dates: March 1 - December 15

Post Time: 7:30 p.m. Tuesday - Saturday
1:30 p.m. Sundays

Track Officials
President:	Joseph J. Ricci
General Manager:	Janis McGrath
Race Secretary:	Denise Herrick
Publicity Director:	TBA

Track Facts
Track Opened:	July 1, 1950
Speed Rating:	2:04 4/5
Length of Homestretch:	440'
Width of Homestretch:	90'
Starters Behind the Gate:	8
Hubrail?:	Yes
General Admission:	$2.00
Clubhouse Admission:	$2.50
General Parking:	Free
Grandstand Capacity:	10,000
Clubhouse Capacity:	1,050
Parking Capacity:	15,000

1990 Attendance and Handle
Number of Race Programs:	207
Gross Handle:	$26,079,123
Gross Attendance:	271,144
Average Handle:	$125,986
Average Attendance:	1,310
Percapita Wagering:	$96.17

Record Business
Handle:	$507,649	September 6, 1987
Attendance:	9,133	June 29, 1980

Leading Drivers
Wins:	Walter Case, Jr.	277
UDR:	Walter Case, Jr.	.438
Purses:	Walter Case, Jr.	$250,540

Leading Trainer
Wins:	Elmer Ballard	100

Scioto Downs (ScD 5/8)

Track located in Columbus, Ohio two and one-half miles south of the Columbus city limits on Route 23.

Address: 6000 South High Street
Columbus, Ohio 43207
Phone: (614) 491-2515
Results "Hotline:" (614) 766-TROT
Fax Number: (614) 491-4626

Sponsored by: Scioto Downs, Inc. and Mid-America Racing Association

Dates: May 4 - September 14

Post Time: 7:30 p.m., Holidays 2:00 p.m.
Dark: Sunday

Track Officials
President:	Robert Steele (Scioto)
President:	LaVerne Hill (MARA)
General Manager:	Robert Steele
Race Secretary:	James Ewart
Publicity Director:	Tom White

Track Facts
Track Opened:	1959
Speed Rating:	2:01 4/5
Length of Homestretch:	539'
Width of Homestretch:	90'
Starters Behind the Gate:	9
Hubrail?:	No
General Admission:	$1.00
Clubhouse Admission:	$2.00
General Parking:	$1.00
Grandstand Capacity:	10,000
Clubhouse Capacity:	2,000
Parking Capacity:	6,000

1990 Attendance and Handle
Number of Race Programs:	115
Gross Handle:	$41,357,703
Gross Attendance:	477,798
Average Handle:	$359,632
Average Attendance:	4,155
Percapita Wagering:	$86.55

Record Business
Handle:	$894,800	September 7, 1985
Attendance:	14,357	April 26, 1986

Leading Drivers
Wins:	Jeff Fout	113
UDR:	"Chip" Noble	.341
Purses:	Jeff Fout	$503,904

Leading Trainers
Wins:	Alan Riegle (Spr.)	15
	"Chip" Noble III (Sum.)	17

TRACKS

Sports Creek Raceway (SpCk 5/8)

Track located in Swartz Creek, Michigan near Flint.

Address: 4290 Morrish Road
Swartz Creek, Michigan 48473

Phone: (313) 635-3333
Results "Hotline:" (313) 635-4519
Fax Number: (313) 635-9711

Sponsored by: Sports Creek Acquisitions

Dates: January 2 - March 30
October 13 - December 31

Post Time: 7:00 p.m.; Sundays 1:30 p.m.

Track Officials
President:	David Tyner
General Manager:	William Crawford
Race Secretary:	Ted Leonard
Publicity Director:	Chris Locking

Track Facts
Track Opened:	November 5, 1986
Speed Rating:	2:03 2/5
Length of Homestretch:	550'
Width of Homestretch:	80'
Starters Behind the Gate:	9
Hubrail?:	Yes
General Admission:	$2.50
Clubhouse Admission:	$3.50
General Parking:	$1.00
Grandstand Capacity:	4,500
Clubhouse Capacity:	2,000
Parking Capacity:	2,400

1990 Attendance and Handle
Number of Race Programs:	134
Gross Handle:	$33,486,952
Gross Attendance:	237,326
Average Handle:	$249,903
Average Attendance:	1,771
Percapita Wagering:	$141.11

Record Business
Handle:	$626,752	March 14, 1990
Attendance:	6,011	November 5, 1986

Leading Drivers
Wins:	Joe Putnam (Win.)	61
	Joe Putnam (Fall)	49
UDR:	Danny Davidson (Win.)	.352
	Jim Miner (Fall)	.466
Purses:	Joe Putnam (Win.)	$95,356
	Peter Wrenn (Fall)	$88,018

Leading Trainer
Not Reported

Sportsman's Park (SPk 5/8)

Track located in Cicero, Illinois, just west of Chicago City limits.

Address: 3301 South Laramie Avenue
Cicero, Illinois 60650

Phone: (312) 242-1121
Results "Hotline:" (708) 976-8200
Fax Number: (708) 452-4709

Sponsored by: Chicago Downs Assn. & Fox Valley Trotting Club, Inc.

Dates: May 17 - October 5

Post Time: 8 p.m.

Track Officials
President:	William H. Johnston, Jr.
Gen. Manager:	William H. Johnston, Jr.
Race Secretary:	Phil Langley
Publicity Director:	Mike Paradise

Track Facts
Track Opened:	1949
Converted to 5/8-Mile:	1956
Speed Rating:	2:00 1/5
Length of Homestretch:	902'
Width of Homestretch:	72'
Starters Behind the Gate:	9
General Admission:	Free
Clubhouse Admission:	$2.00
General Parking:	Free
Grandstand Capacity:	20,000
Clubhouse Capacity:	10,000
Parking Capacity:	10,300

1990 Attendance and Handle
Number of Race Programs:	123
Total Handle:	$87,769,058
Total Attendance:	771,857
Average Handle:	$713,570
Average Attendance:	6,275
Percapita Wagering:	$113.72

Record Business
Handle:	$2,333,058	September 15, 1990
Attendance:	22,832	July 20, 1980

Leading Drivers
Wins:	Ron Marsh	169
UDR:	Ron Marsh	.291
Purses:	Dave Magee	$1,546,975

Leading Trainer
Not Reported

TRACKS

Stampede Park (Clgy 5/8)

Track located on the corners of MacLeod Trail, SE & 25th Ave., SE

Address: 1410 Olympic Way
P.O. Box 1060, Station M
Calgary, Alberta T2P 2K8

Phone: (403) 261-0214
Results "Hotline:" (403) 290-0919
Fax Number: (403) 265-7009

Sponsored by: Calgary Stampede & Exhibition

Dates: January 1 - February 25
June 1 - September 15
December 6 - December 29
Post Times: 6:30 p.m., Sat. & Sun. 1:30 p.m.

Track Officials
General Manager:	Keith Barr
Race Secretary:	Jackson Wittup
Publicity Director:	Deborah Middleton

Track Facts
Track Opened:	1975
Speed Rating:	2:03
Length of Homestretch:	600'
Width of Homestretch:	70'
Starters Behind the Gate:	8
General Admission:	$2.00
Clubhouse Admission:	$4.00
General Parking:	$3.00
Grandstand Capacity:	17,900
Clubhouse Capacity:	2,500
Parking Capacity:	2,400

1990 Attendance and Handle
Number of Race Programs:	100
Gross Handle:	$34,623,365
Gross Attendance:	229,685
Average Handle:	$346,234
Average Attendance:	2,297
Percapita Wagering:	$150.74

Record Business
Handle:	$727,909	August 8, 1982
Attendance:	5,065	August 8, 1982

Leading Drivers
Wins:	Keith Clark (Comb.)	106
UDR:	Clark Beelby (Win.)	.434
	Rod Hennessy (Sum.)	.442
	Clark Beelby (Fall)	.621
Purses:	Keith Clark (Comb.)	$367,188

Leading Trainer
Wins:	Keith Clark	NR

Summerside Raceway (Summ 1/2)

Track located in Summerside, Prince Edward Island.

Address: 477 Notre Dame Street
Summerside, P.E.I. C1N 1T2

Phone: (902) 436-7221/7222

Sponsored by: Prince County Horsemen's Club

Dates: May 1 - December 26

Post Time: 7:30 p.m.

Track Officials
President:	Reg Warren
General Manager:	Gerard Smith
Race Secretary:	Gerard Smith
Publicity Director:	Gerard Smith

Track Facts
Track Opened:	1886
Speed Rating:	2:08 1/5
Length of Homestretch:	440'
Width of Homestretch:	65'
Starters Behind the Gate:	6
Hubrail?:	Yes
General Admission:	$1.00
Clubhouse Admission:	$2.00
General Parking:	Free
Grandstand Capacity:	5,000
Parking Capacity:	600

1990 Attendance and Handle
Number of Race Programs:	36
Gross Handle:	$923,064
Gross Attendance:	9,424
Average Handle:	$25,641
Average Attendance:	262
Percapita Wagering:	$97.95

Record Business
Handle:	$60,333	1955
Attendance:	6,000	July 24, 1981

Leading Drivers
Wins:	Gary Chappell	34
UDR:	Boyd MacDonald	.478
Purses:	Allan Smith	$13,522

Leading Trainer
Not Reported

TRACKS

Tartan Downs (Sydny 1/2)

Track located in Sydney, Nova Scotia.

Address: Upper Prince Street
P.O. Box 941
Sydney, Nova Scotia B1P 6H5

Phone: (902) 564-8465
Results "Hotline:" (902) 562-6666
Fax Number: (902) 539-9784

Sponsored by: Jockey Club of Nova Scotia, Inc.

Dates: January 3 - December 29

Post Times: 7:30 p.m.; Sundays 1:30 p.m.

Track Officials
President:	Louise MacDonald
General Manager:	Louise MacDonald
Race Secretary:	David Kelly
Publicity Director:	David Kelly

Track Facts
Track Opened:	1944
Speed Rating:	2:07 2/5
Length of Homestretch:	660'
Width of Homestretch:	50'
Starters Behind the Gate:	6
Hubrail?	Yes
General Admission:	$1.00
Clubhouse Admission:	$1.00
Grandstand Capacity:	1,300
Clubhouse Capacity:	350
Parking Capacity:	300

1990 Attendance and Handle
Number of Race Programs:	104
Gross Handle:	$4,032,835
Gross Attendance:	35,284
Average Handle:	$38,777
Average Attendance:	339
Percapita Wagering:	$114.30

Record Business
Handle:	$112,984	June 28, 1979
Attendance:	4,500	June 28, 1979

Leading Drivers
Wins:	Harold Youden	112
UDR:	Ken McMaster	.351
Purses:	Doug Rankin	$40,283

Leading Trainer
Not Reported

Truro Raceway (Truro 1/2)

Track located in Truro, Nova Scotia.

Address: Ryland Avenue
P.O. Box 422
Truro, Nova Scotia B2N 5C5

Phone: (902) 893-8075
Results "Hotline:" (902) 893-0505
Fax Number: (902) 897-0069

Sponsored by: Nova Scotia Provincial Exhibition Commission

Dates: January 1 - December 29

Post Times: 7:00 p.m.; Sundays 1:30 p.m.

Track Officials
President:	Donald Legge
General Manager:	Gail MacAvoy
Race Secretary:	Joe Kelly

Track Facts
Track Opened:	1875
Speed Rating:	2:07 1/5
Length of Homestretch:	440'
Width of Homestretch:	70'
Starters Behind the Gate	8
Hubrail?:	No
General Admission:	$2.00
Clubhouse Admission:	Free
General Parking:	Free
Grandstand Capacity:	572
Clubhouse Capacity:	149
Parking Capacity:	300

1990 Attendance and Handle
Number of Race Programs:	111
Gross Handle:	$7,845,529
Gross Attendance:	63,423
Average Handle:	$70,680
Average Attendance:	571
Percapita Wagering:	$123.70

Record Business
Handle:	$102,708	January 29, 1989
Attendance:	1,150	July 31, 1983

Leading Drivers
Wins:	Daniel Romo	129
UDR:	Dave Pinkney	.324
Purses:	Daniel Romo	$98,959

Leading Trainer
Wins	Lynn Privett	87

TRACKS

Vernon Downs (VD 3/4)

Located in Vernon, New York off Rte. 31 (Stuhlman Rd.), close by Route 5 and NY State Thruway (Exit 33) between Utica and Syracuse; 18 miles west of Utica and 32 miles east of Syracuse.

Address: Ruth Street
P.O. Box E
Vernon, New York 13476-0850
Phone: (315) 829-2201
Results "Hotline:" (315) 829-2201
Fax Number: (315) 829-4384

Sponsored by: Mid-State Raceway, Inc.
Dates: April 4 - November 9
Post Time: 7:30 p.m., Sundays 6:30 p.m.; Holidays 1:30 p.m.

Track Officials
President:	Frank White Sr.
Ass't. Gen. Mgr.:	Frank White Jr.
Race Secretary:	Walter Bonafice
Publicity Director:	Jim Moran

Track Facts
Track Opened:	1953
Speed Rating:	2:00
Length of Homestretch:	660'
Width of Homestretch:	100'
Starters Behind the Gate:	8
Hubrail?:	No
General Admission:	$2.00
Clubhouse Admission:	$3.50
General Parking:	$1.00
Grandstand Capacity:	3,500
Clubhouse Capacity:	2,500
Parking Capacity:	5,000

1990 Attendance and Handle
Number of Race Programs:	155
Gross Handle:	$30,452,454
Gross Attendance:	336,451
Average Handle:	$196,467
Average Attendance:	2,171
Percapita Wagering:	$90.50

Record Business
Handle:	$580,311	November 1, 1975
Attendance:	14,169	July 14, 1965

Leading Drivers
Wins:	Brian Allen	145
UDR:	Mickey Bridges	.370
Purses:	Brian Allen	$313,808

Leading Trainer
Wins:	Dave Dewhurst	56

Western Fair Raceway (Lon 1/2)

Located in Queens Park, London, Ontario, ten blocks from downtown.

Address: 900 King Street
P.O. Box 4550, Station "D"
London, Ontario N5W 5K3

Phone: (519) 438-7203
Fax Number: (519) 679-3124

Sponsored by: Western Fair Association
Dates: January 2 - June 17
October 2 - December 31

Post Times: 7:30; Matinees 1:15 p.m.

Track Officials
President:	Gerry Long
Raceway Manager:	Hugh Mitchell
Race Secretary:	Reg Gordon
Publicity Director:	Anne Eadie

Track Facts
Track Opened:	May 6, 1961
Speed Rating:	2:05
Length of Homestretch:	600'
Starters Behind the Gate:	7
Hubrail?:	Yes
General Admission:	$2.75
Clubhouse Admission:	$2.00
General Parking:	Free
Grandstand Capacity:	5,000
Clubhouse Capacity:	500
Parking Capacity:	2,000

1990 Attendance and Handle
Number of Race Programs:	141
Gross Handle:	$20,869,850
Gross Attendance:	235,511
Average Handle:	$148,013
Average Attendance:	1,670
Percapita Wagering:	$88.62

Record Business
Handle:	$415,593	1987
Attendance:	7,258	1967

Leading Drivers
Wins:	Rod Robblee (Win.)	119
	Ross Battin (Fall)	49
UDR:	Dave Wall (Win.)	.352
	Greg Campbell (Fall)	.414
Purses:	Ray McLean (Win.)	$167,216
Purses:	Ray McLean (Fall)	$84,526

Leading Trainer
Not Reported

TRACKS

Windsor Raceway (WR 5/8)

Located in Windsor, Ontario, two miles south of Ambassador Bridge to Detroit, and seven miles from downtown Detroit.

Address: Highway 18 & Sprucewood
P.O. Box 998
Windsor, Ontario N9A 6P6

Phone: (519) 969-8311 Windsor
(313) 961-9545 Detroit
Results "Hotline:" (313) 976-6666
Fax Number: (313) 962-1010 or
(519) 969-4452

Dates: January 2 - March 31
October 13 - December 31
Post Times: 7:00 p.m.; Matinees 1:30 p.m.

Track Officials
President:	B. Thomas Joy
General Manager:	Robert B. Dow
Race Secretary:	Ken Le Drew
Publicity Director:	Frank Salive

Track Facts
Track Opened:	October, 1965
Speed Rating:	2:02 3/5
Length of Homestretch:	520'
Width of Homestretch:	80'
Starters Behind the Gate:	9
Hubrail?:	Yes
General Admission:	$2.00
Clubhouse Admission:	$4.00
General Parking:	$1.50
Grandstand Capacity:	4,600
Clubhouse Capacity:	1,400
Parking Capacity:	4,600

1990 Attendance and Handle
Number of Race Programs:	167
Gross Handle:	$49,164,444
Gross Attendance:	351,047
Average Handle:	$294,398
Average Attendance:	2,102
Percapita Wagering:	$140.05

Record Business
Handle:	$985,151	December 7, 1980
Attendance:	12,057	March 19, 1972

Leading Drivers
Wins:	Danny Johnson (Win.)	114
	Mark Williams (Fall)	91
UDR:	Bill Gale (Win.)	.386
	Don Rankin, Jr. (Fall)	.375
Purses:	Danny Johnson (Win)	$278,921
	Mark Williams (Fall)	$199,632

Leading Trainer
Wins:	Donnie Rankin, Jr.	90

Yonkers Raceway (YR 1/2)

Located in Yonkers, New York at Central and Yonkers Aves., 17 miles from Times Square. Accessible via Subways and special buses. Central Ave. at the New York Thruway

Address: 810 Central Avenue
Yonkers, New York 10704
Phone: (914) 968-4200
Results "Hotline:" (914) 976-6969
Fax Number: (914) 968-1121

Sponsored by: Yonkers Racing Corp.

Dates: January 1 - December 31

Post Times: 8:00 p.m.; Matinees 1:00 p.m.

Track Officials
President:	Timothy Rooney
General Manager:	Robert Galterio
Race Secretary:	Steven Starr
Publicity Director:	Gary Sussman

Track Facts
Track Opened:	1899
Speed Rating:	2:02 1/5
Length of Homestretch:	440'
Width of Homestretch:	90'
Starters Behind the Gate:	8
Hubrail?:	No
General Admission:	$2.25
Clubhouse Admission:	$3.25
General Parking:	$1.50
Grandstand Capacity:	15,000
Clubhouse Capacity:	15,000
Parking Capacity:	9,400

1990 Attendance and Handle
Number of Race Programs:	353
Gross Handle:	$207,404,444
Gross Attendance:	925,213
Average Handle:	$587,548
Average Attendance:	2,621
Percapita Wagering:	$224.17

Record Business
Handle:	$3,220,686	December 15, 1969
Attendance:	40,386	August 16, 1958

Leading Drivers
Wins:	Walter Case, Jr.	390
UDR:	Walter Case, Jr.	.386
Purses:	Herve Filion	$2,648,658

Leading Trainer
Wins:	Tom Salerno	85

TRACKS

Barrie Raceway (Bar 1/2)

Address: Essa Rd.
P.O. Box 365
Barrie, Ont. L4M 4T5
Phone: (705) 726-9400
Results "Hotline:" (705) 726-3631
Fax Number: (705) 726-8364

Track Officials
President:	William Rowe
General Manager:	Jane Hutchins
Race Secretary:	Jean McEachern
Publicity Director:	Al Josey

1990 Attendance and Handle
Number of Race Programs:	119
Gross Handle:	$13,930,966
Gross Attendance:	130,236
Average Handle:	$117,067
Average Attendance:	1,094
Percapita Wagering:	$106.97

Record Business
Handle:	$238,338	January 27, 1990
Attendance:	2,873	July 30, 1977

Leading Drivers
Wins:	Steve Byron	152
UDR:	Steve Byron	.335
Purses:	Derek Newman	$184,529

Cloverdale (Clov 1/2)

Address: 6050 176th St.
P.O. Box 1199, Station "A"
Surrey, British Columbia V3S 5A5
Phone: (604) 576-9141
Results "Hotline:" (604) 574-3311
Fax Number: (604) 576-9821

Track Officials
President:	James Keeling, Sr.
General Manager:	James Keeling, Jr.
Racing Secretary:	Keith Quinlan
Publicity Director:	Bill Saunders

1990 Attendance and Handle
Number of Race Programs:	123
Gross Handle:	$53,722,784
Gross Attendance:	314,100
Average Handle:	$436,771
Average Attendance:	2,554
Percapita Wagering:	$171.04

Record Business
Handle:	$780,050	February 22, 1989
Attendance:	5,760	October 22, 1983

Leading Drivers
Wins:	Joe Hudon, Jr.	104
UDR:	Joe Hudon, Jr.	.397
Purses:	Joe Hudon, Jr.	$336,924

Clinton Raceway (Clntn 1/2)

Address: P.O. Box 778
Clinton, Ontario N0M 1L0
Phone: (519) 482-7729

Track Officials
Chairman:	Bill Fleming
Race Secretary:	Mary Donnelly

1990 Attendance and Handle
Number of Race Programs:	11
Gross Handle:	$644,419
Gross Attendance:	10,517
Average Handle:	$58,584
Average Attendance:	956
Percapita Wagering:	$61.27

Leading Drivers
Wins:	John Muir	18
UDR:	Howard Kennedy	.475
Purses:	Dave Wall	$19,368

Dresden Raceway (Dres 1/2)

Address: P.O. Box 689
Dresden, Ontario N0P 1M0

Phone: (519) 683-4466

Track Officials
President:	Graham Chambers
Race Secretary:	George Deacon
Publicity Director:	Jean Lekavy

1990 Attendance and Handle
Number of Race Programs:	33
Gross Handle:	$1,948,080
Gross Attendance:	31,177
Average Handle:	$59,033
Average Attendance:	945
Percapita Wagering:	$62.48

Record Business
Handle:	$187,252	September 7, 1986
Attendance:	3,347	September 7, 1986

Leading Drivers
Wins:	Dennis DuFord	47
UDR:	Mark Williams	.400
Purses:	Allen Cullen	$38,284

TRACKS

Elmira Raceway (Emira 1/2)

Address: 28 Snyder Ave., P.O. Box 98
Elmira, Ontario N3B 2Z5
Phone: (519) 669-8036
Fax Number: (519) 669-1202

Track Officials
President:	Jim McLeod
General Manager:	Ken Middleton
Race Secretary:	Diane Thaler
Publicity:	Ken Middleton/Diane Thaler

1990 Attendance and Handle
Number of Race Programs:	50
Gross Handle:	$4,286,983
Gross Attendance:	40,717
Average Handle:	$85,740
Average Attendance:	814
Percapita Wagering:	$105.29

Record Business
Handle:	$217,538	May 20, 1985
Attendance:	3,731	August 21, 1981

Leading Drivers
Wins:	Bryan Holmes	52
UDR:	Don Graham	.366
Purses:	Bryan Holmes	$52,880

Hanover Raceway (Hnvr 1/2)

Address: P.O. Box 93
Hanover, Ontario N4N 3C3

Phone: (519) 364-2860

Track Officials
President:	Cahrles Martin
General Manager:	Doug Hopkins
Race Secretary:	Doug Hopkins
Publicity Director:	Doug Hopkins

1990 Attendance and Handle
Number of Race Programs:	31
Gross Handle:	$1,682,911
Gross Attendance:	29,836
Average Handle:	$54,287
Average Attendance:	962
Percapita Wagering:	$56.41

Record Business
Handle:	$101,809	August, 1987
Attendance:	2,176	July 23, 1983

Leading Drivers
Wins:	Terry Fritz	20
UDR:	Paul Walker	.442
Purses:	Mark Estell	$28,379

Goderich Raceway (Godr 1/2)

Address: R.R. #4
P.O. Box 301
Goderich, Ontario N7A 4C6
Phone: (519) 524-6641

Track Officials
General Manager:	Shelly Hartman
Race Secretary:	Mary Donnelly

1990 Attendance and Handle
Number of Race Programs:	10
Gross Handle:	$314,114
Gross Attendance:	9,777
Average Handle:	$31,411
Average Attendance:	978
Percapita Wagering:	$32.13

Leading Drivers
Wins:	John Muir	79
UDR:	John Muir	.379
Purses:	John Muir	$10,947

Inverness Raceway (Invrn 1/2)

Address: P.O. Box 503
Inverness, Nova Scotia B0E 1N0

Phone: (902) 258-2648

Track Officials
General Manager:	Donnie MacLellan
Race Secretary:	Donnie MacLellan

1990 Attendance and Handle
Number of Race Programs:	24
Gross Handle:	$341,390
Gross Attendance:	5,781
Average Handle:	$14,225
Average Attendance:	241
Percapita Wagering:	$59.05

Record Business
Handle:	$37,214	Unknown
Attendance:		Unknown

Leading Drivers
Wins:	Joe Campbell	22
UDR:	Joe Campbell	.596
Purses:	Joe Campbell	$5,224

TRACKS

Kingston Park Raceway (KPR 5/8)

Address: R.R. #8
Kingston, Ontario K7L 4V4

Phone: (613) 549-2314

Track Officials
President:	Fred Gibson
General Manager:	Fred Gibson
Racing Secretary:	Dan Gibson

1990 Attendance and Handle
Number of Race Programs:	53
Gross Handle:	$2,637,312
Gross Attendance:	23,739
Average Handle:	$49,761
Average Attendance:	448
Percapita Wagering:	$111.10

Record Business
Handle:	$117,033	June 2, 1985
Attendance:	1,466	May 30, 1974

Leading Drivers
Wins:	Ed Huntbach	79
UDR:	Ed Huntbach	.379
Purses:	Ed Huntbach	$67,278

Orangeville Raceway (Ornvl 1/2)

Address: P.O. Box 296
Orangeville, Ontario L9W 2Z7
Phone: (519) 941-5321
Results "Hotline:" (519) 941-6964
Fax Number: (519) 942-0108

Track Officials
President:	Ian Hardcastle
General Manager:	Donna Black
Race Secretary:	Chris Bradt

1990 Attendance and Handle
Number of Race Programs:	103
Gross Handle:	$11,301,233
Gross Attendance:	109,620
Average Handle:	$109,721
Average Attendance:	1,064
Percapita Wagering:	$103.09

Record Business
Handle:	$322,700	February 26, 1984
Attendance:	2,900	February 26, 1984

Leading Drivers
Wins:	Jim Ritchie	144
UDR:	Jim Ritchie	.362
Purses:	Jim Ritchie	$154,522

Leamington Raceway (Leam 1/2)

Address: 194 Erie St., North
P.O. Box 646
Leamington, Ontario N8H 3A4
Phone: (519) 326-1885

Track Officials
President:	Richard Myers
General Manager:	Cheryl Harrison
Racing Secretary:	Reg Gordon

1990 Attendance and Handle
Number of Race Programs:	16
Gross Handle:	$1,136,464
Gross Attendance:	16,785
Average Handle:	$71,029
Average Attendance:	1,049
Percapita Wagering:	$67.71

Record Business
Handle:	$98,872	Unknown
Attendance:	1,207	Unknown

Leading Drivers
Wins:	Gord McDonnell	17
UDR:	Doug McIntosh	.529
Purses:	John Brooks	$19,082

Hippodrome de Quebec (Que 1/2)

Address: Exhibition Pk., P.O. Box 2053
Quebec City, Quebec G1K 7M9
Phone: (418) 524-5283
Results "Hotline:" (418) 524-6148
Fax Number: (418) 524-0776

Track Officials
President:	Marcel Jobin
General Manager:	Guy Cloutier
Race Secretary:	Raynald Toupin
Publicity Director:	Lucie Cloutier

1990 Attendance and Handle
Number of Race Programs:	163
Gross Handle:	$24,570,985
Gross Attendance:	259,349
Average Handle:	$150,742
Average Attendance:	1,591
Percapita Wagering:	$94.74

Record Business
Handle:	$347,022	September 1, 1985
Attendance:	10,464	August 31, 1986

Leading Drivers
Wins:	Gabriel Boily	208
UDR:	Jean Marie Potvin	.369
Purses:	Gabriel Boily	$359,552

TRACKS

Queensbury Downs (Reg 1/2)

Address: Elphinstone St. & Exhibition Way
P.O. Box 167
Regina, Saskatchewan S4P 2Z6
Phone: (306) 781-9310
Results "Hotline:" (306) 359-7703
Fax Number: (306) 525-0955

Track Officials
President:	Keith Critchley
General Manager:	Les Butler
Race Secretary:	Bill Teske
Publicity Director:	Les Butler

1990 Attendance and Handle
Number of Race Programs:	71
Gross Handle:	$3,755,659
Gross Attendance:	58,072
Average Handle:	$52,897
Average Attendance:	818
Percapita Wagering:	$64.67

Record Business
Handle:	$135,584	Spetember 3, 1989
Attendance:	3,485	September 3, 1989

Leading Drivers
Wins:	Harris Toole	77
UDR:	Harris Toole	.369
Purses:	Doug Shaw	$91,095

Quinte Raceway (BIVl 1/2)

Address: 18 Yeomans Street
Belleville, Ontario K8P 3X2

Phone: (613) 968-3266

Track Officials
President:	George McNeely
First Vice-President:	R Jarrell
Race Secretary:	Harry Burkitt
Publicity Director:	Vickie Henderson

1990 Attendance and Handle
Number of Race Programs:	27
Gross Handle:	$1,437,849
Gross Attendance:	19,696
Average Handle:	$53,254
Average Attendance:	729
Percapita Wagering:	$73.00

Record Business
Handle:	$73,282	Date not recorded
Attendance:	1,382	Date not recorded

Leading Drivers
Wins:	Ted McDonald	51
UDR:	Ted McDonald	.429
Purses:	Ted McDonald	$30,135

Sandown Harness Raceway (San 5/8)

Address: 1810 Glamorgan Rd.
P.O. Box 2370
Sidney, British Columbia V8L 3Y3
Phone: (604) 656-1631

Track Officials
President:	Jim Keeling, Sr.
General Manager:	Jim Keeling, Sr.
Director of Racing:	Keith Quinlan
Publicity Director:	Jim Keeling, Jr.

1990 Attendance and Handle
Number of Race Programs:	52
Gross Handle:	$6,800,857
Gross Attendance:	85,828
Average Handle:	$130,786
Average Attendance:	1,651
Percapita Wagering:	$79.24

Record Business
Handle:	$221,036	Not Recorded
Attendance:	2,272	Not Recorded

Leading Drivers
Wins:	Tim Brown	54
UDR:	Joe Hudon, Jr.	.505
Purses:	Bill Davis	$104,953

Sudbury Downs (Sudby 1/2)

Address: P.O. Box 1810
Chelmsford, Ontario P0M 1L0
Phone: (705) 855-9001
Race Office: (705) 855-9005
Fax Number: (705) 855-5434

Track Officials
President:	John C. MacIsaac
General Manager:	Mike MacIsaac
Racing Secretary:	Mike MacIssac
Publicity Director:	Dante Sindori

1990 Attendance and Handle
Number of Race Programs:	54
Gross Handle:	$3,904,774
Gross Attendance:	47,352
Average Handle:	$72,311
Average Attendance:	877
Percapita Wagering:	$82.46

Record Business
Handle:	$144,456	September 17, 1977
Attendance:	3,891	June 2, 1974

Leading Drivers
Wins:	Mark Cecile	57
UDR:	Mark Cecile	.374
Purses:	Gary Rivest	$71,834

TRACKS

Hipp. Trois Rivieres (TrRvs 1/2)

Address: 1600 Boulevard des Forges
Trois Rivieres, Quebec G9A 5H3

Phone: (819) 374-6734
Fax Number: (819) 376-4453

Track Officials
President:	Jean-Guy Laferte
General Manager:	Robert Pare
Race Secretary:	Robert Pare

1990 Attendance and Handle
Number of Race Programs:	99
Gross Handle:	$12,610,976
Gross Attendance:	106,314
Average Handle:	$127,384
Average Attendance:	1,074
Percapita Wagering:	$118.62

Record Business
Handle:	$223,188	July 18, 1989
Attendance:	2,968	July 3, 1976

Leading Drivers
Wins:	Gaetan Lamy	194
UDR:	Serge Ouellet	.472
Purses:	Gaetan Lamy	$425,711

Woodstock Raceway (Wodsk 1/2)

Address: P.O. Box 234
Woodstock, Ontario N4S 7W8
Phone: (519) 537-8212
Fax Number: (519) 537-2349

Track Officials
President:	James N. McDowell
General Manger:	W.B. Wallace
Race Secretary:	Teresa Donnelly
Publicity Director:	W.B. Wallace

1990 Attendance and Handle
Number of Race Programs:	25
Gross Handle:	$2,274,562
Gross Attendance:	25,425
Average Handle:	$90,982
Average Attendance:	1,017
Percapita Wagering:	$89.46

Record Business
Handle:	$151,115	July 19, 1988
Attendance:	2,300	August 23, 1983

Leading Drivers
Wins:	Rod Robblee	22
UDR:	John MacCormick	.470
Purses:	Ross Battin	$24,308

Grand Circuit Fairs

TRACKS

Delaware, OH County Fair (Dela 1/2)

Track located on Pennsylvania Ave., one mile west of U.S. Route 23 in Delaware, Ohio.

Address: 263 Pennsylvania Ave.
P.O. Box 100
Delaware, Ohio 43015
Phone: (614) 363-6000
(614) 548-4834 (Columbus)
(614) 362-3851, Ticket Sales

Sponsored by: Delaware Cty. Ag. Society, and The Little Brown Jug Society

Dates: September 15 - September 19
Post Time: 1 p.m. Sunday thru Tuesday
12 Noon Wed. and 11:00 a.m. Thur.

Track Officials
President:	Henry C. Thomson
Race Secretary:	Tom Thomson
Publicity Director:	Wil Kilburger
Secretary of Ticket Sales:	William Lowe

Track Facts
Track Opened:	1939
Speed Rating:	2:02
Length of Homestretch:	380'
Width of Homestretch:	80'
Starters Behind the Gate:	8
Hubrail?:	Yes
General Admission:	$5.00
Jug Day:	$10.00
Jug Day Reserved Stadium Seats:	$23.00
Grandstand Platform Chairs:	$30.00
Ground Chairs:	$23.00
Grandstand, Jugette Day:	$15.00
Grandstand Capacity:	3,200
Chair Seats:	3,000
Stadium Seats:	5,200
Parking Capacity:	12,000

1990 Attendance and Handle
Number of Race Programs:	4 days
Gross Handle:	$2,613,319
Gross Attendance:	62,792
Average Handle:	$522,644
Average Attendance:	15,698
Percapita Wagering:	$43.02

Record Business
Handle:	$1,768,316	September 22, 1988
Attendance:	50,792	September 21, 1989

Leading Drivers
Wins:	Jeff Fout	6
UDR:	Dan Ater	.600
Purses:	John Campbell	$197,472

Du Quoin State Fair (DuQ 1)

Track located on U.S. Route 51, two miles south of Du Quoin, Illinois.

Address: U.S. Rte. 51 South
Du Quoin, Illinois 62832

Phone: (618) 542-3000
Fax Number: (618) 542-3871

Sponsored by: Illinois Dept. of Agriculture

Dates: August 26 - August 31

Post Time: Noon

Track Officials
President:	John Rundquist
General Manager:	Mike DuBois
Racing Secretary:	Eliot Narotsky
Publicity Director:	Mary Jane Dwyer

Track Facts
Track Opened:	1942
Speed Rating:	2:00 1/5
Length of Homestretch:	900'
Width of Homestretch:	75-1/2'
Starters Behind the Gate:	10
Hubrail?:	Yes
General Admission:	Free
General Parking:	$1.00
Grandstand Capacity:	8,228
Bleacher Capacity:	9,792
Parking Capacity:	5,500

1990 Attendance and Handle
Number of Race Programs:	5 days
Gross Handle:	$537,869
Gross Attendance:	(est.) 18,000
Average Handle:	$107,574
Average Attendance:	(est.) 3,600
Percapita Wagering:	(est.) $29.88

Record Business
Handle:	$481,929	August 30, 1980
Attendance:	15,121	August 30, 1980

Leading Drivers
Wins:	John Campbell & Connel Willis	6
UDR:	"Chip" Noble	.514
Purses:	Cat Manzi	$304,350

TRACKS

Historic Track – Goshen (Gosh 1/2)

Track located on Park Place, 10 - 12 miles west of Intersection of New York State Thruway and Route 17. Track opened in 1838, making it the oldest active track in North America.

Address: Park Place
P.O. Box 192
Goshen, New York 10924
Phone: (914) 294-5333

Sponsored by: Goshen Historic Track, Inc.

Dates: June 1, 8, 15, 22; July 4 - July 7
Post Time: 1:30 p.m.

Track Officials
President:	Robert Dickover
Administrator:	Timothy J. Varden
Race Secretary:	Ray Goodness
Publicity Director:	Sherry Skramstad

Track Facts
Track Opened:	1838
Speed Rating:	2:04 1/5
Length of Homestretch:	500'
Width of Homestretch:	90'
Starters Behind the Gate:	8
Hubrail?:	Yes
General Admission:	$2.00
Box Seats:	(Season) $125.00
Grandstand Capacity:	2,323

No Parking Allowed on the Grounds

1990 Attendance
No. of Race Programs	8 days
Gross Attendance:	14,000
Average Attendance:	1,750

No Wagering Allowed at Historic Track

Leading Drivers
Wins:	Herve Filion	5
UDR:	Cat Manzi	.722
Purses:	Herve Filion	$35,946

Indiana State Fair (Ind 1)

Track located at 38th and Fall Creek Boulevard, Indianapolis, Indiana

Address: 1202 East 38th Street
Indianapolis, Indiana 46205-2869

Phone: (317) 927-7589
Fax Number: (317) 927-7578

Sponsored by: Indiana State Fair

Dates: August 19 - 24

Post Time: 11:00 a.m.

Track Officials
Executive Director:	Donald W. Moreau, Sr.
Publicity Coordinator:	Paul Miner

Track Facts
Track Opened:	1892
Speed Rating:	2:01 1/5
Length of Homestretch:	900'
Width of Homestretch:	80'
Starters Behind the Gate:	8
Hubrail?:	Yes
Reserved Seats:	$5.00 (Sat. Only)
Grandstand Capacity:	14,000
Parking Capacity:	14,300

1990 Attendance
Number of Race Programs:	5
Gross Attendance:	(est.) 6,000
Average Attendance:	(est.) 1,200

No Wagering Allowed at Indianapolis

Leading Drivers
Wins:	(Several Drivers)	4
UDR:	"Chip" Noble	.556
Purses:	"Chip" Noble	$64,697

TRACKS

Springfield, Illinois (Spr 1)

Track located on Sangamon and Eighth Aves. One mile east of the intersection of Interstate 55 and Sangamon Ave.

Address: Horse Racing Program -
Illinois Department of Agriculture
801 East Sangamon Avenue
Springfield, Illinois 62794-9281

Phone: (217) 782-2239
Results "Hotline:" (217) 782-4231
Fax Number: (217) 524-6194

Sponsored by: Illinois Dept. of Agriculture

Dates: August 12 - August 16
Post Time: Noon

Track Officials
President:	John Rundquist
General Manager:	Merle S. Miller
Racing Secretary:	Eliot Narotsky
Publicity Director:	Jered Hooker

Track Facts
Track Opened:	1928
Speed Rating:	1:58 3/5
Length of Homestretch:	510'
Width of Homestretch:	73'
Starters Behind the Gate:	9
Hubrail?:	Yes
General Admission:	Free
General Parking:	Free
Grandstand Capacity:	10,000
Bleacher Capacity:	400
Parking Capacity:	5,000

1990 Attendance and Handle
Number of Race Programs:	5
Gross Handle:	$835,457
Gross Attendance:	(est.) 34,500
Average Handle:	$167,091
Average Attendance	(est.) 6,900
Percapita Wagering:	(est.) $24.22

Record Business
Handle:	$218,539	August 21, 1987
Attendance:	(est.) 9,000	August 17, 1987

Leading Drivers
Wins:	Tom Graham	9
UDR:	Berndt Lindstedt	.750
Purses:	Berndt Lindstedt	$105,850

The Syracuse Mile (Sycs 1)

Track located at the New York State Fairgrounds in Syracuse, New York, four miles west of the city, adjacent to Route 690.

Address: c/o Buffalo Raceway
P.O. Box 38, Hamburg, New York 14075

Phone: (716) 649-1280 (Buffalo)
(315) 487-7711 (Fairgrounds)
Fax Number: (315) 487-5711
Sponsored by: Syracuse Mile, Inc.; NY State Industrial Exhibition Authority; Harness Breeders of NY State; Agriculture & NY State Horse Breeding Development Fund; and NY State Fair.
Dates: Aug. 3, 4, 10, 11, 16, 17, 18

Track Officials
President:	Frank O. White
General Manager:	Bruce Munn
Race Secretary:	Sharon Herrmann
Publicity Director:	Darrell Wood

Track Facts
Track Opened:	1890
Speed Rating:	1:59 2/5
Length of Homestretch:	1,260'
Width of Homestretch:	80'
Starters Behind the Gate:	8
Hubrail?:	Yes
General Admission:	$1.50
General Parking:	$1.00
Grandstand Capacity:	15,000
Parking Capacity:	5,000

1990 Attendance and Handle
Number of Race Programs:	7
Gross Handle:	$2,138,983
Gross Attendance:	19,005
Average Handle:	$305,569
Average Attendance:	2,715
Percapita Wagering:	$112.55

Record Business
Handle:	$486,613	August 20, 1989
Attendance:	6,749	August 16, 1980

Leading Drivers
Wins:	Chuck Connor, Jr., Michel Lachance, and Abe Stoltzfus	4
UDR:	Michel Lachance	.436
Purses:	Michel Lachance	$86,044

TRACKS

PROMINENT NORTH AMERICAN TRAINING CENTERS

Florida Training Centers

Ben White Raceway   **(305) 293-8721**
1805 Lee Rd., Orlando, FL 32810

Castletiny Training Center   **(305) 499-5196**
Rte. 1, Box 305, Delray Beach, FL 33446

Pompano Training Center   **(305) 972-5911**
1800 S.W. Third St., Pompano Beach, FL 33069

South Florida Trotting Center   **(305) 967-5911**
7563 St. Rte. 7, Lake Worth, FL 33467

Spring Garden Ranch   **(904) 985-5654**
P.O. Box 367, DeLeon Springs, FL 32028

Sunshine Meadows   **(407) 495-1455**
16668 Winner's Circle, Del Ray Beach, FL 33446

Winter Miles Training Center   **(305) 365-6773**
Highway 476, P.O. Box 1389, Oviedo, FL 32765

Southern Training Centers

Hawkinsville Harness Training Facility   **(912) 892-9463**
P.O. Box 95, Hawkinsville, GA 31036

Little River Farm   **(919) 949-3333**
P.O. Box 3330, Pinehurst, NC 28374

Pinehurst Harness Training Center   **(919) 295-2723**
P.O. Box 41, Pinehurst, NC 28374

Aiken Mile Training Center   **(803) 642-8295**
620 Banks Mills Rd., Aiken, SC 29801

New Jersey Training Centers

Gaitway Farms   **(201) 446-1222, 446-7100**
P.O. Box 204A, R.D. 1, Freehold, NJ 07728

Showplace Farms   **(201) 446-3100**
505 Route 33, Englishtown, NJ 07726

Other Training Centers

Paiement Training Centre   **(416) 659-3301**
210 Campbellville Rd., R.R. #2, Campbellville, ONT L0P 1B0

The Red Mile   **(606) 255-0752**
P.O. Box 420, Lexington, KY 40585

TRACKS

ALPHABETICAL LISTING OF TRACK ABBREVIATIONS

Legend: **1** = Mile Track, **T** = 13/16, **Q** = 3/4, **f** = 5/8, all others 1/2

Abbreviation	Track & Size	Abbreviation	Track & Size
Adrn	Adrian, MI	Brk	Brooklin, ONT
Aftn	Afton, NY	Brkvi	Brockville, ONT
Agawm	Agawam, MA	Brom	Brome, QUE
Ahsk	Ahoskie, NC	Brtn	Barton, QUE
Albn	Albion, IL	Btva	Batavia Downs, NY
Aldo	Aledo, IL	Bucy	Bucyrus, OH
Allgn	Allegan, MI	Burf	Burford, ONT
Alp	Alpena, MI	Burt	Burton, OH
Alsn	Allison, IA	Butlr	Butler, PA
Altmt	Altamont, IL	BvDm	Beaver Dam, WI
Amst	Amherst, WI	Bvdr	Belvidere, IL
Anca	Ancaster, ONT	BwlG	Bowling Green, OH
And	Anderson, IN	ByCy	Bay City, MI
Angel	Angelica, NY	Byd	Buckyland Stables, PA
Anna	Anna, IL	Cald	Caldwell, OH
Arnp	Arnprior, ONT	Camb	Cambridge, IL
AsD	Assiniboia Downs, MAN T	Canon	Cannon Falls, MN
Ashl	Ashland, OH	Cantn	Canton, OH
Athns	Athens, OH	Carlt	Carrollton, IL
Atl	Atlanta, GA	Carmi	Carmi, IL
Atmt	Altamont, NY	Caro	Caro, MI
Attc	Attica, OH	Carr	Carrollton, OH
Aud	Audubon Downs, KY	Cass	Cassopolis, MI
Aust	Austin, MN	Cbls	Cobleskill, NY
Avmr	Avonmore, ONT	CbsJn	Columbus Junction, IA
AxBy	Alexandria Bay, NY f	Cby	Canterbury Downs, MN 1
AyrCl	Ayers Cliff, QUE	Cdiz	Cadiz, OH
BalSp	Ballston Spa, NY	Cdlc	Cadillac, MI
Bang	Bangor Raceway, ME	Cdna	Caledonia, NY
Bar	Barrie Raceway, ONT	CdRp	Cedar Rapids, IA
Bath	Bath, NY	Cel	Celina, OH
BB	Blue Bonnets, QUE f	CHF	Capital Hill Farms, NJ f
BdAx	Bad Axe, MI	Char	Charleston, IL
Bdfd	Bedford, PA	Chey	Cheboygan, MI
Bdstn	Bardstown, KY	Chhs	Chahalis, WA
Beams	Beamsville, ONT	Chil	Chillicothe, OH
Bedf	Bedford, QUE	Chino	Chino, CA
Bent	Benton, KY	Chlt	Charlotte, MI
Ber	Berea, OH	ChP	New Brunswick Downs, N. Brun. f
Bftn	Bellefontaine, OH	Chrtn	Charlottetown, PEI
BgRpd	Big Rapids, MI	Circ	Circleville, OH
BgZ	Big Z Farms, NJ	Clark	Clarksburg, NJ
Bklyn	Brooklyn, CT	Cldn	Caledon, ONT
BlHl	Blue Hill, ME	Clear	Clearfield, PA
Blom	Bloomsburg, PA	Clgy	Stampede Park, ALTA f
Blue	Blue Earth, MN	Clna	Caledonia, ONT
Blvl	Quinte Raceway, ONT	Clntn	Clinton Raceway, Ont
BmlPf	Balmoral Park, IL f	Clov	Cloverdale Raceway, B.C.
BmlPm	Balmoral Park, IL 1	Cmros	Camrose, ALTA
Bnbk	Binbrook, ONT	Cnfld	Canfield, OH
Bnvl	Boonville, NY	Cnsv	Connersville, IN
Bott	Bottineau, ND	Cntck	Contoocook, NH
BR	Buffalo Raceway, NY	Cntrv	Centreville, MI
Brd	Brandywine Raceway, DE f	Cnvr	Converse, IN

TRACKS

Abbreviation	Track & Size		Abbreviation	Track & Size	
Cols	Ohio State Fair		FlmD	Flamboro Downs, ONT	
Conn	Connaught Park, QUE		Fox	Foxboro Raceway, MA	f
Cort	Cortland, OH		FP	Fairmount Park, IL	1
Cosh	Coshocton, OH		Frdtn	Fredericton, N.Brun.	
Crb	Carberry, MAN		Fred	Frederick, MD	
Crlvl	Carlinville, IL		Frfld	Fairfield, IL	
Crm	Carman, MAN		FrmCy	Farmer City, IL	
Crot	Croton, OH		Frnft	Frankfort, IN	
Crswl	Croswell, MI		Frst	Forest, ONT	
Crydn	Corydon, IN		Frybg	Fryeburg, ME	
Csty	Castletiny Farm, FL		FsR	Freestate Raceway, MD	f
Ctm	Chatham, NY		Fwvl	Fowlerville, MI	
Cum	Cumberland, ME		GCTC	Gil Crest Training Center, FL	f
Cvll	Centreville, ONT		Glbr	Glenboro, MAN	
Cwtn	Cowtown, NJ		Gldwn	Gladwin, MI	
Darl	Darlington, WI		Godr	Goderich Raceway, ONT	
Daup	Dauphine, MAN		Gosh	Historic Track, NY	
Dayt	Dayton, OH		Gouv	Gouverneur, NY	
Dctr	Decatur, IL		Grebr	Greenbrier Farms, CA	
DD	Dover Downs, DE	f	Green	Greenville, OH	
Dela	Delaware, OH		Grig	Griggsville, IL	
DelM	Del Mar, CA	1	Grnfd	Greenfield, MA	
Det	Wolverine Raceway, MI	1	GrnPr	Grand Prairie, ALTA	
DLrn	DeLoraine, MAN		Grnup	Greenup, IL	
DLSgn	DeLeon Springs, FL		Grnvl	Greenville, IL	
DLSp	DeLeon Springs, FL	1	Grot	Groton, MA	
DMV	Delmarva Downs, Berlin, MD		GrR	Greenwood Raceway, ONT	f
Dndlk	Dundalk, ONT		Grtz	Gratz, PA	
Dnkrk	Dunkirk, NY		GSP	Garden State Park, NJ	1
Dnlsn	Donnellson, IA		Gshn	Goshen, IN	
Dnsn	Denison, IA		Gtwy	Gaitway Farms, NJ	1
Dorch	Dorchester, ONT		Gty	Gaitway Farms, NJ	1
Dover	Dover, OH		Gwy	Gaitway Farms, NJ	1
Dres	Dresden Raceway, ONT		Gyld	Gaylord, MI	
DsMns	Des Moines, IA		Had	Hadley, MA	
Dund	Dundee, NY		Hale	Hale, MI	
DuQ	DuQuoin, IL		Ham	Hamilton, ND	
Dytn	Dayton, PA		Har	Harrington Raceway, DE	
EA	Egyptian Acres, NJ		Hart	Hart, MI	
Eaton	Eaton, OH		Haw	Hawthorne Park, IL	1
Edm	Northlands Park, ALTA	f	Hdwk	Hardwick Farms, NJ	
ELF	East Lynne Farms, NJ		Hend	Western Kentucky Raceway, KY	
Eldon	Eldon, IA		HhTC	Hollyhurst Training Center, PA	
Elkrn	Elkhorn, WI		Hick	Hicksville, OH	
Elmra	Elmira, NY		Hill	Hilliard, OH	
Emira	Elmira Raceway, ONT		Hin	Hinsdale Raceway, NH	
Emo	Emo, ONT		Hksv	Hawkinsville, GA	1
Enoch	Enoch, ALB		Hldn	Holdens Raceway, MS	
EPR	Exhibition Park, N.Brun		Hlnd	Holland, MI	
EsxJn	Essex Junction, VT		Hlsdl	Hillsdale, MI	
Fairb	Fairbault, MN		Hmlok	Hemlock, NY	
Fair	Fairbury, IL		Hmt	Hemet, CA	
Farm	Farmington, ME		Hndn	Huntingdon, PA	
Fat	Fatima, QUE		Hnry	Henry, IL	
Faye	Fayetteville, TN		Hnvr	Hanover Raceway, ONT	
Fda	Fonda, NY		Hol	Hollywood Park, CA	1
Fhld	Freehold Raceway, NJ		Holln	Holland, MAN	
Find	Findlay, OH		Hone	Honesdale, PA	

Page 47

TRACKS

Abbreviation	Track & Size		Abbreviation	Track & Size	
Hopk	Hopkinsville, KY		Lrn	Laura Lan Farm, NJ	
HP	Hazel Park, MI	f	LSM	Lake Shore Meadows, PA	Q
HR	Hamilton, OH		Lsbn	Lisbon, OH	
Hrsn	Harrison, MI		LtlVy	Little Valley, NY	
Hstng	Hastings, MI		Lud	Ludington, MI	
Hugh	Hughesville, PA		Lwstn	Lewistown, IL	
Humb	Humboldt, IA		Lyd	Lloydminster, SASK	
Hutch	Hutchinson, MN		Lydvl	Lyndonville, VT	
Imad	Havre aux Maisons, QUE		Malon	Malone, NY	
Imlay	Imlay City, MI		Manit	Manitowaning, ONT	
Ind	Indiana State Fair, IN	1	Maq	Maquoketa, IA	
Indna	Indiana, PA		Mari	Marietta, OH	
Invrn	Inverness, N.Scot.		Mar	Marion, IL	
Ionia	Ionia, MI		Marsh	Marshall, IL	
Ipls	Indianapolis, IN		Mart	Martinsville, IL	
Iron	Ironwood, MI		Mary	Marysville, OH	
Ithca	Ithaca, MI		Mason	Mason, MI	
Jack	Jackson Raceway, MI		Mass	Massena, NY	
Jeff	Jefferson, OH		Mayfd	Mayfield, KY	
Jksvl	Jacksonville, IL		May	Maywood Park, IL	
Jrsv	Jerseyville, IL		McCnl	McConnelsville, OH	
KD	Kawartha Downs, ONT	f	Mdlnd	Midland, MI	
Kent	Kentland, IN		Meadv	Meadville, PA	
Keos	Keosauqua, IA		Mea	The Meadows, PA	f
Khka	Kahoka, MO		Med	Medina, OH	
Klmzo	Kalamazoo, MI		Melb	Melbourne, ONT	
Klrny	Killarney, MAN		Memp	Memphis, MO	
Knox	Knoxville, IL		Mend	Mendota, IL	
Knrs	Kinross, MI		Miami	Miami, MAN	
Knton	Kenton, OH		Milt	Milton, ONT	
KPR	Kingston Park Raceway, ONT	f	Minn	Minnedosa, MAN	
LA	Los Alamitos, CA	f	Mkg	Muskegon, MI	
LaCht	LaChute, QUE		Mnch	Manchester, VT	
Lanc	Lancaster, OH		MnlPt	Mineral Point, WI	
Laprt	Laporte, IN		Mnsf	Mansfield, OH	
Lat	Latonia Raceway, KY	1	Mntcl	Monticello, IA	
LB	Liberty Bell Park, PA	f	Mntpl	Mt. Pleasant, MI	
Lbn	Lebanon, KY		Mntwc	Manitowoc, WI	
Lcnt	Lacenter, KY		Moh	Mohawk Raceway, ONT	f
Leam	Leamington Raceway, ONT		Montp	Montpelier, IN	
Leb	Lebanon Raceway, OH		Mor	Morris, NY	
Lehgh	Lehighton, PA		Mphs	Memphis, TN	1
Leth	Lethbridge, ALTA		MqD	Marquis Downs, SASK	f
Lever	Leverett, MA		MRc	Muskegon Racecourse, MI	f
Lewbg	Lewisburg, WV		MR	Monticello Raceway, NY	
Lew	Lewiston Raceway, ME		Mrion	Marion, OH	
Lex	The Red Mile, KY	1	Mrisn	Morrison, IL	
Lima	Lima, OH		Mrkh	Markham, ONT	
Linc	Lincoln, IL		Mrlb	Marlborough, MA	
LkOds	Lake Odessa, MI		Mrn	Marion, MI	
Lncln	Lincoln, IL		Mroe	Monroe, WI	
Lndn	London, OH		Mrsfd	Marshfield, MA	
Lnsdw	Lansdowne, ONT		Mrshl	Marshall, MI	
Logan	Logan, OH		Mrtvl	Martinsville, ONT	
Lomb	Lombardy, ONT		Msfld	Marshfield, WI	
Lon	Western Fair Raceway, ONT		MsJw	Moose Jaw, SASK	f
LouD	Louisville Downs, KY		M	The Meadowlands, NJ	1
Low	Lowville, NY		MtGil	Mount Gilead, OH	

TRACKS

Abbreviation	Track & Size		Abbreviation	Track & Size	
MtJP	Mt. Joli Price, QUE		Plnvl	Plainville, MA	
Mtplr	Montpelier, OH		Pltbg	Plattsburg, NY	
MtStr	Mount Sterling, IL		Ply	Plymouth, NH	
MtVer	Mount Vernon, OH		Pom	Fairplex Park, CA	
Mun	Muncie, IN		Port	Portage LaPrairie, MAN	
Napa	Napanee, ONT		PPk	Pompano Park, FL	f
Nash	Nashua, IA		Ppvl	Papineauille, QUE	
NBD	New Brunswick Downs, N. Brun.	f	Pres	Presque Isle, ME	
NcR	Northcoast Raceway, MI		PrM	Prairie Meadows, IA	1
Neil	Neillsville, WI		Prnc	Princeton, IL	
Nfld	Northfield Park, OH		Proc	Proctorville, OH	
Nor	Northville Downs, MI		PrRoy	Port Royal, PA	
Nouvl	Nouvelle, QUE		PrtPy	Port Perry, ONT	
Npln	Napoleon, OH		Ptlnd	Portland, IN	
Nrwd	Norwood, ONT		Ptsbg	Petersburg, IL	
NtSD	North Side Downs, N.Scot.		PV	Hipp. Sorella, QUE	
Nway	Norway, MI		QCD	Quad City Downs, IL	f
Nwch	Norwich, NY		Que	Hippodrome de Quebec, QUE	
Nwlk	Norwalk, OH		Quyon	Quyon, QUE	
Nwng	Newington, ONT		Rchln	Richland Center, WI	
Nwton	Newton, IL		Rchst	Rochester, NH	
Ocla	Golden Cross Farm, FL	f	Rchwd	Richwood, OH	
OD	Ocean Downs, MD		Rcmnd	Richmond, QUE	
OHbr	Oak Harbor, OH		RcR	Rosecroft Raceway, MD	
Ohs	Ohsweken, ONT		Rdvl	Readville, MA	1
Onkma	Onekama, MI		Reg	Queensbury Downs, SASK	
Oreg	Oregon, IL		Rhin	Rhinebeck, NY	
Orill	Orillia, ONT		Rich	Richelieu Park, QUE	
Orlnd	Orlando, FL		RicLk	Rice Lake, WI	
Orl	Orlando, FL	1	RidC	Rideau Carleton, ONT	f
Ormst	Ormstown, ONT		Ridg	Ridgetown, ONT	
Ornvl	Orangeville Raceway, ONT		RidL	Riviere du Loup, QUE	
Orono	Orono, ONT		Rksp	Rocksprings, OH	
Oskls	Oskaloosa, IA		ROC	Delmarva Downs, MD	
Ott	Ottawa, OH		Roch	Rochester, MN	
Ovdo	Oviedo, FL		Rod	Rodney, ONT	
OWash	Old Washington, OH		RP	Raceway Park, OH	f
Owat	Owatonna, MN		RR	Roosevelt Raceway, NY	
			RSD	Riverside Downs, KY	
Owego	Owego, NY				
Owen	Owensville, OH		Rshvl	Rushville, IL	
Pabos	Pabos, QUE		Russ	Russell, MAN	
Pad	Paducah, KY		Rutln	Rutland, VT	
Pain	Painesville, OH		SA	Santa Anita, CA	1
Pana	Pana, IL		Sack	Sackville Downs, N.Scot.	
Paris	Paris, IL		Sacr	Cal-Expo, CA	1
Park	Parkhill, ONT		Sagy	Hippodrome Saguenay, QUE	
Par	Paris, ONT		Salm	Salem, IL	
Pauld	Paulding, OH		Sand	Sandown Park Raceway, BC	f
PcD	Pocono Downs, PA	f	Sar	Hiawatha Horse Park, ONT	f
Peca	Pecatonica, IL		Sart	Sartigan, QUE	
Perth	Perth, ONT		SBLG	St. Basile le Grand, QUE	
Pet	Petosky, MI		Sbyvl	Shelbyville, IN	
Phila	Philadelphia, MS		Scar	Scarborough Downs, ME	
Pike	Piketon, OH		ScD	Scioto Downs, OH	f
Pilot	Pilot Mound, MAN		Sedal	Sedalia, MO	
Pink	Pinckneyville, IL		Sed	Sedalia, MO	1
Pisc	Piscataway, NJ		SgHr	Saginaw Valley Downs, MI	
PlnCy	Plain City, OH		SgVy	Saginaw Valley Downs, MI	

TRACKS

Abbreviation	Track & Size	Abbreviation	Track & Size
SHEDD	Shedden Center, ONT	TrRvs	Hippodrome Trois Rivieres, QUE
Shedd	Shedden, ONT	TrSp	Trout Springs, ALTA
Sherb	Sherbrooke, QUE	Trum	Trumansburg, NY
Shpl	Showplace Farms, NJ f	Truro	Truro, N.Scot.
Sid	Sidney, OH	Trvs	Traverse City, MI
Sim	Simcoe, ONT	Try	Troy, PA
Skow	Skowhegan, ME	Tunbr	Tunbridge, VT
Smeth	Smethport, PA	Twnr	Towner, MD
Smld	Smithland, KY	Union	Union, ME
Smth	Smithfield, OH	UpSan	Upper Sandusky, OH
Smtvl	Smithville, ONT	Urbna	Urbana, OH
SndCr	Sandy Creek, NY	Urb	Urbana, IL
Sndwh	Sandwich, IL	Vass	Vassar, MI
SnJos	San Jose, CA	Vctvl	Victorville, CA
Snsh	Sunshine Meadows, FL f	VD	Vernon Downs, NY Q
SPk	Sportsman's Park, IL f	Viro	Viroqua, WI
SpCk	Sports Creek Raceway, MI f	VnWrt	Van Wert, OH
Spenc	Spencer, MA	Vrdn	Virden, MAN
Spncr	Spencer, IA	Wake	Wakeeney, KA
Sprng	Springfield, OH	Wapak	Wapakoneta, OH
Spr	Springfield, IL 1	Wapel	Wapello, IA
Squt	Squatec, QUE	Warrn	Warren, OH
Srl	Hipp. Sorella, QUE	War	Warren, IL
Srry	Surrey, BC	WasCH	Washington Court House, OH
SSV	St-Syl Vere, QUE	Wash	Washington, PA
SsM	Sunshine Meadows, FL 1	Water	Waterloo, IA
StBx	Ste. Beatrix, QUE	Watt	Wattsburg, PA
StEd	St. Edouard, QUE	Wausa	Wausau, WI
StGlm	St. Guillaume, QUE	Waw	Wawanesa, MAN
Stga	Saratoga Harness, NY	Wayn	Waynesburg, PA
StHgs	St. Hughes, QUE	Wdna	Wadena, MN
SthMt	South Mountain, ONT	Wdsfd	Woodsfield, OH
StJDl	St.Joseph Delepage, QUE	Wdstk	Woodstock, VA
StJhn	Saint John's, NFLD	Well	Welland, ONT
Stnd	Standish, MI	West	Westport, NY
Stock	Stockton, KA	Wey	Weyauwega, WI
Ston	Stoneboro, PA	What	What Cheer, IA
StPtr	Saint Peter, MN	Whtn	Wheaton, MN
Strgs	Sturgis, KY	Whtny	Whitney Point, NY
Stroy	Strathroy, ONT	Wilm	Wilmington, OH
Sturg	Sturgeon Bay, WI	Wind	Windsor, ME
Sudby	Sudbury Downs, ONT	Wint	Winterburn, ALTA
Summ	Summerside, P.E.I.	Wlctn	Wallacetown, ONT
Sund	Sunderland, ONT	Wlngt	Wellington, OH
Sutt	Sutton, ONT	Wlstn	Wellstown, OH
Swan	Swan River, MAN	Wodsk	Woodstock, ONT
SxC	Sioux Center, IA	Wodst	Woodstock, NB
SxFl	Sioux Falls, SD	Wood	Woodstock, IL
Sycs	Syracuse, NY 1	Wostr	Wooster, OH
Sydny	Sydney, N.Scot.	WR	Windsor Raceway, ONT f
Tara	Tara, ONT	Wseon	Wauseon, OH
Tayvl	Taylorville, IL	Wtfd	Westfield, WI
Tees	Teeswater, ONT	Wtrl	Waterloo, NY
Tiff	Tiffin, OH	Xenia	Xenia, OH
Till	Tillsonburg, ONT	York	York, PA
TinFl	Tinton Falls, NJ	YR	Yonkers Raceway, NY
Tops	Topsham, ME	Yrktn	Yorkton, SASK
Troy	Troy, OH	Zane	Zanesville, OH

TRACKS

TOP TRACKS BY PURSES PAID

Top Ten Tracks by Total Purses		Top Ten Tracks by Average Purse	
Track	Total Purses	Track	Average Purse
The Meadowlands	$39,080,329	Delaware, OH Cty. Fair	$23,891
Yonkers Raceway	29,984,755	Du Quoin St. FairIL	20,006
Blue Bonnets	20,567,250	Syracuse, NY	16,480
Greenwood Raceway	20,248,621	The Meadowlands	15,777
Mohawk Raceway	18,927,497	Mohawk Raceway	14,776
Freehold Raceway	15,384,196	Greenwood Raceway	13,321
Rosecroft Raceway	15,204,165	Sportsman's Park	10,553
Sportsman's Park	14,479,138	Springfield, IL	9,848
Pompano Park	11,810,422	Garden State Park	9,016
Maywood Park	10,527,102	Hawthorne Racecourse	8,840

PURSES PAID AT NORTH AMERICAN TRACKS
(Rank, from among 87 tracks, shown in parentheses)

Track	Races	Total Purses	(Rank)	Avg. Purse	(Rank)
Assiniboia Downs	945	1,457,313	(51)	1,542	(63)
Avalon Raceway (St. John's)	386	88,696	(86)	230	(87)
Balmoral Park	1,052	4,992,334	(22)	4,746	(23)
Bangor Raceway	480	445,081	(72)	927	(77)
Barrie Raceway	1,147	1,966,640	(44)	1,715	(55)
Batavia Downs	1,452	3,607,105	(34)	2,484	(37)
Blue Bonnets	3,149	20,567,250	(3)	6,531	(14)
Buffalo Raceway	1,506	3,678,965	(33)	2,443	(38)
Cal-Expo	603	1,902,374	(45)	3,155	(32)
Charlottetown Raceway	1,334	951,412	(62)	713	(82)
Clinton Raceway	114	202,328	(82)	1,775	(53)
Cloverdale Raceway	1,208	4,007,871	(27)	3,318	(29)
Hippodrome Connaught	1,380	3,186,940	(36)	2,309	(40)
Cumberland Fair	106	121,660	(85)	1,148	(72)
Delaware, OH	72	1,720,125	(47)	23,891	(1)
Delmarva Downs	895	1,589,945	(49)	1,776	(52)
Dover Downs	1,211	1,091,017	(61)	901	(80)
Dresden Raceway	332	638,083	(68)	1,922	(50)
Du Quoin, IL	67	1,340,414	(55)	20,006	(2)
Elmira Raceway	515	805,012	(66)	1,563	(61)
Exhibition Park Raceway	1,038	942,924	(63)	908	(79)
Fairmount Park	844	2,766,509	(39)	3,278	(31)
Flamboro Downs	2,251	6,533,444	(17)	2,902	(34)
Frederickton Raceway	358	352,766	(77)	985	(76)
Freehold Raceway	2,695	15,384,196	(6)	5,708	(17)
Garden State Park	844	7,609,252	(14)	9,016	(9)
Goderich Raceway	100	130,329	(84)	1,303	(68)
Goshen, NY	50	256,057	(80)	5,121	(20)
Greenwood Raceway	1,520	20,248,621	(4)	13,321	(6)
Hanover Raceway	311	424,208	(73)	1,364	(67)
Harrington Raceway	458	477,795	(70)	1,043	(75)
Hawthorne Racecourse	663	5,860,796	(19)	8,840	(10)
Hazel Park	1,965	10,058,399	(11)	5,119	(21)
Hiawatha Horse Park	704	1,449,700	(52)	2,059	(45)
Indianapolis, IN	56	455,902	(71)	8,141	(11)
Inverness Raceway	199	52,817	(87)	265	(86)

TRACKS

Track	Races	Total Purses	(Rank)	Avg. Purse	(Rank)
Jackson Raceway	878	1,363,095	(53)	1,553	(62)
Kawartha Downs	546	1,145,495	(58)	2,098	(44)
Kingston Park Raceway	553	643,734	(67)	1,164	(71)
Leamington Raceway	164	273,724	(79)	1,669	(59)
Lebanon Raceway	1,520	2,684,864	(41)	1,766	(54)
Los Alamitos	1,287	6,941,296	(15)	5,393	(19)
Louisville Downs	1,678	3,810,654	(31)	2,271	(42)
Maywood Park	1,562	10,527,102	(10)	6,740	(13)
The Meadowlands	2,477	36,080,329	(1)	15,777	(4)
The Meadows	2,817	9,358,685	(12)	3,322	(28)
Mohawk Raceway	1,281	18,927,497	(5)	14,776	(5)
Monticello Raceway	2,713	5,331,313	(21)	1,965	(48)
Muskegon Racecourse	1,059	1,584,037	(50)	1,496	(65)
New Brunswick Downs	749	1,278,843	(56)	1,707	(57)
Northfield Park	2,571	8,443,279	(13)	3,284	(30)
Northlands Park	1,003	4,953,025	(23)	4,938	(22)
Northside Downs (Sydney)	1,126	555,929	(69)	494	(85)
Northville Downs	1,780	6,049,841	(18)	3,399	(27)
Orangeville Raceway	1,076	1,772,964	(46)	1,648	(60)
Pocono Downs	1,796	3,811,792	(30)	2,122	(43)
Pompano Park	1,930	11,810,422	(9)	6,119	(15)
Prarie Meadows	316	360,981	(76)	1,142	(73)
Quad City Downs	1,438	2,618,305	(43)	1,821	(51)
Hippodrome de Quebec	1,712	4,553,449	(26)	2,660	(36)
Queensbury Downs	665	825,818	(65)	1,242	(70)
Quinte Raceway	283	368,372	(75)	1,302	(69)
Raceway Park	1,853	3,760,575	(32)	2,029	(46)
The Red Mile	679	3,885,861	(29)	5,723	(16)
Rideau Carlton	1,154	2,620,288	(42)	2,271	(41)
Riverside Downs	367	336,282	(78)	916	(78)
Rosecroft Raceway	2,782	15,204,165	(7)	5,465	(18)
Saginaw Harness Raceway	1,035	1,594,053	(48)	1,540	(64)
Hippodrome Saguenay	300	185,123	(83)	617	(83)
Sandown Raceway	548	1,092,237	(60)	1,993	(47)
Saratoga Raceway	2,017	4,815,290	(24)	2,387	(39)
Scarborough Downs	2,608	2,965,056	(38)	1,137	(74)
Scioto Downs	1,181	5,567,233	(20)	4,714	(24)
Sports Creek Raceway	1,602	2,725,113	(40)	1,701	(58)
Sportsman's Park	1,372	14,479,138	(8)	10,553	(7)
Springfield, IL	119	1,171,937	(57)	9,848	(8)
Stampede Park	1,012	3,906,189	(28)	3,860	(25)
Sudbury Downs	522	891,664	(64)	1,708	(56)
Summerside Raceway	405	241,673	(81)	597	(84)
Syracuse Mile	82	1,351,346	(54)	16,480	(3)
Hippodrome Trois Rivieres	1,201	3,604,077	(35)	3,001	(33)
Truro Raceway	1,284	1,132,519	(59)	882	(81)
Vernon Downs	1,607	4,658,466	(25)	2,899	(35)
Western Fair Raceway	1,572	3,026,710	(37)	1,925	(49)
Windsor Raceway	1,792	6,607,770	(16)	3,687	(26)
Woodstock Raceway	282	413,779	(74)	1,467	(66)
Yonkers Raceway	3,886	29,984,755	(2)	7,716	(12)

There were a total of 108,120 purse races in North America, paying $407,172,871)

TRACKS

TOP TRACKS BY 2:00 AND 1:55 MILES

TOP TEN, 2:00 MILES, ALL-TIME

Track	2:00 Miles All-Time
The Meadowlands	23,896
Pompano Park	8,152
Sportsman's Park	6,926
Yonkers Raceway	6,306
Greenwood Raceway	5,929
Red Mile	5,763
Mohawk Raceway	5,685
Blue Bonnets	5,512
The Meadows	5,357
Vernon Downs	5,354

TOP TEN, 1:55 MILES, ALL-TIME

Track	1:55 Miles All-Time
The Meadowlands	2,548
Garden State Park	448
Red Mile	359
Greenwood Raceway	236
Pompano Park	209
Mohawk Raceway	157
Freestate Raceway	108
Springfield, IL	103
Scioto Downs	84
The Meadows	83

FASTEST MILES, BY TRACK
(Rank, from among the 82 tracks listed, shown in parenthesis)

Track	2:00 Miles All-Time		2:00 Miles in 1990	1:55 Miles All-Time		1:55 Miles in 1990
Assiniboia Downs	84	(67)	36	none		none
Avalon Raceway (St.John's)	none		none	none		none
Balmoral Park	1,033	(32)	337	10	(30)	4
Bangor Raceway	17	(77)	none	none		none
Barrie Raceway	105	(61)	33	none		none
Batavia Downs	472	(44)	135	1	(43)	none
Blue Bonnets	5,512	(8)	1,362	77	(13)	35
Brandywine Raceway	3,404	(20)	none	17	(27)	none
Buffalo Raceway	425	(49)	94	1	(43)	1
Cal-Expo	2,454	(21)	409	32	(20)	11
Charlottetown Driving Pk.	84	(67)	24	none		none
Cloverdale Raceway	105	(61)	41	none		none
Hippodrome Connaught	93	(65)	36	1	(43)	1
Delaware, OH Cty. Fair	468	(45)	41	34	(19)	6
Delmarva Downs	431	(47)	134	none		none
Dover Downs	361	(52)	141	1	(43)	none
Dresden Raceway	71	(70)	4	none		none
Du Quoin, IL	683	(37)	50	71	(15)	9
Exhibition Park	34	(73)	7	none		none
Fairmount Park	930	(36)	290	2	(39)	2
Fairplex Park	376	(50)	none	1	(43)	none
Flamboro Downs	1,353	(29)	343	6	(34)	4
Fredericton Raceway	29	(74)	9	none		none
Freehold Raceway	4,541	(14)	986	30	(21)	12
Freestate Raceway	4,793	(12)	none	108	(7)	none
Garden State Park	4,871	(11)	848	448	(2)	113
Goshen (Historic)	76	(69)	6	none		none
Greenwood Raceway	5,929	(5)	1,227	236	(4)	110
Harrington Raceway	20	(76)	9	none		none
Hawthorne Race Course	1,434	(28)	281	8	(32)	2
Hazel Park	4,397	(15)	858	22	(25)	10
Hiawatha Horse Park	441	(46)	210	4	(35)	2
Indianapolis, IN	496	(42)	35	50	(18)	5
Inverness Raceway	none		none	none		none
Jackson Harness Raceway	101	(64)	22	none		none

TRACKS

Track	2:00 Miles All-Time		2:00 Miles in 1990	1:55 Miles All-Time		1:55 Miles in 1990
Kawartha Downs	500	(41)	176	none		none
Kingston Park Raceway	141	(58)	19	1	(43)	none
Lebanon Raceway	429	(48)	104	none		none
Lewiston Raceway	41	(72)	none	none		none
Los Alamitos	4,014	(17)	817	60	(16)	30
Louisville Downs	1,093	(31)	224	3	(38)	2
Maywood Park	4,144	(16)	572	24	(24)	2
The Meadowlands	23,896	(1)	2,691	2,548	(1)	530
The Meadows	5,357	(9)	1,038	83	(10)	28
Mohawk Raceway	5,685	(7)	1,164	157	(6)	88
Monticello Raceway	656	(38)	111	1	(43)	none
Muskegon Racecourse	161	(56)	104	none		none
New Brunswick Downs	249	(53)	86	4	(35)	1
Northfield Park	1,791	(25)	488	9	(31)	3
Northlands Park	1,881	(24)	351	20	(26)	3
Northville Downs	644	(39)	194	none		none
Orangeville Raceway	102	(63)	22	none		none
Pocono Downs	1,940	(23)	443	2	(39)	2
Pompano Park	8,152	(2)	1,459	209	(5)	92
Prairie Meadows	127	(60)	33	1	(43)	none
Quad City Downs	1,956	(22)	507	8	(32)	none
Hippodrome de Quebec	146	(57)	54	1	(43)	none
Queensbury Downs	70	(71)	32	none		none
Raceway Park	1,593	(27)	331	4	(35)	none
The Red Mile	5,763	(6)	462	359	(3)	50
Rideau Carleton	1,007	(34)	299	15	(28)	6
Riverside Downs	24	(75)	4	none		none
Rosecroft Raceway	3,713	(18)	1,842	81	(11)	69
Saginaw Harness Raceway	476	(43)	111	1	(43)	none
Hippodrome Saguenay	9	(79)	none	none		none
Sandown Park	624	(40)	154	none		none
Saratoga Harness	1,289	(30)	254	2	(39)	none
Scarborough Downs	362	(51)	108	1	(43)	1
Scioto Downs	4,648	(13)	706	84	(9)	16
Sports Creek Raceway	219	(54)	90	1	(43)	none
Sportsman's Park	6,926	(3)	909	81	(11)	21
Springfield, IL	1,008	(33)	73	103	(8)	11
Stampede Park	1,743	(26)	270	11	(29)	none
Summerside Raceway	14	(78)	4	none		none
Syracuse, NY	953	(35)	67	52	(17)	5
Tartan Downs	8	(80)	3	none		none
Hippodrome Trois Rivieres	135	(59)	78	none		none
Truro Raceway	92	(66)	54	none		none
Vernon Downs	5,354	(10)	780	73	(14)	16
Western Fair Raceway	177	(55)	45	none		none
Windsor Raceway	3,679	(19)	619	30	(21)	9
Yonkers Raceway	6,306	(4)	1,248	29	(23)	19

(There were 27,435 2:00 Miles in 1990 - 1,331 of them in 1:55 or better)

> # TRACKS

SPEED RATINGS FOR U.S. TRACKS

These Official Speed Ratings are based on comparisons of individual times at one track with the same horses' times at other tracks at the same time of year over fast tracks, without breaks or parkouts, and at a mile distance:

Mile Tracks (Two turns to the mile)

Track	Location	Time
Balmoral Park	Crete, Illinois	1:59 1/5
Cal-Expo	Sacramento, California	2:02
Du Quoin State Fair	Du Quoin, Illinois	2:00
Fairmount Park	Collinsville, Illinois	2:01 3/5
Garden State Park	Cherry Hill, New Jersey	1:59 2/5
Hawthorne Race Course	Cicero, Illinois	2:01 3/5
Illinois State Fair	Springfield, Illinois	1:58 3/5
Indiana State Fair	Indianapolis, Indiana	2:01
The Meadowlands	East Rutherford, New Jersey	1:58 3/5
The Red Mile	Lexington, Kentucky	2:00 3/5
Syracuse Mile	Syracuse, New York	1:59 2/5
Vernon Downs (3/4-Mile Track)	Vernon, New York	2:00

Five Eighth-Mile Tracks (Three turns to the mile)

Track	Location	Time
Balmoral Park	Crete, Illinois	2:00 3/5
Dover Downs	Dover, Delaware	2:02
Hazel Park Harness	Hazel Park, Michigan	2:03
Los Alamitos Harness	Los Alamitos, California	2:03
The Meadows	Meadow Lands, Pennsylvania	2:02 1/5
Muskegon Racecourse	Muskegon, Michigan	2:03 3/5
Pocono Downs	Wilkes-Barre, Pennsylvania	2:02
Pompano Park	Pompano Beach, Florida	2:01 2/5
Quad City Downs	East Moline, Illinois	2:02 1/5
Raceway Park	Toledo, Ohio	2:02 3/5
Rosecroft Raceway	Ft. Washington, Maryland	2:00 4/5
Scioto Downs	Columbus, Ohio	2:02
Sports Creek Raceway	Swartz Creek, MI	2:03 2/5
Sportsman's Park	Cicero, Illinois	2:00 1/5

Half-Mile Tracks (Four turns to the mile)

Track	Location	Time
Bangor Raceway	Bangor, Maine	2:05
Batavia Downs	Batavia, New York	2:02 3/5
Buffalo Raceway	Hamburg, New York	2:02 3/5
Delaware County Fair	Delaware, Ohio	2:02
Delmarva Downs	Berlin, Maryland	2:02 3/5
Freehold Raceway	Freehold, New Jersey	2:02
Harrington Raceway	Harrington, Delaware	2:03 4/5
Historic Track	Goshen, New York	2:04 2/5
Jackson Harness Raceway	Jackson, Michigan	2:04 4/5
Lebanon Raceway	Lebanon, Ohio	2:03 2/5
Louisville Downs	Louisville, Kentucky	2:03 4/5
Maywood Park	Maywood, Illinois	2:00 1/5
Monticello Raceway	Monticello, New York	2:02 2/5
Northfield Park	Northfield, Ohio	2:02 2/5
Northville Downs	Northville, Michigan	2:03 3/5
Riverside Downs	Henderson, Kentucky	2:04 4/5
Saginaw Harness Raceway	Saginaw, Michigan	2:02 4/5
Saratoga Harness	Saratoga Springs, New York	2:02 1/5
Scarborough Downs	Scarborough, Maine	2:04 4/5
Yonkers Raceway	Yonkers, New York	2:02 1/5

TRACKS

SPEED RATINGS FOR MARITIME TRACKS

Five Eighth-Mile Track (Three turns to the mile)

New Brunswick Downs				Dieppe, New Brunswick 2:03 4/5

Half-Mile Tracks (Four turns to the mile)

Avalon Raceway	Saint Johns, Newfoundland	2:13 4/5
Charlottetown Driving Park	Charlottetown, P.E.I	2:07 4/5
Exhibition Park Raceway	Coldbrook, New Brunswick	2:05
Fredericton Raceway	Fredericton, New Brunswick	2:07 1/5
Inverness Raceway	Inverness, Nova Scotia	2:14
Summerside Raceway	Summerside, P.E.I	2:08 1/5
Tartan Downs	Sydney, Nova Scotia	2:07 2/5
Truro Raceway	Truro, Nova Scotia	2:07 1/5
Woodstock Raceway	Woodstock, New Brunswick	2:11 1/5

SPEED RATINGS FOR C.T.A. TRACKS

The following speed ratings have been issued by the Canadian Trotting Association for the pari-mutuel tracks in Canada.

Thirteen Sixteenths-Mile Track (Three turns to the mile)

Assiniboia Downs				Winnipeg, Manitoba 2:03 4/5

Five Eighth-Mile Tracks (Three turns to the mile)

Hippodrome Blue Bonnets Raceway	Montreal, Quebec	2:01 3/5
Greenwood Raceway	Toronto, Ontario	2:01 3/5
Kawartha Downs	Fraserville, Ontario	2:04
Kingston Park Raceway	Kingston, Ontario	2:04 1/5
Marquis Downs	Saskatoon, Saskatchewan	2:03 2/5
Mohawk Raceway	Campbellville, Ontario	2:01 4/5
Northlands Park	Edmonton, Alberta	2:03 1/5
Rideau Carleton Raceway	Ottawa, Ontario	2:03 3/5
Sandown Park	Sidney, British Columbia	2:03 3/5
Stampede Park	Calgary, Alberta	2:03
Windsor Raceway	Windsor, Ontario	2:02 3/5

Half-Mile Tracks (Four turns to the mile)

Barrie Raceway	Barrie, Ontario	2:05 4/5
Clinton Raceway	Clinton, Ontario	2:05 3/5
Cloverdale Raceway	Surrey, British Columbia	2:05 2/5
Hippodrome Connaught	Lucerne, Quebec	2:04 3/5
Dresden Raceway	Dresden, Ontario	2:05 2/5
Elmira Raceway	Elmira, Ontario	2:05 2/5
Flamboro Downs	Dundas, Ontario	2:03 4/5
Goderich Raceway	Goderich, Ontario	2:06 1/5
Hanover Raceway	Hanover, Ontario	2:04 3/5
Leamington Raceway	Leamington, Ontario	2:04 4/5
Orangeville Raceway	Orangeville, Ontario	2:05 3/5
Hippodrome de Quebec	Quebec City, Quebec	2:04 2/5
Queensbury Downs	Regina, Saskatchewan	2:06
Quinte Raceway	Belleville, Ontario	2:05 3/5
Hippodrome Saguenay	Jonquiere, Quebec	2:05 3/5
Sudbury Downs	Sudbury, Ontario	2:05
Hippodrome Trois-Rivieres	Three Rivers, Quebec	2:04 4/5
Western Fair Raceway	London, Ontario	2:05
Woodstock Raceway	Woodstock, Ontario	2:05 3/5

TRACKS

TRACK RECORDS FOR MAJOR NORTH AMERICAN TRACKS

* - Mile Track   ** - 5/8-Mile Track   # - 3/4-Mile Track   ## - 13/16-Mile Track

Grand Circuit Fairs-Pg. 59   Maritime Tracks-Pg. 59   Other North American Tracks-Pg. 59
U.S. Fair Tracks-Pg. 60   Other Canadian Raceways-Pg. 75   Canadian Fair Tracks-Pg. 76

Assiniboia Downs (Winnipeg, Man.) (AsD)
T- 2:03.2   Maxidale ('76 N. McRann)
2:03.2   Fast Hope ('76 D. Anderson)
P- 1:55.4   Bold Bramble ('90 D.B. Shaw)

* Balmoral Park (Crete, IL)   (BmlP)
T- 1:57.2   King's Hope ('90 F. Finn, Jr.)
P- 1:54.1   Son Of A Gun ('89 A.E. Gregory, Jr.)

** Balmoral Park (Crete, IL)   (BmlP)
T- 1:59.2   Prairieland Clint ('89 M.D. Finn)
Q1:59.2   Thompson Pro ('90 A.D. Gregory, Jr.)
P- 1:54.1   Incredible Finale ('87 T. Harmer)
1:54.1   Snow Sammy ('88 M. Chupp)

Bangor Raceway (Bangor, ME)   (Bang)
T- 2:01.1   Indianapolis ('88 D. Nye)
P- 1:56.4   Michael's All Star ('88 W. Case, Jr.)

Batavia Downs (Batavia, NY)   (Btva)
T- 1:58.2   Shawland Magic ('90 C.C. Hie)
1:58.2   Peach Pit ('90 W. Wellwood)
1:58.2   Kit Lobell ('90 J.E. Johnson)
P- 1:55   Niatross ('80 C. Galbraith)

** Blue Bonnets Rcwy. (Montreal, Que.) (BB)
T- 1:55.4   No Sex Please ('90 R. Waples)
P- 1:52.1   Goalie Jeff ('89 M. Lachance)

Buffalo Raceway (Hamburg, NY)   (BR)
T- 2:00   Tex Kash ('89 C. Galbraith)
P- 1:54.3   Dorunrun Bluegrass ('90 H. Filion)

Cloverdale Raceway (Surrey, BC)   (Clov)
T- 2:08   Rock Dominion ('76 R. Gemmill)
P- 1:56.3   Damaged Goods ('90 B.H. Davis)

Connaught Park (Aylmer, Que.)   (Conn)
T- 2:00.1   Monsieur Loup ('90 S. Ouellet)
P- 1:53.3   Chatham Light ('90 K.R. Sheppard)

Delmarva Downs (Ocean City, MD)   (DMV)
T- 1:59.1   Skeet Load ('89 R.R. Shahan)
P- 1:55.1   Donovan ('87 J. Lare)

** Dover Downs (Dover, DE)   (DD)
T- Q1:59   Lungistics ('90 A.H. Martin)
P- 1:54.4   Forrest Skipper ('86 L. Fontaine)

* Fairmount Park (Collinsville, IL)   (FP)
T- 1:58   Ouchy ('88 J. Finn)
P- 1:55   Dart Victory ('90 J.D. Cross)
1:55   Armada (T.R. Simmons)

Flamboro Downs (Dundas, Ont.)   (FlmD)
T- 1:59   Defrocked ('89 W. Wellwood)
P- 1:54.1   Jate Lobell ('87 M. O'Mara)

Freehold Raceway (Freehold, NJ)   (Fhld)
T- 1:58   Cindy's Action('88 D. Dancer)
P- 1:53.1   Dorunrun Bluegrass ('90 H. Filion)

* Garden State Pk. (Cherry Hill, NJ)   (GSP)
T- 1:55.1   Sugarcane Hanover ('88 G. Eggen)
P- 1:52   Governors Choice ('86 J. Doherty)
1:52   T K's Skipper ('89 M. Lachance)

** Greenwood Rcwy. (Toronto, Ont.)   (GrR)
T- 1:56.2   No Sex Please ('89 R.W. Waples)
1:56.2   Mather's Streak ('89 R.D. Zeron)
P- 1:52.2   Topnotcher ('90 D.S. Brown)
1:52.2   Apaches Fame ('90 W.A. Fritz)

Harrington Raceway (Harrington, DE)   (Har)
T- 1:59.1   Whip It Wood ('86 R. Shahan)
P- 1:58   Missouri Time ('78 D. Staffrey)

* Hawthorne Race Course (Cicero, IL)   (Haw)
T- 1:56.4   Broderick ('89 L.M. Hosteler)
P- 1:54   T K's Skipper ('89 T.G. Harmer)

** Hazel Park (Hazel Park, MI)   (HP)
T- 1:56.3   Jeff's Playboy ('89 K.H. Crawford)
P- 1:53.3   Cimarron ('90 P.M. Wrenn)
1:53.3   Topnotcher ('90 R.D. Pierce)

Jackson Raceway (Jackson, MI)   (Jack)
T- 1:59.3   Den E Two Zip ('88 M. Kakaley)
P- 1:56.1   Stir Fry ('87 M. Baillargeon)
1:56.1   Solid Force ('89 R.J. Lorenzo)
1:56.1   W A Thiamine ('90 M.C. Jordan)

Lebanon Raceway (Lebanon, OH)   (Leb)
T- 1:58.4   Schimitar ('87 D. Ater)
P- 1:55.2   Hilliard Hill ('87 S. Noble III)

** Los Alamitos (Los Alamitos, CA)   (LA)
T- 1:56.4   Magic Moose ('90 R.A. Croghan)
P- 1:51.2   T K's Skipper ('90 J.S. Anderson)

Louisville Downs (Louisville, KY)   (Loud)
T- 1:57.2   Nearly Perfect ('86 M. McNichol)
P- 1:53.3   It's Fritz ('83 M. Allen)

Maywood Park (Maywood, IL)   (May)
T- 1:58.2   Manfred Hanover ('86 M.Jordan)
1:58.2   Billie S ('88 C. Baker)
P- 1:53.1   Falcon Seelster ('86 T. Harmer)

TRACKS

* The Meadowlands (E. Rutherford, NJ) (M)
T- 1:53.3　　　　　Mack Lobell ('87 J. Campbell)
P- 1:49.3　　　　　Nihilator ('85 W. O'Donnell)

** The Meadows (Meadow Lands, PA) (Mea)
T- 1:55.2　　　　　Photo Maker ('87 D. McConnell)
P- 1:50.4　　　　　In The Pocket ('90 J. Campbell)

** Mohawk (Campbellville, Ont.)　　(Moh)
T- 1:56.3　　　　　Super Timken ('90 D.S. Brown)
P- 1:51　　　　　　Matt's Scooter ('89 M. Lachance)

Monticello Raceway (Monticello, NY)　(MR)
T- 1:59.1　　　　　Green Speed ('78 W. Haughton)
P- 1:55　　　　　　Amity Chef ('86 J. Campbell)

** Muskegon Race Course (MI)　　(MRC)
T- 1:59.2　　　　　Steall The Money ('90 L.D. Stalbaum)
P- 1:56.4　　　　　Turbo Twin ('90 C.A. Putnam, Jr.)
　 1:56.4　　　　　Bummer Too ('90 S.J. DeMull)

Northfield Park (Northfield, OH)　　(Nfld)
T- 1:57.4　　　　　Lakewater Glory ('89 V. Tanishin)
P- 1:53　　　　　　Jaguar Spur ('88 R. Stillings)

** Northlands Park (Edmonton, Alta)　(Edm)
T- 2:02.2　　　　　Holridge Alec ('78 J. Baxter)
　 2:02.2　　　　　Jon Coaltown ('81 T. Turcotte)
　 2:02.2　　　　　Daltons Hope ('90 E.J. Tracey)
P- 1:52　　　　　　Matt's Scooter ('89 M. Lachance)

Northville Downs (Northville, MI)　(Nor)
T- 1:59　　　　　　Jeff's Playboy ('90 C.A. Putnam, Jr.)
　 1:59　　　　　　Hey Foxtrot ('90 P.M. Wrenn)
P- 1:55.4　　　　　Sachem ('90 K.H. Crawford)

** Pocono Downs (Wilkes-Barre, PA)　(PcD)
T- 1:57.3　　　　　Probe ('89 J.M. Kvik)
P- 1:54　　　　　　Prince Ebony ('90 W.H. Lambertus)

** Pompano Pk. (Pompano Beach, FL)　(PPk)
T- 1:54.1　　　　　Mack Lobell ('87 J. Campbell)
P- 1:51.1　　　　　Artsplace ('90 J. Campbell)

** Quad City Downs (E. Moline, IL)　(QCD)
T- 1:58.2　MadeForTheBride ('90 D.Bowermaster)
　 1:59　　　　　　Gala Yates ('89 J.R. Reese)
P- 1:53.1　　　　　Pacific ('88 T. Harmer)

** Raceway Park (Toledo, OH)　　(RP)
T- 1:57　　　　　　Mack Lobell ('88 J. Campbell)
P- 1:53.3　　　　　Quite A Sensation ('88 P. Kerr)
　 1:53.3　　　　　Bob's Escort ('89 K.R. Holliday)

* The Red Mile (Lexington, KY)　　(Lex)
T- 1:53　　　　　　Express Ride ('87 B. Lindstedt)
　 T1:54　　　　　Arndon ('82 D. Miller)
P- T1:48.2　　　　Matt's Scooter ('88 M. Lachance)
　 1:49.3　　　　　Call For Rain ('88 C. Galbraith)

** Rideau Carlton (Ottawa, Ont.)　　(RidC)
T- 1:57.2　　　　　A Js Image ('90 R. O'Dwyer)
P- 1:53　　　　　　Apaches Fame ('90 W.A. Fritz)

Riverside Downs (Henderson, KY)　(RSD)
T- 2:01　　　　　　Budgait Libby ('86 R.G. Finn)
P- 1:58　　　　　　Classy Strike ('84 M. Finn)

** Rosecroft (Ft. Washington, MD)　(RcR)
T- 1:56　　　　　　Esquire Spur ('89 D. Irvine, Jr.)
　 1:56　　　　　　Roydon Lad ('90 D. Irvine, Jr.)
P- 1:52.2　　　　　T K's Skipper ('90 R.I. Remmen)

Saginaw Harness Rcwy. (Saginaw, MI)　(SgHr)
T- 1:58.2　　　　　Chicory Wind ('88 G. Sutherland)
P- 1:54.2　　　　　Stir Fry ('88 D. Johnson)

** Sandown Park (Sidney, BC)　　(Sand)
T- 2:07.2　　　　　Tryst ('84 E. Stewart)
P- 1:55.3　　　　　Hy Class Minbar ('85 A. Bowman)

Saratoga Harness (Saratoga Spr., NY)　(Stga)
T- 1:56　　　　　　Mack Lobell ('88 J. Campbell)
P- 1:54.3　　　　　Robust Hanover ('86 W. Gilmour)

Scarborough (Scarborough, ME)　　(Scar)
T- 1:57.3　　　　　Friendly Face ('88 E. Lahtinen)
P- 1:54　　　　　　Prince Ebony ('90 R.D. Pierce)

** Scioto Downs (Columbus, OH)　　(ScD)
T- 1:56　　　　　　Editor In Chief ('88 L. Hostetler)
P- 1:53　　　　　　Global Assault ('90 M.W. Williams)

** Sports Creek (Swartz Creek, MI)　(SpCk)
T- 1:59.3　　　　　Senor Shiaway ('87 S. Sugg)
　 1:59.3　　　　　Red Rhone ('88 S. Demull)
P- 1:55　　　　　　Stir Fry ('87 T. Buter)

** Sportsman's Park (Cicero, IL)　　(SPk)
T- 1:55　　　　　　Express Ride ('87 B. Lindstedt)
P- 1:52.4　　　　　Beach Towel ('90 R.I. Remmen)

** Stampede Park (Calgary, Alta.)　　(Clgy)
T- 2:02.2　　　　　Jon Coaltown ('81 T. Turcotte)
P- 1:53.3　　　　　Falcon Seelster ('85 T. Harmer)

\# Vernon Downs (Vernon, NY)　　(VD)
T- 1:56　　　　　　Prakas ('85 R. Waples)
　 1:56　　　　　　Mack Lobell ('87 J. Campbell)
　 1:56　　　　　　Proximity Three ('88 D. Irvine)
P- 1:51.3　　　　　Dragon's Lair ('87 J. Campbell)

Western Fair Rcwy. (London, Ont.)　(Lon)
T- 2:00.2　　　　　N V Worthy ('87 J. Walker)
P- 1:55.1　　　　　Jagger Hanover ('90 D.W. Wall)

** Windsor Raceway (Windsor, Ont.)　(WR)
T- 1:57　　　　　　Mathers Streak ('89 W.R. Gale)
P- 1:52.3　　　　　Frugal Gourmet ('87 T. Ritchie)

TRACKS

Yonkers Raceway (Yonkers, NY) **(YR)**
T- 1:57.1   Mack Lobell ('88 J. Campbell)
P- 1:53.4   Falcon Seelster ('85 T. Harmer)
   1:53.4   Matt's Scooter ('89 M. Lachance)
   1:53.4   Sea The USA ('90 G.M. Procino)
   1:53.4   Lorryland Butler ('90 G.D. Mosher)

GRAND CIRCUIT FAIR TRACKS

Delaware, OH **(Dela)**
T- 1:56   Peace Corps ('89 J. Campbell)
P- 1:51   Falcon Seelster ('85 T. Harmer)

* Du Quoin, IL **(DuQ)**
T- 1:52.4   Peace Corps ('89 J. Campbell)
P- T1:49.2   T K's Skipper ('90 M. Lachance)
   1:50   Beach Towel ('90 Ray Remmen)

Historic Track (Goshen, NY) **(Gosh)**
T- 1:58.4   Speedy Rodney ('66 P. Corley)
P- 1:55.1   Chairmanoftheboard ('86 B. Gilmour)

* Indianapolis, IN **(Ind)**
T- 1:54.1   Peace Corps ('89 J. Campbell)
T1:54.4   Nevele Pride ('69 S. Dancer)
P- 1:51.4   Drawing Board ('89 W.R. Gale)
   1:51.4   Deal Direct ('90 S. Noble III)

* Springfield, IL **(Spr)**
T- 1:52.1   Mack Lobell ('87 J. Campbell)
P- 1:50.3   Colt Fortysix ('84 C. Boring)
T1:49.3   Camtastic ('89 M. Lachance)

* Syracuse Mile (Syracuse, NY) **(Sycsm)**
T- 1:54.2   Crown's Best ('87 P. Eriksson)
P- T1:51.2   Runnymede Lobell ('89 Y. Filion)

MARITIME TRACK RECORDS

Avalon Raceway (St. John's, Nfld.) **(StJhn)**
T- 2:08.2   Donmar Trinket ('88 D. Ellsworth)
P- 2:02.1   Shadows Norman ('90 G.F. McDonald)

Charlottetown, Price Edward Is. **(Chrtn)**
T- 2:01.2   Rustico Hotshot ('88 A. Pineau)
P- 1:56.4   Waveore ('85 D. Pinkney)
   1:56.4   Sherwood Abe ('89 P.R. Pinkney)

Exhibition Pk. Rcwy. (St.John, N.B.) **(EPR)**
T- 2:02.2   Rustico Hotshot ('88 A. Pineau)
P- 1:57   Angel's Shadow ('85 M. Barrieau)
   1:57   Suthen Guvna ('87 M. MacDonald)

Fredericton, New Brunswick **(Frdtn)**
T- 2:02   Cosmonaut ('90 D.L. Davies)
P- 1:58   Bub ('89 G.L. Chappell)

Inverness, Nova Scotia **(Invrn)**
T- 2:07.2   Dunvegan ('88 D. Rankin, Jr.)
P- 1:59.4   Bye Skipper ('88 D. Rankin, Jr.)

** New Brunswick Downs (Dieppe,NB) **(NBD)**
T- 2:00.4   Maple Leaf Bramble ('86 R. Annear)
   2:00.4   Espoir Good ('88 R. Craig)
P- 1:53.2   Skipper Forrest ('90 H. Filion)

North Side Downs (N. Sydney, N.S.) **(NtSD)**
T- 2:07.1   Glen William ('88 H. Youden)
P- 2:01.1   Lingan Parker ('84 D. Pezzarello)

Summerside (Summerside, PEI) **(Summ)**
T- 2:03.2   Colgan's Comet ('85 R. Craig)
   2:03.2   Oh That Treasure ('88 R. Annear)
P- 1:58.3   Working Overtime ('89 F.J. Fagan, Jr.)

Tartan Downs (Sydney, N.S.) **(Sydny)**
T- 2:04   Flaming Hanover ('83 J. Frison)
P- 1:57.4   Big Gene ('90 D.A. Pinkney)

Truro, N.S. **(Truro)**
T- 2:01.3   Rich Man ('90 C.J. MacDonald)
P- 1:56.2   J K Beauty ('90 J.K. Smallwood)

Woodstock, N.B. **(Wodst)**
T- 2:07-1/2   Calumet Calling ('39 Hunt)
P- 2:00   Maple Grove Shadow ('89 S. Mahar)

OTHER NORTH AMERICAN TRACKS

** Brandywine (Wilmington, DE) **(Brd)**
T- 1:57.1   Lindy's Crown ('80 H. Beissinger)
P- 1:53.4   Pershing Square ('85 W. O'Donnell)

* Cal-Expo (Sacramento, CA) **(Sacr)**
T- 1:57.1   Supernal ('88 J. Olsen)
Q1:57.1   Alfa Star ('90 J.E. Lackey)
P- 1:53   Irresistible Magic ('88 R. Sleeth)

TRACKS

Canterbury Downs (Shakopee, MN) (Cby)
T- 1:59.2 Baroque ('86 R. Pierce)
  1:59.2 Super Flora ('86 R. Waples)
P- 1:53.4 Forrest Skipper ('86 L. Fontaine)

** Fairplex Park (Pomona, CA) (Pom)
T- 1:59.3 Lakoa ('86 Y. Bergeron)
  1:59.3 Petey ('86 G. Vallandingham)
P- 1:54.1 California Blaster ('86 R. Sleeth)

** Foxboro Raceway (Foxboro, MA) (Fox)
T- 2:00 Lively Anne ('75 E. Houle)
P- 1:54.4 Caramore ('85 J. Doherty)

** Freestate Raceway (Laurel, MD) (FsR)
T- 1:55.2 Delray Lobell ('89 D. Irvine, Jr.)
P- 1:52.2 Ring Of Light ('88 J. Morand)

Hinsdale Raceway (Hinsdale, NH) (Hin)
T- 2:02.2 Ten Karat Glen ('85 L. Garwood)
P- 1:55.3 Caramore ('85 J. Doherty)

 # Lake Shore Meadows (Erie, PA) (LSM)
T- 2:01.2 Texas Aggie ('85 D. Ackley)
P- 1:56.3 Seven O'Clock ('85 E. Ryan)

** Liberty Bell Park (Philadelphia, PA) (LB)
T- 1:58 Piggvar ('85 S. Dancer)
P- 1:54.3 Dragon's Lair ('85 J. Mallet)

Northcoast Raceway (Escanaba, MI) (NcR)
T- 2:02.1 Santo Matt ('87 M. Owen)
P- 1:58.2 St Johns Flyer ('88 P. Wrenn)

Lewiston Raceway (Lewiston, ME) (Lew)
T- 2:01.3 Indianapolis ('89 R.A. Goodblood, Jr.)
P- 1:55.2 Out To Score ('89 K.P. Switzer)

* Prairie Meadows (Altoona, IA) (PrM)
T- 1:59.3 Ouchy ('89 J.W. Finn)
  1:59.3 Dawn's Colt ('89 B.C. Gamboe)
P- 1:54.4 Light Foyle N ('89 G. Longo)

Rosecroft (Ft.Washington, MD) (RcR)
T- 1:57.2 Mack Lobell ('87 J. Campbell)
P- 1:54 Forrest Skipper ('86 L. Fontaine)

Roosevelt Raceway (Westbury, NY) (RR)
T- 1:58.2 Grades Singing ('86 H. Filion)
P- 1:54.1 Armbro Emerson ('87 J. Whelan)

Sackville Downs (L. Sackville N.S.) (Sack)
T- 2:03.2 Captain Jamie ('86 E. Bernard)
P- 1:57.1 Witsend's Gypsy ('86 L. Walker)

TRACK RECORDS – U.S. FAIRS

California

* Del Mar (DelM)
T- Q2:01.4 Tansy Tea ('89 R.C. Plano)
P- Q1:58.2 Happy Patron N ('89 R.H. Kuebler)

Sacramento, Greenbrier Farms (Grebr)
P- Q2:01.2 West Side Story ('89 E.S. Desomer)
T- Q1:59.4 Court Of Appeal ('89 J.D. Grundy)

San Jose (SnJos)
T- 2:12 Tanya Tass ('78 M. Toronto)
P- 2:05.1 Fly Man Fly ('85 M. Ruiz)

Connecticut

Brooklyn (Bklyn)
T- 2:13 Ladd Hanover ('65 D. Letendre)
P- 2:08.2 Lucky Gina ('78 S. Wheeler)

Florida

Castletiny Farm (Csty)
T- 2:03.3 Don's Final ('88 R. Dailey)
P- 1:58.4 Casual Rebuff ('87 R. Bridges)

* DeLeon Springs (Dlsp)
T- Q1:57.3 Mack Lobell ('88 N. Boring)
P- Q1:54.3 Keystone Raider ('89 N.C. Boring)

DeLeon Spirngs (DlSgn)
T- 2:13.3 Irish Annie ('85 C. Boring)
P- 2:06.3 Florida Cracker ('85 B.Komers II)

** Gil Crest Training Center (GcTc)
T- 2:05 Artemis Acornis ('87 M. Wellman)
P- 1:58.4 Forceful Strike ('87 W. Adams)

TRACKS

** Golden Cross Farm, Ocala (Ocla)
T- 2:03 Not Recorded
P- 1:59.3 Franks Harem ('90 M.A. Lynch)

* Orlando (Orl)
T- Q2:00 Kerry's Crown ('89 J.H. Cruise, Jr.)
P- Q1:55.1 Jaguar Spur ('89 R.L Stillings)

Orlando (Orlnd)
T- 2:05.3 Flip For Luck ('88 J. Harp)
P- 2:01.4 Fast Approaching ('88 J. Tolson)

Oviedo (Ovdo)
T- 2:06.4 John Quincy ('88 W. Adams)
P- 2:01.2 Casual Rebuff ('88 D. Cooksey)

** Sunshine Meadows (SnSh)
T- 2:01 Irene's Boy ('88 J. Langley)
P- 1:58.4 Youngro J J ('88 J. Young)

* Sunshine Meadows (SSM)
T- 2:00.4 Coast Express ('90 D.D. Harmon)
P- 1:56.3 Cocktail Talk ('90 J.C. Sears)

Georgia

* Atlanta (Atl)
T- 2:01 R D L ('86 M. Todd)
P- 1:59 Single G ('20 Allen)

* Hawkinsville (Hksv)
T- Q2:03.1 Double Tip ('90 J. Dailey)
P- Q1:55.4 Cloonty ('90 J. Larente)

Illinois

Albion (Albn)
T- 2:05.1 Dream Of Gambi ('85 T. Graham)
P- 2:00.1 Cami Ranger ('88 J. Finn)
2:00.1 C Him In Action ('89 R.L. Binkley)

Aledo (Aldo)
T- 2:04 Good Night Irene ('89 H.S. Channick)
P- 2:01.4 Styling ('90 D.M. Insko)

Altamont (Altmt)
T- 1:59 Ouchy ('87 J. Finn)
P- 2:01.3 Sweet Sport ('87 L. Pence)

Anna (Anna)
T- 2:03.1 Never Mess Around ('89 C. Lorance, Sr.)
P- 2:01.1 Altamont Indian ('79 R. Moss)

Belvidere (Bvdr)
T- 2:05.3 Mary M ('45 Hassen)
P- 2:02 Incredible Finale ('86 T. Harmer)

Cambridge (Camb)
T- 2:04 Never Mess Around ('89 C.R. Lorance, Sr.)
P- 2:00.2 Count The Loot ('82 R. Parker)

Carlinville (Crlvl)
T- 2:07 Genie Gal ('80 G. Jacobus)
2:07 Justice Ranger ('88 J. Finn)
P- 2:04 Ole Stoney ('88 A. Bowen)

Carmi (Carmi)
T- 2:02.1 Jano Rose ('89 T.L. Graham)
P- 2:00 Stumptownboy ('90 B. Simpson)

Carrollton (Carlt)
T- 2:03.4 Illini Queen ('88 R. Parker)
2:03.4 Prairieland Clint ('88 V. Espinosa)
P- 2:02 Pronghorn ('80 V. Espinosa)
2:02 Mr Wichita ('87 G. Leonard)

Charleston (Char)
T- 2:01.4 Ouchy ('87 J. Finn)
P- 2:00.3 C Him N Action ('89 R.L. Binkley)

Decatur (Dctr)
T- 2:02 Ouchy ('88 J. Finn)
P- 2:01 Smart Angle ('90 R.J. Finn)

Fairbury (Fair)
T- 2:05.2 Last Deac ('89 J.R. Jones)
P- 2:01.2 Mi Amigo Grande ('89 S.D. Tocco)

Fairfield (Frfld)
T- 2:03 Another Diamond ('86 C. Willis)
P- 2:01 Egyptian Genius ('84 F. Finn)
2:01 C Him In Action ('89 R.L. Binkley)

Farmer City (FrmCy)
T- 2:06 Cardinal Leeds ('48 Shell)
2:06 Nutjammer ('87 J. Reynolds)
P- 2:02.4 Birch Yates ('88 J. Reynolds)

Greenup (Grnup)
T- 2:04.2 Ace Hanover ('63 E. Leonard)
P- 2:02.3 Ghost Painter ('90 D.E. Doughty)

Greenville (Grnvl)
T- 2:04.1 Cami Ranger ('88 J. Finn)
P- 2:03.1 Poplar Mahone ('77 L. Walker)

Griggsville (Grig)
T- 2:05.3 Roxies Flight ('89 P.T. Phillips)
P- 2:05 Dale Adam ('54 R. Parkhurst)

Henry (Hnry)
T- 2:04 W O's Jet ('87 C. Torgerson)
P- 2:02.1 Valen's Song ('84 J. Dennis)

Page 61

TRACKS

Jacksonville (Jksvl)
T- 2:03.3 Picky Picky Pete ('89 N. Robinson)
P- 2:02.2 Illinois Zephyr ('83 D. Freese)

Jerseyville (Jrsv)
T- 2:04.4 Newstar Jane ('89 R.D. Parker)
P- 2:03 Double Grey ('89 R.A. Prather)

Knoxville (Knox)
T- 2:03.3 Never Still ('82 C. Lorance)
2:03.3 Bit's Of Quality ('89 J.A. Schaefer)
P- 2:01 Count The Loot ('82 R. Parker)

Lewistown (Lwstn)
T- 2:05 Never Mess Around ('89 C.R. Lorance, Sr.)
P- 2:06.3 First Dollar ('89 T.H. Busse)

Lincoln (Linc)
T- 2:02 Austin Hanover ('45 Beasley)
P- 1:59 Foolish Eyes ('81 D. O'Dwyer)
1:59 Sweet Society ('87 G. Leonard)

Marion (Mar)
T- 2:03.4 J Hustle ('89 C.A. Finn)
P- 2:02.3 Mister Dizzle ('84 R. Binkley)

Marshall (Marsh)
T- 2:01.4 Jano Rose ('89 T.L. Graham)
P- 1:58.4 Hot Dog Dick ('88 B. Carpenter)

Martinsville (Mart)
T- 1:59.1 Brooklyn Jet ('86 E. Liles)
P- 1:58.3 Jay Time ('72 G. Riegle)

Mendota (Mend)
T- 2:05 Snagged ('86 S. Nessa)
P- 2:03.3 Class E Fellow ('88 R. McKibbon)

Morrison (Mrisn)
T- 2:05 Canton Jubilee ('88 B. Ashby)
P- 2:03 Orchestra ('87 B. Ashby)

Mount Sterling (MtStr)
T- 2:03.1 Rapid Rover ('88 R.J. Walker)
P- 2:00 Styling ('90 D.C. Larsen)

Newton (Nwton)
T- 2:03 Ouchy ('88 H. Finn)
P- 2:00.1 Scotty Y ('82 B. Carpenter)

Oregon (Oreg)
T- 2:05-1/2 Pearl Harbor ('44 P. Amundsen)
P- 2:05.2 Brook King ('52 W. Carney)

Pana (Pana)
T- 2:02 Smart Angle ('90 S.L. Derousse)
P- 2:00 Bretsbac ('89 T.D. Wilson, Jr.)

Paris (Paris)
T- 2:05.1 Billy Corbitt ('53 Wilburn)
P- 2:02.4 Mister Dizzle ('84 R. Binkley)
2:02.4 Lovin Rainbow ('85 L. Avenatti, Jr.)

Pecatonica (Peca)
T- 2:07.4 Wiekers Babe ('73 G. Leonard)
P- 2:04.3 Cobra Star ('90 D.J. Clark)

Petersburg (Ptsbg)
T- 2:05.1 F E Patsy ('87 D. Hein)
P- 2:03.4 Gomer's Time ('85 M. Lewis)

Pinkneyville (Pink)
T- 2:08.4 Augitato ('89 W.E. Haynes, Jr.)
P- 2:08.3 Rebel Rorty ('90 T.S. Barbre)

Princeton (Prnc)
T- 2:05 Tim S. ('39 H. Fitzpatrick)
P- 2:05 Instant Lobell ('71 D.G. Insko)
2:05 Jolly's Bit ('82 R. Thompson)
2:05 Rosie's Rascal ('84 R. Thompson)

Rushville (Rshvl)
T- 2:03.1 J R's Chip ('85 G. Leonard)
P- 2:01.4 Rorty Doodle ('89 D.E. Banks)

Salem (Salm)
T- 2:05 Hillbillie Bully ('87 S.F. Girvin)
P- 1:59.3 Hawthorne Jake ('87 B. Simpson)

Sandwich (Sndwh)
T- 2:05 Randy Randolph ('84 T. Busse)
2:05 Snagged ('86 S. Nessa)
P- 2:02 Song Of Oz ('84 D. Freese)

Taylorville (Tayvl)
T- 2:04.1 Barbie Rengo ('83 D. Banks)
P- 2:03 Mark Time ('87 L. Moyer)

Urbana (Urb)
T- 2:03 Icecapage ('82 O. Tucker)
P- 2:01.2 Arbrator ('90 D.C. Larsen)

Warren (War)
T- 2:06.4 Reddy Butler ('89 J.S. Henry)
P- 2:01.4 Fat Buck ('89 G.A. Rath)

Woodstock (Wood)
T- 2:08.2 Earthquake ('70 M. Bumstead)
P- 2:03.2 Pacing Model ('88 A. Morgan)

Indiana

Anderson (And)
T- 2:04.4 Blaze Blaze ('86 W. Bridges)
P- 2:00.4 Judy's Delight ('90 T.P. Stohler)

Connersville (Cnsv)
T- 2:04 Blaze Blaze ('86 J. Landess)
P- 2:02 Guinea Gold ('51 Hungerford)

TRACKS

Converse (**Cnvr**)
T- 2:03.2 Two ('86 H. Sowash)
P- 2:01.1 Alex Miles ('89 B.T. Barnes)

Corydon (**Crydn**)
T- 2:05 Sis's Brother ('60 R. Parker)
P- 2:01.4 Indestructo ('88 C. Conrad)

Frankfort (**Frnft**)
T- 2:03.2 Hot Dog Matthew ('90 H.E. Barnes)
P- 1:58.2 Hot Dog Dick ('88 B. Carpenter)

Goshen (**Gshn**)
T- 2:03.1 Tryson's Way ('88 J. Landess)
P- 2:00.1 Hathaway High ('88 H. Yoder)
2:00.1 Big Valey ('89 W.D. White)

Indianapolis (**Ipls**)
T- 2:09.2 Billy Ranger ('90 R.L. Wilfong)
P- 2:01.3 Fizz Whiz Lauxmont ('90 J.A. Edwards)

Kendallville (**Kendl**)
T- 2:06 Lakeland Albert ('35 McKeen)
P- 2:05 Ghost Ranger ('78 D. Petty)

Kentland (**Kent**)
T- 2:06.2 The Appraiser ('89 J.A. Kieninger, Jr.)
P- 2:03.3 Barmary Byrd ('89 R.G. Allen)

LaPorte (**LaPrt**)
T- 2:04 The Appraiser ('88 J. Kieninger)
P- 2:02 Barmary Byrd ('88 R. Allen)

Montpelier (**Montp**)
T- 2:05 S B Begonia ('90 E.E. Haynes)
P- 1:59.2 Rayjean Blast ('90 B.A. Lewis)

Muncie (**Mun**)
T- 2:04 Darcy Jo ('88 L. Beeman)
P- 2:02.2 Fizz Whiz Lauxmont ('89 J.A. Edwards)

Portland (**Ptlnd**)
T- 2:02.3 Nat's Luck ('90 R.J. Dever)
P- 2:01.3 Sheal B Abbey ('90 J.G. Landess)

Princeton (**Prntn**)
T- 2:05.3 Darcy Jo ('89 L.L. Beeman)
P- 2:01.3 Special Sojourn ('89 K.D. Mack)

Shelbyville (**Sbyvl**)
T- 2:02.1 Blaze Blaze ('86 J. Landess)
P- 1:59.3 Alex Mills ('89 B.T. Barnes)

Terre Haute (**Tere**)
T- 2:05 Kay Way ('59 M. Taylor)
P- 2:03 Gold Rise ('59 P. Hungerford)

Iowa

Allison (**Alsn**)
T- 2:12.4 Masqueroger ('75 E. Bronkhurst)
P- 2:09 Parker Pierson ('77 B. Feltus)

Cedar Rapids (**Cdrp**)
T- 2:06 Brad Coy ('85 S. Huffman)
P- 2:03 Foxy Hoff ('85 H. Dasen, Jr.)
2:03 JR Girl ('86 R. Weber)

Columbus Junction (**CbsJn**)
T- None Recorded
P- 2:03.2 Orchestra ('83 R. Huffman)

Denison (**Dnsn**)
T- 2:11 Game Try ('85 J. Nessa)
P- 2:04.4 St Patrick ('86 D. McDanel)

Des Moines (**DsMns**)
T- 2:02-1/4 Spintell ('38 Stone)
P- 2:00.4 Attorney General ('87 E. Liles)

Eldon (**Eldon**)
T- 2:03.2 Brooklyn Jet ('86 E. Liles)
P- 2:00.2 Dr Rival ('78 E. Liles)

Humboldt (**Humb**)
T- 2:03.1 Brooklyn Jet ('86 R. Burgess)
P- 2:02 Tina's Two ('84 D. McDanel)
2:02 I Imagine ('85 B. Ennen)

Keosauqua (**Keos**)
T- 2:13.1 Brooklyn Spirit ('89 E.L. Liles)
P- 2:10.1 Powr Broker ('89 R.L. Huffman)

Maquokets (**Maq**)
T- 2:06.2 Canton Jubilee ('89 B.F. Ashby)
P- 2:03.2 Orchestra ('85 J. Kenney)

Monticello (**Mntcl**)
T- 2:06 Artis ('86 B. Ashby)
P- 2:04 Jamy Sun ('77 A. Douglas)
2:04 Orchestra ('86 J. Keeney)
2:04 Orchestra ('87 B. Ashby)

Nashua (**Nash**)
T- 2:08.1 Jodevin's Denise ('85 D. McDanel)
P- 2:04.3 Cajun Sound ('85 K. Nanke)

Oskaloosa (**Oskls**)
T- 2:04 Jodevin ('76 K. Hinshaw)
P- 2:02 Pauls Golden Girl ('89 J.A. Telfer)

Sioux Center (**SxC**)
T- 2:22.3 Mobile Queen ('78 D. Hammer)
P- 2:04.4 Real Deal Skipper ('86 A. Sandbulte)

Spencer (**Spncr**)
T- 2:03.1 Northern Prince ('86 M. McDanel)
P- 1:59.3 Precious Flyer ('86 N. Jenson)

TRACKS

Wapello	**(Wapel)**	**Waterloo**	**(Water)**
T-2:07.2	Miss Morristown ('69 L. Long)	T-2:12.1	Jubilee John ('83 R. Owens)
P-2:01.3	Orchestra ('87 B. Ashby)	P-2:07.2	Andy J ('84 B. Ashby)

What Cheer	**(What)**
T-2:05	Brooklyn Jet ('85 E. Liles)
2:05	Brooklyn Flyer ('88 E. Liles)
P-2:01.4	Raven Run ('85 R. Huffman)

Kansas

Stockton	**(Stock)**	**Wakeeney**	**(Wake)**
T-2:05	Last Deac ('89 J.R. Jones)	T-2:08.2	Counts Best ('84 L. Bunston)
P-2:03.2	Poppin Dandy ('88 M. Saner)	P-2:05.1	Tyrolean Kate ('83 F. Beitlich)

Kentucky

Bardstown	**(Bdstn)**	**Lebanon**	**(Lbn)**
T-2:06.2	Kentucky Winna ('86 M. Finn)	T-2:03.3	On The Air ('87 S. Waller)
P-2:04	Falcon Two Step ('90 J.S. Butler)	P-2:00.2	Night Tracker ('89 R.D. Cullipher)
Benton	**(Bent)**	**Mayfield**	**(Mayfd)**
T-2:04.1	Kwik Trot ('79 E.L. Martin)	T-2:04.3	Lafayette's Queen ('90 T.F. Cullipher)
P-2:01.3	Somkinda Bluegrass ('88 R. Cullipher)	P-2:01	Timber Jack ('89 J.A. Martin)
Hopkinsville	**(Hopk)**	**Paducah**	**(Pad)**
T-2:05.1	Speedy Primo ('88 M. Murphy)	T-2:04.1	Amitillie ('88 D. Armstrong)
P-1:59.2	Dorunrun Bluegrass ('89 A.S. Harris)	P-1:59.4	Dorunrun Bluegrass ('89 A.S. Harris)
Lacenter	**(Lcnt)**	**Smithland**	**(Smld)**
T-2:01	Timber Jack ('89 J.A. Martin)	T-2:04.1	Amitillie ('87 D. Armstrong)
P-2:01.3	Sister Alert ('86 R. Guhy)	P-2:01.1	Dorunrun Bluegrass ('89 A.S. Harris)

Sturgis	**(Strgs)**
T-2:04.3	Amitillie ('89 D.A. Armstrong)
2:04.3	Headed Home ('89 A.S. Harris)
P-2:00	Dorunrun Bluegrass ('89 A.S. Harris)

Maine

Blue Hill	**(BlHl)**	**Presque Isle**	**(Pres)**
T-2:09-1/2	Calumet Euclid ('39 Jordan)	T-2:04.1	Satan's Legend ('90 S.E. Case)
P-2:05.3	Federal ('38 Clukey)	P-2:00.2	Columbo Seelster ('82 W. Carr)
Cumberland	**(Cum)**	**Skowhegan**	**(Skow)**
T-2:03.2	Frankenshew ('86 F. Inman)	T-2:01.2	Bunny R ('90 F.W. Woodbury, Jr.)
P-1:58.3	Chester Baron ('86 F. Withee)	P-1:57	License To Fly ('90 R.W. Sumner)
Farmington	**(Farm)**	**Topsham**	**(Tops)**
T-2:04.2	Kelvin Lobell ('89 K.P. Switzer)	T-2:04.3	Mr Favor ('87 D. Gray)
P-2:00.3	Skip's Chance ('89 P.R. Bresciani)	2:04.3	Brooklyn P L D ('88 W. Case, Jr.)
		2:04.3	Kelvin Lobell ('89 K.P. Switzer)
Fryeburg	**(Frybg)**	P-2:00	French Major ('87 D. Niles, Jr.)
T-2:02	Tryst Spectator ('90 L.W. Fitch)		
P-1:57.4	Tahoe Lobell ('90 J.E. Hardy)		

TRACKS

Union	**(Union)**	**Windsor**	**(Wind)**
T- 2:05	Miss Mandi Hayes ('90 G. Hall)	T- 2:01.3	Keystone Signor ('90 F.E. Parker)
P- 2:00.1	Witsend's Sport ('90 J.D. Mosher)	P- 1:57.1	Witsend's Sport ('89 J.D. Mosher)

Maryland

Frederick **(Fred)**
T- 2:05.2 Keystone Jacque ('86 W. Lineweaver)
P- 2:04.1 Midgie Hanover ('87 J. Offutt)
2:04.1 Maggie's Bay Rum ('90 B.A. Brown)

Massachusetts

Greenfield **(Grnfd)**
T- 2:04 Young Count ('90 R. Tisbert)
2:07 Arch Hanover ('41 Ralston)
P- 2:01.2 Dr Bowens ('86 M. Robillard)

Groton **(Grot)**
T- 2:08.1 Captain Henry ('86 J. Distefano)
P- 2:04 Complete Power ('87 J. Marshall)

** Hadley **(Had)**
T- 2:02.2 Copter Pilot ('88 R. Flanders)
P- 1:59.4 Gentleman's Fancy ('87 B. Mattison)

Leverett **(Lever)**
T- 2:07 Mountain Tip ('87 A. Mason)
P- 2:00 Complete Power ('87 J. Marshall)

Marlborough **(Mrlb)**
T- 2:23 General Sharlu ('90 J.H. Wheeler)
P- 2:15 Young Satellite ('90 L.E. Pickett III)

Marshfield **(Mrsfd)**
T- 2:14.3 Rummy Pete ('78 C. Mattison)
P- 2:10.1 H Pickup ('79 S. LeBlanc)

Northampton **(Nhtn)**
T- 2:14 Naida's Doll ('80 R. Cross)
P- 2:06 Count Down ('80 J. Marshall)

Plainville **(Plnvl)**
T- 2:07 Helen Sharlu ('87 R. Cross)
P- 2:01.2 Complete Power ('87 J. Marshall)

Spencer **(Spenc)**
T- 2:08 Twilight N ('87 A. Nason)
P- 2:03 Diamond Lead ('87 A. Card)

Michigan

Adrian **(Adrn)**
T- 2:01.2 Double Aught ('90 H.P. Wilson)
P- 1:59.1 Shiaway Ö H ('90 S.J. DeMull)

Allegan **(Allgn)**
T- 2:04 Corkeys Blaze ('90 P.F. Otten)
2:04 S F Clean Sweep ('90 L. Sattelberg)
P- 2:01.3 Poorman's Poison ('90 W.T. Schuyler)

Alpena **(Alp)**
T- 2:08 (unknown)
P- 2:06.3 (unknown)

Bad Axe **(BdAx)**
T- 2:03.1 Jeff's Playboy ('87 M. Goldschmidt)
P- 2:00.3 Shiaway Belshah ('88 P. Wrenn)

Bay City **(ByCy)**
T- 2:08.4 Foggie River ('59 J. Rousseau)
P- 2:04 Captain Vance ('86 M. Kakaley)

Big Rapids **(BgRpd)**
T- 2:02.2 Fancy Arbor ('79 C.J. Osborn)
P- 2:00 Mainstreet ('90 R.P. Wrenn)

Cadillac **(Cdlc)**
T- 2:02.3 King O'Windswept ('85 K. Hough)
P- 2:02.1 Tiffany Erin ('90 P.F. Otten)

Caro **(Caro)**
T- 2:01.3 Super Top ('90 R.H. Sampson)
P- 2:01.3 Fleet Gipsy ('84 C.J. Osborn)
2:01.3 C G Major ('85 M. Merriman)

Cassopolis **(Cass)**
T- 2:03.1 Ignitor ('88 L. Smith)
P- 2:02 BJ's Windshadow ('89 A.J. Tomlinson)

Centreville **(Cntrv)**
T- 2:03.1 Fancy Arbor ('79 C.J. Osborn)
P- 2:01 Dreamers Knox ('79 W. McIlmurray)

Charlotte **(Chlt)**
T- 2:06.4 O K's Stance ('87 T. Buter)
2:06.4 K-Z Sheri ('89 L. Street)
P- 2:01.4 Equinox Alba ('88 C. Putnam, Jr.)

TRACKS

Cheboygan (Chey)
T- 2:08 Air Attack ('62 E. Casagranda)
P- 2:05.3 Timely Jubilee ('84 A. Chaffin)

Croswell (Crswl)
T- 2:01 Chicory Wind ('87 G. Sutherland)
2:01 Priority Headliner ('88 P. Wrenn)
P-1.56.4 Crashland ('90 M.C. Jordan)

Fowlerville (Fwvl)
T- 2:01.3 Jeff's Playboy ('87 Goldschmidt)
P- 1:59.1 Solid Force ('88 E. Hennessey)

Gaylord (Gyld)
T- 2:04.3 Four De ('87 J. DeMull)
P- 2:01.4 W A Thiamine ('87 M. Clark)

Gladwin (Gldwn)
T- 2:05.4 Speedin Bambino ('90 M.A. Wrenn)
2:05.4 Wantz To Cruise ('90 T.J. Wantz)
P- 2:02.3 Good N Loyal ('85 C. Faurot, Jr.)

Hale (Hale)
T- 2:08.2 Cindy's Meg A Buck ('90 K.W. Billman)
P- 2:04.2 Bakersfield Glenn ('90 T.L. Buter)

Harrison (Hrsn)
T- 2:02 Bicycle Jim ('83 R. Renner)
P- 1:59 Bakersfield Glenn ('89 L.C. Stone)

Hart (Hart)
T- 2:02 Chillin ('90 R.P. Wrenn)
P- 2:01.1 P V Strike ('89 M.S. Hoover)

Hastings (Hstng)
T- 2:06 Arundel Stout ('46 Winn)
P- 2:05.3 Buskins ('90 T.G. Buter)

Hillsdale (Hlsdl)
T- 2:03-1/4 Coney Azoff ('43 Dispannett)
P- 2:00 Avatara ('86 S. Demull)

Holland (Hlnd)
T- 2:00.1 S F Rambo ('88 T. Buter)
P- 1:57.4 BJ's Windshadow ('89 A.J. Tomlinson)

Imlay City (Imlay)
T- 2:03 Equinox Joie ('90 L.J. Venier)
P- 1:59.4 Mainstreet ('90 R.P. Wrenn)

Ionia (Ionia)
T- 2:02.3 K-Z Sheri ('89 L. Street)
P- 1:59.3 Smokin Jose' ('89 T.E. Boring)

Ironwood (Iron)
T- 2:05.2 Malcolm J. ('74 D. Ackerman)
P- 2:01.3 Hot Tomato ('87 J. Hering)

Ithaca (Ithca)
T- 2:02 Fancy Arbor ('79 C.J. Osborn)
P- 2:00.3 Summerfield ('84 T. Taylor)

Kalamazoo (Klmzo)
T- 2:03 Superman's Ghost ('89 E.V. Hennessey)
P- 2:01 Equinos Alba ('88 C. Putnam, Jr.)

Kinross (Knrs)
T- 2:01.1 Rompaway Henry ('89 D.D. Harmon)
P- 2:00.1 BJ's Windshadow ('90 A.J. Tomlinson)

Lake Odessa (LkOds)
T- 2:03.4 Rompaway Henry ('89 D.D. Harmon)
P- 1:59.2 Smokin Jose' ('89 T.E. Boring)

Lincoln (Lncln)
T- 2:10.1 Superbly Good ('90 P.M. Wrenn)
P- 2:10.2 Shiaway Bruin ('89 R.H. Dean)

Ludington (Lud)
T- 2:04.1 Mr Isaac ('89 D. Longieliere)
P- 2:00.4 Equinox Alba ('88 C. Putnam, Jr.)

Marion (Mrn)
T- 2:03.2 K-Z Sheri ('89 L. Street)
P- 1:58.2 Good By Design ('85 K. Crawford)

Marshall (Mrshl)
T- 2:04 Thor's Tippy Tyler ('88 L. Smith)
P- 2:00.3 Hasty Ed ('73 C. Faurot)

Mason (Mason)
T- 2:06-1/2 Arion Guy Scott ('40 Winn)
P- 2:04 Rusty Range ('62 W. Niles)

Midland (Mdlnd)
T- 2:00 Superman's Ghost ('89 E.V. Hennessey)
P- 1:59 Good By Design ('85 K. Crawford)
1:59 S F Silverspoon ('88 K.Crawford)

Mount Pleasant (MntPl)
T- 2:05 Sweet Serene ('81 J. James)
P- 2:02.1 Turn Key ('81 J. Crandall)

Muskegon (Mkg)
T- 2:07 Bay De ('90 S.J. DeMull)
P- 2:02 Bakersfield Glenn ('89 L.C. Stone)

Norway (Nway)
T- 2:07 Pat Ti Way ('76 W. Jensen)
P- 2:02.3 Bakersfield Glenn ('90 G.L. Miller)

Onekama (Onkma)
T- 2:02.4 Speeding Breeze ('89 K.E. Hough)
P- 1:58.4 Bakersfield Glenn ('90 K.S. Pluta)

Petoskey (Pet)
T- 2:04.2 A Simple Story ('87 D. Lake)
P- 2:01.2 Grande ('90 S.M. Bateson)

Standish (Stnd)
T- 2:04.2 Timothy Earl ('86 R. Rowland)
P- 2:03 O K's Best ('86 B. Searle)

TRACKS

Traverse City	(Trvs)	Vassar	(Vass)
T- 2:03	Super Nonie ('90 J.W. Putnam)	T- 2:04.3	Neville Q ('88 G. Quick)
2:04.1	Vanna ('89 R.J. Edmonds)	P- 2:01.3	Stoney Viking ('88 S. Main)
P- 2:00	Mainstreet ('89 P.M. Wrenn)		

Minnesota

Arlington (Arln)
T- 2:08.3 Halston ('80 B. Budahn)
P- 2:07 Captain's Arion ('59 H. Ward)

Austin (Aust)
T- 2:17.3 Jade Lave ('84 N. Budahn)
P- 2:10.1 Norine Egyptian ('84 H. Jensen)

Blue Earth (Blue)
T- 2:11.2 J J Floridian ('77 B. Budahn)
P- 2:09.3 Egyptian Cash ('76 H. Jensen)

Cannon Falls (Canon)
T- 2:10 Chetwin ('22 McDonald)
P- 2:04 Cardamon Leo ('86 K. Banks)

Fairbault (Farb)
T- 2:14 Honorable Edition ('86 G. Wilson)
P- 2:06.1 Lee's Dream ('86 H. Crawford)

Hutchinson (Hutch)
T- 2:07 Iowa Star ('40 McCoy)
P- 2:01.2 Cardamon Leo ('86 C. Banks)

Owatonna (Owat)
T- 2:07.3 Cardamon Ben ('81 R. Banks)
2:07.3 Miss Who's Who ('87 P. Mouw)
P- 2:03.1 Luan Adios ('82 D. Mattson)

Rochester (Roch)
T- 2:07 Sam Volo ('37 Guernsey)
P- 2:06.3 Kitty Kat ('47 LeRoy)

St. Peter (StPtr)
T- 2:11.2 Cardamon Ben ('81 R. Banks)
P- 2:07 Matching Spirit ('88 P. Vandevelde)
2:07 Sherman's Best ('90 K. Kreykes)

Thief River Falls (TRFls)
T- None Recorded
P- 2:09.3 Sirs Lovely Lady ('83 M. Olson)

Wadena (Wdna)
T- 2:15 Dakota Dee ('90 D.R. Denny)
P- 2:11 Norine Egyptian ('83 G. Budach)
2:11 Night Dance ('87 R. Wilson)

Wheaton (Whtn)
T- 2:08.2 Stardom Andy ('74 J. Budahn)
P- 2:06-1/4 The Great G ('42 Loomis)

Mississippi

Camden (Cmdn)
T- 2:11 Bobby's Trotter ('88 J. Tillman)
P- 2:05.4 Quick A ('89 F.L. Patton, Sr.)

Philadelphia (Phila)
T- 2:08.2 T W Dale ('90 D.J. Donald)
P- 2:00.1 Our Joint Venture ('87 H. Dees)

Missouri

Kahoka (Khka)
T- 2:05 Brooklyn Jet ('86 E. Liles)
2:05 Brooklyn Flyer ('88 E. Liles)
P- 2:03 Rolling Chuck ('64 C. Collar)

Kirksville (Kirk)
T- 2:09 Regina Rose ('78 F. Chandler)
P- 2:07.3 Better Butler ('78 P. Liles)
2:07.3 Cracker Box Kid ('81 D. Freese)

Memphis (Memp)
T- 2:03.2 Game Iowa ('84 R. Doggett)
P- 2:04.3 B F Flicker ('84 J. Rohdy)

* Sedalia (Sed)
T- 1:59 Egan Hanover ('49 Baldwin)
P- 1:57.3 Countess Adios ('60 D. Miller)

Sedalia (Sedal)
T- 2:04 Jano Melody ('88 C. Butler)
P- 1:59.2 Jerico Bluegrass ('86 A. Morgan)

TRACKS

New Hampshire

Contoocook (Cntck)
T- 2:08-1/2   Adam Hanover ('39 R. Smith)
P- 2:04   Searights ('90 R.A. Flanders)

Plymouth (Ply)
T- 2:12.2   Jurgy ('86 B. Schmidt)
P- 2:06.4   Riv-Lea Echo Ridge ('87 Farrell)

Rochester (Rchst)
T- 2:03.2   Frankenshew ('87 F. Inman)
P- 1:59.3   Baystate ('90 G.J. Annaloro)

New Jersey

Big Z Farms (BgZ)
T- 2:01   Skippy's Lady ('85 J. Gluhm)
P- 1:57   Long Ago Blue Chip ('89 L.J. Toscano)

Cowtown (Cwtn)
T- 2:02.4   Impressive Ann ('88 R. Shahan)
P- 1:59.4   Closing ('87 J. Cameron)

** Englishtown - Capital Hill Farms (CHF)
T- 2:01   Bambino's Rocky ('81 D. Wade)
2:01   Stonegate Saunter ('82 A. Day)
P- 1:57   Katie Bobs ('83 H. Filion)

East Lynne Farms - Flemington (ELF)
T- 2:02   Rooster Rouster ('84 D. Wade)
2:02   Garrett Lobell ('85 Her. Filion)
P- 1:57.2   Off My Case ('89 C.R. Manzi)

Egyptian Acres - New Egypt (EA)
T- 2:01.1   Moore Hanover ('84 P. Henriksen)
P- 1:58   Closing ('87 H. Filion)

** Gaitway (Gty)
T- T1:59   Shack ('87 R. Turner)
P- T1:56   Gold Rush ('83 R. Remmen)
1:56   Brand New Dream ('85 J. Cameron)
1:56   Rewarding Skipper ('86 C. Manzi)
1:56   Closing ('87 W. Bresnahan)
1:56   Governor Scooter ('89 J.D. Cameron)

Hardwick (Hdwk)
T- 2:04.3   Stonegate Moors ('85 L. Raae)
P- 2:00.4   Ata Ray ('85 J. Stafford)

Johnson Park - Piscataway (Pisc)
T- 2:03.4   Impressive Ann ('88 J. Schwind)
2:04.2   Camp Haven ('87 V. Puma)
P- 1:59.2   Caramore ('82 C. Manzi)

Laura Lan Farm - Blairstown (Lrn)
T- 2:01.1   Pesach ('90 C.R. Manzi)
P- 1:59.3   Scooterific ('90 J.W. Lancaster)

Millville (Milv)
T- 2:05.4   Stonegate Saunder ('82 A. Day)
P- 2:01.2   Dime A Dozen ('82 L. Telymonde)

Scenic View - Clarksburg (Clark)
T- 2:02.4   H T's Doll ('85 J. Belote)
2:02.4   Lungistics ('88 P. Erikson)
P- 1:59.1   Diggin Machine ('87 E. Seiler)

** Showplace Farms (Shpl)
T- 1:58   Delphi's Jet ('89 P.K. Eriksson)
P- 1:54.4   Nuclear Nightmare ('88 H. Harvey)

Willowbrook - Tinton Falls (TinFl)
T- 2:04.3   Cari Bambina ('83 J. House, Jr.)
2:04.3   H T's Doll ('85 J. Belote)
P- 2:00.4   Caramore ('82 C. Manzi)

New York

Afton (Aftn)
T- 2:04.2   Audie's Flyer ('90 H.H. Westbrook Jr.)
P- 2:03.3   Citizen Cane ('89 H.E. Thornton)

** Alexandria Bay (AxBy)
T- 2:15   Robin Scot ('90 D.R. Chapman)
P- 2:06   Aubrey Hanover ('90 M.F. Capone)

Altamont (Atmt)
T- 2:06   Willsboro Warrior ('87 J. Hargett)
2:06   Holly Smoke ('88 H. Westbrook, Jr.)
P- 2:04.1   Bacon Hill Fox ('84 P. Davis)

Angelica -- Victoria Raceway (Angel)
T- 2:05.4   Mr Yuk ('89 S.S. Cooper)
P- 2:02   Rocky's Rhody ('87 R. Houghtaling)

Ballston Spa (BalSp)
T- 2:06   Jewel's Jewel ('86 C. Burgess)
P- 2:05.2   Precious Don ('83 A. Davignon)

Bath (Bath)
T- 2:07   Harvest High ('39 Hall)
P- 2:04.2   Fiddlechips ('88 B. Sears)

Boonville (Bnvl)
T- 2:06   Breezy Knoll Boy ('89 P. Barkley)
P- 2:00.4   Katie R ('89 J.C. Sears)

TRACKS

Caledonia	**(Cdna)**
T- 2:06	Camilla Hanover ('46 Unknown)
2:06	Provident ('45 Milton)
P- 2:03.1	Miss Sunny ('85 C. Cappotelli)
Chatham	**(Ctm)**
T- 2:07-1/2	More Expense ('39 C. Dill)
P- 2:02-1/2	Newbrook Volo ('39 Munz)
Cobleskill	**(Cbls)**
T- 2:06-1/2	Lee Stout ('37 Forcier)
P- 2:02-1/4	Earl West ('37 Welp)
Dundee	**(Dund)**
T- 2:09-1/2	Hollyrood Darrell ('40 Unknown)
P- 2:07	Cheerful Grattan ('38 Unknown)
Dunkirk	**(Dnkrk)**
T- 2:07.1	Lucky Fire Whiz ('90 K.J. Cummings)
P- 2:03	Jackie's Hartac ('86 C. McClory)
Elmira	**(Elmra)**
T- 2:07.1	Frugal Eddie ('87 S. Lindell)
P- 2:02.3	Avon Seneca ('88 D. Robbins)
Fonda	**(Fda)**
T- 2:04.4	R Super Star ('85 R. Smith)
P- 1:59.4	Just A Gem ('89 H.B. Parttridge)
Gouverneur	**(Gouv)**
T- 2:06-1/2	Volo Mae ('40 Muckle)
P- 2:04-1/4	Torresdale ('42 Bell)
Hemlock	**(Hmlok)**
T- 2:05.2	Wiscoy Topper ('86 G. Kashino)
P- 2:02	Even Up ('87 R. Tisbert)
Little Valley	**(LtlVy)**
T- 2:07.2	Frugal Eddie ('89 S.P. Lindell)
P- 2:06	Rocky's Rhody ('87 R. Houghtaling)
Lowville	**(Low)**
T- 2:06.4	Little Jimmy G ('88 P. Brown)
P- 2:03	Jacsue Kermit ('88 E. Cross)
Malone	**(Malon)**
T- 2:03-1/4	Calumet Evelyn ('36 Fleming)
P- 2:01-1/4	Little Pat ('38 Fleming)
Massena	**(Mass)**
T- 2:10.2	Dawn's Lark ('81 P. Collette)
P- 2:08.1	First Score ('80 W. Delarm)
Morris	**(Mor)**
T- 2:06.2	Bethany Botique ('90 B.J. Russo)
P- 2:04.3	Sundance Betty ('89 F.S. Fiero)
Norwich	**(Nwch)**
T- 2:06.3	Jericho BG ('89 M.P. Clark)
P- 2:02.3	Dosedo ('80 T. Lanpher)
2:02.3	Cypress Miracle ('86 J. Sears)
Owego	**(Owego)**
T- 2:06-1/4	Chestnut Harvester ('31 Murray)
P- 2:02.3	Rocky's Rhody ('87 R. Houghtaling)
Palmyra	**(Plmya)**
T- 2:09.1	Neddie Joe ('88 S. Lindell)
P- 2:05	Quail Ridge Coggy ('88 B. Sears)
Plattsburg	**(Pltbg)**
T- 2:06.4	Gus's Filly ('88 J. Mattison)
P- 2:04.1	Bill Bells ('89 H.F. Smith)
Rhinebeck	**(Rhin)**
T- 2:05.1	Song Guy ('90 B. Belanger)
P- 2:01	Merry Tango ('90 K. DiBenedetto)
Sandy Creek	**(SndCr)**
T- 2:06.3	Demanding ('88 H. Okusko)
P- 2:05	Quail Ridge Coggy ('88 J. Sears)
Trumansburg	**(Trum)**
T- 2:06.3	M B's Best ('90 R.M. Bridges)
P- 2:03.4	Rocky's Rhody ('87 R. Houghtaling)
Waterloo	**(Wtrl)**
T- 2:05.1	Bawdy Yankee ('89 J.C. Sears)
P- 2:03.2	Bye Bye Chance ('88 P. Rapone)
Westport	**(West)**
T- 2:08	Millie Jo Q ('85 J. Hargett)
P- 2:03	Jacsue Kermit ('90 E.F. Cross)
Whitney Point	**(Whtny)**
T- 2:06-3/4	Intruder ('35 Casper)
P- 2:04.1	Citizen Cain ('89 H.E. Thornton)

North Carolina

Ahoskie	**(Ahsk)**
T- 2:10	Hassie Town ('88 C. Daiello)
P- 2:05	Polly's First ('90 H.L. Brown)

North Dakota

Bottineau	**(Bott)**	**Hamilton**	**(Ham)**
T-	None Recorded	T- 2:06	Guy Barnes ('44 F. Feldner, Jr.)
P- 2:03	Gamblers Chips ('90 R.A. Cullen)	P- 2:03.2	Quit Sniveling ('90 B.G. Wiltermuth)

TRACKS

Towner **(Twnr)**
T- None Recorded
P- 2:07 Jake's Lucky Pat ('90 E.T. Berentson)

Ohio

Ashland **(Ashl)**
T- 2:04.2 Arzew ('85 T. Vincent, Jr.)
2:04.2 Mountain Of Faith ('87 E. Kaufman)
P- 2:01.1 P J's Iroc ('90 D.L. McKirgan)

Athens **(Athns)**
T- 2:02.4 Hay Day Ross ('88 D. Guthrie)
P- 2:00.2 Happen A'long ('90 R.J. Newhart)

Attica **(Attc)**
T- 2:05.3 Paper List ('90 M.S. Kendall)
P- 2:01.4 C Lightning ('86 F. Keener)

Bellefontaine **(Bftn)**
T- 2:04.2 Tryson's Way ('88 B. Brown)
P- 2:00.2 Omaha Kid ('76 J. Smith)

Berea **(Ber)**
T- 2:04.3 TNT Macho ('89 S.M. Carter)
P- 2:00.1 Bare Back Writer ('90 R.J. ReVault)

Bowling Green **(BwlG)**
T- 2:04.3 How Merry ('89 G.H. Witty)
P- 2:01.3 Waving Jerry ('84 D. Whitacre)

Bucyrus **(Bucy)**
T- 2:03 Fence Post ('89 P.J. Soehnlen)
P- 2:00.3 I C C ('85 R. Todd)

Burton **(Burt)**
T- 2:01.4 Mountain Of Faith ('87 E. Kaufman)
P- 1:58.3 Bare Back Writer ('90 R.J. DeVault)

Cadiz **(Cdiz)**
T- 2:02.3 Peewee Pancake ('84 T. Smith)
P- 1:59.4 Hi Lo Leven ('84 R. Myers)

Caldwell **(Cald)**
T- 2:02 Wesleys Dream ('89 R.E. Jordan II)
P- 2:02 Ravensfalcon ('90 M.L. Thomas)

Canfield **(Cnfld)**
T- 2:01.3 Dixie's Score ('88 M. McClelland)
P- 1:58.3 Bob's Escort ('89 S.K. Bauder)

Canton **(Cantn)**
T- 2:03.3 Independent Blaze ('88 J. Cox)
P- 2:00.2 Falcon's Mann ('85 T. Holton)

Carrollton **(Carr)**
T- 2:03.2 Stone Queen ('87 P. Soehnlen)
P- 2:01 Hi Lo Leven ('82 D. McKirgan)

Celina **(Cel)**
T- 2:03.2 Dancom ('90 J.G. Landess)
P- 1:58.3 Just Jason ('88 E. Greeno)

Chillicothe **(Chil)**
T- 2:02.1 Becken Becky ('87 D. Ater)
P- 2:00.3 Ruark ('84 J. Barnes)

Circleville **(Circ)**
T- 2:03.3 B T Smoke ('90 F. Todd, Jr.)
2:03.4 Uncle Trotter ('88 H. Miller)
P- 2:00 Falcon's Echo ('86 C. Huber)

Cortland **(Cort)**
T- 2:06.2 R Cornstalk ('90 B.C. Umholtz)
P- 2:04.2 Beacons Fifth (W.P. Popio)

Coshocton **(Cosh)**
T- 2:02.4 Miss Judy Comfort ('89 F. Todd, Jr.)
P- 2:00.2 Hallie's Integrity ('90 G.E. Guy)

Croton **(Crot)**
T- 2:02.3 Mountain Of Faith ('87 E. Kaufman)
P- 1:59 I C C ('85 R. Todd)

Dayton **(Dayt)**
T- 2:05-1/4 Tim S. ('37 Gordon)
P- 2:02 Angies True Tom ('90 R.A. Taubert)

Dover **(Dover)**
T- 2:02.1 Miss Judy Comfort ('89 C.K. Williams)
P- 1:59.2 Abba Marquis ('90 J.L. Hochstetler)

Eaton **(Eaton)**
T- 2:05 Miss Famous Sky ('88 R. Miller)
P- 2:02.1 Noble High Fever ('90 T.J. Hope)

Findlay **(Find)**
T- 2:04.4 Fabio W ('87 J. Konesky III)
P- 2:02.2 Copious ('83 D. Burks)
2:02.2 Billy Delite ('89 J.W. Dailey)

Greenville **(Green)**
T- 2:02.2 Gayn T ('84 F. Todd)
P- 1:59.3 Jay Time ('72 G. Riegle)

Hamilton **(HR)**
T- 2:02 Duke Rodney ('62 W. Haughton)
P- 2:02.4 Whiz Abbe ('61 B. Cote)

Hicksville **(Hick)**
T- 2:04.4 Demon's Dream ('58 D. Greeno)
2:04.4 D V Belle ('83 T. Moore)
2:04.4 Arnies Delite ('88 C. Peter)
P- 1:58.3 Frances Chip ('88 J. Landess)

TRACKS

Hilliard	**(Hill)**
T- 2:03.2	Rachel J ('86 R. Higgins)
2:03.2	Florida Promise ('86 D. Ward)
P- 1:59.2	Tangency ('87 F. Todd, Jr.)

Jefferson	**(Jeff)**
T- 2:03-1/2	Scotland's Comet ('44 Ervin)
P- 2:01	King's Counsel ('44 H. Fitzpatrick)

Kenton	**(Knton)**
T- 2:01	Mad Speed ('84 J. Fout)
P- 1:59.3	Steady Roll ('90 R.S. Burns)

Lancaster	**(Lanc)**
T- 2:03.1	Miss Judy Comfort ('89 T. VanRhoden)
P- 2:01.2	Destination First ('89 D.L. Hawk)

Lima	**(Lima)**
T- 2:03	Odal In Action ('86 J. Fout)
P- 2:00	Windswept Song ('88 T. Bates)

Lisbon	**(Lsbn)**
T- 2:08	Dr Grundy ('68 D. Staffrey)
2:08	Miss Judy Comfort ('88 J. Cox)
P- 2:06	Hobo Special ('85 J. McKenzie)
2:06	Catcando ('90 S.M. Carter)

Logan	**(Logan)**
T- 2:05	Mighty Tara ('88 T. Van Rhoden)
P- 2:01.1	It's A Date ('85 B. Merkel)

London	**(Lndn)**
T- 2:03	Southern Stride ('86 D. High)
P- 2:00.2	Ramblin Champ ('85 D. Roberts)
2:00.2	Bat Mahone ('88 H. Snyder)

Mansfield	**(Mnsf)**
T- 2:02	Miss Judy Comfort ('89 M.K. Bailey)
P- 2:01	Old Blue Rooster ('80 W. Hansen)

Marietta	**(Mari)**
T- 2:04.3	Hey Hey ('89 C.A. Elliott)
P- 1:59.2	Wolf Creek Levi ('90 R.L. Morgan)

Marion	**(Mrion)**
T- 2:04.2	On To Glory ('85 G. Soehnlen)
P- 2:01.4	J J Deer ('88 F. Keener)

Marysville	**(Mary)**
T- 2:03-1/2	Speed King ('43 H. Whitney)
P- 2:00.2	Bye Bye Sleepyhead ('89 E.C. Young)

McConnelsville	**(McCnl)**
T- 2:03.1	Florida Jewel ('88 D. Lowe)
P- 2:00	Strike The Time ('87 R. Potts)

Medina	**(Med)**
T- 2:03	Mr Smooth Move ('90 R.T. Lippiatt)
P- 2:00.2	Governor Gus ('90 J.M. Kiesel)

Montpelier	**(Mtplr)**
T- 2:02.3	Mighty Magoo ('89 S.A. Sugg)
P- 2:02	Rayjean Blast ('85 L. Stantz)

Mount Gilead	**(MtGil)**
T- 2:04.4	Meadow Nile ('90 P.W. Woolison)
P- 2:02.1	Hur Am Quick ('85 B. Colley)
2:02.1	Chocoholic ('90 J.W. Quinn)

Mount Vernon	**(MtVer)**
T- 1:59.4	Meadow Nile ('88 P. Woolison)
P- 1:59.2	J J Deer ('89 R.E. Steck)

Napoleon	**(Npln)**
T- 2:04	Wen Her Finale ('87 H. Dick)
2:04	Magnificent Marv ('89 T.L. Adams)
2:04	Slow Poke ('90 J.A. Konesky III)
P- 1:59	Peglos Dream ('88 M. Morris)

Norwalk	**(Nwlk)**
T- 2:02.4	Southern Stride ('86 D. High)
P- 1:59.2	Instant Little Man ('87 McKirgan)

Oak Harbor	**(OHbr)**
T- 2:02.1	Speedtown's Score ('89 S.J. Brannan)
P- 1:59.4	Lady's Ran A Lite ('89 B.J. Heywood)

Old Washington	**(OWash)**
T- 2:04.4	Robin L ('85 E. Hochstetler)
P- 2:00.4	Hi Lo Leven ('82 D. McKirgan)

Ottawa	**(Ott)**
T- 2:05.3	Hallie Lois ('69 J. Edwards)
P- 2:01	Wen Her Lite ('89 H.R. Dick)

Owensville	**(Owen)**
T- 2:02.2	Gayn T ('84 F. Todd)
P- 1:59.2	Tangency ('87 F. Todd, Jr.)

Painesville	**(Pain)**
T- 2:01.2	Mondo ('87 B. Weaver)
P- 1:59	Tiercel ('89 L.E. Merriman)

Paulding	**(Pauld)**
T- 2:02.4	Noble Score ('87 M. Rosengarten)
P- 2:00	Shock Wave-MC ('87 M. McCarty)
2:00	Wen Her Lite ('89 H.R. Dick)

Piketon	**(Pike)**
T- 2:04.1	Macs Class ('87 C. Harness)
P- 2:01	Homesteader ('84 B. Long)

Plain City	**(PlnCy)**
T- 2:05.4	Fez Hanover ('44 Plaxico)
P- 2:04.1	Chancellor Potamus ('85 B.Farrington)

Proctorville	**(Proc)**
T- 2:06.1	Gigi Can ('86 D. Spencer)
P- 2:01.2	Macs Boy ('87 A. Jones)

TRACKS

Richwood (Rchwd)
T- 2:02.3 Wen Her Finale ('87 H. Dick)
P- 1:59 P J's Iroc ('90 D.S. Miller)

Rock Springs (RkSp)
T- 2:07.3 Hopeful Action ('86 D. Spencer)
P- 2:05.1 Ambitious Abagail ('88T. VanRhoden)

Sidney (Sid)
T- 2:04.4 R U Willing ('85 R. Muntz)
P- 2:01 Steady Roll ('89 B.E. Schmidt)

Smithfield (Smth)
T- 2:05 Star City Printer ('89 G.A. Soehnlen)
P- 2:01 Hobo Special ('85 J. McKenzie)

Springfield (Sprng)
T- 2:03.3 Uncle Trotter ('88 H. Miller)
P- 2:00 C'Mon Ashley ('86 M. Wollan)

Tiffin (Tiff)
T- 2:02.3 C A Winner ('90 B.A. Lewis)
P- 2:00 Rustic Reflection ('90 K.M. Sherman)

Troy (Troy)
T- 2:03.1 Arzew ('85 T. Vincent, Jr.)
P- 1:57.3 Rootbeer Slammer ('87 D.Williams)

Upper Sandusky (UpSan)
T- 2:04.1 Dr J Adonno ('90 R.J. Brown)
P- 1:59.3 Skeets Dream ('90 T.T. Holton)

Urbana (Urbna)
T- 2:00.3 Common Sense ('88 S. Kostura)
P- 1:57.3 Dee's Tuition ('90 B.L. Riegle)

Van Wert (VnWrt)
T- 2:05 Lima Power ('78 H. Dick)
P- 2:00.3 Windswept Song ('89 D.E. Bates)

Wapakoneta (Wapak)
T- 2:05 Peter Astra ('42 Parshall)
2:05 Silent Rage ('85 K. Funk)
2:05 Wen Her Finale ('88 H. Dick)
P- 2:00.4 J T Bret ('90 T.L. Hasis)

Warren (Warrn)
T- 2:02.2 Robud ('85 J. Cox)
P- 1:59 Corner Pocket ('85 D. Harmon)

Washington Court House (WasCH)
T- 2:01.4 Spinning Ranger ('89 D.R. Rankin)
P- 1:59.1 Bare Back Writer ('90 J.D. Fout)

Wauseon (Wseon)
T- 2:03.2 Noble Alice ('89 C.A. Putnam, Jr.)
P- 1:58.4 Honest Chance ('76 D. McIntosh)

Wellington (Wlngt)
T- 2:03.4 College Record ('74 E. Bowman)
P- 2:00 Flying Domitian ('86 E. Kaufman)
2:00 Friendly Chris ('88 L. Gorfido)

Wellston (Wlstn)
T- 2:07 Hey Frosty ('88 D. Rucker)
P- 2:03.1 Falcons Sunburst ('88 D. Spencer)

Wilmington (Wilm)
T- 2:02.4 Truth B Mightier ('87H. Coven, Jr.)
P- 1:58.4 J J Deer ('89 F.A. Keener)

Woodsfield (Wdsfd)
T- 2:03.4 Robin L ('85 E. Hochstetler)
P- 2:00.2 Flying Tiger ('87 L. Leasure)

Wooster (Wostr)
T- 2:04.4 Fence Post ('89 P.J. Soehnlen)
P- 1:58.3 Meadow Dart ('89 T.A. Brinkerhoff)
1:58.3 Governor Gus ('90 F.P. Todd, Jr.)

Xenia (Xenia)
T- 2:03.3 Uncle Trotter ('88 H. Miller)
P- 1:59 Rootbeer Slammer ('87 D. Williams)

Zanesville (Zane)
T- 2:04.1 Mac's Exchange ('89 B.M. Davis)
P- 2:00.3 Image Of Falcon ('83 R. Roberts)

Pennsylvania

Bedford (Bdfd)
T- 2:01.3 Super Fellow ('90 J.D. McMullen)
P- 1:56.3 Keystone Famous ('86 R.R. Hammer)

Bloomsburg (Blom)
T- 1:59.4 Keystone Badger ('88 R.Hammer)
P- 1:58.1 Keystone Rambo ('89 R.R.R. Hammer)

Buckyland Stables (Byd)
T- 2:04 Triple Your Cash ('88 R.R. Hammer)
P- 2:03.3 Toddy D ('88 S. Beegle)

Butler (Butlr)
T- 2:05.1 Armbro Upsala ('79 D. Altmeyer)
P- 2:02.3 Wicked Tobias ('79 D. Altmeyer)

Chester (Wtst)
T- 2:08.3 Santa's Helper ('78 R. Reeser)
P- 2:08 Beltide Boxwood ('70 A. Sleva)

Clearfield (Clear)
T- 2:03.1 Keystone Salute ('90 R.R. Hammer)
P- 2:02.2 Starring Role ('87 D. Wilson II)

TRACKS

Dana Irving Farm **(DIF)**
T- 2:05.1 Gala Pro ('86 J. Offutt)
P- 2:00.1 Toddy D ('86 S. Beegle)

Dayton **(Dytn)**
T- 2:02.4 Shreck Danny Boy ('90 B.K. Weaver)
P- 1:59 Keystone Rambo ('89 R.R. Hammer)

Gratz **(Grtz)**
T- 2:01.4 Keystone Badger ('88 R.R. Hammer)
P- 1:59.4 Keystone Luscious ('90 R.R. Hammer)

** Holly Hurst Training Center **(HHTC)**
T- 1:59.4 Nettie M ('90 P.E. Spears)
P- 1:58 Keystone Famous ('86 R.R.R. Hammer)
 1:58 Keystone Rambo ('89 R.R.R. Hammer)

Honesdale **(Hone)**
T- 2:05 What A Tagger ('90 N.H. Burns)
P- 2:02 David's Fella ('88 A. Brownell)

Hughesville **(Hugh)**
T- 2:04 Keystone Nighthawk ('87 R.R. Hammer)
P- 2:01 Naughty Girl ('90 R.C. Neal)

Huntingdon **(Hndn)**
T- 2:03.3 Keystone Luscious ('90 R.R. Hammer)
 2:04 Landaspeed ('89 R.R.R. Hammer)
P- 2:00.2 Keystone Rambo ('89 R.R. Hammer)

Indiana **(Indna)**
T- 2:00 Keystone Badger ('88 R.R. Hammer)
P- 1:59.3 Keystone Rambo ('89 R.R. Hammer)

Lehighton **(Lehgh)**
T- 2:02.1 Bedford Spirit ('77 C. Hammer)
P- 1:58.1 Impromptu Hanover ('84 C. Connor)

Meadville **(Meadv)**
T- 2:07.1 Justacinch ('77 W. Dunn)
P- 2:03 Keystone Ensign ('89 R.R. Hammer)

Port Royal **(PrRoy)**
T- 2:05 Meadow Sergeant ('90 R.D. Sharbaugh)
P- 2:00.2 Keystone Luscious ('90 R.R. Hammer)

Smethport **(Smeth)**
T- 2:04 Anastasia Andy ('88 L. Urban)
P- 2:04 Silver Storm ('90 W. Dunn)

Stoneboro **(Ston)**
T- 2:02 Laser Almahurst ('86 H. Brocklehurst)
P- 1:59.2 Keystone Rambo ('89 H. Brocklehurst)

Troy **(Try)**
T- 2:02 Triple T Magnum ('87 R.R. Hammer)
P- 2:01.2 Sweet But Sassy ('88 W. Brickell)

Washington **(Wash)**
T- 2:02.4 In Haste ('60 S. Dancer)
P- 2:00.1 Ollie Von ('90 L.L. Beinhauer)

Wattsburg **(Watt)**
T- 2:04 Smokey Crown ('88 D. Brocklehurst)
P- 2:04 Ebony ('80 R.R. Hammer)

Waynesburg **(Wayn)**
T- 2:02.1 Moore Hanover ('83 R.R. Hammer)
P- 2:00 Red-Sota ('84 D. Reese)
 2:00 Toda Mix ('87 S. Johnston)

York **(York)**
T- 2:02.1 Keystone Badger ('88 R.R. Hammer)
P- 1:59 Keystone Famous ('88 R.R. Hammer)

South Carolina

Fountain Inn **(FtIn)**
T- 2:09 Scot's Guard ('58 J. Huggins)
P- 2:06 Blazing Comet ('65 J. King)

South Dakota

Sioux Falls **(SxFl)**
T- None Recorded
P- 2:06.3 RollingCareless ('85 M. VanOtterloo)

Tennessee

Fayetteville **(Faye)**
T- 2:04.2 Speedy Ritz ('88 J. Harry)
P- 1:58.3 Dance Caller ('86 R. Cullipher)

Vermont

Barton **(Brtn)**
T- 2:03-3/4 Kelly ('39 O'Connell)
P- 2:03-3/4 Atlantic Hanover ('38 J. Dill)
 2:03-3/4 Little Pat ('38 D. Maher)
 2:03-3/4 Royal Napoleon ('39 Ackerman)

Essex Junction **(EsxJn)**
T- 2:03-1/4 Hanover Peters ('37 Stuart)
P- 2:01-1/2 Earl West ('37 Welp)
 2:01-1/2 Little Pat ('39 Maher)

Page 73

TRACKS

Lyndonville	**(Lydvl)**	**Rutland**	**(Rutln)**
T- 2:06.1	Tryst Spectator ('90 R.F. Vance)	T- 2:05.4	Millie Jo Q ('88 D. Tuccillo, Jr.)
P- 2:02.2	Char Jon A ('89 C.L. Mosher)	P- 2:01.2	Jacsue Kermit ('90 E.F. Cross)

Manchester	**(Mnch)**	**Tunbridge**	**(Tunbr)**
T- 2:13.3	King Thor ('84 P. Marashio)	T- 2:07.2	Tiny Sota ('90 W.E. White)
P- 2:06.4	Signal Hill Cadet ('87 K. Martin)	P- 2:08.2	Signal Hill Jake ('89 C.E. Fleming)

Virginia

Washington

Woodstock	**(Wdstk)**	**Chahalis**	**(Chhs)**
T- 2:05.1	Keystone Jacque ('87 W. Lineweaver)	T- Q2:17	High Sparkle ('85 J. Russo)
P- 2:03.1	Jefferyu Wil ('89 A.M. Lineweaver)	P- 2:01.2	Wada Hy ('84 T. Brown)
2:03.1	Jeffery Wil ('90 A.M. Lineweaver)		

West Virginia

Lewisburg	**(Lewbg)**
T- 2:04.4	Red Oaks Drew ('85 R. Newhart)
P- 2:00	Happen A'Long ('90 R.L. Morgan)

Wisconsin

Antigo	**(Ant)**	**Monroe**	**(Mroe)**
T- 2:19	Significant Penny ('86 R. Davis)	T- 2:06	Eleanor Volo ('36 McNutt)
P- 2:14	Hypnosis ('86 R. Davis)	2:06	Pearl Harbor ('44 Amundsen)
		2:06	All Spencer ('46 Livingston)
Amherst	**(Amst)**	P- 2:02-1/4	King's Counsel ('44 H. Fitzpatrick)
T- 2:08.4	Dancing Idyll ('85 E.Casagranda)		
P- 2:05.1	Fox Valley Rampage ('90 B. Alexander)	**Neillsville**	**(Neil)**
		T- 2:08	Better Boy ('79 L. Laurent)
Beaver Dam	**(BvDm)**	P- 2:03.2	Norine Egyptian ('79 H. Jensen)
T- 2:06.1	LaVitesse ('48 Hasson)		
P- 2:04.2	Highlawn Dale ('40 Ream)	**Rice Lake**	**(RicLk)**
		T- 2:08.4	Pat Ti Way ('76 W. Jensen)
Darlington	**(Darl)**	P- 2:03.2	Bestdealintown ('90 D.A. Watson)
T- 2:06-1/4	Lovely Lady ('42 H. McNutt)		
2:06-1/4	Pearl Harbor ('44 O. Amundsen)	**Richland Center**	**(Rchln)**
P- 2:05	Delco Smokin Crown ('85 J. DeLong)	T- 2:07-1/2	Athlone Iosola Guy ('37 A.Shaw)
		P- 2:05	Keith K ('90 G.L. Garrels)
Elkhorn	**(Elkrn)**	2:05	GoGo ('90 T.H. Hill)
T- 2:05	Johnnie Jade ('82 D. Insko)		
2:05	Special Reporter ('90 R.J. Schroeder)	**Sturgeon Bay**	**(Sturg)**
P- 2:01	Why Bill ('77 A.G. Shaw)	T- 2:08	Mina Deroche ('37 Unknown)
		P- 2:05.4	Mrs Chancey ('77 L. Turner)
Manitowoc	**(Mntwc)**		
T- 2:07	Quality ('29 McKay)	**Viroqua**	**(Viro)**
P- 2:05-12	The Legionnaire ('45 Newell)	T- 2:06.2	Dancing Idyll ('88 E. Casagranda)
		P- 2:05	Sally's Last ('49 V. Cockroft)
Marshfield	**(Msfld)**	2:05	Brooks Judge ('89 L.E. Brunston)
T- 2:06.3	Reddy Candy ('87 G. Redeker)		
P- 2:02.2	Ideal Rorty ('87 J. Goehring)	**Wausau**	**(Wausa)**
		T- 2:09.1	Better Boy ('79 L. Laurent)
Mineral Point	**(MnlPt)**	2:09.1	Reddy Candy ('90 G.L. Redeker)
T- 2:05.1	Bangor ('56 Hague)	P- 2:04.3	Prairie Badger ('82 R. Yohn)
P- 2:04.3	Jamy Sun ('77 A. Douglas)		
		Westfield	**(Wtfd)**
		T- 2:10	Blue Grass Special ('90 M. Blihovde)
		P- 2:04	Delco Smokin Crown ('89 J.J. DeLong)

TRACKS

Weyauwega (Wey)
T- 2:14.3 Janes Magoo ('89 R.P. Kline)
P- 2:06 Anita's Son ('89 C.D. Frenzel)
2:06 Sycamores Kash ('89 G.A. Rath)

OTHER CANADIAN RACEWAYS

Ontario

Ancaster Raceway, Ancaster (Anca)
T- 2:07 Clickity Clack ('90 W.J. Megens)
P- 2:04.4 Mohawk Spirit ('90 L. Hill)

Barrie Raceway, Barrie (Bar)
T- 2:00.2 The Barn Stormer ('89 N.J. McKnight)
P- 1:56 Mystery Fund ('89 W.R. Gale)

Belleville Raceway, Belleville (Blvl)
T- 2:02 Roger Rascal ('90 S.J. Skene)
P- 1:57.2 Laurstar ('90 J.P. Brooks)

Clinton Raceway, Clinton (Clntn)
T- 2:02 Lou Mac's Dream ('85 G. Gordon)
P- 1:58 Tantallon Wonder ('90 M.G. Etsell)

Dresden Raceway, Dresden (Dres)
T- 1:59.1 Nadirs Pride ('86 J. Walker)
P- 1:56.4 The Brat ('88 D. Wall)

Elmira Raceway, Elmira (Emira)
T- 1:59.3 Delcrest Gambler ('90 D.M. Shadlock)
P- 1:57.2 Silver Reign ('90 W.A. Fritz)

Goderich Raceway, Goderich (Godr)
T- 2:03.2 Kawartha Special ('86 C. Lawson)
P- 1:57.3 Timely Pride ('88 J. Holmes)

Hanover Raceway, Hanover (Hnvr)
T- 2:00.1 A Go Go Lauxmont ('88 D. LeBlanc)
P- 1:57.4 Kinway Heather ('88 L. Kindorney)

* Hiawatha Horse Park, Sarnia (Sar)
T- 1:58.4 A Worthy Lad ('90 W.A. Fritz)
P- 1:53.2 Mystery Fund ('89 W.R. Gale)

** Kawartha Downs, Peterborough (KD)
T- 1:57.1 Nadirs Pride ('86 J. Walker)
P- 1:55.2 Air Force One ('89 A.W. Nicholls)

** Kingston Park Raceway, Kingston (KPR)
T- 2:00.3 Vinaigrette ('87 W. Maertens)
2:00.3 A Worthy Lad ('90 W.A. Fritz)
P- 1:54.4 Armbro Herman ('89 J.R. Kopas)

Leamington Raceway, Leamington (Leam)
T- 2:01.3 Ruby Skye ('88 J. Walker)
P- 1:57.3 Laurstar ('90 J.P. Brooks)

Orangeville Raceway, Orangeville (Ornvl)
T- 1:59.4 A Go Go Lauxmont ('88 D. Leblanc)
1:59.4 Delcrst Gambler ('89 D.M. Shadlock)
P- 1:56.4 Hawkeye Ranger ('88 B. Drury)

Sudbury Downs, Sudbury (Sudby)
T- 2:01.2 N V Worthy ('87 J. Walker)
2:01.2 A Worthy Lad ('90 W.A. Fritz)
P- 1:57 Stonehouse Ryan ('90 G.G. Lamoureux)

Woodstock Raceway, Woodstock (Wodsk)
T- 2:03.2 Antwerp Lobell ('90 J.B. MacCormick)
2:03.2 Twinks Star ('90 W.A. Fritz)
P- 1:58.4 Top Of The Road ('90 J.P. Brooks)

Quebec

Hippodrome de Quebec, Quebec City (Que)
T- 2:00 Super Green ('88 F. Maguire)
P- 1:55 Bomb Rickles ('89 M.R. MacDonald)

Hippodrome Saguenay (Jonquiere) (Sagy)
T- 2:05 Diana Gabe ('89 G. Beaumont)
P- 1:56.2 Au Revoir Grade ('89 C. Corneau)

Hippodrome Trois Rivieres (TrRvs)
T- 2:00.1 Super Green ('90 F. Maguire)
P- 1:55.2 Skipper Forrest ('90 H. Filion)

TRACKS

Saskatchewan

** Marquis Downs, Saskatoon (MqD)
T- 2:06.4 Brontosaurus ('77 W. Urquhart)
P- 1:56.3 Sports Light ('86 C. MacLeod)

Queensbury Downs, Regina (Reg)
T- 2:08.2 Cap Collection ('87 P. Coleman)
P- 1:55.4 Conditional ('87 J. Baxter)

TRACK RECORDS – CANADIAN FAIRS

Alberta

Enoch (Enoch)
T- None Recorded
P- 2:02.1 Minus Magic ('88 P. Barr)

Lethbridge (Leth)
T- None Recorded
P- 2:00.2 (unknown)

Grand Prairie (GrnPr)
T- None Recorded
P- 2:02.1 Happy Scott N ('89 M.D. Adams)
    2:02.1 Take The Night Off ('90 G.K. Baxter)

Winterburn (Wint)
T- None Recorded
P- None Recorded

British Columbia

Surrey (Srry)
T- None Recorded
P- 1:58.2 Hy Mikey ('88 B. Davis)

Manitoba

Carberry (Crb)
T- 2:18 Bedfords Choice ('83 A. Grundy)
P- 2:04.2 Shirleys Tango ('82 G. Isman)

Miami (Miami)
T- 2:05 (unknown)
P- 2:00 C A McCann ('90 R.A. Cullen)

Carman (Crm)
T- 2:09 Rojo Reynard ('76 A. Lamontagne)
P- 2:01.4 Cliffs Transport N ('88 R. Rey)

Minnedosa (Minn)
T- None Recorded
P- 2:01.3 Kara Brewer ('89 G.M. Isman)

Dauphine (DauP)
T- None Recorded
P- 2:01.4 Bogy Doc ('87 G.G. Dunn)

Pilot Mound (Pilot)
T- None Recorded
P- 1:59.2 C A McCann ('90 R.A. Cullen)

Deloraine (Dlrn)
T- 2:11 Brets Cache ('79 J. Forster)
P- 2:00.4 Kara Brewer ('90 G.M. Isman)

Portage La Prairie (Port)
T- 2:14 (unknown)
P- 2:00.1 C A McCann ('90 R.A. Cullen)

Glenboro (Glbr)
T- None Recorded
P- 2:00.2 Cliffs Transport ('88 R. Rey)

Russell (Russ)
T- None Recorded
P- 2:03.3 Kinsmore Tovah ('87 A. Cullen)

Holland (Holln)
T- 2:13.4 Brets Cache ('79 J. Forster)
P- 2:00.4 Bogy Doc ('85 G. Dunn)

Virden (Vrdn)
T- 2:15.2 Brets Cache ('80 J. Forster)
P- 2:01.2 Wonders Streak ('89 R.A. Cullen)

Killarney (Klrny)
T- 2:11.1 Distant Cache ('83 J. Forster)
P- 1:58.2 Cliffs Transport N ('88 R. Rey)

Wawanesa (Waw)
T- None Recorded
P- 2:01 C A McCann ('90 R.A. Cullen)

TRACKS

Ontario

Arnprior **(Arnp)**
T- 2:07 Brisco Ann ('85 D. Forgie)
P- 2:02.4 Bellestar Desiree ('90 E.S. Stewart)

Avonmore **(Avmr)**
T- None Recorded
P- 2:03.2 Larry Micvic ('90 R.G. Hess)

Beamsville **(Beams)**
T- 2:06.4 Command Miss ('88 J. King)
P- 2:05.2 Coal Miner's Girl ('88 F. Roloson)
2:05.2 Executed ('89 J.N. Farrington)

Binbrook **(Bnbk)**
T- 2:12.4 Clickity Clack ('90 W.J. Megens)
P- 2:08.2 Mohawk Spirit ('90 L. Hill)

Brockville **(Brkvi)**
T- 2:09.2 Tough Bunney ('88 O. Coville)
P- 2:04.2 Bradleys Earl ('88 J. Bradley)

Brooklin **(Brk)**
T- 2:05.3 King Of Utopia ('87 K. Klawitter)
P- 2:02.1 Mooreland's Comet ('85 G. Graham)

Burford **(Burf)**
T- 2:08.4 Prince Of Star ('90 D.R. Field)
P- 2:07.1 Executed ('90 J.N. Farrington)

Caledon **(Cldn)**
T- 2:10 (unknown)
P- 2:06.1 Kilcurry Pete ('85 W. McClure)

Caledonia **(Clna)**
T- 2:09.1 Shiaway Ben ('87 J. Farrington)
P- 2:07.2 So Direct ('89 L.L. Plant)

Centreville **(Cvll)**
T- 2:12 Earl E ('86 B. Wemp)
P- 2:03 Roof Vent Dee ('87 L. Huffman)

Dorchester **(Dorch)**
T- 2:04 Dominos Star ('90 D. DiCicco)
P- 2:03.1 Scamp Rip ('88 W. Borth)

Forest **(Frst)**
T- 2:12 River Flat Jake ('89 K. Graham)
P- 2:06 Cruising Jan ('87 T. Cochrane)

Lansdowne **(Lnsdw)**
T- 2:16.4 Surge Adinif ('83 E. Lake)
P- 2:05.2 Ellys Willy ('89 K.H. Lake)

Lombardy **(Lomb)**
T- 2:15 Wolf's Norah ('89 R.J. Thompson)
P- 2:10.3 Dingaling Chris ('90 R.J. Thompson)

Manitowaning **(Manit)**
T- 2:16 Mc Pal ('87 R. Jenkins)
P- 2:07 Dover Cliff ('83 G. Lamoureux)
2:07 Lillimac Talena ('84 M. Safic)
2:07 Hazard County ('86 K. Amand)

Markham **(Mrkh)**
T- 2:09.3 Sam Newton ('89 M.E. Ward)
P- 2:07.3 Overcookie ('89 J.M Fitzgerald)

Martinville **(Mrtvl)**
T- 2:10 Poilu Kempt ('89 J. Sirois)
P- 2:05 Fortunate Jo ('89 L. Cotton)

Melbourne **(Melb)**
T- None Recorded
P- 2:05 Peter Puff ('90 B.J. Graham)

Newington **(Nwng)**
T- 2:12 Harry Zeron ('78 A. Pyke)
2:12 Lincoln's Favorite ('78 W. Strader)
P- 2:09 Chico Boy ('78 B. Alguire)
2:09 Lami Temps ('86 H. Zeron, Jr.)

Norwood **(Nrwd)**
T- 2:18.4 Kawartha Strider ('85 R. Smith)
P- 2:14 Johnny Brooke ('84 G. Larush)
2:14 Morgage Don ('85 J. Robinson)

Ohsweken **(Ohs)**
T- 2:08 Kawartha Rex ('88 F. Macneil)
P- 2:05.3 Victress Hill ('90 P.G. Hamilton)

Orillia **(Orill)**
T- 2:09.2 Vera Bluegrass ('84 S. Goodale)
P- 2:04.2 Good Samaritan ('85 G. Wain)

Orono **(Orono)**
T- 2:07 (unknown)
P- 2:01 Trojan Frosty ('87 D.W. Clements)
2:01 Trojan Frosty ('90 W.F. Nicholls)

Paris **(Par)**
T- 2:10.2 Kim Land ('78 W. Langille)
P- 2:06.3 Executed ('89 A.S. Knill)
2:06.3 Mohawk Spirit ('90 L. Hill)

Parkhill **(Park)**
T- 2:11 Flat River Jake ('89 K. Graham)
P- 2:05 Betty John ('88 K. Gowan)

Perth **(Perth)**
T- 2:06 Settlor CEC ('86 R. Curran)
P- 2:04.1 Penya Princhessa ('86 E. Norris)

Port Perry **(PrtPy)**
T- 2:12 Shi Bob ('89 R.J. Paradis)
P- 2:03.3 Button Swinger ('90 W.J. Dowson)

TRACKS

Ridgetown (Ridg)
T- 2:14.3 Lis Pendens ('77 N. McKnight)
P- 2:05.4 Betty John ('88 K. Gowan)

Rodney (Rod)
T- 2:14 (unknown)
P- 2:05.2 City Vu Earl ('86 J. Wray)

SHEDCen (SHEDC)
T- 2:15.1 Thamesview Time ('80 C. Lilley)
P- 2:06.4 Overcookie ('89 L.E. Dawson)

Simcoe (Sim)
T- 2:07 Shiaway Ben ('87 J. Farrington)
P- 2:03.4 Carols Ranger ('86 J. Farrington)

Smithville (Smtvl)
T- 2:08 Clickity Clack ('90 M.A. Megens)
P- 2:03.2 American Funds ('90 P.R. Miller)

South Mountain (SthMt)
T- 2:10.1 Keystone Rocket ('88 O. Coville)
P- 2:02 Patty Perdo ('85 H. Portelance)

Strathroy (Stroy)
T- 2:11.2 (unknown)
P- 2:08 Chicopee Duchess ('86 R. Djukic)

Sunderland (Sund)
T- 2:09 (unknown)
P- 2:05.4 Stanley Strem ('82 H. Smalley)

Sutton (Sutt)
T- 2:10.4 Secret Lover ('84 R. Cunningham)
P- 2:05.4 Disco Doc ('86 M. Brethour)

Teeswater (Tees)
T- 2:10.3 Campers Son ('87 K. Houston)
P- 2:09 Ilderton Star ('84 H. Kennedy)

Tillsonburg (Till)
T- 2:07.4 Jambo Mercedes ('86 R. Duval)
P- 2:00.4 New Departure ('85 F. List)

Wallacetown (Wlctn)
T- 2:12.1 Nayarch ('88 M. Neff)
P- 2:06.3 Montego Captain ('88 J.Tacij)

Welland (Well)
T- 2:09.1 Busy Bob ('87 P.B. Kiradjian)
P- 2:06.4 Northern Mist ('87 J. Remmerswall)

Quebec

Ayers Cliff (AyrCl)
T- 2:12.4 Luctow's Flame ('89 A. Theroux)
P- 2:05.2 Estragon V L ('90 S. Turenne)

Bedford (Bedf)
T- 2:04 Denys Ga Du ('90 L. Cotton)
P- 2:00.4 Avroum Paul ('89 F. Morrissette)

Brome (Brom)
T- 2:06.3 Rhythm Speed ('89 M.W. Baillargeon)
   2:06.3 Courtice Place ('90 M.G. Dessureault)
P- 2:02.3 Night Colt ('89 M.W. Baillargeon)

Fatima (Fat)
T- None Recorded
P- 2:07.1 Steady Lion ('90 P. Turbide)

Havre aux Maisons (Imad)
T- None Recorded
P- 2:05.2 Riverlea Anne ('90 G. Turbide)

Lachute (Lacht)
T- 2:10 Grimshaw Paul ('89 P. Gabriel)
P- 2:05.1 Ideal Wilco ('89 J. Primeau)

Mount Joli Price (MtJP)
T- 2:16.2 Elgin Drummond ('86 A. Veilleux)
P- 2:03 Truxon Angus ('90 S. Houde)
   2:03 RD's Kitty ('90 C. Dugay)

Nouvelle (Nouvl)
T- None Recorded
P- 2:01 Township Fern ('90 C. Dugay)

Ormstown (Ormst)
T- 2:14.3 Cas El Texas Tee ('90 A.D. McCoy)
P- 2:05.4 Donero ('90 J. Bernert)

Pabos (Pabos)
T- 2:10.4 Poilu Kempt ('89 J. Sirois)
P- 2:05.4 RD's Kitty ('90 G. McKinney)

Papineauville (Ppvl)
T- None Recorded
P- 2:05.1 Karyleine ('86 A. Morin)

Quyon (Quyon)
T- 2:07.2 (unknown)
P- 2:01 Papi Fern ('90 J. Maheu)

Richmond (Rcmnd)
T- 2:13.2 Gee Two ('90 G. Chabot)
P- 2:09.3 La Cocotte ('90 M. Parr)

Riviere du Loup (RidL)
T- 2:08.4 Denys Ga Du ('90 L. Cotton)
P- 2:03.4 Jouffu Grade ('90 S. Fiola)

Saint Augustine (StAug)
T- (None Recorded)
P- 2:07 Credit Note ('87 G.L. Hamel)

TRACKS

Saint Basile Le Grand (SBLG)
T- 2:16.3 (unknown)
P- 2:02.4 Baron Bayama ('85 Y. Filion)

Saint Edouard (StEd)
T- 2:07.4 Kenwood Hoo ('89 P.A. Lavigne)
P- 2:04 La Cocotte ('90 P.A. Lavigne)

Saint Hughes (StHgs)
T- 2:06.4 Bonne Allure ('89 R.J. Grimard)
P- 2:02.1 Myllas ('90 G. Blanchette)

Saint-Syl Vere (SSV)
T- 2:10.4 Denys Ga Du ('90 L. Cotton)
P- 2:07.2 Avroum Paul ('89 F. Morrissette)

Saint Joseph Delepage (StJDl)
T- 2:03.3 Anne Gallon ('62 Unknown)
P- 1:59 Armbro Vienna ('83 G. Gendron)

Sartigan (Sart)
T- 2:11 Bon Premier ('90 R.J. Grimard)
2:11 Level Yankee ('90 J.G. Bergeron)
P- 2:07 London Market ('90 C.D. Chabot)

Sherbrooke (Sherb)
T- 2:13 Keystone Shannon ('83 N. Giard)
P- 2:09.4 Alcatraz T E ('84 P. Deslauriers)
2:09.4 Stello ('85 A. Morin)

Squatec (Squt)
T- 2:08.1 Rob Van Allen ('90 Y. Morin)
P- 2:04 Baroness Paloma ('89 R. Charest)

Saskatchewan

Lloydminster (Lyd)
T- None Recorded
P- 2:02.2 Detergent ('85 R. Federwick)

Yorkton (Yrktn)
T- None Recorded
P- 2:03.4 Relda Rocket ('90 L. Bell)

** Moose Jaw (MsJw)
T- 2:11.4 Guillermito ('77 D. Bell)
P- 1:58.3 Mark Temper ('87 K.D. Anderson)

Page 79

TRACKS

THE BUSINESS OF RACING: 1990

(On-Track at North American Tracks Only *)

State	Dates	Attendance	Mutuel Handle
California	176	516,321	$75,497,809
Delaware	213	311,807	31,805,990
Florida	156	672,479	68,730,814
Iowa	44	64,399	2,200,986
Illinois	647	2,032,159	255,253,911
Kentucky	257	525,322	26,695,184
Maine	249	(est.) 318,638	29,459,774
Maryland	320	898,304	128,291,342
Michigan	705	1,803,129	288,996,973
New Jersey	513	2,885,023	447,232,376
New York	1,178	2,390,563	354,429,963
Ohio	610	1,722,590	195,069,858
Pennsylvania	366	815,093	68,898,483
Sub Total:	**5,434**	**14,955,827**	**$1,972,563,463**

MARITIME PROVINCES

New Brunswick	206	125,614	$11,100,568
Newfoundland	42	13,596	779,772
Nova Scotia	239	104,488	12,219,754
Prince Edward Island	149	79,850	7,006,741
Sub Total:	**636**	**323,548**	**$31,106,835**

C.T.A. PROVINCES

Alberta	202	500,707	$91,337,996
British Columbia	175	399,928	60,523,641
Manitoba	89	118,467	18,246,107
Ontario	1,549	3,659,717	608,485,012
Quebec	661	1,758,881	297,468,165
Saskatchewan	71	58,072	3,755,659
Sub Total:	**2,747**	**6,495,772**	**$1,079,816,580**
Canadian Total:	**3,383**	**6,819,320**	**$1,110,923,415**
GRAND TOTAL:	**8,817**	**21,775,147**	**$3,083,486,878**

LEADING STATES

By Total Attendance		By Average Attendance		By Total Handle	
New Jersey	2,885,023	New Jersey	5,624	New Jersey	$447,232,376
New York	2,390,563	Florida	4,311	New York	354,429,963
Illinois	2,032,139	Illinois	3,141	Michigan	288,996,973
Michigan	1,803,129	California	2,933	Illinois	255,253,911
Ohio	1,722,590	Ohio	2,824	Ohio	195,069,858

* U.S. statistics provided by individual tracks or racing commissions;
Canadian figures courtesy of Canadian Department of Agriculture, Race Track Division

TRACKS

BUSINESS TRENDS: 1990-1989

(On-Track at Extended Pari-Mutuel Meets)

Track	Dates '90	Dates '89	Avg. Attendance 1990	Avg. Attendance 1989	Trend	Avg. Mutuel Handle 1990	Avg. Mutuel Handle 1989	Trend
California	176	131	2,933	3,002	(-2.30%)	$428,965	$560,077	(-23.41%)
Delaware	213	227	1,464	2,254	(-35.05%)	149,324	208,000	(-28.21%)
Florida	156	160	4,311	4,481	(-3.79%)	440,582	449,670	(-2.02%)
Iowa	44	34	1,464	1,959	(-25.27%)	50,022	133,837	(-62.62%)
Illinois	647	583	3,141	3,226	(-2.63%)	394,519	424,564	(-7.08%)
Kentucky	257	230	2,044	2,462	(-16.98%)	103,872	149,148	(-30.36%)
Maine	249	252	1,280	1,443	(-11.32%)	118,312	138,320	(-14.47%)
Maryland	320	317	2,807	3,679	(-23.70%)	400,910	423,600	(-5.36%)
Michigan	705	719	2,558	2,544	(-0.55%)	409,925	404,574	(-1.32%)
New Jersey	513	520	5,624	5,845	(-3.78%)	871,798	883,886	(-1.37%)
New York	1,178	1,202	2,029	2,044	(-0.73%)	300,874	323,286	(-6.93%)
Ohio	610	596	2,824	2,985	(-5.39%)	319,787	331,069	(-3.41%)
Pennsylvania	366	353	2,227	2,215	0.54%	188,247	268,658	(-29.93%)
Sub Total:	**5,434**	**5,324**	**2,752**	**2,921**	**(-5.78%)**	**$363,004**	**$390,552**	**(-7.05%)**

MARITIME PROVINCES

Track	Dates '90	Dates '89	Avg. Attendance 1990	Avg. Attendance 1989	Trend	Avg. Mutuel Handle 1990	Avg. Mutuel Handle 1989	Trend
New Brunswick	206	192	610	621	(-1.77%)	$53,886	$54,665	(-1.43%)
Newfoundland	42	48	324	328	(-1.22%)	18,566	20,072	(-7.50%)
Nova Scotia	239	242	437	456	(-4.17%)	51,129	52,026	(-1.72%)
Prince Edward Island	149	156	536	557	(-3.77%)	47,025	46,047	2.12%
Sub Total:	**636**	**638**	**509**	**521**	**(-2.30%)**	**$48,910**	**$48,954**	**(-0.09%)**

C.T.A. PROVINCES

Track	Dates '90	Dates '89	Avg. Attendance 1990	Avg. Attendance 1989	Trend	Avg. Mutuel Handle 1990	Avg. Mutuel Handle 1989	Trend
Alberta	202	208	2,479	2,531	(-2.05%)	$452,168	$434,702	4.02%
British Columbia	175	178	2,285	2,293	(-0.35%)	345,849	354,329	(-2.39%)
Manitoba	89	87	1,331	1,115	19.37%	205,012	196,313	4.43%
Ontario	1,549	1,588	2,363	2,392	(-1.21%)	392,824	390,838	0.51%
Quebec	661	658	2,661	2,812	(-5.37%)	450,027	457,314	(-1.59%)
Saskatchewan	71	88	818	801	2.12%	52,897	57,555	(-8.09%)
Sub Total:	**2,747**	**2,807**	**2,365**	**2,405**	**(-1.66%)**	**$393,089**	**$390,879**	**0.57%**
Canadian Total:	**3,383**	**3,445**	**2,016**	**2,056**	**(-1.95%)**	**$328,384**	**$327,556**	**0.25%**
GRAND TOTAL:	**8,817**	**8,769**	**2,469**	**2,581**	**(-4.31%)**	**$346,193**	**$365,803**	**(-5.36%)**

TRACKS

TRENDS AND LEADERS, NORTH AMERICAN TRACKS

(Extended Pari-Mutuel Meets Only)

The following comparisons are made without respect to "corresponding" meets, but are based upon the averages drawn from the total on-track attendance and handle recorded by each track during 1989 and 1990. Some meets may have been raced during different times in each year, although the majority are raced during the same period:

Leading Tracks, Avg. Mutuel Increase	
Delmarva Downs	58.44%
Balmoral Park	22.65%
Muskegon Racecourse	16.19%
New Brunswick Downs	8.00%
Northville Downs	7.86%

Leading Tracks, Avg. Attendance Increase	
Balmoral Park	60.04%
Assiniboia Downs	19.37%
Monticello Raceway	8.60%
Northville Downs	8.03%
Pocono Downs	7.32%

Leading Tracks, Average Mutuel Handle	
Greenwood Raceway	$1,697,759
The Meadowlands	1,682,211
Mohawk Raceway	1,406,246
Hippodrome Blue Bonnets	942,737
Hazel Park Harness	770,966

Leading Tracks, Average Daily Attendance	
The Meadowlands	10,321
Greenwood Raceway	7,136
Mohawk Raceway	6,887
Sportsman's Park	6,275
Hippodrome Blue Bonnets	4,856

BUSINESS TRENDS: U.S. EXTENDED PARI-MUTUEL TRACKS

Track	Dates '90	Dates '89	Avg. Attendance 1990	Avg. Attendance 1989	Trend	Avg. Mutuel Handle 1990	Avg. Mutuel Handle 1989	Trend
Balmoral Park	99	44	2,239	1,399	60.04%	$282,891	$230,656	22.65%
Bangor Raceway	42	45	1,131	1,322	(-14.45%)	80,492	94,103	(-14.46%)
Batavia Downs	133	143	1,525	1,523	0.13%	147,085	145,181	1.31%
Buffalo Raceway	128	127	1,767	1,810	(-2.36%)	182,150	187,181	(-2.69%)
Cal-Expo	54	44	2,817	2,657	6.02%	143,147	264,740	(-45.93%)
Delmarva Downs	72	76	2,078	2,008	3.49%	225,472	142,304	58.44%
Dover Downs	100	71	1,217	1,412	(-13.82%)	117,891	141,661	(-16.78%)
Fairmount Park	78	78	1,957	2,476	(-20.96%)	339,212	324,133	4.65%
Freehold Raceway	235	258	2,226	2,123	4.86%	351,588	345,108	1.88%
Garden State Park	76	71	3,645	4,001	(-8.89%)	326,350	369,571	(-11.69%)
Harrington Raceway	41	39	988	1,146	(-13.81%)	92,267	107,188	(-13.92%)
Hawthorne	66	50	3,451	3,593	(-3.95%)	565,176	661,683	(-14.59%)
Hazel Park	168	168	4,292	4,473	(-4.04%)	770,966	786,356	(-1.96%)
Jackson Raceway	144	157	1,926	1,839	4.72%	327,429	329,046	(-0.49%)
Lebanon Raceway	132	128	1,266	1,537	(-17.63%)	207,479	226,820	(-8.53%)
Los Alamitos	122	87	2,985	3,176	(-6.00%)	555,474	709,443	(-21.70%)
Lousiville Downs	160	164	2,199	2,362	(-6.91%)	96,948	140,166	(-30.83%)
Maywood Park	150	172	2,700	3,148	(-14.23%)	405,829	494,098	(-17.86%)
The Meadowlands	202	191	10,321	11,559	(-10.71%)	1,682,211	1,802,844	(-6.69%)
The Meadows	216	203	2,464	2,552	(-3.45%)	198,570	346,425	(-42.68%)
Monticello Raceway	230	211	1,515	1,395	8.60%	194,459	198,551	(-2.06%)
Muskegon Racecourse	88	94	2,384	2,358	1.090%	192,405	165,602	16.19%
Northfield Park	211	213	3,474	3,491	(-0.48%)	430,301	434,999	(-1.08%)
Northville Downs	85	88	2,610	2,416	8.03%	526,759	488,369	7.86%
Pocono Downs	150	150	1,886	1,757	7.32%	173,382	163,413	6.10%
Pompano Park	156	160	4,311	4,481	(-3.80%)	440,582	449,670	(-2.02%)
Prairie Meadows	44	34	1,464	1,959	(-25.29%)	50,022	133,837	(-62.62%)
Quad City Downs	131	144	1,932	1,936	(-0.19%)	136,618	144,533	(-5.48%)

TRACKS

Track	Dates '90	Dates '89	Avg. Attendance 1990	Avg. Attendance 1989	Trend	Avg. Mutuel Handle 1990	Avg. Mutuel Handle 1989	Trend
Raceway Park	152	150	2,267	2,486	(-8.80%)	$233,760	$250,021	(-6.50%)
The Red Mile	58	66	2,472	2,709	(-8.73%)	158,688	171,468	(-7.45%)
Riverside Downs	39		772			50,759		
Rosecroft Raceway	248	140	3,019	3,871	(-22.01%)	451,844	496,308	(-8.96%)
Saginaw Harness	86	86	1,578	1,628	(-3.06%)	199,209	208,457	(-4.44%)
Saratoga Raceway	179	197	1,963	1,948	0.75%	161,844	159,431	1.51%
Scarborough Downs	207	103	1,310	1,499	(-12.62%)	125,986	147,601	(-14.64%)
Scioto Downs	115	115	4,155	4,255	(-2.36%)	359,632	356,496	0.88%
Sports Creek	134	126	1,771	1,701	4.12%	249,903	243,256	2.73%
Sportsman's Park	123	95	6,275	6,588	(-4.75%)	713,570	770,611	(-7.40%)
Vernon Downs	155	159	2,171	2,166	0.21%	196,467	197,212	(-0.38%)
Yonkers Raceway	353	365	2,621	2,703	(-3.03%)	587,548	655,885	(-10.42%)

BUSINESS TRENDS: MARITIME TRACKS

Track	Dates '90	Dates '89	Avg. Attendance 1990	Avg. Attendance 1989	Trend	Avg. Mutuel Handle 1990	Avg. Mutuel Handle 1989	Trend
Avalon Raceway	42	48	324	328	(-1.22%)	$18,566	$20,072	(-7.50%)
Charlottetown	113	121	623	619	0.65%	53,838	52,473	2.60%
Exhibition Park	103	98	579	625	(-7.36%)	54,582	59,143	(-7.71%)
Fredericton	34	36	512	546	(-6.23%)	41,292	42,447	(-2.72%)
Inverness Raceway	24	24	241	273	(-11.72%)	14,225	16,709	(-14.87%)
New Brunswick Downs	69	58	704	662	6.34%	59,053	54,682	8.00%
Summerside	36	35	262	345	(-24.06%)	25,641	23,832	7.59%
Tartan Downs	104	104	339	367	(-7.63%)	38,777	38,627	0.27%
Truro Raceway	111	114	571	575	(-0.70%)	70,680	71,685	(-1.40%)

BUSINESS TRENDS: C.T.A. TRACKS

Track	Dates '90	Dates '89	Avg. Attendance 1990	Avg. Attendance 1989	Trend	Avg. Mutuel Handle 1990	Avg. Mutuel Handle 1989	Trend
Assiniboia Downs	89	87	1,331	1,115	19.37%	$205,012	$196,313	4.43%
Blue Bonnets	253	251	4,856	5,278	(-8.00%)	942,737	960,617	(-1.86%)
Cloverdale Raceway	123	127	2,554	2,562	(-0.31%)	436,771	439,295	(-0.57%)
Connaught Park	116	117	1,243	1,326	(-6.26%)	176,077	187,769	(-6.23%)
Flamboro Downs	215	213	1,772	1,817	(-2.46%)	221,479	225,943	(-1.98%)
Greenwood Raceway	145	142	7,163	7,164	(-0.01%)	1,697,759	1,677,482	1.21%
Hiawatha Horse Park	70	79	1,077	1,180	(-8.73%)	91,737	100,434	(-8.66%)
Mohawk Raceway	119	119	6,887	6,992	(-1.50%)	1,406,246	1,420,074	(-0.97%)
Northlands Park	99	99	2,726	2,915	(-6.48%)	571,787	541,507	5.59%
Rideau Carleton	105	110	1,799	1,811	(-0.66%)	180,635	182,910	(-1.24%)
Sandown	52	51	1,651	1,621	1.85%	130,786	142,748	(-8.38%)
Stampede Park	100	100	2,297	2,342	(-1.92%)	346,234	362,597	(-4.51%)
Western Fair	141	144	1,670	1,740	(-4.02%)	148,013	153,260	(-3.42%)
Windsor Raceway	167	187	2,102	2,353	(-10.67%)	294,398	314,786	(-6.48%)

TRACKS

TOTAL COMPARATIVE ON-TRACK ATTENDANCE
AT U.S. MEETS

1960 through 1990

Year	Dates	Tot. Attendance	Trend	Avg. Attendance	Trend
1990	54340	14,955,827	(-3.83%)	2,752	(-5.78%)
1989	5,324	15,550,871	(-4.70%)	2,921	(-3.66%)
1988	5,381	16,317,560	(-8.05%)	3,032	(-6.45%)
1987	5,475	17,747,029	(-3.53%)	3,241	(-1.13%)
1986	5,613	18,397,142	(-7.67%)	3,278	(-6.29%)
1985	5,696	19,925,399	(-6.17%)	3,498	(-6.24%)
1984	5,692	21,236,074	(-7.01%)	3,731	(-5.45%)
1983	5,673	22,383,270	0.30%	3,946	1.81%
1982	5,758	22,317,406	(-2.48%)	3,876	(-3.37%)
1981	5,706	22,884,716	(-6.21%)	4,011	(-5.78%)
1980	5,731	24,399,868	(-2.79%)	4,257	(-0.33%)
1979	5,877	25,100,568	(-1.30%)	4,271	(-2.64%)
1978	5,797	25,431,195	(-1.75%)	4,387	(-4.75%)
1977	5,619	25,883,920	(-6.57%)	4,606	0.35%
1976	6,036	27,703,184	(-2.69%)	4,590	(-4.36%)
1975	5,853	28,089,984	1.43%	4,799	(-4.08%)
1974	5,392	26,976,122	1.73%	5,003	(-0.79%)
1973	5,258	26,517,729	4.29%	5,043	(-4.56%)
1972	4,812	25,452,367	(-6.54%)	5,284	(-8.61%)
1971	4,705	27,203,645	4.16%	5,782	(-3.94%)
1970	4,339	26,117,742	5.76%	6,019	0.75%
1969	4,134	24,695,063	1.28%	5,974	(-0.91%)
1968	4,044	24,382,885	5.18%	6,029	(-0.45%)
1967	3,828	23,182,870	(-1.69%)	6,056	(-12.81%)
1966	3,395	23,581,760	3.02%	6,946	4.75%
1965	3,452	22,889,203	6.32%	6,631	(-5.23%)
1964	3,007	21,529,780	12.15%	6,997	2.82%
1963	2,821	19,197,066	15.19%	6,805	2.07%
1962	2,498	16,655,471	5.95%	6,667	0.73%
1961	2,375	15,719,479	4.73%	6,619	(-12.90%)
1960	1,975	15,009,569	7.09%	7,599	

TOTAL ATTENDANCE, PREVIOUS YEARS

Year	Total Attendance	Year	Total Attendance	Year	Total Attendance
1959	14,015,020	1954	10,033,203	1948	5,753,803
1958	12,769,494	1953	10,021,578	1947	3,871,485
1957	11,807,547	1952	8,539,117	1946	3,017,800
1956	10,484,133	1951	7,719,922	1945	1,383,966
1955	10,241,101	1950	6,981,578	1944	918,378
		1949	6,687,199		

(Total Attendance, 1944 through 1990 = 811,680,088)

TRACKS

TOTAL COMPARATIVE ON-TRACK MUTUEL HANDLE AT U.S. EXTENDED PARI-MUTUEL MEETS

1960 through 1990

Year	Dates	Total Handle	Trend	Avg. Handle	Trend	Per Capita
1990	5,434	$1,972,563,463	(-5.13%)	$363,004	(-7.05%)	$131.89
1989	5,324	2,079,298,976	(-6.71%)	390,552	(-5.72%)	133.71
1988	5,381	2,228,968,320	(-6.90%)	414,229	(-5.27%)	136.62
1987	5,475	2,394,194,054	(-0.66%)	437,296	1.84%	134.93
1986	5,614	2,410,141,543	(-6.54%)	429,309	(-5.18%)	130.99
1985	5,696	2,578,858,537	(-1.48%)	452,749	(-1.55%)	129.88
1984	5,692	2,617,607,038	(-4.56%)	459,875	(-4.83%)	123.26
1983	5,673	2,742,631,560	0.56%	483,198	2.11%	122.53
1982	5,758	2,724,771,869	(-2.03%)	473,215	(-3.55%)	122.09
1981	5,706	2,799,617,068	(-1.18%)	490,644	(-0.75%)	122.34
1980	5,731	2,833,126,601	0.31%	494,351	2.87%	116.11
1979	5,877	2,824,240,487	3.98%	480,558	1.92%	112.52
1978	5,797	2,733,383,632	5.23%	471,517	2.00%	107.48
1977	5,619	2,597,519,276	(-3.26%)	462,274	3.92%	100.35
1976	6,036	2,684,915,022	3.94%	444,817	0.79%	96.92
1975	5,853	2,583,032,769	6.42%	441,318	(-1.96%)	91.96
1974	5,392	2,427,200,578	5.85%	450,148	3.21%	89.98
1973	5,258	2,293,161,493	10.12%	436,128	0.78%	86.48
1972	4,812	2,082,424,699	1.32%	432,757	(-0.93%)	81.82
1971	4,705	2,055,243,824	6.19%	436,821	(-2.08%)	75.55
1970	4,339	1,935,530,530	6.35%	446,078	1.33%	74.11
1969	4,134	1,819,965,781	9.26%	440,243	6.88%	73.70
1968	4,044	1,665,788,247	9.86%	411,916	4.00%	68.32
1967	3,828	1,516,201,636	3.56%	396,082	(-8.15%)	65.40
1966	3,395	1,464,019,969	7.33%	431,228	9.14%	62.08
1965	3,452	1,363,976,147	8.21%	395,126	(-5.74%)	59.59
1964	3,007	1,260,516,636	18.12%	419,194	10.82%	58.55
1963	2,821	1,067,130,007	14.90%	378,281	1.74%	55.59
1962	2,498	928,740,959	8.30%	371,794	2.96%	55.73
1961	2,375	857,587,384	4.69%	361,089	(-12.94%)	54.56
1960	1,975	819,152,619	5.49%	414,761		54.58

TOTAL HANDLE, PREVIOUS YEARS

Year	Total Handle	Year	Total Handle	Year	Total Handle
1959	$776,487,454	1954	444,845,200	1948	194,771,307
1958	712,872,993	1953	443,637,912	1947	134,066,712
1957	614,920,402	1952	362,662,754	1946	111,569,313
1956	534,857,846	1951	303,986,301	1945	48,919,994
1955	476,728,009	1950	242,835,529	1944	26,569,202
		1949	209,377,545		

(Total Handle, 1944 through 1990 = $70,000,619,197)

TRACKS
CHARTING TRENDS: ON-TRACK ATTENDANCE AND HANDLE

The charts below demonstrate trends in attendance (top), handle (middle) and per-capita wagering (bottom) in Standardbred racing. Only on-track statistics are plotted. No off-track, or county and state fair racing statistics are used:

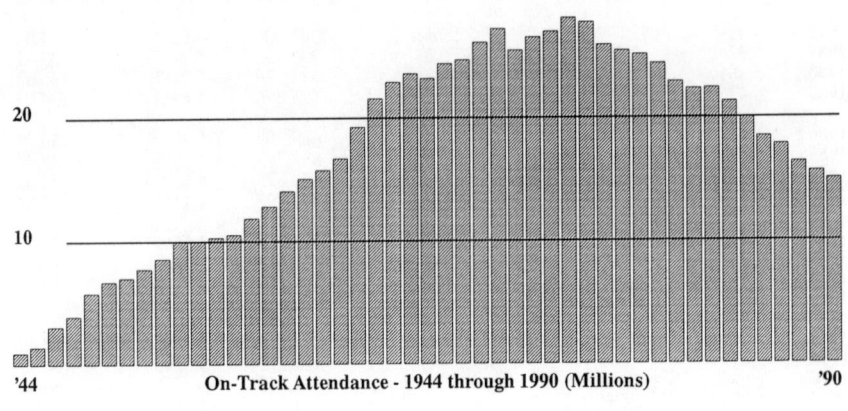

On-Track Attendance - 1944 through 1990 (Millions)

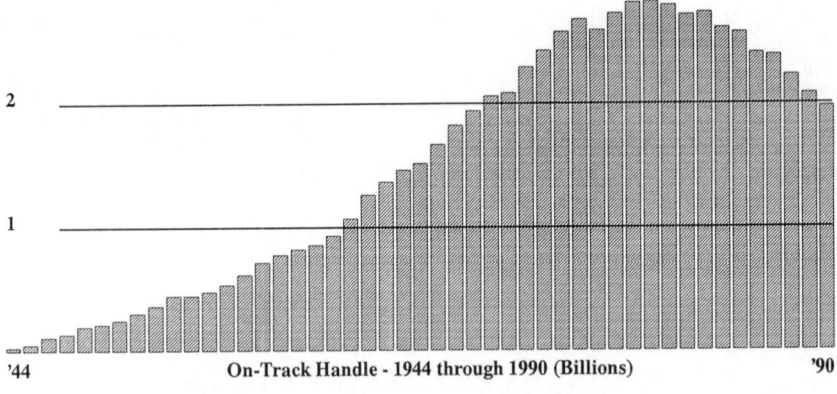

On-Track Handle - 1944 through 1990 (Billions)

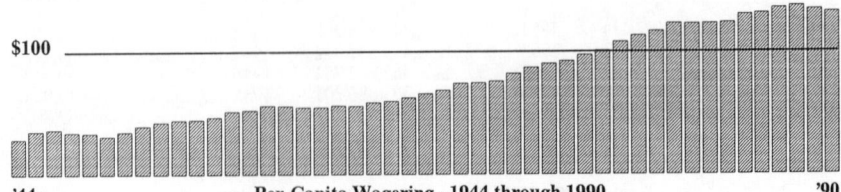

Per-Capita Wagering - 1944 through 1990

TRACKS

CHARTING TRENDS: GROWTH OF THE SPORT IN THE U.S.

The charts below demonstrate trends in horses starting in races (top), total U.S. purses paid (middle), and individual membership in the United States Trotting Association (bottom):

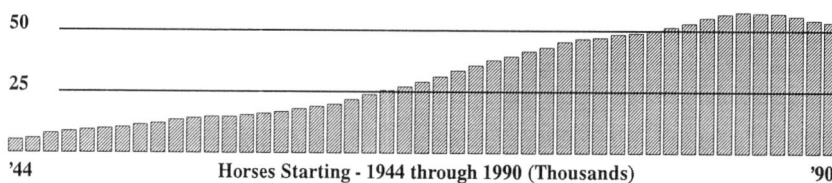

Horses Starting - 1944 through 1990 (Thousands)

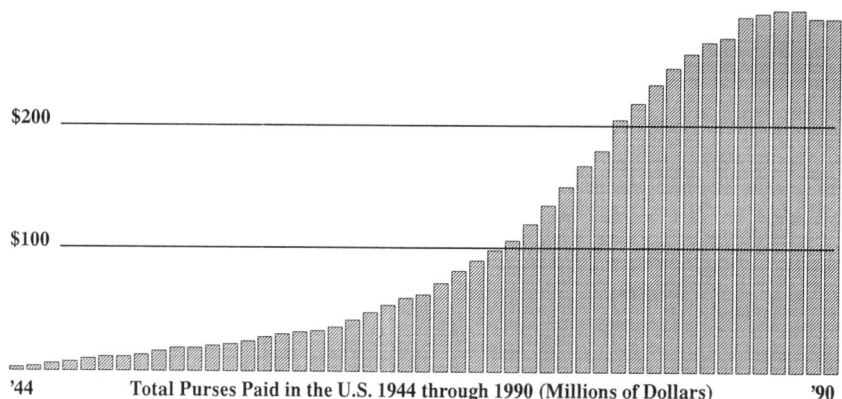

Total Purses Paid in the U.S. 1944 through 1990 (Millions of Dollars)

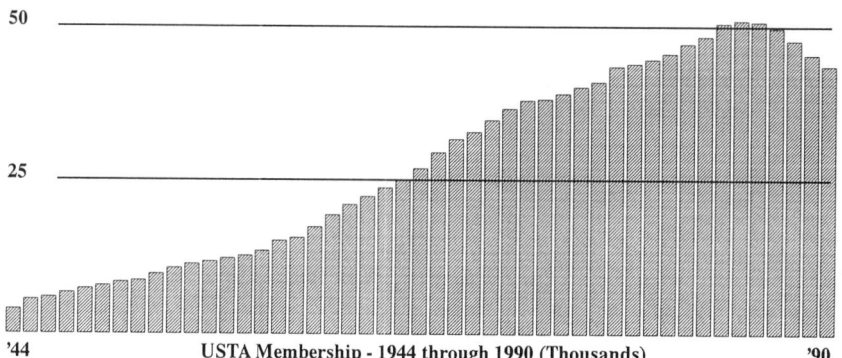

USTA Membership - 1944 through 1990 (Thousands)

TRACKS

PARI-MUTUEL TAX METHODS

Under the pari-mutuel system, wagers are pooled and a percentage of the total pool is set-aside for, generally, three-way distribution - shares going to the state, horsemen, and tracks.

The horsemen's share goes to the purse account, from which purses are paid. Other, smaller shares may also go to "sire stakes" purses (events for horses bred within that state) and the like. The state's share, as the name implies, is paid to the state.

There are, however, as many tax scales as there are states, with percentages constantly reviewed and changed by legislation. The figures presented here, gathered from the 1989 Annual Report of the Association of Racing Commissioners International, show only the gross "takeout" percentages. Percentages may also differ for each breed racing within a state - Standardbred, Thoroughbred, or Quarterhorse - but only percentages for Standardbred racing are presented here:

State	Win, Place, &Show	"Exotic" Wagers
California	16.00%	23.75%
Delaware	18.00%	20.00 - 25.00%
Florida	17.60 - 18.10%	19.00 - 24.00%
Illinois	17.00%	20.50 - 25.00%
Iowa	16.00%	16.00 - 20.00%
Kentucky	18.00%	25.00%
Maine	18.00%	26.00%
Maryland	17.00%	19.00 - 25.00%
Michigan	17.00%	20.50 - 25.00%
New Hampshire	19.00%	25.00%
New Jersey	17.00%	19.00 - 25.00%
New York	17.00 - 18.00%	19.00 - 36.00%
North Dakota	18.25%	18.25%
Ohio	18.00%	22.00%
Pennsylvania	17.00 - 19.00%	21.00 - 36.00%

MINIMUM ATTENDANCE AND WAGERING REGULATIONS

State	Minimum Age to Attend	Conditions	Minimum Age to Wager
California	None	None	18
Delaware	None	Under 18 with adult	18
Florida	None	Under 18 with adult	18
Illinois	None	None	17
Iowa	None	None	18
Kentucky	None	None	18
Maine	None	None	18
Maryland	None	None	18
Michigan	None	Under 12 with adult	18
New Hampshire	None	Under 18 with adult	18
New Jersey	None	None	18
New York	None	Under 18 with adult	21
North Dakota	None	None	18
Ohio	None	None	18
Pennsylvania	None	Under 18 with adult	18

TRACKS

NATIONAL SUMMARY

Year	Total Handle *	State's Share	Attendance *
1990	$1,972,563,463	N/A **	14,955,827
1989	2,079,298,976	$99,213,921	15,550,871
1988	2,228,968,320	87,466,996	16,317,560
1987	2,394,194,054	82,993,095	17,747,029
1986	2,410,141,543	108,321,643	18,397,142
1985	2,578,858,537	93,910,478	19,925,399
1984	2,617,607,038	96,525,251	21,236,074
1983	2,742,631,560	118,709,108	22,383,270
1982	2,724,771,869	118,850,832	22,317,406
1981	2,799,617,068	111,574,842	22,884,716
1980	2,833,126,601	146,861,483	24,399,868
1979	2,824,240,487	148,488,962	25,100,568
1978	2,733,383,632	150,321,429	25,431,195
1977	2,597,519,276	141,620,783	25,883,920
1976	2,684,915,022	176,634,138	27,703,184
1975	2,583,032,769	185,447,595	28,089,984

Year	Horses Starting	N.A. Races Total	U.S. Races Only	N. America Total Purses	U.S. Only Total Purses
1990	53,254	108,120	76,304	$407,172,871	$287,642,307
1989	54,065	108,865	76,228	407,806,255	287,928,217
1988	55,819	110,672	77,247	405,486,921	294,400,399
1987	56,938	110,158	78,485	394,870,181	294,376,467
1986	57,021	112,171	80,500	387,474,745	291,904,107
1985	57,422	112,697	81,475	377,575,134	289,261,893
1984	56,518	110,467	78,648	360,160,671	272,268,666
1983	55,134	110,509	79,575	356,968,689	268,229,336
1982	52,735	106,792	76,883	337,568,691	258,761,424
1981	51,046	N/C ***	N/C	N/C	247,068,152
1980	49,723	"	"	"	233,421,503
1979	48,711	"	"	"	217,848,161
1978	48,177	"	"	"	204,446,636
1977	46,888	"	"	"	179,095,788
1976	46,373	"	"	"	166,774,640
1975	45,048	N/C	N/C	N/C	149,563,698

Year	N. American Starters	Earnings Per Starter in N. America	USTA Members	USTA Tracks	Horses Registered
1990	53,254	$7,645.87	43,455	371	16,576
1989	54,065	7,542.89	45,244	411	16,896
1988	55,819	7,264.32	47,564	426	17,393
1987	56,938	6,935.09	49,650	438	17,579
1986	57,021	6,795.30	50,671	464	17,637
1985	57,422	6,575.44	50,932	504	18,384
1984	56,518	6,372.49	50,459	475	19,795
1983	55,134	6,474.57	48,250	483	20,298
1982	52,735	6,401.23	47,013	473	20,068
1981	51,046	N/C	45,408	467	17,438
1980	49,723	"	44,478	500	14,691
1979	48,711	"	43,747	486	15,865
1978	48,177	"	43,362	486	13,991
1977	46,888	"	40,861	491	13,929
1976	46,373	"	39,981	486	13,184
1975	45,048	N/C	38,905	482	14,592

* On track, at U.S. extended pari-mutuel raceways, includes inter-track and phone bets
** - N/A = Not Available   *** - N/C = Not Calculated

Organizations

ORGANIZATIONS

HARNESS TRACKS OF AMERICA

35 Airport Road, Morristown, New Jersey 07960   (201) 285-9090 - Fax: (201) 285-0867

    Harness Tracks of America, or HTA, is the trade association of 38 major pari-mutuel harness meets in the United States and Canada. Organized in 1954, it is dedicated to the advancement and progress of the sport.

    Association activities include economic and management studies and surveys; position papers; promotions, including the HTA art competition and auction; sponsorship of scholarships; sponsorship of research; production of promotional and advertising materials for its member tracks; preparation of materials for legislative research; periodic meetings and seminars; and issuance of two widely-circulated weekly newsletters, *Track Topics* and *Promotions at HTA Tracks*.

Officers

John A. Cashman, Jr.	President	Stanley Bergstein	Exec. Vice President
Robert E. Mulcahy III	Chmn. of the Board	Charles D. Hill	Vice Chairman
J.H. Kenney	Senior Vice President	Lloyd Arnold	Vice President
Curt Greene	Secretary	William E. "Hap" Hansen	Vice President
Lester McKeever	Treasurer	Harvey S. Fosner	Counsel Emeritus

Executive Committee

Robert E. Mulcahy III	Timothy J. Rooney	Warren DeSantis
Lou Carlo	Lester H. McKeever, Jr.	John A. Cashman, Jr.
James "Chic" Young	Barbara Samberg	David Goodwill
Thomas Aldrich		Harold S. Duris

Staff

Chris McErlean	Executive Assistant	Diane Gauch	Secretary
Ray Gomez	Administrative Assistant		

Member Race Meets

Associates Racing Assn.	Jackson Raceway	Pocono Downs
Atlantic City	Lebanon Raceway	Pompano Harness Track
Batavia Downs	Los Alamitos Racing Assn.	Quad City Downs
Blue Bonnets	Louisville Downs	Raceway Park
Buffalo Raceway	The Meadowlands	The Red Mile
Dover Downs	Ladbroke at the Meadows	Rosecroft Raceway
Edmonton Northlands	Miami Valley Trotting	Saginaw Valley Downs
Fairmount Park	Mid-America Racing Assn.	Saratoga Harness
Freehold Raceway	Mohawk Raceway	Scioto Downs
Freestate Raceway	Muskegon Racecourse	Suburban Downs
Garden State Park	Northfield Park Harness	Vernon Downs
Greenwood Raceway	Northville Downs	Windsor Raceway
Harrington Raceway		Yonkers Raceway

* * * * *

ORGANIZATIONS

HARNESS RACING COMMUNICATIONS

c/o Pompano Pk., 1800 SW 3rd St., Pompano Beach, FL 33069 (305) 972-2000-Fax: (305) 972-7894
New York Office: 3 Barker Ave., White Plains, NY 10601 (914) 428-4227 - Fax: (914) 428-5427

The goal of Harness Racing Communications is to increase public awareness and improve the public image of harness racing, thereby increasing public participation.

Officers

Harold Duris	President	Dominic Frinzi	Secretary
John Cisna	First Vice President	Paul Spears	Treasurer
Dr. J. Glen Brown	Second Vice President		

Board of Directors

Francis X. Ready	Member	Robert Mulcahy	Member
Corwin M. Nixon	Member	John Cashman, Jr.	Member
Hugh A. Grant, Jr.	Member	Anthony Abbatiello	Member
Stanley Bergstein	Member		

New York Office:
Tim O'Leary, Executive Director - John Lipporace, Assistant

THE AMERICAN HORSE COUNCIL

1700 K Street, N.W., Suite 300, Washington, D.C. 20006   (202) 296-4031

The American Horse Council was founded in 1969 as a Washington, D.C.-based trade association for the U.S. horse industry. Its primary purpose was, and remains, the monitoring of all federal legislation that would have an effect on the conduct of the horse business in this country. AHC's initial goals centered on tax legislation, but in recent years its range of activities and services has broadened to include representation of the racing industry at-large, work on health and regulatory issues, land usage matters and other areas affecting horses and the participants in the industry. AHC has compiled statistics and analyses related to all aspects of the American horse business. It has an extensive publications section, which includes regularly updated, comprehensive tax information and an encyclopedic directory of organizations, government agencies and trade journals involved with horses. The Council also conducts conferences and workshops on racing, showing, taxation and state horse council activities. The American Horse Council currently has approximately 180 member organizations and over 2,500 individual members.

Key Personnel

Ogden Mills Phipps	R. Richards Rolapp
Chairman of the Board	President

American Horse Racing Federation

1700 K Street, N.W., Suite 300, Washington, D.C. 20006   (202) 296-4031

The American Horse Racing Federation is a division of the American Horse Council, founded in 1990 to advance horse racing in the United States through industry-wide discussion, decision making and planning. Its objective include, among others: the development of programs of national scope and impact; the promulgation of industry standards with a view to supporting and enhancing the regulatory process; and providing legislative and regulatory support on a state and local level.

Key Personnel

John A. Cashman, Jr.	James P. Heffernan
President	Executive Director

ORGANIZATIONS

THE CANADIAN TROTTING ASSOCIATION

2150 Meadowvale Blvd., Mississaauga, Ontario L5N 6R6   (416) 858-3060 - Fax: (416) 858-3111

The Canadian Trotting Association is a non-profit organization incorporated under the Canadian Companies Act to supervise and promote the racing of trotting and pacing horses and to encourage the breeding of the Standardbred horse.

A need for uniform regulations and central record keeping led to the merger in 1939 of two organizations called the Dominion Trotting Association and the Canadian Trotting and Pacing Association. The result of that merger was the birth of the Canadian Trotting Association.

Early in 1982, the CTA reached an important milestone with the introduction of an on-line computer system with race tracks. In the latest step towards developing greater efficiency for members, electronic eligibility was put into place.

CTA Key Personnel

Executive Committee

David G. Campbell - President

Verne Rea	First Vice President	John Burns	Committee Member
Clare Hauck	2nd V.P./Treasurer	Sten Deneka	Committee Member
Jane Hutchins	Secretary	Marcel Jobin	Committee Member

Administration

Tom Gorman - Executive V.P. & G.M.

Pat Kennedy	Manager of Member Services	Janet Cookson	Data Processing Manager
Barb Brown	Manager of Field Operations	Roseanna So	Asst. Treasurer/Mgr. Finance

Trot Magazine

Harold Howe - Editor

Heather Mackay-Roberts	Associate Editor	Carol Susnik	Executive Assistant
Susan Simmons	Production Coordinator	Tracey Lang	Advertising Assistant
Lise Whitworth	French Editor	Elynne Lewis	Librarian

THE CANADIAN STANDARDBRED HORSE SOCIETY

2150 Meadowvale Blvd., Mississaauga, Ontario L5N 6R6   (416) 858-3060 - Fax: (416) 858-8047

Founded in 1909, the Society established a Canadian registry of Standardbred horses. Incorporated under The Animal Pedigree Act of Canada, the CSHS is responsible to the Federal Agriculture Ministry.

In addition to maintaining the official breed registry, establishing its regulations, governing the registration of horses, and identification of horses in Canada, the CSHS conducts three major horse sales each year and conducts events to encourage both ownership and the breeding of horses. By contract, routine registration and ownership transfer applications are processed by the CTA on behalf of the Society.

Officers

Ted Smith - General Manager/Registrar

Dr. Maurice Stewart	President	Heather Reid	Secretary/Treasurer
Dr. John Thomson	Vice President	Dow Clowater	Assistant Registrar

ORGANIZATIONS

THE BREEDERS CROWN

1 Pear Tree Plaza, 289 Route 33 East, Manalapan, NJ 07726   (908) 446-5151 - Fax: (908) 446-5153

The Certified Vacations Breeders Crown sponsors championship events in each of twelve age, sex, and gait divisions. Over its first six seasons, the Crown has become the unofficial championship series of Harness Racing, with each event having major implications in Horse of the Year balloting. Members of the media who wish to know more may contact the Breeders Crown office to obtain a copy of their comprehensive media guide.

The Breeders Crown is owned and serviced by the Hambletonian Society.

Staff

Tom Charters	Executive Director	Moira Sullivan	Publicist

THE HAMBLETONIAN SOCIETY

P.O. Box 554, Lexington, Kentucky 40586   (606) 255-3689 - Fax: (606) 231-9311

The Hambletonian Society not only administers the stake from which its name is taken, but also rules over many of the most important stakes raced in North America.

Officers

Hugh A. Grant, Jr.	President & CEO	Elbridge T. Gerry, Sr.	Treasurer
Elbridge T. Gerry, Jr.	1st V.P./Asst. Treas.	Norman S. Woolworth	Secretary
Philip J. Baugh	Second Vice President	Gladys Bell	Assistant Secretary

THE GRAND CIRCUIT

P.O. Box 356, Meadow Lands, Pennsylvania 15347   (412) 222-8620

The idea of a racing circuit for Standardbreds originated in 1871 when William Edwards, Lewis J. Powers, and E.A. Buck met in Cleveland, Ohio. They were representatives from three racetracks in different states. The circuit was launched in 1873, when four tracks offered $169,300 in purses.

The Grand Circuit blossomed into a yearly showcase of the finest 2- and 3-year-old harness horses competing in North America, with purses now totaling many millions of dollars at racetracks and fairs in many areas of the continent.

Officers

Delvin Miller	President	Frank O. White	Vice President
Henry C. Thomson	Chairman of the Board	Carol B. Cramer	Steward-at-Large
Tom Thomson	Executive Vice President	Cathy Goetz	Secretary
Joseph A. DeFrank	Senior Vice President	Gladys Bell	Treasurer
Mrs. David R. Johnston	Vice President	Charles Bowen	Assistant to the President.
John A. Cashman, Jr.	Vice President		

Grand Circuit Publicity

Paul Ramlow
c/o The United States Trotting Association
750 Michigan Avenue - Columbus, Ohio 43215
Phone: (614) 224-2291 - Fax: (614) 228-1385

ORGANIZATIONS

THE TROTTING HORSE MUSEUM

240 Main St., P.O. Box 590, Goshen, New York 10924 (914) 294-6330 -Fax: (914) 294-3463

See back cover and inside cover for information concerning the Trotting Horse Museum - home of the Hall of Fame of the Trotter.

Officers of the Museum

Elbridge T. Gerry, Sr.	President
Max C. Hempt	Vice President
Norman S. Woolworth	Vice President
Elbridge T. Gerry, Jr.	Treasurer
Delvin Miller	Secretary

Key Personnel

Philip A. Pines	Director
Gail C. Cunard	Administrator
Walter Latzko	Registrar
Gail C. Cunard	Secretary/Treasurer

THE DELVIN MILLER AMATEUR DRIVERS ASSOCIATION

P.O. Box 339, Route 194 South, Hanover, Pennsylvania 17331 (717) 637-8931 - Fax: (717) 637-6766

Formed in 1985, the Delvin Miller Amateur Drivers Association (DMADA) consists of amateur drivers (i.e., drivers who have not received valuable compensation for their driving services in the last ten years). Eventually, the group would like to unite amateur drivers from around the world in an Olympic-style world championship. The organization is named after Hall of Famer Delvin Miller, a longtime advocate of amateur driving competition.

Officers

Paul Spears	President	Delvin Miller	Chairman of the Board
Max Hempt	Vice President	Bowman A. Brown, Jr.	Director
Shirley Kuhn	Secretary/Treasurer	Peter Gerry	Director
Phil Pines	Publicity		

THE NORTH AMERICAN AMATEUR DRIVERS ASSOCIATION

125-10 Queens Blvd., Kew Gardens, New York 11415 (718) 544-6800 - Fax: (718) 544-0033

Founded in 1986, the North American Amateur Driver's Association was formed to advance competition between the several amateur driving clubs in the United States and Canada. NAADA is also a charter member of the World Amateur Drivers Federation, formed in July of 1986, which sponsors The World Cup Driving Series.

Sponsored in conjunction with FEGAT (Federation Europeenne des Gentlemen Amateurs et Cavalieres du Trot), World Cup competition has been held every fourth year for the last twenty years. It will next be held in 1992 in France, home of the reigning World Amateur Champion, Daniel Foucault.

The group also coordinates the formation of local amateur clubs and encourages their parti-cipation in international amateur events. U.S. Amateurs have also received challenges from Swedish man and Ductch amateurs for 1991.

Directors

Joseph Faraldo	Kew Gardens, NY	Frank Lavigna	East Hampton, NY
Lon Frocione	Syracuse, NY	David Scharf	New York, NY
Ugo Chiola	Hanover, PA	Bob Pare	Trois Rivieres, Canada

ORGANIZATIONS

THE UNITED STATES HARNESS WRITERS ASSOCIATION

P.O. Box 10, Batavia, New York 14020   (716) 343-5900 - Fax: (716) 344-1187

Founded in 1947, the United States Harness Writers' Association is the organization of newspaper, magazine, radio, and television reporters of harness racing news as well as many involved in publicizing and promoting the sport.

USHWA also works with the U.S. Trotting Association Publicity Department in selecting the "Harness Horse of the Year," and in conducting the "Hervey" and "Broadcasters" awards programs.

Officers

John Manzi	President	William F. Brown	Secretary
Marv Bachrad	Vice President	Alan Prince	Treasurer
Leon Zimmerman	Vice President	Allen Finkelson	Chairman of the Board

THE NORTH AMERICAN HARNESS PUBLICISTS ASSOCIATION

c/o Kawartha Downs, Fraserville, Ont., K0L 1V0   (705) 939-6316 - Fax: (705) 939-6342

Founded in 1966, the Harness Publicists' Association has approximately 60 members in the United States and Canada. The group is comprised of harness track publicists, public relations directors, advertising directors, and track management members as well as public relations practitioners from related industry groups.

Officers

Grant Wade	President	Tom White	Treasurer
Jim Moran	Vice President	Roger Huston	Chairman
Joe Hartmann	Secretary		

Directors

Tim O'Leary	Harness Racing Comm.	Jerry Connors	Northfield Park
Steve Wolf	Freehold Raceway	Leon Zimmerman	SBOA New Jersey
Dave Garland	Michigan HHA	Moira Fanning	Breeders Crown
Ellen Harvey	The Meadowlands	Rene Tessier	Blue Bonnets

The HPA meets annually to exchange ideas in the fields of promotion, publicity, and advertising as they relate to the harness racing sport. Also, the HPA annually awards the "Golden Pen" to a member of the association who has made a significant contribution to publicity and public relations skills in the sport of harness racing:

Golden Pen Award Winners

1991	Chuck Burr	1984	Lew Barasch	1979	Chuck Stokes
1990	Jim Moran	1983	Allen Finkelson	1978	Jim Harrison
1989	John Manzi	1982	Jim Lampman	1977	Earl Flora
1988	Marv Bachrad	1981	Dave Herman	1976	Don Evans
1987	Raymond Benoit	1980	Bob Cox	1975	Larry Evans
1986	Bruce Stearns			1974	Phil Pines
1985	Tom White			1973	Stan Bergstein

ORGANIZATIONS
HARNESS HORSEMEN INTERNATIONAL

525 Highway 33, Suite 3, Englishtown, NJ 07726　　　(908) 446-3346 - Fax: (908) 446-3541

    HHI, formed in 1964, was created for the primary purpose of promoting harness racing in the U.S. and Canada. The organization provides and encourages ideas and suggestions aimed at improving the sport. One of its major achievements has been the creation of the International Harness Racing Group Insurance Fund instituted to provide major medical and life insurance protection to members and backstretch employees.

    HHI functions as a clearinghouse of information for its member groups by disseminating federal- and state-level news through a quarterly newsletter. HHI provides several group insurance policies such as a national fire disaster policy, a third-party public liability policy and a term life policy.

Officers

Dominic H. Frinzi, Esq.	President	Joseph A. Faraldo, Esq.	Secretary
Donald P. Booth	First Vice President	Verne Rea	Treasurer
Brooks Wells	Second Vice President	Mike Izzo	Executive Director

Alberta Standardbred Horse Association, Box 1060, Calgary, Alberta, Canada T2P 2K8
    Danny Garinger, Secretary Manager　　　　　　　　　　　　　　(403) 263-8903

British Columbia Standardbred Association, Box 1224, Station A, Surrey, B.C., V3S 2B3
    Marlene Skiba, Secretary/Treasurer　　　　　　　　　　　　　　(604) 574-3633

California Harness Horsemen's Assn., 11132 Winner's Cir. Dr., Suite 208, Los Alamitos, CA 90720
    Alan Horowitz, Executive Secretary　　　　　　　　　　　　　　(213) 493-3729

Cloverleaf SOA, 830 Walker Square, Dover, DE 19901
    Charles B. Lockhart, Executive Vice President　　(302) 678-3058 - Fax: (302) 678-8507

Florida SBOA, 1800 S. W. 3rd St., Pompano Bch., FL 33069
    Jay Sears, President　　　　　　　　　　　　　(305) 972-5400 - Fax: (305) 978-9070

HHA of Central New York, P.O. Box 586, Vernon, NY 13476
    Lon V. Frocione, President　　　　　　　　　　(315) 829-3872 - Fax: (315) 829-4350

Illinois HHA, 15 Spinning Wheel Rd., Suite 406, Hinsdale, IL 60521
    Mickey J. Ezzo, Executive Director　　　　　　(708) 323-0808 - Fax: (708) 323-0761

Kentucky HHA, 1330 Durrett Ln., Louisville, KY 40213
    Norman Smith, Executive Secretary　　　　　　(502) 361-2339 - Fax: (502) 361-5882

Maine HHA, Box 3093, Lewiston, ME 04240
    Kenneth Ronco, Executive Secretary　　　　　　　　　　　　　　(207) 783-2535

Manitoba Harness Horsemen, Inc., Box 102, Postal Station A, Winnipeg, Manitoba R3K 1Z9
    Dr. William Welsh, Secretary/Treasurer　　　　　　　　　　　　(204) 339-4688

Meadows Standardbred Owners Assn., PO Box 253, Meadow Lands, PA 15347
    Sharon Braden, Secretary　　　　　　　　　　　　　　　　　　(412) 228-3644

Michigan HHA, 4650 Moore St., Box 349, Okemos, MI 48864
    Larry Mallar, General Manager　　　　　　　　(517) 349-2920 - Fax: (517) 349-4983

Minnesota Harness Racing, Inc., 3405 Sugarbush Trail North, Brainerd, MN 56401
    John Backlund, Executive Secretary　　　　　　　　　　　　　(218) 829-7515

Monticello HHA, Monticello Raceway, Monticello, NY 12701
    Rocco Yanoti, Executive Secretary　　　　　　　　　　　　　(914) 791-7748

ORGANIZATIONS

Northeastern HHA, P.O. Box 77, Saratoga Springs, NY 12866
    Ingvar Berg, Executive Secretary   (518) 584-2110 - Fax: (518) 583-1240

Ohio HHA, 471 E. Broad St., Suite 1310, Columbus, OH 43215
    James Powers, General Manager   (614) 221-3650 - Fax: (614) 221-8726

Ontario HHA, 35 Crawford Crescent, Box 430, Campbellville, Ontario L0P 1B0
    J.G. (Joe) Burke, Exec. Vice President   (416) 854-2221 - Fax: (416) 854-2691

Pennsylvania HHA, 1300 Plaza West, Suite 303, Lemoyne, PA 17043
    Ron Battoni, Executive Director   (717) 975-0774

Quebec Trotting and Pacing Association, 5375 Rue Pare, Suite 230, Montreal, Quebec H4P 1P7
    Gilles Fortier, Coordinator   (514) 731-9484 - Fax: (514) 731-7687

Saskatchewan Standardbred Horsemens Assn., Inc., Box 4122, Regina, Saskatchewan S4P 3W5
    Chris Belan, President   (306) 757-4755 - Fax: (306) 525-6049

SBOA of New Jersey, P. O. Box 839, Freehold, NJ 07728
    Pat A. Salerno, Administrative Secretary   (908) 462-2357 - Fax: (908) 409-0741

SOA of New England, Box 175, South Walpole, MA 02071
    Andy Lyon, Jr., President   (508) 695-4343

SOA of New York, 750 McLean Ave., Yonkers, New York 10704
    Joseph A. Faraldo, President   (914) 237-2345 - Fax: (914) 237-7393

Washington State Standardbred Association, Box 172, Olympia, Washington 98507
    Claudia Westbrook, Secretary   (206) 786-8121

Western New England HHA, P. O. Box 33, Hinsdale, New Hampshire 03451
    William Faucher, President   (603) 336-5664

Western New York HHA, Box 730, Batavia, NY 14020
    Hugh Bentley, Executive Secretary   (716) 343-5008

Wisconsin Horse Foundation 1216 W. Wisconsin Avenue, PO Box 265, Appleton, WI 54912
    James R. Laird, President   (414) 731-4157

STANDARDBRED BREEDERS AND OWNERS ASSOCIATIONS

American Standardbred Breeders Association, P.O. Box 339, Hanover, Pennsylvania 17331
    John Simpson, Jr., President   (717) 637-8931

Alabama Harness Horsemen's Association, P.O. Box 607, Ardmore, Alabama 35739
    Sam Glossup, President   (205) 423-2666

Atlantic Standardbred Breeders Association, R.R. #5, Tatamagouche, Nova Scotia B0K 1V0
    Jack Ferguson, Manager   (902) 657-3068

California Harness Horse Breeders Association, 11132 Winners Circle Dr., Suite 208, Los Alamitos, CA 90720 - Harris Levin, President   (213) 598-1159 - (714) 826-3322

Illinois Standardbred Owners and Breeders Association, P. O. Box 576, State Fairgrounds, Springfield, IL 62705 - Jay Sundeen, Executive Director   (217) 522-8781

Indiana Trotting & Pacing Horse Association, RR 1, Box 22D, Pittsboro, Indiana 46167
    James A. Garrett, Secretary/Treasurer   (317) 892-3471

Maritime Breeders Association, P.O. Box 1855, Truro, Nova Scotia B2N 6C7
    Ken Starratt, Secretary/Treasurer   (902) 893-2866 - (902) 893-5871

Maryland Standardbred Breeders Association, 5500-A Jefferson Pike, Frederick, Maryland 21701
    Robert Uebel, Sr., President   (301) 473-5053

Michigan Standardbred Breeders, 2764 W. Gier Rd., Adrian, Michigan 49221
    Patti Gira, Secretary/Treasurer   (517) 436-3179

Harness Horse Breeders of New York State, Inc., 90 State Street, Albany, NY 12207
    James Crawford, President   (518) 434-1264

ORGANIZATIONS

Ohio Standardbred Breeders and Owners Association, 6797 N. High St., Suite 321,
Worthington, OH 43085-2533 - John C. Mossbarger, DVM, President (614) 885-8040
Standardbred Breeders of Kentucky, P.O. Box 13280, Lexington, Kentucky 40583
Marth Brown, President (606) 254-4358
Tennessee Harness Horsemen's Association, Route 5, Lewisburg, Tennessee 37091
John E. Brown, President (615) 359-3814
Wisconsin Harness Horse Association, 2074 18th St., Rice Lake, Wisconsin 54868
James R. Laird, President; Kathleen Larson, Secretary (715) 234-7460

THE HARNESS HORSE YOUTH FOUNDATION

14950 Greyhound Ct., Suite 210, Carmel, Indiana 46032   (317) 848-5132 - Fax: (317) 848-5136

The Harness Horse Youth Foundation is a national non-profit organization dedicated to interest and educate young people about harness racing. HHYF hosts camps at racetracks and training centers attracting 400-500 12- to 19-year-olds annually, and awards scholarships totalling $13,000 to students in horse-related programs. These scholarships are funded through special grants that have been contributed to the HHYF in memory of distinguished horsepeople.

HHYF publications include the popular and highly-acclaimed *Equine School and College Directory*, and the mini "Care & Training" manual, *Studying the Standardbred*, which serves as a guide for 4-H projects. The quarterly newsletter, *Futurity*, reports HHYF's far-reaching influence.

In celebration of its 15 years of service to the sport, HHYF has sponsored a series of "Harness Hero Cards" (harness racing's answer to baseball cards), featuring past and present great horses, people, and events.

The operating budget of HHYF comes almost entirely from the proceeds of an annual stallion auction conducted by mail. Owners of stallions contribute one or more breedings. The list of stallions is then advertised and broodmare owners send in their bids. The breeding is awarded to the highest bidder, and, upon production of a live foal, the bid amount is paid to HHYF.

HHYF makes and annual Service to Youth Award to the person who, in the opinion of the Board of Trustees, has over a period of years made a continuing contribution to helping young people get started and pursue careers in any phase of harness racing.

Service to Youth Award

1990	Albert C. Adams	1986	James M. Lynch	1982	Larry Evans
1989	Norman Woolworth	1985	Allen J. Finkelson	1981	Dr. Robert Mairs
1988	Marv Bachrad	1984	Duane Thomas	1980	Delvin Miller
1987	Philip A. Pines	1983	Robert Huff	1979	Stan Bergstein

Officers and Key Personnel

Margot L. Taylor	President	Barbara Galbraith	Secretary
David M. Dolezal	Vice President	Charlotte Maurer	Special Projects
Steven Wolf	Treasurer	Ellen Taylor	Executive Director

Trustees

Joel S. Black	William H. Maddison	George Segal
William S. Brown	Taylor Palmer, Jr.	T.D. Van Camp
John Campbell	Philip A. Pines	Douglas B. Weldon
Nelson E. Wert, DVM		Thurman Downing

ORGANIZATIONS

ASSOCIATION OF RACING COMMISSIONERS, INTERNATIONAL

4067 Iron Works Pk., Lexington, KY 40511-8434   (606) 254-4060 - Fax: (606) 233-4634

Comprised of representatives of all state racing commissions, ARCI serves the industry as a clearinghouse for information and a forum for cooperation between the pari-mutuel jurisdictions.

RCI annually publishes a complete statistical report on the North American pari-mutuel industry - the only one of its kind. it also maintains a computerized record of racing fins and suspensions of all licensees. It sponsors a Drug Testing and Quality Assurance Program involving industry laboratories, the Steward Accreditation Program at the University of Louisville, the Multi-State Licensing Program, and the Thoroughbred Ownership Registry. It is currently working on standardizing the rules of racing.

Officers

Wayne Shumate, Kentucky Harness Racing Commission	President
Joe M. Smreker, Arkansas State Racing Commission	President-Elect
L Erich Braun, Florida Pari-Mutuel Commission	First Vice President
Joseph P. Neglia, New York State Racing & Wagering Board	Second Vice President
Leslie M. Liscom, California Harness Racing Board	Treasurer
Tony Chamblin	Executive Vice President

NORTH AMERICAN JUDGES AND STEWARDS ASSOCIATION

27 Waters Lane, Englishtown, New Jersey 07726   (908) 446-5843 - Fax: (908) 431-4242

Founded in 1987, NAJSA is an organization designed to keep open the lines of communications between racing officials in the many racing jurisdictions. It provides a forum upon which racing officials may discuss topics pertinent to their daily functions.

NAJSA annually sponsors an educational seminar for racing officials. An apprentice program program for judges and stewards, in cooperation with other industry organizations, is conducted each year. A newsletter, *It's Official*, is published throughout the year to keep racing officials informed on regulatory matters.

Officers

Kent Hastings	President	Dennis L. Nolan	Treasurer
Hugh J. Gallagher	Vice President	Jewel N. Klein	Co-Counsel
Arthur A. Gray	Secretary	Salvatore DiMario	Co-Counsel

OTHER HARNESS RACING ORGANIZATIONS

Federation of Ontario Racetracks Marketing, Inc., 6535 Millcreek Dr., Unit #60, Mississauga, Ont. L5N 2M2 - Tom Gorman, President   (416) 826-2520 - Fax: (416) 826-4726

Racetracks of Canada, Inc., 6535 Millcreek Drive, Unit #60, Mississauga, Ont. L5N 2M2
Jane Hutchins, President   (416) 826-2520 - Fax: (416) 826-4726

Canadian Standardbred Amateur Drivers Assn., 1610 Wilfrid Pelletier, Laval, Quebec H7S 1K4
Robert Pare, President   (514) 629-1414

Christian Harness Horsemen's Association, 1846 Ross Rd., Sunbury, OH 43074
Weldon Stockwell, Field Representative   (614) 965-1356

ORGANIZATIONS
STATE AND PROVINCIAL RACING COMMISSIONS

Alberta Racing Commission
#507 Sloane Square; 5920 1A Street, S.W.
P.O. Box 5684, Station "A"
Calgary, Alberta, Canada T2H 1Y2
Phone: (403) 297-6551
Fax: (403) 255-4078
Roy A. Farran, Chairman
Donald J. Buchanan, Vice-Chairman
Donald Stewart, Supervisor of Racing

British Columbia Racing Commission
4595 Canada Way, Suite 200
Burnaby, B.C., Canada V5G 4L9
Phone: (604) 660-7400
Fax: (604) 660-7414
Robert W. Bonner, Q.C., Chairman
Robert E. Collis, Executive Director

California Horse Racing Board
1010 Hurley Way, Room 190
Sacramento, California 95825
Phone: (916) 920-7178
Fax: (916) 920-7658
Henry Chavez, Chairman
Dennis Hutcheson, Exec. Secretary

State of Connecticut
Division of Special Revenue (CT)
555 Russell Road
P.O. Box 11424
Newington, Connecticut 06109
Phone: (203) 566-2756
Fax: (203) 665-1198
William Hickey, Executive Director

Delaware Harness Racing Commission
2320 S. Dupont Highway
Dover, Delaware 19901
Phone: (302) 739-4811
Fax: (302) 697-6287
Anthony Flynn, Chairman

Florida Division of Pari-Mutuel Wagering
8405 NW 53rd St., Suite 250
Miami, Florida 33166
Phone: (305) 470-5675
Fax: (305) 470-5683
Janet E. Ferris, Secretary
Department of Business Regulation
W.N.V. Jones, Director,
Division of Pari-Mutuel Wagering
Joseph Priede-Rodriguez, Chairman

Illinois Racing Board
100 W. Randolph
Chicago, Illinois 60601
Phone: (708) 814-2600
Fax: (708) 814-5062
Gary L. Starkman, Chairman
Joseph Sinopoli, Executive Director

Iowa Racing and Gaming Commission
Lucas State Office Building - 2nd Floor
Des Moines, IA 50319
Phone: (515) 281-7352
L.C. "Bud" Pike, Chairman
Mick Lura, Administrator

Kentucky Harness Racing Commission
4063 Iron Works Pike
Building B
Lexington, Kentucky 40511
Phone: (606) 255-2448
Fax: (606) 252-3538
Wayne Shumate, Chairman
Carl B. Larsen, Executive Director

Maine State Harness Racing Commission
State House Station #28
Augusta, Maine 04333-0028
Phone: (207) 289-3221
Fax: (207) 289-7548
Philip M. Tarr, Executive Director

Manitoba Horse Racing Commission
P.O. Box 40, Postal Station A
Winnipeg, Manitoba, Canada R3K 1Z9
Phone: (204) 885-7770
Fax: (204) 831-0942
Dan Williams, Q.C.
Chairman and Acting Supervisor

Maryland Racing Commission
Dep. of Licensing & Regulations
501 St. Paul Place - 6th Floor
Baltimore, Maryland 21202-2272
Phone: (301) 333-6267
Fax: (301) 333-1229
Dr. Ernest J. Colvin, Chairman
Kenneth Schertle, Executive Director

Massachusetts State Racing Commission
John W. McCormack Building
Room #1313
One Ashburton Place
Boston, Massachusetts 02108
Phone: (617) 727-2581
Fax: (617) 227-6062
Henry O'Donnell, Chairman
James G. Nagle, Secretary

Michigan Office of Racing Commissioner
37650 Professional Center Dr., 105A
Livonia, Michigan 48154-1114
Phone: (313) 462-2400
Fax: (313) 462-2429
Luke Quinn, Commissioner
Kenn Christopher, Executive Secretary

ORGANIZATIONS

Minnesota Racing Commission
11000 W. 78th Street
Suite 201
Eden Prairie, MN 55344
 Phone: (612) 341-7555
 Fax: (612) 341-7563
  Ralph Strangis, Chairman
  Richard Krueger, Executive Director

Missouri Horse Racing Commission
314 E. High Street
P.O. Box 754
Jefferson City, MO 65102
 Phone: (314) 751-3565
 Fax: (314) 751-8722
  Mrs. Betty Weldon, Chairman
  Jane Scheel, Acting Director

New Jersey Racing Commission
CN 088, 200 Woolverton Street
Trenton, New Jersey 08625
 Phone: (609) 292-0613
 Fax: (609) 396-3575
  Dennis O. Dowd, Chairman
  Stuart O. Goldsmith, Commissioner
  Bruce H. Garland, Executive Director

**New York State Racing and
Wagering Board**
400 Broome Street
New York, New York 10013
 Phone: (212) 219-4230
 Fax: (212) 219-4199
  Richard F. Corbisiero, Jr., Chairman

Nova Scotia Horse Racing Commission
P.O. Box 1073
Halifax, Nova Scotia,
Canada B3J 2X1
 Phone: (902) 424-3125 or 26
  Vincent Lambie, Chairman
  Gerald G. Grant, Director of Racing

Ohio State Racing Commission
77 South High Street
18th Floor
Columbus, Ohio 43266-0416
 Phone: (614) 466-2757
 Fax: (614) 466-1900
  Norman I. Barron, Chairman
  Clifford Nelson, Executive Director

Ontario Racing Commission
180 Dundas Street West, 14th Floor
Toronto, Ontario, Canada M5G1Z8
 Phone: (416) 963-0520
 Fax: (416) 324-3478
  Frank Drea, Chairman
  W.R. McDonnell, Director
  T. Stone, Deputy Dir.- Standardbred

**Pennsylvania State Harness
Racing Commission**
2301 N. Cameron Street
Harrisburg, Pennsylvania 17110-9408
 Phone: (717) 787-5196
 Fax: (717) 787-2387
  James B. Eckenrode, Jr., Chairman
  Richard E. Sharbaugh, Exec. Secretary

**Prince Edward Island Horse Racing and
Sports Commission**
P.O. Box 3014
Charlottetown, P.E.I., Canada C1A 7N9
 Phone: (902) 368-4798
  Jack Mulligan, Chairman
  Gordon Carr, Executive Director

**Commission des Courses
du Quebec**
5400 Boulevard des Galleries, 2nd Floor
Quebec City, Que., Canada G2K 2B4
 Phone: (418) 646-1632
 Fax: (418) 646-2528
  Louis Bernard, President
  Leo Bilodeau, Secretary

Vermont Racing Commission
120 State Street
Montpelier, VT 05602
 Phone: (802) 828-3429
  Mrs. Barbara L. Menard, Exec. Sec.

Virginia Racing Commission
P.O. Box 1123
Richmond, VA 23208
 Phone: (804) 371-7363
  John H. Shenefield, Chairman
  Donald R. Price, Executive Secretary

Washington Horse Racing Commission
3700 Martin Way - Suite 101
Olympia, WA 98506
 Phone: (206) 459-6462
 Fax: (206) 459-6461
  John Crowley, Executive Secretary

ORGANIZATIONS

SIRE STAKES INFORMATION SOURCES

Atlantic Sires Stakes
Atlantic Standardbred Breeders Assn.
R.R. #5, Tatamagouche, Nova Scotia,
Canada B0K 1V0
Phone: (902) 657-3068
J.S. Ferguson, Secretary/Treasurer

Florida Breeders Stakes
Florida Standardbred Breeders & Owners
1800 S.W. 3rd Street
Pompano Beach, FL 33069
Phone: (305) 972-5400
Fax: (305) 978-9070
Walter Warrington, Exec. Dir.

Indiana Sires Stakes
Indiana Standardbred Board of Regulations
Commissioner of Agriculture
One North Capitol - Suite 600
Indianapolis, Indiana 46204
Phone: (317) 232-8767
Fax: (317) 232-8766
Kay Roberts

Maine Standardbred Breeders Stakes
Maine State Harness Racing Commission
State House Station #28
Augusta, ME 04333
Phone: (207) 289-3221
Fax: (207) 289-7548
Henry W. Jackson, Pgm. Coordinator

Massachusetts Sire Stakes
Massachusetts Dept. of Food & Agriculture
100 Cambridge Street
Boston, MA 02202
Phone: (617) 727-3018
Robert Bennett, Supervisor

New England Sulky Championships
Pine Hill Terrace - P.O. Box 799
Berwick, ME 03901
Phone: (207) 698-1302
Robert Ferland, Executive Secretary

New York-Bred Events
Harness Breeders of New York State, Inc.
90 State Street
Albany, NY 12207
Phone: (518) 434-1264
Fax: (518) 434-1265
Bruce Hamilton, Executive Secretary

Ontario Sires Stakes
c/o The Ontario Racing Commission
180 Dundas Street West, 14th Floor
Toronto, Ontario, Canada M5G 1Z8
Phone: (416) 963-0520
Fax: (416) 324-3478
Rob Roy, Supervisor

California Sires Stake
Cal. Standardbred Sire Stakes Cmmte.
P.O. Box 13368
Sacramento, California 95813
Phone: (916) 442-2135
Fax: (916) 362-8319
Vicki Desomer, Secretary

Illinois Standardbred Breeders Fund
Illinois Department of Agriculture
Illinois State Fairgrounds
Springfield, Illinois 62794-9281
Phone: (217) 782-4231
Fax: (217) 524-6194
Jered Hooker, Administrator

Kentucky Sires Stake
Kentucky Standardbred Development Fund
4063 Iron Works Pike - Building B
Lexington, KY 40511
Phone: (606) 255-2448
Fax: (606) 252-3538
Penny (Becker) Dailey, Director

Maryland Standardbred Race Fund
6336 Rosecroft Drive
Ft. Washington, MD 20744
Phone: (301) 567-0100
Fax: (301) 567-9267
E. Jane Murray, Administrator

Michigan Sires Stakes
P.O. Box 349
Okemos, MI 48805
Phone: (517) 349-2920
Fax: (517) 349-4983

New Jersey Sire Stake Program
CN 330
Trenton, NJ 08625
(*Note*: Payments ONLY to P.O. Box 479
Newark, NJ 07101)
Phone: (609) 292-8830 or 292-8831
Fax: (609) 984-2508
Bruce Stearns, Executive Director

Ohio Sires Stakes
Ohio Standardbred Development Fund
c/o The Ohio State Racing Commission
77 South High Street, 18th Floor
Columbus, OH 43266-0416
Phone: (614) 466-7437
Fax: (614) 466-1900
Joanna Craig, Public Information

Pennsylvania Sires Stakes
c/o Pennsylvania Harness Racing Comm.
2301 N. Cameron Street
Harrisburg, PA 17110
Phone: (717) 787-3609

ORGANIZATIONS

WORLD TROTTING COUNCILS

Australia
Australian Harness Racing Council
One Queens Road
Melbourne, Victoria, Australia 3004
Phone: 61 32678033
Telex: VTCB AA 32993
Fax: 61 32675059
    Mr. Ken Dyer, Chief Executive

Austria
Zentrale fur Traber-Zucht und
    Renen im Oesterreich
Nibelungengasse 3
1010 Wien, Austria
Telex: 131 411 WRTR
    Kurt Kollross, Secretary General

Belgium
Federation Belge Du Trot
410 Boulevard Lambermont
1030, Bruxelles, Belgium
Telex: 63 081 FDTROT B
Fax: 32 22152192
    Georges Dumont, Secretary General

Denmark
Dansk Travsports Centralforbund
Solendsvej 2
2100, Kobenhavin O, Denmark
Phone: 45 31208802
Fax: 45 31204464
    Eric Mueller, Secretary General
    Carl Anderson, Managing Editor

England
The British Harness Racing Club
Bryn Goleu, Bryniau
Dyserth, Rhyl,
Clwyd LL18 6ER
Phone: (07456)4746
    T.W. Menzies, Chairman
    Miss A.M. Brophy, Secretary

Ente Nazional Per Le
Corse Al Trotto
(ENCAT)
Via Catania 9 A
00161, Roma, Italy
Telex: 680 495 UNIREB I
Fax: 39 6428003
    Dr. Alberto Gaiani, Secretary General
    Franco Mioni, General Manager

European Trotting Union
Union Europeenne Du Trot (UET)
7, rue d'Astorg
75008, Paris, France
Telex: TROT A 290 674
Fax: 33 147420990
    Miss E. Wacker, Secretary
    L.E. Hofstedt, President

Finland
Suomen Hippos ry
Tulkinkuja, 3
02600, Expoo, Finland
Phone: 35 805121411
Fax: 35 805121790
Fax: 35 805121791
Telex: 123 429 TROT SF
    Matti Lakkisto, Secretary General

France
Societe d'Encouragement a
    l'Elevage du Cheval Francais
(S.E.C.F.)
7, rue d'Astorg
75008, Paris, France
Phone: 33 147420770
Fax: 33 147420990
Telex: TRO A 290 674
    P. de Montesson, President
    B. Battistini, Adm. Director
    J. Chartier, Racing Director
    C. Peirre-Bloch, PR Director

Germany
Hauptverband fur Traberzucht
und-Rennen e.v.
Gutenbergstrassse 40
Postfach 2360
4044 Kaarst 2, West Germany
Phone: 49 210151557
Fax: 49 2101511649
Telex: 8517557
    Manfred Peters, Secretary General

ORGANIZATIONS

Holland
Stichting Nederlandse Draf-en
  Rensport
Nieuwe Parklaan 25
Postbus 87950
2508 DJ DEN HAAG, The Netherlands
  Fax: 31 703549923
  Telex: 34573
    J. Govers, Secretary General

Italy
U.N.I.R.E.
Via Catania 9 A
00161, Roma, Italy
  Fax: 39 6428003
  Telex: 680495 UNIREB I
    Dr. Piero Golisano, General Director

Norway
Det Norske Travselskap
Postboks 85 - Arvoll
0515 Oslo 5 Norway
  Phone: 47 2646000
  Fax: 47 2956060
  Telex: 19141
    Bjorn Trandum, President
    Knut Erik Johansen, Gen. Secretary
    Nils O. Krekling, Int'l. Organization

Sweden
Svenska Travsportens
  Centralforbund
161 89 Stockholm, Sweden
  Phone: 46 86272000
  Fax: 46 8292530
  Fax: 46 8987828
  Telex: 10327
    Lars Erik Hofstedt, President
    Anders Tornkvist, General Manager

Zimbabwe
Zimbabwe National Trotting Association
P.O. Box 3456
Salisbury, Rhodesia/Zimbabwe

Ireland
Irish Harness Racing Club
Old Portmarnock
County Dublin, Ireland
  Phone: 35 31462834
    Hugh Richardson, Director

New Zealand
New Zealand Harness Racing Conference
135 Lincoln Road, PO Box 459
Christchurch, 2, New Zealand
  Phone: 64 33385099
  Fax: 64 33388211
    R.I. Mill, Chief Executive Officer

Spain
Real Federacion Nancional
  del Trote
Capitan Salom, 10 Entresuelo
07004 Palma de Mallorca
    Oliver Muntaner, President

Switzerland
Schweizerischer Trabrenn-Verband
Federation Suisse du Trotting
Schaffhauserstrasse 315
8050 Zurich
  Fax: 41 13113651
  Telex: 823506
    Jean-Pierre Kratzer, President

Race Dates

RACE DATES

U.S. RACING DATES FOR 1991

Here's a are race dates for the major in North America; tentative dates carry an asterisk - "*."

CALIFORNIA
February	8	thru	July	27	Los Alamitos Racecourse	Los Alamitos

DELAWARE
January	1	thru	March	23	Dover Downs	Dover
March	24	thru	May	19	Harrington Raceway	Harrington
September	5	thru	November	16	Harrington Raceway	Harrington
November	17	thru	December	31	Dover Downs	Dover

FLORIDA
January	1	thru	April	27	Pompano Harness Track	Pompano Beach
October	* 5	thru	December	* 31	Pompano Harness Track	Pompano Beach

ILLINOIS
January	1	thru	December	31	Balmoral Park	Crete
January	1	thru	April	7	Fairmount Park	Collinsville
January	1	thru	February	18	Hawthorne Racecourse	Cicero
February	19	thru	May	16	Maywood Park	Maywood
April	11	thru	October	27	Quad City Downs	East Moline
May	17	thru	October	5	Sportsman's Park	Cicero
October	7	thru	December	31	Maywood Park	Maywood
December	5	thru	December	31	Fairmount Park	Collinsville

KENTUCKY
March	1	thru	April	25	Louisville Downs	Louisville
April	26	thru	June	29	The Red Mile	Lexington
April	26	thru	June	29	Riverside Downs	Henderson
July	1	thru	September	7	Louisville Downs	Louisville
September	10	thru	October	4	The Red Mile	Lexington
October	1	thru	October	26	Louisville Downs	Louisville
October	25	thru	December	7	Riverside Downs	Henderson

MAINE
March	1	thru	December	15	Scarborough Downs	Scarborough
May	24	thru	July	26	Bangor Raceway	Bangor
October	11	thru	October	27	Bangor Raceway	Bangor

MARYLAND
January	11	thru	December	21	Rosecroft Raceway	Fort Washington
May	24	thru	September	2	Delmarva Downs	Berlin

MICHIGAN
January	2	thru	March	30	Sports Creek Raceway	Swartz Creek
January	3	thru	March	31	Northville Downs	Northville
April	3	thru	October	12	Hazel Park Harness	Hazel Park
April	3	thru	June	23	Jackson Raceway	Jackson
April	10	thru	August	25	Saginaw Harness Raceway	Saginaw
May	3	thru	October	27	Muskegon Race Course	Muskegon
August	21	thru	October	12	Jackson Raceway	Jackson
October	13	thru	December	31	Sports Creek Raceway	Swartz Creek
October	14	thru	December	31	Northville Downs	Northville

RACE DATES

NEW JERSEY

January	1	thru	August	18	The Meadowlands	East Rutherford
January	1	thru	May	27	Freehold Raceway	Freehold
August	16	thru	December	31	Freehold Raceway	Freehold
September	4	thru	December	7	Garden State Park	Cherry Hill
December	26	thru	December	31	The Meadowlands	East Rutherford

NEW YORK

January	1	thru	December	31	Monticello Raceway	Monticello
January	1	thru	December	31	Yonkers Raceway	Yonkers
January	2	thru	February	24	Buffalo Raceway	Hamburg
January	11	thru	November	30	Saratoga Raceway	Saratoga Springs
February	28	thru	April	20	Batavia Downs	Batavia
April	4	thru	November	9	Vernon Downs	Vernon
April	24	thru	July	28	Buffalo Raceway	Hamburg
July	31	thru	November	30	Batavia Downs	Batavia
December	4	thru	December	31	Buffalo Raceway	Hamburg

OHIO

January	1	thru	December	29	Northfield Park	Cleveland
January	4	thru	May	4	Lebanon Raceway	Lebanon
March	16	thru	December	7	Raceway Park	Toledo
May	4	thru	September	14	Scioto Downs	Columbus
September	20	thru	December	28	Lebanon Raceway	Lebanon

PENNSYLVANIA

January	3	thru	December	29	The Meadows	Meadow Lands
March	1	thru	November	30	Pocono Downs	Wilkes-Barre

MARITIME RACING DATES FOR 1991

NEW BRUNSWICK

January	1	through	December	28	Exhibition Park Raceway	St. John
March	30	through	December	31	New Brunswick Downs	Dieppe
May	27	through	September	28	Fredericton Raceway	Fredericton

NOVA SCOTIA

January	1	through	December	29	Truro Raceway	Truro
January	3	through	December	29	Tartan Downs	Sydney
June	9	through	October	13	Inverness Raceway	Inverness

NEWFOUNDLAND

May	12	through	October	27	Avalon Raceway	St. John's

PRINCE EDWARD ISLAND

January	1	through	December	28	Charlottetown Driving Park	Charlottetown
May	1	through	December	26	Summerside Raceway	Summerside

RACE DATES

OTHER CANADIAN RACING DATES FOR 1991
(These dates were correct as of press time, but are subject to change)

ALBERTA
January	1	through	February	25	Stampede Park	Calgary
March	1	through	May	27	Northlands Park	Edmonton
June	1	through	September	15	Stampede Park	Calgary
September	20	through	December	2	Northlands Park	Edmonton
December	6	through	December	29	Stampede Park	Calgary

BRITISH COLUMBIA
January	1	through	April	7	Cloverdale Raceway	Surrey
May	4	through	September	8	Sandown Park	Sidney
October	1	through	December	30	Cloverdale Raceway	Surrey

MANITOBA
January	1	through	April	14	Assiniboia Downs	Winnipeg
October	19	through	December	29	Assiniboia Downs	Winnipeg

ONTARIO
January	1	through	December	30	Flamboro Downs	Dundas
January	1	through	March	16	Greenwood Raceway	Toronto
January	2	through	March	31	Windsor Raceway	Windsor
January	2	through	June	17	Western Fair Raceway	London
January	2	through	December	28	Barrie Raceway	Barrie
January	3	through	December	29	Orangeville Raceway	Orangeville
January	6	through	December	29	Kingston Park Raceway	Kingston
March	17	through	May	26	Mohawk Raceway	Campbellville
April	6	through	November	9	Elmira Raceway	Elmira
April	26	through	October	4	Quinte Raceway	Belleville
April	28	through	September	28	Dresden Raceway	Dresden
May	4	through	November	30	Kawartha Downs	Fraserville
May	10	through	October	6	Leamington Raceway	Leamington
May	11	through	September	28	Hanover Raceway	Hanover
May	27	through	August	31	Greenwood Raceway	Toronto
June	22	through	September	24	Woodstock Raceway	Woodstock
July	1	through	November	30	Rideau Carleton	Ottawa
September	1	through	December	3	Mohawk Raceway	Campbellville
October	2	through	December	31	Western Fair Raceway	London
October	13	through	December	31	Windsor Raceway	Windsor
December	6	through	December	31	Greenwood Raceway	Toronto

QUEBEC
January	1	through	June	30	Hippodrome Connaught	Aylmer
January	2	through	December	29	Hippodrome de Quebec	Quebec City
January	4	through	December	30	Hippodrome Blue Bonnets	Montreal
January	8	through	December	29	Hippodrome Trois Rivieres	Trois Rivieres
April	7	through	November	24	Hippodrome Saguenay	Jonquiere
December	1	through	December	29	Hippodrome Connaught	Aylmer

SASKATCHEWAN
May	3	through	October	26	Queensbury Downs	Regina

RACE DATES

1991 FAIR RACING DATES

Illinois

June 20 - 21	Cambridge	July 16 - 18	Farmer City	August 4 - 8	Altamont
June 26 - 27	Pinckneyville	July 19 - 20, & 22	Henry	August 5 - 7	Albion
June 26 - 27	Marshall	July 22 - 24	Paris	August 6 - 9	Belvidere
June 29	Griggsville	July 22 - 24	Urbana	August 14 - 15	Pecatonia
June 30 - July 3	Newton	July 23 - 24	Carrollton	August 15 - 17	Morrison
July 2 - 4	Rushville	July 24 - 25	Lewistown	August 20 - 23	Greenville
July 6 - 7	Aledo	July 27 - 28	Petersburg	August 20 - 24	Greenup
July 8 - 9	Jerseyville	July 27 - 28	Salem	August 21 - 23	Anna
July 9 - 12	Martinsville	July 28 - 30	Carmi	August 23 - 25	Fairbury
July 11 - 14	Decatur	July 29 - August 2	Charleston	August 30 - Sep. 2	Pana
July 13 - 14	Jacksonville	July 30 - August 1	Knoxville	August 31 - Sep. 2	Mendota
July 14 - 16	Fairfield	July 31 - August 1	Woodstock	September 1 - 2	Oregon
July 15 - 16	Taylorville	July 31 - Aug. 3	Mt. Sterling	September 4 - 5	Sandwich
July 16 - 18	Carlinville	August 1 - 4	Lincoln	September 6 - 7	Marion

Indiana

June 9	Portland	July 13	Kentland	July 29 - 30	Connersville
June 16	Portland	July 13 - 15	Shelbyville	July 31 - August 2	Corydon
June 24 - 27	Converse	July 17 - 19	Frankfort	August 2	Portland
July 6 - 7	Princeton	July 20 - 24	Goshen	TBA	Anderson
		July 24 - 27	La Porte		

Iowa

May 29	What Cheer	July 13 - 14	What Cheer	August 3 - 4	Humboldt
June 9	Oskaloosa	July 20 - 21	Wapello	August 5 - 6	Oskaloosa
June 16	Eldon	July 21	Keosauqua	August 8 - 9	Eldon
July 4	Humboldt	July 26	Monticello	August 15	Des Moines
July 7	Maquoketa	July 27	Sioux Center	September 9 - 10	Spencer

Kentucky

May 31 - June 1	Smithland	June 24 - 25	Paducah	July 20	Bardstown
June 7 - 8	La Center	July 2 - 4	Lebanon	July 26 - 27	Benton
June 14 - 15	Mayfield	July 6 - 7	Sturgis	August 2 - 3	Hopkinsville

Maine

July 27 - Aug. 3	Skowhegan	August 11 - 17	Skowhegan	September 7-21	Farmington
August 4 - 10	Topsham	August 18 - 24	Union	September 22-30	Cumberland
August 3 - 10	Northern Maine	August 25 - Sept. 2	Windsor	October 1 - 6	Fryeburg

Michigan

June 24 - 27	Marion	July 7 - 10	Big Rapids	July 15 - 16	Fowlerville
June 24 - 25, 27, 28	Ithaca	July 9 - 12	Vassar	July 15 - 17	Cassopolis
July 3 - 7	Lake Odessa	July 14 - 19	Croswell	July 15 - 18	Hastings

RACE DATES

July 19 - 20	Muskegon	August 5 - 7	Imlay City	August 19 - 22, 24	Ludington
July 21 - 22	Charlotte	August 5 - 8	Gaylord	August 19 - 23	Kalamazoo
July 21 - 23	Standish	August 6 - 9	Bad Axe	August 22 - 24	Hart
July 22 - 27	Holland	August 9 - 11	Ironwood	August 26 - 28	Traverse City
July 25 - 27	Gladwin	August 11 - 13	Midland	August 28 - 30	Onekama
July 25 - 27	Hale	August 12 - 14	Cadillac	August 30-31, Sep. 2	Kinross
July 29 - August 1	Caro	August 12 - 16	Marshall	September 1 - 2	Norway
July 29 - August 3	Harrison	August 14 - 17	Adrian	September 7, 9-14	Allegan
August 1	Ionia	August 16	Lincoln	September 16 - 21	Centreville
August 2 - 3	Mason	August 19 - 20	Petoskey	September 23 - 28	Hillsdale

Missouri

June 23	Kahoka	July 26 - 28	Kahoka	August 21 - 23	Sedalia

New Jersey

June 15 - 16	Showplace Farm	July 12 - 13	Egyptian Acres	Aug. 17-18	East Lynne Farm
June 22-23	Willowbrook Fm.	July 20 - 21	Lauralan Farm	August 30-31	Garden St. Pk.
June 29 - 30	Gaitway Farm	July 27 - 28	Cream Ridge	September 11	Garden St. Pk.
		August 8 - 9	Cowtown		

New York

(Fair dates; not necessarily racing dates)

July 2 - 7	Sandy Creek	July 23 - 28	Ballston Spa	August 6 - 11	Norwich
July 4 - 7	Goshen	July 23 - 28	Whitney Point	August 9 - 18	Hamburg
July 9 - 14	Weedsport	July 28 - Aug. 4	Little Valley	August 11 - 17	Palmyra
July 15 - 20	Angelica	July 29 - Aug. 23	Morris	August 12 - 18	Altamont
July 15 - 20	Waterloo	July 30 - Aug. 4	Horseheads	August 13 - 17	Westport
July 16 - 20	Penn Yan	July 30 - Aug. 4	Plattsburgh	August 13 - 18	Bath
July 16 - 21	Afton	August 4 - 11	Malone	August 20 - 24	Trumansburg
July 16 - 21	Hemlock	August 6 - 10	Caledonia	August 20 - 25	Rhinebeck
July 16 - 21	Lowville	August 6 - 10	Owego	August 23 - 28	Gouverneur
July 22 - 28	Boonville	August 6 - 11	Cobleskill	August 27 - Sep. 2	Fonda
July 22 - 28	Dunkirk			August 29 - Sep. 2	Chatham

Ohio

(Fair dates; not necessarily racing dates)

June 21 - 27	Circleville	July 15 - 21	Oak Harbor	July 23 - 28	Tallmadge
June 29 - July 4	Ottawa	July 16 - 20	Lebanon	July 23 - 28	Marysville
July 2 - 7	Marion	July 16 - 21	Carrollton	July 23 - 29	Tiffin
July 5 - 14	Cadiz	July 16 - 21	Bellefontaine	July 27 - August 3	Eaton
July 7 - 13	Proctorville	July 17 - 21	New Lexington	July 28 - August 3	Xenia
July 8 - 14	London	July 20 - 26	Springfield	July 28 - August 4	Medina
July 8 - 14	Paulding	July 21 - 26	Hamilton	July 29 - August 3	Gallipolis
July 9 - 14	Cortland	July 21 - 27	Mt. Vernon	July 29 - August 3	Piketon
July 12 - 20	Wellston	July 22 - 27	Owensville	July 29 - August 3	McArthur
July 13 - 20	Hilliard	July 22 - 27	Washington C.H.	July 31 - August 4	Carthage
July 14 - 20	West Union	July 22 - 28	Sidney	August 1 - 7	Bowling Green
July 15 - 21	Bucyrus	July 23 - 28	Maumee	August 2 - 8	Wapakoneta

RACE DATES

August 3 - 9	Urbana	August 17 - 24	Lima
August 4 - 10	Wilmington	August 17 - 24	Hicksville
August 4 - 10	Chillicothe	August 19 - 24	Woodsfield
August 4 - 11	Mansfield	August 19 - 25	Wellington
August 5 - 10	Athens	August 20 - 24	Attica
August 5 - 10	Hartford	August 20 -25	Lisbon
August 5 - 10	Lucasville	August 20 - 25	Painesville
August 5 - 11	Berea	August 20 - 25	Randolph
August 6 - 11	Jefferson	August 20 - 25	Fremont
August 6 - 11	Sandusky	August 27 - 31	Caldwell
August 9 - 15	Napoleon	Aug. 27 - Sep. 1	Mt. Gilead
August 9 - 15	Celina	Aug. 27 - Sep. 2	Canton
August 10 - 15	Troy	Aug. 28 - Sep. 2	Findlay
August 11 - 17	Zanesville	Aug. 28 - Sep. 2	Dayton
August 12 - 17	Pomeroy	Aug. 29 - Sep. 2	Burton
August 12 - 18	Norwalk	Aug. 29 - Sep. 2	Canfield
August 13 - 17	Millersburg	Aug. 29 - Sep. 2	Richwood
August 13 - 18	Smithfield	Aug. 29 - Sep. 4	Van Wert
August 16 - 24	Greenville	Aug. 31 - Sep. 3	Marietta
		Aug. 31 - Sep. 6	Wauseon

September 2 - 7		Hillsboro
Sep. 3 - 7		McConnelsville
September 3 - 8		Kenton
September 4 - 8		St. Clairsville
September 4 - 9		Albany
September 7 - 12		Wooster
September 8 - 14		Logan
September 9 - 14		Montpelier
Sep. 9 - 15		Old Washington
Sep. 10 - 15		Upper Sandusky
Sep. 11 - 14		Bellville
September 14 - 20		Delaware
September 15 - 21		Ashland
September 16 - 22		Dover
Sep. 23 - 28		Georgetown
September 27 - 29		Barlow
Sep. 28 - Oct. 3		Coshochton
October 1 - 2		Loudonville
October 6 - 12		Lancaster

Pennsylvania

July 1 - 3	Butler	August 6 - 9	Honesdale	August 27 - 30	Wattsburg
July 5	Gratz	August 6 - 9	Waynesburg	Aug. 31 - Sept. 2	Stoneboro
July 11 - 12	Wilkes-Barre	August 11-13	Washington	September 3 - 5	Port Royal
July 17 - 19	Hughesville	August 12 - 14	Smethport	Sept. 10 - 13	York Interstate
July 23 - 25	Troy	August 14 - 16	Dayton	September 17 - 19	Gratz
July 29-Aug. 1	Clearfield	August 14-16	Huntingdon	September 23-26	Bloomsburg
August 5 - 7	Bedford	August 20 - 23	Meadville	October 6	Mt. Holly
		August 26 - 28	Indiana		

Vermont

August 16 - 17	Barton	August 28	Essex Junction	August 30 - Sep. 8	Rutland
August 23 - 24	Lyndonville			TBA	Cunbridge

RACE DATES

1991 GRAND CIRCUIT DATES

From	To	Track	Location
June 9	June 16	Raceway Park	Toledo, OH
June 17	June 22	Scioto Downs	Columbus, OH
June 23	June 29	Historic at the Meadowlands	E. Rutherford, NJ
July 4	July 7	Historic Track	Goshen, NY
July 12	July 15	Northfield Park	Northfield, OH
July 16	July 21	Vernon Downs	Vernon, NY
July 29	August 3	The Meadowlands	E. Rutherford, NJ
August 5	August 10	The Meadows	Washington, PA
August 12	August 16	Illinois State Fair	Springfield, IL
August 19	August 24	Indiana State Fair	Indianapolis, IN
August 26	August 31	Du Quoin Fair	Du Quoin, IL
September 1	September 7	Mohawk Raceway	Campbellville, ONT
September 9	September 14	Freehold Racewayt	Freehold, NJ
September 15	September 21	Delaware County Fair	Delaware, OH
September 24	October 4	The Red Mile	Lexington, KY
October 7	October 14	Rosecroft Raceway	Ft. Washington, MD
November 3	December 22	Pompano Park	Pompano Beach, FL

1991 EUROPEAN GRAND CIRCUIT

Date	Event	Track	Country
February 10	Prix de France	Vincennes	France
March 10	Grand Criterium de Vitesse	Cagnes sur Mer	France
April 7	Grand Prix du Sud Ouest	Agen (Bordeax)	France
April 14	Grosser Preis Von Bayern	Munich	Germany
April 28	Finlandia AJO	Helsinki	Finland
May 12	Oslo Grand Prix	Oslo	Norway
May 26	Internationella Elitloppet	Solvalla	Sweden
June 9	Copenhagen Cup	Copenhagen	Denmark
June 21	Gran Premio Duomo	Florence	Italy
July 14	Elite Rennen	Gelsenkirchen	Germany
August 18	Grand Prix d'Aby	Aby	Sweden
September 1	Campionato Europeo	Cesena	Italy
October 13	Grosser Pries von Hamburg	Hamburg	Germany
October 22	Pries der Giganten	Hilversum	The Netherlands
November 16	Gran Premio delle Nazioni	Milano	Italy

* * * * *

RACE DATES

MAJOR STAKE RACES IN 1991

Here is a list of the major races for 1991 as reported to the USTA by press time. We would recommend checking with the track involved to see if there are any updates to the particulars of these events. All Triple Crown races appear in **BOLDFACE CAPS**, and Breeders Crown races appear in **boldface type**:

1991 Calendar

```
      JANUARY                    FEBRUARY                    MARCH
        1  2  3  4  5                          1  2                          1  2
 6  7  8  9 10 11 12      3  4  5  6  7  8  9      3  4  5  6  7  8  9
13 14 15 16 17 18 19     10 11 12 13 14 15 16     10 11 12 13 14 15 16
20 21 22 23 24 25 26     17 18 19 20 21 22 23     17 18 19 20 21 22 23
27 28 29 30 31           24 25 26 27 28           24 25 26 27 28 29 30
                                                  31

       APRIL                        MAY                         JUNE
    1  2  3  4  5  6                 1  2  3  4                             1
 7  8  9 10 11 12 13      5  6  7  8  9 10 11      2  3  4  5  6  7  8
14 15 16 17 18 19 20     12 13 14 15 16 17 18      9 10 11 12 13 14 15
21 22 23 24 25 26 27     19 20 21 22 23 24 25     16 17 18 19 20 21 22
28 29 30                 26 27 28 29 30 31        23 24 25 26 27 28 29
                                                  30

       JULY                       AUGUST                    SEPTEMBER
    1  2  3  4  5  6                    1  2  3      1  2  3  4  5  6  7
 7  8  9 10 11 12 13      4  5  6  7  8  9 10      8  9 10 11 12 13 14
14 15 16 17 18 19 20     11 12 13 14 15 16 17     15 16 17 18 19 20 21
21 22 23 24 25 26 27     18 19 20 21 22 23 24     22 23 24 25 26 27 28
28 29 30 31              25 26 27 28 29 30 31     29 30

      OCTOBER                    NOVEMBER                  DECEMBER
        1  2  3  4  5                          1  2      1  2  3  4  5  6  7
 6  7  8  9 10 11 12      3  4  5  6  7  8  9      8  9 10 11 12 13 14
13 14 15 16 17 18 19     10 11 12 13 14 15 16     15 16 17 18 19 20 21
20 21 22 23 24 25 26     17 18 19 20 21 22 23     22 23 24 25 26 27 28
27 28 29 30 31           24 25 26 27 28 29 30     29 30 31
```

Chronological List of Major Events

Month	Date	Event (Age, Sex, Gait)	Estimated Purse	Track
January	3	Blizzard Series (3&4yo F&M Pace)	$8,000	Greenwood
January	6	Bromont Series (Open Trot) Horsemen's Series (4&up Open Trot)	5,000 20,000	Blue Bonnets Greenwood
January	7	Chill Factor Series (3&4yo H&G Pace)	12,500	The Meadowlands
January	8	Comforter Series (3&4yo F&M Pace)	10,000	The Meadowlands
January	9	Trendsetter Series (3&4yo H&G Pace)	10,000	The Meadowlands
January	10	Blizzard Series (3&4yo F&M Pace) Complex Series (3-5yo Open Pace)	8,000 12,500	Greenwood The Meadowlands
January	11	des Neiges Series (Open Pace) Cape and Cutter Series (Open Pacing Mares)	4,000 20,000	Blue Bonnets The Meadowlands

RACE DATES

Date		Race	Purse	Track
January	12	Presidential Series (FFA Pace)	$35,000	The Meadowlands
January	13	Bromont Series (Open Trot) Horsemen's Series (4&up Open Trot)	5,000 20,000	Blue Bonnets Greenwood
January	14	Chill Factor Series (3&4yo H&G Pace)	12,500	The Meadowlands
January	15	Comforter Series (3&4yo F&M Pace)	10,000	The Meadowlands
January	16	Trendsetter Series (3&4yo H&G Pace)	10,000	The Meadowlands
January	17	Blizzard Series Final (3&4yo F&M Pace) Complex Series (3-5yo Open Pace)	20,000 12,500	Greenwood The Meadowlands
January	18	des Neiges Series (Open Pace) Cape and Cutter Series (Open Pacing Mares)	4,000 20,000	Blue Bonnets The Meadowlands
January	19	Presidential Series (FFA Pace)	35,000	The Meadowlands
January	20	Horsemen's Series Final (4&up Open Trot) Bromont Series Final (Open Trot)	90,000 20,000	Greenwood Blue Bonnets
January	21	Carnaval Series (Open Trot) Chill Factor Series (3&4yo H&G Pace)	4,000 12,500	Blue Bonnets The Meadowlands
January	22	Comforter Series (3&4yo F&M Pace)	10,000	The Meadowlands
January	23	Trendsetter Series (3&4yo H&G Pace)	10,000	The Meadowlands
January	24	Complex Series (3-5yo Open Pace)	12,500	The Meadowlands
January	25	des Neiges Series Final (Open Pace) Cape and Cutter Series (Open Pacing Mares)	20,000 20,000	Blue Bonnets The Meadowlands
January	26	Presidential Series Final (FFA Pace) Battle of Saratoga Series (3-6yo Open Pace) Whizzer R. White (4yo Open Pace)	100,000 10,000 25,000	The Meadowlands Saratoga Raceway Hawthorne
January	27	Damsel Series (3&4yo F&M Pace)	14,000	Greenwood
January	28	Chill Factor Series Final (3&4yo H&G Pace) Carnaval Series (Open Trot)	40,000 4,000	The Meadowlands Blue Bonnets
January	29	Comforter Series Final (3&4yo F&M Pace)	75,000	The Meadowlands
January	30	Trendsetter Series Final (3&4yo H&G Pace)	100,000	The Meadowlands
January	31	Complex Series Final (3-5yo Open Pace) Snowshoe Series (3&4yo Open Pace)	45,000 8,000	The Meadowlands Greenwood
February	1	Cape and Cutter Series Final (Open Pacing Mares)	40,000	The Meadowlands
February	2	Battle of Saratoga Series (3-6yo Open Pace) Pretty Direct (3&up F&M Pace)	10,000 25,000	Saratoga Raceway Hawthorne
February	3	Damsel Series (3&4yo F&M Pace) Aquarius Series (4&5yo Open Pace)	14,000 25,000	Greenwood The Meadowlands
February	4	Carnaval Series Final (Open Trot)	20,000	Blue Bonnets
February	5	Su Mac Lad Series (FFA Trot)	30,000	The Meadowlands

RACE DATES

Date		Race	Purse	Track
February	6	Night Styles Series (3-5yo F&M Pace)	$12,500	The Meadowlands
February	7	Snowshoe Series (3&4yo Open Pace)	8,000	Greenwood
		Exit 16W Series (3-5yo H&G Pace)	12,500	The Meadowlands
February	8	Boucherville Series (3&4yo F&M Pace)	4,000	Blue Bonnets
February	9	Damsel Series Final (3&4yo F&M Pace)	100,000	Greenwood
		Surburban Downs Pacing Derby (Open)	60,000	Hawthorne
		Battle of Saratoga Series (3-6yo Open Pace)	10,000	Saratoga Raceway
		Fort Lauderdale Series (3&4yo Open Pace)	10,000	Pompano Park
February	10	Toronto Series (4&up Open Pace)	25,000	Greenwood
		Aquarius Series (4&5yo Open Pace)	25,000	The Meadowlands
February	12	Su Mac Lad Series (FFA Trot)	30,000	The Meadowlands
February	13	Night Styles Series (3-5yo F&M Pace)	12,500	The Meadowlands
February	14	Snowshoe Series Final (3&4yo Open Pace)	30,000	Greenwood
		Exit 16W Series (3-5yo H&G Pace)	12,500	The Meadowlands
		Hopeful Series (3yofp)	6,000	Yonkers Raceway
February	15	Boucherville Series (3&4yo F&M Pace)	4,000	Blue Bonnets
		Hopeful Series (3yocp)	6,000	Yonkers Raceway
February	16	Erwin F. Dygert Memorial (Open Trot)	75,000	Hawthorne
		Fort Lauderdale Series (3&4yo Open Pace)	10,000	Pompano Park
February	17	Aquarius Series Final (4&5yo Open Pace)	50,000	The Meadowlands
		Toronto Series (4&up Open Pace)	25,000	Greenwood
February	18	Su Mac Lad Series Final (FFA Trot)	75,000	The Meadowlands
		Battle of Saratoga Series Final (3-6yo Open Pace)	15,000	Saratoga Raceway
		Harfang des Nieges Series (3&4yo H&G Pace)	4,000	Blue Bonnets
February	20	Night Styles Series (3-5yo F&M Pace)	12,500	The Meadowlands
February	21	Exit 16W Series (3-5yo H&G Pace)	12,500	The Meadowlands
		Hopeful Series (3yofp)	6,000	Yonkers Raceway
February	22	Boucherville Series Final (3&4yo F&M Pace)	15,000	Blue Bonnets
		Overbid Series (Open Pacing Mares)	20,000	The Meadowlands
		Hopeful Series (3yocp)	6,000	Yonkers Raceway
February	23	Fort Lauderdale Series Final (3&4yo Open Pace)	50,000	Pompano Park
February	24	Toronto Series Final (4&up Open Pace)	90,000	Greenwood
		Four Leaf Clover Series (3-5yo Open Pace)	17,500	The Meadowlands
February	25	Harfang des Nieges Series (3&4yo H&G Pace)	4,000	Blue Bonnets
February	27	Night Styles Series Final (3-5yo F&M Pace)	80,000	The Meadowlands
February	28	Exit 16W Series Final (3-5yo H&G Pace)	75,000	The Meadowlands
		Hopeful Series (3yofp)	6,000	Yonkers Raceway
March	1	St. Patrick Series (3&4yo F&M Pace)	6,000	Blue Bonnets
		Overbid Series (Open Pacing Mares)	20,000	The Meadowlands
		Hopeful Series (3yocp)	6,000	Yonkers Raceway
March	3	Cam Fella Series (3&4yo Open Pace)	14,000	Greenwood

RACE DATES

March	4	Harfang des Nieges Series Final (3&4yo H&G Pace)	$15,000	Blue Bonnets
March	6	Blossom Series (3yofp)	15,000	The Meadowlands
March	7	Hopeful Series Final (3yofp) Hopeful Series Consolation (3yofp)	32,000 12,000	Yonkers Raceway Yonkers Raceway
March	8	Overbid Series Final (Open Pacing Mares) Hopeful Series Final (3yocp) Hopeful Series Consolation (3yocp) Dade County Series (3&4yo Open Trot) St. Patrick Series (3&4yo F&M Pace)	60,000 42,000 12,000 10,000 6,000	The Meadowlands Yonkers Raceway Yonkers Raceway Pompano Park Blue Bonnets
March	9	George Morton Levy Series (Open Pace)	50,000	Yonkers Raceway
March	10	Cam Fella Series (3&4yo Open Pace) Four Leaf Clover Series (3-5yo Open Pace)	14,000 17,500	Greenwood The Meadowlands
March	11	Sucre d'Erable Series (3&4yo H&G Pace)	6,000	Blue Bonnets
March	13	Blossom Series (3yofp)	15,000	The Meadowlands
March	14	Rags to Riches Series ($10,000 Clm. Pace)	5,000	Yonkers Raceway
March	15	New Faces Series (3yocp) St. Patrick Series Final (3&4yo F&M Pace) Rags to Riches Series ($15,000 Clm. Pace)	15,000 25,000 6,000	The Meadowlands Blue Bonnets Yonkers Raceway
March	16	Cam Fella Series Final (3&4yo Open Pace) George Morton Levy Series (Open Pace) North American Series (3&4yo Open Pace)	100,000 50,000 25,000	Greenwood Yonkers Raceway Freehold Raceway
March	17	Four Leaf Clover Series Final (3-5yo Open Pace) Youthful Series (3yo Open Pace)	100,000 8,500	The Meadowlands Mohawk Raceway
March	18	Sucre d'Erable Series (3&4yo H&G Pace)	6,000	Blue Bonnets
March	20	Blossom Series Final (3yofp)	60,000	The Meadowlands
March	21	Rags to Riches Series ($10,000 Clm. Pace)	5,000	Yonkers Raceway
March	22	New Faces Series (3yocp) Rags to Riches Series ($15,000 Clm. Pace) Dade County Series Final (3&4yo Open Trot)	15,000 6,000 50,000	The Meadowlands Yonkers Raceway Pompano Park
March	23	George Morton Levy Series (Open Pace) Battle of Saratoga Series (3-6yo Open Pace)	50,000 15,000	Yonkers Raceway Saratoga Raceway
March	24	Youthful Series (3yo Open Pace)	8,500	Mohawk Raceway
March	25	Sucre d'Erable Series Final (3&4yo H&G Pace)	25,000	Blue Bonnets
March	28	Rags to Riches Series ($10,000 Clm. Pace)	5,000	Yonkers Raceway
March	29	New Faces Series Final (3yocp) Rags to Riches Series ($15,000 Clm. Pace)	60,000 6,000	The Meadowlands Yonkers Raceway
March	30	North American Series (3&4yo Open Pace) George Morton Levy Series (Open Pace) Graduate Series (Open Pace) Battle of Saratoga Series (3-6yo Open Pace)	25,000 50,000 75,000 15,000	Batavia Downs Yonkers Raceway The Meadowlands Saratoga Raceway

RACE DATES

Date		Race	Purse	Track
March	31	Youthful Series (3yo Open Pace)	$8,500	Mohawk Raceway
April	1	Belle Isle Elims (3&4yo Open Pace)	7,500	Hazel Park
April	3	Jersey Girls Series (3-5yo F&M Pace)	12,500	The Meadowlands
April	4	Rags to Riches Series Final ($10,000 Clm. Pace)	20,000	Yonkers Raceway
April	5	Graduate Series (Open Pace) Rags to Riches Series Final ($15,000 Clm. Pace)	75,000 30,000	Rosecroft Raceway Yonkers Raceway
April	6	North American Series (3&4yo Open Pace) George Morton Levy Series (Open Pace) Pompano Beach Series (3yo Open Pace) Battle of Saratoga Series Final (3-6yo Open Pace)	25,000 50,000 8,000 15,000	Freehold Raceway Yonkers Raceway Pompano Park Saratoga Raceway
April	7	Berry's Creek Elims (3yo Open Pace) Youthful Series Final (3yo Open Pace)	12,500 40,000	The Meadowlands Mohawk Raceway
April	8	Belle Isle Final (3&4yo Open Pace) des Nations Series (Open Pace)	20,000 5,700	Hazel Park Blue Bonnets
April	10	Jersey Girls Series (3-5yo F&M Pace)	12,500	The Meadowlands
April	13	Graduate Series (Open Pace) George Morton Levy Series (Open Pace) Pompano Beach Series (3yo Open Pace)	75,000 50,000 8,000	Freehold Raceway Yonkers Raceway Pompano Park
April	14	Berry's Creek Final (3yo Open Pace) les Laureats Series (Open Pace) Princess Series (3yofp)	350,000 6,900 14,000	The Meadowlands Blue Bonnets Mohawk Raceway
April	15	des Nations Series (Open Pace)	5,700	Blue Bonnets
April	17	Jersey Girls Series (3-5yo F&M Pace)	12,500	The Meadowlands
April	19	Hanover Stake (Aged Trot)	20,000	Rosecroft Raceway
April	20	R. Bruce Cornell Memorial (Aged Pace) Pompano Beach Series (3yo Open Pace) Kentucky Sire Stake (3yocp)	100,000 8,000 16,000	Freehold Raceway Pompano Park Louisville Downs
April	21	North American Series (3&4yo Open Pace) Princess Series (3yofp) les Laureats Series (Open Pace)	25,000 14,000 6,900	The Meadowlands Mohawk Raceway Blue Bonnets
April	22	des Nations Series Final (Open Pace)	20,000	Blue Bonnets
April	24	Jersey Girls Series Final (3-5yo F&M Pace)	60,000	The Meadowlands
April	25	Cinderella (3yofp) Pensylvania Sire Stake (3yoft)	100,000 50,000	Maywood Park The Meadows
April	26	Pennsylvania Sire Stake (3yoct)	50,000	The Meadows
April	27	George Morton Levy Series Final (Open Pace) Pompano Beach Series Final (3yo Open Pace) Ohio Sire Stake (4&5yo Open Pace) Pennsylvania Sire Stake (3yocp)	200,000 40,000 28,000 60,000	Yonkers Raceway Pompano Park Lebanon Raceway The Meadows
April	28	Princess Series Final (3yofp) North American Series (3&4yo Open Pace)	75,000 25,000	Mohawk Raceway Rosecroft Raceway

RACE DATES

		les Laureats Series Final (Open Pace)	$28,000	Blue Bonnets
		Pennsylvania Sire Stake (3yofp)	60,000	The Meadows
April	29	Ohio Sire Stake (4&5yo Open Trot)	29,000	Lebanon Raceway
May	2	Ohio Sire Stake (3yoct)	42,000	Lebanon Raceway
May	3	Ohio Sire Stake (3yofp)	44,000	Lebanon Raceway
		Ohio Sire Stake (3yoft)	38,000	Lebanon Raceway
		Maryland Sire Stake (3yoct)	6,000	Rosecroft Raceway
May	4	Graduate Series (Open Pace)	75,000	Buffalo Raceway
		J.W. Miller Memorial Elims (3yofp)	50,000	Rosecroft Raceway
		W.E. Miller Memorial Elims (3yo Open Pace)	75,000	Rosecroft Raceway
May	5	Mohawk Series (3yo Open Pace)	14,000	Mohawk Raceway
		Ohio Sire Stake (3yocp)	44,000	Raceway Park
		Maryland Sire Stake (3yoft)	6,000	Rosecroft Raceway
May	10	Graduate Series (Open Pace)	75,000	Blue Bonnets
		les Quebecoises Series (3yofp)	10,000	Blue Bonnets
		Maryland Sire Stake (3yoct)	6,000	Rosecroft Raceway
May	11	W.E. Miller Memorial Final (3yo Open Pace)	300,000	Rosecroft Raceway
		J.W. Miller Memorial Final (3yofp)	200,000	Rosecroft Raceway
		Guys & Dolls Elims (Pacing Mares)	12,000	Freehold Raceway
		Battle of Saratoga Series (3-6yo Open Pace)	20,000	Saratoga Raceway
May	12	Mohawk Series (3yo Open Pace)	14,000	Mohawk Raceway
		Maryland Sire Stake (3yoft)	6,000	Rosecroft Raceway
May	13	les Quebecoises Series (3yocp)	10,000	Blue Bonnets
May	14	New Jersey Sire Stake (3yofp)	115,000	The Meadowlands
May	15	New Jersey Sire Stake (3yoct)	75,000	The Meadowlands
May	17	Scarlet O'Hara Elims (3yofp)	10,000	Scioto Downs
		New Jersey Sire Stake (3yocp)	125,000	The Meadowlands
		New York-Bred Late-Closer (3yo Open Trot)	10,000	Yonkers Raceway
		Kentucky Sire Stake (3yoft)	16,000	The Red Mile
		Maryland Sire Stake (3yofp)	6,000	Rosecroft Raceway
		les Quebecoises Series (3yofp)	10,000	Blue Bonnets
May	18	Graduate Series (Open Pace)	75,000	The Meadowlands
		Hanover & Hempt (3yocp)	75,000	Vernon Downs
		Guys & Dolls Final (Pacing Mares)	60,000	Freehold Raceway
		Battle of Saratoga Series (3-6yo Open Pace)	20,000	Saratoga Raceway
		Maryland Sire Stake (3yocp)	6,000	Rosecroft Raceway
		New York-Bred Late-Closer (3yo Open Pace)	10,000	Yonkers Raceway
May	19	Mohawk Series Final (3yo Open Pace)	75,000	Mohawk Raceway
		les Sportives Elims (Pacing Mares)	15,000	Blue Bonnets
		Ohio Sire Stake (3yofp)	44,000	Raceway Park
		Maryland Standardbred (3yoct)	75,000	Rosecroft Raceway
May	20	les Quebecoises Series (3yocp)	10,000	Blue Bonnets
May	21	New Jersey Sire Stake (3yofp)	115,000	The Meadowlands
May	22	New Jersey Sire Stake (3yoft)	75,000	The Meadowlands

RACE DATES

May	23	Ohio Sire Stake (3yoft)	$38,000	Scioto Downs
May	24	Scarlet O'Hara Final (3yofp)	50,000	Scioto Downs
		les Quebecoises Series Final (3yofp)	40,000	Blue Bonnets
		Kentucky Sire Stake (3yoft)	15,000	The Red Mile
		Maryland Sire Stake (3yofp)	6,000	Rosecroft Raceway
May	25	Currier & Ives (3yoft)	50,000	The Meadows
		New Jersey Classic Elims (3yo Open Pace)	20,000	The Meadowlands
		New York Sire Stake (3yocp)	85,000	Buffalo Raceway
		Kentucky Sire Stake (3yoct)	16,000	The Red Mile
		Maryland Sire Stake (3yocp)	6,000	Rosecroft Raceway
May	26	Currier & Ives (3yo Open Trot)	125,000	The Meadows
		les Sportives Final (Pacing Mares)	50,000	Blue Bonnets
		Grand Prix du Quebec (Aged Pace)	75,000	Quebec Raceway
		Ohio Sire Stake (4&5yo Open Pace)	28,000	Northfield Park
		Maryland Standardbred (3yoft)	75,000	Rosecroft Raceway
May	27	North American Series (3&4yo Open Pace)	25,000	The Red Mile
		Kentucky Sire Stake (3yofp)	16,000	The Red Mile
		Kentucky Sire Stake (3yocp)	16,000	The Red Mile
		les Quebecoises Series Final (3yocp)	40,000	Blue Bonnets
		New Jersey Sire Stake (3yofp)	115,000	The Meadowlands
		Ohio Sire Stake (4&5yo Open Trot)	29,000	Northfield Park
		Ohio Sire Stake (3yocp)	44,000	Scioto Downs
		New York Sire Stake (3yoct)	58,000	Vernon Downs
		Battle of Saratoga Series Final (3-6yo Open Pace)	15,000	Saratoga Raceway
May	29	New Jersey Sire Stake (3yoft)	75,000	The Meadowlands
May	31	Ohio Sire Stake (3yofp)	44,000	Northfield Park
June	1	Turtle Dove (3yofp)	200,000	Rosecroft Raceway
		MacFarlane Memorial (3yofp)	75,000	Hazel Park
		Burlington Elims (3yo Open Pace)	20,000	Greenwood
		New Jersey Classic Final (3yo Open Pace)	500,000	The Meadowlands
		New York Sire Stake (3yofp)	80,000	Buffalo Raceway
June	2	Challenge Stakes (Aged Pace)	150,000	Blue Bonnets
		Ohio Sire Stake (3yoct)	42,000	Raceway Park
		Maryland Sire Stake Final (3yocp)	50,000	Rosecroft Raceway
		Maryland Sire Stake Final (3yofp)	50,000	Rosecroft Raceway
		Maryland Sire Stake Final (3yoft)	50,000	Rosecroft Raceway
		Maryland Sire Stake Final (3yoct)	50,000	Rosecroft Raceway
June	3	Canadian Trotting Classic Elims (3yo Open)	15,000	Greenwood
June	4	New Jersey Sire Stake (3yofp)	100,000	The Meadowlands
June	5	New Jersey Sire Stake (3yoct)	75,000	The Meadowlands
June	6	Ambassador Series (2yocp)	5,000	Rosecroft Raceway
		Battle of Saratoga Series (3-6yo Open Trot)	15,000	Saratoga Raceway
June	7	Castor Elims (3yocp)	15,000	Blue Bonnets
		New York Sire Stake (3yoft)	73,000	Buffalo Raceway
		New Jersey Sire Stake (3yocp)	125,000	The Meadowlands
June	8	Terrapin (3yocp)	300,000	Rosecroft Raceway
		American-National (3yofp)	200,000	Sportsman's Park
		Burlington Final (3yo Open Pace)	175,000	Greenwood

RACE DATES

		Battle of Lake Erie (4&up Inv. Pace)	$100,000	Northfield Park
		Ohio Sire Stake (4&5yo Open Pace)	28,000	Northfield Park
		Ohio Sire Stake (3yocp)	44,000	Northfield Park
		de la Ste. Jean Series (2yofp)	9,000	Blue Bonnets
June	9	W.N. Reynolds Memorial (3yoft)	45,000	Raceway Park
		W.N. Reynolds Memorial (2yofp)	50,000	Raceway Park
		Hanover Filly Stake (2yofp)	50,000	The Meadowlands
		North American Series (3&4yo Pace)	25,000	Blue Bonnets
		Maryland Sire Stake (3yoct)	1,500	Delmarva Downs
		New York-Bred Late-Closer (3yo Open Trot)	10,000	Vernon Downs
		Pennsylvania Sire Stake (3yofp)	60,000	The Meadows
June	10	American-National (3yoft)	175,000	Sportsman's Park
		Canadian Trotting Classic Final (3yo Open Trot)	80,000	Greenwood
June	11	New Jersey Sire Stake (3yoft)	75,000	The Meadowlands
June	12	W.N. Reynolds Memorial (2yoft)	40,000	Raceway Park
		W.N. Reynolds Memorial (2yoct)	45,000	Raceway Park
		Montreal Series (2yocp)	9,000	Blue Bonnets
		New Jersey Sire Stake (3yoct)	75,000	The Meadowlands
June	13	Flamboro Breeders Stake (3yofp)	20,000	Flamboro Downs
		Battle of Saratoga Series (3-6yo Open Trot)	15,000	Saratoga Raceway
		Miss New Jersey Elims (3yofp)	15,000	The Meadowlands
		Ambassador Series (2yocp)	5,000	Rosecroft Raceway
June	14	W.N. Reynolds Memorial (2yocp)	60,000	Raceway Park
		Castor Final (3yocp)	55,000	Blue Bonnets
		New York Sire Stake (3yoct)	75,000	Buffalo Raceway
		Maryland Sire Stake (3yoft)	1,500	Delmarva Downs
		Maryland Standardbred (3yofp)	75,000	Rosecroft Raceway
		New Jersey Sire Stake (3yocp)	125,000	The Meadowlands
June	15	W.N. Reynolds Memorial (3yofp)	55,000	Raceway Park
		W.N. Reynolds Memorial (3yoct)	50,000	Raceway Park
		North America Cup Elims (3yo Open Pace)	50,000	Greenwood
		Lake Superior (Inv. Pace)	100,000	Hazel Park
		de la Ste. Jean Series (2yofp)	9,000	Blue Bonnets
		Maryland Standardbred (3yocp)	75,000	Rosecroft Raceway
		New York-Bred Late-Closer (3yo Open Pace)	10,000	Buffalo Raceway
June	16	W.N. Reynolds Memorial (3yocp)	75,000	Raceway Park
		Hanover Colt Stake (2yocp)	50,000	The Meadowlands
		Maryland Sire Stake (3yoct)	1,500	Delmarva Downs
		New York Sire Stake (3yoft)	55,000	Vernon Downs
		Pennsylvania Sire Stake (3yoct)	50,000	The Meadows
June	17	Tompkins-Geers (3yoft)	50,000	Scioto Downs
		Tompkins-Geers (2yofp)	82,500	Scioto Downs
		American-National (3yoct)	250,000	Sportsman's Park
		Labatts Invitational (Pace)	35,000	Western Fair
June	18	Tompkins-Geers (2yo Open Trot)	60,000	Scioto Downs
		Kindergarten Series (2yocp)	7,500	Greenwood
		New Jersey Sire Stake (3yoft)	100,000	The Meadowlands
June	19	Tompkins-Geers (2yoft)	65,000	Scioto Downs
		Montreal Series (2yocp)	9,000	Blue Bonnets
		New Jersey Sire Stake (3yoct)	100,000	The Meadowlands

RACE DATES

June	20	Tompkins-Geers (2yo Open Pace)	$80,000	Scioto Downs
		Maiden Series (2yofp)	7,500	Greenwood
		Ambassador Series (2yocp)	5,000	Rosecroft Raceway
		Battle of Saratoga Series (2yo Open Pace)	10,000	Saratoga Raceway
		Miss New Jersey Final (3yofp)	175,000	The Meadowlands
		New Jersey Sire Stake (2yocp)	140,000	The Meadowlands
June	21	Tompkins-Geers (3yofp)	50,000	Scioto Downs
		North America Cup Consolation (3yo Open Pace)	50,000	Greenwood
		Battle of Saratoga Series (3-6yo Open Trot)	15,000	Saratoga Raceway
		New York-Bred Late-Closer (3yo Open Trot)	10,000	Buffalo Raceway
		Maryland Sire Stake (3yofp)	1,500	Delmarva Downs
		Maryland Sire Stake (3yoft)	1,500	Delmarva Downs
		New Jersey Sire Stake (3yocp)	100,000	The Meadowlands
June	22	North America Cup Final (3yo Open Pace)	1,000,000	Greenwood
		Tompkins-Geers (3yo Open Pace)	55,000	Scioto Downs
		Tompkins-Geers (3yo Open Trot)	55,000	Scioto Downs
		Driscoll Series (FFA Pace)	50,000	The Meadowlands
		Dexter Cup Elims (3yo Open Trot)	25,000	Yonkers Raceway
		North American Series (3&4yo Open Pace)	25,000	Delmarva Downs
		Maryland Sire Stake (3yocp)	1,500	Delmarva Downs
		de la Ste. Jean Series Final (2yofp)	50,000	Blue Bonnets
		New York-Bred Late-Closer (3yo Open Pace)	10,000	Vernon Downs
June	23	Historic - Debutante (2yofp)	125,000	The Meadowlands
		Titan Cup (FFA Trot)	40,000	The Meadowlands
		Billings Amateur Trot (Open)	10,000	The Meadowlands
		Hanover Filly Stake (3yofp)	30,000	Rosecroft Raceway
		Hopeful Elims (2yocp)	10,000	Buffalo Raceway
		Pennsylvania Sire Stake (3yoft)	50,000	The Meadows
		New York Sire Stake (3yofp)	125,000	Monticello Raceway
		Ohio Sire Stake (4&5yo Open Trot)	29,000	Raceway Park
June	25	Historic - Harriman Cup (2yoct)	120,000	The Meadowlands
		Hall of Fame Amateur Drivers (Open Trot)	15,000	The Meadowlands
		Kindergarten Series (2yocp)	7,500	Greenwood
June	26	Historic - Acorn (2yoft)	115,000	The Meadowlands
		Historic - Coaching Club Trotting Oaks (3yof)	95,000	The Meadowlands
		Montreal Series Final (2yocp)	50,000	Blue Bonnets
		Ohio Sire Stake (2yofp)	51,500	Northfield Park
June	27	Historic - Goshen Cup (2yocp)	150,000	The Meadowlands
		Maiden Series (2yofp)	7,500	Greenwood
		Ambassador Series Final (2yocp)	25,000	Rosecroft Raceway
		Battle of Saratoga Series (2yo Open Pace)	10,000	Saratoga Raceway
June	28	Historic - Ladyship (3yofp)	75,000	The Meadowlands
		Historic - Dickerson Cup (3yoct)	100,000	The Meadowlands
		MacFarlane Memorial (3yoft)	75,000	Hazel Park
		Maryland Sire Stake (3yofp)	1,500	Delmarva Downs
		New York Sire Stake (3yoct)	120,000	Monticello Raceway
		Ohio Sire Stake (3yoft)	38,000	Northfield Park
		Kentucky Sire Stake (3yoct)	16,000	The Red Mile
June	29	Historic - Jersey Cup (3yocp)	100,000	The Meadowlands
		Driscoll Series (FFA Pace)	75,000	The Meadowlands
		Hanover & Hempt (3yoct)	75,000	Vernon Downs
		American-National (3yocp)	375,000	Sportsman's Park
		Dexter Cup Final (3yo Open Trot)	175,000	Yonkers Raceway
		North American (3&4yo Open Pace)	25,000	Yonkers Raceway

RACE DATES

		First Lady Elims (2yofp)	$50,000	Rosecroft Raceway
		Flamboro Breeders Stake (2yocp)	20,000	Flamboro Downs
		Kentucky Sire Stake (3yofp)	16,000	The Red Mile
		Maryland Sire Stake (3yocp)	1,500	Delmarva Downs
June	30	Hopeful Final (2yocp)	200,000	Buffalo Raceway
		Hopeful Consolation (2yocp)	25,000	Buffalo Raceway
		Flamboro Breeders Stake (3yocp)	20,000	Flamboro Downs
		Pennsylvania Sire Stake (3yocp)	60,000	The Meadows
		Ohio Sire Stake (2yoct)	40,000	Raceway Park
July	2	Kindergarten Series (2yocp)	7,500	Greenwood
		New Jersey Sire Stake (2yoct)	60,000	The Meadowlands
		New Jersey Sire Stake (2yofp)	135,000	The Meadowlands
		Ohio Sire Stake (3yoct)	42,000	Scioto Downs
July	3	Flamboro Breeders Stake (3yoct)	20,000	Flamboro Downs
		New Jersey Sire Stake (2yoft)	58,000	The Meadowlands
		New York Sire Stake (3yocp)	80,000	Saratoga Raceway
		Pennsylvania Sire Stake (2yoft)	60,000	The Meadows
		Pennsylvania Sire Stake (3yoft)	60,000	Pocono Downs
		Ohio Sire Stake (2yocp)	55,000	Northfield Park
July	4	Maiden Series (2yofp)	7,500	Greenwood
		New York-Bred Late-Closer (3yo Open Trot)	10,000	Goshen Historic
		New York-Bred Late-Closer (3yo Open Pace)	10,000	Goshen Historic
		New Jersey Sire Stake (2yocp)	140,000	The Meadowlands
		Pennsylvania Sire Stake (2yoct)	60,000	The Meadows
		Pennsylvania Sire Stake (3yofp)	60,000	The Meadows
		Ohio Sire Stake (2yofp)	51,500	Scioto Downs
		Ohio Sire Stake (4&5yo Open Pace)	28,000	Scioto Downs
July	5	Meadowlands Pace Elims (3yo Open Pace)	35,000	The Meadowlands
		Maryland Sire Stake (2yoct)	1,500	Delmarva Downs
		Maryland Sire Stake (2yofcp)	1,500	Delmarva Downs
		Michigan Sire Stake (3yocp)	10,000	Muskegon
		New York Sire Stake County Fair (2yo Open Pace)	3,000	Goshen Historic
		New York Sire Stake County Fair (3yo Open Pace)	3,000	Goshen Historic
		New York Sire Stake County Fair (3yo Open Trot)	3,000	Goshen Historic
		New York Sire Stake County Fair (2yo Open Trot)	3,000	Goshen Historic
		Ohio Sire Stake (3yocp)	44,000	Northfield Park
		Battle of Saratoga Series (2yo Open Pace)	15,000	Saratoga Raceway
July	6	Driscoll Series Final (Open Pace)	200,000	The Meadowlands
		Potomac (2yocp)	300,000	Rosecroft Raceway
		First Lady Final (2yofp)	200,000	Rosecroft Raceway
		Lady Suffolk (3yoft)	75,000	Yonkers Raceway
		Lady Maud (3yofp)	125,000	Yonkers Raceway
		YONKERS TROT ELIMS (3yo Open Trot)	**30,000**	**Yonkers Raceway**
		La Paloma Elims (2yofp)	20,000	Yonkers Raceway
		North American Series (3&4yo Open Pace)	25,000	Vernon Downs
		Landmark (2yocp)	40,000	Goshen Historic
		Landmark (2yofp)	20,000	Goshen Historic
		Landmark (2yoft)	20,000	Goshen Historic
		Landmark (2yoct)	35,000	Goshen Historic
		Maryland Sire Stake (3yofp)	8,000	Delmarva Downs
		Maryland Sire Stake (3yoct)	8,000	Delmarva Downs
		Maryland Sire Stake (3yocp)	8,000	Delmarva Downs
		Maryland Sire Stake (3yoft)	8,000	Delmarva Downs
		Michigan Sire Stake (3yoct)	10,000	Saginaw Harness
		Pennsylvania Sire Stake (2yocp)	65,000	The Meadows
		Kentucky Sire Stake (3yoct)	16,000	Louisville Downs

RACE DATES

July	7	Jazzman (Open Trot)	$100,000	Blue Bonnets
		Hanover Filly Stake (2yoft)	50,000	The Meadowlands
		Landmark (3yoct)	30,000	Goshen Historic
		Landmark (3yocp)	30,000	Goshen Historic
		Landmark (3yoft)	20,000	Goshen Historic
		Landmark (3yofp)	25,000	Goshen Historic
		Billings Amateur Trot (Open)	10,000	Goshen Historic
		Maryland Sire Stake (2yoft)	1,500	Delmarva Downs
		Maryland Sire Stake (2yocp)	1,500	Delmarva Downs
		Pennsylvania Sire Stake (2yofp)	65,000	The Meadows
		Ohio Sire Stake (2yoft)	40,000	Raceway Park
		Ohio Sire Stake (3yoft)	38,000	Raceway Park
July	8	Roses Are Red Series (3&up F&M Pace)	20,000	Greenwood
		Ohio Sire Stake (2yoct)	40,000	Northfield Park
July	9	Kindergarten Series (2yocp)	7,500	Greenwood
		Ville de Trois Rivieres Elims (2yocp)	40,000	Trois Rivieres
		New Jersey Sire Stake (2yoct)	60,000	The Meadowlands
		New Jersey Sire Stake (2yofp)	135,000	The Meadowlands
July	10	American-National (2yofp)	100,000	Sportsman's Park
		New Jersey Sire Stake (2yoft)	58,000	The Meadowlands
July	11	Maiden Series (2yofp)	7,500	Greenwood
		New Jersey Sire Stake (2yocp)	140,000	The Meadowlands
		New York Sire Stake (3yoft)	120,000	Monticello Raceway
July	12	Meadowlands Pace Final (3yo Open Pace)	1,000,000	The Meadowlands
		Col. Wm. Edwards Memorial (3yoct)	45,500	Northfield Park
		Stephen Phillips Memorial (2yofp)	58,000	Northfield Park
		Maryland Sire Stake (2yoct)	1,500	Delmarva Downs
		Maryland Sire Stake (2yofp)	1,500	Delmarva Downs
		Michigan Sire Stake (3yocp)	100,000	Muskegon
		Pennsylvania Sire Stake (3yoct)	60,000	Pocono Downs
		New York-Bred Late-Closer (3yo Open Trot)	10,000	Saratoga Raceway
July	13	**YONKERS TROT FINAL** (3yo Open Trot)	**300,000**	**Yonkers Raceway**
		La Paloma Final (2yofp)	200,000	Yonkers Raceway
		Bronx Filly Pace (3yofp)	125,000	Yonkers Raceway
		Hudson Filly Trot (3yoft)	75,000	Yonkers Raceway
		Sheppard Elims (2yocp)	30,000	Yonkers Raceway
		New York Sire Stake (3yocp)	200,000	Yonkers Raceway
		Hanover & Hempt (3yofp)	75,000	Vernon Downs
		North Randall Park (3yofp)	36,000	Northfield Park
		Maud S (3yoft)	39,000	Northfield Park
		Molson Canadian Pacing Derby Series (3&up Pace)	95,000	Greenwood
		Kentucky Sire Stake (3yoft)	16,000	Louisville Downs
		Maryland Sire Stake (3yocp)	6,000	Rosecroft Raceway
		Michigan Sire Stake (3yoct)	100,000	Saginaw Harness
July	14	Statue of Liberty (Inv. Trot)	250,000	The Meadowlands
		Hanover Colt Stake (2yoct)	50,000	The Meadowlands
		Founders Gold Cup (3yo Open Trot)	150,000	Vernon Downs
		H.K. Devereaux Memorial (2yoft)	38,000	Northfield Park
		Bret Hanover (3yocp)	39,000	Northfield Park
		de la Moisson elims (3yofp)	25,000	Blue Bonnets
		Maryland Sire Stake (2yoft)	1,500	Delmarva Downs
		Maryland Sire Stake (2yocp)	1,500	Delmarva Downs
		Maryland Sire Stake (3yoct)	6,000	Rosecroft Raceway

RACE DATES

July	15	Rainy Day Sweepstakes (2yoct)	$38,000	Northfield Park
		Forest City Stakes (2yocp)	58,500	Northfield Park
		Rose Are Red Series (3&up F&M Pace)	20,000	Greenwood
July	16	Ville de Trois Rivieres Final (2yocp)	120,000	Trois Rivieres
		Ville de Trois Rivieres Consolation (2yocp)	40,000	Trois Rivieres
		Hanover & Hempt (2yoct)	50,000	Vernon Downs
		Kindergarten Series Final (2yocp)	40,000	Greenwood
		New Jersey Sire Stake (2yoct)	60,000	The Meadowlands
		New Jersey Sire Stake (2yofp)	135,000	The Meadowlands
July	17	Hanover & Hempt (2yoft)	45,000	Vernon Downs
		New Jersey Sire Stake (2yoft)	58,000	The Meadowlands
		New York Sire Stake (2yoct)	60,000	Saratoga Raceway
		Kentucky Sire Stake (2yofp)	16,000	Louisville Downs
July	18	Hanover & Hempt (2yofp)	40,000	Vernon Downs
		Maiden Series Final (2yofp)	40,000	Greenwood
July	19	Hanover & Hempt (3yoft)	65,000	Vernon Downs
		Pink Bonnet Elims (2yofp)	10,000	Scioto Downs
		Maryland Standardbred (2yoct)	15,000	Delmarva Downs
		New Jersey Sire Stake (2yocp)	100,000	The Meadowlands
		Ohio Sire Stake (4&5yo Open Trot)	29,000	Northfield Park
		New York Sire Stake (2yofp)	70,000	Saratoga Raceway
July	20	Sheppard Final (2yocp)	400,000	Yonkers Raceway
		Art Rooney Memorial Elims (3yo Open Pace)	35,000	Yonkers Raceway
		Courageous Lady (3yofp)	132,000	Northfield Park
		Hanover Colt Stake (3yocp)	30,000	Rosecroft Raceway
		Molson Canadian Pacing Derby Series (3&up Pace)	95,000	Greenwood
		Budweiser Beacon Course Elims (3yo Open Trot)	15,000	The Meadowlands
		Motor City Elims (3yo Open Pace)	15,000	Hazel Park
		Maryland Standardbred (3yofp)	15,000	Delmarva Downs
		New York Sire Stake (3yofp)	62,000	Vernon Downs
		Kentucky Sire Stake (2yoft)	16,000	Louisville Downs
		Pennsylvania Sire Stake (2yocp)	70,000	Pocono Downs
		Criterium des Poulains (3yocp)	40,000	Quebec Raceway
July	21	Hanover & Hempt (2yocp)	45,000	Vernon Downs
		de la Moisson Final (3yofp)	100,000	Blue Bonnets
		Canadian Juvenile Elims (2yocp)	20,000	Blue Bonnets
		New York Sire Stake (2yocp)	110,000	Monticello Raceway
		Ohio Sire Stake (2yoft)	40,000	Raceway Park
		Maryland Sire Stake (3yoft)	6,000	Rosecroft Raceway
July	22	Roses Are Red Final (3&up F&M Pace)	100,000	Greenwood
July	23	Peter Haughton Memorial Elims (2yoct)	15,000	The Meadowlands
		New Jersey Sire Stake (2yofp)	100,000	The Meadowlands
		la Trifluvienne Elims (2yofp)	20,000	Trois Rivieres
July	24	Merrie Annabelle Elims (2yoft)	15,000	The Meadowlands
		New York Sire Stake (2yoct)	65,000	Buffalo Raceway
		Ohio Sire Stake (2yoct)	40,000	Scioto Downs
July	25	Nat Ray Elims (FFA Trot)	15,000	The Meadowlands
		Summertime Series (3yo Open Pace)	8,000	Greenwood
		New York Sire Stake (2yoft)	65,000	Buffalo Raceway
		New York Sire Stake (3yoft)	68,000	Saratoga Raceway
		Ohio Sire Stake (2yocp)	55,000	Scioto Downs

RACE DATES

Date		Race	Purse	Track
July	26	Pink Bonnet Final (2yofp)	$120,000	Scioto Downs
		Hanover Filly Stake (3yoft)	30,000	Rosecroft Raceway
		Niatross Elims (2yocp)	15,000	The Meadowlands
		Ohio Sire Stake (2yofp)	44,000	Scioto Downs
		New York Sire Stake (2yofp)	75,000	Buffalo Raceway
		Maryland Sire Stake (2yoct)	8,000	Delmarva Downs
		Maryland Sire Stake (2yoft)	8,000	Delmarva Downs
		Maryland Sire Stake (2yocp)	8,000	Delmarva Downs
		Maryland Sire Stake (2yofp)	8,000	Delmarva Downs
July	27	Art Rooney Memorial Final (3yo Open Pace)	500,000	Yonkers Raceway
		Budweiser Beacon Course Final (3yo Open Trot)	400,000	The Meadowlands
		Molson Canadian Pacing Derby Final (3&up Pace)	240,000	Greenwood
		Thomas P. Gaines Memorial (3yo Open Pace)	190,000	Vernon Downs
		Motor City Final (3yo Open Pace)	75,000	Hazel Park
		Criterium des Poulains Final (3yocp)	60,000	Quebec Raceway
		Maryland Sire Stake (3yocp)	6,000	Rosecroft Raceway
		New York Sire Stake (2yocp)	75,000	Buffalo Raceway
		New York-Bred Late-Closer (3yo Open Pace)	10,000	Monticello Raceway
		Pennsylvania Sire Stake (2yofp)	70,000	Pocono Downs
July	28	North American Series Final (3&4yo Open Pace)	75,000	Buffalo Raceway
		Canadian Juvenile Final (2yocp)	80,000	Blue Bonnets
		Frank Ryan Memorial (Aged Pace)	40,000	Rideau Carleton
		Maryland Sire Stake (3yoct)	6,000	Rosecroft Raceway
		Maryland Sire Stake (3yoft)	6,000	Rosecroft Raceway
		Michigan Sire Stake (2yofp)	10,000	Saginaw Harness
July	30	Peter Haughton Memorial Consolation (2yoct)	35,000	The Meadowlands
		Hambletonain Amateur Drivers (Open Trot)	10,000	The Meadowlands
		la Trifluvienne Final (2yofp)	60,000	Trois Rivieres
		la Trifluvienne Consolation (2yofp)	20,000	Trois Rivieres
July	31	Merrie Annabelle Consolation (2yoft)	35,000	The Meadowlands
		Pride of Ohio (3yoft)	60,000	Scioto Downs
		Ohio Fairs (2yoft)	88,000	Scioto Downs
		New York Sire Stake (2yoct)	65,000	Batavia Downs
August	1	Countess Adios (2yofp)	250,000	The Meadowlands
		Tarport Hap (3yofp)	175,000	The Meadowlands
		State Fair Manager's (2yofp)	90,000	Scioto Downs
		Ohio Fairs (2yoct)	60,000	Scioto Downs
		Miss Henson Creek Series (2yofp)	5,000	Rosecroft Raceway
		Summertime Series (3yo Open Pace)	8,000	Greenwood
		New York Sire Stake (2yoft)	65,000	Batavia Downs
August	2	Oliver Wendell Holmes (3yocp)	250,000	The Meadowlands
		Hambletonian Eligibles Inv. (3yo Open Trot)	35,000	The Meadowlands
		Governor's Cup (3yoct)	70,000	Scioto Downs
		Ohio's First Lady (3yofp)	70,000	Scioto Downs
		New York Sire Stake (2yofp)	75,000	Batavia Downs
		New York Sire Stake (3yoct)	70,000	Saratoga Raceway
		Pennsylvania Sire Stake (2yoct)	65,000	Pocono Downs
		Maryland Sire Stake (2yofp)	6,000	Rosecroft Raceway
August	3	**HAMBLETONIAN** (3yo Open Trot)	**1,200,000**	**The Meadowlands**
		Hambletonian Oaks (3yoft)	300,000	The Meadowlands
		Peter Haughton Memorial Final (2yoct)	600,000	The Meadowlands
		Merrie Annabelle Final (2yoft)	450,000	The Meadowlands
		Nat Ray Final (FFA Trot)	200,000	The Meadowlands
		Niatross Final (2yocp)	400,000	The Meadowlands
		American-National (Aged Pace)	150,000	Sportsman's Park

RACE DATES

		Stars & Stripes Trot (Invitational)	$35,000	Yonkers Raceway
		Director of Agriculture (3yocp)	70,000	Scioto Downs
		Buckeye State (2yocp)	100,000	Scioto Downs
		Criterium des Pouliches Elims (3yofp)	35,000	Quebec Raceway
		Battle of Saratoga Series (3-6yo Open Pace)	30,000	Saratoga Raceway
		Maryland Sire Stake (3yofp)	6,000	Rosecroft Raceway
		New York Sire Stake (2yocp)	75,000	Batavia Downs
		New York Sire Stake (4yo Mare Trot)	20,000	Syracuse Mile
		New York Sire Stake (4yo H&G Trot)	20,000	Syracuse Mile
		New York-Bred Late-Closer (2yo Open Pace)	10,000	Syracuse Mile
		Kentucky Sire Stake (2yocp)	16,000	Louisville Downs
August	4	Prix de l'Avenir (2yocp)	600,000	Blue Bonnets
		Maryland Sire Stake (2yoft)	6,000	Rosecroft Raceway
		Maryland Standardbred (3yoft)	75,000	Rosecroft Raceway
		Michigan Sire Stake (2yofp)	100,000	Saginaw Harness
		New York Sire Stake (4yo H&G Pace)	20,000	Syracuse Mile
		New York Sire Stake (4yo Mare Pace)	20,000	Syracuse Mile
		New York-Bred Late-Closer (2yo Open Trot)	10,000	Syracuse Mile
		Elitist Cup Elims (2yo Open Pace)	10,000	Syracuse Mile
August	6	Arden Downs (2yofp)	75,000	The Meadows
		Arden Downs (2yoft)	50,000	The Meadows
		Billings Amateur Trot (Open)	5,000	The Meadows
		New York Sire Stake (2yoct)	100,000	Monticello Raceway
August	7	les Jouvencelles (2yofp)	10,000	Blue Bonnets
August	8	Adioo Volo (3yofp)	150,000	The Meadows
		Arden Downs (2yoct)	50,000	The Meadows
		Sweetheart Elims (2yofp)	15,000	The Meadowlands
		Summertime Series (3yo Open Pace)	8,000	Greenwood
		Miss Henson Creek Series (2yofp)	5,000	Rosecroft Raceway
		Ohio Sire Stake (4&5yo Open Trot)	29,000	Scioto Downs
		New York Sire Stake (2yoft)	52,000	Vernon Downs
August	9	Arden Downs (3yoct)	50,000	The Meadows
		Arden Downs (3yoft)	50,000	The Meadows
		Kentucky Standardbred Sales (2yoft)	200,000	Rosecroft Raceway
		Maryland Sire Stake (2yofp)	6,000	Rosecroft Raceway
		Woodrow Wilson Elims (2yo Open Pace)	25,000	The Meadowlands
		New York Sire Stake (3yofp)	75,000	Saratoga Raceway
		New York-Bred Late-Closer (3yo Open Trot)	10,000	Batavia Downs
		Maryland Standardbred (3yoct)	15,000	Delmarva Downs
		Ohio Sire Stake (2yofp)	51,500	Raceway Park
August	10	Adios (3yo Open Pace)	500,000	The Meadows
		Arden Downs (2yocp)	100,000	The Meadows
		International Trot (Invitational)	450,000	Yonkers Raceway
		U.S. Pacing Championships (Open)	75,000	Sportsman's Park
		Mistletoe Shalee Elims (3yofp)	25,000	The Meadowlands
		Battle of Saratoga Series (3-6yo Open Pace)	30,000	Saratoga Raceway
		Criterium des Pouliches Final (3yofp)	50,000	Quebec Raceway
		New York Sire Stake (3yocp)	85,000	Batavia Downs
		New York-Bred Late-Closer (2yo Open Trot)	10,000	Syracuse Mile
		New York-Bred Late-Closer (2yo Open Pace)	10,000	Syracuse Mile
		Maryland Standardbred (2yocp)	15,000	Delmarva Downs
		Maryland Sire Stake (3yofp)	6,000	Rosecroft Raceway
		Ohio Sire Stake (3yoct)	42,000	Northfield Park
		Flamboro Breeders Stake (2yofp)	20,000	Flamboro Downs
		Kentucky Sire Stake (2yofp)	16,000	Louisville Downs

RACE DATES

Date	Race	Purse	Track
August 11	Nat Christie Memorial (3yo Open Pace)	$150,000	Stampede Park
	Hanover Colt Stake (3yoct)	30,000	Rosecroft Raceway
	Ohio Sire Stake (2yoct)	40,000	Raceway Park
	Ohio Sire Stake (2yocp)	55,000	Raceway Park
	Maryland Sire Stake (2yoft)	6,000	Rosecroft Raceway
	Elitist Cup Final (2yo Open Pace)	100,000	Syracuse Mile
	New York Sire Stake (3yoct)	62,000	Syracuse Mile
	New York Sire Stake (3yoft)	56,000	Syracuse Mile
August 12	les Jouvenceaux Series (2yocp)	10,000	Blue Bonnets
August 14	Review Stake - The Greyhound (2yo Open Trot)	125,000	Springfield, IL
	Review Stake - The Little Pat (2yo Open Pace)	100,000	Springfield, IL
	Review Stake - The Castleton (2yofp)	85,000	Springfield, IL
	Review Stake - The Castleton (2yoft)	80,000	Springfield, IL
	les Jouvencelles Final (2yofp)	60,000	Blue Bonnets
	Ohio Sire Stake (2yoft)	40,000	Scioto Downs
August 15	Review Stake (3yo Open Pace)	70,000	Springfield, IL
	Review Stake - The Castleton (3yoft)	60,000	Springfield, IL
	Review Stake - The Castleton (3yofp)	65,000	Springfield, IL
	Summertime Series Final (3yo Open Pace)	30,000	Greenwood
	Miss Henson Creek Series (2yofp)	5,000	Rosecroft Raceway
August 16	Woodrow Wilson Final (2yo Open Pace)	1,000,000	The Meadowlands
	Woodrow Wilson Consolation (2yo Open Pace)	50,000	The Meadowlands
	Sweetheart Final (2yofp)	750,000	The Meadowlands
	Sweetheart Consolation (2yofp)	50,000	The Meadowlands
	Mistletoe Shalee Final (3yofp)	400,000	The Meadowlands
	Mistletoe Shalee Consolation (3yofp)	35,000	The Meadowlands
	U.S. Pacing Championships (Open)	75,000	The Meadowlands
	Review Stake - Alexander Mem. (3yo Open Trot)	115,000	Springfield, IL
	New Jersey Sire Stake (2yoft)	100,000	The Meadowlands
	New Jersey Sire Stake (2yoct)	100,000	The Meadowlands
	New Jersey Futurity (2yo Open Pace)	100,000	Freehold Raceway
	New York Sire Stake (3yofp)	71,000	Syracuse Mile
	New York Sire Stake (2yoft)	46,000	Syracuse Mile
	New York Sire Stake (2yofp)	66,000	Syracuse Mile
	Pennsylvania Sire Stake (2yoft)	65,000	Pocono Downs
	Maryland Standardbred (3yoct)	75,000	Rosecroft Raceway
	Ohio Sire Stake (2yofp)	51,500	Scioto Downs
August 17	Maple Leaf Trot (3&up Open)	250,000	Greenwood
	CANE PACE ELIMS (3yo Open Pace)	**35,000**	**Yonkers Raceway**
	Battle of Saratoga Series (3-6yo Open Pace)	30,000	Saratoga Raceway
	New York-Bred Late-Closer (3yo Open Pace)	10,000	Batavia Downs
	New York Sire Stake (2yocp)	64,000	Syracuse Mile
	New York Sire Stake (2yoct)	44,000	Syracuse Mile
	New Jersey Sire Stake (3yofp)	100,000	Freehold Raceway
	Ohio Sire Stake (3yoft)	38,000	Northfield Park
	Maryland Standardbred (3yocp)	75,000	Rosecroft Raceway
	Kentucky Sire Stake (2yocp)	16,000	Louisville Downs
August 18	Prix d'Ete Molson (3yocp)	750,000	Blue Bonnets
	Zweig Memorial (3yo Open Trot)	200,000	Syracuse Mile
	Zweig Memorial Filly Division (3yoft)	25,000	Syracuse Mile
	New York Sire Stake (3yocp)	90,000	Syracuse Mile
	New Jersey Sire Stake (3yocp)	110,000	Freehold Raceway
	Ohio Sire Stake (3yocp)	44,000	Raceway Park
	Ohio Sire Stake (2yocp)	55,000	Raceway Park
	Maryland Sire Stake (2yoct)	6,000	Rosecroft Raceway
	Maryland Sire Stake (2yocp)	6,000	Rosecroft Raceway

RACE DATES

August	19	les Jouvenceaux Series (2yocp)	$10,000	Blue Bonnets
		Ohio Sire Stake (2yoct)	40,000	Northfield Park
August	20	New Jersey Futurity (2yo Open Trot)	50,000	Freehold Raceway
August	21	Parshall Memorial (2yo Open Trot)	15,000	Greenville, OH
		Parshall Memorial (3yo Open Pace)	7,000	Greenville, OH
		New York-Bred Late-Closer (2yo Open Trot)	10,000	Batavia Downs
		New Jersey Futurity (3yo Open Trot)	50,000	Freehold Raceway
		Ohio Sire Stake (2yoft)	40,000	Northfield Park
August	22	Hoosier Futurity (2yocp)	25,000	Indianapolis, IN
		Hoosier Futurity (2yofp)	25,000	Indianapolis, IN
		Horseman Futurity (3yofp)	21,000	Indianapolis, IN
		Parshall Memorial (2yo Open Pace)	15,000	Greenville, OH
		Parshall Memorial (3yo Open Trot)	7,000	Greenville, OH
		Miss Henson Creek Final (2yofp)	25,000	Rosecroft Raceway
		New York Sire Stake (3yoft)	72,000	Batavia Downs
		New York Sire Stake (2yoft)	100,000	Monticello Raceway
		Ohio Sire Stake (3yoct)	42,000	Scioto Downs
August	23	Hoosier Futurity (2yoft)	24,000	Indianapolis, IN
		Horseman Futurity (3yoft)	21,000	Indianapolis, IN
		Horseman Stake (2yo Open Trot)	70,000	Indianapolis, IN
		Provenzano Memorial Elims (Open Trot)	10,000	Batavia Downs
		Maryland Standardbred (2yoft)	15,000	Delmarva Downs
		Maryland Standardbred (3yoft)	15,000	Delmarva Downs
		Ohio Sire Stake (2yofp)	51,500	Northfield Park
		New York-Bred Late-Closer (2yo Open Pace)	10,000	Saratoga Raceway
		New York Sire Stake (2yofp)	61,000	Vernon Downs
August	24	**CANE PACE FINAL (3yo Open Pace)**	**500,000**	**Yonkers Raceway**
		U.S. Pacing Championships Final (Open)	125,000	Yonkers Raceway
		Fox Stake (2yo Open Pace)	175,000	Indianapolis, IN
		Horseman Futurity (3yo Open Trot)	35,000	Indianapolis, IN
		Horseman Futurity (3yo Open Pace)	32,000	Indianapolis, IN
		Hoosier Futurity (2yoct)	25,000	Indianapolis, IN
		Garden State Stake (2yo Open Pace)	370,000	Freehold Raceway
		MacFarlane Memorial (3yo Open Trot)	125,000	Hazel Park
		Fan Hanover Elims (3yofp)	20,000	Greenwood
		Kentucky Pacing Derby Elims (2yo Open Pace)	TBA	Louisville Downs
		Kentucky Sire Stake (2yoct)	16,000	Louisville Downs
		Battle of Saratoga Series Final (3-6yo Open Pace)	50,000	Saratoga Raceway
		New York Sire Stake (3yofp)	80,000	Batavia Downs
		New York Sire Stake (2yocp)	61,000	Vernon Downs
		Maryland Standardbred (2yofp)	15,000	Delmarva Downs
		Maryland Standardbred (3yocp)	15,000	Delmarva Downs
		Maryland Standardbred (3yofp)	75,000	Rosecroft Raceway
		Pennsylvania Sire Stake (3yocp)	65,000	Pocono Downs
		Ohio Sire Stake (2yocp)	55,000	Scioto Downs
August	25	Confederation Cup (3yo Open Pace)	350,000	Flamboro Downs
		Lou Babic Memorial Elims (2yofp)	10,000	Freehold Raceway
		New York Sire Stake (3yocp)	130,000	Monticello Raceway
		Ohio Sire Stake (4&5yo Open Pace)	28,000	Raceway Park
		Maryland Sire Stake (2yocp)	6,000	Rosecroft Raceway
		Maryland Sire Stake (2yoct)	6,000	Rosecroft Raceway
August	26	les Jouvenceaux Final (2yocp)	60,000	Blue Bonnets
August	27	New York Sire Stake (2yoct)	50,000	Vernon Downs

RACE DATES

August	28	New Jersey Sire Stake (2yoct)	$50,000	Freehold Raceway
		New York Sire Stake (2yoft)	62,000	Saratoga Raceway
		Ohio Sire Stake (2yoft)	40,000	Scioto Downs
August	29	Hayes Memorial (3yofp)	60,000	Du Quoin, IL
		Hayes Memorial (3yo Open Pace)	60,000	Du Quoin, IL
		Battle of Saratoga Series (3-6yo Open Trot)	12,500	Saratoga Raceway
August	30	World Filly Trotting Derby (3yoft)	125,000	Du Quoin, IL
		Hayes Memorial (2yofp)	75,000	Du Quoin, IL
		Hayes Memorial (2yoft)	90,000	Du Quoin, IL
		Fan Hanover Final (3yofp)	120,000	Greenwood
		Charles Smith Memorial Elims (3yo Open Trot)	10,000	Freehold Raceway
		New York Sire Stake (3yoct)	110,000	Batavia Downs
		New York Sire Stake (2yofp)	75,000	Monticello Raceway
		Kentucky Sire Stake (2yoft)	16,000	Louisville Downs
		Pennsylvania Sire Stake (2yoft)	60,000	The Meadows
August	31	World Trotting Derby (3yo Open Trot)	550,000	Du Quoin, IL
		Hayes Memorial (2yoct)	90,000	Du Quoin, IL
		Hayes Memorial (2yocp)	100,000	Du Quoin, IL
		Kentucky Pacing Derby Final (2yo Open Pace)	400,000	Louisville Downs
		Kentucky Sire Stake (3yocp)	16,000	Louisville Downs
		James B. Dancer Memorial (3yo Open Pace)	380,000	Freehold Raceway
		Lady Baltimore (2yofp)	200,000	Rosecroft Raceway
		MESSENGER STAKES ELIMS (3yocp)	**90,000**	**Rosecroft Raceway**
		Provenzano Memorial Final (Open Trot)	50,000	Batavia Downs
		Provenzano Memorial Consolation (Open Trot)	10,000	Batavia Downs
		Pennsylvania Sire Stake (2yocp)	65,000	The Meadows
		Ohio Sire Stake Final (2yofp)	100,000	Scioto Downs
		New York Sire Stake (3yofp)	200,000	Yonkers Raceway
September	1	Simcoe Stakes (3yo Open Pace)	180,000	Mohawk Raceway
		Champlain Stakes (2yo Open Pace)	260,000	Mohawk Raceway
		Lou Babic Memorial Final (2yofp)	100,000	Freehold Raceway
		Pennsylvania Sire Stake (2yoct)	60,000	The Meadows
		New York-Bred Late-Closer (3yo Open Trot)	30,000	Monticello Raceway
		Kentucky Sire Stake (3yofp)	16,000	Louisville Downs
September	2	Simcoe Stakes (3yoft)	165,000	Mohawk Raceway
		Helen Dancer Memorial (3yofp)	200,000	Freehold Raceway
		New York-Bred Late-Closer (2yo Open Pace)	10,000	Batavia Downs
		New York-Bred Late-Closer (3yo Open Pace)	30,000	Saratoga Raceway
		New York Sire Stake (2yocp)	70,000	Saratoga Raceway
		New York Sire Stake (3yocp)	77,000	Vernon Downs
		New York Sire Stake (3yoft)	200,000	Yonkers Raceway
		Pennsylvania Sire Stake (2yofp)	65,000	The Meadows
		Ohio Sire Stake Final (2yocp)	100,000	Northfield Park
		Ohio Sire Stake Final (3yoft)	100,000	Scioto Downs
		Ohio Sire Stake Final (2yoct)	100,000	Scioto Downs
		Ohio Sire Stake (3yofp)	44,000	Scioto Downs
		Maryland Sire Stake (2yocp)	50,000	Rosecroft Raceway
		Maryland Sire Stake (2yoct)	50,000	Rosecroft Raceway
		Maryland Sire Stake (2yofp)	50,000	Rosecroft Raceway
		Maryland Sire Stake (2yoft)	50,000	Rosecroft Raceway
		Maryland Sire Stake (3yocp)	50,000	Rosecroft Raceway
		Maryland Sire Stake (3yoct)	50,000	Rosecroft Raceway
		Maryland Sire Stake (3yofp)	50,000	Rosecroft Raceway
		Maryland Sire Stake (3yoft)	50,000	Rosecroft Raceway
September	3	Champlain Stakes (2yoft)	225,000	Mohawk Raceway
		New York Sire Stake (2yoct)	150,000	Yonkers Raceway

RACE DATES

Date	Race	Purse	Track
September 4	New Jersey Sire Stake (2yoct)	$50,000	Freehold Raceway
	New Jersey Sire Stake (3yoft)	50,000	Garden State Park
	Ohio Sire Stake Final (2yoft)	100,000	Northfield Park
	New York-Bred Late-Closer (2yo Open Trot)	10,000	Saratoga Raceway
	New York Sire Stake (2yoft)	150,000	Yonkers Raceway
September 5	Battle of Saratoga Series (3-6yo Open Trot)	12,500	Saratoga Raceway
September 6	Simcoe Stakes (3yo Open Trot)	180,000	Mohawk Raceway
	Champlain Stakes (2yofp)	225,000	Mohawk Raceway
	Charles Smith Memorial Final (3yo Open Trot)	150,000	Freehold Raceway
	Ohio Sire Stake Final (4&5yo Open Trot)	85,000	Northfield Park
	New York Sire Stake (2yofp)	150,000	Yonkers Raceway
September 7	**MESSENGER STAKES FINAL** (3yocp)	**350,000**	**Rosecroft Raceway**
	Kentucky Standardbred Sales (2yofp)	250,000	Rosecroft Raceway
	Champlain Stakes (2yo Open Trot)	255,000	Mohawk Raceway
	Simcoe Stakes (3yofp)	165,000	Mohawk Raceway
	Little Brown Jug Preview (3yo Open Pace)	180,000	Scioto Downs
	Hanover Stake (Aged Pace)	20,000	Rosecroft Raceway
	New Jersey Sire Stake (2yocp)	120,000	Freehold Raceway
	New Jersey Sire Stake (2yofp)	115,000	Garden State Park
	New York Sire Stake (3yoct)	200,000	Yonkers Raceway
	New York Sire Stake (2yocp)	150,000	Yonkers Raceway
	Kentucky Sire Stake (2yoct)	16,000	Louisville Downs
September 8	Nassagaweya (2yo Open Pace)	250,000	Mohawk Raceway
	Des Smith Classic (Aged Pace)	40,000	Rideau Carleton
	New Jersey Futurity (3yo Open Pace)	75,000	Freehold Raceway
	Michigan Sire Stake (3yofp)	10,000	Jackson Raceway
September 9	American-National (2yoct)	100,000	Sportsman's Park
September 10	American-National (2yoft)	100,000	Sportsman's Park
	New Jersey Sire Stake (2yoct)	50,000	Garden State Park
September 11	Billings Amateur Trot (Open)	5,000	Garden State Park
	New Jersey Sire Stake (3yoft)	65,000	Garden State Park
September 12	Flamboro Breeders Stake (3yoft)	20,000	Flamboro Downs
	New Jersey Sire Stake (2yoft)	45,000	Garden State Park
	Pennsylvania Sire Stake (2yoft)	15,000	The Meadows
September 13	MacFarlane Memorial (3yo Open Pace)	200,000	Hazel Park
	Battle of Saratoga Series (3-6yo Open Trot)	15,000	Saratoga Raceway
	New Jersey Sire Stake (3yoct)	65,000	Freehold Raceway
	New Jersey Sire Stake (2yocp)	120,000	Garden State Park
	Pennsylvania Sire Stake Early-Closer (2yoct)	15,000	The Meadows
	Ohio Sire Stake Final (3yofp)	100,000	Northfield Park
	Maryland Standardbred (2yoft)	75,000	Rosecroft Raceway
	Maryland Standardbred (2yoct)	75,000	Rosecroft Raceway
September 14	Metro Elims (2yo Open Pace)	35,000	Mohawk Raceway
	Nadia Lobell Elims (3yofp)	15,000	Garden State Park
	New Jersey Sire Stake (2yofp)	115,000	Freehold Raceway
	Michigan Sire Stake (2yoct)	10,000	Jackson Raceway
	Pennsylvania Sire Stake Early-Closer (2yocp)	15,000	The Meadows
	Kentucky Sire Stake (2yoct)	16,000	The Red Mile
	Maryland Standardbred (2yofp)	75,000	Rosecroft Raceway
	Maryland Standardbred (2yocp)	75,000	Rosecroft Raceway
	Ohio Sire Stake Final (4&5yo Open Pace)	75,000	Scioto Downs
	New York Sire Stake (2yocp)	200,000	Yonkers Raceway

RACE DATES

	New York Sire Stake (2yoct)	$200,000	Yonkers Raceway
	New York Sire Stake (2yofp)	200,000	Yonkers Raceway
	New York Sire Stake (2yoft)	200,000	Yonkers Raceway
	New York Sire Stake (3yocp)	200,000	Yonkers Raceway
	New York Sire Stake (3yoct)	200,000	Yonkers Raceway
	New York Sire Stake (3yofp)	200,000	Yonkers Raceway
	New York Sire Stake (3yoft)	200,000	Yonkers Raceway
September 15	Senior Jug (4&5yo Open Pace)	50,000	Delaware, OH
	Ohio Breeders Championship (2yofp)	70,000	Delaware, OH
	Campbellville (2yo Open Trot)	150,000	Mohawk Raceway
	Michigan Sire Stake (3yofp)	100,000	Jackson Raceway
	Pennsylvania Sire Stake Early-Closer (2yofp)	15,000	The Meadows
	New York-Bred Late Closer (2yo Open Pace)	10,000	Monticello Raceway
	Kentucky Sire Stake (2yofp)	16,000	The Red Mile
September 16	Ohio Breeders Championship (2yoct)	65,000	Delaware, OH
	Ohio Breeders Championship (2yoft)	60,000	Delaware, OH
	Ohio Breeders Championship (3yoft)	50,000	Delaware, OH
	Ohio Breeders Championship (4&5yo Open Pace)	25,000	Delaware, OH
September 17	Standardbred (2yo Open Trot)	100,000	Delaware, OH
	Standardbred (2yoft)	75,000	Delaware, OH
	Ohio Breeders Championship (4&5yo Open Trot)	25,000	Delaware, OH
	Ohio Breeders Championship (3yoct)	50,000	Delaware, OH
	Michigan Sire Stake (3yoft)	10,000	Hazel Park
	New York-Bred Late-Closer (2yo Open Trot)	10,000	Monticello Raceway
	Kentucky Sire Stake (2yoft)	16,000	The Red Mile
September 18	Jugette (3yofp)	400,000	Delaware, OH
	Old Oaken Bucket (3yo Open Trot)	110,000	Delaware, OH
	Standardbred (2yofp)	100,000	Delaware, OH
	Ohio Breeders Championship (2yo Open Pace)	90,000	Delaware, OH
	Billings Amateur Trot (Open)	5,000	Delaware, OH
	New Jersey Sire Stake (2yoct)	60,000	Garden State Park
September 19	**LITTLE BROWN JUG** (3yo Open Pace)	**800,000**	**Delaware, OH**
	Standardbred (2yo Open Pace)	150,000	Delaware, OH
	Buckette (3yoft)	60,000	Delaware, OH
	Ohio Breeders Championship (3yocp)	48,000	Delaware, OH
	Ohio Breeders Championship (3yofp)	50,000	Delaware, OH
	Pensylvania Sire Stake Early-Closer (2yoft)	70,000	The Meadows
September 20	Charles Smith Memorial Elims (3yoft)	10,000	Freehold Raceway
	Milton Elims (3&up F&M Pace)	20,000	Mohawk Raceway
	New Jersey Sire Stake (2yocp)	120,000	Garden State Park
	Michigan Sire Stake (2yocp)	10,000	Hazel Park
	Pennsylvania Sire Stake Early-Closer (2yoct)	70,000	The Meadows
	New York Sire Stake County Fair (2yo Open Trot)	7,500	Saratoga Raceway
September 21	Metro Final (2yo Open Pace)	750,000	Mohawk Raceway
	Nadia Lobell Final (3yofp)	200,000	Garden State Park
	American-National (2yocp)	120,000	Sportsman's Park
	Michigan Sire Stake (2yoct)	100,000	Jackson Raceway
	Pensylvania Sire Stake Early-Closer (2yocp)	70,000	The Meadows
	Kentucky Sire Stake (2yocp)	16,000	The Red Mile
	New York Sire Stake County Fair (2yo Open Pace)	7,500	Vernon Downs
September 22	Molly Pitcher (2yofp)	180,000	Freehold Raceway
	Mohawk Gold Cup Elims (3&up Pace)	25,000	Mohawk Raceway
	Pennsylvania Sire Stake Early-Closer (2yofp)	70,000	The Meadows
	New York Sire Stake County Fair (3yo Open Pace)	7,500	Monticello Raceway

RACE DATES

Date	Race	Purse	Location
	Michigan Sire Stake (2yoft)	$10,000	Muskegon
September 23	Bloomsburg Stake (2yoct)	6,700	Bloomsburg, PA
	Bloomsburg Stake (3yoct)	6,000	Bloomsburg, PA
	New York Sire Stake County Fair (3yo Open Trot)	7,500	Batavia Downs
September 24	Bluegrass (2yofp)	135,000	The Red Mile
	Lexington (2yoct)	10,000	The Red Mile
	Frank Ervin (2yoft)	10,000	The Red Mile
	Bloomsburg Stake (3yoft)	5,600	Bloomsburg, PA
	Bloomsburg Stake (3yocp)	7,300	Bloomsburg, PA
	Bloomsburg Stake (2yoft)	6,000	Bloomsburg, PA
	Bloomsburg Stake (2yofp)	8,100	Bloomsburg, PA
	Michigan Sire Stake (3yoft)	100,000	Hazel Park
September 25	Bluegrass (2yoft)	100,000	The Red Mile
	Herald-Leader (3&4yo F&M Pace)	8,000	The Red Mile
	Rosalind (3&4yo F&M Trot)	6,000	The Red Mile
	Billy Direct (3yocp)	10,000	The Red Mile
	Harold Dancer Memorial Elims (2yoct)	7,500	Garden State Park
	Bloomsburg Stake (3yofp)	6,800	Bloomsburg, PA
	Bloomsburg Stake (2yocp)	6,500	Bloomsburg, PA
	Flamboro Breeders Stake (2yoct)	20,000	Flamboro Downs
	New Jersey Sire Stake (2yoft)	50,000	Freehold Raceway
September 26	Bluegrass (2yoct)	100,000	The Red Mile
	Bluegrass (3yofp)	115,000	The Red Mile
	Peter Manning (3&4yo Trot)	8,500	The Red Mile
	Guiding Beam (2yofp)	8,000	The Red Mile
	Camp Collier (3yo Open Trot)	12,000	The Red Mile
	American-National (Aged Trot)	100,000	Sportsman's Park
September 27	Bluegrass (3yoft)	100,000	The Red Mile
	Bluegrass (3yoct)	100,000	The Red Mile
	Peninsula Farm (2yocp)	7,500	The Red Mile
	Charles Smith Memorial Final (3yoft)	100,000	Freehold Raceway
	New Jersey Sire Stake (3yofp)	100,000	Garden State Park
	Michigan Sire Stake (2yocp)	100,000	Hazel Park
	New York-Vermont Colt Stake (3yocp)	5,000	Saratoga Raceway
	New York-Bred Late Closer (2yo Open Pace)	30,000	Yonkers Raceway
	New York-Bred Late Closer (2yo Open Trot)	30,000	Yonkers Raceway
September 28	Bluegrass (2yocp)	150,000	The Red Mile
	Tattersalls (3yo Open Pace)	150,000	The Red Mile
	Hill Farm (2yo Open Pace)	12,500	The Red Mile
	Meadow Skipper (3yo Open Pace)	15,000	The Red Mile
	Milton Final (3&up F&M Pace)	100,000	Mohawk Raceway
	New Jersey Sire Stake (3yocp)	100,000	Garden State Park
	Ohio Sire Stake Final (3yoct)	100,000	Lebanon Raceway
September 29	Mohawk Gold Cup Final (3&up Pace)	100,000	Mohawk Raceway
	Lou Babic Memorial Elims (2yo Open Pace)	15,000	Freehold Raceway
	Michigan Sire Stake (2yoft)	100,000	Muskegon
October 1	International Stallion Stake (2yofp)	135,000	The Red Mile
	Kerry Way (3&4yo Trot)	7,500	The Red Mile
	Stable of Memories (3&4yo F&M Pace)	8,000	The Red Mile
	New Jersey Sire Stake (2yoft)	45,000	Garden State Park
October 2	International Stallion Stake (2yoft)	100,000	The Red Mile
	Bret Hanover (3&up Pace)	50,000	The Red Mile
	Hunterton Farm (2yofp)	7,500	The Red Mile

RACE DATES

		Harold Dancer Memorial Final (2yoct)	$150,000	Garden State Park
		New Jersey Sire Stake (3yoct)	65,000	Freehold Raceway
October	3	Glen Garnsey Memorial (3yofp)	120,000	The Red Mile
		International Stallion Stake (2yoct)	150,000	The Red Mile
		Speedy Scot (3&up Trot)	50,000	The Red Mile
		Fayette County (3yo Open Pace)	10,000	The Red Mile
October	4	**KENTUCKY FUTURITY** (3yo Open Trot)	**175,000**	**The Red Mile**
		Kentucky Futurity Filly (3yoft)	85,000	The Red Mile
		Bluegrass (3yocp)	110,000	The Red Mile
		International Stallion Stake (2yocp)	175,000	The Red Mile
		Clearview (2yo Open Pace)	12,500	The Red Mile
		Greyhound (3yo Open Trot)	10,000	The Red Mile
		New Jersey Sire Stake (3yoft)	65,000	Freehold Raceway
		Maryland Standardbred (2yofp)	75,000	Rosecroft Raceway
		Night of Champions (2yocp)	15,000	Northfield Park
		Night of Champions (2yoct)	15,000	Northfield Park
		Night of Champions (2yofp)	15,000	Northfield Park
		Night of Champions (2yoft)	15,000	Northfield Park
		Night of Champions (3yocp)	15,000	Northfield Park
		Night of Champions (3yoct)	15,000	Northfield Park
		Night of Champions (3yofp)	15,000	Northfield Park
		Night of Champions (3yoft)	15,000	Northfield Park
October	5	Western Canada Pacing Derby (3yo Open)	150,000	Northlands Park
		Breeders Crown Elims (Aged Mare Trot)	**TBA**	**The Meadows**
		Breeders Crown Elims (Aged Mare Pace)	**TBA**	**The Meadows**
		Breeders Crown Elims (Aged H&G Trot)	**TBA**	**The Meadows**
		Breeders Crown Elims (Aged H&G Pace)	**TBA**	**The Meadows**
		Three Diamonds Elims (2yofp)	12,500	Garden State Park
		New Jersey Sire Stake (3yofp)	115,000	Freehold Raceway
		Ohio Sire Stake Final (3yocp)	100,000	Lebanon Raceway
		Maryland Sire Stake (2yocp)	6,000	Rosecroft Raceway
October	6	Lou Babic Memorial Final (2yo Open Pace)	230,000	Freehold Raceway
		Maryland Sire Stake (2yoct)	6,000	Rosecroft Raceway
		Maryland Sire Stake (2yoft)	6,000	Rosecroft Raceway
October	8	Harold Dancer Memorial Elims (2yoft)	5,000	Garden State Park
October	10	Flamboro Breeders Stake (2yoft)	20,000	Flamboro Downs
October	11	**Breeders Crown Final** (Aged Mare Trot)	**300,000**	**The Meadows**
		Breeders Crown Final (Aged Mare Pace)	**300,000**	**The Meadows**
		Breeders Crown Final (Aged H&G Trot)	**400,000**	**The Meadows**
		Breeders Crown Final (Aged H&G Pace)	**400,000**	**The Meadows**
		Battle of Saratoga Series (3yo Open Pace)	12,500	Saratoga Raceway
		New Jersey Sire Stake (3yocp)	110,000	Garden State Park
		Maryland Sire Stake (2yofp)	6,000	Rosecroft Raceway
October	12	Three Diamonds Final (2yofp)	400,000	Garden State Park
		Cleveland Classic (3yo Open Pace)	300,000	Northfield Park
		Colonial (3yo Open Trot)	225,000	Rosecroft Raceway
		Colonial Filly (3yoft)	125,000	Rosecroft Raceway
		Maryland Standardbred (2yocp)	75,000	Rosecroft Raceway
		Abraham Lincoln (2yo Open Pace)	130,000	Maywood Park
October	13	Harvest (2yofp)	150,000	Mohawk Raceway
		New Jersey Sire Stake (2yofp)	115,000	Freehold Raceway
		Maryland Standardbred (2yoct)	75,000	Rosecroft Raceway
		Maryland Sire Stake (2yoft)	6,000	Rosecroft Raceway

RACE DATES

October	14	Autumn (2yoft)	$100,000	Mohawk Raceway
		Octoberfest Elims (3&4yo Pace)	7,500	Northville Downs
October	15	Harold Dancer Memorial (2yoft)	100,000	Garden State Park
October	18	**Breeders Crown Elims** (3yofp)	**TBA**	**Pompano Park**
		Breeders Crown Elims (3yoft)	**TBA**	**Pompano Park**
		Breeders Crown Elims (2yoct)	**TBA**	**Pompano Park**
		Breeders Crown Elims (2yoft)	**TBA**	**Pompano Park**
		New Jersey Sire Stake (3yoct)	65,000	Garden State Park
		Maryland Sire Stake (2yofp)	6,000	Rosecroft Raceway
		Battle of Saratoga Series (3yo Open Pace)	12,500	Saratoga Raceway
October	19	**Breeders Crown Elims** (3yoct)	**TBA**	**Pompano Park**
		Breeders Crown Elims (2yocp)	**TBA**	**Pompano Park**
		Breeders Crown Elims (2yofp)	**TBA**	**Pompano Park**
		Breeders Crown Elims (3yocp)	**TBA**	**Pompano Park**
		Northlands Filly Stake (3yofp)	100,000	Northlands Park
		New Jersey Sire Stake (2yocp)	60,000	Freehold Raceway
		New Jersey Sire Stake (2yofp)	60,000	Garden State Park
		Maryland Sire Stake (2yocp)	6,000	Rosecroft Raceway
October	20	New Jersey Sire Stake (3yoft)	60,000	Freehold Raceway
		Maryland Standardbred (2yoft)	75,000	Rosecroft Raceway
		Maryland Sire Stake (2yoct)	6,000	Rosecroft Raceway
		Michigan Sire Stake (4yo H&G Trot)	TBA	Sports Creek
October	21	Octoberfest Final (3&4yo Open Pace)	22,500	Northville Downs
October	23	New Jersey Sire Stake (2yoft)	60,000	Freehold Raceway
October	25	**Breeders Crown Final** (3yoct)	**350,000**	**Pompano Park**
		Breeders Crown Final (2yofp)	**360,000**	**Pompano Park**
		Breeders Crown Final (3yofp)	**300,000**	**Pompano Park**
		Breeders Crown Final (3yoft)	**330,000**	**Pompano Park**
		Breeders Crown Final (3yocp)	**360,000**	**Pompano Park**
		Breeders Crown Final (2yocp)	**450,000**	**Pompano Park**
		Breeders Crown Final (2yoft)	**300,000**	**Pompano Park**
		Breeders Crown Final (2yoct)	**300,000**	**Pompano Park**
		New Jersey Sire Stake (3yoct)	60,000	Garden State Park
October	26	Sewart Fraser Memorial (Open Pace)	200,000	Northlands Park
		Battle of Saratoga Series Final (3yo Open Pace)	15,000	Saratoga Harness
October	27	New Jersey Sire Stake (3yocp)	60,000	Freehold Raceway
		Maryland Sire Stake (2yoft)	50,000	Rosecroft Raceway
		Maryland Sire Stake (2yoct)	50,000	Rosecroft Raceway
		Maryland Sire Stake (2yofp)	50,000	Rosecroft Raceway
		Maryland Sire Stake (2yocp)	50,000	Rosecroft Raceway
		Michigan Sire Stake (4H&G Trot)	100,000	Sports Creek
November	1	Matron Stakes Elims (3yo Open Trot)	TBA	Pompano Park
		Ron Hodge Memorial (3yo Open Pace)	20,000	Northville Downs
		Battle of Saratoga Series (Pacing Mares)	10,000	Saratoga Raceway
November	2	Matron Stakes Elims (2yofp)	TBA	Pompano Park
		Presidential Elims (2yo Open Pace)	75,000	Rosecroft Raceway
		New Jersey Sire Stake (3yofp)	60,000	Garden State Park
		Michigan Sire Stake (4yo Mare Trot)	5,000	Northville Downs
November	3	Michigan Sire Stake (4yo Mare Pace)	TBA	Sports Creek

RACE DATES

Date	Event	Purse	Track
November 6	Goldsmith Maid Elims (2yoft)	$15,000	Garden State Park
November 7	Valley Victory Elims (2yoct)	15,000	Garden State Park
November 8	Matron Stakes Final (3yo Open Trot)	125,000	Pompano Park
	Clare Series (Pacing Mares)	25,000	Yonkers Raceway
	Windy City Elims (3yo Open Pace)	25,000	Maywood Park
	Battle of Saratoga Series (Pacing Mares)	10,000	Saratoga Raceway
November 9	Presidential Final (2yo Open Pace)	300,000	Rosecroft Raceway
	Matron Stakes Final (2yofp)	135,000	Pompano Park
	Matron Stakes Elims (3yofp)	TBA	Pompano Park
	On The Road Again (Open Pace)	50,000	Yonkers Raceway
	Michigan Sire Stake (4yo Mare Trot)	100,000	Northville Downs
November 10	Michigan Sire Stake (4yo Mare Pace)	100,000	Sports Creek
November 13	Goldsmith Maid Final (2yoft)	300,000	Garden State Park
November 14	Valley Victory Final (2yoct)	300,000	Garden State Park
November 15	Windy City Final (3yo Open Pace)	350,000	Maywood Park
	Matron Stakes Elims (3yoft)	TBA	Pompano Park
	Clare Series (Pacing Mares)	25,000	Yonkers Raceway
November 16	Matron Stakes Final (3yofp)	100,000	Pompano Park
	Governor's Cup Elims (2yocp)	20,000	Garden State Park
	Wm. Haughton Memorial Series (Open Pace)	35,000	Yonkers Raceway
	Wm. Haughton Memorial Series (3yo Open Pace)	35,000	Yonkers Raceway
	Battle of Saratoga Series Final (Pacing Mares)	10,000	Saratoga Raceway
	Michigan Sire Stake (4yo H&G Pace)	5,000	Northville Downs
November 18	Galt Memorial (3yo Open Trot)	100,000	Maywood Park
November 22	Matron Stakes Final (3yoft)	120,000	Pompano Park
	Matron Stakes Elims (2yoft)	TBA	Pompano Park
	Clare Series (Pacing Mares)	50,000	Yonkers Raceway
November 23	Governor's Cup Final (2yopc)	700,000	Garden State Park
	Matron Stakes Elims (2yo Open Trot)	TBA	Pompano Park
	Wm. Haughton Memorial Series (Open Pace)	35,000	Yonkers Raceway
	Wm. Haughton Memorial Series (3yo Open Pace)	35,000	Yonkers Raceway
	Michigan Sire Stake (4yo H&G Pace)	100,000	Northville Downs
November 24	Provincial Cup (3yo Open Pace)	200,000	Windsor Raceway
November 29	Matron Stakes Final (2yoft)	135,000	Pompano Park
November 30	Matron Stakes Final (2yo Open Trot)	135,000	Pompano Park
	Wm. Haughton Memorial Series Final (Combined)	200,000	Yonkers Raceway
	Harvest Moon Elims (3yo&up Pace)	8,000	Northville Downs
December 6	Matron Stakes Elims (2yo Open Pace)	TBA	Pompano Park
December 7	Harvest Mood Final (3yo&up Pace)	27,500	Northville Downs
	Matron Stakes Elims (3yo Open Pace)	TBA	Pompano Park
December 13	Matron Stakes Final (2yo Open Pace)	150,000	Pompano Park
December 14	Matron Stakes Final (3yo Open Pace)	150,000	Pompano Park

RACE DATES

$100,000 OPEN RACES IN 1991, LISTED BY DIVISION

The following is a list of the major, unrestricted races of 1991, carrying estimated purses of at least $100,000.

The list is broken down by age, sex, and gait, showing the date on which the race is scheduled (subject to change); the name of the race; the estimated purse; the track at which it will be held; the name of last year's winner (or winners when the stake was divided); and the winning time. If the winner was placed first via disqualification, it will be indicated by the use of a "plus sign" (+).

In the case of events which were the finals to a series or eliminations, the time shown is for the final, and where events are contested under the heat plan, the time for the final (deciding) heat is shown below:

2-Year-Old Colt and Gelding Pace

Date	Name of Event	Estimated Purse	Track	'90 Winner(s)	Time(s)
June 27	Historic - Goshen Cup	$150,000	M	Brett's Story	1:57
				Lefty	1:55.3
				Mantese	1:56.1
				Henry Letsgo	1:55
June 30	Hopeful Final	200,000	BR	He's Discreet	1:59.2h
July 6	Potomac	300,000	RcR	Deal Breaker	1:56.2f
				Cambest	1:55.2f
				Gigowatt	1:54.4f
				Razzle Dazzlem	1:56.1f
				Silky Stallone	1:56.1f
July 16	Ville de Trois Rivieres Final	120,000	TrRvs	Bombe Angus	1:59.3h
July 20	Sheppard Final	400,000	YR	June's Baby	1:58.2h
August 3	Niatross Final	400,000	M	Die Laughing	1:54.2
August 4	Prix de l'Avenir	600,000	BB	Jackpot Raider	1:57f
				Nuke Of Earl	1:59.1f
				Shark Almahurst +	TDis
				Silky Stallone	1:57.4f
August 10	Arden Downs	100,000	Mea	Artsplace	1:55.3f
				Gold Glover	1:56.4f
				The Other Guy	1:55.1f
August 14	Review Stake-The Little Pat	100,000	Spr	Mantese	1:53.4
August 16	Woodrow Wilson Final	1,000,000	M	Die Laughing	
August 24	Fox Stake	175,000	Ind	Deal Direct	1:51.4
August 24	Garden State Stake	370,000	Fhld	Cambest	1:56.1h
				Nuclear Legacy	1:57.3h
				Shark Almahurst	1:56.4h
				Three Wizzards	1:56h
August 31	Hayes Memorial	100,000	DuQ	Rebelator	1:55.4
August 31	Kentucky Pacing Derby Final	400,000	LouD	Tooter Scooter	1:57h
September 1	Champlain Stakes	260,000	Moh	Deal Direct	1:56f
				Happy Family	1:56.2f
				Mantese	1:57f
				Prudhomme	1:56.2f
				Silky Stallone	1:55.2f
September 8	Nassagaweya	250,000	Moh	Artsplace	1:55f
				Shipps Commander	1:56.2f
				Happy Family	1:56.1f
				June's Baby	1:55.3f
September 19	Standardbred	150,000	Dela	Deal Breaker	1:56.4h
				W R H	1:54.1h
September 21	American-National	120,000	SPk	Interpretor	1:56.3f
				Mantese	1:55.1f
September 21	Metro Final	750,000	Moh	Artsplace	1:53.4f

RACE DATES

Date	Race	Purse	Track	Winner	Time
September 28	Bluegrass	150,000	Lex	Interpretor	1:53.3
October 4	International Stallion Stake	175,000	Lex	Die Laughing	1:52.1
October 12	Abraham Lincoln	130,000	May	Three Wizzards	1:57.1h
October 25	Breeders Crown Final	450,000	PPk	Artsplace	1:51.1f
November 9	Presidential Final	300,000	RcR	Die Laughing	1:54f
November 23	Governor's Cup Final	700,000	GSP	Artsplace	1:53
December 13	Matron Stakes Final	150,000	PPk	Mantese	1:54.2f

2-Year-Old Filly Pace

Date	Race	Purse	Track	Winner	Time
June 23	Historic - Debutante	$125,000	M	Laugh Line	1:59
				Miss Easy	1:56.3
				Miss Intensity	1:58
July 6	First Lady Final	200,000	RcR	Cams Exotic	1:56.3f
July 10	American-National	100,000	SPk	Start Dialing	1:59.3f
July 13	La Paloma Final	200,000	YR	Perfect Together	1:59.3h
July 26	Pink Bonnet Final	120,000	ScD	Shy Devil	1:57.3f
August 1	Countess Adios	250,000	M	Laugh Line	1:56.3
				Falcon's Secret	1:56.4
				Miss Easy	1:54
August 16	Sweetheart Final	750,000	M	Miss Easy	1:52.3
August 31	Lady Baltimore	200,000	RcR	Miss Easy	1:55.4f
				R M Gee	1:57.3f
				Yankee Co-ed	1:54.4f
September 6	Champlain Stakes	225,000	Moh	Falcon's Secret	1:57.1f
				Laugh Line	1:56.3f
				Jollie Dame	1:58.2f
September 7	Kentucky Standardbred Sales	250,000	RcR	Unreachable	1:57.1f
				Miss Easy	1:55f
September 18	Standardbred	100,000	Dela	Start Dialing	1:57.2h
September 22	Molly Pitcher	180,000	Fhld	Cams Exotic	1:57.3h
				Sunraycer	1:58.2h
				Lexie	1:57.2h
September 24	Bluegrass	135,000	Lex	Shady Daisy	1:55.4
October 1	International Stallion Stake	135,000	Lex	Explosive Legacy	1:55.4
October 12	Three Diamonds Final	400,000	GSP	Miss Easy	1:55.3
October 13	Harvest	150,000	Moh	Jollie Dame	1:56.2f
				Big Bloomer	1:56.3f
				Falcon's Secret	1:59.1f
October 25	Breeders Crown Final	360,000	PPk	Miss Easy	1:54f
November 9	Matron Final	135,000	PPk	Cams Exotic	1:56f

2-Year-Old Colt and Gelding Trot

Date	Race	Purse	Track	Winner	Time
June 25	Historic - Harriman Cup	$120,000	M	Grundy's Mint	2:00.2
				Super Pleasure	2:01.3
				Wall Street Banker	2:01
August 3	Peter Haughton Mem. Final	600,000	M	Charlie Ten Hitch	2:00.2
August 14	Review Stake - The Greyhound	125,000	Spr	Dickerson	1:58.1
September 7	Champlain Stakes	255,000	Moh	Crimson Lobell (DH)	2:04f
				Grundy's Mint (DH)	2:04f
				Super Pleasure	2:01.2f
September 9	American-National	100,000	SPk	Anders Crown	2:02.2f
				Square Rigger	2:02.2f
September 15	Campbellville	150,000	Moh	Tag Team	2:01.4f
				Anders Crown	2:03f
September 17	Standardbred	100,000	Dela	Grundy's Mint	1:59.1h
September 26	Bluegrass	100,000	Lex	Grundy's Mint	1:57.1
October 3	International Stallion Stake	150,000	Lex	Grundy's Mint	1:57.4
October 25	Breeders Crown Final	300,000	PPk	Crysta's Best	2:01f

RACE DATES

November 14	Valley Victory Final	300,000	GSP	Mr Chin	1:58.1
November 30	Matron Stakes Final	135,000	PPk	Mr Chin	2:00.4f

2-Year-Old Filly Trot

June 26	Historic - Acorn	$115,000	M	Another Geisha	2:01.2
				Jean Bi	1:59.3
August 3	Merrie Annabelle Final	450,000	M	Santa Royal	1:58.1
August 9	Kentucky Standardbred Sales	200,000	RcR	Santa Royal	1:59.4f
				Frances Jet Boko	2:01.2f
September 3	Champlain Stakes	225,000	Moh	Frances Jet Boko	2:02f
September 10	American-National	100,000	SPk	Jean Bi	2:00.4f
September 25	Bluegrass	100,000	Lex	Frances Jet Boko	1:58.2
October 2	International Stallion Stake	100,000	Lex	Eternal Flare	1:59.2
October 14	Autumn	100,000	Moh	Collier St Kathy	2:03f
				Shipps Doll	2:03f
October 25	Breeders Crown Final	300,000	PPk	Jean Bi	2:00.3f
November 13	Goldsmith Maid Final	300,000	GSP	Kramer Nobless	2:00.2
November 29	Matron Stakes Final	135,000	PPk	Esprit Spur	1:58f

3-Year-Old Colt and Gelding Pace

April 14	Berry's Creek Final	$350,000	M	Mark Johnathan	1:54
May 11	W.E. Miller Memorial Final	300,000	RcR	Beach Towel	1:52.3f
June 8	Burlington Final	175,000	GrR	Apaches Fame	1:52.2f
June 8	Terrapin	300,000	RcR	Beach Towel	1:54.1f
June 22	North America Cup Final	1,000,000	GrR	Apaches Fame	1:53.4f
June 29	American-National	375,000	SPk	Beach Towel	1:52.4f
June 29	Historic - Jersey Cup	100,000	M	In The Pocket	1:51.2
				Raven Lunatic	1:54.3
July 12	Meadowlands Pace Final	1,000,000	M	Beach Towel	1:52.2
July 27	Art Rooney Memorial Final	500,000	YR	Jake And Elwood	1:55h
July 27	Thomas P. Gaines Memorial	190,000	VD	Till We Meet Again	1:53.3q
August 2	Oliver Wendell Holmes	250,000	M	Brando Hanover	1:51.3
August 10	Adios	500,000	Mea	Beach Towel	1:51.4f
August 11	Nat Christie Memorial	150,000	Clgy	Counterfeit Crown (f)	1:55.1f
August 18	Prix d'Ete Molson	750,000	BB	Beach Towel	1:53.1f
August 24	**Cane Pace Final**	**500,000**	**YR**	**Jake And Elwood**	**1:55.1h**
August 25	Confederation Cup	350,000	Flmd	Apaches Fame	1:55f
August 31	James B. Dancer Memorial	380,000	Fhld	Road Machine	1:54.4h
September 1	Simcoe Stakes	180,000	Moh	Cam's Venture	1:54.2f
				Global Assault	1:54.1f
September 7	Little Brown Jug Preview	180,000	ScD	Apaches Fame	1:53.4f
				Global Assault	1:53f
				Brando Hanover	1:54.2f
September 7	**Messenger Stakes Final**	**350,000**	**RcR**	**Jake And Elwood**	**1:52.3f**
September 13	MacFarlane Memorial	200,000	HP	Brando Hanover	1:57.2f
				Camluck	1:56.3f
September 19	**Little Brown Jug**	**800,000**	**Dela**	**Beach Towel**	**1:53.3h**
September 28	Tattersalls	150,000	Lex	Beach Towel	1:51.1
October 4	Bluegrass	110,000	Lex	Kiev Hanover	1:50.1
October 5	Western Canada Pacing Derby	150,000	Edm	Sky Hagler	1:58.1f
October 12	Cleveland Classic	300,000	Nfld	Jake And Elwood	1:54.4h
				Kiev Hanover	1:55.4h
October 25	Breeders Crown Final	360,000	PPk	Beach Towel	1:51.2f
November 15	Windy City Final	350,000	May	Jake And Elwood	1:57.2h
November 24	Provincial Cup	200,000	WR	Camluck	1:52.4f
December 14	Matron Stakes Final	150,000	PPk	Shipps Schnoops	1:53.2f

RACE DATES

3-Year-Old Filly Pace

Date	Race	Purse	Track	Winner	Time
April 25	Cinderella	$100,000	May	Instant Rebate	1:59h
May 11	J.W. Miller Memorial Final	200,000	RcR	Instant Rebate	1:54.2f
June 1	Turtle Dove	200,000	RcR	Sea Biscuit	1:54.3f
				Choice Yankee	1:54.3f
June 8	American-National	200,000	SPk	Town Pro	1:55.2f
July 6	Lady Maud	125,000	YR	Armbro Ilona	1:57.1h
July 13	Bronx Filly Pace	125,000	YR	Cataclysm	1:57.3h
				Excited	1:58.1h
July 20	Courageous Lady	132,000	Nfld	Excited	1:56.2h
July 21	de la Moisson Final	100,000	BB	Town Pro	1:53.2f
August 1	Tarport Hap	175,000	M	Bruce's Lady	1:53.3
				Town Pro	1:51.4
				Tambourine	1:54.1
August 8	Adioo Volo	150,000	Mea	Lady Genius	1:56f
				Lady Dynamo	1:56.2f
				Yankee Goddess	1:55f
August 16	Mistletoe Shalee Final	400,000	M	Choice Yankee	1:52.4
August 30	Fan Hanover Final	120,000	GrR	Town Pro	1:53.1f
September 2	Helen Dancer Memorial	200,000	Fhld	Excited	1:57.3h
				It's Sunny	1:57.4h
September 7	Simcoe Stakes	165,000	Moh	Town Pro	1:54.4f
				Jonvik Castle	1:56.2f
September 18	Jugette	400,000	Dela	Lady Genius	1:55.3h
September 21	Nadia Lobell Final	200,000	GSP	Crafty Caper	1:53.4
September 26	Bluegrass	115,000	Lex	Delinquent Account	1:53.3
October 3	Glen Garnsey Memorial	120,000	Lex	Rulers Chippie	1:53.2
October 19	Northlands Filly Stake	100,000	Edm	Tylers Royalty	1:55.4f
October 25	Breeders Crown Final	300,000	PPk	Town Pro	1:54.4f
November 16	Matron Stakes Final	100,000	PPk	Rulers Chippie	1:55.3f

3-Year-Old Colt and Gelding Trot

Date	Race	Purse	Track	Winner	Time
May 26	Currier & Ives	$125,000	Mea	Cheyenne Spur	2:00.4f
				King Of The Sea	2:00f
				Zizi's Prakas	1:59.4f
June 17	American-National	250,000	SPk	Armbro Iliad	2:00.1f
June 28	Historic - Dickerson Cup	100,000	M	Star Mystic	2:00.2f
June 29	Dexter Cup Final	175,000	YR	Royal Troubador	1:58.3h
July 13	**Yonkers Trot Final**	**300,000**	**YR**	**Royal Troubador**	**1:59.2h**
July 14	Founders Gold Cup	150,000	VD	Star Mystic	1:57.1q
July 27	Budweiser Beacon Course Fin.	400,000	M	Embassy Lobell	1:56.3
August 3	**Hambletonian**	**1,200,000**	**M**	**Harmonious**	**1:54.1**
August 16	Review Stake-Alexander Mem.	115,000	Spr	Super Arnie	1:54.1
August 18	Zweig Memorial	200,000	Sycs	Embassy Lobell	1:57.3
				Harmonious	1:57.1
				Jeanne's Somolli	1:58.2
August 24	MacFarlane Memorial	125,000	HP	Jeanne's Somolli	1:59.1f
August 31	World Trotting Derby	550,000	DuQ	Harmonious	2:04.3
September 6	Simcoe Stakes	180,000	Moh	Osgood Hanover	2:01.1f
				Roughing It	2:00.1f
September 18	Old Oaken Bucket	110,000	Dela	Lender Hanover	2:02.3h
September 27	Bluegrass	100,000	Lex	Embassy Lobell	1:54.4
October 4	**Kentucky Futurity**	**175,000**	**Lex**	**Star Mystic**	**1:55.3**
October 12	Colonial	225,000	RcR	Jeanne's Somolli	1:56.4f
				Cheyenne Spur	1:56.2f
October 25	Breeders Crown Final	350,000	PPk	Embassy Lobell	1:56.4f
November 8	Matron Final	125,000	PPk	Jeanne's Somolli	1:57.2f
November 18	Galt Memorial	100,000	May	Incredible DJ	1:59.2h

RACE DATES

3-Year-Old Filly Trot

Date	Race	Purse	Track	Winner	Time
June 10	American-National	$175,000	SPk	Spreadsheet	1:59.2f
August 3	Hambletonian Oaks	300,000	M	Working Gal	1:58.1
August 30	World Filly Trotting Derby	125,000	DuQ	Happy Diamonds	2:04.3
September 2	Simcoe Stakes	165,000	Moh	Ashley Jane	2:00.1f
				Armbro Icon	1:59.3f
September 27	Bluegrass	100,000	Lex	Model Home	1:56.3
October 12	Colonial Filly	125,000	RcR	Happy Diamonds	1:57f
				Me Maggie	1:57.2f
				Working Gal	1:57.1f
October 25	Breeders Crown Final	330,000	PPk	Me Maggie	1:57.1f
November 22	Matron Stakes Final	120,000	PPk	Model Home	1:57.4f

Aged Pace

Date	Race	Purse	Track	Winner	Time
January 26	Presidential Series Final	$100,000	M	Barely Visible	1:53.3
January 30	Trendsetter Series Final	100,000	M	Master Scoot	1:55.3
February 9	Damsel Series Final	100,000	GrR	Tinycrombie (m)	1:56.4f
March 16	Cam Fella Series Final	100,000	GrR	Gigalo	1:55.2f
March 17	Four Leaf Clover Final	100,000	M	Trouble Twosum	1:55.1
April 20	R. Bruce Cornell Memorial	100,000	Fhld	Dorunrun Bluegrass	1:53.1h
April 27	Geo. Morton Levy Series Final	200,000	YR	My Guru	1:54.3h
June 2	Challenge Stakes	150,000	BB	Topnotcher	1:53f
June 8	Battle of Lake Erie	100,000	Nfld	Dorunrun Bluegrass	1:54h
June 15	Lake Superior	100,000	HP	Topnotcher	1:53.3f
July 6	Driscoll Series Final	200,000	M	T K's Skipper	1:51.2
July 22	Roses Are Red Final (F&M)	100,000	GrR	Caesars Jackpot	1:52.4f
July 27	Molson Can. Pacing Derby Fin.	240,000	GrR	Topnotcher	1:52.2f
August 3	American-National	150,000	SPk	Keystone Raider	1:53.2f
August 24	U.S. Pacing Championship Fin.	125,000	YR	Dorunrun Bluegrass	1:54h
September 26	Milton Final (F&M)	100,000	Moh	Caesars Jackpot	1:53.3f
September 29	Mohawk Gold Cup Final	100,000	Moh	Topnotcher	1:52.4f
October 11	Breeders Crown Final (H&G)	400,000	Mea	Bay's Fella	1:52.1f
October 11	Breeders Crown Final (Mares)	300,000	Mea	Caesar's Jackpot	1:52.3f
October 26	Sewart Fraser Memorial	200,000	Edm	Topnotcher	1:53.4f
November 30	Wm. Haughton Series Fin.	200,000	YR	Dorunrun Bluegrass	1:55h

Aged Trot

Date	Race	Purse	Track	Winner	Time
July 7	Jazzman	$100,000	BB	No Sex Please	1:55.4f
				Texas Snazzy	1:58.1f
July 14	Statue of Liberty	250,000	M	(Not Raced)	
August 3	Nat Ray Final	200,000	M	Alfresco	1:57
August 10	International Trot 1-1/4 mi.	450,000	YR	Reve d'Udon	2:28.3h
August 17	Maple Leaf Trot	250,000	GrR	No Sex Please	1:57f
September 26	American-National	100,000	SPk	Kit Lobell (m)	1:58.4f
				Peach Pit (m)	1:58.3f
October 11	Breeders Crown Final (H&G)	400,000	Mea	No Sex Please	1:55f
October 11	Breeders Crown Final (Mares)	300,000	Mea	Peace Corps	1:54.2f

* * * * *

World Records

WORLD RECORDS

WORLD CHAMPIONSHIP RECORDS

Official Compilation

This compilation recognized as Champions those horses that have made the fastest time at their gait, age, and sex on the major sizes of tracks, either against time or in a race at one mile. This is the distance upon which the sport of harness racing has been established. New records for 1989 appear in **boldface**:

Trotting on a Mile Track

All-Age

1:52.1	Mack Lobell	br c, 3, by Mystic Park--Matina Hanover (John Campbell) Springfield, IL, August 21, 1987
1:52.4	Peace Corps	b f, 3, by Baltic Speed--Worth Beein (John Campbell) Du Quoin, IL, September 2, 1989
1:54.2	**I'm Impeccable**	**b g, 3, by Coleman Lobell--Impudent (Chip Noble) The Red Mile, Lexington, KY, September 28, 1990**

Two-Year-Olds

1:55.3	Mack Lobell	br c, by Mystic Park--Matina Hanover (John Campbell) The Red Mile, Lexington, KY, October 3, 1986
TT1:55	Noxie Hanover	b f, by Super Bowl--Noble Gal (Jim Simpson) The Red Mile, Lexington, KY September 19, 1988
1:57.2	I'm Impeccable	b g, by Coleman Lobell--Impudent (Dave Rankin) The Red Mile, Lexington, KY, September 28, 1989

Three-Year-Olds

1:52.1	Mack Lobell	br c, by Mystic Park--Matina Hanover (John Campbell) Springfield, IL, August 21, 1987
1:52.4	Peace Corps	b f, by Baltic Speed--Worth Beein (John Campbell) Du Quoin, IL, September 2, 1989
1:54.2	**I'm Impeccable**	**b g, by Coleman Lobell--Impudent (Chip Noble) The Red Mile, Lexington, KY, September 28, 1990**

Four-Year-Olds

1:53	Express Ride	b h, by Super Bowl--Flory Messenger (Berndt Lindstedt) The Red Mile, Lexington, KY, September 25, 1987
TT1:55.2	Classical Way	b m, by Speedy Scot--Kerry Way (John Simpson, Jr.) The Red Mile, Lexington, KY, October 5, 1980
1:56	Delray Lobell	b g, by Speedy Crown--Duchess Faye (John Campbell) The Meadowlands, East Rutherford, NJ, June 20, 1989; and
	War Nickel	**br g, by Copter Lobell--Power Bay (Ray Tremblay) Garden State Park, Cherry Hill, NJ, October 18, 1990**

Five-Year-Olds and Older

1:54.1	Napoletano	b h, 5, by Super Bowl--Noble Sarah (Stig Johansson) The Meadowlands, East Rutherford, NJ, July 1, 1989
1:54.4	**Kit Lobell**	**b m, 5, by Speedy Crown--Keystone Pioneer (Berndt Lindstedt) The Meadowlands, East Rutherford, NJ, June 27, 1990**
1:55	**No Sex Please**	**br g, 5, by Brisco Hanover--Gay Ann Herbert (Ron Waples) The Red Mile, Lexington, KY, October 4, 1990**

WORLD RECORDS

Trotting on a Five Eighths–Mile Track

All-Age

1:54.1	Mack Lobell	br c, 3, by Mystic Park--Matina Hanover (John Campbell) Pompano Park, Pompano Beach, FL, November 13, 1987
1:54.2	**Peace Corps**	**b m, 4, by Baltic Speed--Worth Beein (Stig Johansson) Pompano Park, Pompano Beach, FL, November 2, 1990**
1:55	**No Sex Please**	**br g, 5, by Brisco Hanover--Gay Ann Herbert (Ron Waples) Pompano Park, Pompano Beach, FL, November 2, 1990**

Two-Year-Olds

1:57.3	Royal Troubador	b c, by Super Bowl--Mae Jeans Crown (Carl Allen) Pompano Park, Pompano Beach, FL, December 7, 1989;
1:57.1	Peace Corps	b f, by Baltic Speed--Worth Beein (John Campbell) Pompano Park, Pompano Beach, FL, November 11, 1988
2:00	**Sammy Silk**	**blk g, by Worthy Bowl--Kawartha Pastel (Steve Byron) Windsor Raceway, Windsor, ONT, November 14, 1990**

Three-Year-Olds

1:54.1	Mack Lobell	br c, by Mystic Park--Matina Hanover (John Campbell) Pompano Park, Pompano Beach, FL, November 13, 1987
1:56.1	**Kindava Hush**	**b f, by Arndon--Quiet Elegance (Jan Nordin) Pompano Park, Pompano Beach, FL, October 20, 1990; and**
	Me Maggie	**b f, by Prakas--Grassbed (Berndt Lindstedt) Pompano Park, Pompano Beach, FL, November 9, 1990**
1:57	JJ's Diamond	b g, by Diamond Exchange--Annette W (Roger Mayotte) Mohawk Raceway, Campbellville, ONT, October 24, 1989

Four-Year-Olds

1:54.4	Mack Lobell	br h, by Mystic Park--Matina Hanover (John Campbell) Solvalla, Sweden, May 29, 1988
1:54.2	**Peace Corps**	**b m, by Baltic Speed--Worth Beein (Stig Johansson) Pompano Park, Pompano Beach, FL, November 2, 1990**
1:55.2	Delray Lobell	b g, by Speedy Crown--Duchess Faye (Don Irvine, Jr.) Freestate Raceway, Laurel, MD, August 20, 1989

Five-year-Olds and Older

1:54.3	**Mack Lobell**	**br h, 6, by Mystic Park--Matina Hanover (Thomas Nilsson) Solvalla, Sweden, May 27, 1990**
1:55.3	**Nealy Lobell**	**b m, 6, by Speedy Crown--Normajean Hanover (Jimmy Takter) Biri Racecourse, Norway, June 10, 1990**
1:55	**No Sex Please**	**br g, 5, by Brisco Hanover--Gay Ann Herbert (Ron Waples) Pompano Park, Pompano Beach, FL, November 2, 1990**

Trotting on a Half–Mile Track

All-Age

1:56	Mack Lobell	br h, 4, by Mystic Park--Matina Hanover (John Campbell) Saratoga Raceway, Saratoga Springs, NY, August 5, 1988
1:56	Peace Corps	b f, 3, by Baltic Speed--Worth Beein (John Campbell) Delaware, OH, September 21, 1989
1:58.1	Gentle Stroke	b g, 8, by Noble Gesture--Eydie Hanover (Jorn Kvikstad) Yonkers Raceway, Yonkers, NY, September 8, 1989

WORLD RECORDS

Two-Year-Olds

1:58.1	Royal Troubador	b c, by Super Bowl--Mae Jeans Crown (Carl Allen) Delaware, OH, September 19, 1989
1:59	Lizzie Lee Brook	by Joie De Vie--Joyous Princess (Donald Dancer) Freehold Raceway, Freehold, NJ, October 15, 1987; and
	Kindava Hush	b f, by Arndon--Quiet Elegance (Jan Nordin) Delaware, OH, September 19, 1989
2:01.2	Proud Coate	b g, by Mighty Crown--M J's Queen (Donald Coate) Delaware, OH, September 14, 1987

Three-Year-Olds

1:56.4	Editor In Chief	b c, by Speed In Action--Sequel (John Campbell) Delaware, OH, September 20, 1988
1:56	Peace Corps	b f, by Baltic Speed--Worth Beein (John Campbell) Delaware, OH, September 21, 1989
1:58.3	Op'Art	b g, by Speed In Action--Opalescence (Bruce Riegle) Delaware, OH, September 18, 1984

Four-Year-Olds

1:56	Mack Lobell	br, h, by Mystic Park--Matina Hanover (John Campbell) Sharatoga Raceway, Saratoga Springs, NY, August 5, 1988
1:57.4	Quick Trip	br m, by Quickster--Darby Hill (John Hogan) Delaware, OH, September 17, 1984; and
	Grades Singing	br m, by Texas--Singing Bay (Herve Filion) Yonkers Raceway, Yonkers, NY, July 6, 1986
1:58.2	Billie S	b g, by Hunters Star--X Pert Dot (Charles Baker) Maywood Park, Maywood, IL, September 29, 1988; and
	Arnie's Express	b g, by Lolas Express--Miss Arnie (Don O'Dwyer) Northfield Park, Northfield, OH, September 8, 1989; and
	War Nickel	**br g, by Copter Lobell--Power Bay (Ray Tremblay) Yonkers Raceway, Yonkers, NY, August 17, 1990**

Five-Year-Olds and Older

1:57.4	Lakewater Glory	br h, 5, by On To Glory--Lakewater Mom (Vitaly Tanishin) Northfield Park, Northfield, OH, May 26, 1989
1:57.2	**Kit Lobell**	**b m, 5, by Speedy Crown--Keystone Pioneer (Berndt Lindstedt) Yonkers Raceway, Yonkers, NY, July 29, 1990**
1:58.1	Gentle Stroke	b g, 8, by Noble Gesture--Eydie Hanover (Jorn Kvikstad) Yonkers Raceway, Yonkers, NY, September 8, 1989

Pacing on a Mile Track

All-Age

TT1:48.2	Matt's Scooter	b c, 3, by Direct Scooter--Ellens Glory (Michel Lachance) The Red Mile, Lexington, KY, September 23, 1988
TT1:50.4	Fan Hanover	b m, 4, by Albatross--Farm Norah (Glen Garnsey) The Red Mile, Lexington, KY, October 2, 1982
1:51.1	Indian Alert	b g, 4, by Armbro Alert--Lemons Mill (Jack Moiseyev) The Meadowlands, East Rutherford, NJ, June 17, 1988; and
	Boston Blue Chip	**ch g, 3, by On The Road Again--Backseat Driver (Joe Schwind) The Meadowlands, East Rutherford, NJ, August 4, 1990**

WORLD RECORDS

Two-Year-Olds

1:51.4	Deal Direct	b c, by Direct Scooter--Dee Bee Hitter (Chip Noble) Indianapolis, IN, August 25, 1990
1:51.2	Miss Easy	b f, by Amity Chef--Pleasure Seeker (John Campbell) The Red Mile, Lexington, KY, September 25, 1990
1:54	Mr Gourmet	b g, by Mr Dalrae--Upper (Tom Harmer) The Red Mile, Lexington, KY, October 5, 1990

Three-Year-Olds

TT1:48.2	Matt's Scooter	b c, by Direct Scooter--Ellens Glory (Michel Lachance) The Red Mile, Lexington, KY, September 23, 1988
TT1:51.2	Trini Hanover	b f, by Big Towner--Tara Row Gil (Ron Waples) Springfield, IL, August 17, 1988
1:51.1	Boston Blue Chip	ch g, by On The Road Again--Backseat Driver (Joe Schwind) The Meadowlands, East Rutherford, NJ, August 4, 1990

Four-Year-Olds

TT1:49.2	Jaguar Spur	b h, by Albatross--J D S Bret (Dick Stillings) The Red Mile, Lexington, KY, October 8, 1988
TT1:50.4	Fan Hanover	b m, by Albatross--Farm Norah (Glen Garnsey) The Red Mile, Lexington, KY, October 2, 1982
1:51.1	Indian Alert	b g, by Armbro Alert--Lemons Mill (Jack Moiseyev) The Meadowlands, East Rutherford, NJ, June 17, 1988

Five-Year-Olds and Older

TT1:49.2	T K's Skipper	br h, 5, by Governor Skipper--Shana Hanover (Michel Lachance) DuQuoin, IL, September 1, 1990
1:51.3	Armbro Feather	b m, 5, by Most Happy Fella--Brets Velvet (John Kopas) The Meadowlands, East Rutherford, NJ, August 5, 1989
1:52.1	Intruder Almahurst	b g, 7, by Keystone Ore--Impish Almahurst (Carl Garofalo) The Meadowlands, East Rutherford, NJ, August 6, 1988

Pacing on a Five Eighths-Mile Track

All-Age

1:50.4	In The Pocket	br h, 3, by Direct Scooter--Black Jade (John Campbell) The Meadows, Meadow Lands, PA, August 11, 1990
1:52.2	Caesars Jackpot	b m, 4, by Walton Hanover--Tracys Jackpot (Wally Hennessey) Pompano Park, Pompano Beach, FL, October 20, 1990
1:52.3	Division Street	b g, 5, by Most Happy Fella--Spiked Byrdie (Michel Lachance) Freestate Raceway, Laurel, MD, September 27, 1985; and
	Night Colt	br g, 7, by Abercrombie--Regina Marie (Mario Baillargeon) Greenwood Raceway, Toronto, ONT, July 21, 1990

Two-Year-Olds

1:51.1	Artsplace	b c, by Abercrombie--Miss Elvira (John Campbell) Pompano Park, Pompano Beach, FL, November 30, 1990
1:53.3	Central Park West	b f, by Big Towner--Park Ave Bell (John Campbell) Pompano Park, Pompano Beach, FL, November 18, 1988
1:55.3	Scotch Baker	b g, by Baker Field--Bonnie Lass N (Steve Brannan) Raceway Park, Toledo, OH, July 16, 1989

WORLD RECORDS

Three-Year-Olds

1:50.4	In The Pocket	br h, by Direct Scooter--Black Jade (John Campbell) The Meadows, Meadow Lands, PA, August 11, 1990
1:52.3	Ruler's Chippie	b m, by Radiant Ruler--Falcons Chip (Bruce Ranger) Pompano Park, Pompano Beach, FL, December 29, 1990
TT1:52.3	Rowleyalla	b g, by National Byrd--Sally Alla (Kevin Rivett) Albion Park, Brisbane, Australia, July 9, 1988

Four-Year-Olds

1:51	Matt's Scooter	b h, by Direct Scooter--Ellens Glory (Michel Lachance) Mohawk Raceway, Campbellville, Ont., October 1, 1989
1:52.2	Caesars Jackpot	b m, by Walton Hanover--Tracys Jackpot (Wally Hennessey) Pompano Park, Pompano Beach, FL, October 20, 1990
1:52.4	Eagle Speaker	b g, by Conquered--Timely Trudy (John Holmes) Greenwood Raceway, Toronto, ONT, July 6, 1990

Five-Year-Olds and Older

1:51.2	T.K.'s Skipper	br h, 5, by Governor Skipper--Shana Hanover (Joe Anderson) Los Alamitos, Los Alamitos, CA, September 29, 1990
1:53.1	Armbro Feather	b m, 5, by Most Happy Fella--Brets Velvet (Buddy Gilmour) Greenwood Raceway, Toronto, Ont., July 1, 1989
1:52.3	Division Street	b g, 5, by Most Happy Fella--Spiked Byrdie (Michel Lachance) Freestate Raceway, Laurel, MD, September 27, 1985; and
	Night Colt	br g, 7, by Abercrombie--Regina Marie (Mario Baillargeon) Greenwood Raceway, Toronto, ONT, July 21, 1990

Pacing on a Half-Mile Track

All-Age

1:51	Falcon Seelster	b c, 3, by Warm Breeze--Fashion Trick (Tom Harmer) Delaware, OH, September 19, 1985
1:54.4	Amneris	b f, 3, by Tyler B--Aida Hanover (John Campbell) Delaware, OH, September 18, 1985;
	Town Tattler	blk f, 3, by Big Towner--Tona Hanover (John Campbell) Delaware, OH, September 18, 1985;
	H H Shadow	br f, 3, by Distant Thunder--H H Silhouette (Jody Stafford) Yonkers Raceway, Yonkers, NY, July 27, 1986;
	Crystal Tree	ch m, 4, by Trim The Tree--Sieson Dream (Gerry Bookmyer) Northfield Park, Northfield, OH, August 26, 1989; and
	L Dees Trish	b m, 4, by Merger--Bluegrass Lou (Michel Lachance) Yonkers Raceway, Yonkers, NY, November 23, 1990
1:53.4	Hi Tech Society	b g, 3, by Ideal Society--Lotus Osborne (Merv Chupp) Maywood Park, Maywood, IL, September 26, 1987

Two-Year-Olds

1:54.1	Tooter Scooter	b c, by Direct Scooter--Bloodstocks Bunny (Bill Fahy) Louisville Downs, Louisville, KY, September 1, 1990
	W R H	b c, by Direct Scooter--The Best Move Yet (John Campbell) Delaware, OH, September 20, 1990
1:55.4	L Dees Trish	b f, by Merger--Bluegrass Lou (Herve Filion) Freehold Raceway, Freehold, NJ, September 10, 1988
TT1:55	Rowleyalla	b g, by National Byrd--Sally Alla (Kevin Rivett) Harold Park, Sydney, Australia, May 22, 1987

WORLD RECORDS

Three-Year-Olds

1:51	Falcon Seelster	b c, by Warm Breeze--Fashion Trick (Tom Harmer) Delaware, OH, September 19, 1985
1:54.4	Amneris	b f, by Tyler B--Aida Hanover (John Campbell) Delaware, OH, September 18, 1985;
	Town Tattler	blk f, by Big Towner--Tona Hanover (John Campbell) Delaware, OH, September, 18, 1985; and
	H H Shadow	br f, by Distant Thunder--H H Silhouette (Jody Stafford) Yonkers Raceway, Yonkers, NY, July 27, 1986
1:53.4	Hi Tech Society	b g, by Ideal Society--Lotus Osborne (Merv Chupp) Maywood Park, Maywood, IL, September 9, 1987

Four-Year-Olds

1:53	Jaguar Spur	b h, by Albatross--J.D.'s Bret (Dick Stillings) Northfield Park, Northfield, OH, August 27, 1988
1:54.4	Crystal Tree	ch m, by Trim The Tree--Sieson Dream (Gerry Bookmyer) Northfield Park, Northfield, OH, August 26, 1989; and
	L Dees Trish	**b m, by Merger--Bluegrass Lou (Michel Lachance) Yonkers Raceway, Yonkers, NY, November 23, 1990**
1:54	Cotton Sock	b g, by Temujin--Dalesia Lobell (Walter Paisley) Maywood Park, Maywood, IL, August 12, 1988; and
	Barely Visible	b g, by Tyler B--Twilite Hanover (John Campbell) Delaware, OH, September 17, 1989

Five-Year-Olds and Older

1:53.3	**Chatham Light**	**b h, 5, by Niatross--Miles End Brenda (Kelly Sheppard) Connaught Park, Aylmer, QUE, May 21, 1990**
1:55	Anniecrombie	b m, 5, by Abercrombie--Sparklespray (Dave Magee) Maywood Park, Maywood, IL, September 17, 1988
1:54.1	**Wiregrass Kerrigan**	**br g, 5, by Bit O Fun--Valiant Sarah (Jim Curran) Maywood Park, Maywood, IL, May 6, 1990**

NORTH AMERICAN RACE RECORDS

Trotting on a Mile Track in Races

All-Age

1:52.1	Mack Lobell	br c, 3, by Mystic Park--Matina Hanover (John Campbell) Springfield, IL, August 21, 1987
1:52.4	Peace Corps	b f, 3, by Baltic Speed--Worth Beein (John Campbell) Du Quoin, IL, September 2, 1989
1:54.2	**I'm Impeccable**	**b g, 3, by Coleman Lobell--Impudent (Chip Noble) The Red Mile, Lexington, KY, September 28, 1990**

Two-Year-Olds

1:55.3	Mack Lobell	br c, by Mystic Park--Matina Hanover (John Campbell) The Red Mile, Lexington, KY, October 3, 1986
1:56	Anamosa Hanover	b f, by Speedy Crown--Anders Favorite (Jan Nordin) Springfield, IL, August 19, 1987; and
	Nan's Catch	b f, by Bonefish--Nan Hanover (Berndt Lindstedt) Du Quoin, IL, September 4, 1987
1:57.2	I'm Impeccable	b g, by Coleman Lobell--Impudent (Dave Rankin) The Red Mile, Lexington, KY, September 28, 1989

WORLD RECORDS

Three-Year-Olds

1:52.1	Mack Lobell	br c, by Mystic Park--Matina Hanover (John Campbell) Springfield, IL, August 21, 1987
1:52.4	Peace Corps	b f, by Baltic Speed--Worth Beein (John Campbell) Du Quoin, IL, September 2, 1989
1:54.2	**I'm Impeccable**	**b g, by Coleman Lobell--Impudent (Chip Noble) The Red Mile, Lexington, KY, September 28, 1990**

Four-Year-Olds

1:53	Express Ride	b h, by Super Bowl--Flory Messenger (Berndt Lindstedt) The Red Mile, Lexington, KY, September 25, 1987
1:55.4	Keystone Impala	,b m, by Speedy Crown--Ima Lula (Bill Fahy) The Meadowlands, East Rutherford, NJ, June 21, 1989
1:56	Delray Lobell	b g, by Speedy Crown--Duchess Faye (John Campbell) The Meadowlands, East Rutherford, NJ, June 20, 1989; and
	War Nickel	br g, by Copter Lobell--Power Bay (Ray Tremblay) Garden State Park, Cherry Hill, NJ, October 18, 1990

Five-Year-Olds and Older

1:54.1	Napoletano	b h, 5, by Super Bowl--Noble Sarah (Stig Johansson) The Meadowlands, East Rutherford, NJ, July 1, 1989
1:54.4	**Kit Lobell**	**b m, 5, by Speedy Crown--Keystone Pioneer (Berndt Lindstedt) The Meadowlands, East Rutherford, NJ, June 27, 1990**
1:55	**No Sex Please**	**br g, 5, by Brisco Hanover--Gay Ann Herbert (Ron Waples) The Red Mile, Lexington, KY, October 4, 1990**

Fastest Heats

1st heat - 1:52.1		Mack Lobell, br c, 3, by Mystic Park--Matina Hanover (John Campbell) Springfield, IL, August 21, 1987
2nd heat - 1:52.4		Peace Corps,b f, 3, by Baltic Speed--Worth Beein (John Campbell) Du Quoin, IL, September 2, 1989
3rd Heat - 1:55.3		**Star Mystic, b c, 3, by Mystic Park--Sissy Crown (Jan Johnson) The Red Mile, Lexington, KY, Octocer 5, 1990**

Heat Racing

All-Age

2-heat race - 3:47.3	Mack Lobell, br c, 3, by Mystic Park--Matina Hanover (John Campbell) The Meadowlands, East Rutherford, NJ, August 8, 1987--1:54; 1:53.3
2-heat race - 3:47.3	Keystone Harem, b f, 3, by Super Bowl--Hoot Be Quick (Jan Nordin) Springfield, IL, August 20, 1987--1:53.4; 1:53.4
2-heat-race - 3:52.4	Nuclear Arsenal, b g, 3, by Arsenal--Cardinal Sahbra (Dave Magee) Springfield, IL, August 14, 1989--1:56; 1:56.4
3-heats divided - 5:44.3	**Star Mystic, b c, 3, by Mystic Park--Sissy Crown (Jan Johnson) The Red Mile, Lexington, KY, October 5, 1990 (Jeanne's Somolli won 1st heat) 1:54.2; 1:54.3; 1:55.3**
3-heats divided - 5:46	Keystone Profile, b f, 3, by Speedy Crown--Peridot (Hakan Wallner) Du Quoin, IL, August 30, 1985 (Armbro Devona won 1st heat) 1:55.3; 1:55.1; 1:55.1
3-heats divided - 6:03.3	Pronto Don, ch g, by Donald Truax--Miss Pronto (B.J. Schue) Indianapolis, IN, September 7, 1951 (Star's Pride won 2nd heat) 2:02; 1:59; 2:02.3

WORLD RECORDS

Two-Year-Olds

2-heat race - 3:52.4	Buckfinder, b c, by Super Bowl--Nutmeg Lobell (Bill O'Donnell) The Red Mile, Lexington, KY, September 27, 1986--1:56.3; 1:56.1	
2-heat race - 3:53.1	Nan's Catch, b f, by Bonefish--Nan Hanover (Berndt Lindstedt) DuQuoin, IL, September 4, 1987--1:57.1; 1:56	
2-heat-race - 3:55.3	I'm Impeccable, b g, by Coleman Lobell--Impudent (Dave Rankin) The Red Mile, Lexington, KY, September 28, 1989--1:57.2; 1:58.1	

Three-Year-Olds

2-heat race - 3:47.3 Mack Lobell, br c, by Mystic Park--Matina Hanover (John Campbell) The Meadowlands, East Rutherford, NJ, August 8, 1987--1:54; 1:53.3

2-heat race - 3:47.3 Keystone Harem, b f, by Super Bowl--Hoot Be Quick (Jan Nordin) Springfield, IL, August 20, 1987--1:53.4; 1:53.4

2-heat race - 3:52.4 Nuclear Arsenal, b g, by Arsenal--Cardinal Sahbra (Dave Magee) Springfield, IL, August 14, 1989--1:56; 1:56.4

3-heats divided - 5:44.3 Star Mystic, b c, by Mystic Park--Sissy Crown (Jan Johnson) The Red Mile, Lexington, KY, October 5, 1990 (Jeanne's Somolli won 1st heat) 1:54.2; 1:54.3; 1:55.3

3-heats divided - 5:46 Keystone Profile, b f, by Speedy Crown--Peridot (Hakan Wallner) Du Quoin, IL, August 30, 1985 (Armbro Devona won 1st heat) 1:55.3, 1:55.1, 1:55.1

3-heats divided-6:07 3/4 Greyhound, gr g, by Guy Abbey--Elizabeth (Sep Palin) Syracuse, NY, August 26, 1935 (Lawrence Hanover won 2nd heat) 2:02 1/4, 2:04, 2:01 1/2

Dead Heat

1:58	Tuneful Contest Worthy Bowl	ch c, 2, by Noble Gesture--Fast Tune (Bruce Nickells) and br c, 2, by Super Bowl--Speeding Evening (Billy Haughton) Indianapolis, IN, August 22, 1980

Double-Gaited Performers

3:55.1	Speedy Romeo	ch h, by Romeo Hanover--Worthy Sis (Peter Haughton) The Meadowlands, East Rutherford, NJ, May 24, 1977, 4, 1:59.2; (Terry Morgan) The Meadowlands, East Rutherford, NJ, May 3, 1980 - p, 7, 1:55.4
3:58-3/4	Calumet Evelyn	blk m, by Guy Abbey--Marion Scott (Vic Fleming) The Red Mile, Lexington, KY, September 21, 1935, p, 4, 1:59 1/4; (Vic Fleming) The Red Mile, Lexington, KY, October 2, 1936 - 5, 1:59 1/2
3:56	Tequila Star	b g, by Hunter's Star--Trolley Car (Jack Williams) Hollywood Pk., Inglewood, CA, Sept. 13, 1980, 4,1:59.1; (Jack Williams) Hollywood Pk., Inglewood, CA, Oct. 2, 1982, p, 6, 1:56.1

At Distances Other Than One Mile

1/2 mile - 58-1/4	Temple Harvester, br g, 4, by The Harvester--Zorah Temple (Marvin Childs) Aurora, IL, August 5, 1925
9/16 mile - 1:06.2	Moses, br g, 6, by Spencer--Jochebed (Dee Stover) Fairmount Park, Collinsville, IL, July 24, 1948
5/8 mile - 1:14	Peaceful Abbey, b m, 8, by Guy Abbey--Lady Britton (Charles McGowan) Fairmount Park, Collinsville, IL, June 4, 1948
13/16 mile - 1:39.2	Lots Of Style, b g, 11, by Armbro Express--Bit Of Fashion (Chris Payne) Lake Shore Meadows, Fairview, PA, July 4, 1984
7/8 mile - 1:46-1/4	Truax, b h, 4, by Guy Axworthy--Hollyrood Polly (R.D. McMahon) North Randall, OH, August 18, 1925
1-1/16 miles - 2:05	Jurgy Hanover, b h,5, by Super Bowl--Jes R Hoot (Doug Miller) Hollywood Park, Inglewood, CA, September 15, 1979

WORLD RECORDS

1-1/8 miles - 2:09.4   Mack Lobell, br c, 4, by Mystic Park--Matina Hanover (John Campbell) The Meadowlands, East Rutherford, NJ, June 18, 1988

1-1/4 miles - 2:30.3   Pronto Don, ch g, by Donald Truax--Miss Pronto (B.J. Schue) Hollywood Park, Inglewood, CA, November 24, 1951

1-1/2 miles - 2:57.3   Meadow Road, b h, 6, by Madison Avenue--Francessa (Torbjorn Jansson) The Meadowlands, East Rutherford, NJ, June 17, 1985

Trotting on a Five Eighths-Mile Track in Races

All-Age

1:54.1	Mack Lobell	br c, 3, by Mystic Park--Matina Hanover (John Campbell) Pompano Park, Pompano Beach, FL, November 13, 1987
1:54.2	**Peace Corps**	**b m, 4, by Baltic Speed--Worth Beein (Stig Johansson) Pompano Park, Pompano Beach, FL, November 2, 1990**
1:55	No Sex Please	br g, 5, by Brisco Hanover--Gay Ann Herbert (Ron Waples) Pompano Park, Pompano Beach, FL, November 2, 1990

Two-Year-Olds

1:57.3	Royal Troubador	b c, by Super Bowl--Mae Jeans Crown (Carl Allen) Pompano Park, Pompano Beach, FL, December 7, 1989
1:57.1	Peace Corps	b f, by Baltic Speed--Worth Beein (John Campbell) Pompano Park, Pompano Beach, FL, November 11, 1988
2:00	**Sammy Silk**	**blk g, by Worthy Bowl--Kawartha Pastel (Steve Byron) Windsor Raceway, Windsor, ONT, October 14, 1990**

Three-Year-Olds

1:54.1	Mack Lobell	br c, by Mystic Park--Matina Hanover (John Campbell) Pompano Park, Pompano Beach, FL, November 13, 1987
1:56.1	**Kindava Hush**	**b f, by Arndon--Quiet Elegance (Jan Nordin) Pompano Park, Pompano Beach, FL, October 20, 1990**
	Me Maggie	b f, by Prakas--Grassbed (Berndt Lindstedt) Pompano Park, Pompano Beach, FL, November 9, 1990
1:57	J J's Diamond	b g, by Diamond Exchange--Annette W (Roger Mayotte) Mohawk Raceway, Campbellville, ONT, October 24, 1989

Four-Year-Olds

1:55	Express Ride	b h, by Super Bowl--Flory Messenger (Berndt Lindstedt) Sportsmans Park, Cicero, IL, September 6, 1987
1:54.2	**Peace Corps**	**b m, by Baltic Speed--Worth Beein (Stig Johansson) Pompano Park, Pompano Beach, FL, November 2, 1990**
1:55.2	Delray Lobell	b g, by Speedy Crown--Duchess Faye (Don Irvine Jr.) Freestate Raceway, Laurel, MD, August 20, 1989

Five-Year-Olds and Older

1:55.2	Photo Maker	b h, 9, by Yankee Bambino--Waynette (Dale McConnell) The Meadows, Meadow Lands, PA, May 30, 1987
1:56.1	**Free Token**	**b m, 6, by Jurgy Hanover--Pan Lady J (Joe Pavia Jr.) Pompano Park, Pompano Beach, FL, March 27, 1990**
1:55	**No Sex Please**	**br g, 5, by Brisco Hanover--Gay Ann Herbert (Ron Waples) Pompano Park, Pompano Beach, FL, November 2, 1990**

WORLD RECORDS

Fastest Heats

1st heat - 1:56.2	Mathers Streak, b g, 4, by Sunday Model--Borne Baby (Rick Zeron) Greenwood Raceway, Toronto, ONT, July 8, 1989	
2nd heat - 1:56.2	No Sex Please, br g, 4, by Brisco Hanover--Gay Ann Herbert (Ron Waples) Greenwood Raceway, Toronto, ONT, July 8, 1989	

Heat Racing

Two-Year-Olds

2-heat race - 4:01.2   Swirlabout, b c, by Speed in Action--Chanelette (Gene Riegle) Scioto Downs, Colubus, OH, August 4, 1988--2:01.4; 1:59.3

2 heat race - 4:04.3   Soaring Action, b f, by Speed In Action--Dorothy Lobell (Jim Dailey and Jeff Fout) Scioto Downs, Columbus, OH, August 2, 1989--2:03.4; 2:00.4

2 heat race - 4:09.2   Royal Cold, b g, by Crysta Crown--Snuffles (Mel Turcotte) Scioto Downs, Columbus, OH, August 3, 1989--2:06.3; 2:02.4

Three-Year-Olds

2-heat race - 3:54.4   Editor In Chief, b c, by Speed In Action--Sequel (Lavern Hostetler) Scioto Downs, Columbus, OH, 1988--1:58.4; 1:56

2-heat race - 3:56.3   Busy Life, b f, by Crystas Crown--Kindly Gesture (Don Swick) Scioto Downs, Columbus, OH, August 3, 1988--1:58.1; 1:58.2

2-heat race - 4:00.2   Tarport Ramey, b g, by Florida Pro--Frenzy (Trevor Ritchie) Mohawk Raceway, Campbellville, ONT, September 12, 1987--2:00.1; 2:00.1

Five-Year-Olds and Older

2-heat race - 3:55.4   Franconia, b m, 6, by Nevele Thunder--Maggie Doo Dah (John Campbell) Greenwood Raceway, Toronto, ONT, July 6, 1987--1:58.2; 1:57.2

2-heat race - 3:54   **No Sex Please, br g, 5, by Brisco Hanover--Gay Ann Herbert (Ron Waples) Greenwood Raceway, Toronto, ONT, August 18, 1990--1:57; 1:57**

Dead Heat

1:57.1	Forty-Five Caliber	b g, 7, by Florida Pro--Christmas Eve (Denis Normandin) and;
	Hypersonic	b h, 4, by Arndon--Sostenuto (Jan Johnson) Pompano Park, Pompano Beach, FL, April 13, 1990

Double-Gaited Performers

3:54	Bandit Spur	b g, by Defiant Yankee--Keystone Saffron (Dick Stillings) The Meadows, Meadow Lands, PA, September 20, 1986, 3, 1:55.3; (Dick Stillings) The Meadows, Meadow Lands, PA, August 15, 1987--4, 1:58.2

At Distances Other Than One Mile

5/8 mile - 1:16   Duchess Of Dorwood, br m, 6, by Daley Hanover--Lady Woodworth (Keith Hagen) Phoenix Trotting Park, Phoenix, AZ, November 12, 1966

11/16 mile - 1:23.1   Annette Sue, br m, 4, by Gay Song--Princess Key (Del Insko) Sportsman's Park, Cicero, IL, June 21, 1958

3/4 mile - 1:32   Express Colby, blk h, 8, by Colby Hanover--Florence (Charles Rumley) Sportsman's Park, Cicero, IL, July 21, 1958

WORLD RECORDS

1-1/16 miles - 2:18.3   Dusty Neal, ch g, 5, by Dusty Hanover--Dona Bradford (Paul Wheeler Sr.) Sportsman's Park, Cicero, IL, August 30, 1956
1-1/4 miles - 2:27.4   Sugarcane Hanover, b h, 4, by Florida Pro--Sugar Hanover (Ron Waples) Pompano Park, Pompano Beach, FL, October 30, 1987
1-5/16 miles - 2:38.2   Nobody Told Me, br g, 5, by Camp David--Keystone Darling (Jeff Gregory) Pompano Park, Pompano Beach, FL, December 22, 1989
1-5/8 miles - 3:17.1   Googie, br h, 4, by Sacremento--White Nest Egg (Jim Grundy) Los Alamitos, Los Alamitos, CA, February 10, 1989

Trotting on a Half-Mile Track in Races

All-Age

1:56	Mack Lobell	br h, 4, by Mystic Park--Matina Hanover (John Campbell) Saratoga Raceway, Saratoga Springs, NY, August 5, 1988
1:56	Peace Corps	b f, 3, by Baltic Speed--Worth Beein (John Campbell) Delaware, OH, September 21, 1989
1:58.1	Gentle Stroke	b g, 8, by Noble Gesture--Eydie Hanover (Jorn Kvikstad) Yonkers Raceway, Yonkers, NY, September 8, 1989

Two-Year-Olds

1:58.1	Royal Troubador	b c, by Super Bowl--Mae Jeans Crown (Carl Allen) Delaware, OH, September 19, 1989
1:59	Lizzie Lee Brook	by Joie De Vie--Joyous Princess (Donald Dancer) Freehold Raceway, Freehold, NJ, October 15, 1987
	Kindava Hush	b f, by Arndon--Quiet Elegance (Jan Nordin) Delaware, OH, September 19, 1989
2:01.2	Proud Coate	b g, by Mighty Crown--M J's Queen (Donald Coate) Delaware, OH, September 14, 1987

Three-Year-Olds

1:56.4	Editor In Chief	b c, by Speed In Action--Sequel (John Campbell) Delaware, OH, September 20, 1988
1:56	Peace Corps	b f, by Baltic Speed--Worth Beein (John Campbell) Delaware, OH, September 21, 1989
1:58.3	Op'Art	b g, by Speed In Action--Opalescence (Bruce Riegle) Delaware, OH, September 18, 1984

Four-Year-Olds

1:56	Mack Lobell	br c, by Mystic Park--Matina Hanover (John Campbell) Saratoga Raceway, Saratoga Springs, NY, August 5, 1988
1:57.4	Quick Trip	br m, by Quickster--Darby Hill (John Hogan) Delaware, OH, September 17, 1984; and
	Grades Singing	br m, by Texas--Singing Bay (Herve Filion) Yonkers Raceway, Yonkers, NY, July 6, 1986
1:58.2	Bille S	b g, by Speed In Action--X Pert Dot (Charles Baker) Maywood Park, Maywood, IL, September 29, 1988; and
	Arnie's Express	b g, by Lolas Express--Miss Arnie (Don O'Dwyer) Northfield Park, Northfield, OH, September 8, 1989; and
	War Nickel	**br g, by Copter Lobell--Power Bay (Ray Tremblay) Yonkers Raceway, Yonkers, NY, August 17, 1990**

Five-Year-Olds and Older

1:57.4	Lakewater Glory	br h, 5, by On To Glory--Lakewater Mom (Vitaly Tanishin) Northfield Park, Northfield, OH May 26, 1989
1:57.2	**Kit Lobell**	**b m, 5, by Speedy Crown--Keystone Pioneer (Berndt Lindstedt) Yonkers Raceway, Yonkers, NY, July 29, 1990**

WORLD RECORDS

1:58.1   Gentle Stroke   b g, 8, by Noble Gesture--Eydie Hanover (Jorn Kvikstad) Yonkers Raceway, Yonkers, NY, September 8, 1989

Fastest Heats

1st heat - 1:57.4   Quick Trip, br m, 4, Quickster--Darby Hill (John Hogan) Delaware, OH, September Trip, br m, 4, Quickster--Darby Hill (John Hogan) Delaware, OH, September 17, 1984; and Master Willie, b c, 3, by Super Bowl--Serengeti (Jan Nordin) Delaware, OH, September 18, 1985

2nd heat - 1:56.4   Editor In Chief, b c, 5, by Speed In Action--Sequel (John Campbell) Delaware, OH, September 20, 1988

3rd heat - 2:02-1/2   Scotland's Comet, b h, 5, by Scotland--Iosola's Worthy (Frank Ervin) Greenville, OH, August 24, 1944

Heat Racing

2-heat race - 3:55.3   Editor In Chief, b c, 3, by Speed In Action--Sequel (John Campbell) Delaware, OH, September 20, 1988--1:58.4; 1:56.4

2-heat race - 3:56.2   Erika's Impulse, br f, 3, by Nevele Impulse--Erika Lynn (Jeff Fout) Delaware, OH, September 14, 1987--1:58.2; 1:58

2-heat race - 3:59   Op'Art, b g, 3, by Speed In Action--Opalescence (Bruce Riegle) Delaware, OH, September 18, 1984--1:58.3; 2:00.2

3-heats divided - 6:01.4 Lender Hanover, b c, 3, by Prakas--Laura Hanover (Jan Nordin) Delaware, OH, September 21, 1990 (Meadowbranch Eddy won 1st heat) 2:00;1:59.1;2:02.3

3-heats divided - 6:05   Single Hill, b f, 3, by Nevele Pride--Solo Hill (Joe Adamsky) Delaware, OH, September 23, 1981 (Keystone Sister won 1st heat) 1:59.4; 2:01.3; 2:03.3

3-heats divided - 6:09.1   Sidney Hanover, b g, 7, by Dean Hanover--Charm Hanover (Franklin Safford) Historic Track, Goshen, NY, July 7, 1948 (Proximity won 1st heat) 2:02.2; 2:03; 2:03.4

Two-Year-Olds

2-heat race - 3:58.4   Editor In Chief, b c, by Speed In Action--Sequel (Jeff Fout) Delaware, OH, September 14, 1987--1:59.3; 1:59.1

2-heat race - 3:58.2   Anamosa Hanover, b f, by Speedy Crown--Anders Favorite (Jan Nordin) Delaware, OH, September 15, 1987--1:59.1; 1:59.1

2-heat race - 4:07.3   Royal Cold, b g, by Crystas Crown--Snuffles (Mel Turcotte) Delaware, OH, September 18, 1989--2:03.3; 2:04

Three-Year-Olds

2-heat race - 3:55.3   Editor In Chief, b c, by Speed In Action--Sequel (John Campbell) Deleware, OH, September 20, 1988--1:58.4; 1:56.4

2-heat race - 3:56.2   Erika's Impulse, br f, by Nevele Impulse--Erika Lynn (Jeff Fout) Delaware, OH, September 14, 1987--1:58.2; 1:58

2-heat race - 3:59   Op'Art, b g, by Speed In Action--Opalescence (Bruce Riegle) Delaware, OH, September 18, 1984--1:58.3; 2:00.2

3-heats divided - 6:01.4 Lender Hanover, b c, by Prakas--Laura Hanover (Jan Nordin) Delaware, OH, September 21, 1990 (Meadowbranch Eddy won the first heat) 2:00; 1:59.1; 2:02.3

3-heats divided - 6:05   Single Hill, b f, by Nevele Pride--Solo Hill (Joe Adamsky) Delaware, OH, September 23, 1981 (Keystone Sister won 1st heat) 1:59.4; 2:01.3; 2:03.3

WORLD RECORDS

Dead Heat

2:01.4	Nature Lover	b c, 3, by Speedster--Gay Blossom (Hakan Wallner) and
	Turn For Home	br c, 3, by Nevele Pride--The Dutchess (Jan Johnson)--Louisville Downs, Louisville, KY, September 7, 1979

Double-Gaited Performers

4:00.2	Crockett	b h, by Diller Hanover--Anchora Hanover (Fred Parks) Rosecroft Raceway, Oxon Hill, MD, May 20, 1966 - 4, 2:01.1; and (Fred Parks) Brandywine Raceway, Wilmington, DE, August 9, 1969 - p, 7, 1:59.1
4:04.2	Countess Adios	b m, by Adios--Countess Vivian (Delvin Miller) Delaware, OH, September 19, 1960 - p, 3, 1:59.1; and (Delvin Miller) Maywood Park, Maywood, IL, May 1, 1963 - 6, 2:05.1
4:00.2	Crown Wood	ch g, by Speedy Crown--Sugar Frosting (Buddy Gilmour) Roosevelt Raceway, Westbury, NY, August 27, 1982 - p, 4, 2:00.3; and (Joe Marsh, Jr.) Yonkers Raceway, Yonkers, NY, September 23, 1983 - 5, 1:59.4

At Distances Other Than One Mile

1/2 mile - 1:00	Daylee, b g, 8, by Guy Day--Peggy Lee (Joe Hylan) Freehold Raceway, Freehold, NJ, August 30, 1941
5/8 mile - 1:16	Ragweed Bob, b g, 11, by Hollyrood Bob--Hollyrood Brenda (Carl Scott) Fort Miami Raceway, Toledo, OH, July 28, 1948
3/4 mile - 1:32	Milestone, b g, 4, by Volomite--Pearl Xavier (Curly Smart) Roosevelt Raceway, Westbury, NY, May 30, 1941; and Wee Laird, br h, 7, by Volomite--Bonnie Lassie (Herbert Roth) Buffalo Raceway, Hamburg, NY, July 4, 1944
13/16 mile - 1:37.1	Katie Key, b m, 7, by Long Key--Beulah Gayle (Clint Hodgins) Roosevelt Raceway, Westbury, NY, July 30, 1954
1-1/16 miles - 2:07.2	Nevele Pride, b h, by Star's Pride--Thankful (Stanley Dancer) Roosevelt Raceway, Westbury, NY, August 2, 1969
1-1/8 miles - 2:24.4	Sweet Lollipop, b m, 5, by Speedy Count--Lisa Medium (Leigh Fitch) Rochester, NH, September 18, 1979
1-1/4 miles - 2:28.3	**Reve D Udon, b h, 7, by Ejakval--Mavia Du Vivier (Yves Dreux) Yonkers Raceway, Yonkers, NY, August 5, 1990**
1-1/2 miles - 3:01.3	Kash Minbar, br h, 5, by Egyptian Candor--Lambeth (Earl Cruise) Roosevelt Raceway, Westbury, NY, July 30, 1977

Pacing on a Mile Track in Races

All-Age

1:49.3	Nihilator	b c, 3, by Niatross--Margie's Melody (Bill O'Donnell) The Meadowlands, East Rutherford, NJ, August 3, 1985; and
	Call For Rain	b h, 4, by Storm Damage--Rain Proof (Clint Galbraith) The Red Mile, Lexington, KY, October 1, 1988
1:51.2	**Caesars Jackpot**	**b f, 4, by Walton Hanover--Tracys Jackpot (Bill Fahy) The Meadowlands, East Rutherford, NJ, August 4, 1990**
	Miss Easy	b f, 2, by Amity Chef--Pleasure Seeker (John Campbell) The Red Mile, Lexington, KY, September 25, 1990
1:51.1	Indian Alert	b g, 4, by Armbro Alert--Lemons Mills (Jack Moiseyev), The Meadowlands, East Rutherford, NJ, June 17, 1988
	Boston Blue Chip	ch g, 3, by On The Road Again--Backseat Driver (Joe Schwind) The Meadowlands, East Rutherford, NJ, August 4, 1990

WORLD RECORDS

Two-Year-Olds

1:51.4	Deal Direct	b c, by Direct Scooter--Dee Bee Hitter (Chip Noble) Indianapolis, IN, August 25, 1990
1:51.2	Miss Easy	**b f, by Amity Chef--Pleasure Seeker (John Campbell) The Red Mile, Lexington, KY, September 25, 1990**
1:54	Mr Gourmet	b g, by Mr Dalrae--Upper (Tom Harper) The Red Mile, Lexington, KY, October 5, 1990

Three-Year-Olds

1:49.3	Nihilator	b c, by Niatross--Margie's Melody (Bill O'Donnell) The Meadowlands, East Rutherford, NJ, August 3, 1985
1:51.3	Don't Dally	br f, by Meadow Skipper--Dalliance (John Campbell) Du Quoin, IL, August 30, 1984
1:51.1	**Boston Blue Chip**	ch g, by On The Road Again--Backseat Driver (Joe Schwind) The Meadowlands, East Rutherford, NJ, August 4, 1990

Four-Year-Olds

1:49.3	Call For Rain	b h, by Storm Damage--Rain Proof (Cling Galbraith) The Red Mile, Lexington, KY, October 1, 1988
1:51.2	**Caesars Jackpot**	**b m, by Walton Hanover--Tracys Jackpot (Bill Fahy) The Meadowlands, East Rutherford, NJ, August 4, 1990**
1:51.1	Indian Alert	b g, by Armbro Alert--Lemons Mill (Jack Moiseyev) The Meadowlands, East Rutherford, NJ, June 17, 1988

Five-Year-Olds and Older

1:50.1	Ramblin Storm	b r, 6, by Storm Damage--Elda Belle (Michel Lachance) The Meadowlands, East Rutherford, NJ, July 8, 1988
1:51.3	Armbro Feather	b m, 5, by Most Happy Fella--Brets Velvet (John Kopas) The Meadowlands, East Rutherford, NJ, August 5, 1989
1:52.1	Intruder Almahurst	b g, 7, by Keystone Ore--Impish Almahurst (Carl Garofalo) The Meadowlands, East Rutherford, NJ, August 6, 1988

Fastest Heats

1st heat - 1:50	**Beach Towel, b c, 3, by French Chef--Sunburn (Ray Remmen) DuQuoin, IL, August 30, 1990**
2nd heat - 1:51.1	Run The Table, b c, 3, by Landslide--Hustlers Best (John Campbell) The Meadowlands, East Rutherford, NJ, August 6, 1987
	Camtastic, b c, 3, by Cam Fella--Lushkara (Bill O'Donnell) The Red Mile, Lexington, KY, October 1, 1988
	Beach Towel, b c, 3, by French Chef--Sunburn (Ray Remmen) The Red Mile, Lexington, KY, September 29, 1990
3rd heat - 1:58	Billy Direct, b c, 3, by Napoleon Direct--Gay Forbes (Vic Fleming) The Red Mile, Lexington, KY, September 29, 1937

Heat Racing

All-Age

2-heat race - 3:42.1	Camtastic, br c, 3, by Cam Fella--Lushkara (Bill O'Donnell) The Red Mile, Lexington, KY, Ocotober 1, 1988--1:51; 151.1
2-heat race - 3:45.4	Leah Almahurst, b f, 3, by Abercrombie--Liberated Angel (Bill Fahy) The Red Mile, Lexington, KY, September 29, 1988--1:53.1; 1:52.3
2-heat race - 3:49	Egyptian Wolf, b g, 3, by Armbro Wolf--Egyptian Lin (John Campbell) Du Quoin, IL, September 4, 1987--1:54; 1:55

WORLD RECORDS

3-heats divided - 5:47.1 Super Clint, br c, 3, by Super Wave--St. Patricks Morn (John Kopas) The Red Mile, Lexington, KY, October 7, 1977 (Governor Skipper won 1st heat) 1:54, 1:54, 1:59.1

Two-Year-Olds

2-heat race - 3:44.3	**Deal Direct, b c, by Direct Scooter--Dee Bee Hitter (Chip Noble) Indianapolis, IN, August 25, 1990--1:51.4; 1:52.4**
2-heat race - 3:46.4	Amneris, b f, by Tyler B--Aida Hanover (Jan Nordin) Springfield, IL, August 15, 1984--1:53.3; 1:53.1
2-heat race - 3:53.4	Ann's Society, b g, by Ideal Society--Egyptian Sapphire (Dave Magee) Springfield, IL, August 15, 1988--1:56.3; 1:57.1

Three-Year-Olds

2-heat race - 3:42.1	Camtastic, br c, by Cam Fella--Lushkara (Bill O'Donnell) The Red Mile, Lexington, KY, October 1, 1988--1:51; 1:51.1
2-heat race - 3:45.4	Leah Almahurst, b f, by Abercrombie--Liberated Angel (Bill Fahy) The Red Mile, Lexington, KY, September 29, 1988--1:53.1; 1:52.3
2-heat race - 3:49	Egyptian Wolf, b g, 3, by Armbro Wolf--Egyptian Lin (John Campbell) Du Quoin, IL, September 4, 1987--1:54; 1:55
3-heats divided - 5:47.1	Super Clint, br c, by Super Wave--St. Patricks Morn (John Kopas) The Red Mile, Lexington, KY, October 7, 1977 (Governor Skipper won 1st heat) 1:54, 1:54, 1:59.1
3-heats divided - 6:09.2	Timely Beauty, b f, 3, by Good Time--Lorraine (Frank Ervin) The Red Mile, Lexington, KY, September 28, 1963 (Glad Rags won 2nd heat) 2:01.4, 1:59.3, 2:08

Dead Heat

1:51.2	Jaguar Spur	b c, 3, by Albatross--J D's Bret (Dick Stillings) and
	Laag	gr c, 3, by Abercrombie--Tinsel (Dick Farrington) The Red Mile, Lexington, KY, September 26, 1987

Double-Gaited Performers
(See table for trotters on a mile track in races)

At Distances Other Than One Mile

1/2 mile - :56.1	Todeo Four, b h, 4, by Infiltrator--Romeo Thirty Six (Doug Hamilton) Du Quoin, IL, September 1, 1988
9/16 mile - 1:04.3	Deep Avian, b h, 8, by Deep Adios--Avian Star (Jim Doherty) The Meadowlands, East Rutherford, NJ, October 28, 1976
5/8 mile - 1:06.3	Hecs Shady Lady, b m, 5 by Shady Hill Hec--Sugar Shop (Steve Scrannage) Assiniboia Downs, Winnepeg, CAN, March 31, 1989
11/16 mile - 1:19.2	Frosty Anderson, gr g, 6, by Black Demon--Clever Bernie (James Fisher) Washington Park, Homewood, IL, July 28, 1970
3/4 mile - 1:26.4	**Beechers Brook b g, 10, by Lumber King--Call Girl Donut (Charles Connor) Vernon Downs, Vernon, NY, October 24, 1990**
13/16 mile - 1:36.1	Swinging Andy, b g, 6, by Bye Bye Andy--Sharon Wave (J.C. Miller, Jr.) Lake Shore Meadows, Fairview, PA, June 30, 1984
7/8 mile - 1:44	Adios, b h, 6, by Hal Dale--Adioo Volo (Frank Ervin) Santa Anita, Arcadia, CA, April 27, 1946; and
	Vernon Elkington, blk c, 3, by Vernon Hanover--Miss Volo Majesty (Henry Clukey) Vernon Downs, Vernon, NY, August 31, 1953
15/16 mile - 1:53.3	Gay Harmony, br g, 5, by Abbe Guy--Gayety (Ken Russell) Vernon Downs, Vernon, NY, July 28, 1954
1-1/16 miles - 2:01.2	Persistent, b h, 7, by Meadow Skipper--Sweetest Story (Cat Manzi) The Meadowlands, East Rutherford, NJ, March 28, 1987

WORLD RECORDS

1-1/8 miles - 2:07.3	Niatross, b c, 3, by Albatross--Niagara Dream (Clint Galbraith) Hollywood Park, Inglewood, CA, November 21, 1980
1-3/16 miles - 2:21.1	Igetthepicture, b g, 7, by Direct Scooter--Bottoms Up (Dan Knox) Balmoral Park, Crete, IL, May 6, 1990
1-1/4 miles - 2:30.2	Dr. Stanton, b g, 7, by Bonnycastle--Mary Philistine (W. Lindley Fraser) Santa Anita, Arcadia, CA, May 15, 1948
1-1/2 miles - 2:53.1	What's Next, b h, 5, by Most Happy Fella--Backseat Driver (Mickey McNichol) The Meadowlands, East Rutherford, NJ, May 30, 1987

Pacing on a Five Eighths-Mile Track In Races

All-Age

1:50.4	In The Pocket	br h, 3, by Direct Scooter--Black Jade (John Campbell) The Meadows, Meadow Lands, PA, August 11, 1990
1:52.2	Caesars Jackpot	b m, 4, by Walton Hanover--Tracy's Jackpot (Wally Hennessey) Pompano Park, Pompano Beach, FL, October 20, 1990
1:52.3	Division Street	b g, 5, by Most Happy Fella--Spiked Byrdie (Michel Lachance) Freestate Raceway, Laurel, MD, September 27, 1985
	Night Colt	br g, 7, by Abercrombie--Regina Marie (Mario Baillargeon) Greenwood Raceway, Toronto, ONT, July 21, 1990

Two-Year-Olds

1:51.1	Artsplace	b c, by Abercrombie--Miss Elvira (John Campbell) Pompano Park, Pompano Beach, FL, November 30, 1990
1:53.3	Central Park West	b f, by Big Towner--Park Ave Bell (John Campbell) Pompano Park, Pompano Beach, FL, November 18, 1988
1:55.3	Scotch Baker	b g, by Baker Field--Bonnie Lass N (Steve Brannan) Raceway Park, Toledo, OH, July 16, 1989

Three-Year-Olds

1:50.4	In The Pocket	br h, by Direct Scooter--Black Jade (John Campbell) The Meadows, Meadow Lands, PA, August 11, 1990
1:52.3	Rulers Chippie	b m, by Radiant Ruler--Falcons Chip (Bruce Ranger) Pompano Park, Pompano Beach, FL, December 29, 1990
1:53	Minuteman Hill	b g, by On The Road Again--Dancing Almahurst (Kevin Lare) Rosecroft Raceway, Oxon Hill, MD, July 6, 1990

Four-Year-Olds

1:51	Matt's Scooter	b h, by Direct Scooter--Ellens Glory (Michel Lachance) Mohawk Raceway, Campbellville, ONT, October 1, 1989
1:52.2	Caesars Jackpot	b m, by Walton Hanover--Tracy's Jackpot (Wally Hennessey) Pompano Park, Pompano Beach, FL, October 20, 1990
1:52.4	Eagle Speaker	b g, by Conquered--Timely Trudy (John Holmes) Greenwood Raceway, Toronto, ONT, July 6, 1990

Five-Year-Olds and Older

1:51.2	T.K.'s Skipper	br h, 5, by Governor Skipper--Shana Hanover (Joe Anderson) Los Alamitos, Los Alamitos, CA, September 29, 1990
1:53.1	Armbro Feather	b m, 5, by Most Happy Fella--Brets Velvet (Buddy Gilmour) Greenwood Raceway, Toronto, ONT, July 1, 1989
1:52.3	Division Street	b g, 5, by Most Happy Fella--Spiked Byrdie (Michel Lachance) Freestate Raceway, Laurel, MD, September 27, 1985
	Night Colt	br g, 7, by Abercrombie--Regina Marie (Mario Baillargeon) Greenwood Raceway, Toronto, ONT, July 21, 1990

WORLD RECORDS

Fastest Heats

1st heat - 1:50.4	**In The Pocket, br c, 3, by Direct Scooter--Black Jade (John Campbell) The Meadows, Meadow Lands, PA, August 11, 1990**
2nd heat - 1:51.4	**Beach Towel, b c, 3 by French Chef--Sunburn (Ray Remmen) The Meadows, Meadow Lands, PA, August 11, 1990**
3rd heat - 2:03	Romulus Hanover, ch c, 3, by Dancer Hanover--Romola Hanover (Billy Haughton) The Meadows, Meadow Lands, PA, August 12, 1967

Heat Racing

All-Age

2-heat race - 3:46.3	**Beach Towel, b c, 3, by French Chef--Sunburn (Ray Remmen) Blue Bonnets, Montreal, QUE, August 19, 1990--1:53.1, 1:53.2**
2-heat race - 3:49.3	Just Like Joanna, b f, 3, by Falcon Almahurst--Joannas Time (Jeff Fout) Scioto Downs, Columbus, OH, August 5, 1988--1:55; 1:54.3
2-heat race - 3:51	Indian Alert, b g, 3, by Armbro Alert--Lemons Mill (Mickey McNichol) Greenwood Raceway, Toronto, ONT, July 13, 1987--1:54.3, 1:56.2
3-heats divided - 5:59	Romulus Hanover, ch c, 3, by Dancer Hanover--Romola Hanover (Billy Haughton) The Meadows, Meadow Lands, PA, August 12, 1967 (Best Of All won 1st heat) 1:58.2, 1:57.3, 2:03

Two-Year-Olds

2-heat race - 3:54	Chatham Light, b c, by Niatross--Miles End Brenda (John Campbell) Mohawk Raceway, Campbellville, ONT, September 12, 1987--1:56.4; 1:57.1
2-heat race - 3:56.2	Silver Reign, b f, by Kawartha Skipper--Silver Wraith (Bud Fritz) Mohawk Raceway, Campbellville, ONT, September 11, 1987--1:58.2; 1:58
2-heat race - 3:54.3	Scotch Baker, b g, by Baker Field--Bonnie Lass N (Steve Brannan) Scioto Downs, Columbus, OH, August 5, 1989--1:57.3; 1:57

Three-Year-Olds

2-heat race - 3:46.3	**Beach Towel, b c, by French Chef--Sunburn (Ray Remmen) Blue Bonnets, Montreal, QUE, August 19, 1990--1:53.1, 1:53.2**
2-heat race - 3:49.3	Just Like Joanna, b f, by Falcon Almahurst--Joannas Time (Jeff Fout) Scioto Downs, Columbus, OH, August 5, 1988--1:55; 1:54.3
2-heat race - 3:51	Indian Alert, b g, by Armbro Alert--Lemons Mill (Mickey McNichol) Greenwood Raceway, Toronto, ONT, July 13, 1987--1:54.3, 1:56.2
3-heats divided - 5:59	Romulus Hanover, ch c, by Dancer Hanover--Romola Hanover (Billy Haughton) The Meadows, Meadow Lands, PA, August 12, 1967 (Best Of All won 1st heat) 1:58.2, 1:57.3, 2:03

Dead Heat

1:55	Charge Plate	b g, 3, by Abercrombie--Glorious Georgia (Bill Zendt) and
	S T Due	b c, 3, by Abercrombie--Llllian Grattan (Don Irvine, Jr.) Scioto Downs, Columbus, OH, August 16, 1986

Double-Gaited Performers
(See table for trotters on a five-eighths mile track)

WORLD RECORDS

At Distances Other Than One Mile

5/8 mile - 1:10.3	Pig Whistlen, b g, 4, by Trenton--Adios Patti (Dave Magee) Quad City Downs, East Moline, IL, April 14, 1990
11/16 mile - 1:18.2	Todd N, b g, 6, by Tudor Hanover--Noble Averil (Jim Lackey) Fairplex Park, Pomona, CA, June 21, 1986
3/4 mile - 1:27.1	Chris Time Pick, br h, 11, by Chris Time--Miss Bye Bye (Merv Chupp) Sportsman's Park, Cicero, IL, September 26, 1984
1-1/16 miles - 2:07.4	Jigtime Buddy, ch g, 4, by Angel's Wave--Bon Flash (Barry Fagan) Champlain Raceway, Dieppe, NB, December 6, 1986
1-1/4 miles - 2:27.3	Pack Leader, ch h, 6, by Peter Lobell--Success Angel (Joe Anderson) Los Alamitos, Los Alamitos, CA, March 5, 1988
1-5/16 miles - 2:33.3	Irresistible Magic, b h, 5, by Ray Charles--Irresistible Me (Gene Vallandingham) Los Alamitos, Los Alamitos, CA, January 28, 1989
1-5/8 miles - 3:14.4	**Storm Prince, b h, 6, by Storm Damage--Beauty Parlor (Jim Morand) Los Alamitos, Los Alamitos, CA, March 17, 1990**
1-7/8 miles - 3:45.4	**Storm Prince, b h, 6, by Storm Damage--Beauty Parlor (Jim Morand) Los Alamitos, Los Alamitos, CA, April 14, 1990**

Pacing on a Half-Mile Track in Races

All-Age

1:51	Falcon Seelster	b c, 3, by Warm Breeze--Fashion Trick (Tom Harmer) Delaware, OH, September 19, 1985
1:54.4	Amneris	b f, 3, by Tyler B--Aida Hanover (John Campbell) Delaware, OH, September 18, 1985;
	Town Tattler	blk f, 3, by Big Towner--Tona Hanover (John Campbell) Delaware, OH, September 18, 1985; and
	H H Shadow	br f, 3, by Distant Thunder--H H Silhouette (Jody Stafford) Yonkers Raceway, Yonkers, NY, July 27, 1986; and
	Crystal Tree	ch m, 4, by Trim The Tree--Seilson Dream (Gerry Bookmyer) Northfield Park, Northfield, OH, August 26, 1989; and
	L Dees Trish	**b m, 4, by Merger--Bluegrass Lou (Michel Lachance) Yonkers Raceway, Yonkers, NY, November 23, 1990**
1:53.4	Hi Tech Society	b g, 3, by Ideal Society--Lotus Osborne (Merv Chupp) Maywood Park, Maywood, IL, September 26, 1987

Two-Year-Olds

1:54.1	**Tooter Scooter**	**b c, by Direct Scooter--Bloodstocks Bunny (Bill Fahy) Louisville Downs, Louisville, KY, September 1, 1990**
	W R H	**b c, by Direct Scooter--The Best Move Yet (John Campbell) Delaware, OH, September 20, 1990**
1:55.4	L Dees Trish	b f, by Merger--Bluegrass Lou (Herve Filion) Freehold Raceway, Freehold, NJ, September 10, 1988
1:55.3	Scotch Baker	b g, Baker Field--Bonnie Lass N (Steve Brannan) Delaware, OH, September 20, 1989

Three-Year-Olds

1:51	Falcon Seelster	b c, by Warm Breeze--Fashion Trick (Tom Harmer) Delaware, OH, September 19, 1985
1:54.4	Amneris	b f, by Tyler B--Aida Hanover (John Campbell) Delaware, OH, September 18, 1985;
	Town Tattler	blk f, by Big Towner--Tona Hanover (John Campbell) Delaware, OH, September, 18, 1985; and
	H H Shadow	br f, by Distant Thunder--H H Silhouette (Jody Stafford) Yonkers Raceway, Yonkers, NY, July 27, 1986

WORLD RECORDS

1:53.4	Hi Tech Society	b g, by Ideal Society--Lotus Osborne (Merv Chupp) Maywood Park, Maywood, IL, September 9, 1987

Four-Year-Olds

1:53	Jaguar Spur	b h, by Albatross--J.D.'s Bret (Dick Stillings) Northfield Park, Northfield, OH, August 27, 1988
1:54.4	Crystal Tree	ch m, by Trim The Tree--Seilson Dream (Gerry Bookmyer) Northfield Park, Northfield, OH, August 26, 1989; and
	L Dees Trish	b m, by Merger--Bluegrass Lou (Michel Lachance) **Yonkers Raceway, Yonkers, NY, November 23, 1990**
1:54	Cotton Sock	b g, by Ideal Society--Lotus Osborne (Walter Paisley) Maywood Park, Maywood, IL, August 12, 1988
	Barely Visible	b g, by Tyler B--Twilite Hanover (John Campbell) Delaware, OH, September, 17, 1989

Five-Year-Olds and Older

1:53.3	Chatham Light	b h, 5, by Niatross--Miles End Brenda (Kelly Sheppard) Hippodrome Connaught, Aylmer, QUE, May 21, 1990
1:55	Anniecrombie	b m, 5, by Abercrombie--Sparklespray (Dave Magee) Maywood Park, Maywood, IL, September 17, 1988
1:54.1	**Wiregrass Kerrigan**	**br g, 5, by Bit O Fun--Valiant Sarah (Jim Curran) Maywood Park, Maywood, IL, May 6, 1990**

Fastest Heats

1st heat - 1:52.4	Pershing Square, b c,3, by Niatross--Treasure Blue Chip (Bill O'Donnell) Delaware, OH, September 19, 1985
2nd heat - 1:52.1	Nihilator, b c, 3, by Niatross--Margie's Melody (Bill O'Donnell) Delaware, OH, September 19, 1985
3rd heat - 1:57.3	Most Happy Fella, b c, 3, by Meadow Skipper--Laughing Girl (Stanley Dancer) Delaware, OH, September 24, 1970

Heat Racing

All-Age

2-heat race - 3:45.2	Nihilator, b c, 3, by Niatross--Margie's Melody (Bill O'Donnell) Delaware, OH, September 19, 1985--1:53.1, 1:52.1
2-heat race - 3:50	Amneris, b f, 3, by Tyler B--Aida Hanover (John Campbell) Delaware, OH, September 18, 1985--1:54.4, 1:55.1
2-heat race - 3:52	Righteous Bucks, b g, 3, by Scarlet Skipper--Happy Trick (Michel Lachance) Yonkers Raceway, Yonkers, NY, July 26, 1987--1:56; 1:56
3-heats divided - 5:52.2	Most Happy Fella, b c, 3, by Meadow Skipper--Laughing Girl (Stanley Dancer) Delaware, OH, September 24, 1970 (Columbia George won 2nd heat) 1:57.1, 1:57.3, 1:57.3
3-heats divided - 5:51.1	Naughty But Nice, b f, 3, by Meadow Skipper--Angel Hair (Tom Haughton) Delaware, OH, September 19, 1984 (Hit Parade won 1st heat) 1:55.3, 1:55.2, 2:00.1

Two-Year-Olds

2-heat race - 3:50.4	Albert Albert, br c, by Abercrombie--Lismore (Chris Boring) Louisville Downs, Louisville, KY, September 5, 1987--1:55.1; 1:55.3
2-heat race - 3:54.3	Mean And Green, b f, by Big Towner--Evergreen Becky Su (Bill O'Donnell) Delaware, OH, September 20, 1989--1:57.1; 1:57.2
2-heat race - 3:54.3	Mugshot Special, b g, by Steady Special--Donna Almahurst (Dan Ater) Delaware, OH, September 21, 1990--1:56.4; 1:57.4

WORLD RECORDS

Three-Year-Olds

2-heat race - 3:45.2	Nihilator, b c, by Niatross--Margie's Melody (Bill O'Donnell) Delaware, OH, September 19, 1985--1:53.1, 1:52.1
2-heat race - 3:50	Amneris, b f, by Tyler B--Aida Hanover (John Campbell) Delaware, OH, September 18, 1985--1:54.4, 1:55.1
2-heat race - 3:52	Righteous Bucks, b g, by Scarlet Skipper--Happy Trick (Michel Lachance) Yonkers Raceway, Yonkers, NY, July 26, 1987--1:56; 1:56
3-heats divided - 5:52.2	Most Happy Fella, b c, by Meadow Skipper--Laughing Girl (Stanley Dancer) Delaware, OH, September 24, 1970 (Columbia George won 2nd heat) 1:57.1, 1:57.3, 1:57.3
3-heats divided - 5:51.1	Naughty But Nice, b f, by Meadow Skipper--Angel Hair (Tom Haughton) Delaware, OH, September 19, 1984 (Hit Parade won 1st heat) 1:55.3, 1:55.2, 2:00.1

Dead Heat

1:54.4	On The Road Again, ch h, 4, by Happy Motoring--Bye Bye Mollie (Buddy Gilmour) and
	George S b h, 4, by Thorpe Hanover--Zelda Jay (Walter Case, Jr.) Rosecroft Raceway, Oxon Hill, MD, April 13, 1985

Double-Gaited Performers
(See table for trotters on half-mile track in races)

At Distances Other Than One Mile

1/2 mile - :56.2	Whakaki N, b g, 7, by Redmond Lane--Pretty Happy (Morgan McInnis) Rosecroft Raceway, Oxon Hill, MD, November 25, 1988
9/16 mile - 1:03.3	Palladium, b h, 8 by Abercrombie--Lillian Brooke (Fred Weinkauff) Yonkers Raceway, Yonkers, NY, October 14, 1989; and
	Queens Trunk, b m, 6, by Happy Motoring--Saratoga Princess (Gary Mosher) Yonkers Raceway, Yonkers, NY, October 16, 1989; and
	Stackolee, b g, 7, by Mostly Cheer--Hardwind (Luc Ouellette) Yonkers Raceway, Yonkers, NY, October 21, 1989
5/8 mile - 1:10-1/2	Dudey Patch, b g, 11, by Gilbert Patch--dam unidentified (Joe O'Brien) Dufferin Park, Toronto, ONT, November 7, 1942
3/4 mile - 1:27.1	Hue Kash, b h, 8, by Tropic Song--Brown Paint (William Long) Rosecroft Raceway, Oxon Hill, MD, December 6, 1985
7/8 mile - 1:41.4	Senga Pennant, b g, 7, by Storm--Pebbles Baby (Freddy Gregory) Trout Springs, ALTA, June 12, 1989
13/16 mile - 1:30.2	Busters Dream, b g, 5, by Joltin Jeff--Betting Time Betty (Steve Scrannage) Queensbury Downs, SASK, October 15, 1989
1-1/16 miles - 2:03.4	**Save The Tiger, b g, 6, by Trenton--Feline (Ted Wing) Yonkers Raceway, Yonkers, NY, June 9, 1990;**
	Sterling Escort, blk h, 4, by Happy Escort--Sterla Thorpe (Alan Charles) Yonkers Raceway, Yonkers, NY, June 30, 1990;
	Peace Parley, b g, 5, by Abercrombie--Peace Rose (Carmine Abbatiello) Yonkers Raceway, Yonkers, NY, August 25, 1990
1-1/8 miles - 2:15.2	Sinamon Skip, br g, 3, by Mountain Skipper--Steady Sinamon (Dave Ingraham) Scarborough Downs, Scarborough, ME, August 27, 1989
1-1/4 miles - 2:27.4	Floored, b h, 4, by Silent Majority--Iris Blue Chip (Carmine Abbatiello) Yonkers Raceway, Yonkers, NY, September 30, 1989
1-1/2 Miles - 3:01.4	Handle With Care, b m, 5, by Meadow Skipper--Lady Emily (Billy Haughton) Yonkers Raceway, Yonkers, NY, August 21, 1976
2 miles - 4:08.4	Irvin Paul, b g, 5, by Gene Abbe--Edalena (Charles King) Yonkers Raceway, Yonkers, NY, June 28, 1962

WORLD RECORDS

MILE RECORDS BY THE WORLD CHAMPION TROTTERS

Horse, Color/Sex/Age	Sire; place where taken, year	(Driver)	Mile *
Mack Lobell, br, c, 3	Mystic Park; Springfield, IL, 1987	(John Campbell)	1:52.1
Prakas, b,c,3	Speedy Crown; Du Quoin, IL, 1985	(Bill O'Donnell)	1:53.2
Cornstalk, b,c,3	Lindy's Pride; Springfield, IL, 1984	(Howard Beissinger)	1:53.4
Fancy Crown, b,f,3	ArnieAlmahurst; Springfield, IL, 1984	(Bill O'Donnell)	1:53.4
Arndon, b,c,3	Arnie Almahurst; Lexington, KY, 1982	(Del Miller)	1:54
Lindy's Crown, b,h,4	Lindy's Pride; Du Quoin, IL, 1980	(Howard Beissinger)	1:54.4
Nevele Pride, b,h,4	Star's Pride; Indianapolis, IN, 1969	(Stanley Dancer)	1:54.4
Greyhound, gr,g,6	Guy Abbey; Lexington, KY, 1938	(Sep Palin)	1:55-1/4
Greyhound, gr,g,5	Guy Abbey; Lexington, KY, 1937	(Sep Palin)	1:56
Greyhound, gr,g,5	Guy Abbey; Lexington, KY, 1937	(Sep Palin)	1:56-3/4
Peter Manning, b,g,6	Azoff; Lexington, KY, 1922	(Tom Murphy)	1:56-3/4
Peter Manning, b,g,6	Azoff; Columbus, OH, 1922	(Tom Murphy)	1:57
Peter Manning, b,g,5	Azoff; Lexington, KY, 1921	(Tom Murphy)	1:57-3/4
Peter Manning, b,g,5	Azoff; Syracuse, NY, 1921	(Tom Murphy)	1:58
Uhlan, blk,g,8	Bingen; Lexington, KY, 1912	(Charles Tanner)	1:58
Lou Dillon, ch,m,5	Sidney Dillon; Memphis, TN, 1903	(Millard Sanders)	1:58-1/4
Lou Dillon, ch,m,5	Sidney Dillon; Readville, MA, 1903	(Millard Sanders)	2:00
Cresceus, ch,h,7	Robert McGregor; Columbus, OH, 1901	(George Ketcham)	2:02-1/4
Cresceus, ch,h,7	Robert McGregor; Cleveland, OH, 1901	(George Ketcham)	2:02-3/4
The Abbot, b,g,7	Chimes; Terre Haute, IN, 1900	(Edward Geers)	2:03-1/4
Alix, b,m,6	Patronage; Galesburg, IL, 1894	(Andrew McDowell)	2:03-3/4
Nancy Hanks, b,m,6	Happy Medium; Terre Haute, IN, 1892	(Budd Doble)	2:04
Nancy Hanks, b,m,6	Happy Medium; Independence, IA, 1892	(Budd Doble)	2:05-1/4
Nancy Hanks, b,m,6	Happy Medium; Chicago, IL, 1892	(Budd Doble)	2:07-1/4
Sunol, b,m,5	Electioneer; Stockton, CA, 1891	(Charles Marvin)	2:08-1/4
Maud S., ch,m,11	Harold; Cleveland, OH, 1885	(William Bair)	2:08-3/4
Maud S., ch,m,10	Harold; Lexington, KY, 1884	(William Bair)	2:09-1/4
Maud S., ch,m,10	Harold; Cleveland, OH, 1884	(William Bair)	2:09-3/4
Jay-Eye-See, blk,g,6	Dictator; Providence, RI, 1884	(E.D. Bither)	2:10
Maud S., ch,m,7	Harold; Rochester, NY, 1881	(William Bair)	2:10-1/4
Maud S., ch,m,7	Harold; Pittsburgh, PA, 1881	(William Bair)	2:10-1/4
Maud S., ch,m,6	Harold; Chicago, IL, 1880	(William Bair)	2:10-3/4
St. Julien, b,g,11	Volunteer; Hartford, CT, 1880	(Orrin Hickok)	2:11-1/4
St. Julien, b,g,11	Volunteer; Rochester, NY, 1880	(Orrin Hickok)	2:11-3/4
Maud S., ch,m,6	Harold; Rochester, NY, 1880	(William Bair)	2:11-3/4
St. Julien, b,g,10	Volunteer; Oakland, CA, 1879	(Orrin Hickok)	2:12-3/4
Rarus, b,g,11	Conklin's Abdallah; Buffalo, NY, 1878	(John Splan)	2:13-1/4
Rarus, b,g,11	Conklin's Abdallah; Cleveland, OH, 1878	(John Splan)	2:14
Goldsmith Maid, b,m,17	Abdallah; Boston, MA, 1874	(Budd Doble)	2:14
Goldsmith Maid,b,m,17	Abdallah; Rochester, NY, 1874	(Budd Doble)	2:14-3/4
Goldsmith Maid,b,m,17	Abdallah; Buffalo, NY, 1874	(Budd Doble)	2:15-1/4
Goldsmith Maid,b,m,17	Abdallah; E. Saginaw, MI, 1874	(Budd Doble)	2:16
Goldsmith Maid,b,m,17	Abdallah; E. Saginaw, MI, 1874	(Budd Doble)	2:16-1/4
Occident, br,g,10	Doc; Sacramento, CA, 1873	(George Tennant)	2:16-3/4
Goldsmith Maid,b,m,15	Abdallah; Boston, MA, 1872	(Budd Doble)	2:16-3/4
Goldsmith Maid,b,m,14	Abdallah; Milwaukee, WI, 1871	(Budd Doble)	2:17
Dexter, br,g,9	Hambletonian; Buffalo, NY, 1867	(Budd Doble)	2:17-1/4
Dexter, br,g,9	Hambletonian; Boston, MA, 1867	(Budd Doble)	2:19
Flora Temple, b,m,14	Bogus Hunter; Kalamazoo, MI, 1859	(James McMann)	2:19-3/4
Flora Temple, b,m,14	Bogus Hunter; Cincinnati, OH, 1859	(James McMann)	2:21-1/4
Flora Temple, b,m,14	Bogus Hunter; Centerville, NY, 1859	(James McMann)	2:22
Flora Temple, b,m,14	Bogus Hunter; Centerville, NY, 1859	(James McMann)	2:23-1/4
Flora Temple, b,m,11	Bogus Hunter; Union Course, NY, 1856	(Hiram Woodruff)	2:24-1/4
Flora Temple, b,m,8	Bogus Hunter; Utica, NY, 1853	(Hiram Woodruff)	2:27
Tacony, ro,g,9	Sportsman; Union Course, NY, 1853	(Hiram Woodruff)	2:27
Highland Maid, b,m,6	Saltram; Centerville, NY, 1855	(F.J. Nodine)	2:27
Pelham, b,g,12	unknown; Centerville, NY, 1849	(William Wheelan)	2:28
Lady Suffolk, gr,m,12	Engineer II; Hoboken, NJ, 1845	(David Bryan)	2:29-1/4

WORLD RECORDS

MILE RECORDS BY THE WORLD CHAMPIONSHIP PACERS

Horse, color, sex, age	Sire, place where taken, year, driver	Mile *
Matt's Scooter, b,c,3	Direct Scooter; Lexington, KY, 1988 (Michel Lachance)	1:48.2
Niatross, b,c,3	Albatross; Lexington, KY, 1980 (Clint Galbraith)	1:49.1
Steady Star, b,h,4	Steady Beau; Lexington, KY, 1971 (Joe O'Brien)	1:52
Bret Hanover, b,h,4	Adios; Lexington, KY, 1966 (Frank Ervin)	1:53.3
Bret Hanover, b,h,4	Adios; Vernon, NY, 1966 (Frank Ervin)	1:54
Adios Butler, b,h,4	Adios; Lexington, KY, 1960 (Paige West)	1:54.3
Adios Harry, br,h,4	Adios; Vernon, NY, 1955 (Luther Lyons)	1:55
Billy Direct, b,h,4	Napoleon Direct, Lexington, KY, 1938 (Vic Fleming)	1:55
Dan Patch, br,h,9	Joe Patchen; Lexington, KY, 1905 (Harry Hersey)	1:55-1/4
Dan Patch, br,h,8	Joe Patchen; Memphis, TN, 1904 (Harry Hersey)	1:56
Dan Patch, br,h,7	Joe Patchen; Memphis, TN, 1903 (Myron McHenry)	1:56-1/4
Dan Patch, br,h,7	Joe Patchen; Brighton Beach, NY, 1903 (Myron McHenry)	1:59
Star Pointer, b,h,8	Brown Hal; Readville, MA, 1897 (Dave McClary)	1:59-1/4
John R. Gentry, b,h,7	Ashland Wilkes; Portland, ME, 1896 (W.J. Andrews)	2:00-1/4
John R. Gentry, b,h,7	Ashland Wilkes; Glen Falls, NY, 1896 (W.J. Andrews)	2:01-1/4
Robert J., b,g,6	Hartford; Terre Haute, IN, 1894 (Edward Geers)	2:01-1/4
Robert J., b,g,6	Hartford; Indianapolis, IN, 1894 (Edward Geers)	2:02-1/4
Robert J., b,g,6	Hartford; Ft. Wayne, IN, 1894 (Edward Geers)	2:03-3/4
Flying Jib, b,g,8	Algona; Chicago, IL, 1893 (John Kelly)	2:04
Mascot, b,g,7	Deceive; Terre Haute, IN, 1892 (W.J. Andrews)	2:04
Hal Pointer, b,g,8	Tom Hal; Chicago, IL, 1892 (Edward Geers)	2:05-1/4
Direct, b,h,6	Director; Independence, IA, 1891 (George Starr)	2:06
Johnston, b,g,7	Joe Bassett; Chicago, IL, 1884 (John Splan)	2:06-1/4
Johnston, b,g,6	Joe Bassett; Chicago, IL, 1883 (John Splan)	2:10
Johnston, b,g,6	Joe Bassett; Chicago, IL, 1883 (John Splan)	2:11-3/4
Little Brown Jug, br,g,6	Tom Hal; Hartford, CT, 1881 (W.H. McCarthy)	2:11-3/4
Sleepy Tom, ch,g,11	Tom Rolfe; Chicago, IL, 1879 (Stephen Phillips)	2:12-1/4
Sleepy Tom, ch,g,11	Tom Rolfe; Columbus, OH, 1879 (Stephen Phillips)	2:14
Rowdy Boy, blk,g,10	Bull Pup; E. Saginaw, MI, 1879 (C.W. Forth)	2:15
Sweetzer, gr,g,10	Tom Crowder; Oakland, CA, 1878 (A.M. Wilson)	2:15
Yankee Sam, dn,g	Age, pedigree unknown; Uhrichsville, OH, 1869 (T. Elwood)	2:16-1/4
Pocahontas, ch,m,8	Iron's Cadmus; Union Course, NY, 1885 (James McMann)	2:17-1/2
Pet, ro,g	Age, pedigree unknown; Union Course, NY, 1855 (Unknown)	2:18-1/4
Pet, ro,g	Age, pedigree unknown; Union Course, NY, 1851 (Jas. Whelpley)	2:21-1/4
Dan Miller, ch,g	Age, pedigree unknown; Centerville, NY, 1849 (Jas. Whelpley)	2:23
Unknown, ch,g	Age, pedigree unknown; Beacon Course, NJ, 1844 (Unknown)	2:23
Aggie Down, gr,m	Age, pedigree unknown; Beacon Course, NJ, 1844 (Unknown)	2:29

* - Times, prior to 1947, were recorded in one-quarter second increments, and then in one-fifth second increments thereafter.

"Parked-Out" Computations

Harness racing mathematicians have compiled these figures on the added distance in each mile race that a horse travels when "parked out" (racing outside another horse, five feet out from the point at which the track is measured).

1/2 - mile track (or tracks with four turns to a mile)   A horse must travel 62.832 feet farther

5/8 - mile track (or tracks with three turns to a mile)   A horse must travel 47.124 feet farther

3/4 - mile track with chute and mile track (2 turns to a mile) A horse must travel 31.416 feet farther

WORLD RECORDS

A HISTORY OF WORLD RECORD SPEED: 1890-1990

The following listing is a history of Standardbred speed from 1890 through 1990. The fastest mile (whether a time trial or a race mile) for each age, sex, and gait is charted. The current world record holders are identified in the preceeding pages of this section. In addition, the chart shows the total number of 2:00 miles for each of the years shown:

Trotters

	1990	1980	1970	1960	1950	1940
2yo Colt/Gelding	1:55 3/5	1:57	1:58 2/5	2:00	2:00	2:02
2yo Filly	1:55	1:56 3/5	1:58 3/5	1:59 4/5	2:02	2:02
3yo Colt/Gelding	1:52 1/5	1:55	1:56 3/5	1:58	1:58	1:58 1/2
3yo Filly	1:52 4/5	1:56 3/5	1:58	1:58	1:59 1/4	1:59 1/4
Aged Horse/Gelding	1:53	1:54 4/5	1:54 4/5	1:55 1/4	1:55 1/4	1:55 1/4
Aged Mare	1:54 4/5	1:55 2/5	1:56 3/4	1:56 3/4	1:56 3/4	1:56 3/4
2:00 Miles	1,451	138	19	14	4	2

	1930	1920	1910	1900	1890
2yo Colt/Gelding	2:02 3/4	2:04 1/2	2:09 1/2	2:10 3/4	2:20 3/4
2yo Filly	2:02	2:04 1/4	2:07 3/4	2:14	2:18
3yo Colt/Gelding	1:59 3/4	2:03 1/2	2:04 3/4	2:10 1/2	2:12
3yo Filly	1:59 1/2	2:02 1/4	2:06 1/2	2:08 3/4	2:10 1/2
Aged Horse/Gelding	1:56 3/4	1:58	1:58 3/4	2:03 1/4	2:10
Aged Mare	1:58 1/4	1:58 1/2	1:58 1/2	2:03 3/4	2:08 3/4
2:00 Miles	4	None	1	None	None

Pacers

	1990	1980	1970	1960	1950	1940
2yo Colt/Gelding	1:51 1/5	1:54	1:57	1:57	2:00 2/5	2:00 3/4
2yo Filly	1:51 2/5	1:56 1/5	1:57 1/5	1:58 1/5	2:00 4/5	2:02 1/2
3yo Colt/Gelding	1:48 2/5	1:49 1/5	1:54	1:55 3/5	1:57 3/4	1:57 3/4
3yo Filly	1:51 2/5	1:53 3/5	1:56 2/5	1:57	1:59 3/4	1:59 3/4
Aged Horse/Gelding	1:49 2/5	1:52	1:53 3/5	1:54 3/5	1:55	1:55
Aged Mare	1:50 4/5	1:52 4/5	1:56 3/4	1:56 3/4	1:56 3/4	1:56 3/4
2:00 Miles	27,435	3,760	287	106	22	8

	1930	1920	1910	1900	1890
2yo Colt/Gelding	2:04 1/4	2:07 3/4	2:07 3/4	2:07 3/4	2:16 1/2
2yo Filly	2:04 3/4	2:08 3/4	2:08 3/4	2:10 1/2	2:24 1/2
3yo Colt/Gelding	1:59 1/2	2:01 1/4	2:05 1/2	2:05 1/2	2:14 1/4
3yo Filly	2:00 3/4	2:00 3/4	2:06 1/4	2:09 1/4	2:14
Aged Horse/Gedling	1:55 1/4	1:55 1/4	1:55 1/4	2:00 1/2	2:06 1/4
Aged Mare	1:58 1/4	1:58 1/4	2:00 1/4	2:04 1/2	2:10
2:00 Miles	5	5	5	None	None

98th Kentucky Futurity

The Crowns

THE CROWNS

THE TROTTING TRIPLE CROWN

$424,965 Yonkers Trot
Yonkers Raceway - July 14, 1990

Horse (Driver)	PP	1/4	1/2	3/4	Stretch	Finish	Time	$1.00
$127,489 First Elimination	Times -			:29.1	:59	1:29.2	1:58.3	
Cheyenne Spur (Dick Stillings)	1	1	1	1	1/2	1/2H	1:58.3	.30*
Embassy Lobell (Michel Lachance)	6	5	5o	3	2/2	2/2H	1:59	3.70
The Devil (Bill O'Donnell)	7	6	6	5o	4/3H	3/5H	1:59.3	8.40
Pastel Pastel (Carmine Abbatiello)	5	3	3	4	5/4H	4/7T	2:00.1	10.20
Sambuca Lobell (Pekka Korpi)	8	7	7	6o	6/5Q	x5/9	2:00.2	97.40
Devon's Gait (Herve Filion)	4	2	2	x7	7/dis	6/dis		57.10
Halibut (Harold Kelly)	3	4	4o	2xo	3/2Q	7/dis		89.10
Grundy's Rambo (Jan Nordin)	2x	8	8	8	8/dis	8/dis		52.70
$127,489 Second Elimination	Times -			:28.4	:57.4	1:28.4	1:59.2	
King Of The Sea (Stanley Dancer)	4	1	1	1	1/1H	1/1	1:59.2	4.10
Jacquie's Kosmos (Bill Fahy)	2	4	4	3	2/1H	2/1	1:59.3	55.90
Royal Troubador (Carl Allen)	5x	8	6o	4o	4/3H	3/3	2:00	.30*
Incredible D J (John Patterson, Jr.)	7	3	2o	2o	3/1T	4/4Q	2:00.1	5.40
Gypsy Thief (Michel Lachance)	8	7	7	6o	5/4T	5/4T	2:00.2	21.70e
Clarendon (Pekka Korpi)	6	6	5	7o	6/6	6/5T	2:00.3	120.50
Keller Lobell (Per Henriksen)	1	2	3	5	7/11	7/20	2:03.2	21.70e
Brother Oliver (Ben Steall)	3	5x	8	8	8/dis	8/dis		54.60
$169,986 Final	Times -			:29.1	:59.3	1:29.3	1:59.2	
Royal Troubador (Carl Allen)	5	1	1	1	1/1Q	1/T	1:59.2	1.90
King Of The Sea (Stanley Dancer)	1	2	2	2	2/1Q	2/T	1:59.3	11.20
Embassy Lobell (Michel Lachance)	3	3	3	4o	4/2H	3/1H	1:59.3	6.00
Jacquie's Kosmos (Bill Fahy)	4	4	5	5	5/3H	4/2T	2:00	142.80
The Devil (Bill O'Donnell)	6	5	6	6	6/4T	5/4Q	2:00.1	121.90
Cheyenne Spur (Dick Stillings)	2x	7	4o	3o	3/1Q	6/8H	2:01	.70*
Incredible D J (John Patterson, Jr.)	8	8	8o	8o	8/7H	7/11	2:01.3	96.50
Pastel Pastel (Carmine Abbatiello)	7	6	7o	7o	7/6	8/13	2:02	54.60

Winner: b, c, by Super Bowl -- Mae Jeans Crown -- Speedy Crown
Owner: Carl & Rod Allen Stable, Inc., Ocala, Florida
Trainer: Carl Allen
Breeder: Mae Jean Allen, Ocala, Florida

$1,346,000 Hambletonian
The Meadowlands - August 4, 1990

Horse (Driver)	PP	1/4	1/2	3/4	Stretch	Finish	Time	$1.00
First Heat - First Division	Times-			:28.1	:56.4	1:26.3	1:56.1	
Embassy Lobell (Michel Lachance)	4	5	6	9o	4/5	1/2	1:56.1	.50*
Armbro Iliad (Ron Waples)	9	9o	9o	5oo	1/HD	2/2	1:56.3	21.90
Crown Bones (Berndt Lindstedt)	7	4	4	6	6/6Q	3/6H	1:57.2	11.90
The Devil (Lorenzo Baldi)	6	8	8	10	7/7H	4/6H	1:57.2	16.80
Meadowbranch Eddy (Per Eriksson)	5	7o	7o	7o	5/6	5/10T	1:58.2	63.90
Jeanne's Somolli (Rod Allen)	1	2	1	1	2x/HD	x6x/11	1:58.2	9.20
Backstreet Guy (Ben Webster)	3	3	3	2o	3/3	7/12T	1:58.4	8.50
Roughing It (John Campbell)	x8	6o	5o	4o	9/10H	8/22	2:00.3	31.50
Remus Hanover (John Simpson, Jr.)	2	1o	2	3	8/9H	9/22	2:00.3	9.90
I'm Impeccable (Bill O'Donnell)	10	10	10	8oox	10/15H	10/dis		37.70

Page 167

THE CROWNS

First Heat - Second Divison	Times-			:28.2	:56.4	1:26.1	1:55	
Harmonious (John Campbell)	2	4	3o	2o	1/2	1/3Q	1:55	1.70
King Of The Sea (Stanley Dancer)	3	3	4	5	3/4	2/3Q	1:55.3	28.00
Royal Troubador (Carl Allen)	1	2	1	1	2/2	3/3H	1:55.3	1.30*
Peddler Yorktowne (Mike Saftic)	6	6o	5o	4o	5/5	4/4Q	1:55.4	26.30
Antwerp Hanover (Ron Waples)	5	7	6o	6o	6/6H	5/7H	1:56.2	38.70
Cheyenne Spur (Dick Stillings)	7	1	2	3	4/5	6/10Q	1:57	20.00
Star Mystic (Jan Johnson)	8	8ox	10	9oo	7/9H	7/10H	1:57	8.20
Meadowbranch Elmer (Richie Silverman)	9	9	8o	7o	9x/16	8/23	1:59.3	73.80
Grundy's Rambo (Jan Nordin)	10	10	9	8	8/11	9/24	1:59.4	233.70
Kosar (Ulf Thoresen)	4	5	7x	10	10/dis	10/dis		5.80

Second Heat	Times-			:28.1	:56.2	1:25	1:54.1	
Harmonious (John Campbell)	2	4	4	4o	3/2H	1/1H	1:54.1	1.20
Embassy Lobell (Michel Lachance)	1	3	3	2o	2/1Q	2/1H	1:54.2	1.00*
Royal Troubador (Carl Allen)	6	1	1	1	1/1Q	3/2T	1:54.4	7.70
King Of The Sea (Stanley Dancer)	4	2	2	3	4/3	4/5	1:55.1	23.60
Armbro Iliad (Ron Waples)	3	5	5	5o	5/7	5/7T	1:55.4	14.70
Peddler Yorktowne (Mike Saftic)	7	8o	7o	6o	6/9H	6dh/9	1:56	67.40
The Devil (Lorenzo Baldi)	8	7	8	8	7/9T	6dh/9H	1:56	76.40
Crown Bones (Berndt Lindstedt)	5	6	6	7	8/10H	8/12	1:56.3	44.00
Antwerp Hanover (Jim Simpson, Jr.)	9	10	10	10	10/15H	9/20	1:58.1	237.10
Meadowbranch Eddy (Per Eriksson)	10	9o	9o	9o	9/15H	10/22	1:58.3	381.30

Summary Standings and Purse Distribution

Harmonious	(x-1-1)	$673,000
Embassy Lobell	(1-x-1)	336,500
King Of The Sea	(x-2-4)	161,520
Armbro Iliad	(2-x-5)	107,680
Royal Troubador	(x-3-3)	67,300

Winner: b, c, by Crowning Point -- Rhapsody In Blue -- Super Bowl
Owner: Lindy Racing Stable, Somersville, Connecticut, and Salvatore Garofalo, Boynton Beach, Florida
Trainer: Osvaldo Formia
Breeder: Kentuckiana Farms, Lexington, Kentucky

$180,000 Kentucky Futurity
The Red Mile - October 5, 1990

First Heat - $81,000	Times-			:27.4	:56	1:25.1	1:54.2	
Jeanne's Somolli (Rod Allen)	1	2	2	2	2/1Q	1/HD	1:54.2	14.10
Columnist (Bill Fahy)	3	6	4o	4o	3/2Q	2/HD	1:54.2	.50e*
Cheyenne Spur (Dick Stillings)	6	1	1	1	1/1Q	3/2H	1:54.4	24.90
Harmonious (Cat Manzi)	7	8	7	6o	6/5Q	4/6H	1:55.3	.30e*
Embassy Lobell (Michel Lachance)	4	7	6	5	5/5Q	5/6T	1:55.4	2.40
Lender Hanover (Jan Nordin)	10	3	3	3o	4/4T	6/7T	1:56	17.30
MB Elite (Ron Waples)	x5	11	10	9	7/20Q	7/21T	1:58.4	34.70
Drummer Hanover (Dick Richardson, Jr.)	11	5	5	7	8/21Q	8/dis		206.80
Royal Cold (Mel Turcotte)	9	10	9	8	9/22Q	9/dis		144.00
Star Mystic (Jan Johnson)	2	x4o	11	10	10/24Q	10/dis		70.20
Super Arnie (Berndt Lindstedt)	8	9	8o	x11o	11/dis	11/dis		9.80

(continued)

THE CROWNS

Second Heat - $81,000

	Times-			:27	:55.1	1:24.2	1:54.3	
Star Mystic (Jan Johnson)	10	5	1	2	1/HD	1/1Q	1:54.3	40.20
Super Arnie (Berndt Lindstedt)	11	6	3o	1	2/HD	2/1Q	1:54.4	5.90
Jeanne's Somolli (Rod Allen)	1	3	5	7	3/4	3/1T	1:55	3.30
Cheyenne Spur (Dick Stillings)	3	2	4	6	4/4Q	4/2	1:55	14.40
MB Elite (Ron Waples)	5	7	6o	4o	5/5Q	5/9	1:56.2	25.20
Columnist (Bill Fahy)	2	4	7	5oo	x6/10Q	6/19	1:58.2	.30e*
Harmonious (Cat Manzi)	4	1o	2	3	7/17Q	7/dis		.30e*
Embassy Lobell	Scratched							
Royal Cold	Scratched							
Lender Hanover	Scratched							
Drummer Hanover	Scratched							

Race-off - $18,000

	Times-			:28.1	:57.2	1:27.2	1:55.3	
Star Mystic (Jan Johnson)	1	1	1	1	1/T	1/NK	1:55.3	.70
Jeanne's Somolli (Rod Allen)	2	2	2	2	2/T	2/NK	1:55.3	.50*

Winner: b, c, by Mystic Park -- Sissy Crown -- Speedy Crown
Owner: Gregory S. Coleman, E. Norwich, NY
Trainer: Bjorn Berglund
Breeder: Antonacci Stable, Lindenhurst, NY

THE PACING TRIPLE CROWN

$486,550 Cane Pace
Yonkers Raceway - August 25, 1990

$145,964 First Elimination

	Times -			:27.1	:56.3	1:25.3	1:54.3	
C K S (John Campbell)	3	3	3o	1	1/2	1/3H	1:54.3	26.80
Orange Sovereign (Ted Wing)	1	2	1o	2	2/2	2/3H	1:55.1	2.00
Road Machine (Tony Kerwood)	2	1o	2	4	3/3H	3/3T	1:55.2	4.30
Ballenger Hanover (Joe Marsh, Jr.)	4	4	4	6	6/6Q	4/5H	1:55.3	65.80
Spirited Style (Michel Lachance)	6	6	5o	3o	4/3H	5/7Q	1:56	.60*
Hot Walker (Harold Kelly)	5	5	6	5o	5/5	6/8T	1:56.2	37.90

$145,964 Second Elimination

	Times -			:27.3	:57.1	1:25.2	1:53.4	
Sea The USA (Gerry Procino)	1	2	2	2	2/1Q	1/NK	1:53.4	19.30
Scoot Outa Reach (Ted Wing)	3	1	1	1	1/1Q	2/NK	1:53.4	1.60
Oscarsson (Jim Marohn)	4	4	4o	4	3/2T	3/2	1:54.1	34.60
Jake And Elwood (John Campbell)	5	5	5o	5oo	4/3	4/2	1:54.1	.50*
Drop-Off (Carmine Abbatiello)	2	3	3	3o	5/3H	5/4Q	1:54.3	21.00
Nuclear Flash (Rick Zeron)	7	7	7	6	6/5	6/4Q	1:54.3	132.10
Big Date (Michel Lachance)	6	6	6o	7	7/5	7/7H	1:55.1	25.70

$194,620 Final

	Times -			:27	:55.1	1:25.4	1:55.1	
Jake And Elwood (John Campbell)	8	2o	1	1	1/T	1/2H	1:55.1	1.10e*
Road Machine (Tony Kerwood)	6	7	7o	6o	7/4H	2/2H	1:55.3	18.10
Orange Sovereign (Carmine Abbatiello)	3	5	5o	4o	5/3	3/3H	1:55.4	8.00
Oscarsson (Jim Marohn)	5	6	6	7	6/4Q	4/4Q	1:56	31.00
Sea The USA (Gerry Procino)	1	3	3	5	4/2T	5/4Q	1:56	4.00
Scoot Outa Reach (Ted Wing)	4	1	2	3	3/1H	6/4Q	1:56	1.90
C K S (Michel Lachance)	2	4	4o	2o	2/T	7/6T	1:56.3	1.10e*
Ballenger Hanover (Joe Marsh, Jr.)	7	8	8	8o	x8/6	8/17	1:58.3	84.30

Winner: br, c, by Samadhi -- Lil Pods Fiddle -- Gypsy Fiddle
Owners: LPG Standardbred Associates (Louis P. Guida, et al), Lawrenceville, NJ;
M R F Racing Stable (Susan & Kenneth Seeber), Lowville, NY; and
Bonnie Castle Stables, Alexandria Bay, NY
Trainer: Ken Seeber
Breeder: Robert Eugene Nixon, Fairdale, KY

THE CROWNS

$444,371 Messenger Stakes
Rosecroft Raceway - September 8, 1990

$66,656 First Elimination	Times-			:27.1	:55.4	1:25.1	1:53.4	
In The Pocket (John Campbell)	3	1o	1	1	1/Q	1/T	1:53.4	.30*
Spirited Style (Michel Lachance)	4	5	5o	4o	4/1H	2/T	1:54	15.90
Till We Meet Again (Buddy Gilmour)	5	2o	2	3	3/1Q	3/1Q	1:54	4.30
Oscarsson (Don Irvine, Jr.)	2	4	4o	2o	2/Q	4/2	1:54.1	24.60
Armbro Intercept (Eddie Davis)	6	6	6	6o	6/2T	5/3	1:54.2	43.60
C K S (Jim Morand)	7	7	7	7	7/4H	6/4Q	1:54.3	19.40
Six Day War (Ray Remmen)	1	3	3	5	5/2H	7/5Q	1:54.4	7.90

66,656 Second Elimination	Times-			:27.2	:55.1	1:23.4	1:53	
Kiev Hanover (Jim Morand)	5	7	7	7o	3/T	1/1	1:53	23.70
Beach Towel (Ray Remmen)	4	1o	2	1	1/Q	2/1	1:53.1	.20*
Jake And Elwood (John Campbell)	7	4o	1	2	4/1T	3/2Q	1:53.2	3.00
Big Date (Michel Lachance)	2	5	6o	5o	5/1T	4/5T	1:54.1	23.00e
Corsair (Joe Pavia, Jr.)	3	2	3	4	6/2T	5/6Q	1:54.1	34.20
No Caveats (Don Irvine, Jr.)	6	6o	4o	3o	2/Q	6/6H	1:54.1	23.00e
Fighting Major (Eddie Davis)	1	3	5	6	7/3	7/10	1:55	46.60

$311,059 Final	Times-			:27.4	:56.3	1:24.3	1:52.3	
Jake And Elwood (John Campbell)	4	4o	1	1	1/1	1/1H	1:52.3	1.40e
Beach Towel (Ray Remmen)	5	5	5o	4o	4/1T	2/1H	1:52.4	.60*
Kiev Hanover (Jim Morand)	6	6	7o	6o	6/3	3/2H	1:53	7.50
Till We Meet Again (Buddy Gilmour)	1	2	3o	2o	2/1	4/3H	1:53.1	15.50
Oscarsson (Don Irvine, Jr.)	7	7	6	7	7/4Q	5/4H	1:53.2	81.90
In The Pocket (Michel Lachance)	2	1	2	3	3/1T	6/4H	1:53.2	1.40e
Big Date (Eddie Davis)	3	3	4	5	5/2T	7/4H	1:53.2	115.70
Spirited Style (Joe Pavia, Jr.)	8	8	8o	8o	8/5	8/10H	1:54.3	66.90

Winner: br, c, by Samadhi -- Lil Pods Fiddle -- Gypsy Fiddle
Owners: LPG Standardbred Associates (Louis P. Guida, et al), Lawrenceville, NJ;
M R F Racing Stable (Susan & Kenneth Seeber), Lowville, NY; and
Bonnie Castle Stables, Alexandria Bay, NY
Trainer: Ken Seeber
Breeder: Robert Eugene Nixon, Fairdale, KY

$468,610 Little Brown Jug
Delaware, OH - September 20, 1990

$56,233 First Elimination	Times-			:27.2	:56.2	1:25.4	1:54.3	
In The Pocket (John Campbell)	7	7	6o	4o	4/1T	1/1	1:54.3	1.00*
Brando Hanover (Mickey McNichol)	8	8	7o	6o	6/3T	2/1	1:54.4	9.90
General Knight (Dick Stillings)	3	3	3	5	5/3Q	3/1Q	1:54.4	14.70
Global Assault (Mark Williams)	2	5	4o	2o	2/1H	4/2	1:55	2.30
Road Machine (Tony Kerwood)	6	1o	1	1	1/1H	5/2	1:55	3.40
Ballenger Hanover (Chris Boring)	5	6	8	8o	8/6Q	6/3Q	1:55.1	123.10
Charlie's Thunder (Wally Hennessey)	1	2	2	3	3/1T	7/3Q	1:55.1	56.90
Six Day War (Ray Remmen)	4	4	5	7	7/5Q	8/4Q	1:55.2	45.30

$56,233 Second Elimination	Times-			:27.2	:57.3	1:27.4	1:55.2	
Kiev Hanover (Jim Morand)	2	1	1	1	1/1H	1/1	1:55.2	.50*
Spirited Style (Michel Lachance)	5	3	3	2o	3/1T	2/1	1:55.3	5.60
Big Date (Jay Picciano)	1	2	2	3	2/1H	3/1H	1:55.3	36.90
Colored Storm (Tom Harmer)	6	4	5	6	5/4Q	4/2H	1:55.4	25.60
Bold Hope (Norm McKnight)	3	5	4o	5o	4/3T	5/2H	1:55.4	34.80
C K S (John Campbell)	7	7	7	4oo	6/6Q	6/4T	1:56.2	5.70
Camluck (Bill Gale)	4	6	6	7x	7/11Q	7/15	1:58.2	4.80

(continued)

THE CROWNS

$56,233 Third Elimination	Times-			:27.3	:56.3	1:25.3	1:54	
Beach Towel (Ray Remmen)	2	1o	1	1	1/2	1/4T	1:54	.05*
Rock Legend (Doug Snyder)	6	6	4o	4o	3/3T	2/4T	1:55	51.50
No Caveats (Jay Picciano)	4	5	2o	2o	2x/2	3/6T	1:55.2	30.60
All In Good Time (Tony Kerwood)	3	4	7	7i	5/8	4/7Q	1:55.2	111.00
Scoot Outa Reach (Bill O'Donnell)	5	3	5	5ix	6/11	6pl5/13	1:56.3	5.60
Brace Yourself (Jim Miller)	7	7	6o	6ix	7/18	7pl6/20	1:58	114.20
Shipps Schnoops (Doug Brown)	1	2	3	3x	4/7T	5pl7/10	1:56	14.60
$253,049 Second Heat	**Times-**			**:28.2**	**:56.3**	**1:26**	**1:53.3**	
Beach Towel (Ray Remmen)	3	1	1	1	1/1H	1/1H	1:53.3	.40*
In The Pocket (John Campbell)	2	2o	2	3	2/1H	2/1H	1:53.4	2.60
Kiev Hanover (Jim Morand)	1	3	4	5	4/3	3/3	1:54.1	4.90
Brando Hanover (Mickey McNichol)	4	5	3o	2o	3/2H	4/3H	1:54.1	12.90
Rock Legend (Doug Snyder)	5	6	6	7	5/3T	5/4Q	1:54.2	193.80
Big Date (Jay Picciano)	9	4	5o	4o	6/4T	6/6	1:54.4	83.10e
General Knight (Dick Stillings)	7	8	8	9	7/5T	7/6	1:54.4	144.30
Spirited Style (Michel Lachance)	6	7	7o	6o	8/6Q	8/6	1:54.4	176.70
No Caveats (Jeff Fout)	8	9	9o	8o	9/7T	9/7Q	1:55	83.10e

Beach Towel, the straight-heat winner, also received the 10% ($46,861) set aside for the race winner

Winner: b, c, by French Chef -- Sunburn -- Armbro Nesbit
Owner: Uptown Stable, New York, NY
Trainer: Larry Remmen
Breeder: Stoner Creek Stud, Inc., Paris, KY

THE CROWNS

THE TROTTING TRIPLE CROWN

In order to win the Trotting Triple Crown, a three-year-old must score victories in the Hambletonian, Kentucky Futurity, and Yonkers Trot. The oldest stake is the Kentucky Futurity, which was first raced in 1893. The Hambletonian began in 1926, while the Yonkers Trot (originally called the Yonkers Futurity) was inaugurated in 1955. The six Trotting Triple Crown winners since its inception in 1955 are:

HORSE

1955-SCOTT FROST
(Hoot Mon - Nora)
Owner: S.A.Camp Farms
Breeder: Est. of W.N. Reynolds
Trainer/Driver: Joe O'Brien
Lifetime Record: 71 56--10--4 $310,685

Horse of the Year in 1955 and 1956. First two-minute 2-year-old trotter. An infection resulted in the stallion's sterility in 1962. He died in 1983 in California.

1963-SPEEDY SCOT
(Speedster - Scotch Love)
Owner: Castleton Farms
Breeder: Homebred
Trainer/Driver: Ralph Baldwin
Lifetime Record: 57 44--3--0 $650,909

Horse of the year in 1963. Won first Yonkers Futurity raced at mile distance. Lost first heat of Hambletonian by head in world record 1:57.3 won by Florlis. Won Kentucky Futurity in stakes record time. Died June 14, 1990 at Castleton Farms in Kentucky.

1964-AYRES
(Star's Pride - Arpege)
Owner: Charlotte Sheppard
Breeder: Homebred
Trainer/Driver: John Simpson, Sr.
Lifetime Record: 30 20--4--3 $254,027

Won Yonkers Futurity in stakes record time. Won Hambletonian in stakes and world record equalling time. The morning of the Kentucky Futurity, Ayres got out of his stall unattended and slightly injured a hind ankle, but proved fit to win in second fastest win time. Died January 30, 1900 at age 29.

1968-NEVELE PRIDE
(Star's Pride - Thankful)
Owner: Nevele Acres & Lou Resnick
Breeders: Mr. & Mrs. E.C. Quin
Trainer/Driver: Stanley Dancer
Lifetime Record: 67 57--4--3 $873,238

Horse of the year in 1967, 1968 and 1969. Never headed in either heat of Hambletonian which he won by four and five and one-half lengths. Also dominated Kentucky Futurity, winning by seven and two and three-quarter lengths, establishing a stakes record. Standing at stud at Stoner Creek Stud, in Kentucky

TRIPLE CROWN BOXSCORE

8/3 -- $86,863 Hambletonian (Goshen)
Straight heats: 2:01.3 -- 2:00.3
2nd -- Galophone (3-2)
9/1 -- $73,840 Yonkers Futurity (YR)
Time: 2:12 (at 1-1/16 mi.)
2nd -- Galophone
10/6 -- $62,702 Kentucky Futurity (Lex)
** DNF-1-1 Times: 2:00.3 -- 2:04.2
2nd -- Home Free (1-2-2)
(** accident with Galophone)

8/15 -- $135,127 Yonkers Futurity (YR)
Time: 2:03.3
2nd -- Florlis
8/28 -- $115,549 Hambletonian (DuQ)
2-1-1 Win times: 1:58 -- 1:58.2
2nd -- Florlis (1-2-2)
10/4 -- $61,128 Kentucky Futurity (Lex)
Straight Heats: 1:57.1 -- 1:57.2
2nd -- Florlis (2-2)

7/23 -- $116,691 Yonkers Futurity (YR)
Time: 2:01.3
2nd -- Speedy Count
9/2 -- $115,281 Hambletonian (DuQ)
Straight heats: 1:56.4 -- 1:58.1
2nd -- Big John (2-2)
10/9 -- $57,096 Kentucky Futurity (Lex)
Straight heats: 1:58.1 -- 1:59.2
2nd -- Dashing Rodney (2-3)

8/8 -- $150,000 Yonkers Futurity (YR)
Time: 2:03.3
2nd -- Fashion Hill
8/25 -- $116,190 Hambletonian (DuQ)
Straight heats: 1:59.3 -- 1:59.2
2nd -- Keystone Spartan (2-2)
10/4 -- $57,398 Kentucky Futurity (Lex)
Straight heats: 1:57 -- 1:57
2nd -- Snow Speed (2-2)

THE CROWNS

1969-LINDY'S PRIDE
(Star's Pride - Galena Hanover)
Owner: Lindy Farm, Inc.
Breeder: Hanover Shoe Farms, Inc.
Trainer/Driver: Howard Beissinger
Lifetime Record: 47 25--9--4 $396,209
Narrowly avoided an accident in his first Hambletonian heat. Standing at stud at Castleton Farm in Ohio.

1972-SUPER BOWL
(Star's Pride - Pillow Talk)
Owners: Rachel Dancer & Rose Hild Breeding Farm
Breeder: Stoner Creek Stud
Trainer/Driver: Stanley Dancer
Won the Hambletonian in stakes and world record time. Won both heats of the Kentucky Futurity with a blown-out sulky tire (both the result of damage caused by Songcan during the race). Standing at stud at Hanover Shoe Farms in Pennsylvania.

7/19 -- $100,000 Yonkers Futurity (YR)
Time: 2:03
2nd -- The Prophet
8/27 -- $124,910 Hambletonian (DuQ)
Straight Heats: 1:57.3 -- 1:58.2
2nd -- The Prophet (2-3)
10/3 -- $64,757 Kentucky Futurity (Lex)
Straight Heats: 1:59 -- 1:59.3
2nd -- Nevele Major (2-2)

8/30 -- $119,090 Hambletonian (DuQ)
Straight Heats: 1:57.2 -- 1:56.2
2nd -- Delmonica Hanover (2-2)
9/29 -- $93,097 Yonkers Futurity (YR)
Time: 2:02
2nd -- Delmonica Hanover
10/6 -- $56,210 Kentucky Futurity (Lex)
Straight Heats: 2:00 -- 1:59
2nd -- Spartan Hanover (5-2)

THE PACING TRIPLE CROWN

To win the Pacing Triple Crown, a 3-year-old must score victories in the Cane Pace, Little Brown Jug and Messenger Stake. The oldest stake is the Little Brown Jug, first raced in 1946. The Cane Pace (originally called The Cane Futurity) began in 1955. The Messenger started a year later. The seven Pacing Triple Crown winners since it began in 1956 are detailed below:

HORSE

TRIPLE CROWN BOXSCORE

1959-ADIOS BUTLER
(Adios - Debby Hanover)
Owners: Paige West & Angelo Pellillo
Breeder: R.C. Carpenter
Trainer: Paiage West
Driver: Clint Hodgins
Lifetime Record: 50 37--4--1 $509,844
Horse of the year in 1960 & 1961, but not during his Triple Crown season. He only started nine times at three. Won Messenger in track and stake record time. First horse to win Jug with mile faster than two-minutes and set a world record in the stake. Adios Butler died in 1983 after a long stud career in Ohio.

7/16 -- $54,457 Cane Futurity (YR)
Time: 2:09 (Raced at 1-1/16 miles)
2nd -- Adios Oregon
8/21 -- $110,994 Messenger (RR)
Time: 2:00.1
2nd -- Meadow Al
9/24 -- $67,582 Little Brown Jug (Dela)
Times: (x-1-1) 1:59.2 -- 2:00.4
2nd -- Meadow Al (1-x-2)

1965-BRET HANOVER
(Adios - Brenna Hanover)
Owner: Richard Downing
Breeder: Hanover Shoe Farms
Trainer/Driver: Frank Ervin
Lifetime Record: 68 62--5--1 $922,616
Horse of the year in 1964, 1965 and 1966. Cane win was number 26 in his string of 35 consecutive wins, despite suffering a severe bump in the first turn. Won Jug in stakes and world record times. Standing at stud at Castleton Farm in Kentucky.

5/12 -- $125,235 Cane Futurity (YR)
Time: 2:01
2nd -- Bobby T Knight
9/23 -- $71,447 Little Brown Jug (Dela)
Straight Heats: 1:57 -- 1:57.2
2nd -- Tuxedo Hanover (2-2)
11/19 -- $151,252 Messenger (RR)
Time: 2:02
2nd -- Tuxedo Hanover

THE CROWNS

1966-ROMEO HANOVER
(Dancer Hanover - Romola Hanover)
Owner: Lucky Star Stables & Morton Finder
Breeder: Hanover Shoe Farms
Trainer: Jerry Silverman
Drivers: Wm. Meyer (Cane), George Sholty (Jug & Messenger)
Lifetime Record: 44 36--2--4 $658,505
The tracks for Cane & Jug listed as fast, but were drenched by rain prior to post. Lost only one start in 1966. At Stud in Australia.

5/19 -- $126,915 Cane Futurity (YR)
Time: 1:59.4
2nd -- Buzzy Hanover
9/22 -- $74,616 Brown Jug (Dela)
Straight heats: 2:01.2 -- 1:59.3
2nd -- Good Time Boy (2-2)
10/29 -- $169,885 Messenger (RR)
Time: 2:01
2nd -- Good Time Boy

1968 -- RUM CUSTOMER
(Poplar Byrd - Custom Maid)
Owners: Kennilworth Farms & L.C. Mancuso
Breeder: Mr. & Mrs. R.C. Larkin
Trainer/Driver: William Haughton
Lifetime Record: 141 52--27--25 $1,001,548
Mr. & Mrs. Larkin were given the dam, Custom Maid by Lloyd Lloyds (Kennilworth Farms) in return for the first foal, Rum Customer. The Mancusos became owners in return for the use of their airplane so the Lloyds could follow the colt's career. Currently at stud in New Zealand.

9/19 -- $104,226 Brown Jug (Dela)
x-1-1 Times: 1:59.3 -- 1:59.3
2nd -- Adios Waverly (1-x-7)
10/12 -- $150,000 Cane Futurity (YR)
Time: 1:59.4
2nd -- Fulla Napoleon
10/26 -- $189,018 Messenger (RR)
Time: 2:01.4
2nd -- Tropic Song

1970-MOST HAPPY FELLA
(Meadow Skipper - Laughing Girl)
Owner: Egyptian Acres Stable
Breeder: Stoner Creek Stud
Trainer/Driver: Stanley Dancer
Lifetime Record: 40 22--10--3 $419,033
After winning Cane in stakes record time, Dancer publicly predicted he'd go on to a Triple Triple Crown win. A top sire, he died in 1983 while recuperating from a broken leg.

8/29 -- $102,770 Cane Futurity(YR)
Time: 1:58.3
2nd -- Shreik
9/24 -- $100,110 Brown Jug (Dela)
1-2-1 Times: 1:57.1 -- 1:57.3
2nd -- Columbia George (3-1-2)
11/7 -- $123,450 Messenger (RR)
Time: 2:00.3
2nd -- Truluck

1980-NIATROSS
(Albatross - Niagara Dream)
Owners: Niagara Acres, C. Galbraith and Niatross Stables
Breeder: Niagara Acres
Trainer/Driver: Clint Galbraith
Lifetime Record: 39 37--0--0 $2,019,213
Horse of the year in 1979 & 1980 and first sub-1:50 performer (1:49.1). Won the Little Brown Jug in world record times. Cane win was 19th straight of career and came week before he fell at Saratoga to end the streak. Standing at stud at Walnridge Farm in New Jersey.

6/28 -- $321,365 Cane Pace (YR)
1-x-1 Times: 1:57.3 -- 1:57.4
2nd -- Trenton Time (x-1-2)
9/18 -- $207,361 Brown Jug (Dela)
Straight heats: 1:55 - 1:54.4
2nd -- Storm Damage (4-2)
10/11 -- $173,522 Messenger (RR)
Time: 1:59.3 ("good" track)
2nd -- Tyler B

1983-RALPH HANOVER
(Meadow Skipper - Ravina Hanover)
Owners: Waples Stable, Pointsetta Stable, Grant's Direct Stable & P.J. Baugh
Breeder: Hanover Shoe Farms
Trainer: Stew Firlotte
Driver: Ron Waples
Lifetime Record: 40 27--9--1 $1,828,871
Set stakes records in both the Messenger and the Cane. Established single season's earnings record of $1,711,990. At stud at Almahurst Farm of Kentucky.

6/18 -- $379.004 Messenger (RR)
1-1 Times: 1:59.1 -- 1:57
2nd -- Raffi (1-2)
8/20 -- $559,230 Cane Pace (YR)
2-1 Win time: 1:57
2nd -- Van Kirk (1-2)
9/22 -- $358,800 Brown Jug (Dela)
1-1 Times: 1:58.2 -- 1:55.3
2nd -- Skirt Lifter (2-2)

THE CROWNS

TROTTERS WHO WON TWO LEGS OF THE TRIPLE CROWN

The trotting Triple Crown races have almost always followed the same chronological pattern: Yonkers Trot, Hambletonian, then the Kentucky Futurity.

Year	Yonkers Trot	Hambletonian	Kentucky Futurity
1987	**Mack Lobell**	**Mack Lobell**	Napoletano
1978	**Speedy Somolli**	**Speedy Somolli**	Doublemint
1977	**Green Speed**	**Green Speed**	Texas
1976	**Steve Lobell**	**Steve Lobell**	Quick Pay
1970	Victory Star	**Timothy T**	**Timothy T**
1962	**A C's Viking**	**A C's Viking**	Safe Mission
1961	**Duke Rodney**	Harlan Dean	**Duke Rodney**
1959	John A Hanover	**Diller Hanover**	**Diller Hanover**
1958	Spunky Hanover	**Emily's Pride**	**Emily's Pride**

WINNERS OF THE FIRST TWO LEGS OF THE TRIPLE CROWN

There are five trotters who have won the *first two* legs of the Triple Crown but not the third:

A C's Viking finished fourth and third to Safe Mission, the straight-heat winner.

Steve Lobell lost all three heats by a total margin of less than a half-length --losing by a nose to Soothsayer in the first heat, then falling short by a nose and neck to Quick Pay in the next two heats. He went on to record a "nose" victory in voting for Trotter of the Year, edging Keystone Pioneer by four votes (98-94)!

Green Speed went on to finish 1977 as the Horse of the Year despite not being eligible to the Kentucky Futurity.

Speedy Somolli made breaks in his two heats, finishing sixth and placed seventh, then finishing second and placed fourth to the race winner, Doublemint, in the final. Despite the breaks, voters forgave him and voted him Trotter of the Year for 1978.

Mack Lobell, after winning his first heat in 1:55, was stalked by Napoletano (the eventual winner) in the final. Napoletano trotted a :26.1 final quarter to edge the favorite in the second, and final, heat.

TROTTING TRIPLE CROWN "BRIDESMAIDS"

In the years since the Trotting Triple Crown was formed two horses have had the dubious distinction of finishing second in all three legs - the Hambletonian, Kentucky Futurity and the Yonkers Trot:

In 1961, Duke Rodney, winner of both the Yonkers Trot and Kentucky Futurity, dueled with Harlan Dean, the Hambletonian winner, for honors as the sport's top three-year-old trotter. All the while, Caleb was the bridesmaid, finishing second in each of the classic events.

Two years later, Florlis won the "runner-up triple," just as Duke Rodney had. 1963 was the year of Speedy Scot's Triple Crown victory and Florlis chased him in each of the three classic races.

THE TROTTING TRIPLE CROWN

Event	'91 Date	Stakes Record	(Record-Holder, Year)	1990 Winner
Yonkers Trot	July 13	1:57.4	(Mack Lobell, '87)	Royal Troubador
Hambletonian	August 3	1:53.3	(Mack Lobell, '87)	Harmonious
Kentucky Futurity	October 4	1:54.2	(Peace Corps, '89, and Jeanne's Somolli, '90)	Star Mystic

THE CROWNS

PACERS WHO WON TWO LEGS OF THE TRIPLE CROWN

The pacing Triple Crown events have not always been raced in the same chronological order. The numeral next to the name of the winner shows the sequence for that year.

Year	Cane Pace (Leg)	Messenger (Leg)	Brown Jug (Leg)
1990	Jake And Elwood, 1	Jake And Elwood, 2	Beach Towel, 3
1986	Barberry Spur, 1	Amity Chef, 3	Barberry Spur, 2
1982	Cam Fella, 1	Cam Fella, 3	Merger, 2
1979	Happy Motoring, 1	Hot Hitter, 3	Hot Hitter, 2
1977	Jade Prince, 1	Governor Skipper, 3	Governor Skipper, 2
1976	Keystone Ore, 1	Windshield Wiper, 3	Keystone Ore, 2
1974	Boyden Hanover, 1	Armbro Omaha, 3	Armbro Omaha, 2
1971	Albatross, 2	Albatross, 1	Nansemond, 3
1964	Race Time, 3	Race Time, 1	Vicar Hanover, 2
1963	Meadow Skipper, 1	Overtrick, 3	Overtrick, 2
1960	Countess Adios, 2	Countess Adios, 1	Bullet Hanover, 3
1957	Torpid, 1	Meadow Lands, 3	Torpid, 2
1956	Noble Adios, 2	Belle Acton, 1	Noble Adios, 3

WINNERS OF THE FIRST TWO LEGS OF THE TRIPLE CROWN

Torpid, Countess Adios, Albatross, Keystone Ore, Barberry Spur, and Jake And Elwood are the only pacers to win the *first two* legs of the pacing Triple Crown and fall short in the third:

Torpid finished second in his elimination heat of the Messenger, but bled and was ordered scratched by the track veterinarian prior to the final heat.

Countess Adios was not eligible to the Jug, but set two world records in winning the Walnut Hall Filly Pace at Delaware.

Albatross began Jug Day with a win in the second heat over Nansemond. The latter won the third heat rematch by one length, and then won the Jug by a 3/4 length margin over the favorite in the raceoff between those two and H T Luca. Nansemond's third heat win ended Albatross' 16-heat win skein.

Keystone Ore was simply second best to Windshield Wiper in the one dash of the '76 Messenger. The latter started from post 11 and threaded through heavy traffic in the stretch to win by a 3/4 length upset margin.

Barberry Spur, trying to overcome post position nine, was parked throughout the final half and couldn't overcome Amity Chef -- a 1-3/4 length victor.

Jake And Elwood was not eligible to the Jug, but won the Cane Pace at Yonkers Raceway with a thrilling early move from the number eight post position, and set a stakes record in winning the Messenger Stakes at Rosecroft Raceway.

PACING TRIPLE CROWN "BRIDESMAIDS"

Among pacers, no horse has finished second in each of the races, the Cane Pace, Messenger Stakes, and Little Brown Jug. One horse, however, had the dubious distinction of finishing third in each of these races:

Morris Eden finished third to Torpid in both the Cane Futurity and Little Brown Jug, and again finished third to Meadow Lands in the Messenger Stakes.

THE PACING TRIPLE CROWN

Event	'91 Date	Stakes Record	(Record-Holder, Year)	1990 Winner
Cane Pace	August 24	1:53.4h	(Chairmanoftheboard,'85, and) Sea The USA, '90)	Jake And Elwood
Messenger	September 7	1:52.3f	(Jake And Elwood, '90)	Jake And Elwood
Little Brown Jug	September 19	1:52.1	(Nihilator, '85)	Beach Towel

Page 176

THE CROWNS

THE 1990 BREEDERS CROWN SERIES

Horse (Driver)   PP   1/4   1/2   3/4   Stretch   Finish   Time $1.00

$378,933 Breeders Crown 3-Year-Old Filly Trot
Pompano Park - November 2, 1990

Horse (Driver)	PP	1/4	1/2	3/4	Stretch	Finish	Time	$1.00
	Times-		:27.2	:57.1	1:27.4	1:57.1		
Me Maggie (Berndt Lindstedt)	6	7o	8	4o	3/2H	1/1H	1:57.1	.70e*
Delphi's Lobell (Ron Waples)	4	9o	9	7o	4/4	3p2/1T	1:57.3	15.60
Our First (Michel Lachance)	5	8	7	8o	5/5	4p3/1T	1:57.3	33.90
Camelia Lobell (Jan Johnson)	12	6	6	3o	2/2	5p4/2T	1:57.4	.70e*
Happy Diamonds (John Campbell)	9	11o	11o	6oo	7/6H	6p5/6Q	1:58.2	2.40
Kindava Hush (Bill Fahy)	11	5	4	2o	1x/2	x2xp6/1H	1:57.2	.70e*
Miss Baltic (Jan Nordin)	3	4o	3o	1	6/6	7/11Q	1:59.2	9.00
Caspian (Cat Manzi)	10	x12	12	11	8/10H	8/12	1:59.3	13.70
Sensuous Suspect (Stig Johansson)	2	1	2	9	9/11	9/13H	1:59.4	.70e*
Hawaiian Pua (Ilkka Korpi)	7	10	10	12	10/13	10/15	2:00.1	159.60
Classic Suspense (Pekka Korpi)	8	2o	1	5	11/15	11/20H	2:01.1	125.80
Nivea Hanover (Billy Herman)	1	3	5	x10	12/23	12/dis		8.50

Winner: b, f, by Prakas -- Gassbed -- Bonefish
Owner: Arden Homestead Stable, Goshen, New York
Trainer: Bjorn Berglund
Breeders: New Bond Street Stable, Inc., Chicago, Illinois; Castleton Farm, Lexington, Kentucky; and Hanley Dawson, Jr., Chicago, Illinois

$221,458 Breeders Crown Aged Horse and Gelding Trot
Pompano Park - November 2, 1990

Horse (Driver)	PP	1/4	1/2	3/4	Stretch	Finish	Time	$1.00
	Times-		:27.2	:56.3	1:26.3	1:55		
No Sex Please (Ron Waples)	5	1o	1	1	1/1H	1/2	1:55	.40*
Delray Lobell (John Campbell)	3	5	5	4o	4/2Q	2/2	1:55.2	4.60
Bold Herbert (Michel Lachance)	2	4	4	3o	2/1H	3/2	1:55.2	14.70
Friendly Face (Ilkka Korpi)	4	2	2	2	3/2	4/3	1:55.3	2.60e
Slybowl Hanover (Pekka Korpi)	6	6	6	6	5/3T	5/3H	1:55.3	2.60e
Lodestar Lobell (Mickey McNichol)	1	3	3	5	6/6T	6/12	1:57.2	29.50
Keystone Shiek	Scratched							

Winner: br, g, 5, by Brisco Hanover -- Gay Ann Herbert -- Reflected Way
Owner: Ron Waples, Jr., Belwood, Ontario
Trainer: Ron Waples, Jr.
Breeder: Earl Lennox, Orton, Ontario

$203,458 Breeders Crown Aged Mare Trot
Pompano Park - November 2, 1990

Horse (Driver)	PP	1/4	1/2	3/4	Stretch	Finish	Time	$1.00
	Times-		:27.3	:55.2	1:25.2	1:54.2		
Peace Corps (Stig Johansson)	4	2o	2	1	1/2H	1/6	1:54.2	.40*
Kit Lobell (Berndt Lindstedt)	9	7o	7o	4o	2/2H	2/6	1:55.3	12.80
Free Token (John Campbell)	5	8	8o	5o	3/5	x3x/7	1:55.4	5.40
Scenic Regal (Harold Story)	7	1o	1o	2	4/7	5p4/13H	1:57	10.10
Alissas Beauty (Jim Whelan)	3	6	6	ix7	6/14	6p5/13H	1:57	28.00
Nettie M (Paul Spears)	6	5o	5o	ix8	7/dis	7p6/dis		130.00
Sarah Gal (Wally Hennessey)	8	9	9	9	8/dis	8p7/dis		122.30
Peach Pit (Bill O'Donnell)	2	3	3	3	5/8	4p8/12	1:56.4	36.70
Kerry's Crown (Ron Waples)	1	4	4ix	pu		dnf		5.50

Winner: b, m, 4, by Baltic Speed -- Worth Beein' -- Super Bowl
Owner: Stall Pieder, Karlstad, Sweden
Trainer: Stig Johansson
Breeders: Stanley F. Dancer, Pompano Beach, Florida, and Rosehild Breeding Farm, Inc., New Egypt, New Jersey

THE CROWNS

$396,933 Breeders Crown 3-Year-Old Colt and Gelding Trot
Pompano Park - November 2, 1990

	Times-			:27.2	:56	1:26.1	1:56.4	
Embassy Lobell (Michel Lachance)	6	9	7	6o	2/2	1/1	1:56.4	1.80*
Jeanne's Somolli (Rod Allen)	2	6	5o	5o	3/4	2/1	1:57	3.10
Armbro Iliad (John Campbell)	8	3	3	1o	1/2	3/3	1:57.2	7.50
Columnist (Cat Manzi)	10	5	4	3	4/5	4/4	1:57.3	12.30
Lender Hanover (Jan Nordin)	1	2	2	4	6/6H	5/6	1:58	70.90
Armbro Index (Bill O'Donnell)	7	8	6	7	7/8H	7p6/9Q	1:58.3	73.70
Cheyenne Spur (Dick Stillings)	9	4o	1o	2	5/6	8p7/10	1:58.4	14.30
Star Mystic (Jan Johnson)	3x	x7o	10	8	8x/9H	6p8/8Q	1:58.2	3.70
Meadowbrancy Eddy (Ron Waples)	5x	10	8	9	9/17H	9/20	2:00.4	79.50
Sambuca Lobell (Pekka Korpi)	4	1	x9x	10	10/dis	10/dis		70.60
Super Arnie (Berndt Lindstedt)	11	x11	11	11	11/dis	11/dis		7.40

Winner: b, c, by Speedy Crown -- Elmsford -- Lindy's Pride
Owner: LPG Standardbred Associates, Lawrenceville, NJ
Trainer: Jerry Riordan
Breeders: Lana Lobell Farms of New Jersey, Inc., Bedminster, New Jersey, and H F Farms, Reg'd., St. Luc, Quebec

$200,000 Breeders Crown Aged Mare Pace
Pompano Park - November 2, 1990

	Times-			:28	:55.3	1:24.2	1:52.3	
Caesars Jackpot (Bill Fahy)	1	1	1	1	1/1H	1/T	1:52.3	.30*
L Dees Trish (Michel Lachance)	2	2	2	2	2/1H	2/T	1:52.4	6.20
Windy Answer (Ron Waples)	3	3	3	3	3/2H	3/2T	1:53.1	17.20
Cheery Hello (John Campbell)	4	4	4	4	4/3	4/3T	1:53.2	2.70
Concertina (Harold Kelly)	5	5	5	5	5/6	5/8Q	1:54.1	32.60

Winner: b, m, 4, Walton Hanover -- Tracy's Jackpot -- Albatross
Owner: Coast to Coast Stable, Inc., Summit, New Jersey
Trainer: Michel Bouvrette
Breeders: Harold L. Schwartz, Jr., Boca Raton, Florida

$304,933 Breeders Crown 3-Year-Old Filly Pace
Pompano Park - November 2, 1990

	Times-			:27.3	:55.3	1:25.1	1:54.4	
Town Pro (Doug Brown)	8	5o	2	1	1/2	1/T	1:54.4	.30*
Delinquent Account (John Kopas)	4	7	7	6o	3/3	2/T	1:55	7.00
Lady Genius (Michel Lachance)	2	2	5	7	6/5H	3/1T	1:55.1	5.10
Instant Rebate (Bill Fahy)	3	6	6	5oo	2/2	4/2	1:55.1	42.30
Crafty Caper (Howard Parker)	5	1o	3	4	5/5H	5/3	1:55.2	29.40
Rulers Chippie (Joe Pavia, Jr.)	6	3o	1o	2	4/4H	6/4T	1:55.4	12.60
Smiling Rebecca (Ron Waples)	1	4	4	3o	7/8	7/5T	1:56	12.20
Bruce's Lady (John Campbell)	7	8	8	8	8/9	8/8Q	1:56.2	34.50

Winner: bf, f, by Big Towner -- Programmed -- Bret Hanover
Owner: Pro Group Stable, Toronto, Ontario
Trainer: Stew Firlotte
Breeders: J. Brian Webster, St. George, Ontario, and Raymond S. Bednarz, Brantford, Ontario

THE CROWNS

$273,458 Breeders Crown Aged Horse and Gelding Pace
Pompano Park - November 2, 1990

	Times-				:27.1	:56.2	1:24.3	1:52.1	
Bay's Fella (Paul MacDonell)	5	2	2	2	2/1H	1/H	1:52.1	69.30
Topnotcher (Doug Brown)	8	1o	1	1	1/1H	2/H	1:52.1	.50*
Sandman Hanover (John Campbell)	1	3	3	4	3/3H	3/2	1:52.3	4.20e
Dare You To (Jack Moiseyev)	3	5	5o	5o	5/4T	4/3	1:52.4	3.20
Mystery Fund (Ron Waples)	2	4	4o	3o	4/4T	5/4Q	1:53	8.70
Pilgrim's Patroit (Jay Picciano)	4	6	7	6o	6/5T	6/6Q	1:53.2	4.20e
Line One (Callie Rankin)	7	8	6	7	7/6T	7/7T	1:53.4	70.40
Storm Compensation (Michel Lachance)	6	7	8	8oo	8/8T	8/11H	1:54.2	53.30

Winner: b, h, 5, by Brand New Fella -- Basin Bay -- Tar Boy
Owner: Par-Birdie Stables, Inc., Athol Springs, New York
Trainer: Mike De Manno
Breeder: Louis Picciano, Jr., Endwell, New York

$366,933 Breeders Crown 3-Year-Old Colt and Gelding Pace
Pompano Park - November 2, 1990

	Times-				:26.4	:54.2	1:23.4	1:51.2	
Beach Towel (Ray Remmen)	3	2	1	1	1/2	1/3	1:51.2	.40*
In The Pocket (John Campbell)	8	1o	2	3	2/2	2/3	1:52	4.60*
C K S (Michel Lachance)	1	3	4	5	4/4H	3/3	1:52	4.60*
Kiev Hanover (Jim Morand)	2	5	5o	4o	3/4	4/4	1:52.1	3.00
Shipps Schnoops (Doug Brown)	5	8	8	8o	5/5T	5/4Q	1:52.1	44.20
Brace Yourself (Jim Miller)	4	7	6	7	6/7T	6/5T	1:52.3	52.50
Till We Meet Again (Buddy Gilmour)	7	6o	7o	6o	8/10Q	7/12Q	1:53.4	18.60
Global Assault (Ron Waples)	6	4o	3o	2o	7/9T	8/16T	1:54.4	50.20

Winner: b, c, By French Chef -- Sunburn -- Armbro Nesbit
Owner: Uptown Stable, New York, New York
Trainer: Ray Remmen
Breeders: Stoner Creek Stud, Inc., Paris, Kentucky

$367,403 Breeders Crown 2-Year-Old Filly Trot Final
Pompano Park - November 30, 1990

	Times-				:29.4	:59	1:30.1	2:00.3	
Jean Bi (Jan Nordin)	1	3	4o	4o	1/NS	1/H	2:00.3	5.50
Santa Royal (Cat Manzi)	2	2	3	3	4/T	2/H	2:00.3	4.30
Loosen Up (John Campbell)	8	6o	2o	2o	3/Q	3/1H	2:00.4	13.30
Esprit Spur (Dick Stillings)	3	1	1	1	2/NS	4/1H	2:00.4	1.70
Armbro Jacuzzi (Bill Fahy)	5	ix8	6	5	5/2Q	5/7	2:02	53.20
A-Treat (Howard Beissinger)	6	ix7	5	7	6/9Q	6/9H	2:02.2	31.80
My Wild Irish Rose (Harold Kelly)	7	4o	x7	6	7/12Q	7/12	2:03	24.10
Frances Jet Boko (Hugo Langeweg)	4	x5	8	8	8/22Q	8/20H	2:04.3	1.60*

Winner: br, f, by Super Bowl -- Jean's Gal -- Noble Victory
Owner: Gina Biasuzzi Stable, Inc., Pompano Beach, Florida
Trainer: Danny Collins (Team Nordin)
Breeders: K.D. Owen, Houston, Texas

THE CROWNS

$355,403 Breeders Crown 2-Year-Old Colt & Gelding Trot Final
Pompano Park - November 30, 1990

	Times-			:28.4	1:00.1	1:30.3	2:01	
Crysta's Best (Dick Richardson, Jr.)	5x	7	7o	6o	4/1T	1/NS	2:01	5.40
Carry The Message (John Campbell)	2	1	1	1	1/1H	2/NS	2:01	1.20
Somatic (Tommy Haughton)	6	6	5o	4o	5/2Q	3/1	2:01.1	106.00
Superior's Champ (Carl Allen)	8	4o	3o	2o	2/1H	4/1Q	2:01.1	39.20
Mr Chin (John Patterson, Jr.)	1	2	2	3	3/1T	5/1H	2:01.1	1.00*
Super Pleasure (Dick Stillings)	7	5	4	5	6/2T	6/2Q	2:01.2	17.90
Nonstop Lobell (Pekka Korpi)	3	3x	6	7	7/3Q	7/3Q	2:01.3	44.20
Harlan Lobell (Mario Zuanetti)	x4	8	8	8	8/dis	8/dis		51.70

Winner: b, c, by Crysta's Crown -- Super Laure -- Super Bowl
Owners: J. Patrick Huber, Lima, Ohio; Thomas E. Biddle, Lima, Ohio;
Harold E. Breidenbach, Lima, Ohio; and Kathy Montgomery, Lexington, Kentucky
Trainer: Dick Richardson, Jr.
Breeder: K.D. Owen, Houston, Texas

$514,870 Breeders Crown 2-Year-Old Filly Pace
Pompano Park - November 30, 1990

	Times-			:27.2	:57.1	1:25	1:54	
Miss Easy (John Campbell)	8	6o	3o	1	1/2	1/1	1:54	.40e*
Cams Exotic (Doug Brown)	4	1	1	2	2/2	2/1	1:54.1	2.00
Wedgies (Steve Condren)	5	7	5o	4o	3/5	3/2H	1:54.2	11.50
Goalie Jess (Michel Lachance)	2	3	4	5	4/5H	4/2H	1:54.2	55.90
Miss Intensity (Mickey McNichol)	1	4	6	6	6/8	5/6	1:55.1	116.20
Sara Loren Rd (Ron Waples)	7	2	2	3	5/6	6/6	1:55.1	98.30
Goddess Of Love (Kevin Sizer)	11	10	8o	7	7/11	7/8H	1:55.3	318.00
Caressa (Jacques Hebert)	6	8	9	8	8/11Q	8/9Q	1:55.4	72.70
Maytown Hanover (Wally Hennessey)	3	11	10	9o	9/12Q	9/9T	1:56	.40e*
Big Bloomer (Tony Kerwood)	10	5	7o	10	10/16Q	10/12Q	1:56.2	21.00
Summer Tan (Harold Kelly)	9	9o	11	x11	11/dis	11/dis		25.30

Winner: b, f, by Amity Chef -- Pleasure Seeker -- Bret Hanover
Owners: Rose M. Guida, Lawrenceville, New Jersey, and
Royal Palm Stables, Eden Prairie, Minnesota
Trainer: Bruce Nickells
Breeder: Stoner Creek Stud, Inc., Paris, Kentucky

$605,870 Breeders Crown 2-Year-Old Colt and Gelding Pace
Pompano Park - November 30, 1990

	Times-			:26.2	:53.2	1:23	1:51.1	
Artsplace (John Campbell)	4	1	1	1	1/8	1/8	1:51.1	1.80
Stormin Jesse (Jim Morand)	10	5	5	5	3/10	2/8	1:52.4	101.90
Tooter Scooter (Bill Fahy)	2	3	2	2	2/8	3/8	1:52.4	8.10
Mantese (Michel Lachance)	7	8o	7	6o	4/11	4/8T	1:53	13.80e
Happy Family (Doug Brown)	8	1o	9o	8o	5/11H	5/11Q	1:53.2	125.00
Sablevision (Ron Waples)	1	4	4	3	6/12H	6/12	1:53.3	44.80
Free Flo (Mark O'Mara)	11	6	6	7	7/13	7/12H	1:53.3	323.60
Cambest (Dave Rankin)	9	11	11	10	8/13H	8/13H	1:53.4	18.10
Silky Stallone (Wally Hennessey)	6	9	10	11	9/14	9/13H	1:53.4	13.80e
Stand And Deliver (Bill Gale)	3	7	8	9	10/14Q	10/14	1:54	53.50
Die Laughing (Richard Silverman)	5	2o	3o	4o	11/17Q	11/17Q	1:54.3	.60*

Winner: b, c, by Abercrombie -- Miss Elvira -- Albatross
Owners: George Segal and Brian Monieson, Chicago, Illinois
Trainer: Gene Riegle
Breeder: George Segal & Brian Monieson, Chicago, Illinois

THE CROWNS
BREEDERS CROWN RESULTS AT A GLANCE

Year	Div.	Winner	Driver	Sire	Track	Time
1984	2CP	Dragon's Lair	Jeff Mallet	Tyler B	Mea	1:54.1f
	2FP	Amneris	John Campbell	Tyler B	May	1:57.1h
	3CP	Troublemaker	Bill O'Donnell	Most Happy Fella	Edm	1:56f
	3FP	Naughty But Nice	Tommy Haughton	Meadow Skipper	LB	1:56.4f
	2CT	Workaholic	Berndt Lindstedt	Speedy Crown	Lex	1:57.1m
	2FT	Conifer	George Sholty	Nevele Diamond	Moh	2:01.2f
	3CT	Baltic Speed	Jan Nordin	Speedy Somolli	PPk	1:57.2f
	3FT	Fancy Crown	Bill O'Donnell	Speedy Crown	RcR	1:59.2h
1985	2PC	Robust Hanover	John Campbell	Warm Breeze	RcR	1:56.4h
	2PF	Caressable	Herve Filion	Niatross	YR	2:00h
	3PC	Nihilator	Bill O'Donnell	Niatross	GSP	1:53
	3PF	Stienam	Buddy Gilmour	Falcon Almahurst	Edm	1:55.4f
	2TC	Express Ride	John Campbell	Super Bowl	Mea	2:01.3f
	2TF	JEF's Spice	Mickey McNichol	Super Bowl	GSP	1:58.4
	3TC	Prakas	John Campbell	Speedy Crown	Moh	1:57.1f
	3TF	Armbro Devona	Bill O'Donnell	Speedy Crown	PPk	1:57.3f
	AP	Division Street (g)	Michel Lachance	Most Happy Fella	FsR	1:52.3f
	AT	Sandy Bowl	John Campbell	Super Bowl	SPk	1:56.3f
1986	2CP	Sunset Warrior	Bill Gale	Sundance Skipper	GSP	1:55.3
	2FP	Halcyon	Ray Remmen	Albatross	RcR	1:58h
	3CP	Masquerade	Richard Silverman	Niatross	GSP	1:55
	3FP	Glow Softly	Ron Waples	Storm Damage	GSP	1:56.2
	2CT	Mack Lobell	John Campbell	Mystic Park	PPk	1:59.1f
	2FT	Super Flora	Ron Waples	Super Bowl	Cby	1:59.2
	3CT	Sugarcane Hanover	Ron Waples	Florida Pro	GSP	1:57.1
	3FT	JEF's Spice	Bill O'Donnell	Super Bowl	Fhld	1:59h
	APM	Samshu Bluegrass	Michel Lachance	Silent Majority	GrR	1:56.1f
	ATM	Grades Singing	Herve Filion	Texas	ScD	1:57.4f
	APH	Forrest Skipper	Lucien Fontaine	Scarlet Skipper	LA	1:53.4f
	ATH	Nearly Perfect	Mickey McNichol	Songcan	LouD	1:57.2h
1987	2PC	Camtastic	Bill O'Donnell	Cam Fella	RcR	1:56.2h
	2PF	Leah Almahurst	Bill Fahy	Abercrombie	FsR	2:00.1f
	3PC	Call For Rain	Clint Galbraith	Storm Damage	PPk	1:53f
	3PF	Pacific	Tom Harmer	Seahawk Hanover	PPk	1:55f
	2TC	Defiant One	Howard Beissinger	Defiant Yankee	Moh	2:01.4f
	2TF	Nan's Catch	Berndt Lindstedt	Bonefish	HP	2:00.2f
	3TC	Mack Lobell	John Campbell	Mystic Park	PPk	1:54.1f
	3TF	Armbro Fling	George Sholty	Speedy Crown	PPk	1:57.3f
	APM	Follow My Star	John Campbell	Governor Skipper	Lex	1:53.4
	ATM	Grades Singing	Olle Goop	Texas	Nfld	1:58.3h
	APH	Armbro Emerson	Walter Whelan	Abercrombie	RR	1:54.1h
	ATH	Sugarcane Hanover	Ron Waples	Florida Pro	M	1:54.3
1988	2PC	Kentucky Spur	Dick Stillings	Abercrombie	PPk	1:53.2f
	2PF	Central Park West	John Campbell	Big Towner	PPk	1:53.3f
	3PC	Camtastic	Bill O'Donnell	Cam Fella	Moh	1:55.1f
	3PF	Sweet Reflection	Bill O'Donnell	Big Towner	HP	1:55.4f
	2TC	Valley Victory	Bill O'Donnell	Baltic Speed	PPk	1:58.1f
	2TF	Peace Corps	John Campbell	Baltic Speed	PPk	1:57.1f
	3TC	Firm Tribute	Mark O'Mara	Bonefish	Mea	1:55.3f
	3TF	Nalda Hanover	Mickey McNichol	Super Bowl	RcR	2:02h
	APM	Anniecrombie	Dave Magee	Abercrombie	M	1:52.3
	ATM	Armbro Flori	Larry Walker	Speedy Crown	Btva	1:59.3h
	APH	Call For Rain	Clint Galbraith	Storm Damage	ScD	1:53.2f
	ATH	Mack Lobell	John Campbell	Mystic Park	Stga	1:56h

THE CROWNS

Year	Race	Horse	Driver	Sire	Track	Time
1989	2PC	Till We Meet Again	Mickey McNichol	Sonsam	PPk	1:56.2f
	2PF	Town Pro	Doug Brown	Big Towner	PPk	1:55f
	3PC	Goalie Jeff	Michel Lachance	Cam Fella	PPk	1:54.1f
	3PF	Cheery Hello	John Campbell	Albatross	PPk	1:55.4f
	2TC	Royal Troubador	Carl Allen	Super Bowl	PPk	1:59.2f
	2TF	Delphi's Lobell	Ron Waples	Speedy Crown	PPk	1:59.3f
	3TC	Esquire Spur	Dick Stillings	Joie De Vie	PPk	1:56.1f
	3TF	Peace Corps	John Campbell	Baltic Speed	PPk	1:57f
	APM	Armbro Feather	John Kopas	Most Happy Fella	Nfld	1:56h
	ATM	Grades Singing	Olle Goop	Texas	BB	1:57.3f
	APH	Matt's Scooter	Michel Lachance	Direct Scooter	Fhld	1:53.2h
	ATH	Delray Lobell (g)	John Campbell	Speedy Crown	FsR	1:57.2f
1990	2PC	Artsplace	John Campbell	Abercrombie	PPk	1:51.1f
	2PF	Miss Easy	John Campbell	Amity Chef	PPk	1:54f
	3PC	Beach Towel	Ray Remmen	French Chef	PPk	1:51.2f
	3PF	Town Pro	Doug Brown	Big Towner	PPk	1:54.4f
	2TC	Crysta's Best	Dick Richardson, Jr.	Crysta's Crown	PPk	2:01f
	2TF	Jean Bi	Jan Nordin	Super Bowl	PPk	2:00.3f
	3TC	Embassy Lobell	Michel Lachance	Speedy Crown	PPk	1:56.4f
	3TF	Me Maggie	Berndt Lindstedt	Prakas	PPk	1:57.1f
	APM	Caesars Jackpot	Bill Fahy	Walton Hanover	PPk	1:52.3f
	ATM	Peace Corps	Stig Johansson	Baltic Speed	PPk	1:54.2f
	APH	Bay's Fella	Paul MacDonell	Brand New Fella	PPk	1:52.1f
	ATH	No Sex Please (g)	Ron Waples	Brisco Hanover	PPk	1:55f

BREEDERS CROWN RACE RECORDS AT A GLANCE

Half-Mile Tracks

Race	Horse	Driver	Date	Track	Time
2PC&G	Camtastic	Bill O'Donnell	October 30, 1987	Rosecroft Raceway	1:56.2h
2PF	Amneris	John Campbell	October 19, 1984	Maywood Park	1:57.1h
2TC&G	No Record				
2TF	No Record				
3PC&G	No Record				
3PF	No Record				
3TC&G	No Record				
3TF	JEF's Spice	Bill O'Donnell	October 25, 1985	Freehold Raceway	1:59h
APH&G	Matt's Scooter	Michel Lachance	Septbember 15, 1989	Freehold Raceway	1:53.2h
APM	Armbro Feather	John Kopas	September 1, 1989	Northfield Park	1:56h
ATH&G	Mack Lobell	John Campbell	August 5, 1988	Saratoga Raceway	1:56h
ATM	Grades Singing	Olle Goop	September 4, 1987	Northfield Park	1:58.3h

Five-Eighths Mile Tracks

Race	Horse	Driver	Date	Track	Time
2PC&G	Artsplace	John Campbell	November 30, 1990	Pompano Park	1:51.1f
2PF	Central Park West	John Campbell	November 18, 1988	Pompano Park	1:53.3f
2TC&G	Valley Victory	Bill O'Donnell	November 11, 1988	Pompano Park	1:58.1f
2TF	Peace Corps	John Campbell	November 11, 1988	Pompano Park	1:57.1f
3PC&G	Beach Towel	Ray Remmen	November 2, 1990	Pompano Park	1:51.2f
3PF	Town Pro	Doug Brown	November 2, 1990	Pompano Park	1:54.4f
3TC&G	Mack Lobell	John Campbell	November 13, 1987	Pompano Park	1:54.1f
3TF	Peace Corps	John Campbell	October 27, 1989	Pompano Park	1:57f
APH&G	Bay's Fella	Paul MacDonell	November 2, 1990	Pompano Park	1:52.1f
APM	Caesars Jackpot	Bill Fahy	November 2, 1990	Pompano Park	1:52.3f
ATH&G	No Sex Please	Ron Waples	November 2, 1990	Pompano Park	1:55f
ATM	Peace Corps	Stig Johansson	November 2, 1990	Pompano Park	1:54.2f

(continued)

THE CROWNS

Mile Tracks

2PC&G	Sunset Warrior	Bill Gale	November 14, 1986	Garden State Park	1:55.3m
2PF	No Record				
2TC&G	Workaholic	Berndt Lindstedt	October 5, 1984	The Red Mile	1:57.1m
2TF	JEF's Spice	Mickey McNichol	October 18, 1985	Garden State Park	1:58.4m
3PC&G	Nihilator	Bill O'Donnell	November 29, 1985	Garden State Park	1:53m
3PF	Glow Softly	Ron Waples	November 14, 1986	Garden State Park	1:56.2m
3TC&G	Sugarcane Hanover	Ron Waples	November 14, 1986	Garden State Park	1:57.1m
3TF	No Record				
APH&G	No Record				
APM	Anniecrombie	Dave Magee	August 12, 1988	The Meadowlands	1:52.3m
ATH&G	Sugarcane Hanover	Ron Waples	August 7, 1987	The Meadowlands	1:54.3m
ATM	No Record				

BREEDERS CROWN BUSINESS STATISTICS

The Breeders Crown has had a definite impact upon the attendance and handle of its host tracks. Just how much of an impact is indicated in the following table, where 1990 figures are compared to an average of figures from the same weekday one week earlier, one week later, and the corresponding weekday from one year ago:

Host Track (Event)	Attendance	Trend	Mutuel Handle	Trend
Pompano Park (3yo & Up)	12,296	+145.20%	$1,122,060	+119.70%
Pompano Park (2yos)	7,966	+77.44%	814,057	+66.95%

YEAR-BY-YEAR BREEDERS CROWN ATTENDANCE

Year:	1984	1985	1986	1987	1988	1989	1990
Total Attendance:	61,448	80,099	69,997	78,613	78,219	34,304	20,262
Average Attendance:	7,681	8,900	7,777	7,861	7,822	6,861	10,131

LEADING BREEDERS CROWN DRIVERS, 1990
12 Events (Ranked by Money Won)

Rank	Driver	Earnings	Events	St.	All Heats W-P-S	St.	Final Heats W-P-S
1.	John Campbell	$1,017,785	12	15	3-3-4	12	2-3-4
2.	Michel Lachance	490,791	9	9	1-1-4	9	1-1-4
3.	Ron Waples	243,134	11	11	1-1-1	10	1-1-1
4.	Berndt Lindstedt	240,330	3	3	1-1-0	3	1-1-0
5.	Doug Brown	398,186	5	5	1-2-1	5	1-2-1
6.	Jan Nordin	237,224	4	6	2-0-0	3	1-0-0
7.	Bill Fahy	222,815	5	6	1-0-2	5	1-0-1
8.	Dick Richarson	184,808	1	2	1-0-1	1	1-0-0
9.	Ray Remmen	183,466	1	1	1-0-0	1	1-0-0
10.	Jim Morand	180,821	2	2	0-1-0	2	0-1-0
11.	Cat Manzi	154,220	4	5	1-1-0	3	0-1-0
12.	Paul MacDonell	136,729	1	1	1-0-0	1	1-0-0
13.	Stig Johansson	101,729	2	2	1-0-0	2	1-0-0
14.	Rod Allen	99,233	1	1	0-1-0	1	0-1-0
15.	John Kopas	76,233	1	1	0-1-0	1	0-1-0
16.	Steve Condren	61,784	1	1	0-0-1	1	0-0-1
17.	Tommy Haughton	49,755	1	2	0-0-2	1	0-0-1
18.	Dick Stillings	49,438	3	5	0-1-0	3	0-0-0
19.	John Patterson, Jr.	47,386	1	2	1-0-0	1	0-0-0
20.	Carl Allen	33,170	1	2	0-0-0	1	0-0-0

THE CROWNS
LEADING BREEDERS CROWN DRIVERS, ALL-TIME
1984-1990, 78 Events (Ranked by Money Won)

Rank	Driver	Earnings	Events	St.	All Heats W-P-S	St.	Final Heats W-P-S
1.	John Campbell	$6,136,124	72	98	25-20-14	71	16-14-12
2.	Bill O'Donnell	4,254,157	50	74	16-13-12	49	9-11-7
3.	Ron Waples	2,104,023	43	60	7-6-8	41	6-4-4
4.	Mickey McNichol	1,478,387	23	32	4-6-2	20	4-3-1
5.	Michel Lachance	1,446,292	23	27	5-2-7	22	5-2-6
6.	Berndt Lindstedt	1,415,517	23	28	6-6-4	23	3-5-3
7.	William "Buddy" Gilmour	1,089,497	22	31	1-7-4	22	1-4-1
8.	Doug Brown	797,582	14	18	2-3-3	13	2-2-1
9.	Dick Stillings	753,943	13	17	4-3-0	12	2-2-0
10.	Bill Fahy	752,404	15	25	3-2-4	18	2-2-2
11.	Jan Nordin	647,781	21	27	4-0-3	18	2-0-2
12.	Jan Johnson	600,126	17	21	2-4-2	14	0-3-1
13.	George Sholty	563,658	10	14	2-0-1	8	2-0-1
14.	Herve Filion	557,040	6	6	2-0-1	6	2-0-1
15.	Bill Gale	527,537	9	12	1-1-4	9	1-1-2
16.	Ray Remmen	520,323	9	10	2-1-1	8	2-0-1
17.	Tommy Haughton	456,184	12	19	2-0-4	10	1-0-2
18.	John Kopas	436,875	7	9	2-3-0	7	1-2-0
19.	Clint Galbraith	417,035	5	7	3-1-0	3	2-0-0
20.	Mark O'Mara	399,837	7	9	2-1-2	5	1-1-1
21.	Larry Walker	359,344	5	6	1-2-1	5	1-2-0
22.	Howard Beissinger	357,903	4	6	1-1-1	4	1-1-0
23.	Hakan Wallner	351,050	10	13	0-2-2	9	0-1-2
24.	Richard Silverman	333,896	12	15	2-0-0	9	1-0-0
25.	Jeff Mallet	318,655	1	3	1-1-0	1	1-0-0
26.	Peter Ruscitto	295,928	9	11	0-2-1	8	0-1-1
27.	Tom Harmer	282,071	6	7	2-0-0	5	1-0-0
28.	Ben Webster	267,697	15	24	0-3-4	13	0-0-2
29.	D.R. Ackerman	266,209	5	7	1-1-1	5	0-1-1
30.	Dick Richardson, Jr.	264,878	3	5	1-0-2	3	1-0-0
31.	Olle Goop	259,006	2	2	2-0-0	2	2-0-0
32.	Carl Allen	251,539	4	6	1-0-0	4	1-0-0
33.	Lucien Fontaine	249,289	4	6	2-0-0	4	1-0-0
34.	Bruce Nickells	234,443	4	5	0-2-2	4	0-1-2
35.	Harold Story	212,967	4	4	0-3-0	4	0-3-0
36.	Cat Manzi	199,424	7	8	1-1-0	5	0-1-0
37.	William "Billy" Haughton	197,284	3	4	1-1-0	2	0-1-0
38.	Jim Morand	180,821	2	2	0-1-0	2	0-1-0
39.	Walter Whelan	179,897	2	2	1-0-0	2	1-0-0
40.	Sam "Chip" Noble III	166,629	3	4	0-2-0	2	0-1-0
41.	Dave Magee	153,628	1	1	1-0-0	1	1-0-0
42.	Don Irvine, Jr.	151,354	4	5	0-0-1	4	0-0-1
43.	Jimmy Takter	149,792	5	6	0-2-0	4	0-1-0
44.	Stanley Dancer	140,302	4	5	0-1-1	4	0-1-0
45.	Steve Condren	137,183	3	5	0-1-2	3	0-0-1
46.	Paul MacDonell	136,729	1	1	1-0-0	1	1-0-0
47.	Del Insko	135,870	2	4	1-0-1	1	0-0-1
48.	Rod Allen	104,914	3	4	0-1-0	2	0-1-0

Awards and Earnings
Beach Towel – 1990 Horse of the Year

AWARDS AND EARNINGS

1990 HARNESS HORSE OF THE YEAR

BEACH TOWEL, b, c, 3, by French Chef -- Sunburn -- Armbro Nesbit

Owner: Uptown Stable (Seth Rosenfeld, et al), New York, New York
Trainer: Ray Remmen
Driver: Ray Remmen
Breeder: Stoner Creek Stud, Paris, Kentucky

BEACH TOWEL'S CAREER SUMMARY

Year	Age	Starts	Wins	2nd	3rd	Earnings	Record	Track	Date
1989:	2	13	11	1	0	$ 478,497	1:53.3f	RcR	11-4
1990:	3	23	18	4	0	2,091,860	1:50	DuQ	8-30
Life:		36	29	5	0	$2,570,357	1:50	DuQ	8-30-90

BEACH TOWEL'S 1990 CAMPAIGN

Date	Track	Event	Purse	Finish	Time
April 10	Pompano Park	Qualifier		1^{16}	1:56.2f
April 20	The Meadowlands	Qualifier		1^3	1:57
April 28	Rosecroft Raceway	Open Pace	$8,000	$1^{2-1/4}$	1:52.4f
May 5	Rosecroft Raceway	Wm. E. Miller Memorial Elims	15,000	$1^{1-3/4}$	1:53f
May 12	Rosecroft Raceway	Wm. E. Miller Memorial Final	315,010	$1^{1/2}$	1:52.3f
May 26	Rosecroft Raceway	Hanover Colt Stake (div.)	20,972	$1^{10-1/4}$	1:54.1f
June 9	Rosecroft Raceway	The Terrapin	316,135	1^1	1:54.1f
June 16	Greenwood Raceway	North America Cup Elims	50,750	1^5	1:53f
June 23	Greenwood Raceway	North America Cup Final	1,000,000	9	
June 30	Sportsman's Park	The American-National	347,000	$1^{3-1/2}$	1:52.4f
July 6	The Meadowlands	Meadowlands Pace Elims	35,000	$1^{3/4}$	1:52.3
July 13	The Meadowlands	Meadowlands Pace Final	1,153,500	1^{ns}	1:52.2
August 3	The Meadowlands	Qualifier		1^{22}	1:53.4
August 11	The Meadows	The Adios (elim.)	65,757	2	
August 11	The Meadows	The Adios (final)	295,905	1^2	1:51.4f
August 19	Blue Bonnets	Prix d'Ete (elim.)	199,050	$1^{2-3/4}$	1:53.1f
August 19	Blue Bonnets	Prix d'Ete (final)	265,400	$1^{3-1/4}$	1:53.1f
August 30	Du Quoin, Illinois	Hayes Memorial (1st heat)	25,200	1^{13}	1:50
August 30	Du Quoin, Illinois	Hayes Memorial (2nd heat)	25,200	Scr.	
September 8	Rosecroft Raceway	Messenger Stakes (elim.)	66,656	2	
September 8	Rosecroft Raceway	Messenger Stakes (final)	311,059	$1^{4-3/4}$	1:54h
September 20	Delaware, Ohio	Little Brown Jug (1st heat)	56,233	$1^{1-1/2}$	1:53.3h
September 20	Delaware, Ohio	Little Brown Jug (2nd heat)	253,049	$1^{2-1/2}$	1:51.3
September 29	The Red Mile	The Tattersalls (elim.)	37,020	1^1	1:51.1
September 29	The Red Mile	The Tattersalls (final)	74,040	2	
October 5	The Red Mile	The Bluegrass	130,000	1^{27}	1:54.1f
October 26	Pompano Park	Qualifier		1^3	1:51.2f
November 2	Pompano Park	Breeders Crown	366,933		

BEACH TOWEL b, c, 3, 1:50	French Chef	Meadow Skipper	Dale Frost
			Countess Vivian
		La Pomme Souffle	Nevele Pride
			Pompanette
	Sunburn	Armbro Nesbit	Bye Bye Byrd
			Armbro Impel
		Sunbelle Hanover	Tar Heel
			Suave Hanover

AWARDS AND EARNINGS

HARNESS HORSE OF THE YEAR: 1947-1989

Beach Towel is the 33rd horse (and 17th pacer) to be honored as Horse of the Year in the 44-year history of the balloting as now conducted by the U.S. Trotting Association and U.S. Harness Writers Association. The list below gives performance data for the year in which each was chosen:

Year	Horse	Age	Gait	Sts.	W	P	S	Best Time	Earnings
1989	Matt's Scooter	4	P	30	23	3	1	1:50.1	$1,140,994
1988	Mack Lobell	4	T	19	17	0	2	1:54.4	769,378
1987	Mack Lobell	3	T	16	13	1	1	1:52.1	1,204,133
1986	Forrest Skipper	4	P	15	15	0	0	TT 1:50.3	637,675
1985	Nihilator	3	P	25	23	1	0	1:49.3	1,864,286
1984	Fancy Crown (f)	3	T	21	13	4	2	1:53.4	701,189
1983	Cam Fella	4	P	36	30	4	2	1:53.1	1,144,056
1982	Cam Fella	3	P	33	28	2	0	TT 1:54	879,723
1981	Fan Hanover (f)	3	P	23	17	3	1	1:54.3	497,717
1980	Niatross	3	P	26	24	0	0	TT 1:49.1	1,414,313
1979	Niatross	2	P	13	13	0	0	1:55.4	604,900
1978	Abercrombie	3	P	33	22	6	3	1:54.3	703,260
1977	Green Speed	3	T	21	16	2	0	1:55.3	584,405
1976	Keystone Ore	3	P	33	22	0	1	1:55.2	539,759
1975	Savoir (g)	7	T	21	13	5	3	1:59.2	351,385
1974	Delmonica Hanover (m)	5	T	17	5	4	1	2:00.2h	252,165
1973	Sir Dalrae	4	P	27	20	3	1	1:56f	307,354
1972	Albatross	4	P	26	20	4	1	1:54.3f	459,921
1971	Albatross	3	P	28	25	2	1	1:54.4	338,009
1970	Fresh Yankee (m)	7	T	31	20	11	0	1:58.4	359,002
1969	Nevele Pride	4	T	14	10	2	1	TT 1:54.4	222,875
1968	Nevele Pride	3	T	24	21	2	0	1:56.3	427,440
1967	Nevele Pride	2	T	29	26	2	0	1:58.2	222,923
1966	Bret Hanover	4	P	20	17	2	1	TT 1:53.3	407,534
1965	Bret Hanover	3	P	24	21	3	0	1:55	341,784
1964	Bret Hanover	2	P	24	24	0	0	1:57.2	173,298
1963	Speedy Scot	3	T	15	13	1	0	1:58.4	244,403
1962	Su Mac Lad (g)	8	T	13	7	3	0	1:58.4	112,350
1961	Adios Butler	5	P	14	13	0	0	TT 1:55.3h	180,250
1960	Adios Butler	4	P	17	12	3	0	TT 1:54.3	173,114
1959	Bye Bye Byrd	4	P	20	13	5	0	1:57.4h	199,933
1958	Emily's Pride (f)	3	T	23	16	4	0	TT 1:58	118,830
1957	Torpid	3	P	22	19	1	2	1:58	113,892
1956	Scott Frost	4	T	21	18	3	0	1:58.3	85,851
1955	Scott Frost	3	T	28	23	2	1	1:59.2	186,101
1954	Stenographer (f)	3	T	32	23	2	1	TT 1:59.1	65,137
1953	Hi Lo's Forbes	5	P	17	11	2	1	1:58	52,625
1952	Good Time	6	P	33	23	4	2	1:58	110,299
1951	Pronto Don (g)	6	T	24	16	4	2	1:59.3	80,850
1950	Proximity (m)	8	T	24	18	1	2	2:00.1	87,175
1949	Good Time	3	P	19	15	2	1	TT 1:58.4	58,766
1948	Rodney	4	T	13	12	1	0	TT 1:58	37,782
1947	Victory Song	4	T	20	12	3	0	1:57.3	17,172

(f) - Filly   (g) - Gelding   (m) - Mare

AWARDS AND EARNINGS

2-Year-Old Pacing Colt
Artsplace, p, 2, 1:51.1f
1990: 15 11 - 3 - 0 $1,180,271
Abercrombie - Miss Elvira - Albatross

Owner:	George Segal and Brian Monieson, IL
Breeder:	Homebred
Trainer:	Gene Riegle
Driver:	John Campbell

Divisional Balloting
Artsplace	277
Die Laughing	30

Major Victories
$797,400	Metro Final	1:53.4f
655,600	Governor's Cup Final	1:53
605,870	Breeders Crown	1:51.1f

2-Year-Old Pacing Filly
Miss Easy, p, 2, 1:55f
1990: 17 15 - 1 - 1 $1,128,956
Amity Chef - Pleasure Seeker - Bret Hanover

Owners:	Rose M. Guida, NJ and Royal Palm Stables, MN
Breeder:	Stoner Creek Stud, KY
Trainer:	Bruce Nickells
Driver:	John Campbell

Divisional Balloting
Miss Easy	308
(No others with 4 or more votes)	

Major Victories
$ 80,000	Countess Adios (div.)	1:54
766,000	Sweetheart Final	1:52.3
422,400	Three Diamonds Final	1:55.3
514,870	Breeders Crown	1:54f

3-Year-Old Pacing Colt
Beach Towel, p, 3, 1:50
1990: 23 18 - 4 - 0 $2,091,860
French Chef - Sunburn - Armbro Nesbit

Owners:	Uptown Stable, NY
Breeder:	Stoner Creek Stud, KY
Trainer/Driver:	Ray Remmen

Divisional Balloting
Beach Towel	306
Jake And Elwood	4

Pacer of the Year Balloting
Beach Towel	275
Miss Easy	13

Horse of the Year Balloting
Beach Towel	273
No Sex Please	13

Major Victories
$1,153,500	Meadowlands Pace	1:52.2
493,176	Adios	1:51.4f
663,500	Prix d'Ete	1:53.1f
468,610	Little Brown Jug	1:53.3h
366,933	Breeders Crown	1:51.2f

AWARDS AND EARNINGS

3-Year-Old Pacing Filly
Town Pro, p, 3, 1:51.4
1990: 17 14 - 2 - 1 $634,690
Big Towner - Programmed - Bret Hanover

Owner:	Pro Group Stable, ONT
Breeders:	Brian Webster and Ray Bednarz, ONT
Trainer:	Stew Firlotte
Driver:	Doug Brown

Divisional Balloting
Town Pro	298
Choice Yankee	7
Lady Genius	4

Major Victories
$181,000 American-National	1:55.2f
191,900 Fan Hanover	1:53.1f
109,612 Simcoe (div.)	1:54.4f
304,933 Breeders Crown	1:54.4f

Aged Pacing Horse
Dorunrun Bluegrass, p, 1:51.3
1990: 31 17 - 6 - 2 $851,755
Fortune Richie - Delila Bluegrass - Sir Carlton

Owner:	Luel P. Overstreet, KY
Breeder:	Paul D. Shelton, TN
Trainer:	John Merkel
Driver:	Herve Filion

Divisional Balloting
Dorunrun Bluegrass	193.5
T K's Skipper	73
Topnotcher	39.5

Major Victories
$100,000 R Bruce Cornell Mem.	1:53.1h
205,500 Graduate Series Final	1:51.3
100,000 Battle of Lake Erie	1:54h
146,000 U.S. Pacing Champ.	1:54f
200,000 Haughton Mem. Final	1:55h

Aged Pacing Mare
Caesar's Jackpot, p, 4, 1:51.2
1990: 24 11 - 7 - 0 $353,550
Walton Wanover - Tracys Jackpot - Albatross

Owner:	Coast to Coast Stable, NJ
Breeder:	Harold Schwartz, Jr., FL
Trainer:	Michel Bouvrette
Driver:	Bill Fahy

Divisional Balloting
Armbro Feather	290
L Dees Trish	11

Major Victories
$125,000 Roses Are Red	1:53f
141,250 Milton Final	1:53.3f
200,000 Breeders Crown	1:52.3f

AWARDS AND EARNINGS

2-Year-Old Trotting Colt
Crysta's Best, 2, 1:58.2f
1990: 19 10 - 1 - 0 $319,520
Crystas Crown - Super Laure - Super Bowl

Owners:	Patrick J. Huber, Thomas E. Biddle, Harold E. Breidenbach, OH; and Kathy J. Montgomery, KY
Breeder:	K.D. Owen, TX
Trainer:	Dick Richardson, Jr.
Driver:	Dick Richardson, Jr.

Divisional Balloting
Crysta's Best	109.5
Charlie Ten Hitch	85
Grundy's Mint	48.5
Super Pleasure	26
Mr Chin	17

Major Victories
$	51,090 Horseman Stake	1:58.2
	355,403 Breeders Crown	2:01f

2-Year-Old Trotting Filly
Jean Bi, 2, 1:59.1
1990: 14 9 - 3 - 0 $366,153
Super Bowl - Jean's Gal - Noble Victory

Owner:	Gina Biasuzzi Stable, FL
Breeder:	K.D. Owen, TX
Trainer:	Danny Collins (Team Nordin)
Driver:	Jan Nordin

Divisional Balloting
Jean Bi	129.5
Santa Royal	93
Frances Jet Boko	78.5

Major Victories
$	56,000 Acorn (div.)	1:59.3
	92,600 American-National	2:00.4f
	367,403 Breeders Crown	2:00.3f

3-Year-Old Trotting Colt
Harmonious, 3, 1:53.2
1990: 14 10 - 0 - 0 $1,033,942
Crowning Point - Rhapsody In Blue - Super Bowl

Owners:	Lindy Racing Stable, CN; and Sal Garofalo, FL
Breeder:	Kentuckiana Farms, KY
Trainer:	Jorn Kvikstad
Drivers:	John Campbell/Cat Manzi

Trotter of the Year Balloting
Harmonious	127
No Sex Please	101
Peace Corps	43

Divisional Balloting
Harmonious	231
Embassy Lobell	65

Major Victories
$1,346,000 Hambletonain	1:54.1
600,000 World Trotting Derby	1:53.2

AWARDS AND EARNINGS

3-Year-Old Trotting Filly
Me Maggie, 3, 1:56.1f
1990: 19 10 - 3 - 2 $305,004
Prakas - Grassbed - Bonefish

Owners:	Johan T. Dieden, SWE; and Edward Redner, FL
Breeder:	New Bond Street Stable, IL; and Castleton Farm, KY
Trainer:	Bjorn Berglund (Continental Farms)
Driver:	Berndt Lindstedt

Divisional Balloting
Me Maggie	139
Model Home	63.5
Happy Diamonds	59.5

Major Victories
$ 46,685	Colonial Filly (div.)	1:57.2f
378,933	Breeders Crown	1:57.1f

Aged Trotting Horse
No Sex Please, 5, 1:55f
1990: 28 18 - 4 - 1 $561,169
Brisco Hanover-Gay Ann Herbert-Reflected Way

Owner:	Ron Waples, Jr., ONT
Breeder:	Earl Lennox, ONT
Trainer:	Ron Waples, Jr.
Driver:	Ron Waples, Sr.

Divisional Balloting
No Sex Please	295
Reve d'Udon	9
Mack Lobell	5

Major Victories
$ 73,000	Su Mac Lad Final	1:57.4
43,800	Jazzman (div.)	1:55.4f
293,250	Maple Leaf Trot	1:57f
221,458	Breeders Crown	1:55f

Aged Trotting Mare
Peace Corps, 4, 1:54.2f
1990: 1 1 - 0 - 0 $101,729
Baltic Speed - Worth Beein' - Super Bowl

Owner:	Stall Peider, SWE
Breeder:	Stanley Dancer, NJ
Trainer:	Stig Johansson
Driver:	Stig Johansson

Divisional Balloting
Peace Corps	140
Kit Lobell	114
Scenic Regal	32
Peach Pit	9
Kerry's Crown	8

Major Victories
$203,458	Breeders Crown	1:54.2f

AWARDS AND EARNINGS

PREVIOUS DIVISIONAL WINNERS

	2yo Pacer *	2yo Filly Pacer	3yo Pacer *	3yo Filly Pacer
1989	Till We Meet Again	Town Pro	Goalie Jeff	Cherry Hello
1988	Totally Ruthless	Central Park West	Matt's Scooter	Sweet Reflection
1987	Camtastic	So Cozy	Jate Lobell	Pacific
1986	Jate Lobell	Halcyon	Amity Chef	Anniecrombie
1985	Barberry Spur	Follow My Star	Nihilator	Steinam
1984	Nihilator	Amneris	On The Road Again	Naughty But Nice
1983	Walton Hanover	De Buena Lobell	Ralph Hanover	Turn The Tide
1982	Fortune Teller	Bardot Lobell	Cam Fella	Three Diamonds
1981	McKinzie Almahurst	Three Diamonds	Seahawk Hanover	Fan Hanover
1980	French Chef	Areba Areba	Niatross	Toy Poodle
1979	Niatross	Misty Misty	Hot Hitter	Roses Are Red
1978	Sonsam	Hazel Hanover	Abercrombie	Happy Lady
1977	No No Yankee	Passing Glance	Governor Skipper	Mistletoe Shalee
1976	Jade Prince	Mary Mel	Keystone Ore	Keystone Model
1975	Armbro Ranger	Meadow Wilma	Nero	Silk Stockings
1974	Alert Bret	Silk Stockings	Armbo Omaha	Handle With Care
1973	Boyden Hanover	Handle With Care	Melvin's Woe	All Alert
1972	Ricci Rennie Time	Real Hilarious	Strike Out	Romalie Hanover
1971	Strike Out	Rosalie Hanover	Albatross	Armbro Louann
1970	Albatross	Keystone Memento	Most Happy Fella	Armbro Kerry
1969	Truluck	Majetta	Laverne Hanover	Scotch Jewel
1968	Laverne Hanover	Scotch Jewell	Rum Customer	Sunnie Tar
1967	Fulla Napoleon		Romulus Hanover	
1966	Best Of All		Romeo Hanover	
1965	Romeo Hanover		Bret Hanover	
1964	Bret Hanover		Race Time	
1963	Race Time		Overtrick	
1962	Overtrick		Lehigh Hanover	
1961	Coffee Break		Henry T Adios	
1960	Adios Cleo		Bullet Hanover	
1959	Bullet Hanover		Adios Butler	
1958	Meadow Al		Shadow Wave	
1957	Corsican		Torpid	
1956	Torpid		Noble Adios	
1955	Belle Acton (f)		Quick Chief	
1954	Quick Chief		Adios Boy	
1953	Adios Boy		Keystoner	
1952	Hillsota		Meadow Rice	

* - Regardless of sex prior to 1968

AWARDS AND EARNINGS

Previous Divisional Winners (continued)

	2yo Trotters *	2yo Filly Trotter	3yo Trotters *	3yo Filly Trotter
1989	Royal Troubador	Cayster	Esquire Spur	Peace Corps
1988	Valley Victory	Peace Corps	Armbro Goal	Nan's Catch
1987	Firm Tribute	Anamosa Hanover	Mack Lobell	Armbro Fling
1986	Mack Lobell	Super Flora	Royal Prestige	JEF's Spice
1985	Express Ride	Britelite Lobell	Prakas	Armbro Devona
1984	Workaholic	Davidia Hanover	Baltic Speed	Fancy Crown
1983	Baltic Speed	Arnie's Frilly	Joie De Vie	Duenna
1982	Dancers Crown	Armbro Blush	Jazz Cosmos	Dance Spell
1981	Self Confident	Crevette	Banker Barker	Panty Raid
1980	Smokin Yankee	Delmegan	Final Score	Kading
1979	Noble Hustle	Cranford	Chiola Hanover	Classicay Way
1978	Legend Hanover	Ahhh	Speedy Somolli	Rosemary
1977	Speedy Somolli	Starita Lobell	Green Speed	Superlou
1976	Jodevin	Superlou	Steve Lobell	Ima Lulu
1975	Nevele Thunder	Ima Lulu	Bonefish	Meadow Bright
1974	Bonefish	Meadow Bright	Dream Of Glory	Noble Florie
1973	Christopher T	Starlark Hanover	Flirth	Colonial Charm
1972	Arnie Almahurst	Colonial Charm	Super Bowl	Delmonica Hanover
1971	Super Bowl	Delmonica Hanover	Speedy Crown	Noble Gal
1970	Quick Pride	Keystone Selene	Timothy T	Vanaro
1969	Victory Star	Floribert	Lindy's Pride	Sheer Speed
1968	Nevele Major	Jounce	Nevele Pride	Daring Speed
1967	Nevele Pride		Flamboyant (f)	
1966	Flamboyant (f)		Kerry Way (f)	
1965	Kerry Way (f)		Armbro Flight (f)	
1964	Noble Victory		Ayres	
1963	Speedy Count		Speedy Scot	
1962	Speedy Scot		A C's Viking	
1961	Impish (f)		Harlan Dean	
1960	Meadow Farr (f)		Elaine Rodney (f)	
1959	Blaze Hanover		Diller Hanover	
1958	Merrie Annabelle (f)		Emily's Pride (f)	
1957	Yankee Lass (f)		Hickory Smoke	
1956	Hickory Smoke		Nimble Colby	
1955	Saboteur		Scott Frost	
1954	Scott Frost		Stenographer (f)	
1953	Newport Dream		Kimberly Kid	
1952	Lively Lady (f)		Sharp Note	

* - Regardless of sex prior to 1968

AWARDS AND EARNINGS

Previous Divisional Winners (continued)

	Aged Pacing Horse	**4yo Pacing Champ**	**Aged Pacing Mare**	**4yo Pacing Mare**
1989	Matt's Scooter		Armbro Feather	
1988	Call For Rain		Armbro Feather	
1987	Amrbro Emerson		Follow My Star	
1986	Forrest Skipper		Samshu Bluegrass	
1985	On The Road Again		Green With Envy	
1984	Mr Dalrae		Green With Envy	
1983	Cam Fella		JEF's Eternity	
1982	Genghis Khan		Fan Hanover	
1981	Royce		Toy Poodle	
1980	Direct Scooter		Kris Messenger	
1979	Try Scotch		Tender Loving Care	
1978	Whata Baron		Mistletoe Shalee	
1977	Rambling Willie		Tarport Hap	
1976	Rambling Willie		Meadow Blue Chip	
1975	Rambling Willie	Sly Attorney	Sandra Lil	Handle With Care
1974	Invincible Shadow	Armbro Nesbit	Huff N Puff	Real Hilarious
1973	Mountain Skipper	Sir Dalrae	Becky Hi Win	Pammy Lobell
1972	Isle Of Wight	Albatross	Miss Conna Adios	Thimble
1971	Super Wave	Steady Star	Miss Conna Adios	Lillian Greene
1970	Rum Customer	Laverne Hanover	Sunnie Tar	Tarport Birdie
1969	Overcall	Rum Customer	Meadow Elva	Miss Conna Adios
1968	Cardigan Bay	Best Of All	Reed's Waylay	
1967	Easy Prom	Romeo Hanover		
1966	Bret Hanover			
1965	Cardigan Bay/Race Time (tie)			
1964	Tarquinius			
1963	Henry T Adios			
1962	Henry T Adios			
1961	Adios Butler			
1960	Adios Butler			
1959	Bye Bye Byrd			
1958	Belle Acton (m)			
1957	Diamond Hal			
1956	Adios Harry			
1955	Adios Harry			
1954	Red Sails			
1953	Hi Lo's Forbes			
1952	Good Time			

AWARDS AND EARNINGS

Previous Divisional Winners (continued)

	Aged Trotting Horse	4yo Trotting Champ	Aged Trotting Mare	4yo Trotting Mare
1989	Napoletano		Scenic Regal	
1988	Mack Lobell		Scenic Regal	
1987	Sugarcane Hanover		Scenic Regal	
1986	Nearly Perfect		Grades Singing	
1985	Sandy Bowl		Babe Kosmos	
1984	Spunky Byron		Quick Trip	
1983	Diamond Exchange		Dutchess Faye	
1982	Bobbo		Delmegan	
1981	Final Score		Kading	
1980	Crown's Star		Classical Way	
1979	Doublemint		Keystone Pioneer	
1978	Green Speed		Petite Evander	
1977	Pride Of Carlisle		Ima Lulu	
1976	Dream Of Glory		Keystone Pioneer	
1975	Savior	Dream Of Glory	Lively Anne	Berna Hanover
1974	Savior	Noble Jade	Delmonica Hanover	Colonial Charm
1973	Flower Child	Spartan Hanover	Une De Mai	Delmonica Hanover
1972	Flower Child	Speedy Crown	Fresh Yankee	Gay Blossom
1971	Dayan	Marlu Pride	Fresh Yankee	Egyptian Floral
1970	Grandpa Jim	Dayan	Fresh Yankee	Extra Bonus
1969	Grandpa Jim	Nevele Pride	Fresh Yankee	Noccalula
1968	Carlisle	Keystone Pride	Roquepine	Flamboyant
1967	Perfect Freight	Carlisle		
1966	Noble Victory			
1965	Dartmouth			
1964	Speedy Scot			
1963	Duke Rodney			
1962	Su Mac Lad			
1961	Su Mac Lad			
1960	Su Mac Lad			
1959	Jamin			
1958	Trader Horn			
1957	Galophone			
1956	Scott Frost			
1955	Kimberly Kid			
1954	Kimberly Kid			
1953	Pronto Don			
1952	Star's Pride			

AWARDS AND EARNINGS

Previous Divisional Winners (continued)

	Pacer of the Year	Trotter of the Year	Horse of the Year
1989	Matt's Scooter	Peace Corps	Matt's Scooter
1988	Matt's Scooter	Mack Lobell	Mack Lobell
1987	Camtastic	Mack Lobell	Mack Lobell
1986	Forrest Skipper	Royal Prestige	Forrest Skipper
1985	Nihilator	Prakas	Nihilator
1984	On The Road Again	Fancy Crown	Fancy Crown (f)
1983	Cam Fella	Duenna	Cam Fella
1982	Cam Fella	Jazz Cosmos	Cam Fella
1981	Fan Hanover	Panty Raid	Fan Hanover (f)
1980	Niatross	Classical Way	Niatross
1979	Niatross	Chiola Hanover	Niatross
1978	Abercrombie	Speedy Somolli	Abercrombie
1977	Governor Skipper	Green Speed	Green Speed
1976	Keystone Ore	Steve Lobell	Keystone Ore
1975	Silk Stockings	Savior	Savior (g)
1974	Armbro Nesbit	Delmonica Hanover	Delmonica Hanover (m)
1973	Sir Dalrae	Flirth	Sir Dalrae
1972	Albatross	Super Bowl	Albatross
1971	Albatross	Speedy Crown	Albatross
1970	Most Happy Fella	Fresh Yankee	Fresh Yankee (m)
1969			Nevele Pride
1968			Nevele Pride
1967			Nevele Pride
1966			Bret Hanover
1965			Bret Hanover
1964			Bret Hanover
1963			Speedy Scot
1962			Su Mac Lad (g)
1961			Adios Butler
1960			Adios Butler
1959			Bye Bye Byrd
1958			Emily's Pride (f)
1957			Torpid
1956			Scott Frost
1955			Scott Frost
1954			Stenographer (f)
1953			Hi Lo's Forbes
1952			Good Time
1951			Pronto Don
1950			Proximity (m)
1949			Good Time
1948			Rodney
1947			Victory Song

AWARDS AND EARNINGS

OWNERS OF HORSES OF THE YEAR

1947 through 1989

Year	Horse of the Year	Owner(s)
1989	Matt's Scooter	Gordon & Illa Rumpel and Charles Juravinski
1988	Mack Lobell	John Erik Magnusson, Vislanda, Sweden
1987	Mack Lobell	One More Time Stable and Fair Winds Farm, NJ
1986	Forrest Skipper	Forrest L. Bartlett
1985	Nihilator	Wall Street-Nihilator Syndicate
1984	Fancy Crown	Fancy Crown Stable
1983	Cam Fella	JEF's Standardbred; Norm Clements & Norm Faulkner
1982	Cam Fella	Norm Clements & Norm Faulkner
1981	Fan Hanover	Dr. J. Glen Brown
1980	Niatross	Niatross Synd.; Niagara Acres & Clint Galbraith
1979	Niatross	Niagara Acres & Clint Galbraith
1978	Abercrombie	Shirley Mitchell & L. Keith Bulen
1977	Green Speed	Beverly Lloyds
1976	Keystone Ore	Mr. & Mrs. Stanley Dancer; Rose Hild Farms; & Robert Jones
1975	Savoir	Allwood Stable
1974	Delmonica Hanover	Delvin Miller & W. Arnold Hanger
1973	Sir Dalrae	A La Carte Racing Stable
1972	Albatross	Amicable Stable
1971	Albatross	Albatross Stable
1970	Fresh Yankee	Duncan MacDonald
1969	Nevele Pride	Nevele Acres & Louis Resnick
1968	Nevele Pride	Nevele Acres & Louis Resnick
1967	Nevele Pride	Nevele Acres
1966	Bret Hanover	Richard Downing
1965	Bret Hanover	Richard Downing
1964	Bret Hanover	Richard Downing
1963	Speedy Scot	Castleton Farm
1962	Su Mac Lad	I. W. Berkemeyer
1961	Adios Butler	Adios Butler Syndicate
1960	Adios Butler	Adios Butler Syndicate
1959	Bye Bye Byrd	Mr. & Mrs. Rex Larkin
1958	Emily's Pride	Walnut Hall & Castleton Farms
1957	Torpid	Sherwood Farm
1956	Scott Frost	S.A. Camp Farms
1955	Scott Frost	S.A. Camp Farms
1954	Stenographer	Max Hempt
1953	Hi Lo's Forbes	Mr. & Mrs. Earl Wagner
1952	Good Time	William Cane
1951	Pronto Don	Hayes Fair Acres Stable
1950	Proximity	Ralph & Gordon Verhurst
1949	Good Time	William Cane
1948	Rodney	R. H. Johnston
1947	Victory Song	Castleton Farm

AWARDS AND EARNINGS

DRIVERS AND TRAINERS OF HORSES OF THE YEAR

1947 through 1989

Year	Horse of the Year	Trainer	Driver
1989	Matt's Scooter	Harry Poulton	Michel Lachance
1988	Mack Lobell	Charles Sylvester	John Campbell
1987	Mack Lobell	Charles Sylvester	John Campbell
1986	Forrest Skipper	Marc Fontaine	Lucien Fontaine
1985	Nihilator	William Haughton	Bill O'Donnell
1984	Fancy Crown	Ted Andrews	Bill O'Donnell
1983	Cam Fella	Pat Crowe	Pat Crowe
1982	Cam Fella	Pat Crowe	Pat Crowe
1981	Fan Hanover	Glen Garnsey	Glen Garnsey
1980	Niatross	Clint Galbraith	Clint Galbraith
1979	Niatross	Clint Galbraith	Clint Galbraith
1978	Abercrombie	Glen Garnsey	Glen Garnsey
1977	Green Speed	William Haughton	William Haughton
1976	Keystone Ore	Stanley Dancer	Stanley Dancer
1975	Savoir	Jimmy Arthur	Jimmy Arthur
1974	Delmonica Hanover	Del Miller	John Chapman
1973	Sir Dalrae	Jim Dennis	Jim Dennis
1972	Albatross	Stanley Dancer	Stanley Dancer
1971	Albatross	Stanley Dancer	Stanley Dancer
1970	Fresh Yankee	Joe O'Brien	Joe O'Brien
1969	Nevele Pride	Stanley Dancer	Stanley Dancer
1968	Nevele Pride	Stanley Dancer	Stanley Dancer
1967	Nevele Pride	Stanley Dancer	Stanley Dancer
1966	Bret Hanover	Frank Ervin	Frank Ervin
1965	Bret Hanover	Frank Ervin	Frank Ervin
1964	Bret Hanover	Frank Ervin	Frank Ervin
1963	Speedy Scot	Ralph Baldwin	Ralph Baldwin
1962	Su Mac Lad	Stanley Dancer	Stanley Dancer
1961	Adios Butler	Paige West	Eddie Cobb
1960	Adios Butler	Paige West	Eddie Cobb
1959	Bye Bye Byrd	Clint Hodgins	Clint Hodgins
1958	Emily's Pride	Fred Egan	Flick Nipe
1957	Torpid	John Simpson, Sr.	John Simpson, Sr.
1956	Scott Frost	Joe O'Brien	Joe O'Brien
1955	Scott Frost	Joe O'Brien	Joe O'Brien
1954	Stenographer	Del Miller	Del Miller
1953	Hi Lo's Forbes	Henry Clukey	Henry Clukey
1952	Good Time	Frank Ervin	Frank Ervin
1951	Pronto Don	Faye Fitzpatrick	Benny Schue
1950	Proximity	Clint Hodgins	Clint Hodgins
1949	Good Time	Frank Ervin	Frank Ervin
1948	Rodney	Bion Shively	Bion Shively
1947	Victory Song	Sep Palin	Sep Palin

AWARDS AND EARNINGS

BREEDERS OF HORSES OF THE YEAR
1947 Through 1989

Year	Horse of the Year	Breeder
1989	Matt's Scooter	Max Gerson, New York, New York
1988	Mack Lobell	Lana Lobell Farms of New Jersey
1987	Mack Lobell	Lana Lobell Farms of New Jersey
1986	Forrest Skipper	Elwyn P. Leary, Camden, North Carolina
1985	Nihilator	Robert E. Gangloff, Logansport, Indiana
1984	Fancy Crown	Dale D. and Floyd Miller, Archbold, Ohio
1983	Cam Fella	Wilfred R. Cameron, Washington, Pennsylvania
1982	Cam Fella	Wilfred R. Cameron, Washington, Pennsylvania
1981	Fan Hanover	Hanover Shoe Farms, Inc., Hanover, Pennsylvania
1980	Niatross	Niagara Acres, Grand Island, New York
1979	Niatross	Niagara Acres, Grand Island, New York
1978	Abercrombie	Walnut Hall Farm, Lexington, Kentucky
1977	Green Speed	L.S. Llyods, Palm Beach, Florida
1976	Keystone Ore	Max C. Hempt, Mechanicsburg, Pennsylvania
1975	Savoir	Allwood Farm, Hanover, Pennsylvania
1974	Delmonica Hanover	Hanover Shoe Farms, Inc., Hanover, Pennsylvania
1973	Sir Dalrae	A La Carte Racing Stables, Los Angeles, California
1972	Albatross	John Kenney, Long Valley, NJ; Charles Kenney, Lexington, KY; Elizabeth Peters, Wilmington, DE; Mark Lydon, Abington, MA; and John Wilcutts, Aberdeen, NC
1971	Albatross	John Kenney, Long Valley, NJ; Charles Kenney, Lexington, KY; Elizabeth Peters, Wilmington, DE; Mark Lydon, Abington, MA; and John Wilcutts, Aberdeen, NC
1970	Fresh Yankee	Charles E. Keller, Frederick, Maryland
1969	Nevele Pride	Mr. & Mrs. Edward C. Quin, Blue Bell, Pennsylvania
1968	Nevele Pride	Mr. & Mrs. Edward C. Quin, Blue Bell, Pennsylvania
1967	Nevele Pride	Mr. & Mrs. Edward C. Quin, Blue Bell, Pennsylvania
1966	Bret Hanover	Hanover Shoe Farms, Inc., Hanover Pennsylvania
1965	Bret Hanover	Hanover Shoe Farms, Inc., Hanover Pennsylvania
1964	Bret Hanover	Hanover Shoe Farms, Inc., Hanover Pennsylvania
1963	Speedy Scot	Castleton Farm, Lexington, Kentucky
1962	Su Mac Lad	Mrs. Paul Davis, Henderson, Illinois
1961	Adios Butler	Russell C. Carpenter, Chester, New York
1960	Adios Butler	Russell C. Carpenter, Chester, New York
1959	Bye Bye Byrd	Poplar Hill Farm, Chicago, Illinois
1958	Emily's Pride	Charles W. Phellis, Greenwich, Connecticut
1957	Torpid	Sherwood Farm, Irvington, New Jersey
1956	Scott Frost	Est. of W.N. Reynolds, Winston-Salem, N. Carolina
1955	Scott Frost	Est. of W.N. Reynolds, Winston-Salem, N. Carolina
1954	Stenographer	Est. of George L. Hempt, Camp Hill, Pennsylvania
1953	Hi Lo's Forbes	Mrs. Raye E. Backart, Byron Center, Michigan
1952	Good Time	Good Time Stable, Goshen, New York
1951	Pronto Don	Hayes Fair Acres Stables, Du Quoin, Illinois
1950	Proximity	Walnut Hall Farm, Donerail, Kentucky
1949	Good Time	Good Time Stable, Goshen, New York
1948	Rodney	Hanover Shoe Farms, Inc., Hanover, Pennsylvania
1947	Victory Song	Walnut Hall Farm, Donerail, Kentucky

AWARDS AND EARNINGS

USTA HORSE OF THE MONTH

1981 THROUGH 1990

As selected each month by a vote of the publicity department of the USTA

1981
Jan.	Mac Breton
Feb.	Miller's Scout
Mar.	Rambling Willie
Apr.	Pumping Iron
May	Keystone Famous
June	Cooper Lobell
July	Fan Hanover
Aug.	Landslide
Sep.	Fan Hanover
Oct.	Eastern Skipper
Nov.	Go'in Dancin'
Dec.	Miss Cabert

1982
Jan.	Midas Almahurst
Feb.	Tresspassers W
Mar.	Skip By Night
Apr.	Willow Wiper
May	Beatcha
June	Mystic Park
July	Three Diamonds
Aug.	Fame
Sep.	Bardot Lobell
Oct.	Cam Fella
Nov.	Justin Passing
Dec.	Sconce

1983
Jan.	Tiffany Star
Feb.	Courageous Red
Mar.	Dutchess Faye
Apr.	Trim The Tree
May	Cam Fella
June	Joie De Vie
July	Ralph Hanover
Aug.	Duenna
Sep.	Ralph Hanover
Oct.	Cam Fella
Nov.	Cam Fella
Dec.	Albaquel

1984
Jan.	Riklis
Feb.	Boomer Drummond
Mar.	Boomer Drummond
Apr.	On The Road Again
May	Excel Hanover
June	Speed Merchant
July	On The Road Again
Aug.	Fancy Crown
Sep.	Colt Fortysix
Oct.	Fancy Crown
Nov.	Crown Wood
Dec.	Doc's Fella

1985
Jan.	George S
Feb.	Silver Dollar
Mar.	Tuff Choice
Apr.	Selena Lobell
May	On The Road Again
June	Pershing Square
July	Nihilator
Aug.	Prakas
Sep.	Nihilator
Oct.	Barberry Spur
Nov.	Nihilator
Dec.	Flying Rich

1986
Jan.	Manfred Hanover
Feb.	Manfred Hanover
Mar.	Falcon Seelster
Apr.	Forrest Skipper
May	Incredible Finale
June	Falcon Seelster
July	Grades Singing
Aug.	Royal Prestige
Sep.	Jate Lobell
Oct.	JEF's Spice
Nov.	Saccharum
Dec.	Grades Singing

1987
Jan.	Saute
Feb.	Hurricane Skipper
Mar.	Rubis Ben
Apr.	Whip It Wood
May	Run The Table
June	Jate Lobell
July	Mack Lobell
Aug.	Mack Lobell
Sep.	Napoletano
Oct.	Camtastic
Nov.	Frugal Gourmet
Dec.	Merrilywerollalong

1988
Jan.	Anniecrombie
Feb.	Burnham
Mar.	Nadia Lobell
Apr.	Call For Rain
May	Singing Strings
June	Runnymede Lobell
July	Kassa Branca
Aug.	Mack Lobell
Sep.	Leah Almahurst
Oct.	Camtastic
Nov.	Jaguar Spur
Dec.	Scenic Regal

1989
Jan.	Barely Visible
Feb.	Casino Cowboy
Mar.	Sweet Sharon
Apr.	Matt's Scooter
May	Jaguar Spur
June	Peace Corps
July	Dexter Nukes
Aug.	Goalie Jeff
Sep.	Peace Corps
Oct.	Till We Meet Again
Nov.	Matt's Scooter
Dec.	Gentle Jody

1990
Jan.	Barely Visible
Feb.	No Sex Please
Mar.	Chatham Light
Apr.	Dorunrun Bluegrass
May.	Beach Towel
June	Apaches Fame
July	Beach Towel
Aug.	Beach Towel
Sep.	Miss Easy
Oct.	Topnotcher
Nov.	Artsplace
Dec.	Rulers Chippie

AWARDS AND EARNINGS
LEADING SINGLE-SEASON MONEYWINNERS

The following table shows the leading single-season moneywinning trotters and pacers. Former leaders are shown in **boldface**:

Trotters

Prakas, bc, 3	(1985)	$1,610,608
Armbro Goal, bc, 3	(1988)	1,311,234
Mack Lobell, brc, 3	(1987)	1,204,133
Napoletano, bc, 3	(1987)	1,137,516
Baltic Speed, bc, 3	**(1984)**	**1,062,611**
Royal Pestige, brc, 3	(1986)	1,052,114
Embassy Lobell, bc, 3	(1990)	1,049,175
Harmonious, bc, 3	(1990)	1,033,942
Joie De Vie, bc, 3	**(1983)**	**1,007,705**
Peace Corps, bf, 3	(1989)	1,002,701
Duenna, bf, 3	(1983)	966,709
Express Ride, bc, 2	(1985)	840,328
Nuclear Kosmos, bc, 3	(1986)	839,461
Armbro Fling, bf, 3	(1987)	820,291
Flak Bait, blkc, 3	(1985)	810,321
Mack Lobell, brh, 4	(1988)	769,378
Firm Tribute, bc, 3	(1988)	756,918
Mark Six, bc, 3	(1985)	728,940
Fancy Crown, brf, 3	(1984)	701,189
Park Avenue Joe, blkc, 3	(1989)	666,311
Mack Lobell, brc, 2	(1986)	674,665
Speed Bowl, bc, 3	**(1982)**	**672,084**
Peace Corps, bf, 2	(1988)	668,599
Historic Freight, bc, 3	(1984)	668,392
JEF's Spice, bf, 3	(1986)	632,423
Sugarcane Hanover, bc, 3	(1986)	629,740
Britelite Lobell, brf, 3	(1986)	612,335
Ron B Hanover, brc, 3	(1985)	608,618
Jazz Cosmos, bc, 3	(1982)	608,248
Another Miracle, bc, 2	(1984)	607,872
Grades Singing, brm, 4	(1986)	606,544
Green Speed, brc, 3	**(1977)**	**584,405**
Sandy Bowl, bh, 4	(1985)	578,601
Ditka Hanover, bc, 2	(1986)	565,387
No Sex Please, brg, 5	(1990)	561,169
Sandy Bowl, bc, 3	(1984)	553,707
Chiola Hanover, brc, 3	(1979)	553,058
Royal Troubador, bc, 2	(1989)	541,336
Backstreet Guy, brc, 2	(1989)	524,845
Davidia Hanover, brf, 2	(1984)	525,713
Keyser Lobell, bc, 2	(1988)	515,229
Britelite Lobell, brf, 2	(1985)	507,171
Why Not, brc, 2	(1983)	507,047
Go Get Lost, br4	(1988)	501,564
Workaholic, bc, 3	(1985)	494,645

Pacers

Beach Towel, bc, 3	(1990)	$2,091,860
Nihilator, bc, 3	**(1985)**	**1,864,286**
Matt's Scooter, b, c, 3	(1988)	1,783,558
On The Road Again, chc, 3	**(1984)**	**1,751,695**
Ralph Hanover, bc, 3	(1983)	1,711,990
Goalie Jeff, bc, 3	(1989)	1,682,151
Jate Lobell, bc, 3	(1987)	1,645,598
Niatross, bc, 3	**(1980)**	**1,414,313**
Redskin, chc, 2	(1986)	1,407,263
Nihilator, bc, 2	(1984)	1,361,367
Jake And Elwood, brc, 3	(1990)	1,335,031
Fortune Teller, bc, 2	(1982)	1,313,175
Frugal Gourmet, bc, 3	(1987)	1,283,348
Amity Chef, bc, 3	(1986)	1,244,481
Praised Dignity, bc, 2	(1984)	1,194,715
Artsplace, bc, 2	(1990)	1,180,271
Apaches Fame, bc, 3	(1990)	1,157,732
Chairmanoftheboard, bc, 3	(1985)	1,148,568
Cam Fella, bh, 4	(1983)	1,144,056
Die Laughing, brc, 2	(1990)	1,142,322
Matt's Scooter, bh, 4	(1989)	1,140,994
Camtastic, brc, 3	(1988)	1,133,231
Miss Easy, bf, 2	(1990)	1,128,956
Runnymede Lobell, bc, 2	(1988)	1,108,355
On The Road Again,chh,4	(1985)	1,054,046
Land Grant, bc, 2	(1980)	1,038,490
Dexter Nukes, bc, 3	(1989)	1,027,620
Guts, bc, 3	(1984)	1,024,967
Barberry Spur, bc, 2	(1985)	971,147
Even Odds, chc, 2	(1987)	950,108
Totally Ruthless, bc, 2	(1988)	938,539
Armbro Emerson, bc, 3	(1986)	937,872
McKinzie Almahurst, bc, 2	(1981)	936,418
Run The Table, bc, 3	(1987)	904,022
Carl's Bird, bc, 2	(1983)	901,760
Caressable, brf, 2	(1985)	895,527
Cam Fella, bc, 3	(1982)	879,723
Grade One, bc, 2	(1985)	873,208
Cullin Hanover, brc, 2	(1986)	857,654
Dorunrun Bluegrass, bh, 4	(1990)	851,755
Falcon Seelster, bc, 3	(1985)	843,470
Hot Hitter, bc, 3	**(1979)**	**826,542**
Follow My Star, bf, 2	(1985)	817,526
Troublemaker, bc, 3	(1984)	806,489
Trutone Lobell, chc, 2	(1983)	805,130

AWARDS AND EARNINGS

LEADING MONEYWINNING TROTTERS OF ALL-TIME

	Horse	Age	Record	Color	Sex	Sire	Years Raced	Career Earnings
1.	Ourasi		None at Mile	ch	h	Greyhound (f)	1988 **	$4,408,857
2.	Mack Lobell	3	1:52.1	br	c	Mystic Park	1986-90	3,907,452
3.	Ideal du Gazeau *		None at Mile	br	h	Alexis III (f)	1976-	2,744,777
4.	Grades Singing	4	1:57	br	m	Texas	1984-89	2,607,552
5.	Peace Corps	3	1:52.4	b	f	Baltic Speed	1988-90	2,590,883
6.	Napoletano	5	1:54.1	b	h	Super Bowl	1986-89	2,467,878
7.	JEF's Spice	3	1:55.2	b	f	Super Bowl	1985-90	2,311,271
8.	Reve d'Udon		None at Mile	b	h	Ejakval (f)	1990	2,178,516
9.	Lutin d'Isigny		None at Mile	ch	h	Firstly (f)	1985	2,017,554
10.	Jorky		None at Mile	b	h	Kerjacques (f)	1982	1,970,432
11.	Prakas *	3	1:53.2	b	h	Speedy Crown	1984-85	1,956,056
12.	Une de Mai		None at Mile	ch	m	Kerjacques (f)	1973	1,834,274
13.	Potin d'Amour		None at Mile	b	h	Chambon P (f)	1988	1,828,160
14.	Mon Tourbillon		None at Mile	b	h	Amyot	1986	1,762,216
15.	Sugarcane Hanover	5	1:55.1	b	h	Florida Pro	1985-88	1,706,465
16.	Hollyhurst	3	1:58.3	br	c	Florida Pro	1982-90	1,643,453
17.	Bellino II		None at Mile	b	h	Boum III (f)	1977	1,639,687
18.	Indro Park		None at Mile	b	h	Sharif de Isolo (f)	1983-90	1,621,069
19.	Feystongal		None at Mile	b	h	Keystone Spartan	----	1,602,069
20.	Esotico Prad		None at Mile	b	h	Sharif di Iesolo (f)	1988	1,517,234
21.	Express Ride	4	1:53	b	c	Super Bowl	1985-90	1,456,762
22.	Armbro Goal	3	1:54.3	b	c	Speedy Crown	1987-88	1,442,022
23.	Callit		None at Mile	b	h	Tibur (f)	1988	1,413,589
24.	Friendly Face	4	1:54.1	b	h	Speedy Somolli	1986-90	1,401,135
25.	Savoir *	3	1:58.1	br	g	Stars Pride	1971-78	1,365,145
26.	Fiaccola Effe		None at Mile	br	h	Mustache (f)	----	1,350,278
27.	Armbro Fling	3	1:55.3	b	f	Speedy Crown	1986-87	1,334,936
28.	Mack The Knife		None at Mile	b	h	Pershing	----	1,332,246
29.	Lancaster OM		None at Mile	b	h	Sharif di Iesolo (f)	1988-90	1,315,982
30.	Mint di Jesolo		None at Mile	b	h	Noble Rogue	----	1,311,530
31.	Sandy Bowl	4	TT 1:54.1	b	h	Super Bowl	1983-85	1,299,199
32.	Fresh Yankee *	4	TT 1:57.1	b	m	Hickory Pride	1965-72	1,294,252
33.	Tenor de Baune		None at Mile	ch	h	Le Loir (f)	----	1,289,490
34.	Baltic Speed	3	1:56	b	h	Speedy Somolli	1983-84	1,271,764
35.	No Sex Please	5	1:55f	br	g	Brisco Hanover	1987-91	1,258,897
36.	Royal Prestige	3	1:55.1	br	h	Speedy Crown	1985-86	1,234,279
37.	Firm Tribute	3	1:54.3	b	c	Bonefish	1987-88	1,231,324
38.	Eleazar		None at Mile	b	h	Kerjacques (f)	1978	1,221,800
39.	Go Get Lost	4	1:54.3	b	r	Speedy Somolli	1986-90	1,197,467
40.	Britelite Lobell	3	1:57.2	br	f	Speedy Crown	1985-87	1,161,506
41.	Duenna	3	1:56.3	b	m	Green Speed	1982-85	1,131,920
42.	Davidia Hanover	4	1:56	br	m	Super Bowl	1984-86	1,108,252
43.	Keystone Pioneer	5	1:57.3	b	m	Hickory Pride	1975-80	1,071,927
44.	Hadol du Vivier		None at Mile	b	h	Mitsouko (f)	1978	1,039,262
45.	Harmonious	3	1:53.2	b	c	Crowning Point	1989-90	1,036,942
46.	Ogorek		None at Mile	ch	h	Borgia III (f)	1985	1,028,225
47.	Keystone Patriot	3	1:57.2	b	c	Hickory Pride	1978-86	1,026,725
48.	Scenic Regal	6	1:57.4	b	m	Lindy's Crown	1985-90	1,024,076
49.	Embassy Lobell	3	1:54.4	b	c	Speedy Crown	1989-90	1,049,175
50.	Joie De Vie	3	1:56.3	b	h	Super Bowl	1982-83	1,017,251

LEADING MONEYWINNING PACERS OF ALL-TIME

	Horse	Age	Record	Color	Sex	Sire	Years Raced	Career Earnings
1.	Nihilator	3	1.49.3	b	h	Niatross	1984-85	$3,225,653
2.	Matt's Scooter	4	TT 1:48.2	b	h	Direct Scooter	1987-89	2,944,591

AWARDS AND EARNINGS

3.	On the Road Again *	4		1:51.4	ch	h	Happy Motoring	1983-85	2,819,102
4.	Beach Towel	3		1:50	b	c	Frecnch Chef	1989-90	2,570,357
5.	Jate Lobell	3		1:51.2	b	c	No Nukes	1986-87	2,231,402
6.	Camtastic	4	TT	1:49.3	br	c	Cam Fella	1987-89	2,117,619
7.	Cam Fella *	4		1:53.1	b	h	Most Happy Fella	1981-83	2,041,367
8.	Rambling Willie *	7		1:54.3f	b	g	Rambling Fury	1972-83	2,038,219
9.	Niatross *	3	TT	1:49.1	b	h	Albatross	1979-80	2,019,213
10.	Goalie Jeff	3		1:51.2	b	c	Cam Fella	1988-89	2,003,439
11.	Redskin	2		1:55	ch	h	Storm Damage	1986-87	1,865,702
12.	Ralph Hanover	3		1:53.4	b	h	Meadow Skipper	1982-83	1,828,871
13.	Jaguar Spur	5	TT	1:49.2	b	c	Albatross	1986-89	1,806,473
14.	Fortune Teller	3		1:54.1	b	h	Governor Skipper	1982-83	1,683,639
15.	Jake And Elwood	3		1:52.2	br	c	Samadhi	1990	1,656,604
16.	Guts	4	TT	1:51.3	b	h	Raven Hanover	1983-90	1,650,815
17.	Barberry Spur	3	TT	1:50.3	b	c	Niatross	1985-86	1,634,017
18.	Runnymede Lobell	4	TT	1:51.2	b	h	Nero	1987-89	1,615,125
19.	Robust Hanover	3		1:52.2	b	c	Warm Breeze	1985-90	1,613,667
20.	Follow My Star	2		1:54.4	b	f	Governor Skipper	1985-88	1,537,503
21.	In The Pocket	3	TT	1:49.3	b	c	Direct Scooter	1989-90	1,537,473
22.	McKinzie Almahurst	3		1:54.4	b	h	B. G'S Bunny	1981-82	1,532,870
23.	Armbro Emerson	3		1:53.1	b	c	Abercrombie	1985-87	1,472,590
24.	Armbro Feather	5		1:51.3	b	m	Most Happy Fella	1986-89	1,454,927
25.	Anniecrombie	5		1:52.3	b	m	Abercrombie	1985-90	1,414,477
26.	Armbro Dallas	3		1:52.3	b	g	Abercrombie	1984-90	1,393,155
27.	Laughs	3		1:52.1	b	c	Silent Majority	1985-86	1,383,172
28.	Amity Chef	3		1:51.1	b	c	French Chef	1985-86	1,372,683
29.	Stienam	3		1:53.4	br	m	Falcon Almahurst	1984-85	1,355,474
30.	Frugal Gourmet	3		1:51.3	b	c	French Chef	1986-87	1,349,560
31.	Chairmanoftheboard	3		1:53.2f	b	h	Meadow Skipper	1984-86	1,341,823
32.	Kentucky Spur	3		1:52	b	c	Abercrombie	1988-89	1,341,340
33.	Topnotcher	4		1:52.2f	b	h	Abercrombie	1988-90	1,340,850
34.	Apaches Fame	3		1:52.2f	b	c	Apache Circle	1989-90	1,306,018
35.	Doc's Fella	4		1:54.1	b	g	Most Happy Fella	1981-90	1,267,059
36.	Albert Albert	3		1:52.1	br	c	Abercrombie	1987-88	1,237,070
37.	Division Street	5		1:52.3f	b	g	Most Happy Fella	1982-87	1,222,552
38.	Albatross *	4		1:54.3f	b	h	Meadow Skipper	1970-72	1,201,470
39.	Praised Dignity	2		1:56.4f	b	h	Albatross	1984	1,194,715
40.	Carls Bird	2		1:55.3	b	h	Sundance Skipper	1983-85	1,180,292
41.	Artsplace	2		1:51.1f	b	c	Abercrombie	1990	1,180,271
42.	Anxious Robby	3		1:52.4	b	c	Happy Motoring	1984-91	1,177,633
43.	Run The Table	3		1:51	b	c	Landslide	1986-87	1,171,053
44.	Incredible Finale	4		1:53.2	br	c	Shadows Finale	1985-87	1,165,508
45.	Land Grant	3		1:56.1	b	h	Meadow Skipper	1980-83	1,164,849
46.	Millers Scout	6		1:54.4f	br	h	Tarport Effrat	1978-84	1,162,061
47.	Dorunrun Bluegrass	4		1:51.3	b	h	Fortune Richie	1988-90	1,158,233
48.	J.D's Buck	4		1:54.3	br	h	Adios Vic	1979-85	1,156,532
49.	Totally Ruthless	2		1:55.1f	b	c	Walton Hanover	1988-90	1,150,964
50.	Mr Dalrae	5		1:52.2	b	h	Meadow Skipper	1981-85	1,150,807
51.	Die Laughing	2		1:52.1	br	c	No Nukes	1990	1,142,322
52.	Broadway Express	4		1:56.1	ro	h	Big Towner	1984-87	1,141,726
53.	Caramore	7		1:54.4f	b	h	Jolly Roger	1980-88	1,129,411
54.	Miss Easy	2		1:51.2	b	f	Amity Chef	1990	1,128,956
55.	Falcon Seelster	3		1:51	b	h	Warm Breeze	1984-86	1,121,045
56.	Troublemaker	2	TT	1:54	b	h	Most Happy Fella	1983-84	1,112,103
57.	Hy Class Minbar	6		1:52.4	br	h	My Minbar	1984-88	1,097,341
58.	Time Well Spent	3		1:53.3	b	f	Governor Skipper	1986-88	1,089,933
59.	Sandman Hanover	3		1:53.2f	br	c	Big Towner	1988-90	1,089,005
60.	Dragon's Lair	5		1:51.3	b	h	Tyler B	1984-88	1,085,317
61.	Perfect Out	4		1:54.2	b	h	Escort	1982-89	1,081,300
62.	Tucson Hanover	4		1:51.3	b	h	Albatross	1985-87	1,072,623
63.	Call For Rain	4		1:49.3	b	h	Storm Damage	1986-88	1,065,919
64.	Naughty But Nice	3		1:54f	b	m	Meadow Skipper	1983-84	1,062,197

AWARDS AND EARNINGS

65. Cullin Hanover	3	1:53	br	c	Albatross	1986-90	1,060,813
66. Leah Almahurst	3	1:52.3	b	f	Abercrombie	1987-89	1,053,201
67. Town Pro	3	1:51.4	br	f	Big Towner	1989-90	1,051,448
68. Quite A Sensation	5	1:53.3f	br	g	Chris Time	1985-90	1,048,353
69. Forrest Skipper	4	TT 1:50.3	b	h	Scarlet Skipper	1984-86	1,044,650
70. Governor Skipper	3	1:54	br	c	Meadow Skipper	1976-78	1,039,756
71. Dexter Nukes	3	1:51.3	b	c	No Nukes	1988-89	1,027,620
72. Energy Burner	3	TT 1:53.1	b	c	Oil Burner	1975-77	1,021,732
73. Nadia Lobell	3	1:53.4f	b	f	No Nukes	1986-88	1,007,119
74. Caressable	2	1:55.4	br	f	Niatross	1985-87	1,006,380
75. Sweet Refelction	3	1:53.1	b	f	Big Towner	1987-88	1,004,639
76. Rum Customer *	3	1:56	b	c	Poplar Byrd	1967-71	1,001,548
77. Cardigan Bay *	9	1:57.2	b	g	Hal Tryax	1959-68	1,000,837

* - **Former All-Time Leader**   ** - *Italics show when last raced in North America*

LEADING MONEYWINNING HORSES BY GAIT

1890 - 1990

Trotters		Year	Pacers	
Harmonious	$1,033,942	**1990**	Beach Towel	$2,091,860
Peace Corps	1,002,701	**1989**	Goalie Jeff	1,682,151
Armbro Goal	1,311,234	**1988**	Matt's Scooter	1,783,558
Mack Lobell	1,204,133	**1987**	Jate Lobell	1,645,598
Royal Prestige	1,052,114	**1986**	Redskin	1,407,263
Prakas	1,610,608	**1985**	Nihilator	1,864,286
Baltic Speed	1,062,611	**1984**	On The Road Again	1,751,695
Joie De Vie	1,007,705	**1983**	Ralph Hanover	1,711,990
Speed Bowl	672,084	**1982**	Fortune Teller	1,313,175
Shiaway St. Pat	478,920	**1981**	McKinzie Almahurst	936,418
Classical Way	350,410	**1980**	Niatross	1,414,313
Chiola Hanover	553,058	**1979**	Hot Hitter	826,542
Speedy Somolli	362,404	**1978**	Abercrombie	703,260
Green Speed	584,405	**1977**	Governor Skipper	522,148
Steve Lobell	357,005	**1976**	Keystone Ore	539,759
Savoir	351,385	**1975**	Silk Stockings	336,312
Delmonica Hanover	252,165	**1974**	Armbro Omaha	357,146
Spartan Hanover	262,023	**1973**	Sir Dalrae	307,354
Super Bowl	436,258	**1972**	Albatross	459,921
Fresh Yankee	293,950	**1971**	Albatross	558,009
Fresh Yankee	359,002	**1970**	Most Happy Fella	387,239
Lindy's Pride	323,997	**1969**	Overcall	373,150
Nevele Pride	427,440	**1968**	Rum Customer	355,618
Carlisle	231,243	**1967**	Romulus Hanover	277,636
Noble Victory	210,969	**1966**	Bret Hanover	407,534
Dartmouth	252,348	**1965**	Bret Hanover	341,784
Speedy Scot	235,710	**1964**	Race Time	199,292
Speedy Scot	244,403	**1963**	Overtrick	208,833
Duke Rodney	206,113	**1962**	Henry T Adios	220,302
Su Mac Lad	245,750	**1961**	Adios Butler	180,250
Su Mac Lad	159,662	**1960**	Bye Bye Byrd	187,612
Diller Hanover	149,996	**1959**	Bye Bye Byrd	199,933
Emily's Pride	118,830	**1958**	Belle Acton	167,887
Hoot Song	114,877	**1957**	Torpid	113,982
Scott Frost	85,851	**1956**	Adios Harry	129,912
Scott Frost	186,101	**1955**	Adios Harry	98,900
Katie Key	84,867	**1954**	Red Sails	66,615
Newport Dream	94,933	**1953**	Keystoner	59,131
Sharp Note	101,625	**1952**	Good Time	110,299
Pronto Don	80,850	**1951**	Tar Heel	66,629

AWARDS AND EARNINGS

Proximity	87,175	**1950**	Scottish Pence	73,387	
Bangaway	74,438	**1949**	Good Time	58,766	
Egan Hanover	67,567	**1948**	Dr Stanton	50,550	
Hoot Mon	56,810	**1947**	April Star	51,750	
Victory Song	43,608	**1946**	Ensign Hanover	34,368	
Titan Hanover	35,272	**1945**	Ensign Hanover	31,000	
Yankee Maid	30,865	**1944**	True Chief	24,768	
Volo Song	29,996	**1943**	Attorney	13,308	
The Ambassador	20,559	**1942**	Adios	16,188	
Bill Gallon	29,118	**1941**	Court Jester	20,700	
Spencer Scott	40,981	**1940**	Blackhawk	11,073	
Peter Astra	45,242	**1939**	William Cash	5,951	
McLin Hanover	31,201	**1938**	Blackstone	14,724	
Shirley Hanover	20,023	**1937**	Chief Counsel	11,154	
Rosalind	37,834	**1936**	Dusty Hanover	9,321	
Greyhound	26,712	**1935**	Calumet Evelyn	6,543	
Lord Jim	13,138	**1934**	Calumet Evelyn	9,358	
Mary Reynolds	20,826	**1933**	Laurel Hanover	4,927	
The Marchioness	52,327	**1932**	Zombro Hanover	13,676	
Calumet Butler	38,115	**1931**	Toll Gate	12,029	
Hanover's Bertha	59,887	**1930**	May E Grattan	32,312	
Walter Dear	57,509	**1929**	Laborador	22,190	
Spencer	55,036	**1928**	Grattan Bars	46,915	
Isola Worthy	56,700	**1927**	Bert Abbe	29,812	
Guy McKinney	68,742	**1926**	Jean Grattan	24,285	
Trumpet	29,375	**1925**	Ribbon Cane	27,320	
Mr McElwyn	24,875	**1924**	Baron Worthy	20,095	
Favonian	20,425	**1923**	Anna Bradfords Girl	13,444	
Czar Worthy	22,800	**1922**	Margaret Dillon	12,337	
Jeanette Rankin	28,220	**1921**	Single G	18,975	
Peter Manning	26,550	**1920**	Hal Mahone	11,562	
McGregor The Great	24,947	**1919**	Grace Direct	17,417	
Nella Dillon	15,689	**1918**	Directum J	13,217	
Early Dreams	23,745	**1917**	Ben Ali	10,310	
Mabel Trask	33,720	**1916**	Ben Earl	12,515	
Peter Scott	50,535	**1915**	Hal Boy	35,066	
Peter Volo	33,572	**1914**	King Couchman	15,125	
Etawah	24,498	**1913**	Frank Bogash, Jr.	23,325	
Baden	35,700	**1912**	Joe Patchen II	27,100	
R T C	31,900	**1911**	Branham Baughman	14,630	
Dudie Archdale	29,234	**1910**	The Abbe	17,650	
Margin	27,000	**1909**	George Grano	13,600	
Allen Winter	33,600	**1908**	The Eel	16,300	
Sonoma Girl	28,950	**1907**	Leland Onward	8,820	
Nut Boy	19,403	**1906**	Ardelle	10,977	
Angiola	12,898	**1905**	Bolivar	10,220	
Sweet Marie	23,825	**1904**	Morning Star	15,900	
Billy Buch	33,300	**1903**	Star Hal	11,150	
Lord Derby	57,625	**1902**	Direct Hal	25,550	
Cresceus	22,874	**1901**	Audubon Boy	19,650	
Cresceus	13,250	**1900**	Connor	9,875	
Idolita	18,000	**1899**	Hal B	13,862	
John Nolan	16,500	**1898**	Lady Of The Manor	11,450	
Rilma	14,406	**1897**	Star Pointer	22,875	
Rose Croix	11,000	**1896**	Planet	8,150	
Oakland Baron	11,475	**1895**	Joe Patchen	15,600	
Beuzetta	23,880	**1894**	Robert J	24,250	
Oro Wilkes	13,425	**1893**	May Marshall	9,200	
Nighingale	16,550	**1892**	Flying Jib	13,700	
Little Albert	11,575	**1891**	Hal Pointer	11,375	
McDoel	9,800	**1890**	Cricket	7,100	

AWARDS AND EARNINGS

AVERAGE EARNINGS BY AGE AND GAIT - 1990

Trotters

Age	No. of Starters	No. of Starts	Avg. Sts.	Total Wins	Total 2nds	Total 3rds	Total Earnings	Average Earnings per Start	Season's Average Earnings
2yo	1,928	13,863	7	1,987	2,024	2,023	$19,774,948	$1,426.46	$10,257
3yo	2,493	25,589	10	3,526	3,382	3,346	25,913,164	1,012.67	10,394
4yo	1,742	21,353	12	2,751	2,773	2,756	9,578,098	448.56	5,498
5yo	1,269	18,664	15	2,515	2,426	2,450	9,873,945	529.04	7,781
6yo	874	14,212	16	1,835	1,872	1,929	7,500,958	527.79	8,582
7yo	588	9,647	16	1,289	1,282	1,216	4,699,920	487.19	7,993
8yo	475	7,876	17	1,084	1,026	1,028	3,135,997	398.17	6,602
9yo	331	4,909	15	596	698	653	1,658,775	337.90	5,011
10yo	208	3,0611	14	380	411	428	806,079	267.71	3,875
11yo	117	1,686	14	205	216	242	375,860	222.93	3,212
12yo	71	1,070	15	123	137	148	256,257	239.49	3,609
13yo	35	403	12	56	66	65	101,650	252.23	2,904
14yo	11	121	11	20	15	23	18,317	151.38	1,665
Total:	10,142	122,404	12	16,367	16,328	16,307	$83,693,968	$683.75	$8,252

Pacers

Age	No. of Starters	No. of Starts	Avg. Sts.	Total Wins	Total 2nds	Total 3rds	Total Earnings	Average Earnings per Start	Season's Average Earnings
2yo	6,241	42,035	7	5,976	5,756	5,693	$42,155,120	$1,002.86	$6,755
3yo	9,535	134,638	14	18,135	17,621	17,274	82,652,696	613.89	8,668
4yo	8,075	151,911	19	18,810	19,351	19,086	68,057,865	448.01	8,428
5yo	6,252	129,988	21	16,331	16,483	16,284	54,482,983	419.14	8,714
6yo	4,448	92,711	21	12,078	11,642	11,953	32,781,882	353.59	7,370
7yo	3,144	64,731	21	8,082	8,280	8,453	20,234,487	312.59	6,436
8yo	2,226	44,910	20	5,776	5,626	5,815	12,656,384	281.82	5,686
9yo	1,402	26,521	19	3,266	3,410	3,406	6,172,008	232.72	4,402
10yo	881	16,035	18	1,994	1,978	2,077	3,299,232	205.75	3,745
11yo	474	7,998	17	951	980	1,016	1,520,343	190.09	3,207
12yo	249	4,113	17	492	518	515	659,641	160.38	2,649
13yo	117	1,910	16	247	245	216	269,135	140.91	2,300
14yo	74	1,027	14	104	128	122	120,643	117.47	1,630
Total:	43,118	718,528	17	92,242	92,018	91,910	$325,062,419	$452.40	$7,539
Grand Total:	53,260	840,932	16	108,609	108,346	108,217	$408,756,387	$486.08	$7,675

AVERAGE EARNINGS BY GAIT: 1982-1990

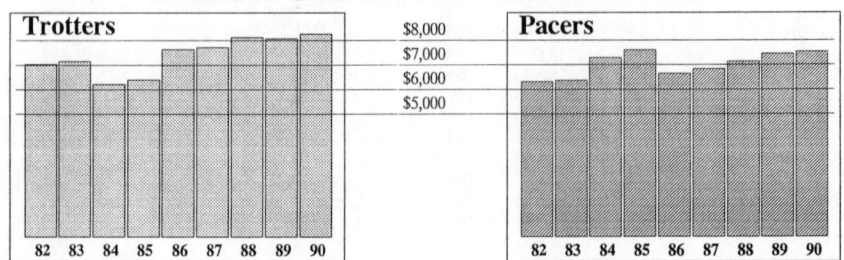

AWARDS AND EARNINGS

LEADING MONEYWINNING TROTTERS IN 1990

Horse	Owner(s)	Earnings
Two-Year-Olds		
Santa Royal	R. Peter Heffering, ONT	$427,154
Charlie Ten Hitch	Mark E. May, VA	366,499
Jean Bi (f)	Gina Biasuzzi Stable, FL	366,153
Super Pleasure	Robert Key, PA & John Glesmann, NJ	349,832
Mr Chin	Paul Nigito, NJ; and Lindy Racing Stable & William Lallier, CT	335,344
Crysta's Best	J. Patrick Huber, Harold Briedenbach, & Thomas Biddle; and Kathy Montgomery, KY	319,520
Frances Jet Boko (f)	John F. Bootsman, SWE	284,849
Gift Box	Clearview Stables, CT	221,601
Kramer Nobless	Johan T. Dieden, SWE	212,586
Carry The Message	Peter & Gail McCann, OH	206,011
Three-Year-Olds		
Embassy Lobell	LPG Standardbred Associates, NJ	$1,049,175
Harmonious	Lindy Racing Stable, CT & Salvatore Garofalo, FL	1,033,942
Jeanne's Somolli	Loren W. Huston, OH	430,115
Armbro Iliad	Peter & Gail McCann, OH	390,290
King Of The Sea	Clearview Stables, CT	346,684
Cheyenne Spur	Roy Davis & Joseph Hardy, Sr., PA	342,023
Royal Troubador	Carl & Rod Allen Stable, FL	340,853
Working Gal (f)	Bjorn Petterson	322,462
Star Mystic	Gregory S. Coleman, NY	305,198
Me Maggie (f)	Arden Homestead Stable, NY	305,004
Aged		
No Sex Please (g)	Ron Waples, Jr., ONT	$561,169
Reve d'Udon	Bernard Dosmontils, FRA	225,000
Florida Jewel	L & L Devisser Partnership, MI	204,062
Kit Lobell (m)	Johan Dieden, SWE	174,330
Scenic Regal (m)	Terrence McGee, MA	156,486
Kerry's Crown (m)	Bjorne Damm, SWE	142,458
Keystone Sheik	Karl Ungerman; Mary Anne Hicks; Stephen Malach; and Tom Artandi Stables, ONT	134,000
Super Timken	Antonio Chiaravalle, ONT	125,054
Mathers Streak	Chang-Racing Dynasty, NY	124,640
Alissas Beauty	K M Equine, ONT	121,207

TOP SINGLE-SEASON MONEYWINNING TROTTERS

2-Year-Old Colts	Express Ride (1985)	$840,328
2-Year-Old Fillies	Peace Corps (1988)	668,599
2-Year-Old Geldings	Sammy Silk (1990)	162,191
3-Year-Old Colts	Prakas (1985)	1,610,608
3-Year-Old Fillies	Peace Corps (1989)	1,002,701
3-Year-Old Geldings	Shiaway St Pat (1981)	480,095
Colts, 2&3-Years-Old, Combined	Prakas (1984-85)	1,956,056
Fillies, 2&3-Years-Old, Combined	Peace Corps (1988-89)	1,671,300
Geldings, 2&3-Years-Old, Combined	Shiaway St Pat (1980-81)	488,745
Aged Stallions	Mack Lobell (1988)	769,378
Aged Mares	Grades Singing (1986)	606,544
Aged Geldings	No Sex Please (1990)	561,169

AWARDS AND EARNINGS

LEADING MONEYWINNING PACERS IN 1990

Horse	Owner(s)	Earnings
	Two-Year-Olds	
Artsplace	George Segal & Brian Monieson, IL	$1,180,271
Die Laughing	Val d'Or Farms, NJ & Alnoff Stable, NY	1,142,322
Miss Easy (f)	Rose Guida, NJ & Royal Palm Stables, MN	1,128,956
June's Baby	Sarah June Racing Stable, NY	582,334
Cams Exotic (f)	Prince Lee Acres, ONT	520,086
Tooter Scooter	L & L Devisser Partnership, MI	461,635
Laugh Line (f)	Armstrong Brothers, ONT	455,917
Cambest	Dan Altmeyer & Jack Piatt II, PA	360,522
Nuclear Legacy	George Segal, IL	349,263
Three Wizzards	Ermen Lanzillotti, Gerald Farber & Fred Esse, MI	323,780
	Three-Year-Olds	
Beach Towel	Uptown Stable, NY	$2,091,860
Jake And Elwood	LPG Standardbred Associates, NJ; M R F Racing Stable, NY; and Bonnie Castle Stables, NY	1,335,031
Apaches Fame	Dovers Venture II, ONT	1,157,732
In The Pocket	LPG Standardbred Associates, NJ; M R F Racing Stable, NY; and Bonnie Castle Stables, NY	1,335,031
Town Pro (f)	Pro Group Stable, ONT	634,690
Mark Johnathan	Gerald Bloch, QUE	604,366
Scoot Outa Reach	Arlene Traub, NY	548,776
Choice Yankee (f)	Yankeeland Farms, Inc., MD	430,112
Kiev Hanover	Andray Farm, PA	428,294
Instant Rebate (f)	George Segal & Brian Monieson, IL	401,865
	Aged	
Dorunrun Bluegrass	Luel P. Overstreet, KY	$851,755
Topnotcher	Alexander Horn & Alan Berk, ONT	800,501
T K's Skipper	Jerebel Stables, NY	601,512
Caesars Jackpot (m)	Coast to Coast Stable, NJ	353,550
Ticket To Heaven	Ronal Michel, CA; and Patrick Lacy & Ted Richter, NY	314,147
My Guru (g)	Daniel J. & Patrick J. Daly, ONT	306,780
Conditional	Roseann Sodano, Norris Barenbaum & Star Studded Stable, NJ	304,910
Chatham Light	Robert K. Waxman, ONT	299,440
Sandman Hanover	LPG Standardbred Associates, NJ; M R F Racing Stable; and Bonnie Castle Stables, NY	297,064
Keystone Raider	LPG Standardbred Associates	266,092

TOP SINGLE-SEASON MONEYWINNING PACERS

2-Year-Old Colts	Redskin (1986)	$1,407,263
2-Year-Old Fillies	Miss Easy (1990)	1,128,956
2-Year-Old Geldings	Dancer's Ideal (1990)	201,899
3-Year-Old Colts	Beach Towel (1990)	2,091,860
3-Year-Old Fillies	Naughty But Nice (1984)	789,165
3-Year-Old Geldings	Armbro Dallas (1985)	641,782
Colts, 2&3-Years-Old, Combined	Nihilator (1984-85)	3,225,653
Fillies, 2&3-Years-Old, Combined	Stienam (1984-85)	1,355,474
Geldings, 2&3-Years-Old, Combined	Armbro Dallas (1984-85)	775,393
Aged Stallions	Cam Fella (1983)	1,144,056
Aged Mares	Armbro Feather (1989)	587,405
Aged Geldings	Division Street (1985)	642,926

Dashes and Speed

DASHES AND SPEED
HISTORY OF THE TWO-MINUTE MILE

The two-minute mile has been the primary standard of excellence in harness racing since 1897, when Star Pointer became the first horse to perform the feat. The next 40 years were remarkable for how little change there was in the number of two-minute miles recorded. Since that time, however, harness racing has experienced explosive growth in "miracle miles." In fact, nearly two-thirds of all the two-minute miles in history have come in the last five years.

Year	Number	Year	Number	Year	Number	Year	Number
1897	1	1921	11	1945	8	1969	209
1898	3	1922	18	1946	10	1970	306
1899	1	1923	10	1947	10	1971	381
1900	none	1924	5	1948	15	1972	445
1901	none	1925	4	1949	23	1973	485
1902	4	1926	4	1950	26	1974	682
1903	13	1927	3	1951	35	1975	714
1904	3	1928	9	1952	49	1976	1,845
1905	10	1929	4	1953	70	1977	2,355
1906	7	1930	9	1954	63	1978	2,849
1907	3	1931	6	1955	60	1979	3,152
1908	3	1932	9	1956	66	1980	3,898
1909	1	1933	1	1957	58	1981	4,929
1910	6	1934	11	1958	77	1982	6,302
1911	4	1935	12	1959	89	1983	8,616
1912	none	1936	21	1960	120	1984	10,899
1913	3	1937	22	1961	125	1985	13,745
1914	10	1938	46	1962	112	1986	14,736
1915	6	1939	23	1963	139	1987	17,483
1916	8	1940	10	1964	134	1988	20,271
1917	1	1941	14	1965	118	1989	23,828
1918	5	1942	6	1966	206	1990	27,435
1919	1	1943	3	1967	181		
1920	5	1944	13	1968	204	**Total:**	**167,935**

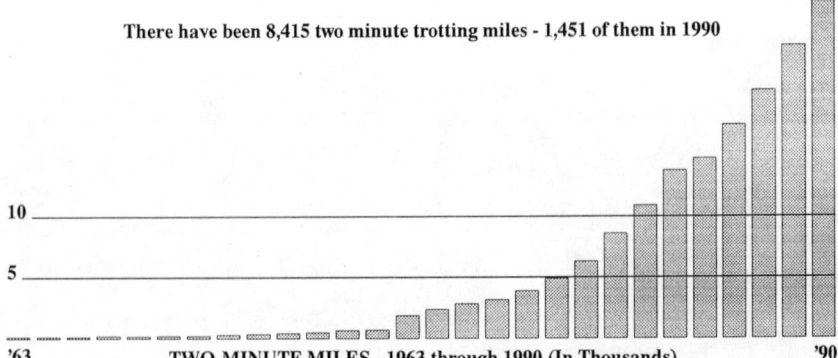

There have been 8,415 two minute trotting miles - 1,451 of them in 1990

TWO-MINUTE MILES - 1963 through 1990 (In Thousands)

DASHES AND SPEED

LEADING DASHWINNING TROTTERS IN 1990

Horse (*), Season Record	Sts.	Wins	Purses	Owner(s)
			Two-Year-Olds	
Sanstone (f), 2:04.1f	28	20	$24,633	Bryce & Cindy Truitt, MD
Jeff's Sister (f), 2:04.1h	20	15	83,551	Joseph Konen; John Sutton; David Jaglois; & Wolverine Acres, MI
Scorella (f), 2:09.1h	27	14	14,636	Ray C. French, OH
Lucky Blaze, 2:00.1f	20	13	45,179	Frank Todd, FL & Pinkney Brewer, OH
M B's Best (g), 2:01.4q	17	13	27,523	Roy M. Bridges, FL & James N. Korines, NY
Sammy Silk (g), 2:00f	15	13	162,191	Shirley Walker, ONT
Super Fellow (g), 2:01.3h	28	12	20,368	J. Donald & John D. McMullen, PA
Gift Box, 1:59.3	17	12	221,601	Clearview Stables, CT
Heather Una (f), 2:02.2	19	12	11,457	Norman Robinson; Irma Dawdy; & Richard Pointer, IL
Chantitown Uzi (g), 2:04.3h	31	11	39,479	Ralph Sherman, NY
Ro Julie (f), 2:08.3h	13	11	14,429	William C. Phillips, OH
Gumcorner Lad (g), 2:01	19	11	37,730	Ruth Burkett & George Knackmuhs, IL
Mathers Yuma (f), 2:02.3f	19	11	114,010	Normand Hogue; Michel Ouellet; Andre Johnson; & Helio Ouellet, QUE
			Three-Year-Olds	
Marilu's Lady (f), 2:05.1f	35	26	$24,895	Rod Newhart, OH
Sreck Danny Boy (g), 2:02.4h	28	16	12,177	Kenneth & Brian Weaver, PA
Incredible D J, 1:55.3	26	14	301,815	Scuderia Noble Stardom, GER
Thief Of Time, 2:01h	21	14	34,179	Pius Soehnlen, OH
OB's Ragtime Annie (f), 2:01.1f	20	13	20,301	Andrew & Olga Corrado, OH
Dembo (g), 2:03h	30	13	17,824	Mary Anne Hicks, OH & Tom Artandi, ONT
Island Kaptain, 2:03.2h	18	13	21,940	Jennie & Emmett Bernard, PEI
A Worthy Lad, 1:57.3f **	13	13	224,848	Bengt Pettersson, SWE
Royal Cold (g), 1:59.4f	25	12	74,996	Rephard Reed & Leonard Fitzpatrick, OH
Simply Spectacular (g), 2:02h	32	12	22,570	Robert Lippiatt; Versie & Joan Ahart, OH
Joya Pride (f), 2:00.3	24	12	59,730	Ivan Sugg, OH; and Harvey Eisman & Steve Serges, MI
Double Aught (g), 2:00.2h	28	12	71,798	Malcom & Debbie Johnston, MI
			Aged	
Larks Crown, 1:59.1h	36	20	$90,325	Frecerick & Anita Fialkow, NY
Hey Foxtrot (g), 1:58f	38	18	81,125	Diane Norris; and Clifford & Seymour Grundy, MI
Speedy Noireau, 2:03h	46	17	24,352	Jean Potvin, QUE
Miss Judy Comfort (m), 2:00f	46	14	37,820	Monroe Weaver, OH
Nothing Ventured, 1:57.2	28	14	77,970	Gratien Deschenes, QUE
Scenic Regal (m), 1:58.2h	25	13	156,486	Terrence McGee, MA
Some Pain (g), 2:01.4h	35	13	46,285	Sonia Bondura, PA
Johnnys Crown (g), 1:59.3f	36	13	33,912	Robert LaLonde, MI
Thunder Cracker (m), 2:01.3f	45	13	22,027	Arthur J. Dortort, PA

(The following aged trotters each had 12 wins. Shown is each performer's season record, number of starts, and 1990 earnings.)

Terrahill Glory (m), 2:04.2h (41)	$14,051	Borne Jupiter (f), 1:58.4f (42)	43,797
Bethany Boutique, 2:00f (34)	4,327	Gauguin Go (g), 1:57.3f (35)	104,688
Whata Notion (g), 2:06.4h (39)	4,388	Home Court (f), 1:57.1 (21)	14,057
Alabaster Hanover, 2:04f (34)	10,116	War Nickel (g), 1:56 (23)	95,486
The Little Prince (g), 1:59.4h (20)	47,760	Keystone Salute, 1:56.1f (24)	35,799

* - "f" denotes filly, "m" denotes mare, "g" denotes gelding; ** - North American performance only

LEADING DASHWINNING TROTTERS, SINGLE-YEAR

2-Year-Old -	Bedford Spirit (1977)	27
3-Year-Old -	Jeffery Hanover (1947)	33
Aged -	Make Believe (1949)	53

DASHES AND SPEED

LEADING DASHWINNING PACERS IN 1990

Horse, Season Record	Sts.	Wins	Purses	Owner(s)
Two-Year-Olds				
My Good Lady (f), 2:02.2h	24	18	$25,249	Wilma Styer, OH
Miss Easy (f), 1:51.2	17	15	1,128,956	Rose Guida, NJ & Royal Palm Stable, MN
Turbo Twin, 1:56.4f	19	15	121,606	Duane Chippi; Richard Sikes; & Allen Tomlinson, MI
Upper Crust (f), 2:01.3f	17	14	17,806	Paul Copsey & Richard Johnson, OH
Avon Breeze, 2:03h	20	13	11,439	Linda Kolnick & Roger Becker, NY
Cambest, 1:54	18	12	360,522	Dan Altmeyer & Jack Piatt II, PA
Alliston Star (f), 1:58.4f	18	12	162,039	Clarence Varcoe, ONT
Bombe Angus, 1:57.1f	15	12	227,530	Ferme Corbeil, QUE

(The following 2-year-old pacers each had 11 wins. Shown is each performer's season record, number of starts, and 1990 earnings.)

Kelly Miles, 1:57.1 (16)		$23,420	Startique, 2:05.1h (20)	10,897
Laugh Line (f), 1:56.1f (17)		455,917	Promise Me K (f), 1:58.4f (20)	112,525
Mantese, 1:53.4 (19)		294,272	Keystone Rambler, 1:56.2f (20)	41,952
Artsplace, 1:51.1f (15)		1,180,271	Gypsy Diamond (f), 2:01.4 (20)	26,633
Nedsbit (g), 1:59 (23)		10,801	Styling (g), 1:55.1 (16)	57,242

Horse, Season Record	Sts.	Wins	Purses	Owner(s)
Three-Year-Olds				
Keystone Luscious (f), 1:54.3f	33	20	$67,107	Roger Hammer, PA
Apaces Fame, 1:52.2f	26	20	1,157,732	Dovers Venture II, ONT
Counterfeit Crown (f), 1:55.1f	24	18	191,697	Jack Beelby; Richard LePage; Bill Mah; and M W Stable, ALTA
Beach Towel, 1:50	23	18	2,091,860	Uptown Stable, NY
Laurstar, 1:54.3f	28	18	235,450	D & H Stable, ONT
Abba Marquis (g), 1:59.1h	40	16	32,446	Roby Hostetler & Martin Yoder, OH
Rulers Chippie (f), 1:52.3f	26	16	183,236	Mervin G. Burke, ONT
Charlott's Buddy, 1:58.1h	25	15	66,906	L. David Ratchford, NS
Dee's Tuition, 1:54.4h	26	15	104,489	John C. Smith, OH
Town Pro (f), 1:51.4	17	14	634,690	Pro Group Stable, ONT
Semalu Fantastic (f), 1:55.4f	31	14	131,720	Semalu, Inc., QUE
Star Of Anzio (g), 2:00.4h	24	14	9,713	Duane & Roger Roland, IA
Jake And Elwood, 1:52.2	24	14		LPG Standardbred Associates, NJ; and M R F Racing Stable & Bonnie Castle Stables, NY
Aged				
Arapa's Hart (m), 2:04.1h	71	20	$10,761	John J. Thompson, PEI
Dusty Trail Beaut (m), 2:03.2h	71	20	9,510	John C. Davies, N.Brun.
Point Dundas A (g), 1:59.2f	49	19	8,298	Joseph E. Campbell, NS
Joy Down (m), 2:04.2h	83	19	9,559	Thomas D. Buckley, N.Brun.
Springing Thru (m), 2:02.3f	45	19	12,046	Denis Kerr, ONT
Simcoe Glencoe, 2:04.1h	54	19	5,165	Arthur P. McVicar, NS
Cliffy T (g), 1:56.3h	38	19	47,359	Lynn Saunders and Brian & William Calvert, ONT
T K's Skipper, 1:49.2	27	19	601,512	Jerebel Stables, NY
Gabby J (m), 2:02.1h	65	18	6,413	Alexander A. MacDonald, NS
Sandy Bel (m), 2:01.4h	32	18	11,562	Guy LaLancette & Rejean Larouche, QUE
Titanic Lobell (g), 1:59f	31	18	21,080	Jim Groff; Bernard O'Brien; and Anthony & Carol Risi, PA

LEADING DASHWINNING PACERS, SINGLE-YEAR

2-Year-Old -	Laddie Boy (1980)	27
3-Year-Old -	Andy's Son (1965)	35
Aged -	Victory Hy (1950)	65

DASHES AND SPEED

LEADING DASHWINNING HORSES: 1946-1990

Most of the records of harness racing are lost in antiquity, but the Trotting & Pacing Guide has kept track of many since first being published in 1947. Here are the leading dashwinning horses, 1946-1989, by gait:

Trotter	Wins	Year	Pacer	Wins
Marilu's Lady	26	1990	Keystone Luscious, Arapa's Hart, Apaches Fame, Dusty Trail Beaut	20
Miss Judy Comfort	24	1989	Newport Skipper	29
Miss Judy Comfort	26	1988	Breeze On J	26
Rock Creek	22	1987	Barney's Birt	24
Grades Singing	23	1986	Rickenfritz	25
Arzew & Manfred Hanover	24	1985	Graduate Boy	30
Eclair Touvent	22	1984	Sure Skipper	34
Incredible Wind & Casey's Dream	19	1983	Niffit	34
Iggy Magoo, Windy Oakie & Peewee Pancake	21	1982	Cam Fella	28
Big Key & Legislator	21	1981	Wooden Spoon	25
Royal Forbes N	23	1980	Rebel Blaze	28
Going Once	23	1979	Sheet Rock	32
Echo Empire, Coleen's Beauty & Smoky's Baldy	19	1978	Greatest Direct	24
Bedford Spirit	27	1977	Solar Eden	44
Lords Champion	23	1975	Malcoms Chief	33
Lucky Laird	24	1974	Chester Judge	42
In Command	30	1973	Count Kef	26
Super Bowl	23	1972	Osborne Creed	23
High Land Bobby	20	1971	That's My David	30
Dottie Du Er	23	1970	Thinks Dream	24
Kendelwood Patty	20	1969	Miss Elktide	27
Kendelwood Patty	26	1968	Lucky V	27
Nevele Pride	26	1967	Amortizer Direct	28
High N Away	23	1966	Onaway	44
Armbro Flight	22	1965	Andy's Son	35
Raunchie B	26	1964	Just Gary	32
Raunchie B & Lucy Frost	22	1963	Jolity Bars	28
B F Coaltown	21	1962	Prompt Reward	29
Great Pleasure	27	1961	Johnny Dale	32
Triona's Scotch	21	1960	Roy McGregor	28
Expresson	28	1959	Vicki's Jet	28
Julia Song & Senator Frost	23	1958	McPhergus	25
Constant Lawrence	27	1957	Danny Lite	31
Paul Jackson	25	1956	Ruth Lybrook	24
Paul Jackson, Scott Frost & Bonnie Lois Volo	23	1955	Josedale Clansman	42
Stenographer & Baron Key C	23	1954	Tom Stuart	27
Jochovolo, Patrick Budlong, & R K Giers	23	1953	Tonymite	45
Gentleman Joe	29	1952	Argyel Grattan	38
Nancy Grimm	24	1951	Turnabout	42
Happy Pegasus	28	1950	Victory Hy	65
Make Believe	53	1949	Amber Grattan	49
Sir Harris	28	1948	Pete Mills	46
Sir Harris, Snappy Kate & Jeffery Hanover	33	1947	Symbol Allen	44
Dynamite	41	1946	Daisy Grattan	40

DASHES AND SPEED

TOP TEN TROTTING MILES BY TRACK SIZE

	Time	Horse, Color, Sex, Age	Sire (Year: Driver)	Where Taken

FASTEST TROTTING MILES, MILE TRACK

	Time	Horse, Color, Sex, Age	Sire (Year: Driver)	Where Taken
	1:52.1	Mack Lobell, br c, 3	Mystic Park (1987: John Campbell)	Spr
	1:52.4	Peace Corps, b, f, 3	Baltic Speed (1989: John Campbell)	DuQ
	1:53	Express Ride, b h, 4	Super Bowl (1987: Berndt Lindstedt)	Lex
	1:53.2	Napoletano, b c, 3	Super Bowl (1987: Bill O'Donnell)	DuQ
	1:53.2	Prakas, b c, 3	Speedy Crown (1985: Bill O'Donnell)	DuQ
	1:53.2	Harmonious, b c, 3	Crowning Point (1990: Cat Manzi)	DuQ
	1:53.3	Supergill, b, c, 3	Super Bowl (1988: Berndt Lindstedt)	Spr
	1:53.3	Mack Lobell, br c, 3	Mystic Park (1987: John Campbell)	M
	1:53.4	Keystone Harem, b f, 3	Super Bowl (1987: Jan Nordin)	Spr
	1:53.4	Keystone Harem, b f, 3	Super Bowl (1987: Jan Nordin)	Spr
TT	1:53.4	Dicks Bell, b h, 4	Cold Comfort (1987: Ray Remmen)	Spr
	1:53.4	Cornstalk, b c, 3	Lindy's Pride (1984: Howard Beissenger)	Spr
	1:53.4	Fancy Crown, br f, 3	Speedy Crown (1984: Bill O'Donnell)	Spr

FASTEST TROTTING MILES, FIVE-EIGHTHS MILE TRACK

	Time	Horse, Color, Sex, Age	Sire (Year: Driver)	Where Taken
	1:54.1	Mack Lobell, br c, 3	Mystic Park (1987: John Campbell)	PPk
	1:54.2	Peace Corps, b m, 4	Baltic Speed (1990: Stig Johannson)	PPk
	1:55	Express Ride, b h, 4	Super Bowl (1987: Berndt Lindstedt)	SPk
	1:55	No Sex Please, br g, 5	Brisco Hanover (1990: Ron Waples)	PPk
	1:55.2	Photo Maker, b h, 8	Yankee Bambino (1987: Dale McConnell)	Mea
	1:55.2	Delray Lobell, b h, 4	Speedy Crown (1989: Don Irvine, Jr.)	FsR
	1:55.3	Firm Tribute, b c, 3	Bonefish (1988: Mark O'Mara)	Mea
	1:55.3	Mack Lobell, br h, 4	Mystic Park (1988: John Campbell)	PPk
	1:55.4	No Sex Please, br g, 5	Brisco Hanover (1990: Ron Waples)	BB
Q	1:56	Schimitar, b h, 6	Yellow Knife (1988: Dan Ater)	ScD
	1:56	Editor In Chief, b c, 3	Speed In Action (1988: Lavern Hostetler)	ScD
	1:56	Esquire Spur, b c, 3	Joie De Vie (1989: Don Irvine, Jr.)	RcR
	1:56	Roydon Lad, b h, 4	Bonefish (1990: Don Irvine, Jr.)	RcR

FASTEST TROTTING MILES, HALF-MILE TRACK

Time	Horse, Color, Sex, Age	Sire (Year: Driver)	Where Taken
1:56	Mack Lobell, br h, 4	Mystic Park (1988: John Campbell)	Stga
1:56	Peace Corps, b f, 3	Baltic Speed (1989: John Campbell)	Dela
1:56.4	Nevele Pride, b h, 4	Star's Pride (1969: Stanley Dancer)	Stga
1:56.4	Editor In Chief, b c, 3	Speed In Action (1988: John Campbell)	Dela
1:57	Armbro Devona, b f, 3	Speedy Crown (1985: Bill O'Donnell)	Dela
1:57	Mack Lobell, br h, 4	Mystic Park (1988: John Campbell)	Dela
1:57.1	Fancy Crown, br f, 3	Speedy Crown (1984: Bill O'Donnell)	Dela
1:57.1	Mack Lobell, br h, 4	Mystic Park (1988: John Campbell)	YR
1:57.2	Sir Taurus, b c, 3	Speedy Crown (1987: Jimmy Takter)	YR
1:57.2	Mack Lobell, br c, 3	Mystic Park (1987: John Campbell)	RcR
1:57.2	Nearly Perfect, b h, 4	Songcan (1986: Mickey McNichol)	LouD
1:57.2	Go Get Lost, b r, 4	Speedy Somolli (1988: Tom Sells)	YR
1:57.2	Kit Lobell, b m, 5	Speedy Crown (1990: Berndt Lindstedt)	YR

DASHES AND SPEED
TOP TEN PACING MILES BY TRACK SIZE

Time	Horse, Color, Sex, Age	Sire (Year: Driver)	Where Taken

FASTEST PACING MILES, MILE TRACK

Time	Horse, Color, Sex, Age	Sire (Year: Driver)	Where Taken
TT 1:48.2	Matt's Scooter, b c, 3	Direct Scooter (1988: Michel Lachance)	Lex
TT 1:49.1	Niatross, b c, 3	Albatross (1980: Clint Galbraith)	Lex
TT 1:49.2	Jaguar Spur, b h, 4	Albatross (1988: Dick Stillings)	Lex
1:49.3	Nihilator, b c, 3	Niatross (1985: Bill O'Donnell)	M
1:49.3	Call For Rain, b h, 4	Storm Damage (1988: Clint Galbraith)	Lex
TT 1:49.3	Camtastic, br h, 4	Cam Fella (1989: Michel Lachance)	Spr
TT 1:49.2	T K's Skipper, br h, 5	Governor Skipper (1990: Michel Lachance)	DuQ
TT 1:49.3	In The Pocket, b c, 3	Direct Scooter (1990: John Campbell)	Lex
1:50	Beach Towel, b c, 3	French Chef (1990: Ray Remmen)	DuQ
1:50.1	Ramblin' Storm, b h, 6	Storm Damage (1988: Michel Lachance)	M
1:50.1	Matt's Scooter, b h, 4	Direct Scooter (1989: Michel Lachance)	M
1:50.1	Kiev Hanover, b c, 3	Albatross (1990: Jim Morand)	Lex

FASTEST PACING MILES, FIVE-EIGHTHS MILE TRACK

Time	Horse, Color, Sex, Age	Sire (Year: Driver)	Where Taken
1:50.4	In The Pocket, b c, 3	Direct Scooter (1990: John Campbell)	Mea
1:51	Matt's Scooter, b h, 4	Direct Scooter (1989: Michel Lachance)	Moh
1:51.1	Artsplace, b c, 2	Abercrombie (1990: John Campbell)	PPk
1:51.2	T K's Skipper, br h, 5	Governor Skipper (1990: Joe Anderson)	LA
1:51.2	Beach Towel, b c, 3	French Chef (1990: Ray Remmen)	PPk
1:51.3	Falcon Seelster, b h, 4	Warm Breeze (1986: Tom Harmer)	Mea
1:51.4	Beach Towel, b c, 3	French Chef (1990: Ray Remmen)	Mea
1:51.4	Dare You To, b h, 5	Abercrombie (1990: Wally Hennessey)	PPk
1:51.4	Shipps Schnoops, gr c, 3	On The Road Again (1990: Tommy Haughton)	PPk
1:52	Matt's Scooter, b h, 4	Direct Scooter (1989: Michel Lachance)	Edm

FASTEST PACING MILES, HALF-MILE TRACK

Time	Horse, Color, Sex, Age	Sire (Year: Driver)	Where Taken
1:51	Falcon Seelster, b c, 3	Warm Breeze (1985: Tom Harmer)	Dela
1:52.1	Nihilator, b c, 3	Niatross (1985: Bill O'Donnell)	Dela
1:52.3	B J Scoot, b c, 3	Falcon Almahurst (1988: Michel Lachance)	Dela
1:52.4	Pershing Square, b c, 3	Niatross (1985: Bill O'Donnell)	Dela
1:52.4	Barberry Spur, b c, 3	Niatross (1986: Bill O'Donnell)	Dela
1:53	Jaguar Spur, b h, 4	Albatross (1988: Dick Stillings)	Nfld
1:53.1	Nihilator, b c, 3	Niatross (1985: Bill O'Donnell)	Dela
1:53.1	Barberry Spur, b c,3	Niatross (1986: Bill O'Donnell)	Dela
1:53.1	Falcon Seelster, b h, 4	Warm Breeze (1986: Tom Harmer)	May
1:53.1	Dorunrun Bluegrass, b h, 4	Fortune Richie (1990: Herve Filion)	Fhld

DASHES AND SPEED

TEN FASTEST MILES BY AGE, SEX AND GAIT
Trotters

Two-Year-Old Colts and Geldings

Mack Lobell	Lex	10-3-86	1:55.3
Buckfinder	Ind	8-22-86	1:55.4
TV Yankee	Lex	10-1-82	1:56
Buckfinder	Lex	9-27-86	1:56.1
Mack Lobell	DuQ	8-30-86	1:56.2
Mack Lobell	Lex	9-27-86	1:56.2
Speed Boots	Spr	8-15-84	1:56.2
Dontellmenomore	Lex	9-25-90	1:56.2
Royal Prestige	Ind	8-23-85	1:56.3
Buckfinder	Lex	9-27-86	1:56.3
Sir Taurus	Sycs	8-15-86	1:56.3
Super Arnie	Spr	8-16-89	1:56.3

Two-Year-Old Fillies

Noxie Hanover	Lex	9-19-88	T	1:55
Fancy Crown	Lex	10-8-83	T	1:55.4
Nan's Catch	DuQ	9-4-87		1:56
Anamosa Hanover	Spr	8-19-87		1:56
Peace Corps	Spr	8-17-88		1:56.2
Star Investment	Lex	10-8-79	T	1:56.3
Armbro Fern	Lex	10-1-86		1:56.4
Peace Corps	Lex	9-28-88		1:56.4
Winkys Gill	Lex	9-29-82		1:57
Newmarket S	DuQ	8-30-85		1:57.1
Nan's Catch	DuQ	9-4-87		1:57.1
Anamosa Hanover	Lex	9-23-87		1:57.1
Peace Corps	PPk	11-11-88		1:57.1f

Three-Year-Old Colts and Geldings

Mack Lobell	Spr	8-21-87		1:52.1
Prakas	DuQ	8-31-85		1:53.2
Napoletano	DuQ	9-5-87		1:53.2
Harmonious	DuQ	9-1-90		1:53.2
Mack Lobell	M	8-8-87		1:53.3
Supergill	Spr	8-6-88		1:53.3
Cornstalk	Spr	8-15-84		1:53.4
Mack Lobell	M	8-8-87		1:54
Mack Lobell	M	7-24-87		1:54
Arndon	Lex	10-6-82	T	1:54
Crowning Point	Spr	8-16-84		1:54

Three-Year-Old Fillies

Peace Corps	DuQ	9-2-89	1:52.4
Fancy Crown	Spr	8-16-84	1:53.4
Keystone Harem	Spr	8-20-87	1:53.4
Keystone Harem	Spr	8-20-87	1:53.4
Peace Corps	Ind	8-25-89	1:54.1
Peace Corps	Lex	10-6-89	1:54.2
Fancy Crown	DuQ	9-1-84	1:54.4
Luicious Almahurst	DuQ	9-4-87	1:54.4
Keystone Harem	DuQ	9-4-87	1:54.4
Nan's Catch	Spr	8-18-88	1:54.4

Aged Horses and Geldings

Express Ride	Lex	9-25-87		1:53
Dicks Bell	Spr	8-19-87	T	1:53.4
Nearly Perfect	M	7-7-86		1:54
Sandy Bowl	Lex	9-29-85	T	1:54.1
Friendly Face	M	5-3-88		1:54.1
Napoletano	M	7-1-89		1:54.1
Meadow Road	M	6-24-85		1:54.2
Sugarcane Hanover	M	8-7-87		1:54.3
Premium Lobell	DuQ	9-1-84		1:54.3
Nearly Perfect	M	6-30-86		1:54.3
Nevele Pride	Ind	8-31-69	T	1:54.4
Lindys Crown	DuQ	8-30-80		1:54.4
Friendly Face	M	5-2-88		1:54.4

Aged Mares

Peace Corps	PPk	11-2-90		1:54.2f
Kit Lobell	M	6-27-90		1:54.4
Franconia	M	7-20-87		1:55
Kerry's Crown	Lex	10-4-90		1:54.1
Kit Lobell	M	6-27-90		1:54.4
Babe Kosmos	GSP	9-10-85		1:55.2
Classical Way	Lex	10-5-80	T	1:55.2
Delmegan	Lex	10-2-82	T	1:55.3
Franconia	M	4-18-88		1:55.3
Keystone Impala	M	6-21-89		1:55.4
China Smoke	Lex	10-5-89	T	1:55.4
Kerry's Crown	Lex	9-28-90		1:55.4

DASHES AND SPEED

TEN FASTEST MILES BY AGE, SEX AND GAIT

Pacers

Two-Year-Old Colts and Geldings

Horse	Track	Date	Time
Artsplace	PPk	11-30-90	1:51.1f
Deal Direct	Ind	8-25-90	1:51.4
Raque Bogart	Lex	10-1-88	1:52.1
Righthand Man	Ind	8-26-89	1:52.1
Die Laughing	M	8-17-90	1:52.1
Die Laughing	Lex	10-5-90	1:52.1
Rumpus Hanover	Lex	9-27-86 T	1:52.3
Kassa Branca	M	7-29-88	1:52.3
Nihilator	M	8-16-84	1:52.4
Albert Albert	Ind	8-29-87	1:52.4
How Bout It	Lex	10-6-88	1:52.4
Deal Direct	Ind	8-25-90	1:52.4

Two-Year-Old Fillies

Horse	Track	Date	Time
Miss Easy	Lex	9-25-90	1:51.2
L Dees Trish	Lex	10-01-88	1:52
Razzle Hanover	Lex	9-29-85 T	1:52.2
Miss Easy	M	8-17-90	1:52.3
Amneris	Spr	8-15-84	1:53.1
Amneris	Spr	8-15-84	1:53.3
Central Park West	PPk	11-18-88	1:53.3f
Hit Parade	DuQ	9-2-83	1:53.4
Tantalize Hanover	Lex	9-28-86 T	1:53.4
Central Park West	Spr	8-17-88	1:53.4

Three-Year-Old Colts and Geldings

Horse	Track	Date	Time
Matt's Scooter	Lex	9-23-88 T	1:48.2
Niatross	Lex	10-1-80 T	1:49.1
Nihilator	M	8-3-85	1:49.3
In The Pocket	Lex	9-28-90 T	1:49.3
Beach Towel	DuQ	8-30-90	1:50
Kiev Hanover	Lex	10-5-90	1:50.1
Barberry Spur	Lex	9-26-86 T	1:50.2
Nihilator	M	7-19-85	1:50.3
Colt Fortysix	Spr	8-16-84	1:50.3
In The Pocket	Mea	8-11-90	1:50.4f

Three-Year-Old Fillies

Horse	Track	Date	Time
Trini Hanover	Spr	8-17-88 T	1:51.2
Dont Dally	DuQ	8-30-84	1:51.3
Town Pro	M	8-4-90	1:51.4
Caesars Jackpot	M	8-5-89	1:52.1
Smiling Rebecca	Lex	9-26-90 T	1:52.1
Rulers Chippie	PPk	12-29-90	1:52.3f
Leah Almahurst	Lex	9-29-88	1:52.3
Cheery Hello	Lex	10-5-89	1:52.3
Town Pro	M	8-11-90	1:52.3
Jolibea Hanover	M	8-8-87	1:52.4
Conquered Quest	M	7-29-88	1:52.4
Stevos' Marcy	M	8-6-88	1:52.4
Choice Yankee	M	8-17-90	1:52.4
Tarport Melody	Spr	8-14-84 T	1:52.4

Aged Horses and Geldings

Horse	Track	Date	Time
Jaguar Spur	Lex	10-8-88 T	1:49.2
T K's Skipper	DuQ	9-1-90 T	1:49.2
Call For Rain	Lex	10-1-88	1:49.3
Camtastic	Spr	8-17-89 T	1:49.3
Ramblin Storm	M	7-8-88	1:50.1
Matt's Scooter	M	7-8-89	1:50.1
Matt's Scooter	M	7-1-89	1:50.2
Forrest Skipper	M	6-13-86 T	1:50.3
Jaguar Spur	M	7-9-88	1:50.3
Jaguar Spur	M	8-6-88	1:50.3
Matt's Scooter	M	8-5-89	1:50.3
T K's Skipper	M	8-17-90	1:50.3

Aged Mares

Horse	Track	Date	Time
Fan Hanover	Lex	10-2-82 T	1:50.4
Forbidden Past	Lex	10-1-86 T	1:51.2
Caesars Jackpot	M	8-4-90	1:51.2
Armbro Feather	M	8-15-89	1:51.3
Caesars Jackpot	M	6-8-90	1:51.4
Caesars Jackpot	PPk	10-20-90	1:52.2f
Tanzy Lobell	Lex	10-6-82 T	1:52.2
Armbro Feather	GSP	9-15-89	1:52.2
Caesars Jackpot	M	6-29-90	1:52.2
Caesars Jackpot	PPk	11-2-90	1:52.3f
May Wine	M	8-3-85	1:52.3
Follow My Star	Lex	10-1-87 T	1:52.3
Anniecrombie	M	8-12-88	1:52.3

DASHES AND SPEED

THE FASTEST MILES OF 1990 ON EACH GAIT

Trotters

Horse	Age	Sex	Time	Driver	Track	Date
Harmonious	3	c	1:53.2	Cat Manzi	Du Quoin, IL	September 1
Harmonious	3	c	1:54.1	John Campbell	The Meadowlands	August 4
Super Arnie	3	c	1:54.1	Berndt Lindstedt	Springfield, IL	August 17
I'm Impeccable	3	g	1:54.2	Sam "Chip" Noble	The Red Mile	September 28
Jeanne's Somolli	3	c	1:54.2	Rod Allen	The Red Mile	October 5
Peace Corps	4	m	1:54.2f	Stig Johannson	Pompano Park	November 2
Star Mystic	3	c	1:54.3	Jan Johnson	The Red Mile	October 5
Super Arnie	3	c	1:54.3	Berndt Lindstedt	Du Quoin, IL	September 1
Embassy Lobell	3	c	1:54.4	Michel Lachance	The Red Mile	September 28
Kit Lobell	5	m	1:54.4	Berndt Lindstedt	The Meadowlands	June 27
Harmonious	3	c	1:55	John Campbell	The Meadowlands	August 4
No Sex Please	5	g	1:55	Ron Waples	The Red Mile	October 4
No Sex Please	5	g	1:55f	Ron Waples	Pompano Park	November 2
Super Arnie	3	c	1:55	Berndt Lindstedt	Springfield, IL	August 17
Columnist	3	c	1:55.1	Cat Manzi	The Red Mile	September 28
Happy Diamonds	3	f	1:55.1	John Campbell	Du Quoin, IL	August 31
Indianapolis	7	g	1:55.1	Bill O'Donnell	The Meadowlands	August 15
Kerry's Crown	5	m	1:55.1	Ron Waples	The Red Mile	October 4
Slybowl Hanover	5	h	1:55.2	Pekka Korpi	The Meadowlands	June 6

Pacers

Horse	Age	Sex		Time	Driver	Track	Date
T K's Skipper	5	h	T	1:49.2	Michel Lachance	Du Quoin, IL	September 1
In The Pocket	3	c	T	1:49.3	John Campbell	The Red Mile	September 28
Beach Towel	3	c		1:50	Ray Remmen	Du Quoin, IL	August 30
Kiev Hanover	3	c		1:50.1	Jim Morand	The Red Mile	October 5
T K's Skipper	5	h		1:50.3	Michel Lachance	The Meadowlands	August 17
In The Pocket	3	c		1:50.4f	John Campbell	The Meadows	August 11
Boston Blue Chip	3	c		1:51.1	Joe Schwind	The Meadowlands	August 4
Kiev Hanover	3	c	T	1:51.1	Bill Fahy	Springfield, IL	August 16
Beach Towel	3	c		1:51.1	Ray Remmen	The Red Mile	September 29
Kiev Hanover	3	c		1:51.1	Jim Morand	The Red Mile	September 29
Artsplace	2	c		1:51.1f	John Campbell	Pompano Park	November 30
In The Pocket	3	c		1:51.2	John Campbell	The Meadowlands	June 30
T K's Skipper	5	h		1:51.2	Michel Lachance	The Meadowlands	July 7
Caesars Jackpot	4	m		1:51.2	Bill Fahy	The Meadowlands	August 4
Miss Easy	2	f		1:51.2	John Campbell	The Red Mile	September 25
T K's Skipper	5	h		1:51.2f	Joe Anderson	Los Alamitos	September 29
Beach Towel	3	c		1:51.2f	Ray Remmen	Pompano Park	November 2
Dorunrun Bluegrass	4	h		1:51.3	Ron Pierce	The Meadowlands	May 19
Cameleon	5	h		1:51.3	Ron Waples	The Meadowlands	June 9
Brando Hanover	3	c		1:51.3	Mickey McNichol	The Meadowlands	August 3
In The Pocket	3	c		1:51.3	John Campbell	The Meadowlands	August 3
Beach Towel	3	c		1:51.3	Ray Remmen	The Red Mile	September 29
Caesars Jackpot	4	m		1:51.4	Bill Fahy	The Meadowlands	June 8
Joe's Scooter	7	h		1:51.4	Joe Schwind	The Meadowlands	June 9
Town Pro	3	f		1:51.4	Doug Brown	The Meadowlands	August 4
Beach Towel	3	c		1:51.4f	Ray Remmen	The Meadows	August 11
Deal Direct	2	c		1:51.4	Sam "Chip" Noble	Indianapolis, IN	August 25
Dare You To	5	h		1:51.4f	Wally Hennessey	Pompano Park	Ocotber 20
Shipps Schnoops	3	c		1:51.4f	Tommy Haughton	Pompano Park	December 29
Even Hand	4	h		1:52	Bill O'Donnell	The Meadowlands	April 27
T K's Skipper	5	h		1:52	Michel Lachance	The Meadowlands	May 26
Too Good	3	c		1:52	Michel Lachance	The Meadowlands	June 2
Tyrannical	5	h		1:52	Joe Schwind	The Meadowlands	June 9
Ticket To Heaven	5	h		1:52	Mickey McNichol	The Meadowlands	June 23
Prince Ebony	7	h		1:52	Ron Pierce	The Meadowlands	August 4

DASHES AND SPEED

THE 1:58 TROTTERS OF 1990

Below are listed the 1:58 trotters of 1990. Given is the name, color, sex, age, sire, and number of 1:58 miles in 1990, then come details on the year's fastest mile.

Horse, color, sex, age	Sire	1:58 Miles	Fastest of 1990, Showing: Track, Date (Driver)	Time
A C Star, gr, h, 5	Armbro Captain	1	GrR, 6/5 (Trevor Ritchie)	1:56.4f
A Js Image, b, g, 6	Balanced Image	4	Ridc, 9/14 (Robert O'Dwyer)	1:57.2f
A Worthy Lad, blk, c, 3	Worthy Bowl	1	KD, 9/29 (Bud Fritz)	1:57.3f
Abdicator, b, c, 3	Speedy Crown	1	PPk, 12/15 (Michel Lachance)	1:57.4f
Alfa Star, blk, h, 5	Hunters Star	1	Sacr, 8/8 (Jim Lackey)	Q 1:57.1
Alfresco, b, h, 4	Arndon	2	M, 7/30 (Ron Waples)	1:57
Alissas Beauty, blk, m, 5	Armbro Agile	1	Moh, 9/10 (Jim Whelan)	1:57.2f
Anastasia Brat, b, m, 6	Coalmoor	3	Mea, 6/27 (Dale McConnell)	1:57.2f
Anken Imperial, b, c, 3	Brisco Hanover	1	Lex, 6/29 (Mike Zeller)	1:57.4
Another Choice, b, m, 5	Lindys Crown	2	RcR, 6/17 (Linda Gentile)	1:57.3f
Antwerp Hanover, b, c, 3	Super Bowl	1	RcR, 7/22 (John Simpson, Jr.)	1:57.3f
Armbro Icon, b, f, 3	Speedy Crown	1	Sycs, 8/12 (Larry Walker)	1:57.3
Armbro Iliad, b, c, 3	Speedy Crown	2	Lex, 10/5 (Ron Waples)	1:55.4
Arndon Glory, b, h, 6	Arndon	1	BB, 6/30 (Yves Gauthier)	1:58f
Arnold's World, b, h, 5	Arndon	1	LA, 9/25 (Jack Parker, Jr.)	1:58f
Backstreet Guy, br, c, 3	Lindys Crown	1	M, 7/28 (John Campbell)	Q 1:58
Bal Maner, b, g, 5	Manero Hanover	1	ScD, 6/15 (Dave Hawk)	1:57.4f
Ballina, b, f, 3	Face To Face	1	Sycs, 8/18 (John Findley)	T 1:57.4
Bloomin Thing, b, m, 7	Speedy Somolli	1	RcR, 4/8 (Bill Long)	1:57.4f
Bold Herbert, br, g, 4	Worthy Bowl	3	PPk, 2/2 (Bruce Ranger)	1:56.3f
Bombed Algebra, b, h, 5	Sherwood Lobell	1	HP, 6/8 (Terry Tomlin)	1:57.1f
Broderick, b, g, 7	Noble Imp	3	DuQ, 8/31 (Ken Crawford)	1:56.2
Brother Oliver, br, c, 3	Niles Hanover	1	VD, 5/28 (Ben Steall)	1:58q
Cabrera Lobell, b, f, 3	Speedy Crown	1	Lex, 9/28 (Billy Herman)	1:56.3
Camelia Lobell, br, f, 3	Speedy Crown	1	Lex, 10/5 (Jan Johnson)	1:56.1
Carry The Message, b, c, 2	Royal Prestige	1	Lex, 9/27 (John Campbell)	1:57.1
Cayster, blk, f, 3	Speedy Somolli	1	M, 6/19 (Bill O'Donnell)	1:57.1
Charlie Somolli, ch, h, 4	Speedy Somolli	1	M, 6/20 (Bill O'Donnell)	1:57.2
Cheyenne Spur, b, c, 3	Super Bowl	2	RcR, 10/13 (Dick Stillings)	1:56.2f
China Smoke, br, m, 5	Diamond Exchange	1	M, 1/9 (John Campbell)	Q 1:58
CMF Bourbon Beau, b, g, 4	Bonefish	2	M, 1/15 (Bill Fahy)	1:57
Cody, b, c, 3	Quigley Hanover	1	Spr, 8/13 (Tom Carey)	1:57
Columnist, b, c, 3	Speedy Crown	4	Lex, 9/28 (Cat Manzi)	1:55.1
Coraopolis, br, g, 9	Florida Pro	1	GSP, 10/9 (Joe Schwind)	1:58
Court Of Appeal, br, m, 5	Big Sur	1	M, 1/29 (Ray Remmen)	1:58
Crown Bones, b, c, 3	Speedy Crown	2	Sycs, 8/12 (Berndt Lindstedt)	1:56.4
Crown's Majesty, b, h, 4	Speedy Crown	1	PPk, 4/20 (Dave Rankin)	1:56.2f
Cumin, b, c, 3	Super Bowl	1	M, 6/1 (Stanley Dancer)	Q 1:57.1
Darby's Pride, br, c, 3	Nevele Pride	1	Lex, 6/29 (Don Swick)	1:58
Defrocked, b, h, 4	Balanced Image	2	Moh, 4/30 (Bill Wellwood)	1:57.2f
Delona Kash, b, f, 3	Uptown	1	Lex, 9/27 (Clint Galbraith)	T 1:57.2
Delphi's Lobell, b, f, 3	Speedy Crown	2	M, 8/3 (Ron Waples)	1:56
Delrary Lobell, b, h, 5	Speedy Crown	1	GSP, 10/25 (Per Henriksen)	1:55.3
Dialect, b, h, 5	Nevele Pride	1	GSP, 10/31 (Ron Waples)	1:58
Dontellmenomore, b, c, 2	Crowning Point	1	Lex, 9/25 (John Campbell)	1:56.2
Double Hill, b, h, 8	Doublemint	2	RcR, 6/24 (Jim Morrill, Jr.)	1:57.3f
Dr Guillotine, b, h, 4	Super Bowl	1	PPk, 3/16 (Chris Boring)	1:57.4f
Embassy Lobell, b, c, 3	Speedy Crown	6	Lex, 9/28 (Michel Lachance)	1:54.4

DASHES AND SPEED

Esprit Spur, b, f, 2	Joie De Vie	1	PPk, 11/9 (Dick Stillings)	1:58f
Essence Bear, b, f, 3	Nevele Pride	1	Lex, 10/5 (Tommy Haughton)	1:58
First Down, ch, h, 8	Chiola Hanover	1	Lex, 9/15 (Tony Patterson)	1:58
Florida Jewel, b, h, 6	Crystas Crown	7	M, 4/9 (John Campbell)	1:55.4
Forever Man, b, h, 4	Speedy Somolli	1	PPk, 11/28 (Jan Nordin)	1:58
Forty-Five Caliber, b, h, 7	Florida Pro	1	PPk, 4/13 (Denis Normandin)	1:57.1f
Frankie Lobell, b, c, 3	Speedy Crown	1	Lex, 9/29 (John Campbell)	1:58
Frederique, br, f, 3	Manfred Hanover	1	Lex, 10/3 (Randy Edmonds)	1:58
Free Throw, b, h, 6	Final Score	1	BB, 10/17 (Serge Ouellet)	1:58f
Free Token, br, m, 6	Jurgy Hanover	9	PPk, 3/27 (Joe Pavia, Jr.)	1:56.1f
French Lieutenant, b, h, 6	Lindys Crown	2	M, 6/11 (Michel Lachance)	1:58
Front Zipper, b, h, 4	Crowntron	1	M, 8/14 (Howard Parker)	1:57.4
Gambi's Bigboy, blk, c, 3	Gambi Lobell	1	Spr, 6/16 (Michael Cox)	1:56
Gauguin Go, b, g, 5	Incredible Nevele	2	BB, 4/27 (Gaetan Lamy)	1:57.3f
General Three, br, h, 4	Mystic Park	1	RcR, 10/7 (Eddie Davis)	1:58f
Gentle Stroke, b, h, 9	Noble Gesture	2	BB, 7/7 (Rick Zeron)	1:57f
Glorious Jazz, b, h, 5	Jazz Cosmos	1	Moh, 5/14 (Tim Twaddle)	1:57f
Grand Marquise, b, h, 4	Diamond Exchange	2	PPk 12/29 (Ed Rudner)	1:57.3f
Granite Stride, br, g, 5	Yankee Bambino	1	M, 5/30 (Ron Pierce)	1:57.4
Grundy's Mint, b, c, 2	Royal Prestige	2	Lex, 9/27 (Jan Nordin)	1:57.1
Happy Diamonds, b, f, 3	Diamond Exchange	5	DuQ, 8/31 (John Campbell)	1:55.1
Happy Home GB, br, g, 7	Homesick	1	VD, 7/8 (Gary Gibson)	1:57.3q
Harmoniuous, b, c, 3	Crowning Point	9	DuQ, 9/1 (Cat Manzi)	1:53.2
Hey Foxtrot, b, g, 8	Heyday	1	PPk, 3/1 (Kevin Wallis)	1:58f
Home Court, b, m, 4	Homesick	1	Lex, 9/27 (Richard Taylor)	1:57.1
However, b, g, 5	Speedy Rodney	1	VD, 6/29 (C. Huckabone, Jr.)	1:57.3q
Hunziker T, b, h, 4	Arndon	2	M, 7/3 (Jan Johnson)	1:57
Hypersonic, b, h, 4	Arndon	1	PPk, 4/13 (Jan Johnson)	1:57.1f
I Envy Noah, b, h, 6	Cold Comfort	1	RcR, 3/11 (Rejean Daigneault)	1:57.2f
I'm Impeccable, b, g, 3	Coleman Lobell	3	Lex, 9/28 (Sam "Chip" Noble)	1:54.2
Incredible D J, b, c, 3	Incredible Nevele	10	Ind, 8/25 (John Campbell)	1:55.3
Incredible M A, b, g, 5	Incredible Nevele	1	PPk, 2/9 (Andre Dagenais)	1:56.4f
Independent Blaze, b, g, 5	Mighty Crown	2	ScD, 6/8 (Jeff Cox)	1:57.4f
Indianapolis, b, g, 7	Dream Of Glory	4	M, 8/15 (Bill O'Donnell)	1:55.1
Jacquie's Kosmos, b, c, 3	Batic Speed	1	M, 6/20 (Bill Fahy)	1:57.3
Jeanne's Somolli, b, c, 3	Speedy Somolli	6	Lex, 10/5 (Rod Allen)	1:54.2
Jeff's Playboy, b, g, 6	Superman	3	PPk, 12/21 (Bruce Ranger)	1:56.4f
Jelly Belly, b, h, 5	Joie De Vie	5	BB, 8/3 (Henri Filion)	1:56.2f
Jet Action, b, g, 5	Speed In Action	2	Moh, 10/7 (Doug Brown)	1:57.3f
Kerry's Crown, br, m, 5	Speedy Crown	5	Lex, 10/4 (Ron Waples)	1:55.1
Keystone Anita, b, f, 3	Speed Bowl	2	Lex, 9/26 (Dick Stillings)	1:57
Keystone Lucas, b, h, 4	Super Bowl	1	GSP, 9/26 (John Patterson, Jr.)	1:58
Keystone Salute, b, h, 4	Florida Pro	2	RcR, 7/15 (Roger Hammer)	1:56.1f
Keystone Sheik, b, g, 5	Lindys Crown	4	Moh, 9/24 (Doug Brown)	1:57f
Keystone Hush, b, f, 3	Arndon	2	PPk, 10/20 (Jan Nordin)	1:56.1f
King Of The Sea, b, c, 3	Bonefish	1	M, 5/9 (Stanley Dancer)	1:58
King's Hope, b, g, 6	Kingfish	2	BmlP, 5/6 (Fred Finn, Jr.)	1:57.2m
Kit Lobell, b, m, 5	Speedy Crown	3	M, 6/27 (Berndt Lindstedt)	1:54.4
Kosar, b, c, 3	Speedy Somolli	2	M, 6/20 (Per Henriksen)	1:56
L V Goldie, b, f, 3	Joie De Vie	1	M, 6/12 (Ron Waples)	1:57.3
Le Fish, b, g, 3	Bonefish	1	M, 3/14 (Jim Doherty)	1:57.4
Lila Lobell, br, f, 3	Speedy Crown	1	M, 6/27 (Jan Johnson)	1:55.4
Linfields Keen, b, g, 5	Worthy Bowl	1	PPk, 10/6 (Kevin Wallis)	1:57.1f
Lodestar Lobell, b, g, 6	Speedy Somolli	1	M, 4/25 (Joe Schwind)	1:56.4

DASHES AND SPEED

Lost Ark, b, g, 5	Lindys Crown	1	PPk, 3/29 (Kevin Wallis)	1:57.4f
Loveable Lemar, b, f, 2	Arnies Exchange	1	Lex, 9/21 (Billy Herman)	T 1:57.3
Luanne Kash, b, m, 4	Uptonw	1	Sycs, 8/4 (Clint Galbraith)	1:56.3
Lungistics, b, g, 5	Lindys Crown	1	RcR, 2/9 (Steve Warrington)	1:57.4f
Magic Moose, b, g, 6	Carl H	4	LA, 10/16 (Ross Croghan)	1:56.4f
Me Maggie, b, f, 3	Prakas	4	PPk, 11/9 (Berndt Lindstedt)	1:56.1f
Meadow Maritime, b, h, 4	Arndon	1	RcR, 6/17 (Don Irvine, Jr.)	1:57.2f
Meadowbranch Eddy, br, c, 3	Prakas	1	Mea, 6/8 (Doug Snyder)	1:57.3
Miss Baltic, ch, f, 3	Baltic Speed	1	GSP, 9/11 (Bill Fahy)	1:57
Mitey Speedy, b, m, 4	Speedy Crown	1	VD, 8/10 (Brian Allen)	1:57.4q
Model Home, ch, f, 3	Homesick	6	DuQ, 8/31 (Berndt Lindstedt)	1:55.3
Mora Chiola, b, g, 4	Chiola Hanover	4	Lex, 9/27 (Bueford Lundsord)	1:56.2
My Wild Irish Rose, b, f, 2	Bonefish	1	GSP, 10/17 (Harold Kelly)	1:57.4
Nashville Lobell, ch, c, 3	Speedy Somolli	1	Lex, 6/8 (Berndt Lindstedt)	1:56.2
Nero Domarr, b, h, 5	Worthy Bowl	1	GrR, 8/2 (Dave Wall)	1:57.3f
Nettie M, b, m, 5	Florida Pro	1	Lex, 9/26 (Paul Spears)	1:57.4
New Legend, br, h, 4	Speedy Crown	1	Sycs, 8/12 (John Campbell)	1:57.2
Nivea Hanover, b, f, 3	Super Bowl	2	Lex, 10/5 (Billy Herman)	1:55.4
No Sex Please, br, g, 5	Brisco Hanover	13	PPk, 11/2 (Ron Waples)	1:55f
Noble You, b, g, 8	Noble Gesture	1	M, 2/5 (Bill O'Donnell)	1:57.4
Nobody Told Me, br, g, 6	Camp David	3	PPk, 10/13 (Jim Gregory)	1:56.4f
Non Negotiable, br, g, 6	Burgomeister	1	M, 2/12 (Ron Pierce)	1:57
Nothing Ventured, b, h, 4	Diamond Exchange	3	Sacr, 8/11 (Nicol Tremblay)	1:58f
Nuclear Arsenal, b, g, 4	Arsenal	1	M, 4/28 (John Campbell)	Q 1:57
Our First, b, f, 3	Speed Bowl	1	Dela, 9/20 (John Campbell)	1:57.3h
Out Of My Way, b, g, 5	Brisco Hanover	1	BB, 8/10 (Mario Baillargeon)	1:57.1f
Pastel Pastel, br, c, 3	Flak Bait	1	M, 6/6 (Carmine Abbatiello)	1:57.4
Peace Corps, b, m, 4	Baltic Speed	1	PPk, 11/2 (Stig Johansson)	1:54.2f
Peach Pit, b, m, 4	Speedy Somolli	3	RcR, 6/2 (Bill Wellwood)	1:57f
Perfect Point, b, f, 3	Crowning Point	1	Ind, 8/24 (Homer Hochstetler)	1:56.4
Perky Crown, b, f, 3	Speedy Crown	1	M, 7/31 (Jan Johnson)	Q 1:57.2
Pesach, b, c, 3	Flak Bait	2	M, 8/2 (Ben Webster)	1:58
Prince Mystic, b, h, 4	Mystic Park	3	M, 6/13 (Ray Remmen)	1:56.3
Princely Fellow, b, c, 3	Crowning Point	1	Lex, 5/26 (Doug Ackerman)	1:57.3
Proud Coate, b, g, 5	Mighty Crown	1	HP, 6/29 (Chris Boring)	1:57.2f
R Pappy, br, g, 3	Gambi Lobell	2	DuQ, 8/28 (Danny Rhodes)	1:56.4
Remus Hanover, b, c, 3	Super Bowl	1	RcR, 7/22 (John Simpson, Jr.)	1:56.4f
Roll'n Oaks Class, b, g, 4	Heyday	2	VD, 6/29 (Mario Pace)	1:58q
Rompaway Henry, b, h, 4	Speedy Claude	1	Lex, 6/1 (David Bartlett)	1:57.3
Roughing It, b, c, 3	Homesick	1	Lex, 9/27 (Tom Durand)	1:57.2
Roydon Lad, b, h, 4	Bonefish	2	RcR, 7/22 (Don Irvine, Jr.)	1:56f
Sambuca Lobell, b, c, 3	Speedy Crown	2	Sycs, 8/12 (Pekka Korpi)	1:57.2
Santa Royal, b, f, 2	Royal Prestige	1	GSP 10/17 (Cat Manzi)	1:58
Sensuous Suspect, b, f, 3	Speedy Crown	1	Lex, 10/5 (Jan Johnson)	1:55.3
Shawland Major, b, g, 6	Worthy Bowl	2	GrR, 6/26 (Steve Condren)	1:57.3f
Sherwood's Chief, b, g, 4	Sherwood Lobell	1	M, 2/21 (John Campbell)	1:57.3
Skeet Load, b, h, 4	Lindys Crown	1	RcR, 5/20 (Bob Shahan)	1:58f
Slybowl Hanover, br, h, 5	Super Bowl	7	M, 6/6 (Pekka Korpi)	1:55.2
Sonny's Jubilee, b, g, 7	Homesick	2	M, 5/23 (Ron Pierce)	1:57.4
Speedy Wings, b, h, 6	Self Confident	1	M, 1/22 (Ron Pierce)	1:57
Star Mystic, b, c, 3	Mystic Park	6	Lex, 10/5 (Jan Johnson)	1:54.3
Super Arnie, b, c, 3	Super Bowl	4	Spr, 8/17 (Berndt Lindstedt)	1:54.1
Super Gleam, b, c, 3	Speed Bowl	1	PPk, 4/27 (Mark O'Mara)	1:57.4f
Super Scotch S J, br, g, 7	Super Juan	9	M, 8/1 (John Campbell)	1:56

DASHES AND SPEED

Super Timken, b, g, 5	Superman	1	Moh, 9/2 (Doug Brown)	1:56.3f
Texas Viking, b, g, 5	Texas	2	VD, 7/13 (Mickey Bridges)	1:58q
Ultimate Kosmos, br, h, 5	Jurgy Hanover	2	M, 5/9 (Carmine Abbatiello)	1:57.1
Uncle Gustaf, b, h, 6	Bonefish	1	POPk, 2/16 (Kevin Wallis)	1:57.2f
Valley Everglades, b, h, 5	Speedy Somolli	1	Lex, 6/15 (Jan Johnson)	1:57.4
Village Kid, b, g, 8	Dream Of Glory	3	GrR, 7/5 (Roger Mayotte)	1:57f
War Nickel, br, g, 4	Copter Lobell	1	GSP, 10/18 (Raymond Tremblay)	1:56
Well Done, b, h, 4	Newsmaker	1	PPk, 3/23 (Frank Todd, Jr.)	1:58f
Whitney Lauxmont, b, f, 3	Workaholic	1	Lex, 10/2 (Ron Waples)	T 1:57.4
Working Gal, blk, f, 3	Speedy Crown	4	RcR, 10/13 (Michel Lachance)	1:57.1f
Yankee Bart, b, g, 6	Defiant Yankee	1	M, 4/14 (John Monaco)	Q 1:57.1
Yourworstnightmare, br, c, 3	Defiant Yankee	1	Mea, 9/3 (Bill Zendt)	1:56.3f
Zip Smiger, br, h, 6	Fossati Hanover	1	GrR, 6/12 (Doug Brown)	1:57.4f

THE 1:54 PACERS OF 1990

Here is a list of the 1:54 pacers of 1990, including details on each performer's fastest mile of the season:

Horse, color, sex, age	Sire	1:54 Miles	Fastest of 1990, Showing: Track, Date (Driver)	Time
A J Storm Honor, b, h, 4	Temujin	2	PPk, 10/27 (Kevin Wallis)	1:52.2f
Able Spring A, b, g, 7	Able Bye Bye	1	M, 6/11 (Michel Lachance)	1:53.3
Agreement, br, c, 3	Walt Hanover	1	GSP, 10/23 (John Plutino)	1:53.4
Ahoy Captain, b, h, 4	Sonsam	1	M, 5/26 (John Campbell)	1:53.4
All Da Time, b, h, 5	Keystone Ore	3	M, 4/28 (Jim Doherty)	1:53.1
Allwin Scotty, br, h, 5	Allwin Steady	1	M, 6/2 (Ray Schnittker)	1:53.2
Anchor U, br, h, 5	Cool Wind	1	M, 4/7 (Ben Webster)	1:54
Apaches Fame, b, c, 3	Apache Circle	7	GrR, 6/9 (Bud Fritz)	1:52.2f
Arbitrator, br, h, 4	No Nukes	1	M, 5/26 (Cat Manzi)	1:53.2
Armbro Galaxy, b, h, 5	Abercrombie	1	M, 8/11 (John Campbell)	1:53.2
Armbro Intercept, b, c, 3	Direct Scooter	1	M, 8/3 (Michel Lachance)	1:54
Artsplace, b, c, 2	Abercrombie	3	PPk, 11/30 (John Campbell)	1:51.1f
Ballenger Hanover, b, c, 3	Tyler B	1	M, 8/10 (Mickey McNichol)	1:53.4
Ballroom Music, b, h, 6	Abercrombie	1	M, 6/23 (Michel Lachance)	1:52.4
Banker Blue Chip, b, h, 6	Brand New Fella	1	M, 7/21 (Cat Manzi)	1:52.1
Barefoot Hanover, b, h, 4	Albatross	1	M, 7/14 (Jim Doherty)	1:53.2
Barely Visible, b, h, 5	Tyler B	3	M, 1/13 (Bill O'Donnell)	1:53.2
Batik Print A, ch, g, 7	Caliburn	1	M, 6/1 (Michel Lachance)	1:53.4
Bay's Fella, b, h, 5	Brand New Fella	3	PPk, 11/2 (Paul MacDonell)	1:52.1f
Beach Towel, b, c, 3	French Chef	17	DuQ, 8/30 (Ray Remmen)	1:50
Big Town Express, br, h, 5	Big Towner	4	M, 4/21 (Joe Offutt)	1:53
Bite Your Tounge, b, g, 4	Raven Hanover	2	M, 4/28 (Michel Lachance)	1:53
Blazing Sahbra, b, h, 4	Walton Hanover	1	M, 3/10 (Michel Lachance)	1:53.4
Bob's Escort, b, g, 5	Happy Escort	2	ScD, 8/25 (Steve Bauder)	1:53.4f
Bomb Rickles, b, h, 6	No Nukes	1	BB, 10/14 (Mike MacDonald)	1:53.3f
Bond Street, b, h, 5	Abercrombie	1	GrR, 7/14 (Bill Gale)	1:53.3f
Bookmaker, b, c, 3	Nihilator	1	M, 6/1 (Harold Kelly)	1:52.4
Boston Blue Chip, ch, c, 3	On The Road Again	1	M, 8/4 (Joe Schwind)	1:51.1
Brando Hanover, b, c, 3	Walton Hanover	3	M, 8/3 (Mickey McNichol)	1:51.3
Bret The Third, b, c, 3	Gypsy Bret	1	M, 6/22 (John Campbell)	1:53.1

DASHES AND SPEED

Bronze Merger, b, h, 6	Merger	1	GSP, 12/1 (Ron Waples)	1:54
Bruce's Lady, b, f, 3	Tyler B	1	M, 8/4 (John Campbell)	1:53.3
C K S, b, c, 3	On The Road Again	2	M, 6/16 (Michel Lachance)	1:53.2
Caesars Jackpot, b, m, 4	Walton Hanover	7	M, 8/4 (Bill Fahy)	1:51.2
Cam's Lucky, b, h, 4	Cam Fella	2	GrR, 7/21 (John Brooks)	1:53.2f
Cambest, br, c, 2	Cam Fella	1	GSP, 10/19 (Dave Rankin)	1:54
Cameleon, br, h, 5	Cam Fella	2	M, 6/9 (Ron Waples)	1:51.3
Cameo, b, c, 3	Cam Fella	1	GSP, 9/29 (Cat Manzi)	1:54
Camluck, b, c, 3	Cam Fella	1	WR, 10/21 (Michel Lachance)	1:52.4f
Cams Exotic, b, f, 2	Cam Fella	1	PPk, 11/23 (Harold Kelly)	1:54f
Canvasback Fella, br, g, 4	Cam Fella	2	M, 6/2 (Joe Schwind)	1:53.2
Champagne Classic, br, h, 4	Samadhi	1	GSP, 9/15 (Ray Remmen)	1:54
Charles Nero N, b, g, 6	Clever Innocence	1	M, 8/16 (Michel Lachance)	1:53.3
Chatham Light, b, h, 5	Niatross	1	Conn, 5/21 (Kelly Sheppard)	1:53.3h
Cheery Hello, b, m, 4	Albatross	2	GSP, 9/7 (John Campbell)	1:53.1
Chefs Magic, b, c, 3	French Chef	1	GrR, 6/16 (Tony Kerwood)	1:52.4f
Chernobyl, b, h, 4	No Nukes	2	M, 6/23 (Jim Doherty)	1:53.1
Choice Yankee, b, f, 3	Colt Fortysix	1	M, 8/17 (Jim Morrill, Jr.)	1:52.4
Cimarron, b, h, 5	Abercrombie	4	M, 4/28 (Jim Doherty)	1:53
Circle Of Light, b, h, 4	Albatross	1	Lex, 9/29 (Ron Waples)	1:52.3
Cognac Hanover, b, h, 6	Tyler B	1	M, 6/2 (Michel Lachance)	1:52.3
Colored Storm, b, c, 3	Storm Damage	1	Lex, 9/29 (Tom Harmer)	1:53.3
Commonwealth, br, g, 5	Sonsam	1	Moh, 10/20 (Doug Brown)	1:53.2
Cool Cash, b, h, 5	Crash	1	HP, 6/30 (John Perttunen)	1:53.4f
Corsair, b, c, 3	Nihilator	3	M, 8/4 (Joe Pavia, Jr.)	1:52.2
Country Beau, b, h, 5	B Gs Bunny	1	M, 6/28 (Ron Pierce)	1:53.3
Courageous Legacy, b, h, 5	Sonsam	2	M, 6/23 (Bill O'Donnell)	1:53.1
Crafty Caper, b, f, 3	Tyler B	1	GSP, 9/15 (Howard Parker)	1:53.4
Crown Rich, b, h, 6	Happy Escort	3	M, 6/22 (Mickey McNichol)	1:53.3
D A Notice, br, g, 4	Legal Notice	1	M, 6/22 (Ron Pierce)	1:53.3
Danforth, b, c, 3	Nihilator	1	M, 6/9 (Jim Meittinis)	1:54
Dare You To, b, h, 5	Abercrombie	3	PPk, 10/20 (Wally Hennessey)	1:51.4f
Deal Direct, b, c, 2	Direct Scooter	2	Ind, 8/25 (Sam "Chip" Noble)	1:51.4
Deer Valley, b, g, 4	Sonsam	1	VD, 7/7 (Jim Gregory)	1:54q
Delinquent Account, b, f, 3	On The Road Again	1	Lex, 9/27 (John Kopas)	1:53.3
Dictionary, br, h, 6	Governor Skipper	1	M, 12/27 (Bill O'Donnell)	1:53.4
Die Laughing, br, c, 2	No Nukes	3	M, 8/17 (Richard Silverman)	1:52.1
Division Title, b, c, 3	Albatross	1	M, 4/7 (Bill Fahy)	1:54
Dorunrun Bluegrass, b, h, 4	Fortune Richie	6	M, 5/19 (Ron Pierce)	1:51.3
Dovers Ranger, br, g, 4	All Time Bret	1	M, 4/20 (Ron Pierce)	1:53.3
Dr No No, blk, c, 3	Storm Damage	1	M, 8/3 (Cat Manzi)	1:53.1
Dumpling Almahurst, br, m, 4	Radiant Ruler	1	Spr, 8/15 (Dan Shetler)	T 1:52.4
E L McKinzie, b, h, 4	McKinzie Almahurst	1	M, 6/30 (Jeff Dauplaise)	1:52.2
Eagle Speaker, b, g, 4	Conquered	1	GrR, 7/6 (John Holmes)	1:52.4f
Echelon, b, h, 4	Troublemaker	2	GSP, 11/24 (J. William Lancaster)	1:53.2
Edson Gold, b, h, 4	Samadhi	1	M, 8/10 (Jim Doherty)	1:53.4
Escortention, b, h, 7	Escort	2	M, 8/3 (John Campbell)	1:54
Even Hand, br, h, 4	No Nukes	2	M, 4/27 (Bill O'Donnell)	1:52
Everything Goes, br, c, 3	No Nukes	2	Lex, 9/27 (Ray Remmen)	T 1:53
Fleetros Rainbow, b, r, 4	Albatross	1	M, 6/30 (John Campbell)	1:52.3
Flexible Computer, br, h, 5	Albatross	1	M, 3/10 (Bill O'Donnell)	1:53.4
Fortitude Hanover, b, h, 8	Tyler B	1	M, 3/16 (Eddie Davis)	1:54
Fortune Leader, b, c, 3	Fortune Teller	1	SPk, 7/7 (Ron Marsh)	1:53.1f
Fortysix Cylinders, b, c, 3	Colt Fortysix	1	Ind, 8/25 (Chris Boring)	1:53

DASHES AND SPEED

Frankiejin, b, h, 4	Temujin	1	M, 8/3 (John Campbell)	1:53.3
General Knight, b, c, 3	Panorama	2	PPk, 11/24 (Dick Stillings)	1:52.2f
Gentry Hanover, b, h, 5	Big Towner	2	PPk, 11/17 (Steve Warrington)	1:53.3f
Global Assault, b, c, 3	Albatross	1	ScD, 9/8 (Mark Williams)	1:53f
Gobot, b, h, 5	G Es Romanero	2	GSP, 9/29 (Cat Manzi)	1:53.4
Gravedigger, br, g, 4	Armbro Venture	1	M, 8/18 (Art Bier)	1:53.3
Hi Lay Tye, b, c, 3	Tylers Brother	1	RcR, 7/28 (Jim Wathen, Jr.)	1:54f
Hicaliber Hanover, b, h, 4	Niatross	2	GSP, 9/29 (Jack Moiseyev)	1:53.1
Hit The Bid, b, h, 4	Albatross	1	M, 8/10 (Bill O'Donnell)	1:53.2
How Bout It, b, h, 4	Trenton	7	M, 7/13 (Mickey McNichol)	1:52.1
Humber Trail, br, g, 3	On The Road Again	1	M, 6/23 (Michel Lachance)	1:53.3
Idlewhiles Mikey, b, g, 4	Icarus Lobell	1	M, 6/2 (Cat Manzi)	1:53.4
Improvisation, b, c, 3	Niatross	1	VD, 9/3 (Richard Wojcio)	1:53.2q
In The Pocket, b, c, 3	Direct Scooter	9	Lex, 9/28 (John Campbell)	T 1:49.3
Incidental Music, b, h, 6	Abercrombie	1	BB, 7/27 (Rick Zeron)	1:53.4f
Instrument Landing, b, h, 9	Flying Bret	4	M, 6/16 (J. William Lancaster)	1:53.3
Interpretor, b, c, 2	Nihilator	1	Lex, 9/29 (D.R. Ackerman)	1:53.3
Jagger Hanover, b, g, 5	Tyler B	1	GrR, 7/7 (Trevor Ritchie)	1:53.4f
Jake And Elwood, br, c, 3	Samadhi	6	Lex, 9/29 (John Campbell)	1:52.2
JEF's Gladiator, b, g, 7	Isle Of Wight	1	M, 4/28 (Ron Pierce)	1:53.3
Jimmy's Buddy, br, g, 4	B Gs Bunny	1	M, 5/19 (Mickey McNichol)	1:53.4
JJ's Ollie, br, c, 3	Colt Fortysix	1	M, 5/25 (Ben Webster)	1:53.4
Joe's Scooter, b, h, 7	Direct Scooter	2	M, 6/9 (Joe Schwind)	1:51.4
Joy, b, f, 3	Andrel	1	M, 6/21 (Bill O'Donnell)	1:53.4
Juan's Boy, b, h, 6	Scarlet Skipper	1	M, 6/21 (Mark Lancaster)	1:54
Key Man Todd, b, c, 3	Lon Todd Hanover	1	Lex, 5/18 (Earl Spalding)	1:54
Keystone Raider, b, h, 5	Big Towner	2	M, 4/28 (Bill O'Donnell)	1:53.1
Kiev Hanover, b, c, 3	Albatross	4	Lex, 10/5 (Jim Morand)	1:50.1
Kimbell Almahurst, b, g, 5	Nero	1	M, 1/27 (Bill Fahy)	1:54
King Charles, b, g, 7	Niatross	3	M, 5/19 (Cat Manzi)	1:53.1
King Gypsy, b, c, 3	Tyler B	1	Mea, 8/11 (Bob Roberts)	1:53f
Krenshaw, b, h, 5	Billy Dart	1	M, 7/13 (Cat Manzi)	1:54
Kuzzin Kat, b, g, 4	Falcon Almahurst	1	M, 6/16 (Jim Doherty)	1:52.3
L Dees Trish, b, m, 4	Merger	1	GrR, 7/16 (Buddy Gilmour)	1:53.3f
Lady Genius, br, f, 3	Tyler B	1	Spr, 8/16 (Jay Picciano)	1:53.2
Land Fire, ch, h, 4	Landslide	2	RcR, 7/21 (Bill Fahy)	1:53.4f
Less Filling, b, h, 6	Direct Scooter	3	M, 5/5 (Mickey McNichol)	1:53.1
Licensed To Kill, b, g, 5	Genghis Khan	1	M, 6/16 (Art Bier)	1:53.3
Lorryland Butler, b, h, 5	Skip By Night	1	YR, 6/9 (Gary Mosher)	1:53.4h
Magna Survivor, b, h, 5	Hunters Star	2	GSP, 11/24 (Jack Parker, Jr.)	1:53.3
Mantese, br, c, 2	Falcon Seelster	1	Spr, 8/15 (Mickey McNichol)	1:53.4
Mark Johnathan, b, c, 3	Big Towner	3	M, 8/3 (Michel Lachance)	1:52.3
Master Scoot, b, h, 4	Direct Scooter	1	M, 8/11 (Michel Lachance)	1:53
Mighty Maradona, b, g, 4	Brigadier General	1	Moh, 9/15 (Dave Smith)	1:54f
Minuteman Hill, b, g, 3	On The Road Again	2	RcR, 7/6 (Kevin Lare)	1:53
Miss Easy, b, f, 2	Amity Chef	4	Lex, 9/25 (John Campbell)	1:51.2
Mister Hanover N, b, g, 8	Mister Hillas	1	M, 6/22 (Bill Fahy)	1:54
Mountain Hideaway, blk, g, 6	Andys Hideaway	2	Moh, 11/3 (Norm McKnight)	1:53.3f
Mr Bagel, b, h, 4	Direct Scooter	3	M, 7/20 (Mickey McNichol)	1:53.3
Mr Gourmet, b, g, 2	Mr Dalrae	1	Lex, 10/5 (Tom Harmer)	1:54
Mr Mallory, b, h, 4	Niatross	1	M, 8/4 (John Campbell)	1:52.4
Mystery Fund, b, h, 4	Fundamentalist	3	Lex, 10/3 (Ron Waples)	1:52.1
Night Colt, br, h, 7	Abercrombie	1	GrR, 7/21 (Mario Baillargeon)	1:52.3f
No Caveats, b, c, 3	Cam Fella	1	VD, 8/4 (Jay Picciano)	1:54q

DASHES AND SPEED

Noble Fella N, b, g, 7	Son Of Afella	2	M, 1/27 (Jack Moiseyev)	1:53.4
Northland Salute, blk, g, 4	Salute Hanover	4	GrR, 7/21 (Paul Sheppard)	1:53f
Nuclear Flash, b, c, 3	No Nukes	1	M, 5/1 (John Campbell)	1:53.3
Nuke Of Earl, br, c, 2	No Nukes	2	DuQ, 8/31 (Michel Lachance)	1:53.3
Odds Against, b, c, 3	Troublemaker	1	M, 6/22 (John Campbell)	1:53.2
Officer Of The Day, b, c, 3	Slapstick	1	M, 4/24 (Cat Manzi)	1:54
On Trial, b, h, 4	Safe Arrival	1	M, 3/16 (John Campbell)	1:53.4
Oscarsson, b, c, 3	Tyler B	2	M, 4/27 (Jim Meittinis)	1:53.4
Our Bucephalus, b, h, 7	Warm Breeze	1	Mea, 6/16 (Dan Altmeyer)	1:54f
Pat's Flagship, b, c, 3	Nihilator	3	GSP, 8/25 (Joe Pavia, Jr.)	1:53.2
Pianist, b, c, 3	French Chef	1	PPk, 4/2 (Mickey McNichol)	1:53.3
Pick Up Your Feet, b, h, 4	Abercrombie	4	M, 6/2 (John Campbell)	1:52.4
Pip Squeek, b, c, 3	Happy Motoring	1	M, 8/11 (Ron Pierce)	1:52.3
Please Please, b, h, 5	Scarlet Skipper	1	M, 6/15 (Bill O'Donnell)	1:53.4
Pocono Fox, b, h, 5	Hot Hitter	1	M, 7/20 (Michel Lachance)	1:53.4
Polo Player, b, h, 4	Cam Fella	1	PPk, 11/10 (Joe Pavia, Jr.)	1:53.3f
Power And Glory N, b, g, 7	Vance Hanover	2	LA, 1/20 (Jim Todd)	1:53.4f
Preview Lobell, br, h, 4	No Nukes	3	M, 6/16 (Mickey McNichol)	1:52.4
Prime Command, b, h, 5	Safe Arrival	1	M, 8/2 (Jim Marshall)	1:54
Primus Almahurst, b, g, 5	Nero	2	Moh, 5/25 (Tony Kerwood)	1:53.3f
Prince Ebony, blk, h, 7	Conquered	6	M, 8/4 (Ron Pierce)	1:52
Prince Lee Cam, b, h, 5	Cam Fella	1	M, 8/6 (John Campbell)	1:53.1
Racy Royce, b, h, 7	Royce	3	M, 8/4 (Mickey McNichol)	1:52.3
Rain Devil, b, h, 4	Storm Damage	1	M, 5/19 (Jim Meittinis)	1:53.1
Rampage Hanover, b, h, 5	Albatross	3	M, 4/7 (Cat Manzi)	1:53.4
Rank Hanover, b, h, 4	Albatross	4	M, 6/9 (Ron Waples)	1:53
Raque Bogart, br, h, 4	Falcon Almahurst	1	ScD, 7/7 (Bruce Riegle)	1:54f
Raven Lunatic, b, c, 3	Tyler B	1	M, 6/23 (Michel Lachance)	1:53
Razzle Dazzlem, b, c, 2	Nihilator	1	M, 8/17 (Ron Pierce)	1:53.3
Resonator, b, h, 4	Tyler B	1	RcR, 9/8 (John Campbell)	1:53.1f
Ribb, b, g, 6	Hymnline	3	M, 4/27 (Bill O'Donnell)	1:53.1
Righthand Man, b, c, 3	Cam Fella	2	GSP, 10/5 (Mickey McNichol)	1:52.3
Robert Lobell, b, h, 4	No Nukes	1	M, 5/19 (Michel Lachance)	1:52.4
Rock Legend, b, c, 3	Silent Majority	1	Mea, 8/4 (Doug Snyder)	1:53.2f
Rudyard Bay, b, h, 4	Conquered	1	M, 6/21 (Bill O'Donnell)	1:53.3
Rulers Chippie, b, f, 3	Radiant Ruler	2	PPk, 12/29 (Bruce Ranger)	1:52.3f
Safe Haven, b, h, 4	Storm Damage	2	M, 4/28 (John Campbell)	1:52.4
Sammy Almahurst, br, h, 5	Big Towner	1	GSP, 11/17 (Joe Schwind)	1:53.3
San Andre, b, h, 4	Albatross	1	M, 6/9 (John Plutino)	1:53
Sandman Hanover, br, g, 4	Big Towner	2	Edm, 10/13 (Jay Picciano)	1:53.3f
Scoot Outa Reach, b, c, 3	Direct Scooter	2	M, 8/8 (Bill O'Donnell)	1:53.2
Scurrilous, b, h, 4	Precious Fella	1	M, 4/21 (Cat Manzi)	1:54
Sea The USA, ch, c, 3	Seahawk Hanover	1	VD, 9/3 (Gerry Procino)	1:53.3q
See You There, b, h, 8	Good To See You	2	M, 5/26 (John Monaco)	1:53
Seeker Almahurst, b, c, 3	Trim The Tree	1	GSP, 9/12 (Rick Farrington)	1:53.2
Seltzer Blue, b, c, 3	Quality Blue Chip	1	M, 5/25 (John Campbell)	1:53.4
Set To Go A, b, m, 5	Three Times One	4	GSP, 8/24 (Michel Lachance)	1:53
Shadydale Special, b, f, 3	B Gs Bunny	1	GSP, 10/5 (Mickey McNichol)	1:54
Shannon Brooks, b, h, 6	Trenton	1	Lex, 6/23 (Jim Cummins)	1:54
Sharvid Fella, b, h, 6	Most Happy Fella	1	GrR, 7/28 (John Holmes)	1:54f
Sherwood Abe, br, h, 6	Abercrombie	3	M, 5/26 (Cat Manzi)	1:53
Shipps Fella, b, h, 5	Cam Fella	1	GrR, 6/15 (Tim Twaddle)	1:54f
Shipps Schnoops, gr, c, 3	On The Road Again	3	PPk, 12/29 (Tommy Haughton)	1:51.4f
Shogun Hanover, b, g, 3	Tyler B	6	M, 8/17 (Ron Waples)	1:52.3

DASHES AND SPEED

Horse	Sire	Wins	Race Info	Time
Skipper Forrest, br, h, 4	Scarlet Skipper	1	NBD, 7/7 (Henri Filion)	1:53.2f
Smiling Rebecca, b, f, 3	Nihilator	1	Lex, 9/26 (Michel Lachance) T	1:52.1
Soaring Falcon, b, h, 4	Falcon Almahurst	1	M, 8/18 (Bill Bresnahan)	1:52.1
Soft Light, b, h, 5	Storm Damage	3	Moh, 10/20 (Mike Saftic)	1:53.2f
Spirited Style, b, c, 3	Walton Hanover	1	Mea, 8/11 (John Campbell)	1:52.4
Star Splash, b, h, 5	Trim The Tree	1	GrR, 7/28 (Dave Wall)	1:53.1f
Stealage, b, h, 4	Legal Notice	1	VD, 7/21 (Wally Hennessey)	1:54q
Stony Ford Nick, b, h, 4	Allwin Steady	2	GrR, 7/28 (Steve Condren)	1:53.3f
Storm Compensation, br, h, 4	Storm Damage	4	M, 7/13 (John Campbell)	1:52.3
Storm Prince, b, h, 6	Storm Damage	2	LA, 1/27 (Jim Morand)	1:53.3f
Super Pickle, b, g, 5	Super Bradshaw	1	M, 8/4 (Howard Parker)	1:53.1
Sweet Sharon, b, m, 6	No Nukes	1	M, 3/9 (Jack Moiseyev)	1:53.3
T K's Skipper, br, h, 5	Governor Skipper	13	DuQ, 9/1 (Michel Lachance) T	1:49.2
Tamarama Rip, b, h, 5	Crosscurrent	3	Moh, 9/9 (Dave Smith)	1:53f
Tax Credit N, b, g, 7	Sir Dalrae	3	M, 4/21 (John Campbell)	1:52.2
Thailand, b, h, 4	Tyler B	1	M, 6/9 (Joe Schwind)	1:53.1
The Chicago Baron, b, h, 7	Whata Baron	1	BB, 7/15 (Henri Filion)	1:53.3f
Three Martinis, b, h, 4	Abercrombie	3	M, 6/23 (Jim Marshall)	1:53
Three Wizzards, b, c, 2	Albatross	1	M, 8/10 (Ben Webster)	1:54
Throned, b, h, 5	Albatross	1	RcR, 6/2 (Don Irvine, Jr.)	1:53.2f
Ticket To Heaven, br, h, 5	No Nukes	2	M, 6/23 (Mickey McNichol)	1:52
Till We Meet Again, br, c, 3	Sonsam	2	GSP, 9/29 (Cat Manzi)	1:53.1
Timber Jack, b, g, 4	Flying Bret	1	M, 1/17 (Ben Webster)	1:54
Tip'n Tax, b, f, 3	Abercrombie	1	DuQ, 8/30 (Tom Harmer)	1:53
Todd's Mark, b, g, 3	Lon Todd Hanover	1	PPk, 4/9 (Don Harmon)	1:53.2f
Token Gesture, b, f, 3	Direct Scooter	1	M, 5/31 (Eldon Harner)	1:54
Too Good, b, c, 3	Direct Scooter	2	M, 6/2 (Michel Lachance)	1:52
Topnotcher, b, h, 4	Abercrombie	10	Moh, 5/27 (Doug Brown)	1:52.2f
Touchdown Pass, b, h, 5	Big Towner	2	PPk, 2/3 (Kevin Wallis)	1:53.2f
Town Pro, br, f, 3	Big Towner	7	M, 8/4 (Doug Brown)	1:51.4
Tranquil Storm, b, h, 5	Storm Damage	3	PPk, 1/6 (Mickey McNichol)	1:53.2f
Trenton Spur, br, h, 4	Trenton	2	PPk, 2/17 (Kevin Wallis)	1:53.1f
Tyler's Best, b, h, 4	Tyler B	1	GSP, 10/13 (Ron Pierce)	1:53.4
Tyler's Point, b, h, 5	Tyler B	1	PPk, 2/17 (Wally Hennessey)	1:53.4f
Tyrannical, b, h, 5	Tyler B	6	M, 6/9 (Joe Schwind)	1:52
Under Siege, b, c, 3	No Nukes	1	M, 6/15 (Donald Dancer)	1:53.4
United Gambler, b, h, 4	No Nukes	2	M, 8/18 (Ben Webster)	1:53.2
Vance Lobell N, b, g, 6	Vance Hanover	1	LA, 10/20 (Ross Croghan)	1:53.4f
W A Thiamine, b, g, 6	Warren Hanover	1	PPk, 3/17 (Ron Waples)	1:53.4f
We The People, br, c, 3	Direct Scooter	1	M, 8/9 (Michel Lachance)	1:53.4
Wellsford Lad N, br, g, 6	Vance Hanover	1	M, 5/12 (Michel Lachance)	1:54
White Ruffles, gr, m, 4	Billy Dart	4	M, 5/25 (John Campbell)	1:53.2
Wightwater Canyon, b, h, 7	Isle Of Wight	1	M, 7/21 (John Campbell)	1:54
Willie Mays, b, h, 6	Hot Hitter	1	M, 6/9 (Michael Fagliarone)	1:53.2
Wondersam, b, h, 7	Sonsam	1	M, 2/9 (Joe Schwind)	1:53.3
Woodie Wright, b, g, 3	Duncans Wright	1	RcR, 6/23 (Jim Morand)	1:53.3f
Woodland, b, c, 3	No Nukes	1	M, 6/22 (John Campbell)	1:53.1
Wrapped, b, h, 4	Signed And Sealed	1	M, 2/24 (Cat Manzi)	1:54

DASHES AND SPEED
THE TOP ALL-TIME 1:55 TROTTERS

Below are listed all the 1:55 trotters in harness racing history. Given is the name of the performer, color, sex, and sire. Next comes the detail on each 1:55 mile, including the age of the performer, age, track, date, driver, and time. 1:55 performances are listed chronologically. Time trials are indicated by a "T."

Horse, color, sex	Sire	Age	Track	Date	Driver		Time
A Go Go Lauxmont, b, c	Balanced Image	3	Lex	9/30/88	Ron Waples	T	1:54.3
Armbro Goal, b, c, 3	Speedy Crown	3	M	7/28/88	John Campbell		1:54.4
		3	M	8/6/88	John Campbell		1:54.3
		3	DuQ	9/3/88	Berndt Lindstedt		1:55
Arndon, b, c	Arnie Almahurst	3	Lex	10/6/82	Delvin Miller	T	1:54
Cornstalk, b, c	Lindys Pride	3	Spr	8/15/84	Howard Beissinger		1:53.4
Crown's Best, b, c	Speedy Crown	3	Sycs	8/16/87	Per Eriksson		1:54.2
Crowning Point, b, c	Speedy Crown	3	Spr	8/16/84	Doug Ackerman		1:54
Diamond Exchange, b, 4	Arnie Almahurst	4	M	7/4/83	Robert Williams		1:55
Dicks Bell, b, h	Cold Comfort	4	Spr	8/19/87	Ray Remmen	T	1:53.4
Embassy Lobell, b, c	Speedy Crown	3	Lex	9/28/90	Michel Lachance		1:54.4
Express Ride, b, h	Super Bowl	4	SPk	9/6/87	Berndt Lindstedt		1:55f
		4	Lex	9/25/87	Berndt Lindstedt		1:53
Fancy Crown, br, f	Speedy Crown	3	Spr	8/16/84	Bill O'Donnell		1:53.4
		3	DuQ	9/1/84	Bill O'Donnell		1:54.4
Firm Tribute, b, c	Bonefish	3	Lex	9/30/88	Mark O'Mara		1:54.3
Florida Pro, br, c	Arnie Almahurst	3	DuQ	9/2/78	George Sholty		1:55
Franconia, b, m	Nevele Thunder	6	M	7/20/87	John Campbell		1:55
Friendly Face, b, h	Speedy Somolli	4	M	5/2/88	Kevin Lare		1:55.4
		4	M	5/30/88	Kevin Lare		1:54.1
Go Get Lost, b, r	Speedy Somolli	4	M	6/25/88	Tom Sells		1:54.3
Harmonious, b, c	Crowning Point	3	M	8/4/90	John Campbell		1:54.1
		3	M	8/4/90	John Campbell		1:55
		3	DuQ	9/1/90	Cat Manzi		1:53.2
Huggie Hanover, br, c	Florida Pro	3	Lex	10/7/88	Ron Waples		1:55
I'm Impeccable, b, g	Coleman Lobell	3	Lex	9/28/90	Sam "Chip" Noble		1:54.2
Jazz Cosmos, b, c	Speedy Crown	3	Lex	10/2/82	Mickey McNichol		1:55
Jeanne's Somolli, b, c	Speedy Somolli	3	Lex	10/5/90	Rod Allen		1:54.2
Keystone Harem, b, f	Super Bowl	3	Spr	8/20/87	Jan Nordin		1:53.4
		3	Spr	8/20/87	Jan Nordin		1:53.4
		3	DuQ	9/4/87	Jan Nordin		1:54.4
Kit Lobell, b, m	Speedy Crown	5	M	6/27/90	Berndt Lindstedt		1:54.4
Lindys Crown, b, h	Lindys Pride	4	DuQ	8/30/80	Howard Beissinger		1:54.4
Lucious Almahurst, b, f	Bonefish	3	DuQ	9/4/87	Ron Waples		1:54.4
Mack Lobell, br, c	Mystic Park	3	M	7/24/87	John Campbell		1:54
		3	M	8/8/87	John Campbell		1:53.3
		3	M	8/8/87	John Campbell		1:54
		3	Spr	8/21/87	John Campbell		1:52.1
		3	Lex	10/2/87	John Campbell		1:55
		3	PPk	11/13/87	John Campbell		1:54.1f
Meadow Road, br, h	Madison Avenue	6	M	6/24/85	Torbjorn Jansson		1:54.2
Nan's Catch, b, f	Bonefish	3	Spr	8/18/88	Berndt Lindstedt		1:54.4
Napoletano, b, c	Super Bowl	3	DuQ	9/5/87	Bill O'Donnell		1:53.2
		3	DuQ	9/5/87	Bill O'Donnell		1:54.4
		3	Lex	9/25/87	Bill O'Donnell		1:54.3
		3	Lex	9/25/87	Bill O'Donnell		1:54.4
		5	M	7/1/89	Stig Johansson		1:54.1
Nearly Perfect, b, h	Songcan	4	M	6/16/86	Mickey McNichol		1:55
		4	M	6/30/86	Mickey McNichol		1:54.3
		4	M	7/7/86	Mickey McNichol		1:54
Nero Domarr, b, c	Worthy Bowl	3	Lex	10/1/88	Ron Waples	T	1:54.4
Nevele Pride, b, h	Stars Pride	4	Ind	8/31/69	Stanley Dancer	T	1:54.4

DASHES AND SPEED

Horse	Sire	Age	Track	Date	Driver		Time
No Sex Please, br, h	Brisco Hanover	5	Lex	10/4/90	Ron Waples		1:55
		3	PPk	11/2/90	Ron Waples		1:55f
Noxie Hanover, b, f	Super Bowl	2	Lex	9/19/88	John Simpson, Jr.	T	1:55
Peace Corps, b, f	Baltic Speed	3	Ind	8/25/89	John Campbell		1:54.1
		3	DuQ	9/2/89	John Campbell		1:52.4
		3	Lex	10/6/89	John Campbell		1:54.2
		4	PPk	11/2/90	Stig Johannson		1:54.2f
Prakas, b, c	Speedy Crown	3	M	8/3/85	Bill O'Donnell		1:54.3
		3	DuQ	8/31/85	Bill O'Donnell		1:53.2
Premium Lobell, b, h	Speedy Crown	4	DuQ	9/1/84	Dan Shetler		1:54.3
Probe, b, c	Super Bowl	3	M	8/5/89	Bill Fahy		1:54.3
Sandy Bowl, b, h	Super Bowl	4	Lex	9/29/85	Jan Nordin	T	1:54.1
Speedy Somolli, b, c	Speedy Crown	3	DuQ	9/2/78	Howard Beissinger		1:55
Spotlite Lobell, b, c	Speedy Somolli	3	Spr	8/21/87	Walter Paisley		1:55
Star Mystic, b, c	Mystic Park	3	Lex	10/5/90	Jan Johnson		1:54.3
Sugarcane Hanover, b, h	Florida Pro	4	M	8/7/87	Ron Waples		1:54.3
Super Arnie, b, c	Super Bowl	3	Spr	8/17/90	Berndt Lindstedt		1:54.1
		3	Spr	8/17/90	Berndt Lindstedt		1:55
		3	DuQ	9/1/90	Berndt Lindstedt		1:54.3
Supergill, b, c	Super Bowl	3	Spr	8/19/88	Berndt Lindstedt		1:53.3

THE ALL-TIME 1:52 PACERS

Below are listed all the 1:52 pacers in harness racing history. Given is the name of the performer, color, sex, and sire. Next comes the detail on each 1:52 mile, including the age of the performer, track, date, driver and time. 1:52 performances are listed chronologically. Time trials are indicated by a "T."

Horse, color, sex	Sire	Age	Track	Date	Driver		Time
Amity Chef, b, c	French Chef	3	Lex	9/27/86	John Campbell		1:51.1
Armbro Aussie, b c	Most Happy Fella	3	Lex	10/2/82	Glen Garnsey		1:51.4
Armbro Emerson, b, h	Abercrombie	4	Lex	9/26/87	Jim Whelan	T	1:51.4
Armbro Feather, b, m	Most Happy Fella	5	M	8/5/89	John Kopas		1:51.3
Artsplace, b, c	Abercrombie	2	PPk	11/30/90	John Campbell		1:51.1f
Banker Blue Chip, b, c	Brand New Fella	3	M	6/13/87	John Campbell		1:51.4
		3	M	6/20/87	John Campbell		1:51.4
		4	M	5/28/88	Bill O'Donnell		1:52
		4	M	7/15/88	Bill O'Donnell		1:52
Barberry Spur, b, c	Niatross	3	Lex	9/26/86	Bill O'Donnell	T	1:50.2
Beach Towel, b, c	French Chef	3	Mea	8/11/90	Ray Remmen		1:51.4f
		3	DuQ	8/30/90	Ray Remmen		1:50
		3	Lex	9/29/90	Ray Remmen		1:51.1
		3	Lex	9/29/90	Ray Remmen		1:51.3
		3	PPk	11/2/90	Ray Remmen		1:51.2
Bond Street, b, h	Abercrombie	4	Lex	10/5/89	Bill Gale	T	1:52
Boston Blue Chip, ch, c	On The Road Again	3	M	8/4/90	Joe Schwind		1:51.1
Brando Hanover, b, c	Walton Hanover	3	M	8/3/90	Mickey McNichol		1:51.3
Caesars Jackpot, b, m	Walton Hanover	4	M	6/8/90	Bill Fahy		1:51.4
		4	M	8/4/90	Bill Fahy		1:51.2
Call For Rain, b, c	Storm Damage	3	Lex	9/26/87	Clint Galbraith		1:52
		4	M	4/2/88	Clint Galbraith		1:52
		4	M	5/14/88	Clint Galbraith		1:51.3
		4	M	7/2/88	Clint Galbraith		1:51.4
		4	M	10/1/88	Clint Galbraith		1:49.3
Cameleon, br, h	Cam Fella	5	M	6/9/90	Ron Waples		1:51.3

DASHES AND SPEED

Name	Sire	Age	Track	Date	Driver	Time
Camtastic, br, c	Cam Fella	3	M	7/8/88	Bill O'Donnell	1:51.3
		3	Lex	10/1/88	Bill O'Donnell	1:51
		3	Lex	10/1/88	Bill O'Donnell	1:51.1
		4	M	5/20/89	John Campbell	1:52
		4	Spr	8/17/89	Michel Lachance T	1:49.3
		4	DuQ	9/2/89	John Campbell	1:52
Colt Fortysix, b, c	Albatross	3	Spr	8/16/84	Chris Boring	1:50.3
Cue Light, b, c	Strike Out	3	Lex	9/26/87	John Campbell	1:51.2
Curragh, b, h	Abercrombie	5	Lex	9/30/88	John Campbell T	1:51.4
Dangarvon, b, h	Bret Hanover	4	M	7/5/86	Ben Webster	1:52
Dare You To, b, h	Abercrombie	5	PPk	10/20/90	Wally Hennessey	1:51.4f
Deal Direct, b, c	Direct Scooter	2	Ind	8/25/90	Sam "Chip" Noble	1:51.4
Dexter Nukes, b, c	No Nukes	3	M	7/7/89	John Campbell	1:51.3
		3	M	7/14/89	John Campbell	1:51.3
Dignatarian, b, h	Tyler B	5	M	6/19/87	Earl Cruise	1:52
Dont Dally, b, f	Meadow Skipper	3	DuQ	8/30/84	John Campbell	1:51.3
Dorunrun Bluegrass, b, h	Fortune Richie	4	M	5/19/90	Ron Pierce	1:51.3
Dragon's Lair, b, h	Tyler B	5	VD	7/11/87	John Campbell	1:51.3q
Drawing Board, br, c	Walton Hanover	3	Ind	8/26/89	Bill Gale	1:51.4
Equitable, blk, b	Governor Skipper	4	M	7/25/86	Jim Doherty	1:51.4
Even Hand, br, h	No Nukes	4	M	4/27/90	Bill O'Donnell	1:52
Falcon Seelster, b, c	Warm Breeze	3	Dela	9/19/85	Tom Harmer	1:51h
		4	Mea	7/4/86	Tom Harmer	1:51.3f
Fan Hanover, b, m	Albatross	4	Lex	10/2/82	Glen Garnsey T	1:50.4
Forbidden Past, b, m	Albatross	4	Lex	10/1/86	Michel Lachance T	1:51.2
Forrest Skipper, b, h	Scarlet Skipper	4	M	5/10/86	Lucien Fontaine	1:51.3
		4	M	5/15/86	Lucien Fontaine	1:51.3
		4	M	6/5/86	Lucien Fontaine	1:51.3
		4	M	6/13/86	Lucien Fontaine T	1:50.3
		4	M	7/26/86	Lucien Fontaine Q	1:51.1
Franz Hanover, b, h	Tyler B	5	M	8/8/87	Billy Herman	1:52
Frugal Gourmet, b, c	French Chef	3	M	7/10/87	Trevor Ritchie	1:51.3
		3	M	7/17/87	Trevor Ritchie	1:52
		3	M	8/6/87	Trevor Ritchie	1:51.3
		3	Lex	9/26/87	Trevor Ritchie	1:52
Genghis Khan, br, h	Meadow Skipper	6	M	8/13/82	Bill O'Donnell	1:51.4
Goalie Jeff, b, c	Cam Fella	3	M	8/4/89	Michel Lachance	1:51.3
		3	M	8/4/89	Michel Lachance	1:51.3
		3	Lex	9/30/89	Michel Lachance	1:51.3
		3	Lex	10/6/89	Michel Lachance	1:51.2
Governors Choice, b, h	Governor Skipper	6	GSP	9/13/86	Jim Doherty	1:52
		7	M	7/3/87	Jim Doherty	1:51.3
Guts, b, c	Raven Hanover	3	Lex	10/5/84	Mike Gagliardi	1:52
		4	DuQ	8/29/85	Bill O'Donnell T	1:51.3
Indian Alert, b, g	Armbro Alert	3	Lex	5/25/87	Larry Noggle	1:51.3
		4	M	6/17/88	Jack Moiseyev	1:51.1
Its Fritz, b, h	Keystone Ore	4	Lex	10/7/83	Martin Allen	1:51.4
In The Pocket, b, c	Direct Scooter	3	M	6/30/90	John Campbell	1:51.2
		3	M	8/3/90/	John Campbell	1:51.3
		3	Mea	8/11/90	John Campbell	1:50.4f
		3	Lex	9/28/90	John Campbell T	1:49.3
Jaguar Spur, b, c	Albatross	3	Lex	9/26/87	Dick Stillings	1:51.2
		3	Lex	9/26/87	Dick Stillings	1:51.3
		4	M	7/9/88	Dick Stillings	1:50.3
		4	M	8/6/88	Dick Stillings	1:50.3
		4	Lex	10/8/88	Dick Stillings T	1:49.2
		5	M	7/15/89	Ray Remmen	1:51.4
		5	Lex	9/30/89	Dick Stillings	1:51
Jate Lobell, b, c	No Nukes	3	M	5/29/87	Mark O'Mara	1:51.4
		3	M	6/6/87	Mark O'Mara	1:51.2
		3	Spr	8/18/87	Mark O'Mara	1:51.3
Joe's Scooter, b, h	Direct Scooter	7	M	6/9/90	Joe Schwind	1:51.4

DASHES AND SPEED

Kentucky Spur, b, c	Abercrombie	3	Lex	9/30/89	Dick Stillings	1:52
Keystone Raider, b, c	Big Towner	3	Lex	10/6/88	Michel Lachance	1:51.4
		4	M	6/3/89	Michel Lachance	1:52
		4	M	6/17/89	Bill O'Donnell	1:51.1
Kiev Hanover, b, c	Albatross	3	Spr	8/16/90	Bill Fahy T	1:51.1
		3	Lex	9/29/90	Jim Morand	1:51.1
		3	Lex	10/5/90	Jim Morand	1:50.1
L Dees Trish, b, f	Merger	2	Lex	10/1/88	Michel Lachance	1:52
Laag, gr, c	Abercrombie	3	M	6/27/87	Bill O'Donnell	1:51.3
		3	Lex	9/26/87	Dick Farrington	1:51.2
Matt's Scooter, b, c	Direct Scooter	3	M	6/11/88	Michel Lachance	1:52
		3	Lex	9/23/88	Michel Lachance T	1:48.2
		4	M	6/24/89	Michel Lachance	1:51
		4	M	7/1/89	Michel Lachance	1:50.2
		4	M	7/8/89	Michel Lachance	1:50.1
		4	M	8/5/89	Michel Lachance	1:50.3
		4	Moh	10/1/89	Michel Lachance	1:51f
		4	Edm	10/14/89	Michel Lachance	1:52f
Miss Easy, b, f	Amity Chef	1	Lex	9/25	John Campbell	1:51.2
Niatross, b, c	Albatross	3	Lex	10/1/80	Clint Galbraith T	1:49.1
Nihilator, b, c	Niatross	3	M	6/29/85	Bill O'Donnell	1:52
		3	M	7/19/85	Bill O'Donnell	1:50.3
		3	M	8/3/85	Bill O'Donnell	1:49.3
		3	Lex	9/28/85	Bill O'Donnell	1:51.2
		3	Lex	10/4/85	Bill O'Donnell	1:51.1
On The Road Again, ch, h	Happy Motoring	4	M	8/3/85	Buddy Gilmour	1:51.4
Pan Am Sam, b, h	Sonsam	5	M	8/12/88	Cat Manzi	1:51.4
Prince Ebony, blk, h	Conquered	7	M	8/4/90	Ron Pierce	1:52
Ramblin' Storm, b, h	Storm Damage	6	M	5/28/88	Bill O'Donnell	1:51.4
		6	M	6/18/88	Michel Lachance	1:51.4
		6	M	6/25/88	Michel Lachance	1:51.3
		6	M	7/8/88	Michel Lachance	1:50.1
		6	M	7/30/88	Michel Lachance	1:51
		7	M	8/5/89	Bill O'Donnell	1:52
		7	M	8/19/89	Michel Lachance	1:52
River Rouge, b, c	Albatross	3	Spr	8/16/84	Dave Rankin	1:52
Run The Table, b, c	Landslide	3	M	5/22/87	John Campbell	1:51
		3	M	7/10/87	John Campbell	1:51.4
		3	M	8/6/87	John Campbell	1:51.1
		3	M	8/6/87	John Campbell	1:51.1
Runnymede Lobell, b, 4	Nero	4	Sycs	8/18/89	Yves Filion T	1:51.2
Save Fuel, b, h	Bret Hanover	4	M	8/17/85	John Campbell	1:51.4
		5	M	5/31/86	John Campbell	1:51.1
Shipps Schnoops, gr, c	On The Road Again	3	PPk	12/29/90	Tommy Haughton	1:51.4f
Steady Star, b, h	Steady Beau	4	Lex	10/1/71	Joe O'Brien T	1:52
Stonebridge Skipper, b, h	Scarlet Skipper	5	M	6/13/87	John Campbell	1:51.3
		5	M	6/20/87	John Campbell	1:51.2
		5	M	8/8/87	John Campbell	1:51.3
T K's Skipper, br, h	Governor Skipper	4	M	5/6/89	Michel Lachance	1:51.4
		4	M	7/22/89	Michel Lachance	1:52
		4	M	8/5/89	Michel Lachance	1:51
		4	GSP	9/16/89	Michel Lachance	1:52
		5	M	5/26/90	Michel Lachance	1:52
		5	M	7/7/90	Michel Lachance	1:51.2
		5	M	8/17/90	Michel Lachance	1:50.3
		5	DuQ	9/1/90	Michel Lachance T	1:49.2
		5	LA	9/29/90	Joe Anderson	1:51.2f
The Denman, b, h	Sonsam	4	M	7/18/86	Peter Ruscitto	1:52
Threefold, br, c	Big Towner	3	Spr	8/18/88	John Campbell	1:51.1
Ticket To Heaven, br, h	No Nukes	4	M	7/22/89	John Campbell	1:52
		5	M	6/23/90	Mickey McNichol	1:52
Too Good, b, c	Direct Scooter	3	M	6/2/90	Michel Lachance	1:52

DASHES AND SPEED

Town Pro, br, f	Big Towner	3	M	8/4/90	Doug Brown		1:51.4
Tranquil Storm, b, h	Storm Damage	4	M	8/12/89	John Plutino		1:52
Trenton, br, c	Meadow Skipper	3	Spr	8/21/82	Tommy Haughton		1:51.3
Trini Hanover, b, c	Big Towner	3	Spr	8/17/88	Ron Waples	T	1:51.2
Tucson Hanover, b, h	Albatross	4	M	8/1/87	Michel Lachance		1:51.3
Tyler's Mark, b, c	Tyler B	3	Lex	9/27/86	John Campbell		1:51.3
Tyrannical, b, h	Tyler B	5	M	6/9/90	Joe Schwind		1:52
Umbrella Fella, b, h	Governor Skipper	4	Lex	10/4/84	Ray Remmen	T	1:52
What's Next, b, h	Most Happy Fella	4	M	6/7/86	Mickey McNichol		1:51.3

(**Note:** More detailed 2:00 information on horses is published annually in the USTA Yearbook, or may be obtained from the USTA's Information and Research Department in Columbus.)

TOP SINGLE-SEASON 2:00 PERFORMERS

Trotters | | | Pacers

2-YEAR-OLDS

Trotters		Category	Pacers	
Mack Lobell (1986)	7	**Colt**	Jate Lobell (1986)	14
Buckfinder (1986)	7			
Backstreet Guy (1989)	7			
Royal Troubador (1989)	7			
Peace Corps (1988)	10	**Filly**	Central Park West (1988)	16
			Miss Easy (1990)	16
Armbro Crouch (1983)	2	**Gelding**	Scotch Baker (1989)	10
Tarport Ramey (1986)	2			
I'm Impeccable (1989)	2			
R Pappy (1989)	2			

3-YEAR-OLDS

Trotters		Category	Pacers	
Mack Lobell (1987)	16	**Colt**	Nihilator (1985)	25
Peace Coprs (1989)	17	**Filly**	Anniecrombie (1986)	18
I'm Impeccable	6	**Gelding**	Quite A Sensation (1986)	16
			Indian Alert (1987)	16
			Ivan (1988)	16

4-YEAR-OLDS

Trotters		Category	Pacers	
Mack Lobell (1988)	14	**Horse**	Cam Fella (1982)	32
Grades Singing (1986)	12	**Mare**	Armbro Feather (1988)	18
Keystone Sheik (1989)	11	**Gelding**	Eagle Speaker (1990)	15

AGED

Trotters		Category	Pacers	
Manfred Hanover (1985)	16	**Horse**	T K's Skipper (1990)	23
Babe Kosmos (1985)	10	**Mare**	Armbro Feather (1989)	22
Scenic Regal (1990)	10			
Free Token (1990)	10			
No Sex Please (1990)	17	**Gelding**	Division Street (1985)	22

DASHES AND SPEED

TOP 2:00 PERFORMERS OF 1990

Trotters

1. No Sex Please — 17
2. Super Scotch S J — 16
3. Incredible D J — 15
4. Nothing Ventured — 11
   Model Home — 11
6. Jeff's Playboy — 10
   Harmonious — 10
   Florida Jewel — 10
   A Js Image — 10
   Slybowl Hanover — 10
   Scenic Regal — 10
   Free Token — 10

Pacers

1. T K's Skipper — 23
2. Beach Towel — 22
3. Apaches Fame — 20
4. Dorunrun Bluegrass — 18
   In The Pocket — 18
   Jake And Elwood — 18
7. Laurstar — 17
8. Millers Aussie — 16
   Miss Easy — 16
   Rulers Chippie — 16
   Topnotcher — 16

TOP 2:00 PERFORMERS, ALL-TIME

Trotters

	Horse	Years Raced	No.
1.	Mack Lobell	(1986-89)	37
2.	Manfred Hanover	(1983-90)	34
3.	Scenic Regal, m	(1985-90)	32
4.	Free Token, m	(1986-1990)	31
5.	Go Get Lost, r	(1986-1990)	28
	Peace Corps, f	(1988-1990)	28
7.	Gentle Stroke, g	(1983-1989)	21
8.	Whip It Wood	(1983-90)	26
9.	Greyhound, g	(1934-40)	25
	No Sex Please, g	(1987-90)	25
11.	Dicks Bell	(1985-89)	24
12.	Ima Lula, m	(1975-80)	22
	Jeff's Playboy, g	(1986-90)	22
	Skullangel, g	(1979-89)	22
15.	Armbro Fling, m	(1986-88)	19
	Crowns Star	(1976-84)	19
	Nevele Pride	(1967-69)	19
	Schimitar	(1984-89)	19
19.	Fancy Crown, m	(1983-85)	18
	Franconia, m	(1983-88)	18
	Future Pro, g	(1983-90)	18
	Keystone Sheik, g	(1987-90)	18
	Napoletano	(1986-89)	18
	Natural Image, g	(1987-89)	18
	Nevele Typhoon, g	(1985-90)	18
	Royal Prestige	(1985-86)	18
	Sandy Bowl	(1983-85)	18
	Slybowl Hanvoer	(1988-90)	18

Pacers

	Horse	Years Raced	No.
1.	Rambling Willie, g	(1972-83)	79
2.	Anniecrombie, m	(1985-90)	67
3.	Courageous Red	(1980-85)	60
4.	Hoosier Hotshot	(1981-90)	57
5.	Ramblin' Storm	(1984-90)	57
6.	Cam Fella	(1981-83)	55
7.	Ironstone Hello	(1982-90)	54
8.	Armbro Feather, m	(1986-1989)	52
9.	Alvoc	(1981-90)	51
	B C Count	(1975-85)	51
	Betrayal	(1983-90)	51
	Doc's Fella, g	(1980-90)	51
	Escortention	(1985-90)	51
	Jaguar Spur	(1986-1989)	51
15.	C'mon Ashley, m	(1985-1990)	49
	Commanche N, g	(1980-89)	49
	Guts	(1983-1990)	49
	Hothead	(1984-90)	49
	Knightwind	(1981-90)	49
20.	Cordon Cordon, g	(1985-1989)	48
	Take A Look	(1984-90)	48
22.	Particular, g	(1984-90)	47
	Sharp Kosmos, g	(1985-90)	47
	Thunder's Image, g	(1986-90)	47
	Ultra Bright, g	(1985-89)	47
26.	Hanover Knight	(1982-90)	46
	Mannart Tornado	(1981-90)	46
	T K's Skipper	(1988-90)	46

TOP 2:00 PERFORMERS OF 1989

Trotters

1. Peace Corps — 17
2. Keystone Sheik — 11
3. Chicory Wind — 10
   Demilo Hanover — 10
   Incredible M A — 10
   Mathers Streak — 10

Pacers

1. Matt's Scooter — 25
2. Armbro Feather — 22
   Barely Visible — 22
4. Dexter Nukes — 19
5. Best Reason — 18

DASHES AND SPEED

TOP 1:55 PERFORMERS OF 1990

	Horse	1:55 Miles		Horse	1:55 Miles
1.	Beach Towel	20	10.	Shogun Hanover (g)	8
2.	T K's Skipper	19	11.	Bay's Fella	7
3.	Apaches Fame	13		Die Laughing	7
	In The Pocket	13		How Bout It	7
5.	Topnotcher	12		Mark Johnathan	7
6.	Dorunrun Bluegrass	10		Prince Ebony	7
7.	Caesars Jackpot (m)	9		Tamarama Rip	7
	Jake And Elwood	9		White Ruffles	7
	Town Pro (f)	9			

TOP 1:55 PERFORMERS, ALL-TIME

	Horse	1:55 Miles		Horse	1:55 Miles
1.	Ramblin' Storm	34	18.	In The Pocket	16
2.	T K's Skipper	30		Save Fuel	16
3.	Jaguar Spur	27	20.	Topnotcher	15
	Matt's Scooter	27	21.	Apaches Fame	14
5.	Beach Towel	25		Caesars Jackpot	14
6.	Camtastic	24		Escortention	14
7.	Banker Blue Chip	22		Fortitude Hanover	14
	Nihilator	22		Tranquil Storm	14
9.	American Freedom	20	26.	Goalie Jeff	13
	Forrest Skipper	20		Incredible Finale	13
	Guts	20		Jate Lobell	13
12.	Falcon Seelster	19		Mystery Fund	13
13.	Governors Choice	18		Niatross	13
	Instrument Landing	18		On The Road Again	13
15.	Cam Fella	17		Saute	13
	Robust Hanover	17		Shannon Brooks	13
	Run The Table	17		Storm Prince	13

TOP 1:55 PERFORMERS OF 1989

	Horse	1:55 Miles		Horse	1:55 Miles
1.	Matt's Scooter	17		Ramblin' Storm	7
2.	Goalie Jeff	13	11.	Banker Blue Chip	6
3.	T K's Skipper	11		Crystal Tree	6
4.	Dexter Nukes	10		Escortention	6
5.	Armbro Feather	8		Money Money Money	6
	Camtastic	8		One Nighter	6
	Mystery Fund	8		Scene Topper	6
8.	Amazing Fella	7		Soft Light	6
	Barefoot Hanover	7			

TOP 1:55 PERFORMERS OF 1988

	Horse	1:55 Miles		Horse	1:55 Miles
1.	Ramblin' Storm	14	9.	Banker Blue Chip	5
2.	Camtastic	13		Fortitude Hanover	5
3.	Jaguar Spur	12		Hothead	5
4.	Matt's Scooter	10		Indian Alert	5
5.	Singing Strings	9		Keystone Raider	5
6.	Call For Rain	8		Kiwi River N	5
7.	Albert Albert	7		Storm Prince	5
8.	Hug A Beat	6		Threefold	5
				Wholesale	5

DASHES AND SPEED

SEASON'S CHAMPION TROTTERS

Track	Div.	Horse	Driver	Track	Date		Time
Mile Track	2yoc	Dontellmenomore	John Campbell	Lex	September 25		1:56.2
	2yof	My Wildirish Rose	Harold Kelly	GSP	October 17		1:57.4
	2yog	United Colors	Tommy Haughton	M	July 17		2:00
	3yoc	Harmonious	Cat Manzi	DuQ	September 1		1:53.2
	3yof	Happy Diamonds	John Campbell	DuQ	August 31		1:55.1
	3yog	I'm Impeccable	Sam "Chip" Noble	Lex	September 28	+	1:54.2
	4yos	Prince Mystic	Ray Remmen	M	June 13		1:56.3
	4yom	Luanne Kash	Clint Galbraith	Sycs	August 4		1:56.3
	4yog	War Nickel	Raymond Tremblay	GSP	October 18	=	1:56
	as	Slybowl Hanover	Pekka Korpi	M	June 6		1:55.2
	am	Kit Lobell	Berndt Lindstedt	M	June 22	+	1:54.4
	ag	No Sex Please	Ron Waples	Lex	October 4	+	1:55
5/8-Mile Track	2yoc	Crysta's Best	Dick Richardson, Jr.	ScD	September 3		1:58.2f
	2yof	Esprit Spur	Dick Stillings	PPk	November 9		1:58f
	2yog	Sammy Silk	Steve Byron	WR	October 14	+	2:00f
	3yoc	Cheyenne Spur	Dick Stillings	RcR	October 13		1:56.2f
	3yof	Kindava Hush	Jan Nordin	PPk	October 20	+	1:56.1f
		Me Maggie	Berndt Lindstedt	PPk	November 9	+	1:56.1f
	3yog	I'm Impeccable	Sam "Chip" Noble	ScD	September 3		1:57.4f
	4yos	Roydon Lad	Don Irvine, Jr.	RcR	July 22		1:56f
	4yom	Peace Corps	Stig Johannson	PPk	November 2	+	1:54.2f
	4yog	Bold Herbert	Bruce Ranger	PPk	February 2		1:56.3f
	as	A C Star	Trevor Ritchie	GrR	June 5		1:56.4f
		Slybowl Hanover	Pekka Korpi	RcR	July 8		1:56.4f
	am	Free Token	Joe Pavia, Jr.	PPk	March 27		1:56.1f
	ag	No Sex Please	Ron Waples	PPk	November 2	+	1:55f
1/2-Mile Track	2yoc	Grundy's Mint	Bill Fahy	Dela	September 18		1:59.1h
	2yof	Frances Jet Boko	Hugo Langeweg	Dela	September 18		1:59.3h
	2yog	Super Fellow	John McMullen	Bdfd	August 6		2:01.3h
	3yoc	Royal Troubador	Carl Allen	YR	July 7		1:58.3h
		Cheyenne Spur	Dick Stillings	YR	July 14		1:58.3h
		Incredible D J	Ron Pierce	Fhld	September 28		1:58.3h
	3yof	Our First	John Campbell	Dela	September 20		1:57.3h
	3yog	Royal Cold	Mel Turcotte	Dela	September 18		2:00.1h
	4yos	Mr Smooth Move	Joe Adamsky	Nfld	June 4		1:59.1h
	4yom	Peach Pit	Buddy Gilmour	Btva	August 24		1:58.2h
	4yog	War Nickel	Raymond Tremblay	YR	August 17	=	1:58.2h
	as	Stoneking	Charles Williams	Nfld	May 5		1:59h
	am	Kit Lobell	Berndt Lindstedt	YR	July 29	+	1:57.2h
	ag	Billie S	Charles Baker	May	April 25		1:58.2h
		Shawland Magic	Carman Hie	Btva	September 1		1:58.2h

"+" - New World Record   = - Equals World Record

DASHES AND SPEED

SEASON'S CHAMPION PACERS

Track	Div.	Horse	Driver	Track	Date		Time
Mile Track	2yoc	Deal Direct	Sam "Chip" Noble	Ind	August 25	+	1:51.4
	2yof	Miss Easy	John Campbell	Lex	September 25	+	1:51.2
	2yog	Mr Gourmet	Tom Harmer	Lex	October 5		1:54
	3yoc	In The Pocket	John Campbell	Lex	September 28	T	1:49.3
	3yof	Town Pro	Doug Brown	M	August 4		1:51.4
	3yog	Boston Blue Chip	Joe Schwind	M	August 4	+	1:51.1
	4yos	Dorunrun Bluegrass	Ron Pierce	M	May 19		1:51.3
	4yom	Caesars Jackpot	Bill Fahy	M	August 4		1:51.2
	4yog	Kuzzin Kat	Jim Doherty	M	June 16		1:52.3
	as	TK's Skipper	Michel Lachance	DuQ	September 1	+ T	1:49.2
	am	Set To Go A	Michel Lachance	GSP	August 24		1:53
	ag	Tax Credit N	John Campbell	M	April 21		1:52.2
5/8-Mile Track	2yoc	Artsplace	John Campbell	PPk	November 2	+	1:51.1f
	2yof	Cams Exotic	Harold Kelly	PPk	November 23		1:54f
		Miss Easy	John Campbell	PPk	November 30		1:54f
	2yog	Henry Wadsworth	Don Harmon	PPk	October 14		1:56.3f
	3yoc	In The Pocket	John Campbell	Mea	August 11	+	1:50.4f
	3yof	Town Pro	Doug Brown	GrR	September 1	+	1:53.1f
	3yog	Minuteman Hill	Kevin Lare	RcR	July 6		1:53f
	4yos	Topnotcher	Doug Brown	Moh	May 27		1:52.2f
		Mystery Fund	Bill Gale	Mea	August 11		1:52.2f
		A J Storm Honor	Kevin Wallis	PPk	October 27		1:52.2f
	4yom	Caesars Jackpot	Wally Hennessey	PPk	October 20	+	1:52.2f
	4yog	Eagle Speaker	John Holmes	GrR	July 6	+	1:52.4f
	as	TK's Skipper	Joe Anderson	LA	September 29	+	1:51.2f
	am	Storm Tossed	Doug Brown	GrR	June 11		1:54.2f
	ag	Night Colt	Mario Baillargeon	GrR	July 21	=	1:52.3f
1/2-Mile Track	2yoc	Tooter Scooter	Bill Fahy	LouD	September 1	+	1:54.1h
		W R H	John Campbell	Dela	September 20	+	1:54.1h
	2yof	Cams Exotic	Harold Kelly	Fhld	August 31		1:56.4h
	2yog	Mugshot Special	Dan Ater	Dela	September 20		1:56.4h
	3yoc	Beach Towel	Ray Remmen	Dela	September 20		1:53.3h
	3yof	Lady Genius	Michel Lachance	Dela	September 21		1:55.2h
	3yog	Camachine	Joe Marsh, Jr.	YR	August 11		1:55.1h
	4yos	Dorunrun Bluegrass	Herve Filion	Fhld	April 21		1:53.1h
	4yom	L Dees Trish	Michel Lachance	YR	November 23	=	1:54.4h
	4yog	Buck And Wing	Walter Paisley	May	April 27		1:54.2h
	as	Chatham Light	Kelly Sheppard	Conn	May 21	+	1:53.3h
	am	C'mon Ashley	Buddy Gilmour	YR	May 19		1:55.4h
	ag	Wiregrass Kerrigan	Jim Curran	May	May 6	+	1:54.1h

"+" - New World Record   = - Equals World Record

Leading Drivers

LEADING DRIVERS

John Campbell

1990 was a typical year for John Campbell: another Hambletonain victory; a couple of Breeders Crown wins; and the top spot in the money standings among drivers. In other words, year-in and year-out you can find the name of John Campbell among the sport's leading drivers; this year you can find the name John Campbell in harness racing's Living Hall of Fame. On July 4, 1991, he will join the other all-time greats, and becomes the second-youngest ever to ascend to the pantheon.

It was inevitable. The 35-year-old has virtually dominated the sport since he left his native London, Ontario in the late 1970s to find fame and fortune at the newly-opened Meadowlands. He has found plenty of both.

Campbell got his start in racing from his father Jim, a respected horseman in the western Ontario region. Campbell had made a reputation for himself at the Detroit area tracks and at Windsor when the Meadowlands opened during the mid-1970s, luring Windsor Raceway secretary Joe DeFrank east. DeFrank remembered the talented Campbell, and urged him to come to the Jersey miler, and now Campbell is the winningest driver in the history of the track.

There is absolutely no truth to the rumor that the United States Trotting Association is going to change the the name of the World Record Table to the "Campbell Chronicles," but if the name *was* changed it would come as no surprise to anyone. Two-time Horse of the Year Mack Lobell has written Campbell's name across the record listings, as have such others as Peace Corps, In The Pocket, Cheery Hello, Franconia, Delray Lobell, Central Park West, and seeming countless others.

While such success sometimes draws the ire and envy of others, the sport is virtually unanimous in it's praise of Campbell. Not only is he a tremendous driver, but he is a valued spokesman for the sport. Because of his glib and generous answers, he is a favorite of the press; because of his great skills and determination, he's a favorite with the betting public; and because of his consumate horsemanship, he's a much sought-after choice of owners and trainers in search of a victory.

An interview after the final Breeders Crown event of 1990 brought out some typical John Campbell. Artsplace had just provided him his latest world record, speeding to an unbelievable 1:51.1f mile, into the teeth of a gale-force wind. Campbell said, "I'd like to take some credit, but I can't." All through the interview, spoken through an easy, wide smile, none among those who heard the simple sentence doubted Campbell's contribution. Great things just happen when he drives.

Year	Starts	Wins	2nd	3rd	UDR	Win Pct.	Purses Won
1972	42	7	5	4	.304	16.67	$4,947
1973	125	19	13	21	.266	15.20	18,311
1974	288	37	34	48	.250	12.85	73,160
1975	353	58	49	43	.282	16.43	170,787
1976	547	80	61	68	.250	14.63	243,335
1977	1,159	188	173	148	.288	16.22	507,634
1978	709	82	93	93	.232	11.57	748,096
1979	1,756	313	278	232	.310	17.82	**3,308,984**
1980	1,881	321	286	221	.294	17.07	**3,732,306**
1981	1,352	217	178	153	.271	16.05	3,166,315
1982	1,407	229	193	186	.283	16.28	4,326,495
1983	1,887	382	297	241	.332	20.24	**6,104,082**
1984	1,921	358	292	242	.313	18.64	7,201,798
1985	2,496	475	381	309	.316	19.03	9,628,116
1986	2,005	406	335	267	.340	20.25	**9,515,055**
1987	2,236	516	337	254	.352	23.08	**10,186,495**
1988	2,088	480	325	257	.357	22.99	**11,148,565**
1989	2,071	425	279	266	.323	20.52	**9,738,450**
1990	2,392	543	385	301	.358	22.70	**11,620,878**
Career:	26,715	5,136	3,994	3,354	.317	19.23	**$91,483,684**

LEADING DRIVERS

HTA DRIVER OF THE YEAR

Each year, Harness Tracks of America presents an award to the driver of the year. The winning driver is not selected by a vote, but is determined by a formula which awards points for finishing in the top 25 in three major driving categories.

These three driving performance categories are: money won, races won, and the Universal Driving Rating System (UDR). A driver must have started at least 1,000 times during the year to qualify for UDR points.

Twenty-five points are awarded for finishing first in each category, 24 for the second, and so on down to one point for 25th place. If a driver finishes in the top 25 in all three categories, he receives a 25 point bonus, thus providing for a potential score of 100 for a driver who wins all three categories. The leading drivers and their point totals are listed below:

Rank	Driver	Purses Earned	(Rank)	Wins	(Rank)	UDR	(Rank)	Points
1.	John Campbell	$11,620,878	(**1st**)	543	(4th)	.358	(5th)	93
2.	Walter Case, Jr.	2,057,184	(25th)	606	(3rd)	.392	(**1st**)	74
3.	Rick Zeron	2,310,374	(21st)	388	(12th)	.376	(3rd)	67
4.	Doug Brown	6,042,217	(3rd)	368	(13th)	.316	(23rd)	64
5.	Walter Paisley	2,942,320	(12th)	340	(16th)	.326	(17th)	58
6.	Mario Baillargeon	2,317,234	(20th)	401	(9th)	.315	(24th)	50
7.	Herve Filion	4,309,598	(5th)	660	(**1st**)	.310	(unpl.)	46
	Cat Manzi	5,511,211	(4th)	641	(2nd)	.286	(unpl.)	46
9.	Dave Palone	1,047,901	(unpl.)	428	(7th)	.381	(2nd)	43
10.	Gaetan Lamy	1,894,118	(unpl.)	460	(6th)	.356	(6th)	40

PREVIOUS HTA DRIVERS OF THE YEAR

(Yearly leaders in each category in **Boldface**)

Year	Driver	Points	Wins	UDRS	Purses
1989	Herve Filion	92	**814**	.340	$5,258,920
1988	John Campbell	94	480	.357	**11,148,565**
1987	Michel Lachance	96	**715**	.369	5,963,008
1986	Michel Lachance	76	**770**	.343	6,473,952
1985	Michel Lachance	93	**592**	.341	5,864,785
1984	William O'Donnell	94	422	.323	**9,059,184**
1983	John Campbell	84	382	.332	**6,104,082**
1982	William O'Donnell	82.5	339	.312	5,755,067
1981	Herve Filion	48	**404**	.296	3,813,996
1980	Ron Waples	81	396	.352	2,099,531
1979	Ron Waples	82	**443**	.355	1,942,454
1978	Carmine Abbatiello and	49	387	.330	**3,344,457**
	Herve Filion	49	**423**	.299	3,256,586
1977	Donald Dancer	68	417	.373	1,166,994
1976	Herve Filion	78	**445**	.326	**2,241,045**
1975	Joe O'Brien	76	219	**.463**	1,288,725
1974	Herve Filion	95	**637**	.360	**3,474,315**
1973	Herve Filion	90	**445**	.350	**2,233,302**
1972	Herve Filion	90	**605**	.373	**2,473,265**
1971	Herve Filion	94	**543**	.393	**1,915,945**
1970	Herve Filion	97	**486**	.400	**1,647,837**
1969	Herve Filion	90	**394**	.397	**1,191,224**
1968	Stanley Dancer	94	215	**.511**	1,488,025

LEADING DRIVERS

LEADING DASHWINNING DRIVERS – 1990

1.	Herve Filion	660	6.	Gaetan Lamy	460
2.	Cat Manzi	641	7.	Dave Palone	428
3.	Walter Case, Jr.	606	8.	Ron Marsh	410
4.	John Campbell	543	9.	Mario Baillargeon	401
5.	Jack Moiseyev	467	10.	Dave Magee	396

TOP 100 DASHWINNING DRIVERS IN 1990
('t' - indicates tied for position)

Rank	Driver	Wins	Rank	Driver	Wins
76. t	Aldrich, Bruce Jr.	189	19.	Magee, Dean	321
99. t	Aubin, Marc	167	24.	Mahar, Steve	284
9.	Baillargeon, Mario	401	2.	Manzi, Cat	641
46.	Battin, Ross	225	17.	Marohn, Jim	334
83. t	Beaudoin, Jacques	184	53. t	Marsh, Joe Jr.	218
44. t	Boily, Gabriel	226	8.	Marsh, Ron	410
96. t	Boring, Troy	168	99. t	Mayotte, Roger	167
13. t	Brown, Doug	368	69. t	McLean, Ray	199
80. t	Busse, Daryl	187	88.	McNeight, Ed Jr.	178
26.	Buter, Terry	262	47. t	McNichol, Mickey	224
51. t	Byron, Steve	219	20.	Miller, David	308
4.	Campbell John	543	5.	Moiseyev, Jack	467
3.	Case, Walter Jr.	606	28.	Morand, Jim	258
39.	Clark, Keith	238	83. t	Morgan, Ed Jr.	184
37. t	Condren, Steve	240	62.	Morgan, Tony	205
27.	Copeland, Vince	260	18.	Mosher, Gary	331
94. t	Coppola, Frank Jr.	170	55.	Ouellette, Luc	217
43.	Crawford, Keith	229	41.	Ouellet, Serge	232
64. t	Crawford, Kim	203	37. t	O'Donnell, Bill	240
91. t	Croghan, Ross	175	16.	Paisley, Walter	340
61.	Cullen, Allan	208	7.	Palone, Dave	428
50.	Cullipher, Roger	221	13. t	Parker, Bill Jr.	368
33.	Dancer, Donald	245	59. t	Pavia, Joe Jr.	210
40.	Danny Johnson	235	44. t	Pierce, Ron	226
23.	Davis, Eddie	285	49.	Plourde, Gilles	223
86.	Dennis, Jim	182	59.t	Portelance, Howard	210
63.	Dube, Daniel	204	34. t	Putnam, Carl, Jr.	243
51. t	Essig, Joe Jr.	219	57. t	Putnam, Joe	212
80. t	Fahy, Bill	187	47. t	Rankin, "Callie"	224
29.	Filion, Henri	256	96. t	Ritchie, Jim	168
1.	Filion, Herve	660	76. t	Robblee, Rod	189
30. t	Fitch, Leigh	252	82.	Saftic, Mike	185
90.	Gale, Bill	176	64. t	Sahely, Mitch	203
67. t	Gilmour, John	201	11.	Schwind, Joe	391
73.	Grundy, Brent	194	74.	Simard, Richard	193
67. t	Harmon, Don	201	96. t	Simmons, Tom	168
25.	Hennesey, Wally	271	89.	Snyder, Doug	177
76. t	Hiteman, Dale	189	94. t	Spinks, Lloyd	170
34. t	Ingraham, Dave	243	87.	Sweeney, Jeff	181
22.	Irvine, Don Jr.	287	57. t	Wagner, John	212
53. t	James, Jeff	218	69. t	Wallis, Kevin	199
85.	Johnston, Chris	183	30. t	Wall, Dave	252
56.	Kerwood, Tony	215	75.	Waples, Ron	190
15.	Lachance, Michel	342	79.	Warrington, Steve	188
36.	Laframboise, Rod	241	42.	Williams, Mark	230
71. t	Lambertus, Bill	198	66.	Wing, Ted	202
6.	Lamy, Gaetan	460	32.	Wojcio, Richard	248
71. t	Long, Bill	198	21.	Wrenn, Peter	296
91. t	MacDonald, Garry	175	93.	Zaimes, Dean	174
10.	Magee, Dave	396	12.	Zeron, Rick	388

LEADING DRIVERS

PREVIOUS LEADING DASHWINNERS – 1946 to 1989

Year	Leading Dashwinner	Wins	Runner-Up	Wins
1989	Herve Filion	814	Cat Manzi	687
1988	Herve Filion	798	Jack Moiseyev	619
1987	Michel Lachance	715	Herve Filion	606
1986	Michel Lachance	770	Herve Filion	462
1985	Michel Lachance	592	John Campbell	475
1984	Michel Lachance	466	Bill O'Donnell	422
1983	Eddie Davis	470	Walter Case, Jr.	429
1982	Herve Filion	495	Walter Case, Jr	471
1981	(TIE) Eddie Davis	404	(TIE) Herve Filion	404
1980	Herve Filion	474	Ron Waples	396
1979	Ron Waples	443	Carmine Abbatiello	393
1978	Herve Filion	423	Carmine Abbatiello	387
1977	Herve Filion	441	Carmine Abbatiello	417
1976	Herve Filion	449	Daryl Busse	354
1975	Daryl Busse	360	Walt Paisley	358
1974	Herve Filion	637	Shelly Goudreau	292
1973	Herve Filion	445	Joe Marsh, Jr.	322
1972	Herve Filion	605	Joe Marsh, Jr.	307
1971	Herve Filion	543	Buddy Gilmour	305
1970	Herve Filion	486	Carmine Abbatiello	295
1969	Herve Filion	394	Del Insko	306
1968	Herve Filion	407	Lucien Fontaine	264
1967	Bob Farrington	277	Del Insko	258
1966	Bob Farrington	306	Del Insko	261
1965	Bob Farrington	310	Billy Haughton	222
1964	Bob Farrington	312	Del Insko	184
1963	Donald Busse	201	Bob Farrington	198
1962	Bob Farrington	203	Del Insko	161
1961	Bob Farrington	201	Harry Burright	183
1960	Del Insko	156	Buddy Gilmour	135
1959	Buddy Gilmour	165	Billy Haughton	157
1958	Billy Haughton	175	Buddy Gilmour	155
1957	Billy Haughton	156	Buddy Gilmour	152
1956	Billy Haughton	167	Stanley Dancer	163
1955	Billy Haughton	168	Stanley Dancer	130
1954	Billy Haughton	153	John Chapman	112
1953	Billy Haughton	116	John Chapman	107
1952	Levi Harner	129	Billy Haughton	110
1951	John Simpson, Sr.	118	W.N. McMillen	98
1950	John Simpson, Sr.	111	Del Miller	108
1949	Clint Hodgins	128	Levi Harner	125
1948	Harry Burright	129	Levi Harner	121
1947	Levi Harner	115	Dr. H.M. Parshall	103
1946	Levi Harner	105	Thomas Winn	101

LEADING DASHWINNING DRIVERS, ALL-TIME
Through, and Including, December 31, 1990

Rank	Driver	Career Wins	Rank	Driver	Career Wins
1.	Herve Filion	12,667	10.	Billy Haughton	4,910
2.	Carmine Abbatiello	7,020	11.	Bill Gale	4,843
3.	Michel Lachance	5,904	12.	Daryl Busse	4,780
4.	Buddy Gilmour	5,352	13.	Gilles Gendron	4,737
5.	Walter Paisley	5,335	14.	Del Insko	4,620
6.	Joe Marsh, Jr.	5,204	15.	Leigh Fitch	4,537
7.	John Campbell	5,136	16.	Bill O'Donnell	4,435
8.	Ron Waples	5,084	17.	Cat Manzi	4,344
9.	Eddie Davis	5,066	18.	Dave Magee	4,340

LEADING DRIVERS

Rank	Driver	Career Wins	Rank	Driver	Career Wins
19.	Doug Brown	4,301	35.	Don Richards	3,525
20.	Walter Case, Jr.	4,295	36.	Jim Curran	3,511
21.	Joe O'Brien	4,285	37.	Jean Paul Morel	3,502
22.	Terry Kerr	4,276	38.	Stan Banks	3,489
23.	Dave Wall	4,171	39.	Lucien Fontaine	3,458
24.	Ben Webster	4,039	40.	Carl Putnam, Jr.	3,440
25.	Freeman Parker	4,022	41.	Don Irvine, Jr.	3,394
26.	Harold Kelly	4,002	42.	Benoit Cote	3,353
27.	John Chapman	3,915	43.	Moiseyev, Jack	3,299
28.	Stanley Dancer	3,750	44.	Yves Filion	3,271
29.	Jim Doherty	3,743	45.	Jack Bailey	3,263
30.	Ted Wing	3,738	46.	Ray McLean	3,255
31.	Jacques Hebert	3,660	47.	John Hogan	3,254
32.	Chris Boring	3,650	48.	Butch Dokey	3,198
33.	Donald Dancer	3,580	49.	Keith Waples	3,171
34.	Bill Parker, Jr.	3,527	50.	Bob Farrington	3,163

LEADING DASHWINNING DRIVERS, ALL-TIME
Through, and Including, December 31, 1990
Mininum - 1,000 Wins - 490 Drivers
('t' - indicates tied for position)

Rank	Driver	Career Wins	Rank	Driver	Career Wins
2.	Abbatiello, Carmine	7,020	84.	Boucher, Andre	2,609
468. t	Abbatiello, Tony	1,029	401.	Boucher, Simon	1,167
223.	Ackerman, Doug	1,686	368.	Boyd, Cliff	1,231
424.	Ackerman, John	1,115	104.	Bresnahan, Bill	2,440
173.	Adamsky, Joe	1,929	473.	Bridges, Roy	1,023
168. t	Allen, Jim	1,947	254.	Brinkerhoff, Tom	1,579
127. t	Altizer, Bob	2,220	302.	Bromley, Don	1,412
234.	Anderson, Joe	1,657	201.	Brown, Bob	1,784
310.	Andrews, Bill	1,392	341.	Brown, Charlie	1,283
97.	Arnold, Mike	2,497	19.	Brown, Doug	4,301
402. t	Arthurs, Bill	1,165	333.	Budd, Bill	1,306
120.	Aubin, Marc	2,276	305.	Burgoyne, Russ	1,407
430. t	Austin, Tom	1,095	78.	Burright, Harry	2,671
485. t	Bach, Fred	1,007	12.	Busse, Daryl	4,780
45.	Bailey, Jack	3,263	488.	Butcher, Matt	1,002
103.	Baillargeon, Mario	2,448	185.	Buter, Terry	1,879
402. t	Baldwin, Ralph	1,165	151.	Buter, Tim	2,035
38.	Banks, Stan	3,489	478. t	Buxton, Branch	1,015
181.	Barrieau, Marcel	1,892	261.	Buxton, Dick	1,562
178.	Battin, Ross	1,903	177.	Callahan, Walter	1,906
58.	Battis, Paul	3,013	322.	Cameron, Del	1,360
421. t	Bauer, Leo	1,117	399. t	Cameron, Warren	1,168
182. t	Baxter, John	1,891	7.	Campbell, John	5,136
481.	Bayless, Stan	1,011	243.	Campbell, Winston	1,609
269.	Beaudoin, Jacques	1,529	202.	Carey, David	1,783
75.	Beckwith, Bert	2,680	428.	Carroll, Dick	1,104
249. t	Bedard, Adrien	1,588	388.	Carr, Willard	1,193
454. t	Beede, Earl	1,061	456. t	Cartnal, Ken	1,057
215.	Beissinger, Howard	1,710	20.	Case, Walter Jr.	4,295
135.	Belanger, Bert	2,165	487.	Cass, William	1,004
363. t	Belanger, Yvon	1,235	313. t	Catellier, Yvon	1,378
205.	Belote, Sam	1,778	27.	Chapman, John	3,915
458.	Blood, Peter	1,054	449.	Chappell, Graham	1,069
88.	Boily, Gabriel	2,579	383.	Charlton, Bernard	1,199
395.	Bolon, Ben	1,179	253.	Charron, Jean Paul	1,582
51.	Bookmyer, Gerry	3,097	216.	Childress, John	1,705
32.	Boring, Chris	3,650	313. t	Clarke, Roy	1,378

LEADING DRIVERS

Rank	Driver	Career Wins
96.	Clark, Keith	2,509
229. t	Clifton, Jerv	1,668
133.	Cobb, Eddie	2,186
268.	Coke, Wes	1,532
390.	Colby, Wayne	1,187
411. t	Coleman, Foster	1,135
60.	Condren, Steve	2,932
126.	Copeland, Leroy	2,221
280.	Coppola, Frank Jr.	1,482
330.	Corbett, Melville	1,323
484.	Coreau, Carol	1,008
288.	Cormier, Real	1,461
42.	Cote, Benoit	3,353
270.	Coven, Herb Jr.	1,528
157.	Coville, Darrell	1,994
199.	Crank, Vern	1,799
114.	Crawford, Keith	2,318
66.	Crawford, Kim	2,858
417. t	Croghan, Ross	1,128
371.	Crowe, Pat	1,223
207.	Cruise, Jimmy	1,767
354.	Cullen, Allan	1,253
273. t	Cullipher, Roger	1,516
36.	Curran, Jim	3,511
214.	Curran, Ross	1,711
263.	Cyrenne, Jean Robert	1,553
59.	Daigneault, Rejean	2,964
33.	Dancer, Donald	3,580
200.	Dancer, Harold	1,793
28.	Dancer, Stanley	3,750
212.	Dancer, Vernon	1,723
220.	Daniels, Frank	1,694
320.	Daniels, Gary	1,362
94.	Dauplaise, Norm	2,517
182. t	Davies, Brent	1,891
434.	Davis, Bill	1,090
9.	Davis, Eddie	5,066
438.	Davis, George	1,082
186.	Davis, Percy	1,878
95.	Day, Al	2,515
448.	DeCample, Syl	1,071
391. t	Demers, Yvon	1,185
360.	Dennis, Jim Sr.	1,239
77.	Dennis, Jim	2,677
142.	Desomer, Steve	2,105
380.	Dessureault, Norm	1,205
413.	Dewbre, Chet	1,134
29.	Doherty, Jim	3,743
48.	Dokey, Butch	3,198
184.	Dolbee, Jim	1,885
266.	Downey, Mike	1,545
464. t	Duford, Jacques	1,038
275.	Duford, Jerry	1,508
477.	Dunn, Walter	1,018
262.	Erdman-Farber, Bea	1,560
374. t	Ervin, Frank	1,213
372. t	Essig, Joe Jr.	1,214
242.	Fagan, Dave	1,611
67. t	Fahy, Bill	2,813
50.	Farrington, Bob	3,163
222.	Farrington, Brad	1,688
281.	Faucher, Billy	1,475
54.	Feagan, Ron	3,063
276.	Fenn, Bryce	1,504
377. t	Ferguson, Marc	1,209
180.	Filion, Gilles	1,895
52.	Filion, Henri	3,095
1.	Filion, Herve	12,667
299.	Filion, Rheo	1,421
44.	Filion, Yves	3,271
343.	Findley, Dr. John	1,276
159.	Finn, Fred Jr.	1,984
338.	Finn, Merle	1,291
319.	Finn, Randy	1,364
451. t	Fisher, Jim	1,067
15.	Fitch, Leigh	4,537
384. t	Fitzpatrick, Charles	1,197
426. t	Foist, Herman	1,105
39.	Fontaine, Lucien	3,458
321.	Foster, Irvin	1,361
166.	Fout, Jeff	1,956
331.	Freese, Don	1,318
224. t	Fritz, William "Bud"	1,683
137.	Gagliardi, Mike	2,157
110.	Galbraith, Clint	2,390
11.	Gale, Bill	4,843
148.	Garnsey, Glen	2,058
162.	Gassien, Reg	1,974
441. t	Gass, Ronnie	1,080
292.	Gauthier, Jean Paul	1,446
13.	Gendron, Gilles	4,738
471.	Gerry, Jovis	1,027
140.	Gibson, Gary	2,129
308.	Gilman, Ed	1,394
4.	Gilmour, Buddy	5,352
206.	Gilmour, George	1,773
70.	Gilmour, John	2,735
101. t	Gilmour, Lloyd	2,460
482.	Gingras, Raymond	1,010
76.	Goodblood, Ruel Jr.	2,679
489.	Gosman, Jesse	1,001
116.	Goudreau, Shelly	2,291
332.	Graham, Jerry	1,317
461.	Graham, Tom	1,050
247.	Gray, Doug	1,602
396. t	Greene, Joe	1,178
464. t	Green, John	1,038
295. t	Grise, Serge	1,440
356. t	Grundy, Brent	1,248
115.	Grundy, Jim	2,304
264.	Guhy, Gary	1,547
86.	Guindon, Gaston	2,591
171.	Hall, Don	1,943
72.	Hamilton, Doug	2,723
456. t	Hammer, Clay	1,057
213.	Hammer, Roger	1,712
459. t	Hanna, Al	1,052
108.	Hardy, Ken	2,400
79.	Harmer, Tom	2,670
396. t	Harmon, Don	1,178
237.	Harner, Eldon	1,630
90.	Harner, Levi	2,574

LEADING DRIVERS

Rank	Driver	Career Wins
414. t	Harp, George, Jr.	1,133
111.	Haslip, Fred	2,384
10.	Haughton, Billy	4,910
106.	Hayter, Ross	2,433
391. t	Hebert, Gerald	1,185
31.	Hebert, Jacues	3,660
112.	Heeney, Ken	2,372
152.	Henderson, Ron	2,029
439. t	Henman, Bill	1,081
337.	Hennessey, Ed	1,294
303.	Hennessey, Joe	1,409
139.	Hennessey, Wally	2,131
245. t	Hennessy, Rod	1,605
327.	Herman, Billy	1,337
176.	Hie, Carman	1,913
258.	Hie, Warren	1,575
55.	Hiteman, Dale	3,046
197.	Hodgins, Clint	1,811
255.	Hodgins, Joe	1,577
47.	Hogan, John	3,254
251.	Holton, Terry	1,586
131. t	Hostetler, Lavern	2,198
127. t	Howard, David	2,220
374. t	Huber, Lou Jr.	1,213
53.	Hudon, Joe Jr.	3,067
295. t	Huntbach, Ed	1,440
450.	Hysell, James	1,068
161.	Ingraham, Dave	1,975
14.	Insko, Del	4,620
485. t	Insko, Delbert G.	1,007
175.	Irvine, Bill	1,920
41.	Irvine, Don Jr.	3,394
463.	Jackson, Hubert	1,044
282.	Jacobs, Randy	1,472
64. t	James, Jeff	2,862
141.	Johnson, Danny	2,107
417. t	Jones, Norman	1,128
313. t	Jordan, Mark	1,378
423.	Jungquist, David	1,116
188.	Kamal, Gary	1,851
451. t	Kash, Keith	1,067
374. t	Kaye, Ken	1,213
221.	Keith, Lewis	1,690
26.	Kelly, Harold	4,002
190.	Kerr, Randy	1,843
22.	Kerr, Terry	4,276
279.	Kerwood, Tony	1,489
419. t	Kidwell, Glen	1,120
245. t	King, Jim Jr.	1,605
425.	Konesky, John III	1,109
144.	Kuebler, Rick	2,096
265.	Lachance, Andre	1,546
69.	Lachance, Gilles	2,784
435.	Lachance, Mario	1,087
3.	Lachance, Michel	5,904
277.	Laframboise, Phil	1,499
170.	Lambertus, Bill	1,944
101. t	Lamy, Gaetan	2,460
134.	Lancaster, Mark	2,168
203.	Landess, Gerry G.E.	1,783
209.	Langille, al	1,754
129.	Larente, James	2,218
294.	Larush, Guy	1,444
121.	Lawson, Charles	2,266
346.	LeBlanc, Steve	1,269
122.	Lighthill, Joe	2,254
98.	Linton, Keith	2,489
441. t	List, Fred	1,080
470.	Litke, Daryl	1,028
138.	Lohmeyer, Eddie	2,155
174.	Longo, Gerry	1,923
381. t	Long, Bill	1,202
472.	Loring, Norton	1,026
372. t	MacDonald, Boyd	1,214
163.	MacDonald, Garry	1,967
419. t	MacDonald, Mike	1,120
430. t	MacDonell, Paul	1,095
235. t	MacKay, Emmons	1,634
444. t	Macomber, Dick	1,078
462.	MacRae, Tony	1,045
350. t	MacTavish, Duncan	1,263
18.	Magee, Dave	4,340
87.	Mahar, Steve	2,580
81.	Maker, Marvin	2,652
287.	Manges, Del	1,462
17.	Manzi, Cat	4,344
398.	Marks, Walter	1,169
107.	Marohn, Jim	2,409
226.	Marshall, David	1,680
6.	Marsh, Joe Jr.	5,204
57.	Marsh, Ron	3,021
240.	Matthews, Paul	1,620
244.	Mattison, Jim	1,607
118.	Maupin, Jim	2,283
339.	Mayes, Jim	1,288
235. t	Mayotte, Roger	1,634
167.	McClure, Jim	1,950
416.	McGarty, Jim	1,130
324.	McIlmurray, Don Sr.	1,353
85.	McIlmurray, Wally	2,604
444. t	McIlmurray, Art	1,078
441. t	McIsaac, Francis	1,080
91.	McKirgan, Don	2,533
348. t	McKnight, Norm	1,265
46.	McLean, Ray	3,255
125.	McNeight, Ed Jr.	2,227
478. t	McNeil, Archie	1,015
92.	McNichol, Mickey	2,532
345.	McNulty, Bob	1,272
459. t	McNutt, Ken	1,052
467.	Megens, Wm. J.	1,033
466.	Megens, Wm. P.	1,034
318.	Merriman, Tom	1,368
301.	Milburn, Phil	1,413
446. t	Miller, Del S.	1,076
105.	Miller, Delvin	2,434
172.	Mills, Gary	1,933
43.	Moiseyev, Jack	3,299
474. t	Mondi, Tony	1,022
358. t	Monkman, Don Jr.	1,243
273. t	Moody, John	1,516
365. t	Moore, Pres Jr.	1,233

LEADING DRIVERS

Rank	Driver	Career Wins
248.	Morand, Jim	1,595
37.	Morel, Jean Paul	3,502
80.	Morgan, Ed Jr.	2,656
267.	Morgan, Tony	1,541
238. t	Morrill, Jim	1,623
64. t	Mosher, Gary	2,531
193.	Myers, Bobby	1,837
340.	Myers, Richard	1,286
93.	Myer, Alan	2,520
191.	Myer, William	1,840
168. t	Nadeau, Fern	1,947
224. t	Nason, Art	1,683
365. t	Nason, John	1,233
453.	Newhart, Ron	1,063
241.	Nicholls, Allan	1,613
272.	Nickells, Bruce	1,519
227.	Nixon, Bob	1,673
365. t	Noble, Mike	1,233
145.	Noble, Sam "Chip" III	2,073
344.	Novick, Mike Jr.	1,275
21.	O'Brien, Joe	4,285
16.	O'Donnell, Bill	4,435
165.	O'Dwyer, Bob	1,958
328.	O'Dwyer, Don	1,334
211.	O'Mara, Frank	1,729
5.	Paisley, Walter	5,335
300.	Palone, Dave	1,419
474. t	Paquet, Fern	1,022
34.	Parker, Bill Jr.	3,527
25.	Parker, Freeman	4,022
454. t	Parker, Howard	1,061
335.	Parker, Howard	1,301
411. t	Parker, Jack Jr.	1,135
73.	Patterson, John Jr.	2,700
256. t	Paver, Ray Sr.	1,576
316.	Paver, Ray, Jr.	1,377
326.	Pavia, Joe Jr.	1,338
147.	Pelchat, Yvon	2,060
158.	Phalen, George	1,991
439. t	Pierce, Ron	1,081
468. t	Pineau, Alyre	1,029
56.	Pinkney, Dave	3,031
283.	Plano, Rick	1,469
289.	Pletcher, Dwayne	1,459
150.	Plourde, Gilles	2,043
405.	Poirier, Yvon	1,154
278.	Popfinger, Bill	1,493
217.	Popfinger, Frank Jr.	1,704
252.	Portelance, Howard	1,583
218.	Porter, Jim	1,700
40.	Putnam, Carl Jr.	3,440
309.	Quessy, Rene	1,393
399. t	Quinlan, Keith	1,168
408.	Quinn, John	1,149
404.	Randall, Jay	1,164
256. t	Ranger, Bruce	1,576
124.	Rankin, Dave	2,236
233.	Rankin, Don Jr.	1,665
100.	Rankin, Doug	2,482
154.	Rankin, "Callie"	2,018
146.	Rapone, Louis	2,068
195.	Rapone, Patsy	1,828
352.	Ratchford, David	1,260
329.	Ratchford, Gus	1,331
384. t	Reese, John	1,197
109.	Remmen, Ray	2,395
325.	Renaud, Herman	1,343
160.	Richards, Del	1,981
35.	Richards, Don	3,525
259.	Riegle, Gene	1,573
229. t	Ritchie, Trevor	1,668
480.	Rivest, Gary	1,014
387.	Roberts, Bib	1,196
306.	Robinson, Jerry	1,403
297. t	Romo, Daniel	1,435
426. t	Ross, Dan	1,105
483.	Ross, Walter H.	1,009
490.	Rothfuss, Don	1,000
284.	Rowe, Scott	1,468
358. t	Russell, Sanders	1,243
377. t	Sadler, Fred	1,209
312.	Samson, Bob	1,382
123.	Sarama, Gerry	2,242
192.	Sattelberg, Lee	1,839
290.	Savignac, Claude	1,457
204.	Schedlosky, Steve	1,780
293.	Schroeder, John	1,445
149.	Schwind, Joe	2,054
446. t	Scrannage, Bob	1,076
369.	Searle, John	1,227
311.	Sears, Jay	1,386
429.	Sells, Tom	1,099
307.	Shahan, Bob	1,399
350. t	Shetler, Dan	1,263
62.	Sholty, George	2,868
384. t	Shuter, Bill	1,197
260.	Simmons, Tom	1,570
355.	Simpson, John Jr.	1,250
285.	Simpson, John Sr.	1,467
231. t	Smallwood, Henry	1,667
187.	Smart, Wayne "Curley"	1,873
323.	Smith, Allan	1,357
437.	Smith, Byron	1,083
370.	Smith, Charles	1,226
136.	Smith, Clark	2,163
409.	Smith, Elmer	1,148
430. t	Smith, Joel	1,095
249. t	Smullin, Wayne	1,588
71.	Snyder, Doug	2,732
117.	Spinks, Lloyd	2,286
304.	Stark, John Jr.	1,408
228.	Stead, Harold	1,670
361. t	Steall, Ben	1,236
271.	Stevenson, Bob	1,521
189.	Stillings, Dick	1,847
342.	Stoltzfus, Abe	1,280
61.	Story, Harold	2,909
156.	Strauss, Tom	2,011
67. t	St. Amour, Andre	2,813
353.	Sumner, Bob	1,256
291.	Swift, Tom	1,450
406. t	Tallman, Jim	1,153

LEADING DRIVERS

Rank	Driver	Career Wins
348. t	Taylor, Charles	1,265
99.	Taylor, Ted	2,484
421. t	Temple, Wayne	1,117
361. t	Tharps, Tom	1,236
196.	Tisbert, Bob	1,812
317.	Tomlin, Terry	1,370
82.	Tracey, Ed	2,629
381. t	Tremere, Boyd	1,202
238. t	Truitt, Bryce	1,623
406. t	Truitt, Charles	1,153
89.	Turcotte, Mel	2,575
410.	Turcotte, Ted Jr.	1,142
119.	Vallandingham, Gene	2,281
131. t	Vance, Dave	2,198
356. t	Wagner, John	1,248
194.	Walker, Larry	1,836
297. t	Wallis, Kevin	1,435
23.	Wall, Dave	4,171
113.	Walsh, Doug	2,352
49.	Waples, Keith	3,171
8.	Waples, Ron	5,084
143.	Warrington, Steve	2,102
394.	Warrington, Walt	1,180
393.	Waugh, Gordon	1,184
24.	Webster, Ben	4,039
74.	Wellwood, Bill	2,692
436.	Wellwood, Harold F.	1,084
347.	Wheeler, Eddie	1,267
198.	Whelan, Jim	1,801
231. t	Wilburn, Tom	1,667
208.	Wilcutts, John	1,755
155.	Williams, Bobby	2,014
286.	Williams, Charles	1,466
389.	Williams, George	1,190
379.	Williams, Jack Jr.	1,207
153.	Williams, Lew	2,023
336.	Williams, Mark	1,301
164.	Willis, Connel	1,962
334.	Wilsey, Dan	1,303
414. t	Winger, Alix	1,133
30.	Wing, Ted	3,738
363. t	Wojcio, Richard	1,235
476.	Worthen, Mike	1,021
130.	Wrenn, Peter	2,211
210.	Wrenn, Ron	1,733
433.	Wright, Darrell	1,094
63.	Wright, Greg	2,864
219.	Zaimes, Dean	1,696
179.	Zendt, Bill	1,899
83.	Zeron, Rick	2,626

LEADING MONEYWINNING DRIVERS IN 1990

1.	John Campbell	$11,620,878
2.	Michel Lachance	7,165,323
3.	Doug Brown	6,042,217
4.	Cat Manzi	5,511,211
5.	Herve Filion	4,309,598
6.	Bill O'Donnell	4,294,221
7.	Bill Fahy	4,034,219
8.	Ron Waples	3,683,735
9.	Dave Magee	3,455,951
10.	Steve Condren	3,243,361

TOP 100 MONEYWINNING DRIVERS IN 1990

Rank	Driver	Earnings
81.	Abbatiello, Carmine	$884,278
70.	Aubin, Marc	1,026,007
20.	Baillargeon, Mario	2,317,234
100.	Barrieau, Marcel	731,629
96.	Battin, Ross	762,206
88.	Boring, Troy	825,671
66.	Brooks, John	1,125,781
3.	Brown, Doug	6,042,217
44.	Busse, DAryl	1,426,045
1.	Campbell, John	11,620,878
25.	Case, Walter Jr.	2,057,184
75.	Clark, Keith	987,124
10.	Condren, Steve	3,243,361
62.	Copeland, Vince	1,130,316
45.	Cote, Benoit	1,417,415
79.	Crawford, Keith	934,506
87.	Croghan, Ross	828,530
63.	Curran, Jim	1,129,274
41.	Dancer, Donald	1,472,801
36.	Davis, Eddie	1,597,729
39.	Doherty, Jim	1,486,663
7.	Fahy, Bill	4,034,219
31.	Filion, Henri	1,784,383
5.	Filion, Herve	4,309,598
92.	Filion, Yves	804,859
51.	Finn, Fred Jr.	1,332,883
72.	Fout, Jeff	1,004,406
33.	Fritz, "Bud"	1,653,331
23.	Gale, Bill	2,219,033
84.	Grundy, Brent	846,148
98.	Harmer, Tom	747,773
85.	Harmon, Don	845,937
74.	Hebert, Jacques	990,705
61.	Hennessey, Wally	1,150,043
32.	Hiteman, Dale	1,677,325
56.	Hostetler, Lavern	1,252,623
40.	Irvine, Don, Jr.	1,476,553
64.	Jacobs, Randy	1,128,049
59.	James, Jeff	1,198,194
47.	Johnson, Jan	1,392,180
30.	Kelly, Harold	1,790,412
95.	Kerr, Terry	764,440
17.	Kerwood, Tony	2,623,532
73.	Knox, Dan	990,846
54.	Kopas, John	1,276,539
89.	Lachance, Mario	816,812

LEADING DRIVERS

Rank	Driver	Earnings
2.	Lachance, Michel	7,165,323
28.	Lamy, Gaetan	1,894,118
48.	Lancaster, Mark	1,373,177
53.	Lindstedt, Berndt	1,284,547
43.	MacDonell, Paul	1,457,662
9.	Magee, Dave	3,455,951
4.	Manzi, Cat	5,511,211
27.	Marohn, Jim	1,942,477
42.	Marsh, Joe Jr.	1,467,065
14.	Marsh, Ron	2,854,896
26.	Mayotte, Roger	2,053,166
52.	McKnight, Norm	1,294,226
24.	McNichol, Mickey	2,178,487
11.	Moiseyev, Jack	2,943,088
99.	Moody, John	737,475
35.	Morand, Jim	1,624,361
49.	Morgan, Tony	1,369,263
82.	Morrill, Jim Jr.	875,718
22.	Mosher, Gary	2,226,588
71.	Noble Sam "Chip" III	1,007,490
37.	Nordin, Jan	1,511,945
57.	Ouellette, Luc	1,215,355
55.	Ouellet, Serge	1,254,598
6.	O'Donnell, Bill	4,294,221
12.	Paisley, Walter	2,942,320
69.	Palone, Dave	1,047,901
93.	Parker, Howard	780,691
60.	Pavia, Joe Jr.	1,167,789
15.	Pierce, Ron	2,779,875
67.	Putnam, Carl Jr.	1,111,921
58.	Rankin, Dave	1,214,327
13.	Remmen, Ray	2,930,725
76.	Ritchie, Trevor	969,534
19.	Saftic, Mike	2,392,575
97.	Schnittker, Ray	750,997
16.	Schwind, Joe	2,741,701
50.	Silverman, Richard	1,354,001
80.	Simard, Richard	902,649
68.	Smith, Dave	1,064,422
94.	Snyder, Doug	767,669
77.	Stillings, Dick	960,966
90.	Twaddle, Tim	811,964
65.	Walker, Larry	1,126,583
83.	Wallis, Kevin	852,671
18.	Wall, Dave	2,467,482
8.	Waples, Ron	3,683,735
78.	Warrington, Steve	958,546
38.	Webster, Ben	1,506,577
86.	Whelan, Jim	834,835
91.	Williams, Mark	810,083
34.	Wing, Ted	1,635,392
29.	Wojcio, Richard	1,818,313
46.	Wrenn, Peter	1,416,618
21.	Zeron, Rick	2,310,374

LEADING MONEYWINNING DRIVERS IN 1989

1.	John Campbell	$9,738,450
2.	Michel Lachance	7,477,749
3.	Herve Filion	5,258,920
4.	Doug Brown	5,135,141
5.	Bill O'Donnell	4,881,195
6.	Bill Fahy	4,801,420
7.	Cat Manzi	4,479,193
8.	Jack Moiseyev	4,122,900
9.	Steve Condren	3,882,893
10.	Ron Waples	3,847,495

PREVIOUS LEADING MONEYWINNING DRIVERS – 1946 to 1988

Year	Leader	Earnings	Runner-up	Earnings
1988	John Campbell	$11,148,565	Bill O'Donnell	$7,113,213
1987	John Campbell	10,186,495	Bill O'Donnell	7,867,495
1986	John Campbell	9,515,055	Bill O'Donnell	8,400,472
1985	Bill O'Donnell	10,207,372	John Campbell	9,621,761
1984	Bill O'Donnell	9,059,184	John Campbell	7,201,798
1983	John Campbell	6,104,082	Bill O'Donnell	5,838,769
1982	Bill O'Donnell	5,755,067	John Campbell	4,326,495
1981	Bill O'Donnell	4,065,608	Herve Filion	3,638,915
1980	John Campbell	3,732,306	Carmine Abbatiello	3,366,615
1979	John Campbell	3,308,984	Herve Filion	3,304,876
1978	Carmine Abbatiello	3,344,457	Herve Filion	3,256,586
1977	Herve Filion	2,551,058	John Chapman	2,469,029
1976	Herve Filion	2,278,634	Merritt Dokey	1,929,967
1975	Carmine Abbatiello	2,275,093	Ben Webster	1,969,819
1974	Herve Filion	3,474,315	Billy Haughton	1,596,475
1973	Herve Filion	2,233,303	Buddy Gilmour	1,918,397
1972	Herve Filion	2,473,265	Del Insko	1,565,417
1971	Herve Filion	1,915,945	Buddy Gilmour	1,550,001
1970	Herve Filion	1,647,837	Del Insko	1,330,737
1969	Del Insko	1,635,463	Stanley Dancer	1,318,201

LEADING DRIVERS

1968	Billy Haughton	1,654,463	Stanley Dancer	1,488,205
1967	Billy Haughton	1,305,773	Stanley Dancer	1,133,772
1966	Stanley Dancer	1,218,403	Billy Haughton	1,062,588
1965	Billy Haughton	889,943	Stanley Dancer	845,479
1964	Stanley Dancer	1,051,538	Billy Haughton	844,558
1963	Billy Haughton	790,086	Stanley Dancer	697,481
1962	Stanley Dancer	760,343	Billy Haughton	670,163
1961	Stanley Dancer	674,723	Billy Haughton	508,944
1960	Delvin Miller	567,282	Stanley Dancer	541,878
1959	Billy Haughton	771,435	Clint Hodgins	609,285
1958	Billy Haughton	816,659	Stanley Dancer	454,881
1957	Billy Haughton	586,950	John Simpson, Sr.	483,164
1956	Billy Haughton	572,945	John Simpson, Sr.	455,301
1955	Billy Haughton	599,455	Joe O'Brien	421,660
1954	Billy Haughton	415,577	Joe O'Brien	307,777
1953	Billy Haughton	374,527	Delvin Miller	288,659
1952	Billy Haughton	311,728	James Jordan	259,839
1951	John Simpson, Sr.	333,316	Billy Haughton	220,816
1950	Delvin Miller	306,813	John Simpson, Sr	234,519
1949	Clint Hodgins	184,108	Frank Ervin	183,656
1948	Ralph Baldwin	153,222	Frank Safford	145,811
1947	H.C. Fitzpatrick	133,675	Sep Palin	121,302
1946	Thomas Berry	121,933	Sep Palin	94,933

LEADING MONEYWINNING DRIVERS, ALL-TIME

Top 50 All-Time Leading Moneywinners

Rank	Driver	Earnings	Rank	Driver	Earnings
1.	John Campbell	$91,481,761	26.	John Patterson, Jr.	22,807,620
2.	Bill O'Donnell	71,093,662	27.	Bill Gale	22,263,781
3.	Herve Filion	71,005,819	28.	John Chapman	21,359,746
4.	Michel Lachance	53,730,189	29.	Lucien Fontaine	21,236,952
5.	Carmine Abbatiello	48,575,379	30.	Butch Dokey	21,076,006
6.	Ron Waples	43,797,245	31.	George Sholty	20,453,412
7.	Buddy Gilmour	43,474,617	32.	Joe O'Brien	20,443,819
8.	Billy Haughton	40,160,336	33.	Jim Curran	20,346,979
9.	Ben Webster	39,742,378	34.	Donald Dancer	20,088,965
10.	Doug Brown	32,931,160	35.	Henri Filion	19,657,529
11.	Joe Marsh, Jr.	31,577,320	36.	Jim Marohn	19,003,481
12.	Cat Manzi	31,488,546	37.	Ron Marsh	18,601,812
13.	Walter Paisley	31,428,879	38.	Jack Moiseyev	18,224,022
14.	Dave Magee	28,971,278	39.	Gillies Gendron	18,108,952
15.	Del Insko	28,166,381	40.	Bill Fahy	17,816,863
16.	Jim Doherty	27,528,543	41.	Norm Dauplaise	17,378,803
17.	Stanley Dancer	27,369,165	42.	Dale Hiteman	17,270,775
18.	Ray Remmen	26,610,776	43.	Stan Banks	17,025,471
19.	Steve Condren	25,177,433	44.	Chris Boring	16,610,859
20.	Rejean Daigneault	24,981,763	45.	Benoit Cote	15,936,488
21.	Mickey McNichol	24,313,023	46.	Yves Filion	15,885,508
22.	Ted Wing	23,709,330	47.	Clint Galbraith	15,844,189
23.	Daryl Busse	23,539,881	48.	Mike Gagliardi	15,717,210
24.	Eddie Davis	23,201,006	49.	Jacques Hebert	15,638,043
25.	Dave Wall	23,166,564	50.	Lavern Hostetler	15,472,728

LEADING DRIVERS

LEADING MONEYWINNING DRIVERS, ALL-TIME

Through, and Including, December 31, 1990
(Alphabetically Listed -- Minimum of $5 Million -- 228 Drivers)

Rank	Driver	Earnings
5.	Abbatiello, Carmine	$48,575,379
178.	Ackerman, Doug	6,170,246
111.	Ackerman, Doug	8,890,421
144.	Adamsky, Joe	7,117,510
165.	Allen, Carl	6,626,013
125.	Anderson, Joe	7,985,565
78.	Aubin, Marc	11,156,188
114.	Bailey, Jack	8,816,360
74.	Baillargeon, Mario	11,317,705
199.	Baldwin, Ralph	5,613,247
227.	Banks, Dwight	5,027,938
43.	Banks, Stan	17,025,471
219.	Baxter, John	5,222,727
193.	Bayless, Stan	5,701,488
228.	Beckwith, Bert	5,007,405
70.	Beissinger, Howard	11,681,621
220.	Belote, Sam	5,199,078
130.	Bookmyer, Gerry	7,738,489
44.	Boring, Chris	16,610,859
108.	Boucher, Andre	8,932,002
107.	Bresnahan, Bill	8,935,675
183.	Brooks, John	5,868,032
10.	Brown, Doug	32,931,160
223.	Burright, Harry	5,069,986
23.	Busse, Daryl	23,539,881
177.	Cameron, Warren	6,175,900
1.	Campbell, John	91,481,761
56.	Case, Walter Jr.	14,276,219
28.	Chapman, John	21,359,746
148.	Charron, Jean Paul	6,952,553
143.	Clark, Keith	7,267,491
146.	Cobb, Eddie	7,003,258
19.	Condren, Steve	25,177,433
173.	Copeland, Leroy	6,315,776
122.	Cormier, Real	8,196,881
45.	Cote, Benoit	15,936,488
198.	Crank, Vern	5,643,004
115.	Crawford, Keith	8,813,544
184.	Crawford, Kim	5,864,973
224.	Croghan, Ross	5,065,622
136.	Crowe, Pat	7,621,083
180.	Cruise, Jimmy	6,134,899
33.	Curran, Jim	20,346,979
20.	Daigneault, Rejean	24,981,763
34.	Dancer, Donald	20,088,965
95.	Dancer, Harold	9,712,194
17.	Dancer, Stanley	27,369,165
106.	Dancer, Vernon	8,957,262
41.	Dauplaise, Norm	17,378,803
194.	Davies, Brent	5,680,648
24.	Davis, Eddie	23,201,006
62.	Dennis, Jim	12,964,222
120.	Desomer, Steve	8,344,528
16.	Doherty, Jim	27,528,543
30.	Dokey, Butch	21,076,006
99.	Dolbee, Jim	9,441,890
129.	Duford, Jerry	7,741,699
131.	Erdman, Bea	7,738,166
40.	Fahy, Bill	17,816,863
105.	Farrington, Bob	9,004,434
164.	Feagan, Ron	6,643,466
35.	Filion, Henri	19,657,529
3.	Filion, Herve	71,005,819
46.	Filion, Yves	15,885,508
215.	Finn, Fred Jr.	5,301,378
29.	Fontaine, Lucien	21,236,952
157.	Fout, Jeff	6,781,418
135.	Fritz, William "Bud"	7,623,343
48.	Gagliardi, Mike	15,717,210
47.	Galbraith, Clint	15,844,189
27.	Gale, Bill	22,263,781
79.	Garnsey, Glen	11,104,977
124.	Gassien, Reg	7,999,741
190.	Gauthier, Jean Paul	5,742,535
39.	Gendron, Gilles	18,108,952
7.	Gilmour, Buddy	43,474,617
196.	Gilmour, John	5,648,863
116.	Gilmour, Lloyd	8,749,950
63.	Goudreau, Shelly	12,931,765
163.	Graham, Jerry	6,702,059
218.	Grise, Serge	5,260,265
112.	Grundy, Jim	8,840,638
205.	Guindon, Gaston	5,513,476
54.	Hamilton, Doug	14,883,997
200.	Hammer, Roger	5,586,788
132.	Hardy, Ken	7,703,906
53.	Harmer, Tom	15,067,504
85.	Harner, Eldon	10,218,422
210.	Haslip, Fred	5,393,778
8.	Haughton, Billy	40,160,336
169.	Haughton, Peter	6,446,491
52.	Haughton, Tommy	15,269,516
142.	Hayes, John Jr.	7,326,268
90.	Hayter, Ross	9,922,721
49.	Hebert, Jacques	15,638,043
161.	Henderson, Ron	6,708,820
207.	Hennessy, Rod	5,471,231
226.	Henriksen, Per	5,037,393
100.	Herman, Billy	9,273,370
119.	Hie, Carman	8,568,313
42.	Hiteman, Dale	17,270,775
175.	Hodgins, Clint	6,277,947
133.	Hogan, John	7,645,495
50.	Hostetler, Lavern	15,472,728
189.	Hudon, Joe Jr.	5,788,072
15.	Insko, Del	28,166,381
155.	Insko, Delvin L.	6,835,160
66.	Irvine, Don Jr.	12,340,407
208.	Irvine, William	5,445,967
126.	Jacobs, Randy	7,871,351
69.	James, Jeff	11,830,946
91.	Johnson, Danny	9,913,699

Page 248

LEADING DRIVERS

Rank	Driver	Earnings
171.	Johnson, Jan	6,345,971
195.	Jordan, Mark	5,650,451
51.	Kelly, Harold	15,313,369
213.	Kerr, Randy	5,320,653
83.	Kerr, Terry	10,375,815
84.	Kerwood, Tony	10,273,465
117.	King, Jim Jr.	8,717,226
188.	Kopas, Jack	5,791,717
98.	Kopas, John	9,446,778
104.	Kuebler, Rick	9,050,153
147.	Lachance, Andre	6,998,806
139.	Lachance, Gilles	7,482,787
191.	Lachance, Mario	5,733,677
4.	Lachance, Michel	53,730,189
222.	Lamy, Gaetan	5,144,711
72.	Lancaster, Mark	11,449,501
128.	Larente, Jim	7,755,747
201.	Levy, Sandy	5,564,919
154.	Lighthill, Joe	6,841,056
59.	Lindstedt, Berndt	13,840,730
71.	Lohmeyer, Ed	11,647,549
127.	Longo, Gerald	7,797,137
118.	MacDonell, Paul	8,713,750
14.	Magee, Dave	28,971,278
102.	Maker, Marvin	9,183,252
12.	Manzi, Cat	31,488,546
36.	Marohn, Jim	19,003,481
11.	Marsh, Joe Jr.	31,577,320
37.	Marsh, Ron	18,601,812
57.	Mayotte, Roger	14,125,402
162.	McIlmurray, Wally	6,708,389
204.	McKirgan, Don	5,525,458
151.	McKnight, Norm	6,865,136
137.	McLean, Ray	7,550,114
21.	McNichol, McNichol	24,313,023
176.	Merriman, Tom	6,188,162
80.	Miller, Delvin	10,958,970
174.	Miller, Jim	6,285,720
141.	Mills, Gary	7,405,835
38.	Moiseyev, Jack	18,224,022
206.	Moody, John	5,497,897
156.	Morand, Jim	6,830,183
170.	Morel, Jean Paul	6,398,618
192.	Morgan, Tony	5,727,637
60.	Mosher, Gary	13,722,290
149.	Myers, Bobby	6,904,169
150.	Myer, Alan	6,882,600
153.	Myer, William	6,851,262
187.	Nickells, Bruce	5,802,155
109.	Noble, Sam "Chip"	8,919,311
65.	Nordin, Jan	12,570,272
32.	O'Brien, Joe	20,443,819
2.	O'Donnell, Bill	71,093,662
87.	O'Mara, Mark	10,051,319
13.	Paisley, Walter	31,428,879
216.	Parker, Howard	5,292,787
76.	Parker, Jack Jr.	11,226,968
26.	Patterson, John Jr.	22,807,620
211.	Pavia, Joe Jr.	5,393,038
214.	Pelling, Brian	5,306,301
97.	Phalen, George	9,484,830
89.	Pierce, Ron	9,954,936
182.	Plutino, John	5,980,348
197.	Poirier, Yvon	5,648,635
68.	Popfinger, Bill	11,845,885
86.	Popfinger, Frank Jr.	10,180,884
185.	Poulin, Rene	5,864,133
81.	Putnam, Carl Jr.	10,938,772
103.	Rankin, Dave	9,073,677
18.	Remmen, Ray	26,610,776
138.	Riegle, Bruce	7,493,365
55.	Ritchie, Trevor	14,780,028
212.	Roberts, "Bib"	5,378,417
203.	Ruscitto, Peter	5,540,251
209.	Samson, Bob	5,423,605
158.	Sattelberg, Lee	6,766,446
61.	Schwind, Joe	13,487,373
221.	Sells, Tom	5,193,148
101.	Shetler, Dan	9,191,081
31.	Sholty, George	20,453,412
110.	Silverman, Richard	8,892,560
96.	Simpson, John Jr.	9,507,795
152.	Snyder, Doug	6,855,588
82.	Srama, Garry	10,439,316
75.	Stead, Harold	11,253,446
64.	Steall, Ben	12,692,034
94.	Stillings, Dick	9,747,722
140.	Stoltzfus, Abe	7,429,686
166.	Story, Harold	6,525,060
73.	Strauss, Tom	11,376,777
186.	Tallman, Jim	5,805,603
160.	Taylor, Ted	6,713,469
179.	Tomlin, Terry	6,141,929
217.	Tracey, Ed	5,292,337
202.	Truitt, Bryce	5,536,882
159.	Turcotte, Mel	6,750,806
92.	Vallandingham, Gene	9,881,870
168.	Vance, David	6,482,187
58.	Walker, Larry	14,030,982
121.	Wallner, Hakan	8,260,160
25.	Wall, Dave	23,166,564
167.	Waples, Keith	6,492,981
6.	Waples. Ron	43,797,245
93.	Warrington, Steve	9,766,714
9.	Webster, Ben	39,742,378
67.	Wellwood, Bill	12,280,761
181.	Whelan, Jim	5,987,564
113.	Williams, Lew	8,833,903
123.	Williams, Robert	8,015,528
145.	Willis, Connel	7,081,839
22.	Wing, Ted	23,709,330
172.	Wojcio, Richard	6,335,464
134.	Wrenn, Peter	7,633,336
77.	Wright, Greg	11,191,970
225.	Zendt, Bill	5,051,799
88.	Zeron, Rick	9,986,394

Page 249

LEADING DRIVERS

LEADING DRIVERS IN 1990 – BY THE U.D.R. SYSTEM

(500 or More Drives)

Rank	Driver	Starts	Wins	Second	Third	UDR
1.	Joe Hudon, Jr.	563	147	123	65	.421
2.	Roger Hammer	503	132	91	67	.407
3.	Walter Case, Jr.	2,337	606	368	314	.392
4.	Bill Davis	694	152	151	98	.387
5.	Sam "Chip" Noble III	587	141	99	90	.385
6.	Kevin Wallis	802	199	136	93	.381
7.	Dave Palone	1,764	428	297	236	.381
8.	Ross Croghan	684	175	105	75	.378
9.	Rick Zeron	1,671	388	285	245	.376
10.	Gilles Plourde	959	223	170	113	.370
11.	Ed Huntbach	557	119	101	88	.367
12.	Keith Clark	1,078	238	175	170	.364
13.	Jacques Beaudoin	858	184	150	130	.362
14.	Bob Sumner	737	166	121	94	.359
15.	John Campbell	2,392	543	385	301	.358
16.	Scott DeMull	540	110	102	79	.357
17.	Gaetan Lamy	2,158	460	359	324	.356
18.	Serge Ouellet	1,083	232	181	149	.353
19.	Gary Hall	657	138	107	100	.351
20.	Mark Williams	1,110	230	206	134	.351

(300 - 499 Drives)

Rank	Driver	Starts	Wins	Second	Third	UDR
1.	Yvon Belanger	306	88	59	39	.437
2.	Roy Bridges	324	80	54	50	.391
3.	Allen Harris	321	68	61	55	.375
4.	Jean Potvin	423	98	71	58	.371
5.	Rod Hennessy	405	84	75	72	.370
6.	Dave Rankin	323	70	55	54	.367
7.	Dan O'Brian	472	103	77	79	.365
8.	Barry Treen	393	84	66	63	.360
9.	Boyd MacDonald	321	67	50	59	.357
10.	Tom Agosti	346	74	61	44	.354

(100 - 299 Drives)

Rank	Driver	Starts	Wins	Second	Third	UDR
1.	Emett Liles	135	43	36	21	.519
2.	Berndt Lindstedt	143	52	27	15	.504
3.	Michel Ouellet	112	41	18	14	.497
4.	William "Bud" Fritz	172	62	23	27	.487
5.	Tom Graham	159	52	32	19	.479
6.	John Muir	183	62	31	20	.469
7.	Joe Smallwood	158	47	36	21	.468
8.	Jan Johnson	238	69	46	29	.438
9.	Henry Wilson	121	30	25	26	.434
10.	Andy Miller	149	47	20	17	.428

CALCULATING THE U.D.R.

$$\frac{(\text{Wins} \times 9) + (\text{Place} \times 5) + (\text{Show} \times 3)}{(\text{Starts} \times 9)} = \text{UDR}$$

LEADING DRIVERS

PREVIOUS U.D.R.S. CHAMPIONS

Year	500 or more Starts Winner / Runner-Up	Avg. / Avg.	300-499 Starts Winner / Runner-Up	Avg. / Avg.	100-299 Starts Winner / Runner-Up	Avg. / Avg.
1989	Walter Case, Jr. / Ross Croghan	.434 / .406	Bill Zendt / Yvon Belanger	.413 / .411	Paul Barkley / Roger Hammer	.562 / .558
1988	Don Rankin, Jr. / Clark Beelby	.429 / .404	Roger Hammer / Dick Stillings	.438 / .397	Tom Graham / Berndt Lindstedt	.534 / .503
1987	Keith Clark / Doug Snyder	.417 / .410	Roger Hammer / Boyd Mac Donald	.544 / .401	Emett Liles / Greg Leonard	.538 / .470
1986	Joe Hudon, Jr. / Bill Davis	.409 / .397	Roger Hammer / Sam Noble III	.470 / .414	Emett Liles / Greg Leonard	.502 / .475
1985	Bill Davis / Joe Hudon, Jr.	.397 / .396	Bruce Riegle / Sten Ericsson	.428 / .415	Emett Liles / Ron Ershler	.610 / .493
1984	Keith Crawford / Leigh Fitch	.385 / .382	Keith Clark / David Pinkney	.407 / .401	Walter Dunn / Dennis Petty	.501 / .499
1983	Sam Noble, III / Walter Case, Jr.	.412 / .398	Percy Davis / William Fritz	.416 / .413	Emett Liles / Roger Hammer	.497 / .440
1982	John Hogan / Keith Linton	.412 / .411	Chris Storms / Robert Coulter	.429 / .400	Roger Hammer / Thomas Graham	.536 / .495

Year	300 or more Starts Winner / Runner-Up	Avg. / Avg.	200-299 Starts Winner / Runner-Up	Avg. / Avg.	100-199 Starts Winner / Runner-Up	Avg. / Avg.
1981	Sam Noble, III / John Hogan	.439 / .403	David Pinkney / Percy Davis	.423 / .421	Roger Hammer / Kenneth Harvey	.511 / .487
1980	Joe Hudon, Jr. / Herb Coven, Jr.	.437 / .432	C.J. Osborn / Sam Noble, III	.548 / .452	Clyde Israel / Royal Roland	.543 / .532
1979	C.J. Osborn / Bea Farber	.566 / .450	George Hawke / Douglas Walsh	.464 / .440	Clay Hammer / K.M. Rutherford	.645 / .552
1978	Sam Noble, III / Bea Farber	.459 / .432	Mark Grismore / Walter Dunn	.455 / .446	Clay Hammer / Buddy Simpson	.571 / .523
1977	David Howard / Lewis Keith	.439 / .434	Walter Dunn / Bea Farber	.462 / .446	Clay Hammer / Buddy Simpson	.605 / .523
1976	Keith Linton / Stanley Dancer	.472 / .451	Glen Garnsey / Walter Dunn	.454 / .446	R.G. Betts / Clay Hammer	.524 / .521
1975	Joe O'Brien / Keith Linton	.463 / .438	John Findley / Roger Violette	.420 / .404	Gerald Ringrose / Delvin Miller	.474 / .461
1974	Joe O'Brien / Andre St. Amour	.413 / .410	Clay Hammer / Glen Garnsey	.494 / .425	Delvin Miller / Robert Neely	.481 / .471
1973	Keith Linton / Neil Karp	.435 / .431	Walter Dunn / Clay Hammer	.468 / .465	David Wade / Russell Doggett	.476 / .460
1972	Gene Riegle / Hugh Wemp	.423 / .410	Stanley Dancer / Glen Garnsey	.448 / .425	Donald Brainard / Walter Dunn	.504 / .481
1971	Dick Buxton / Gene Riegle	.483 / .461	Howard Beissinger / Joe Hennessey	.423 / .413	Sidney Spencer / Robert Cheney	.520 / .517
1970	Harry Harvey / John Findley	.459 / .423	Gene Riegle / Jerry Landess	.461 / .423	Ralph Mapes / Jerry Graham	.555 / .481
1969	John Findley / Stanley Dancer	.440 / .430	Harry Harvey / William Fritz	.508 / .507	Theodore Smith / Thomas Graham	.531 / .526
1968	Stanley Dancer / Brad Farrington	.511 / .424	Ken Vander Schaaf / Charles Lawson	.438 / .423	Clay Hammer / James Moore	.558 / .538
1967	Stanley Dancer / Yves Filion	.488 / .417	Donald Bromley / Thomas Graham	.462 / .449	Nealie Oliver / Paul Pasley	.507 / .506
1966	Stanley Dancer / Jerry Landess	.493 / .428	Gene Riegle / Donald Bromley	.468 / .412	T. Wayne Smart / Ed Dunwoody	.511 / .516
1965	Stanley Dancer / Dick Buxton	.423 / .383	Levi Harner / James Moore	.421 / .413	Leslie Redshaw / Frank Ervin	.602 / .555
1964	Stanley Dancer / Donald Huff	.442 / .425	Donald MacNeill / Dick Buxton	.472 / .419	Howard Parker / Leo Burns	.528 / .504

LEADING DRIVERS

Year	Winner Runner-Up	Avg. Avg.	Winner Runner-Up	Avg. Avg.	Winner Runner-Up	Avg. Avg.
1963	Stanley Dancer	.468	Donald G. MacNeill	.472	Howard Parker	.528
	Jimmy Cruise	.412	Dick Buxton	.419	Leo Burns	.504
1962	Stanley Dancer	.468	Erv Samples	.433	T. Wayne Smart	.493
	Joe O'Brien	.436	Frank Ervin	.404	Tom Graham	.461
1961	Joe O'Brien	.416	Jimmy Arthur	.411	Royce Carey	.587
	Stanley Dancer	.399	Julius Louiso	.387	T. Wayne Smart	.546
1960	Delvin Miller	.438	T. Wayne Smart	.485	Ralph Baldwin	.553
	Levi Harner	.424	James Fisher	.477	Robert Altizer	.469
1959	Levi Harner	.416	T. Wayne Smart	.550	Herman Ross	.531
	Joe O'Brien	.376	James Fisher	.432	Frank Weller	.491
1958	George Sholty	.383	T. Wayne Smart	.539	Ralph Baldwin	.506
	Levi Harner	.379	Dick Buxton	.447	Bill Popfinger	.469
1957	John Simpson, Sr.	.419	John Ackerman	.480	Raymond Moore	.535
	Delvin Miller	.392	Joe O'Brien	.438	Emmett Davidson	.529

	200 or more Starts		**200-299 Starts**		**100 or more starts**	
1956	Joe O'Brien	.417	Bob Cheney	.557	(Not Kept)	
	Clarence Hansen	.383	Arthur Garrigues	.511		
1955	T. Wayne Smart	.477	(Not Kept)		(Not Kept)	
	Julius Louiso	.463				
1954	William Current	.469	(Not Kept)		(Not Kept)	
	Delvin Miller	.410				
1953	T. Wayne Smart	.530	(Not Kept)		(Not Kept)	
	Delvin Miller	.488				
1952	T. Wayne Smart	.469	(Not Kept)		(Not Kept)	
	Lou Huber, Jr.	.461				
1951	W.N. McMillen	.457	Fred Johnson	.696	(Not Kept)	
	B.J. Schue	.454	S.H. Edwards	.547		
1950	Delvin Miller	.501	Lew Howell	.657	(Not Kept)	
	Mel Harmening	.454	E.L. Lowery	.500		
1949	Wm. E. Miller	.629	J.F. Cartnal	.666	(Not Kept)	
	John Simpson, Sr.	.482	Art Shaw	.613		
1948	(Not Kept)		(Not Kept)		J.F. Cartnal	.575
					Joe O'Brien	.561

LEADING DRIVERS

TOP TWO-MINUTE DRIVERS, ALL-TIME

Rank	Driver	Life Total	In 1990	Rank	Driver	Life Total	In 1990
1.	John Campbell	4,207	606	26.	Marc Aubin	874	117
2.	Bill O'Donnell	3,030	250	27.	Joe Pavia, Jr.	862	200
3.	Cat Manzi	1,904	408	28.	Joe Anderson	857	120
4.	Michel Lachance	1,896	378	29.	Ted Wing	808	99
5.	Doug Brown	1,577	328	30.	Rick Kuebler	800	99
6.	Herve Filion	1,533	231	31.	Mike Gagliardi	784	39
7.	Jim Doherty	1,514	125	32.	Dale Hiteman	779	88
8.	Ben Webster	1,500	110	33.	Tony Kerwood	753	194
9.	Jack Moiseyev	1,432	314	34.	Ron Pierce	748	218
10.	Ron Waples	1,378	181	35.	Roger Mayotte	742	147
11.	Eddie Davis	1,301	219	36.	Danny Johnson	740	113
12.	Dave Magee	1,259	211	37.	Jack Parker, Jr.	713	48
13.	Mickey McNichol	1,249	202	38.	Lavern Hostetler	693	88
14.	Steve Condren	1,209	221	39.	Joe O'Brien	685	None
15.	Ray Remmen	1,165	90	40.	Ross Croghan	656	149
16.	Ron Marsh	1,086	235	41.	Tom Harmer	639	42
17.	Joe Schwind	1,070	255	42.	Donald Dancer	633	82
18.	Bill Fahy	1,024	193	43.	Mark Lancaster	631	118
19.	Bill Gale	970	115	44.	Peter Wrenn	628	137
20.	Walter Paisley	961	179	45.	Doug Hamilton	627	11
21.	Walter Case, Jr.	942	141	46.	Doug Snyder	618	102
22.	Steve Warrington	941	151	47.	Joe Marsh, Jr.	582	68
23.	Carmine Abbatiello	932	46	48.	Jim Morand	577	181
24.	Don Irvine, Jr.	912	213	49.	Mario Baillargeon	570	139
25.	Dave Wall	887	154	50.	Rejean Daigneault	566	51

LEADING TWO-MINUTE DRIVERS – 1990

Rank	Driver	2:00 Miles	Rank	Driver	2:00 Miles
1.	John Campbell	606	11.	Eddie Davis	219
2.	Cat Manzi	408	12.	Ron Pierce	218
3.	Michel Lachance	378	13.	Don Irvine, Jr.	213
4.	Doug Brown	328	14.	Dave Magee	211
5.	Jack Moiseyev	314	15.	Rick Zeron	210
6.	Joe Schwind	255	16.	Mickey McNichol	202
7.	Bill O'Donnell	250	17.	Joe Pavia, Jr.	200
8.	Ron Marsh	235		Dave Palone	200
9.	Herve Filion	231	19.	Tony Kerwood	194
10.	Steve Condren	221	20.	Bill Fahy	193

LEADING TWO-MINUTE DRIVERS – 1989

Top 2:00 Drivers – 1989

Rank	Driver	2:00 Miles
1.	John Campbell	481
2.	Cat Manzi	401
3.	Michel Lachance	369
4.	Jack Moiseyev	345
5.	Doug Brown	307
6.	Bill O'Donnell	257
7.	Dave Magee	251
8.	Herve Filion	230
	Bill Fahy	230
10.	Steve Condren	225

Top 2:00 Drivers – 1988

Rank	Driver	2:00 Miles
1.	John Campbell	507
2.	Jack Moiseyev	375
4.	Bill O'Donnell	296
4.	Joe Schwind	274
5.	Cat Manzi	243
6.	Michel Lachance	231
7.	Doug Brown	211
	Herve Filion	211
9.	Peter Wrenn	209
10.	Joe Pavia, Jr.	191

LEADING DRIVERS

TOP 1:55 DRIVERS, ALL-TIME

Rank	Driver	Life Total	In 1990
1.	John Campbell	603	142
2.	Bill O'Donnell	419	52
3.	Michel Lachance	249	92
4.	Jack Moiseyev	160	24
5.	Ron Waples	159	36
6.	Jim Doherty	147	23
	Cat Manzi	147	45
8.	Ben Webster	145	15
9.	Ray Remmen	118	31
10.	Ron Pierce	105	44
11.	Mickey McNichol	102	38
12.	Bill Fahy	98	34
13.	Joe Schwind	85	37
14.	Doug Brown	84	48
15.	Mike Gagliardi	77	4
16.	Eddie Davis	63	10
17.	Tom Harmer	61	5
18.	Richard Silverma	57	7
19.	Walter Case, Jr.	56	1
20.	Ted Wing	47	2

Rank	Driver	Life Total	In 1990
	John Plutino	47	7
22.	Dick Stillings	46	5
23.	Jack Parker, Jr.	42	4
24.	Don Irvine, Jr.	41	12
25.	Howard Parker	38	13
26.	Trevor Ritchie	36	3
	Tommy Haughton	36	6
28.	Joe Pavia, Jr.	35	00
29.	Steve Condren	33	12
30.	Dave Wall	31	8
	Bill Gale	31	10
32.	Buddy Gilmour	30	3
	Tony Kerwood	30	00
34.	Dave Magee	29	5
35.	Clint Galbraith	28	none
	Chris Boring	28	4
37.	Herve Filion	27	7
	Peter Ruscitto	27	none
39.	Kevin Wallis	26	00

TOP 1:55 DRIVERS - 1990

Rank	Driver	1:55 Miles
1.	John Campbell	142
2.	Michel Lachance	92
3.	Bill O'Donnell	52
4.	Doug Brown	48
5.	Cat Manzi	45
6.	Ron Pierce	44
7.	Mickey McNichol	38
8.	Joe Schwind	37
9.	Ron Waples	36
10.	Bill Fahy	34

Rank	Driver	1:55 Miles
11.	Ray Remmen	31
12.	Jack Moiseyev	24
13.	Jim Doherty	23
	Joe Pavia, Jr.	23
15.	Tony Kerwood	18
16.	Mike Saftic	15
	Kevin Wallis	15
	Ben Webster	15
19.	Dave Smith	14

Top 1:55 Drivers - 1989

Rank	Driver	1:55 Miles
1.	John Campbell	85
2.	Michel Lachance	84
3.	Jack Moiseyev	70
4.	Cat Manzi	54
5.	Bill O'Donnell	44
6.	Bill Fahy	43
7.	Ron Pierce	34
8.	Jim Doherty	27
9.	Ron Waples	19
10.	Eddie Davis	18

Top 1:55 Drivers - 1988

Rank	Driver	1:55 Miles
1.	John Campbell	85
2.	Bill O'Donnell	62
3.	Michel Lachance	59
4.	Jack Moiseyev	42
5.	Ben Webster	23
6.	Cat Manzi	22
7.	Ron Pierce	19
	Dick Stillings	19
	Ron Waples	19

LEADING DRIVERS

MAJOR RACES WON BY LEADING DRIVERS IN 1990

Here is a list of major races won by some of the top drivers in North America in 1990. Shown is the date and name of the event; age, sex and gait division; whether the stake was divided or raced under the heat or elimination plan; the purse (showing the total purse for heat or elimination plan events and division purse for divided events); the track where it was raced; the name of the winning horse and the time.

Triple Crown and Breeders Crown events are shown in **boldface**:

Date	Event (Division)	Purse	At	Winner	Time
Abbatiello, Carmine					
5-28	Charles Smith Mem. Final (3yo Open Trot)	$113,565	Fhld	Pastel Pastel	2:00h
9-3	Helen Dancer Memorial (3yofp) (div.)	107,068	Fhld	It's Sunny	1:57.4f
Ackerman, D.R.					
6-8	W.N. Reynolds Memorial (3yoft)	27,900	RP	Gretel T	2:02.1f
6-9	W.N. Reynolds Memorial (2yocp) (div.)	26,385	RP	Interpretor	1:59.3f
6-15	Windsor Riverfront (2yocp) (div.)	25,000	WR	Black Gold Road	1:58.3f
7-15	Hanover-Hempt (2yocp) (div.)	12,500	VD	Interpretor	1:57.4q
9-12	Col. Wm. Edwards Memorial (3yoct) (div.)	22,300	Nfld	Princely Fellow	2:00.4h
9-21	American-National (2yocp) (div.)	55,000	SPk	Interpretor	1:56.3f
9-29	Bluegrass (2yocp)	144,900	Lex	Interpretor	1:53.3
Ackerman, Doug					
6-26	Historic-Harriman (2yoct) (div.)	38,467	M	Wall Street Banker	2:01
8-24	Hoosier Futurity (2yoft)	23,567	Ind	A-Treat	2:00
8-31	The Castleton (2yoft)	55,000	DuQ	A-Treat	1:58.2
Adamsky, Joe					
6-8	W.N. Reynolds Memorial (2yoct)	46,843	RP	Super Pleasure	2:03.2f
6-14	Windsor Riverfront (2yoct)	36,450	WR	Super Pleasure	2:03f
6-26	Historic-Harriman (2yoct) (div.)	38,467	M	Super Pleasure	2:01.3
9-10	Rainy Day Sweepstakes (2yoct)	37,500	Nfld	Taborizer	2:03h
Allen, Carl					
6-6	W.N. Reynolds Memorial (2yoft)	45,313	RP	Grand Encore	2:03.4f
7-7	Dexter Cup (3yo Open Trot)	186,682	YR	Royal Troubador	1:58.3h
7-14	**Yonkers Trot** (3yo Open)	**424,965**	**YR**	**Royal Troubador**	**1:59.2h**
Allen, Rod					
8-19	Zweig Memorial (3yo Open Trot) (div.)	75,300	Sycs	Jeanne's Somolli	1:58.2
8-25	Mac Farlane Memorial (3yo Open Trot)	126,200	HP	Jeanne's Somolli	1:59.1f
10-13	Colonial (3yo Open Trot) (div.)	122,032	RcR	Jeanne's Somolli	1:56.4f
11-17	Matron Stakes (3yo Open Trot)	125,465	PPk	Jeanne's Somolli	1:57.2f
Anderson, Joe					
9-29	American Pacing Classic Final (FFA Pace)	150,000	LA	T K's Skipper	1:51.2f
Bailey, Jim					
6-6	W.N. Reynolds Memorial (2yofp) (div.)	32,872	RP	Goalie Jess	1:59.1f
9-10	Stephen Phillips Memorial (2yofp) (div.)	29,250	Nfld	Goalie Jess	1:57.1h
Baillargeon, Mario					
7-21	Molson Series Final (3&up Open Pace)	108,500	GrR	Night Colt, 7	1:52.3f
Baker, Charles					
2-10	Erwin F. Dygert Memorial (FFA Trot) (div.)	72,700	Haw	Eastridge Star	1:59.2
Bauslaugh, Louis					
6-19	Tompkins-Geers (2yofp) (div.)	20,600	ScD	Shady Daisy	1:58.4f
Beelby, Jack					
8-12	Nat Christie Memorial (3yo Open Pace)	$150,000	Clgy	Counterfeit Crown	1:55.1f
Bolon, Rodney					
8-8	Arden Downs (2yofp) (div.)	22,375	Mea	TLC Mindale	1:57.3f
Bookmyer, Gerry					
9-10	Stephen Phillips Memorial (2yofp) (div.)	28,500	Nfld	Tally Almahurst	2:00.1h
Boring, Chris					
6-9	W.N. Reynolds Memorial (3yoct) (div.)	19,050	RP	Letters From Hill	2:02f
6-10	W.N. Reynolds Memorial (3yocp) (div.)	22,900	RP	Fortysix Extralong	1:58.1f
8-15	The Castleton (2yofp)	62,000	Spr	Shady Daisy	1:56.4

LEADING DRIVERS

8-25	Horseman Futurity (3yo Open Trot)	37,032	Ind	Incredible D J	1:55.4
8-25	Horseman Futurity (3yocp)	27,958	Ind	Fortysix Cylinders	1:53
10-3	International Stallion Stake (2yofp)	95,150	Lex	Explosive Legacy	1:55.4

Boring, Troy
11-2	Ron Hodge Memorial (3yo Open Pace)	13,350	Nor	Fortysix Extralong	1:57.2h

Brocklehurst, Harold
5-26	Currier & Ives (3yo Open Trot) (div.)	38,060	Mea	Zizi's Prakas	1:59.4f

Brooks, John
4-8	Youthful Series Final (3yo Open Pace)	38,800	Moh	Laurstar	1:55.1f

Brown, Doug
5-12	George Morton Levy Series Final (Aged Pace)	240,000	YR	My Guru	1:54.3h
5-20	Mohawk Series Final (3yo Open Pace)	115,100	Moh	Neat Touch	1:56f
6-9	American-National (3yofp)	181,000	SPk	Town Pro	1:55.2f
6-17	Blue Bonnets Challenge (4&up H&G Pace)	130,500	BB	Topnotcher	1:53f
6-29	Historic-The Ladyship (3yofp)	74,355	M	Town Pro	1:53
7-28	Molson Canadian Pacing Derby (3&up Open)	265,250	GrR	Topnotcher	1:52.2f
7-30	de la Moisson Final (3yofp)	102,000	BB	Town Pro	1:53.2f
8-4	Tarport Hap (3yofp) (div.)	56,335	M	Town Pro	1:51.4
9-1	Fan Hanover Final (3yofp)	191,100	GrR	Town Pro	1:53.1f
9-2	Champlain Stakes (2yo Open Pace) (div.)	70,000	Moh	Happy Family	1:56.2f
9-8	Simcoe Stakes (3yofp) (div.)	109,612	Moh	Town Pro	1:54.4f
9-9	Nassagaweya (2yo Open Pace) (div.)	71,150	Moh	Happy Family	1:56.1f
9-30	Mohawk Gold Cup Final (3&up Open Pace)	197,750	Moh	Topnotcher	1:52.4f
10-13	Stewart Fraser Memorial (Open Pace)	230,000	Edm	Topnotcher	1:53.4f
11-2	**Breeders Crown** (3yofp)	**304,933**	**PPk**	**Town Pro**	**1:54.4f**
11-3	First Lady Final (2yofp)	144,701	RcR	Cams Exotic	1:56.3f
12-14	Matron Stakes (2yofp)	131,605	PPk	Cams Exotic	1:56f

Cameron, Jeff
1-30	Comforter Ser. Final (3&4yo F&M Pace)	72,250	M	Sunnie Nukes	1:57.1

Campbell, John
2-2	Cape & Cutter Series Final (Open Mare Pace)	43,000	M	Anniecrombie	1:57.2
2-5	Chill Factor Series Final (3&4yo C&G Pace)	38,000	M	My Tree	1:56.3
4-21	Big Apple Pace (3yo Open Pace) (div.)	40,000	YR	Jake And Elwood	1:55.2h
4-25	Jersey Girls Series Final (3-5yo F&M Pace)	66,800	M	White Ruffles	1:54
5-8	Trendsetter II Series Final (3&4yo C&G Pace)	55,500	M	Odds Against	1:54.2
5-10	The Westwind Series Final (3&4yo Pace)	50,300	M	Positive Cash	1:54.2
6-25	Historic-Debutante (2yofp) (div.)	37,415	M	Miss Easy	1:56.3
6-28	Historic-Goshen Cup (2yocp) (div.)	35,425	M	Henry Letsgo	1:55
6-28	Historic-Goshen Cup (2yocp) (div.)	35,075	M	Lefty	1:55.3
6-30	Historic-Jersey Cup (3yocp) (div.)	48,130	M	In The Pocket	1:51.2
7-7	Lady Maud (3yofp) (div.)	69,020	YR	Armbro Ilona	1:57.1h
7-7	Lady Suffolk (3yoft) (div.)	24,609	YR	Happy Diamonds	2:00.1h
7-7	Lady Suffolk (3yoft) (div.)	24,609	YR	Working Gal	2:00.2h
7-14	Bronx Filly Pace (3yofp) (div.)	$56,792	YR	Cataclysm	1:57.3h
7-14	Hudson Filly Trot (3yoft) (div.)	35,522	YR	Happy Diamonds	1:59.4h
7-28	Art Rooney Memorial Final (3yo Open Pace)	304,127	YR	Jake And Elwood	1:55h
8-2	Countess Adios (2yofp) (div.)	80,000	M	Miss Easy	1:54
8-4	**Hambletonian** (3yo Open Trot)	**1,346,000**	**M**	**Harmonious**	**1:54.1**
8-4	Tarport Hap (3yofp) (div.)	56,335	M	Bruce's Lady	1:53.3
8-17	Sweetheart Final (2yofp)	766,000	M	Miss Easy	1:52.3
8-25	**Cane Pace** (3yo Open Pace)	486,550	YR	Jake And Elwood	1:55.1h
8-31	World Filly Trotting Derby (3yo)	130,000	DuQ	Happy Diamonds	2:04.3
9-1	Lady Baltimore (2yofp) (div.)	77,083	RcR	R M Gee	1:57.3f
9-1	Lady Baltimore (2yofp) (div.)	75,834	RcR	Miss Easy	1:54.4f
9-2	Champlain Stakes (2yo Open Pace) (div.)	70,000	Moh	Silky Stallone	1:55.2f
9-8	**Messenger Stakes** (3yo Open Pace)	444,371	RcR	Jake And Elwood	1:52.3f
9-8	Kentucky Standardbred (2yofp) (div.)	127,650	RcR	Miss Easy	1:55f
9-8	Hanover Stake (Aged Pace)	22,865	RcR	Resonator	1:53.1f
9-9	Nassagaweya (2yo Open Pace) (div.)	69,650	Moh	Shipps Commander	1:56.2f
9-9	Nassagaweya (2yo Open Pace) (div.)	69,650	Moh	Artsplace	1:55f
9-20	Standardbred (2yo Open Pace) (div.)	32,186	Dela	W R H	1:54.1h
9-20	Buckette (3yoft) (div.)	36,255	Dela	Our First	1:57.3h

LEADING DRIVERS

9-21	American-National (2yocp) (div.)	55,000	SPk	Mantese	1:55.1f
9-22	Metro Stakes Final (2yo Open Pace)	797,400	Moh	Artsplace	1:53.4f
9-26	American-National (Aged Trot) (div.)	40,000	SPk	Peach Pit	1:58.3f
10-12	Cleveland Classic (3yo Open Pace) (div.)	150,000	Nfld	Jake And Elwood	1:54.4h
10-13	Three Diamonds Final (2yofp)	422,400	GSP	Miss Easy	1:55.3
11-17	Governor's Cup Final (2yo Open Pace)	655,600	GSP	Artsplace	1:53
11-30	**Breeders Crown** (2yofp)	**514,870**	PPk	**Miss Easy**	**1:54f**
11-30	**Breeders Crown** (2yocp)	**605,870**	PPk	**Artsplace**	**1:51.1f**

Charron, Mario
| 5-26 | Guys & Dolls Final (Open Pacing Mares) | 50,000 | Fhld | Games | 1:57.4h |

Clark, Keith
| 10-27 | Western Canada Pacing Dby. (3yo Open Pace) | 111,790 | Edm | Sky Hagler | 1:58.1f |

Clements, Dan
| 9-2 | Simcoe Stakes (3yo Open Pace) (div.) | 111,707 | Moh | Cam's Venture | 1:54.2f |

Condren, Steve
| 3-17 | Cam Fella Series Final (3&4yo Open Pace) | 152,500 | GrR | Gigalo | 1:55.2f |
| 8-13 | Boardwalk Final (3yofp) | 91,700 | GrR | Smiling Rebecca | 1:55f |

Copeland, Vince
| 6-2 | Mac Farlane Memorial (3yofp) | 77,425 | HP | Temptres Almahurst | 1:57.3f |

Cote, Benoit
| 7-17 | Ville de Trois Rivieres Final (2yocp) | 96,000 | TrRvs | Bombe Angus | 1:59.3h |

Cullipher, Roger
| 9-12 | Forest City Stakes (2yocp) (div.) | 29,500 | Nfld | Alfalad | 1:58.4h |

Daigneault, Rejean
| 7-1 | Landmark (3yofp) (div.) | 6,976 | Gosh | Bradash Pilot | 2:02.1h |

Daisey, Gene
| 8-10 | Arden Downs (3yoft) (div.) | 21,058 | Mea | Caspian | 1:58.2f |

Dancer, Donald
| 5-26 | Hanover Colt Stake (3yocp) (div.) | 21,223 | RcR | Kiev Hanover | 1:56.2f |

Dancer, Stanley
5-26	Currier & Ives (3yo Open Trot) (div.)	$38,060	Mea	King Of The Sea	2:00f
6-20	Tompkins-Geers (2yo Open Trot) (div.)	29,700	ScD	Gift Box	2:02.4f
6-30	Landmark (2yoct) (div.)	10,069	Gosh	Gift Box	2:07.4h

Davis, Eddie
3-21	Blossom Series Final (3yofp)	60,000	M	Yankee Desire	1:56.3
6-30	Turtle Dove (3yofp) (div.)	110,715	RcR	Sea Biscuit	1:54.3f
7-21	Potomac (2yocp) (div.)	66,387	RcR	Razzle Dazzlem	1:56.1f
8-26	Hanover Colt Stake (2yocp) (div.)	13,611	RcR	Thunderball	1:56.2f
9-8	Kentucky Standardbred (2yofp) (div.)	126,650	RcR	Unreachable	1:57.1f
11-2	Ron Hodge Memorial (3yo Open Pace) (div.)	13,350	Nor	My King Pin	1:57.3h

Davis, Tom
| 9-12 | Forest City Stakes (2yocp) (div.) | 28,800 | Nfld | Moravian Hanover | 1:58.3h |

Doherty, Jim
| 4-21 | Big Apple Pace (3yo Open Pace) (div.) | 40,000 | YR | Hubris | 1:57.2h |

Dokey, Merrit "Butch"
6-9	W.N. Reynolds Memorial (2yocp) (div.)	26,385	RP	Isle Of Maui	2:02f
6-21	Tompkins-Geers (2yo Open Pace) (div.)	27,200	ScD	Isle Of Maui	1:58.4f
6-30	Landmark (2yocp) (div.)	7,312	Gosh	Isle Of Maui	2:00h

Downey, Mike
| 8-18 | Gold Cup And Saucer (FFA Inv. Pace) | 20,000 | Chrtn | Tigerbird | 1:58h |

Dreux, Yves
| 8-5 | International Trot (Inv.-1-1/4 mi.) | 450,000 | YR | Reve d'Udon | 2:28.3h |

Durand, Tom
| 9-7 | Simcoe Stakes (3yo Open Trot) (div.) | 111,708 | Moh | Roughing It | 2:00.1f |

Fahy, Bill
5-19	Hanover-Hempt (3yocp) (div.)	32,800	VD	Till We Meet Again	1:54.4q
6-25	Historic-Acorn (2yoft) (div.)	56,000	M	Jean Bi	1:59.3
6-25	Historic-Debutante (2yofp) (div.)	37,415	M	Miss Intensity	1:58
6-25	Historic-Acorn (2yoft) (div.)	56,000	M	Another Geisha	2:01.2
7-14	Bronx Filly Pace (3yofp) (div.)	56,792	YR	Excited	1:58.1h
7-15	Hanover-Hempt (2yocp) (div.)	12,800	VD	Artsplace	1:57.3q
7-21	Potomac (2yocp) (div.)	66,387	RcR	Silky Stallone	1:56.1f

LEADING DRIVERS

7-23	Roses Are Red Series Final (3&up F&M Pace)	125,000	GrR	Caesars Jackpot	1:52.4f
7-28	Thomas P. Gaines Mem. (3yo Open Pace)	184,500	VD	Till We Meet AGain	1:53.3q
8-5	Prix de l'Avenir (2yocp) (div.)	146,125	BB	Shark Almahurst +	TDis
8-5	Prix de l'Avenir (2yocp) (div.)	146,125	BB	Silky Stallone	1:57.4f
8-25	Garden State Stake (2yo Open Pace) (div.)	92,451	Fhld	Shark Almahurst	1:56.4h
8-25	Garden State Stake (2yo Open Pace) (div.)	89,451	Fhld	Nuclear Legacy	1:57.3h
9-3	Helen Dancer Memorial (3yofp) (div.)	107,068	Fhld	Excited	1:57.3h
9-8	Kentucky Pacing Derby Final (2yo Open Pace)	379,553	LouD	Tooter Scooter	1:57h
9-18	Standardbred (2yo Open Trot)	52,150	Dela	Grundy's Mint	1:59.1h
10-7	Milton Final (3&up F&M Elims)	141,250	Moh	Caesars Jackpot	1:53.3f
10-8	Lou Babic Memorial Final (2yo Open Pace)	216,775	Fhld	Nuclear Legacy	1:56.2h
11-2	**Breeders Crown** (Aged Pacing Mares)	**200,000**	**PPk**	**Caesars Jackpot**	**1:52.3f**

Filion, Henri
7-7	Monctonian (FFA Pace)	127,000	NBD	Skipper Forrest	1:53.2f

Filion, Herve
4-21	R. Bruce Cornell Memorial (Open Pace)	100,000	Fhld	Dorunrun Bluegrass	1:53.1h
5-12	Windy City Final (3yo Open Pace)	255,000	May	Jake And Elwood	1:57.2h
6-2	Battle of Lake Erie (FFA Pace)	100,000	Nfld	Dorunrun Bluegrass	1:54h
7-1	Landmark (3yofp) (div.)	6,726	Gosh	No Discussion	2:00.3h
7-1	Landmark (3yocp)	$27,495	Gosh	Bon Nuit Karey	2:00h
7-1	Landmark (3yofp) (div.)	6,976	Gosh	Princess Silver	2:02.4h
7-7	Lady Maud (3yofp) (div.)	69,020	YR	Fiji Hanover	1:58.2h
7-7	Lady Suffolk (3yoft) (div.)	24,609	YR	L V Goldie	1:59.2h
8-11	U.S. Pacing Championships (Open Aged Pace)	75,000	YR	Dorunrun Bluegrass	1:56h
8-25	U.S. Pacing Championships (Aged Pace)	146,000	SPk	Dorunrun Bluegrass	1:54f
12-1	Wm. Haughton Memorial Final (Combined)	200,000	YR	Dorunrun Bluegrass	1:55h

Filion, Sylvain
7-8	Jazzman (Open Trot) (div.)	44,300	BB	Texas Snazzy	1:58.1f

Fout, Jeff
6-19	Tompkins-Geers (2yofp) (div.)	20,600	ScD	Sugar Lorraine	1:59.1f
6-22	Tompkins-Geers (3yofp) (div.)	26,100	ScD	Lady Genius	1:59f
7-21	Courageous Lady (3yofp)	131,500	Nfld	Excited	1:56.2h
7-27	Pink Bonnet Final (2yofp)	115,000	ScD	Shy Devil	1:57.3f
9-12	H.K. Devereux Memorial (2yoft)	38,400	Nfld	Shezatrotnmachine	2:02.4h
9-25	Bluegrass (2yofp)	99,250	Lex	Shady Daisy	1:55.4

Fritz, William "Bud"
6-9	Burlington Final (3yo Open Pace)	214,300	GrR	Apaches Fame	1:52.2f
6-11	Canadian Trotting Classic Final (3yo Open)	207,000	GrR	A Worthy Lad	1:59.4f
6-23	North America Cup Final (3yo Open Pace)	1,000,000	GrR	Apaches Fame	1:53.4f
7-28	Motor City Final (3yo Open Pace)	75,000	HP	Apaches Fame	1:54f
8-26	Confederation Cup (3yo Open Pace)	341,000	FlmD	Apaches Fame	1:55f
9-8	Little Brown Jug Preview (3yo Pace) (div.)	68,000	ScD	Apaches Fame	1:53.4f

Gale, Bill
4-29	Princess Series Final (3yo Filly Pace)	87,100	Moh	Instant Rebate	1:55.4f
5-12	John W. Miller Memorial Final (3yofp)	202,690	RcR	Instant Rebate	1:54.2f
6-6	W.N. Reynolds Memorial (2yofp) (div.)	32,872	RP	Jollie Dame	2:00f
6-13	Windsor Riverfront (2yofp) (div.)	29,250	WR	Jollie Dame	1:58.4f
6-14	Windsor Riverfront (3yoft)	39,100	WR	B Cor Jenny	2:00f
6-15	Windsor Border City (3yoct)	39,700	WR	I'm Impeccable	1:59.2f
8-8	Arden Downs (2yofp) (div.)	22,375	Mea	In Your Dreams	1:57.4f
9-7	Champlain Stakes (2yofp) (div.)	85,690	Moh	Jollie Dame	1:58.2f
9-14	Mac Farlane Memorial (3yo Open Pace) (div.)	76,255	HP	Camluck	1:56.3f
10-13	Abe Lincoln (2yo Open Pace)	130,000	May	Three Wizzards	1:57.1h
10-14	Harvest Stakes (2yofp) (div.)	81,134	Moh	Jollie Dame	1:56.2f

Gatto, Richard
6-30	Landmark (2yocp) (div.)	7,312	Gosh	Could This B Magic	2:02h

Gilmour, William "Buddy"
4-14	Berry's Creek Consolation (3yo Open Pace)	20,000	M	Shipps Schnoops	1:55.1
6-30	Landmark (2yocp) (div.)	7,312	Gosh	Banquet Table	2:01.3h
7-29	Juvenile Canadien Final (2yocp)	79,900	BB	Stand And Deliver	1:56.2f

Hammer, Roger
8-26	Hanover Colt Stake (2yocp) (div.)	13,611	RcR	Hello Almahurst	1:56.3f

LEADING DRIVERS

Harmer, Tom
8-30   Hayes Memorial (3yofp)   35,650   DuQ   Tip 'N Tax   1:53

Haughton, Tommy
5-27   Currier & Ives Filly Trot (3yo) (div.)   14,555   Mea   Essence Bear   2:01.2f
12-22 Matron Stakes (3yo Open Pace)   138,490   PPk   Shipps Schnoops   1:53.2f

Hayes, John Jr.
9-8   Simcoe Stakes (3yofp) (div.)   109,613   Moh   Jonvik Castle   1:56.2f

Henderson, Ron
6-16   Windsor Border City (3yofp) (div.) $32,750   WR   Fiji Hanover   1:54.4f

Hennessy, Rod
9-22 Northlands Filly Stake (3yofp)   82,090   Edm   Tylers Royalty   1:55.4f

Herman, Billy
8-10   Arden Downs (3yoct) (div.)   30,377   Mea   Castleton Magic   1:59.4f
10-5   Ky. Futurity Filly Div. (3yoft)   92,120   Lex   Nivea Hanover   1:58.2

Hewitt, Kevin
6-30   Landmark (2yoct) (div.)   10,069   Gosh   Clovis Mon Ami   2:07.4h

Hie, Carman
1-19   Blizzard Series Final (3&4yo F&M Pace)   25,200   GrR   Town Sweetheart   1:57.4f
9-1   Provenzano Memorial Final (Open Trot)   50,000   Btva   Shawland Magic   1:58.2h

Holloway, Joe
8-23   Hoosier Futurity (2yocp)   24,776   Ind   Endowment   1:57.4

Irvine, Don Jr.
7-27   Hanover Filly Stake (2yofp) (div.)   16,460   RcR   Heather Lane   1:57.3f
7-29   Hanover Filly Stake (2yoft) (div.)   13,055   RcR   Seductive Lass   2:05f
8-26   Hanover Colt Stake (2yocp) (div.)   13,611   RcR   Front View   1:58.1f

James, Jeff
9-14   Mac Farlane Memorial (3yo Open Pace) (div.)   76,255   HP   Brando Hanover   1:57.2f

Johansson, Stig
11-2   **Breeders Crown** (Aged Trotting Mares)   **203,458**   **PPk**   **Peace Corps**   **1:54.2f**

Johnson, Jan
5-27   Currier & Ives Filly Trot (3yo) (div.)   14,405   Mea   Camelia Lobell   1:59.2f
5-27   Currier & Ives Filly Trot (3yo) (div.)   14,555   Mea   Lila Lobell   2:00.3f
6-27   Historic-Coaching Club Oaks (3yoft) (div.)   45,987   M   Lila Lobell   1:55.4
6-29   Historic-Historic Cup (3yoct)   102,955   M   Star Mystic   2:00.2
7-7   Founders Gold Cup (3yo Open Trot)   140,100   VD   Star Mystic   1:57.1q
7-18   Hanover-Hempt (2yofp) (div.)   8,900   VD   Eternal Flare   2:02.3q
7-18   Hanover-Hempt (2yoft) (div.)   8,600   VD   Sweet Adeline   2:01.1q
10-3   International Stallion Stake (2yoft)   121,000   Lex   Eternal Flare   1:59.2
10-24 Goldsmith Maid Final (2yoft)   294,600   GSP   Kramer Nobless   2:00.2
10-5   **Kentucky Futurity** (3yo Open Trot)   **180,000**   **Lex**   **Star Mystic**   **1:55.3**

Kelly, Harold
6-13   Windsor Riverfront (2yoft)   31,050   WR   Good Lookin Mouse   2:01.4f
6-16   Windsor Border City (2yoft)   33,750   WR   Tambourine   1:56f
6-19   Tompkins-Geers (2yoft) (div.)   21,200   ScD   Good Lookin Mouse   2:02.4f
6-23   Tompkins-Geers (3yo Open Pace) (div.)   27,700   ScD   Hot Walker   1:57.2f
6-23   Tompkins-Geers (3yo Open Pace) (div.)   27,700   ScD   Bookmaker   1:54.3f
6-23   Tompkins-Geers (3yo Open Trot) (div.)   28,150   ScD   Downhill Racer   2:01f
8-4   Tarport Hap (3yofp) (div.)   57,335   M   Tambourine   1:54.1
8-31   Lou Babic Memorial Final (2yofp)   121,465   Fhld   Cams Exotic   1:56.4h
9-22   Molly Pitcher (2yofp) (div.)   60,579   Fhld   Cams Exotic   1:57.3h

Kerwood, Tony
2-16   Snowshoe Series Final (3&4yo Open Pace)   35,800   GrR   Stew Almahurst   1:57.3f
9-1   James B. Dancer Mem. (3yo Open Pace)   379,280   Fhld   Road Machine   1:54.4h
10-14 Harvest Stakes (2yofp) (div.)   82,633   Moh   Big Bloomer   1:56.3f

Kopas, John
6-25   Historic-Debutante (2yofp) (div.)   37,415   M   Laugh Line   1:59
8-2   Countess Adios (2yofp) (div.)   79,000   M   Laugh Line   1:56.3
9-7   Champlain Stakes (2yofp) (div.) $83,690   Moh   Laugh Line   1:56.3f
9-27   Bluegrass (3yofp)   96,590   Lex   Delinquent Account   1:53.3

Kvikstad, Jorn
7-1   Landmark (3yoft) (div.)   8,965   Gosh   La Montagna   2:06.2h
8-8   Arden Downs (2yoct) (div.)   17,057   Mea   Beaurina   2:01.1f

LEADING DRIVERS

9-14	Hanover Colt Stake (2yoct) (div.)	14,274	RcR	UConn Don	2:01.2f

Lachance, Michel

1-31	Trendsetter Series Final (3&4yo C&G Pace)	100,000	M	Master Scoot	1:55.3
3-30	New Faces Series Final (3yocp)	104,000	M	Mark Johnathan	1:56.1
4-14	Berry's Creek Final (3yo Open Pace)	323,750	M	Mark Johnathan	1:54
5-7	Hiram Woodruff Series Final (3&4yo Trot)	42,200	M	Incredible D J	1:57
6-28	Historic-Goshen Cup (2yocp) (div.)	35,075	M	Brett's Story	1:57
6-30	Historic-Jersey Cup (3yocp) (div.)	48,130	M	Raven Lunatic	1:54.3
7-7	Driscoll Series Final (FFA Pace)	211,000	M	T K's Skipper	1:51.2
7-28	Beacon Course Final (3yo Open Trot)	401,500	M	Embassy Lobell	1:56.3
8-3	Hambletonian Oaks (3yoft)	441,555	M	Working Gal	1:58.1
8-5	Prix de l'Avenir (2yocp) (div.)	146,125	BB	Nuke Of Earl	1:59.1f
8-17	U.S. Pacing Championships (FFA Pace)	75,000	M	T K's Skipper	1:50.3
8-19	Zweig Memorial (3yo Open Trot) (div.)	75,300	Sycs	Embassy Lobell	1:57.3
8-26	Hanover Colt Stake (2yocp) (div.)	13,611	RcR	Hahn Hanover	1:55.3f
9-20	Buckette (3yoft) (div.)	36,255	Dela	Working Gal	1:59.3h
9-21	Jugette (3yofp)	200,000	Dela	Lady Genius	1:55.3h
9-22	Molly Pitcher (2yofp) (div.)	60,579	Fhld	Sunraycer	1:58.2h
9-28	Bluegrass (3yoct)	119,970	Lex	Embassy Lobell	1:54.4
10-13	Colonial Lady (3yoft) (div.)	46,685	RcR	Working Gal	1:57.1f
10-21	Provincial Cup (3yo Open Pace)	230,500	WR	Camluck	1:52.4f
11-2	**Breeders Crown** (3yoct)	**396,933**	**PPk**	**Embassy Lobell**	**1:56.4f**
11-23	Clare Series Final (Aged Paced Mares)	75,000	YR	L Dees Trish	1:54.4h
12-15	Matron Stakes (2yo Open Pace)	160,005	PPk	Mantese	1:54.2f

Lancaster, Mark

2-1	Complex Series Final (3-5yo Pace)	46,900	M	Storm Compensation	1:53.4

Langeweg, Hugo

7-18	Hanover-Hempt (2yoft) (div.)	8,900	VD	Frances Jet Boko	2:00.3q
9-18	Standardbred (2yoft)	51,472	Dela	Frances Jet Boko	1:59.3h
9-26	Bluegrass (2yoft)	105,630	Lex	Frances Jet Boko	1:58.2

Laurente, Jimmy

6-30	Landmark (2yofp) (div.)	4,591	Gosh	Bossin' Around	2:07h

LeBlanc, Steve

8-8	Arden Downs (2yofp) (div.)	22,775	Mea	Eicarls Carlene	1:59f

Lindstedt, Berndt

6-20	Tompkins-Geers (3yoft) (div.)	24,510	ScD	Lila Lobell	1:59.4f
6-20	Tompkins-Geers (3yoft) (div.)	24,510	ScD	Me Maggie	1:59.1f
7-8	Hanover Filly Stake (3yoft) (div.)	19,041	RcR	Eternal Goddess	2:00.1f
7-20	Hanover-Hempt (3yoft) (div.)	21,600	VD	Me Maggie	1:59.1q
7-20	Hanover-Hempt (3yoft) (div.)	21,100	VD	Model Home	1:58q
7-29	Stars & Stripes (Inv. Trot)	35,000	YR	Kit Lobell	1:57.2h
8-7	Arden Downs (2yoft) (div.)	16,494	Mea	Cookout	2:04.4f
8-10	Arden Downs (3yoft) (div.)	21,058	Mea	Eternal Goddess	2:00.3f
8-10	Arden Downs (3yoct) (div.)	30,727	Mea	Wolfs Degel	1:59.2f
8-10	Arden Downs (3yoft) (div.)	20,708	Mea	Me Maggie	1:57.2f
8-15	The Castleton (2yoft)	62,000	Spr	Cookout	2:00.1
8-16	The Castleton (3yoft)	55,000	Spr	Model Home	1:58.1
8-17	The Alexander Mem. (3yo Trot)	110,000	Spr	Super Arnie	1:54.1
8-19	Zweig Memorial Filly Trot (3yo)	45,000	Sycs	Eternal Goddess	1:59.3
9-26	American-National (Aged Trot) (div.)	40,000	SPk	Kit Lobell	1:58.4f
9-28	Bluegrass (3yoft)	$107,480	Lex	Model Home	1:56.3
10-13	Colonial Lady (3yoft) (div.)	46,685	RcR	Me Maggie	1:57.2f
11-2	**Breeders Crown** (3yoft)	**378,933**	**PPk**	**Me Maggie**	**1:57.1f**
11-16	Matron Stakes Final (3yoft)	75,000	PPk	Model Home	1:57.4f

Longo, Gerald

9-11	American-National (2yoct) (div.)	47,500	SPk	Square Rigger	2:02.2f

MacDonell, Paul

11-2	**Breeders Crown** (Aged H&G Pace)	**273,458**	**PPk**	**Bay's Fella**	**1:52.1f**

Magee, Dave

1-27	Whizzer White (4yo Open Pace)	32,100	Haw	Dark Rye	1:57
2-3	Suburban Downs Pacing Derby (FFA) (div.)	55,300	Haw	Dark Rye	1:56.1
6-18	American-National (3yoct)	272,000	SPk	Armbro Iliad	2:00.1f

LEADING DRIVERS

10-12	Cinderella (3yofp)	100,000	May	Instant Rebate	1:59h	

Mancik, Rich

2-10	Erwin F. Dygert Memorial (FFA Trot) (div.)	72,700	Haw	Teddys Toy	1:58.3

Manzi, Cat

2-17	Aquarius Series Final (4&5yo Open Pace)	58,000	M	Direct Current	1:54.2
6-30	Landmark (2yofp) (div.)	4,592	Gosh	Classic Aussie	2:02.4h
6-30	Landmark (2yofp) (div.)	4,441	Gosh	Another Halo	2:03.4h
7-18	Hanover-Hempt (2yoft) (div.)	8,900	VD	Meadow Heather	2:03.2q
8-1	Merrie Annabelle Consolation (2yoft)	35,000	M	Sherbie's Lady	1:59.3
8-1	Merrie Annabelle Final (2yoft)	464,750	M	Santa Royal	1:58.1
8-10	Kentucky Standardbred (2yoft) (div.)	96,250	RcR	Santa Royal	1:59.4f
8-19	Zweig Memorial (3yo Open Trot) (div.)	75,300	Sycs	Harmonious	1:57.1
9-24	Charles Smith Memorial Final (3yoft)	109,440	Fhld	Caspian	1:59.1h
10-9	Harold Dancer Memorial Final (2yoft)	96,950	GSP	Loosen Up	1:59.1
9-1	World Trotting Derby (3yo Open)	600,000	DuQ	Harmonious	2:04.3

Marsh, Ron

2-2	Pretty Direct (4&up Pacing Mares)	34,300	Haw	Bye Bye Sleepyhead	1:57.1

Mayotte, Roger

2-25	Toronto Series Final (4&up Open Pace)	125,000	GrR	Take A Look	1:55.4f

Mazeroski, Bob

9-14	Hanover Colt Stake (2yoct) (div.)	14,024	RcR	Dontellmenomore	1:59.1f

McGee, Dave

4-9	Belle Isle Final (3&4yo Open Pace)	20,000	HP	Indylator	1:58.1f

McIlmurray, Art

6-13	Windsor Riverfront (2yofp) (div.)	29,250	WR	Phast Madam	1:59.2f
6-15	Windsor Riverfront (2yocp) (div.)	25,000	WR	Fabulious	1:58.2f

McNichol, Mickey

6-28	Historic-Goshen Cup (2yocp) (div.)	35,075	M	Mantese	1:56.1
7-15	Hanover-Hempt (2yocp) (div.)	12,500	VD	Mantese	1:57q
8-3	Oliver Wendell Holmes (3yocp)	258,000	M	Brando Hanover	1:51.3
8-11	Adioo Volo (3yofp) (div.)	48,614	Mea	Lady Dynamo	1:56.2f
8-15	The Little Pat (2yo Open Pace)	74,000	Spr	Mantese	1:53.4
9-2	Champlain Stakes (2yo Open Pace) (div.)	70,000	Moh	Mantese	1:57f
9-8	Little Brown Jug Preview (3yo Pace) (div.)	70,000	ScD	Brando Hanover	1:54.2f
9-22	Molly Pitcher (2yofp) (div.)	62,079	Fhld	Lexie	1:57.2h

Moiseyev, Jack

3-8	Exit 16W Final (3-5yo C&G Pace)	82,100	M	Mr Bagel	1:54.1
3-9	Overbid Series Final (F&M Open Pace)	57,000	M	Sweet Sharon	1:53.3

Morand, Jim

9-14	Bret Hanover (3yocp)	$39,100	Nfld	Kiev Hanover	1:57h
10-5	Bluegrass (3yocp)	130,000	Lex	Kiev Hanover	1:50.1
10-12	Cleveland Classic (3yo Open Pace) (div.)	150,000	Nfld	Kiev Hanover	1:55.4h

Morgan, Anthony

2-3	Suburban Downs Pacing Derby (FFA) (div.)	55,300	Haw	In His Favor	1:57.1

Morrill, Jim Jr.

6-30	Turtle Dove (3yofp) (div.)	112,715	RcR	Choice Yankee	1:54.3f
7-15	Hanover Filly Stake (3yofp) (div.)	20,386	RcR	Choice Yankee	1:55.2f
8-17	Mistletoe Shalee Final (3yofp)	425,250	M	Choice Yankee	1:52.4

Nickells, Bruce

8-25	Hoosier Futurity (2yoct)	21,476	Ind	Ten Pound Bass	2:01.2

Noble, Sam "Chip"

8-25	Fox Stake (2yo Open Pace)	103,362	Ind	Deal Direct	1:52.4
6-9	W.N. Reynolds Memorial (2yocp) (div.)	26,385	RP	Squire Squirt	1:58.4f
6-19	Tompkins-Geers (2yofp) (div.)	20,600	ScD	Gretzky	1:59.3f
8-16	Review Stake (3yo Open Pace)	54,000	Spr	Happy Hoosier	1:55.2
8-30	Hayes Memorial (3yo Open Pace)	50,400	DuQ	Happy Hoosier	1:55
8-31	Hayes Memorial (2yofp)	57,000	DuQ	Gretzky	1:55.3
9-2	Champlain Stakes (2yo Open Pace) (div.)	70,000	Moh	Deal Direct	1:56f

Nordin, Jan

6-26	Historic-Harriman (2yoct) (div.)	38,467	M	Grundy's Mint	2:00.2
7-3	Mac Farlane Memorial (3yoft)	75,000	HP	Miss Baltic	2:00.4f
7-14	Hudson Filly Trot (3yoft) (div.)	35,522	YR	Kindava Hush	2:02h

LEADING DRIVERS

7-17	Hanover-Hempt (2yoct) (div.)	12,400	VD	Baltic Viking	2:02.3q
7-17	Hanover-Hempt (2yoct) (div.)	12,100	VD	Chapman	2:01.4q
7-17	Hanover-Hempt (2yoct) (div.)	12,400	VD	Grundy's Mint	2:00.3q
7-18	Hanover-Hempt (2yoft) (div.)	8,600	VD	Jean Bi	1:59.1q
7-29	Hanover Filly Stake (2yoft) (div.)	12,805	RcR	Frances Jet Boko	2:02.2f
7-29	Hanover Filly Stake (2yoft) (div.)	12,805	RcR	Jean Bi	2:02.3f
8-7	Arden Downs (2yoft) (div.)	16,494	Mea	Granny Smith	2:03f
8-8	Arden Downs (2yoct) (div.)	17,057	Mea	Chapman	2:02.4f
8-8	Arden Downs (2yoct) (div.)	17,057	Mea	Dickerson	2:01.2f
8-10	Kentucky Standardbred (2yoft) (div.)	97,500	RcR	Frances Jet Boko	2:01.2f
8-15	The Greyhound (2yo Open Trot)	110,000	Spr	Dickerson	1:58.1
8-24	Horseman Futurity (3yoft)	22,210	Ind	Kindava Hush	1:57.1
9-1	The Castleton Stake (2yoct)	64,600	DuQ	Dickerson	1:59.2
9-4	Champlain Stakes (2yoft)	221,070	Moh	Frances Jet Boko	2:02f
9-8	Champlain Stakes (2yo Open Trot) (div.)	131,515	Moh	Grundy's Mint (DH)	2:04f
9-11	American-National (2yoct) (div.)	47,500	SPk	Anders Crown	2:02.2f
9-12	American-National (2yoft)	92,600	SPk	Jean Bi	2:00.4f
9-16	Campbellville (2yo Open Trot) (div.)	77,000	Moh	Anders Crown	2:03f
9-16	Campbellville (2yo Open Trot) (div.)	75,500	Moh	Tag Team	2:01.4f
9-21	Old Oaken Bucket (3yo Open Trot)	125,808	Dela	Lender Hanover	2:02.3h
9-27	Bluegrass (2yoct)	106,290	Lex	Grundy's Mint	1:57.1
10-4	International Stallion Stake (2yoct)	135,300	Lex	Grundy's Mint	1:57.4
11-30	**Breeders Crown Final** (2yoft)	**367,403**	PPk	**Jean Bi**	**2:00.3f**

O'Donnell, Bill

1-27	Presidential Series Final (FFA Pace)	100,000	M	Barely Visible	1:53.3
2-19	Su Mac Lad Series Final (FFA Trot)	73,000	M	No Sex Please	1:57.4
2-27	Night Styles Series Final (3-5yo F&M Pace)	81,800	M	Why Wont Ya	1:57.1
3-17	Four Leaf Clover Series Final (3-5yo Pace)	93,500	M	Trouble Twosum	1:55.1
6-11	American-National (3yoft)	185,000	SPk	Spreadsheet	1:59.2f
8-8	Arden Downs (2yoct) (div.)	17,457	Mea	Super Pleasure	1:59.3f
8-17	Sweetheart Consolation (2yofp)	50,000	M	Paper Caper	1:57
9-8	Champlain Stakes (2yo Open Trot) (div.)	133,515	Moh	Super Pleasure	2:01.2f

Ouellet, Michel

6-17	Windsor Border City (3yocp) (div.)	$30,250	WR	Broussard	1:54.2f

Ouellet, Serge

6-24	Grand Prix de Quebec (Invitational)	50,000	Que	Fiorello Blue Chip	1:56.4h

Paisley, Walter

9-1	American-National (Aged Pace)	148,000	SPk	Keystone Raider	1:53.2f
10-20	Galt (3yo Open Trot)	100,000	May	Incredible DJ	1:59.2h

Palone, Dave

8-9	Arden Downs (2yocp) (div.)	23,675	Mea	Artsplace	1:55.3f
8-9	Arden Downs (2yocp) (div.)	23,675	Mea	The Other Guy	1:55.1f

Parker, Howard

9-15	Nadia Lobell Final (3yofp)	220,000	GSP	Crafty Caper	1:53.4

John Patterson, Jr.

10-3	Harold Dancer Mem. Final (2yo Open Trot)	117,575	GSP	Mr Chin	1:59.1
10-25	Valley Victory Final (2yoct)	330,300	GSP	Mr Chin	1:58.1
11-10	Matron Stakes Final (2yo Open Trot)	91,143	PPk	Mr Chin	2:00.4f

Pavia, Joe Jr.

10-4	Tattersalls-Garnsey Mem. (3yofp)	91,100	Lex	Rulers Chippie	1:53.2
12-21	Matron Stakes (3yofp)	91,095	PPk	Rulers Chippie	1:55.3f

Picciano, Jay

8-16	The Castleton (3yofp)	50,000	Spr	Lady Genius	1:54.1
9-10	Maud S (3yoft)	38,850	Nfld	Aspiring Lass	2:00.2h

Pierce, Ron

5-19	Graduate Series Final (4&5yo Open Pace)	205,500	M	Dorunrun Bluegrass	1:51.3
6-9	Lake Superior (FFA)	100,000	HP	Topnotcher	1:53.3f
7-28	Beacon Course Consolation (3yo Open Trot)	15,000	M	Incredible D J	1:56.1
9-2	President's Pace (FFA)	60,000	Scar	Prince Ebony	1:54f
9-9	Des Smith Classic (Aged Pace)	76,000	RidC	Topnotcher	1:55f
9-16	Senior Jug (4&5yo Open Pace)	35,500	Dela	Casino Cowboy	1:54.3h

Plutino, John

LEADING DRIVERS

9-3	North American Ser. Final (3&4yo Open Pace)	67,000	Btva	San Andre	1:56h

Procino, Gerald

4-21	Big Apple Pace (3yo Open Pace) (div.)	40,000	YR	Sea The USA	1:56.4h

Rankin, Dave

6-19	Tompkins-Geers (2yoft) (div.)	21,200	ScD	Con's In Tassel	2:04f
7-12	American-National (2yofp)	86,200	SPk	Start Dialing	1:59.3f
7-21	Potomac (2yocp) (div.)	66,387	RcR	Cambest	1:55.2f
8-9	Arden Downs (2yocp) (div.)	23,675	Mea	Meadow Lucas	1:58.2f
8-23	Hoosier Futurity (2yofp)	26,537	Ind	Start Dialing	1:55.2
8-23	Horseman Futurity (3yofp)	18,374	Ind	Touch Of Silk	1:54.2
8-25	Garden State Stake (2yo Open Pace) (div.)	89,451	Fhld	Cambest	1:56.1h
9-12	North Randall Park (3yofp)	36,350	Nfld	Touch Of Silk	1:58.3h
9-21	Walnut Hall (2yofp)	57,973	Dela	Start Dialing	1:57.2h

Rapone, Patsy

7-1	Hopeful Final (2yocp)	190,000	BR	He's Discreet	1:59.2h

Remmen, Ray

5-12	Wm. E. Miller Memorial Final (3yo Pace)	315,010	RcR	Beach Towel	1:52.3f
5-26	Hanover Colt Stake (3yocp) (div.)	20,972	RcR	Beach Towel	1:54.1f
6-9	Terrapin (3yocp)	316,135	RcR	Beach Towel	1:54.1f
6-30	American-National (3yocp)	$347,000	SPk	Beach Towel	1:52.4f
7-13	Meadowlands Pace Final (3yo Open Pace)	1,153,500	M	Beach Towel	1:52.2
8-11	Adios (3yo Open Pace)	493,176	Mea	Beach Towel	1:51.4f
8-19	Prix d'Ete (3yocp)	663,500	BB	Beach Towel	1:53.1f
9-20	**Little Brown Jug** (3yo Open Pace)	468,610	Dela	Beach Towel	1:53.3h
9-29	Tattersalls (3yo Open Pace)	185,100	Lex	Beach Towel	1:51.1
11-2	**Breeders Crown** (3yocp)	**366,933**	**PPk**	**Beach Towel**	**1:51.2f**

Richards, Del

7-14	Hanover-Hempt (3yofp)	52,300	VD	Dear Dignity	1:57.2q

Richardson, Dick Jr.

6-9	W.N. Reynolds Memorial (3yoct) (div.)	20,050	RP	Drummer Hanover	2:01.2f
6-20	Tompkins-Geers (2yo Open Trot) (div.)	29,200	ScD	Crysta's Best	2:00.1f
6-23	Tompkins-Geers (3yo Open Trot) (div.)	74,400	ScD	Drummer Hanover	2:00.4f
6-30	Hanover-Hempt (3yoct) (div.)	33,200	VD	Drummer Hanover	1:59.4q
8-24	Horseman Stake (2yo Open Trot)	51,090	Ind	Crysta's Best	1:59
11-30	**Breeders Crown Final** (2yoct)	**355,403**	**PPk**	**Crysta's Best**	**2:01f**

Riegle, Bruce

6-19	Tompkins-Geers (2yofp) (div.)	20,600	ScD	Shy Devil	1:58.2f
6-21	Tompkins-Geers (2yo Open Pace) (div.)	27,200	ScD	Master Fund	1:58.4f
6-21	Tompkins-Geers (2yo Open Pace) (div.)	27,200	ScD	Nuclear Legacy	1:58.4f

Roberts, "Bib"

7-27	Hanover Filly Stake (2yofp) (div.)	16,460	RcR	Yankee Co-Ed	1:56.3f
9-1	Lady Baltimore (2yofp) (div.)	77,083	RcR	Yankee Co-ed	1:54.4f

Saftic, Mike

2-17	Damsel Series Final (3&4yo F&M Pace)	135,250	GrR	Tinycrombie	1:56.4f
8-5	Prix de l'Avenir (2yocp) (div.)	146,125	BB	Jackpot Raider	1:57f

Schroeder, Brian

10-15	Autumn Stakes (2yoft) (div.)	76,800	Moh	Collier St Kathy	2:03f

Schwind, Joe

5-11	The Spring Fever Series Final (3&4yo Pace)	37,400	M	Canvasback Fella	1:53.4

Sells, Tom

1-21	Horsemen's Series Final (4&up Open Trot)	125,500	GrR	Go Get Lost	1:59f

Sheppard, Kelly

5-21	Connaught Cup (FFA Pace)	50,000	Conn	Chatham Light	1:53.3h

Sheppard, Paul

7-29	Frank Ryan Memorial (Aged Pacers)	68,500	RidC	Northland Salute	1:53.2f

Silverman, Richard

8-3	Niatross Final (2yocp)	365,600	M	Die Laughing	1:54.2
8-17	Woodrow Wilson Final (2yo Open Pace)	1,043,500	M	Die Laughing	1:52.1
10-5	International Stallion Stake (2yocp)	153,500	Lex	Die Laughing	1:52.1
11-3	Presidential Final (2yo Open Pace)	298,345	RcR	Die Laughing	1:54f

Simpson, John Jr.

7-22	Hanover Colt Stake (3yoct)	19,633	RcR	Antwerp Hanover	1:57.3f

LEADING DRIVERS

Sirtonon, Juha
7-22	Hanover Colt Stake (3yoct)		19,633	RcR Remus Hanover	1:56.4f

Snyder, Doug
6-30	Landmark (2yoft) (div.)		6,588	Gosh Edwina Lobell	2:07.3h
5-19	Hanover-Hempt (3yocp) (div.)		32,800	VD King Gypsy	1:54.1q
8-7	Arden Downs (2yoft) (div.)		$16,494	Mea T-Ball	2:01.4f
8-11	Adioo Volo (3yofp) (div.)		48,614	Mea Yankee Goddess	1:55f

Steall, Ben
9-14	Hanover Colt Stake (2yoct) (div.)		14,274	RcR Anabolic Ben	2:01.2f

Stillings, Dick
5-26	Currier & Ives (3yo Open Trot) (div.)		38,060	Mea Cheyenne Spur	2:00.4f
6-30	Hanover-Hempt (3yoct) (div.)		33,200	VD Cheyenne Spur	1:57.1q
8-11	Adioo Volo (3yofp) (div.)		47,614	Mea Lady Genius	1:56f
10-13	Colonial (3yo Open Trot) (div.)		122,033	RcR Cheyenne Spur	1:56.2f
11-9	Matron Stakes (2yoft)		88,683	PPk Esprit Spur	1:58f

Stults, Leroy
7-1	Landmark (3yoft) (div.)		8,965	Gosh Cabrera Lobell	2:02.2h

Sugg, John
6-15	Windsor Riverfront (2yocp) (div.)		25,000	WR Brett's Story	1:57.2f

Sugg, Kurt
6-10	W.N. Reynolds Memorial (3yocp) (div.)		22,900	RP French Embassy	1:56.3f

Turcotte, Mel
9-12	Col. Wm. Edwards Memorial (3yoct) (div.)		23,300	Nfld Royal Cold	2:01h

Turner, Robert
6-19	Tompkins-Geers (2yoft) (div.)		20,700	ScD Peace Bid	2:03f
7-1	Landmark (3yoct)		25,095	Gosh Wolfs Gaon	2:05.1h

Twaddle, Tim
10-15	Autumn Stakes (2yoft) (div.)		76,800	Moh Shipps Doll	2:03f

Walker, Larry
7-20	Hanover-Hempt (3yoft) (div.)		20,600	VD Armbro Icon	2:00.3q
8-2	Countess Adios (2yofp) (div.)		80,000	M Falcon's Secret	1:56.4
9-3	Simcoe Stakes (3yoft) (div.)		107,613	Moh Armbro Icon	1:59.3f
9-3	Simcoe Stakes (3yoft) (div.)		105,612	Moh Ashley Jane	2:00.1f
9-7	Champlain Stakes (2yofp) (div.)		83,690	Moh Falcon's Secret	1:57.1f
10-14	Harvest Stakes (2yofp) (div.)		82,633	Moh Falcon's Secret	1:59.1f

Wallis, Kevin
6-10	W.N. Reynolds Memorial (3yofp)		32,700	RP Royal Harmony	1:56.4f
6-22	Tompkins-Geers (3yofp) (div.)		26,100	ScD Royal Harmony	1:57.2f

Waples, Ron
6-27	Historic-Coaching Club Oaks (3yoft) (div.)		45,987	M Delphi's Lobell	1:57.3
7-8	Jazzman (Open Trot) (div.)		43,800	BB No Sex Please	1:55.4f
7-14	Sheppard Final (2yocp)		474,500	YR June's Baby	1:58.2h
7-21	Potomac (2yocp) (div.)		64,877	RcR Deal Breaker	1:56.2f
7-21	Potomac (2yocp) (div.)		66,387	RcR Gigowatt	1:54.4f
7-29	Hanover Filly Stake (2yoft) (div.)		13,055	RcR Mal Hana Kaari	2:04.1f
7-30	Nat Rat ('88 & '89 Hambletonian Elig. Trot)		112,000	M Alfresco	1:57
8-7	Arden Downs (2yoft) (div.)		16,494	Mea Malahana Kaari	2:00.3f
8-18	Maple Leaf Trot (3yo&up)		293,250	GrR No Sex Please	1:57f
9-1	Hayes Memorial (2yocp)		72,500	DuQ Rebelator	1:55.4
9-8	Champlain Stakes (2yo Open Trot) (div.)		131,515	Moh Crimson Lobell (DH)	2:04f
9-9	Nassagaweya (2yo Open Pace) (div.)		71,150	Moh June's Baby	1:55.3f
9-20	Standardbred (2yo Open Pace) (div.)		32,186	Dela Deal Breaker	1:56.4h
10-3	Bret Hanover (Open Pace)		63,000	Lex Mystery Fund	1:52.1
10-4	Speedy Scot (Open Trot) (div.)		47,500	Lex No Sex Please	1:55
10-4	Speedy Scot (Open Trot) (div.)		47,500	Lex Kerry's Crown	1:55.1
10-13	Colonial Lady (3yoft) (div.)		$46,685	RcR Happy Diamonds	1:57f
11-2	**Breeders Crown** (Aged H&G Trot)		**221,458**	PPk **No Sex Please**	**1:55f**

Warrington, Steve
7-15	Hanover Filly Stake (3yofp) (div.)		20,386	RcR Fitness Flower	1:55f

Webster, Ben
8-2	Townsend Ackerman ('90 Hambo Eligibles)		35,000	M Pesach	1:58
8-25	Garden State Stake (2yo Open Pace) (div.)		92,451	Fhld Three Wizzards	1:56h

LEADING DRIVERS

Wellwood, Bill
6-2	Hanover Stake (Open Aged Trot)	19,500	RcR	Peach Pit	1:57f
6-30	Landmark (2yoft) (div.)	6,738	Gosh	Turkish Sweet	2:08h

Williams, Dick II
7-8	Hanover Filly Stake (3yoft) (div.)	19,291	RcR	Nivea Hanover	2:00.1f
7-31	Peter Haughton Memorial Final (2yoct)	609,250	M	Charlie Ten Hitch	2:00.2

Williams, Mark
6-17	Windsor Border City (3yocp) (div.)	30,250	WR	Global Assault	1:54.2f
8-9	Arden Downs (2yocp) (div.)	23,675	Mea	Gold Glover	1:56.4f
9-2	Simcoe Stakes (3yo Open Pace) (div.)	113,708	Moh	Global Assault	1:54.1f
9-8	Little Brown Jug Preview (3yo Pace) (div.)	68,000	ScD	Global Assault	1:53f

Wojcio, Richard
7-7	La Paloma Final (2yofp)	219,000	YR	Perfect Together	1:59.3h
7-19	Hanover-Hempt (2yofp)	33,000	VD	Janna Rose	1:57.4q
7-27	Hanover Filly Stake (2yofp) (div.)	16,710	RcR	Perfect Together	1:56.2f
8-8	Arden Downs (2yofp) (div.)	22,375	Mea	Perfect Together	1:56.1f

Zeron, Rick
9-2	Champlain Stakes (2yo Open Pace) (div.)	70,000	Moh	Prudhomme	1:56.2f
9-7	Simcoe Stakes (3yo Open Trot) (div.)	111,707	Moh	Osgood Hanover	2:01.1f

Zuanetti, Mario
5-27	Currier & Ives Filly Trot (3yo) (div.)	14,405	Mea	Atlantic	2:01.2f

LEADING DRIVERS BY NUMBER OF $1 MILLION SEASONS

Number	Driver	Number	Driver	Number	Driver
22	Herve Filion	12	Merritt Dokey	10	Stanley Dancer
19	Billy Haughton	12	Rejean Daigneault	10	Lucien Fontaine
19	Carmine Abbatiello	12	Ted Wing	10	Steve Condren
18	Walter Paisley	12	Dave Magee	10	Jim Marohn
17	Buddy Gilmour	11	Jim Curran	9	Stan Banks
17	Ben Webster	11	Doug Brown	9	Dave Wall
15	Daryl Busse	11	Donald Dancer	9	Bill Gale
14	Del Insko	11	Eddie Davis	9	Mickey McNichol
14	Ron Waples	11	Bill O'Donnell	9	John Chapman
14	Joe Marsh, Jr.	11	Cat Manzi	9	Gilles Gendron
14	Jim Doherty	11	Ray Remmen	9	Michel Lachance

LEADING DRIVERS BY 300-WIN SEASONS

Number	Driver	Number	Driver	Number	Driver
20	Herve Filion	6	Dave Magee	4	Gary Mosher
10	John Campbell	5	Bill Gale	4	Joe Schwind
9	William O'Donnell	5	Terry Kerr	4	Walt Paisley
9	Carmine Abbatiello	5	Ron Marsh	3	Bill Parker, Jr.
8	Ron Waples	5	Dave Wall	3	Donald Dancer
7	Mike Lachance	4	Daryl Busse	3	Eddie Davis
6	Walter Case, Jr.	4	Leigh Fitch	3	Cat Manzi
6	Doug Brown	4	Jack Moiseyev	3	Doug Snyder

YOUNGEST DRIVERS TO REACH WINNING MILESTONES

Milestone	Driver	Age	Milestone	Driver	Age
1,000 wins	Walter Case, Jr.	21	3,500	Herve Filion	31
1,500	Walter Case, Jr.	22	4,000	Herve Filion	32
2,000	Walter Case, Jr.	24	4,500	Herve Filion	33
2,500	Walter Case, Jr.	* 26	5,000	Herve Filion	34
3,000	Walter Case, Jr.	* 27			

(Filion holds all the other records, for 6,000 and above, too.)

* - Both these milestones were passed in 1988.

LEADING DRIVERS

LEADING DRIVERS AT MAJOR TRACKS

Driver	Sts.	Win	2nd	3rd	UDR		Driver	Sts.	Win	2nd	3rd	UDR
Assiniboia Downs (Winter-1990)							**Assiniboia Downs (Fall)**					
Doug Shaw	260	56	49	46	.379	Wins	Doug Shaw	175	38	21	21	.324
Steve Scrannage	322	47	43	52	.270		Greg Manning	156	33	28	26	.367
Garry Schedlosky	233	44	31	29	.304		Garry Schedlosky	140	29	24	16	.341
Gregory Manning	276	40	42	37	.274		Steve Scrannage	182	29	17	18	.244
Ron Cullen	281	40	36	41	.262		Roland Rey	123	28	23	15	.372
Roland Rey	124	37	21	15	.433	UDR	Roland Rey	123	28	23	15	.372
George Isman	109	22	21	26	.388		Greg Manning	156	33	28	26	.367
Doug Shaw	260	56	49	46	.379		Garry Schedlosky	140	29	24	16	.341
Doug Moore	69	15	7	13	.337		Doug Shaw	175	38	21	21	.324
Keith Cullen	112	19	24	10	.319		Steve Scrannage	182	29	17	18	.244
Doug Shaw					$76,792	Money	Greg Manning					$77,224
Steve Scrannage					64,260		Garry Schedlosky					49,278
Gregory Manning					61,488		Ron Cullen					45,431
Kevin Anderson					57,840		Doug Shaw					45,161
Roland Rey					55,988		Roland Rey					41,985
Avalon Raceway							**Balmoral Park (Winter)**					
Gary Mc Donald	163	44	24	20	.393	Wins	Dan Knox	233	49	25	28	.324
Don Howlett	164	24	36	28	.325		Jim Maxwell	225	44	29	26	.306
Jim Barton	138	23	22	39	.349		Brian Carpenter	203	43	23	23	.313
Ron Ershler	102	20	15	20	.343		Gerald Longo	211	41	32	31	.328
Wayne Hafey	122	20	17	22	.302		Tim Curtin	260	38	37	22	.253
Gary Mc Donald	163	44	24	20	.393	UDR	Ernie Adam	50	16	11	1	.449
Jim Barton	138	23	22	39	.349		Fred Finn, Jr.	56	12	9	6	.339
Ron Ershler	102	20	15	20	.343		Gerald Longo	211	41	32	31	.328
Garry Merner	49	9	9	6	.327		Dan Knox	233	49	25	28	.324
Don Howlett	164	24	36	28	.325		Brian Carpenter	203	43	23	23	.313
Gary Mc Donald					$8,965	Money	Dan Knox					$214,873
Don Howlett					5,827		Jim Maxwell					168,311
Jim Barton					6,220		Gerald Longo					156,362
Ron Ershler					4,593		Brian Carpenter					155,541
Wayne Hafey					4,201		Tim Curtin					147,506
Balmoral Park (Fall)							**Bangor Raceway**					
Jim Maxwell	188	38	28	23	.326	Wins	Gary Hall	287	68	51	38	.380
Gerald Longo	160	26	20	22	.278		Bob Sumner	236	67	43	24	.419
Merv Chupp	209	26	28	23	.236		Ger. MacKenzie, Jr.	228	36	36	34	.295
Doug Hamilton	109	22	21	14	.352		Ron Cushing	171	25	28	29	.294
Dan Knox	193	22	35	23	.255		Mike Cushing	247	21	27	20	.173
Doug Hamilton	109	22	21	14	.352	UDR	Bob Sumner	236	67	43	24	.419
Ernie Adam	62	12	11	8	.335		Gary Hall	287	68	51	38	.380
Jim Maxwell	188	38	28	23	.326		Ivan Davies	67	10	16	15	.357
Gary Mills	78	17	9	9	.321		Derryl Niles, Jr.	50	9	10	7	.338
Gerald Longo	160	26	20	22	.278		Ruel Goodblood, Jr.	100	19	14	17	.324
Jim Maxwell					$130,121	Money	Gary Hall					$51,873
Merv Chupp					124,073		Bob Sumner					51,132
Dan Knox					114,793		Gerald MacKenzie, Jr.					30,156
Doug Hamilton					100,608		Ron Cushing					21,876
Gerald Longo					93,031		Mike Cushing					18,762

LEADING DRIVERS

Driver	Sts.	Win	2nd	3rd	UDR		Driver	Sts.	Win	2nd	3rd	UDR
Hippodrome Blue Bonnets							**Batavia Downs (Spring)**					
Rick Zeron	1,591	368	270	238	.375	Wins	Rod Laframboise	267	53	47	43	.350
Mario Baillargeon	1,613	266	262	215	.300		Patsy Rapone	162	32	19	29	.322
Gaetan Lamy	1,076	209	158	156	.324		Ed McNeight, Jr.	193	30	26	27	.277
Henri Filion	1,401	209	203	166	.269		John Flanigen	149	26	20	13	.278
Serge Ouellet	871	174	141	126	.338		Gaston Guindon	134	24	19	19	.305
Rick Zeron	1,591	368	270	238	.375	UDR	Bob Bompczyk	66	17	16	10	.443
Serge Ouellet	871	174	141	126	.338		Sam Schillaci	96	22	18	12	.375
Gaetan Lamy	1,076	209	158	156	.324		Daniel Guindon	61	12	9	14	.355
Mario Baillargeon	1,613	266	262	215	.300		Rod Laframboise	267	53	47	43	.350
Raymond Gingras	507	79	82	65	.288		Patsy Rapone	162	32	19	29	.322
Rick Zeron				$1,941,021		Money	Rod Laframboise				$81,125	
Mario Baillargeon				1,692,473			Ed McNeight, Jr.				56,279	
Henri Filion				1,179,944			Gaston Guindon				50,570	
Gaetan Lamy				1,150,296			Patsy Rapone				46,716	
Serge Ouellet				910,775			Don Rothfuss				42,853	
Batavia Downs (Summer-Fall)							**Buffalo Raceway (Winter - 1990)**					
Sam Schillaci	423	80	61	58	.315	Wins	Rod Laframboise	225	46	40	34	.354
Rod Laframboise	430	62	58	58	.264		Ed McNeight, Jr.	224	39	38	23	.303
Tom Swift	354	58	46	46	.279		Patsy Rapone	223	25	37	27	.245
Don Rothfuss	423	58	58	78	.275		John Flanigen	154	24	21	21	.277
Mike Caprio	357	55	47	44	.268		Mike Caprio	113	20	17	13	.299
Tom Agosti	159	36	24	21	.361	UDR	Tom Agosti	54	12	12	6	.383
Dan Yetman	107	27	8	17	.347		Bruce Tubin	45	11	7	6	.375
Sam Schillaci	423	80	61	58	.315		Rod Laframboise	225	46	40	34	.354
Fred Haslip	110	16	20	19	.304		Betsy Brown	50	14	4	4	.351
David Vance	135	19	26	19	.295		Sam Schillaci	71	13	9	14	.319
Tom Swift				$145,577		Money	Rod Laframboise				$75,290	
Don Rothfuss				141,901			Ed McNeight, Jr.				67,338	
Rod Laframboise				141,733			Don Rothfuss				48,737	
Sam Schillaci				134,785			Patsy Rapone				46,584	
Mike Caprio				116,839			John Flanigen				37,293	
Buffalo Raceway (Summer)							**Cal-Expo**					
Rod Laframboise	475	77	66	76	.293	Wins	Ross Croghan	212	67	37	29	.459
Ed McNeight, Jr.	456	67	65	55	.266		Rick Kuebler	339	53	46	50	.281
Patsy Rapone	403	66	68	56	.304		Bob Sleeth	266	51	37	40	.319
John Flanigen	307	62	43	28	.310		Rick Plano	264	44	34	35	.282
Tom Swift	276	43	31	41	.268		Joe Anderson	180	42	36	20	.382
Gerry Sarama	200	37	32	24	.314	UDR	Ross Croghan	212	67	37	29	.459
John Flanigen	307	62	43	28	.310		Joe Anderson	180	42	36	20	.382
Fred Haslip	171	27	33	22	.308		Bob Sleeth	266	51	37	40	.319
Patsy Rapone	403	66	68	56	.304		Ken Williams	74	10	19	8	.314
Clint Galbraith	93	14	12	21	.298		Mike DiFranco, Jr.	82	17	10	8	.308
Patsy Rapone				$245,905		Money	Ross Croghan				$213,919	
Rod Laframboise				175,623			Rick Plano				184,480	
Ed McNeight, Jr.				132,544			Bob Sleeth				156,693	
Gerry Sarama				107,178			Rick Kuebler				133,330	
Don Rothfuss				89,000			Steve DeSomer				116,829	

LEADING DRIVERS

Driver	Sts.	Win	2nd	3rd	UDR		Driver	Sts.	Win	2nd	3rd	UDR
Charlottetown Driving Park							**Cloverdale Raceway (Winter-1990)**					
Paul MacDonald	436	86	72	67	.340	Wins	Joe Hudon, Jr.	248	57	59	29	.401
Ken Arsenault	473	68	75	78	.287		Bill Davis	239	53	46	24	.362
Walt Cheverie	388	67	64	57	.313		Bill Megens	253	46	36	43	.318
Garry MacDonald	261	61	51	28	.378		Tim Brown	233	45	32	27	.308
Len McGuigan	323	60	45	40	.304		Brent Beelby	211	43	25	17	.297
Joe Smallwood	132	37	29	19	.450	UDR	Barry Treen	131	37	19	19	.411
Garry MacDonald	261	61	51	28	.378		Joe Hudon, Jr.	248	57	59	29	.401
Boyd MacDonald	212	45	28	42	.352		Bill Davis	239	53	46	24	.362
Paul MacDonald	436	86	72	67	.340		Andy Arsenault	204	42	25	29	.321
Emmett Bernard, Jr.	276	52	53	33	.335		Bill Megens	253	46	36	43	.318

Driver	Amount		Driver	Amount
Paul MacDonald	$49,224	Money	Bill Davis	$188,009
Allan Smith	38,987		Joe Hudon, Jr.	158,245
Ken Arsenault	38,323		Tim Brown	130,028
Garry MacDonald	38,108		Gord Abbott	124,985
Walt Cheverie	37,161		Bill Megens	124,639

Driver	Sts.	Win	2nd	3rd	UDR		Driver	Sts.	Win	2nd	3rd	UDR
Cloverdale Raceway (Fall)							**Hippodrome Connaught**					
Joe Hudon, Jr.	188	47	32	26	.391	Wins	Gilles Plourde	585	138	109	72	.380
Bill Davis	191	39	42	31	.381		Darrell Coville	777	114	138	99	.288
Jim Burke	272	39	37	43	.272		Howard Portelance	610	100	79	96	.288
Brent Beelby	150	32	17	18	.316		Bob O'Dwyer	406	71	71	54	.316
Tim Brown	243	32	29	22	.228		Andre St. Amour	544	66	78	70	.244
Joe Hudon, Jr.	188	47	32	26	.391	UDR	Gilles Plourde	585	138	109	72	.380
Bill Davis	191	39	42	31	.381		Doug Forgie	224	55	33	29	.371
Kelly MacMillan	74	20	7	9	.363		Bob O'Dwyer	406	71	71	54	.316
Jim Lackey	100	20	16	20	.356		Ricky Forgie	216	33	32	35	.289
Brent Beelby	150	32	17	18	.316		Howard Portelance	610	100	79	96	.288

Driver	Amount		Driver	Amount
Joe Hudon, Jr.	$178,679	Money	Darrell Coville	$227,884
Jim Burke	164,675		Gilles Plourde	215,656
Bill Davis	142,670		Howard Portelance	163,097
Tim Brown	107,836		Benoit Cote	136,582
Bill Megens	101,769		Bob O'Dwyer	134,218

Driver	Sts.	Win	2nd	3rd	UDR		Driver	Sts.	Win	2nd	3rd	UDR
Delaware, Ohio							**Delmarva Downs**					
Jeff Fout	32	6	2	4	.264	Wins	Bill Long	503	89	66	59	.289
John Campbell	26	5	6	4	.372		Ken Mitchell	386	68	67	47	.313
Jan Nordin	9	4	1	1	.543		Mike Rossi	353	52	53	44	.272
Ray Paver, Jr.	15	4	4	2	.459		Clifton Green	323	46	34	34	.236
Dan Ater	5	3	0	0	.600		George Dennis	374	45	46	63	.245
Dan Ater	5	3	0	0	.600	UDR	Walter Callahan	98	18	18	18	.347
Jan Nordin	9	4	1	1	.543		Leslie Given	142	22	28	22	.316
Bruce Riegle	6	3	0	0	.500		Ken Mitchell	386	68	67	47	.313
Ray Paver, Jr.	15	4	4	2	.459		Bill Long	503	89	66	59	.289
John Campbell	26	5	6	4	.372		Randy Truitt	140	26	13	21	.287

Driver	Amount		Driver	Amount
John Campbell	$197,472	Money	Bill Long	$142,776
Ray Remmen	194,912		Ken Mitchell	115,377
Michel Lachance	126,632		Jim Dennis	79,831
Bill Fahy	80,496		Mike Rossi	79,253
Dave Rankin	79,022		George Dennis	70,298

LEADING DRIVERS

Driver	Sts.	Win	2nd	3rd	UDR		Driver	Sts.	Win	2nd	3rd	UDR
Dover Downs (Winter-1990)							**Dover Downs (Fall)**					
Jim Dennis	480	77	75	84	.306	Wins	Bret Brittingham	79	17	10	15	.349
Mike Rossi	437	64	84	62	.301		Russ Thomas, Jr.	95	16	16	10	.297
Bret Brittingham	234	41	34	24	.290		Eddie Davis	48	13	5	9	.391
Bob Kinsey	271	38	34	34	.252		Ken Mitchell	64	13	9	6	.313
Clifton Green	243	33	38	38	.275		John Childress	86	13	14	8	.273
John Littleton, Jr.	62	18	11	10	.443	UDR	Eddie Davis	48	13	5	9	.391
Eddie Davis	93	23	13	13	.372		Bob Shahan	48	12	9	4	.382
Jim Porter	69	14	12	12	.358		Joe Sullivan	52	12	5	14	.374
Roger Botsch	51	9	13	6	.357		Bret Brittingham	79	17	10	15	.349
Joe Mac Donald	48	10	8	6	.343		Ken Mitchell	64	13	9	6	.313
Jim Dennis					$73,203	Money	Jim Dennis					$12,532
Mike Rossi					58,937		Russ Thomas, Jr.					11,695
Bob Kinsey					32,671		Bret Brittingham					11,383
Clifton Green					32,619		Mike Rossi					9,983
Bret Brittingham					32,027		John Childress					9,919
Du Quoin, Illinois							**Exhibition Park Raceway**					
John Campbell	21	6	5	2	.450	Wins	Steve Mahar	829	158	143	117	.334
Connel Willis	30	6	6	3	.344		Brian Moore	508	101	75	58	.319
Dave Magee	25	4	6	3	.333		John Davidson	642	100	109	108	.306
Sam "Chip" Noble	8	3	2	0	.514		Joe Hennessey	568	100	82	73	.299
Doug Larsen	11	3	1	3	.414		Ross MacDonald	430	77	68	51	.307
Sam "Chip" Noble	8	3	2	0	.514	UDR	Dan O'Brian	150	40	27	17	.404
John Campbell	21	6	5	2	.450		Steve Mahar	829	158	143	117	.334
Doug Larsen	11	3	1	3	.414		Brian Moore	508	101	75	58	.319
Connel Willis	30	6	6	3	.344		Ivan Davies	119	22	19	13	.310
Dave Magee	25	4	6	3	.333		Gilles Barrieau	381	63	57	70	.310
Cat Manzi					$304,350	Money	Steve Mahar					$131,167
Berndt Lindstedt					193,891		John Davidson					73,019
John Campbell					101,234		Joe Hennessey					71,586
Michel Lachance					83,159		Gilles Barrieau					57,958
Chris Boring					67,325		Brian Moore					57,549
Fairmount Park (Winter-1990)							**Fairmount Park (Fall-1990)**					
Dean Magee	384	65	65	40	.298	Wins	Dean Magee	205	47	31	19	.344
John Reese	237	50	30	29	.322		John Reese	140	26	11	20	.277
Greg Haston	254	49	39	30	.318		Jay Cross	127	24	17	14	.300
Tom Simmons	281	34	34	40	.236		Tom Simmons	111	15	10	16	.233
Lemoyne Svendsen	221	24	19	24	.193		Gregg Haston	113	15	11	10	.216
John Reese	237	50	30	29	.322	UDR	Chris Loney	48	11	7	7	.359
Greg Haston	254	49	39	30	.318		Dean Magee	205	47	31	19	.344
Dan Bowermaster	83	12	14	16	.303		Tom Tetrick	34	3	10	7	.320
Dean Magee	384	65	65	40	.298		Jay Cross	127	24	17	14	.300
Jay Cross	83	11	16	8	.272		Steve Martz	37	6	6	5	.297
Dean Magee					$223,753	Money	Dean Magee					$137,985
John Reese					141,853		John Reese					67,805
Greg Haston					167,546		Jay Cross					64,015
Tom Simmons					118,633		Gregg Haston					41,520
Lemoyne Svendsen					85,038		Tom Simmons					37,666

LEADING DRIVERS

Driver	Sts.	Win	2nd	3rd	UDR		Driver	Sts.	Win	2nd	3rd	UDR
Flamboro Downs							**Frederickton Raceway**					
Callie Rankin	1,193	216	225	208	.344	Wins	Steve Mahar	264	63	41	46	.383
Bill Budd	973	141	129	153	.271		Steve Trites	157	38	20	16	.347
Don Graham	965	132	142	121	.260		Mike Downey	216	34	40	41	.324
Paul MacKenzie	582	106	73	93	.305		Brian Moore	100	20	14	20	.344
Paul Matthews	631	105	89	67	.280		John Davidson	129	17	30	17	.305
Callie Rankin	1,193	216	225	208	.344	UDR	Steve Mahar	264	63	41	46	.383
Jim Whelan	283	63	38	39	.343		Steve Trites	157	38	20	16	.347
Paul MacKenzie	582	106	73	93	.305		Brian Moore	100	20	14	20	.344
Curtis Bond	590	93	96	69	.287		Gilles Barrieau	45	8	9	6	.333
Paul Matthews	631	105	89	67	.280		Mike Downey	216	34	40	41	.324
Callie Rankin					$533,395	Money	Steve Mahar					$51,518
Bill Budd					333,800		Steve Trites					28,928
Don Graham					279,531		Mike Downey					25,813
Paul Matthews					237,987		John Davidson					15,603
Paul MacKenzie					200,408		Danny Romo					13,806
Freehold Raceway (Win.-Spr.)							**Freehold Raceway (Sum.-Fall)**					
Cat Manzi	930	199	132	128	.339	Wins	Jack Moiseyev	763	160	107	107	.334
Joe Schwind	766	150	113	108	.325		Herve Filion	899	159	159	112	.317
Herve Filion	553	86	85	82	.290		Cat Manzi	659	134	85	84	.318
Harold Kelly	671	82	96	99	.251		Joe Schwind	616	74	98	101	.263
Jack Moiseyev	437	75	74	49	.303		Bill Bresnahan	421	45	46	56	.212
Cat Manzi	930	199	132	128	.339	UDR	Jack Moiseyev	763	160	107	107	.334
Dave Pinkney, Jr.	213	34	46	34	.333		Cat Manzi	659	134	85	84	.318
Joe Schwind	766	150	113	108	.325		Herve Filion	899	159	159	112	.317
Mark Lancaster	268	41	53	41	.314		Ted Wing	138	25	14	21	.288
Jack Moiseyev	437	75	74	49	.303		Joe Schwind	616	74	98	101	.263
Cat Manzi					$796,875	Money	Herve Filion					$889,685
Joe Schwind					590,622		Jack Moiseyev					731,976
Herve Filion					489,285		Cat Manzi					686,729
Harold Kelly					355,029		Joe Schwind					454,757
Jack Moiseyev					321,755		Bill Fahy					344,050
Garden State Park							**Goshen Historic**					
Jack Moiseyev	569	116	88	78	.336	Wins	Herve Filion	12	5	3	1	.583
Cat Manzi	434	80	52	68	.303		Cat Manzi	4	2	1	1	.722
Joe Schwind	512	67	69	59	.244		Steve Sherman	3	2	0	0	.667
John Plutino	420	59	42	66	.248		Ralph Sherman	4	2	1	0	.639
Ron Pierce	403	48	51	56	.236		H. Westbrook/J. Sears	6	2	1	0	.426
Jack Moiseyev	569	116	88	78	.336	UDR	Cat Manzi	4	2	1	1	.722
Cat Manzi	434	80	52	68	.303		Ralph Sherman	4	2	1	0	.639
Michel Lachance	136	26	14	12	.278		Herve Filion	12	5	3	1	.583
John Plutino	420	59	42	66	.248		Tim Lanpher	5	1	1	3	.511
Mickey McNichol	146	17	23	19	.247		H. Westbrook/J. Sears	6	2	1	0	.426
John Campbell					$813,225	Money	Herve Filion					$35,946
Jack Moiseyev					700,393		Bob Turner					12,547
Cat Manzi					489,115		Clint Galbraith					8,269
Joe Schwind					438,977		Buddy Gilmour					8,008
Ron Pierce					435,662		Cat Manzi					7,076

LEADING DRIVERS

Driver	Sts.	Win	2nd	3rd	UDR		Driver	Sts.	Win	2nd	3rd	UDR
Greenwood Raceway (Winter-1990)							**Greenwood Raceway (Summer)**					
Doug Brown	431	83	52	55	.302	Wins	Doug Brown	476	78	75	55	.290
Tony Kerwood	308	51	62	42	.323		Steve Condren	464	67	64	62	.266
Dave Wall	382	50	46	57	.248		Tony Kerwood	315	65	55	40	.346
Mike Saftic	343	41	44	33	.223		Roger Mayotte	371	46	38	48	.224
Steve Condren	317	39	31	40	.219		Dave Wall	376	38	45	44	.207
Tony Kerwood	308	51	62	42	.323	UDR	Tony Kerwood	315	65	55	40	.346
Doug Brown	431	83	52	55	.302		Doug Brown	476	78	75	55	.290
Bill Gale	62	10	10	6	.283		John Brooks	172	28	24	24	.287
Dave Smith	143	19	22	15	.253		Steve Condren	464	67	64	62	.266
Dave Wall	382	50	46	57	.248		Dave Smith	198	32	23	17	.255
Doug Brown					$909,779	Money	Doug Brown					$1,384,314
Tony Kerwood					580,926		Steve Condren					843,979
Steve Condren					567,707		"Bud" Fritz					805,496
Dave Wall					559,419		Tony Kerwood					752,838
Mike Saftic					517,275		Dave Wall					556,468
Greenwood Raceway (Fall-1990)							**Harrington Raceway**					
Doug Brown	142	36	19	16	.365	Wins	Jim Dennis	276	48	42	41	.308
Steve Condren	121	19	21	13	.289		George Dennis	247	41	31	37	.286
Dave Wall	108	15	14	16	.260		Mike Rossi	209	36	28	22	.282
Mike Saftic	84	13	11	10	.267		Russ Thomas, Jr.	186	35	23	17	.287
Tony Kerwood	50	19	3	4	.260		Joe Sullivan	135	20	19	21	.278
John Holmes	21	5	4	4	.407	UDR	Ray Robinson, Jr.	55	9	13	10	.356
Tom Strauss	21	6	2	2	.370		Roger Botch	63	12	9	13	.339
Doug Brown	142	36	19	16	.365		Jim Dennis	276	48	42	41	.308
Richard McNeill	23	4	4	5	.343		Al Callahan	43	6	9	5	.308
Steve Condren	121	19	21	13	.289		Russ Thomas, Jr.	186	35	23	17	.287
Doug Brown					$277,086	Money	Jim Dennis					$42,328
Steve Condren					185,557		George Dennis					38,977
Dave Wall					125,025		Mike Rossi					32,120
Mike Saftic					108,590		Russ Thomas, Jr.					30,029
Roger Mayotte					97,103		Joe Sullivan					18,603
Hawthorne Racecourse							**Hazel Park**					
Walter Paisley	334	87	62	40	.404	Wins	Peter Wrenn	914	159	152	115	.308
Ron Marsh	422	59	55	53	.254		Vince Copeland	948	133	135	143	.270
Dave Magee	429	54	61	56	.248		John Moody	739	130	126	88	.310
Tony Morgan	184	41	30	17	.344		Keith Crawford	689	122	112	93	.312
Daryl Busse	308	41	33	24	.219		Jeff James	932	113	147	117	.251
Walter Paisley	334	87	62	40	.404	UDR	Kevin Wallis	219	69	45	19	.458
Tony Morgan	184	41	30	17	.344		Keith Crawford	689	122	112	93	.312
Ron Marsh	422	59	55	53	.254		John Moody	739	130	126	88	.310
Dave Magee	429	54	61	56	.248		Peter Wrenn	914	159	152	115	.308
Dale Hiteman	286	36	39	32	.239		Terry Tomlin	168	33	20	22	.306
Walter Paisley					$652,689	Money	Peter Wrenn					$772,931
Dave Magee					532,444		Vince Copeland					712,651
Ron Marsh					477,847		Jeff James					672,811
Tony Morgan					326,363		John Moody					646,578
Daryl Busse					326,213		Keith Crawford					579,787

LEADING DRIVERS

Driver	Sts.	Win	2nd	3rd	UDR		Driver	Sts.	Win	2nd	3rd	UDR
Hiawatha Horse Park							**Indianapolis, Indiana**					
Mark Megens	368	72	40	48	.300	Wins	Sam "Chip" Noble	12	4	3	3	.556
Allan Cullen	432	70	81	69	.319		Trent Stohler	10	4	1	0	.456
Chris Johnston	399	55	71	63	.289		Bill White	14	4	3	2	.452
Bryce Fenn	321	50	45	42	.277		Chris Boring	10	4	0	1	.433
Dennis DuFord	267	37	32	38	.253		Doug Ackerman	12	4	2	0	.426
Danny Johnson	82	18	14	16	.379	UDR	Sam "Chip" Noble	12	4	3	3	.556
Steve Bossence	93	16	25	5	.339		Richard Taylor	5	2	0	1	.467
Allan Cullen	432	70	81	69	.319		Gregg Haston	7	2	1	2	.460
Mark Megens	368	72	40	48	.300		Trent Stohler	10	4	1	0	.456
Chris Johnston	399	55	71	63	.289		Bill White	14	4	3	2	.452
Allan Cullen					$119,573	Money	Sam "Chip" Noble					$64,697
Chris Johnston					88,616		Dick Richardson, Jr.					41,513
Mark Megens					85,121		John Campbell					33,926
Bryce Fenn					82,285		Chris Boring					27,103
Dennis DuFord					60,294		Doug Ackerman					25,030
Inverness Raceway							**Jackson Raceway (Spring)**					
Joe Campbell	49	22	10	5	.596	Wins	Terry Buter	333	83	51	51	.385
Don Gillis, Jr.	78	19	11	15	.386		Bob Harmon	204	34	33	26	.299
Ray Wyrwas	81	13	16	15	.332		Gary Massey	232	20	35	31	.215
Doug MacQuarrie	59	11	5	6	.267		Jim Wright	159	19	16	14	.205
Alex MacQuarrie	125	11	19	23	.234		Jeff Stimer	77	17	20	12	.417
Joe Campbell	49	22	10	5	.596	UDR	Jeff Stimer	77	17	20	12	.417
Ray Deagle	39	10	7	7	.416		Terry Buter	333	83	51	51	.385
Don Gillis, Jr.	78	19	11	15	.386		Randy Edmonds	53	11	12	6	.371
John MacDonald	44	10	9	5	.359		Tim Buter	72	16	12	4	.333
Alex MacDonald	50	7	14	6	.336		John Curran	69	13	11	10	.325
Joe Campbell					$5,224	Money	Terry Buter					$82,386
Don Gillis, Jr.					4,373		Bob Harmon					37,286
Alex MacQuarrie					4,025		Gary Massey					31,821
Ray Wyrwas					3,222		Jim Wright					20,696
Alex MadDonald					2,650		Jeff Stimer					17,699
Jackson Raceway (Summer)							**Jackson at Northville**					
Terry Buter	209	41	33	33	.337	Wins	Vince Copeland	329	59	61	53	.336
Darrell Wright	129	23	16	17	.291		Art McIlmurray	197	58	38	25	.444
Jeff Sweeney	134	16	23	25	.277		Peter Wrenn	192	42	30	23	.346
Dennis Marchand	70	13	12	8	.319		Darrell Wright	244	36	33	37	.273
Mark Hamlet	75	13	13	7	.301		Jeff James	258	36	44	29	.272
Jim Jomes	42	7	13	7	.394	UDR	Art McIlmurray	197	58	38	25	.444
Terry Buter	209	41	33	33	.337		Tim Buter	82	21	11	10	.371
Dennis Marchand	70	13	12	8	.319		Peter Wrenn	192	42	30	23	.346
Mark Hamlet	75	13	13	7	.301		Vince Copeland	329	59	61	53	.336
Gary Massey	43	6	7	9	.300		Ed Hennessey	113	18	26	16	.334
Peter Wrenn					$55,527	Money	Vince Copeland					$190,069
Terry Buter					53,607		Art McIlmurray					149,142
Art McIlmurray					49,197		Jeff James					144,470
Scott DeMull					36,181		Peter Wrenn					137,844
Todd Buter					35,822		Keith Crawford					115,346

LEADING DRIVERS

Driver	Sts.	Win	2nd	3rd	UDR		Driver	Sts.	Win	2nd	3rd	UDR
Kawartha Downs							**Lebanon Raceway (Winter-1990)**					
Allan Nicholls	311	56	44	34	.295	Wins	David Miller	506	103	79	82	.344
Guy Larush	363	50	39	52	.245		Joe Essig, Jr.	456	82	65	54	.299
Murray Brethour	255	47	43	30	.317		Ken Holliday	379	69	55	53	.309
Gord Brown	238	37	34	24	.268		Randy Tharps	210	32	29	24	.267
Jerry Robinson	261	33	38	39	.257		Brent Holland	176	27	20	15	.245
Wayne Dowson	56	14	14	4	.413	UDR	Sam "Chip" Noble	78	22	9	11	.393
Dan Clements	56	15	7	6	.373		David Miller	506	103	79	82	.344
Warren Hie	142	26	18	29	.322		Don Cromer	100	16	20	13	.314
Murray Brethour	255	47	43	30	.317		Ken Holliday	379	69	55	53	.309
Allan Nicholls	311	56	44	34	.295		Joe Essig, Jr.	456	82	65	54	.299
Murray Brethour					$78,089	Money	David Miller					$142,521
Allan Nicholls					72,124		Joe Essig, Jr.					108,144
Guy Larush					69,222		Ken Holliday					85,099
Jerry Robinson					52,181		Randy Tharps					51,809
Gord Brown					51,244		Keith Justice					49,621
Lebanon Raceway (Fall-1990)							**Los Alamitos Racecourse (Winter-1990)**					
David Miller	471	102	72	61	.345	Wins	Ross Croghan	284	68	44	26	.356
Joe Essig, Jr.	342	55	50	40	.281		Rick Kuebler	499	64	56	70	.237
Brent Holland	300	48	44	46	.293		Rick Plano	301	54	37	30	.281
Ken Holliday	233	33	31	26	.253		Peter Wrenn	330	53	43	45	.279
Randy Tharps	210	29	37	27	.279		Jim Morand	325	42	40	49	.248
David Miller	471	102	72	61	.345	UDR	Ross Croghan	284	68	44	26	.356
Jeff Smith	59	15	5	5	.330		Joe Anderson	225	39	33	34	.305
Mike Thomas	78	14	11	11	.305		D.R. Ackerman	128	22	18	15	.289
Brent Holland	300	48	44	46	.293		Steve Hyman	105	16	16	15	.289
Joe Essig, Jr.	342	55	50	40	.281		Robert Reeser	100	14	18	13	.283
David Miller					$112,859	Money	Ross Croghan					$338,814
Joe Essig, Jr.					79,750		Rick Kuebler					283,003
Mark Miller					70,750		Rick Plano					264,388
Brent Holland					64,857		Jim Morand					241,072
Gerry Bookmyer					62,500		Peter Wrenn					213,383
Los Alamitos Racecourse (Fall)							**Louisville Downs (Winter-1990)**					
Joe Anderson	275	61	43	40	.357	Wins	Roger Cullipher	379	87	61	50	.363
Rick Kuebler	265	44	30	33	.270		Ed Morgan, Jr.	516	67	94	75	.280
Ross Croghan	188	40	24	20	.319		Walter Haynes, Jr.	499	63	79	66	.258
Jack Parker, Jr.	161	30	21	21	.302		Rick Mapes	298	53	44	30	.293
Rick Plano	217	29	16	30	.221		Joe Cirasuola	263	47	37	45	.314
Joe Anderson	275	61	43	40	.357	UDR	Roger Cullipher	379	87	61	50	.363
Tim Maier	65	15	8	7	.335		Joe Cirasuola	263	47	37	45	.314
Ross Croghan	188	40	24	20	.319		Everett Pickett	131	24	17	19	.304
Jack Parker, Jr.	161	30	21	21	.302		Jim Robinson	161	26	21	30	.296
Bobby Rosen	64	11	9	9	.297		Rick Mapes	298	53	44	30	.293
Joe Anderson					$378,443	Money	Roger Cullipher					$131,111
Ross Croghan					275,797		Walter Haynes, Jr.					123,779
Rick Kuebler					223,244		Ed Morgan, Jr.					122,336
Rick Plano					193,799		Rick Mapes					89,517
Bob Sleeth					141,054		Joe Cirasuola					73,384

LEADING DRIVERS

Driver   Sts. Win 2nd 3rd UDR   *Driver*   Sts. Win 2nd 3rd UDR

Louisville Downs (Summer)

Roger Cullipher	259	51	35	36	.318
Gregg Haston	293	49	45	35	.292
Steve Martz	223	45	36	24	.327
Ed Morgan, Jr.	332	41	57	49	.268
Walter Haynes, Jr.	223	30	28	27	.245

Allen Harris	104	29	16	15	.412
Jim Robinson	57	13	8	8	.353
Steve Martz	223	45	36	24	.327
Roger Cullipher	259	51	35	36	.318
Everett Pickett	107	17	17	16	.297

Bill Fahy	$200,947
Ed Morgan, Jr.	162,703
Roger Cullipher	136,293
Gregg Haston	114,471
Ron Pierce	99,888

Wins / UDR / Money (column labels)

Louisville Downs (Fall)

Steve Martz	127	28	20	14	.345
Roger Cullipher	97	22	10	15	.336
Gregg Haston	139	19	21	20	.269
Walter Haynes, Jr.	127	19	16	18	.267
Ed Morgan, Jr.	142	15	27	34	.291

Earl Spalding	45	13	11	5	.462
Tom Luther	41	10	7	9	.412
Everett Pickett	52	12	9	10	.391
Mike Neafus	39	8	8	8	.388
Steve Martz	127	28	20	14	.345

Gregg Haston	$32,620
Ed Morgan, Jr.	28,569
Roger Cullipher	27,511
Steve Martz	27,224
Walter Haynes, Jr.	24,496

Maywood Park (Spring)

Dave Magee	631	107	104	86	.307
Ron Marsh	500	103	66	58	.318
Walter Paisley	423	83	61	49	.315
Daryl Busse	310	47	41	41	.269
Tony Morgan	296	45	40	44	.277

Ron Marsh	500	103	66	58	.318
Walter Paisley	423	83	61	49	.315
Dave Magee	631	107	104	86	.307
Tony Morgan	296	45	40	44	.277
Daryl Busse	310	47	41	41	.269

Dave Magee	$680,177
Walter Paisley	592,023
Ron Marsh	584,327
Dale Hiteman	335,872
Daryl Busse	286,282

Maywood Park (Fall)

Dave Magee	457	80	73	59	.307
Ron Marsh	448	73	71	65	.299
Walter Paisley	278	54	38	47	.327
Tony Morgan	277	47	35	23	.268
Dale Hiteman	249	42	24	29	.261

Bea Erdman	83	20	16	8	.380
Walter Paisley	278	54	38	47	.327
Neil Coleman	80	13	16	9	.311
Dave Magee	457	80	73	59	.307
Ron Marsh	448	73	71	65	.299

Dave Magee	$543,787
Ron Marsh	425,260
Walter Paisley	369,931
Dale Hiteman	287,261
Jim Curran	241,421

The Meadowlands

John Campbell	1,890	434	286	223	.353
Michel Lachance	1,930	263	225	222	.239
Bill O'Donnell	1,527	199	174	188	.235
Cat Manzi	1,565	191	182	186	.226
Ron Pierce	1,283	150	122	165	.213

John Campbell	1,890	434	286	223	.353
Jack Moiseyev	641	115	80	52	.276
Mark Lancaster	311	37	42	47	.244
Michel Lachance	1,930	263	225	222	.239
Howard Parker	297	34	40	41	.235

John Campbell	$6,070,474
Michel Lachance	4,608,830
Bill O'Donnell	3,160,844
Cat Manzi	2,547,913
Ron Pierce	1,864,339

Ladbroke at The Meadows

Dave Palone	1,749	427	296	234	.383
Doug Snyder	889	173	136	116	.323
Dean Zaimes	1,172	172	177	180	.282
Richard Myers	1,136	132	123	130	.215
Bob Roberts	747	110	99	100	.266

Dave Palone	1,749	427	296	234	.383
Bill Zendt	404	82	78	54	.355
Roger Hammer	273	58	39	37	.337
Doug Snyder	889	173	136	116	.323
Tom Sells	239	44	32	37	.310

Dave Palone	$1,035,126
Doug Snyder	600,425
Dean Zaimes	469,664
Richard Myers	364,591
Bill Zendt	293,140

Page 274

LEADING DRIVERS

Driver	Sts.	Win	2nd	3rd	UDR		Driver	Sts.	Win	2nd	3rd	UDR
Mohawk Raceway (Spring)							**Mohawk Raceway (Fall)**					
Doug Brown	319	64	39	49	.320	Wins	Doug Brown	366	73	41	50	.307
Steve Condren	356	57	41	35	.257		Steve Condren	407	52	61	54	.255
Roger Mayotte	277	42	35	33	.262		Tony Kerwood	269	47	32	39	.289
Mike Saftic	335	41	43	39	.233		Dave Wall	357	41	41	56	.231
Tony Kerwood	251	38	33	34	.270		Roger Mayotte	320	41	33	42	.229
Doug Brown	319	64	39	49	.320	UDR	Doug Brown	366	73	41	50	.307
John Brooks	125	21	13	24	.290		Dave Smith	192	33	27	23	.290
Larry Walker	98	15	14	11	.270		Tony Kerwood	269	47	32	39	.289
Tony Kerwood	251	38	33	34	.270		Larry Walker	98	14	18	12	.286
Bill Gale	139	25	15	12	.269		Steve Condren	407	52	61	54	.255
Doug Brown					$717,866	Money	Doug Brown					$1,030,840
Steve Condren					594,620		Steve Condren					803,617
Roger Mayotte					504,020		John Campbell					716,106
Mike Saftic					436,229		Tony Kerwood					564,174
Tony Kerwood					392,178		Dave Wall					539,760
Monticello Raceway							**Muskegon Racecourse**					
Bill Parker, Jr.	1,665	339	262	227	.337	Wins	Larry Stalbaum	440	86	80	52	.336
John Gilmour	1,643	201	247	240	.255		Robert Williams, Jr.	526	83	62	84	.277
Kyle DiBenedetto	966	147	133	151	.281		Rick Lake	407	80	61	57	.327
John Desimone	845	120	99	116	.253		Jeff Pugh	496	72	61	58	.253
Ron Coyne, Jr.	713	116	107	100	.293		Peter Otten	346	58	53	43	.294
Bill Parker, Jr.	1,665	339	262	227	.337	UDR	Larry Stalbaum	440	86	80	52	.336
Craig Mosher	368	59	66	50	.305		Larry Smith	167	32	29	20	.328
Ken DeVaux	244	50	25	26	.297		Rick Lake	407	80	61	57	.327
Ron Coyne, Jr.	713	116	107	100	.293		Angus Lake	198	32	36	31	.315
Tony Giovannelli	546	103	71	51	.292		Peter Otten	346	58	53	43	.294
Bill Parker, Jr.					$537,085	Money	Larry Stalbaum					$100,943
John Gilmour					370,606		Robert Williams, Jr.					100,364
Kyle DiBenedetto					236,521		Peter Otten					89,050
Ron Coyne, Jr.					192,059		Rick Lake					84,976
Matt Romano					175,997		Jeff Pugh					80,121
New Brunswick Downs							**Northfield Park**					
Frank Fagan, Jr.	421	68	69	59	.299	Wins	Mitch Sahely	1,013	202	127	119	.308
Dan O'Brian	296	56	48	61	.348		Ray Fisher, Jr.	838	143	131	96	.296
Paul Breau	385	52	55	51	.259		Dan Ross	722	128	105	107	.308
Steve Mahar	297	43	55	42	.295		Bill Irvine	993	110	114	108	.211
Ian Downey	308	39	41	31	.234		Don McKirgan	629	94	79	69	.256
Dan O'Brian	296	56	48	61	.348	UDR	Don O'Dwyer	370	82	63	37	.350
Paul Bernard	74	17	12	6	.347		Kelly O'Donnell	219	43	30	27	.314
Jean Belliveau	71	14	8	11	.311		Mitch Sahely	1,013	202	127	119	.308
Gilles Barrieau	67	9	13	13	.307		Dan Ross	722	128	105	107	.308
Walter Cheverie	62	8	12	12	.301		Joe Adamsky	458	88	57	53	.300
Steve Mahar					$79,983	Money	Mitch Sahely					$460,331
Frank Fagan, Jr.					64,176		Dan Ross					410,696
Paul Breau					62,367		Ray Fisher, Jr.					378,378
Henri Filion					58,500		Bill Irvine					334,710
Dan O'Brian					57,802		Joe Adamsky					275,752

LEADING DRIVERS

Driver   Sts. Win 2nd 3rd UDR

Northlands Park (Spring)

Driver	Sts	Win	2nd	3rd	UDR
Keith Clark	275	51	46	49	.338
Don Monkman, Jr.	229	49	41	29	.356
Brent Grundy	313	38	45	42	.246
John Baxter	138	33	23	24	.390
Bruce Clarke	163	29	18	21	.282
Isaac Tougas	50	11	13	4	.391
John Baxter	138	33	23	24	.390
Rod Hennessy	92	22	14	15	.378
Don Monkman, Jr.	229	49	41	29	.356
Keith Clark	275	51	46	49	.338

Driver	Money
Keith Clark	$228,796
Don Monkman, Jr.	187,782
Brent Grundy	180,420
John Baxter	125,247
Bruce Clarke	96,724

Northlands Park (Fall)

Wins

Driver	Sts	Win	2nd	3rd	UDR
Keith Clark	299	78	48	51	.407
Brent Grundy	372	59	61	55	.299
Bruce Clarke	188	30	29	31	.300
Jerv Clifton	186	29	36	22	.303
Don Monkman, Jr.	211	25	42	21	.262

UDR

Driver	Sts	Win	2nd	3rd	UDR
Keith Clark	299	78	48	51	.407
Rod Hennessy	97	17	22	11	.339
Serge Masse	72	16	13	3	.336
John Baxter	106	13	29	14	.319
Jerv Clifton	186	29	36	22	.303

Money

Driver	Money
Keith Clark	$380,305
Brent Grundy	314,657
Rod Hennessy	186,324
Don Monkman, Jr.	146,900
Bruce Clarke	120,695

Northville Downs

Driver	Sts	Win	2nd	3rd	UDR
Keith Crawford	298	73	62	42	.408
Vince Copeland	322	65	47	46	.331
Troy Boring	318	60	47	36	.309
Jeff James	279	57	46	42	.346
Terry Buter	365	54	40	53	.257
Keith Crawford	298	73	62	42	.408
Jeff James	279	57	46	42	.346
Vince Copeland	322	65	47	46	.331
Troy Boring	318	60	47	36	.309
Ed Hennessey	153	33	16	14	.304

Driver	Money
Keith Crawford	$237,797
Jeff James	215,526
Vince Copeland	196,602
Troy Boring	189,082
Carl Putnam, Jr.	154,366

Pocono Downs

Wins

Driver	Sts	Win	2nd	3rd	UDR
Bill Lambertus	974	192	147	133	.327
Jim Hysell	876	142	128	137	.295
Dale King	516	89	82	53	.295
Bill Mullin	431	80	66	52	.311
Jim Groff	315	65	38	45	.321

UDR

Driver	Sts	Win	2nd	3rd	UDR
Carmine Vitale	228	54	25	29	.340
Bob Nixon	273	52	49	33	.331
Bill Lambertus	974	192	147	133	.327
Jim Groff	315	65	38	45	.321
Bill Mullin	431	80	66	52	.311

Money

Driver	Money
Bill Lambertus	$331,875
Jim Hysell	278,359
Dale King	183,754
Bill Mullin	170,338
Norton Shoemaker III	122,757

Pompano Park (Winter-1990)

Driver	Sts	Win	2nd	3rd	UDR
Don Harmon	703	107	92	74	.260
Wally Hennessey	534	100	87	90	.334
Joe Pavia, Jr.	522	98	76	59	.306
Mickey McNichol	497	91	78	49	.303
Kevin Wallis	295	66	46	40	.356
Kevin Wallis	295	66	46	40	.356
Wally Hennessey	534	100	87	90	.334
Joe Pavia, Jr.	522	98	76	59	.306
Mickey McNichol	497	91	78	49	.303
Ron Waples	376	647	54	52	.296

Driver	Money
Don Harmon	$331,911
Joe Pavia, Jr.	301,524
Wally Hennessey	295,364
Mickey McNichol	254,212
Kevin Wallis	247,260

Pompano Park (Fall-1990)

Wins

Driver	Sts	Win	2nd	3rd	UDR
Wally Hennessey	369	63	59	41	.297
Joe Pavia, Jr.	317	60	67	47	.356
Kevin Wallis	264	55	42	31	.336
Bruce Ranger	311	41	29	49	.236
Don Harmon	304	30	40	36	.211

UDR

Driver	Sts	Win	2nd	3rd	UDR
John Hogan	74	20	8	8	.366
Joe Pavia, Jr.	317	60	67	47	.356
Kevin Wallis	264	55	42	31	.336
Bill Fahy	108	21	17	16	.331
Wally Hennessey	369	63	59	41	.297

Money

Driver	Money
John Campbell	$1,021,815
Michel Lachance	614,372
Doug Brown	474,338
Bill Fahy	342,367
Berndt Lindstedt	309,800

LEADING DRIVERS

Driver	Sts.	Win	2nd	3rd	UDR		Driver	Sts.	Win	2nd	3rd	UDR
Prairie Meadows							**Quad City Downs**					
Craig Banks	190	39	30	27	.340	Wins	Dean Magee	982	205	158	173	.357
Royal Roland	176	33	26	28	.323		Lemoyne Svendsen	593	106	95	79	.312
Mike Murphy	168	31	16	25	.287		Tom Simmons	623	106	104	82	.307
Jim Mitchell	100	17	16	10	.292		Ron Vanderostyne	655	91	77	73	.241
Tim Curtin	81	14	9	17	.305		Steve Searle	545	77	86	88	.283
Duane Roland	62	13	17	8	.405	UDR	Dean Magee	982	205	158	173	.357
Craig Banks	190	39	30	27	.340		Lemoyne Svendsen	593	106	95	79	.312
Mike Morales	38	8	3	9	.333		Tom Simmons	623	106	104	82	.307
Royal Roland	176	33	26	28	.323		Steve Searle	545	77	86	88	.283
Tim Curtin	81	14	9	17	.305		Ron Vanderostyne	655	91	77	73	.241
Craig Banks					$35,114	Money	Dean Magee					$316,180
Royal Roland					29,023		Tom Simmons					183,004
Mike Murphy					25,916		Lemoyne Svendsen					163,599
Jim Mitchell					14,996		Neil Coleman					154,588
Duane Roland					14,423		Ron Vanderostyne					150,797
Hippodrome de Quebec							**Queensbury Downs**					
Gabriel Boily	1,053	208	133	130	.309	Wins	Harris Toole	350	77	63	51	.369
Daniel Dube	1,014	196	153	136	.322		Steve Scrannage	420	74	76	61	.325
Jacques Beaudoin	746	160	129	114	.362		Doug Shaw	379	69	66	53	.325
Yvon Pelchat	811	112	106	123	.261		Robert Scrannage	259	51	37	35	.321
Alain Perrault	891	108	144	147	.266		Kelly Hoerdt	295	47	37	45	.280
Jean Marie Potvin	413	95	69	57	.369	UDR	Harris Toole	350	77	63	51	.369
Jacques Beaudoin	746	160	129	114	.362		Laurie Bell	210	34	43	34	.330
Gaetan Lamy	261	51	53	33	.350		Doug Shaw	379	69	66	53	.325
Raymond Vachon	250	45	51	34	.339		Steve Scrannage	420	74	76	61	.325
Daniel Dube	1,014	196	153	136	.322		Robert Scrannage	259	51	37	35	.321
Gabriel Boily					$359,552	Money	Doug Shaw					$91,095
Jacques Beaudoin					301,444		Steve Scrannage					85,388
Daniel Dube					294,222		Harris Toole					81,454
Gaetan Lamy					276,628		Darren Callaghan					54,349
Alain Perrault					208,416		Laurie Bell					51,541
Raceway Park							**The Red Mile (Spring)**					
Charlie Brown	741	143	104	85	.309	Wins	Jay Picciano	208	46	38	31	.372
Jay Cross	672	106	101	96	.289		Roger Cullipher	204	32	29	23	.273
Mike Wolfe	827	89	107	109	.223		Walter Haynes, Jr.	221	29	29	34	.255
Gord McKnight	494	79	63	67	.276		Chris Loney	100	24	11	15	.351
Russ Swartz	402	66	49	43	.268		Jan Johnson	49	21	9	2	.544
Charlie Brown	741	143	104	85	.309	UDR	Dan Shetler	62	11	19	11	.407
Greg Grismore	336	47	66	44	.293		Jay Picciano	208	46	38	31	.372
Jay Cross	672	106	101	96	.289		Chris Loney	100	24	11	15	.351
Gord McKnight	494	79	63	67	.276		Larry Noggle	53	12	6	9	.346
Tom Marts, Jr.	287	45	37	39	.274		Eric Ledford	55	10	10	5	.313
Jay Cross					$188,315	Money	Jay Picciano					$77,588
Charlie Brown					178,162		Roger Cullipher					66,339
Mike Wolfe					136,061		Chris Loney					63,931
Gord McKnight					118,722		Walter Haynes, Jr.					58,604
Jeff Fout					93,603		Steve Waller					40,313

LEADING DRIVERS

Driver	Sts.	Win	2nd	3rd	UDR		Driver	Sts.	Win	2nd	3rd	UDR
The Red Mile (Fall & G.C.)							**Rideau Carleton**					
John Campbell	74	12	17	4	.308	Wins	Howard Portelance	610	107	99	94	.317
Billy Herman	36	10	8	3	.429		Gilles Plourde	367	84	59	40	.355
Jay Picciano	60	10	10	5	.287		Bob O'Dwyer	345	75	61	45	.359
Jan Johnson	30	9	5	5	.448		Kevin Sizer	354	56	57	55	.299
Gregg Haston	60	9	11	7	.291		Matt DuPuis	333	49	43	43	.262
Jan Johnson	30	9	5	5	.448	UDR	Bob O'Dwyer	345	75	61	45	.359
Billy Herman	36	10	8	3	.429		Gilles Plourde	367	84	59	40	.355
Tommy Haughton	23	4	5	4	.353		Howard Portelance	610	107	99	94	.317
Dave Rankin	24	5	3	4	.333		Kevin Sizer	354	56	57	55	.299
Bruce Riegle	26	5	4	4	.329		Pierre Desjardins	168	30	25	16	.293
Michel Lachance					194,737	Money	Howard Portelance					$181,373
John Campbell					194,482		Gilles Plourde					125,084
Jan Johnson					171,707		Bob O'Dwyer					118,995
Bill Fahy					168,970		Kevin Sizer					116,650
Ron Waples					139,147		Darrell Coville					83,253
Riverside Downs							**Rosecroft Raceway**					
Ed Morgan, Jr.	265	46	38	44	.309	Wins	Don Irvine, Jr.	1,538	281	230	187	.306
Gary Guhy	178	28	28	25	.292		Jim Morand	1,266	207	165	166	.280
Rex Watson	146	21	12	15	.224		John Wagner	1,219	206	172	163	.292
Bobby Wilson	125	16	20	18	.265		Eddie Davis	1,030	189	146	151	.311
Paul Shelton	55	14	7	15	.416		Steve Warrington	637	159	98	68	.371
Paul Shelton	55	14	7	15	.416	UDR	Steve Warrington	637	159	98	68	.371
Mike Pryor	47	13	8	4	.400		Eddie Davis	1,030	189	146	151	.311
Tom Tetrick	43	11	5	6	.367		Don Irvine, Jr.	1,538	281	230	187	.306
Ewell Binkley	52	13	5	8	.355		John Wagner	1,219	206	172	163	.292
Don Conrad	84	9	23	13	.311		Jim Morand	1,266	207	165	166	.280
Ed Morgan, Jr.					$39,184	Money	Don Irvine, Jr.					$1,351,318
Gary Guhy					26,098		Jim Morand					937,966
Rex Watson					15,934		Eddie Davis					852,796
Bobby Wilson					15,079		Steve Warrington					758,716
Tom Smith					13,760		John Wagner					581,949
Sandown Harness Raceway							**Saginaw Harness Raceway**					
Tim Brown	252	54	32	48	.348	Wins	Dan Rathka	590	78	86	89	.264
Bill Davis	232	53	58	37	.421		Mike Sciacca	387	76	45	50	.304
Brent Beelby	195	49	19	21	.341		Jeff Sweeney	621	76	102	83	.258
Joe Hudon, Jr.	127	43	32	10	.505		Brad Kramer	423	67	54	59	.276
Jim Burke	316	35	66	50	.280		Darrell Wright	349	52	62	42	.288
Joe Hudon, Jr.	127	43	32	10	.505	UDR	Clayton Faurot	104	35	14	9	.440
Bill Davis	232	53	58	37	.421		Tim Roach	113	23	18	13	.330
Barry Treen	118	27	24	25	.412		Duane Roach	87	12	17	17	.312
Tim Brown	252	54	32	48	.348		Mike Sciacca	387	76	45	50	.304
Brent Beelby	195	49	19	21	.341		Joe Putnam	228	32	42	32	.290
Bill Davis					$104,953	Money	Joe Putnam					$126,858
Tim Brown					90,195		Jeff Sweeney					104,563
Jim Burke					85,227		Dan Rathka					100,080
Bill Megens					78,139		Mike Sciacca					80,593
Joe Hudon, Jr.					74,187		Darrell Wright					76,471

LEADING DRIVERS

Driver	Sts.	Win	2nd	3rd	UDR		Driver	Sts.	Win	2nd	3rd	UDR
Saratoga Raceway							**Scarborough Downs**					
Kim Crawford	1,045	199	150	136	.314	Wins	Dave Ingraham	1,268	218	201	175	.306
Frank Coppola, Jr.	1,025	166	161	146	.297		Leigh Fitch	1,136	198	179	155	.307
Gary Kamal	779	123	103	120	.283		Bruce Aldrich, Jr.	1,211	186	163	163	.273
Dave Marshall	724	114	121	105	.299		Walter Case, Jr.	634	171	98	86	.401
Dan Cappello	547	98	87	85	.319		Jim Hardy	1,041	142	157	140	.265
Wally Hennessey	380	90	64	57	.380	UDR	Walter Case, Jr.	634	171	98	86	.401
Perry Simser	207	46	28	21	.331		Bob Sumner	360	73	54	50	.332
Dan Cappello	547	98	87	85	.319		Ruel Goodblood, Jr.	518	101	77	81	.330
Kim Crawford	1,045	199	150	136	.314		Leigh Fitch	1,136	198	179	155	.307
John Stark, Jr.	474	92	68	52	.310		Dave Ingraham	1,268	218	201	175	.306
Kim Crawford					$421,849	Money	Dave Ingraham					$222,904
Frank Coppola, Jr.					370,758		Leigh Fitch					213,065
Wally Hennessey					275,749		Bruce Aldrich, Jr.					168,718
Gary Kamal					256,150		Jim Hardy					164,652
Dave Marshall					238,056		Walter Case, Jr.					145,070
Scioto Downs							**Sports Creek Raceway (Winter-1990)**					
Jeff Fout	561	113	86	66	.326	Wins	Joe Putnam	346	61	46	52	.300
Dave Miller	451	63	52	57	.246		Dan Rathka	424	46	62	57	.235
Sam "Chip" Noble	291	57	48	47	.341		Jeff Sweeney	357	43	49	42	.236
Ray Paver, Jr.	372	55	42	61	.265		Brad Kramer	259	42	40	31	.288
Dan Ater	406	49	58	53	.244		Larry Stalbaum	298	33	31	38	.211
Sam "Chip" Noble	291	57	48	47	.341	UDR	Danny Davidson	101	23	16	11	.352
Jeff Fout	561	113	86	66	.326		Joe Putnam	346	61	46	52	.300
Randy Tharps	254	41	39	36	.294		Bob Barella	93	13	20	11	.299
Bruce Riegle	291	45	50	28	.282		Brad Kramer	259	42	40	31	.288
Herb Coven, Jr.	131	21	17	17	.276		Mark Owen	98	17	17	5	.287
Jeff Fout					$503,904	Money	Joe Putnam					$95,356
Sam "Chip" Noble					368,756		Dan Rathka					70,456
Ray Paver, Jr.					230,725		Jeff Sweeney					64,206
Bruce Riegle					222,423		Larry Stalbaum					52,793
Dan Ater					181,091		Dennis Marchand					51,681
Sports Creek Raceway (Fall-1990)							**Sportsman's Park**					
Joe Putnam	276	49	43	26	.296	Wins	Ron Marsh	990	169	137	128	.291
Jeff Sweeney	325	44	38	43	.244		Dave Magee	952	144	133	110	.267
Mark Webster	165	34	20	20	.314		Walter Paisley	638	101	91	89	.284
Brad Kramer	223	30	39	33	.281		Marc Aubin	468	74	56	56	.265
Dennis Marchand	174	28	25	20	.279		Lavern Hostetler	474	62	58	57	.239
Jim Miner	67	19	16	10	.466	UDR	Ron Marsh	990	169	137	128	.291
Clayton Faurot, Jr.	61	22	5	5	.434		Walter Paisley	638	101	91	89	.284
Mark Webster	165	34	20	20	.314		Doug Larsen	139	26	15	14	.281
Joe Putnam	276	49	43	26	.296		Bea Erdman	174	25	25	26	.273
Ron Cushing	96	17	11	14	.289		Dave Magee	952	144	133	110	.267
Peter Wrenn					$88,018	Money	Dave Magee					$1,546,975
Joe Putnam					69,786		Ron Marsh					1,312,584
Troy Boring					62,513		Walter Paisley					1,203,062
Jeff Sweeney					57,578		Lavern Hostetler					700,950
Brad Kramer					45,698		Dale Hiteman					692,722

LEADING DRIVERS

Driver	Sts.	Win	2nd	3rd	UDR
Springfield, IL					
Tom Graham	36	9	5	4	.364
Fred Finn, Jr.	34	7	4	6	.330
Berndt Lindstedt	8	6	0	0	.750
Connel Willis	32	5	6	2	.281
Jay Picciano	10	4	1	0	.456
Berndt Lindstedt	8	6	0	0	.750
Jan Johnson	8	2	4	1	.569
Jan Nordin	8	2	4	0	.528
Jay Picciano	10	4	1	0	.456
Tom Graham	36	9	5	4	.364
Berndt Lindstedt					$105,850
Jan Johnson					69,675
Jan Nordin					64,909
Dave Magee					43,189
Sam "Chip" Noble					40,436

	Driver	Sts.	Win	2nd	3rd	UDR
	Stampede Park (Winter-1990)					
Wins	Brent Grundy	245	42	44	37	.322
	Don Monkman, Jr.	136	35	22	16	.386
	Todd Beelby	145	29	26	16	.336
	Keith Clark	103	20	16	14	.326
	Richard Turcotte	125	16	12	12	.213
UDR	Clark Beelby	52	13	13	7	.434
	Kim Dressler	41	9	9	8	.407
	Don Monkman, Jr.	136	35	22	16	.386
	John Baxter	50	10	10	8	.364
	Rod Hennessy	66	13	8	15	.340
Money	Brent Grundy					$130,272
	Don Monkman, Jr.					90,200
	Todd Beelby					82,651
	Keith Clark					60,765
	Jerv Clifton					52,769

	Driver	Sts.	Win	2nd	3rd	UDR
	Stampede Park (Spr.-Sum.)					
Wins	Keith Clark	289	58	43	43	.333
	Brent Grundy	237	36	29	34	.268
	Don Monkman, Jr.	194	32	31	20	.288
	Rod Hennessy	119	29	28	24	.442
	Bruce Clarke	246	28	46	42	.275
UDR	Rod Hennessy	119	29	28	24	.442
	Clark Beelby	78	15	20	14	.395
	Kim Dressler	94	19	23	14	.388
	Isaac Tougas	66	19	5	8	.370
	Jamie Gray	70	16	12	7	.357
Money	Keith Clark					$220,703
	Don Monkman, Jr.					162,590
	Rod Hennessy					160,405
	Bruce Clarke					132,835
	Brent Grundy					125,928

	Driver	Sts.	Win	2nd	3rd	UDR
	Stampede Park (Fall)					
Wins	Keith Clark	95	28	18	11	.439
	Brent Grundy	98	18	10	13	.285
	Clark Beelby	22	10	6	1	.621
	Jerv Clifton	45	9	8	7	.351
	Todd Beelby	34	8	4	1	.311
UDR	Clark Beelby	22	10	6	1	.621
	Keith Clark	95	28	18	11	.439
	John Glen	16	3	4	3	.389
	Jerv Clifton	45	9	8	7	.351
	Jamie Gray	16	2	4	3	.326
Money	Brent Grundy					$94,171
	Keith Clark					85,720
	Warren Grant					41,378
	Jerv Clifton					39,123
	Bruce Clarke					32,028

	Driver	Sts.	Win	2nd	3rd	UDR
	Summerside Raceway					
Wins	Gary Chappell	154	34	18	22	.333
	Bill MacKay	163	31	17	22	.293
	Bob MacInnis	180	29	24	26	.283
	Walter Cheverie	177	26	36	20	.298
	Dale Sobey	238	23	36	29	.221
UDR	Boyd MacDonald	37	10	12	3	.478
	Elton Millar	56	15	6	10	.387
	Greg MacInnis	71	16	14	11	.387
	Gary Chappell	154	34	18	22	.333
	Walter Cheverie	177	26	36	20	.298
Money	Allan Smith					$13,522
	Walter Cheverie					13,107
	Bob MacInnis					11,291
	Paul MacDonald					11,063
	Gary Chappell					10,397

	Driver	Sts.	Win	2nd	3rd	UDR
	The Syracuse Mile					
Wins	Michel Lachance	13	4	0	5	.436
	Abe Stoltzfus	13	4	1	0	.350
	Chuck Connor, Jr.	23	4	1	3	.242
	Cat Manzi	10	3	0	1	.333
	John Campbell	14	3	1	2	.302
UDR	Michel Lachance	13	4	0	5	.436
	Abe Stoltzfus	13	4	1	0	.350
	Cat Manzi	10	3	0	1	.333
	Ken Ball	8	2	0	2	.333
	John Campbell	14	3	1	2	.302
Money	Michel Lachance					$86,044
	Ron Waples					82,249
	Cat Manzi					69,014
	Ken Ball					59,575
	Clint Galbraith					56,606

LEADING DRIVERS

Driver	Sts.	Win	2nd	3rd	UDR		Driver	Sts.	Win	2nd	3rd	UDR
Tartan Downs							**Hippodrome Trois Rivieres**					
Harold Youden	560	112	96	67	.335	Wins	Gaetan Lamy	788	194	142	132	.402
Doug Rankin	530	102	68	72	.309		Mario Baillargeon	574	120	100	83	.354
Greg Sparling	608	83	81	81	.255		Claude Savignac	580	88	113	102	.319
Ken McMaster	319	65	53	53	.351		Andre Corbin	463	74	71	58	.287
Alex MacQuarrie	366	60	41	44	.266		Henri Filion	236	39	35	26	.284
Ken McMaster	319	65	53	53	.351	UDR	Serge Ouellet	108	36	21	10	.472
Hugh MacInnis	155	35	22	20	.348		Gaetan Lamy	788	194	142	132	.402
Harold Youden	560	112	96	67	.335		Mario Baillargeon	574	120	100	83	.354
Gerald Snow	238	47	40	26	.327		Mario Cote	157	31	20	27	.326
Doug Rankin	530	102	68	72	.309		Claude Savignac	580	88	113	102	.319
Doug Rankin					$40,283	Money	Gaetan Lamy					$425,711
Harold Youden					40,225		Mario Baillargeon					320,532
Greg Sparling					33,836		Henri Filion					235,148
Ken McMaster					25,662		Benoit Cote					211,711
Alex MacQuarrie					19,467		Claude Savignac					136,484
Truro Raceway							**Vernon Downs**					
Dan Romo	680	129	112	85	.323	Wins	Brian Allen	919	145	121	141	.282
David Carey	864	116	133	125	.268		Charles Connor, Jr.	633	113	95	84	.306
Dave Pinkney	511	100	75	71	.324		Gary Gibson	694	105	90	84	.264
Garry MacDonald	685	100	93	105	.273		Jeff Gregory	434	77	78	55	.320
Russ Burgoyne	532	92	96	80	.323		Ron Hill	533	69	86	71	.264
Dave Pinkney	511	100	75	71	.324	UDR	Mickey Bridges	263	61	42	39	.370
Russ Burgoyne	532	92	96	80	.323		Clint Galbraith	161	29	37	21	.351
Dan Romo	680	129	112	85	.323		Jeff Gregory	434	77	78	55	.320
Mike Worthen	267	48	39	24	.291		Charles Connor, Jr.	633	113	95	84	.306
Jimmy Davis	517	84	73	62	.281		Brian Allen	919	145	121	141	.282
Dan Romo					$98,959	Money	Brian Allen					$313,808
David Carey					93,300		Gary Gibson					239,883
Dave Pinkney					83,472		Charles Connor, Jr.					232,755
Russ Burgoyne					82,125		Jeff Gregory					194,616
Garry MacDonald					78,151		Ron Hill					182,433
Western Fair Raceway (Winter-1990)							**Western Fair Raceway (Fall-1990)**					
Rod Robblee	575	119	91	72	.337	Wins	Ross Battin	228	49	22	29	.311
Ray McLean	644	103	82	108	.287		Ray McLean	314	41	33	49	.241
Ross Battin	521	94	93	71	.325		Rod Robblee	273	36	38	43	.262
Ken Quire	433	81	64	59	.315		Fred Sadler	238	35	33	29	.265
Fred Sadler	375	49	58	53	.264		Steve Bossence	152	26	36	31	.371
Dave Wall	153	36	17	25	.352	UDR	Greg Campbell	94	24	22	8	.414
Terry Kerr	192	38	33	29	.344		Steve Bossence	152	26	36	31	.371
Steve Bossence	110	25	14	13	.337		Dave Wall	75	19	8	9	.353
Rod Robblee	575	119	91	72	.337		Ross Battin	228	49	22	29	.311
Ross Battin	521	94	93	71	.325		Crawford McKeen	49	9	6	7	.299
Ray McLean					$167,216	Money	Ray McLean					$84,526
Ross Battin					159,463		Ross Battin					75,853
Rod Robblee					149,857		Rod Robblee					57,014
Ken Quire					114,153		Steve Bossence					54,605
Fred Sadler					80,009		Fred Sadler					51,878

LEADING DRIVERS

Driver   *Sts. Win 2nd 3rd UDR*

Windsor Raceway (Winter-1990)

Driver	Sts.	Win	2nd	3rd	UDR	
Danny Johnson	467	114	65	83	.381	**Wins**
Ron Henderson	439	90	80	63	.354	
Mark Williams	408	69	75	57	.318	
Bill Gale	244	64	40	24	.386	
Randy Kerr	527	64	86	76	.260	
Bill Gale	244	64	40	24	.386	**UDR**
Danny Johnson	467	114	65	83	.381	
Ron Henderson	439	90	80	63	.354	
Ken Hardy	199	43	26	28	.336	
Mark Williams	408	69	75	57	.318	

Driver	Money	
Danny Johnson	$278,921	**Money**
Ron Henderson	275,732	
Bill Gale	267,487	
Randy Kerr	200,314	
Mark Williams	194,572	

Windsor Raceway (Fall-1990)

Driver	Sts.	Win	2nd	3rd	UDR	
Mark Williams	396	91	72	42	.366	**Wins**
Danny Johnson	315	64	40	37	.313	
Don Rankin, Jr.	243	54	46	35	.375	
Ron Henderson	315	48	36	41	.259	
Allen Cullen	316	48	33	38	.250	
Don Rankin, Jr.	243	54	46	35	.375	**UDR**
Mark Williams	396	91	72	42	.366	
Danny Johnson	315	64	40	37	.313	
Randy Kerr	306	45	43	45	.274	
Ron Henderson	315	48	36	41	.259	

Driver	Money	
Mark Williams	$199,632	**Money**
Ron Henderson	152,231	
Danny Johnson	144,669	
Randy Kerr	128,559	
"Bud" Fritz	114,541	

Yonkers Raceway

Driver	Sts.	Win	2nd	3rd	UDR	
Walter Case, Jr.	1,539	390	244	206	.386	**Wins**
Herve Filion	2,105	361	308	309	.302	
Jim Marohn	2,204	334	346	322	.288	
Gary Mosher	2,178	331	319	260	.273	
Richard Wojcio	1,684	229	237	184	.251	
Walter Case, Jr.	1,539	390	244	206	.386	**UDR**
Herve Filion	2,105	361	308	309	.302	
Luc Ouellette	1,399	217	216	222	.294	
Jim Marohn	2,204	334	346	322	.288	
Gary Mosher	2,178	331	319	260	.273	

Driver	Money	
Herve Filion	$2,648,658	**Money**
Gary Mosher	2,207,080	
Jim Marohn	1,942,177	
Walter Case, Jr.	1,863,386	
Richard Wojcio	1,543,860	

LEADING DRIVERS

LEADING DRIVERS AT OTHER NORTH AMERICAN TRACKS

Driver	Sts.	Win	2nd	3rd	UDR		Driver	Sts.	Win	2nd	3rd	UDR
Barrie Raceway							**Clinton Raceway**					
Steve Byron	713	152	101	92	.335	Wins	John Muir	68	18	12	8	.402
Steve Byron	713	152	101	92	.335	UDR	Howard Kennedy	11	4	1	2	.475
Derek Newman				$184,529		Money	Dave Wall				$19,368	
Cumberland Raceway							**Dresen Raceway**					
Dave Ingraham	53	11	8	10	.354	Wins	Dennis DuFord	221	47	44	30	.369
Paul Battis	18	6	2	3	.451	UDR	Mark Williams	127	34	23	12	.400
Dave Ingraham				$11,176		Money	Allen Cullen				$38,284	
Elmira Raceway							**Goderich Raceway**					
Bryan Holmes	257	52	46	30	.341	Wins	John Muir	66	26	10	7	.514
Don Graham	93	23	15	8	.366	UDR	John Muir	66	26	10	7	.514
Bryan Holmes				$52,880		Money	John Muir				$10,947	
Hanover Raceway							**Kingston Park Raceway**					
Terry Fritz	82	20	17	10	.400	Wins	Ed Huntbach	360	79	71	54	.379
Paul Walker	53	18	8	3	.442	UDR	Ed Huntbach	360	79	71	54	.379
Mark Etsell				$28,379		Money	Ed Huntbach				$67,278	
Leamington Raceway							**Orangeville Raceway**					
Gord McDonnell	83	17	11	13	.331	Wins	Jim Ritchie	652	144	112	89	.362
Doug McIntosh	17	5	6	2	.529	UDR	Jim Ritchie	652	144	112	89	.362
John Brooks				$19,082		Money	Jim Ritchie				$154,522	
Presque Isle, Maine							**Quinte Raceway**					
Jim Shaw	70	14	9	9	.314	Wins	Ted McDonald	178	51	33	21	.429
Mark Grant	27	7	8	3	.461	UDR	Ted McDonald	178	51	33	21	.429
Mike Murchison				$7,518		Money	Ted McDonald				$30,135	
Hippodrome Saguenay							**Sudbury Downs**					
Yvon Belanger	224	74	42	27	.475	Wins	Mark Cecile	254	57	45	39	.374
Yvon Belanger	224	74	42	27	.475	UDR	Mark Cecile	254	57	45	39	.374
Yvon Belanger				$34,129		Money	Gary Rivest				$71,834	
Woodstock Raceway, Ontario												
Rod Robblee	150	22	15	22	.251	Wins						
John MacCormick	60	21	10	5	.470	UDR						
Ross Battin				$24,308		Money						

* * * * *

LEADING DRIVERS

THE WORLD DRIVING CHAMPIONSHIP

The World Driving Championship, a biennial event, was last held the summer of 1989 in Canada, and decided on the final night of competition, September 2, at Greenwood Raceway in Toronto. Competition was held at six different venues: Hippodrome Blue Bonnets, in Montreal; Hippodrome Trois Rivieres, in Three Rivers, Quebec; Quebec City Raceway; Rideau Carleton, in Gloucester, Ontario; Barrie Raceway, Barrie, Ontario; and Greenwood Raceway. Horses were drawn in each race by lot, and the event was marked by much pageantry and local color. Ron Pierce, the 33-year-old native of California, proved that in harness racing, consistency is everything. Pierce failed to win any of the six rounds, but edged Maurice McKendry and defending champ Ted Demmler in the final standings. The championship came down to the final race of the series, when Pierce finished second to a hard-charging Ted Demmler while driving 8-1 longshot Tough Kracker. McKendry, meanwhile, could muster only a fifth place finish. Scoring was done on a 17-12-9-7-6-5-4-3-2-1 basis in each race. Here are the final standings, including the round-by-round scoring, with the winning score in each round indicated in **boldface**:

Round-by-Round Results of the 1989 Series

	Driver (Country) Pts. by Round:	One	Two	Three	Four	Five	Six	Total
1.	Ron Pierce (U.S.A.)	41	28	26	20	27	11	**153**
2.	Maurice McKendry (N. Zealand)	27.5	**43**	28	**39**	9	5	151.5
3.	Ted Demmler (Australia)	**43**	26	15	22	26	**15**	148
4.	Tjitse Smeding (Netherlands)	18.5	32	13	35	38	4	140.5
5.	Rick Zeron (Canada)	32	15	31	34	17	6	135
6.	Bartolome Fuster (Spain)	11	15	**47**	21	22	1	117
7.	Adolf Uebleis (Austria)	12	26	18	10	**47**	3	116
8.	Birger Jorgensen (Denmark)	16	31	13	23	20	8	111
9.	Tony Turnbull (Australia)	15	8	33	20	14	2	92

Previous Winners - The World Driving Championship

Year	Venue	Winner	Country
1987	Sweden	Ted Demmler	Australia
1985	Australasia	Tony Herlihy	New Zealand
1983	Asia	Robert Cameron	New Zealand
1981	Europe	Ulf Thoresen	Norway
1979	Australasia	Ulf Thoresen	Norway
1978	North America	Kevin Holmes	New Zealand
1977	Europe	Ulf Thoresen	Norway
1975	Australasia	Keith Addison	Australia
1974	Europe	Joe Marsh, Jr.	United States
1973	Europe	Ulf Thoresen	Norway
1972	North America	Guiseppe Guzzinati	Italy
1971	North America	Adolf Ubleis	Austria
1970	North America	Herve Filion	Canada

THE WORLD CUP OF AMATEUR DRIVING

For the first time since its inception in 1972, the World Cup of Amateur Driving was held on North American soil in 1988. Sponsored by the North American Amateur Drivers Association, the World Cup visited Balmoral Park, Hippodrome Trois Rivieres, Blue Bonnets, Goshen's Historic Track and The Meadowlands. Fourteen drivers representing the United States, Canada and several European countries took part. France's Daniel Foucault, a gynecologist by profession, won two of the six heats contested, including the final at The Meadowlands:

Driver (Country)	Pts.
1. Daniel Foucault (France)	66
2. Hans Johann Stamp (West Germany)	50
3. Gerald Van Pollaert (Belgium)	49
4. Urs Sommer (Switzerland)	41
5. Gerhard Mayr (Austria)	40
6. Oddvar Maeland (Norway)	38
7. Fred Handelaar (The Netherlands)	37
8. Robert Nilsson (Sweden)	35
9. Saul Mendelson (Canada)	32
10. Istvan Kovacs (Hungary)	29
11. Ron Tabas (United States)	26
12. Frank Mikkelson (Denmark)	23
13. Juan Antonia Terrasa Pou (Spain)	17
14. Pier Francesco Mauro (Italy)	11

Breeding and Sales

BREEDING AND SALES

LEADING MONEYWINNING SIRES OF 1990

Sire	Starters	Winners	Wins	Earnings	Top '90 Moneywinner	Earnings
1. Abercrombie	371	293	1,233	$10,180,347	Artsplace	$1,180,271
2. No Nukes	424	284	850	8,774,327	Die Laughing	1,142,322
3. Big Towner	397	298	1,092	7,917,751	Town Pro	634,690
4. Direct Scooter	467	334	1,062	7,848,905	In The Pocket	745,051
5. Tyler B	350	249	976	6,592,138	Conditional	304,910
6. Speedy Crown	178	93	274	5,684,801	Embassy Lobell	1,049,175
7. Niatross	381	269	869	5,613,461	Instant Rebate	401,865
8. Albatross	341	241	843	5,218,386	Kiev Hanover	428,294
9. Cam Fella	202	155	519	4,919,284	Cams Exotic	520,086
10. Storm Damage	332	222	726	4,597,439	Stormin Jesse	322,299
11. Super Bowl	165	94	270	3,829,942	Jean Bi	366,153
12. French Chef	158	121	485	3,828,909	Beach Towel	2,091,860
13. On The Road Again	138	96	307	3,749,210	Road Machine	401,508
14. Walton Hanover	178	145	549	3,696,662	Caesars Jackpot	353,550
15. Landslide	270	208	754	3,459,860	It's Sunny	154,850
16. Nihilator	169	111	332	3,163,850	Silver Almahurst	302,996
17. Sonsam	223	155	574	3,067,885	Till We Meet Again	377,797
18. B Gs Bunny	352	235	860	2,960,662	Shadydale Special	109,789
19. Ideal Society	216	132	430	2,952,309	Gosox	256,472
12. Speedy Somolli	160	92	222	2,881,237	Jeanne's Somolli	430,115

1990 LEADING MONEYWINNING SIRES, BY GAIT

Listed below are the leading moneywinning sires of 1990, divided by gait. The dollar amounts may be smaller than those on the leading sire list, since progeny racing on the opposite gait have been excluded:

TROTTERS

Sire	Starters	Earnings
1. Speedy Crown	170	$5,668,042
2. Super Bowl	156	3,812,703
3. Speedy Somolli	157	2,870,526
4. Worthy Bowl	145	2,526,178
5. Dream Of Glory	199	2,176,562
6. Joie De Vie	170	1,788,027
7. Speed In Action	211	1,723,302
8. Brisco Hanover	135	1,677,190
9. Prakas	97	1,658,770
10. Superman	175	1,631,708
11. Crowning Point	45	1,571,424
12. Florida Pro	117	1,425,741
13. Bonefish	124	1,387,656
14. Crysta's Crown	135	1,295,435
15. Lindys Crown	144	1,291,377
16. Royal Prestige	39	1,231,981
17. Batic Speed	111	1,217,723
18. Jazz Cosmos	139	1,212,505
19. Meadow Road	71	1,100,158
20. Final Score	131	1,019,287

PACERS

Sire	Starters	Earnings
1. Abercrombie	371	$10,180,347
2. No Nukes	424	8,774,327
3. Big Towner	396	7,917,751
4. Direct Scooter	465	7,848,835
5. Tyler B	350	6,592,138
6. Niatross	381	5,613,461
7. Albatross	341	5,218,386
8. Cam Fella	202	4,919,284
9. Storm Damage	331	4,597,439
10. French Chef	156	3,824,598
11. On The Road Again	138	3,749,210
12. Walton Hanover	178	3,696,662
13. Landslide	270	3,459,860
14. Nihilator	169	3,163,850
15. Sonsam	220	3,012,303
16. B Gs Bunny	351	2,960,662
17. Ideal Society	216	2,952,309
18. Falcon Almahurst	324	2,830,985
19. Troublemaker	160	2,781,485
20. Armbro Omaha	265	2,441,820

(continued)

BREEDING AND SALES

21. Balanced Image	80	$1,013,640	21. Fundamentalist	215	$2,392,964
22. Homesick	105	998,970	22. Ralph Hanover	272	2,328,594
23. Arndon	113	982,378	23. Flight Of Fire	131	2,056,181
24. Diamond Exchange	80	981,028	24. Armbro Wolf	211	1,991,350
25. Texas	82	793,147	25. Armbro Aussie	144	1,962,016
26. Mighty Crown	143	776,146	26. Colt Fortysix	123	1,924,689
27. Hunters Star	52	734,047	27. Royce	214	1,908,892
28. Armbro Agile	86	644,576	28. Nero	278	1,900,918
29. Coleman Lobell	79	639,978	29. Precious Fella	241	1,860,954
30. Incredible Nevele	53	628,424	30. Seahawk Hanover	207	1,852,713

LEADING SIRES BY AVERAGE EARNINGS

Listed below are the leading sires (of at least ten starters) by the average earnings of their progeny in 1990. The Index is the result of total earnings divided by the number of starters, regardless of gait. During 1990, the average earnings of all North American Starters was $7,675. Thus, for example, the index shows that the foals of Fortune Richie earned an average of 6.36 times the average of all horses that started in 1990:

TROTTERS

Sire	Avg. Earnings	Earnings Index
1. Crowning Point	$34,912	4.55
2. Speedy Crown	33,341	4.34
3. Roayl Prestige	31,589	4.12
4. Super Bowl	24,440	3.18
5. Garland Lobell	23,264	3.03
6. Noble Gesture	19,275	2.51
7. Darvin	19,080	2.49
8. Speedy Somolli	18,284	2.38
9. Mystic Park	17,959	2.34
10. Worthy Bowl	17,422	2.27
11. Prakas	17,101	2,23
12. Copter Lobell	16,346	2.13
13. Meadow Road	15,495	2.02
14. Self Confident	15,091	1.97
15. Lucky Almahurst	14,748	1.92
16. Nevele Pride	14,424	1.88
17. Hunters Star	14,116	1.84
18. Workaholic	13,846	1.80
19. Nevele Impulse	13,748	1.79
20. Camp David	12,827	1.67

PACERS

Sire	Avg. Earnings	Earnings Index
1. Fortune Richie	$48,845	6.36
2. Apache Circle	36,241	4.72
3. Samadhi	33,089	4.31
4. Lake Hills Tex	30,031	3.91
5. Abercrombie	27,440	3.58
6. On The Road Again	27,168	3.54
7. Amity Chef	26,494	3.45
8. French Chef	24,517	3.19
9. Cam Fella	24,353	3.17
10. Walton Hanover	20,768	2.71
11. No Nukes	20,694	2.70
12. Big Towner	19,994	2.61
13. Bit O Fun	19,7144	2.57
14. Andrel	18,875	2.46
15. Tyler B	18,835	2.45
16. Monkey Wrench	18,727	2.44
17. Nihilator	18,721	2.44
18. Governor Skipper	18,169	2.37
19. Supreme Jade	17,806	2.32
20. Falcon Seelster	17,802	2.32

LEADING MONEYWINNING SIRES: 2- AND 3-YEAR-OLDS

Sire (Foals)	Starters	Winners	Wins	Earnings	Top Juvenile Winner	Earnings
1. No Nukes (374)	267	178	489	$6,348,238	Die Laughting	$1,142,322
2. Direct Scooter (306)	223	160	481	4,881,048	In The Pocket	745,051
3. Speedy Crown (192)	100	52	144	4,817,941	Embassy Lobell	1,049,175
4. On The Road Again (215)	138	96	307	3,749,210	Road Machine	401,508
5. Super Bowl (192)	91	50	128	3,268,820	Jean Bi	366,153

(continued)

BREEDING AND SALES

6. Nihilator (248)	169	111	332	$3,163,850	Silver Almahurst	$302,996
7. Big Towner (185)	139	97	310	3,135,730	Mark Johnathan	604,366
8. Abercrombie (121)	81	56	172	2,952,802	Atsplace	1,180,271
9. Cam Fella (178)	116	84	255	2,870,483	Cams Exotic	520,086
10. Tyler B (228)	165	98	315	2,807,740	Lady Genius	282,496
11. French Chef (64)	34	24	96	2,556,052	Beach Towel	2,091,860
12. Niatross (208)	124	92	258	2,457,264	Instant Rebate	401,865
13. Speedy Somolli (156)	72	38	84	2,152,755	Jeanne's Somolli	430,115
14. Albatross (180)	115	76	219	2,093,287	Kiev Hanover	428,294
15. Walton Hanover (159)	110	90	338	2,078,609	Brando Hanover	306,500
16. Flight Of Fire (190)	131	73	230	2,056,181	Proprietors Choice	301,927
17. Ideal Society (189)	126	74	242	1,970,017	Gosox	256,472
18. Troublemaker (167)	116	74	268	1,952,801	Excited	274,657
19. Prakas (256)	98	46	121	1,659,050	Me Maggie	305,004
20. Worthy Bowl (203)	86	36	114	1,657,466	A Worthy Lad	224,848

LEADING FIRST CROP SIRES – 1990

Sire (Foals)	Starters	Winners	Wins	Earnings	Top Moneywinner	Earnings
1. Amity Chef (102)	47	20	49	$1,245,203	Miss Easy	$1,128,956
2. Royal Prestige (73)	39	21	51	1,231,981	Santa Royal	427,154
3. Falcon Seelster (94)	59	39	113	1,050,337	Mantese	294,272
4. Tyler's Mark (101)	58	31	72	541,923	TP's Express	85,650
5. Energy Burner (90)	50	27	97	526,272	Turbo Twin	121,606
6. Forrest Skipper (176)	86	36	72	484,567	Perfect Together	185,445
7. Nobleland Sam (31)	20	14	47	341,434	Beacon's Star	116,339
8. Barberry Spur (102)	57	26	42	294,232	Prudhomme	67,197
9. On The Take (54)	31	15	36	230,014	Lukes Pheidippides	38,529
10. Armbro Cadet (57)	36	22	52	202,505	Cadeeze	60,445

LEADING FIRST CROP SIRES – 1989

Sire (Foals)	Starters	Winners	Wins	Earnings	Top Moneywinner	Earnings
1. On The Road Again (106)	52	35	94	$1,397,961	Road Machine	$369,164
2. Nihilator (140)	78	42	89	960,992	Jane Ann Almahurst	151,472
3. Flight Of Fire (104)	66	42	118	951,920	Cushion	88,498
4. Praised Dignity (108)	57	30	66	649,628	Lindwood Praise	173,303
5. Prakas (128)	51	19	35	560,628	Meadowbranch Eddy	170,731

LEADING MONEYWINNING SIRES OF 1989

Sire	Starters	Starts	Wins	Earnings	Top '88 Moneywinner	Earnings
1. Big Towner	395	302	1,141	$9,028,125	Sandman Hanover	$767,153
2. Abercrombie	370	298	1,214	8,775,849	Kentucky Spur	723,945
3. Tyler B	345	252	895	7,360,068	Bruce's Lady	628,925
4. Direct Scooter	405	296	973	7,016,847	Matt's Scooter	1,140,994
5. Albatross	368	256	909	6,639,860	Cherry Hello	572,664
6. Storm Damage	335	241	847	6,420,735	Kick Up A Storm	472,169
7. Speedy Crown	199	117	347	6,096,835	Bon Vivant	414,729
8. No Nukes	317	204	641	5,707,968	Dexter Nukes	1,027,620
9. Cam Fella	149	114	428	5,695,082	Goalie Jeff	1,682,151
10. Niatross	396	262	826	5,632,446	Casino Cowboy	570,311
11. Super Bowl	173	89	280	4,540,102	Royal Troubador	541,336
12. Speedy Somolli	172	103	324	3,901,505	Park Avenue Joe	666,311
13. Falcon Almahurst	307	215	778	3,453,599	Raque Bogart	173,128
14. Sonsam	231	159	504	3,445,978	Till We Meet Again	442,994
15. Landslide	259	187	665	3,321,883	Precedent	223,800

BREEDING AND SALES

PREVIOUS LEADING MONEYWINNING SIRES
(Top two shown; former single-year record-holder in **boldface**)

'88	Abercrombie	$9,888,742	'80	**Most Happy Fella**	**8,588,636**
	Big Towner	9,229,855		Albatross	6,308,993
'87	Abercrombie	8,616,906	'79	**Most Happy Fella**	**7,100,055**
	Speedy Crown	7,638,114		Meadow Skipper	4,456,943
'86	Albatross	9,393,122	'78	Meadow Skipper	5,409,872
	Speedy Crown	8,359,367		Most Happy Fella	5,137,896
'85	Speedy Crown	9,762,506	'77	Meadow Skipper	4,565,777
	Niatross	8,632,487		Race Time	3,682,154
'84	Albatross	8,803,245	'76	**Meadow Skipper**	**4,658,019**
	Most Happy Fella	7,743,406		Bret Hanover	3,034,174
'83	Albatross	9,537,399	'75	Meadow Skipper	3,278,753
	Most Happy Fella	9,203,226		Bret Hanover	2,930,175
'82	**Albatross**	**10,322,989**	'74	Bye Bye Byrd	2,763,308
	Most Happy Fella	9,608,961		Shadow Wave	2,265,485
'81	**Albatross**	**10,083,778**	'73	Bye Bye Byrd	2,030,128
	Most Happy Fella	8,098,776		Star's Pride	1,919,873

LEADING MONEYWINNING SIRES, ALL-TIME

	Sire	Gait	First Crop Raced	Total Winnings	Top Moneywinner Performer	Earnings
1.	Albatross	Pace	1976	$97,685,816	Niatross	$2,019,213
2.	Most Happy Fella	Pace	1974	93,455,434	Cam Fella	2,041,367
3.	Speedy Crown	Trot	1976	74,823,407	Prakas	1,956,056
4.	Meadow Skipper	Pace	1969	66,752,726	Ralph Hanover	1,828,871
5.	Bret Hanover	Pace	1970	60,247,457	Even Odds	976,683
6.	Abercrombie	Pace	1983	51,862,201	Armbro Emerson	1,472,590
7.	Super Bowl	Trot	1976	48,318,905	Napoletano	* 2,467,878
8.	Nero	Pace	1980	42,559,083	Runnymede Lobell	1,615,125
9.	Big Towner	Pace	1982	43,969,394	Broadway Express	1,141,726
10.	B Gs Bunny	Pace	1981	39,892,576	McKinzie Almahurst	1,532,870

* - includes some foreign earnings

LEADING STALLIONS BY STUD FEE

Fee	TROTTING Stallion	Standing At:
$50,000	Speedy Crown	Lana Lobell Farms Of NY
30,000	Super Bowl	Hanover Shoe Farms, PA
12,000	Armbro Goal	Castleton Farm, NJ
10,000	Royal Prestige	Castleton Farm, NY
7,500	Baltic Speed	Castleton Farm, NJ
7,500	Prakas	Hanover Shoe Farms, PA
7,500	Valley Victory	Southwind Farm, NJ
6,000	Meadow Road	Blue Chip Farms, NY
6,000	Nevele Pride	Stoner Creek Stud, KY
6,000	Royal Troubador	Upstream Farm, NJ

(continued)

BREEDING AND SALES

Fee	PACING Stallion	Standing At:
$25,000	No Nukes	Upstream Farm, NJ
20,000	Albatross	Hanover Shoe Farms, PA
20,000	Matt's Scooter	Perretti Farms, NJ
15,000	Abercrombie	Castleton Farm, KY
15,000	Jate Lobell	Kentuckiana Farms, NY
12,000	Cam Fella	Dreamaire Stud, NJ
12,000	Direct Scooter	Walnridge Farm, NJ
12,000	Nihilator	Almahurst Farm, NJ
12,000	On The Road Again	Blue Chip Farms, NY
10,000	Big Towner	Hanover Shoe Farms, PA
10,000	Call For Rain	Rodney Farms, NY
10,000	Dragon's Lair	Walnut Hall Farm, KY
10,000	Falcon Almahurst	Hill Farms, OH
10,000	Sonsam	Fair Winds Farm, NJ
10,000	Storm Damage	Castleton Farm, NY

LEADING SIRES OF CAREER $100,000 WINNERS

	Sire	Total $100,000 Winners	Starters in '90	New $100,000 Winners in '90	Top Career Moneywinner	Carreer Earnings
1.	Most Happy Fella	282	162	3	Cam Fella	$2,041,367
2.	Albatross	277	341	12	Niatross	2,019,213
3.	Speedy Crown	201	178	13	Prakas	1,956,056
4.	Meadow Skipper	184	31	none	Ralph Hanover	1,828,871
5.	Bret Hanover	175	173	5	Even Odds	976,683
6.	Nero	119	278	7	Runnymede Lobell	1,615,125
7.	Abercrombie	132	371	24	Armbro Emerson	1,472,590
8.	Super Bowl	119	165	9	Napoletano	* 2,467,878
9.	Big Towner	109	397	21	Broadway Express	1,141,726
10.	Race Time	107	5	1	Dream Maker	746,332
11.	B Gs Bunny	99	352	12	McKinzie Almahurst	1,532,870
12.	Bye Bye Byrd	95	9	none	Armbro Nesbit	625,964
	Tar Heel	95	2	none	Laverne Hanover	868,557
14.	Tyler B	94	350	27	Dragon's Lair	1,085,317
15.	Dream Of Glory	91	215	1	Shipps Dream	652,199
16.	High Ideal	88	166	3	Wizard Almahurst	627,640
	Precious Fella	88	241	7	Red Colt	722,838
18.	Adios Vic	85	18	none	J.D's Buck	1,156,532
	Storm Damage	85	332	11	Redskin	1,865,702
	Niatross	85	381	16	Nihilator	3,225,653

* - Includes some foreign earnings

Leading Sires of $100,000 Winners, 1990 Season

	Sire	Number
1.	No Nukes	17
2.	Speedy Crown	15
3.	Abercrombie	14
4.	Direct Scooter	13
5.	Tyler B	12
6.	Big Towner	10
	Cam Fella	10
	Niatross	10
	Super Bowl	10
10.	On The Road Again	9
11.	Speedy Somolli	8
12.	Nihilator	7

Leading Sires of $100,000 Winners, 1989 Season

	Sire	Number
1.	Speedy Crown	20
2.	Abercrombie	15
	Storm Damage	15
4.	Big Towner	14
5.	Albatross	11
	Super Bowl	11
	Tyler B	11
8.	No Nukes	10
9.	Direct Scooter	9
	Niatross	9
11.	Cam Fella	8
	Dream Of Glory	8
	Speedy Somolli	8

BREEDING AND SALES

LEADING SIRES OF TWO-MINUTE PERFORMERS

Shown is the name of the sire; number of two-minute pacer, trotters, and total number of two-minute offspring; and how many new two-minute performers have been added to his credit in 1990. Next comes that sire's fastest performer, including record. If the credit is on the opposite gait, the fastest performer on the same gait is also shown:

	Trotting Sire	Pace	Trot	Total	New in '90	Fastest Performer(s)	Record
1.	Speedy Crown	19	257	276	29	Prakas	1:53.2
2.	Super Bowl	10	184	194	19	Express Ride	1:53
3.	Speedy Somolli	3	130	133	17	Freindly Face	1:54.1
4.	Florida Pro	11	91	102	8	Huggie Hanover	1:54.3
5.	Bonefish	6	90	96	6	Firm Tribute	1:54.3
6.	Dream Of Glory	8	61	69	9	Indianapolis	1:55.1
7.	Nevele Pride	4	62	66	1	Incredible Nevele	1:56
	Noble Victory	18	48	66	none	Noble Prince, p	T 1:55.2
						& Dallas Lobell	1:56.1
9.	Speedy Scot	12	48	60	1	Classical Way	T 1:55.2
10.	Texas	13	41	54	4	Tex Les Collins, p	1:56.1
						& Derby Tex Whiz	1:56.2
11.	Stars Pride	7	42	49	none	Nevele Pride	T 1:54.4
12.	Brisco Hanover	14	34	48	11	Brisk Fling, p	1:53.3
						& No Sex Please	1:55f
13.	Lindys Crown	2	44	46	10	Crown Agent, p	1:54.4
						& Reunited	1:56.4
14.	Arndon	4	39	43	14	Kindava Hush	1:56.1f
15.	Arnie Almahurst	3	38	41	none	Arndon	T 1:54
	Speed In Action	1	40	41	7	Editor In Chief	1:56f
17.	Homesick	1	36	37	9	Model Home	1:55.3
18.	Noble Gesture	4	32	36	none	Pay Tribute	1:56
19.	Final Score	10	24	34	9	Courtney Charamar	T 1:57.1
20.	Green Speed	5	28	33	1	Witsend's Speedy	1:55.3

	Pacing Sire	Pace	Trot	Total	New in '90	Fastest Performer(s)	Record
1.	Albatross	805	0	805	51	Niatross	T 1:49.1
2.	Most Happy Fella	552	0	552	1	What's Next	1:51.3
						& Armbro Feather	1:51.3
3.	Bret Hanover	502	0	502	20	Save Fuel	1:51.1
4.	Meadow Skipper	453	2	455	1	Trenton Time	
						& Don't Dally	1:51.3
5.	B Gs Bunny	428	0	428	27	Awesome Almahurst	1:52.4
6.	Nero	403	0	403	19	Runnymede Lobell	T 1:51.2
7.	Big Towner	399	0	399	56	Threefold	1:51.1
						& Keystone Raider	1:51.1
8.	Abercrombie	390	0	390	57	Artsplace	1:51.1f
9.	Niatross	375	0	375	63	Nihilator	1:49.3
10.	Tyler B	334	0	334	52	Dragon's Lair	1:51.3
						& Tyler's Mark	1:51.3
11.	Direct Scooter	316	0	316	83	Matt's Scooter	T 1:48.2
12.	Falcon Almahurst	306	0	306	53	Raque Bogart	1:52.1
						& Soaring Falcon	1:52.1
13.	Storm Damage	304	0	304	46	Call For Rain	1:49.3
14.	No Nukes	302	0	302	102	Jate Lobell	1:51.2
	Precious Fella	302	0	302	14	Fiorello Blue Chip	1:53.2
16.	Sonsam	240	1	241	38	Pan Am Sam	1:51.4
17.	Silent Majority	229	0	229	19	Laughs	1:52.1
18.	Oil Burner	228	0	228	8	No Nukes	T 1:52.1
19.	Warm Breeze	227	0	227	17	Falcon Seelster	1:51h
20.	High Ideal	220	0	220	8	Sindav	1:52.4

BREEDING AND SALES

LEADING STALLIONS BY STATE

Listed below are the leading stallions on a state-by-state basis, with the rankings based upon the 1990 earnings of their offspring.

If a stallion has been moved, he is listed by the state where he will stand in 1990. For example, Crystas Crown is listed among the Kentucky stallions, although his racing offspring were mostly sired in Ohio.

California

Denali	$1,061,425
Hunters Star	925,177
Peter Lobell	848,487
Rowdy Yankee	443,862
Jambooger	365,631

Illinois

Ideal Society	$2,952,309
Armbro Wolf	1,993,348
Egyptian Dancer	1,657,926
High Ideal	1,024,672
Rorty Hanover	857,978

Kentucky

Abercrombie	$10,180,347
Silent Majority	1,769,930
Crowning Point	1,571,749
Bret Hanover	1,468,308
Crystas Crown	1,313,331

Maryland

Distant Thunder	$1,344,194
Arties Dream	1,281,960
Conquered	896,610
Icarus Lobell	846,617
Tyler's Mark	541,923

Michigan

Superman	$1,638,102
Good Albatross	1,022,126
Crosscurrent	956,835
Warren Hanover	876,101
Jurgy Hanover	616,149

New Jersey

No Nukes	$8,774,327
Niatross	5,613,461
Cam Fella	4,919,284
Storm Damage	4,597,439
Walton Hanover	3,696,662

New York

Speedy Crown	$5,684,801
On The Road Again	3,749,210
Nero	1,900,918
Precious Fella	1,860,954
Seahwak Hanover	1,852,713

Ohio

Falcon Almahurst	$2,842,642
Speed In Action	1,731,569
Good To See You	1,727,589
Raven Hanover	1,718,287
Set The Style	1,140,710

Ontario

Worthy Bowl	$2,571,984
Armbro Omaha	2,441,820
Fundamentalist	2,392,964
Ralph Hanover	2,328,754
Dream Of Glory	2,271,420

Pennsylvania

Big Towner	$7,917,751
Albatross	5,218,386
Super Bowl	3,829,942
Colt Fortysix	1,924,689
Keystone Ore	1,663,961

Quebec

Flight Of Fire	$2,056,181
Better Heather	851,889
Striking Image	812,831
Bye Bye Pat	687,365
Meadow Weston	617,068

Deceased

Tyler B	$6,592,138
Royce	1,908,892
Scarlet Skipper	1,832,495
Most Happy Fella	1,529,878
Bonefish	1,391,090

* * * * * *

BREEDING AND SALES

LEADING PERCENTAGE SIRES

(15 or more foals)

2:10 2-year-old Trotters

Sire	Foals	Perf.	Pct.
Lucky Almahurst	15	6	.400
Roayl Prestige	73	24	.329
Speedy Crown	90	29	.322
Super Bowl	96	26	.271
Workaholic	54	14	.259
Coleman Lobell	52	13	.250
Arndon	43	10	.233
T V Yankee	37	8	.216
Speedy Somolli	76	16	.211
Garland Lobell	29	6	.207

2:05 2-year-old Pacers

Sire	Foals	Perf.	Pct.
Nihilator	108	50	.463
Big Towner	84	36	.429
No Nukes	213	89	.418
Cam Fella	95	38	.400
Nobleland Sam	31	12	.387
Bret Hanover	26	10	.385
Niafirst	24	9	.375
Falcon Seelster	94	35	.372
Albatross	97	36	.371
Sonsam	62	23	.371

2:05 2-year-old Trotters

Sire	Foals	Perf.	Pct.
Speedy Crown	90	24	.267
Lucky Almahurst	15	4	.267
Super Bowl	96	24	.250
Speedy Somolli	76	15	.197
Royal Prestige	73	14	.192
Crowning Point	43	8	.186
Workaholic	54	10	.185
Arndon	43	7	.163
Florida Pro	31	5	.161
Joie De Vie	127	19	.150

2:00 2-year-old Pacers

Sire	Foals	Perf.	Pct.
Long Fella	15	5	.333
Nihilator	108	34	.315
No Nukes	213	52	.244
Falcon Seelster	94	20	.213
Radiant Ruler	38	8	.211
Abercrombie	72	15	.208
Walton Hanover	69	14	.203
Big Towner	84	17	.202
Sonsam	62	11	.177
Albatross	97	17	.175

2:10 2-year-old Pacers

Sire	Foals	Perf.	Pct.
Warren Hanover	62	32	.516
Satanic	28	14	.500
Nihilator	108	52	.481
Paris Dexter	19	9	.474
Big Towner	84	39	.464
Nobleland Sam	31	14	.452
No Nukes	213	92	.432
Falcon Seelster	94	40	.426
Bret Hanover	26	11	.423
Cam Fella	95	39	.411

1:55 3-Year-Old Pacers

Sire	Foals	Perf.	Pct.
Panorama	16	2	.125
French Chef	34	4	.117
Lon Todd Hanover	21	2	.100
Cam Fella	83	8	.096
On The Road Again	9	106	.084
Tyler B	132	11	.083
No Nukes	161	13	.080
Silent Majority	59	4	.067
Walton Hanover	90	6	.066
Radiant Ruler	45	3	.066

BREEDING AND SALES

2:05 3-year-old Trotters

Sire	Foals	Perf.	Pct.
Workaholic	33	14	.424
Desert Night	29	10	.345
Speedy Crown	102	35	.343
Excel Hanover	23	7	.304
T V Yankee	30	9	.300
Prakas	128	38	.297
Super Bowl	96	28	.292
Dream Of Glory	64	18	.281
Flak Bait	43	12	.279
Speedy Somolli	80	22	.275

2:00 3-year-old Pacers

Sire	Foals	Perf.	Pct.
Panorama	16	8	.500
Abercrombie	49	23	.469
Albatross	83	36	.434
Sonsam	67	29	.433
Troublemaker	81	35	.432
Direct Scooter	177	75	.424
No Nukes	161	67	.416
Big Towner	101	42	.416
Cam Fella	83	34	.410
Bret Hanover	27	11	.407

2:02 3-year-old Trotters

Sire	Foals	Perf.	Pct.
Speedy Crown	102	24	.235
Super Bowl	96	22	.229
Prakas	128	26	.203
Lucky Almahurst	15	3	.200
Garland Lobell	21	4	.190
Flak Bait	43	8	.186
Crowning Point	54	10	.185
Excel Hanover	23	4	.174
T V Yankee	30	5	.167

1:58 3-year-old Pacers

Sire	Foals	Perf.	Pct.
Cam Fella	83	28	.337
Panorama	16	5	.313
No Nukes	161	49	.304
Albatross	83	25	.301
Walton Hanover	90	25	.278
Direct Scooter	177	47	.266
Abercrombie	49	13	.265
French Chef	34	9	.265
On The Road Again	106	28	.264
Troublemaker	81	21	.259

2:05 3-year-old Pacers

Sire	Foals	Perf.	Pct.
Panorama	16	12	.750
Walton Hanover	90	62	.689
Bret Hanover	27	18	.667
Direct Scooter	177	116	.655
Higher Power	22	14	.636
On The Road Again	106	67	.632
Troublemaker	81	51	.630
Big Towner	101	63	.624
Abercrombie	49	30	.612
Good To See You	67	41	.612

2:00 3-year-old Trotters

Sire	Foals	Perf.	Pct.
Speedy Crown	102	22	.215
Super Bowl	96	14	.145
Prakas	128	17	.132
Speedy Somolli	80	9	.112
Crowning Point	54	6	.111
Kawartha Mon Ami	19	2	.105
Desert Night	29	3	.103
Bonebreaker	21	1	.095
Garland Lobell	21	2	.095
Gambi Lobell	32	3	.093
Flak Bait	43	4	.093

BREEDING AND SALES

TOP 'EARLY SPEED' SIRES, BY NUMBER OF PERFORMERS

2:10 2-Year-Old Trotters
Speedy Crown	29
Super Bowl	26
Royal Prestige	24
Joie De Vie	23
Speed In Action	17
Speedy Somolli	16
Baltic Speed	14
Workaholic	14
Coleman Lobell	13
Meadow Road	13
Prakas	13

2:10 2-Year-Old Pacers
No Nukes	92
Nihilator	52
Direct Scooter	46
Forrest Skipper	41
Falcon Seelster	40
Albatross	39
Big Towner	39
Cam Fella	39
Tyler B	36
Praised Dignity	34

2:05 2-Year-Old Trotters
Speedy Crown	24
Super Bowl	24
Joie De Vie	19
Speedy Somolli	15
Royal Prestige	14
Prakas	11
Speed In Action	10
Workaholic	10
Bonefish	9
Batic Speed	8
Crowning Point	8
Meadow Road	8
Worthy Bowl	8

2:05 2-Year-Old Pacers
No Nukes	89
Nihilator	50
Direct Scooter	44
Cam Fella	38
Albatross	36
Big Towner	36
Forrest Skipper	36
Falcon Seelster	35
Tyler B	34
On The Road Again	32

2:00 2-Year-Old Pacers
No Nukes	52
Nihilator	34
Falcon Seelster	20
Albatross	17
Big Towner	17
Direct Scooter	17
Tyler's Mark	17

2:05 3-Year-Old Trotters
Prakas	38
Speedy Crown	35
Joie De Vie	32
Super Bowl	28
Homesick	23
Speedy Somolli	22
Baltic Speed	20
Worthy Bowl	20
Dream Of Glory	18
Final Score	17

2:05 3-Year-Old Pacers
Direct Scooter	116
No Nukes	96
Tyler B	73
Nihilator	69
On The Road Again	67
Slapstick	67
Niatross	65
Ralph Hanover	65
Big Towner	63
Walton Hanover	62

2:02 3-Year-Old Trotters
Prakas	26
Speedy Crown	24
Super Bowl	22
Joie De Vie	20
Baltic Speed	12
Homesick	12
Speedy Somolli	12
Crowning Point	10
Arndon	9
Lindy's Crown	9
Worthy Bowl	9

2:00 3-Year-Old Pacers
Direct Scooter	75
No Nukes	67
Nihilator	45
Tyler B	44
Big Towner	42
Niatross	40
On The Road Again	38
Slapstick	38
Ralph Hanover	37
Albatross	36
Walton Hanover	36

1:58 3-Year-Old Pacers
No Nukes	49
Direct Scooter	47
Nihilator	34
Tyler B	32
Cam Fella	28
On The Road Again	28
Big Towner	26
Albatross	25
Walton Hanover	25

BREEDING AND SALES

LEADING 2:00 BROODMARE SIRES, ALL-TIME

The following lists show leading sires of 2:00 producing broodmares. The list below on the left is that of the overall leaders, while the list on the right gives the leaders among sires of 2:00 trotting dams.

Leading Sires, All 2:00 Dams				Leading Sires, 2:00 Trotting Dams			
Broodmare Sire	Pace	Trot	Total	Broodmare Sire	Pace	Trot	Total
1. Tar Heel	1,101	0	1,101	1. Stars Pride	47	118	165
2. Bret Hanover	1,033	0	1,033	2. Noble Victory	24	139	163
3. Meadow Skipper	934	1	935	3. Speedy Crown	17	130	147
4. Albatross	892	0	892	4. Super Bowl	16	118	134
5. Most Happy Fella	695	0	695	5. Speedster	25	97	122
6. Race Time	658	0	658	6. Hickory Pride	23	86	109
7. Bye Bye Byrd	641	0	641	7. B F Coaltown	12	87	99
8. Overtrick	456	3	459	8. Hoot Mon	40	48	88
9. Adios Vic	447	0	447	9. Speedy Scot	14	71	85
10. Best Of All	407	0	407	10. Nevele Pride	10	74	84

TOP BROODMARE SIRES, ALL-AGE, 1990

Broodmare Sire	Starters	Winners	Dashes	Earnings
1. Albatross	1,133	803	2,866	$21,156,419
2. Meadow Skipper	980	679	2,428	14,000,027
3. Most Happy Fella	1,031	714	2,638	13,882,483
4. Bret Hanover	1,090	712	2,353	12,551,050
5. Race Time	662	464	1,677	7,131,828
6. Tar Heel	678	450	1,491	5,736,349
7. Speedy Crown	401	220	649	5,539,325
8. Best Of All	494	337	1,141	5,311,368
9. Nero	535	372	1,158	5,226,227
10. B Gs Bunny	332	219	789	5,170,285

TOP BROODMARE SIRES, 2- AND 3-YEAR-OLDS, 1990

Broodmare Sire	Starters	Winners	Dashes	Earnings
1. Albatross	544	369	1,151	$12,421,519
2. Bret Hanover	513	306	871	6,965,759
3. Meadow Skipper	371	223	638	5,384,618
4. Most Happy Fella	425	255	722	5,065,350
5. Speedy Crown	214	107	281	4,168,458
6. Super Bowl	153	80	240	3,868,261
7. B Gs Bunny	202	131	416	3,160,482
8. Nero	313	205	590	3,001,308
9. Armbro Nesbit	70	44	153	2,744,743
10. Race Time	224	144	468	2,724,863

TOP BROODMARE SIRES, ALL-AGE, 1989

Broodmare Sire	Starters	Winners	Dashes	Earnings
1. Albatross	966	698	2,560	$20,135,211
2. Meadow Skipper	938	684	2,474	15,833,691
3. Most Happy Fella	923	664	2,495	12,884,612
4. Bret Hanover	982	631	2,088	11,605,372
5. Race Time	699	489	1,841	8,131,923
6. Tar Heel	749	472	1,567	6,989,097
7. Best Of All	478	325	1,183	6,523,310
8. Speedy Crown	385	204	671	6,017,873
9. Adios Vic	549	397	1,505	5,973,778
10. High Ideal	452	315	1,034	5,621,542

BREEDING AND SALES

LEADING 2:00 PRODUCING BROODMARES

Pacing Broodmares

	Dam	Fastest Performer	Record
12	Lacy Hanover	Lear Hanover p, 4,	1:55.3
10	Tarport Cheer	Cheery Hello p, 3,	1:52.3
	Romola Adios	Romola Lobell p, 3,	T 1:55.1
9	Romola Hanover	Irish Jimmy p, 4,	1:53
	Tigers Milk	Tucson Hanover p, 4,	1:51.3
	Duet	Dakota Hanover, p 4,	1:55.2f
	Pammy Lobell	Present Laughter p, 4,	1:54
	Prelude Lobell	Pefecta Lobell p, 4,	1:54.4
8	Anitas Dream	Wolf p, 4, & Another Almahurst p, 4,	1:58f
	Bountiful Bird	Devil's Adversary p, 3,	1:54
	Farmers Hostess	Raging Glory p, 3,	1:55.1
	Farmstead Belle	Franz Hanover p, 5,	1:52
	Gena	Strike Le Ru p, 7,	1:55.4
	Keystone Dixie	Rambling Rudolph p, 5,	1:52.4
	Keystone Sandra	Kiev Hanover p, 3,	1:50.1
	Kitten Hanover	Kammy Hanover p, 2,	T 1:57.4
	Lantern	Save Fuel p, 5,	1:51.1
	Lil Miss Thompson	Lucius Lobell, p, 4,	1:54.2
	Noble Claire	Direct Scooter p, 3, & Nappie Hanover p, 3,	1:54
	Precious Newport	Precious Fella p, 3,	T 1:55
		& Del's Fella p, 3,	1:55
	Pretty Margie	Goodmorningamerica p, 3,	1:54
	Pretty Tricky	Turn The Tide p, 3,	1:53.2
	Quick O'Brien	Sea Quick p, 2,	1:54.4
	R D's Bret	RD's T'groff p, 5,	1:55.4
	Santa Dee	Princess Stephanie p, 5,	1:58
	Sprinkle	Rain God p, 4,	1:53.3
	Steady Miss Karen	Claudius p, 6,	1:53.4
	Surprise Reporter	Oakwood p, 8,	1:56.1
	Sweetie Edie	Keystone Scamp p, 4,	1:54.4
	Sweetsie Hanover	Suitland Hanover p, 4,	1:55.4f
	Worthy Eleda	Be Myself p, 4,	T 1:57

(74 tied with 7 pacing credits)

Trotting Broodmares

	Dam	Fastest Performer	Record
7	Heidi Rodney	Joie De Vie 3,	1:56.3
6	Descent	Demilo Hanover 3,	1:55.1
	Desert Wind	Desert King 3,	T 1:57.3
	Elma	Japa 3,	1:56.3
	Exciting Speed	Panty Raid 3,	1:57
	Noble Gal	Noxie Hanover 2,	T 1:55
	Spry Hanover	Sven Hanover 2,	1:57.2
5	Bourbon Candy	Mighty Crown 3,	1:58.3f
	Crysta Hanover	Arsenal 2,	1:57
	Pompanette	Filet Of Sole 3,	1:57.3
	Somolli	Speedy Somolli 3,	1:55
	Tarport Lady Ann	Model Home 3,	1:55.3
	Tosca	Dr. Guillotine 3,	1:56.1

(21 tied with 4 credits)

NOTE: The leading "double-gaited" broodmares each have six 2:00 credits: Evensong (2 pacers, 4 trotters); Jadda Jet (4 pacers, 2 trotters); and Glad Rags (5 pacers, 1 trotter)

BREEDING AND SALES

LEADING BREEDERS IN 1990, ALL PERFORMERS

Breeder	Starters	Winners	Dashes Won	Earnings
Hanover Shoe Farms, Inc., Hanover, PA	707	508	1,765	$11,187,808
Stoner Creek Stud, Paris, KY	128	96	365	6,024,111
Armstrong Brothers, Inglewood, ONT	322	201	726	4,988,679
Castleton Farm, Lexington, KY	331	221	799	4,796,403
Kentuckiana Farms, Lexington, KY	136	94	380	3,066,775
Ridgedale Farms, Beverly Hills, CA	149	98	313	2,320,889
Max C. Hempt, Mechanicsburg, PA	180	117	481	2,004,545
George Segal & Brian Monieson, Chicago, IL	23	16	58	1,887,292
Yankeeland Farms, Inc., Frederick, MD	115	68	215	1,793,882
Clearview Stables, New Canaan, CT	49	39	165	1,767,777
Robert R. Chapple, Chatham, ONT	84	52	177	1,664,810
Lauxmont Farms, Wrightsville, PA	99	66	247	1,654,441
The Walnut Hall Farm Corp., Lexington, KY	80	62	217	1,497,533
Lana Lobell Farms, Inc., Bedminster, NJ	152	94	303	1,403,812
Estate of Robert E. Nixon, Fairdale, KY	2	2	16	1,336,331
Robert K. Waxman, Ancaster, ONT	11	5	18	1,227,349
George Segal, Chicago, IL	53	32	117	1,191,751
Hugh A. Grant, Jr., NY & Hanley Dawson, Jr., IL	52	32	121	1,163,804
Royal Casino Farms, Inc., Mays Landing, NJ	42	22	102	1,089,571
Lana Lobell Farms, NJ & H F Farms, Reg'd., QUE	3	2	11	1,070,729
Boardwalk Associates, Ltd., Short Hills, NJ	67	50	197	1,065,974
Walnut Hall Farm, Lexington, KY	87	59	195	1,056,190
Dan Gernatt Farms, Collins, NY	150	89	303	1,052,188
Brittany Farms, Versailles, KY	28	13	42	1,018,802
David R. & Fredericka Caldwell, Georgetown, KY	26	18	63	955,904
Joe M. Thomson & Edwin J. Gold, Paoli, PA	62	40	164	947,010

LEADING BREEDERS IN 1990, 2- AND 3-YEAR-OLDS

Breeder	Starters	Winners	Dashes Won	Earnings
Hanover Shoe Farms, Inc., Hanover, PA	290	188	526	$4,877,375
Stoner Creek Stud, Paris, KY	58	42	169	4,440,536
Castleton Farm, Lexington, KY	117	65	195	2,394,102
Armstrong Brothers, Inglewood, ONT	122	74	206	2,323,052
Kentuckiana Farms, Lexington, KY	64	36	136	2,078,858
George Segal & Brian Monieson, Chicago, IL	13	9	46	1,805,586
Yankeeland Farms, Inc., Frederick, MD	57	34	106	1,400,548
Robert R. Chapple, Chatham, ONT	32	18	58	1,344,870
Estate of Robert E. Nixon, Fairdale, KY	2	2	16	1,336,331
Robert K. Waxman, Ancaster, ONT	10	5	18	1,227,349
Clearview Stables, New Canaan, CT	20	16	60	1,179,215
Lana Lobell Farms, NJ & H F Farms, Reg'd., QUE	2	2	11	1,069,513
Brittany Farms, Versailles, KY	28	13	42	1,018,802
Ridgedale Farms, Beverly Hills, CA	59	37	104	892,705
Lauxmont Farms, Wrightsville, PA	37	25	74	865,992
William J. Perretti, Saddle River, NJ	17	12	32	861,581
The Walnut Hall Farm Corp., Lexington, KY	32	24	67	850,870
David R. & Fredericka Caldwell, Georgetown, KY	15	8	33	819,123
George Segal, Chicago, IL	34	20	73	813,644
Royal Casino Farms, Inc., Mays Landing, NJ	28	14	61	809,058
Saratoga Traders, Ballston Spa, NY	5	5	19	782,710
Hugh A. Grant, Jr., NY & Hanley Dawson, Jr., IL	22	11	33	775,310
K.D. Owen, Houston, TX	16	7	28	765,441
J. Brian Webster, & Raymond S. Bednarz, ONT	4	4	22	701,454

BREEDING AND SALES

LEADING BREEDERS IN 1989, ALL PERFORMERS

Breeder	Starters	Winners	Dashes Won	Earnings
Hanover Shoe Farms Inc., Hanover, PA	688	486	1,804	$12,631,255
Armstrong Brothers, Inglewood, ONT	330	236	936	6,814,232
Castleton Farm, Lexington, KY	330	226	785	4,696,795
Stoner Creek Stud, Inc., Paris, KY	123	86	356	4,086,101
Lana Lobell Farms of NJ, Inc., Bedmister, NJ	179	123	433	2,802,646
Ridgedale Farms, Beverly Hills, CA	158	92	341	2,523,133
Max C. Hempt, Mechanicsburg, PA	186	129	439	2,377,477
Clearview Stables, New Canaan, CT	51	44	182	2,095,603
Boardwalk Associates, Ltd., Short Hills, NJ	65	48	207	2,051,886
Yankeeland Farms, Frederick, MD	116	78	243	1,849,906
Charles R. Michael, Woodbridge, CT	28	19	61	1,780,429
Kentuckiana Farms, Lexington, KY	134	87	291	1,735,611
George Segal, Chicago, IL	54	38	130	1,545,350
Lauxmont Farms, Wrightsville, PA	97	66	212	1,363,958
D.C. Johnson Holdings, Inc., Peterborough, ONT	119	86	351	1,308,810
Dan Gernatt Farms, Scottsville, NY	170	99	329	1,264,540
Max Gerson, New York, NY	9	7	42	1,245,291
Hill Farms, Hilliard, OH	108	74	248	1,064,142
Lana Lobell Farms, NJ & Erba Stables, NY	5	4	26	1,045,542
Mr. & Mrs. John Wehle, Scottsville, NY	56	35	142	1,037,123
BeeJay Stables, Reg'd., Beamsville, ONT	103	69	222	1,027,223
Stanley Dancer & Rose Hild Breeding Farm, NJ	3	3	19	1,008,624
The Walnut Hall Farm Corp., KY	68	50	197	991,807
Sterlingbrook Farm, NJ	30	25	84	990,845
Lana Lobell Farms of NJ & Wilrose Farms, FL	60	42	151	986,409
Dreamaire Stable, Rutherford, NJ	23	18	69	983,235

LEADING BREEDERS IN 1989, 2-AND 3-YEAR-OLDS

Breeder	Starters	Winners	Dashes Won	Earnings
Hanover Shoe Farms, Inc., Hanover, PA	257	159	488	$5,702,073
Armstrong Brothers, Inglewood, ONT	111	74	237	2,894,707
Stoner Creek Stud, Paris, KY	57	38	144	2,865,033
Castleton Farm, Lexington, KY	117	66	206	2,101,921
Ridgedale Farms, Beverly Hills, CA	123	69	244	1,878,729
Charles R. Michael, Woodbridge, CT	9	6	29	1,702,667
Clearview Stables, New Canaan, CT	23	19	85	1,423,415
George Segal, Chicago, IL	42	28	92	1,363,021
Yankeeland Farms, Inc., Frederick, MD	52	35	105	1,264,040
Boardwalk Associates, Short Hills, NJ	31	21	78	1,140,718
Lana Lobell Farms, NJ & Erba Stables, NY	4	4	26	1,045,542
Stanley Dancer & Rose Hild Breeding Farm, NJ	1	1	16	1,002,701
Kentuckiana Farms, Lexington, KY	65	37	91	869,134
Max C. Hempt, Mechanicsburg, PA	73	42	133	824,630
Saratoga Traders, Inc. Ballston Spa, NY	3	2	11	811,889
Lana Lobell Farms of NJ, Bedmister, NJ	67	38	120	762,911
Lana Lobell Farms, NJ & Crown Stable, NY	12	6	22	727,710
Sterlingbrook Farm, Pittstown, NJ	16	14	47	701,008
Prudential Bache-Almahurst LPI, KY	21	14	55	686,264
Lana Lobell Farms of NJ & George Segal, IL	29	20	52	677,737
Richard S. Staley, Los Angeles, CA	14	6	34	636,274
Dreamaire Stable, Rutherford, NJ	14	11	33	630,308
Match Maker Stable, Yardley, PA	4	4	17	594,413
Estate of Robert Mumma, Harrisburg, PA	10	5	25	562,736

BREEDING AND SALES

MAJOR STANDARDBRED SALES IN 1990

Sale	Number Sold	Total Sales	Average
Standardbred Horse Sale	1,598	$29,470,000	$18,442
Kentucky Standardbred	567	14,940,000	26,349
Tattersalls (Yearling)	527	12,238,900	23,224
Garden State (February)	621	9,016,900	14,520
Garden State (Fall Classic)	316	6,610,400	20,919
Tattersalls (Mixed)	356	4,859,900	13,651
Garden State (Int'l Bloodstock)	110	3,435,400	31,231
Garden State (August)	304	3,288,600	10,818
Garden State (April)	222	2,735,600	12,323
Canadian Classic	240	2,552,900	10,637
Illinois Standardbred	232	1,807,900	7,793
Tattersalls (Ohio)	250	1,703,700	6,815
Garden State (Octoberfest)	338	1,587,500	4,697
Canadian Standardbred (Fall Mixed)	244	1,178,300	4,829
Canadian Select	87	1,102,800	12,676
Canadian Standardbred (Spring Mixed)	158	1,053,600	6,668

MAJOR SALES, 1990, YEARLINGS ONLY

Sale	Number Sold	Total Sales	Average
Standardbred Horse Sale	821	$18,201,900	$22,170
Kentucky Standardbred	567	14,940,000	26,349
Tattersalls	527	12,238,900	23,224
Garden State (Fall Classic)	316	6,610,400	20,919
Canadian Classic	240	2,552,900	10,637
Illinois Standardbred	232	1,807,900	7,793
Tattersalls (Ohio)	250	1,703,700	6,815
Garden State (Octoberfest)	338	1,587,500	4,697
Garden State (Int'l Bloodstock)	37	1,586,000	42,865
Canadian Select	87	1,102,800	12,676
Michigan Classic	253	996,000	3,937
Buckeye Standardbred	242	862,150	3,563
Royal Blue (August)	132	686,700	5,202
Garden State (February)	112	620,900	5,544
Garden State Park	132	531,600	4,027
Illinois Standardbred Breeders	160	500,435	3,128

MAJOR STANDARDBRED SALES IN 1989

Sale	Number Sold	Total Sales	Average
Standardbred Horse Sale	1,772	$35,186,000	$19,856
Kentucky Standardbred	579	17,388,000	30,031
Tattersalls (Yearling)	498	13,566,700	27,242
Garden State (January)	328	9,222,100	28,116
Garden State (Fall Classic)	281	6,214,800	22,117
Lana Lobell Select Yearlings	156	4,644,500	29,772
Garden State (Summer Mixed)	327	3,728,400	11,402
Canadian Classic (CSHS)	290	3,339,300	11,515
Tattersalls (Int'l Bloodstock)	110	3,327,100	30,246
Garden State (Int'l Bloodstock)	96	3,278,500	34,151

MAJOR SALES, 1989, YEARLINGS ONLY

Sale	Number Sold	Total Sales	Average
Standardbred Horse Sale	1,006	$21,517,200	$21,388
Kentucky Standardbred	579	17,388,000	30,031
Tattersalls (Kentucky)	498	13,566,700	27,242
Garden State (Fall Classic)	281	6,214,800	22,117
Lana Lobell Select Yearlings	156	4,644,500	29,772
Canadian Classic (CSHS)	290	3,339,300	11,515

BREEDING AND SALES
U.S. YEARLING PRICE AVERAGES, 1952 TO 1990

Year	Number Sold	Total Amount	Yearling Average	Pct. Change	Total Purses (U.S.)	Pct. Change
1990	4,742	$64,190,760	$13,537	(-11.82%)	$287,642,307	(-0.10%)
1989	4,785	73,462,920	15,352	(-5.04%)	287,928,217	(-2.20%)
1988	4,823	77,971,425	16,167	+2.3%	294,400,399	+ 0.0%
1987	5,100	80,599,520	15,804	+0.3%	294,376,467	+ .8%
1986	5,138	80,919,950	15,749	+8.9%	291,904,107	+ .9%
1985	4,771	75,885,680	14,467	(-20.5%)	289,261,893	+ 5.9%
1984	5,039	91,718,565	18,202	(-8.2%)	272,268,666	+ 1.5%
1983	5,101	101,106,230	19,821	+19.4%	268,229,336	+ 3.7%
1982	5,011	83,154,110	16,596	(-12.7%)	258,761,424	+ 4.7%
1981	4,443	84,139,523	18,937	+1.0%	247,068,152	+ 5.8%
1980	3,731	69,791,091	18,754	+24.0%	233,421,503	+ 7.1%
1979	3,732	56,425,019	15,119	+11.2%	217,846,161	+ 6.5%
1978	3,526	47,900,650	13,595	+27.7%	204,578,607	+ 14.2%
1977	3,351	35,669,925	10,644	+12.9%	179,095,788	+ 7.4%
1976	2,975	28,048,205	9,427	+12.8%	166,774,640	+ 11.5%
1975	2,959	24,723,935	8,355	+21.0%	149,563,698	+ 11.3%
1974	2,604	17,974,273	6,903	+ .9%	134,387,251	+ 12.6%
1973	2,677	18,320,315	6,844	+21.0%	119,301,985	+ 13.0%
1972	2,758	17,083,400	6,194	+24.5%	105,595,669	+ 8.2%
1971	2,717	13,514,950	4,974	+6.5%	97,593,634	+ 9.3%
1970	2,645	12,353,080	4,670	+7.0%	89,280,537	+ 10.7%
1969	2,631	11,482,344	4,364	(-12.0%)	80,683,497	+ 13.6%
1968	2,258	11,200,085	4,960	+25.5%	71,004,560	+ 14.8%
1967	2,131	8,424,555	3,953	+12.0%	61,851,457	+ 5.4%
1966	2,160	7,625,550	3,530	(-10.1%)	58,679,557	+ 10.5%
1965	1,948	6,421,060	3,926	+13.5%	53,123,148	+ 12.7%
1964	1,647	5,699,525	3,461	(-4.8%)	47,130,980	+ 14.8%
1963	1,439	5,233,925	3,637	+11.5%	41,069,037	+ 15.9%
1962	1,496	4,882,260	3,263	+7.1%	35,427,388	+ 8.6%
1961	1,422	4,331,370	3,046	(-21.2%)	32,635,694	+ 3.3%
1960	1,165	4,505,430	3,867	+21.8%	31,581,923	+ 6.2%
1959	988	3,669,910	3,174	+5.6%	29,748,582	+ 7.9%
1958	1,002	3,011,225	3,005	+15.8%	27,572,830	+ 13.7%
1957	963	2,499,860	2,596	(-10.3%)	24,249,842	+ 10.9%
1956	975	2,816,115	2,894	+8.8%	21,862,611	+ 6.0%
1955	898	2,389,640	2,661	+17.1%	20,626,774	+ 8.8%
1954	888	2,017,908	2,272	+15.2%	18,961,265	+ .6%
1953	946	1,865,380	1,972	(- .2%)	18,832,741	+ 17.3%
1952	990	1,957,200	1,976	------	16,052,773	------

Charting Trends in the U.S. Yearling Averages: 1952-1990

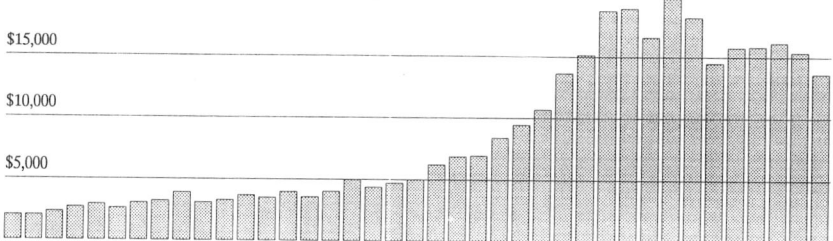

BREEDING AND SALES

THE $200,000 YEARLINGS OF 1990

Horse	Price	Sire	Vendue*	Purchaser
Valley Boss	$320,000	Baltic Speed	Har	Gina Biasuzzi Stable, FL
Personal Thoughts (f)	250,000	Super Bowl	Tat	Tom Harmer, FL (as agent)
Rubenesque (f)	235,000	Super Bowl	Tat	Tom Harmer, FL (as agent)
Royal Strut	215,000	Crowning Point	Ky	Robert K. Waxman, ONT
Savage Hanover	210,000	Super Bowl	Har	Charles Sylvester, FL
J T Lobell	210,000	No Nukes	FC	Robert H. Grand Holdings, ONT
Winky's Trophy (f)	210,000	Super Bowl	Tat	Continental Farm, FL
Molzon Lobell (f)	200,000	Speedy Crown	FC	Team Nordin, FL

* - Vendues:
Tat - Tattersalls; Ky - Kentucky Standardbred; Har - Standardbred Horse Sale; FC - Fall Classic

OTHER $100,000 YEARLINGS SOLD IN 1990

Yearling	Price	Sire	Vendue
Keystone Cobra	$185,000	Super Bowl	Harrisburg
Armbro Kosher	171,000	Speedy Crown	Kentucky Standardbred
Grand Admiral	160,000	No Nukes	Kentucky Standardbred
Jean's Pride (f)	155,000	Super Bowl	Harrisburg
Armbro Kinship	150,000	Speedy Crown	Kentucky Standardbred
That's A Gleam	147,000	Super Bowl	Tattersalls
Living Legend	145,000	Speedy Crown	Kentucky Standardbred
Malahana Max	145,000	Mystic Park	Kentucky Standardbred
Program Speed	145,000	Super Bowl	Tattersalls
Brace Yorself Now	140,000	Direct Scooter	Kentucky Standardbred
Craig Hanover	140,000	Speedy Crown	Harrisburg
Scooter Drive	137,000	Direct Scooter	Tattersalls
Fast Growing	135,000	Speedy Crown	Tattersalls
Keystone Scooter	135,000	Speedy Crown	Harrisburg
Armbro Karril (f)	130,000	Speedy Crown	Kentucky Standardbred
Gorbachev	130,000	No Nukes	Tattersalls
Highest Regards	127,000	Speedy Crown	Kentucky Standardbred
Chin Piece	125,000	Albatross	Tattersalls
Pawn The Silver (f)	125,000	Super Bowl	Tattersalls
Vero Beach (f)	125,000	No Nukes	Tattersalls
Keystone Ludwig	122,000	Speedy Crown	Harrisburg
Hazelette Hanover (f)	120,000	Big Towner	Harrisburg
Herschel Walker	120,000	Super Bowl	Tattersalls
One Tough Town	120,000	No Nukes	Tattersalls
Bax Lobell	110,000	Mystic Park	Garden State (Int'l Bloodstock)
Paris	110,000	Super Bowl	Tattersalls
Surviror Gold	110,000	Abercrombie	Kentucky Standardbred
Singer Lobell (f)	107,000	Speedy Crown	Garden State (Int'l Bloodstock)
Sizzling Crown (f)	107,000	Speedy Crown	Tattersalls
Kipahulu	105,000	Speedy Crown	Tattersalls
Western Hanover	105,000	No Nukes	Harrisburg
Lady Desdemona (f)	102,000	Royal Prestige	Harrisburg

BREEDING AND SALES

Babble Blue Chip	100,000	Albatross	Fall Classic
Bit Part (f)	100,000	Super Bowl	Kentucky Standardbred
Chatham Winds	100,000	Niatross	Kentucky Standardbred
Dale's Delite (f)	100,000	Speedy Crown	Harrisburg
Derick Lobell	100,000	Speedy Somolli	Garden State (Int'l Bloodstock)
Slik Stockings (f)	100,000	Nihilator	Kentucky Standardbred

LEADING SIRES OF 100,000 YEARLINGS IN 1990

Trotting Sires

Sire	Number	Top-Priced Yearling	Price	Vendue
Speedy Crown	14	Molzon Lobell (f)	$200,000	Fall Classic
Super Bowl	12	Personal Thoughts (f)	250,000	Tattersalls
Mystic Park	2	Malahana Max	145,000	Ky. Standardbred
Baltic Speed	1	Valley Boss	320,000	Harrisburg
Crowning Point	1	Royal Strut	215,000	Ky. Standardbred
Royal Prestige	1	Lady Desdemona (f)	102,000	Harrisburg
Speedy Somolli	1	Derrick Lobell	100,000	Garden St.

Pacing Sires

Sire	Number	Top-Priced Yearling	Price	Vendue
No Nukes	6	J T Lobell	$210,000	Fall Classic
Albatross	2	Chin Piece	125,000	Ky. Standardbred
Direct Scooter	2	Brace Yourself Now	140,000	Ky. Standardbred
Abercrombie	1	Survivor Gold	110,000	Ky. Standardbred
Big Towner	1	Hazelette Hanover (f)	120,000	Harrisburg
Niatross	1	Chatham Winds	100,000	Ky. Standardbred
Nihilator	1	Slik Stockings (f)	100,000	Ky. Standardbred

TOP-PRICED YEARLINGS OF 1989

Price	Yearling	Sire	Purchaser
$375,000	Exclusive Flight	Albatross	Mark Loewe, FL (as agent)
315,000	Carry The Message	Royal Prestige	George Sholty, FL (as agent)
270,000	Armbro Jargon	Super Bowl	Continental Farm, FL (as agent)
245,000	Keystone Fantasy (f)	Super Bowl	Roger Hammer, PA (as agent)
215,000	Margit Lobell (f)	Speedy Crown	Jan Nordin, FL
210,000	Top Of List	No Nukes	Richard Staley, CA
200,000	The Watcher	Albatross	Alnoff Stable, NY

TOP-PRICED YEARLINGS OF 1988

Price	Yearling	Sire	Purchaser
$425,000	Moving Forward	Super Bowl	Workaholic Stable & Paul Ewell, MD
350,000	Heaven Made (f)	Albatross	Alnoff Stable, NY
264,000	Keystone Commando	Super Bowl	Rose Guida, NJ (as agent)
220,000	Lord Bentley *	Speedy Crown	Johan Behrn, SWE
200,000	Winky's Valentine (f)	Super Bowl	Douglas Kass, NY
200,000	Speedy Flo Jo (f) **	Speedy Crown	Skip Lewis, NY (as agent)
200,000	Frankie Lobell	Speedy Crown	Louis P. Guida (as agent)
185,000	Armbro Idaho	Speedy Crown	Gail & Peter H. McCann, OH
180,000	Doodles Hanover (f)	Super Bowl	Grant & Pedone, NY; E.Rudner, FL
180,000	Self-Supporting (f)	Prakas	Johan Behrn, SWE

* - Sold as End Around
** - Sold as Yew

BREEDING AND SALES

TOP-PRICED YEARLINGS, 1944-1989

Year	Name (Name Before Change)	Selling Price	Career Earnings	Sire
1989	Exclusive Flight	$375,000	$702	Albatross
1988	Moving Forward	425,000	-----	Super Bowl
1987	Golden Route	500,000	960	Super Bowl
1986	Supergill	500,000	664,194	Super Bowl
1985	Parker Almahurst	350,000	30,643	Niatross
1984	Clear And Crisp	390,000	25,532	Niatross
1983	Laugh A Day	625,000	38,555	Most Happy Fella
1982	Albatrage	400,000	161,163	Albatross
1981	Silk Spats	400,000	1,800	Bret Hanover
1980	Dia Hanover	425,000	3,876	Super Bowl
1979	Landslide (Tammany Hall)	290,000	162,835	Meadow Skipper
1978	Cobra Almahurst	285,000	2,973	Meadow Skipper
1977	Escape Artist	260,000	85,194	Meadow Skipper
1976	Falcon Almahurst	150,000	400,776	Meadow Skipper
1975	Courtney Hanover	140,000	36,855	Star's Pride
1974	Courvoisier	130,000	3,153	Meadow Skipper
1973	Outstanding	175,110	1,648	Good Time
1972	Romette Hanover	110,000	1,332	Dancer Hanover
1971	Good Humor Man	210,000	9,075	Meadow Skipper
1970	Miracle Tip	117,000	106,493	Good Time
1969	Dexter Hanover (Froelich Hanover)	125,000	332,090	Dancer Hanover
1968	Nevele Bigshot (Romunda Hanover)	115,000	29,360	Dancer Hanover
1967	Bart Hanover	105,000	502	Adios
1966	Brad Hanover	100,000	37,621	Adios
1965	Speedy Streak	113,000	95,576	Speedster
1964	Effrat Hanover	65,000	116,265	Adios
1963	Bret Hanover	50,000	922,616	Adios
1962	Frost Ridge (Ilo's Frost)	70,000	8,709	Scott Frost
1961	Rodilo	60,000	21,815	Rodney
1960	Mon Mite	81,000	45,654	Hoot Mon
1959	Bill Hanover	50,000	7,016	Hoot Mon
1958	Dancer Hanover	105,000	87,746	Adios
1957	Ebby Hanover	60,000	------	Hoot Mon
1956	Josie's Victory	42,000	5,265	Victory Song
1955	Junior Executive	55,000	985	Bill Gallon
1954	The Intruder	35,000	66,562	Scotland
1953	American Way	35,000	60,757	King's Counsel
1952	Smashaway	46,000	9,887	Volomite
1951	Gosling	55,000	18,918	Volomite
1950	Voting Trust	26,500	32,870	Volomite
1949	Imperial Hanover	72,000	1,663	Spencer Scott
1948	Mighty Sun	28,000	63,743	Volomite
1947	White Hanover	42,000	5,089	Spencer Scott
1946	Isolandia	28,000	250	Scotland
1945	Mighty Song	30,000	22,496	Volomite
1944	Victory Song	37,000	73,859	Volomite

* * * * *

BREEDING AND SALES

RECORD PRICES FOR HORSES SOLD AT AUCTION

Yearlings

	Price	Name	Sire	Year Sold
Pacing Colts	$430,000	Mustang Almahurst	Niatross	1983
	400,000	Albatrage	Albatross	1982
	400,000	Silk Spats	Bret Hanover	1981
	390,000	Clear And Crisp	Niatross	1984
	385,000	Cobra Almahurst	Meadow Skipper	1978
Pacing Fillies	$625,000	Laugh A Day	Most Happy Fella	1983
	380,000	Wendymae Hanover	Albatross	1984
	370,000	Kristin Almahurst	Bret Hanover	1984
	370,000	Napa Valley	Most Happy Fella	1981
	350,000	Obedient	Bret Hanover	1980
	350,000	Heaven Made	Albatross	1988
Trotting Colts	$500,000	Golden Route	Super Bowl	1987
	500,000	Supergill	Super Bowl	1986
	425,000	Moving Forward	Super Bowl	1988
	375,000	Duran Hanover	Super Bowl	1984
	360,000	To The Gate	Speedy Crown	1987
	350,000	Shane T Hanover	Florida Pro	1981
	350,000	Spellcaster	Florida Pro	1981
Trotting Fillies	$425,000	Dia Hanover	Super Bowl	1980
	425,000	Keystone Profile	Speedy Crown	1983
	380,000	Seascape Lobell	Speedy Crown	1984
	355,000	Crowned Lark	Speedy Crown	1980
	350,000	Delmirage	Noble Victory	1983
	350,000	Mae Jean's Crown	Speedy Crown	1982
	350,000	Zoomin Zula	Speedy Scot	1982

Racehorses

Price	Name	Age, Gait, Sex	Year Sold
$505,000	Bree's Brief	4-year-old pacing mare	1986
380,000	Seven O'Clock	3-year-old pacing filly	1985
375,000	Cheery Hello	4-year-old pacing mare	1990
360,000	Forbidden Past	3-year-old pacing filly	1985
320,000	Division Street	4-year-old pacing gelding	1984
310,000	Skirt Lifter	4-year-old pacing horse	1984

Broodmares

Price	Name	Age, Gait, Sex	Year Sold
$800,000	Winkys Gill	6-year-old trotting mare	1986
430,000	Bardot Lobell	6-year-old pacing mare	1986
400,000	Classical Way	10-year-old trotting mare	1986
375,000	Fancy Donut	7-year-old trotting mare	1983
350,000	Chickadee Newton	4-year-old trotting mare	1987
330,000	Lucious Almahurst	5-year-old trotting mare	1989
325,000	Liberated Angel	6-year-old pacing mare	1984
310,000	Conch	3-year-old trotting filly	1985
305,000	Rabble Rouser	9-year-old pacing mare	1985

BREEDING AND SALES

1991 STANDARDBRED SALE DATES

(Dates are Subject to Change)

Month	Date(s)	Vendue	Type	Location
January	18	Midwest Speed Sale Co.	Mixed	Sprinfield, IL
January	20	Garden State Sale	Mixed	E. Rutherford, NJ
February	2	Freestate Standardbred Sales	Mixed	Timonium, MD
February	4	Garden State Sale	Mixed	E. Rutherford, NJ
February	11	Garden State Sale	Mixed	E. Rutherford, NJ
February	11 & 12	Blooded Horse Sale	Mixed	Delaware, OH
April	8	Garden State Sale	Mixed	E. Rutherford, NJ
April	20	Canadian Standardbred Horse Society	Mixed	Toronto, ONT
May	13 & 14	Blooded Horse Sale	In Training	Delaware, OH
June	15	Royal Blue Standardbred Sale	Mixed	Campbellville, ONT
August	2	Meadowlands Int'l. Trotting	Mixed	E. Rutherford, NJ
August	11	ISBOA Select	Yearlings	Sherman, IL
August	15	ISBOA Annual	Yearlings	Sherman, IL
August	17	Royal Blue Standardbred Sale	Mixed	Campbellville, ONT
August	23	Forest City Sale	Mixed	London, ONT
August	24	Forest City Sale	Yearlings	London, ONT
August	24 & 25	Garden State Sale	Mixed	E. Rutherford, NJ
August	26	Blooded Horse Sale	Yearlings	Delaware, OH
August	27	Blooded Horse Sale	Mixed	Delaware, OH
September	7 & 8	Buckeye Standardbred Sale	Yearlings	Columbus, OH
September	8	Equus Caballus Sale	Yearlings	Maywood, IL
September	12	Canadian Standardbred Horse Society	Yearlings	Toronto, ONT
September	15	Illini Standardbred Sale	Yearlings	Maywood, IL
September	15 & 16	Fall Clasic Select	Yearlings	E. Rutherford, NJ
September	16 - 18	Ohio Tattersalls Sale	Yearlings	Columbus, OH
September	21	Morrisville College Sale	Yearlings	Morrisville, NY
September	22	Morrisville College Sale	Mixed	Morrisville, NY
September	25 - 27 & 29	Kentucky Standardbred Sale	Yearlings	Lexington, KY
September	28 & 30	Tattersalls Grand 500	Yearlings	Lexington, KY
October	1-3	Tattersalls Grand 500	Yearlings	Lexington, KY
October	4 & 5	Tattersalls Int'l. Bloodstock	Mixed	Lexington, KY
October	5	U.S. Breeders Sale	Yearlings	Timonium, MD
October	13 & 14	Octoberfest	Yearlings	Allentown, IL
October	14	D.R. Chambers & Sons Sale	Mixed	Unadilla, NY
October	14	Royal Blue Standardbred Sale	Mixed	Toronto, ONT
October	* 18 & 19	Wolverine Speed Sale	Mixed	Saginaw, MI
October	19	Canadian Standardbred Horse Society	Mixed	Toronto, ONT
October	20 & 21	Atlantic Seaboard Sale	Yearlings	Allentown, NJ
November	4 - 6	Standardbred Horse Sale	Yearlings	Harrisburg, PA
November	7 & 8	Standardbred Horse Sale	Mixed	Harrisburg, PA
November	11 - 14	Blooded Horse Sale	Mixed	Delaware, OH

* - Tentative Date

* * * * *

Chronicles

CHRONICLES
CHRONICLES OF RICH AND HISTORIC EVENTS
The Acorn
Two-Year-Old Filly Trot
Meadowlands, E. Rutherford, NJ June 25, 1990

45	4,854	Deanna (Gibson White)	2:04 m	79	22,785	Allurement (Ross Hayter)	2:04.3m
46	5,475	Nymph Hanover (Thomas Berry)	2:12 1/4h	80	47,065	Keystone Sister (Billy Herman)	2:06.3m
47	6,425	Song Girl (John Caton)	2:12.1h		47,065	Spring Dash (Berndt Lindstedt)	2:07.1m
48	9,539	Martha Doyle (Frank Ervin)	2:10 h	81	52,500	Crevette (Hakan Wallner)	2:03 m
49	8,854	Honor Bright (Henry Myott)	a 2:11.2h		53,500	Princess Crown (Howard Beissinger)	2:03 m
50	9,582	Royal Blood (Paul Vineyard)	2:14.2h	82	50,000	Heloise Lobell (Hakan Wallner)	2:03.2m
51	11,530	Vesta's Worthy (Frank Safford)	2:09.4h		50,000	Laurinda Hanover (Wm. Haughton)	2:04.4m
52	11,777	Lively Lady (Delvin Miller)	2:09.2h		50,000	Winky's Gill (Hakan Wallner)	2:05.2m
53	13,929	Stenographer (Delvin Miller)	2:11.3h	83	77,000	Anthem Hill (Clint Galbraith)	2:03.2m
54	11,875	Wilda Hanover (Frank Ervin)	b 2:11 h		77,000	Grassbed (Hakan Wallner)	2:02.3m
55	12,143	Blythe Hanover (Frank Ervin)	c 2:09.4h	84	55,000	Crown Bias (Abe Stoltzfus)	2:02.2m
56	13,181	Charming Barbara (Wm. Haughton)	2:07 h		55,000	Victory Somolli (Jan Nordin)	2:01.2m
57	13,904	Yankee Lass (Frank Ervin)	2:09 h		55,000	Conch (Hakan Wallner)	1:59.4m
58	14,031	Pompon (Harry Pownall, Sr.)	d 2:11 h	85	58,470	Meadowbranch Ada (John Campbell)	2:01.4m
59	14,147	Farr's Pride (H. Pownall, Sr.)	e 2:09.3h		58,470	Season Champion (William Haughton)	2:01.2m
60	17,592	Gay Fabrina (Howard B. Camden)	f 2:08.1h		57,470	Corvette Lauxmont (Jan Nordin)	2:01.4m
61	14,778	Sprite Rodney (Frank Ervin)	f 2:08.4h	86	71,420	Keystone Harem (M. Vartiainen)	1:59.4m
62	18,003	Delicious (Delvin Miller)	h 2:06.4h		71,420	Armbro Fling (George Sholty)	R 1:59 m
63	18,382	A.C.'s Jennie (Sanders Russell)	2:09 h	87	56,000	Iza Biza (Howard Beissinger)	2:00.1m
64	17,830	Frosty Song (Ralph Baldwin)	2:09.4h		56,000	Speedy Quilt (Mickey McNichol)	1:59.2m
65	18,193	Coalition (Frank Ervin)	2:07 h		57,000	Lady Defiant (Peter Ruscitto)	2:02.1m
66	13,265	Kimberly Dutchess (Ralph Baldwin)	2:06.3h	88	44,500	E D Kash (Clint Galbraith)	2:00.3m
67	14,645	Viv Hanover (Stanley Dancer)	2:07.1h		44,500	Perfect Mate (Bill O'Donnell)	2:00.4m
68	15,213	Dillers Fleur (Malcom Weaver)	i 2:07.4h		44,500	Youve Gotta Friend (P. Ruscitto)	1:59 m
69	9,870	Dancing Flower (Chris Boring)	2:08.4h	89	42,000	Donna Wanna (Eddie Wheeler)	2:01.1m
70	12,202	Keystone Selene (Del Miller)	2:06 h		42,000	Lila Lobell (Berndt Lindstedt)	2:03.4m
71	10,000	Franella Hanover (George Sholty)	2:07.2h		42,000	Whitney Lauxmont (Bill O'Donnell)	2:03.3m
72	13,398	Colonial Charm (Glen Garnsey)	2:07.3h	90	56,000	Amother Geisha (Bill Fahy)	2:01.2m
73	13,760	Starlark Hanover (David Wade)	2:06.3h		56,000	Jean Bi (Bill Fahy)	1:59.3m
74	13,202	Wishmaker (Billy Haughton)	2:10 h	a By Honor Bright & Mysteria.	f By Meadow Farr.		
75	14,445	Summer Madness (Stanley Dancer)	2:08.2h	b By Arvilla Hanover.	g By Sprite Rodney &		
76	12,760	Royal Clown (David Wade)	2:07.3h	c By Nora Frost.	Tercel		
77	11,862	Starita Lobell (Joe O'Brien)	R 2:04.3h	d By Matora Hanover.	h By Buff Hanover.		
78	10,215	Salome (Stanley Dancer)	2:13.4h	e By Elaine Rodney.	i By Quinton Hanover		

The Adioo Volo
Three-Year-Old Filly Pace
The Meadows, Meadow Lands, PA Aug. 11, 1990

72	30,870	Romalie Hanover (R. Beaulieu)	2:00.1f		30,860	Hit Parade (Richard Silverman)	1:55.1f
73	29,925	Armbro Norma (Delvin Miller)	2:01.3f	85	88,390	Stienam (Kelly O'Donnell)	1:57.1f
74	35,830	Handle With Care (Wm. Haughton)	2:00.2f	86	45,508	Anniecrombie (George Sholty)	1:56.3f
75	40,855	Silk Stockings (Pres Burris, Jr.)	1:57.2f		46,008	Loni Almahurst (Ri. Farrington)	1:58.3f
76	31,405	Tarport Crystal (Delvin Miller)	1:59.2f	87	44,068	Legacy Of Love (Steve Waller)	1:57.2f
	30,905	Bret's Amour (Dick Buxton)	1:59.2f		44,068	Quille Lauxmont (Dan Altmeyer)	1:56 f
77	57,510	Mistletoe Shalee (S. Dancer)	a 1:57 f	88	44,988	Huna Buna (Dick Stillings)	1:55.2f
78	50,607	Passing Glance (George Sholty)	1:58 f		44,988	Leah Almahurst (Bill Fahy)	1:54.4f
79	51,075	Sherry Almahurst (Glen Garnsey)	1:58.4f	89	30,220	Cheery Hello (Bill Fahy)	1:56 f
80	55,940	Armbro Vicky (Joe O'Brien)	1:58.3f		30,720	Le Cirque (William Walters)	1:56.4f
81	56,238	Loose News (Harold Dancer)	1:57 f		30,720	Lingerie (Bill Fahy)	1:56.4f
82	41,900	Dreamy Ore (Vernon Crank)	1:56.2f	90	47,614	Lady Genius (Dick Stillings)	1:56 f
	41,900	Three Diamonds (Bruce Riegle)	1:55.3f		48,614	Lady Dynamo (Mickey McNichol)	1:56.2f
83	81,615	Turn The Tide (Bill Fahy)	1:56.4f		48,614	Yankee Goddess (Doug Snyder)	1:55 f
84	31,360	Naughty But Nice (Bill Fahy)	R 1:54 f				
	30,860	Leslie Lobell (George Berkner)	1:56.2f	a By Future Fame.			

The Adios
Three-Year-Old Colt Pace *
The Meadows, Meadow Lands, PA Aug. 11, 1990

67	85,510	Romulus Hanover (William Haughton)	1:57.3f	82	206,000	Higher Power (Mickey McNichol)	1:54 f
68	93,320	Bye And Large (George Sholty)	2:00.1f	83	242,000	Ralph Hanover (Ron Waples)	1:54.4f
69	88,970	Laverne Hanover (William Haughton)	2:01 f	84	250,586	Andrel (John Campbell)	1:54.2f
70	86,740	Most Happy Fella (S. Dancer)	a 1:59.2f	85	242,400	Marauder (D. Richardson, Jr.)	1:52.1f
71	88,800	Albatross (Stanley Dancer)	1:58.3f	86	233,450	Barberry Spur (Dick Stillings)	1:53.3f
72	92,110	-dh- Strike Out (Keith Waples)	b 1:58.1f	87	240,076	Run The Table (John Campbell)	e 1:53.2f
		-dh- Jay Time (Gene Riegle)	b 1:58.1f	88	277,055	Camtastic (Bill O'Donnell)	1:53.3f
73	86,780	Ricci Reenie Time (Harold Dancer)	1:58.4f	89	275,045	Goalie Jeff (Michel Lachance)	1:53.4f
74	104,350	Armbro Omaha (William Haughton)	1:58 f	90	493,176	Beach Towel (Ray Remmen)	Rf 1:50.4f
75	111,645	Nero (Joe O'Brien)	c 1:57.2f	* - Three-Year-Old Open Pace before 1972.			
76	124,141	Armbro Ranger (Joe O'Brien)	d 1:56 f				
77	120,450	Governor Skipper (John Chapman)	1:54.4f	a By Columbia George.	e By Run The Table &		
78	128,633	Abercrombie (Glen Garnsey)	1:55 f	b By Lynden Bye Bye.	Jaguar Spur.		
79	150,000	Hot Hitter (Herve Filion)	1:56.3f	c By Whata Baron.	f By In The Pocket.		
80	150,000	Storm Damage (Joe O'Brien)	1:53.2f	d By Armbro Ranger &			
81	155,000	Landslide (Ed Lohmeyer)	1:56.1f	Keystone Ore.			

The American-National Stake *
Two-Year-Old Colt Trot **
Sportsman's Park, Cicero, IL Sept. 11, 1990

47	8,378	Judge Moore (Delvin Miller)	2:10.3h	51	16,017	Duke Of Lullwater (J.Simpson,Sr.)	2:06 m
48	12,590	Miss Tilly (Fred Egan)	2:04.2m	52	12,237	Simpson Hanover (J. Simpson, Sr.)	2:05.2m
49	9,255	Lusty Song (Doc Parshall)	2:02.2m	53	10,875	Newport Dream (Del Cameron)	2:04.2m
50	17,899	Scotch Rhythm (Ralph Baldwin)	2:04.2m	54	10,599	Butch Hanover (Jake Rodman)	2:03.4m

CHRONICLES

55	10,649 Saboteur (Harry Pownall, Sr.)	a	2:05.3m
56	13,294 Philip Frost (James Arthur)	b	2:09.1f
57	10,000 Mix Hanover (Frank Ervin)	c	2:08.3f
58	10,000 Flight Song (Lou Huber, Jr.)		2:14.3f
59	10,000 Uncle Sam (Lou Huber, Jr.)		2:05.4f
60	10,000 Matastar (Harry Pownall, Sr.)		2:06.1f
61	10,000 Nathaniel (Harry Pownall, Sr.)		2:07.3f
62	10,000 Speedy Scot (Ralph Baldwin)		2:05.2f
63	10,000 Big John (Eddie Wheeler)		2:08 f
64	10,000 Noble Victory (Stanley Dancer)		2:05.1f
65	12,500 Careless Vlado (Joe Marsh, Jr.)		2:08 f
66	12,500 Halifax Hanover (Joe O'Brien)		2:08.4f
67	12,500 Snow Speed (Ralph Baldwin)		2:03.2f
68	7,500 Nevele Major (Stanley Dancer)		2:06.1f
	7,500 Lindys Pride (Howard Beissinger)		2:05 f
69	12,500 Speedy Spin (Frank Ervin)		2:06.3f
70	12,500 Hard Decision (William Haughton)		2:13.3f
71	12,500 Star's Chip (Stanley Dancer)		2:10.1f
72	12,500 South Bend (Mike Zeller)		2:05.1f
73	12,500 Nevele Diamond (Stanley Dancer)		2:06.1f
74	12,500 Surefire Hanover (J. Marsh, Jr.)		2:07.4f
75	12,500 Nevele Thunder (Stanley Dancer)		2:06.2f

76	12,500 Scandal Sheet (D.Richardson, Jr.)	2:06 f
77	15,000 Florida Pro (George Sholty)	2:03.1f
78	15,000 Gridiron Lad (Carl Allen)	2:06.1f
79	20,000 Noble Hustle (Doug Ackerman)	2:05.3f
80	20,000 Graf Zepplin (Gary Lewis)	2:04 f
81	22,500 Self Confident (D.R. Ackerman)	2:00.4f
82	62,900 Jealousy (Stanley Dancer)	2:03.1f
83	36,500 Caleb Lobell (Howard Beissinger)	2:03.3f
	36,500 Desert Ruler (Jimmy Larente)	2:03.1f
84	58,250 John Dory (Doug Ackerman)	2:04.1f
85	62,400 Mr. Novak (Jan Nordin)	2:02.3f
86	92,400 Waikiki Beach (Jim Doherty) R	1:59.4f
87	102,500 Firm Tribute (Mark O'Mara)	2:01.4f
88	63,250 London Hunt (Doug Brown)	2:03 f
	63,250 Rapido (John Campbell)	2:01.2f
89	95,200 Cumin (Stanley Dancer)	2:02 f
90	47,500 Anders Crown (Jan Nordin)	2:02.2f
	47,500 Square Rigger (Gerald Longo)	2:02.2f

* - Raced as The Trotting Club Stake from 1947-1949
** - Two-Year-Old Open Trot before 1968.
a By Lullwater Victory.   c By Anna Dares.
b By Bond Hanover.

The American-National Stake *
Two-Year-Old Colt Pace **
Sportsman's Park, Cicero, IL Sept. 21, 1990

47	9,190 Knight Dream (Frank Safford)		2:06.4h
48	10,597 Good Time (Frank Ervin)		2:02.1m
49	11,407 Beryl Hanover (Gibson White)	a	2:02.3m
50	12,930 Tar Heel (Del Cameron)		2:04 m
51	12,609 Gander (Hugh Bell)	b	2:04 m
52	-- Rain --		
53	13,602 Parker Byrd (Frank Ervin)	c	2:01.1m
54	12,954 Meadow Leo (B.J. Schue)		2:03 m
55	11,397 Buckeye (B.J. Schue)	d	2:01.4m
56	16,164 Adios Express (Joe O'Brien)		2:04 m
57	10,000 Painter (John Simpson, Sr.)		2:05 f
58	10,000 Bristol Hanover (Ned Bower)		2:11 f
59	10,000 Knight Time (James Boring)		2:02.3f
59	Sampson Direct (Lou Huber, Jr.)		2:05.4f
60	10,000 High Test (Frank Ervin)		2:04.3f
60	Scotch Time (Dwayne Pletcher)		2:08 f
61	10,000 Coffee Break (George Sholty)		2:02.1f
62	20,000 Hondo Hanover (Joe O'Brien)		2:07.2f
63	10,000 Torpedo (William Haughton)		2:01.2f
64	10,000 Bret Hanover (Frank Ervin)		2:01.1f
65	12,500 Joanie's Pony (Warren Cameron)		2:02.2f
66	12,500 Best Of All (Jim Hackett)		2:01.1f
67	12,500 Rum Customer (William Haughton)		2:01 f
68	12,500 Armbro Judd (Robert Aumsbaugh)		2:03.4f
69	9,375 Most Happy Fella (Stanley Dancer)		2:01.4f
	9,375 Free Love (Glen Garnsey)		2:03.1f
70	9,500 Albatross (Harry Harvey)		2:04.3f
	9,500 -dh- Flying Bret (Charles Clark)		2:03 f
	-dh- Jolly Roger (Stanley Dancer)		2:03 f
71	12,500 Fast Clip (Bruce Nickells)		2:06 f
72	9,375 Harry Fitz (Herman Graham, Jr.)		2:02.3f
	9,375 Steady Airliner (Glen Johnson)		2:03 f

73	9,500 Boyden Hanover (George Sholty)		2:01 f
	9,500 Timely Objection (H. Lunsford)		2:04 f
	9,500 Reel Heel (Gene Riegle)		2:02.1f
74	9,375 Todaro Hanover (Joe Marsh, Jr.)		2:06.3f
	9,375 Brets Champ (William Haughton)		2:04.2f
75	9,375 Raven Hanover (George Sholty)		2:01 f
	9,375 Late Show (Jerry Graham)		2:03 f
76	12,500 Tremor (Walter Paisley)		2:00.2f
77	15,000 Lime Time (Mike Zeller)		2:01.4f
78	15,000 Plat Du Jour (Dick DeSantis)		1:59.4f
79	20,000 Midas Almahurst (Lew Williams)		1:59.3f
80	20,000 Artie's Dream (Joe Marsh, Jr.)		1:59.3f
81	25,000 Livingston County (Ben Webster)		2:00.1f
82	90,950 Time To Cash (Tom Harmer)		1:57.3f
83	47,700 Anzio Hanover (John Campbell)		1:57.3f
	47,500 Native Ruler (Jim Dennis)		1:59.2f
84	35,200 Good By Design (Keith Crawford)		1:57.2f
	35,200 Marauder (Dick Richardson, Jr.)		2:01.2f
85	47,500 Happy Chatter (Doug Ackerman)		2:00.1f
	47,500 Southern Gentleman (Bruce Riegle)		1:58.2f
86	106,200 Jate Lobell (Mark O'Mara)		1:55.2f
87	75,000 Armbro Getty (Bill Gale)		1:57 f
	75,000 Concussion (Sam Noble III)		1:58 f
88	141,000 Kentucky Spur (Dick Stillings)		1:57.3f
89	127,500 Drop-Off (Tommy Haughton)		1:57.3f
90	55,000 Mantese (John Campbell) R		1:55.1f
	55,000 Interpretor (D.R. Ackerman)		1:56.3f

* - Raced as The Trotting Club Stake from 1947-1949.
** - Two-Year-Old Open Trot before 1968.
a By Our Time.   c By Meadow Pace.
b By Thunderclap.   d By Greentree Adios.

The American-National Stake *
Three-Year-old Colt Trot **
Sportsman's Park, Cicero, IL June 18, 1990

48	16,502 Egan Hanover (Ralph Baldwin)		2:01.2m
49	16,971 Fibber (Harry Pownall, Sr.)		2:03 m
50	13,774 Lusty Song (Delvin Miller)		2:04 m
51	19,071 Spennib (Fay Fitzpatrick)	a	2:04 m
52	-- Rain --		
53	17,245 Kimberly Kid (Thomas Berry)		2:02.2m
54	14,561 Darn Safe (B.J. Schue)	b	2:01.4m
55	13,332 Trump Hanover (H. Pownall, Sr.)		2:03.1m
56	13,322 Moray (Dee Stover)		2:15.4f
57	20,143 Double Scotch (Joe O'Brien)	c	2:03.1f
58	15,000 Great Lullwater (Del Miller)		2:06.3f
	Mr. Saunders (Gene Riegle)		2:07.1f
59	15,000 Diller Hanover (Lawrence Garton)		2:05.1f
60	15,000 In Haste (Stanley Dancer)		2:03.1f
61	15,000 Matastar (Harry Pownall, Sr.)		2:02.3f
62	15,000 Worth Seein (Stanley Dancer)		2:03.1f
63	15,000 Choir Boy (Keith Waples)		2:05.1f
64	25,000 Speedy Count (William Haughton)		2:00.2f
65	25,000 Noble Victory (Stanley Dancer)		2:01.1f
66	25,000 Carlisle (William Haughton)		2:02.1f
67	18,750 Speed Model (Art Hult)		2:03.1f
	18,750 Dazzling Speed (Stanley Dancer)		2:04.4f
68	25,000 Snow Speed (Ralph Baldwin)		2:02.3f
69	25,000 Smokey Morn (Ned Bower)		2:04 f
70	25,000 Paris Air (Howard Beissinger)		2:04.1f

71	25,000 Speedy Crown (Howard Beissinger)	2:02 f
72	25,000 Super Bowl (Stanley Dancer)	2:01 f
73	19,200 Knightly Way (John Simpson, Jr.)	2:02 f
74	19,535 Nevele Diamond (Stanley Dancer)	2:00.3f
75	19,225 Bonefish (Stanley Dancer)	1:59.3f
76	19,000 Lola's Express (Bruce Nickells)	2:03.1f
77	19,000 Slomen (Chris Boring)	2:01.3f
78	24,375 Florida Pro (George Sholty)	2:01.4f
79	21,250 Gridiron Lad (Carl Allen)	2:03.2f
80	20,900 Noble Hustle (D.R. Ackerman)	2:03 f
81	26,400 Banker Barker (Mike Zeller)	2:00.3f
82	108,500 Speed Bowl (Tom Haughton)	2:00 f
83	139,500 Mr. Drew (Buddy Gilmour)	1:59.1f
84	75,200 Coogee (Dick Hogan)	2:00 f
	75,200 Baltic Speed (Jan Nordin)	1:58.4f
85	129,500 Workoholic (Berndt Lindstedt)	1:59.3f
86	207,400 Royal Prestige (Berndt Lindstedt)	2:01 f
87	229,500 Napoletano (Berndt Lindstedt)	R 1:58.1f
	243,500 Somollison' (Rod Allen)	1:58.4f
88	309,000 Egyptian Gentleman (Walt Paisley)	1:58.4f
	272,000 Armbro Iliad (Dave Magee)	2:00.1f

* - Raced as The Trotting Club Stake from 1948-1950.
** - Three-Year-Old Open Trot before 1969.
a By Yankee Hanover a& Spennib.   c By Hoot Song.
b By Harlan.

CHRONICLES

The American-National Stake *
Three-Year-Old Colt Pace **
Sportsman's Park, Cicero, IL June 30, 1990

48	9,240 Knight Dream (Frank Safford)	2:01.3m	
49	12,425 Good Time (Frank Ervin)	1:59.3m	
50	11,920 Quilla Hanover (J. Simpson, Sr.)	2:02.2m	
51	12,828 Tar Heel (Delvin Miller)	2:02 m	
52	10,203 Thunderclap (Hugh Bell)	1:59.4m	
53	10,099 Keystoner (Frank Ervin)	R 1:59.2m	
54	11,172 Diamond Hal (Joe O'Brien)	a 2:00.2m	
55	9,347 Libby's Boy (Delvin Miller)	b 2:00 m	
56	12,486 Adioscot (Delvin Miller)	2:12.3f	
57	16,116 Meadow Rhythm (B.J. Schue)	c 2:03.2f	
58	15,000 Raider Frost (Joe O'Brien)	2:04.2f	
59	15,000 Carloader (Fred Bradbury)	2:14.1f	
60	15,000 Countess Adios (Delvin Miller)	2:00.2f	
61	15,000 Adios Don (Howard Camper)	2:00.2f	
62	15,000 Ranger Knight (Eugene Minniear)	2:01.2f	
63	15,000 Delightful Time (George Sholty)	2:00.3f	
64	25,000 Race Time (James Arthur)	1:59 f	
65	25,000 Bret Hanover (Frank Ervin)	2:00.3f	
66	25,000 Romeo Hanover (George Sholty)	1:56.1f	
67	25,000 Honest Story (Eddie Cobb)	1:58.4f	
68	25,000 Careless Time (Joe Marsh, Jr.)	2:00.4f	
69	25,000 Laverne Hanover (Wm. Haughton)	2:04.2f	
70	25,000 Columbia George (Roland Beaulieu)	1:59.2f	
71	17,500 Nibble Tar (Daryl Busse)	2:02.1f	
	17,500 Paulos Hanover (Howard Camper)	2:00.2f	
72	18,750 Breadwinner (Del Cameron)	1:59.2f	
	18,750 Silent Majority (Vernon Dancer)	1:59.1f	
73	31,000 Gay Skipper (John Ackerman)	1:58.3f	
74	20,000 Timely Archer (Bill Herman)	2:01.2f	
	20,000 Brets Star (Mike Gagliardi)	1:59 f	
75	30,775 Nero (Joe O'Brien)	1:58.1f	
76	31,000 Valerian (Walter Paisley)	1:57.4f	
77	31,000 Thorpe Messenger (Stan Banks)	1:57.2f	
78	50,625 Brittany Road (Bruce Riegle)	2:00.4f	
79	53,750 Penner (Doug Ackerman)	2:00.1f	
80	54,100 Hoot Hanover (John Hayes, Jr.)	1:58.4f	
81	70,000 Artie's Dream (Shelly Goudreau)	1:58 f	
82	200,600 Lon Todd Hanover(J.Simpson, Jr.)d	1:57.3f	
83	102,000 Time To Cash (Mickey McNichol)	1:58 f	
	109,000 Del Cavallo (Doug Ackerman)	1:59.1f	
84	117,500 Walton Hanover (Harold Dancer)	1:56.4f	
	117,500 Farmstead's Fame (Wm. Haughton)	1:56.1f	
85	102,000 Marauder (Dick Richardson, Jr.)	1:55.4f	
	102,000 Falcon Seelster (Tom Harmer)	1:55.4f	
86	425,500 Incredible Finale (Tom Harmer)	1:54.4f	
87	353,700 Jate Lobell (Mark O'Mara)	1:53 f	
88	384,500 Matt's Scooter (Michel Lachance)	1:55.2f	
89	401,000 Sandman Hanover (Bill O'Donnell)	1:54 f	
90	347,000 Beach Towel (Ray Remmen)	R 1:52.4f	

* - Raced as The Trotting Club Stake from 1948-1950.
** - Three-Year-Old Open Pace before 1969.

a By Meadow Gold. c By Amigo Hal.
b By Hundred Proof. d By Solid Fuel.

The American-National Stake
Four-Year-Old and Over Trot
Sportsman's Park, Cicero, IL Sept. 26, 1990

59	68,032 Senator Frost (Dick Buxton)	2:01.3f	
60	61,196 Tie Silk (Philippe Dussault)	2:02.2f	
61	70,848 Merrie Duke (J. Patterson, Sr.)	2:06 f	
62	59,944 Duke Rodney (William Haughton)	2:00.1f	
63	63,639 Tercel (Harry Pownall, Sr.)	2:03 f	
64	66,201 Speedy Scot (Ralph Baldwin)	2:00.3f	
65	59,478 Dartmouth (Ralph Baldwin)	2:02.4f	
66	83,462 Noble Victory (Stanley Dancer)	1:59.3f	
67	89,580 Carlisle (William Haughton)	1:59.3f	
68	69,728 Proven Freight (Jim Dennis)	2:02 f	
69	70,396 Snow Speed (Ralph Baldwin)	1:59.2f	
70	67,324 Armbro Jet (Joe O'Brien)	2:03.1f	
71	65,694 Keystone Brian (Edward Dunnigan)	*	
72	66,645 Savoir (James Arthur)	1:59 f	
73	55,785 Songcan (John Quinn)	2:07.2f	
74	64,637 Noble Jade (Del Insko)	2:01.3f	
75	70,200 Golden Sovereign(D.Richardson,Jr)	2:01.3f	
76	72,450 Songflori (Stanley Banks)	2:01 f	
77	66,750 Zoot Suit (Stanley Dancer)	2:01 f	
78	71,700 Green Speed (William Haughton)	1:57.3f	
79	68,750 Bedford Spirit (Maurice Pusey)	2:00.4f	
80	54,200 Lindy's Crown (Howard Beissinger)	2:00.2f	
81	61,510 Burgomeister (William Haughton)	2:03.3f	
82	57,600 Balanced Image (Walter Paisley)	2:00 f	
83	65,950 Diamond Exchange (Rob. Williams)	1:58.4f	
84	69,100 Coleman Lobell (William Haughton)	2:01 f	
85	80,000 Sandy Bowl (Neal Shapiro)	1:59.1f	
86	50,000 Master Willie (Jan Nordin)	2:00.3f	
87	55,600 Express Ride (Berndt Lindstedt)	R 1:55 f	
88	62,500 Oucho (Fred Finn, Jr.)	1:58.2f	
89	-- Not Raced --		
90	40,000 Kit Lobell (Berndt Lindstedt)	1:58.4f	
	40,000 Peach Pit (John Campbell)	1:58.3f	

* - Time disallowed

The American-National Stake
Four-Year-Old and Over Pace
Sportsman's Park, Cicero, IL Sept. 1, 1990

59	54,879 Bye Bye Byrd (Clint Hodgins)	1:58.2f	
60	61,196 Adios Butler (Eddie Cobb)	2:01.1f	
61	61,222 Merrie Gesture (Edward Kelly)	2:00 f	
62	72,425 Henry T. Adios (Stanley Dancer)	1:59.2f	
63	86,030 Coffee Break (George Sholty)	2:00 f	
64	83,278 Delightful Time (George Sholty)	2:00.3f	
65	80,731 Race Time (Ralph Baldwin)	1:59.1f	
66	71,418 Bret Hanover (Frank Ervin)	1:58.2f	
67	80,719 Song Cycle (Bill Shuter)	1:59.2f	
68	83,612 Best Of All (Robert Williams)	1:57.1f	
69	49,533 Careless Time (Joe Marsh, Jr.)	2:01.1f	
	49,533 Rum Customer (William Haughton)	2:00.1f	
70	39,352 Lightning Wave (Bill Shuter)	2:04.1f	
71	104,000 Kentucky (Bruce Nickells)	1:59.3f	
72	80,425 Albatross (Stanley Dancer)	2:00 f	
73	52,873 Jay Time (Gene Riegle)	2:00.3f	
	52,873 Game Guy (Daryl Busse)	2:02.3f	
74	101,598 Otaro Hanover (Herve Filion)	1:57.4f	
75	111,752 Title Holder (Tom Brinkerhoff)	1:56.2f	
76	107,500 N L Skipper (Jim Dennis)	1:56.4f	
77	108,750 Warm Breeze (Dick Farrington)	1:58.3f	
78	125,725 Governor Skipper (John Chapman)	1:56.2f	
79	101,250 Abercrombie (Glen Garnsey)	1:58.1f	
80	78,600 Penner (D.R. Ackerman)	2:01.3f	
81	100,450 Bandelier (Walter Paisley)	1:56.3f	
82	74,250 Dutch Treat (Joe Adamsky)	1:57.2f	
83	73,400 Cam Fella (Pat Crowe)	1:54.2f	
84	80,000 Mr Dalrae (Dave Magee)	1:55 f	
85	77,500 Mr Dalrae (Dale Hiteman)	1:56.1f	
86	71,200 Hothead (Lavern Hostetler)	1:56 f	
87	76,750 Anniecrombie (Walter Case, Jr.)	1:53.4f	
88	73,200 Stir Fry (Danny Johnson)	1:55.1f	
89	50,000 Keystone Raider (Dave Magee)	1:54 f	
	50,000 Money Lender (Dale Hiteman)	1:54.3f	
90	148,000 Keystone Raider (Walter Paisley)	R 1:53.2f	

The American Pacing Classic Final
Free-For-All
Los Alamitos Racecourse, Los Alamitos, CA Sept. 29, 1990

90	150,000 TK's Skipper (Joe Anderson)	1:51.2f	

The Arden Downs Stake
Two-Year-Old Trot
The Meadows, Meadow Lands, PA Aug. 8, 1990

57	10,095 Sharpshooter (H. Pownall, Sr.)	2:10.1h	
58	13,593 Brogue Hanover (Joe O'Brien)	2:07.1h	
59	15,263 Mystery Song (Jim Hackett)	a 2:07.4h	
60	13,455 Scotch Irish (C.J. Champion)	2:11.2h	
61	10,835 Apex Hanover (James Arthur)	2:06 h	
62	10,596 Frosty Hanover (Stanley Dancer)	b 2:05.3h	

CHRONICLES

63	14,556	Ayres (John Simpson, Sr.)	2:03.3f
64	11,357	Marengo Hanover (J. Simpson, Sr.)	2:05.3f
	11,357	Mr. Magoo (Gordon Larlee)	2:06.3f
65	9,785	Jed (Ralph Baldwin)	2:05.2f
	10,085	Step Right (Ralph Baldwin)	2:06.3f
66	9,386	Halifax Hanover (J.Patterson,Sr.)	2:06.3f
	9,536	Pay Dirt (Earle Avery)	2:05.4f
67	13,400	Nevele Pride (Stanley Dancer)	2:02.4f
68	9,130	Gun Runner (Earle Avery)	2:08.3f
	9,130	Lindys Pride (Howard Beissinger)	2:06.2f
	9,130	Nevele Major (Stanley Dancer)	2:07.1f
69	9,175	Hungry Harry (C.J. Champion)	2:06.4f
	9,475	Victory Star (Vernon Dancer)	2:05.4f
	9,475	Nevele Rascal (Stanley Dancer)	2:05.2f
70	17,205	A.C.'s Orion (William Haughton)	2:04.1f
71	10,129	Songcan (Gilles Lachance)	2:05.2f
	10,127	-dh- Star's Chip (Stanley Dancer)	2:07.1f
		-dh- Flash (William Haughton)	2:07.1f
72	10,648	Burning Speed (Glen Garnsey)	2:07 f
	20,948	Hardy Coaltown (Bruce Nickells)	2:06.1f
73	9,893	Another Hill (David Rankin)	2:06.4f
	10,193	Dream Of Glory (Mel Turcotte)	2:05.4f
74	12,091	Noble Tryst (Vernon Crank)	2:05.4f
	12,091	Bonefish (Stanley Dancer)	2:05.1f
75	12,581	Nevele Thunder (Stanley Dancer)	2:05.1f
	12,281	Quick Pay (William Haughton)	2:04.1f
76	10,581	Haygood (Marcel Lariviere)	2:04.3f
	10,581	Naturally Nevele (Stanley Dancer)	2:04.1f
	10,581	Busy Rob (Courtney Foos, Jr.)	2:04.4f
	10,881	Cold Comfort (William Haughton)	2:03.4f
77	10,677	Noble Move (Glen Garnsey)	2:03.1f
	10,677	Bedford Spirit (Clay Hammer)	2:03.3f
	10,677	Speedy Somolli (Howard Beissinger)	2:01.4f
78	10,102	Legend Hanover (Ray Tripp)	2:04.2f
	9,802	Thaddeus Hanover (J.Simpson, Jr.)	2:04.2f
79	11,025	Flickory Flies (Joe O'Brien)	2:04.2f
80	11,325	Netted (Hakan Wallner)	2:03.1f
	11,548	Smokin Yankee (Stanley Dancer)	2:00.2f
	11,548	Tuneful Contest (Bruce Nickells)	2:02.4f
	11,548	Pay The Yankee (Buddy Gilmour)	2:04.3f
81	10,632	Scottish Wind (Stanley Dancer)	2:01.3f
	10,632	Incredible Nevele (Glen Garnsey)	2:00.4f
	10,932	Jazz Cosmos (Mickey McNichol)	2:02.4f
82	28,340	Keystone Edmund (Tom Haughton)	2:02 f
83	15,495	Coogee (Bill Herman)	2:01.3f
	15,075	Sandy Bowl (Jan Nordin)	R 1:59.1f
84	13,848	Bowl Bid (Bruce Riegle)	2:01.2f
	14,198	Ata Joe Montana (Jan Nordin)	2:01.4f
	14,198	Armbro Demon (Jan Nordin)	2:02 f
	14,198	Super Freddie (Harold Dancer)	2:03.1f
	14,198	Admiral's Walk (Jan Nordin)	2:02 f
85	15,285	Farm King (Hakan Wallner)	2:01.1f
	14,935	Gunslinger Spur (Dick Stillings)	2:01.4f
	15,285	Everglade Hanover (J.Simpson,Jr.)	2:01.2f
	14,935	Barbeque (Tom Haughton)	2:01.4f
86	16,045	Nobleboy Hanover (Jimmy Simpson)	2:02.2f
	16,395	Arnson (Per Eriksson)	2:02.1f
	16,045	Napoletano (Tom Haughton)	2:02 f
87	23,820	Sharpsburg (Bill Zendt)	2:02 f
	23,820	Yankee Ubet (Terry Altmeyer)	2:02 f
88	16,192	Mister Moberg (Maurizio Biasuzzi)	2:03 f
	16,192	Scott S Hanover (George Sholty)	2:02.3f
	16,192	Yankee Class (Doug Snyder)	1:59.4f
89	18,271	Follow My Fire (Mark Christman)	2:03.2f
	18,621	Sully Hanover (Jan Nordin)	2:05.2f
	18,621	Meadowbranch Eddy (Tom Anderson)	2:04.3f
90	17,057	Shaurina (Jorn Kvikstad)	2:01.1f
	17,057	Chapman (Jan Nordin)	2:02.4f
	17,057	Dickerson (Jan Nordin)	2:01.2f
	17,457	Super Pleasure (Bill O'Donnell)	1:59.3f

a By Mystery Song & Lowe Hanover.
b By B F Coaltown

The Arden Downs Stake
Two-Year-Old Pace
The Meadows, Meadow Lands, PA Aug. 9, 1990

57	12,745	Thorpe Hanover (Delvin Miller)	2:06 h
58	14,993	Meadow Al (Joe O'Brien)	2:05.3h
59	14,263	Muncy Hanover (Earle Avery) a	2:04.4h
		Merrie Adios (John Patterson, Jr.)	*
60	12,755	Star Gem (Frank Ervin)	2:04.1h
61	10,985	Lehigh Hanover (Stanley Dancer)	2:08.2h
62	10,746	Country Don (Marcel Dostie)	2:02.3h
63	11,853	Chief Duane (James Michaels)	2:03.3f
	11,853	Calcaneus (Delvin Miller)	2:03 f
64	10,122	Reed's Gold (Del Cote)	2:04.3f
	9,822	Gee Lee Hanover (Harold Dancer)	2:01.4f
	10,122	Bret Hanover (Frank Ervin)	2:01.4f
65	11,260	Clay (William Haughton)	2:03.1f
	11,260	Romeo Hanover (Bill Myer)	2:03 f
66	10,836	Nardin's Byrd (Delvin Miller)	2:04.2f
	10,136	Romulus Hanover (Stanley Dancer)	2:00.1f
67	10,425	Holly Sand (George Sholty)	2:01 f
	10,725	Fulla Napoleon (Richard Thomas)	2:01.1f
68	11,971	Bergen Hanover (William Haughton)	2:03.2f
	12,271	Laverne Hanover (Wm. Haughton)	2:02.1f
69	12,127	Desert Dancer (Jack Bailey)	2:02.1f
	12,427	Ferric Hanover (Ben Webster)	2:02 f
	12,127	Most Happy Fella (Stanley Dancer)	2:01.3f
70	17,370	Paulos Hanover (Howard Camper)	2:02.4f
	17,370	Seton Hanover (Edward Dunnigan)	2:00.2f
71	15,169	Tony The Butler (Eddie Cobb)	2:01.4f
	14,869	Town Leader (Dick Brandt)	2:01.3f
72	14,869	Alley Fighter (John Hayes)	2:03.1f
	19,839	Southern Lehigh (Stanley Dancer)	2:02.1f
	19,839	H.T. Thorpe (Chris Boring)	2:03.1f
73	16,238	Boyden Hanover (Bill Herman)	2:01.1f
	16,238	Lustron Hanover (Harold Dancer)	2:03.1f
	16,238	H.T. Sam (Del Cameron)	2:04.3f
74	16,828	Alert Bret (Bill Herman)	2:04.4f
	16,828	Phil The Bill (Norm Dauplaise)	2:04.1f
	16,828	Keystone Newkirk (Richard Moore)	2:04.3f
	16,238	Nero (Joe O'Brien)	2:06 f
75	15,331	J.J.'s Nino (Bill Zendt)	2:01.4f
	15,331	Armbro Ranger (Joe O'Brien)	2:00.2f
	15,331	Adam Lobell (Harold Dancer)	2:02.1f
	15,331	Bit O Fun (Warren Cameron)	2:01 f
76	13,885	Governor Skipper (Hen. Filion)	1:59.1f
	13,885	Racy Goods (Glen Garnsey)	1:59.1f
	13,885	Kawartha Eagle (Stanley Dancer)	1:58.4f
	13,885	Striking Image (Glen Garnsey)	1:59 f
77	19,021	Balance Of Power (Bill Zendt)	1:58.4f
	19,321	Spicy Charlie (Bill Popfinger)	1:58.4f
78	13,440	Pence Time (Jack Kopas)	2:00.2f
	13,440	Genghis Khan (Eddie Cobb)	1:58.1f
	13,440	Crackers (Bill Popfinger)	1:59.3f
	13,740	Overkill (Don McKirgan)	1:59.2f
79	15,066	Sans Strike (John Chapman)	2:00.2f
	15,066	Storm Damage (William Haughton)	2:00.1f
	15,066	Cool Wind (Glen Garnsey)	2:01.4f
80	14,343	Clansman (Tom Sells)	2:02.4f
	14,343	French Chef (Stanley Dancer)	2:00.4f
	14,343	Skippers Ensign (Glen Garnsey)	2:01.4f
	14,343	Cowboy Spur (Dick Stillings)	2:01.1f
81	16,498	Irish Jimmy (John Simpson, Jr.)	1:57 f
	16,798	Keystone Famous (Roger Hammer)	1:58.1f
	16,798	Le Roan (Ross Hayter)	1:57.4f
82	20,214	Better Heather (William Haughton)	1:58.2f
	20,564	Elwood Hanover (Bill Fahy)	1:57.3f
	20,564	Hamilton R.H. (Howard Beissinger)	1:59.1f
	20,564	Armbro Belmont (Archie McNeil)	1:58.1f
83	14,790	Shady Deal (Don Irvine, Jr.)	1:58.3f
	14,790	Shannon Majority (Tom Haughton)	2:00 f
	14,790	Forest Hanover (John Kopas)	1:59.2f
	15,210	Cadillac (Bill Fahy)	1:58.1f
84	26,760	Fortitude Hanover (Bill Fahy)	1:58.3f
	27,110	Nero's Star (Jeff Mallet)	1:57.3f
	26,760	Stir Fry (Terry Tomlin)	1:57.1f
85	26,248	Audubon Hanover (Wm. Haughton)	1:57.2f
	26,249	Tropic March (Bill O'Donnell)	1:56 f
	26,249	Avalanche Spur (Dick Stillings)	1:59.2f
86	21,322	Simcoe Hanover (Michel Lachance)	1:57.2f
	21,672	Golden Greek (Tom Haughton)	1:57.2f
	21,672	Shannon Brooks (Tom Haughton)	1:57.4f
	21,322	Meadowbranch Bret (Tom Haughton)	1:58 f
87	26,102	Barstow Hanover (Doug Snyder)	1:56 f
	26,102	Cimarron (Don Swick)	1:57 f
	26,102	Flexible Computer (Jim Miller)	1:57.4f
	26,452	Eddie The Quick (Doug Snyder)	R 1:54.4f
88	24,177	Barefoot Hanover (Dave Rankin)	1:57.2f
	24,177	Its Country (Carl Allen)	1:58.3f
	24,177	Keystone Fabulous (Roger Hammer)	1:56.1f
	24,177	Trenton's Image (Ron Waples)	1:57 f
89	21,532	Ballenger Hanover (Sam Noble III)	1:57.2f
	21,532	French Embassy (Bill Fahy)	1:57.4f
	21,532	Rock Legend (Doug Snyder)	1:57.1f
	21,882	Brando Hanover (Sam Noble III)	1:57.3f
90	23,675	Artsplace (Dave Palone)	1:55.3f
	23,675	Gold Glover (Mark Williams)	1:56.4f
	23,675	Meadow Lucas (Dave Rankin)	1:58.2f
	23,675	The Other Guy (Dave Palone)	1:55.1f

* - Time disallowed

CHRONICLES

The Arden Downs Stake
Three-Year-Old Trot
The Meadows, Meadow Lands, PA Aug. 10, 1990

58	9,645	Mc Colby (Dana Cameron)	a	2:07.2h	78	25,186	Count's Pride (Dick Buxton)	2:02.3f
59	11,643	Circo (William Haughton)		2:05.2h	79	25,920	Legend Hanover (Joe O'Brien)	2:04.1f
60	14,463	In Haste (Stanley Dancer)		2:02.4h	80	25,700	Marino Hanover (Jim Miller)	2:02.2f
61	11,955	Matastar (Harry Pownall, Sr.)		2:08 h	81	27,952	Smokin Yankee (Stanley Dancer)	2:01.3f
		Harlan Dean (James Arthur)		2:11.1h	82	26,075	Crysta's Crown (Hakan Wallner)	1:59.4f
62	9,485	A.C.'s Viking (Sanders Russell)		2:04.2h	83	22,533	Micron Hanover (J. Simpson, Jr.)	1:58.2f
63	15,646	Florlis (Harry Pownall, Sr.)		2:02.1f		22,953	Power Seat (Ted Andrews)	2:00 f
64	15,506	Ayres (John Simpson, Sr.)		2:00.2f	84	21,105	Cornstalk (Howard Beissinger)	2:01.4f
65	16,565	Spud Coaltown (Bruce Nickells)		2:04.4f		21,455	Gallant Pro (Tom Haughton)	2:03.4f
66	14,570	Our Rainbow (Stanley Dancer)		2:02.4f	85	26,324	Hollyhurst (Ted Andrews)	1:59.3f
67	14,272	Pomp (Harry Pownall, Sr.)		2:01.2f		26,474	Somolli Star (Howard Beissinger)	1:59.4f
68	13,700	Eric B. (Stanley Dancer)		2:02.4f	86	18,204	Shack (Charles Morgan)	2:00.1f
69	10,495	Lindys Pride (Howard Beissinger)		2:01 f		17,854	Armbro Eldorado (D.Richardson,Jr.)	1:59.3f
	10,495	Hiland Hill (Curly Smart)		2:02.3f		17,854	Barbeque (Berndt Lindstedt)	2:01.1f
70	18,076	Fairbanks Hanover (Jimmy Arthur)		2:03.2f	87	50,011	Cotton Hanover(D.Richardson,Jr.)R	1:58.1f
71	16,955	Hoot Speed (Glen Garnsey)		2:01 f	88	29,673	Carrier (Terry Altmeyer)	1:59.3f
72	15,068	Songcan (George Sholty)		2:04.2f		29,673	Danny Lad (Perry O'Brien)	1:59.2f
73	16,526	South Bend (Mike Zeller)		2:03.2f	89	24,486	Scott S Hanover (George Sholty)	1:59.1f
74	19,910	Nevele Diamond (Stanley Dancer)		2:01.3f		24,836	Swirlabout (Sam Noble III)	1:59.3f
75	18,702	Songflori (Delvin Miller)		2:02 f	90	30,377	Castleton Magic (Billy Herman)	1:59.4f
76	20,126	Lola's Express (Bruce Nickells)		2:00 f		30,727	Wolfs Degel (Berndt LindstedtA)	1:59.2f
77	24,151	Cold Comfort (William Haughton)		1:58.3f				

a By Great Lullwater.

The Arden Downs Stake
Two-Year-Old Filly Trot
The Meadows, Meadow Lands, PA Aug. 7, 1990

57	9,011	Anna Dares (John Simpson, Sr.)		2:10.4h	77	15,246	Starita Lobell (Joe O'Brien)	2:01.4f
58	9,677	Venture (Robert Walker)	a	2:09 h	78	10,634	Arica (William Haughton)	2:05.4f
59	8,943	Elaine Rodney (Clint Hodgins)		2:09.4h		10,934	Ahhhh (Howard Beissinger)	2:05.2f
60	11,256	My Gal Sal (Sanders Russell)		2:07 h	79	9,627	Star Investment (M. Crocco, Jr.)	2:04.3f
		Speedy Princess (Del Cameron)		2:07.3h		9,627	Yankee Mama (Delvin Miller)	2:04.4f
61	9,333	Spry Rodney (James Arthur)		2:12 h	80	10,894	Vase (Dick Richardson, Jr.)	2:03.1f
62	8,683	Graceful Kid (Robert Cherrix)		2:09 h		11,194	Panty Raid (Stanley Dancer)	2:04.1f
63	9,190	Myra (Robert Cherrix)		2:06 f	81	19,923	Sashay Lobell (George Sholty)	2:02.2f
	9,190	Golden Make It (Dana Irving)		2:05.3f	82	13,337	Silky Cedar (William Haughton)	2:06 f
64	9,545	Lansbury Hanover (J.Simpson, Sr.)		2:06 f		13,337	Southern Crown (Joe O'Brien)	2:03.3f
	9,845	Armbro Flight (Joe O'Brien)		2:06.1f		13,687	Tarport Lizzy (Bill Herman)	2:02.4f
65	9,245	My Opinion (William Haughton)		2:07.1f	83	27,075	Maida Hanover (Tom Haughton)	2:03 f
	9,247	Kerry Way (Stanley Dancer)		2:04.3f	84	33,657	Annabel Lobell (Tom Haughton)	2:02.4f
66	8,089	Flamboyant (John Chapman)		2:05.2f	85	13,819	Argyle Socks (Berndt Lindstedt) R	2:00.1f
	8,380	Speed Model (Frank Ervin)		2:05.1f		13,819	Newmarket S (Hakan Wallner) R	2:00.1f
67	8,812	Jostle (John Simpson, Jr.)		2:05.2f		13,819	My Girl's Lindy (H. Beissinger)	2:01.3f
	8,812	Arbida Hanover (J. Simpson, Jr.)		2:06 f	86	14,759	Keystone Harem (Jan Nordin)	2:04 f
68	10,547	Jounce (Clint Hodgins)		2:04.3f		15,109	Icefolly (Doug Snyder)	2:04.2f
	10,247	Maneros Pride (William Haughton)		2:06.1f		15,109	Crown Starlet (Bill Herman)	2:02.2f
69	9,699	Luscious Newport (Del Cameron)		2:08.3f	87	21,270	Calcutta (Jan Johnson)	2:01.4f
	9,699	Sweet Freight (Fred Bradbury)		2:08.2f		21,270	Nan's Catch (Jan Johnson)	2:01.3f
70	9,628	Sonata Hill (William Haughton)		2:04.2f	88	14,725	Glisten Lobell (Jeff Fout)	2:01.4f
	9,628	Keystone Selene (Del Miller)		2:05.4f		14,725	Roz's Lady (Eddie Wheeler)	2:02.4f
71	9,403	Franella Hanover (Glen Garnsey)		2:05.1f		14,725	Triangle Park (Mickey McNichol)	2:01.2f
	9,103	Delmonica Hanover (Del Miller)		2:04 f		14,725	Youve Gotta Friend (Jan Nordin)	2:00.3f
72	9,643	Scandalize (William Haughton)		2:06 f		15,075	On A Cruise (Jimmy Takter)	2:04 f
	9,643	Colonial Charm (Glen Garnsey)		2:06.4f	89	15,216	Bold Gal (Mark O'Mara)	2:00.4f
73	9,623	Noble Florie (Glen Garnsey)		2:07.2f		15,216	Essence Bear (Mel Turcotte)	2:03.4f
	9,623	Berna Hanover (Glen Garnsey)		2:05 f		15,216	Atlantic (Mark O'Mara)	2:02.4f
74	8,972	San Juan (John C. Wingard)		2:06.4f		15,216	Model Home (Berndt Lindstedt)	2:02.2f
	9,272	Brilliance (Stanley Dancer)		2:06 f	90	16,494	Cookout (Berndt Lindstedt)	2:02.4f
	9,272	Victorious Lou (Glen Garnsey)		2:06.1f		16,494	Granny Smith (Jan Nordin)	2:03 f
75	11,057	Starral Hanover (Peter Haughton)		2:05.1f		16,494	Malahana Kaari (Ron Waples)	2:00.3f
	11,057	Japa (James Arthur)		2:06 f		16,494	T-Ball (Doug Snyder)	2:01.1f
76	10,434	Laurna Jean (Carl Allen)		2:05 f				
	10,734	Sail By (Del Cameron)		2:06.1f				

a By Delicia Hanover.

The Arden Downs Stake
Two-Year-Old Filly Pace
The Meadows, Meadow Lands, PA Aug. 8, 1990

57	7,061	High Time (Frank Ervin)		2:10.2h		12,524	Alva (John Simpson, Jr.)	2:05.1f
58	9,777	Kathena (Levi Harner)		2:07 h	70	13,488	Keystone Memento (Stanley Dancer)	2:03.3f
59	9,993	Countess Adios (Delvin Miller)		2:06.1h		13,788	Trucita Blue Chip (S. Dancer)	2:05.2f
60	10,756	Sweet Mirian (Frank Darish)		2:04.1h		13,788	Tarport Helene (Stanley Dancer)	2:04.1f
		Patricia Rhythm (Clint Hodgins)		2:04.3h	71	17,127	Decorum (Stanley Dancer)	2:04 f
61	8,983	Ritzy Hanover (Howard Camper)		2:04.2h		17,127	Queens Blue Chip (Stanley Dancer)	2:02.4f
62	7,883	Adios Susan (Jim Hackett)		2:05 h	72	14,456	Jambo Belle (Merritt Dokey)	2:03.4f
63	15,131	Bit O'Sugar (John Chapman)		2:01.4f		14,456	Lauras Image (James Tallman)	2:03 f
64	10,545	Time Out (Don C. Miller)		2:06.2f		14,756	All Alert (Glen Garnsey)	2:04.4f
	10,545	Bewitch Hanover (J. Simpson, Sr.)		2:03.4f	73	14,712	Tiffy Time (Bill Herman)	2:04.1f
65	9,572	Conga Hanover (Vernon Dancer)		2:03.1f		14,412	Best Of Donut (William Haughton)	2:03.2f
	9,572	Worth Knowing (Joe Lighthill)		2:00.2f		14,712	Missouri Time (Jerry E. Ross)	2:03.1f
66	9,680	Ember Hanover (Richard Thomas)		2:03.3f	74	15,891	Melony Hanover (Delvin Miller)	2:04.3f
	9,680	Armbro Halo (Joe O'Brien)		2:06.2f		15,891	Tarport Hap (Delvin Miller)	2:02.4f
67	8,962	Thorpe Marge (Dick Williams II)		2:04 f		15,891	Sweetie Edie (William Haughton)	2:06.2f
	8,962	Tarport Karen (J. Patterson, Sr.)		2:04.4f	75	15,670	Meadow Wilma (William Haughton)	2:01.1f
68	9,631	Tiger Lily Lobell (Curly Smart)		2:07 f		15,670	Armbro Regret (Joe O'Brien)	2:03.1f
	9,331	Octavia Hanover (J. Simpson, Jr.)		2:04.3f		15,970	Ice Tea (Dick Farrington)	2:02.1f
	9,631	Scotch Jewel (Ralph Baldwin)		2:04.4f	76	14,130	Future Fame (William Haughton)	1:59.4f
69	12,224	Sprinkle (John W. Smith)		*		14,430	Helen's Deal (Peter Haughton)	2:02.1f

CHRONICLES

	14,430 Only Love (Gene Riegle)	2:01.4f		21,518 Seven O'Clock (Ed Ryan)	1:57.4f
77	14,864 Passing Glance (George Sholty)	1:58.4f		21,518 Steal The Show (Herve Filion)	1:57.3f
	14,564 Vala (Bill Herman)	2:01 f	85	36,729 Caressable (Tom Haughton)	R 1:57.1f
78	18,255 Rilda Hanover (J. Simpson, Jr.)	1:59.2f		37,079 Damask Hanover (Ernest Houle)	1:58.2f
	18,255 Roses Are Red (Jack Kopas)	1:59.4f	86	35,356 Simonsays Hi Toots (Ed Lohmeyer)	2:02.1f
79	17,987 Guiding Beam (Glen Garnsey)	2:00.3f		35,356 Tantalize Hanover (D. Stillings)	2:01.3f
	17,987 The Thilly Thavage (Rick Kuebler)	2:01 f	87	26,466 Huna Buna (Dick Stillings)	1:58.2f
80	19,812 Firma Hanover (Stanley Dancer)	2:01.2f		26,466 I Wish (Roger Hammer)	1:58.1f
	20,112 Zula Bird (Mike Allen)	2:01.2f		26,466 Sydra (Doug Snyder)	1:58.4f
81	15,482 Bartross (Jim Miller)	1:58 f	88	38,614 Frilly One (Bill Fahy)	1:58.3f
	15,482 Clint's Lady (Carl Allen)	1:59.1f		38,614 Marietta Lauxmont (W. Ross, Jr.)	1:58.3f
	15,782 Sunny And Fair (George Sholty)	1:59.4f	89	23,109 Heaven Made (Peter Ruscitto)	2:01.3f
82	23,083 Miss Yankee (Bib Roberts)	2:00.3f		23,109 Keystone Luscious (Roger Hammer)	1:59.1f
	23,083 Bardot Lobell (Howard Beissinger)	1:59.3f		23,109 Respectfully Yours (Ron Waples)	1:59.4f
	23,433 Keystone Flamingo (Wm. Haughton)	2:00.1f	90	23,375 Perfect Together (Rich. Wojcio)	R 1:56.1f
83	23,637 Mary B. Skipper (Lew Williams)	2:01.4f		23,375 In Your Dreams (Bill Gale)	1:57.4f
	24,057 Naughty But Nice (Tom Haughton)	2:00.2f		23,375 Thil Mindale (Rodney Bolon)	1:57.3f
84	21,868 Tyler's Fit (Herve Filion)	1:59 f		22,775 Eicarls Carlene (Steve LeBlanc)	1:59 f
	21,518 Wings Of Gold (Herve Filion)	1:59.2f		* - Time disallowed	

The Arden Downs Stake
Three-Year-Old Filly Trot
The Meadows, Meadow Lands, PA Aug. 10, 1990

58	7,011 La Belle (Dick Buxton)	2:05.3h	78	17,676 Rosemary (William Haughton)	1:59.3f
59	7,927 Expresson (Frank Ervin)	2:08 h	79	20,145 Classical Way (J. Simpson, Jr.)	2:00.3f
60	8,743 Elaine Rodney (Clint Hodgins)	2:03 h	80	10,486 Yankee Mama (Delvin Miller)	2:01.1f
61	9,156 Air Medal (Dick Hackett)	2:03.4h		10,486 Alta Moda (Delvin Miller)	2:02.1f
62	8,733 Sprite Rodney (Frank Ervin)	2:03 h	81	24,669 Keystone Sister (Del Miller)	1:58 f
63	12,333 Campus Queen (Ralph Baldwin)	2:05 f	82	27,200 Tiffany Star (Ted Andrews)	1:58.4f
64	15,000 Really Something (Don Miller)	2:04.4f	83	43,641 Tarport Lizzy (Billy Herman)	1:58.1f
65	13,341 Armbro Flight (Joe O'Brien)	2:04.1f	84	30,360 Annie's Frilly (Glen Garnsey)	1:58.2f
66	11,643 Coalition (Art Hult)	2:02.1f	85	22,946 Dash Alone (Berndt Lindstedt)	1:58 f
67	13,010 Flamboyant (William Haughton)	2:02.2f		22,596 Best Wishes Lobell (Jan Nordin)	2:00 f
68	8,162 Daring Speed (Clint Hodgins)	2:04.2f	86	16,968 B.J.'s Pleasure (Doug Snyder)	1:59.4f
	8,462 Arbida Hanover (J. Simpson, Jr.)	2:06 f		16,968 Victorious Tail (B. Lindstedt)	1:59.1f
69	15,892 Speedy American (Del Insko)	2:02.4f		16,617 Newmarket S (Hakan Wallner)	1:58.3f
70	14,848 Lovester (Charlie Clark)	2:03.1f	87	25,834 Keystone Harem (Jan Nordin)	R 1:56.4f
71	16,905 Waverly Hostess (Renald Filion)	2:03 f		26,183 Jazzy Jen (Jan Nordin)	2:00.1f
72	15,318 Speedy Carlene (Harold Dancer)	2:02 f	88	24,070 Joy Of Summer (Jim Gluhm)	1:59.2f
73	15,576 Florinda (Verne Gagnon)	2:02 f		24,070 Namara Hanover (Jan Johnson)	2:00.1f
74	15,460 Berna Hanover (Glen Garnsey)	2:04.4f	89	29,344 Bandee Hanover (Berndt Lindstedt)	2:00.2f
75	10,320 Keystone Pioneer (Dick DeSantis)	2:00.2f		29,344 Snippy Hanover (Jo. Simpson, Jr.)	2:01.2f
	10,320 Fairmaid Hanover (Jimmy Arthur)	2:04.1f	90	20,708 Me Maggie (Berndt Lindstedt)	1:57.2f
76	20,996 Japa (Jimmy Arthur)	2:00 f		21,058 Caspian (Gene Daisey)	1:58.2f
77	20,134 Nobie (Bill Herman)	2:02 f		21,058 Eternal Goddess (Ber. Lindstedt)	2:00.2f

The Autumn Stakes
Two-Year-Old Filly Trot
Mohawk Raceway, Campbellville, ONT Oct. 15, 1990

89	124,800 Cajala (Robert Walker)	R 2:02.2f	76,800 Shipps Doll (Tim Twaddle)	2:03 f
90	76,800 Collier St Kathy (Brian Schroeder)	2:03 f		

The Battle of Lake Erie
Open Aged Pace
Northfield Park, Northfield, OH June 2, 1990

86	50,000 Falcon Seelster (Tom Harmer)	1:55.2h	89	100,000 Jaguar Spur (Dick Stillings)	1:55.2h
87	50,000 Quite A Sensation (Trevor Ritchie)	1:55.1h	90	100,000 Dorunrun Bluegrass (Her. Filion)	R 1:54 h
88	100,000 Jaguar Spur (Dick Stillings)	1:54.4h			

The Budweiser Beacon Course Trot Final
Three-Year-Old Open Trot
Meadowlands, E. Rutherford, NJ July 28, 1990

76	94,000 Tropical Storm (Ralph Baldwin)	2:00 m	85	100,000 Mark Six (John Campbell)	1:59 m
77	100,000 Green Speed (William Haughton)	1:59.1m		100,000 Prakas (Bill O'Donnell)	1:57.2m
78	106,500 Florida Pro (George Sholty)	1:59.4m	86	85,000 Express Ride (Dan Shetler)	1:56.2m
79	109,500 Crown's Cristy (H. Beissinger)	1:57.3m		85,000 Barbeque (Jan Johnson)	1:57 m
80	120,000 Netted (Berndt Lindstedt)	1:56.2m	87	85,500 Beseiged (Per Henriksen)	1:56.1m
81	150,000 Super Juan (Howard Beissinger)	1:57.3m		85,500 Mack Lobell (John Campbell)	R 1:54 m
82	90,000 Self Confident (Doug Ackerman)	1:59.1m	88	70,000 Armbro Goal (John Campbell)	1:54.4m
	90,000 Jazz Cosmos (Mickey McNichol)	1:57 m		70,000 Firm Tribute (Mark O'Mara)	1:56.1m
83	100,000 Joie De Vie (John Campbell)	1:57.3m		70,000 Stable Gait (Carl Allen)	1:56 m
	100,000 Astro Hill (Ray Remmen)	1:57.2m	89	64,000 Bon Vivant (Michel Lachance)	1:57.4m
84	65,000 Crowning Point (Doug Ackerman)	1:56.1m		64,000 Egyptian Gentleman (John Campbell)	1:57 m
	65,000 Speed Merchant (Tony Quartarolo)	1:57.2m		64,000 Probe (Bill Fahy)	1:57 m
	65,000 Historic Freight (Ben Webster)	1:58.1m	90	401,500 Embassy Lobell (Michel Lachance)	1:56.3m

The Berry's Creek Series Final
Three-Year-Old Open Pace
The Meadowlands, E. Rutherford, NJ April 14, 1990

89	309,250 Fiorello Blue Chip (S. Ouellet)	R 1:53.2m	90	323,750 Mark Johnathan (Michel Lachance)	1:54 m

CHRONICLES

The Bluegrass
"The Walnut Hall Cup"
Two-Year-Old Colt Trot
The Red Mile, Lexington, KY Sept. 27, 1990

97	2,500	The Monk (Pop Geers)	2:11 1/2m	50	5,000	Pronto Don (Sep Palin)	2:00.1m
98	3,000	Nico (H. Titer)	2:11 1/4m	51	5,000	Miss Excellency (J. Simpson, Sr.)	2:04 m
99	3,000	Ellert (B. VanBokkelen)	2:15 m	52	4,600	Yankee Hanover (Frank Ervin)	2:00.4m
00	3,000	Chain Shot (George West)	2:15 1/2m	53	5,000	Scotch Victor (Joe O'Brien)	j 1:59.1m
01	3,000	Captor (Charles Marvin)	2:09 3/4m	54	4,200	Jamie (Bob Parkinson)	1:59.2m
02	3,000	Nutbearer (W.O. Foote)	2:09 3/4m	55	5,000	Deckwin (Wilbur Long)	2:02.4m
03	3,000	Billy Buck (Pop Geers)	2:07 3/4m	56	5,000	Lady's First (Charles King)	k 1:58.1m
04	3,000	Redwood (J. Burns)	2:09 3/4m	57	5,300	Empress Rodney (Wm. McMillen)	l 2:02.2m
05	3,000	Turley (Pop Geers)	2:07 1/4m	58	5,000	Fisherman (Dick Buxton)	2:00.3m
06	3,000	Nutboy (Myron E. McHenry)	2:11 3/4m	59	5,000	Morgan Calhoun (S. Dancer)	m 2:00.4m
07	3,000	Jack Leyburn (Pop Geers)	2:08 1/2m	60	5,000	Demon Damsel (Delvin Miller)	n 2:00.1m
08	3,000	Uhlan (R. Proctor)	2:07 1/2m	61	5,000	Hoot Frost (Joe O'Brien)	o 2:00.2m
09	3,000	Penisa Maid (M.D. Shutt)	2:13 3/4m	62	5,000	Behave (Ralph Baldwin)	p 2:01 m
10	3,000	Joan (M. McDevitt)	2:04 3/4m	63	4,250	Pack Hanover (Jim Hackett)	2:00 m
11	3,000	R. T. C. (T.W. Murphy)	2:08 3/4m	64	5,000	Dashing Rodney (Harold Dancer)	q 2:03.2m
12	3,000	Dorsh Medium (Pop Geers)	2:07 1/2m	65	5,790	Short Stop (Ralph Baldwin)	2:01 m
13	3,000	Fan Patch (W.L. Snow)	2:08 m	66	5,000	Speedy Play (Stanley Dancer)	2:05 m
14	3,000	Rhythmell (B.O. Shank)	2:04 1/4m	67	5,000	Garma Alert (A. Walker)	2:01.4m
15	3,000	Peter Scott (T.W. Murphy)	2:05 3/4m	68	5,000	Eric B. (Stanley Dancer)	1:59.4m
16	3,000	Mabel Trask (Walter Cox)	2:07 1/2m	69	5,000	Noccalula (Sanders Russell)	2:04.2m
17	3,000	Early Dreams (A. McDonald)	2:04 1/4m	70	11,201	Hoot Speed (Glen Garnsey)	2:04 m
18	3,000	Ante Guy (T.W. Murphy)	2:03 1/2m	71	11,500	Super Bowl (Stanley Dancer)	1:59.4m
19	3,000	Selka (H. Fleming)	2:06 1/4m	72	13,957	Travelogue (Terry Holton)	2:07 m
	3,000	Baron Cegantle (A. McDonald)	a 2:05 1/2m	73	14,381	My Super Pride (Del Cameron)	2:07.3m
20	3,000	Bonnie Del (T.G. Hinds)	b 2:04 3/4m	74	20,987	Bonefish (Stanley Dancer)	2:02.3m
21	3,000	Jeanette Rankin (A. McDonald)	2:04 1/2m	75	30,401	Tropical Storm (Ralph Baldwin)	2:04.1m
22	3,000	The Great Volo (Walter Cox)	2:03 1/2m	76	24,387	Profit Sharing (Stanley Dancer)	1:59.3m
23	4,000	Favonian (Fred Edman)	c 2:03 1/4m	77	26,306	Dark Eagle (D. Richardson, Jr.)	2:00.1m
24	4,000	Tilly Brooke (T.W. Murphy)	2:01 3/4m	78	27,676	Legend Hanover (Joe O'Brien)	1:59.3m
25	4,000	Crawford (T.W. Murphy)	2:04 1/4m	79	32,250	Rodney's Best (Hakan Wallner)	2:00 m
26	4,000	Guy Ozark (W.K. Dickerson)	2:05 m	80	36,460	Homesick (Bill Herman)	1:58.3m
27	4,000	Hazelton (Walter Cox)	2:03 3/4m	81	42,400	Incredible Nevele (Glen Garnsey)	1:58.1m
28	4,000	Dewey McKinney (Walter Cox)	2:02 1/2m	82	48,500	T V Yankee (Tom Haughton)	1:56 m
29	3,000	Gaylworthy (Harry Stokes)	2:05 1/4m	83	46,100	Gentle Stroke (George Sholty)	1:57.1m
30	3,000	Hollyrood Chief (W.H. Leese)	2:01 m	84	55,067	Affable Crown (John Campbell)	1:58.3m
31	3,000	Allie Pluto (Charles Mabrey)	2:01 1/2m	85	43,240	Barbeque (Berndt Lindstedt)	1:59.2m
32		-- Not Raced --		86	94,070	Nevele Olympian (Geo. Sholty)	Rr 1:55.3m
33	1,500	Vansandt (Earl Pitman)	2:02 1/2m	87	110,855	Grundy's Connection (Jan Nordin)	1:57.4m
34	2,000	Taffy Volo (Ben White)	d 2:01 1/2m	88	107,000	Meadow Gallant (Dave Rankin)	1:58 m
35	1,000	Calumet Durham (Sep Palin)	e 2:01 1/2m	89	123,263	I'm Impeccable (Dave Rankin)	s 1:57.2m
36	2,000	Lee Hanover (Charles Lacey)	2:01 m	90	106,290	Grundy's Mint (Jan Nordin)	t 1:57.1m
37	2,000	Guy Scotland (Will Moore)	f 2:01 3/4m				
38	2,000	Havolina (Will Caton)	g 2:02 1/4m		a By Direct Forbes.		m By Morgan Calhoun &
39	2,000	Senator V. (Robert Vallery)	2:01 3/4m		b By Peter Coley.		Storm Cloud.
40	3,000	Spud Hanover (H. Pownall, Sr.)	2:03 m		c By Cupid's Albingen.		n By Brogue Hanover.
41	3,000	Speed King (Harry Craig)	2:02 1/2m		d By Angel Child.		o By Demon Ros.
42	3,000	Volarion (J.F. Cartnal)	2:03 1/2m		e By General Douglass.		p By Sprite Kid.
43	2,000	Horate (Fred Egan)	2:04 m		f By Purling Brook.		q By Marco Hanover.
44	3,000	Love Song (Tom Berry)	h 2:00 m		g By Gaylmakinnie.		r By Mack Lobell.
45	3,000	Spartan Hanover (Frank Safford)	2:04 3/4m		h By Speed King.		s By I'm Impeccable &
46	3,000	Walter Spencer (H.Pownall,Sr.)	2:02 3/4m		i 2nd dash 2:19.3 (1-1/8 mi.).		Royal Troubador.
47	3,000	Don Scott (Delvin Miller)	i 2:02.2m		j By Katie Key.		t By Carry The Message &
48	3,000	Chris Spencer (Harry Whitney)	2:00.2m		k By Prince Victor.		Grundy's Mint.
49	5,000	Moses (Dee Stover)	2:03 m		l By Lumber Boy.		

The Bluegrass
The Meadow Lands Farm
Two-Year-Old Colt Pace
The Red Mile, Lexington, KY Sept. 30, 1989

75	46,021	Pensive Bret (Joe O'Brien)	2:04.1m	83	69,340	Walton Hanover (J. Simpson, Jr.)	1:55.2m
76	39,072	Jonquil Hanover (George Sholty)	2:00.3m	84	68,137	Witsend's Wizard (Ron Waples)a	1:56 m
77	40,054	Say Hello (Bill Popfinger)	1:56.1m	85	65,790	Talk About Class (John Campbell)	1:59 m
78	44,946	Sonsam (George Sholty)	1:54.2m	86	125,350	Dictionary (John Campbell)	1:53.3m
79	40,620	Niatross (Clint Galbraith)	1:55.4m	87	182,960	Camtastic (Bill O'Donnell)	1:53 m
80	54,401	French Chef (Stanley Dancer)	1:56.2m	88	176,810	How Bout It (Tom Haughton)	R 1:52.4m
81	52,800	Merger (John Campbell)	1:53.4m	89	163,636	Kiev Hanover (Dick Stillings)	1:54 m
82	67,000	Ralph Hanover (Ron Waples)	1:54.1m		a By Pinocchio.		

The Bluegrass
"The Transylvania"
Three-Year-Old Colt Trot
The Red Mile, Lexington, KY Sept. 28, 1990

89	5,000	Jack (Budd Doble)	2:15 m	02	6,000	Ozanam (Ed Benyon)	2:07 1/2m
90	5,000	McDoel (Budd Doble)	2:15 1/2m	03	6,000	Caspian (B. Shank)	2:09 1/2m
91	5,000	Cheyenne (H.J. Dickerson)	2:15 3/4m	04	5,000	Sweet Marie (A.P. McDonald)	2:04 1/2m
92	5,000	Kremlin (E.D. Bither)	2:11 1/2m	05	5,000	Ethel's Pride (W.J. Andrews)	2:04 1/2m
93	5,000	Harrietta (Crit Davis)	2:09 3/4m	06	5,000	Nutboy (Myron McHenry)	2:06 3/4m
94	5,000	Azote (A. McDowell)	2:08 3/4m	07	5,000	Sonoma Girl (Myron McHenry)	2:07 1/4m
95	5,000	Bouncer (W.J. Andrews)	2:10 1/4m	08	5,000	Spanish Queen (Guss Macey)	2:09 1/4m
96	5,000	Senator A. (C.E. Alexander)	2:10 m	09	5,000	Penisa Maid (M.D. Shutt)	2:14 1/4m
97	5,000	Rilma (W.O. Foote)	a 2:08 1/4m	10	5,025	Joan (M. McDevitt)	2:05 3/4m
98	5,000	John Nolan (W.O. Foote)	2:07 3/4m	11	5,025	Charley Mitchell (T.W. Murphy)	2:07 1/4m
99	10,000	Lord Vincent (Charles Doble)	2:08 1/2m	12	5,000	Baden (A.S. Rodney)	2:06 1/4m
00	5,000	Boralma (J.Y. Gatcomb)	2:08 m	13	5,000	Cheeny (J.P. Fleming)	2:04 3/4m
01	6,000	Onward Silver (Pop Geers)	2:09 3/4m	14	5,000	Etawah (Pop Geers)	2:03 1/2m

CHRONICLES

15	5,000 Peter Scott (T.W. Murphy)	2:05 1/4m
16	5,000 Mabel Trask (Walter Cox)	b 2:03 1/4m
17	5,000 Ima Jay (H.D. Ernest)	c 2:04 1/4m
18	5,000 Binland (Frank Hedrick)	d 2:03 1/4m
19	5,000 Prince Loree (M. McDevitt)	2:03 1/4m
20	5,000 Peter Manning (Harry Stokes)	2:02 1/2m
21	5,000 Greyworthy (Walter Cox)	2:03 m
22	5,000 Peter The Brewer (Nat Ray)	2:02 1/2m
23	5,000 Rose Scott (T.W. Murphy)	2:04 1/4m
24	5,000 Tilly Brooke (T.W. Murphy)	2:01 1/4m
25	5,000 Etta Druien (T.W. Murphy)	2:02 1/2m
26	5,000 Guy Trogan (W.K. Dickerson)	2:04 1/4m
27	5,000 Kahla Dillon (Tom Berry)	2:02 1/2m
28	5,000 Doane (C. Becker)	e 2:04 m
29	5,750 Guy Ozark (W.K. Dickerson)	2:02 1/2m
30	4,000 Hollywood Chief (W.H. Leese)	2:05 m
31	4,000 Worthywood (W.N. McMillen)	2:04 1/4m
32	-- Not Raced --	
33	1,500 Vansandt (Earl Pitman)	2:05 m
	Calumet Bush (Henry Thomas)	2:06 1/4m
34	4,300 Prince Hall (Henry Thomas)	2:00 3/4m
35	4,800 Taffy Volo (Ben White)	f 2:01 1/4m
36	3,200 Greyhound (Sep Palin)	2:00 m
37	2,000 Rosalind (Ben White)	1:59 1/4m
38	2,000 Boyne (Dunbar Bostwick)	g 2:00 3/4m
39	2,000 Spintell (Doc Parshall)	2:00 3/4m
40	3,000 Sister Mary (Sep Palin)	h 2:01 1/2m
41	3,000 Earl's Moody Guy (V. Fleming)	2:01 3/4m
42	2,000 Nibble Hanover (H. Whitney)	2:02 3/4m
43	3,000 His Excellency (Tom Berry)	2:01 1/4m
44	3,000 Blue Boy (Henry Thomas)	i 2:03 m
45	3,000 Darnley (Harry Whitney)	2:03 1/4m
46	3,000 The Colonel's Lady (Bi Shively)	2:01 m
47	3,000 Victory Song (Sep Palin)	2:02.1m
48	3,000 Rodney (Bi Shively)	2:01 m
49	3,000 Pronto Don (Curly Smart)	j 2:01.2m
50	3,000 Pronto Don (Delvin Miller)	2:00 m
51	3,200 Pronto Don (B.J. Schue)	2:01.3m
52	5,000 Yankee Hanover (Frank Ervin)	2:00.3m
53	2,000 Pronto Don (B.J. Schue)	2:01 m
54	1,800 Pronto Don (B. J. Schue)	k 2:01.4m
55	2,900 Kimberly Kid (Ned Bower)	l 1:59.2m
56	2,900 Scott Frost (Joe O'Brien)	2:00 m
57	1,600 Galophone (Robert Walker)	2:00.4m
58	2,500 Egyptian Princess (E. Avery)	m 2:03.1m
59	3,000 Senator Frost (Dick Buxton)	1:58.4m
60	2,500 Sharpshooter (H. Pownall, Sr.)	2:01.4m
61	2,500 Senator Frost (Dick Buxton)	2:00.3m
	Tie Silk (Howard Beissinger)	2:01 m
62	2,500 Uncle Sam (Lou Huber, Jr.)	2:02.2m
63	2,500 Pack Hanover (Jim Hackett)	2:02.1m
64	1,600 Lucy's Victory (Jim Hackett)	1:59.2m
65	9,370 Governor Armbro (Joe O'Brien)	2:07.3m
66	8,067 Pay Dirt (Earle Avery)	2:04 m
67	8,267 Nevele Pride (Stanley Dancer)	2:06.1m
68	9,515 Nevele Major (Stanley Dancer)	2:00.1m
69	11,850 Timothy T (John Simpson, Jr.)	2:03.1m
70	12,149 Savoir (James Arthur)	2:00.2m
71	500 Hoot Speed (Glen Garnsey)	1:57.3m
72	3,162 Flower Child (Joe O'Brien)	2:01.3m
73	4,255 Delmonica Hanover (Sonny Graham)	1:59.3m
74	4,830 Colonial Charm (Glen Garnsey)	1:56 m
75	4,887 Dream Of Glory (Archie McNeil)	2:03.3m
76	21,418 Zoot Suit (Stanley Dancer)	2:00.1m
77	28,300 Speed In Action (Delvin Miller)	2:00.1m
78	27,900 Doublemint (Peter Haughton)	1:58.2m
79	28,556 Chiola Hanover (Jimmy Allen)	1:58 m
80	34,310 Final Score (Tom Haughton)	1:56.4m
81	43,000 Graf Zepplin (Gary Lewis)	1:58 m
82	51,000 Speed Bowl (Tom Haughton)	n 1:53.3m
83	56,300 T V Yankee (Tom Haughton)	1:56.2m
84	55,861 Impish Legacy (Pekka Korpi)	1:56.3m
85	57,250 Nearly Perfect (Mickey McNichol)o	1:56 m
86	46,500 Royal Prestige (B. Lindstedt)	p 1:57 m
87	93,623 Napoletano (Bill O'Donnell)	R 1:54.3m
88	123,500 Slybowl Hanover (Dan Shetler)	Rq 1:54.3m
89	125,998 Crown's Majesty (Dave Rankin)	1:56.2m
90	119,970 Embassy Lobell (Michel Lachance)r	1:54.2m

a By The Monk.   j By Rodney.
b By Saint Frisco.   k By Kimberly Kid.
c By Ross B.   l By Prince Victor.
d By Esperanze.   m By Philip Frost.
e By Trumpet.   n By Jazz Cosmos.
f By Hollyrood Phillis.   o By Mark Six.
g By Havoline.   p By Long Legend.
h By Dale Hanover.   q By Firm Tribute.
i By Colby Hanover.   r By I'm Impeccable.

The Bluegrass
Three-Year-Old Colt Pace
The Red Mile, Lexington, KY Oct. 5, 1990

70	16,400 Kentucky (Bruce Nickells)	1:57 m
71	14,600 Springfield (Jack Kopas)	2:06.2m
72	15,100 Silent Majority (Wm. Haughton)	1:56.3m
73	18,600 Osborne Creed (Archie McNeil)	1:56.3m
74	18,600 Pickwick Baron (Mel Turcotte)	1:56.3m
75	16,450 Nero (Joe O'Brien)	2:00 m
76	37,968 Keystone Ore (Stanley Dancer)	1:56 m
77	42,000 Super Clint (John Kopas)	1:55.4m
78	40,614 Abercrombie (Glen Garnsey)	1:54.3m
79	47,510 General Star (Keith Waples)	1:54.3m
80	46,450 Tyler B (Bill Herman)	a 1:54.1m
81	50,800 Armbro Wolf (John Campbell)	b 1:54.4m
82	56,800 Billy Dart (D. Richardson, Jr.)	c 1:55.2m
	Temujin (Bill O'Donnell)	1:55.2m
83	65,520 American Freedom (Bill O'Donnell)	1:53.1m
84	65,285 Guts (Mike Gagliardi)	1:52 m
85	66,250 Nihilator (Bill O'Donnell)	1:51.1m
86	63,910 Tyler's Mark (John Campbell)	1:52.2m
87	102,093 Golden Greek (Tom Haughton)	1:52.1m
88	147,430 Keystone Raider (Michel Lachance)	1:51.4m
89	140,840 Goalie Jeff (Michel Lachance)	1:51.2m
90	130,000 Kiev Hanover (Jim Morand)	R 1:50.1m

a By Storm Damage.   c By Billy Dart & Temujin.
b By Slapstick.

The Bluegrass
"The Johnston Memorial"
Two-Year-Old Filly Trot
The Red Mile, Lexington, KY Sept. 26, 1990

76	23,012 Angel's Flight (William Haughton)	2:03.4m
77	22,730 Starita Lobell (Joe O'Brien)	2:00.2m
78	24,981 Precious Memories (Del Miller)	2:00.2m
79	26,640 Tisha Lobell (Ray Tripp)	2:03.2m
80	29,150 Filet Of Sole (J. Simpson, Jr.)	1:58.3m
81	35,600 Ginger Belle (Harold Dancer)	1:59 m
82	42,600 Luv I (Jack Bailey)	a 1:58 m
83	42,620 Arnie's Frilly (Glen Garnsey)	1:57.4m
84	48,337 Armbro Devona (Joe Marsh, Jr.)	1:58.3m
85	50,500 Breena Almahurst (Archie McNeil)	b 2:00.1m
86	99,730 Super Flora (Ron Waples)	Rc 1:56.4m
87	111,845 Anamosa Hanover (Jan Nordin)	1:57.2m
88	110,480 Peace Corps (John Campbell)	R 1:56.4m
89	119,798 Kindava Hush (Jan Nordin)	d 1:58.1m
90	105,630 Frances Jet Boko (Hugo Langeweg)e	1:58 m

a By Tarport Lizzy.   d By Lila Lobell.
b By Britelite Lobell.   e By Armbro Jacuzzi.
c By Armbro Fern.

The Bluegrass
"The K.D. Owen"
Two-Year-Old Filly Pace
The Red Mile, Lexington, KY Sept. 25, 1990

76	34,397 Tall Oaks Jade (Chris Boring)	1:59.3m
77	33,235 Passing Glance (George Sholty)	1:57.3m
78	39,721 Hazel Hanover (Bill Herman)	1:57.1m
79	42,128 D I Sweetie (Ray Ireland)	1:59.3m
80	45,150 Areba Areba (Jack Kopas)	1:58 m
81	64,600 Sconce (John Simpson, Jr.)	a 1:56.2m
82	63,100 Sabella Lobell (Glen Garnsey)	1:55.2m
83	66,500 Secret Wager (Mike O'Donnell)	1:55 m
84	71,657 Stardrift Hanover (M. McNichol)	b 1:55.2m
85	71,180 Sea Quick (Ben Webster)	1:57.4m
86	119,670 Legacy Of Love (Steven Waller)	c 1:57.3m
87	151,810 Sweet Reflection (Wm.O'Donnell)	1:56 m
88	141,167 Central Park West (J.Campbell)	d 1:54.3m
89	121,888 Delinquent Account (John Kopas)	1:55.4m
90	99,250 Shady Daisy (Jeff Fout)	eR 1:51.2m

a By Bartross.   d By Frilly One.
b By Steinam.   e By Miss Easy.
c By Merci.

CHRONICLES

The Bluegrass
The Holly Lane Stud
Three-Year-Old Filly Trot
The Red Mile, Lexington, KY Sept. 28, 1990

76	19,118 Ima Lula (Joe O'Brien)	2:01.3m	85	55,380 Double Coverage (C. Galbraith)	1:57 m	
77	30,243 Superlou (John Simpson Jr.)	1:57.1m	86	54,440 Armbro Ermine (Larry Walker)	R 1:55.1m	
78	28,615 Rosemary (William Haughton)	1:57.2m	87	87,738 Keystone Harem (Jan Nordin)	b 1:55.3m	
79	26,197 Classical Way (J. Simpson Jr.)	2:00.1m	88	90,950 Proximity Three (Chris Boring)	1:56.1m	
80	33,260 Kading (William Haughton)	1:59.1m	89	98,267 Peace Corps (John Campbell)	1:56.4m	
81	32,800 Filet Of Sole (Stanley Dancer)	1:57 m	90	107,480 Model Home (Berndt Lindstedt)	c 1:56.3m	
82	45,250 Ginger Belle (Harold Dancer)	1:57.3m				
83	47,820 Anders Favorite (Jan Nordin)	1:56.2m		a By Fancy Crown.	c By Model Home &	
84	48,896 Petrolianna (B. Lindstedt)	a 1:57 m		b By Armbro Fling.	Cabrera Lobell.	

The Bluegrass
"The Cuddy Farms"
Three-Year-Old Filly Pace
The Red Mile, Lexington, KY Sept. 27, 1990

76	24,680 Keystone Model (William Haughton)	1:58.3m	85	70,350 Amneris (John Campbell)	a 1:55.2m	
77	26,146 Impatiens (Joe O'Brien)	1:56.3m	86	73,210 Sales Girl (Eddie Davis)	1:53.4m	
78	37,470 Lady Albatross (Harold Dancer)	1:55.3m	87	106,491 Pacific (Tom Harmer)	1:53.4m	
79	36,641 Perette Hanover (Carl Allen)	1:58.2m	88	135,220 Leah Almahurst (Bill Fahy)	1:52.3m	
80	44,150 Guiding Beam (Glen Garnsey)	1:57.2m	89	124,292 Cheery Hello (John Campbell)	b 1:53.4m	
81	44,800 Fan Hanover (Glen Garnsey)	1:54.3m	90	96,590 Delinquent Account (John Kopas)	1:53.3m	
82	62,700 Three Diamonds (Bruce Riegle)	R 1:53.1m				
83	61,460 Turn The Tide (Bill O'Donnell)	1:53.2m		a By Town Tattler.	b By Cheery Hello &	
84	74,120 Hit Parade (Bill O'Donnell)	1:54.4m			U Drive It.	

The Breeders Crown
Two-Year-Old Colt Trot
Pompano Park, Pompano Beach, FL Nov. 30, 1990

84	600,750 Workaholic (Berndt Lindstedt)	R 1:57.1m	88	488,218 Valley Victory (Bill O'Donnell)	R 1:58.1f	
85	474,804 Express Ride (John Campbell)	2:01.3f	89	475,212 Royal Troubador (Carl Allen)	1:59.2f	
86	496,850 Mack Lobell (John Campbell)	1:59.1f	90	473,870 Crysta's Best (Dick Richardson)	2:01 f	
87	560,000 Defiant One (Howard Beissinger)	a 2:01.2f		a By Firm Tribute.		

The Breeders Crown
Two-Year-Old Filly Trot
Pompano Park, Pompano Beach, FL Nov. 30, 1990

84	539,825 Conifer (George Sholty)	2:01.2f	88	459,219 Peace Corps (John Campbell)	R 1:57.1f	
85	514,303 JEF's Spice (Mickey McNichol)	R 1:58.4m	89	420,213 Delphi's Lobell (Ron Waples)	1:59.3f	
86	472,850 Super Flora (Ron Waples)	1:59.2m	90	489,870 Jean Bi (Jan Nordin)	2:00.3f	
87	385,912 Nan's Catch (Berndt Lindstedt)	2:00.2f				

The Breeders Crown
Two-Year-Old Colt Pace
Pompano Park, Pompano Beach, FL Nov. 30, 1990

84	772,500 Dragon's Lair (Jeff Mallet)	1:54.1f	88	661,218 Kentucky Spur (Dick Stillings)	1:53.2f	
85	673,553 Robust Hanover (John Campbell)	1:56.4h	89	567,213 Till We Meet Again (M. McNichol)	1:56.2f	
86	819,600 Sunset Warrior (Bill Gale)	1:55.3m	90	605,870 Artsplace (John Campbell)	R 1:51.1f	
87	623,912 Camtastic (Bill O'Donnell)	R 1:56.2h				

The Breeders Crown
Two-Year-Old Filly Pace
Pompano Park, Pompano Beach, FL Nov. 30, 1990

84	555,000 Amneris (John Campbell)	R 1:57.1h	88	573,218 Central Park West (J. Campbell)	R 1:53.3f	
85	632,803 Caressable (Herve Filion)	2:00 h	89	438,213 Town Pro (Doug Brown)	1:55 f	
86	536,100 Halcyon (Ray Remmen)	1:58 h	90	514,870 Miss Easy (John Campbell)	1:54 f	
87	573,912 Leah Almahurst (Bill Fahy)	1:59.4f				

The Breeders Crown
Three-Year-Old Colt Trot
Pompano Park, Pompano Beach, FL Nov. 2, 1990

84	558,000 Baltic Speed (Jan Nordin)	1:57.2f	88	393,506 Firm Tribute (Mark O'Mara)	1:55.3f	
85	613,209 Prakas (John Campbell)	1:57.1f	89	429,700 Esquire Spur (Dick Stillings)	1:56.1f	
86	460,350 Sugarcane Hanover (Ron Waples)	R 1:57.1m	90	396,933 Embassy Lobell (Michel Lachance)	1:56.4f	
87	442,662 Mack Lobell (John Campbell)	R 1:54.1f				

The Breeders Crown
Three-Year-Old Filly Trot
Pompano Park, Pompano Beach, FL Nov. 2, 1990

84	365,000 Fancy Crown (Bill O'Donnell)	1:59.2h	88	351,506 Nalda Hanover (Mickey McNichol)	2:02 h	
85	418,553 Armbro Devona (Bill O'Donnell)	1:57.3f	89	335,701 Peace Corps (John Campbell)	R 1:57 f	
86	470,850 JEF's Spice (Bill O'Donnell)	R 1:59 h	90	378,933 Me Maggie (Berndt Lindstedt)	1:57.1f	
87	390,662 Armbro Fling (George Sholty)	1:57.3f				

CHRONICLES

The Breeders Crown
Three-Year-Old Colt Pace
Pompano Park, Pompano Beach, FL Nov. 2, 1990

84	670,000	Troublemaker (Bill O'Donnell)	1:56 f		88	604,364	Camtastic (Bill O'Donnell)	1:55.1f
85	565,053	Nihilator (Bill O'Donnell)	R 1:53 m		89	377,701	Goalie Jeff (Michel Lachance)	1:54.1f
86	543,850	Masquerade (Richard Silverman)	1:55 m		90	366,933	Beach Towel (Ray Remmen)	R 1:51.2f
87	566,662	Call For Rain (C. Galbraith)	a 1:53 f			a By Call For Rain & Run The Table.		

The Breeders Crown
Three-Year-Old Filly Pace
Pompano Park, Pompano Beach, FL Nov. 2, 1990

84	465,000	Naughty But Nice (Tom Haughton)	1:56.4f		88	357,506	Sweet Refelection (Wm. O'Donnell)	1:55.4f
85	558,333	Stienam (Buddy Gilmour)	1:55.4f		89	285,701	Cheery Hello (John Campbell)	1:55.4f
86	549,849	Glow Softly (Ron Waples)	R 1:56 m		90	304,933	Town Pro (Doug Brown)	R 1:54.4f
87	568,162	Pacific (Tom Harmer)	1:55 f			a By Follow My Star		

The Breeders Crown
Aged Horse Trot *
Pompano Park, Pompano Beach, FL Nov. 2, 1990

85	354,553	Sandy Bowl (John Campbell)	1:56.3f		89	249,738	Delray Lobell (John Campbell)	1:57.2f
86	258,350	Nearly Perfect (Mickey McNichol)	1:57.2h		90	221,458	No Sex Please (Ron Waples)	R 1:55 f
87	219,662	Sugarcane Hanover (Ron Waples)	R 1:54.3m					
88	223,756	Mack Lobell (John Campbell)	R 1:56 h				* - Open Trot in 1985.	

The Breeders Crown
Aged Mare Trot
Pompano Park, Pompano Beach, FL Nov. 2, 1990

86	242,290	Grades Singing (Herve Filion)	1:57.4f		89	289,850	Grades Singing (Olle Goop)	1:57.3f
87	228,162	Grades Singing (Olle Goop)	R 1:58.3h		90	203,458	Peace Corps (Stig Johansson)	R 1:54.2f
88	268,756	Armbro Flori (Larry Walker)	1:59.3h					

The Breeders Crown
Aged Horse Pace *
Pompano Park, Pompano Beach, FL Nov. 2, 1990

85	309,553	Division Street (M. Lachance)	1:52.3f		89	278,238	Matt's Scooter (M. Lachance)	R 1:53.2h
86	301,350	Forrest Skipper (Lucien Fontaine)	1:53.4f		90	273,458	Bay's Fella (Paul Macdonell)	R 1:52.1f
87	359,794	Armbro Emerson (Walter Whelan)	1:54.1h					
88	316,256	Call For Rain (Clint Galbraith)	1:53.2f				* - Open Pace in 1985	

The Breeders Crown
Aged Mare Pace
Pompano Park, Pompano Beach, FL Nov. 2, 1990

86	367,041	Samshu Bluegrass (M. Lachance)	1:56.1f		89	287,686	Armbro Feather (John Kopas)	R 1:56 h
87	307,662	Follow My Star (John Campbell)	1:53.4m		90	200,000	Caesars Jackpot (Bill Fahy)	R 1:52.3f
88	307,256	Anniecrombie (Dave Magee)	R 1:52.3m					

The Bronx Filly Pace
Three-Year-Old Filly Pace *
Yonkers Raceway, Yonkers, NY July 14, 1990

57	22,947	Newport Judy (Del Cameron)	2:13 h		81	54,321	Fan Hanover (Glen Garnsey)	1:59.1h
58	25,163	Kwik (C.J. Fitzpatrick, Jr.)	2:10.4h		82	53,235	Albaquel (D.R. Ackerman)	1:59 h
59	23,352	Honick Rainbow (Stanley Dancer)	2:11.1h			53,235	Yankee Cest (Ron Waples)	2:01.1h
60	25,765	Rapid Transit (Hugh Bell)	2:12.4h		83	49,800	Sudden Urge (Michel Lachance)	1:58.2h
61	45,470	Sweet Miriam (Frank Darish)	2:11 h			50,800	Turn The Tide (Herve Filion)	1:59.1h
62	44,402	Stand By (William Haughton)	2:10.4h		84	40,560	My Melissa (Catello Manzi)	1:58 h
63	54,702	Harry's Laura (Clint Hodgins)	2:02.4h			41,560	Leslie Lobell (J. Patterson, Jr.)	1:58.1h
64	39,791	Bit O'Sugar (William Haughton)	2:05.1h			41,560	Lightning Beach (James Conine)	2:00.2h
65	39,933	Balenzano (George Phalen)	2:03.4h		85	111,020	Semalu D'Amour (Benoit Cote)	1:58.1h
66	35,407	Bonjour Hanover (Stanley Dancer)	2:02.1h		86	57,294	-dh- Sarcastick (Ray Remmen)	1:59.1h
67	25,000	Meadow Elva (John Chapman)	2:01.3h				-dh- MusicalHanover(J.Simpson,Jr.)	1:59.1h
68	35,000	Quickie Hanover (Clint Hodgins)	2:03.3h			58,294	Scamper Hanover (Michel Lachance)	1:59.4h
69	35,000	Scotch Jewel (Glen Garnsey)	2:07.1h		87	41,343	Armbro Feather (John Kopas)	1:59.1h
70	26,660	Timely News (Buddy Gilmour)	2:03.1h			41,343	Shop Till Ya Drop (M. Lachance)	1:59.1h
71	27,247	Overdrawn (Warren Cameron)	2:02.3h			41,343	Time Well Spent (Wm. O'Donnell)	R 1:56.2h
72	27,700	Pammy Lobell (William Haughton)	2:01.1h		88	44,900	Mardi's Crown (Michel Lachance)	1:57.2h
73	24,800	Armbro Norma (William Haughton)	2:04.3h			44,900	Storm Tossed (Frank Popfinger)	1:57.3h
74	44,250	Joannas Time (Ed Lohmeyer)	2:01 h			44,900	Sweet Reflection (Bill O'Donnell)	1:58.1h
75	18,300	Native Amber (Buddy Gilmour)	2:01.4h		89	58,885	L Dees Trish (Michel Lachance)	1:58.1h
76	22,300	Bonjour Karey (Real Cormier)	2:01.3h			58,885	Uptown Swell (Bill O'Donnell)	1:58.1h
77	18,400	Luanne's Jewel (Merritt Dokey)	1:59.3h		90	56,792	Cataclysm (John Campbell)	1:57.3h
78	16,660	Passing Glance (George Sholty)	1:59.2h			56,792	Excited (Bill Fahy)	1:58.1h
79	12,700	Sherry Almahurst (Glen Garnsey)	2:00 h					
80	48,200	Shy Dawn (Lucien Fontaine)	2:00.4h				* - 1-1/16 mile before 1963.	

CHRONICLES

The Campbellville
Two-Year-Old Trot
Mohawk Raceway, Campbellville, ONT Sept. 16, 1990

88	72,625 Rapido (Jorn Kvikstad)	2:02 f			71,000 Nashville Lobell (Ber. Lindstedt)	2:00.4f
	72,625 Ride The Wave (Bill Wellwood)	R 2:00.1f		90	75,500 Tag Team (Jan Nordin)	2:01.4f
89	71,000 Columnist (Jorn Kvikstad)	2:02.1f			77,000 Anders Crown (Jan Nordin)	2:03 f

The Molson Canadian Pacing Derby
Three-Year-Old & Up Pace
Greenwood Raceway, Toronto, ONT July 28, 1990

65	15,280 Jerry Hall (Wally McIlmurray)	* 2:37.2f	78	89,500 Dream Maker (Ron Waples)	1:56.1f
66	14,760 H. A. Meadowlands (Ron Feagan)	2:00.1f	79	100,000 Try Scotch (Shelly Goudreau)	1:57.2f
67	18,900 Good Time Boy (Jimmy Larente)	1:59.4f	80	100,000 Direct Scooter (Warren Cameron)	1:57.3f
68	13,500 Timely Knight (Roger White)	2:01.1f	81	102,500 Royce (Walter Paisley)	1:56.1f
69	41,800 Overcall (Del Insko)	2:00.2f	82	134,500 Willow Wiper (Ray McLean)	1:55.3f
70	49,000 Horton Hanover (Joe O'Brien)	1:59.3f	83	125,500 Cam Fella (Pat Crowe)	1:54.4f
71	55,400 Kentucky (Bruce Nickells)	1:59.3f	84	138,000 Mr. Dalrae (Dave Magee)	1:54 f
72	59,400 Albatross (Stanley Dancer)	1:58.2f	85	124,000 On The Road Again (Buddy Gilmour)	1:55.3f
73	58,300 Sir Dalrae (Jim Dennis)	1:57.3f	86	181,500 Witsend's Gypsy (Larry Walker)	1:53.3f
74	59,700 Otaro Hanover (Herve Filion)	1:58.2f	87	189,900 Indian Alert (Mickey McNichol)	1:54.3f
75	46,150 Rambling Willie (Bob Farrington)	1:58.4f	88	226,750 Indian Alert (Mickey McNichol)	1:54 f
	46,150 Pickwick Baron (Mel Turcotte)	1:58.4f	89	237,500 Camtastic (Tom Harmer)	1:52.4f
76	61,600 Rambling Willie (Bob Farrington)	1:57.4f	90	265,250 Topnotcher (Doug Brown)	R 1:52.2f
77	86,500 Rambling Willie (Bob Farrington)	1:57.1f		* - Raced at 1-3/16 mile.	

The Canadian Trotting Classic
Three-Year-Old Open Trot
Greenwood Raceway, Toronto, ONT June 11, 1990

76	28,100 Keystone Pioneer (Wm. Haughton)	2:01.1f	84	326,000 Sandy Bowl (Ulf Nordin)	1:59.2f
77	61,500 Ima Lula (Joe O'Brien)	2:01.3f	85	241,500 Mark Six (Jan Nordin)	1:59.2f
78	61,500 Glencoe Pride (Percy Robillard)	2:00.4f	86	265,500 Traveling Salesman (Wm. Haughton)	2:00.3f
79	75,000 Doublemint (Peter Haughton)	1:59.4f	87	270,500 N V Worthy (Robert Walker)	1:58.4f
80	75,000 Devil Hanover (Delvin Miller)	2:03.4f	88	311,000 Armbro Goal (Berndt Lindstedt)	R 1:57.2f
81	75,000 Snack Bar (Hakan Wallner)	2:01.4f	89	310,000 Bon Vivant (Michel Lachance)	R 1:57.2f
82	241,500 Incredible Nevele (Glen Garnsey)	2:00.3f	90	207,000 A Worthy Lad (Wm. "Bud" Fritz)	1:59.4f
83	314,000 Joie De Vie (John Campbell)	1:58.3f			

The Cane Pace *
Three-Year-Old **
Yonkers Raceway, Yonkers, NY Aug. 25, 1990

Yr	Purse	Winner	Driver	Time	Starters	Heats	Second ***	Third
55	71,040	Quick Chief	William Haughton	2:11.1h	10	1	Meadow Ace	Libby's Boy
56	71,570	Noble Adios	John Simpson, Sr.	2:09.2h	12	1	Bachelor Hanover	Flourish
57	66,952	Torpid	John Simpson, Sr.	2:09.1h	17	2	Adios Express	Morris Eden
58	60,457	Raider Frost	Hugh Bell	2:08.1h	10	1	Bye Bye Byrd	Thorpe Hanover
59	64,457	Adios Butler	Clint Hodgins	2:09 h	15	1	Adios Oregon	Import Freight
60	65,245	Countess Adios (f)	Delvin Miller	2:08 h	9	1	Betting Time	Bright Knight
61	110,950	Cold Front	Clint Hodgins	2:08.3h	11	1	Henry T Adios	Flying Baker
62	117,542	Ranger Knight	Clint Hodgins	2:13.1h	13	1	Lehigh Hanover	Ritzy Hanover
63	163,187	Meadow Skipper	Earle Avery	1:58.4h	12	1	Overtrick	Timely Beauty
64	123,191	Race Time	Stanley Dancer	2:01.4h	7	1	Bengazi Hanover	Vicar Hanover
65	125,236	Bret Hanover	Frank Ervin	2:01 h	8	1	Bobby T Knight	Scarlet Wave
66	126,915	Romeo Hanover	Bill Myer	1:59.4h	11	1	Buzzy Hanover	Chris Time
67	150,000	Meadow Paige	William Haughton	2:03 h	7	1	Best Of All	King Omaha
68	150,000	Rum Customer	William Haughton	1:59.4h	9	1	Fulla Napoleon	Preferred Time
69	100,000	Kat Byrd	Eldon Harner	2:02.2h	8	1	Hammerin Hank	Bye Bye Sam
70	102,770	Most Happy Fella	Stanley Dancer	1:58.3h	6	1	Shriek	Columbia George
71	106,795	Albatross	Stanley Dancer	2:00 h	7	1	H T Luca	High Ideal
72	107,097	Hilarious Way	John Simpson, Jr.	2:02.2h	12	1	Strike Out	Keystone Pebble
73	100,000	Smog	Vernon Dancer	1:58.4h	9	1	Armbro Nesbit	Valiant Bret
74	121,822	Boyden Hanover	Billy Herman	a 1:59.4h	14	2	Bret's Star	Armbro Omaha
75	200,000	Nero	Joe O'Brien	1:58.4h	13	2	Albert's Star	Tarport Hap
76	200,000	Keystone Ore	Stanley Dancer	1:57.1h	7	1	Raven Hanover	Windshield Wiper
77	286,500	Jade Prince	Jack Kopas	b 1:58.2h	14	2	Nat Lobell	Big Towner
78	307,594	Armbro Tiger	Herve Filion	c 1:58.1h	15	2	Falcon Almahurst	Timely's Best Man
79	336,420	Happy Motoring	Bill Popfinger	1:57.3h	14	2	Hot Hitter	Most Happy Collins
80	321,365	Niatross	Clint Galbraith	1:57.3h	15	2	Trenton Time	Stone Racer
81	373,650	Wildwood Jeb	Jimmy Marohn	1:58.1h	14	2	Eastern Skipper DH/w	Brand New Fella
82	513,500	Cam Fella	Pat Crowe	1:57.3h	19	2	Merger	Lon Todd Hanover
83	559,230	Ralph Hanover	Ron Waples	1:57 h	15	2	Vankirk	Jo-Nathan
84	600,000	On The Road Again	Buddy Gilmour	1:56.4h	23	2	Holmes Hanover	Farmsteads Fame
85	600,000	Chairmanoftheboard	John Campbell	d 1:53.4h	15	2	Falcon Seelster	Niafirst
86	542,764	Barberry Spur	Bill O'Donnell	1:55.1h	20	2	H H Shadow	Amity Chef
87	581,540	Righteous Bucks	M. Lachance	e 1:55.3h	24	2	Golden Greek	Simcoe Hanover
88	583,790	Runnymede Lobell	Yves Filion	1:55.2h	19	2	Squirter	Cameleon
89	621,210	Dancing Master	John Campbell	1:56.2h	21	2	Sandman Hanover	Topnotcher
90	486,550	Jake And Elwood	John Campbell Rg	1:53.4h	13	2	Road Machine	Orange Sovereign

* - Raced as the "William H. Cane Futurity," 1955-1974; As the "Cane Pace," 1975 to present.
** - Raced at 1-1/16 miles before 1963.
*** - Based upon order of finish in final heat.

a By Bret's Star.
b By Big Towner.
c By Abercrombie.
d By Falcon Seelster.
e By Golden Greek.
f By Topnotcher.
g By Sea The USA.

CHRONICLES

The Castleton Farm Stake
Two-Year-Old Trot
Du Quoin State Fair, Du Quoin, IL Sept. 1, 1990

46	12,042	Way Yonder (Thomas Berry)	2:05 1/4m	73	32,185	Anvil (Ned Bower)	2:02 m
47	19,773	Adeline Hanover (Gibson White)	2:05.3m	74	27,362	Bonefish (Stanley Dancer)	j 2:01.2m
48	25,446	Miss Tilly (Fred Egan)	2:05 m	75	31,112	Nevele Thunder (Stanley Dancer)	2:00.3m
49	23,540	Florican (Harry Pownall, Sr.)	a 2:04 m	76	22,987	Jodevin (Joe O'Brien)	2:01 m
50	32,398	Scotch Rhythm (Ralph Baldwin)	2:06 m	77	26,622	Speedy Somolli (H. Beissinger)	k 1:57 m
51	32,119	Duke Of Lullwater (J.Simpson,Sr.)	2:04.2m	78	20,204	Courtly (Hakan Wallner)	2:01.1m
52	26,070	Elby Hanover (Hugh Bell)	2:03.2m	79	27,170	Noble Hustle (Doug Ackerman)	2:00.1m
53	26,186	Newport Dream (Del Cameron)	2:01.3m	80	34,305	Worthy Bowl (William Haughton)	l 1:58.1m
54	23,589	Butch Hanover (Joe O'Brien)	b 2:03.4m	81	49,310	Speed Bowl (Tom Haughton)	1:58.2m
55	22,356	Saboteur (Curly Smart)	2:03.3m	82	126,410	Cape Canaveral (Doug Ackerman)	1:58.1m
56	22,703	Major Newport (Del Cameron)	c 2:04.1m	83	100,344	Excel Hanover (J. Simpson, Jr.)	m 1:58.4m
57	24,366	Mix Hanover (Frank Ervin)	2:04.1m	84	111,793	Ata Joe Montana (Jan Nordin)	n 1:58.2m
58	27,455	Diller Hanover (John Chapman)	2:04.1m	85	90,231	Express Ride (George Sholty)	1:58.2m
59	27,398	Blaze Hanover (Joe O'Brien)	2:03.2m	86	98,365	Ditka Hanover (Jan Nordin)	Ro 1:56.2m
60	23,945	Matastar (Harry Pownall, Sr.)	d 2:02.1m	87	83,066	Bolla (Bill O'Donnell)	1:57.2m
61	25,715	Gallant Hanover (Lou Huber, Jr.)	2:01.3m	88	79,400	Grundy's Kruger (Jan Nordin)	2:01.2m
62	23,314	Florlis (Harry Pownall, Sr.)	e 2:01.1m	89	79,660	Elliotts Express (Wm.O'Donnell)	p 1:57.1m
63	22,282	Big John (Eddie Wheeler)	f 2:02.3m	90	64,600	Dickerson (Jan Nordin)	q 1:59.2m
64	25,289	Noble Victory (Stanley Dancer)	2:00.2m				
65	28,011	Kerry Way (Frank Ervin)	2:08 m				
		Amastar (Gordon Larlee)	2:10 m				
66	22,186	Cardinal Jamie (George Sholty)	2:03.4m				
		Kimberly Dutchess (R. Baldwin)	2:06.2m				
67	23,599	Nevele Pride (Stanley Dancer)	1:58.4m				
68	29,858	Nardins Gayblade (Wm. Haughton)	g 2:04.4m				
69	30,365	Victory Star (Vernon Dancer)	2:02.1m				
70	28,377	Hoot Speed (Glen Garnsey)	h 1:59.1m				
71	25,604	Songcan (Gilles Lachance)	2:00 m				
72	28,961	South Bend (Howard Beissinger)	i 2:01 m				

a By Lusty Song.
b By Scott Frost.
c By Bond Hanover.
d By Peter Frost.
e By Speedy Scot.
f By Dartmouth.
g By Nevele Major & Lindys Pride.
h By Noble Gesture.
i By Blitzen.
j By Skipper Walt.
k By Brisco Hanover.
l By Defiant Yankee.
m By Sandy Bowl & Father Heads Off.
n By Ata Joe Montana & Mack Lobell.
o By Mack Lobell.
p By Armbro Iliad.
q By Dickerson & Torsion.

The Champlain Pace
Two-Year-Old Colt Pace
Mohawk Raceway, Campbellville, ONT Sept. 2, 1990

61	3,431	Armbro Canuck (Howard Beissinger)	2:10 q	79	44,605	Alberton (John Kopas)	2:01.1f
62	2,626	Lynden Chief (A. Holmes)	2:09 q	80	34,822	Armbro Wabash (Ron Waples)	2:01.1f
63	3,682	June Dale Chips (L. Haryett)	2:09.2f		34,822	Kawartha Pace On (Keith Waples)	2:01.4f
64	4,182	Opeongo (Dr. John Findley)	2:07 f	81	130,950	Mr. Dalrae (Jim Dennis)	1:59.4f
65	6,845	Oneida Howard (M. Picard)	2:05.4f	82	113,350	Elwood Hanover (Bill Fahy)	1:57.3f
66	8,645	Sharp'n Smart (John Hayes, Sr.)	2:05.1f	83	126,880	Shogun Almahurst (Ron Waples)	1:58.3f
67	9,895	Maxie Mir (Gilles Gendron)	2:10.1f	84	166,495	Dignatarian (Earl Cruise)	1:58.2f
68	8,853	La Chance Mir (Marcel Dostie)	2:05.4f	85	176,980	Amity Chef (Blair Burgess)	1:57 f
	8,853	Chocolate Eclair (J. Geisel Jr.)	*	86	196,780	Rumpus Hanover (Paul MacDonell)	1:58 f
69	10,021	Countess Mir (Marcel Dostie)	2:09.4f	87	212,375	Chatham Light (John Campbell)	1:56.4f
	10,021	Mr. Terrific (K. Galbraith)	2:06.3f	88	82,974	Call Me Bruce (Ron Waples)	1:59.1f
70	13,975	Rob Ron Tarios (Ron Waples)	2:04.3f		82,974	Happy Paysak (Doug Brown)	1:57.2f
71	13,455	Lynden Bye Bye (Hal McKinley)	2:07.2f		82,974	Shippa Scorch (Larry Walker)	1:58.2f
72	13,952	Rob Ron Ritzar (Keith Waples)	2:04.2f	89	92,295	Till We Meet Again (T. Ritchie)	R 1:53.4f
73	10,901	Dave Hamilton (Garth Workman)	2:07.1f		94,295	Brace Yourself (Jim Miller)	1:55.3f
74	17,515	Pat's Bye Bye (Harold Wellwood)	2:05.4f		94,295	Road Machine (Trevor Ritchie)	1:55.4f
75	13,703	Kojak (Chris Storms)	2:06.2f	90	70,000	Deal Direct (Sam "Chip" Noble)	1:56 f
	13,803	Mr. Bohana (Jerry Duford)	2:05.2f		70,000	Happy Family (Doug Brown)	1:56.2f
76	30,150	Super Clint (Jack Kopas)	2:02.2f		70,000	Mantese (Mickey McNichol)	1:57 f
77	33,818	Mike Seiling (Gord Waples)	2:04 f		70,000	Prudhomme (Rick Zeron)	1:56.2f
78	22,572	Springer (Dave Wall)	2:01.2f		70,000	Silky Stallone (John Campbell)	1:55.2f
	22,773	Bold Zip (D. Mitchell)	2:02.3f			* - Time disallowed	

The Champlain Pace
Two-Year-Old Filly Pace
Mohawk Raceway, Campbellville, ONT Sept. 7, 1990

82	116,214	Armbro Bala (Tom Strauss)	1:58.4f	89	78,696	Stayon Purpose (Michel Lachance)	1:57.1f
83	130,710	Milynn Hanover (Dick Macomber)	2:01 f		78,697	Town Pro (Doug Brown)	R 1:56.3f
84	151,385	Trudy Almahurst (Pete Ruscitto)	a 1:59.1f		80,697	Royal Notice (Carman Hie)	1:57 f
85	171,372	Cher-A-Like (Buddy Gilmour)	2:00.1f	90	83,690	Falcon's Secret (Larry Walker)	1:57.1f
86	165,307	No No Abby (Ron Waples)	1:57.2f		83,690	Laugh Line (John Kopas)	R 1:56.3f
87	181,585	Silver Reign (Bud Fritz)	1:58 f		85,690	Jollie Dame (Bill Gale)	1:58.2f
88	103,480	Keystone Wallis (John Kopas)	1:58.3f				
	103,480	Windy Answer (Ron Waples)	1:58.1f				

a By Hannalee Hanover.

The Champlain Trot
Two-Year-Old Colt Trot
Mohawk Raceway, Campbellville, ONT Sept. 8, 1990

61	3,431	Miss Riddell (E. Rowe)	2:11.1q	73	13,202	LeLand Song (Ken Carmichael)	2:07.1f
62	3,355	Niagara Chance (A. Holmes)	2:12.4q	74	13,907	Diller's Demon (Scott Rowe)	2:09.3f
63	5,215	Sis Herbert (William Herbert)	2:08.1f		14,007	Shawland Belle (Brent Davies)	2:12.1f
64	4,057	Doc Fin (Dr. John Findley)	2:10.4f	75	13,703	Dusty Acclaim (Ron Feagan)	2:11.2f
65	6,795	Stemwinder (Edward Langille)	2:10.4f		13,803	Happy Cindy (Scott Rowe)	2:09.3f
66	8,520	Sharp Hoot (G. Campbell)	2:09.3f	76	29,550	Armbro Sonnet (Larry Walker)	2:09.4f
67	9,895	Davey Mir (Marcel Dostie)	2:11.1f	77	33,617	Demon Tad (Don McKirgan)	2:09.2f
68	12,007	Kawartha Dent (P. Dussault)	2:11.4f	78	22,573	Grand Bucky (Charles Lawson)	2:10.2f
69	10,027	Merrywood Malone (Don Larkin)	2:13.4f		22,773	Gayety Herbert (Jack Herbert)	2:09 f
	10,021	Spring Mir (Marcel Dostie)	2:11 f	79	26,152	Surrogate (John Kopas)	2:07 f
70	13,775	Prince Ezra (Ken Carmichael)	2:10.3f		26,353	No Ma's Model (Ron Waples)	2:06.4f
71	13,465	Garma Fiery (Larry Walker)	2:08.1f	80	34,022	All Candor (Terry Kerr)	2:09.1f
72	13,352	Jahil Devil (Bill Habkirk)	2:16 f		34,223	Verseau Model (Simon Boucher)	2:08.2f

CHRONICLES

81	129,950	Jazz Cosmos (Mickey McNichol)	a 2:03.1f
82	108,850	Crysta's Star (Hakan Wallner)	2:01.2f
83	125,380	Baltic Speed (Trevor Ritchie)	2:01.4f
84	160,495	Nearly Perfect (M. McNichol)	b 2:03.2f
85	179,980	Royal Prestige (Hakan Wallner)	R 2:00 f
86	174,280	Sir Taurus (Steve Condren)	2:01.1f
87	201,875	Continental Spirit (Jan Johnson)	2:02.1f
88	122,460	Ride The Wave (Bill Wellwood)	2:01 f

	122,460	Speedy G B (Doug Brown)	2:02.3f
89	129,442	Antwerp Hanover (J. Simpson, Jr.)	2:02.4f
	131,400	Royal Troubador (Carl Allen)	*
90	131,515	-dh- Crimson Lobell (Ron Waples)	2:04 f
		-dh- Grundy's Mint (Jan Nordin)	2:04 f
	133,515	Super Pleasure (Bill O'Donnell)	2:01.2f

* - Time disallowed

a By Speed Bowl.   b By Ata Joe Montana.

The Champlain Trot
Two-Year-Old Filly Trot
Mohawk Raceway, Campbellville, ONT   Sept. 4, 1990

82	108,850	Armbro Blush (Glen Garnsey)	2:02.2f
83	124,710	Arnie's Frilly (Glen Garnsey)	2:03.3f
84	140,885	Double Coverage (C. Galbraith)	2:03.2f
85	175,872	Britelite Lobell (John Campbell)	2:00.3f
86	165,308	Armbro Fling (George Sholty)	2:00.4f
87	171,085	Anamosa Hanover (Jan Nordin)	2:05.1f
88	74,986	Colette Lobell (Ben Webster)	2:01.4f

	74,986	On A Cruise (Jimmy Takter)	2:03.1f
	74,986	Reeling (Mickey McNichol)	2:02.1f
89	78,696	Armbro Icon (Larry Walker)	R 2:00.1f
	78,697	Goosey Cathy (Jim Whelan)	2:01.3f
	80,697	Cajala (Bob Walker)	2:01.3f
90	221,070	Frances Jet Boko (Jan Nordin)	2:02 f

The Cinderella
Three-Year-Old Filly Pace
Maywood Park, Maywood, IL   Oct. 12, 1990

85	66,000	Bree's Brief (Doug Brown)	R 1:53.4m
	65,000	Seven O'Clock (Ray Remmen)	R 1:53.4m
86	82,600	Annie's Surprise (Mark O'Mara)	1:57.1h
87	81,600	Bit Of Good News (Tom Harmer)	2:00 h
88	40,000	Gotta Get On (James Larente)	1:58.4h
	40,000	Sabra Almahurst (Tom Harmer)	R 1:55.3h

	40,000	Stevos' Marcy (Ron Waples)	1:56 h
89	40,000	Bye Bye Sleepyhead (Dale Hiteman)	1:56.4h
	40,000	Frilly One (Dave Magee)	1:56.4h
	40,000	Labyrinth (Jim Takter)	1:58.2h
90	100,000	Instate Rebate (Dave Magee)	1:59 h

The Clevland Classic *
Three-Year-Old Colt Pace
Northfield Park, Cleveland, OH   Oct. 12, 1990

85	242,370	Chairmanoftheboard (J.Campbell)	1:55.2h
86	292,158	Amity Chef (John Campbell)	1:55 h
87	350,130	Call For Rain (Clint Galbraith)	1:56.1h
88	329,000	Albert Albert (Chris Boring)	1:55.2h
89	276,395	Dorunrun Bluegrass(J.Patterson,Jr)1:56.1h

90	150,000	Jake And Elwood (John Campbell)	R 1:54.4h
	150,000	Kiev Hanover (Jim Morand)	1:55.4h

* - Formerly named the Slutsky Memorial, and raced at Monticello Raceway.

The Coaching Club Trotting Oaks
Three-Year-Old Fillies
Meadowlands, E. Rutherford, NJ   June 27, 1990

41	5,845	Florimel (Harry Pownall, Sr.)	2:10 3/4h
42	4,061	Follow Me (Eddie Havens)	2:11 3/4h
43	7,657	Barbara Babcock (Ben White)	2:04 3/4m
44	7,791	Emily Scott (Fred Egan)	2:06 1/4m
45	10,007	Beatrice Hanover(H.Pownall,Sr.)	2:04 3/4m
46	11,443	Onolee Hanover (F. Safford)	2:08 1/4h
47	10,034	Nymph Hanover (Thomas Berry)	2:09.1h
48	14,011	Adeline Hanover (G. White)	a 2:08.1h
49	15,299	Martha Doyle (Frank Ervin)	2:05 h
50	14,935	Honor Bright (J. Simpson, Sr.)	2:08.1h
51	17,911	Betsy Volo (Delvin Miller)	2:06.3h
52	18,485	Crystal Hanover (Henry Myott)	2:07.1h
53	15,284	Bewitch (Henry Myott)	2:05 h
54	18,299	Stenographer (Delvin Miller)	2:06 h
55	15,819	Arvilla Hanover (Wm. Haughton)	2:07 h
56	14,404	Egyptian Princess (Earl Avery)	2:04 h
57	17,018	Charming Barbara(Wm. Haughton)	2:05.1h
58	19,019	Anna Dares (J. Simpson, Sr.)	2:05 h
59	18,028	Matora Hanover(J.Simpson, Sr.)	b 2:05.2h
60	17,746	Elaine Rodney (Clint Hodgins)	2:03.4h
61	22,212	Meadow Farr (Delvin Miller)	2:04 h
62	15,921	Impish (Frank Ervin)	2:02.4h
63	14,208	Kentucky Belle (Ralph Baldwin)	2:04.3h
64	14,760	A.C.'s Jennie (Sanders Russell)	c 2:06.3h
65	16,278	Armbro Flight (Joe O'Brien)	2:03.2h
66	14,053	Mary Donner (Frank Ervin)	2:03.1h
67	12,978	Flamboyant (William Haughton)	2:04 h
68	11,942	Daring Speed (Clint Hodgins)	2:05.4h
69	14,981	Flowing Speed (John Chapman)	2:03.4h
70	10,736	Vanaro (Bill Popfinger)	2:02.1h

71	10,000	My Own Star (Ralph Baldwin)	2:05.3h
72	10,000	Franella Hanover (George Sholty)	2:06 h
73	11,998	Colonial Charm (Glen Garnsey)	R 2:02 h
74	11,910	Devona Hanover (Henri Filion)	2:03.2h
75	11,058	Brilliance (Stanley Dancer)	2:03.2h
76	13,833	Hilary Almahurst (Delvin Miller)	2:02.3h
77	11,988	Royal Clown (David Wade)	2:05 h
78	12,121	Descent (James Arthur)	2:05 h
79	23,210	Soozie Babe (Walt Warrington)	2:03.3m
80	30,000	Rhododendron (Delvin Miller)	2:02.2m
81	72,500	Spring Dash (Hakan Wallner)	2:00.2m
	72,500	One Flash (Hakan Wallner)	2:00.4m
82	79,130	Lucretia's Kash (C. Galbraith)	2:04.1m
	79,130	Dance Spell (Howard Beissinger)	2:07 m
83	83,000	Winky's Gill (Hakan Wallner)	1:57.3m
	80,003	Luv I (Jack Bailey)	1:58.4m
84	86,040	Worth Beein (Stanley Dancer)	1:58.3m
85	90,000	Conch (Hakan Wallner)	1:58.1m
86	75,200	Newmarket S (Bill O'Donnell)	1:57.2m
	73,700	Chickadee Newton (John Campbell)	1:58 m
87	63,000	Armbro Fling (George Sholty)	1:56.4m
	63,000	Armbro Flori (George Sholty)	1:57.4m
88	56,718	Anamosa Hanover (Jan Nordin)	1:57.4m
	58,218	Nan's Catch (Berndt Lindstedt)	1:56 m
89	42,875	Maralie Lobell (Berndt Lindstedt)	1:57.1m
	42,875	Peace Corps (John Campbell)	R 1:55.4m
90	45,987	Delphi's Lobell (Ron Waples)	1:57.3m
	45,987	Lila Lobell (Jan Johnson)	R 1:55.4m

a By Mighty Sister.   c By Speedy Victory.
b By Lady Belvedere.

The Colonial
Three-Year-Old Trot
Rosecroft Raceway, Ft Washington, MD   Oct. 13, 1990

68	100,000	Nevele Pride (Stanley Dancer)	1:59 f
69	100,000	Lindys Pride (Howard Beissinger)	2:00.1f
70	102,275	Timothy T. (John Simpson, Jr.)	2:03.1f
71	103,120	Savoir (James Arthur)	1:59.1f
72	100,000	Super Bowl (Stanley Dancer)	2:02 f
73	103,495	Flirth (Ralph Baldwin)	2:01.2f
74	117,095	Keystone Gabriel (Peter Haughton)	2:01.3f
75	122,970	Meadow Bright (Delvin Miller)	2:02 f

76	124,765	Armbro Regina (Joe O'Brien)	2:00.4f
77	118,495	Green Speed (William Haughton)	1:58.4f
78	113,350	Florida Pro (George Sholty)	1:58.1f
79	112,755	Chiola Hanover (Jimmy Allen)	2:02.1f
80	131,740	Noble Hustle (Doug Ackerman)	2:00.1f
81	132,363	Keystone Triton (Eldon Harner)	2:01 f
82	160,730	Jazz Cosmos (Mickey McNichol)	1:58.1f
83	150,000	Power Seat (Bill O'Donnell)	1:59.1f

CHRONICLES

84	196,480 Why Not (Mickey McNichol)	1:58.3f		
85	190,385 Piggvar (Stanley Dancer)	1:58 f		
86	80,349 Everglade Hanover (Hakan Wallner)	1:59.4h		
	82,349 Jersey Blizzard (Jody Stafford)	2:01.2h		
87	142,455 Mack Lobell (John Campbell)	1:57.2h		
88	103,190 Huggie Hanover (Ron Waples)	2:02.4h		

	103,190 Somollison (Rod Allen)	1:59.4h
89	105,228 Esquire Spur (Don Irvine, Jr.) R	1:56 f
	105,228 Flying Irishman (Harold Kelly)	1:58.2f
90	122,032 Jeanne's Somolli (Rod Allen)	1:56.4f
	122,033 Cheyenne Spur (Dick Stillings) R	1:56.2f

The Colonial Lady *
Three-Year-Old Filly Trot
Rosecroft Raceway, Ft Washington, MD Oct. 13, 1990

82	35,855 Lady Bowl (Jan Nordin)	2:00.2f
83	43,350 Duenna (Stanley Dancer)	2:00.1f
84	27,678 Selena Lobell (Mickey McNichol)	1:58.1f
	27,678 Harmony Lobell (Berndt Lindstedt)	2:01.3f
85	28,763 Davidia Hanover (Gary Lewis)	2:00 f
	28,763 Narva Hanover (Marvin Maker)	2:01 f
86	52,649 Tropical Star (John Campbell)	2:00.1h
87	49,045 Jazzy Jen (John Campbell)	1:59.3h

88	51,177 China Smoke (Richard Silverman)	2:02.2h
	51,177 Kit Lobell (Berndt Lindstedt) R	1:59.2h
89	48,780 Wish For Speed (Tommy Haughton)	1:57.3f
	48,780 Peach Pit (Bill Wellwood)	1:58.3f
90	46,685 Happy Diamonds (Ron Waples) R	1:57 f
	46,685 Me Maggie (Berndt Lindstedt)	1:57.2f
	46,685 Working Gal (Michel Lachance)	1:57.1f
	* - Raced as Cradle Of Liberty prior to 1987	

The Confederation Cup
Three-Year-Old Pace
Flamboro Downs, Dundas, ONT Aug. 26, 1990

77	72,500 Governor Skipper (John Chapman)	1:58.2h
78	93,000 Abercrombie (Glen Garnsey)	1:56.4h
79	110,500 Hot Hitter (Henri Filion)	1:57.3h
80	100,000 Justin Passing (Doug Arthur)	1:58 h
81	100,000 Conquered (John Hayes, Jr.)	1:58 h
82	125,000 Cam Fella (Pat Crowe)	1:58.1h
83	210,000 Time To Cash (M. McNichol)	1:57.3h
84	202,500 On The Road Again (Buddy Gilmour)	1:56.1h

85	250,000 What's Next (John Plutino)	*
86	230,000 Nobleland Sam (Sam Noble III)	1:55.1h
87	378,500 Jate Lobell (Mark O'Mara) R	1:54.1h
88	318,500 Matt's Scooter (Michel Lachance)	1:55 h
89	311,500 Mystery Fund (Bill Gale)	1:56.3h
90	341,000 Apaches Fame (Wm. "Bud" Fritz) a	1:54.2h
a By No Taste.		
	* - Time disallowed	

The Countess Adios
Two-Year-Old Filly Pace
Meadowlands, E. Rutherford, NJ Aug. 2, 1990

77	25,875 JEF's Super Bird (Doug Ackerman)	2:01 m
	25,875 Lady Ferman (Roger Hammer)	2:02.4m
78	38,325 Roses Are Red (Jack Kopas)	1:58 m
	38,325 Hazel Hanover (Billy Herman)	1:58 m
79	63,700 Cool Heel (Peter Haughton)	1:58.3m
	43,525 Thithter Thavage(Shelly Goudreau)	1:59 m
80	43,525 Side By Side (Ben Webster)	1:59.4m
81	55,000 Savilla Lobell (John Kopas)	1:58.1m
	55,000 Classic Tale (Don Harmon)	1:57.2m
	55,000 Three Diamonds (Bruce Riegle)	1:56 m
82	86,500 Turn The Tide (Herve Filion)	1:57.2m
	86,500 Miss Yankee (Ray Remmen)	1:58.2m
	86,500 Armbro Bala (Jack Kopas)	1:58.1m
83	161,000 Hit Parade (Catello Manzi)	1:56.3m
	162,000 DeBuena Lobell (H. Beissinger)	1:56 m
84	114,000 Amneris (Jan Nordin)	1:55.1m
	114,000 Stormy Flo (Ben Webster)	1:56.1m

	114,000 Rodine Hanover (Bill O'Donnell)	1:54.4m
85	150,000 Follow My Star (John Campbell)	1:55.4m
	150,000 Caressable (Bill O'Donnell)	1:56.3m
86	90,000 Valleygirl Hanover (J. Campbell)	1:59 m
	90,000 Nadia Lobell (John Campbell)	1:59.1m
	90,000 Halcyon (John Campbell)	1:58.1m
87	142,000 Dawn Michele (Richard Silverman)	1:56.3m
	142,000 So Cozy (John Campbell)	1:55.2m
88	94,000 Amy Rocklin (John Campbell)	1:56.1m
	94,000 Central Park West (John Campbell)	1:56 m
	94,000 Terri S (D.R. Ackerman)	1:56.2m
89	111,000 Vassar Hanover (Ron Waples)	1:55.4m
	112,000 Lukes Ophelia (Michel Lachance)	1:55 m
90	80,000 Miss Easy (John Campbell) R	1:54 m
	79,000 Laugh Line (John Kopas)	1:56.3m
	80,000 Falcon's Secret (Larry Walker)	1:56.4m

The Courageous Lady *
Three-Year-Old Filly Pace
Northfield Park, Northfield, OH July 21, 1990

85	92,895 Everglade Mitzie (Ed Hysell) R	1:57 h
86	67,807 Queens Over (John Campbell)	1:57.2h
	66,307 Laney B (Mickey McNichol)	2:01 h
87	66,540 Midi A Semalu (Benoit Cote)	1:59 h
	66,540 Kittiwake (Norman Bradbury)	1:58.1h
88	69,605 Conquered Quest (John Campbell)	1:57.2h

	69,605 Sweet Reflection (Bill O'Donnell)	1:58 h
89	119,075 Tyler Town (Peter Ruscitto)	1:57.1h
90	131,500 Excited (Jeff Fout) R	1:56.2h
* - Formerly named the Lady Catskill, and		
raced at Monticello Raceway		

The Currier and Ives
Three-Year-Old Open Trot
The Meadows, Meadow Lands, PA May 26, 1990

75	23,050 Excellent Tad (George Mueller)	2:03.3f
	23,050 Surefire Hanover (Stanley Dancer)	2:00.4f
76	40,000 Steve Lobell (Peter Haughton)	2:02.3f
77	50,000 Green Speed (William Haughton)	2:00.1f
78	50,000 Doublemint (Peter Haughton)	2:02.4f
79	61,815 Dorian's Music (Pius Soehnlen) a	2:02.3f
80	30,255 Burgomeister (William Haughton)	2:01.4f
	30,255 Nevele Impulse (Dick Macomber)	2:03.2f
81	32,216 Mo Bandy (Mike Allen)	2:03.3f
	32,216 Nut Jammer (Danita Harvey)	2:02.3f
82	39,600 -dh- Bone Meal (Bill Zendt)	2:01 f
	-dh- Crysta's Crown (Jan Johnson)	2:01 f
	39,600 Yankee Predator (J. MacDonald)	2:01 f
83	45,850 Joie De Vie (Billy Herman)	1:58.1f
	45,850 Duenna (Stanley Dancer)	1:59.4f
84	46,025 Excel Hanover (Del Miller)	1:57.4f

	46,025 Record Bowl (Tom Haughton)	1:59.3f
85	87,025 Master Willie (Soren Nordin)	1:58.2f
86	50,000 Shane Scottseth (Tom Haughton)	1:59 f
87	65,000 Crown's Best (Per Eriksson)	1:58.1f
	65,000 Porsche Kosmos (Steve Warrington)	1:58.3f
88	42,000 Sir Scot (Per Erikson)	1:59.3f
	42,000 Somollison (Rod Allen)	1:59.3f
	42,000 Stable Gait (Rod Allen)	1:58 f
89	36,623 Classic Air (Jimmy Takter)	1:57.4f
	36,623 Scott S Hanover (George Sholty) R	1:57.3f
	37,123 Sheet Load (Bob Shahan)	1:58.3f
90	38,060 Cheyenne Spur (Dick Stillings)	2:00.4f
	38,060 King Of The Sea (Stanley Dancer)	2:00 f
	38,060 Zizi's Prakas (Har. Brockelhurst)	1:59.4f
a By Chiola Hanover.		

Page 321

CHRONICLES

The Helen Dancer Memorial
Three-Year-Old Filly Pace
Freehold Raceway, Freehold, NJ Sept. 3, 1990

76	16,875	Bonjour Karey (Real Cormier)	2:00.2h	85	88,221	Amneris (John Campbell)	R 1:55 h
	16,875	Sampson's Del Ida (S. Dancer)	2:01 h		88,221	Town Tattler (John Campbell)	1:55.4h
77	29,818	Au Clair (Preston Burris, Jr.)	1:59.4h	86	102,622	Searchparty (Mike Gagliardi)	1:57.4h
78	34,717	Passing Glance (John Chapman)	2:00 h		104,622	Musical Hanover (Harold Dancer)	1:59.1h
79	37,285	Roses Are Red (Jack Kopas)	1:59.3h	87	101,104	Quille Lauxmont (S. Warrington)	1:57.2h
80	50,000	Fast Tracker (Herve Filion)	2:01.3h		101,104	Time Well Spent (Bill O'Donnell)	1:56.4h
81	55,540	Loose News (Harold Dancer)	1:58.4h	88	110,419	Lakers Fortune (Rich. Silverman)	1:56.2h
82	70,195	Three Diamonds (Bruce Riegle)	1:56.1h		110,419	Sweet Reflection (Bill O'Donnell)	1:56.1h
83	65,770	Napa Valley (John Campbell)	1:56.4h	89	195,585	Tyler Town (Peter Ruscitto)	1:57 h
	65,770	Valley Jewel (Donald Dancer)	1:58.2h	90	107,068	Excited (Bill Fahy)	1:57.3h
84	76,278	Naughty But Nice (Tom Haughton)	1:57 h		107,068	It's Sunny (Carmine Abbatiello)	1:57.4h
	76,278	Margaret Turner (Herve Filion)	1:58 h				

The James B. Dancer Memorial
Three-Year-Old Pace
Freehold Raceway, Freehold, NJ Sept. 1, 1990

76	44,300	Windshield Wiper (Wm.Haughton)	1:57 h	84	268,281	Troublemaker (Bill O'Donnell)	1:54.4h
77	54,143	Kawartha Eagle (Stanley Dancer)	1:58.1h	85	300,000	Nihilator (Bill O'Donnell)	R 1:52.2h
78	66,633	Abercrombie (Glen Garnsey)	1:56.3h	86	328,357	Armbro Emerson (Walt Whelan)	a 1:54.2h
79	70,000	Hot Hitter (Herve Filion)	1:55.4h	87	334,887	Simcoe Hanover (Bill O'Donnell)	1:54.4h
80	10,000	Niatross (Clint Galbriath)	1:56.2h	88	357,188	Keystone Raider (Michel Lachance)	1:55.1h
81	118,469	Eastern Skipper (Herve Filion)	1:56.2h	89	377,650	Goalie Jeff (Michel Lachance)	b 1:55
82	140,705	McKinzie Almahurst (Wm. Haughton)	1:56.2h	90	379,280	Road Machine (Tony Kerwood)	1:54.4h
83	269,080	F Troop (Ron Waples)	1:56.1h				

a By Barberry Spur.   b By Resonator.

The Debutante Stake
Two-Year-Old Filly Pace
Meadowlands, E. Rutherford, NJ June 25, 1990

47	2,546	Marion Direct (Paul Vineyard)	2:13.2h		48,750	Sugar Move (Dick Farrington)	1:58.3m
48	5,074	Television (C.P. Chappell)	2:11.1h		49,750	Bambi Almahurst (Ben Webster)	1:57.3m
49	4,989	Our Time (Frank Ervin)	2:09.4h		49,750	Heida Hanover (Carl Lecause)	1:58.1m
50	7,933	Gay Sadie (Frank Safford)	2:09.2h	82	51,000	J.D.'s Annette (Ben Webster)	2:01.2m
51	8,736	Galleta (Delvin Miller)	2:08.1h		51,000	Tango Almahurst (G. Daisey, Sr.)	1:59 m
52	11,394	Precious Hal (Ralph Baldwin)	a 2:07.4h		51,000	Kala Lobell (Bill O'Donnell)	1:59.1m
53	10,225	Phantom Lady (Frank Ervin)	2:08 h	83	65,000	Whe A Dump (Stanley Dancer)	1:59.3m
54	10,291	Poplar Juliann (Delvin Miller)	b 2:07.2h		65,000	Bermuda Dunes (Ben Webster)	1:59.4m
55	10,449	Elizabeth D. (Curly Smart)	2:06 h		65,000	Maeling Hanover (Bill O'Donnell)	1:58.2m
56	9,663	Adios Fancy (Frank Safford)	c 2:06.2h		65,000	De Buena Lobell (H. Beissinger)	1:58.2m
57	9,505	Traffic Lady (John Simpson, Sr.)	2:08 h	84	72,700	Dazzle Almahurst (Tom Haughton)	1:58.3m
58	10,565	Wonderful Time (Frank Ervin)	2:06 h		72,700	Tyler's Fit (Herve Filion)	1:59.4m
59	11,262	Jan Hanover (William Haughton)	2:04.1h		72,700	Rodine Hanover (Catello Manzi)	1:57 m
60	12,110	Vivian's Adios (Delvin Miller)	2:05.1h	85	74,000	H.H. Silk (Bill O'Donnell)	1:57.4m
61	13,231	Ritzy Hanover (Howard Camper)	2:06 h		74,000	Valentana (William Haughton)	1:57.4m
62	12,517	Timely Beauty (Frank Ervin)	2:04.2h		75,000	Follow My Star (Prince Nickells)	1:57 m
63	15,053	Poplar Wick (Del Insko)	d 2:07.2h	86	59,335	Dawn's Debut (Richard Silverman)	1:58.2m
64	19,015	Beloved Hanover (Stanley Dancer)	2:03.4h		60,335	Naidi Lobell (Peter Ruscitto)	1:56.4m
65	14,800	Bonjour Hanover (Stanley Dancer)	2:03.4h		60,335	Diahn Lynn Lobell (John Campbell)	1:58.2m
66	15,542	Ember Hanover (Richard Thomas)	2:02.3h		60,335	Cheerful Maiden (Tom Haughton)	1:58 m
67	15,617	Mildred Pierce (Earl Avery)	e 2:05.1h	87	64,260	Monterey Almahurst (Tom Haughton)	1:58.3m
68	18,576	Scotch Jewel (Ralph Baldwin)	2:04.2h		65,260	French Dressing(C.Warrington,Jr.)	1:57 m
69	18,497	Betty Hanover (Stanley Dancer)	2:03.1h		65,260	So Cozy (John Campbell)	1:58 m
70	16,170	Keystone Memento (Stanely Dancer)	2:03 h	88	52,500	Central Park West (John Campbell)	1:57 m
71	12,422	Saucy Wave (Harry Harvey)	2:04.4h		52,500	Nadia's Sister (John Campbell)	1:57.4m
72	14,894	All Alert (Glen Garnsey)	f 2:04.3h		52,500	Terri S (Doug Ackerman)	R 1:56.2m
73	16,185	Joannas Time (George Sholty)	2:03.3h	89	47,000	Before Hours (John Campbell)	2:02.4m
74	14,702	Bret's Nicki (John Chapman)	2:04.4h		47,000	Excited (John Campbell)	1:57.2m
75	15,995	Toplady Almahurst (Abe Stoltzfus)	2:02.4h		47,000	Jane Ann Almahurst (Jo. Campbell)	1:57.1m
76	14,510	Gravel Pit (Stanley Dancer)	Rg 2:02 h	90	37,415	Laugh Line (John Kopas)	1:59 m
77	12,711	Angela Hanover (Delvin Miller)	2:03.2h		37,415	Miss Easy (John Campbell)	1:56.3m
78	13,015	Baby Dumpling (Stanley Dancer)	2:02.2h		37,415	Miss Intensity (Bill Fahy)	1:58 m
79	19,542	Cool Heel (Peter Haughton)	2:02.3m				
	19,292	Aldona Ironstone (Syl King, Jr.)	2:01.4m				
80	53,365	Inside Joke (William Haughton)	2:02.3m				
	53,365	Friendly Gift (William Haughton)	2:02 m				
81	48,750	Three Diamonds (Bruce Riegle)	1:58.2m				

a By Adios Ann.   d By Timely Choice.
b By Big Bertha &   e By Scuse Me.
  Bunny Chief.   f By Real Hilarious.
c By Maxine's Dream.   g By Chappaqua Hanover.

The Dexter Cup
Three-Year-Old Trot *
Yonkers Raceway, Yonkers, NY July 7, 1990

60	73,129	Quick Song (Ralph Baldwin)	2:10.4h	72	100,000	Songcan (George Sholty)	2:02.4h
61	83,175	Matastar (Harry Pownall, Sr.)	2:10.1h	73	101,563	Knightly Way (John Simpson, Jr.)	2:03.2h
62	89,721	Lord Gordon (J. Patterson, Sr.)	2:11 h	74	112,380	Surge Hanover (Bill Wellwood)	2:03.4h
63	80,376	Speedy Scot (Ralph Baldwin)	2:11.2h	75	118,525	Songflori (Delvin Miller)	2:02 h
64	78,222	Dartmouth (Stanley Dancer)	2:08.4h	76	166,290	Soothsayer (Delvin Miller)	2:02.4h
65	79,886	Armbro Flight (Joe O'Brien)	2:03.3h	77	166,655	Cold Comfort (Peter Haughton)	2:01.3h
66	87,180	Carlisle (William Haughton)	2:07.2h	78	170,362	Brisco Hanover (Jim Miller)	2:01 h
67	183,463	Flamboyant (William Haughton)	2:04.3h	79	175,225	Chiola Hanover (Jimmy Allen)	2:02.2h
68	166,746	Nevele Pride (Stanley Dancer)	2:02.2h	80	186,022	Nevele Impulse (Dick Macomber)	2:02.2h
69	173,455	Lindys Pride (Howard Beissinger)	2:03.3h	81	233,955	Defiant Yankee (H. Beissinger)	2:01 h
70	111,514	Marlu Pride (Herve Filion)	2:01.2h	82	273,578	Mystic Park (Frank O'Mara)	2:01.2h
71	107,686	Quick Pride (Stanley Dancer)	2:03 h	83	376,004	Joie De Vie (Buddy Gilmour)	1:59.2h

CHRONICLES

84	388,341	Speed Merchant (Tony Quartarolo)	1:59.2h	88	221,366	Armbro Goal (Berndt Lindstedt)	1:59.4h
85	362,560	Master Willie (Jan Nordin)	2:00 h	89	138,479	H H Killington (Jody Stafford)	2:02.1h
86	348,537	Mangrove (Stanley Dancer)	2:00 h	90	186,682	Royal Troubador (Carl Allen)	R 1:58.3h
87	167,962	Crown's Best (John Campbell)	2:00.3h			* - 1-1/16 mile before 1965.	

The Governor Alfred E. Driscoll Final
Free-For-All Pace
Meadowlands, E. Rutherford, NJ July 7, 1990

77	186,000	Rambling Willie (Bob Farrington)	1:55.1m	84	203,000	Glen Almahurst (Eddie Davis)	1:52.1m
78	152,000	Whata Baron (Lew Williams)	1:54.4m	85	174,000	Tuff Choice (John Campbell)	1:53 m
79	171,000	Dream Maker (Ron Waples)	1:54.3m	86	180,000	Forrest Skipper (Lucien Fontaine)	1:51.3m
80	167,000	Tijuana Taxi (Jim Miller)	1:54.3m	87	178,000	Governors Choice (Jim Doherty)	1:51.3m
81	193,000	Royce (John Campbell)	1:53.4m	88	200,000	Jaguar Spur (Dick Stillings)	1:50.3m
82	164,000	Genghis Khan (Bill O'Donnell)	1:53.4m	89	196,000	Matt's Scooter (Mich. Lachance)	R 1:50.1m
83	183,000	Cam Fella (Pat Crowe)	1:53.2m	90	211,000	T K's Skipper (Michel Lachance)	1:51.2m

The First Lady
(Filly Division of the Presidential Stakes)
Two-Year-Old Filly Pace
Rosecroft Raceway, Oxon Hill, MD Nov. 3, 1990

85	125,775	Caressable (William Haughton)	2:00 h	88	175,505	Southtown (Bill Fahy)	1:59 h
86	171,306	Halcyon (Ray Remmen)	1:57.4h	89	167,825	Yankee Goddess (Doug Snyder)	R 1:55.3f
87	153,790	Sweet Reflection (Wm. O'Donnell) R	1:57.3h	90	144,701	Cams Exotic (Doug Brown)	1:56.3f

The Founders Gold Cup
Three-Year-Old Trot
Vernon Downs, Vernon, NY July 7, 1990

67	25,000	Keystone Pride (William Haughton)	2:02 q	82	147,500	Mystic Park (Frank O'Mara)	c 1:56.4q
68	25,000	Nevele Pride (Stanley Dancer)	1:58.4q	83	160,000	Play Action (Marty Allen)	d 1:59.1q
69	30,000	Dayan (Fred Bradbury)	2:03.1q	84	171,000	Baltic Speed (Jan Nordin)	1:56.3q
70	30,000	Timothy T. (John Simpson, Jr.)	1:58.4q	85	155,000	Prakas (Ron Waples)	R 1:56 q
71	57,530	Keystone Hilliard (V. Dancer)	a 1:59.3q	86	149,000	Royal Prestige (Berndt Lindstedt)	1:57.4q
72	46,015	Super Bowl (Stanley Dancer)	1:58.3q	87	160,000	Buckfinder (Bill O'Donnell)	Re 1:56 q
73	52,329	Knightly Way (J. Simpson, Jr.)	2:05.4q	88	125,000	Firm Tribute (Mark O'Mara)	1:57 q
74	63,665	Buckeye Count (Hakan Wallner)	b 1:58.4q	89	165,000	Demilo Hanover (Bern. Lindstedt)	f 1:57.3q
75	68,000	Bonefish (Stanley Dancer)	1:59 q	90	140,100	Star Mystic (Jan Johnson)	1:57.1q
76	75,000	Quick Pay (Richard DeSantis)	2:05.2q				
77	100,000	Speed In Action (Delvin Miller)	1:57.2q		a By Speedy Crown.	e By Mack Lobell.	
78	85,000	Speedy Somolli (H. Beissinger)	1:57.4q		b By Anvil.	f By Fortunate One.	
79	107,500	Chiola Hanover (Jimmy Allen)	1:57.4q		c By Arndon.		
80	110,000	Burgomeister (William Haughton)	1:57.4q		d By Play Action &		
81	157,500	Graf Zepplin (Gary Lewis)	1:59 q		Bone Breaker.		

The Fox Stake
Two-Year-Old Pace
Indiana State Fair, Indianapolis, IN Aug. 25, 1990

27	14,887	Red Pluto (Sep Palin)	2:06 m	65	58,559	Romeo Hanover (Bill Myer)	1:59 m
28	11,841	Baron Hall (John Case)	2:09 1/2m	66	61,718	Best Of All (Jim Hackett)	1:59.2m
29	11,996	Capital Stock (W.J. Hodson)	2:06 1/2m	67	67,037	Golden Money Maker (Harold Dancer)	1:58.4m
30	8,568	Corporal Lee (Lyman Brusie)	2:06 1/2m	68	67,341	Laverne Hanover (Wm. Haughton)	j 1:59.4m
31	8,352	Calumet Cheater (Thomas Berry)	2:02 1/2m	69	71,327	Truluck (George Sholty)	1:57.4m
32	6,447	Logan Scott (W.T. Britenfield)	a2:02 m	70	71,030	Albatross (Harry Harvey)	1:58.3m
33	3,325	Laurel Hanover (Thomas Berry)	2:08 m	71	68,112	Strike Out (John Hayes)	1:58 m
34	4,303	The Auctioneer (Sep Palin)	2:12 1/2m	72	76,492	Ricci Reenie Time (Harold Dancer)	1:57.2m
35	7,076	Worthy Grattan (Warren Dennis)	2:04 1/2m			Faraway Bay (Dick Buxton)	1:57.4m
36	9,051	Dusty Hanover (Henry Thomas)	2:04 m	73	70,528	Boyden Hanover (George Sholty)	k 1:59 m
37	9,450	The Widower (Vic Fleming)	2:05 1/2m	74	100,000	Alert Bret (Glen Garnsey)	l 1:58 m
38	10,495	Blackstone (Doc Parshall)	2:04 m	75	100,000	Bit O Fun (Warren Cameron)	1:57.4m
39	11,980	William Cash (W.T. Britenfield)	2:05 m	76	105,721	Crash (William Haughton)	m 1:55.3m
40	14,920	Blackhawk (Delvin Miller)	b 2:03 1/4m	77	100,000	Say Hello (Bill Popfinger)	1:56 m
41	16,965	Court Jester (Rupert Parker)	2:04 1/4m			Spicy Charlie (Frank Popfinger)	1:56.2m
42	16,240	Adios (Rupert Parker)	2:05 3/4h	78	113,681	Crackers (Peter Haughton)	n 1:55.3m
43	12,703	Attorney (Earnest Smith)	2:06 1/4h	79	127,477	Storm Damage (William Haughton)	1:57 m
44	15,690	True Chief (Thomas Berry)	2:06 1/2h	80	171,416	Slapstick (Jack Parker Jr.)	1:55.4m
45	19,651	Ensign Hanover (Sep Palin)	2:09 1/2h	81	161,247	Temujin (Clarence Martin, Sr.)	o 1:54.2m
46	20,585	Poplar Byrd (Thomas Berry)	c 2:02 m	82	167,492	Fame (Bill O'Donnell)	1:55.3m
47	29,019	Knight Dream (Frank Safford)	2:01.2m	83	185,390	Radiant Ruler (John Campbell)	p 1:54.3m
48	32,159	Good Time (Frank Ervin)	2:03.2m	84	188,492	Marauder (Dick Richardson, Jr.)	1:53.4m
49	29,358	Our Time (Frank Ervin)	2:03.2m	85	160,380	Happy Chatter (Doug Ackerman)	q 1:55 m
50	33,477	Solicitor (Delvin Miller)	d 2:03.1m	86	190,600	Jate Lobell (Mark O'Mara)	1:54.1m
51	33,680	Thunderclap (Edgar Leonard)	e 2:04.4m	87	222,155	Albert Albert (Chris Boring)	1:52.4m
52	32,942	Iosola's Ensign (Curly Smart)	2:03 m	88	164,412	Beach Walker (Tom Haughton)	1:53.3m
53	41,137	Meadow Pace (Joe O'Brien)	f 2:01.2m	89	159,666	Till We Meet Again (M.McNichol)	r 1:52.1m
54	29,444	Captain Adios (Delvin Miller)	g 2:02 m	90	103,362	Deal Direct (Sam "Chip" Noble)	R 1:51.4m
55	26,578	Bachelor Hanover (Wm.Haughton)	h 2:00.4m		a By His Majesty.	j By Santas Fury.	
56	34,815	Torpid (J. Simpson, Sr.)	1:59.4m		b By Victorious Hal.	k By Romanline.	
57	42,131	Thorpe Hanover (Delvin Miller)	i 2:00.2m		c By Goose Bay.	l By Broadcaster B.	
58	46,436	Meadow Al (Joe O'Brien)	2:00.3m		d By Tar Heel.	m By Racy Goods.	
59	50,469	Bullet Hanover (J. Simpson, Sr.)	1:57 m		e By Thunderclap &	n By Sonsam.	
60	42,193	Adios Cleo (J. Simpson, Sr.)	1:59.2m		Silent Waters.	o By Icarus Lobell.	
61	55,635	Coffee Break (George Sholty)	1:58.1m		f By Excellent Chief.	p By Panorama.	
62		-- Rain --			g By American Way.	q By Freight Saver.	
63	57,351	Race Time (Ralph Baldwin)	1:58 m		h By Greentree Adios.	r By Righthand Man.	
64	54,308	Bret Hanover (Frank Ervin)	1:58 m		i By Raider Frost.		

CHRONICLES

The Stewart Fraser Memorial
Open Pace
Edmonton Northlands, Edmonton, ALTA Oct. 13, 1990

81	125,000	Dorado Hanover (G. Gendron)	1:56.3f	87	200,000	Armbro Emerson (Walter Whelan)	1:54.3f
82	175,000	Justin Passing (Pat Crowe)	1:57.3f	88	200,000	E Jay Bullet (Don Monkman, Jr.)	1:55.3f
83	81,500	Cam Fella (Pat Crowe)	1:55 f	89	200,000	Matt's Scooter (Mich. Lachance) R	1:52 f
84	200,000	Energy Burner (Tom Merriman)	1:56. f	90	230,000	Topnotcher (Doug Brown)	a 1:53.3f
85	200,000	On The Road Again (Buddy Gilmour)	1:54.3f				
86	200,000	Hy Class Minbar (Alvin Bowman)	1:54.2f		a By Sandman Hanover.		

The Thomas P. Gaines Memorial
Three-Year-Old Pace
Vernon Downs, Vernon, NY July 28, 1990

72	57,325	Strike Out (Keith Waples)	1:58 q			-dh- Hamilton RH (Dg. Ackerman) c	1:55.2q
73	54,624	Ricci Reenie Time(Harold Dancer)a	1:56.4q	84	200,000	Walton Hanover (Harold Dancer)	1:54 q
74	73,910	Boyden Hanover (Billy Herman)	1:56 q	85	182,000	Flight of Fire (Mickey McNichol)	1:53.3q
75	81,500	Nero (Joe O'Brien)	1:56.3q	86	175,000	Miraculous Moment (M. Barrieau)	1:54.3q
76	93,500	Windshield Wiper (P. Haughton) b	1:58 q	87	191,000	Jaguar Spur (Dick Stillings)	1:54.1q
77	109,000	Kawartha Eagle (Stanley Dancer)	1:55.4q	88	206,000	Camtastic (Bill. O'Donnell)	1:54 q
78	107,000	Flight Director (Joe O'Brien)	1:57.4q	89	224,500	Dexter Nukes (John Campbell) R	1:52.3q
79	120,000	Sonsam (George Sholty)	1:54 q	90	184,500	Till We Meet Again (Bill Fahy) d	1:53.3q
80	137,500	Niatross (Clint Galbraith)	1:53.3q				
81	145,000	Computer (Jack Parker, Jr.)	1:54.3q		a By J.R. Skipper.	d By Brando Hanover &	
82	150,500	Rompin Home (Bill O'Donnell)	1:56.1q		b By Richmond.	Till We Meet Again	
83	192,000	-dh- Better Heather (T.Haughton)c	1:55.2q		c BY Power Bunny.		

The Garden State Pace
Two-Year-Old Open
Freehold Raceway, Freehold, NJ Aug. 25, 1990

82	188,994	Big Band Sound (William Haughton)	1:58.1h		108,895	Prince Royce (Ted Wing)	1:58.3h
83	111,651	Jariz (Bill O'Donnell)	1:59.1h		111,895	Folio (Ron Waples)	1:59 h
	111,651	Walton Hanover (J. Simpson, Jr.)	1:57.2h		111,895	Money Lender (John Campbell)	1:58.2h
84	105,201	Praised Dignity (Bill Popfinger)	1:59 h	88	114,698	Beach Walker (Michel Lachance)	1:58.2h
	105,201	Witsend's Wizard (Ron Waples)	1:57.4h		114,698	Nukes Image (Mickey McNichol)	1:56.2h
	105,201	Devil's Adversary (Abe Stoltzfus)	1:58 h		117,698	King Cam (Michel Lachance)	1:57.4h
85	188,035	Tijuana Blue Chip (W. Case, Jr.)	1:54.2h	89	133,598	Captain Scooter (Mickey McNichol)	1:58.2h
	188,035	Laughs (Michel Lachance) R	1:55.1h		133,598	Kiev Hanover (Dick Stillings)	1:57.1h
86	93,950	Golden Greek (Tom Haughton)	1:57.2h	90	89,451	Cambest (Dave Rankin)	1:56.1h
	90,950	Ezra Almahurst (Mickey McNichol)	1:58.3h		89,451	Nuclear Legacy (Bill Fahy)	1:57.3h
	93,950	Nukem (Richard Silverman)	1:56.4h		92,451	Shark Almahurst (Bill Fahy)	1:56.4h
	93,950	Dictionary (Bill O'Donnell)	1:58.4h		92,451	Three Wizzards (Ben Webster)	1:56 h
87	108,895	Pied Piper (C. Warrington, Jr.)	1:57.4h				

The Goldsmith Maid Final
Two-Year-Old Filly Trot
Garden State Park, Cherry Hill, NJ October 24, 1990

90	294,600	Kramer Nobless (Jan Johnson)	2:00.2m

The Goshen Cup
Two-Year-Old Pace
Meadowlands, E. Rutherford, NJ June 28, 1990

49	10,000	Irish Hal (H.C. Fitzpatrick)	2:08.3h		44,582	Bo Bo (Ben Steall)	2:00 m
50	10,000	Tar Heel (William Haughton)	2:07.2h		44,582	Steady Card (George Phalen)	2:01.1m
51	10,000	Gander (Hugh Bell)	a 2:06.4h	81	51,000	J.J.'s Biltmore (Jack Bailey)	1:59 m
52	12,850	Knight Star (Frank Safford)	b 2:07.1h		51,000	Deerfield (Bruce Riegle)	1:59.2m
53	16,450	Parker Byrd (Frank Ervin)	2:05 h		50,000	No Nukes (Ben Webster)	1:56.3m
54	10,000	Adios Evret (Robert Myer)	2:04.3h		50,000	Icarus Lobell (Henri Filion)	1:57.3m
55	11,950	Queen's Knight (Frank Safford)	2:04.4h	82	48,000	Rashad (Bill Popfinger)	1:59.2m
56	13,950	Airliner (Ned Bower)	2:07.3h		48,000	Torino Lobell (Ben Webster)	1:58.4m
57	13,350	Pat Rainbow (Clint Hodgins)	2:07 h		48,000	C.F. Magnum (Carl Allen)	1:57.4m
58	13,800	Adios Day (Ned Bower)	c 2:04.4h		48,000	Fortune Teller (Eldon Harner)	1:58 m
59	16,350	Muncy Hanover (Earle Avery)	2:04.1h		48,000	Carafe (Bill O'Donnell)	1:56.3m
60	15,450	Henry T Adios (S. Dancer)	d 2:03.1h	83	55,500	Grand Duke (Bill Popfinger)	1:58.2m
61	13,350	Play Bill (Frank Ervin)	2:04.3h		55,500	First Attraction (Wm. Haughton)	1:58 m
62	15,300	Majestic Hanover (Stanley Dancer)	2:04.1h		55,500	Andy's Popeye (Herve Filion)	1:58.1m
63	17,400	Vicar Hanover (William Haughton)	2:04.1h		55,500	Farmstead's Fame (Tom Haughton)	1:58.2m
64	17,700	Bret Hanover (Don C. Miller)	2:03 h		55,500	Southern Style (William Haughton)	1:59.3m
65	21,300	Overcall (John Patterson, Jr.)	2:01.4h		55,500	Sky Tracer (Tom Haughton)	1:59.1m
66	14,323	Romulus Hanover (Wm. Haughton) R	2:01.2h	84	71,270	Ramblin' Storm (Walter Case, Jr.)	1:56.4m
67	13,090	Fulla Napoleon (Richard Thomas)	2:02 h		71,270	Town Council (William Haughton)	1:57.2m
68	18,559	Laverne Hanover (Wm. Haughton)	2:04.2h		71,270	Nihilator (William Haughton)	1:57.2m
69	20,357	Sir Carlton (Leroy Copeland)	e 2:03.3h		71,270	Devil's Adversary (Abe Stoltzfus)	1:57.1m
70	17,481	Count Bret (Herve Filion)	2:03.4h	85	65,500	Tropic March (Eddie Davis)	1:57.2m
71	11,922	Cory (George Sholty)	2:03.2h		65,500	Freight Saver (Ben Webster)	1:57.4m
72	16,212	Valiant Bret (John Wilcutts)	2:03.1h		65,500	Boone And Crockett (J.Parker,Jr.)	1:56.1m
73	16,956	Southampton V (Herve Filion)	f 2:03 h		65,500	Prairie Lobell (John Plutino)	1:57.2m
74	16,065	John V. (Roland Beaulieu)	2:04.2h	86	59,068	Nukem (Richard Silverman)	1:56.2m
75	14,445	Henson Hanover (William Haughton)	2:02.4h		59,068	Golden Greek (Tom Haughton)	1:58 m
76	12,748	Governor Skipper (John Chapman)	2:01.4h		59,068	Dictionary (Bill O'Donnell)	R 1:54.2m
77	11,074	Vaudeville (Stanley Dancer)	2:03.2h		59,068	Laag (Bill O'Donnell)	1:55.3m
78	11,190	Plat Du Jour (Stanley Dancer)	2:06.2h		59,068	Casino Gambler (Ron Waples)	1:55.4m
79	20,611	Whamo (Charlie Clark)	1:59.2m	87	54,540	Barbara's Prince (D.R. Ackerman)	1:58 m
	20,611	Brets Reign (Herve Filion)	1:59.4m		54,540	Chatham Light (Bill O'Donnell)	1:56.3m
80	42,982	Skipper's Ensign (S. Goudreau)	2:01.2m		54,540	Curbside (Tom Haughton)	1:57 m
	42,982	French Chef (Stanley Dancer)	2:00.3m		54,540	No Direction (John Plutino)	1:57.4m

CHRONICLES

	54,540	Pied Piper (C. Warrington, Jr.)	1:55.2m		55,500	Secret Asset (Bill O'Donnell)	1:55.4m
	54,540	Pops Punch (John Plutino)	1:56.2m		55,500	Talon Almahurst (John Campbell)	1:54.3m
	54,540	Video Dancer (Ron Waples)	1:55.4m	90	35,075	Brett's Story (Michel Lachance)	1:57 m
88	43,218	Hit The Bid (Bill O'Donnell)	1:55.1m		35,075	Lefty (John Campbell)	1:55.3m
	43,218	Jamboree (Norm Dauplaise)	1:57.4m		35,075	Mantese (Mickey McNichol)	1:56.1m
	43,218	Nukes Image (Mickey McNichol)	1:57.4m		35,425	Henry Letsgo (John Campbell)	1:55 m
	43,218	Subway (Jack Moiseyev)	1:57.1m		a By David Caudle. d By Adios Don.	
	43,218	Totally Ruthless (John Campbell)	1:57.1m		b By Iosola's Ensign. e By Ideal Donut.	
89	55,500	Sea The USA (Michel Lachance)	1:56.2m		c By Adios Chief. f By Bestman Hanover.	

The Governor's Cup
Two-Year-Old Colt Pace
Garden State Park, Cherry Hill, NJ Nov. 17, 1990

85	1,357,500	Barberry Spur (Bill O'Donnell)	1:54.1m	88	705,100	How Bout It (Tom Haughton)	1:54.3m
86	1,513,500	Redskin (Bill O'Donnell)	1:55 m	89	681,100	In The Pocket (John Campbell)	1:54.2m
87		-- Not Raced --		90	655,600	Artsplace (John Campbell)	R 1:53

The Graduate Pacing Series Final
Four- and Five-Year-Olds
Meadowlands, E. Rutherford, NJ May 19, 1990

78	125,000	Dream Maker (Ron Waples)	1:55.3m	85	128,000	Mystery Skipper (John Campbell)	1:54.1m
79	112,500	Double Splendor (Archie McNeil)	1:56 m	86	139,000	Forrest Skipper (L. Fontaine)	R 1:51.3m
80	122,500	Direct Scooter (Warren Cameron)	1:56.2m	87	157,000	Quite A Sensation (J. Campbell)	1:53.3m
81	12,546	Safe Arrival (Ron Waples)	1:54.1m	88	161,500	Call For Rain (Clint Galbraith)	R 1:51.3m
82	127,000	Willow Wiper (John Campbell)	1:57.1m	89	152,500	Jaguar Spur (Bill Fahy)	1:52.1m
83	130,500	Cam Fella (Pat Crowe)	1:53.4m	90	205,500	Dorunrun Bluegrass (Her. Filion)	R 1:51.3m
84	130,500	Boomer Drummond (John Campbell)	1:53.2m				

The Greyhound
Two-Year-Old Trot - Review Stake
Illinois St. Fair, Springfield, IL Aug. 15, 1990

42	5,018	Volo Song (Ben White)	2:08 3/4h	70	33,050	Hoot Speed (Glen Garnsey)	2:01.2m
43	4,825	Enac (Rupert Parker)	2:12 3/4h	71	28,070	Super Bowl (Vernon Dancer)	2:04.3m
44	9,823	Algiers (H.C. Fitzpatrick)	2:07 m	72	35,440	Volstar Hanover (Joe O'Brien)	2:01 m
45	12,546	Bombs Away (Sep Palin)	2:05 1/2m	73	28,120	Moot Point (Ralph Baldwin)	f 2:03.4m
46	14,234	Way Yonder (Thomas Berry)	2:06 m	74	28,340	Bonefish (Stanley Dancer)	2:00.4m
47	14,368	Rollo (Del Cameron)	a 2:06.2m	75		-- Rain --	
48	20,650	Miss Tilly (Fred Egan)	2:05.3m	76	47,120	Speed In Action (Delvin Miller)	g 2:01.1m
49	16,809	Florican (H. Pownall, Sr.)	b 2:06.2m	77	39,230	Speedy Somolli (H. Beissinger)	1:59.3m
50	23,162	Mighty Fine (Delvin Miller)	2:04.4m	78	75,488	Legend Hanover (Joe O'Brien)	h 2:00.1m
51	21,840	Duke Of Lullwater(J.Simpson,Sr.)	c 2:04.3m	79	80,594	Netted (Hakan Wallner)	1:59 m
52	16,664	Elby Hanover (Hugh Bell)	2:05.3m	80	102,028	Smokin Yankee (Stanley Dancer)	i 1:59.1m
53	22,628	Newport Dream (Del Cameron)	2:02.3m	81	97,259	Self Confident (Doug Ackerman)	1:57.3m
54	18,358	Childs Hanover (Frank Ervin)	2:04.1m	82	50,000	Desert Night (Jan Nordin)	2:00 m
55	16,250	Saboteur (Curly Smart)	2:03.1m		50,000	Yankee (Tom Haughton)	1:58.4m
56	17,114	Double Scotch (Gene Mattucci)	d 2:03.4m	83	112,383	Arsenal (Hakan Wallner)	1:57 m
57	20,030	Way Cloud (Robert Walker)	2:03.4m	84	152,432	Myles Hanover (B. Lindstedt)	Rj 1:56.2m
58	23,288	Diller Hanover (John Chapman)	2:06 m	85		-- Rain --	
59	23,719	Blaze Hanover (Joe O'Brien)	2:03 m	86	130,740	Buckfinder (Bill O'Donnell)	1:57.1m
60	18,311	Matastar (Harry Pownall, Sr.)	2:02.3m	87	125,620	Firm Tribute (Mark O'Mara)	1:57.1m
61	22,307	Gallant Hanover (Lou Huber, Jr.)	2:03.1m	88	113,000	Keystone Dominator (J. Campbell)	k 2:00 m
62	19,483	Speedy Scot (Ralph Baldwin)	2:01.4m	89	122,000	Super Arnie (Berndt Lindstedt)	1:56.3m
63	17,842	Dartmouth (Lawrence Garton)	2:03.3m	90	110,000	Dickerson (Jan Nordin)	1:58.1m
64	20,300	Marengo Hanover (J. Simpson, Sr)	2:03.3m		a By Adeline Hanover. f By My Super Pride.	
65	26,127	Amastar (Gordon Larlee)	e 2:02.3m		b By Lusty Song. g By Jodevin.	
66	23,230	Speedy Streak (Frank Ervin)	2:04.3m		c By Hardy Hanover. h By Saint Francis.	
67	26,244	Nevele Pride (Stanley Dancer)	2:00.1m		d By Double Scotch & i By Worthy Bowl.	
68	32,480	Lindys Pride (Howard Beissinger)	2:01.1m		Hoot Song. j By Speed Boots.	
69	37,150	Timothy T. (John Simpson, Sr.)	2:02.1m		e By Governor Armbro. k By Grundy's Kruger.	

The Hambletonian
Three-Year-Old Trot
Meadowlands, E. Rutherford, NJ Aug. 4, 1990

Yr	Purse	Winner (f - filly)	Driver	Time	Starters	Heats	Second *	Third
26	73,451	Guy McKinney	Nat Ray	2:04 3/4	14	2	Guy Dean	Ellie Trabue
27	54,694	Iosola's Worthy (f)	Marv Childs	2:03 3/4	7	2	Nescopec	Benelwyn
28	66,226	Spencer	W.H. Lessee	2:02 1/2	10	2	Guy Abbey	Scotland
29	60,309	Walter Dear	Walter Cox	2:02 3/4	8	2	Volomite	Sir Guy Mac
30	56,859	Hanover's Bertha (f)	Tom Berry	2:03 m	10	3	Larkspur	Guy Day
31	50,921	Calumet Butler	R.D. McMahon	2:03 1/4	6	3	Keno	Calumet Belricka
32	49,489	The Marchioness (f)	Will Caton	a 2:01 1/4	7	4r **	Invader	Hollyrood Dennis
33	40,459	Mary Reynolds (f)	Ben White	2:03 3/4	12	3	Brown Berry	Meurice
34	25,845	Lord Jim	Doc Parshall	2:02 3/4	8	4r	Muscletone	Princess Peg
35	33,321	Greyhound	Sep Palin	2:02 1/4	9	2	Warwell Worthy	Pedro Tipton
36	35,643	Rosalind (f)	Ben White	2:01 3/4	10	2	Brownie Hanover	Ed Lasater
37	37,912	Shirley Hanover (f)	Henry Thomas	2:01 1/2	12	2	DeSota	Farr
38	37,962	McLin Hanover	Henry Thomas	2:02 1/4	10	2	Earl's Princess Martha	Champlain
39	40,502	Peter Astra	Doc Parshall	2:02 1/4	10	2	Gauntlet	Sir Walter
40	43,658	Spencer Scott	Fred Egan	2:02 m	9	2	Remus	Kuno
41	38,729	Bill Gallon	Lee Smith	2:05 m	9	2	His Excellency	Merwynna
42	38,954	The Ambassador	Ben White	2:04 m	11	3	Pay Up	Scotland's Comet
43	42,298	Volo Song	Ben White	2:02 1/2m	10	3	Worthy Boy	Phonograph
44	33,577	Yankee Maid (f)	Henry Thomas	2:04 m	11	2	Emily Scott	Enac
45	50,196	Titan Hanover	Harry Pownall, Sr	2:04 m	19	2	Kimberly Hanover	Axomite
46	50,995	Chestertown	Thomas Berry	2:02 1/2m	11	3	Victory Song	Deanna
47	46,267	Hoot Mon	Sep Palin	2:00 m	13	3	Rodney	Way Yonder

Page 325

CHRONICLES

48	59,941	Demon Hanover	Harrison Hoyt	2:02 m	11	2	Rollo	Egan Hanover
49	69,791	Miss Tilly (f)	Fred Egan	2:01.2m	18	2	Volume	Rocco Hanover
50	75,209	Lusty Song	Delvin Miller	2:02 m	13	2	Star's Pride	Lord Steward
51	95,263	Mainliner	Guy Crippen	2:02.3m	20	2	Spennib	Scotch Rhythm
52	87,637	Sharp Note	Bion Shively	2:02.3m	16	3	Hit Song	Duke Of Lullwater
53	117,117	Helicopter (f)	Harry Harvey	b 2:01.3m	23	3	Morse Hanover	Singing Sword
54	106,830	Newport Dream	Del Cameron	2:02.4m	16	2	Princess Rodney	Harlan
55	86,863	Scott Frost	Joe O'Brien	2:00.3m	11	2	Galophone	Leopold Hanover
56	100,603	The Intruder	Ned Bower	2:01.2m	18	3	Valiant Rodney	Nimble Colby
57	111,126	Hickory Smoke	John Simpson, Sr.	2:00.1m	21	3	Hoot Song	Buckeye Demon
58	106,719	Emily's Pride (f)	Flave Nipe	1:59.4m	14	3	Little Rocky	Mr Saunders
59	125,283	Diller Hanover	Frank Ervin	2:01.1m	15	2	Tie Silk	Circo
60	147,481	Blaze Hanover	Joe O'Brien	c 1:59.3m	19	4r	Quick Song	Hoot Frost
61	131,573	Harlan Dean	James Arthur	1:58.2m	13	2	Caleb	Matastar
62	116,612	A.C.'s Viking	Sanders Russell	1:59.3m	15	2	Isaac	Safe Mission
63	115,549	Speedy Scot	Ralph Baldwin	d 1:57.3m	14	3	Florlis	Elma
64	115,281	Ayres	John Simpson, Sr.	2:02.4m	9	2	Big John	Speedy Count
65	122,245	Egyptian Candor	Del Cameron	e 2:03.4m	11	4r	Armbro Flight	Short Stop
66	122,540	Kerry Way (f)	Frank Ervin	1:58.4m	12	2	Polaris	Shatter Way
67	122,650	Speedy Streak	Del Cameron	2:00 m	12	2	Keystone Pride	Speed Model
68	116,190	Nevele Pride	Stanley Dancer	1:59.2m	9	2	Keystone Spartan	Dart Hanover
69	124,910	Lindys Pride	Howard Beissinger	1:57.3m	9	2	The Prophet	Smokey Morn
70	143,630	Timothy T	John Simpson, Jr.	f 1:58.2m	15	3	Formal Notice	Flower Child
71	129,770	Speedy Crown	Howard Beissinger	1:57.2m	9	2	Savoir	AC's Orion
72	119,090	Super Bowl	Stanley Dancer	1:56.2m	7	2	Delmonica Hanover	***
73	144,710	Flirth	Ralph Baldwin	1:57.1m	16	2	Florinda	Noble Jade
74	160,150	Christopher T	William Haughton	1:58.3m	22	2	Nevele Diamond	Noble Sovereign
75	232,192	Bonefish	Stanley Dancer	g 1:59 m	13	4r	Yankee Bambino	Noble Rogue
76	263,524	Steve Lobell	William Haughton	1:56.2m	18	4r	Zoot Suit	Armbro Regina
77	284,131	Green Speed	William Haughton	1:55.3m	16	2	Texas	Native Starlight
78	241,280	Speedy Somolli	Howard Beissinger	h 1:55 m	8	3	Florida Pro	Brisco Hanover
79	300,000	Legend Hanover	George Sholty	1:56.1m	12	2	Chiola Hanover	Butch Lobell
80	293,570	Burgomeister	William Haughton	1:56.3m	19	2	Final Score	Devil Hanover
81	838,000	Shiaway St Pat	Ray Remmen	i 2:01.1m	24	3r	Super Juan	Olaf
82	875,000	Speed Bowl	Tom Haughton	1:56.4m	21	2	Jazz Cosmos	Roz T Collins
83	1,080,000	Duenna (f)	Stanley Dancer	1:57.2m	25	2	Joie De Vie	Winky's Gill
84	1,219,000	Historic Freight	Ben Webster	j 1:56.2m	23	3r	Delvin G Hanover	Gentle Stroke
85	1,272,000	Prakas	Bill O'Donnell	1:54.3m	17	2	Torway	Ron B Hanover
86	1,172,082	Nuclear Kosmos	Ulf Thoresen	k 1:55.2m	29	2	Royal Prestige	Britelite Lobell
87	1,046,300	Mack Lobell	John Campbell	R 1:53.3m	15	2	Napoletano	Spotlite Lobell
88	1,156,800	Armbro Goal	John Campbell	1:54.3m	13	2	Firm Tribute	Rule The Wind
89	1,131,000	Park Avenue Joe/Probe ****		l 1:54.3m	11	3r	DH for win	Peace Corps
90	1,346,000	Harmonious	John Campbell	1:54.1	20	2	Embassy Lobell	King Of The Sea

* - Second- and third-place finishers determined by best in summary.
** - "r" next to number of heats indicates there was a race-off.
*** - Flush and Spartan Hanover divided third and fourth monies.
**** - Park Avenue Joe (Ron Waples driving) finished in a dead heat with Probe (Bill Fahy) in the race-off. They were later declared co-winners, but Park Avenue Joe, based upon a 2-1-1 summary, as opposed to Probe's 1-9-1 summary, was awarded first money.

a By Hollyrood Dennis.
b By Morse Hanover.
c By Quick Song & Hoot Frost.
d By Florlis.
e By Armbro Flight.
f By Formal Notice.
g By Yankee Bambino.
h By Speedy Somolli & Florida Pro.
i By Super Juan.
j By Delvin G. Hanover.
k By Royal Prestige.
l By Probe.

Raced at The New York State Fairgrounds, Syracuse, NY .... 1926 & 1928
Raced at The Red Mile, Lexington, KY .... 1927 & 1929
Raced at Good Time Park, Goshen, NY 1930-1942; 1944-1956
Raced at Empire City, Yonkers, NY 1943
Raced at The Du Quoin State Fair, Du Quoin, IL 1957-1980
Raced at The Meadowlands, E. Rutherford, NJ .... 1981 until present

The Hambletonian Oaks
Three-Year-Old Filly Trot
Meadowlands, E. Rutherford, NJ Aug. 3, 1990

71	31,500	Gay Blossom (Glen Garnsey)	2:00 m		83	313,825	Tarport Frenzy (Jan Nordin)	1:57.4m
72	32,480	Sara Lane Hanover (Joe O'Brien)	2:00.1m		84	354,000	Fancy Crown (Bill O'Donnell)	R 1:55.3m
73	32,685	Colonial Charm (Glen Garnsey)	2:01.2m		85	401,000	Conch (Hakan Wallner)	d 1:56.4m
74	34,865	Berna Hanover (Glen Garnsey)	2:03.3m		86	397,000	JEF's Spice (Mickey McNichol)	1:56 m
75	57,692	Keystone Pioneer (Dick DeSantis)	1:59 m		87	338,780	Armbro Fling (George Sholty)	1:56 m
76	60,474	Ima Lula (Joe O'Brien)	a 1:56.3m		88	395,300	Man's Catch (Berndt Lindstedt)	1:55.3m
77	65,686	Elmsford (Henri Filion)	1:57.3m		89	423,000	Park Avenue Kathy (B.Nickells)	eR 1:55.3m
78	70,000	Cora T (Billy Herman)	b 1:57.3m		90	441,555	Working Gal (Michel Lachance)	f 1:56 m
79	140,000	Pagan Princess (Peter Haughton)	c 1:58.3m					
80	74,820	Princess Glory (Bill Popfinger)	1:57.4m				a By Japa.	d By Dash Alone.
81	219,000	Spring Dash (Berndt Lindstedt)	2:02.4m				b By Rosemary.	e By Peach Pit.
82	256,000	Dance Spell (Howard Beissinger)	1:58.3m				c By Superior Sweep.	f By Delphi's Lobell.

The Hanover Colt Stake*
Two-Year-Old Trot
Rosecroft Raceway, Oxon Hill, MD Sep. 14, 1990

65	16,277	Governor Armbro (Joe O'Brien)	2:07.1f		71	27,391	Super Bowl (Vernon Dancer)	2:01.4f
	16,477	Proud Vic (Marcel Dostie)	2:05.4f		72	26,487	Arnie Almahurst (Gene Riegle)	2:05 f
66	28,228	Keystone Pride (William Haughton)	2:05.2f		73	29,015	Surge Hanover (Bill Wellwood)	2:06 f
67	26,277	Nevele Pride (Stanley Dancer)	2:03.3f		74	30,035	Yankee Bambino (Walter H. Ross)	2:02.1f
68	17,011	Dayan (John Wilcutts)	2:03.4f		75	25,360	Nevele Thunder (Stanley Dancer)	2:02.2f
	17,011	Gun Runner (Earle Avery)	2:03.1f		76	27,585	Green Speed (William Haughton)	2:01 f
69	29,854	Victory Star (Vernon Dancer)	2:03.4f		77	24,635	Noble Art (Delvin Miller)	2:04.4f
70	26,202	Quick Pride (Delvin Miller)	2:04.3f		78	25,148	Scotty Graduate (Syl King, Jr.)	2:06.1f

Page 326

CHRONICLES

79	24,787	Flickory Flies (Donald Dancer)	2:03.3f		15,500	Buckfinder (Jan Nordin)	1:59.3f
80	25,442	Nathan Lobell (James Dancer)	2:03.3f	87	20,615	Huggie Hanover (Ron Waples)	2:01.2f
81	28,020	Scottish Wind (Stanley Dancer)	2:02 f		20,615	Sports Idol (Ron Waples)	2:02.2f
82	29,907	Lass Quick (Soren Nordin)	2:05 f	88	17,735	Demilo Hanover (John Campbell)	2:00.4f
83	27,018	Delvin G Hanover (Hakan Wallner)	2:01.3f		18,052	Egyptian Gentleman (Jorn Kvikstad)	2:01.4f
84	18,484	Torway (Paul Ruhl)	2:02.2f	89	29,170	Grundy's Rambo (Walter Ross, Sr.)	2:01.4f
	18,484	Flak Bait (Ben Webster)	2:01.3f	90	14,274	UConn Don (Jorn Kvikstad)	2:01.2f
85	18,233	Sir Cronos (Ross Hayter)	2:01.4f		14,024	Dontellmenomore (Bob Mazeroski) R	1:59.1f
	17,983	Mangrove (Stanley Dancer)	2:03.2f		14,274	Anabolic Ben (Ben Steall)	2:01.2f
86	15,500	C Lewis Lauxmont (Jan Nordin)	1:59.4f				
	15,750	Sir Taurus (Jan Nordin)	2:00 f		* - Raced at Freestate Raceway prior to 1990		

The Hanover Colt Stake *
Two-Year-Old Pace
Rosecroft Raceway, Oxon Hill, MD Aug. 26, 1990

65	16,785	Overcall (John Patterson)	2:01.4f	83	23,146	Farmstead's Fame (Tom Haughton)	1:58.3f
	16,785	Effrat Hanover (Joe O'Brien)	2:02.2f		22,896	Electric Guitar (Stanley Dancer)	1:56.3f
	16,785	Tarport Paul (Delvin Miller)	2:03.1f	84	19,622	Meadow Aussie (Billy Herman)	1:59 f
66	22,314	Romulus Hanover (Wm. Haughton)	2:02 f		19,872	Dragon's Lair (Jeff Mallet)	1:56.4f
	22,314	Nardins Byrd (William Haughton)	2:01.1f		19,622	Town Council (Marvin Maker)	1:59.3f
67	40,027	Batman (Del Cameron)	2:06 f	85	15,391	Boone And Crockett (J.Parker,Jr)	2:01.2f
68	23,826	Hammerin Hank (George Sholty)	2:02 f		15,641	Freight Saver (Marvin Maker)	1:58.1f
	23,826	Laverne Hanover (Wm. Haughton)	2:00.1f		15,641	Singer's Star (William Haughton)	1:57 f
69	23,782	Columbia George (Roland Beaulieu)	1:59.3f		15,641	Maritime Hanover (W. Case, Jr.)	1:57.3f
	23,982	Truluck (George Sholty)	1:59 f	86	14,230	Ima Fool Too (Kim Vincent)	2:00.3f
70	21,593	Nansemond (Herve Filion)	2:00.1f		14,230	Keep It Up (Don Irvine, Jr.)	1:58.4f
	21,593	Veri Special (Herve Filion)	1:59.2f		14,230	Zaxson (Ron Waples)	2:01 f
71	22,190	Strike Out (Buddy Gilmour)	1:59.1f		14,230	Crimson (Jody Stafford)	1:57.2f
	22,190	Berry Hanover (Vernon Dancer)	2:01 f		14,230	Jiffy Pop (Norm Parker)	1:58.3f
72	40,222	Valiant Bret (Harry Tudor)	2:01.3f	87	17,370	Barstow Hanover (Doug Snyder)	1:56.3f
73	23,662	Boyden Hanover (Billy Herman)	2:00 f		17,620	Big Eyes (Ted Wing) R	1:55.4f
	23,662	Southampton V. (Herve Filion)	1:59.3f		17,620	Eddie The Quick (Ben Webster)	1:58.4f
74	25,065	Scarsdale (Jimmy Larente)	2:00.2f		17,620	Pied Piper (C. Warrington, Jr.)	1:56.2f
	25,315	Nero (Joe O'Brien)	1:58.4f	88	17,900	Keystone Rambo (Roger Hammer)	1:57.3f
75	21,492	Windshield Wiper (Peter Haughton)	2:00.1f		17,900	Mizner (Don Irvine, Jr.)	2:00.4f
	21,492	Bit O Fun (Warren Cameron)	1:58.4f		17,900	Platoon Leader (Don Irvine, Jr.)	1:59.2f
76	20,557	Jonquil Hanover (George Sholty)	2:01.1f	89	15,242	-dh- Danforth (Tom Haughton)	1:59.3f
	20,807	Jade Prince (Jack Kopas)	1:59.1f			-dh- Dr No No (Bill Popfinger)	1:59 f
77	33,915	Spicy Charlie (Bill Popfinger)	1:58.3f		15,242	Havoc Hanover (Bruce Ranger)	1:58.2f
78	21,381	J Js Metro (William Haughton)	1:59.3f		15,242	Spirited Style (Jim Brittingham)	1:58.1f
	21,381	Mostest Yankee (Billy Herman)	1:58.3f		15,492	Chefs Magic (Steve Warrington)	1:57.1f
79	35,317	Jiffy Boy (Marvin Maker)	1:58.1f	90	13,611	Front View (Don Irvine, Jr.)	1:58.1f
80	40,992	Center Square (John Kopas)	1:58.3f		13,611	Hahn Hanover (Michel Lachance)	1:55.3f
81	42,049	Keystone Icy (Clint Warrington)	2:01.1f		13,611	Hello Almahurst (Roger Hammer)	1:56.3f
82	23,788	Doctor Nero (William Andrews)	2:00 f		13,611	Thunderball (Eddie Davis)	1:56.2f
	23,788	Jules Hanover (Mickey McNichol)	2:00.3f		* - Raced at Freestate Raceway prior to 1990		

The Hanover Colt Stake *
Three-Year-Old Trot
Rosecroft Raceway, Oxon Hill, MD July 22, 1990

66	24,605	Carlisle (William Haughton)	2:02.2f	83	18,153	Micron Hanover (J. Simpson, Jr.)	2:01.4f
67	27,378	Keystone Pride (William Haughton)	2:02.1f		18,153	Joie De Vie (Billy Herman)	2:00 f
68	24,371	Snow Speed (Ralph Baldwin)	1:59.3f	84	24,043	Artificial Bait (Billy Herman)	1:58.3f
69	25,981	Dayan (Fred Bradbury)	2:02.2f	85	19,184	Somolli Star (Eldon Harner)	2:01.4f
70	22,876	Timothy T (John Simpson, Jr.)	2:03.4f		19,184	Piggvar (Stanley Dancer)	2:01.3f
71	22,102	Speedy Crown (Howard Beissinger)	1:59.4f	86	19,111	Mr Novak (Soren Nordin)	2:01.1f
72	19,741	Super Bowl (Stanley Dancer)	2:01.3f		19,361	Buck Newton (N. Shoemaker III)	1:58 f
73	21,887	Artie Almahurst (Gene Riegle)	2:02.2f	87	21,650	Crown Sweep (Rod Allen)	1:58.4f
74	25,575	Nevele Diamond (Stanley Dancer)	2:01.3f		21,650	Sir Taurus (Jimmy Takter)	1:58 f
75	23,614	Noble Rogue (Billy Herman)	2:03.4f	88	18,000	Stable Gait (Rod Allen)	1:58.4f
76	24,485	Quick Pay (Richard DeSantis)	2:00 f		18,250	Armbro Gaylord (Tom Sells)	1:59.2f
77	24,695	Green Speed (William Haughton)	1:59.3f		18,250	Southern Newton (Jan Johnson)	1:59 f
78	23,045	Doublemint (Peter Haughton)	2:01.1f	89	19,515	Egyptian Gentleman (J. Kvikstad)	1:59.1f
79	14,364	Getting Even (Ben Steall)	2:01.4f		19,765	Skeet Load (Tom Sells)	1:58.3f
	14,364	Crown's Cristy (H. Beissinger)	2:00.4f	90	19,633	Antwerp Hanover (Jo.Simpson,Jr.)	1:57.3f
80	20,566	Marino Hanover (Scott Forbes)	2:02.2f		19,633	Remus Hanover (Jo.Simpson,Jr.) R	1:56.4f
81	24,544	Uptown (Clint Galbraith)	2:01.3f				
82	17,210	Arndon (Delvin Miller)	2:01 f		* - Raced at Liberty Bell prior to 1986; and		
	17,210	Jazz Cosmos (Mickey McNichol)	2:02.1f		Raced at Freestate Raceway priot to 1990		

The Hanover Colt Stake *
Three-Year-Old Pace
Rosecroft Raceway, Oxon Hill, MD May 26, 1990

66	29,705	Romeo Hanover (George Sholty)	2:01.2f	81	24,593	Artie's Dream (Shelly Goudreau)	1:56.2f
67	31,878	Meadow Paige (Herve Filion)	1:59.1f	82	19,142	Solid Fuel (Shelly Goudreau)	1:59.1f
68	35,839	Fulla Napoleon (R. Thomas)	2:01.2f		18,892	Elitist (Jack Parker Jr.)	1:58 f
69	36,036	Laverne Hanover (Wm. Haughton)	2:00 f	83	19,458	Ciudad Trujillo (Donald Dancer)	1:58.1f
70	33,521	Truluck (Jim Wilcutts)	1:57.3f		19,208	Keystone Exceller (Jim Miller)	1:57.3f
71	27,252	Nansemond (Herve Filion)	1:58.1f	84	20,921	Electric Guitar (S. Dancer)	1:57.4f
72	26,166	Strike Out (John Hayes)	2:01.3f		20,921	Holmes Hanover (Carl Lecause)	1:59 f
73	27,847	Armbro Nesbit (John Wilcutts)	1:58.3f	85	17,922	Stonebridge Skipper(S.War'gton)	1:55.3f
74	29,040	Bye Bye T. (C. Galbraith)	1:59 f		17,922	Stargell (V. Copeland)	1:57.1f
75	27,945	Sirocco Hanover (Robert Samson)	2:00.3f		17,922	Seminole Lobell (Lou Sperendi)	1:57.3f
76	29,820	Keystone Ore (Stanley Dancer)	1:58.4f	86	20,000	Cash Asset (Tom Haughton)	1:55.2f
77	28,240	Seedling Herbert (Wm. Haughton)	1:58 f		20,000	Uncut Jade (Bill O'Donnell)	1:57.4f
78	27,835	Abercrombie (Glen Garnsey)	1:59.1f		20,000	Barberry Spur (Bill O'Donnell)	1:57.3f
79	30,495	Oil Strike (John Hayes Jr.)	1:56.4f	87	25,000	Golden Greek (Tom Haughton)	1:55.3f
80	27,315	Niatross (C. Galbraith)	1:56.1f		25,000	Team Hanover (D. Pinkney Jr)	1:55 f

CHRONICLES

88	18,014 Guida (Jay Picciano)	1:55.2f	
	18,264 Big Eyes (John Hogan)	1:54.3f	
	18,264 Nero's Chariot (Steve Warrington)	1:55.1f	
	18,264 Timothy Lobell (John Hogan)	R 1:54 f	
89	23,165 Mr Mallory (Don Irvine, Jr.)	1:57 f	
90	23,165 Totally Ruthless (Steve Elliott)	1:56 f	
	20,972 Beach Towel (Ray Remmen)	1:54.1f	
	21,223 Kiev Hanover (Donald Dancer)	1:56.2f	

* – Raced at Liberty Bell prior to 1986; and Raced at Freestate Raceway 1987-1989

The Hanover Filly Stake *
Two-Year-Old Trot
Rosecroft Raceway, Oxon Hill, MD July 29, 1990

47	10,079 Tilly Trott (Sep Palin)	2:08.2m	
48	11,826 Martha Doyle (Frank Ervin)	2:12 m	
49	11,166 Mysteria (Delvin Miller)	2:13.3m	
50	13,324 Betsy Volo (Delvin Miller)	2:03.3m	
51	16,041 Kimberly Mine (J. Simpson, Sr.)	2:04.3m	
52	15,164 Earl's Song (Curly Smart)	2:03.1m	
53	19,159 Stenographer (Delvin Miller)	2:03.1m	
54	16,167 Columbia Hanover(J.Simpson,Sr.) a	2:03 m	
55	16,953 Egyptian Princess (Earle Avery)	2:02 m	
56	16,452 Cassin Hanover (Fred Egan)	2:02.3m	
57	18,628 Yankee Lass (Frank Ervin)	2:02.4m	
58	17,096 Merrie Annabelle(J.Patterson,Sr.)	2:00 m	
59	17,625 Carlene Hanover (Ralph Baldwin)	2:02 m	
60	20,053 Florikash (Curly Smart)	2:01.4m	
61	18,155 Impish (Frank Ervin)	R 1:58.3m	
62	20,321 Star Act (Joe O'Brien)	2:01.3m	
63	20,685 A.C.'s Jennie (Sanders Russell)	2:03 m	
64	23,013 Armbro Flight (Joe O'Brien)	2:06.4m	
65	16,860 Mary Donner (Frank Ervin)	2:06.4f	
	16,860 Kerry Way (Frank Ervin)	2:07.1f	
66	26,337 Flamboyant (William Haughton)	2:04.4f	
67	27,412 Ole Hanover (Jim Hackett)	2:09.1f	
68	26,229 Sparkling Molly (John Chapman)	2:03 f	
69	16,478 Lovester (Charlie Clark)	2:05 f	
	16,278 Misty Ayres (Jerry Graham)	2:06 f	
70	25,250 Keystone Selene (Delvin Miller)	2:04.1f	
71	25,901 Killbuck Mary (Dick Buxton)	2:03.3f	
72	26,143 Colonial Charm (Glen Garnsey)	2:04.2f	
73	24,491 Berna Hanover (Glen Garnsey)	2:06.1f	
74	17,687 Edith Lobell (Joe O'Brien)	2:05.1f	
	17,687 Meadow Bright (Delvin Miller)	2:05.1f	
75	24,923 Lindys Super Star (Yves Filion)	2:04.2f	
76	24,882 Countess Star (Glen Garnsey)	2:05.4f	
77	24,056 Speedy Talk (Peter Haughton)	2:03.2f	
78	24,972 Armbro Upsala (Daniel Altmeyer)	2:05.2f	
79	22,234 Saroya (Jan Johnson)	2:06.1f	
80	23,931 Keystone Sister (Marvin Maker)	2:05.1f	
81	26,648 Ginger Belle (Harold Dancer)	2:04.4f	
82	30,706 Montesquieu (William Parker)	2:02.3f	
83	18,058 Tambee's Florette (Eddie Davis)	2:02.3f	
	18,058 Desdemona Hanover (J.Simpson,Jr.)	2:02.3f	
84	16,756 Davidia Hanover (John Campbell)	2:01.4f	
	16,506 Keystone Request (Joe Marsh Jr)	2:02.2f	
85	12,768 Vawn Almahurst (R.M. Roberts)	2:04.3f	
	12,768 Castleton Memo (Joe Marsh, Jr.)	2:02.1f	
	12,518 Why Indeed (H. Beissinger)	2:03.2f	
	12,518 Geisha (Stanley Dancer)	2:04.1f	
86	18,650 Genuine Comfort (Jimmy Takter)	2:04 f	
	18,650 Lucious Almahurst (Rheo Filion)	2:04.3f	
87	18,168 Nanuet Hanover (Per Eriksson)	2:04 f	
	18,418 Proximity Three (C. Foster)	2:02.4f	
88	18,816 Roz's Lady (Eddie Wheeler)	2:05.1f	
	19,066 On A Cruise (Jimmy Takter)	R 2:01.3f	
89	14,459 Bardot Bi (Walter Ross, Sr.)	2:05 f	
	14,459 Camelia Lobell (Per Eriksson)	2:02.2f	
	14,459 Yankee Twilite (Bib Roberts)	2:03.1f	
90	12,805 Frances Jet Boko (Jan Nordin)	2:02.2f	
	12,805 Jean Bi (Jan Nordin)	2:02.3f	
	13,055 Malhana Kaari (Ron Waples)	2:04.1f	
	13,055 Seductive Lass (Don Irvine, Jr.)	2:05 f	

* – Raced at Freestate Raceway prior to 1990
a By Sweet Talk.

The Hanover Filly Stake *
Two-Year-Old Pace
Rosecroft Raceway, Oxon Hill, MD July 27, 1990

47	8,527 Marion Direct (Paul Vineyard)	2:08 m	
48	10,273 Miss Morris Chief (Joe O'Brien) a	2:07.1m	
49	12,316 Beryl Hanover (Gibson White)	R 2:11.1h	
50	12,576 Floating Dream (McKinley Kirk)	2:00.4m	
51	15,178 Silent Waters (J. Simpson, Sr.)	2:03 m	
52	15,049 Pleasant Surprise (M. Kirk)	2:02 m	
53	19,389 Adios Betty (Delvin Miller)	2:01.3m	
54	18,295 Step Lively (Joe O'Brien)	2:02.2m	
55	18,678 Flaming Arrow (Eddie Cobb)	b 2:02 m	
56	18,102 Good Counsel (Frank Ervin)	2:02 m	
57	18,578 Traffic Lady (J. Simpson, Sr.)	2:02 m	
58	18,596 Great Pleasure (Robert Altizer)	2:01.4m	
59	18,175 Countess Adios (Delvin Miller)	R 1:59.2m	
60	16,853 Way Wave (Ralph Baldwin)	2:02 m	
61	19,455 Stancy Hanover (Curly Smart)	c 2:00 m	
62	17,971 Timely Beauty (Frank Ervin)	2:02 m	
63	20,185 Poplar Wick (Del Insko)	1:59.3m	
64	27,713 Bewitch Hanover (J.Simpson, Sr.)	2:02.3m	
65	18,910 Tarport Lib (Delvin Miller)	2:02.3m	
	18,910 Bonjour Hanover (Stanley Dancer)	2:02 f	
66	33,237 Meadow Elva (William Haughton)	2:03.2f	
67	19,406 Armbro Indigo (Joe O'Brien)	2:03.2f	
	19,606 Keystone Widow (Wm. Riddick)	2:04 f	
68	21,295 Adiola Hanover (H. Beissinger)	2:02 f	
	21,295 Shadow Mir (Herve Filion)	2:01.2f	
69	20,654 Fanny Hail (Edward Dunnigan)	2:03.2f	
	20,454 Bardot Hanover (Keith Waples)	2:05.2f	
70	16,093 Jo Hanover (C.J. Fitzpatrick)	2:02.2f	
	16,093 Good Bret (Harold Dancer)	2:03 f	
	16,093 Truthful Waverly (Herve Filion)	2:02.2f	
71	20,825 Myrtle Direct (H. Graham, Jr.)	2:02.1f	
	20,825 Romalie Hanover (Art Hult)	2:00.1f	
72	33,643 Shifting Scene (Charlie Clark)	2:01.4f	
73	36,246 Handle With Care (Wm. Haughton)	2:00.2f	
74	23,057 Silk Stockings (Pres Burris, Jr.)	2:00.2f	
	23,057 Tarport Hap (Delvin Miller)	2:01.1f	
75	32,253 Keystone Model (Peter Haughton)	2:00.1f	
76	21,553 Future Fame (William Haughton)	2:00.1f	
	21,803 Tall Oak's Jade (Joe Adamsky)	1:59.4f	
77	19,778 Funny Bunnie (Norman Dauplaise)	2:02.4f	
	20,028 Happy Blue Chip (Del Insko)	2:01.1f	
78	31,537 Lismore (Harry Harvey)	1:59.4f	
79	18,813 Broom Hilda (Dick Buxton)	2:01.4f	
	18,563 Bunnie Hanover (Stanley Dancer)	2:01.4f	
80	34,906 Fan Hanover (Glen Garnsey)	1:56.4f	
81	41,649 Amorous Wil (Catello Manzi)	2:01 f	
82	40,556 Turn The Tide (Herve Filion)	1:58.2f	
83	15,560 Garbo (Marvin Maker)	2:02.4f	
	15,810 My Melissa (Lew Williams)	2:01.4f	
	15,560 Security First (Lew Williams)	2:02 f	
	13,810 Tracy Sarnel (Lew Williams)	2:04.3f	
84	43,212 Seven O'Clock (Ed Ryan)	1:58.1f	
85	15,955 Angela Ty (Doug Snyder)	1:59.2f	
	15,955 Joy Hanover (Billy Herman)	1:59.3f	
	15,955 Razzle Hanover (Billy Herman)	1:58.4f	
	15,955 Nunny Nanny (Cosmo DePinto)	2:02 f	
86	18,500 Romantic Mood (Ray Remmen)	2:00.2f	
	18,250 Valleygirl Hanover (G. Gendron)	2:00 f	
	18,500 Edith's Girl (Jim Doherty)	1:59.2f	
87	15,000 Eva Marie Semalu (Benoit Cote)	1:58.3f	
	15,000 High Ty (Bill O'Donnell)	1:59.2f	
	15,000 Paulette Rivenoak (Ron Waples)	1:58.2f	
	15,000 So Cozy (John Campbell)	1:58.3f	
	15,250 Sweet Reflection (Wm.O'Donnell)	1:58.3f	
88	14,500 Amy Rocklin (Ron Waples)	1:57.4f	
	14,500 Cafe Mariposa (Paul MacDonell)	1:58.4f	
	14,500 Small Treasure (Ron Waples)	1:59 f	
	14,500 Southtown (Ron Waples)	1:57.4f	
	14,750 Presumed Innocence (Bobby Meyers)	1:58.1f	
89	16,375 Yankee Goddess (Doug Snyder)	1:58 f	
	16,375 Choice Yankee (Jim Morrill, Jr.)	1:56.3f	
	16,625 Lady Dynamo (John Hogan)	1:57.3f	
90	16,460 Heather Lane (Don Irvine, Jr.)	1:57.3f	
	16,460 Yankee Co-ed (Bib Roberts)	1:56.3f	
	16,710 Perfect Together (Rich. Wojcio)	R 1:56.2f	

* – Raced at Freestate Raceway prior to 1990
a Dotty Direct.   c By Ritzy Hanover.
b By Princess Adios.

The Hanover Filly Stake *
Three-Year-Old Trot
Rosecroft Raceway, Oxon Hill, MD July 8, 1990

48	10,884 Voluptuous (Thomas Berry)	2:05 m	49	12,688 Lady Jeritza (Del Cameron)	a 2:03.3m

CHRONICLES

50	11,051	Honor Bright (J. Simpson, Sr.)	2:04.1m	75	21,170	Meadow Bright (Delvin Miller)	2:00.4f
51	14,186	Neola Hanover (Wilbur Ehlen)	2:12.4m	76	22,813	Ima Lula (Joe O'Brien)	2:00.3f
52	16,374	Lu Peck (H.C. Fitzpatrick)	2:02.1m	77	22,632	Elmsford (Henri Filion)	2:00.3f
53	15,451	Earl's Song (Curly Smart)	2:00.2m	78	21,661	Bernadette Lobell (P. Haughton)	2:01.3f
54	18,986	Stenographer (Delvin Miller)	2:00.4m	79	22,617	Pagan Princess (Peter Haughton)	2:00.2f
55	14,960	Sweet Talk (Curly Smart)	2:02 m	80	20,153	Kading (William Haughton)	2:03.1f
56	14,078	Nimble Colby (Ralph Baldwin)	2:00.2m	81	21,850	Keystone Sister (Delvin Miller)	2:04.3f
57	14,652	Charming Barbara (Wm. Haughton)	2:00.3m	82	25,331	Tiffany Star (Ted Andrews)	1:59.3f
58	16,028	Emily's Pride (Flave Nipe) b	2:00.1m	83	17,920	Tarport Lizzy (Billy Herman)	2:01.1f
59	16,946	Sara Black (Robert Walker)	2:00 m		18,170	Lady Lexington (Jan Johnson)	2:01.3f
60	13,925	Carlene Hanover (Ralph Baldwin) c	2:01 m	84	18,471	Mae Jean's Crown (Carl Allen)	2:01.1f
61	16,353	Meadow Farr (Joe O'Brien) Rd	1:59.4m		18,471	Petrolianna (Hakan Wallner)	2:00 f
62	14,205	Worth Seein (Ralph Baldwin)	2:01.1m	85	17,681	Maxine Lobell (Berndt Lidnstedt)	2:00.4f
63	15,271	Elma (J. Simpson, Sr.)	2:01.1m		17,681	Davidia Hanover (Gary Lewis)	1:58.4f
64	17,635	Golden Make It (Joe O'Brien) e	2:01.1m	86	17,862	Meadowmiss Hanover (Jas. Simpson)	2:00 f
65	22,113	Armbro Flight (Joe O'Brien)	2:02.1f		18,112	JEF's Spice (Mickey McNichol)	1:59.2f
66	21,620	Fresh Yankee (Sanders Russell)	2:04 f	87	20,668	Armbro Fling (George Sholty) R	1:58 f
67	24,037	Lana Hanover (Vernon Dancer)	2:05.4f		20,668	Spinning (Jimmy Takter)	1:58.3f
68	19,445	Arbida Hanover (J. Simpson, Sr.)	2:04.1f	88	30,000	Nalda Hanover (Jan Nordin)	2:01.1f
	19,445	Daring Speed (Clint Hodgins)	2:04 f	89	18,553	On A Cruise (Jimmy Takter)	1:58.3f
69	17,509	Extra Bonus (Clifford Boyd)	2:04.1f		18,803	Wolfs Moshava (Robert Turner)	2:00 f
	17,709	Tarport Farr (Buddy Gilmour)	2:05.2f	90	19,041	Eternal Goddess (Bern. Lindstedt)	2:00.1f
70	24,492	Vanaro (Bill Popfinger)	2:02.3f		19,291	Nivea Hanover (Dick Williams II)	2:00.1f
71	20,020	Noble Gal (Herman Graham Jr.)	2:02.2f			* - Raced at Freestate Raceway prior to 1990	
72	20,326	Delmonica Hanover (J.Simpson,Jr.)	2:04.4f		a By Rosamond.		d By Air Medal.
73	20,168	Honeysuckle Rose (Vernon Dancer)	2:03 f		b By Sandalwood.		e By Speedy Victory.
74	21,641	Starlark Hanover (Warren Cameron)	2:02.3f		c By Elaine Rodney.		

The Hanover Filly Stake *
Three-Year-Old Pace
Rosecorft Raceway, Oxon Hill, MD   July 15, 1990

48	9,619	Marion Direct (Paul Vineyard)	2:11.1m	75	24,200	Tarport Hap (Delvin Miller)	2:01 f
49	12,688	Romola Hal (Del Cameron)	2:02.3m	76	25,838	Keystone Model (William Haughton)	1:59.4f
50	11,396	Direct Gal (John Caton)	2:01.3m	77	26,627	Mistletoe Shalee (Stanley Dancer)	2:02 f
51	12,634	Meda Volo (Delvin Miller)	2:00.3m	78	25,911	Proposal (John Hayes, Jr.)	1:59.1f
52	15,512	Silent Waters (Delvin Miller)	2:03 m	79	23,579	Roses Are Red (Jack Kopas)	1:59.2f
53	12,404	Pleasant Surprise (McKinley Kirk)	2:01 m	80	22,403	Guiding Beam (Glen Garnsey)	1:59.1f
54	13,226	Phantom Lady (Frank Ervin)	1:59.4m	81	26,684	Tanzy Lobell (Bill O'Donnell)	1:58.3f
55	15,305	Dottie's Pick (Delvin Miller) a	2:00.4m	82	19,183	Bio Prelude (Jim Miller)	2:00.1f
56	15,228	Flaming Arrow (Eddie Cobb) R	1:58.2m		19,183	Adore (Jim Miller)	1:58.1f
57	14,652	Quick Pick Up (J. Simpson, Sr.)	1:59.3m	83	19,090	Lucky Lady (Richard Hogan)	2:00 f
58	16,228	Sunbelle (Joe O'Brien)	1:59.4m		19,340	Yankee Mistress (Robert Myers)	1:59.3f
59	17,546	Quick Lady (Olin Davis)	1:58.4m	84	19,971	Margaret Turner (Jim Conine)	2:01.1f
60	15,225	Countess Adios (Delvin Miller)	1:59.4m		20,221	Lightning Beach (Jim Conine)	2:00.1f
61	15,453	Way Wave (Ralph Baldwin)	1:58.3m	85	20,456	Seven O'Clock (Delvin Miller)	1:58.4f
62	15,605	Stand By (William Haughton)	2:00.3m		20,456	Amneris (Jan Nordin)	1:57.3f
63	14,471	Timely Beauty (Frank Ervin) b	1:59.3m	86	30,500	Loni Almahurst (Rick Farrington)	1:57 f
64	16,535	Adiolia (George Sholty)	2:03.1m	87	20,000	Diana Lynn Lobell (Gil. Gendron)	1:56.4f
65	14,506	Rescued (James Arthur)	2:02 f		20,000	Halcyon (Ted Wing)	1:57.2f
	14,506	Colleen Napoleon (Richard Thomas)	2:03 f		20,000	Jolibea Hanover (Joe Pavia, Jr.)	1:57 f
66	23,720	Bonjour Hanover (Stanley Dancer)	2:02 f	88	21,742	Haifa (Bob Shahan)	1:59 f
67	27,237	Meadow Elva (William Haughton)	2:01.1f		22,092	Easy Answer (Eddie Lohmeyer)	1:58.4f
68	20,568	Sunnie Tar (Joe O'Brien)	1:59.2f	89	19,700	Cheery Hello (Jim Miller)	1:57.2f
	20,568	Trotwood Tootie (Delvin Miller)	2:01.3f		19,700	Happy Sapphire (Billy Herman)	1:56.2f
69	29,640	Nevele Dream (J. Simpson, Jr.)	2:00.4f		19,700	Kimmy B (Ben Steall)	1:57.1f
70	30,872	Bardot Hanover (Herve Filion)	2:01 f	90	20,386	Choice Yankee (Jim Morrill, Jr.)	1:55.2f
71	24,525	Keystone Memento (Ronald Dancer)	2:01 f		20,386	Fitness Flower (St. Warrington) R	1:55 f
72	24,155	Romalie Hanover (Roland Beaulieu)	1:59.2f			* Raced at Freestate Raceway prior to 1990	
73	22,768	Real Hilarious (Lew Williams)	2:01.2f				
74	24,431	Joannas Time (John Wilcutts)	1:59.1f		a By Amber Rodney.		b By Glad Rags.

The Hanover-Hempt Farm Stake
Two-Year-Old Colt Trot
Vernon Downs, Vernon, NY   July 17, 1990

60	12,935	Harlan Dean (James Arthur)	2:07.1h		11,300	Haygood (Marcel Lariviere)	2:06.1q
61	12,912	A.C.'s Viking (Sanders Russell)	2:08.1h		11,300	Delvin Hanover (William Haughton)	2:03.4q
62	12,102	Frosty Hanover (M.J. Duer Jr.) R	2:07 h		11,300	Meadow Frank (Delvin Miller)	2:03 q
63	15,670	Speedy Count (William Haughton) R	2:03 f	77	14,200	Noble Move (Glen Garnsey)	2:02.4q
64	10,940	Marengo Hanover (J. Simpson, Sr.)	2:03.2f		13,900	Wide Acclaim (Glen Garnsey)	2:03.2q
	10,640	Atlanta Georgia (James Arthur)	2:05.2f	78	11,900	Gridiron Lad (Carl Allen)	2:03 q
65	10,236	Governor Armbro (Joe O'Brien)	2:06.4f		12,200	Courtly (Hakan Wallner)	2:04.2q
	10,236	Gay Sam (Joe Lighthill)	2:05.2f		12,200	Super Way (J. Simpson, Jr.)	2:03.4q
66	14,324	Pomp (Harry Pownall Sr.)	2:06 f	79	12,700	Noble Hustle (Doug Ackerman)	2:03.1q
67	14,723	Nevele Pride (Stanley Dancer)	2:02.3f		12,400	Choctaw Brave (Howard Beissinger)	2:01.3q
68	10,023	Thats Great (William Haughton)	2:08.2f		12,700	Rodney's Best (Jan Johnson)	2:02.3q
	10,023	Voltaire Hanover (Harold Dancer)	2:05.4f	80	16,300	Snack Bar (Hakan Wallner)	2:08.4q
69	11,197	Victory Star (Vernon Dancer)	2:05.1f		16,600	Keystone Triton (Eldon Harner)	2:09.4q
	11,497	Mustapha (Clifford Boyd)	2:06.4f		16,600	Smokin Yankee (Stanley Dancer)	2:07 q
70	11,618	Noble Gesture (Herman Graham,Jr.)	2:04.3f	81	14,300	Speed Bowl (Tom Haughton)	2:04.2q
	11,318	Quick Pride (Delvin Miller)	2:05.4f		14,300	Self Confident (Doug Ackerman)	2:04.4q
71	10,426	Hambo Hope (John Schroeder)	2:05 f		14,300	Newfi Hanover (J. Simpson, Jr.)	2:05.1q
	11,026	Songcan (Gilles Lachance)	2:07.4f	82	13,800	Mr. Drew (Jan Nordin)	2:00.4q
72	10,483	Jumbo Rainbow (Stanley Dancer)	2:08.4f		13,800	Dancer's Crown (Stanley Dancer)	2:00.1q
	10,783	Keystone Gyro (Harry Harvey)	2:09.4f		14,100	Keystone Edmund (Tom Haughton)	2:02.1q
73	10,462	Meadow Grant (William Haughton)	2:10.1f	83	10,700	Frederic Hanover (J. Simpson,Jr.)	2:01.4q
	10,462	Spitfire Hanover (John Smith,Jr.)	2:09.2f		10,700	Roydon Boy (Delvin Miller)	2:01.3q
74	18,684	Bonefish (Stanley Dancer)	2:03 q		10,700	Excel Hanover (J. Simpson, Jr.)	2:02.1q
75	11,900	Tropical Storm (Ralph Baldwin)	2:04 q		11,000	Desert Ruler (Jimmy Larente)	2:02.3q
	12,500	Nevele Thunder (Stanley Dancer)	2:01.2q	84	10,800	Workaholic (Jan Johnson)	2:02.1q
76	11,300	Cold Comfort (William Haughton)	2:04.4q		11,100	Armbro Demon (Neal Shapiro)	2:01.3q

CHRONICLES

	11,000	Speed Boots (Mickey McNichol)	2:01.3q	88	7,550	Delphi's Jet (Per Eriksson)	2:02.2q
	11,000	Keystone Signal (Wm. Haughton)	2:02.2q		7,550	Warning Signal (Jan Johnson)	2:01.2q
85	13,600	Spanish Pro (Lloyd Gilmour)	2:05.3q		7,550	Flying Irishman (Harold Kelly)	2:00.2q
	14,200	Elgin Almahurst (Ulf Nordin)	2:05.3q		7,850	Bachelor Button (Harold Kelly)	2:02.1q
	14,200	Street Price (Ulf Nordin)	2:04 q		7,850	Classic Air (Jimmy Takter)	2:03.2q
86	12,250	Dancing Bill (Neal Shapiro)	2:03.4q		7,850	Sure Fact (Doug Ackerman)	2:00.3q
	11,950	Waikiki Beach (Jim Doherty)	2:03.1q		7,850	Yankee Cougar (Per Henriksen)	2:01.2q
	11,950	BJ's Superstar (Jimmy Takter)	2:02.2q	89	10,500	Armbro Iliad (George Sholty)	2:01.4q
	12,250	Moment Of Magic (Jim Doherty)	2:03.4q		10,500	Continental Racer (B. Lindstedt)	2:02 q
87	9,155	Super Chuzz (J. Simpson, Jr.)	2:02.4q		10,500	Cumin (Stanley Dancer) R	1:58 q
	9,155	Yankee Yankee (D.R. Ackerman)	2:00.2q		10,800	Drummer Hanover (Dick Richardson)	2:03 q
	9,455	King Of Broline (Jan Johnson)	2:01.1q	90	12,100	Chapman (Jan Nordin)	2:01.4q
	9,455	Slocum Hanover (J. Simpson, Jr.)	2:01 q		12,400	Baltic Viking (Jan Nordin)	2:02.3q
	9,455	Valley Everglades (Jan Nordin)	1:59.4q		12,400	Grundy's Mint (Jan Nordin)	2:00.3q
	9,455	Yankee Ubet (Terry Altmeyer)	1:59.3q				

The Hanover-Hempt Farm Stake
Two-Year-Old Colt Pace
Vernon Downs, Vernon, NY July 15, 1990

60	14,535	Hogan Hanover (William Hudson)	2:03.1h		12,000	Wellwood Hanover (Wm. Haughton)	1:58.1q
61	14,112	Lehigh Hanover (Stanley Dancer)	2:04.2h		12,000	Say Hello (Bill Popfinger)	1:57.3q
62	14,002	Chapel Chief (William Haughton)	2:04.4h	78	11,600	Alaskan Strike (Eddie Cobb)	1:58.4q
63	11,485	Bengazi Hanover (James Arthur) R	2:01.2h		11,900	Keith Lobell (John Kopas)	2:00.2q
	11,485	Iron Rail (Vernon Dancer)	2:02.2f		11,600	Eli Hanover (John Simpson, Jr.)	2:01.3q
64	11,565	Toreador Hanover (J. Simpson,Sr.)	2:06.3f	79	16,100	Niatross (C. Galbraith)	1:57.3q
	11,565	Steady Move (Howard Camden)	2:03.1f		16,400	Whamo (Charlie Clark)	1:57.1q
65	10,286	Good Time Boy (Del Cote)	2:03.1f	80	14,600	Transtar (Ron Waples)	1:57.2q
	10,586	Peppy Rainbow (Alix Winger)	2:03 f		14,600	Center Square (John Kopas)	2:01.3q
66	8,725	Recneps Jack (John W. Smith)	2:02.3f		14,600	No No Nero (Abe Stoltzfus)	1:59.4q
	9,025	Zero Dares (William Pocza)	2:06.1f		14,300	Set The Style (William Haughton)	2:01.3q
	9,025	Schatzie Byrd (Hugh Bell)	2:03.2f	81	13,900	Irish Jimmy (John Simpson, Jr.)	2:01 q
67	10,362	Fulla Napoleon (Richard Thomas)	2:00.4f		13,900	Lon Todd Hanover (J. Simpson,Jr.)	2:02 q
	10,662	Rebel Grey (Charles Norris, Jr.)	2:04.3f		13,900	Temujin (Clarence Martin, Sr.)	2:01.3q
68	12,598	Kat Byrd (Levi Harner)	2:01 f	82	13,400	Doctor Nero (William Andrews)	2:01 q
	12,598	Penn Hanover (Murray Waples)	2:02 f		13,700	Flying Rich (Abe Stolfus)	1:58.3q
69	12,290	Columbia George (Roland Beaulieu)	2:02 f		13,700	Trim The Tree (Roland Macomber)	1:58 q
	12,290	Truluck (George Sholty)	2:00 f	83	18,500	Community State (Abe Stoltzfus)	1:57.2q
	12,290	Trojan Hanover (Bill Popfinger)	2:03.4f		18,500	Handsome Devil (Abe Stoltzfus)	1:58.4q
70	11,145	Scot Time (Howard Camper)	2:03 f	84	13,700	Pinocchio (Neal Shapiro)	1:58.2q
	11,145	Seton Hanover (Edward Dunnigan)	2:00.2f		13,700	Broadway Express (M. McNichol)	1:58.2q
	11,445	Albatross (Harry Harvey) R	1:59.1f		13,400	Niafirst (Clint Galbraith)	1:57.3q
71	10,681	No Error (James Arthur)	2:03.2f	85	19,200	Mr. Rodeo Drive (Nicol Tremblay)	1:57 q
	10,381	Dancer George (Jim Dennis)	2:05 f		19,200	Gi Gi's Fella (Jan Nordin)	1:57.2q
	10,981	Lord Hanover (William Haughton)	2:03.4f	86	15,100	Merrilywerollalong (R. Silverman)	1:58.2q
	10,681	Strike Out (John Hayes)	2:01.3f		14,800	Fit To Rule (Abe Stoltzfus)	1:58.3q
72	12,516	Armbro Nesbit (Duncan MacDonald)	2:04 f		15,100	Rush For Gold (Mickey Bridges) R	1:55.4q
	12,516	Jewell Mir (Marcel Dostie)	2:05.3f	87	9,450	Ever So Rich (D.R. Ackerman)	1:57 q
	12,516	Steady Special (Glen Johnson)	2:03.3f		9,450	Ironstone Tornado (Robert Rankin)	1:57.4q
73	15,667	Trial And Error (Mike Gagliardi)	2:03.3f		9,450	Money Lender (James Larente)	1:57.3q
	15,967	Nevele Bret (Vernon Dancer)	2:02.1f		9,450	Pied Piper (Clint Warrington Jr.)	1:57 q
74	15,917	Keystone Newkirk (Richard Moore)	2:01.4q		9,450	Simon Says Sail On (Ed Lohmeyer)	1:57 q
	15,917	Good Knight Star (Peter Haughton)	2:02 q		9,450	Skipper's Hawk (Robert Rankin)	1:57.1q
75	10,300	Timely Proposal (Glen Garnsey)	2:01.2q	88	13,850	Frazer (Mickey Bridges)	1:57.3q
	10,900	Armbro Ranger (Joe O'Brien)	1:59.2q		14,150	MacDuff Hanover (Delvin Miller)	2:00 q
	10,900	Adam Lobell (Harold Dancer)	2:00.3q		14,450	Savoyard (Ron Waples)	1:58.3q
	10,600	J.J.'s Nino (Wilbur Zendt)	2:01.3q	89	10,100	Chefs Magic (Jack Bailey)	1:56.4q
76	10,200	Armbro Splurge (J. Simpson, Jr.)	1:59.2q		10,100	Radical Ruler (Bill Fahy)	1:56.3q
	9,900	Striking Image (Glen Garnsey)	1:59.1q		10,400	French Embassy (Bill Fahy) R	1:55.4q
	10,200	Governor Skipper (Henri Filion)	1:58.4q		10,400	Till We Meet Again (A.Stoltzfus)R	1:55.4q
	10,200	Racy Goods (Glen Garnsey)	1:58.4q	90	12,500	Interpreter (D.R. Ackerman)	1:57.4q
	10,200	Kawartha Eagle (Stanley Dancer)	1:58.2q		12,500	Mantese (Mickey McNichol)	1:57 q
77	12,000	No No Yankee (Walter Ross)	1:57.3q		12,800	Artsplace (Bill Fahy)	1:57.3q

The Hanover-Hempt Farm Stake
Three-Year-Old Colt Trot
Vernon Downs, Vernon, NY June 30, 1990

61	11,985	Mr Pride (Clarence Martin)	2:05.2h	80	29,800	Noble Hustle (D.R. Ackerman)	1:59.2q
62	10,237	A.C.'s Viking (Sanders Russell) R	2:03.2h		29,300	Rodney's Best (Hakan Wallner)	1:58.3q
63	12,002	Donner Hanover (Joe O'Brien)	2:03 f	81	32,200	Saturated (Raymond Tripp)	2:00.2q
64	11,370	Ayres (J. Simpson, Sr.) R	2:00.1f		32,200	Interception (Soren Nordin)	2:01 q
65	15,830	Marengo Hanover (Thomas Wilburn)	2:00.3f	82	36,500	Arndon (Delvin Miller)	1:58.3q
66	15,075	Polaris (George Sholty)	2:02.4f		36,000	Self Confident (D.R. Ackerman)	1:58.3q
67	12,386	Blaze Frost (John Wilcutts)	2:04.4f	83	58,800	Brookside Pride (John Walker)	1:58.2q
68	22,772	Eric B. (Stanley Dancer)	2:01.3f	84	57,200	Wholly Arnie (Tom Haughton)	2:00.2q
69	16,073	Tarport Reward (Gary Cameron)	2:03.3f	85	64,700	R D L (Robert Todd)	1:59.3q
	16,373	Smokey Morn (Ned Bower)	2:02.2f		64,700	Anglers Line (Hakan Wallner)	2:01.2q
70	24,345	Gil Hanover (William Haughton)	2:03.3f	86	33,525	Shannon Bright (Berndt Lindstedt)	1:58 q
71	22,136	Quick Pride (Del Cameron)	2:06.1f		33,525	Nevele Typhoon (Buddy Gilmour)	1:59 q
72	23,290	Songcan (George Sholty)	2:03.2f	87	26,000	Beseiged (Per Henriksen)	1:58.4q
73	25,967	Knightly Way (J. Simpson, Jr.)	2:01.4f		26,000	Mack Lobell (John Campbell)	1:57.1q
74	26,897	Way To Reason (Thomas V. Staker)	2:04.3q		26,000	Napoletano (Bill O'Donnell) R	1:56.1q
75	24,700	Surefire Hanover (Stanley Dancer)	2:08.1q	88	39,000	Bolla (Bruce Nickells)	1:58.2q
	15,800	Nevele Thunder (Stanley Dancer)	2:00.3q		39,000	Grundy's Ebony (Peter Ruscitto)	1:59.1q
	16,100	Quick Pay (Richard DeSantis)	2:01 q	89	26,900	Demilo Hanover (Berndt Lindstedt)	1:57.2q
77	23,800	Yankee Poncho (Doug Miller)	2:03.3q		26,900	Lemoyne Square (Jan Johnson)	1:58.3q
	24,100	Texas (Billy Herman)	2:05 q		26,900	Scott S Hanover (George Sholty)	1:58.3q
78	36,300	Brisco Hanover (Jim Miller)	2:00.3q	90	33,200	Cheyenne Spur (Dick Stillings)	1:57.1q
79	59,900	Crown's Cristy (H. Beissinger)	2:01.1q		33,200	Drummer Hanover (Dick Richardson)	1:59.4q
	59,900	Gridiron Lad (Carl Allen)	1:58.3q				

CHRONICLES

The Hanover-Hempt Farm Stake
Three-Year-Old Colt Pace
Vernon Downs, Vernon, NY May 19, 1990

61	10,685 Henry T. Adios (Stanley Dancer)	2:02.2h			18,400 Armbro Ranger (Joe O'Brien)	1:56.4q
62	12,737 Buxton Hanover (William Haughton)	2:00 h			27,500 Racy Goods (Glen Garnsey)	2:01.2q
	Lehigh Hanover (Stanley Dancer)	2:03.4h			27,800 Naval Affaire (Robert McNulty)	2:01.3q
63	14,402 Overtrick (J. Patterson Sr.)	2:00 f		78	43,000 Flight Director (Joe O'Brien)	1:56.1q
64	15,070 Iron Rail (Stanley Dancer)	2:00.1f		79	58,000 Sonsam (George Sholty)	1:54.3q
65	17,400 Bret Hanover (Frank Ervin)	1:57.2f		80	55,000 Niatross (Clint Galbraith)	1:56.1q
66	14,275 Romeo Hanover (Bill Myer)	1:58 f		81	60,000 Armbro Wolf (Steven Norris)	2:04.2q
67	10,193 Im The Judge (Dick Brandt)	2:02.1f		82	66,300 Coal Harbor (Ron Waples)	1:59.1q
	10,493 Best Of All (Jim Hackett)	2:00.2f		83	33,800 Mountain Fella (Jim Miller)	1:57 q
68	26,322 Rum Customer (William Haughton)	1:59.3f			33,800 Jo-Nathan (Jimmy Marohn)	1:56.2q
69	26,896 Laverne Hanover (Wm. Haughton)	1:56.3f		84	59,100 Southern Style (Robert Vitrano)	1:56.1q
70	26,295 Columbia George (Roland Beaulieu)	1:58.1f		85	63,900 Nero's Star (Jack Bailey)	1:56.1q
71	17,793 Paulos Hanover (Howard Camper)	1:59.3f		86	61,000 Barberry Spur (Dick Stillings)	1:54.1q
	17,793 Nansemond (Herve Filion)	2:00.1f		87	36,050 All's Great (Clint Galbraith)	1:57 q
72	27,240 Shadow Star (Jack Kopas)	2:00 q			36,050 Jaguar Spur (Dick Stillings)	1:55.2q
73	27,417 Keystone Smartie (Wm. Vaughan)	2:00 q		88	39,850 American Storm (Peter Ruscitto)	1:55.3q
74	30,396 Boyden Hanover (Billy Herman)	1:56 q			39,850 Threefold (Peter Ruscitto)	1:56.1q
75	17,200 Alberts Star (Keith Waples)	2:00 q		89	68,200 Mr Mallory (Jeff Cameron)	R 1:53.4q
	17,500 H.A. Taylor (Preston Burris, Jr.)	1:58.2q		90	32,800 King Gypsy (Doug Snyder)	1:54.1q
76	18,400 Keystone Ore (Stanley Dancer)	1:57.1q			32,800 Till We Meet Again (Bill Fahy)	1:54.4q

The E.H. Harriman Challenge Trophy
Two-Year-Old Trot
Meadowlands, E. Rutherford, NJ June 26, 1990

24	2,000 Spatfast (W.L. Snow)	2:15 1/4h		68	13,183 Nevele Major (Stanley Dancer)	2:06.1h
25	3,000 Peter Maltby (W.K. Dickerson)	2:10 3/4h		69	15,397 Nevele Rascal (Stanley Dancer)	2:05.3h
26	3,000 Ruth M. Chenault (Ben White)	2:12 3/4h		70	10,000 A.C.'s Orion (William Haughton)	2:06.1h
27	2,000 Plucky (Ed Kirby)	2:12 3/4h		71	10,000 Songcan (Gilles Lachance)	2:08.3h
28	3,000 Egan (Fred Egan)	2:13 1/4h		72	11,937 Wyatt Dill (Jacques Hebert)	2:06.2f
29	3,000 Due Return (W.K. Dickerson)	2:13 1/4h		73	11,031 Journalist (William Haughton)	2:08.3h
30	3,000 Chestnut Burr (W.Britenfield)	2:09 1/2h		74	14,215 Surefire Hanover(Wm. Haughton)	f 2:06.2h
31	3,000 Hollyrood Robin (Wm.Crozier)	2:10 1/2h		75	11,295 Zoot Suit (Stanley Dancer)	2:07.2h
32	-- Not Raced --			76	12,898 Naturally Nevele (Stanley Dancer)	2:04.1h
33	1,000 Sturdy (Harry Brusie)	2:11 1/2h		77	11,284 Noble Move (Glen Garnsey)	R 2:03.3h
34	600 Snowdown (Alfred Drinkwater)	2:14 h		78	11,440 Legend Hanover (Ray Tripp)	2:08.1h
35	1,000 Clever Hanover (Vic Fleming)	2:15 1/4h		79	18,761 Flickory Flies (Mark Schwartz)	2:05.4m
36	1,500 Mr.Watt [Dean Hanover] (T.Berry)2:08 h				19,001 Armbro Vanguard (Ross Hayter)	2:06 m
37	1,500 Royal Spencer (Chas. Lacey)	2:10 h		80	49,815 Tarry's Boy (Billy Herman)	2:03.2m
38	1,500 Peter Astra (Doc Parshall)	2:11 1/4h			48,215 Smokin Yankee (Stanley Dancer)	2:03.3m
39	2,000 Kuno (Harry Whitney)	2:09 h		81	59,000 Spirits Supreme (Jan Nordin)	2:00.2m
40	2,000 Florimel (Harry Pownall, Sr.)	2:12 1/2h			60,000 Self Confident (D.R. Ackerman)	2:00.3m
41	2,000 Cannon Ball (Harry Whitney)	2:11 1/2h		82	51,340 Jersey Cup (Ed Morris)	2:03.3m
42	2,000 Scarlet Hanover (W.E. Miller)	2:12 h			51,340 Dancer's Crown (Stanley Dancer)	2:02.4m
43	3,000 Eva's Boy (Curly Smart)	2:11 1/2h			51,340 Mr. Drew (Jan Nordin)	2:01.4m
44	5,000 Titan Hanover (H. Pownall, Sr.)	2:09 m		83	64,000 Delvin Kosmos (Heikki Korpi)	2:02 m
45	5,000 Scotch Fez (Frank Safford)	2:08 3/4h			64,000 Yankee Renegade (Ben Webster)	2:01.4m
46	5,000 Flying Dutchess (Frank Ervin)	2:13 h			64,000 Excel Hanover (Stanley Dancer)	2:00.3m
47	5,000 Judge Moore (Delvin Miller)	2:09.4h		84	80,300 Workaholic (Jan Johnson)	2:01 m
48	5,000 Scotch Pal (Doc Parshall)	a 2:10.1h			80,800 Bon Sport (Stanley Dancer)	2:01.2m
49	10,000 Lusty Song (Doc Parshall)	2:09.4h		85	79,000 Farm King (Hakan Wallner)	2:00 m
50	10,000 Mahlon Hanover (S.L. Caton)	2:09.4h			79,000 Mr. Novak (Jan Nordin)	2:00 m
51	10,000 Diplomat Hanover (Frank Ervin)	2:07.4h		86	63,615 Ditka Hanover (Jan Nordin)	1:59.2m
52	11,500 Worthy Coburn (Hugh Bell)	2:12 h			64,615 Friendly Face (Jan Johnson)	1:59.2m
53	14,200 Newport Dream (Del Cameron)	2:08 h			64,615 Manor Victory (M. Vartiainen)	1:59.4m
54	8,800 Childs Hanover (Frank Ervin)	2:06.1h		87	57,590 Yankee Yankee (Doug Ackerman)	2:00.3m
55	13,300 Saboteur (Harry Pownall, Sr.)	2:08 h			58,590 Lenox Lobell (Jan Nordin)	2:00.4m
56	13,200 Hickory Smoke (Delvin Miller)	2:06.4h			58,590 Rising Chief (Bob Roberts)	2:00.4m
57	11,550 Mix Hanover (Frank Ervin)	b 2:10 h		88	45,200 Bon Vivant (Neal Shapiro)	2:01.4m
58	13,050 Anvil Chorus (H. Pownall, Sr.)	2:10.4h			45,200 Demilo Hanover (John Campbell)	1:58.3m
59	18,300 Blaze Hanover (Joe O'Brien)	2:07 h			45,200 Keyser Lobell (Ray Remmen)	1:59.3m
60	17,850 Matastar (H. Pownall, Sr.)	c 2:06.4h		89	69,500 Cumin (Stanley Dancer)	R 1:58 m
61	19,950 Gallant Hanover(L. Huber, Jr.)	d 2:07.2h			69,500 Royal Troubador (Carl Allen)	1:58.4m
62	17,400 Speedy Scot (Ralph Baldwin)	e 2:06.2h		90	38,467 Grundy's Mint (Jan Nordin)	2:00.2m
63	15,600 Speedy Count (William Haughton)	2:07 h			38,467 Super Pleasure (Joe Adamsky)	2:01.3m
64	19,229 Egyptian Candor (Stanley Dancer)	2:06.2h			38,467 Wall Street Banker (Dg. Ackerman)	2:01 m
65	18,600 Carlisle (William Haughton)	2:06.3h			a By Volo A.C. b By Great Lullwater. c By Matastar.	
66	11,707 Hickory Blaze (William Haughton)	2:06.1h			d By Safe Mission. e By Florlis.	
67	9,548 Nevele Pride (Stanley Dancer)	2:04.4h			f By Surefire Hanover & Skipper Walt.	

The Peter Haughton Memorial
Two-Year-Old Colt Trot
Meadowlands, E. Rutherford, NJ July 31, 1990

81	75,000 Incredible Nevele (Glen Garnsey)	2:00.2m		85	1,000,000 Express Ride (George Sholty)	1:57.4m
	75,000 Triplemint (Tom Haughton)	2:01.1m		86	879,250 Ditka Hanover (Jan Nordin)	R 1:57.3m
	75,000 Self Confident (Doug Ackerman)	2:00.3m		87	600,750 Supergill (Berndt Lindstedt)	1:58.2m
82	653,250 Dancer's Crown (Stanley Dancer)	1:58 m		88	682,250 Keyser Lobell (Ray Remmen)	1:58.4m
83	875,000 Why Not (Mickey McNichol)	2:00.1m		89	639,250 Backstreet Guy (John Campbell)	1:58 m
84	1,000,000 Another Miracle (Mickey McNichol)	1:58.4m		90	609,250 Charlie Ten Hitch (D.Williams II)	2:00.2m

The William Haughton Memorial Series Final *
Pace, Four-Year-Olds and Up **
Yonkers Raceway, December 1, 1990

85	250,000 On The Road Again (Wm. Gilmour)	1:55.1h		87	250,000 Armbro Emerson (Walter Whelan)	1:56.1h
86	250,000 Saccharum (Richie Silverman)	1:57.4h		88	250,000 Jaguar Spur (Dick Stillings)	1:55.2h

CHRONICLES

89   250,000 Matt's Scooter (Michel Lachance)R 1:53.4h
90   200,000 Dorunrun Bluegrass (Herve Filion) 1:55 f
* - Innaugurated as the Fall Championship Series, and given its present name in 1986

** - Winners of the Clare Series (F&M, 3&up) also invited to race in the Haughton Series Final

The Hayes Memorial Stake
Two-Year-Old Pace
Du Quoin State Fair, Du Quoin, IL Sept. 1, 1990

74	31,562	Alert Bret (Glen Garnsey)	1:58.1m	84	86,097	Marauder (D. Richardson, Jr.)	R 1:53.3m
75	33,287	Armbro Ranger (Joe O'Brien)	a 1:58.2m	85	91,016	Talk About Class (John Campbell)	1:54 m
76	22,907	Racy Goods (Joe O'Brien)	1:55.4m	86	98,833	Sticky Two Step (Chris Loney)	1:54 m
77	21,686	Skipper's Subject (Archie McNeil)	1:57.1m	87	94,334	Only Mine (Bill O'Donnell)	1:54.1m
78	30,653	Sonsam (George Sholty)	1:57.3m	88	104,600	Barefoot Hanover (Dave Rankin)	1:56.2m
79	28,335	Midas Almahurst (Archie McNeil)	1:56 m	89	93,150	A'nutter Butter (Bill Fahy)	1:54 m
80	34,240	Artie's Dream (Joe March)	1:57 m	90	72,500	Mr Tuff Guy (D. Richardson, Jr.)	1:55.1m
81	49,610	On Around (Archie McNeil)	b 1:56.2m				
82	108,655	Fame (Bill O'Donnell)	1:56.1m		a By Armbro Ranger & Grand Abe Lee.		
83	96,444	Radiant Ruler (David Magee)	1:55.2m		b By Solid Fuel.		

The Historic-Dickerson Cup
Three-Year-Old Trot
Meadowlands, E. Rutherford, NJ June 29, 1990

10	1,200	Chatty Direct (Norm Tallman)	2:16 1/2h	57	6,300	Silver Way (Wm. S. Brown)	d 2:04.1h
11	2,000	Mamie Guy (C.W. Lasell)	2:16 1/2h	58	5,700	Sharpshooter (H. Pownall, Sr.)	2:05.1h
12	2,000	Junior Watts (Darnaby)	2:15 1/2h	59	7,350	Hickory Pride (Delvin Miller)	2:05 h
13	2,000	Howdie Mowdie Girl (C.W. Lasell)	2:13 3/4h	60	9,150	Manton Hanover (Howard Camper)	e 2:03.3h
14	2,000	W.J.Leyburn (W.H. McCarthy)	a 2:13 1/2h	61	7,050	Duke Rodney (Eddie Wheeler)	2:01.3h
15	2,000	Henry Todd (C.W. Lasell)	2:16 h	62	5,500	AC's Viking (Sanders Russell)	2:04 h
16	2,000	Lotto Watts (Ross Stout)	2:14 1/4h	63	5,500	Speedy Scot (Ralph Baldwin)	2:04 h
17	2,000	Labe Riddell (Packer)	2:14 1/4h	64	4,800	Big John (Eddie Wheeler)	f 2:06.1h
18	1,000	Miriam Guy (F. Hyde)	2:13 3/4h	65	6,450	Nimble Boy (Ralph Baldwin)	2:06 h
19	2,000	Let Fly (Earl Pitman)	2:14 1/4h	66	5,775	Bonus Boy (Del Cameron)	2:04.3h
20	2,000	Lady Mozart (Norm Tallman)	2:13 3/4h	67	11,304	Dazzling Speed (Stanley Dancer)	2:03.4h
21	2,000	Czar Worthy (G. Slaughter)	2:11 3/4h	68	10,000	Nevele Pride (Stanley Dancer)	2:02.3h
22	2,000	Edith Worthy (Lyman Brusie)	2:12 h	69	11,458	Nardins Gayblade (Wm. Haughton)	g 2:04.1h
23	2,000	Trumpet (S.S. Post)	2:09 1/4h	70	10,819	Nevele Rascal (Stanley Dancer)	2:05.1h
24	2,000	Lucera Dillon (Fred Hyde)	2:11 1/2h	71	10,000	Circus (Ralph Baldwin)	2:01.3h
25	3,000	Guy Ozark (W.K. Dickerson)	2:09 1/4h	72	8,000	Sparkling Norman (George Sholty)	2:08.1h
26	3,000	Cinema (W.K. Dickerson)	2:09 1/4h	73	10,387	Flirth (Ralph Baldwin)	2:05.4h
27	3,000	Doane (C. Becker)	2:08 1/2h	74	9,881	Spitfire Hanover (Delvin Miller)	2:03 h
28	3,000	Shirley Harvester (E. McGrath)	2:08 3/4h			Journalist (William Haughton)	2:08.1h
29	3,000	Caretaker (W.K. Dickerson)	2:09 3/4h	75	11,512	Songflori (Delvin Miller)	2:03.2h
30	3,000	Peter Ingomar (Harry Goodhart)	2:07 1/2h	76	11,607	Nevele Thunder (Stanley Dancer)	2:02.1h
31	3,000	Mac Aubrey (Harry Stokes)	2:10 1/2h			Soothsayer (Delvin Miller)	2:02.2h
32		-- No Meeting --		77	10,261	Glencoe Pride (Tom Miller)	2:06.1h
33	1,000	Calumet Delco (Lyman Brusie)	2:08 3/4h	78	10,425	Noble Move (Glen Garnsey)	2:03 h
34	600	Calumet Epson (Marty Brennan)	2:09 1/4h	79	25,420	Gin Tonic (Peter Haughton)	2:00.3m
35	1,000	Countess Zabetta (H. Crossman)	2:09 h	80	32,000	Burgomeister (William Haughton)	1:59.2m
36	1,500	Ed Lasater (Sep Palin)	2:06 3/4h	81	131,000	Arnie's Aim (Greg Wright)	1:59.1m
37	1,500	Dean Hanover (Karl Recor)	2:05 h	82	92,500	Arndon (Delvin Miller)	1:57.2m
38	1,500	Balkan Hanover (Harry Short)	2:06 1/4h		92,500	Mystic Park (Frank O'Mara)	1:57 m
39	2,000	Peter Astra (Doc Parshall)	2:08 h	83	95,500	Florida Sun (Howard Beissinger)	1:59.3m
40	2,000	Milestone (Curly Smart)	2:05 3/4h		95,500	Dancer's Crown (Stanley Dancer)	1:57.3m
41	1,500	Perpetual (Sep Palin)	2:09 3/4h	84	80,820	Speed Merchant (Tony Quartarolo)	1:56.4m
42	2,000	Paxton Hanover (Dar. Parshall)	2:09 1/4h		80,820	Delvin G. Hanover (Hakan Wallner)	1:58.4m
43		-- No Meeting --		85	70,000	Mark Six (Bill O'Donnell)	1:57 m
44		-- No Meeting --			68,500	Prakas (Bill O'Donnell)	R 1:56 m
45		-- No Meeting --		86	71,750	Jet Ahead (Jan Nordin)	1:57.3m
46	5,000	Walter Spencer(H. Pownall, Sr.)	2:08 1/4h		70,250	Pamela's Pride (R. Silverman)	1:58.3m
47	5,000	Rodney (Bion Shively)	2:05 h	87	100,025	Buckfinder (Bill O'Donnell)	1:56.2m
48	5,000	Demon Hanover (Harrison Hoyt)	2:05.4h	88	67,418	Firm Tribute (Mark O'Mara)	1:57 m
49	10,000	Bangaway (Ralph Baldwin)	2:05.1h		68,918	Grundys Cohnection (Jan Nordin)	1:56.3m
50	10,000	Star's Pride (John Simpson, Sr.)	2:05 h	89	47,150	Shogun Lobell (Howard Beissinger)	1:56.4m
51	10,000	Mighty Fine (B.J. Schue)	2:06 h		47,900	Demilo Hanover (Berndt Lindstedt)	1:56.1m
52	5,650	Hit Song (H. Pownall, Sr.)	2:05.2h	90	102,955	Star Mystic (Jan Johnson)	2:00.2m
53	7,900	Jamie (Charles McKinley)	2:05.3h	a By Billy Bing.		e By Darn Valley.	
54	5,200	Lord Pick (Frank Ervin)	b 2:05 h	b By Cronus.		f By Dartmouth.	
55	5,200	Scott Frost (Joe O'Brien)	c 2:04.3h	c By Childs Hanover.		g By Lindys Pride.	
56	6,750	Saboteur (H. Pownall, Sr.)	2:06 h	d By Demon Rum.			

The Hoosier Futurity
Two-Year-Old Colt Trot *
Indiana State Fair, Indianapolis, IN Aug. 25, 1990

37	984	Kitty O'Kane (J.D. Mahoney)	2:15 1/4h	52	11,062	Peter Lind (H. Pownall, Sr.)	c 2:06.2m
38	1,025	Allenmite (Houston Stone)	2:19 h	53	12,049	Harlan (Delvin Miller)	2:06.4m
39	1,232	Pay Off (Sep Palin)	2:16 h	54	12,941	Scott Frost (Joe O'Brien)	2:03.4m
40	1,469	Jane Long (Roscoe Carlock)	2:15 h	55	13,367	Newport Del (Del Cameron)	2:06.1m
41	1,504	Ruth Spencer (Houston Stone)	2:15 1/2h	56	11,394	Double Scotch (Joe O'Brien)	2:05.4m
42	1,752	Silver Keppie (R.W. Wright)	2:13 1/4h	57	11,436	Winter Wonderland (Frank Ervin)	d 2:05.1m
43	2,000	Gene Buck (Fred Swaim)	2:14 3/4h	58	11,196	Merrie Annabelle (J.Patterson,Sr)	2:04.2m
44	2,056	Voltite (Sep Palin)	2:13 h	59	13,065	Family Man (H. Pownall, Sr.)	2:03.3m
45	1,898	Walter Spencer (Don Taylor)	2:11 3/4h	60	11,471	Miss Demon Song (Dave McClain)	e 2:03 m
46	2,003	Way Yonder (Thomas Berry)	2:14 3/4h	61	16,871	Impish (Frank Ervin)	2:02.3m
47	6,128	Pronto Don (Doc Parshall)	2:06.3m	62		-- Rain --	
48	7,577	Tidewater (Clay Hasch)	2:09.3m	63	17,691	Speedy Count (William Haughton)	2:01 m
49	8,364	Dalzell (Roy Riegle)	2:07.2m			Ayres (John Simpson, Sr.)	2:02.3m
50	10,545	Seneca (B.J. Schue)	a 2:06.3m	64	18,403	Spinning Song (Lou Huber, Jr.)	2:04.2m
51	13,289	Joy Hanover (R. Bullington)	b 2:09.3m			Intent Way (Frank Ervin)	2:04.4m

CHRONICLES

65	17,540	Mary Donner (Frank Ervin)	2:03 m	82	26,431	Power Seat (Ted Andrews)	2:01 m
66	13,817	Faybill (Delvin Miller)	f 2:05.1m	83	24,955	Gentle Stroke (George Sholty)	1:58.4m
67	11,179	Fashion Hill (Del Cameron)	2:02.3m	84	23,225	John Dory (Doug Ackerman)	1:59.4m
68	13,132	Arnie Blaze (Howard Beissinger)	g 2:07 m	85	24,800	Shannon Bright (Jan Johnson)	1:59 m
69	15,588	Timothy T. (John Simpson, Sr.)	2:04 m	86	26,395	Skywatch Lobell (Hakan Wallner)	R 1:58.3m
		Coachman (Art Hult)	2:02.2m	87	27,440	Defiant One (Howard Beissinger)	1:59.3m
70	14,212	Lansdowne (Charlie Clark)	2:03.1m	88	54,952	Baltic Spirit (Jan Nordin)	** 2:00.3m
71	13,732	Exciting Record (Glen Garnsey)	h 2:04.3m			Grundy's Kruger (M. McNichol)	** 2:00.3m
72	14,057	Fairmont Hanover (J.Simpson,Jr.)	2:04.4m	89	21,984	Sesquistar (John Campbell)	1:59.1m
		MacArthur (Mike Zeller)	2:09 m	90	21,476	Ten Pound Bass (Bruce Nickells)	k 2:01.1m
73	16,872	Buckeye Count(H.Anders Wallner)	i 2:04.3m			* Two-Year-Old Open Trot before 1967.	
74	17,159	Ways To Win (Glen Garnsey)	j 2:04.2m			** Both Baltic Spirit (1-2) and Grundy's Kruger (2-1)	
75	19,292	Tropical Storm (Ralph Baldwin)	2:03.3m			tied in summary, and won in identical time.	
76	18,345	Jodevin (Kermit Hinshaw)	1:59 m	a By Mainliner.		g By Hiland Hill.	
77	18,211	Speedy Somolli (H. Beissinger)	2:01 m	b By My Precious.		h By Sparking Norman.	
78	20,958	Turn For Home (Joe O'Brien)	2:02.1m	c By Fiesta Hanover.		i By Christopher T.	
79	15,930	Noble Spirit (Art Hult)	2:04.2m	d By La Belle.		j By Ways to Win &	
80	18,433	Malibu Hanover (Archie McNeil)	2:01.2m	e By Scotch Irish.		Thornhill.	
81	22,674	Summit Hill (William Haughton)	1:59.3m	f By Miss Marker.		k By Primrose Lane.	

The Hoosier Futurity
Two-Year-Old Colt Pace
Indiana State Fair, Indianapolis, IN Aug. 23, 1990

37	647	Myrtella Henley (McCord)	2:15 1/2h	69	20,198	Adover Rainbow (Stanley Dancer)	1:57.4m
38	1,025	Miss Highland (H. Beattie)	a 2:07 1/4h			Banner Ranger (Joe Marsh, Jr.)	1:59.4m
39	1,282	Highland Wayne (H. Beattie)	2:01 h	70	17,372	Smart Lobell (Warren Cameron)	2:03.1m
40	1,519	Victorious Hal (George Keys)	2:11 3/4h	71	18,532	Kit Hanover (Gene Riegle)	e 2:00.2m
41	1,654	Eddie D. (Ralph Baldwin)	2:09 h	72	18,782	Steady Airliner (Joe O'Brien)	1:58.4m
42	1,752	Purdue Hal (Sep Palin)	2:13 h	73	20,146	Title Holder (Archie McNeil)	2:00.4m
43	2,000	Direct Brewer (Doc Parshall)	2:13 3/4h	74	21,359	H.A.'s Pet (Lou Huber, Jr.)	2:00.3m
44	2,106	Jimmy Creed (Homer Walton)	2:06 1/4h			Worthy Master (William Haughton)	2:02 m
45	1,948	Royal Chief (Thomas Berry)	2:10 h	75	24,440	Racing Time (Robert Todd)	f 1:59.3m
46	2,303	Forbes Chief (Del Cameron)	2:10 1/2h	76	21,170	Doc's Tuck (Roland Beaulieu)	1:58.4m
47	6,458	E.J. Hal (H.C. Fitzpatrick)	2:05 m	77	20,986	Skip Hanover (Peter Haughton)	1:58 m
48	8,062	Theo A. Abbe (J.F. Cartnal)	b 2:06 m	78	21,283	Mostest Yankee (Billy Herman)	1:56.4m
49	9,419	Mighty Grattan (Doc Parshall)	2:06.2m	79	20,005	Surfer Scott (William Haughton)	g 1:58.4m
50		-- Rain --		80	19,683	Tabb Hanover (Delvin Miller)	R 1:54 m
51	13,459	Meadow Rice (Curly Smart)	2:02.4m	81	25,200	Apollo's Way (Shelly Goudreau)	2:00.1m
52	11,862	Knox Hanover (Hugh Bell)	2:03.3m	82	26,406	Thurston Hanover (Chris Boring)	h 1:57.2m
53	13,199	The Tippler (Frank Ervin)	2:02.4m	83	28,255	Passionate Prince(R. Williams II)	1:56 m
54	13,486	Libby's Boy (Houston Stone)	2:03 m	84	27,625	Mighty Mouse (Mike O'Donnell)	1:57.1m
55	14,077	Canny Scot (Frank Ervin)	c 2:03.3m	85	24,900	Corporate Ruler (Don Irvine, Jr.)	1:57.4m
56	13,039	Nyland Hanover (Ralph Baldwin)	2:02.4m	86	32,020	JJ's Somerset(D.Richardson,Jr.)	i 1:54.3m
57	12,136	Painter (John Simpson, Sr.)	2:03.1m	87	16,237	Hearty Welcome (Bill Fahy)	1:58.3m
58	12,536	Right Time (John Patterson, Sr.)	2:03 m	88	17,267	Reebok (Sam Noble III)	1:59.2m
59	12,265	Gene Direct (Gene Riegle)	2:02.4m	88	32,140	Raque Bogart (Bill Fahy)	j 1:55.1m
60	11,480	Keystoner's Tip (Frank Ervin)	2:02.4m	89	25,334	Harpo (Mike O'Donnell)	1:55.3m
61	15,261	Next Knight (William Haughton)	2:02.1m	90	24,776	Endowment (Joe Holloway)	1:57 m
62		-- Rain --				* Two-Year-Old Open Pace before 1967.	
63	19,576	Don Parker (Gene Riegle)	2:00 m	a By Kent Scott.		f By Hickory Express.	
64	19,592	Scarlet Wave (Clarence Martin)	2:00.2m	b By Larry Grattan.		g By Dear Star.	
65	18,175	Bonjour Hanover (Del Cameron)	2:00 m	c By Adioway.		h By Keystone Chief.	
66	18,287	Mighty Ad (Stanley Dancer)	d 2:00 m	d By Mighty Ad & Coral Ridge.		i By War Horse.	
67	15,609	Bye And Large (George Sholty)	1:59.2m	e By Uncle Kenny.		j By Raque Bogart &	
68	15,692	Shiaway Lad (Chris Boring)	2:03.4m			Shannon Intruder.	

The Hopeful
Two-Year-Old Colt Pace
Buffalo Raceway, Hamburg, NY July 1, 1990

89	200,000	Farley Almahurst (Ken Hardy)	2:00.3h	90	190,000	He's Discreet (Patsy Rapone)	R 1:59.2h

The Horseman Futurity
Three-Year-Old Trot
Indiana State Fair, Indianapolis, IN Aug. 25, 1990

07	4,000	Kentucky Todd (Harry Stinson)	2:09 m	32	6,105	The Marchioness (William Caton)	2:02 m
09	4,000	Baroness Virginia (Sam Fleming)	2:13 1/4m	33	6,805	Brown Berry (Fred Egan)	2:03 1/4m
10		-- Not Raced --		34	4,293	Vitamine (William Caton)	2:01 3/4m
11	6,500	Mainleaf (Richard Curtis)	2:09 1/4m	35	3,088	Greyhound (Sep Palin)	2:05 m
12		-- Not Raced --		36	3,235	Bill Strang (W.K. Dickerson)	2:02 3/4m
13	6,277	Etawah (Pop Geers)	2:01 3/4m	37	3,141	Southland (Fred Egan)	2:03 1/2m
14	6,625	Ortolan Axworthy (A. McDonald)	2:08 1/4m	38	5,155	McLin (Henry Thomas)	2:01 3/4m
15	6,552	Native Spirit (Bert Shank)	2:08 1/4m	39	3,160	Lyrmite (Thomas Berry)	2:07 m
16	4,900	Bingen Silk (J.B. Chandler)	2:07 1/4m	40	4,480	Spencer Scott (Fred Egan)	2:01 1/4m
17	3,598	Harvest Gale (Walter Cox)	2:08 3/4m	41	4,792	Bill Gallon (Lee Smith)	2:01 m
18	4,188	Peter June (Pop Geers)	2:05 1/2m	42	5,979	Pay Up (Lee Smith)	2:07 1/4h
19	4,839	Periscope (John Dodge)	2:06 1/4m	43	7,084	Darnley (Harry Whitney)	2:04 3/4h
20	6,406	Arion Guy (Harry Stokes)	2:05 1/4m	44	4,290	Yankee Song (Henry Thomas)	2:05 1/4h
21	5,500	Nelson Dillon (Joe Serrill)	2:05 1/2m	45	3,755	Voltite (Sep Palin)	2:05 1/4h
22	5,242	Peter Earl (Nat Ray)	2:05 1/4m	46	5,475	Victory Maid (Sep Palin)	2:01 3/4m
23	4,902	The Senator (Alonzo McDonald)	2:07 1/2m	47	6,465	Way Hanover (Del Cameron)	2:03.2m
24	4,379	Mr.McElwyn (Ben White)	2:03 3/4m	48	12,130	Egan Hanover (Ralph Baldwin)	2:02.3m
25	4,394	Sam Williams (Walter Cox)	2:06 1/4m	49	15,493	Magnany (Ralph Baldwin)	2:05 m
26	5,933	Charm (Ben White)	2:08 1/4m	50	12,803	Lusty Song (Delvin Miller)	2:02 m
27	7,665	Iosola's Worthy (Tom Berry)	2:05 3/4m	51	23,685	Scotch Rhythm (Ralph Baldwin)	2:04.4m
28	7,712	Etta Volo (W.K. Dickerson)	2:04 1/2m	52	24,707	Sharp Note (Bion Shively)	2:01 m
29	8,468	Volomite (Walter Cox)	2:04 1/2m	53	24,456	Kimberly Kid (Thomas Berry)	2:01.3m
30	7,454	Legality (Doc Parshall)	2:06 1/2m	54	22,502	Darn Safe (B.J. Schue)	2:00.3m
31	6,428	Protector (William Caton)	2:02 1/4m	55	20,741	Galophone (William Haughton)	2:01 m

Page 333

CHRONICLES

56	20,656 Nimble Colby (Ralph Baldwin)	2:03.3m
57	20,489 Hoot Song (Ralph Baldwin)	2:01.4m
58	22,708 Sandalwood (Ralph Baldwin)	2:01.2m
59	26,251 Expressum (Frank Ervin)	2:01.4m
60	32,265 Quick Song (Ralph Baldwin)	2:00.3m
61	36,895 Spectator (Ralph Baldwin)	1:59.4m
62	37,517 Safe Mission (Joe O'Brien)	a 2:03 m
63	39,549 Speedy Scot (Ralph Baldwin)	1:59.1m
64	36,843 Dartmouth (Ralph Baldwin)	2:00.2m
65	38,496 Armbro Flight (Joe O'Brien)	b 1:57.2m
66	36,879 Carlisle (William Haughton)	c 2:00.2m
67	35,303 Dazzling Speed (Stanley Dancer)	d 2:00.2m
68	34,737 Nevele Pride (Stanley Dancer)	1:56.3m
69	41,563 Nevele Major (Stanley Dancer)	2:02.4m
70	38,365 Formal Notice (James Arthur)	2:00.4m
71	35,737 Hoot Speed (Glen Garnsey)	1:59.3m
72	32,080 Super Bowl (Stanley Dancer)	1:59.3m
73	34,280 Arnie Almahurst (Gene Riegle)	2:00.3m
74	50,329 Anvil (Glen Garnsey)	e 1:59.2m
75	40,528 Glasgow (William Haughton)	1:59 m
	Surefire Hanover (Ronald Dancer)	1:59.1m
76	39,592 Pershing (Billy Herman)	1:58 m
77	42,813 Reprise (Joe O'Brien)	1:58 m
78	33,479 Way To Gain (John Simpson, Jr.)	1:59.4m
79	31,588 Gator Bowl (John Simpson, Jr.)	1:59.1m
80	35,956 Noble Hustle (D.R. Ackerman)	1:58 m
81	33,707 Noble Traveler (Doug Ackerman)	f 1:57.3m
82	32,788 Jazz Cosmos (Mickey McNichol)	1:56.3m
83	37,951 Astro Hill (Howard Beissinger)	1:57.2m
84	36,010 Op Art (Bruce Riegle)	1:56.2m
85	35,404 Nearly Perfect (S. Warrington)	R 1:55.2m
86	37,906 ArmbroEldorado(D.Richardson,Jr)	g 1:55.3m
87	40,068 Crown Speed (Carl Allen)	h 1:56.3m
88	40,870 Defiant One (Howard Beissinger)	i 1:55.4m
89	37,510 Scott S Hanover (George Sholty)	j 1:56.1m
90	37,032 Incredible D J (Chris Boring)	1:55.3m

a By Lord Gordon.   f By Snack Bar.
b By Noble Victory.   g By Long Legend.
c By Polaris.   h By Mack Lobell.
d By Speed Model.   i By Armbro Garnsey.
e By Stock Split.   j By Dr Guillotine.

The Horseman Futurity
Three-Year-Old Pace
Indiana State Fair, Indianapolis, IN Aug. 25, 1990

07	2,100 Betty Brent (Vance Nuckols)	2:12 1/2m
08	-- Not Raced --	
09	2,000 Maggie Winder (Henry Jones)	2:06 1/2m
10	-- Not Raced --	
11	3,366 Miss De Forest (A. McDonald)	2:07 3/4m
12	-- Not Raced --	
13	3,381 Homer Baughman (Crit Davis)	2:12 1/4m
14	3,567 Bud Elliott (Frank Jones)	2:14 1/4m
15	3,528 General Todd (Guy Rea)	2:04 1/4m
16	2,670 Alice Jolla (C.A. Valentine)	2:17 1/4m
17	1,983 Rex De Forest (Walter Cox)	2:11 1/2m
18	2,370 Liberty Mac (William Hasch)	2:09 1/4m
19	2,598 Goldie King (T.W. Murphy)	2:10 3/4m
20	2,362 Tramp Safe (Harry Stokes)	2:04 1/4m
21	2,000 Peter Henley (T.W. Murphy)	2:08 1/4m
22	2,056 Peter Etawah (T.W. Murphy)	2:06 3/4m
23	1,859 Anna Bradford's Girl (B. White)	2:05 3/4m
24	1,791 Marion C. (W.T. Candler)	2:11 1/2m
25	1,876 Hollyrood Abigail (J.L. Dodge)	2:12 1/4m
26	2,358 Highland Scott (T.W. Murphy)	2:06 1/2m
27	4,127 Hollyrood Jacqueline (H.Stokes)	2:03 3/4m
28	3,448 Trumpination (Marvin Childs)	2:07 1/4m
29	3,719 Petroguy (Sep Palin)	2:06 3/4m
30	3,606 Calumet Adam (R.D. McMahon)	2:07 1/2m
31	3,134 Calumet Brownie (Fred Egan)	2:02 m
32	3,338 Raider (Fred Egan)	2:03 m
33	2,449 Daniel Hanover (Tom Berry)	2:03 m
34	1,875 Calumet Evelyn (Vic Fleming)	2:07 1/2m
35	1,749 Calumet Fingo (R. Nohlechek)	a 2:09 1/2m
36	1,469 Jack Orr (W.K. Dickerson)	2:02 m
37	1,689 Frisco Dale (Homer Walton)	2:04 3/4m
38	1,839 Chief Counsel (Doc Parshall)	2:01 3/4m
39	1,327 Alban (Harry Whitney)	2:07 1/4m
40	2,385 William Cash (W. Britenfield)	2:01 1/4m
41	2,151 Wilmington (H.C. Fitzpatrick)	2:04 1/4m
42	2,591 Margamite (John Simpson, Sr.)	2:08 h
43	3,043 King's Counsel (Doc Parshall)	2:09 1/2h
44	2,350 Filly Direct (Curly Smart)	2:08 3/4h
45	1,829 Jimmy Creed (Claude Wright)	2:09 1/2h
46	4,025 Honest Truth (McKinley Kirk)	2:05 3/4m
47	5,265 Norris Hanover (Henry Myott)	2:02.4m
48	9,730 Knight Dream (Frank Safford)	2:01.3m
49	11,593 Stormyway (Ralph Baldwin)	2:02.4m
50	14,604 Quilla Hanover (J. Simpson, Sr.)	2:00.4m
51	15,385 Floating Dream (McKinley Kirk)	2:01 m
52	17,103 Thunderclap (Hugh Bell)	
53	19,356 Keystoner (Frank Ervin)	2:00 m
54	19,922 Diamond Hal (Joe O'Brien)	b 2:00.3m
55	19,741 Meadow Ace (Del Cameron)	1:59 m
56	14,898 Adioscot (James Arthur)	c 2:00.3m
57	21,187 Torpid (John Simpson, Sr.)	1:59.3m
58	18,332 Bye Bye Byrd (Donald Taylor)	1:59.3m
59	26,558 Newport Admiral (Del Cameron)	1:59.1m
60	24,394 Bullet Hanover (J. Simpson, Sr.)	1:59.2m
61	32,402 Tarport Jimmy (James Arthur)	d 2:00.3m
62	-- Rain --	
63	28,991 Sly Yankee (Stanley Dancer)	e 1:58.3m
64	29,689 McHoe (Jim Hackett)	f 2:00.3m
65	34,838 Adios Vic (Jim Dennis)	g 1:55 m
66	30,329 Romeo Hanover (George Sholty)	1:58.4m
67	32,053 Best Of All (Jim Hackett)	1:57.2m
68	40,437 Rum Customer (William Haughton)	1:56.3m
69	37,913 Laverne Hanover (Wm. Haughton)	1:59 m
70	38,515 Columbia George (Roland Beaulieu)	1:56.4m
71	40,507 Gamely (George Sholty)	1:56.4m
72	37,030 Hilarious Way (John Simpson, Jr.)	1:55.3m
73	31,896 Melvin's Woe (Joe O'Brien)	1:57.4m
74	44,829 Peter Lobell (Lou Huber, Jr.)	1:57.4m
75	40,979 Bo Bo Arrow (Joe O'Brien)	1:57 m
76	33,542 Warm Breeze (Dick Farrington)	h 1:57.1m
77	34,343 Lightning Strikes (Wm. Haughton)	1:56.3m
78	30,850 Regal Rogue (Doug Ackerman)	1:57.4m
79	40,058 Scarlet Skipper (Billy Herman)	1:58 m
80	29,300 Flash Almahurst (George Sholty)	1:57.2m
81	28,152 Tiger Almahurst (S. Goudreau)	i 1:57.2m
82	34,713 Temujin (Howard Beissinger)	1:55.1m
83	32,121 Crosscurrent (John Campbell)	1:53.4m
	Umbrella Fella (Glen Garnsey)	1:55.2m
84	36,725 Colt Fortysix (Chris Boring)	1:54 m
85	31,390 Nero's Star (Steve Warrington)	1:58.3m
86	15,790 Smartest Remark (Bill O'Donnell)	1:55.3m
	15,790 Our Bucephalus (Dan Altmeyer)	1:55.1m
87	35,118 Scene Topper (Dan Shetler, Jr.)	j 1:53.4m
88	45,654 Smooth George (John Campbell)	k 1:52.1m
89	41,724 Drawing Board (Bill Gale)	R 1:51.4m
90	27,958 Fortysix Cylinders (Chris Boring)	1:53 m

a By Kent Bumpas.   g By Bret Hanover.
b By Queen's Adios.   h By Welk Hanover.
c By Noble Adios.   i By Slipstream.
d By Adios Cleo.   j By Meadowbranch Bret.
e By Meadow Russ.   k By Albert Albert.
f By Torpedo.

The Horseman Stake
Two-Year-Old Trot
Indiana State Fair, Indianapolis, IN Aug. 24, 1990

38	8,335 Peter Astra (Doc Parshall)	2:05 1/4m
39	9,375 Kuno (Harry Whitney)	a 2:05 m
40	15,495 Bill Gallon (Lee Smith)	2:04 m
41	14,875 Colby Hanover (Fred Egan)	2:05 1/2m
42	13,335 Volo Song (Ben White)	2:06 1/4h
43	13,120 Eva's Boy (Curly Smart)	2:09 1/4h
44	17,480 Titan Hanover (H. Pownall, Sr.)	2:05 3/4h
45	18,311 Deanna (Ben White)	2:07 h
46	17,556 Hoot Mon (Fred Egan)	2:04 1/4m
47	26,405 Rollo (Del Cameron)	2:06.2m
48	33,846 Miss Tilly (Fred Egan)	2:04 m
49	32,992 Floricam (H. Pownall, Sr.)	b 2:02.1m
50	40,748 Mighty Fine (Delvin Miller)	2:04.2m
51	34,716 Duke Of Lullwater (J.Simpson,Sr.)	2:03.4m
52	30,695 Newport Star (Del Cameron)	2:06.1m
53	32,484 Newport Dream (Del Cameron)	2:03.4m
54	28,041 Galophone (Houston Stone)	c 2:04.3m
55	26,276 Saboteur (H. Pownall, Sr.)	2:05.2m
56	23,770 Bond Hanover (Joe O'Brien)	d 2:04 m
57	41,598 Sharpshooter (H. Pownall, Sr.)	e 2:05.1m
58	41,598 Diller Hanover (John Chapman)	2:03.1m
59	43,701 Blaze Hanover (Joe O'Brien)	f 2:01.2m
60	42,469 Harlan Dean (Delvin Miller)	2:01.2m
61	51,927 Safe Mission (Joe O'Brien)	g 2:03.3m
62	-- Rain --	
63	47,173 Smart Rodney (William Haughton)	2:03.3m
64	51,643 Noble Victory (Stanley Dancer)	2:00.1m
65	47,291 Kerry Way (Frank Ervin)	2:02.4m
66	41,308 Kimberly Dutchess (R. Baldwin)	h 2:04.3m
67	36,858 Nevele Pride (Stanley Dancer)	2:02.1m

Page 334

CHRONICLES

68	47,435	Nevele Major (Stanley Dancer)	i 2:02.2m	83	66,073	Coogee (Glen Garnsey)	k 1:58.4m
69	44,589	Nevele Rascal (Stanley Dancer)	2:03.1m	84	75,643	Another Miracle (Jim Gluhm)	l 1:58.4m
70	44,262	Noble Gesture (H. Graham, Jr.)	2:01.1m	85	71,807	Royal Prestige (Jan Johnson)	1:56.3m
71	34,084	Star's Chip (Stanley Dancer)	2:03 m	86	71,030	Buckfinder (Bill O'Donnell)	R 1:55.4m
		Super Bowl (Vernon Dancer)	2:04 m	87	38,555	Yankee Yankee (Doug Ackerman)	2:03.1m
72	46,320	Blitzen (Herman Graham, Jr.)	2:02.1m		38,555	Arnover (Bob Roberts)	2:01.3m
73	41,588	Armbro Ouzo (Glen Garnsey)	j 2:04.3m	88	22,500	To The Gate (Jan Nordin)	1:59.3m
74	48,160	Bonefish (Stanley Dancer)	2:01.3m	89	57,530	Royal Troubador (Carl Allen)	m 1:58.3m
75	45,868	Nevele Thunder (Stanley Dancer)	2:02.3m	90	51,090	Crysta's Best (DickRichardsonJr.)	1:58.2m
		Quick Pay (William Haughton)	2:04.1m	a By Spencer Scott.		h By Halifax Hanover.	
76	62,014	Speed In Action (Delvin Miller)	2:00.2m	b By Lusty Song.		i By The Prophet.	
77	60,346	Brisco Hanover (Jim Miller)	2:00.1m	c By Butch Hanover.		j By Spitfire Hanover.	
78	54,010	Courtly (Hakan Wallner)	1:59 m	d By Major Newport.		k By Crowning Point.	
79	60,174	Armbro Vanguard (Joe O'Brien)	2:00.4m	e By Gang Awa.		l By Super Freddie.	
80	61,817	Tuneful Contest (Bruce Nickels)	1:58 m	f By Uncle Sam.		m By Armbro Iliad.	
81	60,872	Speed Bowl (Shelly Goudreau)	2:00.3m	g By Gallant Hanover &			
82	70,460	Premium Lobell (Joe O'Brien)	1:59 m	Safe Mission.			

The Hudson Filly Trot
Three-Year-Old Filly Trot *
Yonkers Raceway, Yonkers, NY July 14, 1990

57	21,117	Taffy Hanover (S.L. Caton)	2:16.4h	80	28,980	Kading (Ben Steall)	2:04.3h
58	24,762	Lumber Along (Philip Corley)	2:17.2h	81	35,039	Gretchen Hanover (J.Simpson,Jr.)	2:04.4h
59	23,122	Thalia Hanover (J. Simpson, Sr.)	2:15.3h	82	29,447	Northern Princess (Ron Waples)	2:03.1h
60	26,405	Darcie Hanover (Levi Harner)	2:15.2h		29,447	Front Page Lady (Frank O'Mara)	2:04 h
61	44,780	Speedy Princess (Earle Avery)	2:13 h	83	34,107	-dh- Crown Jennefer (Wm. Gilmour)	2:02 h
62	45,882	Worth Seein (Stanley Dancer)	2:19 h			-dh- Color of Money (H. McNichol)	2:02 h
63	47,372	Cheer Honey (Don C. Miller)	2:04.2h		34,107	Emma Lobell (Berndt Lindstedt)	2:02.2h
64	35,131	Golden Make It (George Sholty)	2:04.1h	84	62,340	Arnie's Frilly (Glen Garnsey)	2:02.2h
65	35,783	Armbro Flight (Joe O'Brien)	2:06.4h	85	24,600	Honor Crown (John Patterson, Jr.)	2:03 h
66	32,947	Coalition (Olof Widell)	2:06.4h		24,600	Nitefilte Lobell (B. Lindstedt)	2:02.4h
67	25,000	Flamboyant (William Haughton)	2:08.1h		24,600	Davidia Hanover (Gary Lewis)	2:01.4h
68	17,500	Partys Over (Richard Thomas)	2:05.2h	86	22,898	JEF's Spice (Mickey McNichol)	2:01.3h
	17,500	Daring Speed (Clint Hodgins)	2:04.2h		22,898	Sunglow Lobell (Berndt Lindstedt)	2:02.3h
69	35,000	CharmetteHanover(J.Patterson,Sr.)	2:04.3h		22,898	Castleton Memo (Bill O'Donnell)	2:01.3h
70	25,160	Sweet Freight (George Sholty)	2:05.4h		22,898	Newmarket S (Hakan Wallner)	R 1:59 h
71	25,747	Waverly Hostess (Herve Filion)	2:06.3h	87	61,530	Lucious Almahurst (Ben Webster)	1:59.1h
72	24,200	Speedy Carlene (Stanley Dancer)	2:05 h	88	37,360	Acupuncture (Carmine Abbatiello)	2:01.4h
73	23,800	Honeysuckle Rose (Vernon Dancer)	2:04.2h		37,360	Tarport Bridget (Jan Johnson)	2:00.2h
74	41,750	Noble Florie (Glen Garnsey)	2:04.4h	89	70,710	Clarisse Lobell (Eldon Harner)	2:02.4h
75	18,700	Meadow Bright (Delvin Miller)	2:03.3h		70,710	Peach Pit (Buddy Gilmour)	2:01.1h
76	21,700	Tall Tale (Glen Garnsey)	2:03.1h	90	35,522	Happy Diamonds (John Campbell)	1:59.4h
77	16,400	Elmsford (Henri Filion)	2:08.2h		35,522	Kindava Hush (Jan Nordin)	2:02 h
78	14,000	Imagery (Stanley Dancer)	2:03.2h			* 1-1/16 mile before 1963.	
79	9,700	Countess Advocate (Real Cormier)	a2:10.2h	a Walkover.			

The International Stallion Stakes *
"The Castleton Cup"
Two-Year-Old Trot
The Red Mile, Lexington, KY Oct. 4, 1990

71	33,403	Super Bowl (Vernon Dancer)	1:59.4m	82	68,450	Micron Hanover (J. Simpson, Jr.)	1:57.2m
		Flush (George Sholty)	2:02.2m	83	83,000	Gentle Stroke (George Sholty)	1:57 m
72	36,190	South Bend (Mike Zeller)	2:03.3m	84	89,000	Nearly Perfect (Mickey McNichol)	2:00 m
		Arnie Almahurst (Gene Riegle)	2:01.2m	85	80,150	Royal Prestige (Hakan Wallner)	1:57.2m
73	39,564	Christopher T. (William Haughton)	2:01.4m	86	84,150	Buckfinder (Bill O'Donnell)	R 1:56.1m
74	39,600	Ways To Win (Glen Garnsey)	a 2:01 m	87	149,875	Defiant One (Howard Beissinger)	1:58.3m
75	43,596	Nevele Thunder (Stanley Dancer)	2:01.1m	88	157,850	Scott S Hanover (George Sholty)	e 1:54.3m
76	47,520	Speed In Action (Delvin Miller)	2:05 m	89	153,480	Super Arnie (Berndt Lindstedt)	1:57.3m
77	51,370	Florida Pro (George Sholty)	2:01.1m	90	135,300	Grundy's Mint (Jan Nordin)	1:57.4m
78	51,315	Chiola Hanover (Jimmy Allen)	b 2:01 m	* - Replaced the Lexington, contested 1875 to 1970			
79	58,355	Noble Hustle (Doug Ackerman)	2:00.3m	a By Skipper Walt.		d By Arndon.	
80	64,750	Homesick (Billy Herman)	c 1:59.4m	b By Legend Hanover.		e By Ziggy Hanover.	
81	65,000	Jazz Cosmos (Mickey McNichol)	d 1:57.2m	c By Worthy Bowl.			

The International Stallion Stakes
"The International Pace"
Two-Year-Old Pace
The Red Mile, Lexington, KY Oct. 5, 1990

71	43,963	Kit Hanover (Joe O'Brien)	a 1:57.2m	83	98,500	Walton Hanover (J. Simpson, Jr.)	1:54.1m
72	52,470	Ricci Reenie Time (H. Dancer)	b 2:01.1m	84	98,560	Niafirst (Clint Galbraith)	e 1:53.2m
73	54,633	Nevele Bret (Vernon Dancer)	c 1:58.1m	85	76,850	Happy Chatter (Doug Ackerman)	1:56 m
74	53,890	Alert Bret (Glen Garnsey)	1:55.4m	86	104,350	Jate Lobell (Mark O'Mara)	1:53 m
75	68,348	Armbro Ranger (Joe O'Brien)	1:56.3m	87	210,375	Concussion (Sam Noble III)	f 1:53.3m
76	62,755	Jade Prince (Jack Kopas)	1:54.1m	88	176,810	How Bout It (Tom Haughton)	1:52.4m
77	64,075	Say Hello (Bill Popfinger)	1:55.4m	89	183,180	A'nutter Butter (Bill Fahy)	g 1:55 m
78	65,175	Happy Motoring (Bill Popfinger)	d 1:55.3m	90	153,500	Die Laughing (Richie Silverman)	R 1:52.1m
79	59,455	Niatross (Clint Galbraith)	1:56.2m	a By Entrepreneur.		e By Nihilator.	
80	76,400	French Chef (Stanley Dancer)	1:55.3m	b By Valiant Bret.		f By Albert Albert.	
81	72,800	Elitist (Jack Parker, Jr.)	1:56.1m	c By Boyden Hanover.		g By Raven Lunatic &	
82	79,700	Trim The Tree (Dick Macomber)	1:53.3m	d By Sonsam.		A'nutter Butter.	

The International Stallion Stakes *
"The Almahurst Stud"
Two-Year-Old Filly Pace
The Red Mile, Lexington, KY Oct. 3, 1990

64	16,645	Bewitch Hanover (J. Simpson, Sr.)	2:01 m	65	13,093	Worth Knowing (Howard Beissinger)	2:04 m

CHRONICLES

66	17,863	Meadow Elva (Billy Haughton)	2:00.3m	81	66,000	Adore (J. Miller)	1:57.3m
67	18,513	Quickie Hanover (Clint Hodgins)	2:07.1m	82	67,000	Rita Almahurst (Dave Rankin)	1:56.3m
68	22,231	Scotch Jewel (R. Baldwin)	1:59.2m	83	72,800	Secret Wager (M. O'Donnell) b	1:56 m
69	23,082	Majette (Art Hult)	1:59.3m	84	79,060	Stienam (Buddy Gilmour)	1:56.2m
70	26,930	Thimble (Hess)	2:00.1m	85	80,000	Musical Hanover (J.Simpson,Jr.) c	1:56.1m
71	32,465	Decorum (Stanley Dancer)	1:57.1m	86	68,260	No No Abby (Ron Waples)	1:54.4m
72	30,464	Laura's Image (Jim Tallman) a	2:02.1m	87	153,175	Sweet Reflection (Bill O'Donnell)	1:58.2m
73	33,737	High Score (Billy Haughton)	2:01.1m	88	152,350	Central Park West (J. Campbell) R	1:54.3m
74	34,402	Armbro Penny (Joe O'Brien)	2:01.2m	89	109,025	Vassar Hanover (Ron Waples)	1:55.4m
75	35,019	Armbro Renown (Joe O'Brien)	2:02.4m	90	95,150	Explosive Legacy (Chris Boring)	1:55.4m
76	34,724	Racing Bretta (Billy Haughton)	1:59.2m			* Prior to 1987, was part of the	
77	38,479	Cher Hanover (Billy Haughton)	1:57.3m			Lexington Filly Stakes.	
78	41,132	High Finesse (Joe O'Brien)	1:56.3m				
79	39,115	Cool Heel (Peter Haughton)	2:00.4m	a By Joannie's Time.		c By Lightning Beach.	
80	44,350	Karril Hanover (Wm. Popfinger)	1:57.2m	b By Scent Of Heather.			

The International Stallion Stakes *
"The Stoner Creek Stud"
Two-Year-Old Filly Trot
The Red Mile, Lexington, KY Oct. 3, 1990

64	16,645	Armbro Flight (Joe O'Brien)	2:07.2m	80	25,160	Panty Raid (Stanley Dancer) a	2:00 m
65	17,743	Mary Donner (F. Ervin/J. O'Brien)	2:01.2m	81	32,900	Crevette (Hakan Wallner)	1:58.1m
66	15,715	Flamboyant (Billy Haughton)	2:04.2m	82	40,250	Winky's Gill (Hakan Wallner) R	1:57 m
67	14,163	Ole Hanover (Joe O'Brien)	2:07.4m	83	39,390	Desdemona Hanover (J.Simpson,Jr.)	1:58.3m
68	18,910	Sparkling Molly (David Begin)	2:02.2m	84	42,750	Harmony Broline (Bern. Lindstedt)	1:59 m
69	16,283	Floribert (Glen Garnsey)	2:03.4m	85	52,560	Castleton Memo (Jeff Fout) b	1:58.4m
70	19,082	Real Cool (T. Taylor)	1:59.1m	86	45,100	Calm Down (George Sholty)	2:00.2m
71	18,913	Delmonica Hanover (Del Miller)	2:02.3m	87	131,175	Anamosa Hanover (Jan Nordin) c	1:59 m
72	19,195	Colonial Charm (Glen Garnsey)	2:02 m	88	127,600	Peace Corps (John Campbell)	1:57.3m
73	19,870	Noble Image (Archie McNeil)	2:03.3m	89	129,730	Kindava Hush (Jan Nordin)	1:58.2m
74	23,175	Edith Lobell (Joe O'Brien)	2:03.3m	90	121,000	Eternal Flare (Jan Johnson)	1:59.2m
75	21,236	Garden Path (Clark)	2:08 m			* - Prior to 1987, was part of the	
76	24,054	Superlou (John Simpson, Jr.)	2:03.2m			Lexington Filly Stakes	
77	21,581	Cami Almahurst (Bruce Riegle)	2:00.1m				
78	23,587	Classical Way (John Simpson, Jr.)	2:00.2m	a By Delmegan.		c By Wharton.	
79	24,760	Princess Glory (Wm. Popfinger)	2:00.2m	b By Newmarket S.			

The International Trot
Invitational
Yonkers Raceway, Yonkers, NY Aug. 5, 1990

59	50,000	Jamin (Fra) (Jean Riaud) a	3:08.3h	76	200,000	Equileo (Fra) (Bernard Froger)	2:33.3h
60	50,000	Hairos II (Neth.) (Wm.Geersen) b	2:34 h	77	200,000	Delfo (Ita) (Sergio Brighenti)	2:34.3h
61	50,000	Su Mac Lad (USA) (Stanley Dancer)	2:34.2h	78	200,000	Cold Comfort (USA) (P. Haughton)	2:31.3h
62	50,000	Tie Silk (Can) (Keith Waples)	2:34.1h	79	200,000	Doublemint (USA) (Peter Haughton)	2:38.3h
63	50,000	Su Mac Lad (USA) (Stanley Dancer)	2:34 h	80	250,000	Classical Way (US)(J.Simpson,Jr.)	2:35.2h
64	50,000	Speedy Scot (USA) (Ralph Baldwin)	2:32.3h	81	250,000	Ideal du Gazeau (Fra) (E.Lefevre)	2:32.3h
65	100,000	Pluvier III (Swe) (Gunnar Nordin)	2:36.2h	82	250,000	Ideal du Gazeau (Fra) (E.Lefevre)	2:36 h
66	100,000	Armbro Flight (Can) (Joe O'Brien)	2:31.3h	83	250,000	Ideal du Gazeau (Fra) (E.Lefevre)	2:35.2h
67	100,000	Roquepine (Fra) (Henry Levesque)	2:43.4h	84	250,000	Lutin d'Isigny (Fra) (J.P.Andre)	2:30 h
68	100,000	Roquepine (Fra) (J.R. Gougeon)	2:38.3h	85	250,000	Lutin d'Isigny (Fra) (J.P.Andre)	2:31 h
69	100,000	Une De Mai (Fra) (J.R. Gougeon)	2:33.2h	86	250,000	Habib (Den) (Ulf Thoresen)	2:33 h
70	125,000	Fresh Yankee (Can) (Joe O'Brien)	2:35.1h	87	200,000	Callit (Swe) (Karl Johansson)	2:33.4h
71	125,000	Une De Mai (Fra) (J.R. Gougeon)	2:34.4h	88	200,000	Mack Lobell (USA) (John Campbell)	2:30.4h
72	125,000	Speedy Crown (USA)(H. Beissinger)	2:35.1h	89	350,000	Kit Lobell (USA)(Ber. Lindstedt)	2:31.1h
73	150,000	Delmonica Hanover (US)(J.Chapman)	2:34.2h	90	450,000	Reve d'Udon (FRA) (Yves Dreux) R	2:28.3h
74	200,000	Delmonica Hanover (US)(J.Chapman)	2:34.4h				
75	200,000	Savoir (USA) (Del Insko)	2:32.1h	a 1-1/2 mile.		b 1-1/4 mile since 1960.	

The Jersey Cup
Three-Year-Old Pace
Meadowlands, E. Rutherford, NJ June 30, 1990

79	23,920	Overkill (Shelly Goudreau)	1:57.4m		75,650	Ogden Lobell (John Campbell)	1:53.2m
80	35,060	Bruce Gimble (Glen Garnsey)	1:56.3m	87	74,513	Laag (Bill O'Donnell)	1:51.3m
81	130,000	Seahawk Hanover (Ben Webster)	1:55.2m		73,013	Frugal Gourmet (Trevor Ritchie)	1:53.1m
82	160,000	No Nukes (Glen Garnsey)	1:55.2m	88	71,018	Prime Royce (Ben Webster)	1:53 m
83	202,000	Jamuga (Bill O'Donnell)	1:55 m		72,518	Camtastic (Bill O'Donnell)	1:52.4m
84	72,000	Electric Guitar (Stanley Dancer)	1:56.1m	89	51,000	Dancer Nukes (John Campbell)	1:53.1m
		Native Seahawk (Bill O'Donnell)	1:55.1m		51,000	Hit The Bid (Bill O'Donnell)	1:53.3m
85	80,000	Nihilator (Bill O'Donnell)	1:54.3m	90	48,130	In The Pocket (John Campbell) R	1:51.2m
	80,000	Nero's Star (Bill O'Donnell)	1:54.1m		48,130	Raven Lunatic (Michel Lachance)	1:54.3m
86	74,150	Towner's Big Guy (S. Warrington)	1:53 m				

The Jugette
Three-Year-Old Filly Pace
Delaware County Fair, Delaware, OH Sept. 21, 1990

71	30,414	Jefferson Time (Ben Webster)	2:00.1h	80	90,877	Toy Poodle (Billy Herman) b	1:58.3h
72	35,460	Romalie Hanover (R. Beaulieu) a	1:57.4h	81	86,398	Watering Can (Stanley Dancer) c	1:58.1h
73	36,684	All Alert (Glen Garnsey)	2:01.1h	82	140,114	Three Diamonds (Bruce Riegle)	1:57.3h
74	45,558	Handle With Care (Wm. Haughton)	1:57.4h	83	119,886	Turn The Tide (Bill O'Donnell)	1:57.1h
75	40,883	Silk Stockings (Pres Burris, Jr.)	1:57.2h	84	158,353	Naughty But Nice (Tom Haughton) R	1:55.2h
76	60,060	Misty Raquel (Jerry Graham)	1:58.2h	85	157,170	Amneris (John Campbell) d	1:54.4h
77	58,452	Mistletoe Shalee (Stanley Dancer)	1:58.3h	86	208,300	Anniecrombie (George Sholty) e	1:56.2h
78	78,633	Passing Glance (George Sholty)	1:56.4h	87	200,000	Armbro Feather (John Kopas)	1:56.1h
79	75,257	Roses Are Red (Jack Kopas)	1:56.3h	88	221,460	Leah Almahurst (Bill Fahy)	1:56.2h

CHRONICLES

89	200,709 Cheery Hello (John Campbell)	R 1:55.2h	b By Armbro Vicky.		Town Tattler.	
90	200,000 Lady Genius (Michel Lachance)	R 1:55.2h	c By Watering Can &		e By Bonniebelle Hanover.	
a By Brets Pet.	d By Amneris &		Loose News.			

The Kentucky Futurity
Three-Year-Old Trot
The Red Mile, Lexington, KY Oct. 5, 1990

Yr	Purse	Winner	Driver	Time	Starters	Heats	Second *	Third
93	11,850	Oro Wilkes	John A. Goldsmith	2:14 1/2m	11	5	Medio	The Conqueror
94	27,480	Beuzetta (f)	Gus Macey	2:14 1/2m	9	3	Futurity	Celaya
95	20,000	Oakland Baron	W.W. Milam	2:16 1/2m	7	4	Katrina Belle	Scourine
96	25,000	Rose Croix (f)	Myron E. McHenry	2:14 m	11	4	Fred S. Moody	Baronaise
97	10,000	Thorn (f)	Orin A. Hickok	2:13 1/4m	8	6r **	Preston	China Silk
98	10,000	Peter The Great	P.V. Johnson	2:12 1/2m	6	3	***	
99	10,000	Boralma	Guss Macey	2:11 1/2m	10	6	Extasy	The Bondsman
00	16,000	Fereno (f)	Ed Benyon	2:10 3/4m	9	3	Susie J.	Lady Thisbe
01	16,000	Peter Stirling	J.B. Chandler	2:11 1/2m	6	3	Walnut Hall	Hawthorne
02	14,000	Nella Jay (f)	F.D. McKey	2:14 1/4m	11	5	Gail Hamilton	John Mc.
03	20,000	Sadie Mac (f)	A. McDonald	2:12 3/4m	10	3	Barongale	Katherine A.
04	21,000	Grace Bond (f)	W.J. Andrews	2:09 1/4m	7	5	Alta Axworthy	Totara
05	21,000	Miss Adbell (f)	A. McDonald	2:09 3/4m	8	4	Susie N.	Marecheale
06	14,000	Siliko	Myron McHenry/W. McCarthy	2:11 1/4m	9	4	Lightsome	Ed Custer
07	14,000	General Watts	M. Bowerman	2:11 m	7	3	Bisa	Baron McKinney
08	14,000	The Harvester	Pop Geers	2:08 3/4m	8	3	Binvolo	The Leading Lady
09	14,000	Baroness Virginia (f)	Tom W. Murphy	2:07 1/4m	10	6r	Czarevna	Bertha C.
10	14,000	Grace (f)	M.C. McDevitt	2:08 m	6	5	Colorado E.	Emily Ellen
11	14,000	Peter Thompson	Jos. L. Serrill	2:07 1/2m	7	6r	Mainleaf	Atlantic Express
12	14,000	Manrico B.	W.G. Durfee	2:07 1/4m	9	6r	Rhythmell	Baldy McGregor
13	14,000	Etawah	Pop Geers	2:05 3/4m	8	5r	Peter Johnson	Bonington
14	14,000	Peter Volo	Thomas W. Murphy	2:03 1/2m	4	3	Lee Axworthy	Lady Wanetka
15	14,000	Mary Putney (f)	R.D. McMahon	2:05 1/2m	8	2	Humfast	Colorado Range
16	14,000	Volga (f)	Ben White	2:04 1/2m	6	3	Harrod's Creek	Expressive Lou
17	14,000	The Real Lady (f)	Thomas W. Murphy	2:03 3/4m	7	3	Harvest Gale	Bertha Maguire
18	14,000	Nella Dillon (f)	Jos. L. Serrill	2:05 1/4m	5	3	Petrex	Miriam Guy
19	14,000	Periscope (f)	J.L. Dodge	2:04 1/2m	7	5r	Brusiloff	Abbie Putney
20	14,000	Arion Guy	Harry Stokes	2:04 3/4m	6	3	Sister Bertha	Natalie The Great
21	14,000	Rose Scott (f)	T.W. Murphy	2:03 1/2m	11	2	Nelson Dillon	****
22	14,000	Lee Worthy	Ben White	2:03 3/4m	7	2	Bunter	Edith Worthy
23	14,000	Ethelinda (f)	Walter Cox	2:03 1/2m	7	4r	Hollywood Leonard	The Senator
24	14,000	Mr. McElwyn	Ben White	2:02 m	4	2	Guy Richard	Erla Guy
25	14,000	Aileen Guy (f)	Ben White	2:03 3/4m	6	2	Guy Ozark	Sam Williams
26	14,000	Guy McKinney	Nat Ray	2:06 3/4m	8	2	Catherine	Charm
27	14,000	Iosola's Worthy (f)	Marvin Childs	2:05 1/4m	7	2	Signal Flash	Hot Pluto
28	14,000	Spencer	W.H. Leese	2:05 m	8	2	Etta Volo	Nelly Signal
29	12,000	Walter Dear	Walter Cox	2:02 3/4m	7	2	Miss Woerner	Hollywood Harrier
30	14,000	Hanover's Bertha (f)	Tom Berry	2:00 m	9	2	Legality	Jessamine
31	14,000	Protector	William Caton	1:59 1/4m	6	2	Mac Aubrey	Charlotte Hanover
32	14,000	The Marchioness (f)	William Caton	2:02 m	4	2	Calumet Chuck	Kashmary
33	14,000	Meda (f)	Ben White	2:03 1/4m	11	2	Taffy Volo	Hollywood Portia
34	14,000	Princess Peg (f)	Sep Palin	2:00 3/4m	6	4r	Vitamine	Lord Jim
35	12,000	Lawrence Hanover	Henry Thomas	2:00 3/4m	7	2	Miss Kate B.	Volo Arion
36	10,000	Rosalind (f)	Ben White	2:03 m	6	2	Ed Lasater	Ruth M. Mac
37	9,295	Twilight Song (f)	Ben White	2:01 1/2m	10	2	Delphia Hanover	DeSota
38	9,570	McLin Hanover	Henry Thomas	2:00 3/4m	11	2	Long Key	Vesta Hanover
39	9,000	Peter Astra	Doc Parshall	2:02 1/2m	6	2	The Abbott	Bagpiper
40	9,075	Spencer Scott	Fred Egan	2:02 m	7	4r	Kuno	Eton
41	8,330	Bill Gallon	Lee Smith	2:02 1/4m	6	2	Lucy Hanover	Fast Train
42		-- Not Raced --						
43		-- Not Raced --						
44		-- Not Raced --						
45		-- Not Raced --						
46	25,781	Victory Song	Sep Palin	2:00 1/2m	9	2	*****	
47	36,905	Hoot Mon	Sep Palin	2:04.1m	6	2	Way Yonder	Joe's Pride
48	50,071	Egan Hanover	Ralph Baldwin	2:03.2m	7	2	Laurelite	Madison Hanover
49	57,154	Bangaway	Ralph Baldwin	2:05.2m	13	2	Martha Doyle	Guy Ambassador
50	54,665	Star's Pride	Harry Pownall, Sr.	2:02 m	6	2	Malcom	Scotch Dean
51	66,659	Ford Hanover	John Simpson, Sr.	2:01.2m	11	2	Candy Man	Scotch Rhythm
52	66,231	Sharp Note	Bion Shively	2:00 m	9	3	Duke Of Lullwater	Lu Peck
53	67,485	Kimberly Kid	Thomas Berry	2:00.3m	11	2	Faber Hanover	Singing Sword
54	63,121	Harlan	Delvin Miller	2:01 m	9	2	Pronto Boy	Darn Safe
55	62,702	Scott Frost	Joe O'Brien	2:00.3m	7	3	Home Free	Way Ahead
56	53,731	Nimble Colby	Ralph Baldwin	2:02 m	15	3	Barlow Hanover	Bold Rodney
57	50,460	Cassin Hanover (f)	Fred Egan	2:02.1m	13	4r	Storm Cloud	Double Scotch
58	53,330	Emily's Pride (f)	Flave Nipe	a 1:59.1m	11	3	Senator Frost	Mr Saunders
59	53,810	Diller Hanover	Ralph Baldwin	2:01.1m	10	2	Tie Silk	Lady Belvedere
60	64,040	Elaine Rodney (f)	Clint Hodgins	1:58.3m	12	2	Quick Song	Blaze Hanover
61	59,330	Duke Rodney	Eddie Wheeler	b 1:58.1m	8	3	Caleb	Matastar
62	55,230	Safe Mission	Joe O'Brien	1:59.1m	11	2	Impish	Lord Gordon
63	61,128	Speedy Scot	Ralph Baldwin	1:57.1m	8	2	Florlis	Cheer Honey
64	57,096	Ayres	John Simpson, Sr.	1:58.1m	7	2	Dashing Rodney	Dartmouth
65	65,133	Armbro Flight (f)	Joe O'Brien	1:59.3m	6	2	Noble Victory	Egyptian Candor
66	61,602	Governor Armbro	Joe O'Brien	2:00.3m	9	2	Gay Sam	Shatter Way
67	58,642	Speed Model (f)	Art Hult	c 1:59.2m	9	3	Rocket Speed	Halifax Hanover
68	57,398	Nevele Pride	Stanley Dancer	1:57 m	7	2	Snow Speed	Larengo Hanover
69	64,757	Lindys Pride	Howard Beissinger	1:59 m	9	2	Nevele Major	Sheer Speed
70	76,351	Timothy T.	John Simpson, Jr.	1:59.4m	12	3	Paris Air	Formal Notice
71	63,415	Savoir	James Arthur	1:58.1m	7	2	Keystone Hilliard	Hoot Speed
72	56,219	Super Bowl	Stanley Dancer	1:59 m	5	2	Spartan Hanover	Songcan
73	64,173	Arnie Almahurst	Joe O'Brien	d 1:59.1m	8	3	Knightly Way	Flirth
74	100,000	Waymaker	John Simpson, Jr.	e 1:58.1m	13	4r	Dancing Party	Nevele Diamond
75	100,000	Noble Rogue	Billy Herman	f 1:59.3m	12	3	Ways To Win	Songflori

Page 337

CHRONICLES

76	100,000	Quick Pay	Peter Haughton	1:59 m	9	3	Steve Lobell	Soothsayer
77	100,000	Texas	Billy Herman	1:57.3m	10	3	Scandal Sheet	Sugarbowl Hanover
78	100,000	Doublemint	Peter Haughton	1:58.3m	8	2	Way To Gain	Count's Pride
79	100,000	Classical Way (f)	John Simpson, Jr.	1:57.4m	10	2	Chiola Hanover	Lindy's Crown
80	100,000	Final Score	Tom Haughton	1:58 m	10	4r	Noble Hustle	Marino Hanover
81	124,311	Filet Of Sole (f)	John Simpson, Jr.	1:57.3m	15	3	Spice Island	Chauncey Lobell
82	116,200	Jazz Cosmos	Mickey McNichol	1:57 m	8	2	Speed Bowl	Messerschmitt
83	150,200	Power Seat	Bill O'Donnell	1:55.4m	10	3	T V Yankee	Tarport Lizzy
84	184,800	Fancy Crown (f)	Bill O'Donnell g	1:55.3m	15	2	Armbro Crouch	Giorgio D
85	185,500	Flak Bait	Ben Webster h	1:55.2m	14	3r	Nearly Perfect	Armbro Devona
86	160,530	Sugarcane Hanover	Ron Waples	1:55.2m	13	2	Victorious Tail	Royal Prestige
87	166,837	Napoletano	Bill O'Donnell i	1:55 m	13	2	Mack Lobell	Waikiki Beach
88	170,910	Huggie Hanover	Ron Waples	1:55 m	10	2	Firm Tribute	Slybowl Hanover
89	177,230	Peace Corps (f)	John Campbell R	1:54.2m	14	2	Demilo Hanover	Flying Irishman
90	180,000	Star Mystic	Jan Johnson Rj	1:54.2m	11	3r	Jeanne's Somolli	Columnist

* - In races after 1974, second and third finishers in deciding heat, or summary standings where there is a race-off. Prior years show summary standing only. From 18993 to 1920, race-winner had to win three heats, and then two heats thereafter.
** - "x" next to number of heats indicates there was a race-off.
*** - Limerick, Charley Herr & Seraphima divided second, third and fourth monies.
**** - Sterling (3-5) and The Great Rose (5-3) split third and fourth monies.
***** - Chestertown (3-2) and Walter Spencer (2-3) divided second and third monies.

a By Senator Frost. d By Knightly Way. g By Garland Lobell i By Mack Lobell.
b By Caleb. e By Dancing Party. h By Flak Bait & j By Jeanne's Somolli.
c By Rocket Speed. f By Exclusive Way. Nearly Perfect.

The Kentucky Futurity Filly Division *
Three-Year-Old Filly Trot
The Red Mile, Lexington, KY Oct. 5, 1990

65	13,242	Armbro Flight (Joe O'Brien)	2:00.2m	80	25,040	Kading (Billy Haughton)	1:57.3m
66	10,593	Kerry Way (Frank Ervin)	2:02.4m	81	25,600	Panty Raid (Stanley Dancer)	1:57.3m
67	13,315	Speed Model (Art Hult)	2:02.3m	82	32,600	Ginger Belle (Harold Dancer, Jr.)	1:56.2m
68	13,863	Valorama (Sanders Russell)	2:01.3m	83	35,020	Ander's Favorite (Jan Nordin)	1:56.4m
69	15,460	Sheer Speed (Joe O'Brien)	2:01.3m	84	34,324	Petroliana (Berndt Lindstedt)	1:56.2m
70	15,283	Misty Ayres (J. Graham)	2:02 m	85	41,100	Double Coverage (C. Galbraith) a	1:58.2m
71	17,982	Noble Gay (H. Graham)	1:58.2m	86	77,929	Armbro Ermine (Larry Walker) bR	1:56.1m
72	15,913	Delmonica Hanover (Del Miller)	2:01.3m	87	76,087	Treasure Me (Ron Waples) c	1:56.3m
73	15,595	Colonial Charm (Glen Garnsey)	2:00.4m	88	72,870	Nan's Catch (Berndt Lindstedt) R	1:56.1m
74	15,185	Berna Hanover (Glen Garnsey)	1:59.4m	89	83,870	Park Avenue Kathy (Br.Nickells) d	1:57.4m
75	19,475	Keystone Pioneer (Dick DeSantis)	1:59.3m	90	92,120	Nivea Hanover (Billy Herman)	1:55.4m
76	21,436	Gayette Hanover (J. Simpson, Jr.)	2:00 m			* - Named the Chestnut Farm prior to 1986	
77	25,156	Elmsford (John Chapman)	1:57.2m			a By Davidia Hanover.	d By Triangle Park &
78	22,310	Rosemary (Billy Haughton)	1:58.2m			b By Chickadee Newton.	Snippy Hanover.
79	21,843	Superior Sweep (Carl Allen)	2:00.2m			c By Lucious Almahust.	

The Kentucky Pacing Derby
Two-Year-Olds
Louisville Downs, Louisville, KY Sept. 8, 1990

78	183,755	Scarlet Skipper (Billy Herman)	1:58.4h	85	367,850	Sherman Almahurst (Doug Brown)	1:56.2h
79	204,000	Niatross (Clint Galbraith)	1:58.3h	86	434,570	Jate Lobell (Mark O'Mara)	1:55.2h
80	200,000	French Chef (Stanley Dancer)	1:57.3h	87	572,340	Albert Albert (Chris Boring)	R 1:55.1h
81	209,200	Temujin (Clarence Martin Sr.)	1:56.1h	88	436,410	Totally Ruthless (Jo. Campbell) a	1:55.1h
82	312,220	Tim The Tree (Dick Macomber)	1:57.4h	89	329,913	Jake And Elwood (Ed Morgan, Jr.)	1:59 h
83	347,580	Signed N Sealed (Bill O'Donnell)	1:56.1h	90	379,553	Tooter Scooter (Bill Fahy)	1:57 h
84	349,310	Witsend's Wizard (Ron Waples)	1:57.2h			a By Kentucky Spur.	

The Kentucky Standardbred Sale Company
Two-Year-Old Filly Trot
Rosecroft Raceway, Oxon Hill, MD Aug. 10, 1990

90	96,250	Santa Royal (Catello Manzi)	1:59.4f		97,500	Frances Jet Boko (Jan Nordin)	2:01.2f

The Kentucky Standardbred Sale Company
Two-Year-Old Filly Pace
Rosecroft Raceway, Oxon Hill, MD Sept. 8, 1990

89	106,933	Bruce's Lady (John Campbell)	1:57.2f	90	126,650	Unreachable (Eddie Davis)	1:57.1f
	106,933	DelinquentAccount (Bill O'Donnell)	1:56.2f		127,650	Miss Easy (John Campbell)	R 1:55 f
	106,933	Mean And Green (Bill O'Donnell)	1:57.2f			* - Raced at Freestate Raceway in 1989	

The Lady Baltimore *
Two-Year-Old-Filly Pace
Rosecroft Raceway, Oxon Hill, MD Sept. 1, 1990

82	53,750	Miss Yankee (Bib Roberts)	1:59.1f		100,000	Follow My Star (Bruce Nickells)	1:59.1f
	53,750	Farmstead's Future (Wayne Smullin)	**	86	110,000	Simonsays Hi Toots (W. O'Donnell)	1:58.4f
83	112,925	Peachbottom (John Campbell)	1:57.2f		110,000	Halcyon (Ray Remmen)	1:58.4f
	112,075	Leslie Lobell (Catello Manzi)	1:58.3f		110,000	Tantalize Hanover (John Campbell)	1:59.1f
84	87,813	Shimmer Hanover (Roger Hammer)	2:00.3f	87	123,750	Huna Buna (John Campbell)	1:58.2f
	87,813	Steinam (Buddy Gilmour)	1:58.2f		125,000	Marcasite (John Campbell)	1:57.4f
	86,563	Dear Dorothy (John Campbell)	1:58.3f		125,000	So Cozy (John Campbell)	R 1:56.4f
	87,813	Semalu D'Amour (Benoit Cote)	1:58.2f	88	87,413	Double Deception (Leo Harvey)	1:58.2f
85	101,250	Joy Hanover (Tom Sells)	1:59.2f		87,413	Kimmy B (Ben Steall)	1:57.2f
	101,250	Caressable (William Haughton)	1:57.2f		88,663	Central Park West (John Campbell)	1:57 f
	100,000	Valentina (William Haughton)	1:59.2f		88,663	Lingerie (Ben Steall)	1:58.4f

CHRONICLES

89	82,384	Bruce's Lady (John Campbell)	1:57.3f		77,083	R M Gee (John Campbell)	1:57.3f
	82,384	Dave D's Hurricane (M. Lachance)	1:57.3f		77,083	Yankee Co-ed (Wm. "Bib" Roberts)R	1:54.4f
	82,384	Warm Ways (Ben Webster)	1:57.1f		* - Raced at Freestate Raceway prior to 1990		
90	75,834	Miss Easy (John Campbell)	1:55.4f		** - Time disallowed		

The Lady Maud
Three-Year-Old Filly Pace
Yonkers Raceway, Yonkers, NY   July 7, 1990

60	26,972	Hodge Podge (Alfred Thomas)	2:03.1h		80	52,717	After The Fact (Bill O'Donnell)	1:59.4h
61	28,776	Truly Rainbow (Walter Welch)	2:07.1h		81	59,929	Fan Hanover (Glen Garnsey)	1:58.4h
62	38,810	Cathy J. Hanover (Stanley Dancer)	2:02.2h		82	40,915	Albaquel (Doug Ackerman)	1:57.1h
63	33,831	Harry's Laura (Clint Hodgins)	2:05.3h			40,915	Sunny And Fair (Michel Lachance)	1:58.4h
64	39,315	Bit O' Sugar (William Haughton)	2:03.4h		83	104,394	Turn The Tide (Bill O'Donnell)	2:00.4h
65	50,639	Woodlawn Drummond (Ke. Waples)	2:04.2h		84	58,615	Don't Dally (Merritt Dokey)	1:58.1h
66	37,321	Bonjour Hanover (Stanley Dancer)	2:01.3h			58,615	Naughty But Nice (Tom Haughton)	1:56.4h
67	38,716	Poplar Evalynda (George Sholty)	2:03.2h		85	41,909	Peppermint Candy (J.Marsh, Jr.)	1:57.4h
68	40,254	Thorpe Marge (William Haughton)	2:03.3h			41,909	Dazzle Almahurst(J.Patterson,Jr.)	1:59.4h
69	44,344	Supple Yankee (Stanley Dancer)	2:03.3h			42,659	Semalu Damour (Benoit Cote)	1:58.1h
70	44,083	Betty Hanover (Harold Dancer)	2:01.2h		86	64,317	Follow My Star (Buddy Gilmour)	1:58 h
71	44,992	Jefferson Time (Ben Webster)	2:05 h			64,317	Annie's Surprise (Mark O'Mara)	1:59.1h
72	46,177	Romalie Hanover (Roland Beaulieu)	2:01.4h		87	67,526	Jolibea Hanover (Ben Webster)	1:58.4h
73	52,177	Skippers Dream (John Chapman)	2:04.2h			67,526	Time Well Spent (W. O'Donnell)	1:59.2h
74	51,281	Handle With Care (Wm.Haughton)	2:01.4h		88	130,468	Sweel Reflection (W. O'Donnell) R	1:55.4h
75	52,517	Beckilyn Hanover (Rol. Beaulieu)	2:00.4h		89	42,257	L Dees Trish (Michel Lachance)	1:58.1h
76	52,001	Misty Raquel (Jerry Graham)	2:02.2h			42,257	Tyler Town (Peter Ruscitto)	1:57.4h
77	54,684	Mistletoe Shalee (Stanley Dancer)	2:01.4h			42,257	Uptown Swell (J. Patterson, Jr.)	1:58.2h
78	59,517	Happy Lady (Jim Rankin)	1:58.4h		90	69,020	Armbro Ilona (John Campbell)	1:57.1h
79	56,036	Roses Are Red (Jack Kopas)	1:59.4h			69,020	Fiji Hanover (Herve Filion)	1:58.2h

The Lady Suffolk
Three-Year-Old Filly Trot *
Yonkers Raceway, Yonkers, NY   July 7, 1990

60	20,175	Elaine Rodney (Clint Hodgins)	2:13.2h			39,814	Panty Raid (Stanley Dancer)	2:03.2h
61	26,325	Speedy Princess (Earle Avery)	2:12.2h		82	39,715	Lucretia's Kash (Don Galbraith)	2:03.4h
62	27,723	Impish (Frank Ervin)	2:12.1h			39,715	Ginger Belle (Harold Dancer)	2:04.1h
63	25,461	Campus Queen (Ralph Baldwin)	2:14.1h		83	56,072	Color Of Money (Mickey McNichol)	2:03.2h
64	28,574	Speedy Victory (Robert Walker)	2:12.4h			56,822	Tarport Frenzy (Jan Nordin)	2:01.4h
65	27,062	Arabesque (Del Insko)	2:07 h		84	57,146	Maiden Yankee (Bib Roberts)	2:02 h
66	30,060	Starlight Way (George Sholty)	2:05.1h			56,396	Mae Jean's Crown (Carl Allen)	2:00.3h
67	36,053	Lana Hanover (Vernon Dancer)	2:07.3h		85	45,742	Super Samantha (Doug Ackerman)	2:03.2h
68	33,890	Jostle (John Simpson, Sr.)	2:06.2h			45,742	Double Coverage (Buddy Gilmour)	2:02 h
69	44,988	Flowing Speed (John Chapman)	2:04.2h			45,742	Grades Singing (Gilles Gendron)	2:02.2h
70	38,571	Tammie Hill (George Sholty)	2:03.3h		86	60,442	Armbro Ermine (Larry Walker)	2:03 h
71	39,962	Egyptian Jody (Stanley Dancer)	2:04.4h			60,442	JEF's Spice (Bill O'Donnell)	2:01.2h
72	35,000	Delmonica Hanover (John Chapman)	2:02.4h		87	58,654	Lucious Almahurst (Ben Webster)	2:00 h
73	36,121	Meadow Flower (John Chapman)	2:05.3h		88	31,027	Tarport Bridget (Jay Randall)	2:01.2h
74	39,510	Noble Florie (Delvin Miller)	2:05.2h			31,027	Kerry's Crown (Joe Marsh, Jr.)	2:03.1h
75	39,175	Meadow Bright (Delvin Miller)	2:04.1h		89	21,514	Clarisse Lobell (Eldon Harner)	2:02.2h
76	52,601	Social Scandal (Merritt Dokey)	2:02.4h			21,514	E D Kash (Clint Galbraith)	2:01.4h
77	36,242	Angel's Flight (John Chapman)	2:02.4h			22,114	Express Courier (J.Patterson,Jr.)	2:02.2h
	35,642	Superlou (John Simpson, Jr.)	2:03.3h		90	24,609	Happy Diamonds (John Campbell)	2:00.5h
78	47,511	Imagery (Stanley Dancer)	2:03.4h			24,609	L V Goldie (Herve Filion)	R 1:59.2h
79	50,036	Superior Sweep (Carl Allen)	2:00.3h			24,609	Working Gal (John Campbell)	2:00.2h
80	50,316	Kading (Ben Steall)	2:04 h					
81	39,814	Spring Dash (Hakan Wallner)	2:03.1h			* 1-1/16 mile before 1965.		

The La Paloma Pace
Two-Year-Old Fillies
Yonkers Raceway, Yonkers, NY   July 7, 1990

64	21,207	Balenzano (Del Insko)	2:05.3h		78	31,500	Lismore (Harry Harvey)	2:00.2h
65	25,000	Bonjour Hanover (Stanley Dancer)	2:11.2h		79	33,700	D I Sweetie (Ray Ireland)	2:06.4h
66	25,000	Meadow Elva (Stanley Dancer)	2:03.3h		80	42,250	Areba Areba (Jack Kopas)	1:59.2h
67	25,000	Berinda Hanover (J. Simpson, Jr.)	2:07 h		81	50,500	Nut House (William Haughton)	2:01.3h
68	12,500	Evalina Lobell (Bill Myer)	2:07.2h		82	66,500	Napa Valley (Bruce Riegle)	2:02.2h
	12,500	Fiesta Lobell (Stanley Dancer)	2:06.2h			67,500	Tango Almahurst (Gene Daisey)	2:03 h
69	25,660	Revolve (Del Insko)	2:05.3h		83	78,125	Peachbottom (John Campbell)	2:00.2h
70	25,247	Evelyn Hanover (Del Insko)	2:04.3h			79,125	De Buena Lobell (H. Beissinger)	2:00.1h
71	28,448	Romalie Hanover (Art Hult)	2:02.3h		84	62,500	Steal The Show (John Campbell)	2:00.2h
72	29,971	Jambo Belle (Merritt Dokey)	2:03.2h			62,500	Funny Honey (Rejean Daigneault)	2:02.1h
73	44,536	Handle With Care (Wm. Haughton)	2:04.3h			61,500	Stormy Flo (Joe Marsh, Jr.)	2:02 h
74	9,312	Ata Whitney (Herve Filion)	2:07.1h		85	300,000	Valentina (William Haughton)	R 1:58.2h
	9,312	Tarport Hap (Delvin Miller)	2:07 h		86	233,500	Halcyon (John Campbell)	2:00.2h
75	10,976	Romantic Princess (Paul Battis)	2:06 h		87	200,000	Glider (Mark O'Mara)	2:01.1h
	10,876	Toplady Almahurst (Abe Stoltzfus)	2:04.4h		88	157,000	Southtown (Michel Lachance)	2:00 h
76	17,993	Sirup Time (George Sholty)	2:03.2h		89	218,500	Mean And Green (Jim Marohn)	2:01 h
	17,993	Helen's Deal (Dick DeSantis)	2:04.2h		90	219,000	Perfect Together (Richard Wojcio)	1:59.3h
77	29,138	Passing Glance (George Sholty)	2:00.2h					

The George Morton Levy Memorial Final
Open Aged Pace
Yonkers Raceway, Yonkers, NY   May 12, 1990

78	200,000	Sirota Anderson (N. Dauplaise)	1:58 h		83	156,000	My Bill Forwood (J.Patterson,Jr.)	1:56.4h
79	200,000	Try Scotch (Shelly Goudreau)	1:56.3h		84	182,000	Caramore (Buddy Gilmour)	1:57.1h
80	200,000	Pat's Gypsy (Lew Williams)	2:01.3h		85	145,000	On The Road Again (Wm. Gilmour) R	1:55.2h
81	154,000	Newt Lobell (Carmine Abbatiello)	1:56.4h		86	119,000	Falcon Seelster (Tom Harmer)	1:55.2h
82	148,000	Skip By Night (Ted Wing)	1:57 h		87	149,000	Dignatarian (Buddy Gilmour)	1:58.1h

CHRONICLES

88	145,000	Dragon's Lair (Donald Dancer)	1:56.1h				
89	200,000	Jaguar Spur (Bill Fahy)	1:55.2h				
				90	240,000	My Guru (Doug Brown)	R 1:54.3h

The Little Brown Jug
Three-Year-Old Pace
Delaware County Fair, Delaware, OH Sept. 20, 1990

Yr	Purse	Winner	Driver	Time	Starters	Heats	Second *	Third
46	35,358	Ensign Hanover	"Curly" Smart a	2:02 3/4h	9	4r **	His Lady	Royal Chief
47	38,200	Forbes Chief	Adelbert Cameron	2:05 h	11	2	Goose Bay	Marcellus
48	47,528	Knight Dream	Frank Safford	2:07.1h	7	2	Poplar Volo	Navy Hal
49	58,281	Good Time	Frank Ervin	2:03.2h	16	2	Stormyway	Golden Chief
50	56,525	Dudley Hanover	Delvin Miller	2:02.3h	11	3	Thomas Hat	Quilla Hanover
51	66,280	Tar Heel	Adelbert Cameron	2:00 h	14	2	Solicitor	H D Hanover
52	60,463	Meadow Rice	Wayne "Curly" Smart	2:01.3h	12	3	Wilmington's Star	Adio Abe
53	54,972	Keystonter	Frank Ervin b	2:02.3h	13	4r	Hillsota	Newport Chief
54	69,332	Adios Harry	Morris MacDonald c	2:02.2h	15	3r	Queen's Adios	Phantom Lady
55	66,608	Quick Chief	William Haughton d	2:00 h	17	2	Dottie's Pick	Meadow Ace
56	52,666	Noble Adios	John Simpson, Sr.	2:00.4h	10	2	Adioscot	Adioway
57	73,528	Torpid	John Simpson, Sr.	2:00.4h	16	2	Meadow Lands	Morris Eden
58	65,252	Shadow Wave	Joe O'Brien	2:01 h	12	2	Thorpe Hanover	O'Brien Hanover
59	76,582	Adios Butler	Clint Hodgins	1:59.2h	18	2	Meadow Al	Culver Pick
60	66,510	Bullet Hanover	John Simpson, Sr. e	1:58.3h	11	3	Muncy Hanover	Betting Time
61	70,069	Henry T.Adios	Stanley Dancer	1:58.4h	19	3r	Way Wave	Lang Hanover
62	75,038	Lehigh Hanover	Stanley Dancer	1:58.4h	13	2	Coffee Break	Gamecock
63	68,294	Overtrick	John Patterson, Sr.	1:57.1h	11	2	Meadow Skipper	Country Don
64	66,590	Vicar Hanover	William Haughton f	2:00.4h	13	2	Combat Time	Sheer Genius
65	71,447	Bret Hanover	Frank Ervin	1:57 h	7	2	Tuxedo Hanover	Rivaltime
66	74,616	Romeo Hanover	George Sholty	1:59.3h	12	2	Good Time Boy	Bonjour Hanover
67	84,778	Best Of All	Jim Hackett g	1:59 h	8	3	Nardins Byrd	Meadow Paige
68	104,226	Rum Customer	William Haughton	1:59.3h	17	2	Adios Waverly	Good Time Knight
69	109,731	Laverne Hanover	William Haughton	2:00.2h	16	2	Lightning Wave	Nardins Grand Slam
70	100,110	Most Happy Fella	Stanley Dancer	1:57.1h	11	3	Columbia George	Ferric Hanover
71	102,994	Nansemond	Herve Filion	1:57.2h	15	3r	Albatross	H T Luca
72	104,916	Strike Out	Keith Waples	1:56.3h	12	2	Good Bye Columbus	Fast Clip
73	120,000	Melvin's Woe	Joe O'Brien	1:57.3h	17	2	Faraway Bay	Armbro Nesbit
74	132,638	Armbro Omaha	William Haughton	1:57 h	17	2	Bret's Star	Boyden Hanover
75	147,813	Seatrain	Ben Webster h	1:56.4h	19	2	Albert's Star	Polaris Lobell
76	153,799	Keystone Ore	Stanley Dancer i	1:56.4h	16	2	Armbro Ranger	Precious Fella
77	150,000	Governor Skipper	John Chapman	1:56.1h	11	2	Crash	Jambooger
78	186,760	Happy Escort	Bill Popfinger j	1:55.2h	12	3r	Flight Director	Falcon Almahurst
79	226,455	Hot Hitter	Herve Filion	1:55.3h	17	2	Tijuana Taxi	Set Point
80	207,361	Niatross	Clint Galbraith	1:54.4h	8	2	Storm Damage	Trenton Time
81	243,799	Fan Hanover (f)	Glen Garnsey k	1:56 h	19	2	Seahawk Hanover	New York Motoring
82	328,900	Merger	John Campbell l	1:54.3h	25	2	Temujin	Icarus Lobell
83	358,800	Ralph Hanover	Ron Waples	1:55.3h	23	2	Skirt Lifter	Fortune Teller
84	366,717	Colt Fortysix	Chris Boring m	1:53.3h	21	2	Legal Notice	Troublemaker
85	350,730	Nihilator	Bill O'Donnell R	1:52.1h	13	2	Pershing Square	Dignatarian
86	407,684	Barberry Spur	Bill O'Donnell	1:52.4h	18	2	Amity Chef	Souffle
87	412,330	Jaguar Spur	Dick Stillings	1:54 h	23	2	Z Twenty Eight	Redskin
88	486,050	B J Scoot	Michel Lachance	1:52.3h	25	2	Camtastic	Albert Albert
89	500,200	Goalie Jeff	Michel Lachance n	1:54.1h	28	2	Barefoot Hanover	Tyler's Best
90	468,610	Beach Towel	Ray Remmen	1:53.3h	22	2	In The Pocket	Kiev Hanover

* - Second and third based on total purse money won.
** - "r" next to number of heats indicates there was a race-off

a By Royal Chief.
b By Newport Chief.
c By Phantom Lady.
d By Dottie's Pick.
e By Bullet Hanover & Muncy Hanover
f By Combat Time.
g By Nardins Byrd.
h By Albert's Star.
i By Armbro Ranger.
j By Falcon Almahurst.
k Seahawk Hanover.
l By Temujin.
m By Legal Notice.
n By Goalie Jeff & Barefoot Hanover.

The Little Brown Jug Preview
Three-Year-Old Pace
Scioto Downs, Columbus, OH Sept. 8, 1990

72	25,000	Hilarious Way (John Simpson, Jr.)	1:59.1f			40,150	Colt Fortysix (Chris Boring)	1:54.4f
73	26,400	Ricci Reenie Time (So. Dancer)	1:58.2f		85	152,350	Chairmanoftheboard(J.Campbell)	1:53.2f
74	26,000	Title Holder (Tom Brinkerhoff)	1:57.4f		86	166,000	Nobleland Sam (Sam Noble III)	1:54.2f
75	26,750	Nero (Joe O'Brien)	1:58.1f		87	82,000	Laag (Dick Farrington)	1:54.1f
76	30,000	Dream Maker (Glen Garnsey)	2:03.3f			84,000	Run The Table (John Campbell)	1:55.1f
77	26,000	Super Clint (John Quinn)	1:56.1f		88	70,000	Archie Almahurst (William Bailey)	1:54 f
78	27,000	Falcon Almahurst (Wm.Haughton)	1:55.2f			70,000	Spiked Bunny (Richard Silverman)	1:54.2f
79	27,500	Black Ace (Jimmy Larente)	1:57.3f			70,000	Threefold (Jay Picciano)	1:54.1f
80	37,000	Fundamentalist (Gene Riegel)	1:58 f		89	90,500	Barefoot Hanover (Dave Rankin)	1:54.2f
81	35,000	Wildwood Jeb (Larry Rolla)	1:57.1f			90,500	Dorunrun Bluegrass (J.Essig,Jr.)	1:54.1f
82	27,325	Billy Dart (Dick Richardson Jr)	1:57.3f		90	68,000	Apaches Fame (Wm. "Bud" Fritz)	1:53.4f
	27,075	Shannon Fella (Sam Noble III)	1:56.2f			68,000	Global Assault (Mark Williams)	R 1:53 f
83	50,600	Sydney Hill (Don Irvine, Jr.)	1:56.4f			70,000	Brando Hanover (Mickey McNichol)	1:54.2f
84	40,150	Cagey Hero (Tom Brinkerhoff)	1:57.3f					

The Little Pat
Two-Year-Old Pace -- Review Stake
Illinois State Fair, Springfield, IL Aug. 15, 1990

42	5,378	King's Counsel (Doc Parshall)	2:07 h		47	14,374	Friscoway (H.C. Fitzpatrick)	2:02.4m
43	3,389	Attorney (Art Blackwell)	2:10 h		48	15,727	Good Time (K.R. Cartnal)	2:04 m
44	7,973	True Chief (Thomas Berry)	2:05 m		49	16,923	Our Time (Frank Ervin)	2:06.4m
45	8,936	Ensign Hanover (Sep Palin)	2:04 1/4m		50	18,737	Tar Heel (Del Cameron)	2:03.2m
46	12,851	Poplar Byrd (Thomas Berry)	2:04 3/4m		51	19,515	Thunderclap (Hugh Bell)	a 2:02.1m

CHRONICLES

52	17,402 Iosola's Ensign (Curly Smart)	2:03.4m
53	21,883 Queen's Adios (Curly Smart)	b 2:01 m
54	17,022 Captain Adios (Del Miller)	c 2:04.1m
55	15,301 Buckeye (James Fitzpatrick)	d 2:01.1m
56	20,020 Adios Express (Joe O'Brien)	e 2:02.1m
57	16,130 Thorpe Hanover (Delvin Miller)	2:00.3m
58	21,213 Adios Day (Delvin Miller)	f 2:01.2m
59	17,473 Bullet Hanover (J. Simpson, Sr.)	1:59.1m
60	16,264 Lang Hanover (Jim Hackett)	g 2:01.4m
61	15,171 Coffee Break (George Sholty)	2:00.2m
62	15,505 Overtrick (John Patterson, Sr.)	2:01.1m
63	16,362 Ripping Good (Frank Ervin)	h 2:02.1m
64	19,570 Bret Hanover (Frank Ervin)	1:58.2m
65	20,388 Overcall (John Patterson, Sr.)	2:01.4m
66	21,822 Armbro Hurricane (Jim Dennis)	2:00 m
67	28,869 Rum Customer (William Haughton)	i 1:58.4m
68	30,880 Laverne Hanover (Wm. Haughton)	1:59.2m
69	42,350 Ideal Donut (Joe O'Brien)	j 1:58.4m
70	33,650 Winning Worthy (H. Graham, Jr.)	1:59.1m
	Race Byrd (Glen Garnsey)	2:00 m
71	34,670 Hilarious Way (John Simpson, Jr.)	1:59.1m
72	37,040 Ricci Reenie Time (Harold Dancer)	1:58.2m
73	36,370 Boyden Hanover (Billy Herman)	2:01 m
74	38,840 Alert Bret (Glen Garnsey)	k 1:58 m
75	-- Rain --	
76	49,370 Striking Image (Glen Garnsey)	1:55 m
77	41,680 Say Hello (Bill Popfinger)	1:57 m
78	45,388 Scarlet Skipper (Billy Herman)	l 1:56.2m
79	45,094 Cool Wind (Glen Garnsey)	m 1:55.4m
80	59,128 French Chef (Stanley Dancer)	n 1:55.2m
81	61,769 Paulsboro (Howard Beissinger)	o 1:55.3m
82	30,000 Carafe (Saverio Villante)	1:58.3m
	30,000 Del Cavallo (Doug Ackerman)	1:55.4m
83	58,483 Panorama (Tom Haughton)	1:55 m
84	63,632 Lake Hills Jeb (Tom Harmer)	p 1:53.4m
85	-- Rain --	
86	103,940 Jate Lobell (Mark O'Mara)	1:53.3m
87	108,020 All Da Time (Billy Herman)	q 1:53.4m
88	106,460 Hostile Takeover (Dg. Ackerman)	s 1:53.4m
89	88,500 Charlie's Thunder (Bill Fahy)	Rt 1:53.2m
90	74,000 Mantese (Mickey McNichol)	1:53.4m

a By Meadow Rice.
b By Parker Byrd.
c By Libby's Boy.
d By Adioscot.
e By Devastator.
f By Adios Chief.
g By High Test.
h By Lancelot Hanover.
i By Meadow Brick.
j By Race Time.
j By Race Time Boy.
k By Broadcaster B.
l By Sonsam.
m By Storm Damage.
n By Cowboy Spur.
o By Ideal Society.
q By Shannon Traffic.
s By King Cam.
t By Till We Meet Again.

The Maple Leaf Trotting Classic
Three-Year-Old & Up Trot *
Greenwood Raceway, Toronto, ONT Aug. 18, 1990

50	5,000 Morris Mite (E. L'Heureux)	2:08.2
	Adeline Hanover (H. Wellwood)	2:13.2
51	3,000 Projectile (P. Dussuatt)	2:14
52	3,000 Celia's Counsel (E. Rowe)	2:08
53	2,500 Vanduzen (J. Mehlenbacher)	2:07
54	3,500 Ben Boy (Keith Waples)	2:10 f
55	-- Did Not Fill --	
56	-- Not Raced --	
57	4,730 In Free (Harold McKinley)	2:07.2f
58	5,120 Mr. Baldridge (P. Dussuatt)	2:02.1f
59	6,150 Mr. Baldridge (Russ VallesKey)	2:03.4f
60	4,095 Selka Song (Harold McKinley)	2:07.3f
61	11,680 Tie Silk (Howard Beissinger)	2:07 q
62	14,110 Duke Of Decatur (Keith Waples)	2:04 q
63	12,800 Tie Silk (F. Baise)	2:28 f
64	12,700 Tie Silk (Marcel Dostie)	2:31.1f
65	13,050 Duke Rodney (D. Huff)	2:29.4f
66	12,100 Sprite Kid (Roger White)	2:02 f
67	19,000 Critic's Choice (Ron Feagan)	2:02.2f
68	32,800 Earl Laird (Jimmy Cruise, Sr.)	2:02 f
69	41,000 Grandpa Jim (Bob Farrington)	2:01.3f
70	49,500 Grandpa Jim (Bob Farrington)	2:00.4f
71	57,100 Grandpa Jim (Dick Farrington)	2:01.2f
72	60,400 Speedy Crown (Howard Beissinger)	2:00.3f
73	62,800 Flower Child (Joe O'Brien)	2:00.2f
74	64,600 Colonial Charm (Jack Bailey)	2:01.1f
75	47,450 Savoir (John Chapman)	2:01.4f
	47,450 Delmonica Hanover (John Chapman)	2:02.2f
76	27,160 Savoir (Ben Steall)	2:04.1f
77	100,000 Ima Lula (Joe O'Brien)	1:59.2f
78	90,000 Cold Comfort (Peter Haughton)	2:01.1f
79	100,000 Cold Comfort (William Haughton)	1:59.3f
80	104,000 Lindy's Crown (Larry Walker)	2:00.4f
81	102,500 Super Marty (Herman Hylkema)	2:00.1f
82	136,500 Bobbo (Norm Jones)	1:59.3f
83	143,000 Bridger (John Campbell)	1:58.2f
84	143,000 Bridger (Ron Waples)	1:57.2f
85	140,500 Manfred Hanover (Patsy Rapone)	1:58.1f
86	174,600 Grades Singing (Herve Filion)	1:57.2f
87	192,100 Franconia (John Campbell)	1:57.2f
88	209,000 Natural Image (Steve Condren)	1:56.3f
89	241,600 No Sex Please (Ron Waples)	Ra 1:56.2f
90	293,250 No Sex Please (Ron Waples)	1:57 f

* 1-1/16 mile in 1950-52; 1-1/8 mile in 1963;
1-3/16 mile in 1964-65.
a by Mathers Streak & No Sex Please.

The Matron Stake
Three-Year-Old Trot
Pompano Park, Pompano Beach, FL Nov. 17, 1990

10	6,274 Colorado E. (Guss Macey)	2:07 1/4m
11	6,166 Peter Thompson (Joe Serrill)	2:08 1/4m
12	5,491 Baldy McGregor (W.J. Andrews)	2:08 m
13	6,835 Dillon Axworthy (Joe Serrill)	2:10 1/4m
14	5,252 Peter Volo (T.W. Murphy)	2:13 3/4m
15	7,443 Rusticoat (W.J. Andrews)	2:08 1/4m
16	5,888 Expressive Lou (T.W. Murphy)	2:11 m
17	5,851 Miss Bertha Dillon(J. Serrill)	2:03 1/4m
18	5,977 David Guy (T.W. Murphy)	2:05 1/4m
19	6,925 Periscope (John Dodge)	2:04 1/2m
20	6,700 Sister Bertha (Joe Serrill)	2:06 3/4m
21	9,000 Guardian Trust (R.D. McMahon)	2:06 1/4m
22	7,350 Lee Worthy (Ben White)	2:05 1/2m
23	7,380 Hollyrood Leonard (N. Tallman)	2:05 1/4m
24	6,080 Mr. McElwyn (Ben White)	2:03 1/2m
25	7,265 Sam Williams (Walter Cox)	2:05 3/4m
26	8,505 Guy McKinney (Nat Ray)	2:14 1/2m
27	8,700 Kashmir (Ben White)	2:05 1/4m
28	8,230 Nelly Signal (Nat Ray)	2:04 1/2m
29	7,970 Volomite (Walter Cox)	2:05 m
30	6,720 Hanover's Bertha (Tom Berry)	2:05 1/2m
31	6,165 Protector (Will Caton)	2:03 3/4m
32	6,370 Brevere (Ben White)	2:04 1/4m
33	5,300 Spencer McElwyn (M. Childs)	a 2:04 1/4m
34	2,880 Emily Stokes (Fred Egan)	b 2:03 1/4m
35	4,105 Greyhound (Sep Palin)	2:03 1/4m
36	4,060 Rosalind (Ben White)	2:04 1/4m
37	3,300 Schnapps (Will Caton)	2:04 1/2m
38	4,085 Professor (George Bennett)	2:02 3/4m
39	5,150 Peter Astra (Doc Parshall)	2:05 m
40	4,427 Spencer Scott (Fred Egan)	2:03 m
41	5,638 Perpetual (Doc Parshall)	2:04 1/4m
42	6,506 Pay Up (Lee Smith)	2:08 1/2m
43	5,430 Volo Song (Ben White)	2:05 1/2m
44	3,856 Yankee Maid (Henry Thomas)	2:05 m
45	3,376 Tompkins Hanover(A.S. Rodney) *	2:08 3/4m
46	4,349 Chestertown (Thomas Berry)	2:04 1/2m
47	7,771 Nymph Hanover (Thomas Berry)	2:09 h
48	9,749 Demon Hanover (Harrison Hoyt)	2:10.4h
49	8,229 Guy Ambassador (H.C. Fitzpatrick)	c 2:04.3m
50	6,629 Star's Pride (H. Pownall, Sr.)	2:11.4m
51	10,777 Scotch Rhythm (Ralph Baldwin)	2:04.4m
52	12,248 Scotch Victor (Joe O'Brien)	2:06.3m
53	17,856 Kimberly Kid (Thomas Berry)	2:01.3m
54	19,542 Prince Victor (H. Pownall, Sr.)	d 2:00.3m
55	18,079 Childs Hanover (Frank Ervin)	2:03.2m
56	19,049 Nimble Colby (Ralph Baldwin)	2:03.1m
57	20,523 Hoot Song (Ralph Baldwin)	2:01.3m
58	20,477 Sandalwood (Ralph Baldwin)	2:02 m
59	19,344 Diller Hanover (Frank Ervin)	e 2:00.2m
60	21,441 Uncle Sam (Lou Huber, Jr.)	1:59.3m
61	17,262 Caleb (John Simpson, Sr.)	2:05 h
62	26,525 Sprite Rodney (Frank Ervin)	2:07.3h
63	20,825 Speedy Scot (Ralph Baldwin)	2:02.2h
64	20,892 Dartmouth (Ralph Baldwin)	2:07 h
65	24,998 Egyptian Candor (Stanley Dancer)	2:06.3h
66	24,680 Bonus Boy (Del Cameron)	2:07 h
67	22,137 Halifax Hanover (Joe O'Brien)	2:09.3h
68	17,278 Master Yankee (Jimmy Larente)	2:10.3h
69	25,000 Wealthy (Stanley Dancer)	2:09.1h
70	25,000 Gallant Prince (Stanley Dancer)	2:06.2m
71	25,000 Noble Gesture (H. Graham, Jr.)	2:00.3m
72	25,000 Mr. Colwell (Chas. Norris, Jr.)	2:02.3m
73	45,755 Walter Be Good (Ben Webster)	2:01.2m
74	53,940 Nevele Diamond (Stanley Dancer)	f 2:01 m
75	40,000 Noble Rogue (James Arthur)	2:02.3m

Page 341

CHRONICLES

76	23,250 Closed Circuit (Frank O'Mara)	2:00.3m	
	23,250 Steve Lobell (Peter Haughton)	2:00.4m	
77	21,900 William Vee (D. Richardson, Jr.)	2:01.2m	
	21,900 Cold Comfort (William Haughton)	2:00.2m	
78	43,249 Doublemint (Peter Haughton)	1:59.4m	
79	41,845 Courtly (Hakan Wallner)	1:59.1m	
80	42,795 Final Score (Tom Haughton)	1:59.2m	
81	24,451 Banker Barker (Mike Zeller)	2:02 m	
	24,251 Mo Bandy (Mike Allen)	2:00.4m	
82	39,525 Self Confident (D.R. Ackerman)	2:02.1m	
83	43,260 Darvin (Maurice Goldschmidt)	1:59.4m	
84	24,535 Op'Art (Bruce Riegle)	1:58.2m	

	25,035 Sandy Bowl (Jan Nordin)	1:59 m	
85	60,000 Ron B. Hanover (Jan Nordin)	1:59.3f	
86	103,802 Mangrove (Stanley Dancer)	1:57.4m	
87	88,650 Napoletano (Bill O'Donnell)	1:57.4f	
88	94,015 Somollison (Rod Allen)	R 1:56.1f	
89	80,835 Esquire Spur (Dick Stillings)	1:56.4f	
90	125,465 Jeanne's Beauty (Rod Allen)	1:57.2f	
	* Walkover.		

a By King Ben.   d By Darn Safe.
b By Reynolda.   e By Tie Silk.
c By Guy Ambassador &   f By Dream Of Glory.
    Atomic Maid.

The Matron Stake
Three-Year-Old Pace
Pompano Park, Pompano Beach, FL Dec. 22, 1990

10	2,166 Leftwich (James Healey)	2:12 m	
11	2,043 Miss DeForest (A. McDonald)	2:10 m	
12	1,938 Herman Wenger (T.W. Murphy)	2:13-1/4m	
13	2,155 Tilly Tipton (T.W. Murphy)	2:13-1/2m	
14	1,050 Anna Bradford (T.W. Murphy)	2:12 m	
15	1,269 General Todd (Guy Rea)	2:06 m	
16	1,046 Rose Magee (T.W. Murphy)	2:22 m	
17	898 Donna Lola (Robert Wright)	2:10-1/4m	
18	793 Direct The Work (J.McAllister)	2:06-1/2m	
19	Not raced from 1919 through 1930.		
31	1,405 Calumet Brownie (Daniel)	2:04 m	
32	1,080 Raider (Fred Egan)	2:04 m	
33	925 Calumet Dubuque (H. Stokes)	2:03-1/2m	
34	556 Laurel Hanover (NR)	*	
35	870 George Washington (W. Caton)	2:06 m	
36	1,350 Erla (Victor Fleming)	2:04 m	
37	1,295 Fred Hamer (Harry McKay)	2:05 m	
38	1,460 Chief Counsel (Doc Parshall)	2:03 1/2m	
39	1,760 Blackstone (Doc Parshall)	2:03 3/4m	
40	1,815 Fearless Peter (Doc Parshall)	2:04 1/4m	
41	1,406 Bell Boy (Victor Fleming)	2:04 m	
42	1,965 Supreme Hal (Frank Safford)	2:07 h	
43	1,879 Adios (Rupert Parker)	2:06 1/4m	
44	2,484 Attorney (Art Blackwell)	2:04 1/2m	
45	1,561 True Chief (Thomas Berry)	2:03 1/2m	
46	1,854 Ensign Hanover (Sep Palin)	2:03 1/4m	
47	5,179 Goose Bay (J.D. Mahoney)	a 2:04.3h	
48	5,429 E.J. Hal (Neal Houslet)	2:07.4h	
49	6,903 Good Time (Frank Ervin)	2:01.3m	
50	6,870 Dudley Hanover (H. Pownall, Sr.)	2:09 m	
51	6,920 Tar Heel (Delvin Miller)	2:02.2h	
52	7,875 Meadow Rice (Delvin Miller)	2:03 h	
53	16,731 Keystoner (Frank Ervin)	2:00.3m	
54	14,248 Meadow Pace (Joe O'Brien)	1:59.4m	
55	13,526 Sea Eagle (H.C. Fitzpatrick)	2:01.2m	
56	14,534 Adioway (Joe O'Brien)	b 2:01 m	
57	17,806 Meadow Rhythm (B.J. Schue)	c 2:03 m	
58	10,379 Bye Bye Byrd (Donald Taylor)	2:00 m	
59	16,005 Newport Admiral (Del Cameron)	2:02.1m	

60	8,796 Bullet Hanover (J. Simpson, Sr.)	1:59 m	
61	9,608 High Test (Frank Ervin)	2:03 h	
62	18,894 Coffee Break (George Sholty)	2:01.4h	
63	20,575 -dh- Delightful Time (Geo.Sholty)	2:02.2h	
	-dh- James B. Hanover (Del Insko)	2:02.2h	
64	20,755 Race Time (Ralph Baldwin)	2:04.4h	
65	21,434 Bret Hanover (Frank Ervin)	2:02.4h	
66	23,211 Carry Man (Philip Corley)	2:03.1h	
67	29,302 Nevele Dancer (Stanley Dancer)	2:04.1h	
68	23,858 Batman (Bruce Nickells)	2:04 h	
69	25,000 Laverne Hanover (Wm. Haughton)	2:02.1h	
70	25,000 Most Happy Fella (Stanley Dancer)	1:59 m	
71	25,000 Albatross (Stanley Dancer)	1:58.2m	
72	25,000 Breadwinner (Del Cameron)	1:59.2m	
73	57,105 Keystone Smartie (Don E. Hall)	1:57.4m	
74	70,270 Bret's Star (Mike Gagliardi)	1:58.3m	
75	49,000 Osbornes Bret (Tom Brinkerhoff)	1:56 m	
76	25,600 Pensive Bret (Delvin Miller)	1:58.2m	
	25,400 Warm Breeze (Dick Farrington)	1:59 m	
77	48,000 River Captain (John Campbell)	1:58.4m	
78	44,200 Flight Director (Joe O'Brien)	1:56.1m	
79	46,795 Composite (Ron Waples)	1:57.1m	
80	52,045 Storm Damage (Joe O'Brien)	1:55.2m	
81	46,952 Conquered (John Hayes, Jr.)	1:56.3m	
82	30,000 Ideal Society (George Sholty)	1:55.3m	
	30,000 Macatross (Archie McNeil)	1:55.4m	
83	44,510 Savvy Almahurst (Bill Gale)	1:57.1m	
84	28,035 Prize Sarnel (Troy Boring)	1:54.3m	
	28,036 Shady Deal (Don Irvine)	1:54.2m	
85	75,000 Next Knight Out (S. Condren)	1:57.2f	
86	160,552 JJ's Citation (Ron Waples)	R d 1:53 f	
87	123,550 Merrilyweerollalong(R.Silverman)	1:54 f	
88	144,415 Tranquil Storm (Mickey McNichol)	1:56.4f	
89	195,475 Tyler's Best (Jeff Fout)	1:54.3f	
90	138,490 Shipps Schnoops (Tommy Haughton)	1:53.2f	
	* Walkover.		

a By Shamrock Joe.   c By Cheyenne Goose.
b By Steamin' Demon.   d By Barberry Spur.

The Meadowlands Pace
Three-Year-Old
Meadowlands, E. Rutherford, NJ July 13, 1990

77	425,000 Escort (Carl LeCause)	a 1:54 m	
78	560,000 Falcon Almahurst (Wm. Haughton)	1:54.2m	
79	750,000 Sonsam (George Sholty)	1:53.2m	
80	1,011,000 Niatross (Clint Galbraith)	1:53.1m	
81	1,000,000 Conquered (John Hayes, Jr.)	1:54.3m	
82	1,000,000 Hilarion (John Campbell)	1:54.1m	
83	1,251,000 Ralph Hanover (Ron Waples)	1:54.1m	
84	1,293,000 On The Road Again (Wm. Gilmour)	1:53.3m	

85	1,018,000 Nihilator (Bill O'Donnell)	R 1:50.3m	
86	1,025,500 Laverne Hanover (Buddy Gilmour)	1:52.1m	
87	902,500 Frugal Gourmet (Trevor Ritchie)	1:52 m	
88	1,039,000 Matt's Scooter (Michel Lachance)	1:52.1m	
89	852,000 Dexter Nukes (John Campbell)	1:51.3m	
90	1,153,500 Beach Towel (Ray Remmen)	1:52.2m	

a By B.G.'s Bunny.

The Merrie Annabelle
Two-Year-Old Filly Trot
Meadowlands, E. Rutherford, NJ August 1, 1990

77	30,000 Rosemary (Peter Haughton)	2:04.3m	
78	41,250 Ahhhh (Howard Beissinger)	2:04 m	
79	37,050 Super Flower (Chris Boring)	2:03.4m	
80	35,475 Delmegan (Steve Waller)	2:00.2m	
	35,475 Highland Bridget (J. Parker, Jr.)	2:00.4m	
81	50,000 Worth Saving (Perry Simser)	2:02.4m	
	50,000 Sashay Lobell (Howard Beissinger)	2:03.1m	
	50,000 Dance Spell (Billy Herman)	2:03 m	
82	67,500 Tarport Lizzy (Billy Herman)	2:01.1m	
	67,500 Winky's Gill (Hakan Wallner)	2:01.1m	

	67,500 Armbro Blush (Glen Garnsey)	1:59.3m	
83	510,250 Geraldine Broline (B. Lindstedt)	1:59.3m	
84	595,750 Davidia Hanover (John Campbell)	1:58.1m	
85	627,250 Britelite Lobell (J. Campbell)	R 1:58.1m	
86	594,250 Armbro Fling (George Sholty)	1:59.3m	
87	437,500 Stage Entrance (Mickey McNichol)	1:59 m	
88	474,500 Peace Corps (Michel Lachance)	1:59.2m	
89	433,750 Cayster (Bill O'Donnell)	1:57.4m	
90	464,750 Santa Royal (Cat Manzi)	1:58.1m	

CHRONICLES

The Messenger Stakes *
Three-Year-Old Pace
Freestate Raceway, Laurel, MD Sept. 8, 1990

Yr	Purse	Winner	Driver	Time	Starters	Heats	Second **	Third
56	71,500	Belle Acton (f)	William Haughton	2:01.2h	17	2	Bachelor Hanover	Knight Patrol
57	100,084	Meadow Lands	Delvin Miller	a 2:04.4h	14	2	Adios Express	Morris Eden
58	108,565	O'Brien Hanover	James Jordan	2:01.4h	10	1	Flying Time	Thorpe Hanover
59	110,950	Adios Butler	Clint Hodgins	2:00.1h	9	1	Meadow Al	Adios Oregon
60	142,786	Countess Adios (f)	Delvin Miller	2:02.1h	10	1	Major Goose	Betting Time
61	145,377	Adios Don	Howard Camper	2:02.4h	9	1	Henry T Adios	Lang Hanover
62	169,430	Thor Hanover	John Simpson, Sr.	2:01.1h	10	1	Adora's Dream	Lehigh Hanover
63	146,324	Overtrick	John Patterson, Sr.	2:00.4h	8	1	Meadow Skipper	Country Don
64	150,960	Race Time	Ralph Baldwin	2:01.2h	9	1	Bengazi Hanover	Lyss Hanover
65	151,252	Bret Hanover	Frank Ervin	2:02 h	7	1	Tuxedo Hanover	Rivaltime
66	169,885	Romeo Hanover	George Sholty	2:01 h	8	1	Good Time Boy	Silent Byrd
67	178,064	Romulus Hanover	William Haughton	1:59.1h	8	1	Best Of All	Nardin's Byrd
68	189,018	Rum Customer	William Haughton	2:01.4h	8	1	Tropic Song	Isolator Hanover
69	182,976	Bye Bye Sam	Stanley Dancer	2:02.3h	8	1	Tempered Yankee	Laverne Hanover
70	123,450	Most Happy Fella	Stanley Dancer	2:02.3h	6	1	Truluck	Columbia George
71	114,977	Albatross	Stanley Dancer	2:00.2h	8	1	Nansemond	Tarport Skipper
72	154,733	Silent Majority	William Haughton	2:01.4h	11	1	Good Bye Columbus	Tarport Adios
73	122,732	Valiant Bret	Lucien Fontaine	2:00.3h	11	1	Bret Over Again	J R Skipper
74	151,043	Armbro Omaha	William Haughton	1:59.3h	9	1	Tarport Low	Nevele Bret
75	154,222	Brets Champ	William Haughton	1:59.1h	10	1	Seatrain	Polaris Lobell
76	161,290	Windshield Wipe	William Haughton	2:00 h	11	1	Keystone Ore	Raven Hanover
77	159,155	Governor Skipper	John Chapman	1:59.1h	9	1	Crash	Jonquil Hanover
78	167,862	Abercrombie	Glen Garnsey	1:58.2h	9	1	Happy Escort	League Leader
79	180,225	Hot Hitter	Henri Filion	1:59.4h	10	1	Striking Force	Black Ace
80	173,522	Niatross	Clint Galbraith	1:59.3h	7	1	Tyler B	Trenton Time
81	224,955	Seahawk Hanover	Ben Webster	1:58 h	13	2	Eastern Skipper	Slapstick
82	259,578	Cam Fella	Pat Crowe	1:57.3h	12	2	Icarus Lobell	Sokys Atom
83	379,004	Ralph Hanover	Ron Waples	1:57 h	27	2	Raffi	Keystone Exceller
84	379,343	Troublemaker	Bill O'Donnell	1:57.3h	10	1	Long Fella	Present Laughter
85	483,560	Pershing Square	Bill O'Donnell	1:55.2h	21	2	Dragon's Lair	Falcon Seelster
86	363,762	Amity Chef	John Campbell	1:55.4h	8	1	Barberry Spur	Armbro Emerson
87	447,310	Redskin	John Campbell	1:58 h	11	1	Jate Lobell	Simcoe Hanover
88	461,404	Matt's Scooter	Michel Lachance	1:56.3h	6	1	Bay's Fella	Cameleon
89	451,069	Sandman Hanover	Bill O'Donnell	1:53.2f	12	2	Goalie Jeff	Arbitrator
90	444,371	Jake And Elwood	John Campbell	R 1:52.3f	14	2	Beach Towel	Kiev Hanover

* - Raced at Roosevelt Raceway, 1956-1987; Raced at Yonkers Raceway, 1988;
Raced at Freestate Raceway, 1989; Raced at Roscroft Raceway, 1990 -
** - Raced on summary plan in 1956 and 1957. Second- and third-place, 1958-present, shown for final heat.

a By Adios Express.

The Metro Series Final
2-Year-Old Open Pace
Greenwood Raceway, Toronto, ONT Sept. 22, 1990

| 88 | 491,100 | Totally Ruthless (Bill O'Donnell) | 1:55.3f | 90 | 797,400 | Artsplace (John Campbell) | R 1:53.4f |
| 89 | 491,500 | Road Machine (Trevor Ritchie) | 1:56.1f | | | | |

The John W. Miller Memorial *
Three-Year-Old Filly Pace
Rosecroft Raceway, Oxon Hill, MD May 12, 1990

70	6,062	Armbro Kerry (Joe O'Brien)	2:06:3h	80	14,000	Vestalba Rainbow (Doug Arthur)	2:04 h
		Lana Hill (William Haughton)	2:08 h			Ridgewood Express (John Suffel)	2:03.2h
71	10,000	Naomi's Best (J.D. Dennis, Sr.)	2:04.2h	81	40,000	Side By Side (Bill Arthurs)	2:02.1h
72	6,000	Leigh's Sugar (Charles Pitts)	2:03.4h	82	51,525	Three Diamonds (Bruce Riegle)	1:57.1h
		To Ri Molly (Eddie Davis)	2:06.3h	83	29,143	Poetic Justice (Pres Moore, Jr.)	1:57.3h
73	10,000	Candyline (Vernon Dancer)	2:03.3h			Turn The Tide (Herve Filion)	1:57.1h
74	12,800	Deb Lobell (Don Milby)	2:02.3h	84	60,000	Leslie Lobell (George Berkner)	1:58.3h
75	7,500	Pam Ryan (Harry Harvey)	2:04.3h	85	110,000	Amneris (Jan Nordin)	1:59.1h
		Miss Chanel (D.Richardson, Jr.)	2:04.4h	86	160,750	Follow My Star (Buddy Gilmour)	1:58.4h
76	9,050	Afella Rainbow (Vern Crank)	2:05:1h	87	167,550	Quille Lauxmont (Ed Tracey)	1:58.4h
77	10,200	Come On Fred (Bob Uebel)	2:01 h	88	180,000	Sweet Reflection (Wm. O'Donnell)	1:57.1h
		Uncle Dick (Millard Jennings)	2:02.1h	89	192,295	Tyler Town (Peter Ruscitto)	R 1:57 h
78	10,400	Quaker Bill (Eddie Davis)	2:02.4h	90	202,690	Instant Rebate (Bill Gale)	R 1:54.2f
79	22,250	Mostest Yankee (Wayne Smullin)	2:01 h			* Raced as Three-Year-Old Colt Pace 1976-1980.	

The William E. Miller Memorial
Three-Year-Old Pace *
Rosecroft Raceway, Oxon Hill, MD May 12, 1990

55	17,280	Knight Patrol (Delvin Miller)	2:07.2h	68	13,575	Caroldon Lehigh (Herve Filion)	2:01.4h
56	21,340	Adios Pick (William Haughton)	2:08 h		13,575	Nevele Romeo (Vernon Dancer)	2:01.2h
57	18,200	Silk Byrd (K.R. Cartnal)	2:04.2h	69	16,000	Tempered Yankee (Vernon Dancer)	2:01.1h
58	17,400	Senator Spangler (Phil Dussault)	2:03.4h		16,000	Kat Byrd (Levi Harner)	1:58.4h
59	22,000	Adios Oregon (Thomas Crank III)	2:04.2h	70	30,000	Don Baker (Charles Smith, Jr.)	2:01.2h
60	18,000	Betting Time (Clint Hodgins)	2:03 h	71	15,000	Proper Time (D. Richardson, Jr.)	2:02 h
61	23,940	Knight Champ (John Wilcutts)	2:03 h		15,000	Scioto Star (D. Richardson, Jr.)	2:02 h
62	16,500	Lieutenant Gray (Cliff Boyd)	2:06 h	72	15,000	Baron Gerard (Lew Williams)	1:59.3h
63	15,000	Chapel Chief (William Haughton)	2:02.2h		15,000	Bob Hilton (Yves Filion)	2:03.2h
64	15,000	Senator Burton (Herve Filion)	2:03.4h	73	30,000	Smog (Stanley Dancer)	2:00 h
65	29,640	High Level (Earle Avery)	2:00.4h	74	30,000	Bret's Star (Mike Gagliardi)	2:02 h
66	20,000	Shadydale Hymn (Herve Filion)	2:00.4h	75	30,000	Currituck Star (Vernon Crank)	2:01.4h
67	20,000	Nevele Dancer (Stanley Dancer)	2:00.2h	76	30,000	Hunter's Chief (Victor White)	2:00.4h

Page 343

CHRONICLES

77	20,000	Jazzy Spark (Roger Hammer)	1:58.2h	84	65,000	Christmas List (Coleman Foster)	1:58.1h
	20,000	Nat Lobell (Jack Kopas)	1:59.1h		65,000	Mannart Maple Leaf (Rheo Filion)	1:58.1h
78	50,000	No No Yankee (Walter Ross)	2:01.2h	85	115,000	Penetrate (Jim Miller)	1:57 h
79	75,000	Tijuana Taxi (Jim Miller)	1:59.1h		115,000	Meadow Ro Mar (Joe Scorsone)	1:58.1h
80	56,250	Trusty Tough Guy (Tom Edler)	1:59.1h	86	213,914	Cash Asset (Tom Haughton)	1:55.3h
	56,250	Honorable Winner (Lloyd Gilmour)	1:58.3h	87	265,165	Dennis Seelster (Bob Barella)	1:58.3h
81	75,000	Seahawk Hanover (Ben Webster)	1:58.2h	88	305,610	Store Wars (Ben Webster)	1:57 h
82	100,000	Rabbit Road (Merritt Dokey)	1:57 h	89	315,550	Kick Up A Storm (Ron Waples)	R 1:55 h
83	51,595	Sweet Meadow Doc (Jerry Sarama)	1:59 h	90	315,010	Beach Towel (Ray Remmen)	R 1:52.3f
	51,595	G.E.'s Romanero (Gary Ewing)	1:59.2h		* - Two-Year-Old Pace in 1955-56.		

The Milton Stakes Final
Three-Year-Olds and up, Fillies and Mares
Mohawk Raceway, Campbellville, ONT Oct. 7, 1990

63	1,815	Rocky Herbert (J. Herbert)	2:10.2f	78	43,500	Courageous Lady (Lew Williams)	1:58.1f
64	3,640	Fleetwood E (Keith Waples)	2:02.2f	79	50,000	Tender Loving Care (Sh. Goudreau)	1:58.3f
65	3,600	Angelic Wick (John Findley)	2:05.1f	80	75,000	Southgate Pride (R. Taylor)	1:58.1f
66	4,250	High Patch (A. Walker)	2:06 f	81	75,000	Armbro Vibrant (Bill Wellwood)	1:59.4f
67	4,650	Gay Reel (Keith Waples)	2:08.1f	82	75,000	Fan Hanover (Glen Garnsey)	1:57 f
68	6,895	Armbro Gambol (K. Galbraith)	2:05.3f	83	81,000	Programmed (Doug Brown)	a 1:57.1f
69	8,500	Blossom Time (M. Dostie)	2:04.2f	84	79,500	How Nice (Trevor Ritchie)	1:56.4f
70	8,600	Chocolate Eclair (J. Geisel, Jr.)	2:07 f	85	71,000	Green With Envy (Walter Case, Jr)	1:55.3f
71	8,750	Adios Susie (J. Muttart)	2:06 f	86	107,000	Misty Silver (Wm. "Bud" Fritz)	1:58 f
72	9,450	Meadow Lisa (D. Pierce)	2:06 f	87	109,000	Glenns Super Star (Doug Brown)	1:57.1f
73	8,950	Twinkles Belle (D. Larkin)	2:04 f	88	109,500	Anniecrombie (Dave Magee)	1:55.4f
74	11,200	Lobro Countess (R. Feagan)	2:06.4f	89	129,000	Armbro Feather (John Kopas)	R 1:53.3f
75	11,250	Speed King N (Dr. John Hayes)	2:05 f	90	141,250	Caesars Jackpot (Bill Fahy)	R 1:53.3f
76	11,300	Lobro Countess (R. Feagan)	2:02.4f	a By Programmed &			
77	44,200	Silk Stockings (Pres. Burris, Jr)	2:01.3f	Armbro Bramble.			

The Mistletoe Shalee
Three-Year-Old Filly Pace
Meadowlands, E. Rutherford, NJ Aug. 17, 1990

79	35,500	Roses Are Red (John Kopas)	2:01.3m	85	600,000	Semalu D'Amour (Benoit Cote)	1:54 m
80	50,000	Miles End Dianne (Ben Webster)	1:57.2m	86	593,250	Angela Ty (Ron Waples)	1:55.2m
81	330,750	JEF's Eternity (John Campbell)	1:56.2m	87	468,250	Pacific (Tom Harmer)	1:53.4m
82	427,500	Three Diamonds (Bruce Riegle)	1:54.4m	88	421,000	Conquered Quest (John Campbell)	R 1:52.4m
83	566,250	Lucky Lady (Dick Hogan)	1:55 m	89	242,250	Caesars Jackpot (Mickey McNichol)	1:54.4m
84	590,750	Naughty But Nice (Tom Haughton)	1:55.1m	90	425,250	Choice Yankee (Jim Morrill, Jr)	R 1:52.4m

The Mohawk Gold Cup Final
Three-Year-Old and Up Open Pace
Mohawk Raceway, Campbellville, ONT Sept. 30, 1990

76	29,000	Jambo Dancer (Charles Lawson)	2:00.1f	84	75,000	Mr Dalrae (Dave Magee)	1:54.1f
77	59,000	Jambo Dancer (Charles Lawson)	1:59.1f	85	75,000	On The Road Again (Buddy Gilmour)	1:58 f
78	59,800	Dream Maker (Ron Waples)	1:58 f	86	107,000	Armbro Dallas (Ron Waples)	1:54.3f
79	75,000	Try Scotch (Shelly Goudreau)	1:56.2f	87	105,000	Dragon's Lair (John Campbell)	1:55 f
80	75,000	Le Baron Rouge (Ron Waples)	1:56.2f	88	117,000	Jaguar Spur (Dick Stillings)	1:54 f
81	75,000	Lime Time (Doug Brown)	1:57.1f	89	154,500	Matt's Scooter (Mich. Lachance)	R 1:51 f
82	75,000	Fan Hanover (Glen Garnsey)	1:56 f	90	197,750	Topnotcher (Doug Brown)	1:52.4f
83	75,000	Cam Fella (Pat Crowe)	1:55.3f				

The Molly Pitcher
Two-Year-Old Filly Pace
Freehold Raceway, Freehold, NJ Sept. 22, 1990

82	43,909	Bardot Lobell (Ray Remmen)	1:57 h	87	59,183	Lady Longlegs (Herve Filion)	1:59.3h
	44,659	Turn The Tide (Herve Filion)	1:59.3h		59,183	Sweet Reflection (Bill O'Donnell)	1:57.1h
83	37,861	Milynn Hanover (Dick Macomber)	1:59.4h		59,183	So Cozy (John Campbell)	2:00.2h
	37,861	Lady Larouche (Jimmy Marohn)	2:01 h	88	60,058	Amy Rocklin (Ben Webster)	1:58.4h
	37,861	Margaret Turner (Tom Sells)	1:57.2h		60,058	L Dees Trish (Herve Filion)	1:55.4h
84	59,281	Bunny's Wish (Bill O'Donnell)	1:59.3h		60,058	Witsends Cinny (Bill O'Donnell)	1:58.4h
	60,281	Wings Of Gold (John Campbell)	2:01.1h	89	75,878	Respectfully Yours (M. Lachance)	1:59.2h
85	96,000	Caressable (Bill O'Donnell)	1:55.4m		75,878	Warm Ways (Ben Webster)	1:58.4h
	96,000	Follow My Star (Buddy Gilmour)	R 1:55.2m	90	60,579	Cams Exotic (Harold Kelly)	1:57.3h
86	65,305	Halcyon (Ray Remmen)	1:58.3h		60,579	Sunraycer (Michel Lachance)	1:58.2h
	65,305	Time Well Spent (Bill O'Donnell)	2:00.2h		62,079	Lexie (Mickey McNichol)	1:57.2h

The Nadia Lobell Final
Three-Year-Old Filly Pace
Garden State Park, Cherry Hill, NJ Sept. 15, 1990

90	220,000	Crafty Caper (Howard Parker)	1:53.4m

The Nassagaweya
Two-Year-Old Open Pace
Mohawk Raceway, Campbellville, ONT Sept. 9, 1990

89	109,850	Road Machine (Trevor Ritchie)	*		69,650	Artsplace (John Campbell)	R 1:55 f
	111,350	Hubris (Jim Doherty)	1:56.4f		69,650	June's Baby (Ron Waples)	1:55.3f
90	69,650	Shipps Commander (John Campbell)	1:56.2f				
	71,150	Happy Family (Doug Brown)	1:56.1f		* - Time Disallowed		

CHRONICLES

The Nat Ray
Four- & Five-Year-Old Trot
The Meadowlands, E. Rutherford, NJ July 30, 1990

81	80,000 Final Score (Tom Haughton)	1:58.1m	86	114,000 Nearly Perfect (M. McNichol)	R 1:55.1m
82	100,000 Banker Barker (Mike Zeller)	1:58.1m	87	102,000 Sugarcane Hanover (Ron Waples)	R 1:55.1m
83	125,000 Diamond Exchange (Rob. Williams)	1:55.4m	88	100,000 Mack Lobell (John Campbell)	R 1:55.1m
84	112,000 Shane T Hanover (Per Henriksen)	1:56 m	89	101,000 Chadwick Hanover (Paul Spears)	1:56.3m
85	126,000 Crowning Point (Doug Ackerman)	1:55.2m	90	112,000 Alfresco (Ron Waples)	1:57 m

The Niatross
Two-Year-Old Pace
The Meadowlands, E. Rutherford, NJ August 3, 1990

90   365,300 Die Laughing (Richard Silverman)   1:54.2m

The North America Cup
Three-Year-Old Colt Pace
Greenwood Raceway, Toronto, ONT June 23, 1990

84	596,500 Legal Notice (John Hayes, Jr.)	a 1:55.1f	88	1,043,000 Runnymede Lobell (Yves Filion)	1:54.4f
85	387,500 Staff Director (Dave Wall)	1:55.2f	89	1,000,000 Goalie Jeff (Steve Condren)	1:53.2f
86	488,000 Quite A Sensation (Trevor Ritchie)	1:54.2f	90	1,000,000 Apaches Fame (Wm. "Bud" Fritz)	1:53.4f
87	1,000,000 Jate Lobell (Mark O'Mara)	R 1:52.3f		a By Long Fella.	

The North American Pacing Series Final *
Three-and Four-Year-Old Pace, Conditioned
Batavia Downs, Batavia, NY Sept. 3, 1990

66	17,600 Shadydale Hymn (Herve Filion)	2:02 f	79	100,000 Rowdy Yankee (Dick Hogan)	1:58.1h
67	29,146 Nevele Dancer (Stanley Dancer)	2:01.3f	80	100,000 Safe Arrival (Buddy Gilmour)	R 1:55.1m
68	19,400 Hal Painter (John Patterson, Jr.)	1:59.2q	81	100,000 Nordic Almahurst (Ray Remmen)	1:59.1m
69	24,000 Hals Jay (William Spriggs)	2:03.4f	82	100,000 Bo Dublin (Bill O'Donnell)	1:56 m
70	20,000 Bye Bye Max (Jack Bailey)	2:08.1f	83	75,000 Tyler's Brother (W. Popfinger)	1:56.2h
71	30,000 Daring Knight (Dick Buxton)	2:01.4f	84	72,000 Robbie's Fella (Bill O'Donnell)	1:56.1q
72	36,000 Mr. Peter Ray (Ray McLean)	2:04.4h	85	100,000 Ring Of Light (Dan Johnson)	1:56.1h
73	50,300 Smog (Stanley Dancer)	1:59.4f	86	67,500 Le Courrier (Walter Case, Jr.)	R 1:56 h
74	50,000 Cheyenne Tomahawk (Herve Filion)	2:03 h	87	80,000 Avenging Eagle (John Campbell)	1:58.1h
75	60,000 Right Tie (Keith Waples)	1:59.2f	88	76,000 Willie Mays (Norm Dauplaise)	R 1:55.3f
76	50,000 Skedaddle N. (Edward Dunnigan)	1:59 h	89	82,000 Shipps Fella (Tim Twaddle)	1:56.3h
77	62,866 Saville Row (Stanley Dancer)	1:59.4f	90	67,500 San Andre (John Plutino)	R 1:56 h
78	88,000 Timely's Best Man (Frank O'Mara)	2:00 h		* Raced as the Can-Am Final 1966-1982.	

Northfield Park Grand Circuit
"The Forest City Stakes"
2-Year-Old Colt Pace
Northfield Park, Northfield, OH Sept. 12, 1990

88	20,000 Just The Ticket (D.R. Ackerman)	1:58.1h	90	28,800 Moravian Hanover (Tom Davis)	1:58.3h
	20,000 Married In Style (Craig Stein)	2:00.4h		29,500 Alfalad (Roger Culliper)	1:58.4h
89	48,000 Kiev Hanover (Dick Stillings)	R 1:57.4h			

Northfield Park Grand Circuit
"The Rainy Day Sweepstakes"
2-Year-Old Colt Trot
Northfield Park, Northfield, OH Sept. 10, 1990

88	17,750 Somolli Park (Terry Altmeyer)	2:07.2h		22,000 Corporate (Steve Sugg)	2:05.1h
	17,750 Sure Fact (Doug Ackerman)	2:05.3h	90	37,500 Taborizor (Joe Adamsky)	R 2:03 h
89	22,000 Anastasia Amos (Clair Umholtz)	2:06.4h			

Northfield Park Grand Circuit
"The Stephen Phillips Memorial"
2-Year-Old Filly Pace
Northfield Park, Northfield, OH Sept. 10, 1990

88	19,100 George's Melanie (D. Stillings)	2:01 h	90	28,500 Tally Almahurst (Gerry Bookmyer)	2:00.1h
	19,100 Tangy B (Jim Dailey)	2:01 h		29,250 Goalie Jess (Jim Bailey)	R 1:57.1h
89	43,000 Yankee Goddess (Doug Snyder)	1:58.1h			

Northfield Park Grand Circuit
"The H.K. Devereux Memorial"
2-Year-Old Filly Trot
Northfield Park, Northfield, OH Sept. 12, 1990

88	16,175 Bahama Spur (Dick Stillings)	2:04 h		22,950 What's Love (Mark O'Mara)	2:03.1h
	16,925 Lily White (Dick Stillings)	2:08.1h	90	38,400 Shezatrotnmachine (Jeff Fout)	2:02.4h
89	22,200 Perfect Point (Doug Ackerman)	R 2:02.2h			

Northfield Park Grand Circuit
"The Bret Hanover"
3-Year-Old Colt Pace
Northfield Park, Northfield, OH Sept. 14, 1990

88	46,000 Cameleon (Ron Waples)	R 1:56 h	90	39,100 Kiev Hanover (Jim Morand)	1:57 h
89	31,500 Sachem (Gerry Bookmyer)	1:57.4h			

CHRONICLES

Northfield Park Grand Circuit
"The Colonel William Edwards Memorial"
3-Year-Old Colt Trot
Northfield Park, Northfield, OH Sept. 12, 1990

88	36,500	Defiant One (Howard Beissinger)	R 2:00.1h	90	22,300 Princely Fellow (D.R. Ackerman)	2:00.4h
89	33,500	Sure Fact (Doug Ackerman)	2:01 h		23,300 Royal Cold (Mel Turcotte)	2:01 h

Northfield Park Grand Circuit
"The North Randall Park"
3-Year-Old Filly Pace
Northfield Park, Northfield, OH Sept. 12, 1990

88	40,000	Leah Almahurst (Bill Fahy)	R 1:57 h	90	36,350 Touch Of Silk (Dave Rankin)	1:58.3h
89	32,000	Romance Hanover (Dean Zaimes)	R 1:57 h			

Northfield Park Grand Circuit
"The Maud S"
3-Year-Old Filly Trot
Northfield Park, Northfield, OH Sept. 10, 1990

88	30,500	Busy Life (Don Swick)	R 1:59.4h	90	38,850 Aspiring Lass (Jay Picciano)	2:00.2h
89	28,500	Melody Bowl (D.R. Ackerman)	2:03 h			

The Old Oaken Bucket
Three-Year-Old Trot
Delaware County Fair, Delaware, OH Sept. 21, 1990

68	19,520	Snow Speed (Clint Hodgins)	2:00.2h	81	46,015	Tarry's Boy (Billy Herman)	c 2:00.2h
69	22,477	Crain Hanover (Harry Harvey)	2:06 h	82	43,596	Happy Crown (John Campbell)	2:01.3h
70	23,033	Paris Air (Joe O'Brien)	2:02.2h	83	81,841	Tarport Frenzy (Jan Nordin)	2:02.3h
71	25,223	Speedy Crown (Howard Beissinger)	1:59.2h	84	85,150	Nevele Express (Jan Nordin)	1:59.2h
72	20,404	Songcan (George Sholty)	1:58.3h	85	81,132	Master Willie (Jan Nordin)	R 1:57.4h
73	28,188	Macarthur (Howard Beissinger)	2:03 h	86	82,142	Everglade Hanover(J.Simpson,Jr.)	R 1:57.4h
74	31,715	Dream Of Glory (Pius Soehnlen)	2:00 h	87	76,845	Mack Lobell (John Campbell)	R 1:57.4h
75	33,169	Skipper Walt (Roland Beaulieu)	2:02.3h	88	80,794	Armbro Gold (John Campbell)	1:58.2h
76	38,798	Japa (Billy Herman)	a 2:02.4h	89	112,608	Dr Guillotine (Chris Boring)	R 1:57.4h
77	33,412	Jurgy Hanover (J. Simpson, Jr.)	2:04.3h	90	116,490	Lender Hanover (Jan Nordin)	1:59.1h
78	34,044	Cami Almahurst (Bruce Riegle)	1:59.1h				
79	39,084	Superior Sweep (Carl Allen)	b 2:01.2h		a By Japa & White Knight.	c By Uptown.	
80	39,714	Yankee Mama (Delvin Miller)	2:04.3h		b By Dorian's Music.		

The Oliver Wendell Holmes
Three-Year-Old Pace
Meadowlands, E. Rutherford, NJ Aug. 3, 1990

76	101,000	Oil Burner (Ben Webster)	1:55.1m	86	236,500	Robust Hanover (Bill O'Donnell)	1:54.4m
77	113,000	Nat Lobell (John Kopas)	a 1:55.4m	87	287,000	Run The Table (John Campbell)	R 1:51.1m
78	120,000	Jargon (Lew Williams)	b 1:56 m	88	284,500	Albert Albert (Chris Boring)	e 1:53.3m
79	108,000	Merry Isle (John Campbell)	1:56.3m	89	252,000	Goalie Jeff (Michel Lachance)	1:51.3m
80	125,000	Niatross (Clint Galbraith)	1:53 m	90	258,000	Brando Hanover (Mickey McNichol)f	1:51.3m
81	250,000	Freedom Fella (Shelly Goudreau)	1:54.4m				
82	300,000	McKenzie Almahurst(W. Haughton)	c 1:53.4m		a By Governor Skipper.	e By Albert Albert & Armbro Global.	
83	350,000	Fortune Teller (Eldon Harner)	1:54.1m		b By Lime Time.		
84	326,520	Guts (Bill O'Donnell)	1:53.3m		c By No Nukes.	f By In The Pocket & Brando Hanover.	
85	300,000	Handsome Sum (Ben Webster)	d 1:52.4m		d By Anxious Robby.		

The Pink Bonnet Final
Two-Year-Old Filly Pace
Scioto Downs, Columbus, OH July 27, 1990

90	115,000	Shy Devil (Jeff Fout)	1:57.3f

The Potomac
Two-Year-Old Colt Pace
Rosecroft Raceway, Oxon Hill, MD July 21, 1990

82	58,000	Fozzie Bear (Wayne Smullin)	1:59.4f	86	84,700	Trigger's Star (John Campbell)	2:00.1f
	58,000	Hampton Court (Bruce Riegle)	2:01.1f		84,700	Surfer Lobell (Jim Dolbee)	1:58.4f
83	63,875	Comacina (Wayne Smullin)	1:59.4f		84,700	Classy Model (Bill O'Donnell)	2:00.2f
	63,875	Walton Hanover (J. Simpson, Jr.)	1:59 f		84,700	Dictionary (John Campbell)	1:56 f
	63,875	Nat's Falcon (Jimmy Larente)	1:59.4f		86,200	Meadowbranch Bret(Bill O'Donnell)	1:59 f
	64,725	Signed N Sealed (Wm. Haughton)	1:59 f	87	83,100	Happy Tree (Peter Ruscitto)	1:56.1f
	63,875	Holmes Hanover (Carl LeCause)	2.00.2f		84,600	Only Mine (Tom Haughton)	1:56.1f
84	71,072	Koala Hanover (Herve Filion)	1:58.2f		83,100	Money Lender (Jim Larente)	1:57.2f
	72,322	Marauder (Dick Richardson, Jr.)	1:59 f		83,100	Pied Piper (C. Warrington, Jr.)	1:57.4f
	72,322	Devil's Adversary (Abe Stoltzfus)	1:58 f		83,100	Barstow Hanover (Doug Snyder)	1:57 f
	71,072	Pershing Square (Tom Haughton)	1:57 f		83,100	Hamlet Lobell (Richard Silverman)	1:57.3f
	71,072	Nihilator (William Haughton)	1:57 f	88	74,137	Beach Walker (Tom Haughton)	1:57.1f
	72,322	Praised Dignity (Wm. Popfinger)	1:56.4f		74,137	Its Country (Carl Callen)	1:58 f
	71,072	Anxious Robby (Herve Filion)	1:59.2f		75,637	Alert Move (Ron Waples)	1:58.1f
85	76,500	Singer's Star (William Haughton)	1:57.2f		75,637	Keystone Fabulous (Roger Hammer)	1:55.1f
	75,000	Smartest Remark (Don Irvine, Jr.)	1:57.3f		75,637	Shipps Scorch (Don Irvine, Jr.)	1:56.3f
	76,500	Tucson Hanover (Bruce Riegle)	1:58.1f	89	83,246	Six Day War (Ray Remmen)	1:57.4f
	76,500	Southern Gentleman (Bruce Riegle)	1:57 f		84,746	Talon Almahurst (John Campbell)	1:57.2f
	75,000	Maritime Hanover (W. Case, Jr.)	1:58 f		84,746	Two Manhattons (Don Irvine, Jr.)	1:57.1f
	75,000	Sherman Almahurst (Doug Brown)	1:57.2f		86,246	Beach Towel (Ray Remmen)	1:56.4f

CHRONICLES

90	64,877 Deal Breaker (Ron Waples)	1:56.2f		66,387 Razzle Dazzlem (Eddie Davis)		1:56.1f
	66,387 Cambest (Dave Rankin)	1:55.2f		66,387 Silky Stallone (Bill Fahy)		1:56.1f
	66,387 Gigowatt (Ron Waples)	R 1:54.4f				

The Presidential Stakes
Two-Year-Old Open Pace
Rosecroft Raceway, Oxon Hill, MD Nov. 3, 1990

85	190,075 Uncut Jade (Dick Stillings)	1:58.3h	88	311,005 Totally Ruthless (John Campbell)	1:57.2h
86	296,406 Redskin (Bill O'Donnell)	1:58.1h	89	335,325 Beach Towel (Ray Remmen)	R 1:53.3f
87	363,690 Camtastic (Bob Bencal)	R 1:57 h	90	298,345 Die Laughing (Richie Silverman)	1:54 f

The Prix de l'Avenir
Two-Year-Old Colt Pace
Blue Bonnets Raceway, Montreal, QUE Aug. 5, 1990

81	77,450 Coal Harbor (John Kopas)	1:57.3f		192,000 Mannart Tempo (Trevor Ritchie)	1:58.1f
	78,700 Royal Rally (Mike Metcalfe)	1:57.4f	87	217,000 Folio (Ron Waples)	1:57.3f
82	98,625 Silent Al (Jacques Hebert)	2:00.4f		220,000 Runnymede Lobell (Yves Filion)	1:57.2f
	100,125 Keystone Exceller (Jim Miller)	1:59.1f	88	184,166 Armbro Hunch (Benoit Cote)	R 1:55 f
83	99,416 Walton Hanover (J. Simpson, Jr.)	1:58.1f		184,166 Rank Hanover (Ron Waples)	1:56 f
	100,916 Forest Hanover (John Kopas)	1:58 f		184,166 Totally Ruthless (John Campbell)	1:56.3f
	100,916 Farmstead's Fame (Tom Haughton)	1:57.2f	89	251,250 Fighting Major (John Campbell)	1:58 f
84	60,937 Marauder (Dick Richardson, Jr.)	1:57.3f		254,250 Jake And Elwood (John Campbell)	1:57.1f
	62,437 Dragon's Lair (Jeff Mallet)	1:57.3f	90	146,125 Jackpot Raider (Mike Saftic)	1:57 f
	60,937 Walkabout (Gilles Gendron)	1:59.3f		146,125 Shark Almahurst (Bill Fahy)	*
	62,437 Armbro Dallas (Archie McNeil)	1:59.1f		146,125 Silky Stallone (Bill Fahy)	1:57.4f
85	168,500 Laughs (Michel Lachance)	1:57.1f		146,125 Nuke Of Earl (Michel Lachance)	1:59.1f
86	192,000 Casino Gambler (Bill O'Donnell)	2:00.4f		* - Time Disallowed	

The Prix d'Ete
Three-Year-Old Pace *
Blue Bonnets Raceway, Montreal, QUE Aug. 19, 1990

68	50,000 True Duane (Chris Boring)	1:58 f	81	226,100 Seahawk Hanover (Ben Webster)	1:55.3f
69	-- Not Raced --		82	377,000 Cam Fella (Pat Crowe)	1:55.1f
70	75,000 Laverne Hanover (George Sholty)	1:57.2f	83	411,500 Ralph Hanover (Ron Waples)	1:54 f
71	75,000 Albatross (Stanley Dancer)	1:57.2f	84	411,500 Butler B.G. (Ted Wing)	1:53.4f
72	100,000 Strike Out (Keith Waples)	1:58.2f	85	358,000 Falcon Seelster (Tom Harmer)	1:53.2f
73	130,000 Armbro Nadir (Nelson White)	1:56.1f	86	527,500 Armbro Emerson (Walt Whelan)	c 1:56 f
74	150,000 Armbro Omaha (Peter Haughton)	a 1:57.4f	87	548,000 Frugal Gourmet (Trevor Ritchie)	d 1:53.3f
75	140,000 Alberts Star (Keith Waples)	1:58 f	88	582,000 Matt's Scooter (Michel Lachance)	1:54.4f
76	163,700 Precious Fella (Gary Cameron)	b 1:56.4f	89	632,500 Goalie Jeff (Michel Lachance)	R 1:52.1f
77	154,750 Governor Skipper (John Chapman)	1:54.3f	90	663,500 Beach Towel (Ray Remmen)	1:53.1f
78	150,750 Abercrombie (Glen Garnsey)	1:55 f		* Invitational Free-For-All 1968-1970.	
79	181,150 Hot Hitter (Herve Filion)	1:54 f		a By Dorado Almahurst.	c By Amity Chef.
80	161,650 Niatross (Clint Galbraith)	1:53.4f		b By Wolf Pack.	d By Laag.

The Provincial Cup
3-Year-Old Open Pace *
Windsor Raceway, Windsor, ONT Oct. 21, 1990

66	15,000 Dancing David (Charles Goins)	2:02.4f	79	50,000 Try Scotch (Shelly Goudreau)	1:55.4f
67	25,000 Cardigan Bay (Stanley Dancer)	2:01 f	80	50,000 Pat's Gypsy (Lew Williams)	1:57.1f
68	30,000 Cardigan Bay (Stanley Dancer)	2:00.1f	81	50,000 Lime Time (Doug Brown)	1:57 f
69	35,000 W W Smith (Carmine Abbatiello)	2:00.4f	82	100,000 Cam Fella (Pat Crowe)	1:55.4f
70	40,000 Good Chase (Del Insko)	2:01 f	83	103,000 Boomer Drummond (J.P. Charron)	1:56.4f
71	40,000 James Darren (Carmine Abbatiello)	2:01.2f	84	105,000 On The Road Again (Buddy Gilmour)	1:53.4f
72	50,000 Isle Of Wight (Herve Filion)	1:59.4f	85	103,000 Falcon Seelster (Tom Harmer)	1:53.4f
73	50,000 Isle Of Wight (Herve Filion)	2:03.2f	86	177,500 Wholesale (John Brooks)	1:54 f
74	50,000 Armbro Nesbit (Joe O'Brien)	2:00 f	87	197,000 Frugal Gourmet (Trevor Ritchie)	R 1:52.3f
75	50,000 Young Quinn (Dick Williams II)	1:56.3f	88	204,400 Bond Street (Bill Gale)	1:55.4f
76	50,000 Young Quinn (Joe Marsh, Jr.)	1:59.3f	89	206,000 Mystery Fund (Bill Gale)	1:54 f
77	50,000 Armbro Ranger (Joe O'Brien)	2:01.1f	90	230,500 Camluck (Michel Lachance)	1:52.4f
78	50,000 Dream Maker (Ron Waples)	2:04.1f		* Invitational Pace prior to 1988	

The Review Stake
"The Alexander Memorial"
Three-Year-Old Trot
Illinois State Fair, Springfield, IL Aug. 17, 1990

94	21,575 B B P (Frank Loomis)	2:13 3/4m	12	6,500 Adlon (John Dickerson)		2:08 1/4m
95	-- Not Raced --		13	9,000 Don Chenault (H.C. Stinson)		2:06 1/4m
96	-- Not Raced --		14	8,500 Peter Volo (T.W. Murphy)		2:07 1/4m
97	-- Not Raced --		15	8,500 Mary Putney (R.D. McMahon)		2:08 1/4m
98	-- Not Raced --		16	8,500 Volga E. (Ben White)		2:07 1/4m
99	20,000 Idolita (Thomas Marsh)	2:12 1/2m	17	6,500 The Real Lady (T.W. Murphy)		2:04 1/4m
00	5,000 Mobel (Edward Benyon)	2:16 3/4m	18	6,000 David Guy (T.W. Murphy)		2:05 3/4m
01	5,000 The Rowellan (James Golden)	2:16 1/4m	19	6,000 Periscope (John Dodge)		2:07 1/4m
02	5,000 The Rajah (Charles Lyons)	2:14 3/4m	20	6,000 Sister Bertha (Joe Serrill)		2:05 1/4m
03	5,000 Ethel's Pride (Scott Hudson)	2:15 m	21	6,000 Rose Scott (T.W. Murphy)		2:04 1/4m
04	7,000 Alta Axworthy (A.L. Thomas)	2:10 1/2m	22	6,000 Peter Earl (Nat Ray)		2:04 1/4m
05	7,000 Susie N. (T.W. Murphy)	2:11 m	23	6,000 The Senator (Alonzo McDonald)		2:04 1/4m
06	7,000 Governor Francis (W.O. Foote)	2:11 1/2m	24	6,235 Mr. McElwyn (Ben White)		2:05 1/4m
07	7,000 General Watts (M. Bowerman)	2:09 1/2m	25	6,235 Alleen Gay (Ben White)		2:04 3/4m
08	7,000 The Harvester (Pop Geers)	2:10 1/2m	26	6,235 Guy McKinney (Nat Ray)		2:05 1/2m
09	7,000 Czarevna (Thomas Nolan)	2:09 1/2m	27	6,235 Isosola's Worthy (Marv Childs)		2:04 3/4m
10	6,500 Native Belle (T.W. Murphy)	2:07 3/4m	28	6,235 Guy Abbey (Victor Fleming)		2:04 3/4m
11	6,500 Atlantic Express (J. Dickerson)	2:08 1/4m	29	6,235 Walter Dear (Walter Cox)		2:05 1/2m

Page 347

CHRONICLES

30	8,500 Hanover's Bertha (Tom Berry)	2:01 1/4m	
31	8,500 Protector (Will Caton)	2:03 1/4m	
32	3,525 The Marchioness (Will Caton)	2:02 m	
33	1,160 Calumet Delco (Doc Parshall)	2:05 3/4m	
34	1,560 Lord Jim (Doc Parshall)	2:04 1/2m	
35	1,610 Greyhound (Sep Palin)	2:00 m	
36	1,700 Ruth M. Mac (Thomas Berry)	2:04 1/4m	
37	1,475 Delphia Hanover (Henry Thomas)	2:05 1/4m	
38	1,740 Earl's Mr. Will (Tom Berry)	2:03 3/4m	
39	1,815 Peter Astra (Doc Parshall)	2:05 m	
40	1,825 Earl's Moody Guy (Tom Berry)	2:02 1/4m	
41	2,210 Bill Gallon (Lee Smith)	2:04 3/4m	
42	3,882 Cannon Ball (Harry Whitney)	2:05 1/2h	
43	4,013 Volo Song (Ben White)	2:08 1/4h	
44	5,726 Pearl Harbor (Omer Amundsen)	2:05 h	
45	5,573 Doctor Spencer (Henry Thomas)	2:00 1/2m	
46	-- Rain --		
47	7,274 Way Yonder (Houston Stone)	2:04.1m	
48	11,039 Egan Hanover (Ralph Baldwin)	2:02.4m	
49	15,128 Bangaway (Ralph Baldwin)	2:03 m	
50	14,135 Lusty Song (Delvin Miller)	2:03.2m	
51	17,138 Spennib (Fay Fitzpatrick)	a 2:02.3m	
52	15,679 Hit Song (Harry Pownall, Sr.)	2:01.2m	
53	17,190 Kimberly Kid (Thomas Berry)	2:01 m	
54	18,277 Prince Victor (Jim Hackett)	2:01.2m	
55	17,600 Scott Frost (Joe O'Brien)	2:01.3m	
56	15,889 Bold Rodney (Robert Parkinson)	2:01 m	
57	19,174 Double Scotch (Joe O'Brien)	2:01.2m	
58	17,518 Mc Colby (Dana Cameron)	b 2:01.2h	
59	18,742 Diller Hanover (Ralph Baldwin)	2:01 m	
60	22,794 Uncle Sam (Lou Huber, Jr.)	2:00.1m	
61	18,533 Caleb (John Simpson, Sr.)	1:58.3m	
62	21,528 Nathaniel (Harry Pownall, Sr.)	2:01.1m	
	Safe Mission (Joe O'Brien)	2:03 m	
63	24,125 Glidden Hanover (Eddie Wheeler)	1:59.4m	
	Cheer Honey (Frank Ervin)	2:00.2m	
64	20,660 Ayres (John Simpson, Sr.)	1:59 m	
65	21,512 Noble Victory (Stanley Dancer)	1:59.3m	
66	18,171 Kerry Way (Frank Ervin)	2:00.1m	
67	20,931 Dazzling Speed (Stanley Dancer) c	1:59.4m	
68	16,730 Snow Speed (Ralph Baldwin) d	1:58.3m	
69	22,000 Lindys Pride (Howard Beissinger)	2:00.3m	
70	26,900 Timothy T. (John Simpson, Jr.)	2:01.1m	
71	29,250 Hoot Speed (Glen Garnsey) e	1:58.1m	
72	21,970 Super Bowl (Stanley Dancer)	1:59.3m	
73	28,140 Arnie Almahurst (Gene Riegle)	2:00 m	
74	34,010 Golden Sovereign(D. Richardson) f	1:58.4m	
75	-- Rain --		
76	40,734 Lola's Express (Bruce Nickells)	1:58.4m	
77	45,520 Scandal Sheet(D. Richardson, Jr.)	1:58.2m	
78	38,629 Speedy Somolli (H. Beissinger)	1:59.1m	
79	33,588 Gator Bowl (J. Simpson, Jr.)	1:59.1m	
80	-- Rain --		
81	97,528 Super Juan (Howard Beissinger)	1:56.1m	
	Snack Bar (Hakan Wallner)	1:56.1m	
82	80,000 Crysta's Crown (Hakan Wallner) g	1:56 m	
83	87,140 Winky's Gill (Hakan Wallner)	1:55.2m	
84	93,583 Crowning Point (Doug Ackerman)	1:54 m	
85	-- Rain --		
86	105,738 Royal Prestige (Berndt Lindstedt)	1:56 m	
87	110,000 Spotlite Lobell (Walt Paisley) Rh	1:52.1m	
88	110,220 Power Beam (Ted Andrews) i	1:53.3m	
89	102,000 Shogun Lobell (How. Beissinger) j	1:55.1m	
90	110,000 Super Arnie (Berndt Lindstedt)	1:54.1m	

a By Scotch Rhythm.   g By Incredible Nevele.
b By Great Lullwater.   h By Mack Lobell.
c By Speedy Streak.   i By Supergill.
d By Nevele Pride.   j By Demilo Hanover.
e By Quick Pride.
f By Golden Soverign & Nevele Diamond.

The Review Stake
Three-Year-Old Pace
Illinois State Fair, Springfield, IL Aug. 16, 1990

29	1,500 Axworthy Pride (Frank Cares) a	2:07 m	
30	2,000 Calumet Adam (R.D. McMahon)	2:01 1/4m	
31	2,150 Lady Vonian (Doc Parshall)	2:03 1/2m	
32	1,175 Raider (Fred Egan)	2:02 1/2m	
33	1,030 Gene Volo (H.C. Fitzpatrick)	2:06 1/4 m	
34	800 Highland Millie (Ben White)	2:07 3/4m	
35	1,420 Wedgemere Volo (Doc Parshall)	2:03 1/4m	
36	1,550 Little Pat (Charles Lacey)	2:01 m	
37	1,545 Hal Cochato (Sep Palin)	2:00 1/2m	
38	1,330 Chief Counsel (Doc Parshall)	1:58 1/4m	
39	1,385 Blackstone (Doc Parshall)	2:00 m	
40	1,525 Fearless Peter (Doc Parshall)	2:01 1/4m	
41	1,525 Bell Boy (Doc Parshall)	2:04 1/4m	
42	3,632 Voloway (Henry Thomas) b	2:05 h	
43	2,463 Purdue Hal (Sep Palin)	2:02 1/4h	
44	4,127 Attorney (Art Blackwell)	2:05 1/2h	
45	3,872 True Chief (Thomas Berry)	2:01 1/4m	
46	-- Rain --		
47	7,327 Forbes Chief (Del Cameron)	2:01.3m	
48	9,335 Atomic Bomb (Delvin Miller) c	2:01.4m	
49	12,903 Good Time (Frank Ervin)	2:01.2m	
50	12,502 Quilla Hanover (J. Simpson, Sr.)	2:01.4m	
51	11,509 Tar Heel (Delvin Miller)	1:59.4m	
52	10,745 Voting Trust (B.J. Schue)	2:01 m	
53	12,254 Dutch Dandy (Curly Smart) d	1:59.1m	
54	15,241 Diamond Hall (Joe O'Brien)	2:01 m	
	Meadow Gold (James Arthur)	2:01 m	
55	15,202 Sea Eagle (H.C. Fitzpatrick)	2:00.3m	
56	13,411 Adioscot (Delvin Miller)	2:00.2m	
57	14,864 Torpid (John Simpson, Sr.)	1:59.4m	
58	14,638 Thorpe Hanover (Delvin Miller)	1:59.2m	
59	19,470 Bristol Hanover (Delvin Miller)	1:59 m	
60	12,286 Dancer Hanover (Delvin Miller)	2:00 m	
61	15,720 Adios Don (Howard Camper) e	1:57.4m	
62	16,765 Coffee Break (George Sholty)	1:57 m	
63	14,486 James B. Hanover (Del Insko)	2:00.1m	
64	17,810 Race Time (Ralph Baldwin)	2:00.2m	
65	15,562 Bret Hanover (Frank Ervin)	1:59.2m	
	Adios Vic (Jim Dennis)	2:00 m	
66	12,821 Fashion Tip (Jim Dennis)	1:58.2m	
67	13,681 Best Of All (Jim Hackett)	1:57 m	
68	16,150 Ozzie Hanover (Gene Riegle)	1:58.4m	
	Nevele Romeo (Stanley Dancer)	1:58.4m	
69	16,280 Bye Bye Sam (Stanley Dancer)	2:03 m	
70	22,650 Race Time Boy (Wm. Haughton) f	1:59 m	
71	25,350 Winning Worthy (H. Graham, Jr.)	1:57.2m	
72	17,170 Hilarious Way (J. Simpson, Jr.)	1:55.2m	
73	27,840 Melvin's Woe (Joe O'Brien)	1:57 m	
74	27,712 Starred By Bret (Stan Bayless)	1:57 m	
75	-- Rain --		
76	35,934 Warm Breeze (Dick Farrington)	1:54.4m	
77	40,620 Lightning Strikes (Joe O'Brien)	1:55 m	
78	31,829 Skipper's Subject (Archie McNeil)	1:55 m	
79	39,088 Scarlet Skipper (Billy Herman)	1:56.2m	
80	-- Rain --		
81	44,328 Landslide (Ed Lohmeyer)	1:55.1m	
82	50,000 Irish Jimmy (Joe O'Brien) g	1:51.3m	
83	45,740 Umbrella Fella (Glen Garnsey)	1:53.1m	
84	50,984 River Rouge (Dave Rankin) Rh	1:50.3m	
85	-- Rain --		
86	42,938 Towner's Big Guy (S. Warrington)	1:52.1m	
87	31,520 Cue Light (John Campbell)	1:53.4m	
	31,520 Z Twenty Eight (Bill Fahy)	1:52.2m	
88	70,820 Threefold (John Campbell)	1:51.1m	
89	67,000 Barefoot Hanover (Dave Rankin)	1:52.3m	
90	54,000 Happy Hoosier (Sam "Chip" Noble)	1:55.2m	

a By Lee Strathmore & Axloretta (four-heat race).   e By Lang Hanover.
b By Lilydale.   f By Toliver Hanover.
c By E.J. Hal.   g By Trenton.
d By Marvel Way.   h By Colt Fortysix.

The W.N. Reynolds Memorial
Two-Year-Old Trot
Raceway Park, Toledo, Ohio June 8, 1990

51	11,092 Theme Song (B.J. Schue)	2:12.4h	
52	13,920 Singing Sword (Delvin Miller) a	2:14 h	
53	12,505 Brevity Hanover (Delvin Miller)	2:10 h	
54	12,597 Colby Mite (Ralph Baldwin)	2:09.4h	
55	12,269 Valiant Rodney (Dana Cameron)	2:07.3h	
56	17,067 Demon Rum (C.J. Champion)	2:12.4h	
57	10,007 Sharpshooter (H. Pownall, Sr.)	2:10 h	
58	12,075 Larue Hanover (S.L. Caton)	2:12.3h	
59	14,986 Blaze Hanover (Joe O'Brien)	2:08.4h	
60	13,633 Mr. Pride (William Haughton)	2:08.2h	
61	17,043 Hickory Hill (William Haughton)	2:08.1h	
62	8,989 B.F. Coaltown (Harry Short)	2:08 h	
	8,989 Incorporator (William Haughton)	2:13.4h	
63	8,831 Late Frost (Delvin Miller)	2:10 h	
	8,831 Space Freight (J. Simpson, Jr.)	2:11.4h	
64	9,415 Ben Hur (Don C. Miller)	2:11.3h	
	9,415 Egyptian Candor (Stanley Dancer)	2:09.3h	
65	18,493 Ideal Rodney (William Haughton)	2:09 h	
66	19,429 Drummond R.C. (Keith Waples)	2:09.1h	
67	18,360 Nevele Pride (Stanley Dancer)	2:07.4h	

CHRONICLES

68	19,729 Nevele Major (Stanley Dancer)	2:06.4h	
69	20,385 Victory Star (Vernon Dancer)	2:06.4h	
70	12,108 A.C.'s Orion (William Haughton)	2:13 h	
	12,008 Thai (Joe O'Brien)	2:15 h	
71	12,475 Songcan (Gilles Lachance)	2:14.3h	
	12,475 Hambo Hope (John Schroeder)	2:14 h	
72	25,050 Walter Be Good (Ben Webster)	2:07.3h	
73	15,600 Journalist (William Haughton)	2:09.1h	
	15,850 Off The Record (Ben Webster)	2:09.1h	
74	12,050 Spearmint (William Haughton)	2:08.4h	
	12,050 Skipper Walt (Roland Beaulieu)	2:06.1h	
75	11,750 Pride And Hope (Peter Haughton)	2:08.4h	
	11,750 Peridot Pride (Peter Haughton)	2:04.4h	
76	11,850 Naturally Nevele (Stanley Dancer)	2:09.2h	
	11,850 A.B.C. Freight (Clint Galbraith)	2:09.4h	
77	19,000 Hecan (Bill Myer)	2:09.2h	
78	22,500 Political Party (J. Schroeder)	2:07.1h	
79	22,000 Nevele Impulse (Gerry Sarama)	2:08.1h	
80	13,750 Liam Almahurst (Clint Galbraith)	2:09 h	
	14,000 Smokin Yankee (Stanley Dancer)	2:04.2h	
81	25,000 Cooper Lobell (Raymond Tripp)	R 2:03.1h	
82	22,000 Quick In Action (Paul Chambers)	2:08.3h	
	22,000 Dancer's Crown (Stanley Dancer)	2:04 h	
83	25,750 Meadow Prize (Paul Chambers)	2:08.4h	
	26,000 Folding Green (Robert Altizer)	2:07.1h	
84	22,500 Hockey Broline (Hakan Wallner)	2:06.1h	
	22,750 Devil's Victory (Abe Stoltzfus)	2:07 h	
	22,750 Kash Exempt (Clint Galbraith)	2:08.4h	
85	22,000 Salem Lobell (Jan Johnson)	2:06.3h	
	22,250 Elgin Almahurst (Jan Nordin)	2:05.4h	
86	19,300 Eighty Four USA (Don Rothfuss)	2:09 h	
	19,600 Manor Victory (Jan Nordin)	2:05.4h	
87	-- Not Raced --		
88	-- Not Raced --		
89	25,450 Florida Power (Rod Allen)	2:03.4f	
	25,450 Letters From Hill (Chris Boring)	2:03.4f	
90	46,843 Super Pleasure (Joe Adamsky)	R 2:03.2f	

a By Lee Gallon.

The W.N. Reynolds Memorial
Two-Year-Old Pace
Raceway Park, Toledo, Ohio June 9, 1990

51	10,592 Voting Trust (B.J. Schue)	a 2:07.4h	
52	13,620 Newport Chief (Del Cameron)	2:08.4h	
53	13,605 Scotch Byrd (Alix Winger)	2:05.4h	
54	12,047 Treasure Island (Henry Myott)	2:08.1h	
55	10,469 Newport Frisco (Del Cameron)	2:05.1h	
56	18,717 Torpid (John Simpson, Sr.)	b 2:04.3h	
57	11,225 Thorpe Hanover (James Arthur)	2:04.1h	
58	13,675 Adios Chief (James Arthur)	2:06 h	
59	16,086 Mifflin Hanover (Vernon Dancer)	2:05.4h	
60	15,733 Magic Adios (Eldon Harner)	c 2:06 h	
61	20,943 Mighty Tar Heel (Alix Winger)	2:04.2h	
62	9,864 Max Hanover (Clarence Martin)	2:06.2h	
	9,864 Vogel Hanover (Buddy Gilmour)	2:05.2h	
63	9,981 Meadow Lou (Louis Rapone)	2:06.1h	
	9,981 Torpedo (William Haughton)	2:03.4h	
64	8,752 Yellowbird (Waldo McIlmurray)	2:07 h	
	8,752 Rivaltime (George Sholty)	2:05.1h	
	8,752 Bret Hanover (Don C. Miller)	2:03.2h	
65	21,643 Deputy Hanover (Eldon Harner)	2:04.1h	
66	26,149 Toledo Hanover (George Sholty)d	2:06.1h	
67	14,007 Fulla Napoleon (Richard Thomas)	2:03.4h	
	14,007 Bye Bye Pat (Clint Bodgins)	2:03.2h	
68	13,384 Laverne Hanover (Wm. Haughton)	2:04 h	
	13,384 Penn Hanover (Keith Waples)	2:02.4h	
69	9,550 Most Happy Fella (Stanley Dancer)	2:03.3h	
	9,550 Columbia George (Roland Beaulieu)	2:04.4h	
	9,550 The Great One (Harold Dancer)	2:06 h	
70	14,741 Tarport Skipper (Delvin Miller)	2:05 h	
	14,741 Jolly Roger (Stanley Dancer)	2:05 h	
71	10,600 Racy Prince (Robert Parkinson)	2:05 h	
	10,400 Strike Out (John Hayes)	2:03.4h	
	10,500 Shadow Star (Jack Kopas)	2:05.4h	
72	16,000 Thor Almahurst (Jack Kopas)	2:05.2h	
	15,900 Steady Airliner (Joe O'Brien)	2:02 h	
73	14,050 Bestman Hanover (Ben Webster)	2:04.2h	
	14,250 Trial And Error (Ben Webster)	2:05 h	
	14,050 National Byrd (William Haughton)	2:05.4h	
74	13,950 Broadcaster B. (William Haughton)	2:05.3h	
	13,950 Armbro Petch (Jack Kopas)	2:05.3h	
	14,750 Dar Hanover (Bill Wellwood)	2:05.2h	
75	12,800 Puppet (Peter Haughton)	2:02.4h	
	12,800 Bit O Fun (Warren Cameron)	2:04.4h	
	12,800 Keith Drummond (Keith Waples)	2:04.2h	
76	13,000 Sure Winner (Dick Farrington)	2:05.1h	
	14,200 River Captain (Doug Arthur)	2:03 h	
	14,200 Rockwell Hanover (D.MacTavish,Sr.)	2:02.4h	
	14,200 Nat Lobell (Jack Kopas)	2:02.4h	
77	12,300 Charles Hanover (D.MacTavish,Sr.)	2:04.3h	
	12,100 Skip Hanover (Peter Haughton)	2:02.4h	
	12,100 J R Power (Tom Strauss)	2:03.1h	
78	17,500 Peace Time (Jack Kopas)	*	
	17,750 Whata Monster (Del Insko)	2:03.2h	
	18,000 Kawartha Skipper (Stanley Dancer)	2:02.2h	
79	35,750 Midas Almahurst (Sal Gati)	2:01.4h	
80	17,500 Eastern Skipper (Stanley Dancer)	2:01.4h	
	17,500 Blizzard Almahurst (Jack Kopas)	2:02 h	
	17,250 French Chef (Stanley Dancer)	R 2:00 h	
	17,250 Bonzo Hanover (Rejean Daigneault)	2:01.4h	
81	26,000 Most Happy Marco (John Kopas)	2:01.3h	
	26,000 Ima Bright Boy (Ted Jacobs)	2:01.4h	
82	32,500 Thurston Hanover (Chris Boring)	2:02.4h	
	32,500 Bret's Hurricane (Frank O'Mara)	2:05 h	
	32,500 Elarfus (Jack Bailey)	2:04.4h	
83	30,250 White Tiger (Bill Popfinger)	2:02.1h	
	30,000 Apache Circle (Gaston Guindon)	2:00.3h	
	30,250 Troublemaker (Bruce Riegle)	R 2:00 h	
84	26,750 Czar Nicholas (John Hayes, Jr.)	2:00.1h	
	26,750 Bounty Blue Chip (Ron Waples)	*	
	27,000 Praised Dignity (Wm. Popfinger)	2:04.2h	
	27,000 Chairmanoftheboard (W. Haughton)	2:05.4h	
85	28,750 El Greco (Gaston Guindon)	2:01 h	
	29,000 The Big Wiz (Jay Sears)	2:01 h	
86	13,350 Surfer Lobell (Jim Dolbee)	2:01.4h	
	13,350 Grand Marshal (Tom Barabasz)	2:03.1h	
	13,350 Supreme Towner (Gaston Guindon)	2:02 h	
87	-- Not Raced --		
88	-- Not Raced --		
89	25,250 Keystone Throng (Jeff Fout)	R 1:58 f	
	26,000 Fortysix Extralong (Chris Boring)	1:59.1f	
	26,000 Friendly Trio (Veral Bowman)	2:02.1f	
90	26,385 Interpretory (D.R. Ackerman)	1:59.3f	
	26,385 Isle Of Maui (Butch Dokey)	2:02 f	
	26,385 Squire Squirt (Sam "Chip" Noble)	1:58.4f	

* Time disallowed

a By Ensign Mite. c By Adios Don.
b By Adios Express. d By Tudor Hanover.

The W.N. Reynolds Memorial
Three-Year-Old Trot
Raceway Park, Toledo Ohio June 9, 1990

52	9,642 Dallas Hanover (Joe O'Brien)	a 2:08.2h	
53	11,620 Bewitch (Henry Myott)	2:06.4h	
54	12,305 Bunny Hanover (Henry Myott)	2:08 h	
55	10,797 Lyman Hanover (C.J. Champion)	b 2:07 h	
56	9,519 Scotty Hanover (Ned Bower)	2:08.1h	
57	17,067 Demon Rum (C.J. Champion)	2:05 h	
58	8,711 Spunky Hanover (Howard Camper)	2:04.1h	
	McColby (Dana Cameron)	2:08.1h	
59	11,625 Brogue Hanover (Joe O'Brien)	2:05.2h	
60	14,611 Manton Hanover (Howard Camper)	2:05.1h	
61	12,865 Merrie Gaston (J. Patterson, Sr.)	2:09.2h	
62	12,818 A.C.'s Viking (Sanders Russell)	2:04.3h	
63	15,178 Rodilo (Stanley Dancer)	2:05 h	
64	13,362 Bold Viking (Stanley Dancer)	2:05.2h	
65	13,906 Crockett (Fred Parks)	2:04.3h	
66	10,600 Polaris (Donald Huff)	2:04.1h	
67	9,640 Armbro Harold (Robt. Silliphant)	2:08.1h	
68	5,040 Nevele Pride (Stanley Dancer)	2:02.2h	
69	8,760 Crain Hanover (James Arthur)	2:05.3h	
70	7,500 Clayt Hanover (Stanley Dancer)	2:05.3h	
71	8,400 Cap D'Antibes (Edward Dunnigan)	2:04.4h	
72	8,200 Dunnigan Lobell (Wm. Haughton)	2:05.3h	
73	12,450 Keystone Wart (C.J. Champion)	2:07.2h	
74	8,600 Surge Hanover (Bill Wellwood)	2:06 h	
75	23,300 Spitfire Hanover (Delvin Miller)	2:07.1h	
76	13,750 Surefire Hanover (Stanley Dancer)	2:02.2h	
	13,750 Steve Lobell (Peter Haughton)	2:02.1h	
	13,750 Quick Pay (Peter Haughton)	2:02.2h	
77	15,000 Speed In Action (Delvin Miller)	2:02.4h	
	15,200 Haygood (William Haughton)	2:04 h	
78	25,000 Doublemint (Peter Haughton)	2:04 h	
79	21,000 Crown's Cristy(Howard Beissinger)	2:03.3h	
80	13,500 Nevele Impulse (Dick Macomber)	2:04 h	
	14,000 Super Split (Doug Arthur)	2:04.4h	
81	27,000 Sigo Hanover (Raymond Tripp)	2:02 h	
82	26,000 Happy Crown (Jan Nordin)	2:03 h	
83	18,750 Sea Chanty (Clint Galbraith)	2:02.4h	
	19,000 Quick In Action (Paul Chambers)	2:02.1h	
84	36,000 Eric Kosmos (John Andersen)	R 2:01.2h	
85	37,500 Piggvar (Stanley Dancer)	2:03.3h	

Page 349

CHRONICLES

86		33,200 Kash Dare (Bob Bloodgood)	2:04.1h			28,500 Rompaway Henry (Don Harmon)	R 1:58.4f
87		53,150 Midnight Clear (David Vance)	2:03.4h	90		19,050 Letters From Hill (Chris Boring)	2:02 f
88		-- Not Raced --				20,050 Drummer Hanover (Dick Richardson)	2:01.2f
89		28,500 Long And Straight (Sam Noble III)	2:00.2f	a By Theme Song.		b By Carla Hanover.	

The W.N. Reynolds Memorial
Three-Year-Old Pace
Raceway Park, Toledo, Ohio June 10, 1990

52	10,142 Mighty Brewer (Don Hayes)	a 2:07 h		17,000 Bret's Champ (Ben Steall)		2:01 h
53	10,320 Knight Star (Franklin Safford)	2:05.4h		17,000 Osborne's Bret (Tom Brinkerhoff)		2:00.4h
54	10,355 Excellent Chief (Ralph Baldwin)	2:04.1h	76	50,000 Smooth Fella (Gerald Sarama)		1:58.3h
55	9,097 Reed's Knight (James Arthur)	2:03.4h	77	25,000 Seedling Herbert (Wm. Haughton)		2:00.1h
56	7,169 Steamin' Demon (Edwin Boyer)	2:04.2h		25,000 Nat Lobell (John Kopas)		1:59.2h
57	12,917 Torpid (John Simpson, Sr.)	2:05.3h	78	50,000 Abercrombie (Glen Garnsey)		2:00 h
58	10,679 Shadow Wave (Joe O'Brien)	2:02.1h	79	50,000 Composite (Ron Waples)		2:01 h
59	11,725 Meadow Al (Joe O'Brien)	2:12 h	80	50,000 Niatross (Clint Galbraith)	R	1:56.2h
60	13,661 Kashworthy (Alfred Thomas)	2:03.2h	81	50,000 Artie's Dream (Shelly Goudreau)		1:58 h
61	17,615 Speedy Time (J. Patterson, Sr.)	2:03 h	82	50,000 Coal Harbor (Ron Waples)		1:59.1h
62	17,018 Buxton Hanover (William Haughton)	2:01.1h	83	50,000 F. Troop (Ron Waples)		1:58 h
63	16,528 Diamond Sam (Lou Huber, Jr.)	2:02.4h	84	50,000 Coloton Collins (Dave Vance)		2:00.2h
64	15,662 Vicar Hanover (William Haughton)	2:01 h	85	25,000 Cedarwood George (Jerry Duford)		2:00.2h
65	17,206 Bret Hanover (Frank Ervin)	2:00.2h		25,000 Staff Director (David Wall)		1:57.1h
66	12,933 Romeo Hanover (David Tovim)	2:11 h	86	25,000 Mr Rodeo Drive (Buddy Gilmour)		1:59.1h
67	12,680 Best Of All (Jim Hackett)	2:03.3h		25,000 Nathan Almahurst (Buddy Gilmour)		1:59.2h
68	13,040 Batman (Bruce Nickells)	2:01.4h	87	28,100 Dakota Killean (Lyle MacArthur)		1:59 h
69	11,620 Kat Byrd (Levi Harner)	2:00 h		28,100 Determined Chase (R. Davis, Jr.)		1:57 h
70	13,220 Keystone Pat (John Hayes)	2:01.4h	88	-- Not Raced --		
71	14,040 Scioto Star (D. Richardson, Jr.)	2:02.1h	89	30,400 Armbro Harrier (Sam Noble III)		1:56.1f
72	8,250 Shadow Star (Jack Kopas)	2:02.4h		30,400 Dancing Master (Chris Boring)		1:57.1f
	8,250 Strike Out (Keith Waples)	2:02.1h		30,400 Over The Wall (Chris Boring)	R	1:55.1f
73	24,350 J.R.Skipper (Ron Waples)	2:00.1h	90	22,900 Fortysix Extralong (Chris Boring)		1:58.1f
74	23,600 Boyden Hanover (Billy Herman)	2:01.1h		22,900 French Embassy (Kurt Sugg)		1:56.3f
75	17,000 John V.(Gerald Sarama)	2:00.4h	a By Claude Hanover.			

The W.N. Reynolds Memorial
Two-Year-Old Filly Trot
Raceway Park, Toledo, Ohio June 6, 1990

57	8,495 Anna Dares (John Simpson, Sr.)	2:13.1h	75	18,200 Garden Path (Charlie Clark)		2:09.4h
58	10,175 Hoot N Toot (Buddy Gilmour)	2:15.4h	76	10,350 El Silcar (Gerald Procino)		2:09.4h
59	11,361 Elaine Rodney (Clint Hodgins)	2:08.1h		10,350 Elmsford (Paul Grenier)		2:11.3h
60	12,383 Just Precious (Eddie Wheeler)	2:09.2h	77	10,200 Love Touch (Richard Hogan)		2:07.2h
61	15,618 Sprite Rodney (Frank Ervin)	2:07.3h		10,400 Dearest (Stanley Dancer)		2:06.4h
62	13,403 First Frost (Benoit Cote)	2:12.1h	78	12,250 Hard To Beat (Howard Beissinger)		2:10 h
63	7,868 Starlette Hill (Carl Larsen)	2:11 h		12,250 Ahhhh (Howard Beissinger)		2:07.2h
	7,868 Vickie Hill (Carl Larsen)	2:12.2h	79	19,600 Allurement (Frank Ervin)	R	2:05.1h
64	8,228 Merrie Flower (Howard Beissinger)	2:12.4h	80	13,000 Filet Of Sole (Stanley Dancer)		2:08 h
	8,228 Armbro Flight (Joe O'Brien)	2:10.4h		13,250 Snuffles (Glen Garnsey)		2:07.3h
	10,221 La Mere (Stanley Dancer)	2:09 h	81	25,000 Truffle Lobell (Ben Steall)		2:06.1h
	10,221 Tarport Toni (Stanley Dancer)	2:09.2h	82	24,000 Color Of Money (Cammie Haughton)		2:05.4h
65	14,959 Floral Hanover (Delvin Miller)	2:08.3h		24,000 Excella Hanover (Gene Riegle)		2:05.4h
66	16,920 Fantasia Hanover (Frank Ervin)	2:07 h	83	26,750 Gratis Yankee (Bib Roberts)		2:10.4h
67	9,126 Medal Frost (Joe O'Brien)	2:10.4h		27,000 Maiden Yankee (Bib Roberts)		2:09.4h
68	9,126 Jounce (Clint Hodgins)	2:11 h	84	25,000 Tenderly (Tom Haughton)		2:06.2h
69	15,045 Sweet Freight (Fred Bradbury)	2:11 h		25,000 Magic Hope (Archie McNeil)		2:06.2h
70	10,332 Keystone Selene (Delvin Miller)	2:06.4h	85	22,250 Psycho (Frank Popfinger)		2:07.1h
	10,232 Meadow Split (Delvin Miller)	2:10 h		22,250 Tearose Lobell (Hakan Wallner)		2:07 h
71	10,018 First Star (Jack Kopas)	2:08.4h	86	18,100 Keystone Harem (M. Vartiainen)		2:08.3h
	10,018 Modern Yankee (Delvin Miller)	2:07.4h		17,800 Meadow Love (Delvin Miller)		2:11 h
72	10,800 Colonial Charm (Glen Garnsey)	2:08.4h	87	-- Not Raced --		
	11,000 Desirade (Charlie Clark)	2:12.4h	88	-- Not Raced --		
73	15,100 Starlark Hanover (David Wade)	2:06.2h	89	21,050 B T Smoke (Frank Todd, Jr.)	R	2:00.4f
	15,100 Berna Hanover (Glen Garnsey)	2:09.3h		21,050 Perfect Point (D.R. Ackerman)		2:04.1f
74	11,400 Brilliance (Stanley Dancer)	2:09.2h	90	45,313 Grand Encore (Carl Allen)		2:03.4f
	11,400 Lincolns Squaw (Jacques Bruyere)	2:09.4h				

The W.N. Reynolds Memorial
Two-Year-Old Filly Pace
Raceway Park, Toledo, Ohio June 6, 1990

57	9,071 Kwik (C.J. Fitzpatrick, Jr.)	2:07.3h		11,913 Jefferson Time (Leroy Copeland)		2:09.3h
58	9,125 Trim Freight (Fred Bradbury)	2:06.3h	71	8,035 Saucy Wave (Harry Harvey)		2:07.3h
59	12,111 Jan Hanover (William Haughton)	2:04.4h		8,035 Hail To Bret (George Gilmour)		2:06.4h
60	12,133 Patricia Rhythm (H. Wellwood)	2:06.1h		8,135 Decorum (Stanley Dancer)		2:07.2h
61	15,468 Juno Hanover (Clint Hodgins)	a 2:06.1h	72	13,000 Real Hilarious (Bruce Nickells)		2:03.4h
62	7,926 Moon Glitter (Clint Hodgins)	2:09 h		12,900 Armbro Norma (Delvin Miller)		2:06.3h
	7,926 Harry's Laura (Clint Hodgins)	2:06.3h	73	11,800 Hilarious Sister (M. Metcalfe)		2:06.3h
63	8,218 Charlotte Adios (Frank Ervin)	2:09.4h		11,600 Jaunty Barmin (Ben Webster)		2:07.4h
	8,218 Angelic Wick (Eugene Minniear)	2:08 h		11,600 DeBuena Fuente (J.W. Smith, Sr.)		2:04.2h
64	7,260 Mindy (John Caton)	2:08.4h	74	14,100 Ata Whitney (Jack Kopas)		2:07.2h
	7,260 Freight Target (Clint Hodgins)	2:09.3h		13,900 Hurricane Wave (Jack Kopas)		2:07 h
	7,260 Taffy Apple (Don C. Miller)	2:08.3h	75	13,100 Captivate (Robert N. Smith, Jr.)		2:06.2h
65	9,296 Worth Knowing (Howard Beissinger)	2:07 h		13,300 Meadow Wilma (William Haughton)		2:06 h
	9,296 Armbro Gambol (Benoit Cote)	2:08.1h		13,100 Toplady Almahurst (Abe Stoltzfus)		2:05.3h
66	17,859 Ember Hanover (Richard Thomas)	2:06 h	76	12,500 Timely Bret (Richard Thomas)		2:06.1h
67	17,880 Trotwood Tootie (Harold Warner)	2:09 h		12,500 Chappaqua Hanover (Wm. Haughton)		2:03.2h
68	10,361 Queen Omaha (Lucien Fontaine)	2:05.3h		12,500 Luanne's Jewel (Peter Haughton)		2:04.3h
	10,361 Supple Yankee (Mehrle Wachter)	2:05.4h	77	13,500 Ata Connie (William Haughton)		2:04.3h
69	17,745 Timely News (Stanley Dancer)	2:06.1h		13,700 Happy Lady (Jim Rankin)		2:03.4h
70	11,913 Brets Blue Chip (Stanley Dancer)	2:11.2h	78	18,700 Lismore (Harry Harvey)		2:04 h

CHRONICLES

	18,700	Roses Are Red (John Kopas)	2:02.4h
79	25,000	Bunnie Hanover (Stanley Dancer)	2:04 h
80	19,000	Keystone Madeira (Jim Rankin)	2:05.1h
	19,000	Areba Areba (Jack Kopas) R	2:01.1h
81	38,000	Harmonica (Stanley Dancer)	2:02.2h
82	50,000	Keystone Flamingo (Wm. Haughton)	2:03.2h
83	35,000	Tabatros Rainbow (Butch Dokey)	2:03.1h
	35,250	Kelly Rocklin (Abe Stoltzfus)	2:01.3h
84	32,500	Borne Ideal (Jack Bailey)	2:02.3h
	32,500	Imatross (Clint Galbraith)	2:03.3h
85	24,000	Samdoe (Trevor Ritchie)	2:02.2h

	24,250	Miss Emily Hanover (Ted Jacobs)	2:03 h
	24,000	Armbro Evita (John Kopas)	2:02.3h
86	35,300	La Toya (Wayne Nickells)	2:04.1h
87		-- Not Raced --	
88		-- Not Raced --	
89	25,550	Excited (Sam Noble III)	2:00.2f
	26,300	Smoochin (D.R. Ackerman)	2:00.2f
90	32,872	Goalie Jess (Jim Bailey) R	1:59.1f
	32,872	Jollie Dame (Bill Gale)	2:00 f

a By Adios Scarlet.

The W.N. Reynolds Memorial
Three-Year-Old Filly Trot
Raceway Park, Toledo, Ohio   June 8, 1990

58	8,279	Anna Dares (John Simpson, Sr.)	2:07.3h
59	10,025	Matora Hanover (J. Simpson, Sr.)	2:07.1h
60	9,311	Elaine Rodney (Clint Hodgins)	2:04.1h
61	9,665	Claire Sampson (Lou Huber, Jr.)	2:06.2h
62	11,318	Sprite Rodney (Frank Ervin)	2:08.4h
63	11,078	Gay Frost (William Haughton)	2:08 h
64	8,031	Speedy Victory (Robert Walker)	2:06 h
	8,031	Golden Make It (Dana Irving)	2:05.3h
	12,206	Armbro Flight (Joe O'Brien)	2:05.3h
65	7,500	Coalition (Art Hult)	2:06 h
66	6,260	Speed Model (Art Hult)	2:03.4h
67	8,000	Arbida Hanover (Delbert Manges)	2:05.3h
68	8,500	Tarport Farr (Delvin Miller)	2:06.2h
69	7,100	Vanaro (Bill Popfinger)	2:06 h
70	8,200	Real Cool (Ben Steall)	2:09.3h
71	8,300	Speedy Carlene (Stanley Dancer)	2:03 h
72	9,900	Colonial Charm (Glen Garnsey)	2:06.1h
73	13,300	Starlark Hanover (David Wade)	2:06 h
74	21,750	Meadow Bright (Delvin Miller)	2:05 h

76	14,100	Portia Lobell (Ron Waples)	2:06.3h
	14,100	Connie Lobell (Ron Waples)	2:07.2h
77	22,600	Laurna Jean (Carl Allen)	2:05 h
78	24,000	Imagery (Stanley Dancer)	2:03.2h
79	21,500	Her Bias (Abe Stoltzfus)	2:06.4h
80	20,000	Kading (Ben Steall)	2:04.2h
81	24,000	Filet Of Sole (Stanley Dancer)	2:03.4h
82	23,000	Northern Princess (Ron Waples)	2:03 h
	23,000	Lucretia's Kash (Clint Galbraith)	2:01.4h
83	36,000	Segriff (Gordon Waples) R	2:01.1h
84	28,600	Maiden Yankee (Bib Roberts)	2:02.1h
85	37,500	Double Coverage (Clint Galbraith)	2:02.2h
86	17,000	Keystone Tussle (Jack Kopas)	2:08 h
	17,000	Armbro Elusive (Jay Sears)	2:07.1h
87	47,650	Jazzy Jen (Markku Vartiainen)	2:04.3h
88		-- Not Raced --	
89	26,150	Stormont Easygoing (Norm Jones)	2:03.1f
	26,150	Speedtown's Score (S. Brannan) R	2:02.1f
90	27,900	Gretel T (D.R. Ackerman) R	2:02.1f

The W.N. Reynolds Memorial
Three-Year-Old Filly Pace
Raceway Park, Toledo, Ohio   June 10, 1990

58	8,999	Kwik (C.J. Fitzpatrick, Jr.)	2:05.3h
59	9,325	Friendly Hal (Louis Rapone)	2:05 h
60	11,111	Countess Adios (Delvin Miller)	2:02.3h
61	10,815	Miss Blue Jay (Clifford Boyd)	2:07.2h
62	11,818	Ritzy Hanover (George Phalen)	2:03 h
63	11,878	Tarport Rose (Delvin Miller)	2:04.2h
64	8,031	Sand Tart (Marvin Parshall)	2:06.3h
	8,031	Poplar Wick (Del Insko)	2:04.3h
65	8,653	Fredrika Byrd (Buddy Gilmour)	2:05.3h
	8,653	Mindy (Raymond Ross)	2:05.1h
66	7,750	Good Candy (Bill Myer)	2:04 h
67	8,460	Meadow Elva (William Haughton)	2:05 h
68	10,580	Shadydale Carol (Elden Turcotte)	2:04.3h
69	5,375	Tarport Birdie (Delbert Manges)	2:03.3h
	5,375	Armbro Jodie (Delbert Manges)	2:04.1h
70	5,417	Fanny Hall (William Haughton)	2:04 h
	5,567	Waltz Time (Stanley Dancer)	2:06.3h
71	9,210	Armbro Louann (Joe O'Brien)	2:04 h
72	10,500	Decorum (Walter Welch)	2:02.3h
73	11,250	All Alert (Glen Garnsey)	2:03.3h
74	7,900	Lantern (Glen Garnsey)	2:04.4h
	8,300	Hilarious Lynn (Lew Williams)	2:05.3h

75	14,000	Gambit Almahurst (Doug Arthur)	2:06.3h
	14,000	Steady Ellie T. (D. Williams II)	2:04 h
76	17,500	Basha (Gerald Sarama)	1:59.3h
	17,500	Bonjour Karey (Real Cormier)	2:01.3h
77	24,000	Au Clair (Preston Burris, Jr.)	2:05.4h
78	25,000	Proposal (John Hayes, Jr.)	2:01 h
79	22,500	Roses Are Red (Jack Kopas)	2:02 h
80	27,500	Armbro Vibrant (Bill Wellwood)	2:01.1h
81	32,000	Fan Hanover (Glen Garnsey)	1:59.3h
82	20,000	Sconce (Phil Laframboise)	1:59.4h
	20,000	Savilla Lobell (Jack Kopas)	1:59.4h
83	36,000	Armbro Bramble (Jack Kopas)	1:59.1h
84	23,250	Inflation Collins (Tom Swift)	1:59.3h
	23,000	Rose Routh (John Kopas)	1:59.4h
85	38,650	Borne Ideal (Jack Bailey)	2:00.4h
86	37,500	Scamper Hanover (J. Hayes, Jr.)	2:00.2h
87	49,600	Armbro Feather (John Kopas) R	1:59 h
88		-- Not Raced --	
89	31,750	Bye Bye Sleepyhead (Jim Dailey)	1:57 f
	32,750	Heather And Lace (Vince Copeland)	1:57.2f
90	32,700	Royal Harmony (Kevin Wallis) R	1:56.4f

The Art Rooney Memorial Final
Three-Year-Old Open Pace
Yonkers Raceway, Yonkers, NY   July 28, 1990

89	300,000	Kick Up A Storm (Ron Waples)	1:56.1h	90	304,127	Jake And Elwood (John Campbell) R	1:55 h

The Roses Are Red
Filly and Mare Pace, Three-Year-Olds and up *
Greenwood Raceway, Toronto, ONT   July 23, 1990

80	42,600	Kris Messenger (Greg Wright)	1:58.4f
81	42,800	Toy Poodle (Billy Herman)	1:57.4f
82	61,100	Fan Hanover (Glen Garnsey)	1:56 f
83	81,500	Programmed (Doug Brown)	1:56.3f
84	74,500	Green With Envy (Jim Doherty)	1:56.1f
85	76,500	Brees Brief (Doug Brown)	1:56.4f

86	116,000	Enroute (Bill O'Donnell)	1:56 f
87	115,500	Follow My Star (Bruce Nickells)	1:55.2f
88	109,500	Armbro Feather (John Kopas)	1:57.1f
89	184,100	Armbro Feather (Buddy Gilmour)	1:53.1f
90	125,000	Caesars Jackpot (Bill Fahy) R	1:52.4f

* 3- and 4-year-old fillies and maries prior to 1989

The Senior Jug
Jug Eligibles From Prior Year
Delaware County Fair, Delaware, OH   Sept. 17, 1990

89	24,500	Barely Visible (John Campbell)	1:54 h	90	35,500	Casino Cowboy (Ron Pierce)	1:54.3h

Page 351

CHRONICLES

The Lawrence B. Sheppard
Two-Year-Old Pace
Yonkers Raceway, Yonkers, NY July 14, 1990

64	57,622	Bret Hanover (Frank Ervin)	2:02.1h	77	52,638	Wellwood Hanover (Wm. Haughton)	2:00.2h
65	100,000	Romeo Hanover (Bill Myer)	2:01 h	78	43,575	Hot Hitter (Herve Filion)	2:02.2h
66	100,000	Nardins Byrd (Del Insko)	2:03.2h		44,325	Bob Lobell (John Kopas)	2:01.1h
67	100,000	Fulla Napoleon (Richard Thomas)	2:01.2h	79	72,450	Jiffy Boy (Joe Marsh, Jr.)	1:59.1h
68	50,000	Hammerin Hank (George Sholty)	2:03 h	80	126,000	Seahawk Hanover (Ben Webster)	2:00.4h
69	49,320	Columbia George (R. Beaulieu)	1:58.4h		126,000	Bo Bo (Ben Steall)	2:01.2h
70	53,495	Albatross (Harry Harvey)	2:02 h		123,500	Slapstack (Jack Parker, Jr.)	2:01 h
71	44,948	Shadow Star (Jack Kopas)	2:02 h	81	463,000	Icarus Lobell (Herve Filion)	1:59 h
72	25,985	Valiant Bret (John Chapman)	2:02 h	82	543,500	Fortune Teller (Eldon Harner)	2:00.1h
	24,985	Armbro Nesbit (Duncan MacDonald)	1:59.4h	83	666,800	Trutone Lobell (Catello Manzi)	1:58.3h
73	49,536	Southampton V. (Herve Filion)	2:03.3h	84	643,000	Praised Dignity (Wm. Popfinger)	1:59.3h
74	20,612	Nero (Herve Filion)	2:02.1h	85	600,000	Laughs (Michel Lachance)	1:58.2h
	20,612	All In One (Carmine Abbatiello)	2:02.2h	86	433,000	Simcoe Hanover (Michel Lachance)	1:59.4h
75	14,668	Smooth Fella (Carmine Abbatiello)	2:03.2h	87	518,000	Chatham Light (Mickey McNichol)	1:58.1h
	14,668	Jorge Hanover (Peter Haughton)	2:04.3h	88	308,500	Count N Sheep (John Campbell) R	1:57.1h
	14,668	Raven Hanover (George Sholty)	2:04 h	89	321,500	Sea The USA (Michel Lachance)	1:59 h
76	33,393	Revenue Skipper (Gene Daisey)	2:04.1h	90	474,500	June's Baby (Ron Waples)	1:58.2h
	33,983	Rockwell Hanover (Henri Filion)	2:01.4h				

The Simcoe Pace
Three-Year-Old Colt Pace
Mohawk Raceway, Campbellville, ONT Sept. 2, 1990

62	2,835	Armbro Canuck (Keith Waples)	2:04 q	78	56,700	Armbro Taurus (Ron Feagan)	1:59.2f
63	2,839	Amos Johnston (W. McIlmurray)	2:04.1f	79	30,300	Devon's Scout (Larry Walker)	2:00.2f
64	3,252	Chief Saint (Wes Coke)	2:07.1f		30,300	Dangerfield Bruce (Hal Stead)	1:59 f
65	3,355	Twinkle's Adios (Don Larkin)	2:04.3f	80	44,675	Goldie Omaha (Doug Brown)	2:00 f
66	3,791	Kino Herbert (Jack Herbert)	2:05 f	81	36,880	Johnny Lus (Normand Masse)	1:58.2f
67	6,288	Sharp 'N Smart (John Hayes)	2:02.4f		36,880	Skeeter Herbert (Dave Wall)	1:57.4f
68	11,860	Tanya Herbert (Jack Herbert)	2:03.2f	82	130,055	Icarus Lobell (Herve Filion)	1:57 f
69	12,865	Vanguard Mir (Gilles Gendron)	2:03.3f	83	109,160	Ralph Hanover (Ron Waples)	1:57.1f
70	13,600	Rob Ron Robbie (Keith Waples)	2:09.1f	84	129,230	Legal Notice (John Hayes, Jr.)	1:55 f
71	11,631	Gay Royal (Bill Wellwood)	2:04 f	85	135,400	Twin B Playboy (Dave Wall)	1:58 f
	11,631	Rob Ron Tarios (Keith Waples)	2:01.1f	86	140,675	Amity Chef (John Campbell)	1:55.1f
72	11,631	Rob Ron Tarios (Keith Waples)	2:01.2f	87	157,843	Frugal Gourmet (Trevor Ritchie) R	1:54.1f
	14,685	Skipper Thorpe (Clint Hodgins)	2:01.2f	88	86,337	Just Bold (Tony Kerwood)	1:55.4f
73	15,827	Rob Ron Ritzrar (Keith Waples)	2:01 f		86,837	Allied Hanover (Mickey McNichol)	1:58 f
	15,827	Moon Magic (Dr. John Findley)	2:03.4f	89	70,271	Jessee Purkey (Michel Lachance)	1:56.3f
74	23,828	Paula's Peanut (Bill Wellwood)	2:04 f		72,272	Armbro Herman (John Kopas)	1:56.3f
	23,828	Montsanto (Ron Feagan)	2:05.2f		72,272	Topnotcher (Doug Brown)	1:55.2f
75	29,432	Merrywood Susie (Ron Waples)	2:01.3f	90	111,707	Cam's Venture (Dan Clements)	1:54.2f
	29,432	Pat's Bye Bye (D. Hodgins)	2:04 f		113,708	Global Assault (Mark Williams)	1:54.1f
76	38,205	Mr. Bohana (Jerry Duford)	2:01.2f				
77	45,130	Super Clint (Jack Kopas)	1:59.4f				

The Simcoe Pace
Three-Year-Old Filly Pace
Mohawk Raceway, Campbellville, ONT Sept. 8, 1990

83	111,960	Armbro Bramble (Jack Kopas)	1:56.4f		75,187	Worth More (Lyle MacArthur)	1:57.4f
84	116,780	Silky Almahurst (Jim Conine)	2:01 f	89	173,205	Concertina (Harold Kelly)	1:55.1f
85	124,475	Bree's Brief (Doug Brown)	1:55.4f	90	109,612	Town Pro (Doug Brown) R	1:54.4f
86	141,265	Misty Silver (William Fritz)	1:58 f		109,613	Jonvick Castle (John Hayes, Jr.)	1:56.2f
87	143,720	Time Well Spent (Wm. O'Donnell) a	1:56 f		a By Time Well Spent &		
88	75,187	Town Skip (Tom Strauss)	1:56.4f		Village Jig.		

The Simcoe Trot
Three-Year-Old Filly Trot
Mohawk Raceway, Campbellville, ONT Sept. 3, 1990

83	111,960	Armbro Blush (Glen Garnsey) a	2:01.4f	78	187	Nalda Hanover (Jan Nordin)	2:00.4f
84	116,780	Head Hunter (Berndt Lindstedt)	2:00.4f	89	89,602	Armbro Hinter (Lyle MacArthur)	1:59 f
85	130,475	Maxine Lobell (Berndt Lindstedt)	1:59.3f		91,663	Peach Pit (Bill Wellwood) R	1:58 f
86	141,265	Shipps Dream (Steve Condren)	1:58.4f	90	105,612	Ashley Jane (Larry Walker)	2:00.1f
87	137,720	Armbro Fling (George Sholty)	1:59 f		107,613	Armbro Icon (Larry Walker)	1:59.3f
88	76,688	Stage Entrance (John Campbell)	1:59 f		a By Winky's Gill.		

The Simcoe Trot
Three-Year-Old Colt Trot
Mohawk Raceway, Campbellville, ONT Sept. 7, 1990

62	2,710	Captain Riddell (William Rowe)	2:11.3q	76	37,805	Armstead Don (Bill Wellwood)	2:09.1f
63	3,228	Niagara Chance (A. Holmes)	2:06 f	77	46,330	Armbro Sonnet (Joe O'Brien)	2:05 f
64	3,177	Johnnie Laird (Clure Archdekin)	2:10.3f	78	57,200	Jet Sky (Paul Matthews)	2:03.4f
65	3,130	Jimmy Frost (Bev Kingston)	2:09 f	79	30,900	Highland Delvin (M. MacDonald)	2:06 f
66	3,716	Armbro Gazelle (Robt. Silliphant)	2:09 f		30,620	Grayfriars Jock (H. Leatherdale)	2:05 f
67	6,213	Kinnel Lodge (Dr. John Findley)	2:11.2f	80	30,237	G. G. George (Bud Fritz)	2:03.4f
68	11,885	Kawartha Calls (J. McIntyre)	2:08 f		30,438	Kawartha Onestep (D. Morrissey)	2:04.1f
69	12,465	Bradley Song (K. Galbraith)	2:07.3f	81	54,660	Mayonnaise (Bill Wellwood)	2:04.2f
70	13,700	Ezra Dnalel (J. Gordon)	2:07 f	82	126,955	Little League (Hakan Wallner)	1:59.3f
71	15,162	Prince Ezra (Keith Waples)	2:08.1f	83	107,660	Desert Night (Per Eriksson)	2:00.2f
72	14,285	Dnalel Blue (Ron Waples)	2:05 f	84	117,230	Armbro Crouch (Glen Garnsey)	1:59.2f
73	18,445	Wellesley Girl (Keith Waples)	2:10.2f	85	136,900	Another Miracle (Ron Waples)	1:59 f
74	27,257	Lynden Victory (Gary Cameron)	2:06.3f	86	143,675	Mr Novak (John Campbell)	2:00.3f
75	33,365	Snegem Flight (Bill Megens)	2:04.2f	87	153,342	Tarport Ramey (Trevor Ritchie)	2:00.1f

CHRONICLES

88	83,838	No Sex Please (Ron Waples)	1:59.3f		99,407	Demilo Hanover (Berndt Lindstedt)	1:59.4f
	85,338	Petri Kosmos (Jan Nordin)	2:00.2f	90	111,707	Osgood Hanover (Rick Zeron)	2:01.1f
89	99,407	Defrocked (William Wellwood)	R 1:58 f		111,708	Roughing It (Tom Durand)	2:00.1f

The Standardbred
Two-Year-Old & Gelding Trot *
Delaware County Fair, Delaware, OH Sept. 18, 1990

43	3,100	Enac (Harry Whitney)	2:08 3/4h	71	19,047	Spartan Hanover (Wm. Haughton) g	2:05.1h
44	3,825	Axomite (Fenner Hawkins)	2:10 1/2h	72	22,384	Arnie Almahurst (Gene Riegle)	2:03.2h
45	5,987	Deanna (Ben White)	2:16 1/2h	73	20,792	Dream Of Glory (Mel Turcotte)	2:03.3h
46	5,109	Flying Dutchess (Frank Ervin) a	2:11 h	74	19,972	Highmark (Frank Todd, Sr.) h	2:03.4h
47	6,386	Rollo (Del Cameron)	2:11 h	75	22,287	Soothsayer (Glen Garnsey)	2:04.3h
48	8,519	Guy Ambassador(H. Fitzpatrick) b	2:09.2h	76	22,131	Sloman (Chris Boring)	2:04.2h
49	8,487	Lusty Song (Doc Parshall)	2:11 h	77	21,337	Speedy Somolli (H. Beissinger)	2:02.4h
50	10,236	Mighty Fine (B.J. Schue)	2:08.2h	78	19,413	Unexpected Guest (Billy Herman)	2:01.1h
51	10,197	Diplomat Hanover (Frank Ervin) c	2:09.3h	79	20,175	Desert King (Stanley Dancer) i	2:03.1h
52	10,387	Newport Star (Del Cameron)	2:05.3h	80	21,707	Defiant Yankee (Joe O'Brien)	2:02 h
53	10,925	Newport Dream (Del Cameron)	2:06.2h	81	22,434	Incredible Nevele (Glen Garnsey)	2:00 h
54	9,637	Scott Frost (Joe O'Brien)	2:06 h	82	40,210	Jealousy (Stanley Dancer)	2:03.3h
55	9,992	Newport Del (Del Cameron) d	2:06.3h			Springfest (Jim King, Jr.)	2:03.1h
56	10,036	Bond Hanover (Joe O'Brien)	2:06.1h	83	40,560	Coogee (John Campbell) j	2:01.2h
57	10,960	Record Mat (Frank Ervin)	2:07 h	84	41,760	Super Freddie (Harold Dancer)	2:00.3h
58	11,890	Diller Hanover (John Chapman)	2:06.4h			Ata Joe Montana (Jan Nordin)	2:02 h
59	12,340	Mystery Song (Jim Hackett)	2:05.1h	85	41,810	Sassy Gesture (Richard Midden)	2:03.3h
60	11,670	Orbiter (Ralph Baldwin)	2:04.1h	86	53,152	Mack Lobell (John Campbell)	1:59.1h
61	12,262	Impish (Frank Ervin)	2:03.3h	87	65,605	Bolla (Bill O'Donnell) k	1:58.3h
62	14,148	Filter (Thomas Graham) e	2:04 h	88	76,674	Meadow Gallant (Dan Alatmeyer)	1:59.4h
63	12,677	Smart Rodney (William Haughton) f	2:00.1h	89	64,123	Castleton Magic (Del Miller) Rl	1:58.1h
64	13,614	Victory Cadet (J. Patterson, Sr.)	2:08.3h	90	52,172	Grundy's Mint (Bill Fahy)	1:59.1h
65	14,081	Kerry Way (Frank Ervin)	2:05.1h			* Two-Year-Old Open Trot before 1974.	
66	13,256	Blaze Frost (John Wilcutts)	2:15 h				
67	14,567	Keystone Spartan (Delvin Miller)	2:03.4h			a By Patrick Hanover. b By Bangaway. c By Theme Song.	
		Nevele Pride (Stanley Dancer)	2:04.2h			d By Magnus Hanover. e By B.F. Coaltown.	
68	17,373	Lindys Pride (Howard Beissinger)	2:05.3h			f By Ayres. g By Spartan Hanover & The Black Streak.	
69	15,121	Art Hill (John Edmunds)	2:08.3h			h By Skipper Walt. i By Noble Hustle.	
70	11,951	Soda Hill (Art Hult)	2:05 h			j By Classic Cast. k By Petri Kosmos.	
		Frosted Yankee (Joe O'Brien)	2:07.1h			l By Royal Troubador.	

The Standardbred
Two-Year-Old Colt Pace *
Delaware County Fair, Delaware, OH Sept. 20, 1990

43	3,215	Eddie Havens (Curly Smart)	2:08 1/2h	72	30,000	J.R. Skipper (Greg Wright)	1:58.4h
44	3,475	True Chief (Thomas Berry)	2:09 1/2h	73	28,797	Southampton V. (Herve Filion) g	2:00.2h
45	5,987	DeSota Hanover (Sep Palin)	2:10 h	74	27,472	Nero (Joe O'Brien) h	1:59.4h
46	5,339	Goose Bay (J.D. Mahoney)	2:07 h	75	30,486	Armbro Ranger (Joe O'Brien)	1:58.4h
47	6,811	Judge Martin (Robert Vallery)	2:08.1h	76	27,781	Crash (William Haughton)	1:59 h
48	8,549	Theo A. Abbe (J.F. Cartnal)	2:07.3h	77	24,536	Abercrombie (Glen Garnsey)	1:59 h
49	8,977	His Brother (William Fleming)	2:09.2h	78	24,014	Keith Lobell (Joe O'Brien)	1:59 h
50	10,271	Stanton Hal (Murel Walters)	2:11 h	79	23,175	Dear Star (Glen Garnsey)	1:58.3h
51	10,167	Thunderclap (Hugh Bell)	2:06.1h	80	27,508	Dutch Treat (Joe Adamsky)	1:58 h
52	11,227	Keystoner (Harry Harvey) a	2:07.2h	81	26,734	Solid Fuel (Dick Farrington)	1:57 h
53	11,980	Meadow Pace (Joe O'Brien)	2:04 h	82	52,960	Armbro Belmont (Archie McNeil)	1:58 h
54	10,427	Meadow Ace (Del Cameron)	2:05 h	83	36,160	Forest Hanover (John Kopas)	2:01.3h
55	11,217	Buckeye (James Fitzpatrick) b	2:04.1h	84	51,650	Keystone Martial (Gerry Bookmyer)	1:56.4h
56	11,871	Devastator (James Arthur) c	2:02.3h	85	27,905	Barberry Spur (Dick Stillings)	1:55.2h
57	11,925	Painter (John Simpson, Sr.)	2:04 h		27,905	Insufficient Funds (Ron Waples)	1:57 h
58	13,740	Meadow Al (Joe O'Brien)	2:06.1h	86	67,542	Leverage Buyout (Tom Haughton)	1:58.2h
59	13,490	Muncy Hanover (Earle Avery)	2:00.4h	87	98,855	Albert Albert (Chris Boring)	1:55.3h
60	12,770	Brooks Hanover (Joe O'Brien)	2:03.3h	88	129,395	Chairman Spur (Dick Stillings) i	1:57.4h
61	13,262	Knight Latch (Dwayne Pletcher)	2:01.3h	89	34,686	Fighting Major (Michel Lachance)	1:57 h
62	14,098	Overtrick (John Patterson, Sr.)	2:01.3h		34,686	Johnnys Scooter (John Campbell)	1:56.4h
63	13,527	Vicar Hanover (William Haughton)	2:00.3h	90	32,186	Deal Breaker (Ron Waples)	1:56.4h
64	14,814	Bret Hanover (Frank Ervin)	2:02.4h		32,186	W R H (John Campbell)	1:54.1h
65	15,431	Mr. Lucifer (John Wilcutts) d	2:04.1h			* Two-Year-Old Open Pace before 1974.	
66	15,556	Honest Story (Eddie Cobb)	2:07 h				
67	16,067	Bye And Large (Del Insko) e	2:02.4h			a By Keystoner & f By Ferric Hanover &	
68	20,173	Arrival Time (Earl Bowman)	2:03.3h			Knox Hanover. Columbia George.	
		Lightning Wave (Joe O'Brien)	2:03.3h			b By Queen's Knight. g By Boyden Hanover.	
69	22,371	Ferric Hanover (Ben Webster) f	2:03 h			c By Adios Express. h By Alert Bret.	
70	16,351	Smart Lobell (Curly Smart)	2:01 h			d By Newport Robbi. i By How Bout It.	
71	22,947	Jay Time (Gene Riegle)	2:01.3h			e By Meadow Brick.	

The Statue of Liberty Trot
Free-For-All Trot
Last raced at The Meadowlands, E. Rutherford, NJ July 1, 1989

85	135,000	Meadow Road (Torbjorn Jansson) a	2:57.3m	88	100,000	Mack Lobell (John Campbell) b	2:09.4m
	185,000	Meadow Road (Torbjorn Jansson)	1:54.2m		125,000	Go Get Lost (Tom Sells)	1:54.3m
86		-- Not Raced --		89	250,000	Napoletano (Stig Johansson) R	1:54.1m
87	100,000	Go Get Lost (John Hogan)	1:56 m	90		-- Not Raced --	
	125,000	Buck Newton (Ron Waples)	1:55.3m			a Raced at 1-1/2 Miles. b Raced at 1-1/16 Miles.	

The Sweetheart
Two-Year-Old Filly Pace
Meadowlands, E. Rutherford, NJ August 17, 1990

79	49,000	Cool Heel (Peter Haughton)	1:59 m	81	700,000	Savilla Lobell (John Kopas)	1:57.4m
80	56,600	Heather's Feather (S. Goudreau)	1:57.3m	82	723,250	Kala Lobell (Bill O'Donnell)	1:58.2m

Page 353

CHRONICLES

83	1,062,000	Shannon Fancy (Ron Waples)	1:55.4m	87	796,750	So Cozy (John Campbell)	1:55.1m
84	1,030,000	Armbro Dazzler (John Campbell)	1:55.4m	88	863,250	Concertina (Harold Kelly)	1:56 m
85	1,000,000	Follow My Star (John Campbell)	1:55 m	89	669,000	Before Hours (Bill Fahy)	1:57.1m
86	915,500	Nadia Lobell (John Campbell)	1:55.1m	90	766,000	Miss Easy (John Campbell)	1:52.3m

The Tarport Hap
Three-Year-Old Filly Pace
Meadowlands, E. Rutherford, NJ Aug. 4, 1990

77	30,250	Mistletoe Shalee (Stanley Dancer)	1:57.3m		101,000	Enroute (Eldon Harner)	1:55 m
	30,250	Future Fame (William Haughton)	1:56.4m	86	192,000	Shocking Secret (R. Silverman)	1:55.2m
78	50,000	Courageous Lady (Lew Williams)	1:55.2m		96,000	Anniecrombie (George Sholty)	1:55.4m
79	43,000	Sherry Almahurst (Glen Garnsey)	1:55.2m	87	67,000	Jolibea Hanover (Ben Webster)	1:52.4m
80	52,500	Willow Bret (Shelly Goudreau)	1:56.2m		68,000	Lady Niatrose (Michel Lachance)	1:53.1m
81	100,000	Fan Hanover (Glen Garnsey)	1:56.1m		68,000	Time Well Spent (Bill O'Donnell)	1:54.1m
	100,000	Robin Almahurst (Wm. Haughton)	1:57 m	88	64,000	Conquered Quest (John Campbell)	1:53.4m
82	66,675	Three Diamonds (Bruce Riegle)	1:54.1m		64,000	Stevos' Marcy (Ron Waples)	1:52.4m
	66,675	Albaquel (Doug Ackerman)	1:55.2m		64,000	Sweet Reflection (Bill O'Donnell)	1:53.1m
	66,675	Kay Ellen Hanover (W. Popfinger)	1:55.3m	89	88,500	Caesars Jackpot (M. McNichol)	1:52.1m
83	112,500	Lucky Lady (Dick Hogan)	1:55.2m		89,500	Heather And Lace (Vince Copeland)	1:53.1m
	112,500	Turn The Tide (Herve Filion)	1:55.1m	90	56,335	Town Pro (Doug Brown)	R 1:51.4m
84	95,500	My Melissa (Mike Gagliardi)	1:55.2m		56,335	Bruce's Lady (John Campbell)	1:53.3m
	95,500	Milynn Hanover (Dick Macomber)	1:53 m		57,335	Tambourine (Harold Kelly)	1:54.1m
85	100,000	Stienam (Buddy Gilmour)	1:53.4m				

The Tattersalls Pace
Three-Year-Olds
The Red Mile, Lexington, KY Sept. 29, 1990

71	52,866	Albatross (Stanley Dancer)	1:54.4m	83	134,520	Walton Hanover (Harold Dancer)	1:53.2m
72	46,141	Strike Out (Keith Waples)	1:58.2m	85	192,700	Nihilator (Bill O'Donnell)	1:51.2m
73	43,920	Keystone Smartie (Joe O'Brien)	2:00.4m	86	158,600	Tyler's Mark (John Campbell)	1:51.3m
74	48,370	Keystone Presto (Peter Haughton)	1:57 m	87	162,980	-dh- Jaguar Spur (Dick Stillings)	1:51.2m
75	47,435	Nero (Joe O'Brien)	2:00 m			-dh- Laag (Richard Farrington)	1:51.2m
76	52,535	Keystone Ore (Stanley Dancer)	1:55.2m	88	164,900	Camtastic (Bill O'Donnell)	R 1:51 m
77	51,805	Super Clint (John Kopas)	a 1:54 m	89	176,870	Goalie Jeff (Michel Lachance)	1:51.3m
78	50,500	Falcon Almahurst (Wm. Haughton)	1:55 m	90	185,100	Beach Towel (Ray Remmen)	1:51.1m
79	56,810	General Star (Keith Waples)	1:56.1m				
80	43,440	Bruce Gimble (Glen Garnsey)	1:56.1m	a By Super Clint &		c By Armbro Aussie.	
81	63,000	Armbro Wolf (John Campbell)	b 1:54.1m	Governor Skipper.			
82	78,700	Icarus Lobell (Herve Filion)	c 1:51.4m	b By Armbro Wolf &			
83	134,760	Ralph Hanover (Ron Waples)	1:51.4m	Landslide.			

The Tattersalls Pace *
"The Glen Garnsey Memorial"
Three-Year-Old Filly Pace
The Red Mile, Lexington, KY Oct. 4, 1990

65	11,742	Balenzano (George Phalen)	2:00 m	80	33,570	Guiding Beam (Glen Garnsey)	1:56.4m
66	10,593	Tarport Lib (Howard Beissinger)	2:01.3m	81	34,300	Watering Can (Stanley Dancer)	1:54.2m
67	12,515	Nemma Hanover (D.W. Pletcher)	2:01.1m	82	48,400	Albaquel (Doug Ackerman)	1:53.3m
68	14,563	Sunnie Tar (Joe O'Brien)	1:56.4m	83	47,670	Sudden Urge (Tommy Haughton)	1:53.3m
69	15,260	Cupid's Arrow (Billy Haughton)	1:58.1m	84	58,604	Hit Parade (Bill O'Donnell)	1:54 m
70	18,283	Armbro Kerry (Joe O'Brien)	1:59.3m	85	85,340	Stienam (Buddy Gilmour)	1:55 m
71	19,982	Princess Sam (George Sholty)	1:59.1m	86	112,670	Anniecrombie (George Sholty)	1:55.2m
72	23,005	Romalie Hanover (Roland Beaulieu)	1:59.3m	87	91,113	Time Well Spent (Bill O'Donnell)	1:54.1m
73	18,595	All Alert (Glen Garnsey)	1:59.2m	88	94,840	Refreshing Touch (Ron Waples)	1:54.3m
74	20,485	Lyn's Beauty (Joe O'Brien)	1:58 m	89	98,095	Cheery Hello (Bill O'Donnell)	R 1:52.3m
75	20,575	Leather Jacket (Bruce Nickells)	1:57.1m	90	91,100	Rulers Choice (Joe Pavia, Jr.)	1:53.2m
76	24,680	Keystone Model (Billy Haughton)	1:58.3m				
77	26,146	Impatiens (Richard Buxton)	1:56.1m	* - Prior to 1985, was part of the Lexington			
78	31,000	Chartist (Bruce Riegle)	1:57.2m	Filly Stakes; In 1985 became the filly division of			
79	33,047	Hazel Hanover (Billy Herman)	1:58.3m	the Tattersalls for 3-year-old colt pacers.			

The Terrapin
Three-Year-Old Colt Pace
Rosecroft Raceway, Oxon Hill, MD June 9, 1990

83	70,275	Great Nero (Bob Myers)	1:55.1f		102,500	Dennis Seelster (Bob Barella)	1:55.2f
	70,275	Division Street (Tom Sells)	1:56.2f		102,500	Dictionary (Bill O'Donnell)	1:54.1f
84	118,870	Embrace Me (Herve Filion)	1:55.4f		100,000	Typhoon B (Ron Waples)	1:54.4f
	121,370	Carls Bird (Carl Allen)	1:58 f	88	132,690	Guida (Bill O'Donnell)	1:55 f
85	136,235	Handsome Sum (Bill O'Donnell)	1:57.1f		132,690	Timothy Lobell (John Campbell)	1:54.3f
	136,235	Nihilator (Bill O'Donnell)	1:57.1f		135,190	Camtastic (Bill O'Donnell)	1:54.4f
86	101,505	Telemon Hanover (Frank Sherren)	1:55.2f	89	114,412	Explorador (Ray Remmen)	1:55 f
	104,005	Amity Chef (John Campbell)	R 1:53.1f		116,912	Kentucky Spur (Don Irvine, Jr.)	R 1:53.1f
	101,505	Tassel Lobell (John Campbell)	1:54.4f		116,912	Pilgrim's Patroit (Mike Borys)	1:55 f
87	100,000	Happy Affair (John Campbell)	R 1:53.1f	90	316,135	Beach Towel (Ray Remmen)	1:54.1f

The Three Diamonds Final
2-Year-Old Filly Pace
Garden State Park, Cherry Hill, NJ Oct. 13, 1990

89	429,500	Choice Yankee (Jim Morrill, Jr.)	R 1:55.2m	90	422,400	Miss Easy (John Campbell)	1:55.3m

CHRONICLES

The Titan Cup
Free-For-All Trot
Last raced at The Meadowlands, E. Rutherford, NJ June 26, 1989

46	5,000	Titan Hanover (H. Pownall, Sr.)	2:04.3h			Noccalula (Saunders Russell)	2:04.1h
47	10,000	Algiers (H.C. Fitzpatrick)	2:02.1h	71	12,295	Fresh Yankee (Joe O'Brien)	f 2:00.4h
48	10,000	Sidney Hanover (Frank Safford)	a 2:02.2h	72		-- Not Raced --	
49	10,000	Proximity (Clint Hodgins)	2:01.3h	73	13,800	Flower Child (Joe O'Brien)	2:01 h
50	10,000	Proximity (Clint Hodgins)	2:03.2h	74	13,450	Delmonica Hanover (John Chapman)	2:00.2h
51	10,000	Star's Pride (H. Pownall, Jr.)	2:01.1h	75	14,300	Savoir (John Chapman)	1:59.4h
52	5,800	Pronto Don (B.J. Schue)	2:02.3h	76	13,200	Dream Of Glory (Joe O'Brien)	2:02.1h
53	7,450	Sharp Note (Bion Shively)	b 2:03 h	77	13,250	Tropical Storm (Ralph Baldwin)	2:02.2h
54	6,400	Kimberly Kid (Ned Bower)	2:05 h	78	13,500	Savior (John Chapman)	2:01 h
55	7,000	Kimberly Kid (Ned Bower)	2:03.2h	79	35,000	Keystone Pioneer (Wm. Haughton)	1:59.1m
56	8,600	Galophone (Robert Walker)	2:05.2h	80	37,500	Calvert (Ted Wing)	2:02 m
57	7,700	Galophone (Robert Walker)	2:01 h	81	35,000	Super Marty (Herman Hylkema)	1:58 m
58	8,000	Darn Safe (William Rouse)	2:01.3h	82	40,000	Iris De Vandel (J.P. Dubois)	1:57.2m
59	32,200	Trader Horn (William Haughton)	c 2:03.1h	83	40,000	Iris De Vandel (Ron Turcotte)	1:57 m
60	13,600	Darn Safe (Delvin Miller)	2:01.4h	84	40,000	Spunky Byron (Bill Gale)	1:56.1m
61	14,500	Elaine Rodney (Clint Hodgins)	2:02 h	85	40,000	Manfred Hanover (Patsy Rapone)	1:55.4m
62	13,900	Matastar (H. Pownall, Sr.)	2:02 h	86		-- Not Raced --	
63	13,900	Duke Rodney (William Haughton)	2:01.2h	87	35,000	Dicks Bell (Ray Remmen)	R 1:55.2m
64	14,200	Speedy Scot (Ralph Baldwin)	d 2:00.3h	88		-- Not Raced --	
65	12,700	Dartmouth (Ralph Baldwin)	2:00.1h	89	40,000	No Sex Please (Ron Waples)	1:58 m
66	13,575	Speedy Rodney (Philip Corley)	R 1:58.4h	90		-- Not Raced --	
67	14,800	Lord Gordon (J.Patterson, Jr.)	2:00.4h				
68	14,700	Pomp (H. Pownall, Sr.)	2:01.2h	a By Proximity.		d By Duke Rodney.	
69	14,225	Lady B. Fast (Bill Popfinger)	e 2:00.1h	b By Pronto Don.		e By Snow Speed.	
70	12,725	Extra Bonus (Glen Garnsey)	2:01.3h	c By Sharpshooter.		f By Marlu Pride.	

The Tompkins-Geers Stake *
Two-Year-Old Trot
Scioto Downs, Columbus, OH June 20, 1990

27	14,700	Spencer (Alonzo McDonald)	2:07 3/4h	66	12,150	Floral Hanover (Delvin Miller)	2:10.4h
28		-- Rain --		67	11,475	Mata Gay (Carl E. Quinn)	2:13 h
29	8,950	Main McElwyn (Ben White)	2:07 3/4h	68	13,150	Tarport Devlin (Delvin Miller)	2:05.1f
30	5,000	Chestnut Burr (W. Britenfield)	2:08 1/4m	69	23,980	Keystone Brian (William Haughton)	2:06.1f
31	4,000	Hollyrood Robin (Fred Egan)	2:06 1/4m	70	16,592	A.C.'s Orion (William Haughton)	2:09.2f
32	4,000	Hollyrood Portia (W. Crozier)	a 2:07 1/4m	71	15,622	Star's Chip (Stanley Dancer)	2:08.1f
33	2,000	Sturdy (Harry Brusie)	2:04 3/4m	72	25,072	Super Bowl (Stanley Dancer)	2:02.4f
34	1,800	Greyhound (Sep Palin)	2:06 3/4m	73	13,118	Christopher T. (William Haughton)	2:07 f
35	1,800	Rosalind (Ben White)	2:04 3/4m		13,368	My Super Pride (Del Cameron)	2:06.1f
36	2,500	Schnapps (Ben White)	2:07 1/2m	74	19,363	Skipper Walt (Roland Beaulieu)	2:09 h
37	2,500	Blair (Vic Fleming)	2:05 1/2m	75	19,583	Match Hill (Gene Riegle)	2:12.2f
38	3,000	Nibble Hanover (H. Whitney)	b 2:05 1/2m	76	30,425	Speed In Action (Delvin Miller)	2:03.4f
39	4,000	Earl's Moody Guy (Tom Berry)	2:09 3/4m	77	26,165	Hassie Scot (Gene Riegle)	2:09.3f
40	4,000	Bill Gallon (Lee Smith)	2:07 m	78	26,098	Gridiron Lad (Mike Allen)	2:03 f
41	4,000	Cannon Ball (Harry Whitney)	2:07 m	79	25,815	Noble Hustle (Doug Ackerman)	2:05.2f
42	4,000	Volo Song (Ben White)	2:07 1/4m	80	18,615	Buckeye Mark (C. Jordan)	2:08.3f
43	4,000	Yankee Maid (Henry Thomas)	2:09 1/2m	81	29,000	Self Confident (D.R. Ackerman)	2:02.1f
44	5,000	Titan Hanover (H. Pownall, Sr.)	2:07 m	82	27,000	T.V.Yankee (Tom Haughton)	2:04.1f
45	5,000	Bombs Away (Sep Palin)	2:07 1/4m	83	20,580	Sandy Bowl (Jan Nordin)	2:05.3f
46	5,000	Rodney (Bion Shively)	2:07 1/2m		20,580	Cavort (Heikka Korpi)	2:05.3f
47	5,000	Judge Moore (Eugene Pownall)	c 2:05.3m	84	25,633	John Dory (Doug Ackerman)	2:04.4f
48	5,000	Miss Tilly (Fred Egan)	2:07.4m	85	25,367	Shane Scottseth (Tom Haughton)	2:01.2m
49	5,000	Lusty Song (Doc Parshall)	2:03.2m		26,167	Mangrove (Stanley Dancer)	R 1:58.4m
50	10,000	Scotch Rhythm (Ralph Baldwin)	2:06.1m	86	70,814	Manor Victory (Jan Nordin)	1:59.3m
51	10,000	Hit Song (H. Pownall, Sr.)	2:06 m		69,814	B J's Super Star (John Campbell)	1:58.4m
52	19,400	Singing Sword (Harry Harvey)	d 2:08.2m	87	78,550	Yankee Yankee (Doug Ackerman)	2:03.3f
53	22,200	Newport Dream (Del Cameron)	R 2:03 m	88	21,206	Extreme Hanover (Jan Nordin)	2:04.3f
54	11,800	Galophone (William Haughton)	2:03.4m		21,206	Hypersonic (Berndt Lindstedt)	2:02.4f
55	21,200	Charlotte Frost (Thomas Berry)	2:04.3m		21,206	Lieutenant Kiji (Jim Dailey)	2:02 f
56	15,600	Bond Hanover (Joe O'Brien)	e 2:06.3m	89	35,300	King Of The Sea (Harold Kelly)	2:01 f
57	16,039	Mix Hanover (Frank Ervin)	f 2:06.3m		35,300	Letters From Hill (Troy Boring)	2:02.3f
58	14,119	Diller Hanover (Ralph Baldwin)	2:06 m	90	77,900	Gift Box (Stanley Dancer)	1:58.4m
59	14,076	Uncle Sam (Lou Huber, Jr.)	2:04 m		29,200	Crysta's Best (Dick Richardson)	R 2:00.1f
60	9,742	Caleb (John Simpson, Sr.)	g 2:04.1m	* Raced as Arthur S. Tompkins Memorial through 1984			
61	10,543	Gallant Hanover (Lou Huber, Jr.)	2:08 h	a By Sir Raleigh.		e By Hoot Song.	
62	17,175	Speedy Scot (Ralph Baldwin)	R 2:05.3h	b By Peter Astra.		f By Gang Awa.	
63	13,275	Dartmouth (Ralph Baldwin)	2:06.3h	c By Madison Hanover.		g By Spectator.	
64	13,150	Florican Flash (Gene Riegle)	2:13.2h	d By Singing Sword &			
65	13,150	Carlisle (William Haughton)	2:10.2h	Kimberly Kid.			

The Tompkins-Geers Stake *
Two-Year-Old Pace
Scioto Downs, Columbus, OH June 21, 1990

35	4,088	Jack Orr (Thomas Berry)	2:04 1/2m	49	14,132	Our Time (Frank Ervin)	a 2:05.2m
36	4,180	Dusty Hanover (Henry Thomas)	2:10 m	50	14,480	Tar Heel (William Haughton)	2:03 m
37	4,631	Chief Counsel (Doc Parshall)	2:09 m	51	15,604	Meadow Rice (Curly Smart)	2:04 m
38	4,693	Blackstone (Doc Parshall)	2:07 1/2m	52	15,368	Keystoner (Delvin Miller)	b 2:01.1m
39	4,222	Countess Hanover (H. Thomas)	2:06 m	53	19,364	Dale Frost (Delvin Miller)	2:01.1m
40	5,825	Blackhawk (Delvin Miller)	2:05 1/4m	54	17,480	Adios Evret (Robert Myer)	c 2:03.3m
41	6,625	Court Jester (Rupert Parker)	2:04 1/2m	55	15,895	Buckeye (James Fitzpatrick)	2:01.1m
42	6,816	Adios (Rupert Parker)	2:02 m	56	20,566	Good Counsel (Frank Ervin)	2:01.3m
43	5,106	Attorney (Art Blackwell)	2:05 m	57	16,504	Painter (John Simpson, Sr.)	d 2:03.1m
44	5,818	True Chief (Thomas Berry)	2:07 m	58	15,262	Adios Day (Delvin Miller)	2:02.3m
45	6,777	Ensign Hanover (Sep Palin)	2:09 3/4m	59	14,931	Bullet Hanover (J. Simpson, Sr.)	R 1:59.1m
46	9,395	Goose Bay (J.D. Mahoney)	2:05 1/4m	60	9,466	Henry T. Adios (Stanley Dancer)	e 2:01 m
47	13,039	Friscoway (H.C. Fitzpatrick)	2:03.2m	61	5,906	Ted Woodley (Lou Huber, Jr.)	2:08.2m
48	12,392	White Mountain Boy (Don Miller)	2:04.1h	62	14,350	Hondo Hanover (Joe O'Brien)	2:07.1h

Page 355

CHRONICLES

63	13,775	Race Time (Ralph Baldwin)	R 2:04.4h		11,707	Dine Alone (D.R. Ackerman)	2:03.3f
64	8,987	Irv's Boy (Thomas Winn)	2:09.2h	81	25,000	Mr. Dalrae (Jim Dennis)	1:58.1f
	8,987	Bullet Van (George VanCamp)	2:10.1h	82	40,000	Del Cavallo (Doug Ackerman)	2:00.3f
65	16,325	The Big Bear (Waldo McIlmurray)	2:09.3h	83	27,440	Ring Of Light (Greg Wright)	1:59.4f
66	11,357	Berry Hill (William Haughton)	2:06.4h		27,440	Crash Town (Norm Cohen)	1:59.4f
	11,357	Blaze Pick (Jack Williams, Jr.)	2:07 h	84	46,973	Armbro Dallas (Ron Waples)	2:00 f
67	18,603	Zip Tar (Keith Waples)	2:08.4h	85	29,565	Corner Stone (Richard Silverman)	1:57.4m
68	25,043	Laverne Hanover (Wm. Haughton)	2:00.3f		29,565	Robust Hanover (Ben Webster)	R 1:55.1m
69	16,165	Banner Ranger (Joe Marsh, Jr.)	2:03 f		29,565	Towner's Big Guy (Ron Waples)	R 1:55.1m
	16,165	Race Time Boy (William Haughton)	2:05.1h	86	76,543	Simcoe Hanover (Bill O'Donnell)	1:56.2m
70	13,550	Albatross (Harry Harvey)	2:06.3f		77,543	Redskin (Bill O'Donnell)	1:56.3m
	13,550	High Ideal (Pat Crowe)	2:04.1f		77,543	Dictionary (John Campbell)	1:55.4m
71	25,067	Strike Out (John Hayes)	2:03.2f	87	55,275	Chatham Light (Jan Nordin)	1:57.3f
72	21,242	J.R. Skipper (Greg Wright)	2:04.3f		54,275	Pied Piper (C. Warrington, Jr.)	1:57.4f
	20,992	Keystone Smartie (Wm. Haughton)	2:08.2f	88	28,206	Keystone Fabulous (Rog. Hammer)	R 1:57 f
73	24,013	Boyden Hanover (George Sholty)	2:00.3f		28,206	Keystone Rambo (Roger Hammer)	1:57.1f
	24,013	Romanline (Jerry Graham)	2:02.3f		28,206	Shipps Scorch (Terry Holton)	1:58.1f
74	18,102	J.R. Call (Greg Wright)	2:04.4f	89	26,100	Bookmaker (Harold Kelly)	1:57.1f
	18,602	Hasty Reply (Arthur Bier)	2:04 f		26,100	French Embassy (Steve Sugg)	1:57.3f
75	13,450	Puppet (Peter Haughton)	2:04.2f		26,100	Radical Ruler (Steve Sugg)	1:57.3f
	13,700	Special Almahurst (R. Williams)	2:03.3f	90	27,200	Isle Of Maui (Butch Dokey)	1:58.4f
	13,700	Shiaway Chatham (Chris Boring)	2:04 f		27,200	Master Fund (Bruce Riegle)	1:58.4f
76	41,893	Rorty Hanover (D.Richardson,Jr.)	2:00.1f		27,200	Nuclear Legacy (Bruce Riegle)	1:58.4f
77	40,000	Balance Of Power (Bill Zendt)	2:04.4f			* Raced as The Geers Stake through 1984.	
78	22,294	Sonsam (George Sholty)	1:58.1f				
	22,294	Composite (Ron Waples)	2:01.2f		a By Irish Hal.	d By Thorpe Hanover.	
79	37,395	Tyler B. (Delvin Miller)	2:01 f		b By Hillsota.	e By Henry T. Adios &	
80	11,707	Bret's Advantage (Ross Roselle)	2:02.3f		c By Meadow Ace.	Lang Hanover.	

The Tompkins-Geers *
Three-Year-Old Pace
Scioto Downs, Columbus, OH June 23, 1990

36	3,842	Little Pat (Charles Lacey)	2:04 1/2m	67	13,463	Coral Ridge (Joe O'Brien)	c 1:57 m
37	3,253	Billy Direct (Victor Fleming)	2:06 m	68	14,152	Rum Customer (William Haughton)	2:01 m
38	3,800	Chief Counsel (Doc Parshall)	2:02 m	69	17,742	Laverne Hanover (Wm. Haughton)	1:58.2m
39	3,372	Brookdale (Harry Whitney)	a 2:02 1/2m	70	19,530	Toliver Hanover (George Sholty)	1:58.3f
40	4,930	Fearless Peter (Doc Parshall)	2:01 m	71		-- Rain --	
41	3,420	Saratoga (Paul Vineyard)	2:03 1/2m	72	20,233	Fast Clip (Bruce Nickells)	1:59.3m
42	4,750	Lilydale (Thomas Berry)	2:00 3/4m	73	21,277	Gay Skipper (John Ackerman)	1:59.4m
43	1,995	Adios (Rupert Parker)	2:02 3/4m	74	24,321	Mirror Image (Jack Bailey)	d 1:56.3m
44	5,177	Eddie Havens (Curly Smart)	2:02 1/2m	75	22,770	Bo Bo Arrow (Joe O'Brien)	1:57.3m
45	5,093	Jimmy Creed (Henry Thomas)	2:01 1/2m	76	22,795	Dream Maker (Dick Oldfield)	1:56.3m
46	5,360	Direct Express (Paul Vineyard)	2:02 m	77	50,000	Crash (William Haughton)	1:57.2f
47	6,755	Goose Bay (J.D. Mahoney)	2:00.2m	78	43,295	Abercrombie (Glen Garnsey)	1:56.2f
48	8,351	Knight Dream (Frank Safford)	b 2:00.3m	79	50,000	Striking Force (John Hayes, Jr.)	1:59.1f
49	8,950	Good Time (Frank Ervin)	1:59.2m	80	50,000	Denali (Doug Ackerman)	1:58.4f
50	9,742	Mighty Sun (Joe O'Brien)	2:01.1m	81	41,000	Nero's B.B. (Joe O'Brien)	1:59.1f
51	7,494	Tar Heel (Del Cameron)	2:01 m	82	55,000	Armbro Aussie (Glen Garnsey)	2:01.4f
52	7,119	Adio Abe (James Jordan)	2:03 m	83	25,000	Time To Cash (Jeff James)	1:56.3f
53	8,139	Torrid (Eugene Minniear)	2:00.4m		25,000	Ralph Hanover (Ron Waples)	1:59.1f
54	11,525	Diamond Hal (Joe O'Brien)	2:00.2m	84	44,350	Mannart Maple Leaf (Bill Gale)	1:57.1f
55	10,378	Libby's Boy (Clint Hodgins)	1:59.2m	85	75,000	Armbro Dallas (Ron Waples)	1:57.2f
56	9,286	Gold Worthy (Curly Smart)	1:59.3m	86	112,998	Armbro Emerson (Walter Whelan)	R 1:53.1m
57	11,363	Torpid (J. Simpson, Sr.)	1:59.4m	87	80,225	Lasting Image (Don Irvine, Jr.)	1:54.4f
58	7,176	Bye Bye Byrd (Donald Taylor)	1:57.4m	88	67,355	Best Of Them (Sam Noble III)	1:56.1f
59	8,335	Newport Admiral (Del Cameron)	1:59.1m	89	20,850	Barefoot Hanover (Dave Rankin)	1:54.4f
60	3,201	Bullet Hanover (J. Simpson, Sr.)	1:57.2m		21,600	Arbitrator (Tom Merriman)	R 1:54.3f
61	5,464	Lang Hanover (Jim Hackett)	1:58.4m		21,600	Echelon (Tom Coddington)	R 1:54 f
62	6,267	Meadow Battles (Delvin Miller)	1:58.1m	90	27,700	Bookmaker (Harold Kelly)	1:54.3f
63	7,200	Overtrick (J. Patterson Sr.)	1:57.3m		27,700	Hot Walker (Harold Kelly)	1:57.2f
64	6,950	Lyss Hanover (Vernon Dancer)	1:59.4m			* Formerly raced as the Geers Stakes	
65	9,075	Bret Hanover (Frank Ervin)	2:03.2m		a By Saint George.	c By Coral Ridge.	
66	11,575	Silent Byrd (Stanley Dancer)	1:58 m		b By Atomic Bomb.	d By Armbro Ontario.	

The Turtle Dove
Three-Year-Old Filly Pace
Rosecroft Raceway, Oxon Hill, MD June 30, 1990

83	26,050	Mrs. Yankee (Bib Roberts)	1:57.3f	87	81,000	Time Well Spent (Jeff Fout)	1:58.2f
	26,050	Leda Hanover (Jim Miller)	1:58.4f		81,000	Jolibea Hanover (Ted Wing)	1:59.1f
84	70,900	Milynn Hanover (Dick Macomber)	1:57.3f		81,000	Armbro Feather (John Kopas)	1:58.2f
	70,900	Intowin Frost (Chris Boring)	1:57.4f	88	118,028	Leah Almahurst (Bill Fahy)	1:55.4f
85	70,333	Forbidden Past (Abe Stoltzfus)	1:56.1f		118,028	Storm Tossed (Bill Popfinger)	1:56.3f
	72,333	Amneris (Jan Nordin)	1:56.3f	89	111,743	Cheery Hello (Bill Fahy)	R 1:53.2f
	72,333	Stardrift Hanover (Herve Filion)	1:55.3f		111,743	Tyler Town (Peter Ruscitto)	1:56 f
86	104,000	Shocking Secret (Tom Haughton)	1:57.4f	90	110,715	Sea Biscuit (Eddie Davis)	1:54.3f
	106,000	Razzle Hanover (G. Gendron)	1:55.3f		112,715	Choice Yankee (Jim Morrill, Jr.)	1:54.3f

The U.S. Pacing Championship
Free-For-All *
1990 Dates: YR - Aug. 11; M - Aug. 17; SPk - Aug. 19 **

73	50,000	Sir Dalrae (Jim Dennis)	S	1:56 f		50,000	Young Quinn (Charles Hunter)	H 1:57.3m
	50,000	Sir Dalrae (Jim Dennis)	R	1:57.4h	76	40,000	Rambling Willie (B. Far'gton)	S 1:57.1f
	50,000	SIR DALRAE (Jim Dennis)	M	1:57.3m		40,000	Shirley's Beau (W. Popfinger)	S 1:55.1f
74	52,500	Sir Dalrae (Jim Dennis)	R	1:59 h		50,000	Tarport Hap (John Chapman)	R 1:57 h
	50,000	Armbro Nesbit (Walt Paisley)	S	1:57 f		50,000	RAMBLING WILLIE (B. Far'gton)	H 2:02.1m
	52,500	SIR DALRAE (Jim Dennis)	H	1:59 m	77	50,000	Rambling Willie (B. Far'gton)	S 1:58.3f
75	50,000	Handle With Care (P.Haughton)	S	1:58 f		50,000	Armbro Ranger (Joe O'Brien)	R 1:57.3h
	50,000	SIR DALRAE (Jim Dennis)	R	1:57.4h		50,000	DREAM MAKER (S. Goudreau)	H 1:55.1m

CHRONICLES

78	50,000	Governor Skipper (J. Chapman)	M	1:55 m		60,000	On The Road Again (W.Gilmour)	M	1:51.4m
	50,000	Big Towner (C. Abbatiello)	R	1:57.3h		60,000	MR DALRAE (Dale Hiteman)	S	1:55.1f
	50,000	GOVERNOR SKIPPER (J. Chapman)	S	1:55.2f	86	60,000	Forrest Skipper (L. Fontaine)	M	1:53.3m
79	50,000	Try Scotch (Shelly Goudreau)	R	1:57.2h		60,000	Forrest Skipper (L. Fontaine)	S	1:54.1f
	50,000	Abercrombie (Glen Garnsey)	M	1:53 m		60,000	FORREST SKIPPER (L. Fontaine)	R	1:55.2h
	50,000	TRY SCOTCH (Shelly Goudreau)	S	1:56 f	87	60,000	Franz Hanover (Wm. Herman)	M	1:52 m
80	50,000	Sample Fella (Ben Webster)	M	1:55.1m		60,000	Franz Hanover (Wm. Herman)	R	1:55 h
	50,000	SAMPLE FELLA (Ben Webster)	R	1:57.4h		60,000	FRANZ HANOVER (Wm. Herman)	S	1:54.3f
	50,000	Direct Scooter (War. Cameron)	S	1:56.3f	88	75,000	Jaguar Spur (Dick Stillings)	M R	1:50.3m
81	60,000	Royce (John Campbell)	M	1:53.4m		75,000	PLAY THE PALACE (Don Dancer)	Y R	1:54.4h
	60,000	Secret Service (Jim Marohn)	R	1:58 h		75,000	Stir Fry (Danny Johnson)	S	1:54.4f
	60,000	ROYCE (Walter Paisley)	S	1:57 f	89	75,000	Matt's Scooter (M. Lachance)	M R	1:50.3m
82	60,000	Genghis Khan (Bill O'Donnell)	M	1:53 m		75,000	RUNNYMEDE LOBELL (Y. Filion)	Y	1:57.1h
	60,000	MILLER'S SCOUT (Wm. Gilmour)	R	1:57.3h		75,000	Keystone Raider (Dave Magee)	S	1:54.3f
83	60,000	Cam Fella (Pat Crowe)	M	1:56.2h	90	75,000	Dorunrun Bluegrass (H.Filion)	Y	1:56 h
	60,000	Cam Fella (Pat Crowe)	R	1:53.2m		75,000	T K's Skipper (M. Lachance)	M R	1:50.3m
	60,000	CAM FELLA (Pat Crowe)	S R	1:54 f		146,000	DORUNRUN BLUEGRASS (H.Filion)	S R	1:54 f
84	60,000	Mr Dalrae (Dave Magee)	M	1:52.2m		* Event winner, by points earned, in BOLDFACE
	60,000	MR DALRAE (Dave Magee)	R	1:56.2h		** H - Hollywood Pk.; M - The Meadowlands;
	60,000	Umbrella Fella (Ray Remmen)	S	1:56 f		S - Sportsman's Park;
85	60,000	On The Road Again (W.Gilmour)	R	1:55.3h		R - Roosevelt Raceway; Y - Yonkers Raceway.

The Valley Victory Final
Two-Year-Old Colt Trot
Garden State Park, Cherry Hill, NJ Oct. 25, 1990

90	330,300	Mr Chin (John Patterson, Jr.)	1:58.1m

The Windy City Pace
Three-Year-Old -Colt Pace
Maywood Park, Maywood, IL May 12, 1990

83	202,000	Trim The Tree (Dick Macomber)		1:57.1h	87	200,000	Bomb Rickles (Neal Shapiro)	1:56.2h
84	262,000	Carls Bird (Carl Allen)		1:56.3h	88	228,000	Wealthy Skipper (Walter Paisley)	1:55 h
85	280,000	Pinocchio (Neal Shapiro)		1:56 h	89	250,000	Just The Ticket (Lavern Hostetler)	1:56.1h
86	284,000	Incredible Finale (Tom Harmer)	R	1:53.3h	90	255,000	Jake And Elwood (Herve Filion)	1:57.2h

The Woodrow Wilson
Two-Year-Old Pace
Meadowlands, E. Rutherford, NJ Aug. 17, 1990

77	280,000	No No Yankee (Walter Ross)		1:57.4m	84	2,161,000	Nihilator (Bill O'Donnell)	1:52.4m
78	481,250	Scarlet Skipper (Billy Herman)		1:57.3m	85	1,344,000	Grade One (Ray Remmen)	1:54.3m
79	862,750	Niatross (Clint Galbraith)		1:55.4m	86	1,561,000	Cullin Hanover (Buddy Gilmour)	1:54.4m
80	2,011,000	Land Grant (Del Insko)		1:56.4m	87	1,422,500	Even Odds (Ben Webster)	1:54.1m
81	1,760,000	McKinzie Almahurst (Wm. Haughton)		1:56.1m	88	1,041,000	Kassa Branca (John Campbell)	1:52.3m
82	1,957,500	Fortune Teller (Eldon Harner)		1:55.3m	89	907,000	Sam Francisco Ben (Ron Pierce)	1:56 m
83	1,700,000	Carls Bird (Carl Allen)		1:55.3m	90	1,043,500	Die Laughing (Rich. Silverman)	R 1:52.1m

The World Trotting Derby
Three-Year-Olds
Du Quoin State Fair, Du Quoin, IL Sept. 1, 1990

81	540,870	Panty Raid (J. Simpson, Jr.)	a	1:56.2m	87	501,870	Napoletano (Bill O'Donnell)	1:53.2m
82	494,260	Diamond Exchange (R. Williams)	b	1:56 m	88	550,690	Armbro Goal (Berndt Lindstedt)	1:55 m
83	580,090	Power Seat (George Sholty)		1:56.1m	89	600,000	Peace Corps (John Campbell)	R 1:52.4m
84	601,950	Baltic Speed (Jan Nordin)	c	1:54.4m	90	600,000	Harmonious (Catello Manzi)	1:53.2m
85	553,750	Prakas (Bill O'Donnell)		1:53.2m		a By Banker Barker.		c By Fancy Crown.
86	630,000	Royal Prestige (Berndt Lindstedt)		1:55.1m		b By Jazz Cosmos.		

World Trotting Derby Filly Division
Three-Year-Old Filly
Du Quoin State Fair, Du Quoin, IL Aug. 31, 1990

81	96,325	Duchess Faye (Don McIlmurray)		1:56.2m	87	120,840	Keystone Harem (Jan Nordin)	Rb 1:54.4m
82	88,825	Dance Spell (Ray Remmen)		1:57.3m	88	126,350	Nan's Catch (Berndt Lindstedt)	1:56.3m
83	108,031	Lady Lexington (Jan Johnson)		1:56.3m	89	123,050	Park Avenue Kathy (Br. Nickells)	1:57.4m
84	107,062	Dem Bones (John Campbell)		1:58 m	90	130,000	Happy Diamonds (John Campbell)	1:55.1m
85	128,626	Keystone Profile (Hakan Wallner)		1:55.1m		a Budgait Libby		b By Keystone Harem &
86	129,523	Britelite Lobell (John Campbell)	a	1:54.1m				Lucious Almahurst.

The Yonkers Trot *
Three-Year-Olds **
Yonkers Raceway, Yonkers, NY July 14, 1990

Yr	Purse	Winner	Driver	Time	Starters	Heats	Second ***	Third
55	73,840	Scott Frost	Joe O'Brien	2:12 h	8	1	Galophone	Black Rico
56	77,170	Add Hanover	John Simpson, Sr.	2:12.4h	8	1	Ego Hanover	Go
57	57,812	Hoot Song	Ralph Baldwin	2:16.1h	7	1	Silver Way	Time Me
58	56,157	Spunky Hanover	Howard Camper	2:13.3h	6	1	McColby	Demon's Dream
59	56,397	John A. Hanover	Stanley Dancer	2:11 h	8	1	Diller Hanover	Farand Hanover
60	74,265	Duke Of Decatur	Delvin Miller	2:13.3h	16	2	Volo Man	Duke Demon
61	100,330	Duke Rodney	Eddie Wheeler	2:10.3h	8	1	Caleb	Spectator
62	105,422	A.C.'s Viking	Sanders Russell	2:10.4h	9	1	Sprite Rodney	Isaac
63	135,127	Speedy Scot	Ralph Baldwin	2:03.3h	9	1	Florlis	Valid Hanover
64	116,691	Ayres	John Simpson, Sr.	2:01.3h	8	1	Speedy Count	Dartmouth
65	122,236	Noble Victory	Stanley Dancer	2:02 h	9	1	Perfect Freight	Short Stop

Page 357

CHRONICLES

66	123,375	Polaris	George Sholty	2:06 h	8	1	Governor Armbro		Kerry Way
67	150,000	Pomp	Harry Pownall, Sr.	2:04.4h	13	1	Dazzling Speed		Keystone Pride
68	150,000	Nevele Pride	Stanley Dancer	2:03.3h	6	1	Fashion Hill		Dart Hanover
69	100,000	Lindys Pride	Howard Beissinger	2:03 h	9	1	The Prophet		Nevele Major
70	106,770	Victory Star	Vernon Dancer	2:03.4h	8	1	Gil Hanover		Luther Hanover
71	110,795	Quick Pride	Stanley Dancer	2:02.4h	9	1	Savior		Keystone Hilliard
72	93,097	Super Bowl	Stanley Dancer	2:02 h	5	1	Delmonica Hanover		Songcan
73	93,242	Tamerlane	Charlie Clark	2:04.4h	6	1	Knightly Way		Manuel
74	125,821	Spitfire Hanover	Delvin Miller	2:05.2h	16	2	Armbro Oxford		Keystone Gabriel
75	200,000	Surefire Hanover	Stanley Dancer	2:03 h	9	1	Fashion Blaze		Skipper Walt
76	202,040	Steve Lobell	William Haughton	2:01.4h	8	1	Quick Pay		Zoot Suit
77	239,000	Green Speed	William Haughton	1:59 h	7	1	Sugarbowl Hanover		Elmsford
78	233,594	Speedy Somolli	Howard Beissinger	1:59.3h	7	1	Doublemint		Count's Pride
79	237,765	Chiola Hanover	Jimmy Allen	2:04 h	8	1	Butch Lobell		Count's Cristy
80	261,040	Nevele Impulse	Dick Macomber	2:03.2h	14	2	Desert King		Marino Hanover
81	284,701	Mo Bandy	Carl Allen	2:02.1h	16	2	Keystone Triton		Smokin Yankee
82	415,160	Mystic Park	Frank O'Mara	2:00.3h	18	2	Messerschmitt		Little League
83	486,150	Joie De Vie	Buddy Gilmour	2:00.3h	23	2	Riklis		Sherwood Lobell
84	431,780	Baltic Speed	Jan Nordin	2:01.3h	23	2	Sandy Bowl		Why Not
85	440,840	Master Willie	Jan Nordin	1:59.3h	25	2	Mark Six		Another Miracle
86	372,503	Gunslinger Spur	Dick Stillings	2:00.4h	17	2	Traveling Salesman		Farm King
87	324,115	Mack Lobell	John Campbell	R 1:57.4h	10	1	Sir Taurus		Go Get Lost
88	431,495	Southern Newton	Berndt Lindstedt	2:00 h	19	2	Stage Entrance		Continental Spirit
89	418,810	Valley Victory	Bill O'Donnell	1:58.3h	18	2	Bon Vivant		Classic Air
90	424,965	Royal Troubador	Carl Allen	a 1:58.2h	16	2	King Of The Sea		Embassy Lobell

* - Raced as "The Yonkers," 1955-59; as the "Quad Futurity," 1960; as the "Yonkers Futurity," 1961-74; and as the "Yonkers Trot," 1975 to present.
** - Raced at 1-1/16 miles, 1955-62.
*** - Best in summary in 1960; In other years, is based upon order of finish in final heat.

a By Cheyenne Spur.

The Dr. Harry Zweig Memorial *
Three-Year-Old Trot
Syracuse, NY Aug. 19, 1990

75	111,000	Bonefish (Stanley Dancer)	1:58.1m	85	150,000 Ron B. Hanover (Jan Nordin)	1:56.4m
76	147,000	Tropical Storm (Ralph Baldwin)	1:57.3m	86	185,000 Tabor Lobell (Per Henriksen)	R 1:55.4m
77	126,000	Cold Comfort (Peter Haughton)	1:57.4m	87	95,000 Crown Sweep (Carl Allen)	1:59.2m
78	120,000	Count's Pride (William Haughton)	1:56 m		97,000 Napoletano (Bill O'Donnell)	1:56.4m
79	121,000	Chiola Hanover (Jimmy Allen)	2:05.2m	88	113,500 Armbro Goal (Berndt Lindstedt)	1:56.1m
80	120,000	Final Score (Tom Haughton)	1:57.2m		113,500 Huggie Hanover (Ron Waples)	1:58.2m
81	140,000	Hot Blooded (Richard DeSantis)	1:57 m	89	99,300 Park Avenue Joe (Ron Waples)	1:57 m
82	75,000	Little League (Hakan Wallner)	1:58 m		112,300 Flying Irishman (William Gilmour)	1:58.1m
	77,000	Jazz Cosmos (Mickey McNichol)	1:57.4m	90	75,300 Embassy Lobell (Michel Lachance)	1:57.3m
83	152,000	Duenna (Stanley Dancer)	1:56.3m		75,300 Jeanne's Somolli (Rod Allen)	1:58.2m
84	82,500	Selena Lobell (Mickey McNichol)	1:58.2m		75,300 Harmonious (Catello Manzi)	1:57.1m
	82,500	Bold Vigil (Jan Nordin)	1:57.3m			

* Raced as The Empire State before 1977.

Page 358

CHRONICLES
RESULTS OF MAJOR RACES IN 1990 – CHRONOLOGICAL

The following is a chronological list of major open stakes, late-closers, series and stakes for 1990. Each entry shows the date, name of event, division (age, sex and gait), and whether it is a division, elimination or heat. Next, the purse, winning horse and time are shown. A "DH" indicates there was a dead heat for win and a " + " indicates that the winner was moved up to that position because of the disqualification of another horse:

Date	Event (Division)	Purse	At	Winner	Time
1-5	Blizzard Series (3&4yo F&M Pace) (div.)	$10,000	GrR	All Included, 4	2:00.1f
1-5	Blizzard Series (3&4yo F&M Pace) (div.)	10,000	GrR	Hornby Salem, 3	1:59.4f
1-5	Blizzard Series (3&4yo F&M Pace) (div.)	10,000	GrR	Stepping Tigeress, 4	2:00.1f
1-5	Blizzard Series (3&4yo F&M Pace) (div.)	10,000	GrR	Town Sweetheart, 4	1:59f
1-7	Horsemen's Series (4&up Open Trot) (div.)	25,000	GrR	A Js Speed	2:00.3f
1-7	Horsemen's Series (4&up Open Trot) (div.)	25,000	GrR	Go Get Lost	1:58.4f
1-8	Chill Factor Series (3&4yo C&G Pace)	12,500	M	(Postponed - Weather)	
1-9	Comforter Series (3&4yo F&M Pace) (div.)	10,000	M	Dime A Dip, 3	1:58.1
1-9	Comforter Series (3&4yo F&M Pace) (div.)	10,000	M	Double Your Luck, 4	1:58.2
1-9	Comforter Series (3&4yo F&M Pace) (div.)	10,000	M	Dumpling Almahrust,4	1:57.1
1-9	Comforter Series (3&4yo F&M Pace) (div.)	10,000	M	Real Happy, 4	1:59
1-9	Comforter Series (3&4yo F&M Pace) (div.)	10,000	M	Rittenhouse Square,3	1:59.1
1-9	Comforter Series (3&4yo F&M Pace) (div.)	10,000	M	Sam's Chick, 3	1:57.1
1-9	Comforter Series (3&4yo F&M Pace) (div.)	10,000	M	Super Sea Quick, 3	1:57.3
1-9	Comforter Series (3&4yo F&M Pace) (div.)	10,000	M	Talent Hanover, 4	1:59.3
1-10	Trendsetter Series (3&4yo C&G Pace) (div.)	10,000	M	A Mond, 4	1:57.4
1-10	Trendsetter Series (3&4yo C&G Pace) (div.)	10,000	M	Balcony Blue Chip, 4	1:57.3
1-10	Trendsetter Series (3&4yo C&G Pace) (div.)	10,000	M	Canvasback Fella, 4	1:56.1
1-10	Trendsetter Series (3&4yo C&G Pace) (div.)	10,000	M	Dovers Ranger, 4	1:56.4
1-10	Trendsetter Series (3&4yo C&G Pace) (div.)	10,000	M	Kay El Khan, 4	1:57
1-10	Trendsetter Series (3&4yo C&G Pace) (div.)	10,000	M	Lescort, 4	1:57.3
1-10	Trendsetter Series (3&4yo C&G Pace) (div.)	10,000	M	Mark Johnathan, 3	1:56
1-10	Trendsetter Series (3&4yo C&G Pace) (div.)	10,000	M	No Taste, 3	1:56.3
1-10	Trendsetter Series (3&4yo C&G Pace) (div.)	10,000	M	Pebbles Lauxmont, 4	1:56.2
1-10	Trendsetter Series (3&4yo C&G Pace) (div.)	10,000	M	Rain Devil, 4	1:56.1
1-10	Trendsetter Series (3&4yo C&G Pace) (div.)	10,000	M	The Porter Bay, 3	1:56.2
1-10	Trendsetter Series (3&4yo C&G Pace) (div.)	10,000	M	Timber Jack, 4	1:57
1-10	Trendsetter Series (3&4yo C&G Pace) (div.)	10,000	M	William S, 3	1:57.1
1-11	Complex Series (3-5yo Pace) (div.)	12,500	M	Belmondo, 4	1:55.2
1-11	Complex Series (3-5yo Pace) (div.)	12,500	M	Blazing Sahbra, 4	1:54.2
1-11	Complex Series (3-5yo Pace) (div.)	12,500	M	Mirabilis, 4	1:55.1
1-11	Complex Series (3-5yo Pace) (div.)	12,500	M	Storm Compensation,4	1:54
1-12	Blizzard Series (3&4yo F&M Pace) (div.)	10,000	GrR	Tinycrombie, 4	1:58.4f
1-12	Blizzard Series (3&4yo F&M Pace) (div.)	10,000	GrR	Town Sweetheart, 4	1:58.4f
1-12	Cape & Cutter Series (Open Mare Pace) (div.)	20,000	M	Anniecrombie	1:55.3
1-12	Cape & Cutter Series (Open Mare Pace) (div.)	20,000	M	Sweet Sharon	1:56.1
1-13	Presidential Series (FFA Pace)	35,000	M	Barely Visible	1:53.2
1-14	Horsemen's Series (4&up Open Trot)	25,000	GrR	Alissas Beauty	2:00f
1-14	Horsemen's Series (4&up Open Trot)	25,000	GrR	You Or Me	1:59.2f
1-15	Chill Factor Series (3&4yo C&G Pace) (div.)	12,500	M	Champagne Kingston,3	1:56.1
1-15	Chill Factor Series (3&4yo C&G Pace) (div.)	12,500	M	Edson Gold, 4	1:56.4
1-15	Chill Factor Series (3&4yo C&G Pace) (div.)	12,500	M	Phantom Ruler, 4	1:56.2
1-15	Chill Factor Series (3&4yo C&G Pace) (div.)	12,500	M	Yo Lenape, 4	1:56.4
1-16	Comforter Series (3&4yo F&M Pace) (div.)	10,000	M	Classify, 3	1:57.2
1-16	Comforter Series (3&4yo F&M Pace) (div.)	10,000	M	Dumpling Almahurst,4	1:56.3
1-16	Comforter Series (3&4yo F&M Pace) (div.)	10,000	M	Fudge On French, 4	1:58.4
1-16	Comforter Series (3&4yo F&M Pace) (div.)	10,000	M	Mafi, 3	1:57.1
1-16	Comforter Series (3&4yo F&M Pace) (div.)	10,000	M	Reggie's Nine W, 3	1:57.2
1-16	Comforter Series (3&4yo F&M Pace) (div.)	10,000	M	Sea Star Amy, 4	1:56.4
1-16	Comforter Series (3&4yo F&M Pace) (div.)	10,000	M	Silver Disk, 3	1:59
1-16	Comforter Series (3&4yo F&M Pace) (div.)	10,000	M	Sunnie Nukes, 3	1:56.3
1-17	Trendsetter Series (3&4yo C&G Pace) (div.)	10,000	M	Asphalt Jungle, 4	1:57.2

CHRONICLES

Date	Event	Purse	Track	Winner	Time
1-17	Trendsetter Series (3&4yo C&G Pace) (div.)	$10,000	M	Ballybunion, 3	1:55.1
1-17	Trendsetter Series (3&4yo C&G Pace) (div.)	10,000	M	Canvasback Fella, 4	1:56.1
1-17	Trendsetter Series (3&4yo C&G Pace) (div.)	10,000	M	Champagne Magician, 3	1:55.4
1-17	Trendsetter Series (3&4yo C&G Pace) (div.)	10,000	M	Kings Full, 3	1:57
1-17	Trendsetter Series (3&4yo C&G Pace) (div.)	10,000	M	Lescort, 4	1:55
1-17	Trendsetter Series (3&4yo C&G Pace) (div.)	10,000	M	Mark Johnathan, 3	1:54.1
1-17	Trendsetter Series (3&4yo C&G Pace) (div.)	10,000	M	No Taste, 3	1:56
1-17	Trendsetter Series (3&4yo C&G Pace) (div.)	10,000	M	Rain Devil, 4	1:55.3
1-17	Trendsetter Series (3&4yo C&G Pace) (div.)	10,000	M	Sir Charles N, 4	1:56
1-17	Trendsetter Series (3&4yo C&G Pace) (div.)	10,000	M	Timber Jack, 4	1:54
1-17	Trendsetter Series (3&4yo C&G Pace) (div.)	10,000	M	Woodie Wright, 3	1:56.2
1-18	Complex Series (3-5yo Pace) (div.)	12,500	M	Mirabilis, 4	1:54.4
1-18	Complex Series (3-5yo Pace) (div.)	12,500	M	Peace Parley, 5	1:55
1-18	Complex Series (3-5yo Pace) (div.)	12,500	M	Three Martinis, 4	1:55.4
1-19	Blizzard Series Final (3&4yo F&M Pace)	25,200	GrR	Town Sweetheart, 4	1:57.4f
1-19	Cape & Cutter Series (Open Mare Pace) (div.)	20,000	M	Anniecrombie	1:55.2
1-19	Cape & Cutter Series (Open Mare Pace) (div.)	20,000	M	Lakers Fortune	1:55.2
1-20	Presidential Series (FFA Pace)	35,000	M	Barely Visible	1:54.3
1-21	Horsemen's Series Final (4&up Open Trot)	125,500	GrR	Go Get Lost	1:59f
1-22	Chill Factor Series (3&4yo C&G Pace) (div.)	12,500	M	Champagne Kingston, 3	1:56.4
1-22	Chill Factor Series (3&4yo C&G Pace) (div.)	12,500	M	Last President, 4	1:55.3
1-22	Chill Factor Series (3&4yo C&G Pace) (div.)	12,500	M	Stellar Yankee, 4	1:56.2
1-23	Comforter Series (3&4yo F&M Pace) (div.)	10,000	M	Classify, 3	1:56
1-23	Comforter Series (3&4yo F&M Pace) (div.)	10,000	M	Come On Skippy, 4	1:58.2
1-23	Comforter Series (3&4yo F&M Pace) (div.)	10,000	M	Dime A Dip, 3	1:57.4
1-23	Comforter Series (3&4yo F&M Pace) (div.)	10,000	M	Dumpling Almahurst, 4	1:58
1-23	Comforter Series (3&4yo F&M Pace) (div.)	10,000	M	Island Girl, 4	1:58.2
1-23	Comforter Series (3&4yo F&M Pace) (div.)	10,000	M	Talent Hanover, 4	1:57
1-24	Trendsetter Series (3&4yo C&G Pace) (div.)	10,000	M	A Mond, 4	1:55.2
1-24	Trendsetter Series (3&4yo C&G Pace) (div.)	10,000	M	Mark Johnathan, 3	1:55
1-24	Trendsetter Series (3&4yo C&G Pace) (div.)	10,000	M	Master Scoot, 4	1:57.1
1-24	Trendsetter Series (3&4yo C&G Pace) (div.)	10,000	M	No Taste, 3	1:55.4
1-24	Trendsetter Series (3&4yo C&G Pace) (div.)	10,000	M	Rain Devil, 4	1:55.3
1-24	Trendsetter Series (3&4yo C&G Pace) (div.)	10,000	M	Timber Jack, 4	1:55.4
1-24	Trendsetter Series (3&4yo C&G Pace) (div.)	10,000	M	Woodie Wright, 3	1:56.1
1-25	Complex Series (3-5yo Pace) (div.)	12,500	M	Mirabilis, 4	1:54.4
1-25	Complex Series (3-5yo Pace) (div.)	12,500	M	Storm Compensation, 4	1:54.1
1-26	Cape & Cutter Series (Open Pacing Mares)	20,000	M	Toylee Hanover	1:55.3
1-27	Presidential Series Final (FFA Pace)	100,000	M	Barely Visible	1:53.3
1-27	Whizzer White (4yo Open Pace)	32,100	Haw	Dark Rye	1:57
1-29	Chill Factor Series (3&4yo C&G Pace) (div.)	12,500	M	Demon Lover, 4	1:57
1-29	Chill Factor Series (3&4yo C&G Pace) (div.)	12,500	M	My Tree, 4	1:56.3
1-29	Chill Factor Series (3&4yo C&G Pace) (div.)	12,500	M	Yo Lenape, 4	1:58.4
1-30	Comforter Ser. Consol. (3&4yo F&M Pace) (div.)	10,000	M	Shoo Fly Dahrlin, 4	1:59
1-30	Comforter Ser. Consol. (3&4yo F&M Pace) (div.)	15,000	M	Island Girl, 4	1:58
1-30	Comforter Ser. Final (3&4yo F&M Pace)	72,250	M	Sunnie Nukes, 3	1:57.1
1-31	Trendsetter Series Consol. (3&4yo C&G Pace)	10,000	M	JJ's Ollie, 3	1:56.4
1-31	Trendsetter Series Consol. (3&4yo C&G Pace)	15,000	M	William S, 3	1:56.1
1-31	Trendsetter Series Final (3&4yo C&G Pace)	100,000	M	Master Scoot, 4	1:55.3
2-1	Complex Series Consol. (3-5yo Pace)	15,000	M	San Andre, 4	1:55.1
2-1	Complex Series Final (3-5yo Pace)	46,900	M	Storm Compensation, 4	1:53.4
2-2	Cape & Cutter Series Final (Open Mare Pace)	43,000	M	Anniecrombie	1:57.2
2-2	Pretty Direct (4&up Pacing Mares)	34,300	Haw	Bye Bye Sleepyhead	1:57.1
2-2	Snowshoe Series (3&4yo Open Pace) (div.)	10,000	GrR	Road To Vegas, 3	2:00f
2-2	Snowshoe Series (3&4yo Open Pace) (div.)	10,000	GrR	Rough Gravel, 4	1:58.1f
2-2	Snowshoe Series (3&4yo Open Pace) (div.)	10,000	GrR	Roy Rocklin, 3	1:58.4f
2-2	Snowshoe Series (3&4yo Open Pace) (div.)	10,000	GrR	Total Control, 4	1:58.3f
2-3	Aquarius Series (4&5yo Open Pace)	25,000	M	Pilgrim's Patroit	1:56.2
2-3	Suburban Downs Pacing Derby (FFA) (div.)	55,300	Haw	Dark Rye	1:56.1
2-3	Suburban Downs Pacing Derby (FFA) (div.)	55,300	Haw	In His Favor	1:57.1
2-4	Damsel Series (3&4yo F&M Pace) (div.)	16,000	GrR	Pleasing Girl, 4	1:59.2f
2-4	Damsel Series (3&4yo F&M Pace) (div.)	16,000	GrR	Potasium, 4	1:58.3f

CHRONICLES

Date	Event	Purse	Sex	Horse	Time
2-4	Damsel Series (3&4yo F&M Pace) (div.)	$16,000	GrR	Tinycrombie, 4	1:59.1f
2-5	Chill Factor Series Consol. (3&4yo C&G Pace)	12,500	M	Walt Hand, 4	1:57.3
2-5	Chill Factor Series Final (3&4yo C&G Pace)	38,000	M	My Tree, 4	1:56.3
2-5	Su Mac Lad Series (FFA Trot) (div.)	30,000	M	No Sex Please	1:57.3
2-5	Su Mac Lad Series (FFA Trot) (div.)	30,000	M	Noble You	1:57.4
2-6	Night Styles Series (3-5yo F&M Pace) (div.)	12,500	M	It's Sunny, 3	1:57.2
2-6	Night Styles Series (3-5yo F&M Pace) (div.)	12,500	M	Miss Marpole, 4	1:58
2-6	Night Styles Series (3-5yo F&M Pace) (div.)	12,500	M	Modern Day Lady, 3	1:57.4
2-6	Night Styles Series (3-5yo F&M Pace) (div.)	12,500	M	Sea Star Amy, 4	1:57.3
2-6	Night Styles Series (3-5yo F&M Pace) (div.)	12,500	M	Steel City Woman, 4	1:57.4
2-9	Snowshoe Series (3&4yo Open Pace) (div.)	10,000	GrR	Lorryland Dandy, 4	2:00.1f
2-9	Snowshoe Series (3&4yo Open Pace) (div.)	10,000	GrR	Stew Almahurst, 4	1:58.1f
2-9	Snowshoe Series (3&4yo Open Pace) (div.)	10,000	GrR	Total Control, 4	1:57.4f
2-10	Aquarius Series (4&5yo Open Pace)	25,000	M	Storm Compensation	1:55.4
2-10	Damsel Series (3&4yo F&M Pace) (div.)	16,000	GrR	All Included, 4	2:00.4f
2-10	Damsel Series (3&4yo F&M Pace) (div.)	16,000	GrR	Jesta Lobell, 4	2:00.2f
2-10	Damsel Series (3&4yo F&M Pace) (div.)	16,000	GrR	Nine Across, 3	1:59.2f
2-10	Erwin F. Dygert Memorial (FFA Trot) (div.)	72,700	Haw	Eastridge Star	1:59.2
2-10	Erwin F. Dygert Memorial (FFA Trot) (div.)	72,700	Haw	Teddys Toy	1:58.3
2-11	Toronto Series (4&up Open Pace) (div.)	25,000	GrR	Commonwealth	1:55.2f
2-11	Toronto Series (4&up Open Pace) (div.)	25,000	GrR	My Guru, 4	1:56f
2-12	Su Mac Lad Series (FFA Trot) (div.)	30,000	M	No Sex Please	1:57.1
2-12	Su Mac Lad Series (FFA Trot) (div.)	30,000	M	Non Negotiable	1:57
2-13	Night Styles Series (3-5yo F&M Pace) (div.)	12,500	M	Hallview Harmony, 4	1:58.1
2-13	Night Styles Series (3-5yo F&M Pace) (div.)	12,500	M	It's Sunny, 3	1:56.3
2-13	Night Styles Series (3-5yo F&M Pace) (div.)	12,500	M	Keystone Hermit, 5	1:57.2
2-13	Night Styles Series (3-5yo F&M Pace) (div.)	12,500	M	Miss Marpole, 4	1:57.3
2-13	Night Styles Series (3-5yo F&M Pace) (div.)	12,500	M	Modern Day Lady, 3	1:56.2
2-15	Exit 16W Series (3-5yo C&G Pace) (div.)	12,500	M	Billy Bignose, 4	1:58.2
2-15	Exit 16W Series (3-5yo C&G Pace) (div.)	12,500	M	Even Hand, 4	1:57
2-15	Exit 16W Series (3-5yo C&G Pace) (div.)	12,500	M	Fiddler Blue Chip, 4	1:57
2-15	Exit 16W Series (3-5yo C&G Pace) (div.)	12,500	M	Licensed To Kill, 5	1:58.1
2-15	Exit 16W Series (3-5yo C&G Pace) (div.)	12,500	M	Mr Bagel, 4	1:57.3
2-15	Exit 16W Series (3-5yo C&G Pace) (div.)	12,500	M	My Tree, 4	1:58.1
2-16	Snowshoe Series Final (3&4yo Open Pace)	35,800	GrR	Stew Almahurst, 4	1:57.3f
2-17	Aquarius Series Final (4&5yo Open Pace)	58,000	M	Direct Current	1:54.2
2-17	Damsel Series Final (3&4yo F&M Pace)	135,250	GrR	Tinycrombie, 4	1:56.4f
2-18	Toronto Series (4&up Open Pace) (div.)	25,000	GrR	Take A Look	1:56.1f
2-19	Su Mac Lad Series Final (FFA Trot)	73,000	M	No Sex Please	1:57.4
2-20	Night Styles Series (3-5yo F&M Pace) (div.)	12,500	M	Armbro Ilona, 3	1:56.4
2-20	Night Styles Series (3-5yo F&M Pace) (div.)	12,500	M	Eds Lil Girl, 4	1:59
2-20	Night Styles Series (3-5yo F&M Pace) (div.)	12,500	M	Everything Goes, 3	1:56.1
2-20	Night Styles Series (3-5yo F&M Pace) (div.)	12,500	M	Kiss My Face, 3	1:57.2
2-20	Night Styles Series (3-5yo F&M Pace) (div.)	12,500	M	Slippery Slide, 4	1:56.4
2-22	Exit 16W Series (3-5yo C&G Pace) (div.)	12,500	M	Master Scoot, 4	1:56.1
2-22	Exit 16W Series (3-5yo C&G Pace) (div.)	12,500	M	My Tree, 4	1:55.3
2-22	Exit 16W Series (3-5yo C&G Pace) (div.)	12,500	M	TE's Mac, 4	1:57.3
2-22	Exit 16W Series (3-5yo C&G Pace) (div.)	12,500	M	Timber Jack, 4	1:56.2
2-22	Exit 16W Series (3-5yo C&G Pace) (div.)	12,500	M	United Gambler, 4	1:56.4
2-23	Overbid Series (F&M Open Pace) (div.)	20,000	M	Lauren B, 5	1:55.2
2-23	Overbid Series (F&M Open Pace) (div.)	20,000	M	Storm Tossed, 5	1:56.3
2-25	Toronto Series Final (4&up Open Pace)	125,000	GrR	Take A Look	1:55.4f
2-27	Night Styles Series Final (3-5yo F&M Pace)	81,800	M	Why Wont Ya, 4	1:57.1
3-1	Exit 16W Series (3-5yo C&G Pace) (div.)	12,500	M	Bone Of Contention, 4	1:56
3-1	Exit 16W Series (3-5yo C&G Pace) (div.)	12,500	M	Harpo, 3	1:55.2
3-1	Exit 16W Series (3-5yo C&G Pace) (div.)	12,500	M	Master Scoot, 4	1:56
3-1	Exit 16W Series (3-5yo C&G Pace) (div.)	12,500	M	Yo Lenape, 4	1:56.3
3-2	Overbid Series (F&M Open Pace) (div.)	20,000	M	Sweet Sharon, 6	1:55.3
3-3	Four Leaf Clover Series (3-5yo Pace) (div.)	17,500	M	Chernobyl, 4	1:54
3-3	Four Leaf Clover Series (3-5yo Pace) (div.)	17,500	M	Rain Devil, 4	1:55.1
3-3	Four Leaf Clover Series (3-5yo Pace) (div.)	17,500	M	Trouble Twosum, 4	1:55.4
3-4	Cam Fella Series (3&4yo Open Pace) (div.)	16,000	GrR	Gigalo, 4	1:57f

CHRONICLES

Date	Event	Purse	Track	Winner	Time
3-4	Cam Fella Series (3&4yo Open Pace) (div.)	$16,000	GrR	My Guru, 4	1:56.3f
3-4	Cam Fella Series (3&4yo Open Pace) (div.)	16,000	GrR	Storm Compensation, 4	1:56.3f
3-7	Blossom Series (3yofp) (div.)	15,000	M	It's Sunny	1:57.2
3-7	Blossom Series (3yofp) (div.)	15,000	M	Miss Tyler Beach	1:57.4
3-8	Exit 16W Consol. (3-5yo C&G Pace)	12,500	M	United Gambler, 4	1:55
3-8	Exit 16W Final (3-5yo C&G Pace)	82,100	M	Mr Bagel, 4	1:54.1
3-9	Overbid Series Final (F&M Open Pace)	57,000	M	Sweet Sharon, 6	1:53.3
3-10	Four Leaf Clover Series (3-5yo Pace) (div.)	17,500	M	Blazing Sahbra, 4	1:53.4
3-10	Four Leaf Clover Series (3-5yo Pace) (div.)	17,500	M	Prince Lee Cam, 5	1:54.4
3-10	George Morton Levy Series (Aged Pace) (div.)	50,000	YR	Chatham Light	1:56.1h
3-10	George Morton Levy Series (Aged Pace) (div.)	50,000	YR	Sandman Hanover	1:57.2h
3-11	Cam Fella Series (3&4yo Open Pace) (div.)	16,000	GrR	Carey's Pride, 4	1:58.1f
3-11	Cam Fella Series (3&4yo Open Pace) (div.)	16,000	GrR	Gigalo, 4	1:57.1f
3-14	Blossom Series (3yofp) (div.)	15,000	M	It's Sunny	1:55.4
3-14	Blossom Series (3yofp) (div.)	15,000	M	Kiss My Face	1:56
3-16	New Faces Series (3yocp) (div.)	15,000	M	JJ's Rebel	1:55.2
3-16	New Faces Series (3yocp) (div.)	15,000	M	Mark Johnathan	1:55.1
3-16	New Faces Series (3yocp) (div.)	15,000	M	Sand Key	1:55
3-16	New Faces Series (3yocp) (div.)	15,000	M	Yankee Tradition	1:54.3
3-17	Cam Fella Series Final (3&4yo Open Pace)	152,500	GrR	Gigalo, 4	1:55.2f
3-17	Four Leaf Clover Series Final (3-5yo Pace)	93,500	M	Trouble Twosum, 4	1:55.1
3-17	George Morton Levy Series (Aged Pace) (div.)	50,000	YR	Chatham Light	1:57h
3-17	George Morton Levy Series (Aged Pace) (div.)	50,000	YR	Sandman Hanover	1:57.3h
3-18	Youthful Series (3yo Open Pace) (div.)	10,000	Moh	Cemetery Ridge	1:56.3f
3-18	Youthful Series (3yo Open Pace) (div.)	10,000	Moh	Keystone Mark	1:58.1f
3-18	Youthful Series (3yo Open Pace) (div.)	10,000	Moh	Nukes Himself	1:57.1f
3-18	Youthful Series (3yo Open Pace) (div.)	10,000	Moh	Wendalator	1:57f
3-21	Blossom Series Final (3yofp)	60,000	M	Yankee Desire	1:56.3
3-23	New Faces Series (3yocp) (div.)	15,000	M	Further Notice	1:55.4
3-23	New Faces Series (3yocp) (div.)	15,000	M	Mark Johnathan	1:56
3-23	New Faces Series (3yocp) (div.)	15,000	M	Napsugar	1:56.4
3-24	George Morton Levy Series (Aged Pace) (div.)	50,000	YR	Chatham Light	1:57.1h
3-24	George Morton Levy Series (Aged Pace) (div.)	50,000	YR	Dorunrun Bluegrass	1:55.2h
3-25	Youthful Series (3yo Open Pace) (div.)	10,000	Moh	Abdul Kerim	1:57.2f
3-25	Youthful Series (3yo Open Pace) (div.)	10,000	Moh	General Trull	1:56.1f
3-25	Youthful Series (3yo Open Pace) (div.)	10,000	Moh	Laurstar	1:56.2f
3-30	New Faces Series Consol. (3yocp)	15,000	M	No Taste	1:57.3
3-30	New Faces Series Final (3yocp)	104,000	M	Mark Johnathan	1:56.1
3-31	George Morton Levy Series (Aged Pace) (div.)	50,000	YR	Dorunrun Bluegrass	1:56.1h
3-31	George Morton Levy Series (Aged Pace) (div.)	50,000	YR	Sandman Hanover	1:58h
3-31	Graduate Series (4&5yo Pace) (div.)	75,000	M	Prince Lee Cam	1:54.1
3-31	Graduate Series (4&5yo Pace) (div.)	75,000	M	T K's Skipper	1:53.3
4-1	Youthful Series (3yo Open Pace) (div.)	10,000	Moh	Minor Violation	1:56.3f
4-1	Youthful Series (3yo Open Pace) (div.)	10,000	Moh	Road To Vegas	1:57.2f
4-2	Belle Isle Elims (3&4yo Open Pace) (div.)	7,500	HP	Fulcrom, 4	1:59.1f
4-2	Belle Isle Elims (3&4yo Open Pace) (div.)	7,500	HP	Oakland Avenue, 3	1:59.1f
4-2	Belle Isle Elims (3&4yo Open Pace) (div.)	7,500	HP	Shopper, 4	1:59.3f
4-4	Jersey Girls Series (3-5yo F&M Pace) (div.)	12,500	M	Dime A Dip, 3	1:59.2
4-4	Jersey Girls Series (3-5yo F&M Pace) (div.)	12,500	M	It's Sunny, 3	1:57.3
4-4	Jersey Girls Series (3-5yo F&M Pace) (div.)	12,500	M	White Ruffles, 4	1:56.4
4-7	Berry's Creek Elims (3yo Open Pace) (div.)	12,500	M	Division Title	1:54
4-7	Berry's Creek Elims (3yo Open Pace) (div.)	12,500	M	Seltzer Blue	1:55.1
4-7	Berry's Creek Elims (3yo Open Pace) (div.)	12,500	M	Ultra Jet	1:55
4-7	George Morton Levy Series (Aged Pace) (div.)	50,000	YR	Dorunrun Bluegrass	1:54.3h
4-7	George Morton Levy Series (Aged Pace) (div.)	50,000	YR	Gold Town	1:57h
4-7	North American Series (3&4yo Pace) (div.)	18,750	Fhld	Power Swing, 4	1:57h
4-7	North American Series (3&4yo Pace) (div.)	18,750	Fhld	San Andre, 4	1:56.4h
4-7	North American Series (3&4yo Pace) (div.)	18,750	Fhld	Scurrilous, 4	1:57.2h
4-8	Graduate Series (4&5yo Pace) (div.)	56,250	RcR	Fiorello Blue Chip	1:54.3f
4-8	Graduate Series (4&5yo Pace) (div.)	56,250	RcR	T K's Skipper	1:52.4f
4-8	Graduate Series (4&5yo Pace) (div.)	56,250	RcR	Ticket To Heaven	1:54.3f
4-8	Youthful Series Final (3yo Open Pace)	38,800	Moh	Laurstar	1:55.1f

CHRONICLES

Date	Event	Purse	Track	Winner	Time
4-9	Belle Isle Final (3&4yo Open Pace)	$20,000	HP	Indylator, 4	1:58.1f
4-11	Jersey Girls Series (3-5yo F&M Pace) (div.)	12,500	M	Dumpling Almahurst, 4	1:56.2
4-11	Jersey Girls Series (3-5yo F&M Pace) (div.)	12,500	M	Five O'Clock Cindy, 3	1:56
4-11	Jersey Girls Series (3-5yo F&M Pace) (div.)	12,500	M	White Ruffles, 4	1:57.4
4-14	Berry's Creek Consolation (3yo Open Pace)	20,000	M	Shipps Schnoops	1:55.1
4-14	Berry's Creek Final (3yo Open Pace)	323,750	M	Mark Johnathan	1:54
4-14	George Morton Levy Series (Aged Pace) (div.)	50,000	YR	Chatham Light	1:55h
4-14	George Morton Levy Series (Aged Pace) (div.)	50,000	YR	My Guru	1:54.3h
4-14	Graduate Series (4&5yo Open Pace) (div.)	56,250	Fhld	Dorunrun Bluegrass	1:53.2h
4-14	Graduate Series (4&5yo Open Pace) (div.)	56,250	Fhld	Ticket To Heaven	1:54.4h
4-14	North American Series (3&4yo Pace) (div.)	18,750	RcR	Campaign Boss, 4	1:55.3f
4-14	North American Series (3&4yo Pace) (div.)	18,750	RcR	T K Rainbow, 4	1:54.2f
4-14	Princess Series (3yo Filly Pace) (div.)	16,000	Moh	Instant Rebate	1:59.2f
4-14	Princess Series (3yo Filly Pace) (div.)	16,000	Moh	Shipps Margitross	1:58.3f
4-14	Princess Series (3yo Filly Pace) (div.)	16,000	Moh	Til Friday	1:58.4f
4-16	Hiram Woodruff Series (3&4yo Trot) (div.)	10,000	M	Daily Review, 3	1:59.4
4-16	Hiram Woodruff Series (3&4yo Trot) (div.)	10,000	M	Hunziker T, 4	2:00.1
4-16	Hiram Woodruff Series (3&4yo Trot) (div.)	10,000	M	January, 3	1:59.4
4-17	Trendsetter II Series (3&4yo C&G Pace)(div.)	10,000	M	Candrel, 3	1:56.2
4-17	Trendsetter II Series (3&4yo C&G Pace)(div.)	10,000	M	Mingooch, 4	1:57.2
4-17	Trendsetter II Series (3&4yo C&G Pace)(div.)	10,000	M	Odds Against, 3	1:56
4-17	Trendsetter II Series (3&4yo C&G Pace)(div.)	10,000	M	P L Express, 3	1:58.1
4-17	Trendsetter II Series (3&4yo C&G Pace)(div.)	10,000	M	Pat's Flagship, 3	1:56
4-17	Trendsetter II Series (3&4yo C&G Pace)(div.)	10,000	M	Pip Squeek, 3	1:57.4
4-17	Trendsetter II Series (3&4yo C&G Pace)(div.)	10,000	M	Windsong Lobell, 3	1:56.1
4-18	Jersey Girls Series (3-5yo F&M Pace) (div.)	12,500	M	White Ruffles, 4	1:54.1
4-18	Jersey Girls Series (3-5yo F&M Pace) (div.)	12,500	M	Why Wont Ya, 4	1:56
4-19	The Westwind Series (3&4yo Pace) (div.)	12,500	M	A Mond, 4	1:55.3
4-19	The Westwind Series (3&4yo Pace) (div.)	12,500	M	Dixie's Fella, 3	1:56.2
4-19	The Westwind Series (3&4yo Pace) (div.)	12,500	M	Slugger Hanover, 4	1:55.3
4-19	The Westwind Series (3&4yo Pace) (div.)	12,500	M	T K Rainbow, 4	1:56.1
4-20	The Spring Fever Series (3&4yo Pace) (div.)	15,000	M	Dovers Ranger, 4	1:53.3
4-20	The Spring Fever Series (3&4yo Pace) (div.)	15,000	M	United Gambler, 4	1:54
4-21	Big Apple Pace (3yo Open Pace) (div.)	40,000	YR	Hubris	1:57.2h
4-21	Big Apple Pace (3yo Open Pace) (div.)	40,000	YR	Jake And Elwood	1:55.2h
4-21	Big Apple Pace (3yo Open Pace) (div.)	40,000	YR	Sea The USA	1:56.4h
4-21	North American Series (3&4yo Pace)	25,000	M	Scurrilous, 4	1:54
4-21	Princess Series (3yo Filly Pace) (div.)	16,000	Moh	Instate Rebate	1:57.2f
4-21	Princess Series (3yo Filly Pace) (div.)	16,000	Moh	Legal Possession	1:56.1f
4-21	Princess Series (3yo Filly Pace) (div.)	16,000	Moh	Parafe	1:58.1f
4-21	R. Bruce Cornell Memorial (Open Pace)	100,000	Fhld	Dorunrun Bluegrass	1:53.1h
4-23	Hiram Woodruff Series (3&4yo Trot) (div.)	10,000	M	Atkinson Ridge, 3	1:58.4
4-23	Hiram Woodruff Series (3&4yo Trot) (div.)	10,000	M	Incredible D J, 3	1:56.4
4-23	Hiram Woodruff Series (3&4yo Trot) (div.)	10,000	M	Mystic Marvel, 4	1:58.1
4-24	Trendsetter II Series (3&4yo C&G Pace)(div.)	10,000	M	Acoustical, 3	1:54.2
4-24	Trendsetter II Series (3&4yo C&G Pace)(div.)	10,000	M	Officer Of The Day, 3	1:54
4-24	Trendsetter II Series (3&4yo C&G Pace)(div.)	10,000	M	Onefiftyonerum, 3	1:55.1
4-24	Trendsetter II Series (3&4yo C&G Pace)(div.)	10,000	M	Pat's Flagship, 3	1:53.4
4-24	Trendsetter II Series (3&4yo C&G Pace)(div.)	10,000	M	Retribution, 4	1:54.2
4-24	Trendsetter II Series (3&4yo C&G Pace)(div.)	10,000	M	Super Service, 3	1:54.4
4-25	Jersey Girls Series Final (3-5yo F&M Pace)	66,800	M	White Ruffles, 4	1:54
4-26	The Westwind Series (3&4yo Pace) (div.)	12,500	M	A Mond, 4	1:55.1
4-26	The Westwind Series (3&4yo Pace) (div.)	12,500	M	Incognito, 4	1:54.4
4-26	The Westwind Series (3&4yo Pace) (div.)	12,500	M	Nice Try, 3	1:54.3
4-26	The Westwind Series (3&4yo Pace) (div.)	12,500	M	Positive Cash, 4	1:54.2
4-27	The Spring Fever Series (3&4yo Pace)	15,000	M	Even Hand, 4	1:52
4-27	The Spring Fever Series (3&4yo Pace)	15,000	M	Oscarsson, 3	1:53.4
4-28	George Morton Levy Series (Aged Pace)	50,000	YR	My Guru	1:55h
4-28	Graduate Series (4&5yo Open Pace)	75,000	BR	Dorunrun Bluegrass	1:54.3h
4-28	North American Series (3&4yo Pace) (div.)	18,750	Fhld	Piks By Day, 3	1:58h
4-28	North American Series (3&4yo Pace) (div.)	18,750	Fhld	San Andre, 4	1:56.1h
4-29	Princess Series Final (3yo Filly Pace)	87,100	Moh	Instant Rebate	1:55.4f

CHRONICLES

Date	Event	Purse	Track	Winner	Time
4-30	Hiram Woodruff Series (3&4yo Trot) (div.)	$10,000	M	Daily Review, 3	1:58.2
5-1	Trendsetter II Series (3&4yo C&G Pace)(div.)	10,000	M	Nuclear Flash, 3	1:53.3
5-1	Trendsetter II Series (3&4yo C&G Pace)(div.)	10,000	M	Pat's Flagship, 3	1:53.4
5-1	Trendsetter II Series (3&4yo C&G Pace)(div.)	10,000	M	Pip Squeek, 3	1:55.2
5-3	The Westwind Series (3&4yo Pace) (div.)	12,500	M	A Mond, 4	1:54.4
5-3	The Westwind Series (3&4yo Pace) (div.)	12,500	M	Positive Cash, 4	1:55.1
5-3	The Westwind Series (3&4yo Pace) (div.)	12,500	M	Sam Breeze, 4	1:55
5-4	Graduate Series (4&5yo Open Pace) (div.)	56,250	Moh	Dare You To	1:56f
5-4	Graduate Series (4&5yo Open Pace) (div.)	56,250	Moh	Fiorello Blue Chip	1:56.2f
5-4	The Spring Fever Series (3&4yo Pace) (div.)	15,000	M	Even Hand, 4	1:55.1
5-4	The Spring Fever Series (3&4yo Pace) (div.)	15,000	M	United Gambler, 4	1:56.4
5-5	George Morton Levy Series (Aged Pace)	50,000	YR	Dorunrun Bluegrass	1:54h
5-5	John W. Miller Memorial Elims (3yofp) (div.)	10,000	RcR	Choice Yankee	1:55f
5-5	John W. Miller Memorial Elims (3yofp) (div.)	10,000	RcR	Instant Rebate	1:55.3f
5-5	Mohawk Series (3yo Open Pace) (div.)	16,000	Moh	Dak	1:56.4f
5-5	Mohawk Series (3yo Open Pace) (div.)	16,000	Moh	Global Assault	1:56.2f
5-5	Mohawk Series (3yo Open Pace) (div.)	16,000	Moh	Teen Idol	1:56.2f
5-5	Mohawk Series (3yo Open Pace) (div.)	16,000	Moh	Wendalator	1:56.2f
5-5	Windy City Elims (3yo Open Pace) (div.)	20,000	May	Center Strip	1:57.1h
5-5	Windy City Elims (3yo Open Pace) (div.)	20,000	May	Jake And Elwood	1:57.4h
5-5	Windy City Elims (3yo Open Pace) (div.)	20,000	May	Ultra Jet	1:57.1h
5-5	Wm. E. Miller Mem. Elims (3yo Pace) (div.)	15,000	RcR	Beach Towel	1:53f
5-5	Wm. E. Miller Mem. Elims (3yo Pace) (div.)	15,000	RcR	In The Pocket	1:53.3f
5-7	Hiram Woodruff Series Final (3&4yo Trot)	42,200	M	Incredible D J, 3	1:57
5-8	Trendsetter II Series Final (3&4yo C&G Pace)	55,500	M	Odds Against, 3	1:54.2
5-10	The Westwind Series Consol. (3&4yo Pace)	12,500	M	Idlewhiles Mikey, 4	1:57.1
5-10	The Westwind Series Final (3&4yo Pace)	50,300	M	Positive Cash, 4	1:54.2
5-11	The Spring Fever Series Final (3&4yo Pace)	37,400	M	Canvasback Fella, 4	1:53.4
5-11	Windy City Consolation (3yo Open Pace)	20,000	May	Seltzer Blue	1:55.1h
5-12	George Morton Levy Series Final (Aged Pace)	240,000	YR	My Guru	1:54.3h
5-12	John W. Miller Memorial Final (3yofp)	202,690	RcR	Instant Rebate	1:54.2f
5-12	Mohawk Series (3yo Open Pace) (div.)	16,000	Moh	Neat Touch	1:55.1f
5-12	Mohawk Series (3yo Open Pace) (div.)	16,000	Moh	Teen Idol	1:57.1f
5-12	Mohawk Series (3yo Open Pace) (div.)	16,000	Moh	Wendalator	1:57f
5-12	Windy City Final (3yo Open Pace)	255,000	May	Jake And Elwood	1:57.2h
5-12	Wm. E. Miller Memorial Final (3yo Pace)	315,010	RcR	Beach Towel	1:52.3f
5-19	Graduate Series Final (4&5yo Open Pace)	205,500	M	Dorunrun Bluegrass	1:51.3
5-19	Guys & Dolls Elims (Open Pacing Mares)(div.)	10,000	Fhld	Cassandra Seelster	1:58.1h
5-19	Guys & Dolls Elims (Open Pacing Mares)(div.)	10,000	Fhld	Gentle Jody	1:58.2h
5-19	Guys & Dolls Elims (Open Pacing Mares)(div.)	10,000	Fhld	Yankee Caroline	1:58.1h
5-19	Hanover-Hempt (3yocp) (div.)	32,800	VD	King Gypsy	1:54.1q
5-19	Hanover-Hempt (3yocp) (div.)	32,800	VD	Till We Meet Again	1:54.4q
5-20	Mohawk Series Final (3yo Open Pace)	115,100	Moh	Neat Touch	1:56f
5-21	Connaught Cup (FFA Pace)	50,000	Conn	Chatham Light	1:53.3h
5-26	Currier & Ives (3yo Open Trot) (div.)	38,060	Mea	Cheyenne Spur	2:00.4f
5-26	Currier & Ives (3yo Open Trot) (div.)	38,060	Mea	King Of The Sea	2:00f
5-26	Currier & Ives (3yo Open Trot) (div.)	38,060	Mea	Zizi's Prakas	1:59.4f
5-26	Guys & Dolls Final (Open Pacing Mares)	50,000	Fhld	Games	1:57.4h
5-26	Hanover Colt Stake (3yocp) (div.)	20,972	RcR	Beach Towel	1:54.1f
5-26	Hanover Colt Stake (3yocp) (div.)	21,223	RcR	Kiev Hanover	1:56.2f
5-27	Currier & Ives Filly Trot (3yo) (div.)	14,405	Mea	Atlantic	2:01.2f
5-27	Currier & Ives Filly Trot (3yo) (div.)	14,405	Mea	Camelia Lobell	1:59.2f
5-27	Currier & Ives Filly Trot (3yo) (div.)	14,555	Mea	Essence Bear	2:01.2f
5-27	Currier & Ives Filly Trot (3yo) (div.)	14,555	Mea	Lila Lobell	2:00.3f
5-27	Elitloppet (Open Trot) (elim.)	48,592	Solv	Florida Jewel	1:57.2f
5-27	Elitloppet (Open Trot) (elim.)	48,592	Solv	Mack Lobell	1:57.2f
5-27	Elitloppet (Open Trot) (final)	243,815	Solv	Mack Lobell	1:54.2f
5-28	North American Series (3&4yo Pace)	25,000	Lex	Central Processing, 4	1:56.2
6-2	Battle of Lake Erie (FFA Pace)	100,000	Nfld	Dorunrun Bluegrass	1:54h
6-2	Burlington Elims (3yo Open Pace) (div.)	25,000	GrR	Apaches Fame	1:54.1f
6-2	Burlington Elims (3yo Open Pace) (div.)	25,000	GrR	Chefs Magic	1:55.1f
6-2	Burlington Elims (3yo Open Pace) (div.)	25,000	GrR	Jake And Elwood	1:53.2f

CHRONICLES

Date	Race	Purse	Track	Winner	Time
6-2	Burlington Elims (3yo Open Pace) (div.)	$25,000	GrR	No Taste	1:55.2f
6-2	Hanover Stake (Open Aged Trot)	19,500	RcR	Peach Pit	1:57f
6-2	Mac Farlane Memorial (3yofp)	77,425	HP	Temptres Almahurst	1:57.3f
6-4	Can. Trotting Classic Elims (3yo Open)(div.)	30,000	GrR	A Worthy Lad	1:58.2f
6-4	Can. Trotting Classic Elims (3yo Open)(div.)	30,000	GrR	Cheyenne Spur	1:59.3f
6-6	W.N. Reynolds Memorial (2yofp) (div.)	32,872	RP	Goalie Jess	1:59.1f
6-6	W.N. Reynolds Memorial (2yofp) (div.)	32,872	RP	Jollie Dame	2:00f
6-6	W.N. Reynolds Memorial (2yoft)	45,313	RP	Grand Encore	2:03.4f
6-8	W.N. Reynolds Memorial (2yoct)	46,843	RP	Super Pleasure	2:03.2f
6-8	W.N. Reynolds Memorial (3yoft)	27,900	RP	Gretel T	2:02.1f
6-9	American-National (3yofp)	181,000	SPk	Town Pro	1:55.2f
6-9	Burlington Final (3yo Open Pace)	214,300	GrR	Apaches Fame	1:52.2f
6-9	Lake Superior (FFA)	100,000	HP	Topnotcher	1:53.3f
6-9	Terrapin (3yocp)	316,135	RcR	Beach Towel	1:54.1f
6-9	W.N. Reynolds Memorial (2yocp) (div.)	26,385	RP	Interpretor	1:59.3f
6-9	W.N. Reynolds Memorial (2yocp) (div.)	26,385	RP	Isle Of Maui	2:02f
6-9	W.N. Reynolds Memorial (2yocp) (div.)	26,385	RP	Squire Squirt	1:58.4f
6-9	W.N. Reynolds Memorial (3yoct) (div.)	19,050	RP	Letters From Hill	2:02f
6-9	W.N. Reynolds Memorial (3yoct) (div.)	20,050	RP	Drummer Hanover	2:01.2f
6-10	North American Series (3&4yo Pace)	25,000	BB	Total Control, 4	1:58.4f
6-10	W.N. Reynolds Memorial (3yocp) (div.)	22,900	RP	Fortysix Extralong	1:58.1f
6-10	W.N. Reynolds Memorial (3yocp) (div.)	22,900	RP	French Embassy	1:56.3f
6-10	W.N. Reynolds Memorial (3yofp)	32,700	RP	Royal Harmony	1:56.4f
6-11	American-National (3yoft)	185,000	SPk	Spreadsheet	1:59.2f
6-11	Canadian Trotting Classic Final (3yo Open)	207,000	GrR	A Worthy Lad	1:59.4f
6-13	Windsor Riverfront (2yofp) (div.)	29,250	WR	Jollie Dame	1:58.4f
6-13	Windsor Riverfront (2yofp) (div.)	29,250	WR	Phast Madam	1:59.2f
6-13	Windsor Riverfront (2yoft)	31,050	WR	Good Lookin Mouse	2:01.4f
6-14	Windsor Riverfront (2yoct)	36,450	WR	Super Pleasure	2:03f
6-14	Windsor Riverfront (3yoft)	39,100	WR	B Cor Jenny	2:00f
6-15	Windsor Border City (3yoct)	39,700	WR	I'm Impeccable	1:59.2f
6-15	Windsor Riverfront (2yocp) (div.)	25,000	WR	Black Gold Road	1:58.3f
6-15	Windsor Riverfront (2yocp) (div.)	25,000	WR	Brett's Story	1:57.2f
6-15	Windsor Riverfront (2yocp) (div.)	25,000	WR	Fabulious	1:58.2f
6-16	North America Cup Elim (3yo Open Pace)(div.)	50,750	GrR	Beach Towel	1:53f
6-16	North America Cup Elim (3yo Open Pace)(div.)	50,750	GrR	Chefs Magic	1:52.4f
6-16	North America Cup Elim (3yo Open Pace)(div.)	50,750	GrR	Jake And Elwood	1:53f
6-16	Windsor Border City (3yofp) (div.)	32,750	WR	Fiji Hanover	1:54.4f
6-16	Windsor Border City (3yofp) (div.)	33,750	WR	Tambourine	1:56f
6-17	Blue Bonnets Challenge (4&up H&G Pace)	130,500	BB	Topnotcher	1:53f
6-17	Windsor Border City (3yocp) (div.)	30,250	WR	Broussard	1:54.2f
6-17	Windsor Border City (3yocp) (div.)	30,250	WR	Global Assault	1:54.2f
6-18	American-National (3yoct)	272,000	SPk	Armbro Iliad	2:00.1f
6-19	Tompkins-Geers (2yofp) (div.)	20,600	ScD	Gretzky	1:59.3f
6-19	Tompkins-Geers (2yofp) (div.)	20,600	ScD	Shady Daisy	1:58.4f
6-19	Tompkins-Geers (2yofp) (div.)	20,600	ScD	Shy Devil	1:58.2f
6-19	Tompkins-Geers (2yofp) (div.)	20,600	ScD	Sugar Lorraine	1:59.1f
6-19	Tompkins-Geers (2yoft) (div.)	20,700	ScD	Peace Bid	2:03f
6-19	Tompkins-Geers (2yoft) (div.)	21,200	ScD	Con's In Tassel	2:04f
6-19	Tompkins-Geers (2yoft) (div.)	21,200	ScD	Good Lookin Mouse	2:02.4f
6-20	Tompkins-Geers (2yo Open Trot) (div.)	29,200	ScD	Crysta's Best	2:00.1f
6-20	Tompkins-Geers (2yo Open Trot) (div.)	29,700	ScD	Gift Box	2:02.4f
6-20	Tompkins-Geers (3yoft) (div.)	24,510	ScD	Lila Lobell	1:59.4f
6-20	Tompkins-Geers (3yoft) (div.)	24,510	ScD	Me Maggie	1:59.1f
6-21	Tompkins-Geers (2yo Open Pace) (div.)	27,200	ScD	Isle Of Maui	1:58.4f
6-21	Tompkins-Geers (2yo Open Pace) (div.)	27,200	ScD	Master Fund	1:58.4f
6-21	Tompkins-Geers (2yo Open Pace) (div.)	27,200	ScD	Nuclear Legacy	1:58.4f
6-22	North America Cup Consol. (3yo Open Pace)	50,750	GrR	Orange Sovereign	1:56f
6-22	Tompkins-Geers (3yofp) (div.)	26,100	ScD	Lady Genius	1:59f
6-22	Tompkins-Geers (3yofp) (div.)	26,100	ScD	Royal Harmony	1:57.2f
6-23	Driscoll Series (FFA Pace)	50,000	M	Ticket To Heaven	1:52
6-23	North America Cup Final (3yo Open Pace)	1,000,000	GrR	Apaches Fame	1:53.4f

CHRONICLES

Date	Event	Purse	Track	Winner	Time
6-23	Tompkins-Geers (3yo Open Pace) (div.)	$27,700	ScD	Bookmaker	1:54.3f
6-23	Tompkins-Geers (3yo Open Pace) (div.)	27,700	ScD	Hot Walker	1:57.2f
6-23	Tompkins-Geers (3yo Open Trot) (div.)	28,150	ScD	Downhill Racer	2:01f
6-23	Tompkins-Geers (3yo Open Trot) (div.)	74,400	ScD	Drummer Hanover	2:00.4f
6-24	Grand Prix de Quebec (Invitational)	50,000	Que	Fiorello Blue Chip	1:56.4h
6-24	Hopeful Elims (2yo Colt Pace) (div.)	10,000	BR	Black Gold Road	2:00h
6-24	Hopeful Elims (2yo Colt Pace) (div.)	10,000	BR	Cambest	1:59.3h
6-24	Hopeful Elims (2yo Colt Pace) (div.)	10,000	BR	Interpretor	2:00h
6-24	Hopeful Elims (2yo Colt Pace) (div.)	10,000	BR	Three Wizzards	2:00.1h
6-24	Hopeful Elims (2yo Colt Pace) (div.)	10,000	BR	W R H	2:00h
6-25	Historic-Acorn (2yoft) (div.)	56,000	M	Another Geisha	2:01.2
6-25	Historic-Acorn (2yoft) (div.)	56,000	M	Jean Bi	1:59.3
6-25	Historic-Debutante (2yofp) (div.)	37,415	M	Laugh Line	1:59
6-25	Historic-Debutante (2yofp) (div.)	37,415	M	Miss Easy	1:56.3
6-25	Historic-Debutante (2yofp) (div.)	37,415	M	Miss Intensity	1:58
6-26	Hall of Fame Drivers (Open Trot)	7,500	M	Struttin Time	1:59
6-26	Historic-Harriman (2yoct) (div.)	38,467	M	Grundy's Mint	2:00.2
6-26	Historic-Harriman (2yoct) (div.)	38,467	M	Super Pleasure	2:01.3
6-26	Historic-Harriman (2yoct) (div.)	38,467	M	Wall Street Banker	2:01
6-27	Historic-Coaching Club Oaks (3yoft) (div.)	45,987	M	Delphi's Lobell	1:57.3
6-27	Historic-Coaching Club Oaks (3yoft) (div.)	45,987	M	Lila Lobell	1:55.4
6-28	Historic-Goshen Cup (2yocp) (div.)	35,075	M	Brett's Story	1:57
6-28	Historic-Goshen Cup (2yocp) (div.)	35,075	M	Lefty	1:55.3
6-28	Historic-Goshen Cup (2yocp) (div.)	35,075	M	Mantese	1:56.1
6-28	Historic-Goshen Cup (2yocp) (div.)	35,425	M	Henry Letsgo	1:55
6-29	Historic-Historic Cup (3yoct)	102,955	M	Star Mystic	2:00.2
6-29	Historic-The Ladyship (3yofp)	74,355	M	Town Pro	1:53
6-30	American-National (3yocp)	347,000	SPk	Beach Towel	1:52.4f
6-30	Driscoll Series (FFA Pace)	75,000	M	T K's Skipper	1:53
6-30	Hanover-Hempt (3yoct) (div.)	33,200	VD	Cheyenne Spur	1:57.1q
6-30	Hanover-Hempt (3yoct) (div.)	33,200	VD	Drummer Hanover	1:59.4q
6-30	Historic-Jersey Cup (3yocp) (div.)	48,130	M	In The Pocket	1:51.2
6-30	Historic-Jersey Cup (3yocp) (div.)	48,130	M	Raven Lunatic	1:54.3
6-30	La Paloma Elims (2yofp) (div.)	20,000	YR	Janna Rose	2:01.1h
6-30	La Paloma Elims (2yofp) (div.)	20,000	YR	Perfect Together	1:58.2h
6-30	La Paloma Elims (2yofp) (div.)	20,000	YR	Pretty Polly	1:59.2h
6-30	Landmark (2yocp) (div.)	7,312	Gosh	Banquet Table	2:01.3h
6-30	Landmark (2yocp) (div.)	7,312	Gosh	Could This B Magic	2:02h
6-30	Landmark (2yocp) (div.)	7,312	Gosh	Isle Of Maui	2:00.4h
6-30	Landmark (2yoct) (div.)	10,069	Gosh	Clovis Mon Ami	2:07.4h
6-30	Landmark (2yoct) (div.)	10,069	Gosh	Gift Box	2:07.4h
6-30	Landmark (2yofp) (div.)	4,441	Gosh	Another Halo	2:03.4h
6-30	Landmark (2yofp) (div.)	4,591	Gosh	Bossin' Around	2:07h
6-30	Landmark (2yofp) (div.)	4,592	Gosh	Classic Aussie	2:02.4h
6-30	Landmark (2yoft) (div.)	6,588	Gosh	Edwina Lobell	2:07.3h
6-30	Landmark (2yoft) (div.)	6,738	Gosh	Turkish Sweet	2:08h
6-30	Turtle Dove (3yofp) (div.)	110,715	RcR	Sea Biscuit	1:54.4f
6-30	Turtle Dove (3yofp) (div.)	112,715	RcR	Choice Yankee	1:54.3f
7-1	Hopeful Final (2yocp)	190,000	BR	He's Discreet	1:59.2h
7-1	Landmark (3yocp)	27,495	Gosh	Bon Nuit Karey	2:00h
7-1	Landmark (3yoct)	25,095	Gosh	Wolfs Gaon	2:05.1h
7-1	Landmark (3yofp) (div.)	6,726	Gosh	No Discussion	2:00.3h
7-1	Landmark (3yofp) (div.)	6,976	Gosh	Bradash Pilot	2:02.1h
7-1	Landmark (3yofp) (div.)	6,976	Gosh	Princess Silver	2:02.4h
7-1	Landmark (3yoft) (div.)	8,965	Gosh	Cabrera Lobell	2:02.2h
7-1	Landmark (3yoft) (div.)	8,965	Gosh	La Montagna	2:06.2h
7-1	North American Series (3&4yo Pace) (div.)	18,750	VD	San Andre, 4	1:55.4q
7-1	North American Series (3&4yo Pace) (div.)	18,750	VD	Total Control, 4	1:54.2q
7-3	Mac Farlane Memorial (3yoft)	75,000	HP	Miss Baltic	2:00.4f
7-6	Meadowlands Pace Elims (3yo Open Pace)(div.)	35,000	M	Beach Towel	1:52.3
7-6	Meadowlands Pace Elims (3yo Open Pace)(div.)	35,000	M	Jake And Elwood	1:53.1
7-6	Meadowlands Pace Elims (3yo Open Pace)(div.)	35,000	M	Scoot Outa Reach	1:53.2

CHRONICLES

Date	Event	Purse	Track	Winner	Time
7-7	Dexter Cup (3yo Open Trot)	$186,682	YR	Royal Troubador	1:58.3h
7-7	Driscoll Series Final (FFA Pace)	211,000	M	T K's Skipper	1:51.2
7-7	Founders Gold Cup (3yo Open Trot) (elim.)	41,850	VD	Crown Bones	2:00.1q
7-7	Founders Gold Cup (3yo Open Trot) (elim.)	41,850	VD	Star Mystic	1:58q
7-7	Founders Gold Cup (3yo Open Trot) (final)	56,400	VD	Star Mystic	1:57.1q
7-7	La Paloma Final (2yofp)	219,000	YR	Perfect Together	1:59.3h
7-7	Lady Maud (3yofp) (div.)	69,020	YR	Armbro Ilona	1:57.1h
7-7	Lady Maud (3yofp) (div.)	69,020	YR	Fiji Hanover	1:58.2h
7-7	Lady Suffolk (3yoft) (div.)	24,609	YR	Happy Diamonds	2:00.1h
7-7	Lady Suffolk (3yoft) (div.)	24,609	YR	L V Goldie	1:59.2h
7-7	Lady Suffolk (3yoft) (div.)	24,609	YR	Working Gal	2:00.2h
7-7	Monctonian (FFA Pace)	127,000	NBD	Skipper Forrest	1:53.2f
7-7	Sheppard Elims (2yocp) (div.)	30,000	YR	June's Baby	1:59.4h
7-7	Sheppard Elims (2yocp) (div.)	30,000	YR	Squire Gary	1:58.1h
7-7	Sheppard Elims (2yocp) (div.)	30,000	YR	Three Wizzards	1:58.3h
7-8	Hanover Filly Stake (3yoft) (div.)	19,041	RcR	Eternal Goddess	2:00.1f
7-8	Hanover Filly Stake (3yoft) (div.)	19,291	RcR	Nivea Hanover	2:00.1f
7-8	Jazzman (Open Trot) (div.)	43,800	BB	No Sex Please	1:55.4f
7-8	Jazzman (Open Trot) (div.)	44,300	BB	Texas Snazzy	1:58.1f
7-9	Roses Are Red Series (3&up F&M Pace) (div.)	20,000	GrR	Caesars Jackpot, 4	1:54.2f
7-9	Roses Are Red Series (3&up F&M Pace) (div.)	20,000	GrR	Madagascar Hanover,5	1:54.3f
7-9	Roses Are Red Series (3&up F&M Pace) (div.)	20,000	GrR	Rulers Chippie, 3	1:55.1f
7-10	Ville de Trois Rivieres Elims (2yocp) (div.)	10,566	TrRvs	Bombe Angus	2:01.3h
7-10	Ville de Trois Rivieres Elims (2yocp) (div.)	10,566	TrRvs	Bye Bye Angus	2:02.3h
7-10	Ville de Trois Rivieres Elims (2yocp) (div.)	10,566	TrRvs	Force Dix	2:02.3h
7-12	American-National (2yofp)	86,200	SPk	Start Dialing	1:59.3f
7-13	Meadowlands Pace Final (3yo Open Pace)	1,153,500	M	Beach Towel	1:52.2
7-14	Bronx Filly Pace (3yofp) (div.)	56,792	YR	Cataclysm ⁄	1:57.3h
7-14	Bronx Filly Pace (3yofp) (div.)	56,792	YR	Excited	1:58.1h
7-14	Hanover-Hempt (3yofp)	52,300	VD	Dear Dignity	1:57.2q
7-14	Hudson Filly Trot (3yof) (div.)	35,522	YR	Happy Diamonds	1:59.4h
7-14	Hudson Filly Trot (3yof) (div.)	35,522	YR	Kindava Hush	2:02h
7-14	Molson Series (3&up Open Pace) (div.)	83,250	GrR	Topnotcher	1:53.2f
7-14	Molson Series (3&up Open Pace) (div.)	84,750	GrR	Ticket To Heaven	1:53.1f
7-14	Sheppard Final (2yocp)	474,500	YR	June's Baby	1:58.2h
7-14	**Yonkers Trot** (3yo Open) (elim.)	**127,489**	**YR**	**Cheyenne Spur**	**1:58.3h**
7-14	**Yonkers Trot** (3yo Open) (elim.)	**127,489**	**YR**	**King Of The Sea**	**1:59.2h**
7-14	**Yonkers Trot** (3yo Open) (final)	**169,986**	**YR**	**Royal Troubador**	**1:59.2h**
7-15	Hanover Filly Stake (3yoft) (div.)	20,386	RcR	Choice Yankee	1:55.2f
7-15	Hanover Filly Stake (3yofp) (div.)	20,386	RcR	Fitness Flower	1:55f
7-15	Hanover-Hempt (2yocp) (div.)	12,500	VD	Interpretor	1:57.4q
7-15	Hanover-Hempt (2yocp) (div.)	12,500	VD	Mantese	1:57q
7-15	Hanover-Hempt (3yoft) (div.)	12,800	VD	Artsplace	1:57.3q
7-16	Roses Are Red Series (3&up F&M Pace) (div.)	20,000	GrR	L Dees Trish, 4	1:53.3f
7-16	Roses Are Red Series (3&up F&M Pace) (div.)	20,000	GrR	Rulers Chippie, 3	1:54.3f
7-17	Hanover-Hempt (2yoct) (div.)	12,100	VD	Chapman	2:01.4q
7-17	Hanover-Hempt (2yoct) (div.)	12,400	VD	Baltic Viking	2:02.3q
7-17	Hanover-Hempt (2yoct) (div.)	12,400	VD	Grundy's Mint	2:00.3q
7-17	Ville de Trois Rivieres Final (2yocp)	96,000	TrRvs	Bombe Angus	1:59.3h
7-18	Hanover-Hempt (2yoft) (div.)	8,600	VD	Jean Bi	1:59.1q
7-18	Hanover-Hempt (2yoft) (div.)	8,600	VD	Sweet Adeline	2:01.1q
7-18	Hanover-Hempt (2yoft) (div.)	8,900	VD	Eternal Flare	2:02.3q
7-18	Hanover-Hempt (2yoft) (div.)	8,900	VD	Frances Jet Boko	2:00.3q
7-18	Hanover-Hempt (2yoft) (div.)	8,900	VD	Meadow Heather	2:03.2q
7-19	Hanover-Hempt (2yofp)	33,000	VD	Janna Rose	1:57.4q
7-20	Hanover-Hempt (3yoft) (div.)	20,600	VD	Armbro Icon	2:00.3q
7-20	Hanover-Hempt (3yoft) (div.)	21,100	VD	Model Home	1:58q
7-20	Hanover-Hempt (3yoft) (div.)	21,600	VD	Me Maggie	1:59.1q
7-20	Pink Bonnet Elims (2yofp) (div.)	10,000	ScD	Gretzky	2:00f
7-20	Pink Bonnet Elims (2yofp) (div.)	10,000	ScD	Shy Devil	1:57.2f
7-20	Pink Bonnet Elims (2yofp) (div.)	10,000	ScD	Tamifay Bluegrass	1:59.1f
7-21	Art Rooney Mem. Elims (3yo Open Pace) (div.)	33,791	YR	Drop-Off	1:54.4h

CHRONICLES

Date	Event	Purse	Track	Winner	Time
7-21	Art Rooney Mem. Elims (3yo Open Pace) (div.)	$33,791	YR	Jake And Elwood	1:54.2h
7-21	Art Rooney Mem. Elims (3yo Open Pace) (div.)	33,791	YR	Scoot Outa Reach	1:54.1h
7-21	Beacon Course Elims (3yo Open Trot) (div.)	15,000	M	Crown Bones	1:57.1
7-21	Beacon Course Elims (3yo Open Trot) (div.)	15,000	M	Jeanne's Somolli	1:56
7-21	Courageous Lady (3yofp)	131,500	Nfld	Excited	1:56.2h
7-21	Molson Series (3&up Open Pace)	108,500	GrR	Night Colt, 7	1:52.3f
7-21	Motor City Elims (3yo Open Pace) (div.)	15,000	HP	Apaches Fame	1:54.3f
7-21	Motor City Elims (3yo Open Pace) (div.)	15,000	HP	Camluck	1:54.2f
7-21	Motor City Elims (3yo Open Pace) (div.)	15,000	HP	Global Assault	1:56.2f
7-21	Potomac (2yocp) (div.)	64,877	RcR	Deal Breaker	1:56.2f
7-21	Potomac (2yocp) (div.)	66,387	RcR	Cambest	1:55.2f
7-21	Potomac (2yocp) (div.)	66,387	RcR	Gigowatt	1:54.4f
7-21	Potomac (2yocp) (div.)	66,387	RcR	Razzle Dazzlem	1:56.1f
7-21	Potomac (2yocp) (div.)	66,387	RcR	Silky Stallone	1:56.1f
7-22	Hanover Colt Stake (3yoct)	19,633	RcR	Antwerp Hanover	1:57.3f
7-22	Hanover Colt Stake (3yoct)	19,633	RcR	Remus Hanover	1:56.4f
7-22	Juvenile Canadien Elims (2yocp) (div.)	20,000	BB	Happy Family	1:57.2f
7-22	Juvenile Canadien Elims (2yocp) (div.)	20,000	BB	Stand And Deliver	1:58f
7-23	de la Moisson Elims (3yofp) (div.)	25,000	BB	Dandy Promise	1:57.2f
7-23	de la Moisson Elims (3yofp) (div.)	25,000	BB	Fiji Hanover	1:58f
7-23	de la Moisson Elims (3yofp) (div.)	25,000	BB	Town Pro	1:55.1f
7-23	Roses Are Red Series Final (3&up F&M Pace)	125,000	GrR	Caesars Jackpot, 4	1:52.4f
7-24	Peter Haughton Memorial Elims (2yoct) (div.)	15,000	M	Charlie Ten Hitch	2:00.1
7-24	Peter Haughton Memorial Elims (2yoct) (div.)	15,000	M	Super Pleasure	1:59.4
7-24	Peter Haughton Memorial Elims (2yoct) (div.)	15,000	M	Tyrannosaurus Rex	1:59.1
7-25	Merrie Annabelle Elims (2yoft)	15,000	M	BJ's Cinderella	2:00
7-25	Merrie Annabelle Elims (2yoft)	15,000	M	Gutsy Lobell	2:00.2
7-25	Merrie Annabelle Elims (2yoft)	15,000	M	Santa Royal	2:00
7-27	Hanover Filly Stake (2yofp) (div.)	16,460	RcR	Heather Lane	1:57.3f
7-27	Hanover Filly Stake (2yofp) (div.)	16,460	RcR	Yankee Co-Ed	1:56.3f
7-27	Hanover Filly Stake (2yofp) (div.)	16,710	RcR	Perfect Together	1:56.2f
7-27	Niatross Elims (2yocp) (div.)	20,000	M	Die Laughing	1:55.3
7-27	Niatross Elims (2yocp) (div.)	20,000	M	June's Baby	1:55.4
7-27	Niatross Elims (2yocp) (div.)	20,000	M	Rashad Bay	1:56
7-27	Niatross Elims (2yocp) (div.)	20,000	M	Razzle Dazzlem	1:55.4
7-27	Niatross Elims (2yocp) (div.)	20,000	M	Thunderball	1:56.2
7-27	Pink Bonnet Final (2yofp)	115,000	ScD	Shy Devil	1:57.3f
7-28	Art Rooney Memorial Final (3yo Open Pace)	304,127	YR	Jake And Elwood	1:55h
7-28	Beacon Course Consolation (3yo Open Trot)	15,000	M	Incredible D J	1:56.1
7-28	Beacon Course Final (3yo Open Trot)	401,500	M	Embassy Lobell	1:56.3
7-28	Molson Canadian Pacing Derby (3&up Open)	265,250	GrR	Topnotcher	1:52.2f
7-28	Motor City Final (3yo Open Pace)	75,000	HP	Apaches Fame	1:54f
7-28	Thomas P. Gaines Mem. (3yo Open Pace)(elim.)	36,900	VD	Brando Hanover	1:53.3q
7-28	Thomas P. Gaines Mem. (3yo Open Pace)(elim.)	36,900	VD	Orange Sovereign	1:55.1q
7-28	Thomas P. Gaines Mem. (3yo Open Pace)(elim.)	36,900	VD	Till We Meet Again	1:54.4q
7-28	Thomas P. Gaines Mem. (3yo Open Pace)(final)	73,800	VD	Till We Meet AGain	1:53.3q
7-29	Frank Ryan Memorial (Aged Pacers)	68,500	RidC	Northland Salute	1:53.2f
7-29	Hanover Filly Stake (2yoft) (div.)	12,805	RcR	Frances Jet Boko	2:02.2f
7-29	Hanover Filly Stake (2yoft) (div.)	12,805	RcR	Jean Bi	2:02.3f
7-29	Hanover Filly Stake (2yoft) (div.)	13,055	RcR	Mal Hana Kaari	2:04.1f
7-29	Hanover Filly Stake (2yoft) (div.)	13,055	RcR	Seductive Lass	2:05f
7-29	Juvenile Canadien Final (2yocp)	79,900	BB	Stand And Deliver	1:56.2f
7-29	North American Series (3&4yo Pace)	25,000	BR	Power Swing, 4	1:57.2h
7-29	Stars & Stripes (Inv. Trot)	35,000	YR	Kit Lobell	1:57.2h
7-30	de la Moisson Final (3yofp)	102,000	BB	Town Pro	1:53.2f
7-30	Nat Rat ('88 & '89 Hambletonian Elig. Trot)	112,000	M	Alfresco	1:57
7-31	Peter Haughton Memorial Consolation (2yoct)	50,000	M	Carry The Message	2:02.2
7-31	Peter Haughton Memorial Final (2yoct)	609,250	M	Charlie Ten Hitch	2:00.2
8-1	Hambletonian Amateur Drivers (Open Trot)	10,000	M	Nettie M	1:58.4
8-1	Merrie Annabelle Consolation (2yoft)	35,000	M	Sherbie's Lady	1:59.3
8-1	Merrie Annabelle Final (2yoft)	464,750	M	Santa Royal	1:58.1
8-2	Countess Adios (2yofp) (div.)	79,000	M	Laugh Line	1:56.3

CHRONICLES

8-2	Countess Adios (2yofp) (div.)	$80,000	M	Falcon's Secret	1:56.4
8-2	Countess Adios (2yofp) (div.)	80,000	M	Miss Easy	1:54
8-2	Townsend Ackerman ('90 Hambo Eligibles)	35,000	M	Pesach	1:58
8-3	Hambletonian Oaks (3yoft) (1st heat)	0	M	Happy Diamonds	1:56.3
8-3	Hambletonian Oaks (3yoft) (1st heat)	0	M	Working Gal	1:58
8-3	Hambletonian Oaks (3yoft) (2nd Heat)	0	M	Delphi's Lobell	1:56
8-3	Hambletonian Oaks (3yoft) (race-off)	441,555	M	Working Gal	1:58.1
8-3	Niatross Final (2yocp)	365,600	M	Die Laughing	1:54.2
8-3	Oliver Wendell Holmes (3yocp) (elim.)	64,500	M	In The Pocket	1:51.3
8-3	Oliver Wendell Holmes (3yocp) (elim.)	64,500	M	Mark Johnathan	1:52.3
8-3	Oliver Wendell Holmes (3yocp) (final)	129,000	M	Brando Hanover	1:51.3
8-4	**Hambletonian** (3yo Open Trot) (1st heat)	**0**	**M**	**Embassy Lobell**	**1:56.1**
8-4	**Hambletonian** (3yo Open Trot) (1st heat)	**0**	**M**	**Harmonious**	**1:55.1**
8-4	**Hambletonian** (3yo Open Trot) (2nd heat)	**1,346,000**	**M**	**Harmonious**	**1:54.1**
8-4	North American Series (3&4yo Pace)	25,000	YR	San Andre, 4	1:55.4h
8-4	Tarport Hap (3yofp) (div.)	56,335	M	Bruce's Lady	1:53.3
8-4	Tarport Hap (3yofp) (div.)	56,335	M	Town Pro	1:51.4
8-4	Tarport Hap (3yofp) (div.)	57,335	M	Tambourine	1:54.1
8-5	International Trot (Inv. -1-1/4 mi.)	450,000	YR	Reve d'Udon	2:28.3h
8-5	Prix de l'Avenir (2yocp) (div.)	146,125	BB	Jackpot Raider	1:57f
8-5	Prix de l'Avenir (2yocp) (div.)	146,125	BB	Nuke Of Earl	1:59.1f
8-5	Prix de l'Avenir (2yocp) (div.)	146,125	BB	Shark Almahurst +	TDis
8-5	Prix de l'Avenir (2yocp) (div.)	146,125	BB	Silky Stallone	1:57.4f
8-6	Boardwalk Elims (3yofp) (div.)	15,000	GrR	Fiji Hanover	1:57.1f
8-6	Boardwalk Elims (3yofp) (div.)	15,000	GrR	Lady Silver	1:56.2f
8-7	Arden Downs (2yoft) (div.)	16,494	Mea	Cookout	2:02.4f
8-7	Arden Downs (2yoft) (div.)	16,494	Mea	Granny Smith	2:03f
8-7	Arden Downs (2yoft) (div.)	16,494	Mea	Malahana Kaari	2:00.3f
8-7	Arden Downs (2yoft) (div.)	16,494	Mea	T-Ball	2:01.4f
8-8	Arden Downs (2yoct) (div.)	17,057	Mea	Beaurina	2:01.1f
8-8	Arden Downs (2yoct) (div.)	17,057	Mea	Chapman	2:02.4f
8-8	Arden Downs (2yoct) (div.)	17,057	Mea	Dickerson	2:01.2f
8-8	Arden Downs (2yoct) (div.)	17,457	Mea	Super Pleasure	1:59.3f
8-8	Arden Downs (2yofp) (div.)	22,375	Mea	In Your Dreams	1:57.4f
8-8	Arden Downs (2yofp) (div.)	22,375	Mea	Perfect Together	1:56.1f
8-8	Arden Downs (2yofp) (div.)	22,375	Mea	TLC Mindale	1:57.3f
8-8	Arden Downs (2yofp) (div.)	22,775	Mea	Eicarls Carlene	1:59f
8-9	Arden Downs (2yocp) (div.)	23,675	Mea	Artsplace	1:55.3f
8-9	Arden Downs (2yocp) (div.)	23,675	Mea	Gold Glover	1:56.4f
8-9	Arden Downs (2yocp) (div.)	23,675	Mea	Meadow Lucas	1:58.2f
8-9	Arden Downs (2yocp) (div.)	23,675	Mea	The Other Guy	1:55.1f
8-9	Sweetheart Elims (2yofp) (div.)	15,000	M	Miss Easy	1:54.1
8-9	Sweetheart Elims (2yofp) (div.)	15,000	M	Yankee Co-ed	1:55.2
8-10	Arden Downs (3yoct) (div.)	30,377	Mea	Castleton Magic	1:59.4f
8-10	Arden Downs (3yoct) (div.)	30,727	Mea	Wolfs Degel	1:59.2f
8-10	Arden Downs (3yoft) (div.)	20,708	Mea	Me Maggie	1:57.2f
8-10	Arden Downs (3yoft) (div.)	21,058	Mea	Caspian	1:58.2f
8-10	Arden Downs (3yoft) (div.)	21,058	Mea	Eternal Goddess	2:00.3f
8-10	Kentucky Standardbred (2yoft) (div.)	96,250	RcR	Santa Royal	1:59.4f
8-10	Kentucky Standardbred (2yoft) (div.)	97,500	RcR	Frances Jet Boko	2:01.2f
8-10	Woodrow Wilson Elims (2yo Open Pace) (div.)	25,000	M	Cambest	1:55
8-10	Woodrow Wilson Elims (2yo Open Pace) (div.)	25,000	M	June's Baby	1:54.3
8-10	Woodrow Wilson Elims (2yo Open Pace) (div.)	25,000	M	Stormin Jesse	1:54.2
8-10	Woodrow Wilson Elims (2yo Open Pace) (div.)	25,000	M	Three Wizzards	1:54
8-10	Woodrow Wilson Elims (2yo Open Pace) (div.)	25,000	M	Tooter Scooter	1:54.2
8-11	Adioo Volo (3yofp) (div.)	47,614	Mea	Lady Genius	1:56f
8-11	Adioo Volo (3yofp) (div.)	48,614	Mea	Lady Dynamo	1:56.2f
8-11	Adioo Volo (3yofp) (div.)	48,614	Mea	Yankee Goddess	1:55f
8-11	Adios (3yo Open Pace) (elim.)	65,757	Mea	In The Pocket	1:50.4f
8-11	Adios (3yo Open Pace) (elim.)	65,757	Mea	King Gypsy	1:53f
8-11	Adios (3yo Open Pace) (elim.)	65,757	Mea	Spirited Style	1:52.4f
8-11	Adios (3yo Open Pace) (final)	295,905	Mea	Beach Towel	1:51.4f

CHRONICLES

Date	Event	Purse	Track	Winner	Time
8-11	Mistletoe Shalee Elims (3yofp) (div.)	$25,000	M	Choice Yankee	1:54.1
8-11	Mistletoe Shalee Elims (3yofp) (div.)	25,000	M	Town Pro	1:52.3
8-11	U.S. Pacing Championships (Open Aged)	75,000	YR	Dorunrun Bluegrass	1:56h
8-12	Nat Christie Memorial (3yo Open Pace)(elim.)	30,000	Clgy	Atlas Hanover	1:56.4f
8-12	Nat Christie Memorial (3yo Open Pace)(elim.)	30,000	Clgy	Center Strip	1:56.3f
8-12	Nat Christie Memorial (3yo Open Pace)(final)	90,000	Clgy	Counterfeit Crown	1:55.1f
8-13	Boardwalk Final (3yofp)	91,700	GrR	Smiling Rebecca	1:55f
8-15	The Castleton (2yofp) (1st heat)	31,000	Spr	Shady Daisy	1:54.4
8-15	The Castleton (2yofp) (2nd heat)	31,000	Spr	Shady Daisy	1:56.4
8-15	The Castleton (2yoft) (elim.)	18,600	Spr	Cookout	2:00.1
8-15	The Castleton (2yoft) (elim.)	18,600	Spr	Eternal Flare	2:01.2
8-15	The Castleton (2yoft) (final)	24,800	Spr	Cookout	2:00.1
8-15	The Greyhound (2yo Open Trot) (elim.)	33,000	Spr	Chapman	2:03.1
8-15	The Greyhound (2yo Open Trot) (elim.)	33,000	Spr	Torsion	2:01.1
8-15	The Greyhound (2yo Open Trot) (final)	44,000	Spr	Dickerson	1:58.1
8-15	The Little Pat (2yo Open Pace) (elim.)	22,200	Spr	Mantese	1:56.3
8-15	The Little Pat (2yo Open Pace) (elim.)	22,200	Spr	Mr Gourmet	1:56
8-15	The Little Pat (2yo Open Pace) (final)	29,600	Spr	Mantese	1:53.4
8-16	Review Stake (3yo Open Pace) (1st heat)	27,000	Spr	Happy Hoosier	1:55.2
8-16	Review Stake (3yo Open Pace) (2nd heat)	27,000	Spr	Happy Hoosier	1:55.2
8-16	The Castleton (3yofp) (1st heat)	25,000	Spr	Lady Genius	1:53.2
8-16	The Castleton (3yofp) (2nd heat)	25,000	Spr	Lady Genius	1:54.1
8-16	The Castleton (3yoft) (1st heat)	27,500	Spr	Model Home	1:55.4
8-16	The Castleton (3yoft) (2nd heat)	27,500	Spr	Model Home	1:58.1
8-17	Mistletoe Shalee Final (3yofp)	425,250	M	Choice Yankee	1:52.4
8-17	Sweetheart Consolation (2yofp)	50,000	M	Paper Caper	1:57
8-17	Sweetheart Final (2yofp)	766,000	M	Miss Easy	1:52.3
8-17	The Alexander Mem. (3yo Trot) (1st heat)	55,000	Spr	Super Arnie	1:55
8-17	The Alexander Mem. (3yo Trot) (2nd heat)	55,000	Spr	Super Arnie	1:54.1
8-17	U.S. Pacing Championships (FFA)	75,000	M	T K's Skipper	1:50.3
8-17	Woodrow Wilson Consol. (2yo Open Pace)	20,000	M	Artie's Best	1:55.2
8-17	Woodrow Wilson Consol. (2yo Open Pace)	50,000	M	Razzle Dazzlem	1:53.3
8-17	Woodrow Wilson Final (2yo Open Pace)	1,043,500	M	Die Laughing	1:52.1
8-18	Cane Pace Prep (3yo Open Pace)	35,000	YR	Spirited Style	1:55.3h
8-18	Gold Cup And Saucer (FFA Inv. Pace)	20,000	Chrtn	Tigerbird	1:58h
8-18	Maple Leaf Trot (3yo&up) (elim.)	58,650	GrR	Florida Jewel	1:58.4f
8-18	Maple Leaf Trot (3yo&up) (elim.)	58,650	GrR	No Sex Please	1:57f
8-18	Maple Leaf Trot (3yo&up) (final)	175,950	GrR	No Sex Please	1:57f
8-19	North American Series (3&4yo Pace)	25,000	RidC	Total Control, 4	1:54.1f
8-19	Prix d'Ete (3yocp) (elim.)	199,050	BB	Apaches Fame	1:53.2f
8-19	Prix d'Ete (3yocp) (elim.)	199,050	BB	Beach Towel	1:53.1f
8-19	Prix d'Ete (3yocp) (final)	265,400	BB	Beach Towel	1:53.1f
8-19	Zweig Memorial (3yo Open Trot) (div.)	75,300	Sycs	Embassy Lobell	1:57.3
8-19	Zweig Memorial (3yo Open Trot) (div.)	75,300	Sycs	Harmonious	1:57.1
8-19	Zweig Memorial (3yo Open Trot) (div.)	75,300	Sycs	Jeanne's Somolli	1:58.2
8-19	Zweig Memorial Filly Trot (3yo)	45,000	Sycs	Eternal Goddess	1:59.3
8-23	Hoosier Futurity (2yocp) (1st heat)	12,388	Ind	Endowment	1:57
8-23	Hoosier Futurity (2yocp) (2nd heat)	12,388	Ind	Endowment	1:57.4
8-23	Hoosier Futurity (2yofp) (elim.)	7,961	Ind	Gretzky	1:57
8-23	Hoosier Futurity (2yofp) (elim.)	7,961	Ind	Shady Daisy	1:55.2
8-23	Hoosier Futurity (2yofp) (final)	10,615	Ind	Start Dialing	1:55.2
8-23	Horseman Futurity (3yofp) (1st heat)	9,187	Ind	Touch Of Silk	1:55.2
8-23	Horseman Futurity (3yofp) (2nd heat)	9,187	Ind	Touch Of Silk	1:54.2
8-24	Hoosier Futurity (2yoft) (elim.)	7,070	Ind	A-Treat	2:00
8-24	Hoosier Futurity (2yoft) (elim.)	7,070	Ind	Granny Smith	2:01.1
8-24	Hoosier Futurity (2yoft) (final)	9,427	Ind	A-Treat	2:00
8-24	Horseman Futurity (3yoft) (1st heat)	11,105	Ind	Perfect Point	1:56.4
8-24	Horseman Futurity (3yoft) (2nd heat)	11,105	Ind	Kindava Hush	1:57.1
8-24	Horseman Stake (2yo Open Trot) (1st heat)	25,545	Ind	Chysta's Best	1:58.2
8-24	Horseman Stake (2yo Open Trot) (2nd heat)	25,545	Ind	Crysta's Best	1:59
8-24	Provenzano Memorial Elims (Open Trot) (div.)	10,000	Btva	Donikash	1:59.1h
8-24	Provenzano Memorial Elims (Open Trot) (div.)	10,000	Btva	Kit Lobell	1:58.2h

CHRONICLES

Date	Race	Purse	Track	Winner	Time
8-24	Provenzano Memorial Elims (Open Trot) (div.)	$10,000	Btva	Peach Pit	1:58.2h
8-24	Provenzano Memorial Elims (Open Trot) (div.)	10,000	Btva	Super Speedy	2:00h
8-25	**Cane Pace** (3yo Open Pace) (elim.)	**145,965**	YR	**C K S**	**1:55.3h**
8-25	**Cane Pace** (3yo Open Pace) (elim.)	**145,965**	YR	**Sea The USA**	**1:53.4h**
8-25	**Cane Pace** (3yo Open Pace) (final)	**194,620**	YR	**Jake And Elwood**	**1:55.1h**
8-25	Fan Hanover Elims (3yofp) (div.)	20,000	GrR	B The Wind	1:56.3f
8-25	Fan Hanover Elims (3yofp) (div.)	20,000	GrR	Town Pro	1:55.1f
8-25	Fox Stake (2yo Open Pace) (1st heat)	51,681	Ind	Deal Direct	1:51.4
8-25	Fox Stake (2yo Open Pace) (2nd heat)	51,681	Ind	Deal Direct	1:52.4
8-25	Garden State Stake (2yo Open Pace) (div.)	89,451	Fhld	Cambest	1:56.1h
8-25	Garden State Stake (2yo Open Pace) (div.)	89,451	Fhld	Nuclear Legacy	1:57.3h
8-25	Garden State Stake (2yo Open Pace) (div.)	92,451	Fhld	Shark Almahurst	1:56.4h
8-25	Garden State Stake (2yo Open Pace) (div.)	92,451	Fhld	Three Wizzards	1:56h
8-25	Hoosier Futurity (2yoct) (1st heat)	10,738	Ind	Primrose Lane	2:01.1
8-25	Hoosier Futurity (2yoct) (2nd heat)	10,738	Ind	Ten Pound Bass	2:01.2
8-25	Horseman Futurity (3yo Open Trot) (1st heat)	18,516	Ind	Incredible D J	1:55.3
8-25	Horseman Futurity (3yo Open Trot) (2nd heat)	18,516	Ind	Incredible D J	1:55.4
8-25	Horseman Futurity (3yocp) (1st heat)	13,979	Ind	Fortysix Cylinders	1:53.1
8-25	Horseman Futurity (3yocp) (2nd heat)	13,979	Ind	Fortysix Cylinders	1:53
8-25	Mac Farlane Memorial (3yo Open Trot)	126,200	HP	Jeanne's Somolli	1:59.1f
8-25	U.S. Pacing Championships (Aged)	146,000	SPk	Dorunrun Bluegrass	1:54f
8-26	Confederation Cup (3yo Open Pace) (elim.)	85,250	FlmD	Center Strip	1:54.3f
8-26	Confederation Cup (3yo Open Pace) (elim.)	85,250	FlmD	No Taste	1:54.2f
8-26	Confederation Cup (3yo Open Pace) (final)	170,500	FlmD	Apaches Fame	1:55f
8-26	Hanover Colt Stake (2yocp) (div.)	13,611	RcR	Front View	1:58.1h
8-26	Hanover Colt Stake (2yocp) (div.)	13,611	RcR	Hahn Hanover	1:55.3f
8-26	Hanover Colt Stake (2yocp) (div.)	13,611	RcR	Hello Almahurst	1:56.3f
8-26	Hanover Colt Stake (2yocp) (div.)	13,611	RcR	Thunderball	1:56.2f
8-30	Hayes Memorial (3yo Open Pace) (1st heat)	25,200	DuQ	Beach Towel	1:50
8-30	Hayes Memorial (3yo Open Pace) (2nd heat)	25,200	DuQ	Happy Hoosier	1:55
8-30	Hayes Memorial (3yofp)	35,650	DuQ	Tip 'N Tax	1:53
8-31	Hayes Memorial (2yofp) (1st heat)	28,500	DuQ	Gretzky	1:56.1
8-31	Hayes Memorial (2yofp) (2nd heat)	28,500	DuQ	Gretzky	1:55.3
8-31	The Castleton (2yoft) (1st heat)	27,500	DuQ	Hopeland Lady	1:59.3
8-31	The Castleton (2yoft) (2nd heat)	27,500	DuQ	A-Treat	1:58.2
8-31	World Filly Trotting Derby (3yo) (1st heat)	0	DuQ	Model Home	1:55.3
8-31	World Filly Trotting Derby (3yo) (2nd heat)	0	DuQ	Happy Diamonds	1:55.1
8-31	World Filly Trotting Derby (3yo) (race-off)	130,000	DuQ	Happy Diamonds	2:04.3
9-1	American-National (Aged Pace)	148,000	SPk	Keystone Raider	1:53.2f
9-1	Fan Hanover Final (3yofp)	191,100	GrR	Town Pro	1:53.1f
9-1	Hayes Memorial (2yocp) (1st heat)	36,250	DuQ	Mr Tuff Guy	1:55.1
9-1	Hayes Memorial (2yocp) (2nd heat)	36,250	DuQ	Rebelator	1:55.4
9-1	James B. Dancer Mem. (3yo Open Pace) (elim.)	113,784	Fhld	In The Pocket	1:55h
9-1	James B. Dancer Mem. (3yo Open Pace) (elim.)	113,784	Fhld	Road Machine	1:55h
9-1	James B. Dancer Mem. (3yo Open Pace) (final)	151,712	Fhld	Road Machine	1:54.4h
9-1	Kentucky Pacing Derby Prep (2yo Open)	5,000	LouD	Tooter Scooter	1:54.1h
9-1	Lady Baltimore (2yofp) (div.)	75,834	RcR	Miss Easy	1:55.4f
9-1	Lady Baltimore (2yofp) (div.)	77,083	RcR	R M Gee	1:57.3f
9-1	Lady Baltimore (2yofp) (div.)	77,083	RcR	Yankee Co-ed	1:54.4f
9-1	Provenzano Memorial Final (Open Trot)	50,000	Btva	Shawland Magic	1:58.2h
9-1	The Castleton Stake (2yoct) (1st heat)	32,300	DuQ	Torsion	1:59.2
9-1	The Castleton Stake (2yoct) (2nd heat)	32,300	DuQ	Dickerson	1:59.2
9-1	World Trotting Derby (3yo Open) (1st heat)	0	DuQ	Super Arnie	1:54.3
9-1	World Trotting Derby (3yo Open) (2nd heat)	0	DuQ	Harmonious	1:53.2
9-1	World Trotting Derby (3yo Open) (race-off)	600,000	DuQ	Harmonious	2:04.3
9-2	Champlain Stakes (2yo Open Pace) (div.)	70,000	Moh	Deal Direct	1:56f
9-2	Champlain Stakes (2yo Open Pace) (div.)	70,000	Moh	Happy Family	1:56.2f
9-2	Champlain Stakes (2yo Open Pace) (div.)	70,000	Moh	Mantese	1:57f
9-2	Champlain Stakes (2yo Open Pace) (div.)	70,000	Moh	Prudhomme	1:56.2f
9-2	Champlain Stakes (2yo Open Pace) (div.)	70,000	Moh	Silky Stallone	1:55.2f
9-2	President's Pace (FFA)	60,000	Scar	Prince Ebony	1:54f
9-2	Simcoe Stakes (3yo Open Pace) (div.)	111,707	Moh	Cam's Venture	1:54.2f

CHRONICLES

Date	Race	Purse	Track	Winner	Time
9-2	Simcoe Stakes (3yo Open Pace) (div.)	$113,708	Moh	Global Assault	1:54.1f
9-3	Helen Dancer Memorial (3yofp) (div.)	107,068	Fhld	Excited	1:57.3h
9-3	Helen Dancer Memorial (3yofp) (div.)	107,068	Fhld	It's Sunny	1:57.4h
9-3	North American Ser. Final (3&4yo Open Pace)	67,000	Btva	San Andre, 4	1:56h
9-3	Simcoe Stakes (3yoft) (div.)	105,612	Moh	Ashley Jane	2:00.1f
9-3	Simcoe Stakes (3yoft) (div.)	107,613	Moh	Armbro Icon	1:59.3f
9-4	Champlain Stakes (2yoft)	221,070	Moh	Frances Jet Boko	2:02f
9-7	Champlain Stakes (2yofp) (div.)	83,690	Moh	Falcon's Secret	1:57.1f
9-7	Champlain Stakes (2yofp) (div.)	83,690	Moh	Laugh Line	1:56.3f
9-7	Champlain Stakes (2yofp) (div.)	85,690	Moh	Jollie Dame	1:58.2f
9-7	Simcoe Stakes (3yo Open Trot) (div.)	111,707	Moh	Osgood Hanover	2:01.1f
9-7	Simcoe Stakes (3yo Open Trot) (div.)	111,708	Moh	Roughing It	2:00.1f
9-8	American Pacing Classic (FFA)	35,000	LA	Riviera Hanover	1:55f
9-8	Champlain Stakes (2yo Open Trot) (div.)	131,515	Moh	(DH) Crimson Lobell	2:04f
				(DH) Grundy's Mint	2:04f
9-8	Champlain Stakes (2yo Open Trot) (div.)	133,515	Moh	Super Pleasure	2:01.2f
9-8	Hanover Stake (Aged Pace)	22,865	RcR	Resonator	1:53.1f
9-8	Kentucky Pacing Derby Final (2yo Open)	379,553	LouD	Tooter Scooter	1:57h
9-8	Kentucky Standardbred (2yofp) (div.)	126,650	RcR	Unreachable	1:57.1f
9-8	Kentucky Standardbred (2yofp) (div.)	127,650	RcR	Miss Easy	1:55f
9-8	Little Brown Jug Preview (3yo Pace) (div.)	68,000	ScD	Apaches Fame	1:53.4f
9-8	Little Brown Jug Preview (3yo Pace) (div.)	68,000	ScD	Global Assault	1:53f
9-8	Little Brown Jug Preview (3yo Pace) (div.)	70,000	ScD	Brando Hanover	1:54.2f
9-8	**Messenger Stakes** (3yo Open Pace) (elim.)	**66,656**	**RcR**	**In The Pocket**	**1:53.4f**
9-8	**Messenger Stakes** (3yo Open Pace) (elim.)	**66,656**	**RcR**	**Kiev Hanover**	**1:53f**
9-8	**Messenger Stakes** (3yo Open Pace) (final)	**311,059**	**RcR**	**Jake And Elwood**	**1:52.3f**
9-8	Nadia Lobell Elims (3yofp) (div.)	15,000	GSP	Crafty Caper	1:54.4
9-8	Nadia Lobell Elims (3yofp) (div.)	15,000	GSP	Token Gesture	1:55.2
9-8	Simcoe Stakes (3yofp) (div.)	109,612	Moh	Town Pro	1:54.4f
9-8	Simcoe Stakes (3yofp) (div.)	109,613	Moh	Jonvik Castle	1:56.2f
9-9	Des Smith Classic (Aged Pace)	76,000	RidC	Topnotcher	1:55f
9-9	Nassagaweya (2yo Open Pace) (div.)	69,650	Moh	Artsplace	1:55f
9-9	Nassagaweya (2yo Open Pace) (div.)	69,650	Moh	Shipps Commander	1:56.2f
9-9	Nassagaweya (2yo Open Pace) (div.)	71,150	Moh	Happy Family	1:56.1f
9-9	Nassagaweya (2yo Open Pace) (div.)	71,150	Moh	June's Baby	1:55.3f
9-10	Maud S (3yoft)	38,850	Nfld	Aspiring Lass	2:00.2h
9-10	Rainy Day Sweepstakes (2yoct)	37,500	Nfld	Taborizer	2:03h
9-10	Stephen Phillips Memorial (2yofp) (div.)	28,500	Nfld	Tally Almahurst	2:00.1h
9-10	Stephen Phillips Memorial (2yofp) (div.)	29,250	Nfld	Goalie Jess	1:57.1h
9-11	American-National (2yoct) (div.)	47,500	SPk	Anders Crown	2:02.2f
9-11	American-National (2yoct) (div.)	47,500	SPk	Square Rigger	2:02.2f
9-12	American-National (2yoft)	92,600	SPk	Jean Bi	2:00.4f
9-12	Col. Wm. Edwards Memorial (3yoct) (div.)	22,300	Nfld	Princely Fellow	2:00.4h
9-12	Col. Wm. Edwards Memorial (3yoct) (div.)	23,300	Nfld	Royal Cold	2:01h
9-12	Forest City Stakes (2yocp) (div.)	28,800	Nfld	Moravian Hanover	1:58.3h
9-12	Forest City Stakes (2yocp) (div.)	29,500	Nfld	Alfalad	1:58.4h
9-12	H.K. Devereux Memorial (2yoft)	38,400	Nfld	Shezatrotnmachine	2:02.4h
9-12	North Randall Park (3yofp)	36,350	Nfld	Touch Of Silk	1:58.3h
9-14	Bret Hanover (3yocp)	39,100	Nfld	Kiev Hanover	1:57h
9-14	Hanover Colt Stake (2yoct) (div.)	14,024	RcR	Dontellmenomore	1:59.1f
9-14	Hanover Colt Stake (2yoct) (div.)	14,274	RcR	Anabolic Ben	2:01.2f
9-14	Hanover Colt Stake (2yoct) (div.)	14,274	RcR	UConn Don	2:01.2f
9-14	Mac Farlane Memorial (3yo Open Pace) (div.)	76,255	HP	Brando Hanover	1:57.2f
9-14	Mac Farlane Memorial (3yo Open Pace) (div.)	76,255	HP	Camluck	1:56.3f
9-15	American Pacing Classic (FFA)	35,000	LA	T K's Skipper	1:52.3f
9-15	Metro Stakes Elims (2yo Open Pace) (div.)	40,000	Moh	Artsplace	1:54.3f
9-15	Metro Stakes Elims (2yo Open Pace) (div.)	40,000	Moh	June's Baby	1:54.1f
9-15	Metro Stakes Elims (2yo Open Pace) (div.)	40,000	Moh	Silky Stallone	1:55.4f
9-15	Nadia Lobell Final (3yofp)	220,000	GSP	Crafty Caper	1:53.4
9-16	Campbellville (2yo Open Trot) (div.)	75,500	Moh	Tag Team	2:01.4f
9-16	Campbellville (2yo Open Trot) (div.)	77,000	Moh	Anders Crown	2:03f
9-16	Senior Jug (4&5yo Open Pace)	35,500	Dela	Casino Cowboy	1:54.3h

CHRONICLES

Date	Race	Purse	Track	Winner	Time
9-16	Senior Jugette (4&5yo Pacing Mares)	$25,000	Dela	(Did not fill)	
9-18	Standardbred (2yo Open Trot) (1st heat)	26,085	Dela	Dickerson	2:06.1h
9-18	Standardbred (2yo Open Trot) (2nd heat)	26,085	Dela	Grundy's Mint	1:59.1h
9-18	Standardbred (2yoft) (1st heat)	25,736	Dela	Frances Jet Boko	1:59.4h
9-18	Standardbred (2yoft) (2nd heat)	25,736	Dela	Frances Jet Boko	1:59.3h
9-20	Buckette (3yoft) (div.)	36,255	Dela	Our First	1:57.3h
9-20	Buckette (3yoft) (div.)	36,255	Dela	Working Gal	1:59.3h
9-20	**Little Brown Jug** (3yo Open Pace) (1st heat)	**56,233**	**Dela**	**Beach Towel**	**1:54h**
9-20	**Little Brown Jug** (3yo Open Pace) (1st heat)	**56,233**	**Dela**	**In The Pocket**	**1:54.3h**
9-20	**Little Brown Jug** (3yo Open Pace) (1st heat)	**56,233**	**Dela**	**Kiev Hanover**	**1:55.2h**
9-20	**Little Brown Jug** (3yo Open Pace) (2nd heat)	**299,910**	**Dela**	**Beach Towel**	**1:53.3h**
9-20	Standardbred (2yo Open Pace) (div.)	32,186	Dela	Deal Breaker	1:56.4h
9-20	Standardbred (2yo Open Pace) (div.)	32,186	Dela	W R H	1:54.1h
9-21	American-National (2yocp) (div.)	55,000	SPk	Interpretor	1:56.3f
9-21	American-National (2yocp) (div.)	55,000	SPk	Mantese	1:55.1f
9-21	Jugette (3yofp) (1st heat)	36,000	Dela	Instant Rebate	1:55.4h
9-21	Jugette (3yofp) (1st heat)	36,000	Dela	Lady Genius	1:55.2h
9-21	Jugette (3yofp) (2nd heat)	128,000	Dela	Lady Genius	1:55.3h
9-21	Old Oaken Bucket (3yo Open Trot) (1st heat)	20,968	Dela	Meadowbranch Eddy	2:00h
9-21	Old Oaken Bucket (3yo Open Trot) (1st heat)	20,968	Dela	Riptide Hanover	2:00.1h
9-21	Old Oaken Bucket (3yo Open Trot) (2nd heat)	62,904	Dela	Lender Hanover	1:59.1h
9-21	Old Oaken Bucket (3yo Open Trot) (race-off)	20,968	Dela	Lender Hanover	2:02.3h
9-21	Walnut Hall (2yofp)	57,973	Dela	Start Dialing	1:57.2h
9-22	American Pacing Classic (FFA)	35,000	LA	T K's Skipper	1:52.2f
9-22	Metro Stakes Final (2yo Open Pace)	797,400	Moh	Artsplace	1:53.4f
9-22	Molly Pitcher (2yofp) (div.)	60,579	Fhld	Cams Exotic	1:57.3h
9-22	Molly Pitcher (2yofp) (div.)	60,579	Fhld	Sunraycer	1:58.2h
9-22	Molly Pitcher (2yofp) (div.)	62,079	Fhld	Lexie	1:57.2h
9-22	Northlands Filly Stake (3yofp)	82,090	Edm	Tylers Royalty	1:55.4f
9-23	Mohawk Gold Cup Elims (3&up Open Pace)	30,000	Moh	Topnotcher	1:53.4f
9-24	Charles Smith Memorial Final (3yoft)	109,400	Fhld	Caspian	1:59.1h
9-25	Bluegrass (2yofp) (elim.)	29,775	Lex	Maytown Hanover	1:56.3
9-25	Bluegrass (2yofp) (elim.)	29,775	Lex	Miss Easy	1:51.2
9-25	Bluegrass (2yofp) (final)	39,700	Lex	Shady Daisy	1:55.4
9-26	American-National (Aged Trot) (div.)	40,000	SPk	Kit Lobell	1:58.4f
9-26	American-National (Aged Trot) (div.)	40,000	SPk	Peach Pit	1:58.3f
9-26	Bluegrass (2yoft) (elim.)	31,189	Lex	Frances Jet Boko	1:58.2
9-26	Bluegrass (2yoft) (elim.)	32,189	Lex	Armbro Jacuzzi	1:58.1
9-26	Bluegrass (2yoft) (final)	42,252	Lex	Frances Jet Boko	1:58.2
9-27	Bluegrass (2yoct) (elim.)	31,387	Lex	Carry The Message	1:57.1
9-27	Bluegrass (2yoct) (elim.)	32,387	Lex	Honkin Hanover	1:58.1
9-27	Bluegrass (2yoct) (final)	42,516	Lex	Grundy's Mint	1:57.1
9-27	Bluegrass (3yofp)	96,590	Lex	Delinquent Account	1:53.3
9-28	Bluegrass (3yoct) (elim.)	35,491	Lex	I'm Impeccable	1:54.2
9-28	Bluegrass (3yoct) (elim.)	36,491	Lex	Columnist	1:55.1
9-28	Bluegrass (3yoct) (final)	47,988	Lex	Embassy Lobell	1:54.4
9-28	Bluegrass (3yoft) (elim.)	32,244	Lex	Cabrera Lobell	1:56.3
9-28	Bluegrass (3yoft) (elim.)	32,244	Lex	Model Home	1:56.4
9-28	Bluegrass (3yoft) (final)	42,992	Lex	Model Home	1:56.3
9-29	American Pacing Classic Final (FFA)	150,000	LA	T K's Skipper	1:51.2f
9-29	Bluegrass (2yocp) (eilm.)	42,970	Lex	Nuke Of Earl	1:53.4
9-29	Bluegrass (2yocp) (eilm.)	43,970	Lex	Mr Tuff Guy	1:54.4
9-29	Bluegrass (2yocp) (final)	57,960	Lex	Interpretor	1:53.3
9-29	Milton Elims (3&up F&M Elims) (div.)	20,000	Moh	Cherry Hello, 4	1:57.4f
9-29	Milton Elims (3&up F&M Elims) (div.)	20,000	Moh	Madagascar Hanover, 5	1:56f
9-29	Milton Elims (3&up F&M Elims) (div.)	20,000	Moh	Viewstar, 4	1:56.3f
9-29	Tattersalls (3yo Open Pace) (elim.)	37,020	Lex	Beach Towel	1:51.3
9-29	Tattersalls (3yo Open Pace) (elim.)	37,020	Lex	Colored Storm	1:53.3
9-29	Tattersalls (3yo Open Pace) (elim.)	37,020	Lex	Kiev Hanover	1:51.1
9-29	Tattersalls (3yo Open Pace) (final)	74,040	Lex	Beach Towel	1:51.1
9-30	Mohawk Gold Cup Final (3&up Open Pace)	197,750	Moh	Topnotcher, 4	1:52.4f
10-3	Bret Hanover (Open Pace)	63,000	Lex	Mystery Fund	1:52.1

CHRONICLES

Date	Race	Purse	Track	Winner	Time
10-3	International Stallion Stake (2yofp)	$95,150	Lex	Explosive Legacy	1:55.4
10-3	International Stallion Stake (2yoft) (elim.)	36,300	Lex	Armbro Jacuzzi	1:58.3
10-3	International Stallion Stake (2yoft) (elim.)	36,300	Lex	Whiteland Janice	1:59.1
10-3	International Stallion Stake (2yoft) (final)	48,400	Lex	Eternal Flare	1:59.2
10-4	International Stallion Stake (2yoct) (elim.)	40,090	Lex	Grundy's Mint	1:58.1
10-4	International Stallion Stake (2yoct) (elim.)	41,090	Lex	Aerostar One	1:59.2
10-4	International Stallion Stake (2yoct) (final)	54,120	Lex	Grundy's Mint	1:57.4
10-4	Speedy Scot (Open Trot) (div.)	47,500	Lex	Kerry's Crown	1:55.1
10-4	Speedy Scot (Open Trot) (div.)	47,500	Lex	No Sex Please	1:55
10-4	Tattersalls - Garnsey Mem. (3yofp) (elim.)	27,330	Lex	Lady Genius	1:54.2
10-4	Tattersalls - Garnsey Mem. (3yofp) (elim.)	27,330	Lex	Smiling Rebecca	1:54.3
10-4	Tattersalls - Garnsey Mem. (3yofp) (final)	36,440	Lex	Rulers Chippie	1:53.2
10-5	Bluegrass (3yocp)	130,000	Lex	Kiev Hanover	1:50.1
10-5	International Stallion Stake (2yocp)	153,500	Lex	Die Laughing	1:52.1
10-5	**Kentucky Futurity** (3yo Open Trot) (1st heat)	**81,000**	**Lex**	**Jeanne's Somolli**	**1:54.2**
10-5	**Kentucky Futurity** (3yo Open Trot) (2nd heat)	**81,000**	**Lex**	**Star Mystic**	**1:54.3**
10-5	**Kentucky Futurity** (3yo Open Trot) (race-off)	**18,000**	**Lex**	**Star Mystic**	**1:55.3**
10-5	Ky. Futurity Filly Div. (3yoft) (1st heat)	27,636	Lex	Essence Bear	1:58
10-5	Ky. Futurity Filly Div. (3yoft) (1st heat)	27,636	Lex	Nivea Hanover	1:55.4
10-5	Ky. Futurity Filly Div. (3yoft) (2nd heat)	27,636	Lex	Camelia Lobell	1:56.1
10-5	Ky. Futurity Filly Div. (3yoft) (race-off)	9,212	Lex	Nivea Hanover	1:58.2
10-6	Three Diamonds Elims (2yofp) (div.)	12,500	GSP	R M Gee	1:55.4
10-6	Three Diamonds Elims (2yofp) (div.)	12,500	GSP	Yankee Co-ed	1:54.1
10-7	Milton Final (3&up F&M Elims)	141,250	Moh	Caesars Jackpot	1:53.3f
10-12	Cinderella (3yofp)	100,000	May	Instant Rebate	1:59h
10-12	Cleveland Classic (3yo Open Pace) (div.)	150,000	Nfld	Jake And Elwood	1:54.4h
10-12	Cleveland Classic (3yo Open Pace) (div.)	150,000	Nfld	Kiev Hanover	1:55.4h
10-13	Abe Lincoln (2yo Open Pace)	130,000	May	Three Wizzards	1:57.1h
10-13	Colonial (3yo Open Trot) (div.)	122,032	RcR	Jeanne's Somolli	1:56.4f
10-13	Colonial (3yo Open Trot) (div.)	122,033	RcR	Cheyenne Spur	1:56.2f
10-13	Colonial Lady (3yoft) (div.)	46,685	RcR	Happy Diamonds	1:57f
10-13	Colonial Lady (3yoft) (div.)	46,685	RcR	Me Maggie	1:57.2f
10-13	Colonial Lady (3yoft) (div.)	46,685	RcR	Working Gal	1:57.1f
10-13	Stewart Fraser Memorial (Open Pace) (elim.)	15,000	Edm	Sandman Hanover	1:53.3f
10-13	Stewart Fraser Memorial (Open Pace) (elim.)	15,000	Edm	Topnotcher	1:55.1f
10-13	Stewart Fraser Memorial (Open Pace) (final)	200,000	Edm	Topnotcher	1:53.4f
10-13	Three Diamonds Final (2yofp)	422,400	GSP	Miss Easy	1:55.3
10-14	Harvest Stakes (2yofp) (div.)	81,134	Moh	Jollie Dame	1:56.2f
10-14	Harvest Stakes (2yofp) (div.)	82,633	Moh	Big Bloomer	1:56.3f
10-14	Harvest Stakes (2yofp) (div.)	82,633	Moh	Falcon's Secret	1:59.1f
10-15	Autumn Stakes (2yoft) (div.)	76,800	Moh	Collier St Kathy	2:03f
10-15	Autumn Stakes (2yoft) (div.)	76,800	Moh	Shipps Doll	2:03f
10-17	Goldsmith Maid Elims (2yoft) (div.)	10,000	GSP	Kramer Nobless	1:59.3
10-17	Goldsmith Maid Elims (2yoft) (div.)	10,000	GSP	Santa Royal	1:58
10-18	Valley Victory Elims (2yoct) (div.)	15,000	GSP	Crimson Lobell	2:01.4
10-18	Valley Victory Elims (2yoct) (div.)	15,000	GSP	Gift Box	1:59.3
10-18	Valley Victory Elims (2yoct) (div.)	15,000	GSP	No Commotion	1:59.1
10-20	Galt (3yo Open Trot)	100,000	May	Incredible DJ	1:59.2h
10-21	Provincial Cup (3yo Open Pace) (elim.)	69,150	WR	Apaches Fame	1:53.2f
10-21	Provincial Cup (3yo Open Pace) (elim.)	69,150	WR	Jake And Elwood	1:53.1f
10-21	Provincial Cup (3yo Open Pace) (final)	92,200	WR	Camluck	1:52.4f
10-24	Goldsmith Maid Final (2yoft)	294,600	GSP	Kramer Nobless	2:00.2
10-25	Valley Victory Final (2yoct)	330,300	GSP	Mr Chin	1:58.1
10-27	First Lady Elims (2yofp) (div.)	16,078	RcR	Sara Loren Rd	1:57f
10-27	First Lady Elims (2yofp) (div.)	16,078	RcR	Yankee Co-ed	1:56.2f
10-27	First Lady Elims (2yofp) (div.)	16,078	RcR	Yankee Shuffle	1:58.2f
10-27	Presidential Elims (2yo Open Pace) (div.)	33,150	RcR	Cambest	1:54.3f
10-27	Presidential Elims (2yo Open Pace) (div.)	33,150	RcR	Die Laughing	1:54.2f
10-27	Presidential Elims (2yo Open Pace) (div.)	33,150	RcR	Razzle Dazzlem	1:56.3f
10-27	Western Canada Pacing Derby (3yo Open)	111,790	Edm	Sky Hagler	1:58.1f
11-2	**Breeders Crown** (3yocp)	**366,933**	**PPk**	**Beach Towel**	**1:51.2f**
11-2	**Breeders Crown** (3yoct)	**396,933**	**PPk**	**Embassy Lobell**	**1:56.4f**

CHRONICLES

Date	Event	Purse	Track	Winner	Time
11-2	**Breeders Crown** (3yofp)	$304,933	PPk	Town Pro	1:54.4f
11-2	**Breeders Crown** (3yoft)	378,933	PPk	Me Maggie	1:57.1f
11-2	**Breeders Crown** (Aged H&G Pace)	273,458	PPk	Bay's Fella	1:52.1f
11-2	**Breeders Crown** (Aged H&G Trot)	221,458	PPk	No Sex Please	1:55f
11-2	**Breeders Crown** (Aged Pacing Mares)	200,000	PPk	Caesars Jackpot	1:52.3f
11-2	**Breeders Crown** (Aged Trotting Mares)	203,458	PPk	Peace Corps	1:54.2f
11-2	Ron Hodge Memorial (3yo Open Pace) (div.)	13,350	Nor	Fortysix Extralong	1:57.2h
11-2	Ron Hodge Memorial (3yo Open Pace) (div.)	13,350	Nor	My King Pin	1:57.3h
11-3	First Lady Final (2yofp)	144,701	RcR	Cams Exotic	1:56.3f
11-3	Matron Stakes Elims (2yo Open Trot) (div.)	30,381	PPk	Aerostar One	1:59.3f
11-3	Matron Stakes Elims (2yo Open Trot) (div.)	30,381	PPk	Mr Chin	1:59.3f
11-3	Matron Stakes Elims (2yoft) (div.)	29,321	PPk	Esprit Spur	1:59f
11-3	Matron Stakes Elims (2yoft) (div.)	29,801	PPk	Frances Jet Boko	2:00.3f
11-3	Presidential Final (2yo Open Pace)	298,345	RcR	Die Laughing	1:54f
11-9	Clare Series (Aged Pacing Mares)	17,500	YR	Kittwake	1:57h
11-9	Matron Stakes (2yoft)	88,683	PPk	Esprit Spur	1:58f
11-9	Matron Stakes Elims (3yoft) (div.)	24,641	PPk	Me Maggie	1:56.1f
11-9	Matron Stakes Elims (3yoft) (div.)	24,641	PPk	Model Home	1:59.1f
11-10	Governor's Cup Elims (2yo Open Pace) (div.)	25,000	GSP	Artsplace	1:55
11-10	Governor's Cup Elims (2yo Open Pace) (div.)	25,000	GSP	Die Laughing	1:54.3
11-10	Matron Stakes Final (2yo Open Trot)	91,143	PPk	Mr Chin	2:00.4f
11-10	On The Road Again (Open Pace)	100,000	YR	(Did not fill)	
11-16	Clare Series (Aged Pacing Mares)	17,500	YR	L Dees Trish	1:55.1h
11-16	Matron Stakes Final (3yoft)	75,000	PPk	Model Home	1:57.4f
11-17	Governor's Cup Final (2yo Open Pace)	655,600	GSP	Artsplace	1:53
11-17	Matron Stakes (3yo Open Trot)	125,465	PPk	Jeanne's Somolli	1:57.2f
11-17	Wm. Haughton Memorial (3yocp)	35,000	YR	(Did not fill)	
11-17	Wm. Haughton Memorial (Aged H&G Pace)	35,000	YR	Dorunrun Bluegrass	1:55.1h
11-23	Clare Series Final (Aged Paced Mares)	75,000	YR	L Dees Trish	1:54.4h
11-24	**Breeders Crown Elims** (2yoct) (div.)	59,233	PPk	Mr Chin	1:59.4f
11-24	**Breeders Crown Elims** (2yoct) (div.)	59,233	PPk	Carry The Message	1:59.1f
11-24	**Breeders Crown Elims** (2yoft) (div.)	61,233	PPk	Jean Bi	1:59.1f
11-24	**Breeders Crown Elims** (2yoft) (div.)	61,233	PPk	Santa Royal	1:58.2f
11-24	Wm. Haughton Memorial (3yocp)	35,000	YR	(Did not fill)	
11-24	Wm. Haughton Memorial (Aged H&G Pace)	35,000	YR	(Did not fill)	
11-30	**Breeders Crown** (2yocp)	605,870	PPk	Artsplace	1:51.1f
11-30	**Breeders Crown Final** (2yoct)	355,403	PPk	Crysta's Best	2:01 f
11-30	**Breeders Crown** (2yofp)	514,870	PPk	Miss Easy	1:54 f
11-30	**Breeders Crown Final** (2yoft)	367,403	PPk	Jean Bi	2:00.3f
12-1	Wm. Haughton Memorial Final (Combined)	200,000	YR	Dorunrun Bluegrass	1:55 h
12-14	Matron Stakes (2yofp)	131,605	PPk	Cams Exotic	1:56 f
12-15	Matron Stakes (2yo Open Pace)	160,005	PPk	Mantese	1:54.2f
12-21	Matron Stakes (3yofp)	91,095	PPk	Rulers Chippie	1:55.3f
12-22	Matron Stakes (3yo Open Pace)	138,490	PPk	Shipps Schnoops	1:53.2f

CHRONICLES

THE RICHEST OPEN PACING EVENTS OF 1990

Event	(Division)	Purse	At	Winner *	Time
7-13	Meadowlands Pace Final (3yo Open Pace)	$1,153,500	M	Beach Towel	1:52.2
8-17	Woodrow Wilson Final (2yo Open Pace)	1,043,500	M	Die Laughing	1:52.1
6-23	North America Cup Final (3yo Open Pace)	1,000,000	GrR	Apaches Fame	1:53.4f
9-22	Metro Stakes Final (2yo Open Pace)	797,400	Moh	Artsplace	1:54f
8-17	Sweetheart Final (2yofp)	766,000	M	Miss Easy	1:52.3
8-19	Prix d'Ete (3yocp)	663,500	BB	Beach Towel	1:53.1f
11-17	Governor's Cup Final (2yo Open Pace)	655,600	GSP	Artsplace	1:53
11-30	Breeders Crown Final (2yocp)	605,870	PPk	Artsplace	1:51.1f
8-5	Prix de l'Avenir (2yocp)	584,500	BB	Jackpot Raider *	1:57f
11-30	Breeders Crown Final (2yofp)	514,870	PPk	Miss Easy	1:54f
8-11	Adios (3yo Open Pace)	493,176	Mea	Beach Towel	1:51.4f
8-25	Cane Pace (3yo Open Pace)	486,550	YR	Jake And Elwood	1:55.1h
9-20	Little Brown Jug (3yo Open Pace)	468,610		Beach Towel	1:53.3h
9-8	Messenger Stakes (3yo Open Pace)	444,371	RcR	Jake And Elwood	1:52.3f
8-17	Mistletoe Shalee Final (3yofp)	425,250	M	Choice Yankee	1:52.4
10-13	Three Diamonds Final (2yofp)	422,400	GSP	Miss Easy	1:55.3
9-1	James B. Dancer Memorial (3yo Open Pace)	379,712	Fhld	Road Machine	1:54.4h
9-8	Kentucky Pacing Derby Final (2yo Open Pace)	379,553	LouD	Tooter Scooter	1:57h
11-2	Breeders Crown Final (3yocp)	366,933	PPk	Beach Towel	1:51.2f
8-3	Niatross Final (2yocp)	365,600	M	Die Laughing	1:54.2
8-25	Garden State Stake (2yo Open Pace)	363,804	Fhld	Three Wizzards *	1:56h
9-2	Champlain Stakes (2yo Open Pace)	350,000	Moh	Silky Stallone *	1:55.2f
6-30	American-National (3yocp)	347,000	SPk	Beach Towel	1:52.4f
8-26	Confederation Cup (3yo Open Pace)	341,000	FlmD	Apaches Fame	1:55f
7-21	Potomac (2yocp)	330,425	RcR	Gigowatt *	1:54.4f
4-14	Berry's Creek Final (3yo Open Pace)	323,750	M	Mark Johnathan	1:54
6-9	Terrapin (3yocp)	316,135	RcR	Beach Towel	1:54.1f
5-12	Wm. E. Miller Memorial Final (3yo Pace)	315,010	RcR	Beach Towel	1:52.3f
11-2	Breeders Crown Final (3yofp)	304,933	PPk	Town Pro	1:54.4f
7-28	Art Rooney Memorial Final (3yo Open Pace)	304,127	YR	Jake And Elwood	1:55h
10-12	Cleveland Classic (3yo Open Pace)	300,000	Nfld	Jake And Elwood *	1:54.4h
11-3	Presidential Final (2yo Open Pace)	298,345	RcR	Die Laughing	1:54h
9-9	Nassagaweya (2yo Open Pace)	281,600	Moh	Artsplace *	1:55.1f
11-2	Breeders Crown Final (Aged H&G Pace)	273,458	PPk	Bay's Fella	1:52.1f
7-28	Molson Canadian Pacing Derby (3&up Open)	265,250	GrR	Topnotcher	1:52.3f

THE RICHEST OPEN TROTTING EVENTS OF 1990

8-4	Hambletonian (3yo Open Trot)	$1,346,000	M	Harmonious	1:54.1
7-31	Peter Haughton Memorial Final (2yoct)	609,250	M	Charlie Ten Hitch	2:00.2
9-1	World Trotting Derby (3yo Open)	600,000	DuQ	Harmonious	2:04.3
8-1	Merrie Annabelle Final (2yoft)	464,750	M	Santa Royal	1:58.1
8-5	International Trot 1-1/4 mi (Inv.)	450,000	YR	Reve d'Udon	2:28.3h
8-3	Hambletonian Oaks (3yoft)	441,555	M	Working Gal	1:58.1
7-14	Yonkers Trot (3yo Open)	424,964	YR	Royal Troubador	1:59.2h
7-28	Beacon Course Final (3yo Open Trot)	401,500	M	Embassy Lobell	1:56.3
11-2	Breeders Crown (3yocp)	396,933	PPk	Jeanne's Somolli	1:57.2f
9-8	Champlain Stakes (2yo Open Trot)	396,545	Moh	Super Pleasure *	2:01.2f
11-2	Breeders Crown Final (3yoft)	378,933	PPk	Me Maggie	1:57.1f
11-30	Breeders Crown Final (2yoft)	367,403	PPk	Jean Bi	2:00.1f
11-30	Breeders Crown Final (2yoct)	355,403	PPk	Crysta's Best	2:01f
10-25	Valley Victory Final (2yoct)	330,300	GSP	Mr Chin	1:58.1
10-24	Goldsmith Maid Final (2yoft)	294,600	GSP	Kramer Nobless	2:00.2
8-18	Maple Leaf Trot (3yo&up)	293,250	GrR	No Sex Please	1:57f
6-18	American-National (3yoct)	272,000	SPk	Armbro Iliad	2:00.1f

* -Divided stakes -winner of fastest division shown; Times shown are for deciding heats

CHRONICLES

THE RICHEST OPEN PACING EVENTS OF ALL-TIME

Year	Event (Division)	Purse	At	Winner	Time*
1984	Woodrow Wilson (2yo Open)	$2,161,000	M	Nihilator	1:52.4
1980	Woodrow Wilson (2yo Open)	2,011,000	M	Land Grant	1:56.4
1982	Woodrow Wilson (2yo Open)	1,957,500	M	Fortune Teller	1:55.3
1981	Woodrow Wilson (2yo Open)	1,760,000	M	McKinzie Almahurst	1:56.1
1983	Woodrow Wilson (2yo Open)	1,700,000	M	Carls Bird	1:55.3
1986	Woodrow Wilson (2yo Open)	1,561,500	M	Cullin Hanover	1:54.4
1987	Woodrow Wilson (2yo Open)	1,422,500	M	Even Odds	1:54.1
1990	Hambletonian (3yo Open Trot)	1,346,000	M	Harmonious	1:54.1
1985	Woodrow Wilson (2yo Open)	1,344,000	M	Grade One	1:54.3
1984	Meadowlands Pace Final (3yo Open)	1,293,000	M	On The Road Again	1:53.3
1983	Meadowlands Pace Final (3yo Open)	1,252,000	M	Ralph Hanover	1:54.1
1990	Meadowlands Pace Final (3yo Open Pace)	1,153,500	M	Beach Towel	1:52.2
1990	Meadowlands Pace Final (2yo Open Pace)	1,043,500	M	Die Laughing	1:52.1
1988	North America Cup Final (3yo Open)	1,043,000	GrR	Runnymede Lobell	1:54.4f
1988	Woodrow Wilson Final (2yo Open)	1,041,000	M	Kassa Branca	1:52.3
1988	Meadowlands Pace Final (3yo Open)	1,039,000	M	Matt's Scooter	1:52.1
1986	Meadowlands Pace Final (3yo Open)	1,025,500	M	Laughs	1:52.1
1985	Meadowlands Pace Final (3yo Open)	1,018,000	M	Nihilator	1:50.3
1980	Meadowlands Pace Final (3yo Open)	1,011,000	M	Niatross	1:53.1
1981	Meadowlands Pace Final (3yo Open)	1,000,000	M	Conquered	1:54.3
1982	Meadowlands Pace Final (3yo Open)	1,000,000	M	Hilarion	1:54.1
1989	North America Cup Final (3yo Open)	1,000,000	GrR	Goalie Jeff	1:53.2f
1987	North America Cup Final (3yo Open)	1,000,000	GrR	Jate Lobell	1:52.3f
1990	North America Cup Final (3yo Open Pace)	1,000,000	GrR	Apaches Fame	1:53.4f
1989	Woodrow Wilson Final (2yo Open)	907,000	M	Sam Francisco Ben	1:56
1987	Meadowlands Pace Final (3yo)	902,500	M	Frugal Gourmet	1:52
1988	Sweetheart Final (2yofp)	863,250	M	Concertina	1:56
1989	Meadowlands Pace (3yo Open)	852,000	M	Dexter Nukes	1:51.3
1986	Breeders Crown (2yocp)	819,600	GSP	Sunset Warrior	1:55.3
1990	Metro Stakes Final (2yo Open Pace)	797,400	Moh	Artsplace	1:54f
1987	Sweetheart Final (2yofp)	796,750	M	So Cozy	1:55.1
1984	Breeders Crown (2yocp)	772,500	Mea	Dragon's Lair	1:54.1f
1990	Sweetheart Final (2yofp)	766,000	M	Miss Easy	1:52.3
1988	Governor's Cup Final (2yo Open)	705,100	GSP	How Bout It	1:54.3
1989	Governor's Cup Final (2yo Open Pace)	681,100	GSP	In The Pocket	1:54.2
1985	Breeders Crown (2yocp)	673,553	RcR	Robust Hanover	1:56.4h

THE RICHEST OPEN TROTTING EVENTS OF ALL-TIME

Year	Event (Division)	Purse	At	Winner	Time*
1990	Hambletonian (3yo Open Trot)	$1,346,000	M	Harmonious	1:54.1
1985	Hambletonian (3yo Open)	1,272,000	M	Prakas	1:54.3
1984	Hambletonian (3yo Open)	1,219,000	M	Historic Freight	1:59.3
1986	Hambletonian (3yo Open)	1,172,082	M	Nuclear Kosmos	1:56.1
1988	Hambletonian (3yo Open)	1,156,800	M	Armbro Goal	1:55.1
1989	Hambletonian (3yo Open)	1,131,000	M	Park Avenue Joe	2:00.2
1983	Hambletonian (3yo Open)	1,080,000	M	Duenna	1:57.2
1987	Hambletonian (3yo Open)	1,046,300	M	Mack Lobell	1:53.3
1984	Haughton Memorial Final (2yo Open)	1,000,000	M	Another Miracle	1:58.4
1985	Haughton Memorial Final (2yo Open)	1,000,000	M	Express Ride	1:57.4
1986	Haughton Memorial Final (2yo Open)	879,250	M	Ditka Hanover	1:57.3
1983	Haughton Memorial Final (2yo Open)	875,000	M	Why Not	2:00.1
1982	Hambletonian (3yo Open)	875,000	M	Speed Bowl	1:56.4
1981	Hambletonian (3yo Open)	838,000	M	Shiaway St Pat	2:01.1
1988	Peter Haughton Memorial Final (2yoct)	682,250	M	Keyser Lobell	1:58.4
1982	Haughton Memorial Final (2yo Open)	653,250	M	Dancers Crown	1:58

*-Times shown are for deciding heat

CHRONICLES
1990 EUROPEAN GRAND CIRCUIT RESULTS

Date	Event Purse	Distance	Winner	Time *	Track Driver
2-11	Prix de France 1,500,000 francs	2,100m	Pussy Cat	1:14.3	Vincennes, France Jean Raffin
3-11	Grand Criterium de Vitesse 800,000 francs	1,609m	Express Ride	1:12.5	Cagnes Sur Mer, France Pekka Korpi
4-8	Grand Prix du Sud-Ouest 800,000 francs	2,400m	Pussy Cat	1:15.3	Beaumont, France Jean Raffin
4-15	Grosser Preis von Bayern 200,000 marks	2,100m	Quinio Des Bordes	1:16	Dafling, West Germany Jean Gaborit
4-29	Finlandia-AJO 465,000 marks	1,609m	Florida Jewel	1:13	Helsinki, Finland Bill Fahy
5-13	SAS Oslo Grand Prix 1,040,000 crowns	2,100m	Meadow Roland	1:13.8	Bjerke, Norway Preben Kjarsgaard
5-27	Solvalla Elitlopp 1,430,000 kronen	1,609m	Mack Lobell	1:11	Solvalla, Sweden Thomas Nilsson
6-10	Copenhagen Cup 500,000 kronen	2,011m	Meadow Roland	1:13.5	Charlottelund, Denmark Preben Kjarsgaard
6-22	Gran Premio Duomo 200,000,000 lire	1,660m	Mr Lucken	1:13.5	Florence, Italy Orjan Kihlstrom
7-22	Elite-Rennen 200,000 marks	2,011m	Reve d'Udon	1:14.1	Gelsenkirchen, Germany Yves Dreux
8-19	Aby Stora-Pris 1,750,000 kronen	2,140m	Reve d'Udon	1:14.6	Aby, Sweden Yves Dreux
9-2	Campionato Europeo 200,000,000 lire	1,660m	Nealy Lobell	1:15.5	Cesena, Italy Jorma Kontio
10-14	Grosser Pries von Bild 150,000 marks	1,609m	Mack Lobell	1:13	Bahrenfeld, Germany Thomas Nilsson
10-23	Prijs der Giganten 110,000 guilders	1,609m	Friendly Face	1:14.1	Hilversum, The Netherlands Pekka Korpi
11-17	Gran Premio delle Nazioni 330,000,000 lire	2,100m	Peace Corps	1:13.8	Milan, Italy Stig H. Johansson

* **NOTE:** All times in kilometer rates, in tenths. A rate of 1:14.6 is approximately equivalent to a 2:00 mile. Mack Lobell trotted to a 1:11 kilometer rate in the 1990 Elitlopp. His 1:54.1 for the 1,609 meters was the fastest "metric mile" ever trotted outside North America.

Kilometer Rate Conversion Table

U.S.	Metric
1:55.3 -	1:11.84
1:55.4 -	1:11.97
1:56 -	1:12.09
1:56.1 -	1:12.21
1:56.2 -	1:12.34
1:56.3 -	1:12.46
1:56.4 -	1:12.59
1:57 -	1:12.71
1:57.1 -	1:12.83
1:57.2 -	1:12.96
1:57.3 -	1:13.08
1:57.4 -	1:13.21
1:58 -	1:13.33
1:58.1 -	1:13.45
1:58.2 -	1:13.58
1:58.3 -	1:13.70
1:58.4 -	1:13.83
1:59 -	1:13.95
1:59.1 -	1:14.08
1:59.2 -	1:14.20
1:59.3 -	1:14.33
1:59.4 -	1:14.45
2:00 -	1:14.58
2:00.1 -	1:14.70
2:00.2 -	1:14.83
2:00.3 -	1:14.95
2:00.4 -	1:15.08
2:01 -	1:15.20
2:01.1 -	1:15.32
2:01.2 -	1:15.45
2:01.3 -	1:15.57
2:01.4 -	1:15.70
2:02 -	1:15.83
2:02.1 -	1:15.94

CHRONICLES

CHRONICLES OF DISCONTINUED EVENTS
The following events, raced during the 1980s, are no longer contested

The American Classics
Invitational Trot *
Last raced at Hollywood Park, Inglewood, CA

55	75,000	Scott Frost (Joe O'Brien)	a 1:59.3m	70	100,000	Dayan (William Myer)	2:13.2m
56	75,000	Scott Frost (Joe O'Brien)	1:58.3m	71	100,000	Fresh Yankee (Joe O'Brien)	2:20.4m
57	75,000	Galophone (W.R. Walker)	2:00.2m	72	100,000	Dayan (William Myer)	2:19.4m
58	75,000	Charming Barbara (Billy Haughton)	2:00.1m	73	100,000	Elesnar (Percy Robillard)	2:16 m
59	85,000	Senator Frost (Richard Buxton)	1:57.3m	74	109,550	Savior (James Dennis)	2:13.3m
60	85,000	Silver Song (Howard Camden)	1:59.1m	75	104,900	Savior (James Dennis)	2:14.1m
61	80,000	Air Record (George Sholty)	1:58.2m	76	109,800	Keystone Pioneer (Billy Haughton)	2:12.3m
62	50,000	Duke Rodney (Billy Haughton)	2:16.1m	77	100,750	Ima Lula (Joe O'Brien)	2:13.4m
63	50,000	Porterhouse (Earle Avery)	2:15 m	78	100,800	Keystone Pioneer (Billy Haughton)	2:15.2m
64	50,000	Marco Hanover (Richard Buxton)	2:14 m	79	92,000	Jurgy Hanover (Peter Haughton)	2:12.3m
65	50,000	Armbro Flight (Joe O'Brien)	2:15.3m	80	94,000	Classical Way (J. Simpson, Jr.) R	2:11.3m
66	50,000	Earl Laird (Robt. J. Williams)	2:13.2m	81	123,500	Dante Jay (Steve Desomer)	2:12.2m
67	60,000	Grandpa Jim (Bob Farrington)	2:13.4m			* - 1-1/8 mi. dash 1962-1981	
68	75,000	Lady B Fast (William Popfinger)	2:15.2m				
69	100,000	Fresh Yankee (Joe O'Brien)	2:15 m			a By Gayleway.	

The American Classics
Invitational Pace *
Last raced at Hollywood Park, Inglewood, CA

55	75,000	**	a 1:57.2m	71	100,000	Albatross (Stanley Dancer)	2:13.4m
56	75,000	Dottie's Pick (Delvin Miller)	1:57.4m	72	100,000	Albatross (Stanley Dancer)	2:11.3m
57	75,000	Widower Creed (Jimmy Wingfield)	1:58.3m	73	114,110	Invincible Shadow (James Miller)	2:11.3m
58	75,000	Gold Worthy (Wayne Smart)	b 1:56.3m	74	113,350	Keystone Smartie (Peter Haughton)	2:11.1m
59	75,000	Sunbelle (Joe O'Brien)	1:57.2m	75	100,000	Young Quinn (Joe O'Brien)	2:12.3m
60	75,000	Adios Butler (Edward Cobb)	1:55.3m	76	113,750	Oil Burner (Ben Webster)	2:10 m
61	80,000	Adios Butler (Paige West)	1:57.3m	77	110,250	Le Baron Rouge (Bernard Gervais)	2:10.3m
62	50,000	Irvin Paul (Charles L. King)	2:11.1m	78	111,750	Rambling Willie (Bob Farrington)	2:11 m
63	50,000	Gamecock (Joe O'Brien)	2:13.3m	79	96,900	Flight Director (Joe O'Brien)	2:12 m
64	50,000	Meadow Skipper (Earle Avery)	2:11.3m	80	98,500	Niatross (Clint Galbraith) R	2:07.3m
65	50,000	Cardigan Bay (Stanley Dancer)	2:12.3m	81	288,000	Genghis Khan (Shelly Goudreau)	2:09 m
66	50,000	True Duane (Chris Boring)	2:09.1m			* - 1-1/8 mi dash 1962-1981	
67	60,000	Easy Prom (Bob Farrington)	2:13.3m			** - Time's Square (McKinley Kirk) finished 4-3-1;	
68	75,000	Overcall (Delmer Insko)	2:15.3m			Hillsota (Earle Avery) finished 1-4-3	
69	100,000	Overcall (Delmer Insko)	2:11.1m				
70	100,000	Laverne Hanover (George Sholty)	2:14.4m			a by Diamond Hal.	b By Shadow Wave.

The American Trotting Championship
Invitational *
Yonkers Raceway, Yonkers, NY - Not Raced in 1990

46	25,000	Doctor Spencer(H.C. Fitzpatrick)	2:03 h	69	50,000	Nevele Pride (Stanley Dancer)	2:33 h
47	25,000	Proximity (Clint Hodgins)	2:02.2h	70	50,000	Dayan (Bill Myer)	2:32.1h
48	25,000	Sidney Hanover (Frank Safford)	2:03.2h	71	50,000	Dart Hanover (Herve Filion)	2:34 h
49	25,000	Chris Spencer (Harry Whitney)	2:04.1h	72	50,000	Speedy Crown (Howard Beissinger)	2:34 h
50	25,000	Proximity (Clint Hodgins)	2:03.2h	73	50,000	Spartan Hanover (Wm. Haughton)	2:34 h
51	25,000	Demon Hanover (Harrison Hoyt)	2:03.1h	74	50,000	Savoir (James Arthur)	2:34 h
52	25,000	Silver Riddle (Clint Hodgins)	2:37.2h	75	50,000	Savoir (Del Insko)	2:32.1h
53	25,000	Florican (Harold Miller)	2:33 h	76	50,000	Meadow Bright (Delvin Miller)	2:01.4h
54	25,000	Royal Pastime (C.J. Champion)	2:36.3h	77	50,000	Kash Minbar (Earl Cruise)	1:58.3h
55	25,000	Jamie (Robert Parkinson)	2:33.3h	78	50,000	Kash Minbar (Jimmy Cruise)	1:59.1h
56	25,000	Galophone (Robert Walker)	2:33.1h	79	50,000	Doubleminit (Peter Haughton)	2:01.4h
57	25,000	Trader Horn (William Haughton)	2:36 h	80	100,000	Classical Way (J. Simpson, Jr.)	2:01 h
58	25,000	Demon Rum (C.J. Champion)	2:36.1h	81	100,000	Kading (Ron Waples)	2:00.1h
59	50,000	Jamin (Jean Riaud)	2:34.1h	82	100,000	Mystic Park (Frank O'Mara)	2:00.4h
60	50,000	Silver Song (Howard Camden)	2:33.2h	83	100,000	Bobbo (Norm Jones)	2:00.1h
61	50,000	Merrie Duke (J. Patterson, Sr.)	2:33.3h	84	100,000	Crown Wood (Joe Marsh, Jr.)	2:00.1h
62	50,000	Porterhouse (Earle Avery)	2:32.3h	85	100,000	Sandy Bowl (John Campbell)	1:58.4h
63	50,000	Su Mac Lad (Stanley Dancer)	2:33.1h	86	100,000	Grade's Singing (Herve Filion)	1:58.2h
64	50,000	Speedy Scot (Ralph Baldwin)	2:31.2h	87	100,000	Whip It Wood(John Patterson, Jr.)	1:59.4h
65	50,000	Speedy Scot (Ralph Baldwin)	2:34 h	88	100,000	Go Get Lost (Tom Sells) R	1:57.2h
66	50,000	Noble Victory (Stanley Dancer)	2:31.2h	89		-Not Raced-	
67	50,000	Perfect Freight (Jim Dennis)	2:33 h			* - 1-1/4 mile from 1952-1975.	
68	50,000	Carlisle (William Haughton)	2:34.2h				

The Batavia Downs Colt & Filly Stake
Two-Year-Old Colt Trot *
Last raced at Batavia Downs, Batavia, NY

52	3,720	Dayton Hanover (Gene Pownall)	2:15.4h	65	18,501	Ideal Rodney (William Haughton)	2:07.3h
53	4,100	Brevity Hanover (Garl.Garnsey)	2:12.2h	66	14,100	Mar Con Demon (Anthony MacRae)	2:10.2h
54	6,750	Jeanie May (Levi Harner)	2:17.4h	67	12,500	Valiant Jimmie (Donald Wiest)	2:07.3h
55	9,377	Charletta Hanover (Fred Parks)	2:13.2h	68	15,800	Adam Eden (Delbert Manges)	2:07.1h
56	10,584	Dolph Hanover (Buddy Gilmour)	2:13.1h	69	15,800	Manana (Irving Roberts)	2:08.4h
57		-- Not Raced --		70	13,300	Arch Hill (Robert N. Smith)	2:07.4h
58	8,135	The Lodger (C.J. Champion)	2:13.3h	71	17,000	Songcan (Gilles Lachance)	2:08.1h
59	11,663	Willowood (Dick Richardson, Jr.)	2:09 h	72	18,500	Burning Speed (Glen Garnsey)	2:05.1h
60	7,738	Henry (John Bedell)	2:08.3h	73	19,300	Surge Hanover (Bill Wellwood)	2:09.4h
61	12,395	Oh You Kid (Alan Myer)	2:07.4h	74	23,700	Rob Roy Hanover (George Gilmour)	2:06 h
62	12,873	Floris (Harry Pownall, Sr.)	2:07.4h	75	12,100	Nevele Thunder (Stanley Dancer) R	2:04.3h
63	13,153	Master Rodney (Wilbur Long)	2:09.4h		12,100	Tropical Storm (Ralph Baldwin)	2:06.3h
64	17,850	Jean Sampson (Murel Walters)	2:07.1h	76	12,550	Naturally Nevele (Wm. Lambertus)	2:07.2h

CHRONICLES

	12,650 Speed In Action (H. Graham, Jr.)	2:11.1h
77	21,000 Sommelier (Delvin Miller)	2:06.3h
78	21,500 Scotty Graduate (Syl King, Jr.)	2:08.2h
79	24,600 Wonder Child (Bud Parshall)	2:07 h
80	22,400 Nathan Lobell (James Dancer)	2:06.1h
81	18,200 Cub Run (Soren Nordin)	2:06 h
	18,500 Scottish Wind (Stanley Dancer)	R 2:04.3h

82	31,000 Green Apple (Paul Doherty)	**
83	31,700 Delvin G Hanover (B. Lindstedt)	R 2:04.3h
84	32,300 Perfect Solution (David Vance)	R 2:04.3h
85	31,070 Tory Sweep (Bill Wellwood)	2:05.4h
86	27,300 Block Party (Ben Steall)	2:05.3h

* - Two-Year-Old Open Trot before 1967.
** - Time disallowed

The Batavia Downs Colt & Filly Stake
Two-Year-Old Colt Pace *
Last raced at Batavia Downs, Batavia, NY

52	3,630 Torrid (Hilda Heydt)	2:21.2h
53	4,000 Chief Ensign (Ward Storum)	2:12.1h
54	7,050 Meadow Leo (William Haughton)	2:16.2h
55	9,277 Bachelor Hanover (Wm. Haughton)	2:12 h
56	10,784 Great Adios (James Arthur)	2:08 h
	-- Not Raced --	
58	8,435 Meadow Cheer (Ned Bower)	2:05 h
59	11,567 Jan Hanover (William Haughton)	2:07.1h
60	12,297 Magic Adios (Eldon Harner)	2:05 h
61	13,195 Mighty Tar Heel (Alix Winger) a	2:04.3h
62	12,973 King Sherry (Eugene Minniear)	2:05 h
63	12,953 Bengazi Hanover (Robert Frame)	2:05 h
64	18,250 Adios Vic (Jim Dennis)	2:05.4h
65	18,101 Philip The Great (Wm. Haughton)	2:07 h
66	12,100 Berry Hill (John Schroeder)	2:07 h
	12,100 Toledo Hanover (Bill Myer)	2:04 h
67	11,710 Drummond Hanover (Keith Waples)	2:05.1h
	11,710 Bye Bye Pat (Clint Hodgins)	2:04.4h
68	12,800 Bergen Hanover (William Haughton)	2:03.4h
	12,700 Super Wave (Jack Kopas)	2:02 h
69	9,200 Truluck (George Sholty)	2:01.3h
	9,200 Can Tar Chief (Archie Young)	2:03.1h
	9,100 Most Happy Fella (Stanley Dancer)	2:03.1h
70	11,000 Michael Hanover (Wm. Haughton)	2:05.2h
	11,000 Count Bret (Herve Filion)	2:03.3h
71	13,800 Scream (Howard Camper)	2:04.1h

	13,700 Shadow Star (Jack Kopas)	2:03.2h
72	26,900 JR Skipper (Greg Wright)	2:04.1h
73	29,300 Florida Almahurst (Ron Feagan)	2:02.3h
74	33,600 Armbro Petch (Jack Kopas)	2:04.1h
75	17,800 Raven Hanover (George Sholty)	2:01.1h
	17,800 Pensive Bret (Joe O'Brien)	2:01.4h
76	19,150 Armbro Splurge (J. Simpson, Jr.)	2:05 h
	19,050 Nat Lobell (Jack Kopas)	2:02.2h
77	16,400 Trampas Hanover (D.MacTavish,Sr.)	2:02.2h
	16,400 Wellwood Hanover (Doug Miller)	2:01.1h
78	35,200 Happy Motoring (Bill Popfinger)	2:02.1h
79	37,000 Mr. Newt (Shelly Goudreau)	2:02.4h
80	20,700 Bit O Cheer (Jim Rankin)	2:05.2h
	20,800 Bret's Advantage (Ross Roselle)	2:01.4h
81	35,200 Larch Hanover (Jim Rankin)	2:00 h
82	43,200 Kawartha Robust (Bill Popfinger)	2:03.4h
83	23,700 Precious Energy (N.McKnight,Jr.)	2:00 h
	23,700 Mannart Overdrive (M. Lancaster)	2:01 h
84	21,500 Major Force (Norman Dauplaise)	2:00.2h
	21,800 Niafirst (Clint Galbraith)	1:59.3h
85	21,535 Fit To Fight (Gilles Gendren)	2:03.4h
	21,835 Our Bucephalus (Dan Altmeyer)	2:03.2h
86	20,050 Crimson (Mickey McNichol)	R 1:59.2h
	19,750 Rumpus Hanover (Paul MacDonell)	2:01.3h

* - Two-Year-Old Open Pace before 1967.
a By Knight Latch.

Batavia Downs Colt & Filly Stake
Three-Year-Old Colt Trot *
Last raced at Batavia Downs, Batavia, NY

57	11,160 Speedster (J. Davis Smith)	2:06.1h
58	9,047 Chapel Call (William Haughton)	2:06.3h
59	9,610 Farand Hanover (S. Russell)	2:06.4h
60	14,450 Darcie Hanover (Levi Harner)	2:03.2h
61	14,677 Matastar (Harry Pownall, Sr.)	2:06.1h
62	14,558 AC's Viking (Sanders Russell)	2:03.4h
63	14,186 Just Jamie (John Mongeon)	2:07 h
64	16,890 Dartmouth (Ralph Baldwin)	2:03 h
65	14,187 Mr Hunter (Sanders Russell)	2:07.2h
66	14,315 Eileen Eden (Stanley Dancer)	2:05.1h
67	14,000 Keystone Pride (William Haughton)	2:03.4h
68	13,800 Dart Hanover (Sanders Russell)	2:04.3h
69	16,750 Gun Runner (Earle Avery)	2:03.4h
70	14,500 Art Hill (John Edmunds)	2:05 h
71	14,000 Sharp Pride (William Haughton)	2:07.4h
72	17,800 Spartan Hanover (William Haughton)	2:07.3h
73	18,800 Imperial Yankee (William Haughton)	2:05.3h

74	19,550 Express Pride (Denzil Berry)	2:04.3h
75	19,800 In Control (Roger Hammer)	2:04.2h
76	21,750 Nevele Thunder (Stanley Dancer)	2:03.1h
77	23,700 Green Speed (Peter Haughton)	2:02.1h
78	17,750 Doublemint (Peter Haughton)	2:03 h
79	22,200 Calvados (Bernard Gervais)	2:05 h
80	12,250 That's Terrific (Wm.Popfinger)	2:03.4h
	12,400 Desert King (Stanley Dancer)	2:01.3h
81	26,900 Chauncey Lobell (Sam Smith)	2:05.1h
82	65,000 Armbro Acadian (Larry Walker)	2:01.1h
83	44,300 Sea Chanty (Clint Galbraith)	2:01.4h
84	58,000 Delvin G Hanover (Hakan Wallner)	2:02.1h
85	50,000 Loaded Yankee (Tom Haughton)	2:05.1h
86	50,000 Shane Scottseth (Tom Haughton)	2:03.2h
87	57,532 Napoletano (Bill O'Donnell)	R 1:59.3h

* - Three-Year-Old Open Trot before 1968.

The Batavia Downs Colt & Filly Stake
Three-Year-Old Colt Pace *
Last raced at Batavia Downs, Batavia, NY

57	10,560 Nyland Hanover (Fred Bradbury)	2:03.2h
58	9,047 Widow's Dream (Alix Winger)	2:04.4h
59	9,610 Import Freight (J. Simpson, Sr.)	2:04.1h
60	14,150 Knight Time (James Boring)	2:02.3h
61	14,677 Adios Don (Howard Camper)	2:02 h
62	14,108 Lehigh Hanover (Stanley Dancer)	2:01.3h
63	14,486 Country Don (Marcel Dostie)	2:01 h
64	14,790 Race Time (Ralph Baldwin)	2:02.2h
65	13,587 Danny Row Gil (Eldon Harner)	2:02 h
66	15,265 Romeo Hanover (George Sholty)	2:00.3h
67	16,100 Nevele Dancer (Harold Dancer)	2:02 h
68	17,800 Bye Bye Pat (Clint Hodgins)	2:01.4h
69	20,400 Super Wave (Jack Kopas)	2:04.4h
70	20,900 Keystone Pat (John Hayes)	2:04.4h
71	20,800 High Ideal (Ron Waples)	2:00.1h
72	24,000 Cory (Gene Sears)	2:01.1h
73	23,500 Armbro Nesbit (Joe O'Brien)	2:00.1h

74	25,450 Tarport Low (Delvin Miller)	2:03 h
75	28,200 Seatrain (Ben Webster)	1:59.1h
76	26,350 Raven Hanover (George Sholty)	2:02.1h
77	24,300 No Hitter (John Hayes, Jr.)	2:01.1h
78	24,550 Distant Thunder (Jimmy Allen)	2:02.4h
79	27,700 Oil Strike (Carman Hie)	2:02.1h
80	50,000 Niatross (Clint Galbraith)	R 1:55 h
81	25,500 Doc's Fella (Gary Payne)	1:59.2h
82	65,400 Soky's Atom (Doug Brown)	1:57.1h
83	66,700 Kawartha Robust (Kim Crawford)	1:57.4h
84	62,600 Farmstead's Fame (Wm. Haughton)	1:59.1h
85	63,400 Armbro Dallas (Ron Waples, Jr.)	**
86	30,250 Flight King (Robin Murphy)	2:00.2h
	30,250 Nathan Almahurst (Ray Remmen)	1:58.3h
87	62,832 Call For Rain (Clint Galbraith)	2:00.1h

* - Three-Year-Old Open Pace before 1968.
** - Time disallowed

The Battle of the Brandywine
Three-Year-Old Pace
Brandywine Raceway, Wilmington, DE May 28, 1989

60	29,800 Knight Time (James Boring)	2:01.4h
	29,800 Betting Time (Clint Hodgins)	2:02.2h
61	28,000 Adios Don (Howard Camper)	2:00.2h

	28,000 Al Sam (Earl Beede)	2:02.1h
62	32,000 Adora's Dream (J. Williams, Jr.)	2:00.1h
63	29,700 Country Don (Marcel Dostie)	2:02.2h

CHRONICLES

64	30,900 Vicar Hanover (William Haughton)	2:01 h
65	33,800 Rivaltime (George Sholty)	2:01.3h
66	24,300 Money Wise (William Riddick)	2:04 h
	24,300 Overcall (John Patterson, Sr.)	2:03.1h
67	34,500 Romulus Hanover (Wm. Haughton)	2:00 h
68	33,100 Fulla Napoleon (Richard Thomas)	2:00.1h
69	33,900 Super Wave (Jack Kopas)	1:59.4h
70	35,900 Columbia George (Roland Beaulieu)	1:58.4f
71	50,000 Albatross (Stanley Dancer)	1:57.1f
72	37,500 Shadow Star (Jack Kopas)	1:59.2f
	37,500 Silent Majority (Vernon Dancer)	1:57.2f
73	50,000 Valiant Bret (John Chapman)	2:00.1f
74	56,250 Barons Boy (Michael Guitard)	1:58.3f
	56,250 Taro Hanover (Vernon Dancer)	1:59.2f
75	56,250 Nero (Joe O'Brien)	2:00.3f
	56,250 Bret's Champ (William Haughton)	1:59.3f
76	56,250 Wolf Pack (Eldon Harner)	1:58.4f
	56,250 Keystone Ore (Stanley Dancer)	1:58.4f
77	100,000 Nat Lobell (John Kopas)	*
78	100,000 No No Yankee (Walter Ross)	1:56.3f
79	100,000 Sonsam (George Sholty)	1:57.4f
80	100,000 Niatross (Clint Galbraith)	1:57.1f
81	100,000 Artie's Dream (Shelly Goudreau)	1:55.1f
82	100,000 Icarus Lobell (Herve Filion)	1:56.2f
83	100,000 Vankirk (Steve Warrington)	1:55 f
84	100,000 Guts (Bill O'Donnell)	1:54.2f
85	100,000 Pershing Square (Bill O'Donnell)	R1:53.4f
86	100,000 Wilcos Data (Ted Wing)	1:54.2f
87	100,000 Racing Machine (Ben Webster)	1:55.2f
88	100,000 Eddie The Quick (Eddie Davis)	1:56.4f
89	100,000 Au Crombie (Tommy Haughton)	1:55.4f

* - Time disallowed

The Battle of Saratoga
E. Roland Harriman Memorial
Three-Year-Old Colt and Gelding Trot
Last raced at Saratoga Harness, Saratoga Springs, NY

63	14,341 Queen's Maplecroft (James Jordan)	2:02.2h
64	16,201 Speedy Count (William Haughton)	2:02.1h
65	16,337 Noble Victory (Stanley Dancer)	2:02.2h
66	17,800 Bonus Boy (Adelbert Cameron)	2:01.4h
67	17,380 Keystone Pride (William Haughton)	2:04.3h
68	15,100 Nevele Pride (Stanley Dancer)	2:01 h
69	15,160 Gun Runner (Earle Avery)	2:03.1h
70	14,800 Marlu Pride (Herve Filion)	2:01 h
71	17,400 Lightning Larry (Harold Dancer)	2:09 h
72	24,100 Songcan (George Sholty)	2:02 h
73	15,100 Nick (James Jordan)	2:08.1h
74	18,000 Spirfire Hanover (Delvin Miller)	2:03.4h
75	20,230 Surefire Hanover (Stanley Dancer)	2:00.3h
76	19,010 Jolly Holiday (Ralph Baldwin)	2:03.1h
77	21,525 Cold Comfort (William Haughton)	1:59.3h
78	18,750 Brisco Hanover (Jim Miller)	2:01 h
79	100,000 Chiola Hanover (James Allen)	2:01.1h
80	100,000 Desert King (Stanley Dancer) a	1:59 h
81	105,650 Keystone Triton (Eldon Harner) b	1:59.4h
82	126,750 Incredible Nevele (Glen Garnsey)R	1:58 h
83	112,795 Nevele Action (Glen Garnsey)	2:00.4h
84	125,000 Baltic Speed (Jan Nordin)	2:00.1h

a By Rodney's Best.   b By Camp David.

The Battle of Saratoga
Harold M. Haswell Memorial
Three-Year-Old Colt and Gelding Pace
Last raced at Saratoga Harness, Saratoga Springs, NY

63	16,566 Overtrick (John Patterson, Sr.)	1:59 h
64	19,201 Vicar Hanover (William Haughton)	2:00 h
65	16,962 Bret Hanover (Frank Ervin)	2:02.1h
66	16,900 Romeo Hanover (William Myer)	1:59.3h
67	16,420 Romulus Hanover (Wm. Haughton)	1:58.2h
68	17,000 Rum Customer (John Chapman)	2:06.1h
69	15,860 Cicero (Arthur Hult)	2:03 h
70	15,300 Columbia George (Roland Beaulieu)	2:01.3h
71	15,800 Nansemond (Herve Filion)	2:01 h
72	15,300 Strike Out (John Hayes, Sr.)	1:59.1h
	15,300 Fortune George (Louis Fanelli)	2:01 h
73	25,000 Otaro Hanover (Herve Filion)	1:57 h
74	25,000 Mirror Image (Glen Garnsey)	1:58 h
75	40,000 Whata Baron (Lewis Williams)	1:57.1h
76	23,305 Keystone Ore (Stanley Dancer)	1:56.2h
77	22,225 Seedling Herbert (R. DeSantis)	1:58.1h
78	23,200 Sundance Skipper (Mike Allen) R	1:56 h
79	100,000 Set Point (William Haughton)	1:56.4h
80	100,000 Trenton Time (William Haughton)	1:59.3h
81	100,000 Seahowak Hanover (Ben Webster)	1:58.2h
82	121,570 Elitist (Jack Parker, Jr.)	1:57.1h
83	110,000 Jo-Nathan (William Gilmour)	1:58 h
84	125,000 Farmstead's Fame (Wm. Haughton)	2:01.3h

The Betsy Ross
Three-Year-Old Filly Pace
Last raced at Brandywine Raceway, Wilmington, DE

62	22,400 Stand By (Jack Williams, Jr.)	2:03 h
63	22,300 Ricci Rennie (Harold Dancer)	2:02 h
64	21,500 Flying Gypsy (Joseph Greene)	2:04 h
65	14,900 Bonnie Duane (Willaim Haughton)	2:03.2h
	14,900 Balenzano (George Phalen)	2:01.3h
66	20,900 Bonjour Hanover (Stanley Dancer)	2:02 h
67	21,100 Klara Bye Bye (Herve Filion)	2:03.3h
68	14,500 Berinda Hanover (J. Simpson, Jr.)	2:04.4h
	14,500 Trotwood Tootie (Delvin Miller)	2:06.3h
	14,750 Little Mother (Alan Myer)	2:05.2h
69	15,800 Rebel Lu (Vern Crank)	2:03.4h
	15,600 Tarport Birdie (James Arthur)	2:05 h
70	15,950 Armbro Kerry (Joe O'Brien)	2:00.3f
	15,750 Timely News (Vernon Dancer)	2:03.2f
71	16,800 Truthful Waverly (Yves Filion)	2:00.4f
	16,800 Jefferson Time (Ben Webster)	2:00.4f
72	14,750 Saucy Wave (Merritt Dokey)	2:03.3f
	14,750 Pammy Lobell (William Haughton)	2:00.1f
73	15,900 Noreen Napoleon (Eddie Wheeler)	2:02 f
74	15,900 Skippers Dream (Clifford Boyd)	2:03.2f
	18,825 Hilarious Lynn (Lew Williams)	1:59.3f
	19,075 Joannas Time (John Wilcutts)	1:59.1f
75	17,200 Tarport Hap (Delvin Miller)	1:59.1f
	17,200 Silk Stockings (P. Burris, Jr.)	1:57.4f
76	26,850 Skipper Dexter (Eddie Lohmeyer) R	1:57.3f
77	18,750 Farm Winner (Vernon Dancer)	2:03 f
	18,750 Future Fame (Peter Haughton)	2:02.4f
78	18,525 Cher Hanover (William Haughton)	1:59 f
	18,525 Ladona Hanover (William Haughton)	2:00.1f
79	22,500 Hazel Hanover (William Herman)	2:00.2f
80	24,900 Prudence Collins (Wm. Haughton)	1:59.3f
81	23,250 Watering Can (Stanley Dancer)	1:57.4f
82	18,825 Bambi Almahurst (Ben Webster)	2:01.4f
	19,125 Adore (Jim Miller)	1:59 f
83	29,250 Lucky Lady (Dick Hogan)	1:58.4f
84	20,265 Three O One (Sam Belote)	1:58.4f
	20,265 Homemade Lovin (Walter Ross)	1:58.3f

The Blue Bonnets Challenge
Invitational Pace
Last raced at Hippodrome Blue Bonnets, Montreal, Que.

76	54,700 Tarport Hap (John Chapman)	1:56.3f
77	56,200 Warm Breeze (Dick Farrington)	1:55.3f
78	50,000 Governor Skipper (John Chapman)	1:55.3f
79	75,000 Try Scotch (Shelly Goudreau)	1:55.3f
80	75,000 Direct Scooter (Warren Cameron)	2:00.1f
81	-- Not Raced --	
82	-- Not Raced --	
83	75,000 Cam Fella (Pat Crowe)	1:54.4f
84	100,000 Soky's Atom (Steve Condren)	1:56 f
85	133,000 On The Road Again (Buddy Gilmour)	R1:53.4f

CHRONICLES

The Challenge Cup Trot
Open *
Last raced at Yonkers Raceway, Yonkers, NY

59	25,000 Trader Horn (William Haughton)	2:40.2h
60	25,000 Hairos II (Willem Geersen)	2:33.3h
61	40,000 Merrie Duke (John Patterson)	2:33.3h
62	25,000 Su Mac Lad (Stanley Dancer)	2:33.3h
63	25,000 Elaine Rodney (John Chapman)	2:34 h
64	25,000 Ozo (Hans Fromming)	3:06.1h
65	25,000 Speedy Scot (Ralph Baldwin)	3:07.3h
66	25,000 Lord Gordon (John Patterson)	3:07.4h
67	25,000 Perfect Freight (Jim Dennis)	3:09.4h
68	25,000 Grandpa Jim (Archie Niles, Jr.)	3:11.2h
69	40,000 Fresh Yankee (Joe O'Brien)	3:15.4h
70	30,000 Fresh Yankee (Joe O'Brien)	2:34.2h
71	30,000 Une De Mai (Jean Rene Gougeon)	2:33.3h
72	150,000 Speedy Crown (Howard Beissinger)	2:32.1h
73	30,000 Une De Mai (Jean Rene Gougeon)	2:34 h
74	50,000 Dosson (Giancarlo Baldi)	2:33.4h
75	50,000 Savoir (Del Insko)	2:33.1h
76	50,000 Dream Of Glory (Joe O'Brien)	3:05.2h
77	50,000 Kash Minbar (Earl Cruise)	R 3:01.3h
78	50,000 Lola's Express (Ted Taylor)	3:06 h
79	50,000 Hillion Brillouard (P. Allaire)	3:12.2h
80	100,000 Classical Way (J. Simpson, Jr.)	3:07.1h
81	100,000 -dh- Ideal Du Gazeau (E. Lefevre)	3:05.2h
	-dh- Jorky (Leopold Verroken)	3:05.2h
82	100,000 Jorky (Leopold Verroken)	3:06.2h
83	100,000 Ideal Du Gazeau (Eugene Lefevre)	3:03.4h
84	100,000 Lutin d'Isigny (J.P. Andre)	3:05 h
85	100,000 Lutin d'Isigny (J.P. Andre)	3:03.1h
86	100,000 Piggvar (Stanley Dancer)	3:02.3h
87	100,000 Tabor Lobell (Buddy Gilmour)	3:03.3h
88	100,000 Mack Lobell (John Campbell)	1:57.1h
89	100,000 Mack Lobell (Viejo Hiesknen)	2:30.4h

* - 1-1/4 mile 1959-1963; 1970-1975; and 1989;
1-1/2 mile 1964-1969; 1976-1986;
1 mile; 1988.

The Peter Haughton Memorial
Two-Year-Old Colt Pace
Last raced at Roosevelt Raceway, Westbury, NY

81	512,000 Soky's Atom (Archie McNeil)	2:00.2h		83	559,800 Apache Circle (Eldon Harner)	1:59.3h
82	510,400 Fame (William O'Donnell)	1:59.2h		84	611,800 Broadway Express (M. McNichol)	R 1:58 h

The Lou Dillon
Two-Year-Old Filly Trot
Last raced at Yonkers Raceway, Yonkers, NY

64	19,707 Armbro Flight (Joe O'Brien)	2:07.3h		75	10,876 Lindy's Super Star (J. Bruyere)	2:10.1h
65	18,750 Justly Scottish (Donald Niccum)	2:07.3h			10,776 Starrral Hanover (P. Haughton)	2:09.2h
	18,750 Little Miss Mitzie (W. Haughton)	2:08.2h		76	16,793 Superlou (John Simpson, Jr.)	2:06.2h
66	25,000 Flamboyant (John Chapman)	2:07.1h			16,793 Elmsford (Henri Filion)	2:07 h
67	25,000 Ole Hanover (James Hackett)	2:09.4h		77	28,138 Imagery (Stanley Dancer)	2:04.1h
68	25,000 Jounce (John Chapman)	2:08.4h		78	23,100 Pagan Princess (J. Simpson, Jr.)	2:05 h
69	25,660 Little Victory (Ted Dennis)	2:09.1h		79	18,200 Princess Glory (Wm. Popfinger)	2:09 h
70	26,747 Sonata Hill (Edward Dunnigan)	2:05.3h		80	15,000 Panty Raid (Stanley Dancer)	2:06.1h
71	27,448 Delmonica Hanover (John Chapman)	2:04.2h			15,000 Camelia Rose (Howard Beissinger)	2:08.1h
72	26,971 Honeysuckle Rose (Har. McKinley)	2:12 h		81	21,500 Worth Saving (Perry Simser)	2:07.3h
73	44,036 Starlark Hanover (David Wade)	R 2:04 h		82	24,750 Southern Crown (Joe O'Brien)	2:07.1h
74	9,612 Mithe (Ralph Baldwin)	2:09.4h		83	37,500 Harmony Lobell (Hakan Wallner)	2:07.1h
	9,512 Exclusive Way (J. Simpson, Jr.)	2:09.4h		84	32,250 Sonora Lobell (Hakan Wallner)	2:04.3h

The Midwest Derby
Three- and Four-Year-Old Pace
Last raced at Sportsman's Park, Cicero, IL

65	50,000 Adios Marches (William Shuter)	1:59.3f		76	50,000 Keystone Accent (Frank O'Mara)	1:58.1f
66	50,000 Transient (Dwayne Pletcher)	2:00.3f		77	50,000 Thorpe Messenger (Stanley Banks)	1:58.4f
67	50,000 Star Carrier (Rich. Farrington)	2:00.4f		78	50,000 C R's Dream (Jerry Graham)	1:57 f
68	50,000 Careless Time (Joe Marsh, Jr.)	2:02.1f		79	50,000 Tarport Express (Jerry Graham)	1:59 f
69	50,000 Tanner (Alvin Stanke)	1:59.2f		80	60,000 Bret's Courage (Joe O'Brien)	2:01.3f
70	50,000 Teffe (Dwayne Pletcher)	2:03.2f		81	60,000 Tarport Boss (Dan Shetler)	1:57.3f
71	50,000 Michigan Mack (Ralph Mapes)	2:04.3f		82	60,000 Elicit Affair (Jim Dolbee)	1:59.1f
72	50,000 Game Guy (Daryl Busse)	2:02.4f		83	50,000 Perfect Blue Chip (Tom Harmer)	R 1:56.2f
73	50,000 Overcast (Dwayne Pletcher)	1:59.2f		84	50,000 Bonjon (Ron Marsh)	*
74	50,000 Braidwood (Walter Paisley)	1:57.4f				
75	50,000 Renees Boy (Delmer Pletcher)	2:04 f			* - Time disallowed	

The Monticello Classic
Three-Year-Old Pace
Last raced at Monticello Raceway, Monticello, NY

75	230,251 Silk Stockings (P. Burris, Jr.)	1:57.3h		80	306,160 Tyler B (William Haughton)	1:58.2h
76	236,250 Oil Burner (Ben Webster)	1:59.1h		81	210,000 Freedom Fella (Shelly Goudreau)	R 1:55.4h
77	254,200 Big Towner (John Chapman)	1:58.3h		82	221,350 Bo Scot's Blue Chip (Jim Allen)	1:56.1h
78	266,165 Happy Lady (Jim Rankin)	1:59 h		83	210,000 Division Street (Bruce Riegle)	1:58.1h
79	250,000 Happy Motoring (Wm. Popfinger)	1:57.3h		84	241,161 Long Fella (Tom Harmer)	1:57.1h

The Montreal Trot
Three-Year-Old Colt Trot
Last raced at Blue Bonnets Raceway, Montreal, Que.

79	59,800 Legend Hanover (Joe O'Brien)	2:00 f		84	172,750 Sandy Bowl (Jan Nordin)	R 1:57.4f
80	60,200 Thor Viking (Berndt Lindstedt)	2:01.3f		85	152,900 Bon Sport (Benoit Cote)	2:02.4f
81	116,000 Smokin Yankee (Stanley Dancer)	1:58.4f		86	173,000 Dance Marathon (Henri Filion)	2:01.1f
82	143,100 Arndon (Delvin Miller)	1:57.2f		87	186,000 Classic Jazz (Mickey McNichol)	1:58.1f
83	154,900 Speedy Claude (Eldon Harner)	1:59.2f				

CHRONICLES

The Nancy Hanks
Two-Year-Old Filly Trot
Last raced at Brandywine Raceway, Wilmington, DE

60	13,800	Miss Sarah Rodney (Jim Jordan)	2:08.2h		10,525 Dulcinea Hanover (Richard Hogan)	2:09.3f
61	16,300	Worth Seein (Stanley Dancer)	2:08.4h	73	16,700 Starlark Hanover (David Wade)	2:02.3f
62	15,900	Elma (John Simpson, Sr.)	2:09.3h	74	19,100 Exclusive Way (John Simpson, Jr.)	2:06 f
63	19,300	Myra (Robert Cherrix)	2:07.4h	75	12,000 Sunsweet Hanover (James Arthur)	2:07.3f
	19,300	Lively Rodney (Vernon Dancer)	2:09 h		12,000 Garden Path (Charles W. Clark)	2:06.2f
64	14,250	Arabesque (Stanley Dancer)	2:07.3h	76	19,900 Superlou (John Simpson, Jr.)	2:03 f
65	9,950	Fresh Yankee (Sanders Russell)	2:06.4h	77	18,900 Imagery (Stanley Dancer)	2:04.4f
	9,800	Formal Yankee (Joseph Eyler)	2:08.3h	78	16,600 Songlark (Frank Albertson)	2:08 f
66	13,050	Flamboyant (John Chapman)	2:07 h	79	20,000 Cranford (Hakan Wallner)	2:05.2f
67	15,000	Dagmar Hanover (J. Simpson, Sr.)	2:07.3h	80	13,850 Panty Raid (Stanley Dancer)	2:04.4f
68	10,025	Tarport Farr (Stanely Dancer)	2:12.2h		13,850 Hot Dog Suzanne (Raymond Tripp)	2:06.2f
	10,025	Miss Regal (Austin Galentine)	2:09.1h	81	14,350 Arnie's Likeness (Jan Johnson) R	2:02.1f
69	13,050	Vanaro (William Popfinger)	2:12.3h		14,650 Perla (Jan Johnson)	2:04 f
70	15,500	Keystone Selene (Delvin Miller)	2:04 f	82	14,700 Montesequieu (William Parker)	2:07 f
71	10,600	Modern Yankee (Delvin Miller)	2:06.3f	83	-- Not Raced --	
	10,750	Franella Hanover (George Sholty)	2:05 f	84	19,100 Lovely Lassie (Stanley Dancer)	2:05 f
72	10,625	Star Of Stars (Glen Garnsey)	2:06.2f			

The Pilgrim
Three-Year-Old Colt Pace
Last raced at Garden State Park, Cherry Hill, NJ

85	770,000	Armbro Dallas (Ron Waples)	R 1:52.3m	86	635,000 Robust Hanover (Bill O'Donnell)	1:53.2m

The Pocahontas
Two-Year-Old Filly Pace
Last raced at Brandywine Raceway, Wilmington, DE

62	17,450	Harry's Laura (Clint Hodgins)	2:04.4h		13,766 Tarport Hap (Delvin Miller)	2:04 f
63	12,100	Christmas Time (John Fox)	2:06 h		13,766 Ben Hanover (Roger Hammer)	2:06.4f
	12,100	Mitzy Hanover (John Simpson, Sr.)	2:05.2h	75	12,833 Skipper Dexter (Ed Lohmeyer, Jr.)	2:04 f
64	11,625	Balenzano (Delmer Insko)	2:05.4h		12,833 Dancers Joy (Gary Cameron)	2:04 f
	11,625	Colleen Napoleon (Richard Thomas)	2:05 h		12,833 Toplady Almahurst (Abe Stoltsfus)	2:01.1f
65	16,250	Aline (Warren Cameron)	2:03.4h	76	15,500 I'm Precious (Adelbert Cameron)	2:02.2f
66	16,800	Ember Hanover (Richard Thomas)	2:04 h		15,800 Sedalia (James Laurente)	2:02.2f
67	11,250	Newport Tarlet (Adelbert Cameron)	2:07.2h	77	15,900 JEF's Super Bird (Doug Ackerman)	2:01 f
	11,250	Mildred Pierce (C.J. Fitzpatrick)	2:09.1h		16,200 Double Judy (Ross Hayter)	2:02.2f
68	10,950	Moonglo Hanover (Robert Myers)	2:08.4h	78	14,250 Our Prize Byrd (D.MacTavish,Jr.)	2:04.2f
	11,100	Friendly Folly (Adelbert Cameron)	2:06.2h		13,950 Our Hap (William Haughton)	2:04.4f
69	10,500	Aphrodite Lobell (Ralph Mecouch)	2:06 h	79	16,250 Star Born (William Haughton)	2:05.3f
	10,500	Taps (Earle Avery)	2:07 h		16,250 Tomboy Blue Chip (Delvin Miller)	2:07.1f
70	11,500	Overdrawn (Warren Cameron)	2:04 f	80	14,800 Firma Hanover (Stanley Dancer)	2:02.1f
	11,500	Wind Dust (William Pocza)	2:02.2f		14,800 Friendly Gift (William Haughton)	2:01.4f
71	12,750	Decorum (Stanley Dancer)	2:02.2f	81	15,766 Harmonica (Stanley Dancer) R	1:59.2f
	12,750	Romalie Hanover (Stanley Dancer)	2:04.4f		15,766 J D's Fancy (Abe Stoltzfus)	2:00.1f
72	11,350	Noreen Napoleon (George Sholty)	2:03.1f		16,066 Nuthouse (William Haughton)	2:01.3f
	11,350	All Alert (Glen Garnsey)	2:04.3f	82	16,600 Farmstead Future (Wm. Haughton)	2:03.2f
	11,350	Skippers Dream (John Wilcutts)	2:04 f		16,300 Keystone Flamingo (Wm. Haughton)	2:02.4f
73	13,450	G String (Warren Cameron)	2:02.3f	83	18,360 Perfect Rendezvous (D. Dancer)	2:01.3f
	13,450	Best Of Donut (William Haughton)	2:02.4f		18,650 Scarlet Meema (Joe O'Brien)	2:01.2f
74	13,766	Silk Stockings (P. Burris, Jr.)	2:01.2f	84	28,800 Tri State Baby (Frederick Grant)	2:01.4f

The Queen City Stakes
Three-Year-Old Open Pace *
Last Raced at Greenwood Raceway, Toronto, ONT

64	9,750	Timely Knight (R. White)	2:16.1f	76	29,000 Windshield Wiper (P. Haughton)	2:00 f
65	9,550	Jerry Hal (W. McIlmurray)	2:29 f	77	31,900 Nat Lobell (John Kopas)	1:59 f
66	8,950	H A Meadowland (Ron Feagan)	2:00.4f	78	78,200 Abercrombie (Glen Garnsey)	1:56.4f
67	13,225	Lynden Dodger (Robt. Silliphant)	2:01.1f	79	130,000 Composite (Ron Waples)	a 1:58.2f
68	19,700	Rum Customer (Alix Winger)	2:01 f	80	130,000 Trenton Time (Billy Haughton)	b 1:58.3f
69	17,700	Super Wave (John Kopas)	2:02.1f	81	215,500 Conquered (John Hayes, Jr.)	1:57.4f
70	27,100	Columbia George (Roland Beaulieu)	1:57.4f	82	303,500 Cam Fella (Pat Crowe)	R 1:56 f
71	24,800	Albatross (Stanley Dancer)	2:00.4f	83	390,000 Ralph Hanover (Ron Waples)	1:56.3f
72	26,500	Lynden Bye Bye (Harold McKinley)	1:59.2f		* - Raced at 1-1/8 mi. in 1964;	
73	25,600	Melvins Woe (Joe O'Brien)	1:59.2f		Raced at 1-1/4 mi. in 1965;	
74	25,150	Mirror Image (Glen Garnsey)	2:00.1f			
	25,150	Armbro Ontario (Joe O'Brien)	1:59.1f		a By Tijuana Taxi.	
75	24,950	Albert's Star (Keith Waples)	1:59.4f		b By Trenton Time &	
	25,250	Bret's Champ (Ben Steall)	2:01.2f		Alberton.	

The Shamrock
Three-Year-Old Colt Trot
Last raced at Garden State Park, Cherry Hill, NJ

85	587,000	Flak Bait (Ben Webster)	R 1:56.2m	86	502,000 Sugarcane Hanover (Ron Waples)	1:57.4m

The L.K. Shapiro Stake
Three- and Four-Year-Old Pace *
Last raced at Hollywood Park, Inglewood, CA

70	75,000	Most Happy Fella (Stanley Dancer)	1:58 m	74	100,300 Armbro Omaha (Billy Haughton)	1:56.1m
71	100,000	Albatross (Stanely Dancer)	1:58.2m	75	100,000 H A's Pet (Joseph Lighthill)	1:57.1m
72	106,500	Silent Majority (Billy Haughton)	1:59 m	76	101,500 Plaza Bret (Lew Williams)	1:57.1m
73	101,200	Armbro Nesbit (Joe O'Brien)	1:57.2m	77	100,000 Governor Skipper (John Chapman) R	1:55.4m

CHRONICLES

78	113,900 Flight Director (Joe O'Brien) R	1:55.4m	
79	100,000 Direct Scooter (Warren Cameron)	1:57.1m	
80	62,000 Cordon Argent (D.R. Ackerman)	1:58.3m	
	* - Three-year-old pace prior to 1980		

The Sophompre Pacing Championship
Three-Year-Old Pace
Last Raced at Mohawk Raceway, Campbellville, ONT

77	64,500 Governor Skipper (John Chapman)	1:58.2f
78	63,600 Abercrombie (Glen Garnsey)	1:56.2f
79	75,000 Striking Force (Dr. John Hayes)	1:58.4f
80	75,000 J D's Buck (Tom Strauss)	1:57.3f
81	75,000 Johnny Lus (Benoit Cote)	2:02 f
82	80,000 Cam Fella (Pat Crowe)	1:55.4f
83	80,000 Savvy Almahurst (Trevor Ritchie)	1:58.4f
84	78,500 Lustra's Big Guy (Trevor Ritchie)	1:56 f
85	78,000 Falcon Seelster (Tom Harmer) R	1:53.4f
86	108,500 Incredible Finale (Tom Harmer)	1:56.3f
87	126,000 Frugal Gourmet (Trevor Ritchie)	1:55.2f

The Leland Stanford Trot
Three- and Four-Year-Olds *
Last raced at Hollywood Park, Inglewood, CA

71	50,000 Speedy Crown (Howard Beissinger)	2:01.4m
72	50,000 Super Bowl (Stanley Dancer)	1:59.4m
73	50,000 Arnie Almahurst (Joe O'Brien)	2:05.2m
74	50,000 Dream Of Glory (Pius Soehnlen)	1:59.4m
75	50,000 Meadow Bright (Joe O'Brien)	2:02.1m
76	50,000 Quick Pay (Billy Haughton)	1:59.1m
77	58,575 Green Speed (Billy Haughton) R	1:57.2m
78	60,675 Doublemint (Peter Haughton)	1:59.1m
79	57,125 Lindy's Crown (Howard Beissinger)	2:00.1m
80	59,200 Noble Hustle (Doug Ackerman)	2:01.3m

* - Three-year-old trot prior to 1980

The Tom Hal
Two-Year-Old Colt and Gelding Pace
Last raced at Brandywine Raceway, Wilmington, DE

62	12,200 Uncle Alex (Clifford Boyd)	*
	12,200 Sly Yankee (Stanley Dancer)	2:02.1h
63	13,525 Bengazi Hanover (Robert Frame)	2:03.3h
	13,525 Chipman's Thorpe (Alan Myer)	2:05.1h
64	12,500 Gee Lee Hanover (Har. J. Dancer)	2:02.4h
	12,500 Reed's Gold (John Wilcutts)	2:06.2h
65	16,600 Good Time Boy (Deleston Cote)	2:06.2h
66	17,350 Tudor Hanover (C.J. Fitzpatrick)	2:04 h
67	12,100 Bye Bye Pat (Clint Hodgins)	2:04.3h
	12,150 Fully Napoleon (Richard Thomas)	2:03.4h
68	12,125 Estes Minbar (Stanley Dancer)	2:07.2h
	12,125 Laverne Hanover (Wm. Haughton)	2:04.4h
69	11,000 Adover Rainbow (Warren Cameron)	2:04.3h
	10,850 Dangerous Wave (Wm. Haughton)	2:08 h
70	11,500 Nansemond (Herve Filion)	2:01.4f
	11,350 The Skipper (John W. Smith)	2:03.1f
71	11,112 Royal Don (Joseph Greene)	2:02.3f
	11,262 Beau Rivage (Clarence Martin)	2:00.2f
	11,112 Strike Out (John Hayes)	2:01.4f
	11,262 Berry Hanover (Vernon Dancer)	2:02.2f
72	10,612 Valiant Bret (John Wilcutts)	2:03.2f
	10,612 Tutti Fruiti (Clint Galbraith)	2:05 f
	10,612 Southern Lehigh (George Sholty)	2:05.3f
	10,612 Lyron Hanover (Stanley Dancer)	2:06.1f
73	13,200 Tarville Joe (Joe O'Brien)	2:03.1f
	13,200 Nevele Bret (Vernon Dancer)	2:02.2f
74	15,000 Ricky Joe (Robert H. Myers)	2:04.2f
	15,000 Broadcaster B (William Haughton)	2:02.3f
75	15,000 Hasty Reply (Arthur Lance Bier)	2:02.3f
	15,033 Puppet (Peter Haughton)	2:02.4f
	13,233 Hunters Chief (Victor White)	2:01 f
	13,033 Race Ace (Adelbert Cameron)	2:04.4f
76	17,400 Thunder Bret (James Larente)	2:02 f
	17,700 Governor Skipper (Henri Filion)	2:00.3f
77	15,550 Widow's Super (Herb Scott)	2:00.3f
	15,250 Columbia Brooks (Roland Beaulieu)	1:59.4f
78	16,550 Sky Writer (Warren Cameron)	2:01.3f
	16,850 Valiant Leader (Jack Parker, Jr.)	2:00.3f
79	15,750 Cool Wind (Stanley Dancer)	2:01.3f
	16,050 Whamo (Charles W. Clark)	1:59.4f
80	15,233 Skipper's Ensign (Ross Hayter)	2:02.3f
	15,233 Lincoln Center (Wayne Smullin)	2:02.2f
	15,234 French Chef (Stanley Dancer)	2:02 f
81	14,750 Striking Scot (William Gilmour)	2:04.2f
	15,050 McKinzie Almahurst (T. Haughton)	2:00.2f
	14,750 Sold Fuel (Richard Farrington)	2:02.2f
	15,050 Royal Rally (Joe O'Brien)	2:00.4f
82	18,250 Skipbar (Tommy Haughton)	2:02.2f
	18,250 C F Magnum (Carl Allen)	1:59.2f
83	19,250 Scarlet Attraction (Tom Sells)	2:00.1f
	19,550 Governor Thunder (Jim King, Jr.)	2:00.1f
84	14,900 Devil's Adversary (A. Stolzfus) R	1:58.4f
	15,200 Silent Target (Rich. Farrington)	2:00.1f
	14,900 Escape Forever (Herve Filion)	2:00.2f
	14,900 Double Bubba (Jim Gluhm)	1:59.2f

* - Time disallowed

Trot des Nations
Invitational Trot
Last raced at Blue Bonnets Raceway, Montreal, Que.

83	100,000 Diamond Exchange (R.Williams,Sr.)R1	1:57.2f
84	100,000 Bobbo (Norm Jones)	1:57.3f

The General George Washington
Three-Year-Old Colt and Gelding Trot
Last raced at Brandywine Raceway, Wilmington, DE

60	18,500 Hickory Fire (William Haughton)	2:05.1h
61	16,700 Caleb (John Simpson, Sr.)	2:04.4h
62	14,600 A C's Viking (Sanders Russell)	2:05.2h
63	15,300 Express Rodney (Jimmy Cruise)	2:05 h
64	13,150 Argo Kid (Charles King)	2:04.4h
65	15,900 Lord Worthy (Ramon Adams)	2:04.1h
66	15,950 Mustard Seed (Herve Filion)	2:05.1h
67	15,500 Aztec (John Simson, Sr.)	2:05.4h
68	15,650 Nevele Pride (Stanley Dancer)	2:01.4h
69	14,750 Dayan (Fred Bradbury)	2:03.4h
70	11,300 Meadow Malchin (Delvin Miller)	2:02.4f
	11,300 Gallant Prince (Adelbert Cameron)	2:01.4f
71	16,350 A C's Orion (Edward Dunnigan)	2:03.2f
72	15,800 Super Bowl (Stanley Dancer)	2:00 f
	12,300 South Bend (Michael Zeller)	2:03 f
	12,300 Walter Be Good (Ben Webster)	2:01.2f
74	13,575 Armbro Ouzo (Duncan MacDonald)	2:01.1f
75	13,775 Nevele Diamond (Stanley Dancer)	1:59.4f
	13,625 Glasgow (William Haughton)	2:02.3f
	13,625 Songflori (Delvin Miller)	2:01.4f
76	18,200 Way To Fame (Harold Dancer, Sr.)	2:04.4f
77	20,600 Kenwood Hampton (Eddie Davis)	2:03.2f
78	10,000 Noble Art (Delvin Miller)	2:02.2f
79	16,400 Chiola Hanover (James Allen)	2:02.1f
	16,400 Gin Tonic (William Haughton)	2:01.1f
80	17,175 Super Crown (Howard Beissinger)	2:03 f
	17,475 Desert King (Stanley Dancer)	2:02.1f
81	17,775 Smokin Yankee (Stanley Dancer)	2:00.1f
	17,775 Day Care (William Wellwood)	2:01.4f
82	15,600 Triplement (Tom Haughton)	2:02.3f
	15,300 Jazz Cosmos (Mickey McNichol)	1:59.4f
83	27,000 Mr Drew (Glen Garnsey)	2:02.1f
84	20,625 Why Not (Mickey McNichol)	2:01 f
	20,625 Limbo Joe (Gerald Procino) R	1:59.2f

CHRONICLES

The Martha Washington
Three-Year-Old Filly Trot
Last raced at Brandywine Raceway, Wilmington, DE

62	14,200 Worth Seein (Stanley Dancer)	2:05.4h	
63	17,300 Prudence N (James Jordan)	2:04.4h	74 18,500 Noble Florie (Delvin Miller) 2:02.2f
64	13,600 Golden Make It (Dana Irving)	2:04.4h	75 12,625 Meadow Bright (Delvin Miller) 2:05 f
65	15,600 Louanna Sampson (Billy Haughton)	2:07 h	12,425 Exclusive Way (J. Simpson, Jr.) 2:02.3f
66	15,800 -dh- Coalition (Warren Cameron)	2:04.2h	76 19,200 Summer Madness (Vernon Dancer) R 2:00.4f
	-dh- Lady Jamie (James Arthur)		77 18,900 Flowering Beauty (Ross Hayter) 2:05.3f
67	14,600 Lady B Fast (William Popfinger)	2:06 h	78 20,800 Love Touch (Delvin Miller) 2:03.4f
68	11,625 Dagmar Hanover (J. Simpson, Jr.)	2:06.2h	79 21,600 Classical Way (J. Simpson, Jr.) 2:01.4f
	11,775 Endearing (James Arthur)	2:07.4h	80 24,000 Alta Moda (Gene Riegle) 2:02.1f
69	15,450 Cathy Lee (John Schroeder)	2:07 h	81 17,325 Panty Raid (Stanley Dancer) R 2:00.4f
70	16,300 Witch Of Endor (Harry Harvey)	2:01.3f	17,625 Flory Messenger (Raymond Tripp) 2:02.2f
71	16,050 Waverly Hostess (Yves Filion)	2:06 f	82 17,250 Speedrise Coaltown (Terry Holton) 2:02.2f
72	15,600 Rodneys Prize (Ben Webster)	2:02.2f	17,250 Perfect Plus (Joe O'Brien) 2:02.4f
73	11,975 Honeysuckle Rose (Vernon Dancer)	2:02.4f	83 28,500 Perfect Beauty (Ross Hayter) 2:01.1f
	11,975 Lumber Starlet (J. Williams, Jr.)	2:04.3f	

The Westchester *
Two-Year-Old Colt & Gelding Trot
Last raced at Yonkers Raceway, Yonkers, NY

64	57,622 Noble Victory (Stanley Dancer)	2:05.2h	
65	75,000 Governor Armbro (Joe O'Brien)	2:07.2h	9,412 Thornhill (Harry M. Harvey) 2:07.3h
	75,000 Bonus Boy (Adelbert Cameron)	2:06.4h	75 22,552 Steve Lobell (William Haughton) 2:07.1h
66	100,000 Flamboyant (William Haughton)	2:09.2h	76 17,693 Kenwood Hampton (Henri Filion) 2:08 h
67	100,000 Nevele Pride (Stanley Dancer)	2:05.2h	17,693 Green Speed (William Haughton) 2:06.2h
68	37,500 Gun Runner (Earle Avery)	2:06.2h	77 28,638 Noble Move (Glen Garnsey) 2:06.4h
	37,500 Adam Eden (William Myer)	2:08 h	78 19,300 Chiola Hanover (James Allen) 2:04.4h
69	50,320 Victory Star (Vernon Dancer)	2:07.2h	79 22,800 A J Ringer (William Popfinger) 2:07.3h
70	49,495 Quick Pride (Delvin Miller)	2:04 h	80 25,250 Mo Bandy (Carl Allen) 2:06.3h
71	45,498 Super Bowl (Vernon Dancer)	R 2:02.3h	81 36,000 Duke Diamond (William Popfinger) 2:07.1h
72	41,971 Colonial Charm (Glen Garnsey)	2:06 h	82 24,500 What's In A Name (Rick Nuhn) 2:07.4h
73	52,536 Starlark Hanover (David Wade)	2:06.4h	83 38,750 Socrates Lobell (Per Eriksson) 2:04.3h
74	9,312 Spearmint (William Haughton)	2:07 h	84 24,500 Loaded Yankee (William Haughton) 2:07.2h

* - Named the E. Roland Harriman before 1975

The Walt Whitman
Three-Year-Old Colt and Gelding Pace
Last Raced at Garden State Park, Cherry Hill, NJ

85   225,000 Nihilator (Bill O'Donnell)   R 1:52.4m

The General George Wilkes
Two-Year-Old Colt and Gelding Trot
Last raced at Brandywine Raceway, Wilmington, DE

61	16,650 Apex Hanover (Jimmy Arthur)	2:09.3h	
62	15,650 Devilish Song (William Haughton)	2:07.3h	73 11,150 Rising Wind (Peter Haughton) 2:10.4f
63	16,150 Ayres (John Simpson, Sr.)	2:05 h	74 13,400 College Star (Glen Garnsey) 2:06.3f
64	-- Not Raced --		13,400 Skipper Walt (Roland Beaulieu) 2:04.3f
65	14,000 Dean Gimble (James Jordan)	2:10.2h	75 16,800 Nevele Thunder (Stanley Dancer) 2:04.4f
66	14,200 Keystone Pride (William Haughton)	*	76 22,200 Profit Sharing (Ben Webster) 2:05 f
67	13,850 Dart Hanover (Sanders Russell)	2:07.2h	77 19,700 Surgy Hanover (Stanley Dancer) 2:04.3f
68	10,100 Nevele Major (Stanley Dancer)	2:08 h	78 19,200 Scotty Graduate (Syl King, Jr.) 2:08.1f
	10,100 Nimble Diller (Adelbert Cameron)	2:10 h	79 14,000 Armbro Vanguard (Duane Mitchell) 2:07.2f
69	13,700 Gil Hanover (William Haughton)	2:09 h	14,000 Bambino's Rocky (David Wade) 2:11.3f
70	14,850 A C's Orion (William Haughton)	2:04.4h	80 19,500 Sigo Hanover (Raymond Tripp) 2:03.3f
71	11,350 Mr. Regal (Austin Galentimer)	2:05 f	81 17,900 Cooper Lobell (Raymond Tripp) 2:04.2f
	11,350 Star's Chip (Stanley Dancer)	2:04.3f	82 18,500 Dancer's Crown (Stanley Dancer) R 2:02.4f
72	15,500 Burning Speed (William Herman)	2:10 f	83 21,500 Baltic Speed (Soren Nordin) 2:04.1f

* - Time disallowed

The Hiram Woodruff
Free-For-All Trot
Last raced at The Meadowlands, East Rutherford, NJ

77	61,000 Pride of Carlisle (Ben Webster)	1:56.3m	82 126,000 Delmegan (Bill O'Donnell) 1:56.3m
78	75,000 Cold Comfort (Eddie Lohmeyer)	1:58 m	83 129,000 Diamond Exchange(R.Williams,Sr.) 1:56 m
79	78,500 Glencoe Pride (John Campbell)	1:58.4m	84 138,000 Neil Hanover (R.Richardson,Jr.) R 1:55.5m
80	116,000 Crowns Star (William Herman)	1:56.3m	85 152,000 Sandy Bowl (John Campbell) 1:56.1m
81	103,000 Final Score (Tommy Haughton)	1:57.3m	

The World Cup International Pace
Invitational
Last raced at The Meadowlands, East Rutherford, NJ

82	100,000 Beatcha (John Campbell)	e	2:09.1m	125,000 Silver Dollar (Herve Filion) h R 2:53.3m
	125,000 Beatcha (John Campbell)	h	2:56.1m	150,000 Raffi (Mike Gagliardi) m 1:54.2m
	150,000 Genghis Khan (Bill O'Donnell)	m	1:53.1m	85 100,000 On The Road Again (W.Gilmour) e R 2:08.1m
83	100,000 Perfect Out (Doug Brown)	e	2:09 m	125,000 On The Road Again (W.Gilmour) h 2:54.1m
	125,000 Cam Fella (Pat Crowe)	h	2:58.2m	150,000 On The Road Again (W.Gilmour) m R 1:52.2m
	150,000 Cam Fella (Pat Crowe)	m	1:55 m	e Raced at 1-1/8 miles. h Raced at 1-1/2 miles.
84	100,000 Energy Burner (Tom Merriman)	e R	2:08.1m	m Raced at 1 mile.

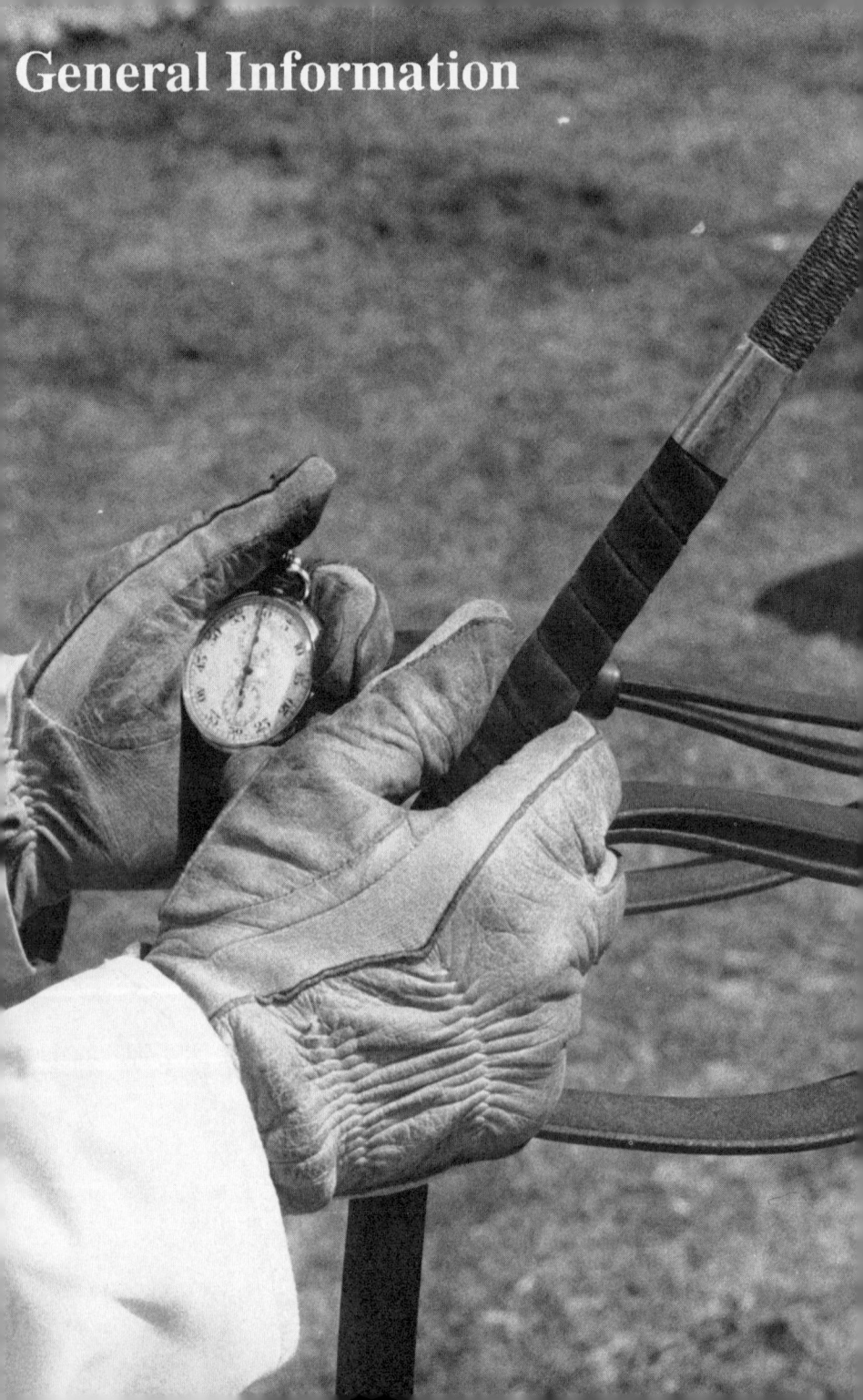

General Information

GENERAL INFORMATION

THE LIVING HALL OF FAME

Election of the Living Hall of Fame is the most prestigious honor a participant in harness racing can attain. The idea for the Living Hall of Fame was originated by the U.S. Harness Writers Association in 1958.

To gain entry, candidates for election must receive seventy-five percent of the votes cast by USHWA members. Only writers and broadcasters who have covered the sport for ten or more years are eligible to participate in the election. Distinctive, life-like statuettes, crafted in the image of each member of the Living Hall of Fame, are on display at the Trotting Horse Museaum, located in Goshen, New York.

Year Voted	Name of Inductee	Born - Died	Achievement
1961	E. Roland Harriman	1896 - 1978	Owner - Breeder
	Stephen G. Phillips	1887 - 1973	Inventor of starting gate
1966	George Morton Levy	1888 - 1977	Track Executive
	Walter J. Michael	1900 - 1977	President of USTA
1967	Octave Blake	1896 - 1969	President of Grand Circuit
	Lawrence B. Sheppard	1897 - 1968	USTA President - Breeder
	Bion Shively	1878 - 1970	Trainer - Driver
1968	Frank Ervin	1904 -	Trainer - Driver
	William Haughton	1923 - 1986	Trainer - Driver
	Delvin Miller	1913 -	Trainer - Driver
1969	Stanley F. Dancer	1927 -	Trainer - Driver
	Thurman Wayne Smart	1904 - 1976	Trainer - Driver
1970	Joseph C. O'Brien	1917 - 1984	Trainer - Driver
	Harry E. Pownall	1902 - 1979	Trainer - Driver
	Sanders Russell	1900 - 1982	Trainer - Driver
1971	Ralph Baldwin	1916 - 1982	Trainer - Driver
	John F. Simpson, Sr.	1919 -	Trainer - Driver
1972	Clint Hodgins	1907 - 1979	Trainer - Driver
1974	Howard Beissinger	1923 -	Trainer - Driver
	Adelbert "Del" Cameron	1920 - 1979	Trainer - Driver
	James J. Dunnigan, Sr.	1912 - 1983	Track Executive
	Frederick L. Van Lennep	1911 - 1987	Owner - Breeder
1975	Herve Filion	1940 -	Trainer - Driver
	Elbridge T. Gerry	1909 -	Owner - Breeder
1977	Earle B. Avery	1894 - 1977	Trainer - Driver
1979	John Chapman	1928 - 1980	Trainer - Driver
	Robert Farrington	1929 -	Trainer - Driver
	Max C. Hempt	1919 -	Owner - Breeder
1980	Clarence F. Gaines	1897 - 1985	Owner - Breeder
	A.E. "Ted" Gibbons	1901 -	Racing Secretary
	Delmer M. Insko	1931 -	Trainer - Driver
1981	Norman Woolworth	1926 -	Owner - Breeder
1982	Glen G. Garnsey	1933 - 1985	Trainer - Driver
1984	George Sholty	1932 -	Trainer - Driver
1985	Carmine Abbatiello	1936 -	Trainer - Driver
	Levi Harner	1909 -	Trainer - Driver
	James M. Lynch	1921 -	Racing Official
1986	Keith Waples	1923 -	Trainer - Driver
	Jimmy Cruise	1917 -	Trainer - Driver
	William Connors	1913 -	Race Secretary
	Theodore J. Zornow	1907 -	Breeder - USTA President
1987	Stanley F. Bergstein	1924 -	HTA Executive V.P.
	Ernest B. Morris	1908 -	Track Executive/USTA Counsel
	Kenneth Dale "K.D." Owen	1903 -	Owner - Breeder
1988	Henry Clay Thomson	1907 -	Co-founder, "Little Brown Jug"
	Dunbar W. Bostwick	1908 -	Owner/Driver/Trainer
1989	William D. "Buddy"Gilmour	1932 -	Trainer - Driver
	Clint Galbraith	1937 -	Trainer - Driver
1990	John D. Campbell	1955 -	Driver
	William A. O'Donnell	1948 -	Driver

GENERAL INFORMATION

IMMORTALS OF THE HALL OF FAME

Men and Women

Name	Year	Name	Year	Name	Year
Townsend Ackerman	1985	Edward F. Geers	1958	William E. Miller	1976
George Alexander	1990	Walter Gibbons	1979	John J. Mooney	1976
Ed Allen	1979	Irvin Gleasson	1959	John Trotwood Moore	1978
W.J. Andrews	1958	William H. Gocher	1979	Walter Moore	1978
J. Elgin Armstrong	1981	John H. Goldsmith	1959	George Ford Morris	1978
Catherine Ault	1981	Shelly Goudreau	1984	P.W. Moser	1979
Earle Avery	1978	Percy Gray	1978	Thomas W. Murphy	1967
Charles Backman	1958	James Hackett	1985	Clinton N. Myers	1976
W.W. Bair	1959	C.J. Hamlin	1958	Joseph Neville	1975
E.J. Baker	1959	Ted Hansom	1978	Katherine H.E. Nichols	1988
William Barefoot	1978	Lamon V. Harkness	1958	H. Willis Nichols	1988
John C. Bauer	1979	E. H. Harriman	1958	Septimus Palin	1958
Tom Berry	1964	E. Roland Harriman	1978	Walter Palmer	1978
C.K.G. Billings	1958	Gladys Harriman	1985	H.M. Parshall	1958
I.O. Blake	1960	Hap Haswell	1979	C.W. Phellis	1958
Octave Blake	1969	Peter D. Haughton	1981	Stephen C. Phillips	1974
Robert Bonner	1967	William R. Haughton	1986	Harry Pownall	1979
Allen Brewer, Jr.	1979	Eugene J. Hayes	1975	Nat Ray	1978
Bowman A. Brown	1975	W.R. Hayes	1976	W.N. Reynolds	1958
Harry Brusie	1978	Dr. Levi Herr	1976	Richard Ricketts	1990
Leonard J. Buck	1974	Harry Hersey	1979	Aubrey Rodney	1978
William Bull	1981	John Hervey	1962	Elizabeth Rorty	1978
Donald H. Busse	1981	Orrin Hickok	1959	William Rysdyk	1958
Del Cameron	1979	Clint Hodgins	1979	Franklin E. Safford	1981
Sol Camp	1959	Scott Hudson	1979	Monroe Salisbury	1959
Walter Candler	1976	Samuel Huttenbauer	1989	Al Sanders	1979
William H. Cane	1958	David R. Johnston	1984	Millard Sanders	1959
Gabe Cartnal	1985	R. Horace Johnston	1981	Marion W. Savage	1974
Jerome I. Case	1990	Frank C. Jones	1958	Ben Schue	1979
William Caton	1958	Edwin T. Keller	1981	Charlotte N. Sheppard	1988
John Chapman	1980	Henry Knauf	1976	Lawrence B. Sheppard	1968
Marvin Childs	1977	Henry Knight	1959	Joseph Sherrill	1958
Walter Cox	1958	Charley Lacey	1979	Bion Shively	1974
A.B. Coxe	1967	Mrs. Rex C. Larkin	1976	Thurman Wayne Smart	1978
Currier & Ives	1976	Rex C. Larkin	1976	John Splan	1958
Jack Curry	1959	George M. Levy	1978	Leland Stanford	1958
Charles Dean	1977	David Look	1958	George Starr	1959
H.K. Devereux	1958	Dan Mace	1977	Harry Stokes	1976
Watson B. Dickerman	1976	Gus Macey	1958	Charles (Doc) Tanner	1978
John H. Dickerson	1958	Donald MacFarlane	1985	Milton Taylor	1985
Robert L. Dickey	1978	John E. Madden	1958	Fred Terry	1979
Budd Doble	1958	Joseph I. Markey	1978	Henry Thomas	1960
John L. Dodge	1958	Charles Marvin	1958	Edward Tipton	1959
Leon G. Duffy	1978	William T. Maybury	1976	Gen. Benjamin Tracy	1990
Roger Duncan	1990	Kenneth McCarr	1979	Charles Valentine	1979
Jim Dunnigan Sr.	1981	Ned McCarr	1976	June VanGundy	1985
Dr. Ogden Edwards, Jr.	1962	W.H. McCarthy	1958	Frances Van Lennep	1971
Col. William Edwards	1976	David McClarey	1959	Frederick Van Lennep	1987
Fred Egan	1960	Mary McCune	1966	Frank Walker	1979
Gage Ellis	1977	Michael McDevitt	1958	John Wallace	1968
Harry Fleming	1958	Lon McDonald	1958	Kay R. Ward	1990
Vic Fleming	1958	Andrew McDowell	1959	Benjamin White	1958
Stoughton Fletcher	1959	Joseph McGraw	1975	Henry Ten Eyck White	1979
J. Malcolm Forbes	1958	Myron McHenry	1958	C.W. Williams	1958
Thomas Gahagan	1960	Richard McMahon	1958	Walter Winans	1981
William Gahagan	1959	Wm. "Doc" McMillen	1985	Frank L. Wiswall	1973
Clarence F. Gaines	1985	Leo McNamara	1959	Frank Woodland	1979
Glen G. Garnsey	1985	Walter Michael	1978	Hiram Woodruff	1958
Walter S. Garrison	1976	Roy Miller	1979	William M. Wright	1976

GENERAL INFORMATION

Horses

Name	Year	Name	Year	Name	Year
Abbedale	1955	Grattan Bars	1976	Nancy Hanks	1955
Abdallah	1967	Greyhound	1965	Napoleon Direct	1955
Adios	1965	Guy Abbey	1957	Nervolo Belle	1966
Adios Butler	1990	Guy Axworthy	1953	Nibble Hanover	1975
Arion	1956	Guy McKinney	1988	Peter Manning	1955
Arion Guy	1957	Hal Direct	1956	Peter Scott	1981
Arnie Almahurst	1984	Hambletonian	1953	Peter The Brewer	1976
Axtell	1955	Hamburg Belle	1957	Peter The Great	1953
Axworthy	1953	Hanover's Bertha	1957	Peter Volo	1953
Beautiful Bells	1976	Happy Medium	1955	Pocahontas	1990
Belle Mahone	1974	Her Ladyship	1973	Poplar Byrd	1976
Belwin	1973	Hickory Pride	1982	Protector	1962
Betty G.	1977	Hickory Smoke	1982	Proximity	1975
Bill Gallon	1984	Highland Scott	1959	Rarus	1978
Billy Direct	1956	Hoot Mon	1966	Rodney	1963
Bingen	1955	Isotta	1975	Romola Hanover	1984
Blue Bull	1981	J. Malcolm Forbes	1959	Rosalind	1973
Brown Hal	1955	Jay-Eye-See	1990	Roya McKinney	1974
Bye Bye Byrd	1982	Jessie Pepper	1969	Ruth M. Chenault	1984
Calumet Chuck	1959	Joe Patchen	1954	St. Julien	1990
Calumet Evelyn	1976	John R. Gentry	1955	San Francisco	1975
Cardigan Bay	1989	Justin Morgan	1976	Scotland	1956
Chimes	1979	Justissima	1975	Scott Frost	1984
Chris Spencer	1979	Kerry Way	1984	Shadow Wave	1977
Countess Vivian	1975	King's Counsel	1975	Sharpshooter	1977
Dale Frost	1977	La Paloma	1973	Single G	1954
Dan Patch	1953	Lady Suffolk	1967	Speedster	1981
Darnley	1960	Lee Axworthy	1955	Spencer	1957
Dean Hanover	1962	Leta Long	1974	Spencer Scott	1956
Dillon Axworthy	1955	Little Pat	1974	Spinster	1981
Direct	1955	Lou Dillon	1955	Star Pointer	1954
Directum	1956	Maggie Counsel	1974	Star's Pride	1979
Directum I	1955	Margaret Castleton	1974	Su Mac Lad	1988
Dottie's Pick	1982	Margaret Parrish	1984	Sunol	1957
Dr. Stanton	1976	Margaret Spangler	1975	Tarport Hap	1978
Electioneer	1955	Maud S.	1955	The Laurel Hall	1959
Emily Ellen	1966	Mc I Win	1976	The Old Maid	1974
Evensong	1957	McKinney	1956	Tilly Brooke	1957
Flora Temple	1955	Meadow Skipper	1983	Titan Hanover	1968
Florican	1976	Merrie Annabelle	1959	Uhlan	1955
Flying Cloud	1985	Messenger	1964	Victory Song	1966
Gene Abbe	1979	Minor Heir	1955	Volo Song	1957
George Wilkes	1955	Miss Bertha Dillon	1966	Volomite	1956
Goldsmith Maid	1953	Misty Hanover	1976	Worthy Boy	1971
Good Time	1978	Most Happy Fella	1984	Zombrewer	1976
		Mr. McElwyn	1956		

THE WRITERS' CORNER OF THE HALL OF FAME

The Writers' Corner of The Hall of Fame honors those who have made contributions to the sport via the written or spoken word. All USHWA members vote on the award.

Name	Year	Name	Year	Name	Year
Stanley Bergstein	1986	Larry Evans	1984	Philip A. Pines	1990
Edward C. Binneweg	1983	James Harrison	1986	Jack Schultz	1983
William F. Brown, Jr.	1990	Clyde Hirt	1987	Tom Shehan	1987
Michael Cipriani	1988	John Hugerich, Jr.	1988	Roy Shudt	1983
Leonard Cohen	1985	Edwin T. Keller	1983	Anthony W. Sisti	1988
Al DeSantis	1989	Mike Lee	1983	Chuck Stokes	1983
Louis Effrat	1985	Lou Miller	1989	Bob Zellner	1987

GENERAL INFORMATION

MEMBERS OF THE U.S. HARNESS WRITERS ASSOCIATION

California Chapter

Steve Schuelein - President
(LA Times) Arcadia
Dick Feinberg - Secretary
(Los Alamitos) Los Alamitos

Antonucci, Jerry
(Orange County Register) Monterey Park
Berry, Peter (Racing Times) Cerritos
Bortstein, Larry
(Orange County Register) Monrovia
Christine, Bill (LA Times) Inglewood
Horowitz, Alan (Pacesetter Brokerage) Anaheim
Leanse, Joel
(Champion Trotter Museum) Sherman Oaks
Lowry, "Biff" (C.A.R.F.) Pomona
McGregor, Ann
(California Breeders Assn.) Rancho Santa Fe
Menges, Jack (Retired) Oakland
Privman, Jay (Racing Times) Santa Monica
Reiss, David
(Del Mar Racing Assn.) San Diego
Simpson, James (*) Sacramento
Wasserman, Bernard (Retired) San Diego

Chicago Chapter

Frinzi, Dominic - President & Secretary
(HHI) Milwaukee

Boudreau, Lou (WGN) Chicago
Brown, John (Daily Racing Form) Chicago
Milbert, Neil (Tribune) Chicago
Polzin, Elmer (Retired) Chicago
Rein, Joseph (Daily News) Chicago
Tinsley, John (Daily Racing Form) Chicago
Walsh, Ed (Maywood Park) Maywood

Delaware Valley Chapter

Marv Bachrad - President
(Times: In Harness) Norristown, PA
Izzy Katzman - Secretary
(Retired) Wilmington

Alpert, Mark (Brandywine Raceway TV) Wilmington
Alpert, Sid (Brandywine Raceway TV) Wilmington
Barton, Jack (Village News) Elverson, PA
Barton, John Reed (Village News) Coatesville, NJ
Dougherty, Richard
(Bucks Cty. Courier-Times) Levittown
Goodman, Isobel (Inquirer) Philadelphia
Hogan, Ed (Retired) Philadelphia
Ireland, Jack (News-Journal) Wilmington
Kiser, Jack (Retired) Philadelphia
Lapos, John III (Evening Chronicle) Allentown
Leaming, Jim (Retired) Philadelphia
McAdams, John (WSSJ) Glendora, PA
Mitchell, Alan (Inquirer) Philadelphia
Newman, Chuck (Inquirer) Philadelphia

Saponara, Nicholas (Retired) Philadelphia
Torrance, Ted (Daily Local News) W. Chester, PA

Florida Chapter

Joe Hartmann - President
(Pompano Park) Pompano Beach
Jean Emerson - Secretary
(Northeast Harness News) Pompano Beach

Andrews, John (Retired) Ft. Myers Beach
Barnes, Craig (Sun-Sentinel) Pompano Beach
Berry, John (*) Coconut Creek
Bonem, Seymour
(Inside Boardwalk) Pompano Beach
Day, Stanley (Wynmoor Voice) Coconut Creek
Dempsey, Kathleen
(Fla. Racing Review) Pompano Beach
Finkelson, Allen (Pompano Park) Pompano Beach
Gawlas, Dan (Pompano Park) Pompano Beach
Hinkle, Chuck (*) Orlando
Hurzler, Robert (*) Delray Beach
Loewe, Denise (The Harness Horse) Boca Raton
Mariotti, Debbie
(Phelps Photography) Pompano Beach
Miller, Connie (*) Lake Worth
Perry, Michael (*) Cooper City
Poirier, Alfred (Pompano Park) Pompano Beach
Prince, Alan (Herald) Miami
Ralby, Herbert (*) Miami Beach
Ransom, Ed (Pompano Park) Pompano Beach
Saltzlman, Philip (WINZ & WIOD) Margate
Santoro, John (Herald) Miami
Fred Segal (Florida Racing Review) Pompano Beach
Siebel, Gary (Pompano Park) Pompano Beach
Strauss, Michael (Retired) New York Times
Thors, Monica (*) Pompano Beach

Monticello-Goshen Chapter

Ed Palladino - President
(Daily Freeman) Kingston
John Manzi - Secretary
(Monticello Raceway) Monticello

Brewer, Christine (Brewer Agcy.) Highland Mills
Burr, William (Times Herald Recrod) Middletown
Burton, Paul (Daily Freeman) Kingston
DeSantis, Al (Times Herald) Middletown
Edwards, Jay (WSUS) Franklin, NJ
Fasman, Donald (Monticello Raceway) Monticello
Finch, Amos (WDLA) Walton
Fusfeld, Ira (Daily Freeman) Kingston
Gould, Wayne (WSUS) Sussex, NJ
Groth, Donald (Catskill OTB) Pomona
Lehman, Charles (Equine geneology) South Falls
Lewis, Barry(Tri-State Gazette)
Mancuso, Sam (Carbondale News) Carbondale
Morelli, Jerry (WSUS) Franklin, NJ
Oil, Howard (Monticello Raceway) Monticello

GENERAL INFORMATION

Outer, Robert (WBNY) Beacon
Pandolfo, Bob (Sports Eye) Delhi
Pines, Phil (Hall of Fame) Goshen
Raskin, Richard (WGNY) Newburgh
Reynolds, William (WSUS) Monticello
Shapiro, Arnold (WLAE-TV) Warwick
Skramstad, Sherry (Historic Track) Goshen
Stogel, Chuck (*) White Plains
Tiano, Charles (Daily Freeman) Kingston
Tunick, Earle (Historic Track) Goshen
Tunick, Julian (Retired) Monticello
Valvano, Guy (Tribune) Scranton
Watson, Earl (Independent) Wilkes-Barre
Wein, Oscar (WDLC) Port Jervis
Wein, Robert (WDLC) Port Jervis
Williams, Al Tribune & Scrantonian) Wilkes-Barre
Wright, Eugene (Goshen Independent) Goshen
Zimich, John (Pocono Downs) Wilkes-Barre, PA

New England Chapter

Vaccaro, Joe - President & Secretary
(Retired) Boston

Berube, Tom (Herald) Boston
Brogna, Sam (Record-American) Boston
Carey, Mike (Herald) Boston
Cohen, Michael (Herald) Newton
Dyer, Frank (Herald) Boston
Ellis, William (Foxboro Raceway) Foxboro
Farley, Peter (Enterprise-Times) Brockton
Gillooly, Ed (Associated Press) Boston
Ginnetti, John Jr. (*) Marlboro
Giuliotti, Joseph (Herald) Boston
Grasso, Ralph T. (Retired) Marlboro
Greenglass, Milton (Herald-American) Boston
Hannon, Jim (Suffolk Downs) Boston
Kelley, Charles
  (Record-American Advertiser) Boston
Kelley, Bob (Herald-American) Boston
Kokernak, Robert (*) Ashburnham
LaChance, Earl (Patriot Ledger) Quincy
Lieberman, Robert (*) Norwood
O'Hara, David (AP) Boston
Olum, Harry (Daily Sun) Lewiston
Poirier, Raymond (*) Salem
Scrivener, Carl (Retired) Quincy
Shehan, Tom (*) Scarborough, ME
Smith, Clayton (*) Cumberland, ME
Sullivan, George (Suffolk Downs) Boston
Sundberg, Cliff (*) Winchester
Temple, Robert(*) Bridgewater
Thomson, Richard (Herald) Boston
Varey, Robert (Retired) Woburn
Ward, Kenneth (Daily News) Bangor
Wheelwright, Hugh (*) Brookline

New Jersey Chapter

Steve Wolf - President
(Freehold Raceway) Freehold
Ellen Harvey - Secretary
(The Meadowlands) East Rutherford

Anzalone, Sam (Meadowlands) East Rutherford
Bergstein, Stanley (HTA) Morristown
Blackton, William (Retired) Phillipsburg
Bradley, John (*) Bedminster
Charters, Tom (Breeders Crown) Manalapan
Doolin, Anne (The Meadowlands) East Rutherford
Dubrowsky, Geoff (Video Knowledge) Middletown
Fanning, Moira (Breeders Crown) Manalapan
Farrar, Jay (Garden State Pk.) Cherry Hill
Farrell, Mike (Record) Bergen
Goldberg, Jane (*) Hawthorne
Goldsmith, Art (*) Titusville
Goodman, Murray (*) River Vale
Gutterman, Allen (Meadowlands) East Rutherford
Heyden, Bob (The Meadowlands) East Rutherford
Hodes, Carol (Meadowlands) East Rutherford
Katz, Steve (Lana Lobell) Long Branch
Kuhnel, George (Courier-Post) Camden
Lawrence, Peter (Harness Horse) Freehold
Lee, Jack E. (Freehold Raceway) Freehold
Leaming, Jim (Retired) Haddonfield
Lerner, Sid (Hoof Beats) Jersey City
Macchia, Paul (*) East Rutherford
McErlean, Chris (HTA) Morristown
Pantalone, John
  (World Wide Racing Photos) Audubon
Putaski, Kelly (Freehold Raceway) Freehold
Rashkow, Mike (2:00 Communications) Freehold
Scutri, Lucille (*) Jersey City
Setola, Christine (Freehold Raceway) Freehold
Singer, Charles (Meadowlands) East Rutherford
Smugar, Craig (Freehold) Freehold
Spellman, Mary Pat (Breeders Crown) Englishtown
Stearns, Bruce (NJSS) West Trenton
Thomas, W. Russell (Retired) West Trenton
Zimmerman, Leon (Public Relations) Trenton

New York City Chapter

Tom Cosentino - President
(Pub. Relations) New York
Kay Cisco - Secretary
(Sports Eye) Port Washington

Alagia, Dom (Dispatch) Hudson
Ansell, Leonard (Retired) New York City
Anthony, George (Teletrack) Manhasset
Baer, Edwin (WHN) New York
Barasch, Lew (Retired) Westbury
Carpenito, Steven (Sports Eye) Pt. Washington
Cirillo, Nick (NYCOTB) New York
Cohen, Irwin (Sports Eye) Port Washington
Cohen, Jack (Sports Eye) Port Washington
Cohen, Mike (Retired) Westbury
Cohen, Steve (Times) Coney Island
DeNonno, Jerry (Retired) New York
Dunnigan, Jim Jr. (Yankees) Bronx
Epstein, Paul (Sports Bulletin) New York
Fensterstock, Howard (Doc Robins) Yonkers
Finley, Bill (Daily News) New York
Gaffer, Wes (*) Nyack
Gallo, John (selections) Woodmere

GENERAL INFORMATION

Gockley, Robert	(Retired) Glen Head
Goldstein, Joseph	(*) New York
Gordon, Michael	(Sports Eye) Port Washington
Gossett, Steve	(Gannett-Westchester) Tarrytown
Grober, Bill	(Harness World) New York
Grossman, Fred	(Triangle Publications) New York
Handler, Eric	(Yonkers Raceway) Yonkers
Hanna, Linda	(Sports Eye) Port Washington
Hirt, Clyde	(Sports Eye) Port Washington
Lefkowitz, Barry	(*) New York
Lewin, Leonard	(Post) New York
Liporace, John	(HRC) White Plains
Little, Dave	(Post) New York
Mastellone, Gerry	(Yonkers Raceway) Yonkers
Miller, Lou	(NYCOTB) New York
O'Day, Joseph	(Retired) New York
Pandolfo, Bob	(Sports Eye) Port Washington
Quinn, Mike	(Quinn Comm.) New York
Robins, M.I. "Doc"	(Doc Robins) Westbury
Sajkowicz, Stan	(Armstrong Daily) NYC
Secolsky, Herman	(Track Facts) Crawford
Sisti, Tony	(Newsday) Garden City
Sussman, Gary	(Yonkers Raceway) Yonkers
Tannenbaum, Harold	(Morning Telegraph) Brooklyn
Tuite, Jim	(Retired) Dix Hills
Walters, Ken	(Sports Eye) Pt. Washington
Watkins, Tom	(Daily Challenger) Brooklyn
Wolf, Joe	(Retired) Port Washington
Zellner, Robert	(Retired) Stony Brook

Ohio Chapter

John Pawlak - President	(USTA) Columbus
Paul Ramlow - Secretary	(USTA) Columbus
Baumgartner, Paul	(The Plain Dealer) Cleveland
Carlton, Ardith	(Hoof Beats) Columbus
Carr, David	(USTA) Columbus
Cowden, Joe	(Retired) Medina
Craig, Joanna	(OSDF) Columbus
Cramer, Carol	(USTA) Columbus
Crum, James	(WCMH-TV) Columbus
Dakin, Dick	(Hoof Beats) Columbus
Darrow, Jack	(Daily Times) Niles
Davis, James J.	(*) Columbus
Evans, Larry	(*) Columbus
Fleming, Paul	(Retired) Columbus
Gilbert, Jenny	(Hoof Beats) Columbus
Grant, Tom	(Journal-News) Hamilton
Hall, Mark	(USTA) Columbus
Harmon, Pat	(Retired) Cincinnati
Hartman, Phil	(Retired) Columbus
Hoffman, Dean	(Hoof Beats) Columbus
Jones, Richard	(Hoof Beats) Columbus
Keckstein, Paul	(Retired) Columbus
Kessler, Kaye	(Retired) Columbus
Keys, Edward	(USTA) Columbus
Kilburger, Wil	(Brown Jug) Columbus
Mann, Stephen	(Retired) Burton
Maurer, Charlotte	(HHYF) Yellow Springs
Millar, Don	(Retired) Columbus
Mindlin, Pacey	(*) Franklin
Moreland, Greg	(Buckeye Harness Horseman) Belleville, MI
Murray, Jack	(Enquirer) Cincinnati
Nardiello, Jerry	(Journal) Middletown
Pastorius, Tom	(Retired) Columbus
Rolfes, Paul	(Dispatch) Columbus
Schiffman, Bill	(*) Columbus
Schmaltz, Brad	(Dispatch) Columbus
Sharpe, Barb	(Buckeye Harness Horseman)
Stewart, John	(Dispatch) Columbus
Strode, George	(Dispatch) Columbus
Sullivan, Robert	(Retired) Springfield
Thomson, Henry	(Gazette) Delaware
Thomson, Tom	(Gazette) Delaware
Verban, George	(Retired) Elyria
Warkentin, Ken	(Northfield Park) Northfield
White, Tom	(Scioto Downs) Columbus
Wilson, Richard	(Beulah Park) Grove City

Saratoga Chapter

Virginia O'Brien - President	(Saratoga Hall Of Fame) Saratoga Springs
George Thompson - Secretary	(Leader-Herald) Gloversville
Bonifacio, John	(Retired) Albany
Butler, Tony	(Retired) Ft. Myers, FL
Carlson, Skip	(Saratoga Raceway) Saratoga Springs
Cooley, Joe	(Times-Record) Troy
Dale, Dean	(Recorder) Amsterdam
Giorgio, Greg	(Capital Dist. OTB) Albany
Gizara, Chester	(Mohawk Valley Democrat) Amsterdam
Graves, Matt	(Times-Record) Troy
Heller, Bill	(Times-Union) Albany
Hugerich, John	(Retired) Schenectady
Lapos, Edward	(Retired) Gloversville
LaRouche, John	(Post Star) Glens Falls
Martin, Ralph, Jr.	(Times-Union) Albany
Meyer, Mike	(*) Schenectady
Miller, George	(Retired) Saratoga Springs
Perkins, Ralph	(Journal) Greenwich
Quinn, James	(Times-Record) Troy
Rowan, William "Rip"	(WTEN) Albany
Smith, Edwin	(Retired) Albany
Sokol, Henry	(NYS Breeders) Amsterdam
Spencer, Phil	(WCSS) Amsterdam
Stellrecht, Richard	(Gazette) Schenectady
Swalsky, Ralph	(Saratoga Harness) Saratoga Spr.
Walker, Cecil	(Gazette) Schenectady
Wildy, Warren "Red"	(Gazette) Schenectady

Vernon, NY Chapter

Leo Pinckney - President	(Retired) Auburn
Jim Moran - Secretary	(Vernon Downs) Vernon
Andrews, John T.	(Retired) Ft. Myers Beach, FL
Burdick, Arnold	(Retired) Hilton Head Island, SC
Caruso, John	(WKTV) Utica
Cerio, George	("Life") East Syracuse

GENERAL INFORMATION

Cimino, Stephen	(City of Utica)
Diliberto, James	(Herald-Journal) Syracuse
Fredericks, Jack	(WKTV) Utica
Fusco, Daniel	(WBVM) Utica
Fusco, Michael	(Retired) Utica
Glasso, Frank	(Retired) Rome
Gryska, Mark	(WKTV) Utica
Heyman, Fred	(Retired) Syracuse
Hobaica, Leo	(Retired) Utica
Keyes, Ed Jr.	(*) Rome
Lawler, Dick	(WKTV) Utica
Malin, Patricia	(Observer-Dispatch) Utica
Milmoe, Michael	(Canastota Publishing) Canastota
Parton, Claude	(*) Syracuse
Reddy, Edward	(Retired) Syracuse
Smith, Gary L.	(Vernon Downs) Canastota
Spartano, Phil	(Retired) Utica
Taylor, Mike	(*) Vernon
Trela, Phillip	(WRNY) Rome
Trimboli, Nick	(Herald-Journal) Herkimer
VanderVeer, Bud	(Herald Journal) Syracuse
Van Sickle, Ken	(Retired) Ithaca
Ventura, John	(Mohawk Valley Times) Utica
Wortley, George III	(Eagle Bulletin) Fayetteville

Western New York Chapter

Bob Summers - President (News) Buffalo

Abbey, Harlan	(*) Buffalo
Brown, William Jr.	(Retired) Batavia
Burr, Chuck	(Buffalo Raceway) Hamburg
Mangefrida, Frank	(WBTA) Batavia
Maussner, Richard	(Metro News) Buffalo
May, Maury	(Buffalo News) Buffalo
McDonald, Michael	(Batavia Downs) Batavia
Morgan, Daniel	(*) Rochester
Sorenson, Michael	(*) Rochester
Szymanski, Peter	(Buffalo Raceway) Hamburg
Thompson, James	(*) Niagara Falls
Valiquette, Gaston	(Consultant) Hamburg
Winegar, Daniel	(Daily News) Batavia
Wood, Darryl	(Buffalo Raceway) Hamburg

At-Large

Brown, Bowman A. Jr. - Director
(Harness Horse) Harrisburg, PA
Ford, Leslie - Director
(Harness Horse) Harrisburg, PA

Batchelar, Lynn	(Horseman & Fair World) Lexington
Barella, Evelyn	(*) Margate, FL
Bisman, Ron	(*) Macau, Hong Kong
Black, Ted	(Bowie Blade News) Lanham, MD
Burke, Phil	(Retired) Springfield, VA
Connors, Jerry	(Rosecroft Raceway) Oxon Hill, MD
Cotolo, Frank	(Times: In Harness) Harrisburg, PA
Davidson, Lyle	(*) Minnetonka, MN
DiRocco, Charles	(Sports Form) Las Vegas, NV
Eddy, Veda	(*) Columbus, IN
Garland, Dave	(HHI) Williamston, MI
Gill, Wes	(Retired), New Windsor, NY
Goldstein, Rob	(Lana Lobell) Whitehouse, NJ
Grant, Tom	(Journal-News) Hamilton, OH
Hackett, Robert A.	(Retired) Tubac, AZ
Harrison, James	(Retired) Hanover, PA
Huston, Roger	(The Meadows) Meadow Lands, PA
Janoff, Murray	(Retired) Boca Raton, FL
Jones, Ralph, Jr.	(PA Race Comm.) Harrisburg, PA
Josey, Al	(Barrie Raceway) Barrie, ONT
King, William H.	Louisville, KY
Kirker, John	(Herald Star) Steubenville, OH
Kyle, Joe	(Horseman & Fair World) Lexington, KY
Miller, George	(Retired) Berryville, AK
Monaghan, Harold	(Retired) Louisville
Roberts, Ernest	(Retired) Hobe Sound, FL
Robinson, Max	(Retired) North Port, FL
Robinson, Maxwell	(Herald) Haines City, FL
Rose, Van	(Times-Leader) Wilkes-Barre, PA
Salive, Frank	(Windsor Raceway) Windsor, ONT
Schuler, Greg	(Horseman & Fair World) Lexington, KY
Sprow, James	(Castleton Farms) Lexington, KY
Sucee, Ralph	(The Standardbred) Toronto, ONT
Tenczar, Rick	(Harness Horse) Harrisburg, PA
Trudelle, Andre	(La Presse) Montreal, QUE
Wallace, Edward	(Retired) Hanover, PA

* - Freelance

Page 393

GENERAL INFORMATION

PROXIMITY ACHIEVEMENT AWARD WINNERS

Given annually by the U.S. Harness Writers Association to an individual or organization for outstanding service to the sport.

Year	Honoree	Year	Honoree
1990	The *Trotting & Pacing Guide*	1970	James C. Harrison
1989	John A. Cashman, Jr.	1969	*Hoof Beats*
1988	Charles F. Russo	1968	Thurman W. Smart
1987	Hugh "Andy" Grant	1967	Frank Ervin
1986	William F. Brown, Jr.	1966	The Hall of Fame of the Trotter
1985	The Breeders Crown	1965	Stanley Dancer
1984	Rambling Willie	1964	Little Brown Jug Society
1983	Allen J. Finkelson	1963	U.S. Trotting Association
1982	George Smallsreed	1962	George M. Levy, Sr.
1981	Alan J. Leavitt	1961	Harness Tracks of America
1980	T.J. (Ted) Zornow	1960	Delvin Miller
1979	The Meadowlands	1959	Hayes Fair Acres (Gene & Don Hayes)
1978	John F. Simpson	1958	Billy Haughton
1977	The Hambletonian Society	1957	Walter J. Michael
1976	Stanley F. Bergstein	1956	E. R. Harriman
1975	Mike Lee	1955	M.I. (Doc) Robins Program
1974	Roy Shudt	1954	Octave Blake
1973	Herve Filion	1953	William H. Cane
1972	The Grand Circuit	1952	Steve Philips, Starting Gate
1971	Dr. LeRoy Coggins	1951	The Old Country Trotting Assn.

HTA CARETAKER OF THE YEAR
The Red Smith Award

Harness Tracks of America, in co-operation with Delvin and Mary Lib Miller, presents annual awards to the Caretakers of the Year. In 1983 the categories were divided into two: the groom of a horse earning over $100,000, and the groom of a horse earning under $100,000.

Year	Winner (Horse)	Money Division
1990	Cheryl Bloomfield (Town Pro)	over $100,000
	Mary Barrett (Valscore)	under $100,000
1989	Paul D. "Huey" Clark (Matt's Scooter)	over $100,000
	Alice Allen (Pat Tarsio)	under $100,000
1988:	Bob Core (Editor In Chief)	over $100,000
	Pam King (Georgina Seelster)	under $100,000
1987:	Ron Molendyk (Frugal Gourmet)	over $100,000
	Sheryl Kolb (Lake Tahoe/Charlie Hustle)	under $100,000
1986:	Charlie Coleman (Sugarcane Hanover)	over $100,000
	Sherry Ford (Scott T Collins)	under $100,000
1985:	Tina Lindgren (Prakas)	over $100,000
	Diane Moser (Shenango Ayres)	under $100,000
1984:	Marcia Hamilton (Baltic Speed)	over $100,000
	Jill Parker (Emperor Virgo)	under $100,000
1983:	Dan Riddell (Ralph Hanover)	over $100,000
	Joan Crain (Valley Jewel)	under $100,000
1982:	Odell Short (Fan Hanover)	(Single division only)

GENERAL INFORMATION

THE JOHN HERVEY JOURNALISM AWARDS

In 1962 the John Hervey Writing Awards were created to honor outstanding print journalism.

In 1980, recognizing the very different styles and requirements of newspaper and magazine journalism, the award was divided into two categories.

1989	(newspaper)	Maryjean Wall, Lexington Herald-Leader
	(magazine)	Gary L. Smith, freelance
1988	(newspaper)	Phil Pines, "On the Rail," syndicated column
	(magazine)	Bill Heller, freelance
1987	(newspaper)	Dave Joseph, Ft. Lauderdale Sun-Sentinel
	(magazine)	Veda Eddy, freelance
1986	(newspaper)	Clyde Hirt, Sports Eye
	(magazine)	Bill Heller, freelance
1985	(newspaper)	Steve Lowery, Los Angeles Times
	(magazine)	Jerry Shively, freelance
1984	(newspaper)	Jay Bergman, Sports Eye
	(magazine)	Steve Schuelein, freelance
1983	(newspaper)	Chuck Slater, New York Daily News
	(magazine)	Steve Schuelein, freelance
1982	(newspaper)	Clyde Hirt, Sports Eye
	(magazine)	Phil Straw, freelance
1981	(newspaper)	Mark Schwartz, Middletown (NY) Times-Herald-Record
	(magazine)	Patty Hillis Carro, Columbus Monthly
1980	(newspaper)	Mark Schwartz, Middletown (NY) Times-Herald-Record
	(magazine)	Phil Von Borries, The Red Mile/Louisville Downs
1979		John Berry, SOANJ
1978		Doug Looney, *Sports Illustrated*
1977		Craig Barnes, Pompano Beach Sun-Sentinel
1976		Jack Kiser, Philadelphia Daily News
1975		Lynn Simross, Los Angeles Times
1974		Maryjean Wall, Lexington Herald-Leader
1967 through 1973		no award given
1966		Pat Ryan, *Sports Illustrated*
1965		Gerald Eskenazi, New York Times
1964		Jack Kiser, Philadelphia Daily News
1963 & 1962		No grand winner; seven "divisional" winners

THE BROADCASTERS AWARDS

In 1984, awards designed to honor radio and TV journalists were begun:

1989	(television)	"The Breeders Crown Finale" - TWI (Chuck Howard, Producer)
	(radio)	"The Great American Pastime" - Syndicated (Philip A. Pines, Producer)
1988	(television)	"From Foal to Finish Line" - WCSH-TV (Bill Green, Producer)
	(radio)	"Racing in New Brunswick" - CBC Radio (Tony Doucette, Writer, Producer)
1987	(television)	"Breeders Crown from Roosevelt Raceway (Bob Rosburg, Jr., Producer)
	(radio)	"Live From Yonkers Raceway" (Norman Weil, Producder)
1986	(television)	William H. King Productions (Pompano Harness Weekly)
	(radio)	The Trotting Horse Museum ("The Great American Pasttime")
1985	(television)	Kentucky Production Center (Breeders Crown Highlights Show)
	(radio)	The Trotting Horse Museum ("The Great American Pasttime")
1984	(television)	WTVQ-TV, Lexington KY (Kenny Rice, on air)
	(radio) (tie)	KYW Newsradio, Philadelphia (Marv Bachrad)
	(tie)	Eastern Racing Network, Hinsdale, NH (Carleton Metcalf)

GENERAL INFORMATION
HARNESS RACING PUBLICATIONS

The following publications are offered by the United States Trotting Association. The prices quoted are in U.S. Funds and include postage and handling.

Please direct all inquiries and orders to: USTA, 750 Michigan Ave., Columbus, OH 43215. Please send checks or money orders, only, and make them payable to: USTA. When ordering, please note that publications are issued at various times of the year.

The Year Book Contains statistical information, world records, alphabetical list of all horses, their breeding, earnings, records, etc. Published annually in March. $15 a copy.

Sires and Dams Register Statistical tables on new and reduced standard record performers of the preceding year. Tables of sires and dams of such performers and a roster of all 2:00 performers. Published annually in April. $60 a copy.

Index of Sires and Index of Broodmares not in the Sires and Dams This publication identifies all of the sires and dams which appeared in the *Sires and Dams* between 1949 and 1986, but are not carried in the 1987 or later editions. The index lists more than 12,000 sires and 82,000 dams and the last year in which each appeared in the *Sires and Dams*. $12.00 per copy. Published every five years. Last published in 1988.

Total Performance Library - Microfiche Complete past performance lines for each horse racing in North America during the past year. Published annually in February. $125 per set. $155 per set with easel binder and filing panels.

USTA Chart Book - Microfiche A library of every race in Canada and U.S., indexed and listed by track. Published in February. $125 per set. $155 with easel binder and filing panels.

Care and Training of the Trotter and Pacer James C. Harrison's comprehensive and authoritative book on all phases of preparing and racing a standardbred. Chapters by 16 leading horsemen. $10 to USTA members; $15 to non-members.

Trotting and Pacing Guide Statistical publication designed for sports writers and sportscasters to assist their reporting of harness racing. Published annually in March. $7.50 per copy.

Hoof Beats The USTA's colorful official monthly magazine. To USTA members, $10 per year ($14.50 if residing outside the U.S.). To non-members, $18 per year ($29.50 outside U.S.) Air mail (both member and non-member) $40.00 additional.

Stakes Guide Contains detailed conditions and payments for stakes and futurities; payment schedules; chronological list of major stakes and feature races with purse values; and racing calendar. Published annually in January. $15 per copy.

Names of Registered Horses Unavailable for reuse - Microfiche Annual product available at the end of March at $10 a set.

Racing, Farm, Corporate, and Stable Names Registered with USTA List of those registered, with addresses, officers, stockholders, etc. Published annually in February. $10 per copy.

Driver Roster Annual listing of drivers in purse races during the past year. Alphabetical arrangement, giving starts, 1sts, 2nds, 3rds, U.D.R.S average, and earnings for each. Published annually in March. $5.00 per copy.

Membership Roster Annual list of names and addresses of USTA members, arranged alphabetically by state within USTA districts. Published annually November 15. $5 per copy.

Harness Handbook Contains profiles and statistics of leading drivers and horses. Published annually in April. $8 per copy.

Handicapping Beyond the Basics A handicapping primer with more than 80 examples using actual races from tracks around North America. $3.50 per copy.

GENERAL INFORMATION

OTHER NORTH AMERICAN HARNESS RACING PUBLICATIONS

U.S.-Based Publications

The Harness Horse Published weekly by The Harness Horse, Inc., P.O. Box 10779, Harrisburg, PA 17105. Phone: (717) 234-5099. Subscription Rates: $78 yearly; $86 Canada; $296 foreign (U.S. funds). Editor: Les Ford.

The Horseman and Fair World Published weekly by The Horseman Publishing Co., 904 N. Broadway, Lexington, KY 40505. Phone: (606) 254-4026. Subscription Rates: $60 yearly; $75 Canada & Foreign (U.S. funds). Editor: Chip Diehl

Harness Eye Published daily (execpt Christmas) by Sports Eye, Inc., 18 Industrial Park Dr., Pt. Washington, NY 11050. Phone: (516) 484-3300. $435/yr. Ed. In Chief: Jay Bergman.

Times: In Harness Published bi-weekly by Times: Standard, Inc., 8125 Jonestown Rd., Harrisburg, PA 17105. Phone: (717) 469-2000. Subscription Rates: $65 yearly; $75 in Canada (U.S. Funds); $225 Foreign Air-Mail. Single copy $3.00. Executive Editor: Frank Cotolo

Canadian-Based Publications

The Canadian Sportsman (Weekly May-Oct, Bi-weekly Nov.-April) 25 Old Plank Rd., P.O. Box 129, Straffordville, Ont., Canada N0J 1Y0. Telephone (519) 866-5558. Canada: $40 yearly ($70 2 years); U.S.: $55 yearly (U.S. Funds). Single copies: $2. Editor: Gary Foerster.

The Standardbred (Bi-weekly) Box 150, Acton, Ont., Canada L7J 2M3. Telephone: (519) 856-9524. Canada: $35 ($55 2 years, $70 3 years); U.S.: $50; Foreign: $60 yearly. Editor and Publisher: Paul A. Nolan.

TROT! (Monthly) Published by CTA, and is the official publication of the Canadian Trotting Association, with offices located at 233 Evans Ave., Toronto, Ont., Canada M8Z 1J6. Telephone: (416) 252-3565. CTA members automatically receive a subscription at a cost of $3.60; Others $18 yearly; $30 for two years. U.S. & Foreign: $30 yearly; $50 for two years. Editor: Harold Howe

Atlantic Post Calls (Weekly March-October, Bi-weekly November-February) P. O. Box 824, Amherst, N.S., Canada B4H 3J9. Telephone: (902) 667-3469. Canada: $40 yearly; U.S.: $70 (U.S. Funds) yearly. Publisher/Editor: Doug Harkness

Publications of Regional Interest

The Buckeye Harness Horseman (Quarterly) 471 E. Broad St., Suite 1308, Columbus, Ohio 43215. Telephone: (614) 221-3650. $10/yr; $18 (U.S.) Canadian & Foreign. Editor: Marty Evans.

Florida Racing Review (Weekly) 8091 NW 13th Street, Margate, FL 33063. Telephone: (305) $26 yearly. Publisher: Fred Segal.

Illinois Standardbred and Sulky News (Monthly) 111 Shore Dr., Hinsdale, IL 60521. Telelephone (708) 887-7722. $24 yearly. Editor: Kimberly Rinker.

The Michigan Harness Horseman (Monthly) Published by the Michigan Harness Horsemen's Association, 4650 Moore St., P.O. Box 349, Okemos, MI 48805. Telephone (517) 349-2920. Editor: Sandy Paesens.

Midwest Harness Horse (Monthly) 3235 S. 53rd Ave., Cicero, IL 60650. Telephone (708) 656-9443. Editor & Publisher: Dan Poprawski.

New Jersey Standardbred (Quarterly) P. O. Box 839, Freehold, NJ 07728. Telephone (201) 462-2357. Subscription: $6 yearly. Editor: Leon Zimmerman.

Northeast Harness News 456 Boom Rd., Saco, ME 04072. Telephone: (207) 282-9295. $10 yearly. Editor: Jean Emerson.

Ohio Standardbred (Weekly) 19 S. Main St., Rittman, Ohio 44270. Telephone: (216) 925-3040. $35 per year. Editor and Publisher: Bruce M. Trogdon.

GENERAL INFORMATION

HARNESS RACING BOOKS

This listing does not guarantee that all titles are available in local bookstores or, necessarily, even in print.

Further information on these publications can be obtained through the publisher or various book dealers serving the sport.

Title by Tom Ainslie
Published by Simon & Schuster
-- **Ainsle's New Complete Guide to Harness Racing**

Title by Barbara Berry
Published by A.S. Barnes & Co.
-- **The Standardbreds**

Title by Ron Bisman
Published by Bisman Publications, Ltd.
-- **Globetrotting Simpson**

Title by Donald P. Evans & Philip S. Pikelny
Published by A.S. Barnes & Co.
-- **Rambling Willie: The Horse That God Loved**

Title by Walter Farley
Published by Random House
-- **The Black Stallion's Sulky Colt**

Titles by Marguerite Henry
Published by Rand McNally & Co.
-- **Born to Trot**
-- **One Man's Horse**

Titles by John Hervey
Published by Coward McCann, Inc.
-- **American Harness Racing**
-- **Lady Suffolk**
-- **Messenger**
-- **The American Trotter**

Title By Paul A. Wilkes, Jr.
Published by Exposition Press
-- **Happiness Is Being In The Winner's Circle**

Title by Marie Hill
Published by Arco
-- **Gentleman Joe: The Story of** Harness Driver Joe O'Brien

Title by Tom Ivers
Published by Esprit Racing Team Limited
-- **The Fit Racehorse**

Title by M. Phyllis Lose, DVM
Published by Arco
-- **Blessed Are The Broodmares**

Title by Ken McCarr
Published by The University of Kentucky
-- **The Kentucy Harness Horse**

Title by R.A. McKenzie
Published by Roydon Lodge Stud
-- **The Roydon Heritage**

Title by Philip A. Pines
Published by Arco
-- **The Complete Book of Harness Racing - Fourth Edition**

Title by E.C. Spaulding, DVM
Published by Rodale Press
-- **A Veterinary Guide For Animal Owners**

Title by Alice Scales
Published by KNI, Inc.
-- **Koko's Filly**

For a more complete listing of harness or horse books, we suggest you contact the Trotting Book Shop, 130 Peachcroft Drive, Bernardsville, NJ 07924, (201) 766-6111, or other harness book dealers.

GENERAL INFORMATION

AN ALBUM OF 'POP' RECORDS

Drivers

Most Wins, One Day, One Track
12 .... Mike Lachance .... Yonkers Raceway, NY, June 23, 1987
11 .... Clint Hodgins .... Dufferin Park, Toronto, Nov. 25, 1939
11 .... Joe O'Brien .... Truro Raceway, Truro, NS, Sept. 16, 1942

Most Wins, One Raceway Program, Single Dashes
8 .... Herve Filion .... Hinsdale Raceway, Hinsdale, NH, Sept. 10, 1978
8 .... Pat Crowe .... Kingston Park Raceway, Kingston, Ont., Dec. 30, 1984
8 .... John Campbell .... Freehold Raceway, Freehold, NJ, October 25, 1986
8 .... Allen Cullen .... Assiniboia Downs, Winnipeg, Alta, February 4, 1989

Consecutive Wins, One Raceway Program, Single Dashes
7 .... Augustine "Gus" Ratchford .... Sackville Downs, Halifax, NS, Feb. 21, 1976
7 .... Ross Croghan .... Cal-Expo Raceway, Sacramento, CA, June 23, 1989

Most Wins, One Driver, One Track, Single Year
487 .... Herve Filion .... Yonkers Raceway, Yonkers, NY, 1989

Three Stakes Wins - Three Tracks - One Day
Michel Lachance - March 25, 1989
No No No - Div. of a leg of the North American Pacing Series - Freehold Raceway
Sweet Sharon - Overbid Pacing Series Final - The Meadowlands
Matt's Scooter - Leg of the George Morton Levy Memorial Pacing Series - Yonkers Raceway

Only Father and Son Duo To Win National Dashwinning Championships
Don Busse (1963) and Daryl Busse (1975)

Only Father and Son Duo to win National UDRS Titles
Gene Riegle (Father: 1966, '70, & '72) and Bruce Riegle (Son: 1985)

Most Dead Heats, One Driver, One Night
2 .... Jean Paul Morel .... Saratoga Harness, Saratoga, NY, June 26, 1978
2 .... Harold Stead .... Greenwood Raceway, Toronto, January 18, 1980
2 .... Tom Swift .... Batavia Downs, Batavia, NY, March 15, 1987
2 .... Scott Robbins .... Quad City Downs, E. Moline, IL, June 14, 1989

Fastest Dead Heat For Win Between Male and Female Driver
1:57.4 - Mickey McNichol (Loubred A J) and Debbie Evilsizor (Bowers Hanover)
Pompano Park, Pompano Beach, FL, January 17, 1986

Most Money Won, One Driver, One Meeting
$6,391,003 - John Campbell, The Meadowlands, E. Rutherford, NJ, - 1988

First Woman to Win a Track Driving Championship
Bea Farber - 1973, Northville Downs, Northville, MI - .536 UDR

Fastest Female Driver
1:54.4 - Jacqueline Ingrassia, driving Followme Holly, The Meadowlands, July 25, 1986
1:55 - Diane Williams, driving Rootbeer Slammer, Scioto Downs, May 14, 1988

Most 2:00 Miles, One Raceway Program
7 - John Campbell, Freehold Raceway - Freehold, NJ, October 25, 1986
7 - John Campbell, The Meadowlands - East Rutherford, NJ, August 7, 1987
7 - John Campbell, The Meadowlands - East Rutherford, NJ, February 6, 1988

Youngest Driver of a 2:00 Mile
TT1:58-1/2 - 12-year-old Alma Sheppard with Dean Hanover - Lexington, KY, Sept. 24 1937

Fastest Miles by an Amateur Driver
1:56.3 .... Trot .... Paul Spears with Chadwick Hanover, The Meadowlands, July 31, 1989
1:54.2 .... Pace .... Ed Ryan with Seven O'Clock, Lexington, Sept. 28, 1985

Most Drivers Accomplishing Following Milestones, Single Season
400 wins	7 (1988)	$3,000,000	12 (1988)
300 wins	17 (1987)	$2,000,000	29 (1988)
200 wins	62 (1987)	$1,000,000	71 (1988)

GENERAL INFORMATION

Horses

Most Dashes or Heats Won, Lifetime
350 .... (Historic Record) .... Goldsmith Maid .... Trotter 1864-77
262 .... (Historic Record) .... Single G .... Pacer .... 19 -26
241 .... (Modern record) .... Symbol Allen .... Pacer 1943-58

Longest Winning Streak
41 .... Carty Nagle, 1937-38

Longest Losing Streak
166 .... New Express, 1977-84
161 ... (N. Am.) .... Shiaway Moses, 1978-87

Most Wins, One Season
65 .... Victory Hy, 1950

Most 2:00 Miles, Lifetime
79 .... Rambling Willie, 1972-83

Most 2:00 Miles, Season
32 .... Pacer .... Cam Fella, 1983 (includes three qualifiers)
16 .... Trotter .... Mack Lobell, 1987 (includes three qualifiers)

Most 2:00 Miles, Consecutive
27 .... Cam Fella, 1983

Most 2:00 Miles, One Raceway Meet
2,348 .... The Meadowlands, 1987

Most Wins in $100,000 Races, One Year
Pacer .... 9, Niatross, 1980   Trotter .... 6, Chiola Hanover, 1979

Only Twin Foals to Face Each Other in a Pari-Mutuel Race
Mr Heckle (c) & Mrs Jeckle (f) .... Fairplex Park, CA, June 12, 1987
Both 2-year-old pacing foals of 1985, by Skippers Subject out of Waltzing Breta
(Mr Heckle finished third, Mrs Jeckle finished sixth)

Triple Dead Heats to Win
Freehold Raceway, October 3, 1953	Patchover, Payne Hal, Penny Maid
Buffalo Raceway, May 18, 1957	Adios Queen, Clever Counsel, Crescendo
Roosevelt Raceway, November 27, 1957	Flaxey Dream, Great Knight, Navy Song
Santa Anita, March 26, 1958	General Thompse, Joyce Rosecroft, McKinley Mahone
Windsor Raceway, October 14, 1970	Arnold Gem, Banjo Phil, Bervaldo
Midwest Harness (now Riverside Downs), May 24, 1974	Poplar Breeze, Ragin Rival, Kimberly Sue
Rockingham Park, April 14, 1975	Bellnow, Turn On, Splendid Splinter
Pocono Downs, July 12, 1977	Booty's Dizzy, Jeff Crain, Royal Grant
Bay Meadows, January 11, 1978	Rapid Canny, Royal Rick's Way, James Gem
Pocono Downs, May 13, 1980	Fulla Promise, Quite Guy, Ron
Greenwood Raceway, August 22, 1981	Baron Reve, Blizzard Almahurst, Happy Hoot
Greenwood Raceway, September 2, 1982	Close Encounter, JayAnn, Sully's Bar
Rideau Carleton, November 9, 1983	Fascination Grade, Nathalie's Presto, Speedy Valiant
Raceway Park, August 2, 1984	Chip Shot, Delajay, Marietta Touress
Hippodrome Trois' Rivieres, May 2, 1988	Kingwood Tog, Jack Des Rivieres, H F Elaine
Hiawatha Horse Park, October 7, 1990	Armbro Indeed, Greystone Alicia, Too Sharp

Dead Heats to Win by Mutuel Entry
Clip Along and Chuck's Comet   at Buffalo Raceway, June 9, 1976 -- 2:08.1
Mars Sharp and Mars Judith   at Blue Bonnets, Oct. 2, 1976 -- 2:05

Dead Heats - Consecutive Races, Same Horses
JC's Pippiniello & Skipper's Victor   Vernon Downs, April 3 & 11, 1987 (2:02.3, 2:00.0)

Fastest Dead Heat, All-Time
1:51.2 .... Laag (Dick Farrington) & Jaguar Spur (Dick Stillings)
The Red Mile, Lexington, KY, Sep. 26, 1987

GENERAL INFORMATION

Business

Record $2 Win Payoff
$1,365.80 .... Rod's Faybill, Scarborough Downs, Scarborough, ME, June 23, 1981

Record $2 Place Payoff
$373.20 .... Aston Wight, Delmarva Downs, Berlin, MD, September 3, 1987

Record $2 Show Payoff
$340.80 .... Armbro Haggart, Freehold Raceway, Freehold, NJ, October 22, 1988

Record $2 Daily Double Payoff
$8,505.80 .... Pilot Me & Shadydale Impact (7-2), Pompano Pk., Pompano Bch., FL, March 4, 1968

Record $2 Payoff - Any Type Wager
$1,243,053 .... Hazel Park, Hazel Park, Mi, September 17, 1988
("Twin-Super" wager, for selecting the first four finishers in two races)

Record Single-Night Mutuel Handle
$4,612,013 .... The Meadowlands, East Rutherford, NJ, July 19, 1985
(Meadowlands Pace Night)

Record Single-Race Handle
$1,168,010 .... The Meadowlands, East Rutherford, NJ, July 19, 1985
(Meadowlands Pace Night)

Record Single-Race Minus Pool
$171,011.15 .... The Meadowlands, East Rutherford, NJ, July 19, 1985
(Meadowlands Pace Night)

Record Attendance - Nighttime Card
54,861 .... Roosevelt Raceway, Westbury, NY, August 20, 1960
(2nd Edition of the Roosevelt International Trot - won by Hairos II)

Record Attendance - Daytime Card
50,792 .... Delaware County Fair, Delaware, OH, September 21, 1989
(44th Little Brown Jug Pacing Classic - won by Goalie Jeff)

The Fastest Single Day in Harness Racing History

The Meadowlands - Friday, July 8, 1988 - Average time for 11 races: 1:52.4

Race	Condition	Winner	Driver	Time
1.	NW 15,500 Last 7 Pace	Windsor's Honor	Jack Moiseyev	1:53.2
2.	WO 15,000 Lifetime	Dictionary	Bill O'Donnell	1:52.4
3.	$50,000 Claiming Hcp	Happy Alche	Ben Webster	1:53.2
4.	NW 4 Races Lifetime	American Storm	Peter Ruscitto	1:53.4
5.	NW 4 Races Lifetime	Aberpass	Cat Manzi	1:53.3
6.	Open	Ramblin' Storm	Mike Lachance	1:50.1 a
7.	Meadowlands Pace Elim.	Paladium Lobell	Richard Silverman	1:52.3
8.	Meadowlands Pace Elim.	Camtastic	Bill O'Donnell	1:51.3
9.	$75,000 Clmg./Cond.	Tautitaw Bluegrass	Mike Lachance	1:53.4
10.	Meadowlands Pace Elim.	Armbro Global	John Campbell	1:53.1
11.	NW 4 Races Lifetime	H A's Pace Setter	Mike Lachance	1:52.1

a - At the Time, the Fastest Mile Ever Paced Under The Lights

GENERAL INFORMATION

FASTEST PERFORMERS BY AGE

Age	Fastest in 1990	Time	Fastest of All-Time	Time	(Year)
14	Van Rhet	1:59.2	Baron Barnum	1:57.2f	(1989)
13	Lord Neutrino	1:58.3	Seatrain	1:57.1	(1985)
12	Extraordinary	1:57.1f	Seatrain	1:55	(1984)
11	Hanover Knight	1:55.1	Black Armbro N	1:55.1f	(1988)
			Newt Lobell	1:55.1	(1985)
			Fancy A Toliver A	1:55.1	(1987)
			Hanover Knight	1:55.1	(1990)
10	Shannon Dee J	1:55	Remarkable N	1:53.1	(1987)
9	Instrument Landing	1:53.3	Same		
8	See You There	1:53	Skipper Vantar N	1:52.4	(1989)
7	Joe's Scooter	1:51.4	Same		
6	Banker Blue Chip	1:52.1	Ramblin' Storm	1:50.1	(1988)
5	T K's Skipper	T 1:49.2	Same		
4	Ceasars Jackpot	1:51.2	Jaguar Spur	T 1:49.2	(1988)
3	In The Pocket	T 1:49.3	Matt's Scooter	T 1:48.2	(1988)
2	Artsplace	1:51.1	Same		

THE LEADING DOUBLE-GAITED PERFORMERS OF ALL-TIME

While it extremely rare to see a Standardbred perform with equal alacrity on both gaits, a number of horses have demonstrated such ability. Here is a list of the most outstanding "double-gaited" performers of all-time; the complete list of individuals who have combined marks of four minutes or faster:

Performer, Sex, Sire (Year Foaled)	Age	Trotting Record	Age	Pacing Record	Total
Bandit Spur, g, by Defiant Yankee (1983)	4	1:58.2f	3	1:55.3f	3:54
Scully, h, by Noble Victory (1977)	6	T 1:58	7	1:56.3	3:54.3
Brisk Fling, g, by Brisco Hanover (1982)	3	2:01.2f	5	1:53.3	3:55
Speedy Romeo, h, by Romeo Hanover (1973)	4	1:59.2	7	1:55.4	3:55.1
Tequila Star, g, by Hunters Star (1976)	4	1:59.4	6	1:56.1	3:56
Skipper Walt, h, by Meadow Skipper (1972)	4	T 1:58.2	4	T 1:57.4	3:56.1
Noble Prince, h, by Noble Victory (1972)	6	T 2:00.4	6	T 1:55.2	3:56.1
Logan Speed, g, by Speed In Action (1980)	2	2:00.2	4	1:57f	3:57.2
Crown Wood, g, by Speedy Crown (1978)	6	1:57.4	4	1:59.4	3:57.3
Armbro Worthy, h, by Dream Of Glory (1978)	7	1:59.1	5	1:59f	3:58
Steamin' Demon, h, by Demon Hanover (1953)	6	1:59.1	4	T 1:58.4	3:58
Twistum, g, by Dream Maker (1984)	6	1:58.2f	4	1:59.4h	3:58.1
Provenance, g, by Dream Of Glory (1980)	8	1:58.2f	7	2:00f	3:58.2
No Gimmicks, m, by Bo Bo Arrow (1986)	3	1:59.1	4	1:59.2f	3:58.3
Calumet Evelyn, m, by Guy Abbey (1931)	5	1:59-1/2	4	1:59-1/4	3:58-3/4
Cabonga Lobell, h, by Speedy Crown (1979)	4	Q 2:00.4	4	1:58q	3:58.4
Southern Sheena, m, by South Bend (1983)	5	1:59.4q	4	1:59.1q	3:59
Countess Adios, m, by Adios (1957)	6	T 2:01.2	3	1:57.3	3:59
Horton's Miss, m, by Horton Hanover (1975)	7	1:59.1	3	2:00.1f	3:59.2
Circuit, h, by Lindys Pride (1980)	5	1:59.4	4	1:59.4f	3:59.3
Gerry Mir, h, by Rodney (1960)	3	T 2:00	7	1:59.3	3:59.3
Crockett, h, by Diller Hanover (1962)	4	2:00.3f	7	1:59.1h	3:59.4
My Credentials, h, by Noble Gesture (1979)	3	T 2:00.3	5	1:59.2f	4:00

GENERAL INFORMATION

USTA SERVICES TO THE MEDIA

The top 3-year-olds are coming to the local track for a major stake this week. How can I get information about how they have done so far this year?

The United States Trotting Association collects and maintains current racing records on all of the harness horses in the U.S. and Canada. Your local track may be the best source of information, but if you need to supplement what they give you, just give the USTA Publicity Department a call. We will be glad to provide you with summary statistics and detailed lines of a horse's previous starts.

Each year, we publish the *Harness Handbook*, which contains extensive racing and background information about the top horses currently racing. The Handbook is provided without charge to the media.

The Publicity Department also sends out frequent news releases on the leading horses in North America, including advances on major stakes events.

I need some background information about a local horse that is not one of the superstars in racing. Can you help?

In addition to the horse's race records, we can provide such information as the breeder, past and current owner, and in many cases the sale price. If that would help your story, give us a call.

We are trying to find out something about a horse that stopped racing several years ago. Is there anything you can dig up?

Between the sophisticated USTA computer and reference books, such as the *Year Book* and the *Sires and Dams*, published by the Association, we can locate information concerning just about any horse ever registered.

Do you have photos of any of these horses?

The USTA has an extensive collection of photos, including those of more than 1,000 horses currently racing. In addition, photos are available of many horses whose racing careers have been completed. These photos, most in black and white but some in color, are offered to the general media without charge. We can also assist television stations in tracking down video tapes of important races.

I am pretty well set with the records of horses. What can you tell me about drivers?

Just as with the horses, the USTA keeps records on all drivers racing in North America. We can provide up-to-date information on these drivers, plus their annual statistics back to 1952. The annual *Harness Handbook* contains a section on the leading drivers. Each entry provides a short biography, the driver's annual statistics, victories in major races, and 2:00 mile production. Photos on many of these drivers are available from the USTA Photo Department.

I am particularly proud of an article I wrote recently about harness racing. Are there any writing awards?

Each year, the USTA, in co-operation with the U.S. Harness Writers Association, presents the John Hervey Awards, with cash prizes, for excellence in the reporting of harness racing. In addition, there are also Broadcasters Awards for excellence in radio and television reporting. Contact the USTA Publicity Department for more details:

USTA Publicity Department: (614) 224-2291 - Fax: (614) 228-1385

GENERAL INFORMATION

NEED TO KNOW MORE?

United States Trotting Association, 750 Michigan Avenue, Columbus, OH 43215-1107. Francis X. Ready, Executive Vice President. For all departments: .... **(614) 224-2291**

American Standardbred Breeders Association, c/o Hanover Shoe Farms, P.O. Box 339, Hanover, PA 17331. John F. Simpson, Jr. President:......................... **(606) 254-4358**

American Harness Racing Secretaries, c/o Maywood Park, 8600 W. North Ave., Maywood, IL 60153. Eliot "Doc" Narotsky, President: .... **(416) 698-3131**

American Horse Council, 1700 K St., N.W., Suite 300, Washington, D.C. 20006. R. Richards Rolapp, President: .... **(202) 296-4031**

Association of Racing Commissioners International, 4067 Ironworks Pike, Lexington, KY 40511. Tony Chamblin, Executive V.P.: .... **(606) 254-4060**

Breeders Crown, 1 Pear Tree Plaza, 289 Rte. 33 East, Manalapan, NJ 07726. Tom Charters, Executive Director: .... **(908) 446-5151**

Canadian Standardbred Horse Society, 2150 Meadowvale Blvd., Mississauga, Ontario, Canada L5N 6R6. Ted Smith, Secretary/Manager: .... **(416) 858-3060**

Canadian Trotting Association, 2150 Meadowvale Blvd., Mississauga, Ontario L5N 6R6. Tom Gorman, Executive V.P. & Gen. Manager: .... **(416) 858-3060**

Delvin Miller Amateur Drivers Association, P.O. Box 339, State Route 194 South Hanover, PA 17331: .... **(717) 637-8931**

Grand Circuit, Meadow Lands Farm, P.O. Box 356, Meadow Lands PA 15347. Delvin Miller, President: .... **(412) 222-8620**

Hambletonian Society, P.O. Box 554, Lexington, KY 40586. Mrs. Gladys Bell, Assistant Secretary: .... **(606) 255-3689**

Harness Horsemen International, 525 Highway 33, Suite 3, Englishtown, NJ 07726 06067. Executive Mike Izzo: .... **(201) 446-3346**

Harness Horse Youth Foundation, 14950 Greyhound Court, Suite 210, Carmel, IN 46032. Margot Taylor, President:.. **(317) 848-5132**

Harness Publicists Association, c/o Kawartha Downs, Fraserville, ONT. K0L 1V0. Grant Wade, President: .... **(412) 225-9300**

Harness Racing Communications, c/o Pompano Park, 1800 SW 3rd St., Pompano Beach, FL 33069. Harold Duris, President: .... **(305) 972-2000**

Harness Racing Hotline, 24-hr. harness results. Updated daily, 1:00 a.m. on weekends from May thru October; 9 a.m. other days: .... **(614) 228-1821**

Harness Tracks of America, 35 Airport Rd, Morristown, NJ 07960. "Chic" Young, President; Stan Bergstein, Executive Vice President: .... **(201) 285-9090**

North American Amateur Drivers Association, 125-10 Queens Blvd., Kew Gardens, NY 11415. Joseph A. Faraldo, Director: .... **(718) 544-6800**

The Trotting Horse Museum, P.O. Box 590, Goshen, NY 10924. Philip A. Pines, Director: .... **(914) 294-6330**

United States Harness Writers Association, P. O. Box 10, Batavia, NY 14020. William F. Brown, Jr., Secretary: .... **(716) 343-5900**

GENERAL INFORMATION

EXCERPTS FROM THE USTA RULE BOOK

The following excerpts are taken from the current edition of the *Charter, By-Laws, Rules and Regulations of the United States Trotting Association.* The rules and regulations quoted below were in effect at the time this book was published. Any changes to these rules become effective after May 1 of this year.

This is not meant to be a complete copy of the current USTA Rules, but rather a compendium of the most important rules and regulations covering racing, licensing and the Standardbred registry. The USTA rules are updated annually in March and published each spring. Updated copies of the USTA rule book may be obtained by contacting the Association.

Rule 4. - Definitions.

Section 1. Added Money Early Closing Event. - An event closing in the same year in which it is to be contested in which all entrance and declaration fees received are added to the purse.

2. Age, How Reckoned. - The age of a horse shall be reckoned from the first day of January of the year of foaling, except that for foals born in November and December of any year in which case the age shall be reckoned from January 1 of the succeeding year effective November 1, 1970 and thereafter. Provided further that for foals foaled after December 31, 1980, the exception for foals of November and December shall not apply.

3. Appeal. - A request for the Board of Review to investigate, consider, and review any decisions or ruling of Judges or officials of a meeting. The appeal may deal with placing, penalties, interpretations of the rules or other questions dealing with conduct of races.

4. Claiming Race. - One in which any horse starting therein may be claimed for a designated amount in conformance with the rules.

5. Classified Race. - A race regardless of the eligibility of horses, entries being selected on the basis of ability or performance.

6. Conditioned Race. - An overnight event to which eligibility is determined according to specified qualifications. Such qualifications may be based upon, among other things:

(a) Horses' money winnings in a specified number of previous races or during a specified previous time.

(b) A horse's finishing position in a specified number of previous races or during a specified period of time.

(c) Age.

(d) Sex.

(e) Number of starts during a specified period of time.

(f) Special qualifications for foreign horses that do not have a representative number of starts in the United States or Canada.

(g) Or any one or more combinations of the qualifications herein listed.

(h) Use of records or time bars as a condition is prohibited.

7. Dash. - A race decided in a single trial. Dashes may be given in a series of two or three governed by one entry fee for the series, in which even a horse must start in all dashes. Positions may be drawn for each dash. The number of premiums awarded shall not exceed the number of starters in the dash.

8. Declaration. - A declaration is the naming of a particular horse to a particular race as a starter.

9. Declarations, When Taken. - Declarations shall be taken not more than three days in advance for all races except those for which qualifying dashes are provided.

10. Disqualification. - It shall be construed to mean that the person disqualified is debarred from acting as an official or from starting or driving a horse in a race, or in the case of a disqualified horse, it shall not be allowed to start.

11. Early Closing Race. - A race for a definite amount to which entries close at least six weeks preceding the race. The entrance fee may be on the installment plan or otherwise, and all payments are forfeits.

12. Elimination Heats or Two Divisions. - Heats of a race split according to Rule 13, Sections 2 and 3, to qualify the contestants for a final heat.

13. Coupled Entry. - Two or more horses starting in a race when owned or trained by the same person, or trained in the same stable or by the same management.

14. Expulsion. - Whenever the penalty of expulsion is prescribed in these rules, it shall be construed to mean unconditional exclusion and the disqualification from any participation, either directly or indirectly, in the privileges and uses of the course and grounds of a member.

15. Extended Pari-Mutuel Meetings. - An extended pari-mutuel meeting is a meeting or meetings, at which no agricultural fair is in progress with an annual total of more than ten days durations with pari-mutuel wagering.

16. Futurity. - A stake in which the dam of the competing animal is nominated either when in foal or during the year of foaling.

GENERAL INFORMATION

17. Green Horse. - One that has never trotted or paced in a race or against time.

18. Guaranteed Stake. - Same as a stake, with a guarantee by the party opening it that the sum shall not be less than the amount named.

19. Handicap. - A race in which performance, sex or distance allowance is made. Post positions for a handicap may be assigned by the Racing Secretary. Post positions in a handicap claiming race may be determined by claiming price.

20. Heat. - A single trial in a race two in three, or three heat plan.

21. In Harness. - When a race is made to go "in harness" it shall be construed to mean that the performance shall be to a sulky as defined in section 38 of this rule.

22. Late Closing Race. - A race for a fixed amount to which entries close less than six weeks and more than three days before the race is to be contested.

23. Length of Race and Number of Heats. - Races or dashes shall be given at a stated distance in units not shorter than a sixteenth of a mile. The length of a race and the number of heats shall be stated in the conditions. If no distance or number of heats are specified all races shall be a single mile dash except at fairs and meetings of a duration of 10 days or less, where the race will be conducted in two dashes at one mile distance.

24. Maiden. - A stallion, mare or gelding that has never won a heat or race at the gait at which it is entered to start and for which a purse if offered. Races or purse money awarded to a horse after the "official sign" has been posted shall not be considered winning performance or affect status as a maiden.

25. Match Race. - A race which has been arranged and the conditions thereof agreed upon between the contestants.

26. Matinee Race. - A race where an entrance fee may be charged and where the premiums, if any, are other than money.

27. Nomination. - The naming of a horse or in the event of a futurity, the naming of foal in utero to a certain race or series of races, eligibility of which is conditioned on the payment of a fee at the time of naming and the payment of subsequent sustaining fees and/or starting fees.

28. Overnight Event. - A race for which declarations close not more than three days (omitting Sundays) or less than one day before such race is to be contested. In the absence of conditions or notice to the contrary, all entries in overnight events must close not laster than 12:00 noon the day preceding the race.

29. Protest. - An objection, properly sworn to, charging that a horse is ineligible to a race, alleging improper entry or declaration, or citing any act of an owner, driver, or official prohibited by the rules, and which, if true, should exclude the hor or driver from the race.

30. Record. - The fastest time made by a horse in a hear or dash which he won. A Standard Record is a record of 2:20 or faster for two-year-olds and 2:15 or faster for all other ages.

31. Stake. - A race which will be contested in a year subsequent to its closing in which the money given by the track conducting the same is added to the money contributed by the nominators, all of which except deductions for the cost of promotion, breeders or nominators award belongs to the winner or winners. In any event, except as provided in Rule 11, Section 7, all of the money contributed in nominating, sustaining, and starting payments must be paid to the winner or winners.

32. Two in Three. - In a two in three race a horse must win two heats to be entitled to first money.

33. Two-Year-Olds. - No two-year-old shall be permitted to start in a dash or heat exceeding one mile in distance and no two-year-old shall be permitted to race in more than two heats or dashes in any single day. Starting any two-year-old in violation of this rule shall subject the member track to a fine of not less than $25.00 and the winning of such two-year-old shall be declared unlawful. Provided, however, that for any two-year-old events where nominations for same have closed prior to January 1, 1971, the provisions of the 1970 version of Rule 4, Section 33 shall govern.

34. Walk Over. - When only horses in the same interest start, it constitutes a walk over. In a "stake race" a "walk over" is entitled to all the stake money and forfeits. To claim the purse the entry must start and go once over the course.

35 Winner. - The whose nose reaches the wire first. If there is a dead heat for first, both horses shall be considered winners. Where to horses are tied in the summary, the winner of the longer dash or heat shall be entitled to the trophy. Where the dashes or heats are of the same distance and the horses are tied in the summary, the winner of the faster dash or heat shall be entitled to the trophy. Where the dashes or heats are of the same distance and the horses are tied in the summary and the time, both horses shall be considered the winners.

36. Wire. - The wire is a real or imaginary line from the center of the judges' stand to a point immediately across, and at right angles to the track.

37. Contract Track. - A pari-mutuel track, not a member of this Association, which receives data and services pursuant to Article VII, Section 7 (c) of the Association's By-Laws.

38. Sulky Defined. - For the purpose of these rules a sulky shall be defined as a dual-shaft, dual-wheel racing vehicle.

GENERAL INFORMATION

39. Race Winner. - (a) A horse shall be deemed the winner of a race as soon as the Judges have determined the official placings and the "Official" sign has been posted. Pari-mutuel pools shall be distributed according to the official placings. Purse money shall be awarded according to the official placings except as provided in Section (b) below.

(b) In the event of a change in the official placing by the Judges or other Review Board due to an appeal, protest, positive test or other finding, the purse money shall be distributed among those horses entitled to such, but no horse shall be considered the winner of a race or receive a win race record by virtue of such change in the official placings unless said horse had finished first in the race in question and such first place finish is affirmed upon review.

Rule 16. - Starting

Section 1. (d) - Speed of the Gate - Allowing Sufficient time so that the speed of the gate can be increased gradually, the following minimum speeds will be maintained.

(1) For the first 1/8 mile, not less than 11 miles per hour.

(2) For the next 1/16 of a mile not less than 18 miles per hour.

(3) From that point to the starting point, the speed will be gradually increased to the maximum speed.

(g) When a speed has be reached in the course of a start there shall be no decrease except in the case of a recall.

(h) **Recall Notice.** - In case of a recall, a light plainly visible to the driver shall be flashed and a recall sounded, but the starting gate shall proceed out of the path of the horses. At extended pari-mutuel tracks in the case of a recall, wherever possible, the starter shall leave the wings of the gate extended and gradually slow the speed of the gate to assist in stopping the field of horses. In an emergency, however, the starter shall use his discretion to close the wings of the gate.

(i) There shall be no recall after the word "go" has been given and any horse, regardless of his position or accident, shall be deemed a starter from the time he entered into the Starter's control unless dismissed by the Starter.

(j) **Breaking Horse.** - The starter shall endeavor to get all horses away in position and on gait but not recall shall be had for a breaking horse.

(k) **Recall-Reasons For.** - The starter may sound a recall only for the following reasons:

(1) A horse scores ahead of the gate.
(2) There is interference
(3) A horse has broken equipment.
(4) There is a malfunction of the starting gate.
(5) A horse falls before the word "go" is given.

(l) **Penalties.** - A fine not to exceed $100, or suspension from driving not to exceed 15 days, or both, may be applied to any driver, by the Starter for:

(1) Delaying the start.
(2) Failure to obey the Starter's instruction.
(3) Rushing ahead of the inside or outside wing of the gate.
(4) Coming to the starting gate out of position.
(5) Crossing over before reaching the starting point.
(6) Interference with another driver during the start.
(7) Failure to come up into position.

A hearing must be granted before any penalty is imposed.

2. Holding Horses Before Start. - Horses may be held on the backstretch not to exceed two minutes awaiting post time, except when delayed by an emergency.

3. Two Tiers. - In the event there are two tiers of horses, the withdrawing of a horse that has drawn or earned a position in the front tier shall not affect the position of the horses that have drawn or earned positions in the second tier.

Whenever a horse is drawn from any tier, horses on the outside move in to fill up the vacancy. Where a horse has drawn a post position in the second tier, the driver of such horse may elect to score out behind any horse in the first tier so long as he does not thereby interfere with another trailing horse or deprive another trailing horse of a drawn position.

4. Starting Without Gate. - When horses are started without a gate the Starter shall have control of the horses from the formation of the parade until he gives the word "go." He shall be located at the wire or other point of start of the race at which point as nearly as possible the word "go" shall be given. No driver shall cause unnecessary delay after the horses are called. After two preliminary warming up scores, the Starter shall notify the drivers to form in parade.

5. The driver of any horse refusing or failing to follow the instructions of the Starter as to the parade or scoring ahead of the pole horse may be set down for the heat in which the offense occurs, or for such other period as the Starter shall determine, and may be fined form $10 to $100. Whenever a driver is taken down the substitute shall be permitted to score the horse once.

A horse delaying the race may be started regardless of his position or gait and there shall not be a recall on account of a bad actor. If the

GENERAL INFORMATION

word is not given, all the horses in the race shall immediately turn at the tap of the bell or other signal, and jog back to their parade positions for a fresh start. There shall be no recall after the starting word has been given.

6. Starters. - The horses shall be deemed to have started when the word "go" if given by the Starter and all the horses must go the course except in case of an accident, broken equipment, or any other reason in which it is the opinion of the Judges that it is impossible to go the course.

7. Unmanageable Horse. - If in the opinion of the Judges or Starter a horse is unmanageable or liable to cause accidents or injury to any other horse or to any driver it may be sent to the bar. When this action is taken the Starter will notify the Judges who will in turn notify the public.

8. Bad Acting Horse. - At meeting where there is no wagering, the Starter may place a bad acting horse on the outside at his discretion. At pari-mutuel meetings such action may be taken only where there is time for the Starter to notify the Judges who will in turn notify the public prior to the sale of tickets on such a race. If tickets have been sold, the bad acting horse must be scratched under the provision of Section 8 herein.

9. Post Positions - Heat Racing. - The horse winning a heat shall take the pole (or inside position) the succeeding heat, unless otherwise specified in the published conditions, and all others shall take their positions in the order they were placed the last heat. When two or more horses shall have made a dead heat, their positions shall be settled by lot.

10. Shield - The arms of all starting gates shall be provided with a screen or shield in front of the position for each horse, and such arms shall be perpendicular to the rail.

11. Every licensed starter is required to check his starting gate for malfunctions before commencing any meeting, and to practice the procedure to be followed in event of a malfunction. Both the starter and the driver of the gate must know and practice emergency procedures, and the starter is responsible for the training is such procedures of drivers.

Rule 17. – Drivers, Trainers and Agents.

Section 1. Licensing of Drivers. - No person shall drive a horse in any race on a track in membership with this Association without have first obtained from this Association an Active Membership including a driver's license. The proper license shall be presented to the Clerk of the Course before driving. Any person violating this rule may be fined $10.00 for each offense and no license shall be issued thereafter until such fines shall have been paid. In addition, thereto, the track member may be fined the sum of $5.00 for permitting a driver to start without a license. In the event of a driver's license being lost or destroyed, a replacement may be obtained upon payment of a fee in the sum of $1.00.

(a) **Trainer Driver/Trainer License Fee.** - Applicants for a trainer or driver/trainer license other than a Matinee driver license shall pay a fee in the amount of $35.00 in addition to their regular annual membership fee of $30.00 for an original license, and $25.00 for renewal licenses annually thereafter.

Provided, however, that the driver's license fee for foreign driver, other than those residing in the Maritime Provinces of Canada, shall be $100.00 for an original license, unless the applicant is already licensed as a driver by the licensing authority of a foreign country in which he resides, in which latter case the fee shall be $30.00. The fee for a renewal of such a license shall be $25.00 annually thereafter.

2. Contents of Application. - The Executive Vice-President shall require the applicant to:

(a) Submit evidence of good moral character.

(b) Except for a Matinee or amateur license, submit written evidence of employment or experience as a groom or other related experience along with the application and resume for either a driver or trainer license.

(c) Be at least 12 years of age for an (MA) or (M) license and 16 years of age for an (F) license or a (Q) license.

(d) Be at least 16 years of age for a (P) license.

(e) Furnish completed application forms. Applicants for a driver's license other than a Matinee license must submit the name of a sponsor who shall have at least five years experience as an "A" licensed driver, and the names of at least three other active licensed "A" drivers for reference. Provided, however, that where an applicant for a driver's license resides in a state where there are fewer than 120 days of extended pari-mutuel racing annually, the three supporting references may come from active drivers licensed in an (F) (Fair) capacity or higher.

(f) Submit satisfactory evidence of an eye examination indicating 20/40 corrected vision in both eyes; or if one eye blind, at least 20/30 corrected vision in the other eye; and when requested submit evidence of physical and mental ability and/or submit to a physical examination.

(g) Applicants, other than for an M, MA or amateur license shall submit to a written examination at a designated time and place to deter-

GENERAL INFORMATION

mine his qualifications to drive or train and his knowledge of racing and the rules. In addition any driver who presently holds a license and wishes to obtain a license in a higher category who has not previously submitted to such written tests shall be required to take a written test before becoming eligible to obtain a license in a higher category.

Any applicant required to submit to a written examination under this sub-section shall be required to demonstrate his or her ability to harness and equip a horse properly and to establish his or her proficiency in handling the animal; such examination to be administered by the local District Track Committee.

3. Categories of Licenses. - Driver and trainer licenses shall be issued in the following categories:

(a) (M) (Matinee) A license valid for matinee meetings only.

(b) (MA) (Matinee-Amateur) A license valid for matinee meetings and amateur racing at other meeting provided the licensee is an amateur at the time of the race.

(c) (SL) (Special License) A license valid for amateur racing at all meetings. Such license shall be issued at the direction of the Executive Vice-President upon the filing of an application therefor.

(d) (F) (Fair) A license valid for fairs and all meetings with the exception of extended pari-mutuel meetings.

Drivers holding a license valid for fairs only who have driven at fairs must demonstrate an ability to drive satisfactorily before they will be granted a (Q) license valid for qualifying races. Drivers holding a Fair license will not be considered for advancement to a "Q" license until he or she has met the following criteria: Had at least six months driving experience while holding an "F" (Fair) license, plus 25 satisfactory fair drives within a consecutive 24 month period, and the approval of the Presiding Judge and the local District Track Committee appointed by the USTA District Directors.

(e) (Q) (Qualifying) A license valid for fairs and a license for qualifying and non-wagering races at extended pari-mutuel meetings with the approval of the Presiding Judge. It shall be the responsibility of the Presiding Judge to fill out the requisite form evaluating each drive made by a "Q" driver in a qualifying, fair or amateur race and to forward such written evaluation to USTA. The Horsemen's Committee may appoint an Advisory Committee of three drivers at any meeting to observe the qualifications, demeanor and general conduct of all drivers and report in regard thereto the Presiding Judge, copy of any such report to be in writing and forwarded to the Association. Applicants for Qualifying licenses must be at least 16 years of age. At the discretion of the USTA and a Pari-Mutuel Presiding Judge, a Qualifying driver who has had satisfactory drives at fairs or in amateur races may be given credit for not more than three-fourths of those drives toward the requisite number of qualifying drives required for advancement to a Provisional license. Drivers holding a Qualifying license will not be considered for advancement to a "P" (Provisional) license until he or she has met the following criteria: Had at least six months driving experience while holding a "Q" (Qualifying) license plus at least 12 satisfactory qualifying drives within a consecutive 12 month period, and the approval of the Presiding Judge and the local District Track Committee appointed by the USTA District Directors. A qualifying drive shall not be deemed unsatisfactory based solely upon the failure of the horse to go qualifying time.

In all cases an individual must have demonstrated professional competence at all times and a licensed pari-mutuel Presiding Judge must have submitted a satisfactory written report certifying to such performance.

(f) (P) (Provisional) A license valid for fairs and for extended pari-mutuel meetings subject to satisfactory performance.

Drivers holding a provisional license will not be considered for advancement to an "A" (full) license until he or she has qualified in one of the three following categories:

1. Had at least one year's driving experience while holding a "P" (Provisional) license plus 25 satisfactory pari-mutuel starts in the twelve-month period beginning with the issuance of the Provisional license, and the approval of the Presiding Judge and the local District Track Committee appointed by the USTA District Directors.

2. Or had less than one year's driving experience while holding a "P" (Provisional) license, but with at least 50 satisfactory pari-mutuel starts and the approval of the Presiding Judge and the local District Track Committee appointed by the USTA District Directors.

3. Or made 25 satisfactory starts at extended pari-mutuel or Grand Circuit meetings in the two-year calendar period preceding the date of application provided he or she has at least 50 satisfactory Fair starts and the approval of the Presiding Judge and the local District Track Committee appointed by the USTA District Directors.

In all cases and individual must have demonstrated professional competence at all times and a licensed pari-mutuel Presiding Judge must have submitted a satisfactory written report certifying to such performance.

(g) (A) (Full) A full license valid for all meetings.

(h) (V) (Probationary) A probationary license indicating that the driver has been guilty

GENERAL INFORMATION

of rule violations and has been warned against repetition of such violations. When a driver with a probationary license commits more than one rule violation, or one major violation, proceeding may be started and he will be given a hearing either before the Executive Vice-President or the District Board of Review in the District where the last penalty was imposed, to determine if his license should be revoked.

Repeated rule violations shall be considered grounds for revocation of any driver's license. A provisional, qualifying, or fair license may be revoked for one or more rule violations, or other indications of lack of qualifications, and the qualifications of drivers in these categories may be reviewed at any time, with written examinations if necessary, to determine if a drive is competent.

(i) (T) (Trainer) A license to enable the holder to train horses and be programmed as a Trainer at all member tracks of this Association.

(j) (Probationary Trainer) A probationary license indicating that the trainer has been guilty of rule violations and has been warned against repetition of such violations.

An applicant for a license as a trainer must satisfy the Executive Vice-president that he possesses the necessary qualifications, both mental and physical, to perform the duties required. Elements to be considered, among others, shall be character, reputation, temperament, experience, knowledge of the rules of racing, and duties of a trainer in the preparation, training, entering and managing horses for racing. A trainer's license shall be either General or Probationary, or it may be issued valid for the horses owned wholly or in part by the trainer only. All trainers participating at tracks located in District 120 must be licensed as such.

An applicant shall be required to:

(1) Submit evidence of good moral character.

(2) Be at least 18 years of age.

(3) Furnish Complete application form including photographs.

(4) Submit Evidence of his ability to train and manage a racing stable which shall include at least three years experience working as a groom or second trainer, and satisfactory completion of a written examination.

(5) When requested, submit evidence of physical ability and/or submit to a physical examination.

(6) When requested, submit three copies of his fingerprints.

(k) Subsequent to the issuance of a "Q" driver's license, "P" driver's license, or a General Trainer's License, the applicant must have prior approval of a licensed Presiding Judge to drive and/or train; said approval to be withheld until the license applicant has met the following minimum requirements:

(1) A personal interview with the Presiding Judge and local District Track Committee.

(2) The Presiding Judge and the local District Track Committee to observe the individual capably handling a horse on the track.

(3) The Presiding Judge and the Local District Track Committee to observe the individual satisfactorily rating a horse during a warm-up or training mile.

4. License Requirements in District 10. - At tracks located in District 10, it shall be the responsibility of all drivers and/or trainers who utilize persons in capacities which require them to be licensed, to be certain that such persons are so licensed. A fine not exceeding $100.00 may be imposed for violation of this rule.

5. Any licensed driver who shall participate in a meeting or drive a horse at a meeting not in membership with this Association or the Canadian Trotting Association shall be fined not to exceed $100 for each such offense; PROVIDED HOWEVER, that nothing herin contained shall prevent any person from driving at a contract track or from participating in a meeting conducted at such a track.

(a) Physical Examination. - An applicant for a driver's license 65 years of age or over may be required to submit annually, with his application for a driver's license, a report of a physical examination on forms supplied by the Association. If the Association so desires, it may designate the physician to perform such examination. However, in such event, the cost thereof shall be paid by the Association. No applicant who has previously held any type of driver's license shall be subsequently denied a driver's license solely on the basis of age.

(b) In the event any person is involved in an accident on the track, the Association may order such person to submit to a physical examination and such examination must be completed within 30 days from such request or the license may be suspended until compliance therewith.

6. The License of any driver or trainer may be revoked or suspended at any time after a hearing by the President or Executive Vice-President for violation of the rules, failure to obey the instructions of any official, or for any misconduct or act detrimental to the sport. The President or Executive Vice-President may designate a proper person as a hearing officer who will conduct a hearing and furnish a transcript to the President or Executive Vice-President. The license may be reinstated by the President or Executive Vice-president in his discretion upon application made to him and upon such terms as he may prescribe. Any suspension or revocation of license made hereunder may be reviewed as provided in Article IX of the By-Laws.

GENERAL INFORMATION

7. The following shall constitute disorderly conduct and be reason for a fine, suspension, or revocation of a driver's or trainer's license:

(a) Failure to obey the Judges' orders that are expressly authorized by the rules of this Association.

(b) Failure to drive when programmed unless excused by the Judges.

(c) Drinking intoxicating beverages within four hours of the first post time of the program on which he is carded to drive.

(d) Appearing in the paddock in an unfit condition to drive.

(e) Fighting.

(f) Assaults.

(g) Offensive and profane language.

(h) Smoking on the track in silks during actual racing hours.

(i) Warming up a horse prior to racing without silks.

(j) Disturbing the peace.

(k) Refusal to take a breath analyzer test when directed by the Presiding Judge.

8. Drivers must wear distinguishing colors and clean white pants, and shall not be allowed to start in a race or other public performance unless in the opinion of the Judges they are properly dressed.

No personal shall drive a horse during the time when colors are required on the race track unless wearing a protective helmet, painted as registered with compatible colors, and a chin strap in place. Where applicable, that helmet shall be as required by the rules or regulations of the appropriate State Racing Commission.

9. Any driver wearing colors who shall appear at a betting window or at a bar or in a restaurant dispensing alcoholic beverages shall be bined not to exceed $100 fo each such offense.

10. No driver can, without good and sufficient reasons, decline to be substituted by Judges. Any driver who refuses to be so substituted may be fined or suspended, or both, by order of the Judges. Provided further that whenever a driver is programmed to drive a particular horse in a race and is removed as the driver for that horse at the driver's request, said driver shall not be permitted to drive another horse in that same race.

11. An amateur driver is one who has never accepted any valuable consideration by way of or in lieu of compensation for his services as a driver during the past ten years.

12. Drivers holding a USTA "A" driver's license, and drivers holding a "V" driver's license who formerly held an "A" driver's license shall register their driving color design with this Association. Residents of foreign countries who hold an equivalent license with a foreign association shall not be bound by this Section until they have driven 25 starts in a year in The United States.

Any person in membership with this Association or any stable, farm, or corporate name registered with this Association may register driving color designs. No person, registered stable, farm or corporation may register more than one design, and no two designs may be registered the same. All disputes as to the rights to particular designs shall be settled by this Association.

The fee for registration of driving color design shall be $100.00 The fee for a duplicate color card shall be $10.00 and the fee for modifying a design which is registered shall be $50.00.

Driving color designs registered with this Association may be released for re-registration if the person, registered stable, farm or corporation is inactive for a period of five consicutive years. Inactivity shall mean not in membership withis this Association or racing under the provisions of Rule 1, Section 3 of these rules.

13. Any person racing a horse at a meeting where registered colors are required by Section 12 herein, using colors registered by any person or persons except himself or his employer without special permission of the Presiding Judge may be fined in an amount not to exceed $100.00

Rule 18.–Racing & Track Rules.

Section 1. Although a leading horse is entitled to any part of the track except after selecting his position in the home stretch, neither the driver of the first horse or any other driver in the race shall do any of the following things, which shall be considered violation of driving rules:

(a) Change either to the right or left during any part of the race when another horse is so near him that in altering his position he compels the horse behind him to shorten his stride, or causes the driver of such other horse to pull him out of his stride.

(b) Jostle, strike, hook wheels, or interfere with another horse or driver.

(c) Cross sharply in front of a horse or cross over in front of a field of horses in a reckless manner, endangering other drivers.

(d) Swerve in and out or pull up quickly.

(e) Crowd a horse or driver by "putting a wheel under him."

(f) Carry a horse out.

(g) Sit down in front of a horse to take up abruptly in front of other horses so as to cause confusion or interference among trailing horses.

(h) Let a horse pass inside needlessly or otherwise help another horse to improve his position in the race.

GENERAL INFORMATION

(i) Commit any act which shall impede the progress of another horse or cause him to break.

(j) Change course after selecting a position in the home stretch or swerve in and out, or beat in and out, in such a manner as to interfere with another horse or cause him to change course or take back.

(k) To drive in a careless or reckless manner.

(l) Whipping under the arch of the sulky, the penalty for which shall be no less than 10 days suspension.

(m) Kicking the horse, the penalty for which shall be not less than 10 days suspension.

2. All complaints by drivers of any foul driving or other misconduct during the heat must be made at the termination of the heat, unless the driver is prevented from doing so by an accident or injury. Any driver desiring to enter a claim of four or other complaint of violation of the rules, must before dismounting indicate to the Judges or Barrier Judge his desire to enter such claim or complaint and forthwith upon dismounting shall proceed to the telephone or Judges' stand where and when such claim, objection, or complaint shall be immediately entered. The Judges shall not cause the official sign to be displayed until such claim, objection, or complaint shall have been entered and considered.

3. If any of the above violations are committed by a person driving a horse coupled as an entry in the betting, the Judges shall set the offending horse back. The horse coupled in the entry with the offending horse shall also be set back if the Judges find that it improved its finishing position as a direct result of the offense committed by the offending horse.

4. In case of interference, collision, or violation of any of the above restrictions, whether occurring before of after the start, the Judges may place the offending horse back one or more positions in that heat or dash, and in the event such collision or interference prevents any horse from finishing the heat or dash, the offending horse may be disqualified from receiving any winnings; and the driver may be fined not to exceed the amount of the purse or stake contended for, or may be suspended or expelled. In the event a horse is set back, under the provisions hereof, he must be placed behind the horse with whom he interfered.

5. (a) Every heat in a race must be contested by every horse in the race and every horse must be driven to the finish. If the Judges believe that a horse is being driven, or has been driven heretofore, with design to prevent his winning a heat or dash which he was evidently able to win, or is being raced in an inconsistent manner, or to perpetrate or to aid a fraud, they shall consider it a violation and the driver, and anyone in concert with him, to so affect the outcome of the race or races, shall be fined, suspended, or expelled. The Judges may substitute a competent and reliable driver at any time. The substituted driver shall be paid at the discretion of the Judges and the fee retained from the purse money due the horse, if any.

(b) In the event a drive is unsatisfactory due to lack of effort or carelessness, and the Judges believe that there is no fraud, gross carelessness, or a deliberated inconsistent driver they shall impose a penalty under this subsection, including, but not limited to a fine, suspension or revocation.

6. If in the opinion of the Judges a driver is for any reason unfit or incompetent to drive or refuses to comply with the directions of the Judges, or is reckless in his conduct and endangers the safety of horses or other drivers in the race, he may be removed and another driver substituted at any time after the positions have been assigned in a race, and the offending driver shall be fined, suspended or expelled. The substitute driver shall be properly compensated.

7. If for any cause other than being interfered with or broken equipment, a horse fails to finish after starting in a heat, that horse will be ruled out.

8. Loud shouting or other improper conduct is forbidden in a race.

After the word "go" is given both feet must be kept in the stirrups until after the finish of the race.

9. Drivers will be allowed whips not to exceed 4 feet, 8 inches, plus a snapper not longer than eight inches.

10. The use of any goading device, chain, or mechanical devices or appliances, other than the ordinary whip or crop upon any horse in any race shall constitute a violation of this rule.

11. The brutal use of a whip or crop or excessive or indiscriminate use of the whip or crop shall be considered a violation and shall be punished by a fine of not to exceed $100.00 or suspension.

12. No horse shall wear hopples in a race unless he starts in the same in the first heat, and having so started, he shall continue to wear them to the finish of the race, and any person found guilty of removing or altering a horse's hopples during a race, or between races for the purpose of fraud, shall be suspended or expelled. Any horse habitually wearing hopples shall not be permitted to start in a race without them except by the permission of the Judges. Any horse habitually raced free legged shall not be permitted to wear hopples in a race except with the permission of the Judges. No horse shall be permitted to wear a head pole protruding beyond its nose.

13. **Breaking** - (a) When any horse or horses break from their gait in trotting or pacing, their

GENERAL INFORMATION

drivers shall at once, where clearance exists, take such horse to the outside and pull it to its gait.

(b) The following shall be considered violations of Section 13 (a):

(1) Failure to properly attempt to pull the horse to its gait.

(2) Failure to take to the outside where clearance exists.

(3) Failure to lose ground by the break.

(c) Any breaking horse shall be set back when a contending horse on its gait is lapped on the hind quarter of the breaking horse at the finish.

(d) Any horse making a break which causes interference to other contending horses may be placed behind all offending horses; if there has been no failure on the part of the driver of the breaking horse in complying with subsection (b) of this rule, no fine or suspension shall be imposed on the driver as a consequence of the interference.

(e) The Judges may set any horse back one or more places if in their judgement any of the above violations have been committed.

14. If in the opinion of the Judges, a driver allows his horse to break for the purpose of fraudulently losing a heat, he shall be liable to the penalties elsewhere provided for fraud and fouls.

15. To assist in determining the matters contained in Section 13 and 14, it shall be the duty of one of the Judges to call out every break made, and the clerk shall at once note the break and character of it in writing.

16. The time between separate heats of a single race shall be no less than 40 minutes. No heat shall be called after sunset where the track is not lighted for night racing.

17. Horses called for a race shall have the exclusive right of the course, and all other horses shall vacate the track at once, unless permitted to remain by the Judges.

18. In the case of accidents, only so much time shall be allowed as the Judges may deem necessary and proper.

19. A driver must be mounted in his sulky at the finish of the race or the horse must be placed as not finishing.

20. It shall be the responsibility of the owner and trainer to provide every sulky used in a raced with unicolored or colorless wheel discs on the inside and outside of the wheel of a type approved by the Executive Vice President or by a Harness Racing Commission. In his discretion, the Presiding Judge may order the use of mud guards at pari-mutuel tracks.

21. A trainer who trains and races a horse knowing said horse to be owned wholly or in part by a person or persons barred or otherwise disqualified from participating in racing shall be suspended from membership in this Association for a minimum of one year.

22. Excessive and/or unnecessary conversation between and among drivers while on the racetrack during the time when colors are required is prohibited. Any violation of this rule may be punished by a fine, suspension or combination thereof.

23. Any violation of any sections of Rule 18 above, unless otherwise provided, may be punished by a fine or suspension, or both, of by expulsion. Provided, however, that where a penalty is to be imposed or an act of interference, said penalty shall be in days suspended.

Rule 21. – Stimulants, Drugs.

Section 6. - A trainer shall be responsible at all times for the condition of all horses trained by him. No trainer shall start a horse or permit a horse in his custody to be started if he knows, or if by the exercise of reasonable care he might have know or have cause to believe, that the horse has received any drug, stimulant, sedative, depressant, medicine, or other substance that could result in a positive test. Every trainer must guard or cause to guarded each horse trained by him in such manner and for such period of time prior to racing the horse so as to prevent any person not employed by or connected with the owner or trainer from administering any drug, stimulant, sedative, depressant, or other substance resulting in a post-race positive test.

8. All winning of such horse in a race in which an offense was detected under any section of this rule shall be forfeited and paid over to this Association for re-distribution among the remaining horses in the race entitled to same. The Judges shall notify this Association in writing of the re-distribution of winnings, giving the following information:

(a) The name and eligibility certificate number of the horse charged with the positive test.

(b) Names of the horses and eligibility certificate numbers of all horses affected by the re-distribution of purse.

(c) The amount of money to be added or subtracted from each horse's earnings.

When the positive test is charged to the winner of the race, the Clerk of the Course shall make the following corrections on the eligibility certificates of all horses competing in the race:

(a) The time of the race shall be corrected to read "time disallowed" (TDIS).

(b) The actual time of the horse finishing first shall be corrected to read "time disallowed" (TDIS).

(c) On the next available performance line of the eligibility certificate the following statement shall be entered in red ink: "Corrections and/or redistribution of purse due to positive test on

GENERAL INFORMATION

(date of race)." Then enter the amount of money to be added or subtracted from each horse's earnings to include both the season and lifetime totals.

When the positive test does not affect the winner of the race, the foregoing provisions relative to the disallowance of time shall not apply.

No forfeiture and re-distribution of winnings shall affect distribution of the pari-mutuel pools at tracks where pari-mutuel wagering is conducted when such distribution of pools is made upon the official placing at the conclusion of the race.

Rule 22. – Fines, Suspensions, & Expulsion.

Section 14. Penalty of Racing Commissions. - All penalties imposed by the Racing Commissions of the various states shall be recognized and enforced by this Association upon notice from the Commission to the Executive Vice-President, except as provided in Section 15 of this rule 22.

15. Reciprocity of Penalties. - All persons and horses under suspension of expulsion by any State Racing Commission or by a reputable Trotting Association or foreign country shall upon notice from such commission or association to the Executive Vice-President, be suspended or expelled by this Association. Provided, however, that, for good cause show, the Board of Appeals may, upon consideration of the record of the proceedings mold the penalty imposed to define the applicability thereof beyond the jurisdiction of the State Commission or foreign Association. Provided further that, whether or not a penalty has been imposed by a State Racing Commission, the District Board may make original inquiry and take original jurisdiction in any case as provided in Sections 2 and 15 of Article IV of the By-Laws.

Rule 24. – Time and Records.

Section 1. - Timing Races. - In every race, the time of each heat shall be accurately taken by three Timers or an approved electric timing device, in which case there shall be one Timer, and placed in the record in minutes, seconds and fifths of seconds, and upon the decision of each heat, the time thereof shall be publicly announced or posted. No unofficial timing shall be announced or admitted to the record, and when the Timers fail to act no time shall be announced or recorded for that heat.

2. - Error in Reported Time. - In any case of alleged error in the record, announcement of publication of the time made by a horse, the time so questioned shall not be changed to favor said horse or owner, except upon the sworn statement of the Judges and Timers who officiated in the race, and then only by order of the District Board of Review or the Executive Vice-President.

3. - Track Measurement Certificate. - In order that the performances thereon may be recognized and/or published as official every track member not having do so heretofore and since January 1st, 1939, shall forthwith caused to be filed withe the Executive Vice-president the certificate of a duly licensed civil engineer or land surveyor that he has subsequently to January 1st, 1939, measured the said track from wire to wire three feet out from the pole or inside hub rail thereof and certifying in linear feet the result of such measurement. Each track shall be measured and recertified in the event of any changes or relocation of the hub rail.

4. Time Where Lapped On. - The leading horse shall be timed and his time only shall be announced. No horse shall obtain a win race record by reason of the disqualification of another horse unless the horse's actual race time can be determined by photo finish or electronic timing.

5. Time for Dead Heat. - In the case of a dead heat, the time shall constitute a record for the horses making the dead heat and both shall be considered winners.

8. Time Performances. - Time performances are permitted subject to the following:

(a) Urine and saliva tests are required for all horses starting for a time performance. The provisions of Rule 21, with the exception of Section 4, relative to stimulants and drugs shall apply to time trial performances, and a violation of any section of that rule shall result in a disallowance of the time trial performance. In addition, further penalties may be imposed under the provisions of Rule 21, Section 10.

(b) An approved electronic timer is required for all time performances. In the event of a failure of a timer during the progress of a time performance, no time trial performance record will be obtained.

(c) Time trial performances may be permitted by the Executive Vice-President immediately prior to or following a regularly scheduled meeting provided of full complement of licensed officials are in the Judges' Stand and provided a separate application is filed with the Executive Vice-President, thirty days in advance, listing the officials and the number of days requested.

(d) Time trial performances are limited for two-year-olds who go to equal or to beat 2:10 and three-year-olds and over who go to equal or beat 2:05.

(e) In any race or performance against time

GENERAL INFORMATION

excessive use of the whip shall be considered a violation.

(f) Any consignor, agent or sales organization or other person may be fined or suspended for selling or advertising a horse with a time trial record without designating it as a time trial.

(g) Time trial performance records shall not be included in the performance lines in a race program.

(h) Time trial performances shall be designated by preceding the time with two capital T's.

(i) When a horse performs against time it shall be proper to allow another horse or horses to accompany him in the performance but not to precede or to be harnessed with or in any way attached to him. Provided however, that a mechanical device acceptable to the President or Executive Vice-President of this Association may be used. Provided, further, that a horse may not be used as a prompter for more than two time trial performances each time he is hitched, and may not be hitched more than three times in a single day, with at least forty minutes between each such use. It shall be the responsibility of the Presiding Judge to see that the prompters are not abused.

(j) A break during a Time Trial is a losing effort and a losing performance shall not constitute a record.

(k) If there is a failure or malfunction of the electric timing device and it is discovered prior to the completion of the first half-mile of the trial, there shall be a recall and it is the responsibility of the tracks sponsoring time performances to provide a signal plainly visible and distinguishable to the driver at or near the quarter and half-mile poles, which shall be flashed when a recall is in order.

9. No time record shall be recognized as a world record if obtained on a track without an inside hub rail or other fixed marker.

10. For horse bred in the United States and subsequently exported from the United States, a winning performance at one mile (1600 meters) by such a horse outside the United States shall receive recognition as the horse's record (expressed in kilometer time where so noted or in mile time where so noted), provided the drug testing program in the country in which the record was taken is accepted by USTA, and the horse is registered in on of the foreign registries recognized by USTA under Rule 26, Section 2(g) as having met the requisite standards. Provided further that foreign earning for such a horse shall be converted to U.S. dollars and credited to the horse on USTA records.

Rule 25. – International Registration

Section 1. – The Executive Vice-President may appoint export agents at various ports of shipping who shall upon examination and identification of the horse to be exported, endorse the application for export certificate. Every application for an export certificate must be accompanied by a certificate of registration in the current ownership and a fee in the sum of $300.00. The export certificate shall be issued and signed by the Executive Vice-President or Registrar of the Association and the corporate seal affixed thereto. No such certificate will be issued for the export of any horse under expulsion nor for any horse currently under suspension by this Association. The fee for a duplicate certificate shall be $10.00.

Except for foals under 17 months of age, no export certificate will be granted to any horse that is not tattooed. Where an export certificate is to be issued pursuant to this rule to a horse that is not tattooed the horse shall nevertheless be further identified with appropriate color photographs depicting color and white markings.

Provided further, that in the case of the export of mares which have been bred, a properly executed mating certificate shall be furnished in addition to the aforementioned requirements.

3. If any horse registered with the Association is exported from the United States or Canada to any other country without making application for an export certificate, then the said horse will be stricken from the records of the United States Trotting Association.

4. Imported Horses. – Horses imported into the United States from countries other than Canada, Australia, New Zealand, Norway, Sweden, Finland and France may be registered with the Association Non-Standard, provided the following requirements are complied with by the person or persons seeking such registration:

(a) Horse must be registered in the country of birth and certificate of such registration must accompany application.

(b) Complete history of breeding including sire, and 1st, 2nd and 3rd dams and chain of ownership must accompany application if not fully set forth on registration of origin.

(c) Clearance or export certificate from country of origin including markings, positive identification of horse, and veterinarian certificate, must accompany application.

(d) If horse is leased, a valid executed lease signed by all parties must accompany application. If lease is signed by agents, written authorization from their principals must be sub-

GENERAL INFORMATION

mitted.

(e) Person or persons seeking such registration must be members of this Association and fee of $25.00 in the case of horses which have not raced previously, and $50.00 in the case of horses which have previously raced, must accompany the application.

(f) A standard USTA application for registration must be filed, signed by the person to whose ownership the horse was cleared from the foreign registry.

Rule 26. – Registration of Horses.

Section 1. - In order to register a horse the owner thereof must be a member of this Association. Provided, however, that in the case of a registered farm or stable owned by a limited partnership the requirement with respect to the registration of horses shall be met if all general partners of such partnership and the Corresponding Officer of such farm or stable is in membership. Any person authorized to sign a mating certificate, an application for registration or any of the required breeding or registration reports must be a member of this Association.

2. Standard Bred. - Horses may be registered as Standard bred with any of the following qualifications:

(a) The progeny of a registered Standard horse and a registered Standard mare.

(b) A stallion sired by a registered Standard horse, provided his dam and granddam were sired by registered Standard horses and he himself has a Standard record and is the sire of three performers with Standard records from different mares.

(c) A mare whose sire is a registered Standard horse, and whose dam and granddam were sired by a registered Standard horse, provided she herself has a Standard record.

(d) A mare sired by a registered Standard horse, provided she is the dam of two performers with Standard records.

(e) A mare or horse sired by a registered Standard horse, provided its first, second and third dams are each sired by a registered Standard horse.

(f) No horse over four years of age is eligible for registration. For foals of 1976, no horse over three years of age is eligible for registration. For foals of 1977 and thereafter, no horse two years of age or older is eligible for registration. For foals of 1989 and thereafter, in order for a foal to be registered the application for registration, the mating certificate, and the fee for registration must be submitted to the Association no later than July 1 of the yearling year.

(g) Horses registered Standard with the Canadian Standardbred Horse Society, the New Zealand Trotting Conference, the Australian Stud Book, the Stud Books of Norway, Finland, Sweden and France or the Stud Books of other selected European countries may be re-registered Standard with this Association provided their records and/or qualifications meet the standards of this Association and are approved by the President, Executive Vice-President or Registration Committee.

(h) The Standing Committee on Registration may register as Standard any horse which does not qualify under the above sections, if in their opinion he or she should be registered Standard.

3. Non-Standard Bred. - Any horse may be registered as Non-Standard upon filing application showing satisfactory identification of the horse for racing purposed. This identification may be accomplished by furnishing the name, age, sex, sire, dam, color and markings and history of the previous owners. A mating certificate must accompany this application, showing the sire to be some type of registered horse. Any owner standing a non-standard stallion for service must include the fact that it is non-standard in all advertisements of such service.

For foals of 1973 and thereafter, prior approval must be obtained from the Standing Committee on Registration before breeding any horse not meeting the requirements for Standard registration in Rule 26, Section 2 above except for foals of mares registered non-standard prior to November 1972. Provided further that no horse or mare shall be approved for non-standard registration unless it has been gelded or spayed.

6. Artificial Insemination. - A foal conceived by semen which is frozen, desiccated, transported off the premises where it is produced or not implanted on the same day collected is not eligible for registration.

7. Breeding Requirements. - Before using a stallion at stud, the owner must register the stallion for breeding purposes with this Association, and the person responsible for maintaining the breeding records for the stallion may be required to establish his qualifications for same by successfully completing a written or oral examination.

It shall be the responsibility of stallion owners to have each stallion properly blood-typed and to furnish this Association with a blood-typing report from a recognized laboratory. Failure to comply with this requirement may subject the stallion owner or lessee of a stallion to suspension and/or a fine not to exceed $5,000, and applications for registration may be refused from any person not complying with this requirement.

Stallion owners shall keep a stallion record

GENERAL INFORMATION

showing the mare's name, sire and dam; color, markings, owner, breeding dates, and color, sex and foaling date of any foals born on the stallion owner's premises. The records shall be available for inspection by officers or authorized representatives of The United States Trotting Association, and shall be kept at least ten years of filed with The United States Trotting Association.

All persons standing a stallion at either public or private service shall file with this Association a list of all mares bred to each stallion, together with the dates of service. This list must be filed by September 1st of the year of breeding. In addition to the service report, a list of standardbred foals dropped on the farm with foaling dates and markings must be filed by August 1st. Failure to comply with this provision may subject the owner or lessee of the stallion to a fine of not less than $10.00 nor more than $50.00. Application for registration may be refused from any person not complying with this rule.

Beginning with the 1987 breeding season, all brood mares must be blood-typed by a laboratory approved by U.S.T.A. and the blood type of the mare must be on file with U.S.T.A. before any foal of 1988 and thereafter may be registered.

8. Names. - (a) Names for proposed registration shall be limited to four words and a total of 18 spaces.

(b) Horses may not be registered under a name of an animal previously registered and active unless fifteen years have elapsed since any such activity, except where the applicant is able to establish to the satisfaction of the Registrar that one of the other of the following circumstances has occurred:

(1) That the horse has died of had its name changed prior to becoming two years of age.

(2) That the horse has died or had its named changed before racing or being used for breeding purposes.

(c) Names of outstanding horses may not be used again, nor may they be used as a prefix or suffix unless the name is part of the name of the sire or dam. A prefix or a suffix such as Junior, etc., is not acceptable.

(d) Use of a farm name in registration of horses is reserved for the farm that has registered that name.

(e) Names of living persons will not be used unless the written permission to use their name is filed with the application for registration.

(f) No horse shall be registered under names if spelling or pronunciation is similar to names already in use.

(g) Names of famous or notorious persons, trade names, or names claimed for advertising purposes, except names, or parts of a name, of a registered breeding farm will not be used.

(h) The United States Trotting Association reserves the right to refuse any name indicating a family or strain which may be misleading, or any name which may be misleading as to the origin or relationship or sex of an animal, or any name which might be considered offensive, vulgar or suggestive.

(i) Horses may be named by January 1st, subsequent to their foaling without penalty.

(j) The foregoing provisions of this section notwithstanding, foals may be registered unnamed provided an application for a name is submitted prior to January 1st of the two-year-old year.

(k) When nominating, advertising, cataloging, selling, or otherwise representing an unregistered horse, the use of a name for the horse in identifying said horse is prohibited. Whoever violates this rule may be punished by a fine or suspension or both.

13. Fees for Re-Registration to Change the Name. - The fee for re-registration of a yearling prior to January 1st when it shall become two years old, which re-registration is solely for the purpose of a change of name, shall be $5.00. After a horse becomes a two-year-old, the fee for change of name shall be $15.00. No change of name will be permitted once a horse has raced, nor will any change of name be permitted for stallions or mares that have been used for breeding purposes.

16. Penalty for Executing False Application for Registration or Transfer. - The President, Executive Vice-President, Registration Committee or District Board of Review may summon persons who have executed applications for registration or transfer or alterations of registration certificates that have become subject to question, as well as any other person who may have knowledge thereof. Failure to respond to such summons may be punished by a fine, suspension or expulsion. If the investigation reveals that an application for registration or transfer contains false or misleading information, the person or persons responsible may be fined, suspended or expelled, and in addition may be barred from further registration or transfer of horses in the Association as such animal may be barred from registration. The decision of the President, Executive Vice-President, Registration Committee or District Board of Review, as the case may be, shall be reduced to writing and shall be final unless the person or persons aggrieved thereby shall, within then (10) days appeal in writing to the Board of Appeals as provided in Article IX of the By-Laws.

22. The registration of foals produced by the ovum transplant method is prohibited.

27. No horse that is conceived by transported or frozen semen, embryo transplant, or by arti-

GENERAL INFORMATION

ficial insemination not meeting the requirements or restrictions as set forth in Rule 26, Section 6, shall be registered with USTA. Furthermore, no foal of 1987 or thereafter, will be issued an eligibility or validation certificate unless first registered with the USTA.

28. Beginning with foals of 1989 and thereafter, the parentage of all foals shall be verified by either a Parentage Verification Blood Test or a DNA positive identification conducted by a recognized laboratory after the permanent identification (tattooing or freeze branding) of the foal and prior to the issuance of an eligibility certificate, or the use of the foal for breeding purposes, which ever occurs first.

GENERAL INFORMATION
THE USTA HARNESS RACING HOTLINE

The USTA's "Harness Racing Hotline" provides a daily summary of feature race results from the last seven days, from tracks around the U.S. and Canada, plus news items of general interest, and daily statistical updates on leading horses and drivers.

The Hotline is updated at 9 a.m. eastern, every Monday through Thursday. Friday and Saturday schedules vary by time of the year, with results being updated at 1 a.m. eastern from Memorial Day through the first week in October. At other times of the year, the Friday and Saturday reports are updated at 9 a.m. We invite you to join the more than 150,000 persons who call the Harness Racing Hotline each year. Beyond toll charges, if any, it's a FREE call.

For 24-hour feature race results and news call:

(614) 228-1821

Recording updated at 9 a.m. (eastern)
every day, or at 1 a.m. each
Saturday and Sunday from Memorial Day
through the first Saturday in October

TRACK HOTLINES

While the USTA's Harness Racing Hotline specializes in news and events of national importance, many tracks have established similar services devoted to the nightly reporting of their own results. Virtually all of the phone numbers listed below involve charges to the caller when dialed from outside the immediate area of the track, and some result in additional charges -- even when dialed locally:

Track	(Area Code) Number	Track	(Area Code) Number
Assiniboia Downs	(204) 831-0321	New Brunswick Downs	(506) 857-RACE
Balmoral Park	(708) 672-4550	Edmonton Northlands	(403) 493-9000
Barrie Raceway	(705) 726-3631	Northville Downs	(313) 349-1528
Hippodrome Blue Bonnets	(514) 340-2018	Orangeville Raceway	(519) 941-6964
Charlottetown Driving Pk.	(902) 566-4408	Pocono Downs	(717) 824-7511
Cloverdale Raceway	(604) 574-3311	Pompano Park	(900) 820-1777
Dover Downs	(302) 678-3212	Quad City Downs	(309) 792-3557
Exhibition Park Raceway	(506) 633-2054	Queensbury Downs	(306) 359-7703
Fairmount Park	(314) 721-7200	Hippodrome de Quebec	(418) 524-6148
Flamboro Downs	(416) 525-2426	Raceway Park	(419) 476-7759
Freehold Raceway	(900) 740-5555	Rideau Carleton	(613) 822-2260
Garden State Park	(900) 786-8880	Rosecroft Raceway	(301) 567-5800
Harrington Raceway	(302) 398-5038	Saginaw Harness Raceway	(517) 752-2464
Hawthorne	(708) 976-8200	Scioto Downs	(614) 766-8768
Hazel Park	(313) 546-0155	Sports Creek	(313) 635-4519
Jackson Raceway	(517) 783-3783	Sportsman's Park	(708) 976-2121
Los Alamitos	(714) 995-2222	Springfield State Fair	(217) 782-4231
(stretch calls)	(900) 370-2121	Stampede Park	(403) 265-7009
Louisville Downs	(900) 420-6789	Tartan Downs	(902) 562-6666
Maywood Park	(708) 976-2121	Truro Raceway	(902) 893-0505
The Meadowlands	(201) 460-4002	Vernon Downs	(315) 829-2201
The Meadows	(900) 420-5444	Windsor Raceway	(313) 976-6666
Monticello Raceway	(900) 976-8883	Yonkers Raceway	(914) 976-6969

GENERAL INFORMATION
A HANDY LIST OF FACSIMILE ("FAX") NUMBERS
Breeding and Bloodstock

Almahurst Farm, KY	(606) 887-1495	Killean Acres, ONT	(519) 485-6573
Almahurst Farm, NJ	(609) 397-1817	Kosmos Horse Breeders, PA	(717) 359-9226
Armstrong Brothers, ONT	(416) 383-2107	Lana Lobell Farm, NY	(914) 472-2121
Blue Chip Farms, NY	(914) 895-2110	Little Farm, NY	(518) 465-4043
Bradford Bloodstock, NY	(212) 861-1643	Marveland Farm, NJ	(201) 584-2901
Bradley Stndb. Agency, NJ	(609) 953-7819	Meadowbranch Farm, PA	(717) 624-3592
Cantario Farms, ONT	(416) 854-0650	Perretti Farms, NJ	(609) 259-3649
Canvasback Farm, MD	(301) 658-4815	Pickwick Farm, OH	(419) 562-2565
Castleton Farm, KY	(606) 281-6284	Pin Oak Lane Farm, PA	(717) 235-8190
Fair Winds Farm, NJ	(609) 259-9654	Preferred Equine Mkt., NY	(914) 241-1333
Ferme Windsor, ONT	(819) 826-6497	Seelster Farms, ONT	(519) 227-1366
Fox Den Farm, MD	(301) 775-0247	Upstream Farm, NJ	(201) 209-8051
Hankins Stndb. Agency, IL	(708) 972-1907	Walnridge Farm, NJ	(609) 758-8308
Hanover Shoe Farms, PA	(717) 637-6766	Walnut Hall Farm, KY	(606) 281-6409
Ideal Farms, NJ	(201) 875-8214	Whitehorse Farms, PA	(215) 640-0350
Kentuckiana Farms, NY	(502) 863-3994	Woodstock Stud, NY	(914) 796-1652

Foreign Organizations

(The numbers below appear with the international access code)

Australian HR Council	61 32675059	Germany (H.T.R.)	49 2101511649
Belgium (F.B.T.)	32 22152192	Italy (U.N.I.R.E.)	39 6428003
Denmark (D.T.C.)	45 31204464	Netherlands (S.N.D.R.)	31 703549923
E.N.C.A.T. (Italy)	39 6428003	New Zealand HR Conf.	64 33388211
European Trotting Union	33 147420990	Norway (D.N.T.)	47 2956060
Finland	35 805121790	Sweden (S.T.C.)	46 8292530
France (S.E.C.F)	33 147420990	Switzerland (S.T.V.F.S.T.)	41 13113651

Racetracks

Assiniboia Downs	(204) 831-5348	Kawartha Downs	(705) 939-6342
Balmoral Park	(708) 672-5932	Lebanon Raceway	(513) 932-5358
Barrie Raceway	(705) 726-8364	Los Alamitos	(714) 995-6276
Batavia Downs	(716) 343-7773	Louisville Downs	(502) 969-3735
Blue Bonnets	(514) 340-2025	Maywood Park (ext. 352)	(708) 343-4800
Buffalo Raceway	(716) 649-0033	Meadowlands, The	(201) 460-4080
Charlottetown Raceway	(902) 368-8856	Meadows, The	(412) 225-0298
Cloverdale Raceway	(604) 576-9821	Mohawk Raceway	(416) 854-2255
Connaught, Hippodrome	(819) 778-1708	Monticello Raceway	(914) 794-0523
Delmarva Downs	(301) 641-2711	Muskegon Racecourse	(616) 798-3997
Dover Downs	(302) 734-3124	New Brunswick Downs	(506) 857-9940
Du Quoin State Fair	(618) 542-3871	Northfield Park	(216) 468-2628
Elmira Raceway	(519) 669-1202	Northlands Park	(403) 471-7134
Exhibition Park Raceway	(506) 633-0802	Northville Downs	(313) 348-8955
Fairmount Park	(618) 344-8218	Orangeville Raceway	(519) 942-0108
Flamboro Downs	(416) 627-3561	Pocono Downs	(717) 823-9407
Fredericton Raceway	(506) 458-9294	Pompano Park	(305) 972-7894
Freehold Raceway	(201) 462-3807	Quad City Downs	(309) 792-4143
Garden State Park	(609) 488-3776	Quebec, Hippodrome de	(418) 524-0776
Greenwood Raceway	(416) 698-1230	Queensbury Downs	(306) 525-0955
Harrington Raceway	(302) 398-5030	Raceway Park	(419) 476-7979
Hazel Park	(313) 398-5236	Red Mile, The	(606) 231-0217
Hiawatha Horse Park	(519) 542-3538	Rideau Carleton	(613) 822-1586
Indiana State Fair	(317) 927-7578	Riverside Downs	(502) 827-1120
Jackson Harness Raceway	(517) 788-6772	Rosecroft Raceway	(301) 567-9267

GENERAL INFORMATION

Saginaw Harness Raceway	(517) 755-1300	Syracuse Mile	(315) 487-5711
Saratoga Harness	(518) 583-2169	Tartan Downs	(902) 539-9784
Scarborough Downs	(207) 883-9521	Hippodrome Trois Rivieres	(819) 376-4453
Scioto Downs	(614) 491-4626	Truro Raceway	(902) 897-0069
Sports Creek Raceway	(313) 635-9711	Vernon Downs	(315) 829-4384
Sportsman's Park	(708) 452-4709	Western Fair Raceway	(519) 679-3124
Springfield, IL	(217) 524-6194	Windsor Raceway	(519) 969-4452
Stampede Park, Calgary	(403) 265-7009	Woodstock Raceway	(519) 537-2349
Sudbury Downs	(705) 855-5434	Yonkers Raceway	(914) 968-1121

Racing Commissions

Alberta	(403) 255-4078	Michigan	(313) 462-2429
British Columbia	(604) 660-7414	Missouri	(314) 751-8722
California	(916) 920-7658	New Jersey	(609) 396-3575
Delaware	(302) 697-6287	New York	(212) 219-4199
Florida	(305) 470-5683	Ohio	(614) 466-1900
Illinois	(312) 917-5062	Ontario	(416) 324-3478
Kentucky	(606) 252-3538	Pennsylvania	(717) 787-2387
Maine	(207) 289-7548	Quebec	(418) 646-2528
Manitoba	(204) 931-0942	Saskatchewan	(306) 343-1088
Maryland	(301) 333-1229	Wisconsin	(608) 267-4879

Sire Stake Sponsors

California	(916) 362-8319	Michigan	(517) 349-4983
Florida	(305) 978-9070	New Jersey	(609) 984-2508
Illinois	(217) 524-6194	New York	(518) 434-1265
Indiana	(317) 232-8766	Ohio	(614) 466-1900
Kentucky	(606) 252-3538	Ontario	(416) 324-3478
Maine	(207) 289-7548	Wisconsin	(608) 267-4879
Maryland	(301) 567-9267		

Trade Organizations

Agriculture Canada	(613) 952-7466	Illinois HHA	(708) 323-0761
Ass. Race Commissioners Int'l.	(606) 233-4634	Kentucky HHA	(502) 361-5882
Breeders Crown	(908) 446-5153	Michigan HHA	(517) 349-4983
Cloverleaf SOA	(302) 678-8507	N.Am. Amateur Drivers	(718) 544-0033
Can. Stnd. Horse Society	(416) 858-8047	N.Am. Judges & Stewards	(908) 431-4242
Canadian Trotting Association	(416) 858-3111	Northeastern HHA	(518) 583-1240
Del Miller Am. Drivers Assn.	(717) 637-6766	Ohio HHA	(614) 221-8726
Florida SBOA	(305) 978-9070	Ontario HHA	(416) 854-2691
Hambletonian Society	(606) 231-9311	Quebec T&P Association	(514) 731-7687
HHA of Central NY	(315) 829-4350	Racetracks of Canada	(416) 826-4726
Harness Horse Youth Found.	(317) 848-5136	Saskatchewan Stnd. Assn.	(306) 525-6049
Harness Horsemen Int'l.	(908) 446-3541	SBOA of New Jersey	(201) 409-0741
Harness Publicists Assn.	(705) 939-6342	SOA New York	(914) 237-7393
Harness Racing Comm.	(914) 428-5427	Trotting Horse Museum	(914) 294-3463
Harness Tracks of America	(201) 285-0867	U.S. Harness Writers Assn.	(716) 344-1187

Trade Publications

Atlantic Post Calls	(902) 667-0377	Sports Eye	(800) 444-6146
Canadian Sportsman	(519) 866-5596	The Standardbred	(519) 856-2347
Harness Horse	(717) 233-7411	Times: In Harness	(717) 469-2005
Hoof Beats	(614) 228-1385	Trot Magazine	(416) 858-3111
Horseman & Fair World	(606) 231-0656		

GENERAL INFORMATION

EQUIPMENT COMMONLY WORN BY STANDARDBREDS

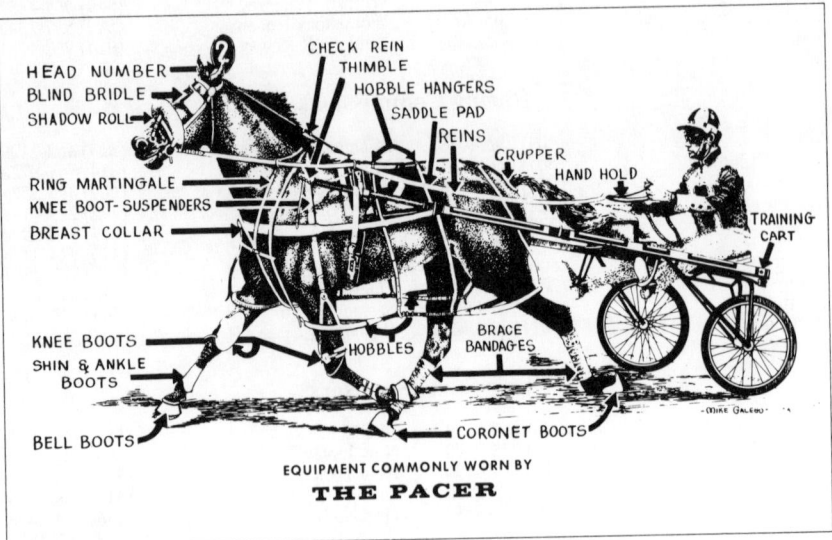

EQUIPMENT COMMONLY WORN BY
THE PACER

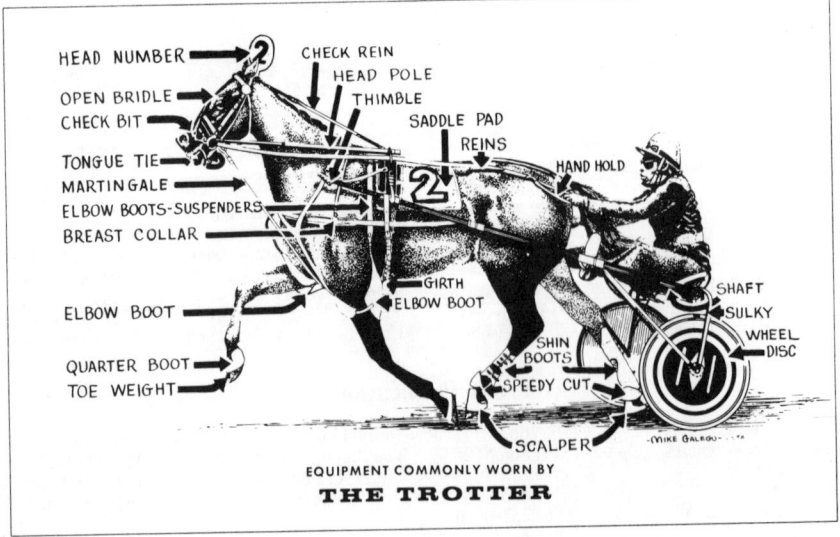

EQUIPMENT COMMONLY WORN BY
THE TROTTER

Notes

Notes